MICROSOFT® PROFESSIONAL EDITIONS

Microsoft® Windows NT® Workstation Resource Kit

Microsoft® Press

PUBLISHED BY
Microsoft Press
A Division of Microsoft Corporation
One Microsoft Way
Redmond, Washington 98052-6399

Library of Congress Cataloging-in-Publication Data
Microsoft Windows NT workstation resource kit : comprehensive resource
guide and utilities for Windows NT workstation version 4.0 /
Microsoft Corporation.
p. cm.
Includes index.
ISBN 1-57231-343-9
1. Microsoft Windows NT. 2. Operating systems (Computers)
I. Microsoft Corporation.
QA76.76.O63M52465 1996
005.4'469--dc20 96-33381
CIP

Printed and bound in the United States of America.

1 2 3 4 5 6 7 8 9 Rand-T 1 0 9 8 7 6

Distributed to the book trade in Canada by Macmillan of Canada, a division of Canada Publishing Corporation.

A CIP catalogue record for this book is available from the British Library.

Microsoft Press books are available through booksellers and distributors worldwide. For further information about international editions, contact your local Microsoft Corporation office. Or contact Microsoft Press International directly at fax (206) 936-7329.

Acquisitions Editor: Casey Doyle
Project Editor: Stuart J. Stuple

This book is dedicated to creating customer self-sufficiency!

Contributors to this book include the following:

Managing Editor
Sonia Marie Moore
Lead Technical Editor
Pamela Miller
Technical Editors
John Andrilla, J. Elise Ellinghausen, Kate Robinson, Megan Sheppard
Proofreader
Kimberly O'Neal
Writing Manager
Peggy Etchevers
Technical Writers
Janet Anderson, June Blender Cahn, Janice Breyer, Maureen Carmichael, Peter Costantini, Chris Dragich, J. Elise Ellinghausen, Peggy Etchevers, Marc Genty, Jeff Howard, Sharon Kay, Edward Lafferty, Peter Lovejoy, Cary Reinstein, Maureen Sullivan
Software Program Managers
Louis Kahn, Ryan Marshall
Software Developer
Martin Holladay
Production Manager
Karye Cattrell
Production Lead
Nikole Faith
Production Team
Jay French, Patrick Ngo, Cathy Pfarr, Keri Segna, Jeff Weaver, Todd White
Indexers
Jane Dow, Ronnie Maier, Barbara Sherman
Lead Graphic Designer
Chris Blanton
Design Support Team
Johnni Cutler, Flora Goldthwaite, Amy Iffland, Casey McGahan, Wendy Salvatori, Gabriel Varela, Sue Wyble, Jan Yeager
Technical Consultants
Reza Baghai, Eugene Baucom, Russ Blake, Matthew Bradburn, Peter Brundrett, Steven Carr, Phillip Carver, Joseph Dadzie, Allen Denver, Bodin Dresevic, Scott Field, Eric Flo, Patrick Franklin, Michele Freed, Jerry Gallagher, Joseph Holman, Terence Hosken, Eric Hough, Cliff Hudson, John Jacobs, Doug Klopfenstein, Eric Kutter, Richard Lerz, Tom Lindley, Jim Livingston, Janice Marsh, Lonny McMichael, Tom Miller, Oshoma Momoh, JosephPagano, Lou Perazzoli, Dave Plummer, Patrick Questembert, Bob Rinne, Dan Ruder, Mark Ryland, John Scarborough, Karol Russell Stubbs, Jim Truchon, Andre Vachon, Brad Waters, Robert Watson, Tom White, Peter Wieland, David Winkler, Steve Wood, David Xu, and numerous other hardworking Windows NT Developers, Program Managers, and Product Support Specialists
Product Support Liaisons
Roger Bruist, Todd Hafer
Technical Marketing Liaisons
Patrick Franklin, Jonathan Perera

Contents

Part II About Windows NT Workstation

Part III Optimizing Windows NT Workstation

Part V Windows NT Registry

Part VII Networking with Windows NT Workstation

Part IX Appendixes

Figures and Tables

Figures

Tables

Introduction

Welcome to the *Microsoft® Windows NT® Workstation Resource Kit: Windows NT Workstation Resource Guide*.

The *Microsoft Windows NT Workstation Resource Kit* for version 4.0 consists of this new, comprehensive volume and a single compact disc (CD) containing utilities that make it easier for you to get the most out of Windows NT Workstation. For information and utilities specific to working with Windows NT Server and/or large networks, you need to purchase the *Microsoft Windows NT Server Resource Kit* for version 4.0.

The *Windows NT Workstation Resource Guide* presents detailed information on the Windows NT Workstation operating system, plus topics that are either new for version 4.0 or reflect issues that our Product Support people consider timely and important. You should consider this information to be an in-depth, technical supplement to the printed and online documentation included as part of the Windows NT Workstation version 4.0 product. It does not replace that information as the source for learning how to use the product features and programs.

This Introduction includes the following types of information you can use to get started:

- The first section outlines the contents of this book, so that you can quickly find pertinent technical details.
- The second section introduces the *Windows NT Workstation Resource Kit* CD.
- The third section describes the support policy for the *Windows NT Workstation Resource Kit*.

About the Windows NT Workstation Resource Guide

This book includes the following chapters.

Part I, Windows NT Workstation Deployment

Chapter 1, "Deployment Strategy and Details," provides an overview of the steps involved in deploying Windows NT Workstation 4.0 throughout an organization. These steps include assembling the teams, choosing and testing the configurations of Windows NT Workstation to be used in an organization, and testing and performing the deployment process.

Chapter 2, "Customizing Setup," tells administrators how to provide their users with an unattended, customized installation. They can include applications, third-party device drivers, and even organization-specific Help files. End users can get right to work with an easy to use, powerful operating system, and all the applications, files, and tools they need.

Chapter 3, "Deploying Windows NT Workstation on an Existing Client-Server Network," discusses tools such as Systems Management Server that administrators can use to make the deployment of Windows NT Workstation 4.0 across an existing network even easier —or administrators, for users, and for help desk personnel.

Chapter 4, "Planning for a Mixed Environment," discusses the tools available to manage a network that includes both Windows NT Workstation and Windows 95. It also discusses factors to consider when deciding which operating system to install on which computers in an organization.

Part II, About Windows NT Workstation

Chapter 5, "Windows NT 4.0 Workstation Architecture," describes the architecture of Windows NT and its components. It also includes information on the improvements that were made in the architecture for Windows NT version 4.0.

Chapter 6, "Windows NT Security," provides a detailed description of the security architecture, which is pervasive throughout the operating system. It also gives detailed examples of how security can be implemented in Windows NT and provides practical suggestions for implementing different levels of security. The chapter concludes with a description of C2 security and the status of Windows NT in the certification process.

Chapter 7, "Printing," describes the Windows NT printing architecture and flow of control, including printing from all possible network clients. Descriptions of each printing component, including the spooler and print server services, are included, as well as a printing troubleshooting guide.

Chapter 8, "Fonts," presents technical information about the font technologies supported by Windows NT and focuses on TrueType fonts. This chapter also provides detailed information about printer fonts, installing fonts, and the expanded support for multiple character sets.

Part III, Optimizing Windows NT Workstation

Chapter 9, "The Art of Performance Monitoring," is an overview of the elements of performance monitoring on Windows NT.

Chapter 10, "About Performance Monitor," is a detailed description of Performance Monitor, the monitoring tool designed for Windows NT, from its most basic level to the subtle details of mastering the tool.

Chapter 11, "Performance Monitoring Tools," is a review of additional tools for monitoring the performance of Windows NT, including many of those that are included on the *Windows NT Workstation Resource Kit* CD.

Chapter 12, "Detecting Memory Bottlenecks," describes tests you can use to monitor your computer's physical memory and its role in the Windows NT virtual memory system. The chapter also includes tests to help you determine how efficiently your applications use the virtual memory system.

Chapter 13, "Detecting Processor Bottlenecks," guides you through the steps of recognizing a processor bottleneck, tracing it to its source, and eliminating it.

Chapter 14, "Detecting Disk Bottlenecks," describes different disk testing methods, and shows you how to measure the efficiency of your disks and your application's use of them. The chapter also includes a guide to testing and analyzing the performance of stripe sets using Performance Monitor logs included on the *Windows NT Workstation Resource Kit* CD.

Chapter 15, "Detecting Cache Bottlenecks," demonstrates how a memory shortage affects the Windows NT file system cache and shows you how to use cache activity indicators to analyze application I/O.

Chapter 16, "Monitoring Multiple Processor Computers," describes the performance issues unique to a symmetric multiprocessing system and how to monitor them.

Part IV, Reliability and Recoverability

Chapter 17, "Disk and File System Basics," describes the organization, contents, and purpose of the information on hard disks, and includes a description of disk hardware. Understanding the information in this chapter will help you to troubleshoot disk problems effectively and recover from them.

Chapter 18, "Choosing a File System," provides an overview of the capabilities and limitations of the File Allocation Table (FAT) file system and the Windows NT file system (NTFS). The previous chapter describes the structure of FAT and NTFS partitions from the perspective of how each file system organizes the data on the disk. This chapter focuses on the user aspects of each file system.

Chapter 19, "What Happens When You Start Your Computer," describes what happens at each step in the process when the computer starts successfully with Windows NT installed as one of the operating systems. It also describes dual-booting and triple-booting other operating systems, such as Windows 95 and MS-DOS®. It provides information on the contents of the Boot.ini file on x86-based computers and describes the firmware menus and how to use them on RISC-based computers.

Chapter 20, "Preparing for and Performing Recovery," describes what information you should back up and how to use those backups to recover from problems.

Chapter 21, "Troubleshooting Startup and Disk Problems," discusses what you can do to isolate startup problems, along with possible causes of and how to recover from disk problems.

Chapter 22, "Disk, File System, and Backup Utilities," describes each of the utilities mentioned in the previous chapters and how to use them.

Part V, Windows NT Registry

Chapter 23, "Overview of the Windows NT Registry," describes the Windows NT Registry, which is the configuration database for Windows NT.

Chapter 24, "Registry Editors and Registry Administration," describes the two Registry editors included with Windows NT, with an emphasis on protecting the Registry contents and using Registry editors to monitor and maintain the system configuration on local and remote computers.

Chapter 25, "Configuration Management and the Registry," provides examples of investigative and problem-solving techniques using the Registry and Registry editors.

Chapter 26, "Initialization Files and the Registry," describes how .ini files and other configuration files are used under Windows NT and how these values are stored in the Registry.

Part VI, Compatibility

Chapter 27, "Windows Compatibility and Migration," provides a technical discussion of the Win16 subsystem for running Win16 and MS-DOS applications under Windows NT. The chapter also presents a discussion about running a mixed environment of Windows operating systems, and a detailed comparison of system architecture, reliability, security, and features between Windows NT and Windows 95.

Chapter 28, "OS/2 Compatibility," describes the implementation of the OS/2 subsystem, the application programming interface, and how to run OS/2 applications under Windows NT.

Chapter 29, "POSIX Compatibility," describes POSIX and its levels of conformance. The chapter also describes the implementation of the POSIX subsystem and how to run POSIX applications under Windows NT.

Part VII, Networking with Windows NT Workstation

Chapter 30, "Microsoft TCP/IP and Related Services for Windows NT," provides an overview of the networking services and TCP/IP transport used in Windows NT networking.

Chapter 31, "Microsoft TCP/IP Architecture," provides a general description of the architecture of TCP/IP in Windows NT.

Chapter 32, "Networking Name Resolution and Registration," describes the name resolution and registration services provided with Windows NT to enable locating and connecting to remote computers on an intranet or the Internet.

Chapter 33, "Using LMHOSTS Files," provides information about the LMHOSTS file that contains static mappings of "friendly" NetBIOS computer names to IP addresses to enable computers to locate resources on the Internet or on routed, TCP/IP intranets.

Chapter 34, "Managing User Work Environments," describes the following tools that you can use to manage user work environments: user profiles, System Policy Editor, logon scripts, and environment variables.

Chapter 35, "Using Windows NT Workstation on the Internet," introduces the components that enable a computer running Windows NT Workstation to access the Internet or to publish using Peer Web Services.

Part VIII, Windows NT Workstation Troubleshooting

Chapter 36, "General Troubleshooting," identifies tools that are available in Windows NT to help you troubleshoot problems. The chapter also contains information about troubleshooting hardware problems and how to use the information in the Registry to determine why services are not working correctly.

Chapter 37, "Monitoring Events," describes the three types of Windows NT events (application, system, and security) and the tool that you use to view them.

Chapter 38, "Windows NT Executive Messages," discusses the various types of messages generated by the Windows NT Executive and categorizes them by their type and severity.

Chapter 39, "Windows NT Debugger," provides information on how to troubleshoot blue screens and Executive STOP messages by configuring the computer for a local or remote debugging session.

Part IX, Appendixes

Appendix A, "Answer Files and UDFs," is a reference for creating the answer files and associated Uniqueness Database Files (UDFs) that enable a completely unattended setup for each user in an organization.

Appendix B, "Security in a Software Development Environment," provides detailed information on protecting and auditing objects that are not normally accessed by anything other than the Windows NT operating system itself. This appendix is of use in a software development environment, or in situations where custom software shares the system with sensitive data. This appendix also describes special cases of auditing that might be of interest to administrators of high-level security installations.

Appendix C, "Port Reference for Microsoft TCP/IP," describes the well-known and registered port assignments that are supported by Microsoft TCP/IP for Windows NT.

Glossary in printed form for Windows NT.

Index to this *Windows NT Workstation Resource Guide*.

Resource Kit Compact Disc

The CD that accompanies the *Windows NT Workstation Resource Kit* contains utilities that apply to information in the *Windows NT Workstation Resource Guide.* This new CD replaces all previous ones. It includes a collection of information resources, tools, and utilities that can make networking and working with the Windows NT platform even easier.

Note The utilities on this CD are designed and tested for the U.S. version of Windows NT version 4.0. Use of these utilities on any other version of Windows NT may cause unpredictable results.

A large Help file with explanations and user actions for the majority of the messages included in Windows NT version 4.0, and a large Help file of Performance Counter Definitions are just two of the major items included on the *Windows NT Workstation Resource Kit* CD. Updates to these files and others will be provided, when available, on the Microsoft Internet web site for the Windows NT Resource Kits. See the Rktools.hlp file for the exact site address, as well as the addresses of other Microsoft information sites.

After installing the *Windows NT Workstation Resource Kit,* please refer first to the following three files:

- The Readme.wri file, which contains a complete list of all the tools and utilities on the *Windows NT Workstation Resource Kit* CD and additional setup instructions for some of them.
- Either the Rkdocw.hlp (for Windows NT Workstation) or the Rkdocs.hlp (for Windows NT Server) file, which provides a single entry point for all of the major components of the Resource Kit's online documentation.
- The Rktools.hlp file, which provides an overview of the Resource Kit tools and utilities and basic instructions on how to use many of them, along with links to additional documentation and, in some cases, to the actual program files.

The most current corrections to those tools and utilities and their documentation, as well as the POSIX and Perl source code files, are available on the Internet at the following Microsoft FTP site:

ftp://ftp.microsoft.com/bussys/winnt/winnt-public/reskit/nt40/

The *Windows NT Workstation Resource Kit* CD includes a wide variety of tools and utilities to help you work more efficiently with Windows NT Workstation. The following notes describe some of the enhancements made to the existing tools and utilities and introduce new ones that have been added for this version 4.0 release.

Computer Administration/Configuration Tools

- SrvInstW is a wizard for installing and deleting services and device drivers. This is a GUI form of the Instsrv.exe application that now also has increased functionality for detailing service parameters.

Computer Diagnostic Tools

- Remote Kill is a service with both GUI and command-line clients. It enables a user to enumerate and kill a process on a remote computer. It also combines some of the functionality of Tlist.exe and Kill.exe.
- ShowAcls is a utility that enumerates the access rights for files, folders, and trees. It also allows masking to enumerate only specific ACLs.

Desktop Tools

- Desktop Themes from the Windows 95 Plus Pack are included now along with several new Windows NT-specific themes. These themes include a variety of visual, sound, and symbolic components that can enhance the look and feel of your Windows NT 4.0 desktop. Each desktop theme includes a background wallpaper, a screen saver, a color scheme, and a set of sounds, cursors, icons, and fonts.
- MultiDesk, Multidsk.exe, is a desktop switching program for Windows NT 4.0. It customizes the desktop wallpaper and colors, and separates executing programs into new desk spaces.

Disk/Fault Tolerance Tools

- DiskProbe, Dskprobe.exe, is a sector editor for Windows NT Workstation and Windows NT Server that enables a user with local Administrator rights to edit, save, and copy data directly on the physical hard drive that is not accessible in any other way.
- DiskMap produces a detailed report on the configuration of the hard disk that you specify. It provides information from the Registry about disk characteristics and geometry, the Master Boot Record, and the Partition Table for all the partitions on the disk.

File Tools

- ForFiles is a utility that enables batch processing of files in a folder or tree. You can run a command or give arguments to certain files. For example, you can run the **type** command on all files in a tree with the *.txt extension. Or you could execute every batch file (*.bat) on the C:\ drive with the "myinput.txt" filename as the first argument.
- LogTime is a utility that logs the date and time stamp for batch file calls.
- SetX is a utility that sets User vs. System environment variables.

Internet and TCP/IP Services/Tools

- The Beta version of our Telnet Server, Telnetd.exe. You can use it to run command-line utilities, scripts, and batch files from operating system-independent clients. It is not intended to be a full, commercial-grade Telnet solution.

Network/Server Administration Tools

- Remote Console is a client/server application that enables you to run a command-line session remotely, within which you may launch any other application. Few tools besides Remote Console run applications remotely. REMOTE is not a service, but simply redirects standard input and output, so console programs that take control of the video memory and the keyboard do not work with REMOTE. Along with RCMD and RSH, Remote Console offers you a new way to run consoles remotely and to take control of a CMD session.

Registry Tools

- The Registry Entries Help file, Regentry.hlp, has been updated again for this newest version. The chapter in the *Windows NT Workstation Resource Guide* that corresponded to this Help file has been discontinued.
- Over 10 new command-line Registry programs have also been added for searching, retrieving, and replacing keys in both local and remote Registries.

Tools for Developers

- PULIST is a utility that enumerates system processes and dumps process owners and IDs. You can use it against local or remote computers.
- Api Monitor, APIMON, is a utility that enables you to monitor the API calls that a process is making. This utility incorporates the functionality of the Application Profiler that will no longer ship with the *Windows NT Workstation Resource Kit.*
- CpuStress is a utility that loads down the processor, which is useful for evaluating how a system performs under heavy usage.
- Heap Monitor, HEAPMON, is a utility that enables you to view system heap information.

User Account Administration Tools

- SU now includes a GUI interface along with other major additions. SU enables you to start a process that is running as an arbitrary user.

Resource Kit Support Policy

The SOFTWARE supplied in the *Windows NT Workstation Resource Kit* is not officially supported. Microsoft does not guarantee the performance of the *Window NT Workstation Resource Kit* tools, response times for answering questions, or bug fixes to the tools. However, we do provide a way for customers who purchase the *Windows NT Workstation Resource Kit* to report bugs and receive possible fixes for their issues. You can do this by either sending Internet mail to RKINPUT@MICROSOFT.COM or by referring to one of the options listed in the *Start Here* book, which is included with your Windows NT Workstation product. This mail address is only for *Windows NT Workstation Resource Kit* related issues.

The SOFTWARE (including instructions for its use and all printed and online documentation) is provided "AS IS" without warranty of any kind. Microsoft further disclaims all implied warranties, including, without limitation, any implied warranties of merchantability or of fitness for a particular purpose. The entire risk arising out of the use or performance of the SOFTWARE and documentation remains with you.

In no event shall Microsoft, its authors, or anyone else involved in the creation, production, or delivery of the SOFTWARE be liable for any damages whatsoever (including, without limitation, damages for loss of business profits, business interruption, loss of business information, or other pecuniary loss) arising out of the use of or inability to use the SOFTWARE or documentation, even if Microsoft has been advised of the possibility of such damages.

PART I

Windows NT Workstation Deployment

CHAPTER 1

Deployment Strategy and Details

The deployment process for Windows NT Workstation 4.0 consists of several distinct phases, including the following:

- Assemble executive and planning teams
- Review Windows NT Workstation 4.0
- Identify the preferred network-client configuration
- Prepare the planning and support teams
- Perform lab tests of the client configuration
- Plan the pilot rollout
- Conduct the pilot rollout
- Finalize the rollout plan
- Roll out Windows NT Workstation 4.0

Not all of these tasks may be necessary for your organization.

Acquiring Resources

This phase involves gathering the resources, including equipment, software, and staff, to properly plan for testing and evaluating Windows NT Workstation 4.0. Members of the support team should receive training during this phase.

Assemble the Teams

The steps involved in deploying Windows NT Workstation are performed by the following teams:

Executive Team
: The executive team includes the deployment project manager (usually the head of the Information Systems department) and members of the executive committee of the corporation. This team must include one or more individuals with decision-making authority for organization policies and procedures.

Planning Team
: The planning team includes the deployment project manager, key installation team members, and a representative from the support and training teams.

Installation Team
: The installation team includes technicians and individuals who will be conducting the installation. This team must include a specialist in 32-bit applications who can evaluate the proposed Windows NT Workstation 4.0 configuration for compatibility.

Training Team
: The training team includes individuals responsible for user training.

Support Team
: The support team includes staff from the help desk or support department, and select individuals from the planning team. This team develops a plan for supporting Windows NT Workstation 4.0 during and after deployment, integrating new methods and processes as needed into the existing support scheme.

In many cases, team members must continue with their regular work, in addition to working with their assigned deployment teams. Make sure you have the support of their managers, and that adjustments can be made to their regular work loads as needed.

The composition of the installation, training, and support teams depends in large part on the early decisions made by the executive and planning teams. Therefore, the first teams to be assembled are the executive and planning teams.

Executive and Planning Teams

The deployment project manager participates on the executive team and leads the planning team. This individual is usually the head of the Information Systems (IS) department; however, the executive committee may find another individual to be more appropriate, depending on the organization.

When setting up the planning team, it is important to include a set of individuals representing the groups involved in the deployment process. This includes people from the corporate support and employee training departments, the corporate standards committee, and key installation team members. Individuals from the finance and accounting groups will need to take part in planning and evaluation later on, but need not be assigned to the team for the full duration of the deployment process.

The executive and planning teams make top-level decisions, including the decision to purchase and deploy Windows NT Workstation. They may also decide which computers should have Windows NT Workstation installed on them, and which computers should run other operating systems, such as Windows 95. Once these decisions are made, these teams can assemble the remaining teams, and continue to oversee the deployment process.

Installation Team

The installation team is busy long before the final deployment. This team sets up the lab, and then uses it to test the deployment process. During this phase, the installation team, together with the planning team, has the opportunity to fine-tune the chosen configurations of Windows NT Workstation.

While testing the deployment process in the lab, the installation team creates a detailed checklist that can be used during the pilot and final deployments. Because the installation team is likely to increase in size for the final rollout, the checklist should include enough information to be useful to those who did not participate in the testing phase.

The Installation team should include an applications expert who can evaluate 32-bit applications running with Windows NT Workstation 4.0.

Training Team

For the deployment to be successful, the users need to know the advantages of the new operating system, and how to use its features to make their jobs easier. The training team is responsible for providing this knowledge to the users.

You can either hire a training vendor to act as the training team, or assemble the team from employees in your organization. Let this team know what configuration of Windows NT Workstation you have chosen, and keep them informed of any refinements you make to that configuration during the lab test phase.

Your Training team can use the materials provided by Microsoft Authorized Technical Education Centers (ATECs) as a basis for their user training course. In addition to developing and presenting the training class, the training team also sets up the lab or classroom with computers for training.

Support Team

The support team develops a plan for supporting Windows NT Workstation 4.0 during and after deployment. The Support team should become familiar with the Windows NT Workstation product documentation and the *Windows NT Workstation 4.0 Resource Kit* before Windows NT Workstation is actually deployed. Team members can receive instruction at a Microsoft Authorized Technical Education Center and participate the Certified Professional program. Call (800) SOLPROV (or (800) 765-7768) for information about authorized training offered for Windows NT Workstation 4.0 and the Certified Professional program, and for referral to a local Microsoft Solution Provider Authorized Technical Education Center (ATEC).

If Microsoft Systems Management Server is available, the support team should also be familiar with the Help Desk and Diagnostics features of Systems Management Server. Systems Management Server is a separate product available from Microsoft.

Conduct a Sample Inventory

You will need to survey a representative sample of your organization to identify the hardware and software typically used on client and server computers. By doing this sample inventory of your organization's active equipment, you can accurately simulate the organizational environment in the lab. Such a simulation helps you make broad decisions about your organization's computing infrastructure, such as which network protocols to use, or which desktop configuration best fits the applications used in your organization. Simulating the network environment also helps you configure client computers for use in a mixed environment of operating systems, servers, and network protocols.

When you are ready for final deployment, you will need a more complete inventory of the computers in your organization. The longer the time between inventory and deployment, the more chance there is for components to be replaced, or disk space filled, in the interim. These changes could cause the installation of Windows NT Workstation to fail. For best results, a complete and accurate inventory should be performed just before deployment.

Software management tools are available to help you ascertain the hardware and software configurations of computers on your network. For detailed information about a large number of computers on a network, use a system management program such as the Microsoft Systems Management Server to conduct the inventory.

Test Lab

The test lab is used to test the deployment process. It can also be used to test the configurations you have chosen for various groups of computers in your organization, including any applications.

Set aside a physical space for this lab, and acquire a mix of computers that accurately reflects your organization's computing environment. Be sure there are computers to represent every kind of hardware used in the computers to which you will deploy Windows NT Workstation – for example, if your organization uses five different models of computer, from two different manufacturers, include all five models in the lab. If you are currently running Windows for Workgroups on some computers and another operating system on others, make sure that both operating systems are represented in the lab. Likewise, make sure that the peripherals used with the computers to which you will deploy Windows NT Workstation are present in the lab. In addition, try to duplicate variables such as free disk space.

If your organization uses portable computers that dial in from remote locations, or if you use additional servers or mainframe computers for business data, give the lab computers full access to the network and an analog phone line.

You'll also want to make sure you have enough disk space on a test server to implement the rollout.

Test Windows NT Workstation 4.0 features in the lab with all of the applications used in your organization, before performing the pilot installation. Maintain a complete list of any problems found in the testing lab.

Executive Review of Windows NT Workstation

The executive and planning teams need to make informed decisions as to when Windows NT Workstation will be deployed in the organization. They also need to decide whether to install Windows NT Workstation on all computers, or only on certain computers. The product documentation for Windows NT Workstation and the Windows NT Workstation Resource Kit provide much of the information these teams need. In addition, they should review information available online, including the following:

Online service	How to access
World Wide Web on the Internet	Point your WWW browser to **http://www.microsoft.com/NTWorkstation**
WinNTNews	Point your WWW browser to **http://www.microsoft.com**
CompuServe	Go to the Windows NT forum.
America Online	Use the Windows NT Workstation folders under software/operating systems/Windows/Windows NT
FTP on the Internet	Type **ftp://ftp.microsoft.com/bussys/winnt**
GEnie	Download files from the WinNTnews area under the Windows NT Workstation 4.0 RTC.

Note especially the *Windows NT Workstation Advantage* paper, published by the Microsoft Windows NT Product Team. This is available on http://www.microsoft.com. It can also be faxed to you from Microsoft's sales department. Call 1-800-936-4200 and ask for part number 098-60928.

The executive and planning teams might also want to review the total cost of ownership, migration, and productivity studies published by analysts such as Gartner Group, Inc. and the Meta Group.

Decide on the Preferred Client Configuration

With the planning and installation teams assembled and educated about Windows NT Workstation 4.0 capabilities, determine the preferred network configuration and preferred feature set for these client computers. The teams will use this configuration for evaluation and testing, prior to full implementation of Windows NT Workstation 4.0 in your organization.

Starting with the ideal configuration, which uses the most functional and best-performing client software, evaluate each feature against your organization's needs and environment to determine whether the feature is appropriate and compatible.

You may want different configurations for different groups. For example, the marketing group might need different features and applications than the human resources. If you are considering different configuration alternatives, repeat the evaluation for each configuration.

The following sections describe feature options and decisions to evaluate in specifying the network client configuration.

User Interface

Use the new Windows NT Workstation 4.0 user interface to provide ease of use and maximum functionality in accessing Windows NT Workstation 4.0 features. Because this interface is the same as that for Windows 95, users can move easily between the two operating systems. The new interface offers significantly more functionality and efficiency, and is installed by default.

However, if a rapid migration is required, and training is not immediately available, you might prefer to use the Windows 3.x Program Manager Interface. To do so, install the Windows 3.x File Manager and Program Manager.

Network Protocols

For best performance, all networking protocols and services in Windows NT Workstation are completely 32-bit. These include TCP/IP, support for the Internet, Dial-Up networking, NetBEUI, peer-to-peer networking, Client Services for NetWare (with support for NetWare NDS networks), and more. Organizations can enjoy the following benefits from this rich set of integrated networking support:

- Easy installation and integration with existing network systems.
- Faster data I/O across the network — ideal for taking advantage of client-server applications.
- Greater stability than real-mode redirectors.
- More than one redirector can be run at one time, thereby enabling access to servers for multiple networks without having to reload the operating system for a new network client. For example, a Microsoft Windows NT Workstation client can access both NetWare servers and existing mainframe servers at the same time.
- Seamless networking in the Windows NT Workstation 4.0 user interface; users can browse the server for multiple networks in Network Neighborhood, all within the same name space—users don't need to know which type of network they are browsing.

TCP/IP

To provide the best network interoperability over WANs and network routers, include TCP/IP in your ideal configuration. The 32-bit TCP/IP stack included with Windows NT Workstation incorporates both SLIP and PPP. Microsoft TCP/IP, in combination with Windows NT Workstation, provides a scalable solution for enterprise networks that include a mix of system types.

When TCP/IP is used as the enterprise networking protocol, an IP addressing scheme is needed for your organization. If your servers run Windows NT Server, you can use Dynamic Host Control Protocol (DHCP) and Windows Internet Naming Service (WINS) for easy TCP/IP address management. With DHCP, administrators can centrally define global and subnet TCP/IP parameters for interconnected networks. The DHCP service dynamically configures the IP address and subnet mask of each workstation. For name resolution on TCP/IP internetworks, use WINS Servers or LMHosts files.

Windows NT Workstation allows users to run with more than a single IP address at the same time when using Remote Access Services.

When TCP/IP is used as a transport protocol with Windows NT Workstation, computers can communicate with other kinds of systems such as UNIX workstations and servers, or an IP configured printer, without additional networking software.

NetBEUI (NetBIOS Extended User Interface)

NetBEUI is a small, efficient, and fast protocol tuned for small LANs. It is designed to support department-sized LANs consisting of 20 to 200 workstations. NetBEUI does not support traffic across routers, but provides for both connectionless and connection-oriented traffic on a single network segment. NetBEUI is self-configuring and self-tuning. It can be installed and bound to a network card automatically when Windows NT is installed.

NWLink IPX/SPX

Windows NT includes the NWLink protocol, which is an implementation of the internetworking packet exchange (IPX) and sequenced packet exchange (SPX) transport protocols used by NetWare. NWLink NetBIOS is a Microsoft-enhanced implementation of Novell NetBIOS, and transmits Novell NetBIOS packets between a NetWare server running Novell NetBIOS and a Windows NT computer, or between two Windows NT computers.

The Microsoft implementations of the IPX, SPX, and Novell NetBIOS protocols can seamlessly coexist with other protocols on the same network adapter card.

For instructions on configuring NWLink, see Help.

DLC (Data Link Control)

The DLC protocol provided with Windows NT is used primarily to access IBM mainframe computers, rather than for general networking on Windows NT. For example, Microsoft SNA Server for Windows NT uses the DLC protocol device driver when communicating with mainframes on the token ring interface. DLC is also used to connect to printers that are connected directly to a LAN, rather than to a specific computer.

Windows NT DLC allows Windows NT computers to connect to IBM mainframes using 3270 emulators. You can also connect to IBM AS/400 computers using 5250 emulators. DLC works with either token ring or ethernet media access control (MAC) drivers.

The DLC protocol works with Windows NT-based programs and with MS-DOS-based and 16-bit Windows-based programs.

AppleTalk Protocol

The AppleTalk protocol is used to deliver data to a network destination when a Windows NT Server computer configured with Windows NT Services for Macintosh is available on the network. This makes it possible for PCs and Apple Macintosh workstations to share files and printers.

The AppleTalk protocol is also used by software application developers who are creating cross-platform applications for Windows NT and the Macintosh. When used for transferring files across Ethernet or for remote debugging in this way, Windows NT Server Services for Macintosh is not required on the network.

Other 32-Bit Network Protocols

If you are using another type of network, contact your network vendor regarding the availability of 32-bit, protected-mode network client software. Solutions are available for Banyan Vines networks, and several vendors distribute NFS (network file system) solutions for better integration with UNIX-based systems.

Remote Access Service (RAS)

Windows NT Remote Access Service (RAS) client software gives the user access to server-based dial-in packages such as Windows NT Server Remote Access Service, Novell NetWare Connect, and Shiva NetModem. Once the connection is made from the RAS client to the server-based dial-in package, users at remote sites can use the network as if their computers were directly connected to the network. RAS can also be used to connect to remote client computers that have inbound modems.

With some additional configuration of protocols and software on the client computer, RAS provides additional security for remote dial-up connections. The Point-to-Point Protocol (PPP) and Serial Line Internet Protocol (SLIP) are supported in RAS.

Remote Access Service contains the following components:

- Remote Access client, which allows a computer to dial in to a remote access server and use the resource on a LAN. This component can be installed on a Windows NT Workstation computer.
- Remote dial-in functionality, which allows one inbound remote connection at a time. This component can be installed on a computer running Windows NT Workstation 4.0 that has a modem configured for inbound calls.
- PPP, which is a set of industry-standard framing and authentication protocols. Computers running Windows NT Workstation 4.0 can dial into remote networks through any server that complies with the PPP standard.
- SLIP, which is an older protocol that does not support authentication as part of the protocol. SLIP connections typically rely on text-based logon sessions. Encryption and automatic network parameter negotiations are not supported.

Mobile Computing Features

Windows NT Workstation 4.0 has features that support mobile computing and also allow users to switch between portable and docking-station configurations. The features you choose will depend on the particular hardware and working needs of your mobile-computing users. Some of these features are not installed by default, but can be specified in the installation process during Network Setup. Or, they can be configured later, using control panel network settings.

The following mobile computing features might be useful in your organization:

- Hardware Profiles
- Remote Access Service client software for dial-up connection to the organization's network
- Windows NT Workstation 4.0 Briefcase for synchronizing files between computers
- Direct Cable Connection for directly linking two computers
- Remote mail and deferred printing, for working away from the main office
- Broader support for PCMCIA cards
- User profiles to provide a custom desktop for each user, no matter where users log on to the network

Network Monitor Agent

The Network Monitor Agent on a Windows NT computer collects and displays statistics about activity detected by the network card in the computer. Users can then view these statistics at a computer running Network Monitor Agent. Administrators can use SMS and Network Monitor to collect statistics from computers that are running Network Monitor Agent. This data helps administrators perform routine troubleshooting tasks, such as locating a server that is down or that is receiving a disproportionate number of work requests.

Recommended Features for Network Clients

The following optional features define how Windows NT Workstation 4.0 will be installed and administered in your organization. These features are recommended for your preferred configuration.

- User-Level Security
- User Manager
- User Profile Editor
- Remote Administration
- Peer Resource Sharing Services
- Windows Messaging
- Separate Memory Spaces For 16-Bit Applications

User-Level Security

User-level security is based on user account lists stored on servers running Windows NT Server or Novell NetWare. The user accounts specify which users have access rights on the network. Windows NT Workstation 4.0 passes on a user's request for access to the servers for validation. Pass-through user-level security protects shared network resources by requiring that a security provider authenticate a user's request to access resources.

Users and groups have access to local shared resources (including the Registry). User-level security is required for remote administration of the Registry and for network access to full user profiles. User-level security includes the following features:

- Users can specify access rights for individuals and groups to shared resources.
- User access is validated based on user accounts on a Windows NT domain, or on a Novell NetWare server, via the bindery.
- User-level security is required for remote administration of the Registry and for network access to full user profiles.

- Optionally, share-level security can be used to protect files on Windows NT networks or Windows NT Workstation 4.0 peer networks to protect an individual's data on a computer that is used by more than one person.
- Protection for line-of-business applications is provided to keep users from accidentally — or purposely — installing their own applications, or modifying existing ones.

User Manager

User Manager allows you to edit and control individual user accounts and policies from a central location. A user with Administrative privileges can use the User Rights Policy Editor to define policies for the local workstation, such as which user accounts can be used to access the local workstation from the network.

Use the Account Policy Editor to set password restrictions and account lockouts.

User Profile Editor

User profiles allow multiple users sharing a single computer to customize their desktops and have those custom settings loaded at logon. Conversely, a single user can move between computers using the same profile if the administrator stores that profile on the server.

The administrator can control whether the users can change profile settings (that is, the appearance of the desktop, automatic network connections, etc.). An administrator can also use profiles to require that a mandatory desktop configuration be loaded each time a user logs on.

A local profile is created by default when a workstation user account is created. User profiles are not needed when only one person uses the computer, or when a custom desktop adds no value. If user profiles are not enabled, the logon process is shortened slightly, because the system does not need to locate and load the profile.

To use the User Profile Editor, a Windows NT Server must be available.

Remote Administration

To administer a computer's Registry from a remote computer, you must join a Windows NT Domain and log on with an account that is part of a Domain Admins group. Remote administration capabilities allow you to conduct a variety of tasks remotely over the network. These include administering the file system, sharing or restricting directories, and querying and making changes to the Registry.

Only members of the Domain Admins Group can use the Remote Registry service of Windows NT Workstation 4.0.

Peer Resource Sharing Services

Peer resource sharing services allow a client computer to share files and resources such as printers and CD-ROM drives with other computers. Peer resource sharing can reduce the traffic and disk space required on central servers by leveraging the power of individual computers. If users are allowed to share local resources on their computers, then peer resource sharing can save network traffic and hard disk space on the server. Remember, however, that Windows NT Workstation has a limit of 10 possible inbound connections to other client computers.

Whether to use peer resource sharing services depends on your site's security needs. For central control, or to prevent users from turning on this feature, use the User Rights Policy Editor.

Security for peer resource sharing services takes the form of user-level security based on the user accounts on a Windows NT Server or NetWare network. If you don't have servers to provide security validation or don't want to use user-level security, you can use share-level security, with each user implementing security and a password scheme on the local computer. Share-level security is set on a directory-by-directory basis.

A Microsoft Windows NT Client Access License is required if the computer will be connecting to servers running Windows NT Server. For information on client access licenses, contact your Microsoft reseller.

If you want, you can maintain centralized control. You can prevent users from turning on peer-to-peer networking. To do so, use the following procedure to disable peer resource sharing.

► **To disable peer resource sharing**

1. On the Windows NT Server, start the User Rights Policy Editor in the User Manager for Domains Utility.
2. Select the Show Advanced User Rights checkbox.
3. Select Create Permanent Shared Objects.
4. Remove any groups from the Grant To box.
5. Click OK.

Windows Messaging

The new Windows Messaging feature in Windows NT Workstation 4.0 manages all messaging information in one place, with a single inbox for electronic mail and other messages. In addition, Windows NT Workstation 4.0 comes with a complete small-business mail system—that is, a mail client and a post office—which allows users to exchange electronic mail through a single post office. This mail client integrates well with Microsoft Mail servers, and the post office can be upgraded to provide an enterprise-wide mail system.

You can also use a variety of other mail or messaging systems through Windows Messaging, as long as they use a MAPI 1.0 driver. If you have an existing mail system that doesn't use a MAPI 1.0 driver, you can continue to use that mail system without running the Windows Messaging capability.

Separate Memory Spaces for 16-Bit Applications

Windows NT Workstation allows you to run all 16-bit applications in Multiple Virtual DOS Machines (MVDMs). This ensures that an error in one application will not affect other applications, or bring down the entire operating system.

For compatibility issues, some older applications may need to run in shared memory spaces. Test your older line of business applications against MVDMs to decide whether to keep this feature in your ideal client configuration.

Set Up the Test Lab

Using the preferred client configuration specified in the previous phase, proceed with installing the configuration in the lab for testing and evaluation. Because only the client-computer configuration is being installed, this test only determines whether the preferred configuration performs as expected. If you are upgrading an existing network, determine whether the preferred configuration is compatible with your current line-of-business applications and processes.

Depending on how the test installation proceeds, it may be necessary to modify the configuration, by either adding or removing selected features. If more than one configuration is being considered, side-by-side evaluations of different configurations can be performed to help determine which one works best.

This phase in the deployment process involves four significant efforts:

- Preparing the test lab
- Installing Windows NT Workstation on a test computer
- Testing the preferred client configuration
- Restoring the system to test the restoration process

Prepare the Test Site and Equipment

In the space allotted for the test lab, the installation team should perform the following tasks:

1. Make sure the test computer meets your organization's standards and the Windows NT Workstation 4.0 minimum standards for operation: a 486 or higher processor with 12 MB RAM and 90 MB of free disk space. If not, perform the hardware upgrades now.
2. Defragment the hard disk and scan it for viruses.
3. Back up and verify key data and configuration files, such as INI, Autoexec.bat, and Config.sys files. Also back up the Windows and DOS directories, and all files in the root directory. Make a system startup disk containing Command.com, Sys.com, and Fdisk.exe.

Install Windows NT Workstation on Test Computers

Once the test computers are in place and have been prepared for the installation of Windows NT Workstation, the installation team should proceed with the following steps:

1. Make sure that the current network client software and connections are functioning properly. Working from a checklist of inventoried applications, make sure that all important applications operate correctly on the test computers before installing Windows NT Workstation.
2. Install Windows NT Workstation on one or more test computers, following the directions in the product documentation and using the preferred client configuration identified in the previous phase.

Test the Preferred Configuration

After you've set up your test computers with Windows NT Workstation 4.0, you'll need to run a variety of tests to make sure that the operating system runs correctly on your network and that you can still perform all of your usual tasks. The planning and installation teams should both be involved in this step.

Use your own testing methodology or test the following to verify correct system operation:

- Can you connect to and browse the network?
- Can you print both locally and across the network?
- Can you perform the core operations of each line of business application locally and on the network (including opening, closing, and printing)? Test all mission-critical applications for proper function.
- Can you shut down successfully?

If you have several test computers, compare your old client configuration from your previous operating system and your new preferred configuration running Windows NT Workstation 4.0. Compare the two in terms of the following:

- Functionality for administering the computer
- Performance for local disk/network/application actions
- Ease of use for performing common tasks
- Stability of the computer under stress
- Compatibility with applications and hardware

If the specified client configuration did not work as expected, modify and document the differences until a working preferred client configuration is installed. Try removing related features from the proposed configuration as a solution. Document any changes made to the original configuration.

If the preferred client configuration works as expected, you may also want to conduct additional testing of the optional software features and components in Windows NT Workstation 4.0. This can help you determine whether you are running Windows NT Workstation 4.0 optimally. For this kind of testing, conduct side-by-side evaluations on two computers, changing individual features on each one, to determine the following:

- Performance in terms of responsiveness and throughput
- Ease of use
- Stability
- Compatibility
- Functionality

Ensure that you have identified a configuration that meets the needs of all the different hardware configurations used in your organization. Note which options you want to predefine as entries for an answer file. The answer file can then be used to automate the installation process.

Test the Restoration Process

After thorough testing of the preferred client configuration, completely restore all test computers to the previous client configuration and document the process. The degree to which you need to test and restore the computer depends on the tools available.

1. Perform a complete restoration of operating system files and system capabilities for your old client configuration on the computer running Windows NT Workstation 4.0. If you need to automate the restoration, consider using a commercial backup program, instead of using File Manager or MS-DOS commands to copy files.
2. Evaluate the restoration process for problems. Document the process and the modifications made.
3. Have all members of the installation team participate in installing the preferred configuration on a variety of hardware.

Plan the Pilot Rollout

Once you have identified ideal client configurations for Windows NT Workstation, you will need to plan your pilot rollout. This will include planning and lab-testing work. This phase involves three major efforts:

- Deciding how to automate the installation
- Determining pilot rollout logistics
- Preparing the user training plan

Automating Installation

Automating the installation is a key step in reducing the cost of migration. The method of setup automation will depend upon the existing network infrastructure, the number and variety of computers to be upgraded, and the schedule for deployment, among other factors. Based on these criteria, the following options can help you smoothly deploy Windows NT Workstation:

- Use Setup Manager to create unattended answer files.

  By creating an unattended answer file with predetermined answers for installation questions, the installation process can run from start to finish with limited or no user intervention.

- Use management software such as Microsoft's Systems Management Server.

  Management software allows you to "push" the installation from the server, so that you can install Windows NT Workstation 4.0 on an individual personal computer without ever touching the computer. This allows a small Installation team to deploy Windows NT Workstation to a large number of computers in a short period of time. In addition, this method requires little or no work on the part of the end users, allowing them to stay focused on productive work for the organization. Relieving the end users of the installation task also eliminates a potential source of installation errors.

  This method is only possible with a system management program such as Microsoft Systems Management Server. If you plan to use system management software in automating the installation, make sure this has been acquired and tested.

  Since you can use Systems Management Server to gather the detailed information about the resources already in use on your network, you might want to begin using it during the earliest stages of the deployment process. You can then use it later to simplify the pilot and final rollouts.

- Modify login scripts, or send embedded setup scripts in e-mail.

  You can automate the installation process by editing the login script for the user, or sending a link in electronic mail to a batch file that runs Windows NT Workstation 4.0 Setup. In these cases, the user only needs to log on or double-click an icon to start the installation.

- Use the Sysdiff utility.

  The Sysdiff utility allows you to record the variations between a standard retail installation of Windows NT Workstation and a customized version. If the difference file created by Sysdiff is available during setup, the Setup program applies the differences automatically.

  Use Sysdiff to include applications in your customized installation of Windows NT Workstation. The Sysdiff utility is discussed in Chapter 2, "Customizing Setup."

- Use third-party solutions (including OEM pre-installation).

  Your organization may choose a third party solution for deploying Windows NT Workstation. These include custom solutions made available through a Microsoft Solution Provider, or pre-installation of the operating system by an Original Equipment Manufacturer.

Unattended Answer Files for Windows NT Workstation 4.0 Setup

Unattended answer files allow you to predefine responses to prompts that appear during Windows NT Workstation 4.0 Setup. If you need to conduct a similar installation more than five times, this is a good option. Begin planning for unattended installations while you are specifying the preferred client configuration. Make sure that you document each feature needed, so that you can automate the selection of these features. The chapters that follow provide detailed information on using unattended mode setup to deploy Windows NT Workstation, with or without an existing client-server network. Answer files are discussed in Chapter 2, "Customizing Setup."

"Push" Installations for Windows NT Workstation 4.0 Setup

You need to understand and plan in advance how the push installation process will work for a given computer. There are several alternatives for remotely initiating the installation, ranging from the use of a system management program to sending a setup script as an embedded link in electronic mail. You will want to consider how to push the installation for each computer and make sure that the client computers are configured to support this process.

For organizations with 50 or more computers, being physically present to install each client computer is not cost effective. An administrative software solution such as Microsoft's Systems Management Server can save you money and increase productivity. When using administrative software tools, additional client-side software may be needed. Be sure to include this software in the installation plan.

For more information, see Chapter 3, "Deploying Windows NT Workstation on an Existing Client-Server Network."

Test the Rollout

Test the deployment method you choose in the lab before performing the pilot rollout. This will help you compose a complete checklist to use during rollout and will help you identify potential problems. To perform the test, the planning and installation teams will need to perform the following steps:

1. Install Windows NT Workstation 4.0 source files on a distribution server. This can be a dedicated server in the lab, or one of the servers used in daily operations in your organization. Make setup choices based on your preferred client configuration tested in the lab.
2. Create and test an automated installation by creating an unattended answer file, using Setup Manager, to predefine answers for Setup. Document the key parts of the setup file that vary depending on which computers are receiving the installation.
3. Determine and test how you will deploy Windows NT Workstation from the server, without having to touch the client computers. Your options include the following:
    - Use management software such as Microsoft Systems Management Server.
    - For smaller LANs, use Unattended Setup in conjunction with Setup Manager.
    - Modify the login scripts on the server.
    - Send a setup script (batch file) that runs Windows NT Workstation 4.0.
    - Send Setup as an embedded link in an electronic mail message.
4. Install Windows NT Workstation on one or more computers in the lab, using the files on the distribution server and your chosen method of deployment.
5. Document the process for the rest of the installation team.

Determine Pilot Rollout Logistics

Although it is a test, the first pilot rollout sets the tone and presents an example of the final rollout. You need to be completely prepared for all aspects of the rollout. This requires that you determine the time it will take for installation, the personnel and tools needed to facilitate the process, and the overall schedule.

The installation and planning teams should create a checklist for the pilot rollout. The checklist should cover, in detail, the following general topics:

- Who will perform the deployment?

  In addition to the installation team members, be sure to assign a system administrator with full rights on the server, including the right to administer mail or database server passwords.

- Who are the pilot users?

  Choose a pilot user group or department that is willing and able to accommodate the rollout. This group, ranging from 15 to 50 persons, should be representative of your overall user base. Try not to select a department that is attempting to meet a schedule deadline during the rollout, or a group that is traditionally slow in adopting new technology.

- What installation process will be used? Does the deployment methodology meet automation goals?
- What new software or tools must be purchased, and on what schedule?
- Has a verified backup been performed for each of the target computers?
- Have passwords been reset for CMOS, the network, and applications?
- Have virus checking and disk defragmentation been performed?
- What is the schedule for pilot installations?

  When determining the installation time for the pilot rollout, base the projections on how long it takes for installation of an individual computer; remember to schedule the downtime for each user.

- How many systems will be installed per day?

  Start with a conservative estimate and then increase or decrease the number, based on your experiences with the initial installations.

- At what time of day should the installations occur?

  You may want to schedule installations to occur on weekdays after normal business hours or on weekends.

As you develop the checklist of logistics, consider your goals for the pilot rollout and the factors that define its success. For example, you might set a percentage for successful upgrades or for automated installations that, if achieved, would indicate that the rollout had been successful. Or you might set a threshold of end-user downtime. If downtime stays below this threshold, another indicator of success has been met. Document these goals and criteria, so that teams can monitor performance against them during the rollout.

Develop User Training

The steps in developing a training plan include acquiring a training lab, setting up computers in the lab, and appointing a team member as instructor. (If in-house resources are not available, use a vendor to develop and conduct the training.) The instructor will be responsible for creating and testing the training program.

There are a number of training approaches and a variety of tools you can use. The materials provided by Microsoft Authorized Technical Education Centers (ATECs) are a good place to start.

A recommended approach is to divide the training into sessions corresponding to three distinct topics: The Basics, Corporate-Specific Applications, and Customization.

The "Basics" session includes the top ten functions any user needs to know to accomplish daily work, such as the following:

Function	To do the function, use this
Run programs, load documents, find a file	Start button
Change settings	Control Panel
Get help on a specific topic	F1 or Help command
Switch between applications	Taskbar
Minimize, maximize, and close windows	Window buttons
Browse your hard disk	My Computer and Windows Explorer
Connect to a network drive	Network Neighborhood
Print a document	Point and Print

The Windows NT Workstation 4.0 online Help files and the System Guide included with the product provide the information you need to train users in the basics. Schedule training sessions of no more than 30 minutes each; in each session, users receive information that is *sufficient to be productive* using Windows NT Workstation 4.0.

The "Corporate-Specific Applications" session varies according to your network environment and the types of applications that are run on your network. This session should focus on the top five to ten functions that will change because of the upgrade to Windows NT Workstation 4.0.

The "Customization" session is intended for more experienced users. The purpose of this session is to provide information and guidance that will help these users learn on their own after the training, and teach them how to work more productively with Windows NT Workstation 4.0. Some of these topics could include:

- Adding items to the Start button
- Adding items to the desktop (move, copy, shortcut)
- Using options controlled by the right mouse button
- Adding a new device (for example, a printer)
- Changing the desktop (for example, screen saver settings)

After creating and testing the program, schedule training sessions to occur immediately before the rollout so that the users will retain most of what they learn by putting it to use right away.

Develop the Support Plan

The support plan must be ready the first day you begin performing Windows NT Workstation 4.0 installations. Because the quality of support available during the pilot rollout will be seen as an indicator of the quality of the rollout as a whole, it is important that you plan carefully to make sure effective support is available.

Staff the support team for your pilot rollout with some of your best technicians, and dedicate their time solely to the pilot group for the first few weeks. The assigned technicians should carry pagers or be available by phone at all times, to give immediate assistance to users. Make sure the users have the names and phone numbers of persons to contact for assistance, as well as a short list of the top questions and answers, and troubleshooting tips.

To help your users help themselves, edit Windows NT Workstation 4.0 Help with organization-specific information on applications or features they will be using with Windows NT Workstation. Doing so requires placing an Oem.cnt file and your custom help file in the user's Windows directory. For information about Oem.cnt and the format of Windows NT Workstation 4.0 help files, see the *Win32 Software Development Kit for Windows 95 and Windows NT*.

Notify Users of the Rollout

Another step at this stage is informing users about the pilot rollout plan. You can use a videotape presentation, an interoffice memo, informal lunch seminars, or an organization-wide meeting as the means for communicating with users about the rollout. Regardless of the form used, the message must explain to users the benefits of moving to Windows NT Workstation 4.0, and describe the overall plan and process by which each group or department will make the move. This makes it easier for your users to plan for and accept the migration to Windows NT Workstation 4.0 as part of their schedules.

Conduct the Pilot Rollout

The schedule for the pilot rollout should simulate—on a smaller scale—the schedule of the final rollout. In this phase you test the capabilities and performance of the system and gather feedback from the users affected by the pilot deployment.

As you conduct the pilot rollout, you may find that certain tasks take more or less time than expected, that some tasks need to be added, or that some tasks can be left out. Be prepared to modify the pilot rollout schedule to account for such changes, and use the pilot schedule for projecting the final rollout timetable.

The following is a summary of the tasks involved in conducting the pilot rollout:

1. Select a pilot user group that is willing and able (particularly in terms of their workload) to handle the installation process. Typically, "power users" provide the ideal target groups for the pilot rollout.
2. Train the users.
3. Back up the Windows and DOS directories and the files on the root directory of the target computers.
4. Following the logistics checklist prepared in the previous phase, perform the installation in the same manner that you expect to install Windows NT Workstation 4.0 throughout the organization. Compare your results against goals and evaluation criteria (developed in the previous task) for this process.
5. Have your technicians on-site for the initial installations, to document the process and problems and to support the users. Have other technicians monitor time and all measurable factors in the installation process. The measurable factors might include the number of attempted installations, the number of successful installations, the elapsed time for each installation (user downtime), and the number of support calls regarding installation. Record these measurements for later evaluation.

6. Make sure that all computers are "up and running" as expected. Make note of possible improvements to the installation, training, or support, where appropriate.
7. Survey members of the pilot user group about their satisfaction with the installation process and take feedback on what could have been done better.
8. Continue to monitor the pilot installation for a week to make sure that everything continues to run smoothly.
9. Prepare a checklist of issues to resolve for the final rollout. Include in this checklist the areas identified in Step 6 as needing improvement, along with comments from the user survey, and the results of comparing your rollout goals and evaluation criteria against actual performance.
10. If the pilot program did not run smoothly or user feedback was poor, conduct additional pilot installations until the process works well.

Test Performance and Capabilities

In addition to the technicians responsible for conducting the pilot installation, extra technicians should be assigned to measure, observe, and test the installation. As this information is gathered and analyzed, areas for improvement or automation become apparent. Consequently, these extra technicians help ensure the success of both the pilot and final rollouts by making the installation more efficient. In addition, after Windows NT Workstation 4.0 is installed, these technicians can test system capabilities, such as remote administration, for proper operation.

Make sure that all computers are "up and running" as expected. Make note of possible improvements to the installation, training, or support, where appropriate. Monitor the client computers for performance, stability, and functionality. Make sure the deployed installations match the lab configurations.

Continue to monitor the pilot installation for a week to make sure that everything continues to run smoothly.

Survey Users for Feedback

The final part of the pilot rollout involves surveying the users to gauge their satisfaction with the new installation, and to evaluate the level of training and support provided.

Survey members of the pilot user group about their satisfaction with the installation process and ask for their suggestions on what could have been done better. Test the users' proficiency by having them perform a few common tasks or ask them to use several of the new features in Windows NT Workstation 4.0—for example, have them register their survey results on the server.

When collected, combine the survey results with the ideas for improvements identified by the planning and installation teams during the pilot rollout. Use this information to prepare a checklist of open issues that must be resolved prior to the final rollout. Then assign to individual team members the actions for solving problems or making improvements. Indicate on the checklist how and when each item was resolved, adjusting the deployment plan if appropriate.

If the pilot program did not run smoothly or if user feedback was poor, conduct additional pilot installations until the process works well.

Finalize the Rollout Plan

The results of the pilot installation provide the basis for developing a final plan for rollout. Using the actual time and resource requirements from the smaller-scale pilot rollout, the installation, training, and support teams can make projections for time and resources, scaled to the organization-wide scope of the final rollout. If additional resources are required, identify these and acquire them at this time. Also, create a template for a central database in which the configuration and uses of each computer on the network can be tracked.

This is a good time to update organization policies and standards regarding computer and network use, to accommodate Windows NT Workstation 4.0.

Complete the Rollout Logistics and Budget

The executive and planning teams now have the information to schedule the final rollout. The planning team can then budget the resources, in terms of personnel and tools, required to meet these goals.

To do this, estimate the number of computers involved in the final deployment, and the time it will require. List the resources needed to complete the process within the stated timeframe. You may need to hire and train additional Installation team members, or purchase additional software or tools.

The executive team might propose a formal budget for the organization-wide implementation, and present it to management for approval. The budget should include the costs for personnel and resources such as system management software.

After obtaining any necessary approval, purchase the resources required for deployment. If you need additional staff, be sure to hire experienced and qualified individuals for the team, and train them extensively before getting started.

Update the Policies and Practices Guidelines

Prior to final rollout, update organization policies regarding the use of the network and computers by employees. Include items such as password length and expiration requirements, and the level of approval needed to obtain remote dial-up privileges.

Update the corporate standards lists for hardware and software usage, and bring all computers into compliance with the updated list prior to deployment. Use the Windows NT 4.0 Hardware Compatibility List (HCL) to update your organization's hardware requirements. The HCL is updated regularly, and is available on the Microsoft web site at **http://www.microsoft.com**.

Tell the users the new standards. Make sure they know that these standards will be enforced prior to the installation, and that they must bring their computers into compliance.

Create a Template for the Rollout Database

Use a central database to track the progress of each computer involved in the deployment, and to document any areas requiring further action.

If you are using Systems Management Server for the deployment, the status of each computer involved in the deployment is automatically maintained in an SQL database. Information from this database can be incorporated into reports or other databases as needed.

If you are not using Systems Management Server for the deployment, create a template for the database before the full deployment. Populate the database with configuration information for every computer and user in the organization, and place the template on the server.

During final deployment, the installation team compiles the data for each computer and user, indicating whether any additional work is needed. The team can then use the template to track open items following the rollout, and to measure actual progress against original objectives.

Roll Out Windows NT Workstation 4.0

After the extensive research, planning, testing, and analysis performed in the previous phases, the deployment teams arrive at the final phase—rolling out the Windows NT Workstation 4.0 installation to the entire organization. Although each prior phase was critical to the overall success of the deployment process, only this phase can fulfill the purpose of the entire planning process, by delivering the substantial new benefits of Windows NT Workstation 4.0 to your broadest base of users. At this phase, weeks of preparation pay off in a smooth migration of all your users to an operating system that is more powerful, more robust, and easier to use.

The steps involved in the final deployment are essentially the same as those for the pilot deployment. Briefly, they are as follows:

1. Set up the distribution servers. (Or use the distribution servers from the pilot rollout.)
2. Customize the server installation. (Or use the files from the pilot rollout.)
3. Notify the users of the upcoming installation.
4. Train the users on Windows NT Workstation 4.0.
5. If needed, upgrade the hardware on the client computers, and remove any software not complying with the organization policy.
6. If needed, back up critical data and configuration files on the client computers.
7. If needed, defragment the client hard disks.
8. Optionally, temporarily reset the user password and ID for each computer. This allows technicians easy access to the client computer so they can make sure that the login scripts and environment operate correctly.
9. Make sure that the client computers are fully operational and the network is running.
10. Prepare for the installation process. Depending on your deployment method, this would involve one or more of the following:
    - Edit the login scripts.
    - Run the queries and send the package files in the management software.
    - Send the setup script, by electronic mail, to the user.
11. Initiate the deployment by the means appropriate to your method of deployment. For example, have the users log on, or leave their computers on, at the end of the business day for an overnight installation.

Troubleshooting Problems With Logon Scripts

Use this list to troubleshoot the most common problems with logon scripts:

- Make sure the logon script is in the directory specified in the Server option of Control Panel. When Windows NT is installed, the logon script directory is as follows:

  ```
  systemroot\system32\repl\import\scripts
  ```

  The only valid path option is a subdirectory of the default logon script directory. If the path is any other directory or it uses the environment variable **%homepath%**, the logon script fails.

- If the logon script is on an NTFS partition, make sure the user has Read permission for the logon script directory. If no permissions have been explicitly assigned, the logon script might fail without providing an error message.
- Make sure the logon script has a filename extension of either .cmd or .bat. The .exe extension is also supported, but only for genuine executable programs. If you use a nondefault file extension for your processor, be sure to specify it with the filename of the logon script.

  Attempting to use the .exe extension for a script file results in the following error message:

  ```
  NTVDM CPU has encountered an illegal instruction.
  ```

  If this error message appears, close the window in which the logon script is running.

- If the logon script is to run on a Windows for Workgroups computer, make sure the Windows NT domain name is specified as a startup option in the Network option of Control Panel.
- Make sure any new or modified logon scripts have been replicated to all domain controllers. Replication of logon scripts happens periodically, not immediately. To manually force replication, use Server Manager. See the Server Manager chapter of the *Windows NT Server System Guide* for detailed information.

CHAPTER 2

Customizing Setup

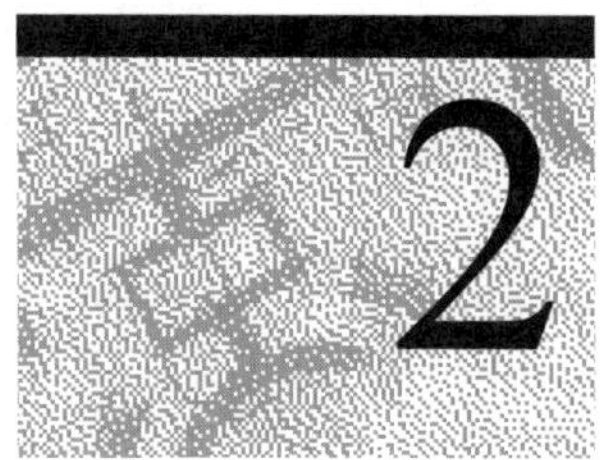

You can customize the installation of Windows NT Workstation that you distribute to your users. Customization can be as simple as specifying which features in the retail product you want to use. Or, you can include applications or additional files, such as corporate-specific help files, along with the installation of Windows NT Workstation. You can even tailor the customized setup so that different computers get different configurations. And with Unattended Setup, you can supply answers to all the prompts the user would normally need to respond to during setup. Even the computername and username for each computer can be supplied via Unattended Setup.

This chapter is loosely organized according to the features you will most likely need to implement, and the order in which you would perform the tasks. It does not parallel the order of the setup process.

Overview of the Setup Process

The key to deploying Windows NT Workstation is the **winnt** or **winnt32** command. These commands use a network connection to access the installation files, which are in one central location. This central location is called the distribution sharepoint. The **winnt** command is used to install Windows NT Workstation on a computer currently running a 16-bit Windows operating system, such as Windows 3.1 or Windows for Workgroups 3.1, MS-DOS, or Windows 95. The **winnt32** command is used to upgrade from an earlier version of Windows NT Workstation. Either of these commands can be issued directly from the keyboard, or as a line in a .bat file, or via Systems Management Server.

When you use the **winnt** or **winnt32** command, all the files needed to complete the installation are copied over the network to a temporary directory. Then Setup continues as it would if you were performing the installation from a local drive, going through first text mode setup, and then GUI mode setup.

In text mode setup, all the files required for installation are copied from the temporary directory into the installation directory on the hard disk of the target computer. After text mode setup is complete, GUI mode begins. In GUI mode, the user is presented with a Graphical User Interface (GUI), and is prompted for information used to customize the setup. For example, the user may be given the opportunity to choose components to install. During GUI mode Setup, computer-specific information such as the computername and username are supplied.

The winnt and winnt32 Commands

Before using the **winnt** or **winnt32** command, there must be a network connection between the computer being upgraded (the destination computer) and the distribution sharepoint. If the destination computer is already using networking software, the connection can be made in the usual way. If the computer is not yet running networking software, you can use a Network Installation Startup Disk to start the computer and make the network connection. See "Network Installation Startup Disks," later in this chapter, for information on creating and using a Network Installation Startup Disk.

The **winnt** or **winnt32** command is run from the destination computer. The command can be issued in any of the following ways:

- Typed from the keyboard
- Run from a batch file
- Included in the Network Installation Startup Disk
- Issued via Systems Management Server

The syntax of the **winnt** command is as follows:

```
winnt [/s:sourcepath] [/i:inf_file] [/t:drive_letter] [/x] [/b] [/o[x]]
[/u:answer_file] [/udf:id, [UDF_file]]
```

The syntax of the **winnt32** command is as follows:

```
winnt32 [/s:sourcepath] [/i:inf_file] [/t:drive_letter] [/x] [/b]
[/o[x]] [/u:answer_file] [/udf:id, [UDF_file]]
```

where:

/s:*sourcepath*
: Specifies the location of the Windows NT files.

/i:*inf_file*
: Specifies the filename (no path) of the setup information file. The default is DOSNET.INF.

/t:*drive_letter*
: Forces Setup to place temporary files on the specified drive.

/x

Prevents Setup from creating Setup boot floppies. Use this when you already have Setup boot floppies (from your administrator, for example).

/b

Causes the boot files to be loaded on the system's hard drive rather than on floppy disks, so that floppy disks do not need to be loaded or removed by the user.

/o

Specifies that Setup only create boot floppies.

/ox

Specifies that Setup create boot floppies for CD-ROM or floppy-based installation.

/u:*answer_file*

Specifies the location of an answer file that provides answers the user would otherwise be prompted for during Setup.

/udf:*id* [,*UDF_file*]

Specifies the identifier that is to be used by the Setup program to apply sections of the UDF_file in place of the same section in the answer file. If no UDF is specified, the Setup program will prompt the user to insert a disk that contains a file called $UNIQUE$.UDF. If a UDF is specified, Setup will look for the identifier in that file.

Computers running an earlier version of Windows NT Workstation can upgrade to Windows NT Workstation 4.0 using the **winnt32** command. These computers do not need a Network Installation Startup Disk, because they can connect to the network using the built-in networking features of Windows NT Workstation. The options for **winnt32** are the same as those for **winnt**.

Note If you are using **winnt** to install Windows NT Workstation, and you want convert to the NTFS file system, you must do the conversion as a separate step, after installing Windows NT Workstation.

After Windows NT Workstation is installed, restart the computer and use the command **convert /fs:ntfs** to change the file system.

Options for Customizing Setup

The tools for customizing setup include the following:

- Answer files (Unattend.txt)
- Uniqueness Database Files (UDFs)
- The OEM directory and its subdirectories
- The OEM\$$ directory, added to your distribution sharepoint and referenced from the OEM\Cmdlines.txt file
- The **sysdiff** utility

Answer Files (Unattend.txt)

Answer files are text files that provide the answers to some or all of the prompts that the end user would otherwise need to respond to during Setup. The answer file is specified with the **/u** option to the **winnt** or **winnt32** command.

The simplest way to use this feature is to specify in the answer file those features of the Windows NT Workstation retail product that you want to include in the installation. However, you can also use the answer file to display company information during GUI-mode setup, to specify a keyboard layout, to join a domain or workgroup, and to install device drivers, protocols, or network adapters.

A sample answer file, Unatttend.txt, is included on the Windows NT Workstation 4.0 product CD. Using this file as a template, you can create one or more answer files to customize your installation of Windows NT Workstation. For a general discussion of answer files see "Answer Files (Unattend.txt)," later in this chapter. See Appendix A, "Answer Files and UDFs," for a discussion of the sections and syntax you can use in your answer files.

Note The options available in Unattend.txt have changed since earlier versions of Windows NT Workstation.

Uniqueness Database Files (UDFs)

Uniqueness Database Files (UDFs) are an extension of the answer file functionality. A UDF has a structure similar to that of an answer file. However, the UDF begins with an additional section in which uniqueness IDs are specified and mapped to sections in the UDF. If a uniqueness ID is specified in the **winnt** or **winnt32** command, any values specified in the sections associated with that uniqueness ID override the values in the sections in the answer file that have the same section names.

One UDF can have numerous uniqueness IDs, and each uniqueness ID can specify a slightly different configuration. For example, you can have a uniqueness ID for each computer in your organization, with a different computername for each uniqueness ID— all in one UDF.

The OEM Directory

To install components, files, or applications that are not included with the Windows NT Workstation retail product, the required files must be added to subdirectories of the OEM directory on the distribution sharepoint.

Place hardware-dependent files that are loaded during text mode setup in subdirectories of OEM\Textmode. Create one directory for each device.

Place files that replace or supplement the system files included with the retail product in subdirectories of OEM\$$.

Place files for network components, such as protocols, adapters, or network services, in subdirectories of OEM\Net. Create one directory for each component.

Place files for applications that support a scripted (silent) installation, and any other files you want to copy to the destination computers, in subdirectories of OEM*drive_letter*, where *drive_letter* is the drive on the destination computer in which the application is to be installed. For example, if you want Microsoft Office to be installed on drive C of the destination computers, you would put the installation files in OEM\C\MSOffice.

To include in your installation of Windows NT Workstation applications that must be installed interactively, use **sysdiff**.

About Sysdiff

To pre-install applications that do not support a scripted installation, you must use **sysdiff**. You can also use **sysdiff** to install other applications.

To use **sysdiff**, first create a snapsho*t* of a reference system. Then install the applications you want to distribute. After you've installed the applications, create a difference file. The information in the difference file includes all the binary files for the applications, as well as the initialization file settings and registry settings for the applications.

A command in the OEM\Cmdlines.txt file is used to apply the difference file to new installations of Windows NT Workstation. Or, the difference file can be applied to a computer that is already running Windows NT Workstation 4.0 by issuing the same command from the command line.

Because the difference file includes all the files and all the initialization and registry settings for the applications, it can be a very large package, depending on the number and complexity of the applications you have added. Applying such a large package can increase the time required for setup considerably. As an alternative, you can create an information file (INF) from the difference file, which contains only registry and initialization file directives. The command that creates the INF also creates a directory tree within the OEM directory structure, that contains all the files contained in the difference file package. These files are then copied along with other files required by setup during the early phases of setup, and are in place when the INF is invoked from the OEM\Cmdlines.txt file.

Adding Applications

You can install any number of applications along with Windows NT Workstation, using the procedure that follows.

▶ **To use unattended setup to distribute applications with the Windows NT Workstation installation**

1. If any of the applications you want to preinstall require an interactive installation, prepare the snapshot and difference files, and optionally an INF file generated from the difference file, as described under "Using Sysdiff," later in this chapter. Install the applications after creating the snapshot file and before creating the difference file. Place the difference file (or, if you prefer, the INF file and directory structure generated from the difference file) on the distribution sharepoint.
2. For each application that has not been installed in step 1, create a subdirectory of the OEM\$$ directory on your distribution sharepoint. Copy all the installation files (including any directory structure) to this directory you have created.
3. Edit Unattend.txt, adding the line **OemPreinstall = Yes** to the **[Unattended]** section. The edited file is the answer file.
4. Add the installation commands to the OEM\cmdlines.txt file.
5. If you created a difference file as described in step one, add the **sysdiff /apply** command to the OEM\Cmdlines.txt file. This command is described under "Using Sysdiff," later in this chapter. Or, if you generated an INF from the difference file, add the command to apply the INF to the OEM\Cmdlines.txt file.
6. Optionally, create a UDF to further customize the sections of the answer file for individuals or groups. The use and format of the UDF is discussed in the section, "Using Uniqueness Database Files" later in this chapter.
7. With all the required files in place on the distribution share, use the **winnt** or **winnt32** command at the destination computer to perform the installation. The **winnt** and **winnt32** commands are discussed earlier in this chapter, under "The winnt and winnt32 Commands."

Using Sysdiff

Sysdiff is used in several steps.

1. First, run **sysdiff /snap** to take a snapshot of the Windows NT retail version of the system after it has been installed on a reference computer. The reference computer needs to be of the same general hardware type (x86, MIPS, Alpha, or PowerPC) as the destination computers. The %systemroot% (for example, C:\Winnt) must be the same on the reference and destination computers.
2. Then, after the system has been customized by installing applications, run **sysdiff /diff** again to create the difference file.
3. Finally, run **sysdiff /apply** as part of an Unattended Setup to apply the difference file to a new installation. The **sysdiff /apply** command can also be run at any time after installation is complete.

   Alternately, run **sysdiff /inf** to create an INF and add the files included in the difference file to the OEM directory tree. Then invoke the INF with a command in the OEM\Cmdlines.txt file, or at any time after installation is complete.
4. Optionally, you can run **sysdiff /dump** to dump the difference file information in a form that you can read. Use the **sysdiff /dump** command to review the contents of the difference file.

If you want to distribute computers or hard disks that are ready for GUI-mode setup, use the **winnt /u** or **winnt32 /u** command to install your customized version of Windows NT Workstation, including the difference file — but stop the process after text mode Setup is complete by turning off the computer. Then duplicate the hard disk, using the **xcopy** command. The duplicated disks will include all the information copied during text mode, including the contents of the OEM directory and its subdirectories. These directories will be deleted, along with other temporary directories used by Setup, after GUI mode setup is completed. GUI mode setup proceeds the first time the computer is turned on.

The sysdiff process is shown in the following illustrations (Figures 2.1 and 2.2).

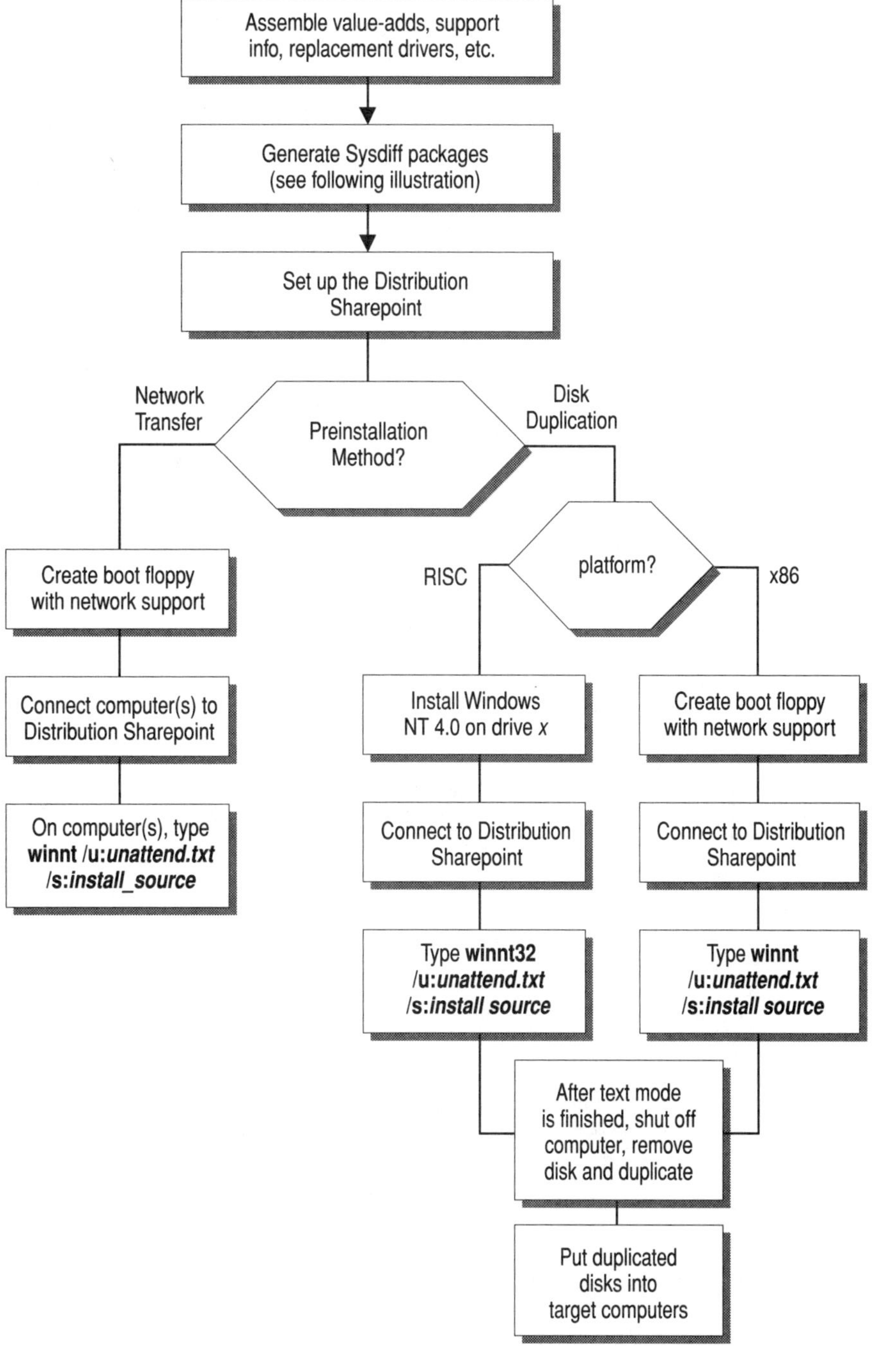

Figure 2.1 Pre-installation using sysdiff

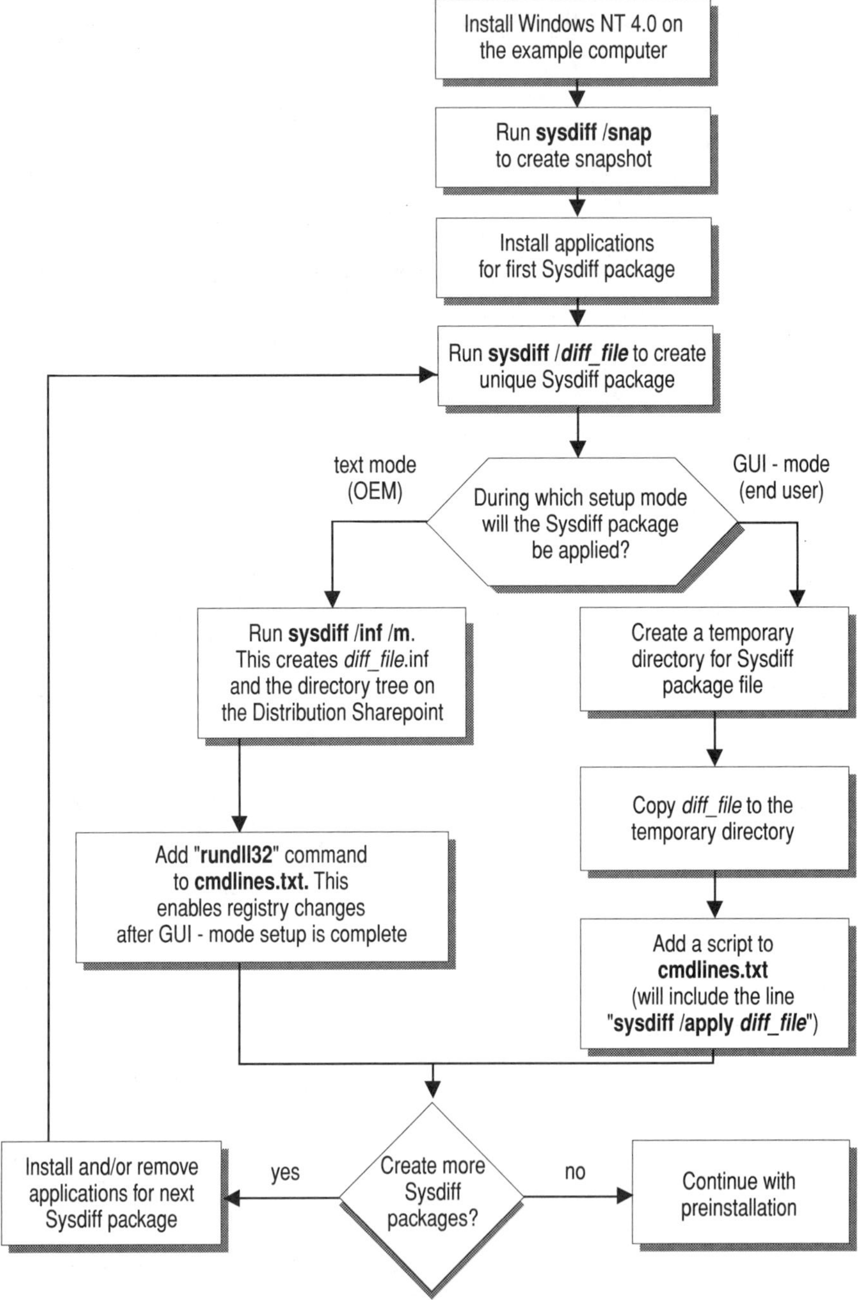

Figure 2.2 Creating and applying a sysdiff package

▶ **To create the snapshot file**

1. Install the retail version of Windows NT Workstation or Windows NT Server on a computer of the same general type (x86, Alpha, MIPS, or PowerPC) as the destination computers.
2. At the command prompt, type the following command:

```
sysdiff /snap [/log:log_file] snapshot_file
```

where:

log_file
: is the name of an optional log file created by **sysdiff**.

snapshot_file
: is the name of the file containing the snapshot of the system. Specify any valid Win32-based filename.

▶ **To create the difference file**

1. After the snapshot file has been created, install the applications that you want to include in the distributed version of the system.
2. At the command prompt, type the following command:

```
sysdiff /diff [/c:title] [/log:log_file] snapshot_file
difference_file
```

where:

/c:*title*
: specifies a title for the difference package

log_file
: is the name of an optional log file created by **sysdiff**.

snapshot_file
: is the name of the file containing the snapshot of the system. This file must be created from the same installation as you modified in step one. If you use a file created on another computer or from another installation, **sysdiff** will fail.

difference_file
: is the name of the file containing the differences between the system as it existed when the snapshot file was created and the system as it currently exists. Specify any valid Win32®-based filename.

▶ To apply the difference file

1. Place the difference file in a subdirectory of the OEM\$$ directory.
2. Add the following command to the OEM\Cmdlines.txt file:

```
sysdiff /apply /m [/log:log_file ] difference_file
```

where:

/m
: causes the file changes in the per-user profile structure to be mapped to the Default User profile structure, rather than to the profile structure for the user logged on when the difference file was created.

For example, if you were logged on as Administrator when you installed the applications to be included in the difference file, then the .lnk files and other user profile files would be created in the %WinDir%\Profiles\Administrator directory (where %WinDir%\ is the value of the %USERPROFILE% environment variable). But this directory does not yet exist when the files are copied during GUI-mode setup. For a preinstallation, these files should be placed into %WinDir%\Profiles\Default User instead of %WinDir%\Profiles\Administrator. By using the **/m** switch to place the files in the Default User profile structure, you ensure that the applications are available to all users when they first log in.

log_file
: is the name of a log file to which **sysdiff** writes information describing its actions. This parameter is optional.

difference_file
: specifies a file generated by an earlier invocation of **sysdiff /diff**. The %SystemRoot% must be the same as it was on the system that was used to generate the original *difference_file*. For example, if a difference file was generated on a Windows NT Workstation installation in C:\Winnt, then that difference file can be applied on other computers only if those computers are running Windows NT installed in C:\Winnt.

Note You can also run the **sysdiff /apply** command from the command line. For example, you can use this command to apply a difference file that contains applications to an existing installation of Windows NT Workstation 4.0.

▶ To create an INF

Run the following command:

```
SYSDIFF /inf /m [/u] sysdiff_file oem_root
```

where:

/m

causes the file changes in the per-user profile structure to be mapped to the Default User profile structure, rather than to the profile structure for the user logged on when the difference file was created.

For example, if you were logged on as Administrator when you installed the applications to be included in the difference file, then the .lnk files and other user profile files would be created in the %WinDir%\Profiles\Administrator directory (where %WinDir%\ is the value of the %USERPROFILE% environment variable). But this directory does not yet exist when the files are copied during GUI-mode setup. For a preinstallation, these files should be placed into %WinDir%\Profiles\Default User instead of %WinDir%\Profiles\Administrator. By using the **/m** switch to place the files in the Default User profile structure, you ensure that the applications are available to all users when they first log in.

/u

specifies that the INF file be generated as a Unicode text file. By default, the file is generated using the system ANSI codepage.

sysdiff_file

is a Win32 path to a file that was created by sysdiff's difference mode.

oem_root

is the Win32 path of a directory. The OEM structure will be created in this directory, and the INF will be placed there with the name Instapp.inf.

The output of this command is a file with the name *dif_file*.inf, where *dif_file* is the name of the difference file (without the three character filename extension). If the difference filename is more than eight characters long, it will be truncated to eight characters. For example, if *sysdiff_file* was named Custom.dif, the INF created by the **sysdiff /inf** command will be Custom.inf. If *sysdiff_file* was named Marketing.dif, the INF created by the **sysdiff /inf** command will be Custom_m.inf.

Because the INF file is copied during text mode Setup, it should be placed in the OEM\Textmode directory and listed in the Txtsetup.oem file in that directory. On x86 machines, Txtsetup.oem and all files listed in it must also be listed in the [OEMBootFiles] section of the answer file.

▶ **To invoke the INF**

Add a line to OEM\Cmdlines.txt to invoke the INF you created from the sysdff difference file. The command is of the same form as you would use to invoke any Windows 95-style INF. The format is as follows:

```
"RUNDLL32 syssetup,SetupInfObjectInstallAction section 128 inf"
```

where:

Section
specifies the name of the section in the INF file.

Inf
specifies the name of the INF file. This should be specified as a relative path to avoid invoking Setup's default INF rules, which look for an unqualified filename in the system inf directory instead of the current directory. For example, specify **..\newtools.inf**, not just **newtools.inf**.

The command is always enclosed in double quotation marks.

▶ **To dump the contents of a difference file**

- Use the command,

```
sysdiff /dump difference_file dump_file
```

This creates a text file with the name specified in the dump_file parameter that contains information regarding the contents of the difference file.

Sysdiff.inf

When sysdiff is run, it looks for a file called Sysdiff.inf in the directory containing Sysdiff.exe. This file contains information used by sysdiff to exclude certain files and registry entries from snapshots or difference files. The Sysdiff.inf file can be customized, but you should use at least a basic Sysdiff.inf when performing the **sysdiff /snap** and **sysdiff /diff** commands. Otherwise, **sysdiff** will attempt to include such files as Pagefile.sys, which will almost certainly cause **sysdiff** to fail.

Example Sysdiff.inf File

The following is an example of a typical Sysdiff.inf file. It is heavily commented to serve as a guide if you choose to customize the file.

```
[Version]
;
; This section is required, as it identifies the file as
; a Win4-style INF. Just leave this section as-is.
;
Signature = $chicago$
```

```
;
; General notes for file/dir exclusion sections:
;
; *: refers to all drives.
; ?: refers to the drive with the system on it.
; :: is substituted with %systemroot%
;
; Lines that are not in valid format (such as those that
; don't start with *:\, ?:\, ::, or <x>:\) are ignored.
;

[ExcludeDrives]
;
; By default, all valid local hard drives are scanned from the root
during
; snapshots and diffs. This section can be used to exclude entire
drives.
; The first character on each line is the drive letter of a hard drive
to exclude.
;

[ExcludeDirectoryTrees]
;
; By default, all directories on a drive are scanned during
snapshots/diffs.
; This section allows entire directory trees to be excluded.
; Each line is a fully-qualified path of a tree to be excluded -- the
directory
; and all of its subtrees are excluded from the snapshot or diff.
;
*:\recycled
*:\recycler

[ExcludeSingleDirectories]
;
; Each line is a fully-qualified path of a directory to be
; excluded. The directory's subdirs are NOT excluded.
;
::\system32\config

[ExcludeFiles]
;
; By default, all files in all directories are included in
snapshots/diffs.
; This section allows exclusion of individual files.
; Each line is a fully-qualified path of a file to be excluded.
; If it does not start with x:\ then we assume it's a filename part
; for a file to be excluded whereever it is found.
;
*:\pagefile.sys
```

```
ntuser.dat
ntuser.dat.log

[IncludeFilesInDir]
;
; Each line in here is a fully qualified path of a directory
; whose files are all to be included in a diff (marked as
; added/changed). Use this if you want to include files in the diff
; that might not have actually been changed.
;

[ExcludeRegistryTrees]
;
; By default, all registry keys in HKEY_LOCAL_MACHINE\System,
; HKEY_LOCAL_MACHINE\Software, and HKEY_CURRENT_USER are scanned during
; snapshots and diffs. This section allows exclusion of entire registry
subkeys.
; Each line indicates a registry key and subkeys to be excluded.
; The first field is one of HKLM or HKCU
; The second field is the subkey, which must NOT start with a \.
;
HKLM,SYSTEM\ControlSet001
HKLM,SYSTEM\ControlSet002
HKLM,SYSTEM\ControlSet003
HKLM,SYSTEM\ControlSet004
HKLM,SYSTEM\ControlSet005
HKLM,SYSTEM\ControlSet006
HKLM,SYSTEM\ControlSet007
HKLM,SYSTEM\ControlSet008
HKLM,SYSTEM\ControlSet009

[ExcludeRegistryKeys]
;
; Each line indicates a single registry key to be excluded.
; Subkeys of this key are not excluded.
;
; The first field is one of HKLM or HKCU
; The second field is the subkey, which must NOT start with a \.
;
HKCU,Software\Microsoft\Windows\CurrentVersion\Explorer\RunMRU

[ExcludeRegistryValues]
;
; Each line indicates a registry value entry to be excluded.
;
; The first field is one of HKLM or HKCU.
; The second field is the subkey, which must NOT start with \.
; The third field is the value entry name.
;
```

Answer Files (Unattend.txt)

You can make unattended answer files for the various setup configurations used in your organization, and then customize them with UDFs as needed. For example, you can make one answer file for each geographic location, or for each division. To tailor the information to individual users, create a UDF with a section for each user or computer that specifies the user name and computer name. Each user can then receive a tailored installation by specifying both the answer file and the UDF in the **winnt** or **winnt32** command.

Answer files and UDFs are text files with specific section names and keys. For a description of these sections and keys, and the customizations you can perform through these files, see Appendix A, "Answer Files and UDFs."

If you are using Microsoft Systems Management Server (SMS) to manage computer resources in your organization, you can use package definition files (PDFs) to install or upgrade Windows NT. See the Microsoft Systems Management Server documentation for information on using PDFs to install operating systems.

Creating an Unattended Answer File

You can create one or more unattended answer files for your organization by editing a copy of the Unattend.txt included with the Windows NT Workstation 4.0 Resource Kit. Use any text editor to modify the file, and save the modified copy as a text file. The modified Unattend.txt can be given any legal filename.

The options available in answer files and UDFs are documented Appendix A, "Answer Files and UDFs."

Using Uniqueness Database Files

When you are deploying a complete, unattended installation of Windows NT Workstation to numerous computers, some of the information you need to supply via answer files (such as the computername) must be unique to each computer. With Windows NT Workstation 4.0, you can use a single answer file for the information that applies to all users, and one or more uniqueness database files (UDFs) to supply information that is specific to a single computer or a small group of computers.

Uniqueness database files (UDFs) are used to provide replacements for sections of the answer file, or supply additional sections. The replacement sections are specified in a text file similar to the answer file. This file is indexed via strings called uniqueness IDs.

The uniqueness database file is used to specify a set of sections that should be merged into the answer file at the start of GUI Setup. This merging takes place before any affected components actually read the internal representation of the answer file. Thus this entire mechanism is totally transparent.

For a discussion of the sections and keys used in answer files and UDFs, see Appendix A, "Answer Files and UDFs."

Creating the UDF

The first section of the UDF is the [UniqueIds] section. This section lists all uniqueness ids that are supported by this database. The left hand side is a uniqueness ID. The uniqueness ID can be any string but must not contain the star (*), space ( ), comma (,), or equals (=) character. The right hand side is a list of sections, each of which should match the name of a section in the answer file. The format is as follows:

```
[UniqueIds]
id1 = section1,section2
id2 = section1,section2
id3 = section1,section3,section4
```

For example, if you were using computernames for the uniqueness IDs, this section might look like this:

```
[UniqueIds]
janeayer = UserData,Unattended
emilybr = UserData,Unattended
jconrad = UserData,KeyboardDrivers, PointingDeviceDrivers
```

Following the [UniqueIds] section are the sections referenced in [UniqueIds]. These section names can take either of two forms: They can be exactly like the section name in the answer file (for example, [Unattended]); or, the section name can be preceded with the uniqueness ID and a colon (for example, [janeayer:UserData]). This allows you to create specialized replacement sections for each computer name.

If both a general section (such as [Unattended]) and an ID-specific section (such as [jconrad:Unattended]) are available, Setup will use the section for the uniqueness ID specified in the **winnt** or **winnt32** command line.

The sections in the UDF can contain any keys and values that the same-named sections could contain in the answer file. During setup, each key specified in a referenced section overrides the value for the same key in the answer file. Values are substituted as follows.

- If a key is specified in the answer file but not in the UDF section referenced by the uniqueness ID, the value specified in the answer file is used.
- If a key is specified in the UDF section referenced by the uniqueness ID, the value specified in the UDF is used.
- If a key is specified in the answer file, and it appears in the UDF section referenced by the uniqueness ID with no value to the right of the equals sign, the default value will be used. This is equivalent to commenting out the key in the answer file.
- If a key is specified in the UDF, but the value is left blank, no value will be used for that key. This might result in the user being prompted for the information.
- If a section or key is used in the UDF, but there is no section by that name in the answer file, the section will be created and used by Setup.
- If a section is referenced in the [UniqueIds] section but does not exist, the user will be prompted to insert a floppy with a valid uniqueness database on it.

Specifying a UDF During Installation

To specify a uniqueness ID during setup, the user must run the **winnt** or **winnt32** command with the following parameter:

```
/UDF:ID[,database_filename]
```

where:

ID
: is the uniqueness ID to use while installing Windows NT Workstation on this computer.

database_filename
: is the filename, including the full path, of the UDF.

If both the uniqueness ID and the filename of the UDF are specified, the UDF is copied to the local drive during text-mode Setup, and is used during GUI Setup without user intervention. The UDF can have any legal filename.

If only the uniqueness ID is specified on the **winnt** or **winnt32** command line, Setup requires a floppy disk with a UDF file named $Unique$.udf. This disk must be prepared by the administrator and made available to the user in advance. The user is prompted for this disk during GUI mode setup.

In either case, if the supplied UDF is corrupt or if Setup cannot locate the specified uniqueness ID in it, the user is prompted either to insert a floppy with the fixed UDF, or Cancel. If the user chooses Cancel, the values in the answer file will be used. These values might not be appropriate for the computer.

The OEM Directory and its Subdirectories

To install components, files, or applications that are not included with the Windows NT Workstation retail product, the required files must be added to subdirectories of the OEM directory on the distribution sharepoint.

The OEM directory includes the following subdirectories:

- OEM
- OEM\Textmode
- OEM\$$
- OEM\NET
- OEM*drive_letter*
- OEM*drive_letter*

The following sections discuss these directories and their uses.

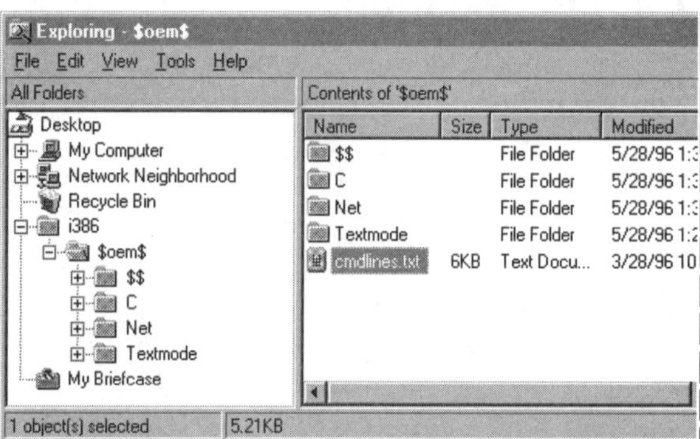

The OEM\Cmdlines.txt File

To install files located in the subdirectories of OEM, list the installation commands in a text file named Cmdlines.txt. Place the Cmdlines.txt file in the OEM directory of the distribution sharepoint. The syntax is as follows:

```
[Commands]
"command 1"
"command 2"
"command 3"
    .
    .
    .
```

Enter the entire command line, in double quotation marks. The following is an example of a Cmdlines.txt file with a single command:

```
[Commands]
"Rundll32 setupapi,InstallHinfSection sectionname 128 ..\newtool.inf"
```

The OEM\Textmode Directory

The OEM\Textmode directory contains all of the files that the Setup Loader needs to load, and that Text Mode Setup needs to copy to the target computer, so that the system can boot into GUI setup.

If you are installing SCSI, keyboard, video, or pointer device drivers, or HALs, that are not included with the Windows NT Workstation 4.0 retail version, this directory should also contain a standard Txtsetup.oem file. This file contains pointers to all the files required by the Setup Loader and Text Mode Setup to load and install these components. On x86 machines, Txtsetup.oem and all files listed in it (HALs and drivers), must also be listed in the [OEMBootFiles] section of the answer file.

The OEM\$$ Directory

This directory contains system files (either new files or replacements to files included in the retail product) that need to be copied to the various subdirectories in the Windows NT system directory. Maintain the directory structure used in the retail product. In each subdirectory, place the files that need to be copied to the corresponding system directory on the destination computer. If some of the files use long filenames, add the file OEM\$$\$$Rename.txt. This file lists all files that have long names, and their corresponding short names.

The OEM\Net Directory

This directory contains only subdirectories. In each subdirectory place the files for a particular network component, such as network cards, network services, and network protocols. Files in this directory will be used by the network setup module.

The OEM*drive_letter* Directories

The OEM*drive_letter* directories are used to hold files that are to be copied by the Setup program to corresponding drives on the destination computers. For example, files in the OEM\C directory will be copied to drive C on the destination computer during text mode setup.

Place files for applications that you want to install along with Windows NT Workstation in subdirectories of the OEM*drive_letter* directories on the distribution sharepoint. The files in these subdirectories must have short filenames. To rename them with long filenames after they have been copied to the destination computer, list them in a file named $$rename.txt, in the same directory.

Applications included in the OEM*drive_letter* directories must support a scripted (silent) installation; to include applications that require interactive installation, use the **sysdiff** utility.

Setup uses commands specified in the OEM\Cmdlines.txt file to install applications or copy files that are available in subdirectories of OEM*drive_letter* on the distribution sharepoint. You can use these commands to invoke a Win95-style INF file, run the **sysdiff** command, or perform other actions.

For example, to install MS Office on the C drive, in the \MSOffice directory, place the files in OEM\C\MSOffice. Then specify the command to install the application in the OEM\Cmdlines.txt file.

You can also place files that you only want copied (but not "installed") in subdirectories of OEM*drive_letter*. For example, if you have written help files that cover policies and procedures used in your organization, you can place them in a subdirectory of OEM\C. Then use a command in the OEM\Cmdlines.txt file to copy them to the destination computers.

The $$Rename.txt Files

To map short filenames used in subdirectories of OEM to long filenames that should be assigned to those files after they are copied to the destination computers, list them in a $$Rename.txt file. Each subdirectory of OEM requires its own $$Rename.txt file, if the files in that directory need to be assigned long filenames on the destination computer. For example, if some of the system files in OEM\$$ use long filenames, they must be mapped in the file OEM\$$\$$Rename.txt. If some of the application files in OEM\C use long filenames, they must be mapped in the file OEM\C\$$Rename.txt. The format for the $$Rename.txt file is as follows:

```
[section name]
short name 1 = "long name 1"
short name 2 = "long name 2"
```

where:

section name
: is the path to the directory that contains the files. To indicate that the section contains the names of files or subdirectories that are on the root of the drive, use a backslash as the section name, as follows:

```
[\]
```

short name
: is the name of the file or subdirectory in this directory, to be renamed.

"long name"
: is the new name of the file or subdirectory. This name must be in double quotes.

Network Installation Startup Disks

To deploy Windows NT Workstation to computers that are not currently running networking software, you need to provide some way for them to connect to the distribution sharepoint and begin the installation process. This is done with a Network Installation Startup Disk.

A Network Installation Startup Disk is a bootable MS-DOS system disk containing just enough network client software to connect to the distribution server. You can then use the **winnt** command to install Windows NT Workstation over the network. You can include the **winnt** command line in the Autoexec.bat file on the disk, so that installation begins automatically when the computer is started with the Network Installation Startup Disk in the drive.

This disk can be used to do additional tasks, by adding lines to the Autoexec.bat file on the disk. For example, a series of Network Installation Startup Disks can be produced for an entire division or organization, with each disk specifying a different uniqueness ID in a common UDF. The end users can simply insert the disk into their primary floppy drive , turn on the computer, and walk away, returning to a completed custom installation of Windows NT Workstation.

Creating a Network Installation Startup Disk

Before you create a Network Installation Startup Disk, you need to determine the following:

- The name to be assigned to the computer.
- The username to be used. The username identifies a member of the workgroup or domain. Choose a unique name within the workgroup or domain.
- The name of the user's workgroup and/or domain.
- The manufacturer and model of the network adapter.
- The network protocol used on this network.

▶ **To create a Network Installation Startup Disk**

1. Make sure that the disk has been formatted using the MS-DOS operating system. Use a high-density system disk that fits the destination computer's primary floppy drive. (On most computers this will be drive A. If your system is configured differently, substitute the drive name which acts as your primary floppy drive.) Insert this disk in drive A of a computer running the MS-DOS operating system.
2. At the MS-DOS command prompt, type **sys a:** and then press ENTER to copy the hidden MS-DOS system files (Io.sys and Msdos.sys) and the MS-DOS command interpreter (Command.com) to the network installation startup disk.

3. On the Windows NT Server computer, double-click on the Network Client Administrator Utility in the Network Administration program group. Follow the directions displayed on the screen to create a Network Installation Startup Disk.
4. When prompted to insert a disk, insert the disk created in step 2 in the floppy drive.
5. Continue following the directions displayed on the screen. You now have a Network Installation Startup Disk.
6. The Network Client Administrator utility configures the Network Installation Startup Disk with default settings for the network adapter. Verify that the default settings are correct for your network adapter and modify them if necessary. (The settings are in the A:\Net\protocol.ini file.)

Using the Network Installation Startup Disk

Once the answer files, along with any UDFs or other customization files, are available on the distribution sharepoint, your technicians or end users can use the Network Installation Startup Disk to install Windows NT Workstation over the network.

▶ **To use the Network Installation Startup Disk**

1. Insert the Network Installation Startup Disk in drive A of the destination computer.
2. Turn on the destination computer. The MS-DOS Network Client installation program is run automatically if the Network Installation Startup Disk is in drive A.
3. When prompted for a username and password, supply the username and password for an account with permission to connect to the directory on the Windows NT Server computer where Windows NT Workstation Setup files are stored. When the computer displays a message about creating a password-list file, type **n** and then press **ENTER**.

4. The client computer must now make a connection to the shared directory on the Windows NT Server computer. To do so, type the following at the command prompt:

   ```
   net use x: \\corpnet\ver4.0
   cd x:
   ```

   where:

   x:

   is the letter assigned to the network drive, *corpnet* is the name of the distribution server, and *ver4.0* is the shared directory containing the Windows NT installation files.

5. Use the command **winnt /u:*answer_file*** to run the setup program.

For more information, see the guidelines for Computers Running MS-DOS Network Client in Chapter 3, "Deploying Windows NT Workstation on an Existing Client-Server Network."

Troubleshooting

If the computer displays an error message saying that "the specified shared directory cannot be found," make sure that the directory containing the Windows NT installation files is indeed shared on the Windows NT Server computer.

The NetBEUI protocol can only be used in a LAN or a setup staging area because NetBEUI does not support traffic across routers. Both IPX and TCP/IP can be used in a WAN with Setup Manager. However, not all companies route IPX, so you may need to create boot floppies with TCP/IP for use in a WAN environment.

If the computer displays an error message about lack of memory, modify the Config.sys file on the network installation startup disk to use extended memory. For example, Emm386.exe and Himem.sys provide extended memory for MS-DOS 5.0 and later. If you do not have extended memory, use the NetBEUI or IPX protocols instead of TCP/IP.

Creating .inf Files

Device information (INF) files provide information used by the Windows NT Workstation Setup program to install software that supports a given hardware device. INF files may also be created to permit scripted installations of applications.

Some Windows NT Workstation 4.0 .inf files use the same format as Windows 95 .inf files. Other .inf files use the format used in earlier versions of Windows NT Workstation. See the *Windows 95 Resource Kit* for a discussion of Windows 95-style INFs.

Using Windows 95-style .inf Files

You can use a Windows 95-style .inf file to install applications and other components into Windows NT. For complete details about the syntax and use of statements in Windows 95 INF files, see the *Win32 Software Development Kit for Windows 95 and Windows NT.*

The command line to invoke a Win95-style INF in Windows NT 4.0 is:

```
RUNDLL32 syssetup,SetupInfObjectInstallAction section 128 inf
```

where:

section
: specifies the name of the section in the INF.

inf
: specifies the name of the INF file. This should be specified as a relative path to avoid invoking Setup's default INF rules, which look for an unqualified filename in the system inf directory instead of the current directory. For example, specify **..\newtools.inf**, not just **newtools.inf**.

For example if you want to install MyGame application into Windows NT, create a Mygame.inf file, such as the following, and place it in the OEM directory.

```
 This inf is a sample win95 style INF
 mygame.inf
 installs a game program into Windows NT

[version]
signature="$Windows NT$"
ClassGUID={00000000-0000-0000-0000-000000000000}

Destination Directories for CopyFiles Sections

[DestinationDirs]
BaseCopyProgramFiles            = 24,%INSTALL_DIR%
MygameDeleteFiles                    = 24,%INSTALL_DIR%
```

```
MygameCopyFilesHelp            = 18 LDID_HELP

[BaseWinOptions]
BaseSection

[Optional Components]
Mygame

[BaseSection]
AddReg                  = BaseAddReg

[Mygame]
OptionDesc              = %MYGAME_Desc%
Tip                     = %MYGAME_TIP%
IconIndex               = 64            Windows mini-icon for dialogs
Parent                  = Games
InstallType             = 0             Manual only.
CopyFiles               = BaseCopyProgramFiles, MygameCopyFilesHelp
AddReg                  = MYGAME.AddReg
UpdateInis              = MYGAME.Inis
Uninstall               = MYGAME.Remove
Upgrade                 = MYGAME.Upgrade
Detect                  = %24%\%INSTALL_DIR%\mygame.exe

[MYGAME.Remove]
AddReg                  = MYGAME.DelReg
DelReg          = MYGAME.DelPath
DelFiles                = BaseCopyProgramFiles, MygameCopyFilesHelp,
MygameDeleteFiles
UpdateInis              = MYGAME.Rem.Inis
Reboot=0

[MYGAME.Upgrade]
CopyFiles               = BaseCopyProgramFiles, MygameCopyFilesHelp
DelFiles                = MygameDeleteFiles
AddReg                  = MYGAME.AddReg

[MYGAME.Inis]
setup.ini, progman.groups,, "group15=%GAMES_DESC%"         creates
folder
setup.ini, group15,,
"""%MYGAME_Desc%""","""""""%24%\%INSTALL_DIR%\mygame.exe""""""",,,,""%24%\%
INSTALL_DIR%"""

[MYGAME.Rem.Inis]
setup.ini, progman.groups,, "group15=%GAMES_DESC%"
folder
setup.ini, group15,, """%MYGAME_Desc%"""
deletes link
```

```
[MYGAME.AddReg]
HKLM,%KEY_OPTIONAL%\Mygame,Installed,,"1"
HKLM,"%KEY_APP_PATH%\mygame.exe",,,"%24%\%INSTALL_DIR%\mygame.exe"

[MYGAME.DelPath]
HKLM,"%KEY_APP_PATH%\mygame.exe"

[MYGAME.DelReg]
HKLM,%KEY_OPTIONAL%\Mygame,Installed,,"0"

[BaseAddReg]
Create entries for Maint Mode Setup, set all initially to uninstalled:
HKLM,%KEY_OPTIONAL%,"Mygame",,"Mygame"
HKLM,%KEY_OPTIONAL%\Mygame,INF,,"mygame.inf"
HKLM,%KEY_OPTIONAL%\Mygame,Section,,"Mygame"
HKLM,%KEY_OPTIONAL%\Mygame,Installed,,"0"

[BaseCopyProgramFiles]
FONT.DAT
MYGAME.DAT
MYGAME.EXE
MYGAME.MID
MYGAME2.MID
SOUND1.WAV
SOUND2.WAV
SOUND3.WAV

table.bmp
wavemix.inf

[MygameDeleteFiles]
mygame.cnt
mygame.hlp
mygame.inf

[MygameCopyFilesHelp]
mygame.cnt
mygame.hlp

[Strings]
KEY_APP_PATH= "SOFTWARE\Microsoft\Windows\CurrentVersion\App Paths"
KEY_OPTIONAL    =
"SOFTWARE\Microsoft\Windows\CurrentVersion\Setup\OptionalComponents"
GAMES_DESC      = "Accessories\Games"
MYGAME_Desc     = "Mygame"
MYGAME_TIP      = "Company X 3-D mygame game"
INSTALL_DIR     = "Program Files\Windows NT\Mygame"
```

To install MyGame, you would include the following command line in the OEM\Cmdlines.txt file on your distribution sharepoint.

```
"RUNDLL32 syssetup,SetupInfObjectInstallAction Version 128
..\mygame.inf"
```

Note All the files needed for this application should be placed in the distribution share point.

Special Issues: Dual Boot Computers

In the deployment lab, you might want to set up some computers to run either Windows NT Workstation 3.51 or Windows NT Workstation 4.0, with the choice of operating system to be made during system startup. This is referred to as dual booting. The following considerations apply in this case:

- If the configurations using Windows NT Workstation 3.51 and Windows NT Workstation 4.0 are members of the same domain, they must have different computernames.
- The installation of Windows NT Workstation 4.0 must be done interactively, without using the **winnt /u** or **winnt32** command.

CHAPTER 3

Deploying Windows NT Workstation on an Existing Client-Server Network

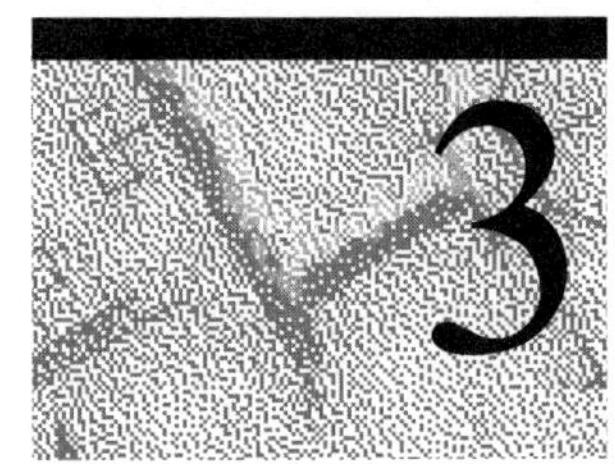

There are several methods for upgrading your existing network clients to Windows NT Workstation 4.0.

- Microsoft Systems Management Server (SMS) provides the most control, speed, security, and flexibility.
- On smaller LANs, users or technicians can run unattended setup from individual computers, using an answer file. Control of the process is shared with the users or technicians who initiate the unattended setup.
- Administrators can modify logon scripts so that unattended setup runs automatically when a user logs on to the network.
- Administrators can create a batch (.bat) file to run unattended setup from individual desktops. They can then send the batch file as an embedded link in e-mail, and the users can run the batch file at their convenience.

"Pull" installations are those in which the user performs the upgrade, using tools provided by the administrator. "Push" installations are those in which the upgrade is performed for the user by the administrator or technicians, either directly or through software such as Systems Management Server. The choice of which type to use depends on several factors, including the corporate culture, the willingness of users to perform the upgrade, and scheduling. For example, if you need all the computers in a department to be upgraded on a certain day, a push installation might be required, since some users might be out of the office that day, or simply might not have a chance to perform the upgrade that day. Push installations can often be done outside regular business hours to minimize the disruption of the users' workday. In many cases, you can ask users to perform an upgrade within a certain time period, after which the upgrade will be mandatory and will be performed for them. This approach is especially easy with Systems Management Server. This chapter discusses how you can use Systems Management Server to deploy Windows NT Workstation 4.0 throughout an existing client-server network.

Using Systems Management Server for Deployment

Systems Management Server helps you deploy Windows NT Workstation, or any software package, in the following ways.

- Systems Management Server inventories the computers on the network as the computers log on, at the specific time interval you set. The software and hardware detected on each computer is then listed in an SQL database. This means you can have an up-to-date inventory of the computers in your network at all times, without the expense and disruptions of a manual inventory.
- With Systems Management Server, you create SMS packages for the configurations that you want to install. Each package contains all the files and information required to install one or more configurations. Packages can be edited, stored, and re-used as often as needed. This means you can be sure that the same package you perfect in the lab and in pilot tests is used to deploy Windows NT Workstation throughout your production network.
- Query functions in Systems Management Server let you determine which computers meet the criteria for upgrade. You can also use any application that uses SQL to query the database that Systems Management Server creates.
- You can use queries to identify the computers that are not ready for Windows NT Workstation, and perform necessary hardware upgrades (or delete files to free required disk space) before the scheduled upgrade.
- Systems Management Server *jobs* deliver the package you created to the computers you specify. You can specify that Systems Management Server perform the installation on only the computers that meet the requirements of a query. Or, perform the query in a separate step, and create a Machine Group from the results of the query. Then send the job to the computers in that Machine Group.
- After deployment, you can quickly identify and correct any problems, using information from the job statistics produced by Systems Management Server , and the updated inventory.
- Systems Management Server help desk functions let your support staff provide on-the-spot assistance to your end users, without leaving their own desks.

Systems Management Server gives administrators of large networks an inventory of the computers on the network, which they can query to compile a list of the computers that are capable of running Windows NT Workstation 4.0. Systems Management Server also allows remote administration of utilities to prepare each computer for the installation or upgrade. Systems Management Server can then be used to create a package of installation procedures and a job to execute the package on each workstation with the ability to monitor and evaluate the process while it's carried out.

At this point, it is assumed you have defined your preferred client configurations and set up a LAN in the lab that simulates your production LAN. You should have at least one computer in the lab for each platform (x86, MIPS, Alpha, or PowerPC) you are using in your organization. If you have not already installed Systems Management Server, do so at this time, before proceeding with the lab tests.

Systems Management Server requires an NTFS partition and at least 100 MB of free disk space. You should allow at least 1 GB of disk space for the deployment of Windows NT Workstation. If you did not choose to have Setup convert a partition to NTFS, convert it before beginning the Systems Management Server Setup program. For more information on setting up Systems Management Server, refer to the *Systems Management Server Administrator's Guide*.

Use Systems Management Server to perform a test deployment in the lab. This involves the following steps, which are discussed in greater detail in the remainder of this chapter:

1. Copy the Windows NT Workstation 4.0 setup files, including any customization files, to a shared directory on the distribution server. This will be the distribution sharepoint.
2. Use Systems Management Server queries to determine which computers on the network can support Windows NT Workstation 4.0.
3. Create Machine Groups of these computers.
4. Create a Systems Management Server package to install Windows NT Workstation on the computers in the Machine Groups.
5. Create a Systems Management Server job to execute the package.
6. Monitor the Systems Management Server job status.
7. Evaluate distribution results.

Copy the Setup Files

The setup files for each platform (x86, MIPS, Alpha, or PowerPC) are located in their corresponding directory on the Windows NT Workstation and Windows NT Server Installation CDs. Copy each directory needed for the platforms running on your production LAN to the distribution sharepoint. For convenience, keep the names of the directories on the distribution sharepoint the same for each platform (for example, \i386 copied to \i386). Add any customization files to the distribution sharepoint, as discussed in Chapter 2, "Customizing Setup."

Be sure the directory on the distribution sharepoint is a shared directory.

Inventory the Test Lab

After Systems Management Server has been installed in your lab or on your production network, it can begin adding computers to its inventory database as the individual computers log on. You can then use the information in the database to determine which computers are ready for the upgrade to Windows NT Workstation 4.0, and which ones need hardware upgrades. Systems Management Server provides an interface in which you can construct queries to the database. The queries you create can be saved, edited, and copied to other sites as needed. They can then be re-used to perform the pilot and final deployments.

Create a "Windows NT Workstation Capable" Query

To identify the computers that have the hardware requirements to run the Windows NT Workstation operating system, create a query from within Systems Management Server. After you run the query, you can create a Machine Group with the results. Then create jobs to run virus detection software and to install Windows NT Workstation on the computers in that Machine Group. Later, you can run queries against the computers in the Machine Group to make sure that all the computers in the group were upgraded as planned.

To create a query

1. Open the Query window in Systems Management Server Administrator.
2. From the File menu, choose New. The Query Properties dialog appears.
3. In the Query Name text box, type the name for the query. The Query Name must be unique within the site.
4. Optionally, in the Comment box, type a comment for the query.
5. In the Architecture box, select Personal Computer, which is the default.
6. Define the criteria for the query by adding expressions to the Find All Personal Computer Items Where box.
7. Click OK to close the Query Properties dialog box.

Once you have created a query to suit your needs, you are ready to run it. The query is run against the contents of the Systems Management Server database that has been populated by Systems Management Server as individual computers logged on.

To run the query

1. From the File menu of the Systems Management Server Administrator window choose Execute Query. The Queries dialog box appears.
2. Drag the query to the site (in the Sites window) on which you want it to run.

By running the query and dragging or pasting the query results into a Machine Group window, you can create a group of all the computers that you want to upgrade to Windows NT Workstation. This group can then be used in subsequent steps.

You might want to create several different machine groups to deploy different configurations. Use variations of the query to create different groups. All the queries should be tested before proceeding further, to make sure you are selecting only those computers you really want to target.

See Chapter 7, "Queries," in the *Systems Management Server Administrator's Guide* for more information on creating and executing queries. Also see Chapter 14, "Machine Groups and Site Groups," in the *Systems Management Server Administrator's Guide* for more information on machine groups.

Create a Package to Install Windows NT Workstation

Windows NT Workstation allows the use of special information files (.inf files), that can specify all possible custom settings. The format and parameters for these files are described in Chapter 2, "Customizing Setup."

Systems Management Server can use these information files for automated installations of the software. The vehicle for this is the Package Definition File, or PDF. A PDF is an ASCII file that specifies setup programs, installation options, and execution command lines for the software you will install. If the PDF contains a reference to an .inf file, then the .inf file is made available to the destination computers when the package is delivered through a Systems Management Server job. In fact, several .inf files can be included in a single package.

Since the PDF has options for installing Windows NT Workstation on computers currently running MS-DOS, Windows 3.1, or Windows for Workgroups 3.11, the queries need to target each platform individually.

In order to install Windows NT Workstation on the target computers, for MS-DOS-, Windows 3.1–, and Windows for Workgroups 3.11–based systems, the **winnt** command must be used to install the operating system. For computers that are running an earlier version of Windows NT Workstation, use the **winnt32** command to install the operating system. Both the **winnt** and the **winnt32** commands include a complete set of command-line switches that can further help automate the setup process. For more information on this, see Chapter 2, "Customizing Setup." Systems Management Server Distribution Packages can be used to run these commands locally on targeted workstations.

Each package is completely self-contained: It has all the files needed for the task or tasks it is designed to do. Furthermore, a single package can contain several different sets of helper files, EXEs, and INFs. The command you want is chosen when you create a job using the package.

▶ **To create a package to deploy Windows NT Workstation**

1. In the Packages window of Systems Management Server, choose New from the File menu. The Package Properties dialog box appears.
2. Choose Import, and then select the file *servername*\import.src\enu\nt40.pdf, where *servername* is the name of the server to which you copied the PDF.

   After you select the file, you are returned to the Package Properties dialog box.
3. Choose Windows NT Workstation. The Setup Package for Windows NT Workstation dialog box appears.

   Enter the full UNC name of your distribution sharepoint in the Source Directory text box. If you choose to browse for the files, edit the resulting path so that it shows the UNC name (which would begin with *servername*) rather than the relative name (which would begin with the drive letter you have assigned to the server during the current session). Be sure to choose the "Automated Setup for Windows NT Workstation" command line.
4. If you want, you can examine the command line for the package by choosing Properties in the Setup Package for Windows NT Workstations dialog box.

   You might also choose to view the inventory properties for the package by choosing Inventory in the Setup Package for Windows NT Workstations dialog box.
5. When you are satisfied with the package, click OK until the Package Properties dialog box is closed.

   Once the package has been created and appears in the Packages window, you can include it in a job.

For more information on creating packages, see Chapter 10, "Packages," in the *Systems Management Server Administrator's Guide*.

Create a Job to Execute the Package

In order for the **winnt** or **winnt32** command in the "setup" package to be run on the destination computers, it must be made available in a Run Command on Workstation job. The job is created by dragging the package to the machine group on the site and filling in the Job Details dialog that appears as a result. You might also choose to take advantage of the job scheduling and configuration options.

After you have set up the job, it appears in the Jobs window as a pending job.

Monitor the Systems Management Server Job Status

Monitor the status of the job by selecting that job in the Job Properties dialog box, clicking on the Status button, and viewing the Sending and Working columns in the Job Status dialog box.

After the job has had a chance to propagate, you can check on details of the job. In the small network you have set up in the lab, this could take as little as 30 minutes. In your production network, you'll need to allow more time. To view the details of the job, select Details from the Job Status dialog box. The Job Status Details dialog box appears.

When the Status column changes to Complete, the job has been distributed. The total duration of the job depends on a number of factors, including the parameters set for the job and the behavior of your users (who must log on to accept the Systems Management Server Package).

For more information on jobs, see Chapter 11, "Jobs," in the *Systems Management Server Administrator's Guide*.

Evaluate Distribution Results

A "complete" job status does not necessarily indicate successful deployment of the operating system. You must perform additional analysis to determine results.

First, make sure the inventory has been updated for all computers in the target group of workstations. Then run queries against the Machine Group to which you sent the Windows NT Workstation installation job. For example, you might create "Successful Windows NT Workstation" and "Unsuccessful Windows NT Workstation" queries.

Examine the computers that were not successfully upgraded on a case-by-case basis. Check, for example, whether there were changes in available disk space or in the availability of some other resource between the time the computer was added to the target group and the time the upgrade was performed.

The computers that were successfully upgraded should be tested to make sure the configuration you specified works as expected.

Job Events

You can check details of job events to troubleshoot problems. For example, if a job has failed, perhaps because the .inf file was not available where it was expected, this would be reported in the job events.

To view the job events

1. From the Systems Management Server Administrator window, choose Jobs. The Jobs window appears.
2. Select the job.
3. From the File menu, choose Properties. The Job Properties dialog box appears.
4. Choose Status. The Job Status dialog box appears.
5. Choose Details.

Viewing job events is further described in the section, "Viewing Job Events and Status" in Chapter 11, "Jobs," of the *Systems Management Server Administrator's Guide*.

Job Logs

A log is created as each job progresses; each task is logged to a log file as it is performed. This log file can be examined if the job failed or produced unexpected results, to help you pinpoint the source of the problem.

Use Trace.exe, which you copied to your Systems Management Server server while setting up the lab, to view log files of jobs that have been run. When you start this program, the Systems Management Server Tracer window appears.

You can open a log file by choosing Open from the File menu, and view the contents of the log file.

Additional Help

If you need to contact Microsoft Product Support for help with the deployment, be sure you have copies of the following files for the test or deployment attempt for which you need help:

- Registry dump
- Trace logs, including:
  - Root\Systems Management Server\logs*.log
  - Root\Scanman.log
- All the files, including the PDF, used in your deployment of Windows NT Workstation

Modifying Logon Scripts

Logon scripts for existing network clients can be modified to include a mandatory upgrade. (Logon scripts point to a batch file that runs automatically every time a user logs on.) One example of a logon script might include the command **net time *servername*** to set the time on all workstations in the domain to be the same as the server time.

Existing logon scripts can be modified to include the **winnt** or **winnt32** command, providing a forced upgrade when a user logs on. A prompt could be included in the logon script to give the user the option to postpone the upgrade. The user will be prompted for information unless you specify an answer file with the **/u** option and possibly a UDF with the **/udf** option. (For example, if the computername for this particular computer is not specified in an answer file or the UDF that you specify on the command line, the user will be prompted for the computername.) For information on these options to the **winnt** and **winnt32** commands, see Chapter 2, "Customizing Setup."

Note This method is only viable for smaller LANs. If undue stress is placed on the network from hundreds of concurrent upgrades, the entire network can fail. However, it is a useful alternative in some situations, as when Systems Management Server is not available, staffing resources for deployment are limited, or only a few users typically log on at any one time.

Remember that any time the **winnt** or **winnt32** command is used, the setup files must be placed on a distribution sharepoint. If necessary, answer files may be included and, if used, must be included in the logon script syntax.

Sending a Batch File as an Embedded Link in an e-mail Message

This option is only useful in a small LAN with users who have sufficient expertise to comfortably initiate the upgrade. Users who are given responsibility for their upgrades can introduce variables (such as when each upgrade takes place or what options are included) that can disrupt your planned deployment. To avoid unnecessary stress on the network, send only about 25 setup batch files at one time. Monitor the users who have been given the option to upgrade to keep track of which workstations are upgraded. The files must be kept in place until all users have performed the upgrade. In some cases, you might need to remind users to perform the upgrade so that you can go on to the next group of users, or remove the installation files from the distribution sharepoint.

CHAPTER 4

Planning for a Mixed Environment

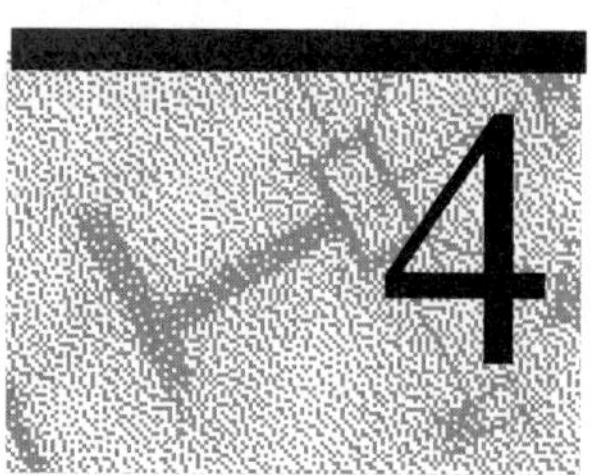

By using both Windows NT Workstation and Windows 95 in your organization's computing environment, you can meet all the needs of your users and the organization as a whole, while providing for efficient network management. These two operating systems enable organizations to take advantage of a new generation of 32-bit applications and technologies, and realize the advantages of a more reliable and manageable operating system. Use the tools and information in this chapter to help manage your migration to a mixed environment of Windows NT Workstation and Windows 95.

This chapter includes information on the following:

- Deploying a mixed environment of Windows NT Workstation and Windows 95.
- Administrative tools to help manage a mixed environment.
- Networking differences between Windows NT Workstation and Windows 95.

Determining Where to Deploy Windows 95 and Windows NT Workstation

The most important decision an organization needs to make is where to deploy Windows NT Workstation and Windows 95 in its computing environment. The primary criteria for this decision are hardware requirements, device driver support, and software compatibility.

Hardware Requirements

When choosing where to deploy Windows 95 and Windows NT Workstation, you must make sure that destination computers meet the hardware requirements for the operating system they will be using. Also, make sure that the operating system provides support for all of the hardware devices (such as video cards, network adapters, etc.) being used on the destination computer. In many cases, your existing hardware inventory will determine where each operating system is deployed.

Windows 95 is designed to have less demanding hardware requirements, and will work very well with existing hardware. You can run Windows 95 on a computer with the following minimum hardware configuration:

- 386DX or higher processor
- 4 MB of memory (8 MB recommended)
- 35–40 MB of free hard disk space
- VGA or higher resolution graphics card

Windows NT Workstation 4.0 has higher hardware requirements for Intel-based platforms:

- 486/33 or higher processor
- 12 MB of memory (16 MB recommended)
- 120 MB of free disk space
- CD-ROM drive (or access to CD-ROM drive over the network)
- VGA or higher resolution graphics card

Windows NT Workstation also supports symmetric multiprocessing (SMP) configurations and RISC-based platforms such as MIPS, Alpha, and the PowerPC.

Windows 95 provides a broader set of device driver support. Check the Windows NT Hardware Compatibility List (HCL) to ensure that Windows NT drivers exist for all of your devices.

Software Compatibility

Windows NT Workstation provides a standard, comprehensive set of protected environment subsystems that include the following:

- MS-DOS
- 16-bit Windows-based applications
- 32-bit Windows-based applications
- OS/2 applications [1]
- POSIX

These environment subsystems support most applications available today.

Windows NT Workstation supports most legacy applications, except where the methods used by those applications for accessing system resources would compromise security or reliability. This includes applications that require direct access to system hardware, a virtual device driver (VXD), or a Terminate and Stay Resident program (TSR).

Windows 95 was designed to provide the broadest range of software compatibility, and is often the best choice for older legacy applications. You should test your applications on both Windows 95 and Windows NT Workstation.

---

1 OS/2 support is compatible with OS/2 version 1.3 for 16-bit applications. As a separate product available at a nominal cost, Microsoft also offers an additional 16-bit OS/2 Presentation Manager subsystem for Intel-based systems.

Installation Considerations for Windows NT Workstation and Windows 95

After you determine where to deploy both operating systems, review the installation options for Windows NT Workstation and Windows 95. When determining the ideal client configurations for computers in a network that will use both operating systems, be aware of the following installation issues:

- Server-based setup
- Upgrading from Windows 95 to Windows NT Workstation and dual-boot scenarios
- Networking and security options

For detailed information on how to roll-out Windows NT Workstation, see Chapter 1, "Deployment Strategy and Details," and Chapter 2, "Customizing Setup," in this deployment guide. For detailed information on how to roll out Windows 95, see Chapters 1 through 6 in the *Windows 95 Resource Kit.*

Server-Based Setup

The term server-based setup refers to running the operating system from the server, rather than locally, on the client computer's hard disk. When server-based setup is used, the client computer starts with only the files needed to connect to the network and access the operating system files on the server.

Windows NT Workstation does not support server-based setup, due to reliability and security implementations of the operating system. However, Windows 95 can be installed on a server to run as a shared copy on client computers. The benefits of a shared installation include the following:

- Little or no hard disk space is required on the local computer.
- Updating drivers for multiple computers is easier.
- The workstation is more secure and operation is safer for novice users because network logon is required and access to system files is limited. (However, you can also use system policies to enforce the same restrictions for local installations)

There are also some disadvantages to running operating systems from the server:

- A shared configuration means more network traffic.
- Larger servers are required.
- Performance is better when the operating system is installed on the local hard disk.
- The server must be available for the operating system to work.

Upgrading from Windows 95 to Windows NT Workstation

Differences in the system registries and hardware device support preclude a software upgrade path from Windows 95 to Windows NT Workstation 4.0. Microsoft plans to provide a Windows 95–to–Windows NT Workstation upgrade path in the release following Windows NT Workstation 4.0.

To install Windows NT Workstation on a computer that is currently running Windows 95, you must perform a fresh installation, rather than upgrading Windows 95 with system settings intact. Applications will also need to be re-installed.

Customers planning to upgrade Windows 95 must use the following manual upgrade path:

1. Check to see if all Windows 95 devices and applications are supported by Windows NT Workstation 4.0.
2. Install Windows NT Workstation 4.0 into a separate directory on your hard drive. This will create a "dual boot" system.
3. Re-install all applications.
4. (Optional) Manually delete the Windows 95 directory.

You can upgrade to Windows NT Workstation version 4.0 from any of the following operating systems, keeping applications and system settings as you do so:

- Any previous version of Windows NT (versions 3.1, 3.5, and 3.51)
- MS-DOS
- Windows 3.1
- Windows for Workgroups 3.11

Dual Booting Between Windows NT Workstation and Windows 95

It is not recommended to set up a computer to dual-boot (giving the user a choice between Windows NT Workstation and Windows 95 when the computer is started). To avoid problems with hardware settings and application installation, choose one operating system for each computer.

If you require a dual-boot configuration, install applications while running Windows NT Workstation and again while running Windows 95, to ensure that the applications are included in the Registries of both operating systems.

Networking Windows NT Workstation and Windows 95

When determining ideal client configurations for a mixed environment of Windows NT Workstation and Windows 95, consider what types of networks these systems will need to support. Both Windows NT Workstation and Windows 95 provide network and protocol support for the following:

- Client services for NetWare
- Remote networking
- TCP/IP, including PPP, SLIP, DHCP, and WINS
- NetBEUI Protocol
- NWLink IPX/SPX Compatible Transport
- Windows Sockets Standard used by popular Internet applications
- OSF, DCE, and RPC available for advanced client-server applications and used extensively by Windows NT
- Peer-to-peer networking
- Internet connectivity

The networking implementation for Windows 95 is slightly different than that for Windows NT Workstation. In order to support all Microsoft networking products that use the Server Message Block (SMB) protocol, install the Client for Microsoft Networks redirector (Vredir.vxd). This allows Windows 95 computers to connect to computers running any of the following networking software:

- Windows 95
- Windows NT
- Windows for Workgroups
- LAN Manager
- Workgroup Add-on for MS-DOS

Refer to, "Decide on the Preferred Client Configuration" in Chapter 1 for more information on network protocol support and configuration.

Network Connections

In Windows NT Workstation, a user can always connect to any network resource he or she has permission to access. If the current logon session is for a different account, the user can fill in his or her domain name and username in the Connect As text box in the Connect Network Drive dialog box.

In Windows 95, this "connect as" feature is not available. To connect to a network resource from Windows 95, the user must log on with an account that has access to that resource.

In either operating system, the **net view** command can also be used to map a network drive. For syntax and usage, use the **net help** command.

Persistent Connections

In Windows NT Workstation, persistent network connections are enabled by default. To disable persistent connections, clear the "Reconnect at Logon" checkbox in the Connect Network Drive dialog box.

In Windows 95, Quick Logon is enabled by default. This network logon option restores the mapping of drive letters to network resources, without actually establishing a session for each persistent network connection. If you want to establish sessions for persistent connections during logon, you can enable Logon and Restore Network Connections. For information on how to do so, see chapter 8, "Windows 95 on Microsoft Networks," of the *Windows 95 Resource Kit.*

For persistent connections from Windows 95, select the "Reconnect at logon" checkbox.

Resource Sharing

Windows NT operating systems allow users to set security permissions on directories, individual files, printers, and other resources. Windows 95 does not support security on individual files.

Before a user can share a resource on a computer running Windows 95, the computer must be configured for share-level or user-level security. Also, File and Printer Sharing services must be installed, using the Network option in Control Panel. The Printers dialog box is used to set access rights to printers in a similar manner.

For computers to share resources such as printers, volumes, CD-ROM drives, and directories, all the computers must be running a common protocol.

Security and Data Protection

Windows NT Workstation was designed to provide the highest levels of system security. Administrators should be aware of the differences in security implementations between Windows NT Workstation and Windows 95 when setting up both peer-to-peer networks and client-server networks.

One of the elements at the core of the Windows NT architecture is integrated security. In its simplest form, Windows NT Workstation includes a secure logon sequence (using the CTRL+ALT+DEL key sequence). This sequence prevents rogue applications from trapping the username and password sequence. In addition, the account lockout feature lets you specify the maximum number of logon attempts. If the correct password is not supplied within this number of attempts, the account cannot be used until an administrator unlocks the account, or a specified period of time has passed. This deters attempts to break into an account by guessing a password.

Windows NT Workstation ensures data and system protection through its ability to define the level of discretionary access control that users can have to the system. The Windows NT security model[2] allows users to apply security to networking, and to all system objects. Administrators can "lock-down" Windows NT Workstation systems to ensure that end users do not damage key system files or change system configurations. The native Windows NT file system (NTFS) provides this security down to the file level.

Windows NT Workstation also supports multi-user capabilities while retaining a high level of security. Several users can share a single computer system while still maintaining total access control over their personal files. Further, multi-user capabilities allow multiple users to have unique desktops, program groups, and other capabilities.

Windows 95 was not designed to meet such high levels of security and data protection. When specifying a Windows 95 client configuration, administrators need to ensure that user-level security is provided by either Windows NT Server or NetWare, in order to provide pass-through authentication for users accessing resources on remote computers.

---

[2] Windows NT was designed to meet C-2 level security specifications, as defined by the United States National Security Agency.

Remote Administration

Several tools are available to help you manage networks using Windows NT Workstation and Windows 95 together. These include the following:

- System policies and the System Policy Editor
- User Profiles
- Systems Management Server or other systems manager software
- Logon scripts
- Performance Monitor

For detailed information on system policies, user profiles, and logon scripts, see Chapter 3, "Managing User Work Environments," in *Windows NT 4.0 Concepts and Planning*. In addition to providing extensive information on the implementation of these features in Windows NT Workstation and Windows NT Server, this chapter includes information on using Windows 95 user profiles on Windows NT Server networks.

System Policies

Like Windows 95, Windows NT Workstation 4.0 now includes system policies, and the System Policy Editor. These are powerful tools for managing a mixed environment network.

System policies allow you to override local registry values for user or computer settings. When a user logs on, system policy settings overwrite the current settings in the user's registry. This allows administrators to control individual desktop and registry settings.

In Windows 95, however, the following apply:

- System policies are only stored on the logon server rather than the local computer.
- Group policies, if used, must be enabled on each computer running Windows 95. You can do so when you install Windows 95, using a custom setup script. Or, use the Add/Remove Programs option in Control Panel after Windows 95 is installed.

System Policy Editor

To centrally manage both Windows NT Workstation and Windows 95 computers, use the System Policy Editor. This tool lets you manage groups of computers by configuring the registry settings of those computers. The alternative is to edit the registry on each computer, using Regedt.exe (for Windows 95) or Regedt32.exe (for Windows NT Workstation). System Policy Editor is easier to use, since it does not require a understanding of the registry structure and syntax.

When you use the System Policy Editor on a computer running Windows NT Workstation or Windows NT Server, a Ntconfig.pol file is created. This file is read and interpreted by the Windows NT Workstation client software, overriding any conflicting information in that computer's registry. When you use the System Policy Editor on a computer running Windows 95, a Config.pol file is created. This file is similar to the Ntconfig.pol file, but has a different file format and reflects differences in the registries of the two operating systems. Place these files on the logon share.

To apply system policies to a network that uses both Windows 95 and Windows NT Workstation, run the System Policy Editor once from each platform, to produce the two different files.

The System Policy Editor cannot be used to set binary values. Hardware component information is often stored as binary data. If you look at a Windows NT registry using RegEdit32.exe, you will see binary value entries marked with data type REG_BINARY. If you look at a Windows 95 registry using RegEdit.exe, you will see binary value entries marked with an icon showing 0s and 1s, rather than the letters ab. These values cannot be set using System Policy Editor. Use the Registry Editor, or make changes on a per-computer basis via the user interface.

You can use the System Policy Editor to edit the HKeyLocalMachine and HKeyCurrentUser portions of the interface. If you need to access a different part of the registry, such as HKeyDynData, use the Registry Editor.

Registry Editor

The alternative to using the System Policy Editor is using the Registry Editor. Both Windows 95 and Windows NT Workstation allow administrators to view and edit the registry on individual remote systems.

You can edit the registry on each computer by using RegEdit.exe (for Windows 95) or RegEdt32.exe (for Windows NT Workstation). For information on the registry and the Registry Editor, see Part 5, "Windows NT Registry."

User Profiles

User profiles are useful for configuring or managing custom desktops on a Microsoft network (that is, one that uses Microsoft products for networking functionality). A user who logs on from different computers at different times can see the same desktop at every logon. Any changes the user makes to the profile appear the next time the user logs on.

In Windows NT Workstation, a user's computing environment is determined primarily by the user profile. Windows NT security requires a user profile for each account that has access to the system. User profiles are created by default when a Windows NT user logs on for the first time. You can also create and modify user profiles on a computer running Windows NT Server. To do so, select System from the Control Panel, and select the User Profile tab.

In Windows 95, user profiles are not created by default; they must be enabled by an administrator. For information on setting up User Profiles for Windows 95 computers on a Windows NT Network, see Chapter 15, "User Profiles and System Policies," in the *Windows 95 Resource Kit*. Also, to take advantage of user profiles from a computer running Windows 95, you must specify Client for Microsoft Networks as the Primary Network Logon client.

Profiles for computers running Windows NT Workstation or Windows NT Server are stored in the "Profile Path" directory on a Windows NT server. The "Profile Path" directory can be found in the user's account in User Manager for Domains. Windows 95 does not use this directory. Windows 95 profiles are stored in the home directory.

If a user works at a computer running Windows NT Workstation part of the time and at a computer running Windows 95 other times, that user can have two different profiles, one for each operating system. Changes to the settings for one operating system will not affect the settings for the other operating system. (Also, the profiles used by Windows NT Workstation 3.51 and Windows NT Workstation 4.0 differ, reflecting the differences in the interfaces. Users who move between versions of Windows NT Workstation will have different profiles for the two versions of the operating system.)

Because these operating systems use different profiles, some elements of the user environment are easier to control in a mixed environment by creating logon scripts.

Using Logon Scripts

Logon scripts are batch files or executable files that run automatically when a user logs on. They can be used when logging on to a computer running any of the following operating systems:

- Windows NT Workstation
- Windows NT Server
- Windows 95
- MS-DOS

Logon scripts can configure users' working environments by making network connections and starting applications. You might want to use logon scripts to manage part of the user environment (such as network connections) without managing or dictating the entire environment. Or, you can use logon scripts to create common network connections for multiple users. If you are using LAN Manager 2.x logon scripts, you can continue using them after upgrading to Windows NT Workstation or Windows 95.

Note It is important that logon scripts are in place for every user if you are planning to use a system management software such as Microsoft's Systems Management Server. Logon scripts are modified by the management software in order to take inventory of all the computers on the network.

You can assign a different logon script for each user, or create logon scripts for use by multiple users. To assign a user a logon script, designate the path name of the logon script file in the user's account information on the domain controller. Then, whenever that user logs on, the logon script is downloaded and run.

A logon script is always downloaded from the server that validates a user's logon request. To ensure that logon scripts always work for users, logon scripts for all user accounts in a domain should be maintained on every primary domain controller (PDC) and backup domain controller (BDC) in the domain.

Systems Management Server

The best overall method of remote administration is a systems management program such as Microsoft's Systems Management Server (SMS). With SMS you can manage Windows NT Workstation and Windows 95 clients in much the same manner. Each computer on the network must be configured as an SMS client in order to enable remote administration. Logon scripts must be in place on each computer to be automatically included in the SMS database—otherwise you will have to configure each workstation manually. Windows NT diagnostics and Server Manager functionality are included in SMS for remote administration of Windows NT Workstations and Servers. For more information, see your Systems Management Server documentation.

The alternatives for remote administration are to manage Windows 95 clients from computers running Windows 95, and manage Windows NT Workstation clients from computer running Windows NT Server. For Windows 95 clients, see Chapter 16, "Remote Administration," in *The Windows 95 Resource Kit.*

Server Manager, included with Windows NT Server, is automatically configured for all computers on the network running Windows NT Workstation. Server Manager cannot view or modify computer properties, shared directories, or services on a Windows 95 client. However, it can list the Windows 95 clients on the network. For information on using the Server Manager application, see *Windows NT Server Concepts and Planning*.

Remote Control Agent and Help Desk Options for SMS must be configured on each Windows 95 Client to allow remote administration.

Performance Monitor

Performance Monitor, included with Windows NT Workstation and Windows NT Server, is a graphical tool for measuring the performance of Windows NT computers on the network.

Windows 95 includes a similar tool, System Monitor. These tools are used by administrators to identify bottlenecks or potential problems.

You can use Performance Monitor to monitor the activity on any computer on the network that is running either Windows NT Workstation or Windows NT Server. However, Performance Monitor cannot view the activity on a computer running Windows 95. Likewise, System Monitor can be used to monitor the activity on any computer on the network that is running Windows 95, but it will not view the activity on a computer running Windows NT Workstation or Windows NT Server. A network administrator should have access to a computer running Windows 95, in order to use System Monitor, as well as the computer running Windows NT Workstation or Windows NT Server, in order to use Performance Monitor.

Logon Process

In networks in which the servers run Windows NT Server, user account information can be stored in one of two places: either in a private local user accounts database, or in a domain user accounts database that is shared by all the Windows NT Server computers in the domain.

This section addresses some of the issues involved in logging on to a Microsoft network from computers running Windows NT Workstation and from computers running Windows 95.

Windows NT Workstation

To prepare for account logons from a Windows NT Workstation, use User Manager on the computer running Windows NT Workstation to set up local access to the Windows NT Workstation operating system. Then use the User Manager for Domains on the domain controller to set up access to the specific domain.

When a user logs on to a workgroup computer, that user's logon information is compared with the local user accounts database. When a user logs on to a computer that participates in a domain, that user can choose whether to log on locally, or log on to the domain. (If the domain trusts another domain, the user can alternately choose to log on to the trusted domain.)

If a user's local password doesn't match the password for the domain account, and that user tries to browse the domain or connect to a resource in the domain, access is denied. While tools such as Windows NT Explorer prompt for a valid password, the command-line interface and some applications simply deny access. It is always a better idea to have one set of credentials that apply everywhere in a trusted enterprise.

For a complete discussion of logon scenarios on a Windows NT Network, see the Chapter 2, "Network Security and Domain Planning," in the *Windows NT Server Networking Guide*.

Windows 95

If you want Windows 95 to validate user logons by checking the domain database, logon validation must be enabled on each computer running Windows 95.

▶ **To enable logon validation**

1. In the Network option in Control Panel on the computer running Windows 95, double-click Client for Microsoft Network in the list of network components.
2. In General Properties, check the Log On to Windows NT Domain option if you want to log on to a Windows NT or LAN Manager domain automatically when starting Windows 95. Otherwise, make sure this option is cleared.
3. When you select logon validation, you must also specify the domain to be used for validation. To do so, type or select a name in the Windows NT Domain box.

   Although Windows NT networks allow multiple domains, a computer running Windows 95 can specify only one domain for user-level security. For information on using trust relationships to access multiple domains, see *Windows NT Server 4.0 Concepts and Planning,* which is part of the Windows NT Server documentation set.

For more information, see Chapter 8, "Windows 95 on Microsoft Networks" in the *Windows 95 Resource Kit.*

Password Caching

By default, password caching and unified user logon are enabled in Windows 95. These features work as follows:

When the user supplies a password in order to connect to a resource, that password is saved in a password list file. The next time the user accesses that resource, the password is supplied from the password list. The user only needs to remember one password, the one to log on to the user account.

Password caching and unified user logon are useful when the user needs to log on to multiple networks (for example Windows NT and Novell NetWare networks). To use unified logon, a user account must be available on the network and must contain user account information for the user.

PART II

About Windows NT Workstation

CHAPTER 5

Windows NT 4.0 Workstation Architecture

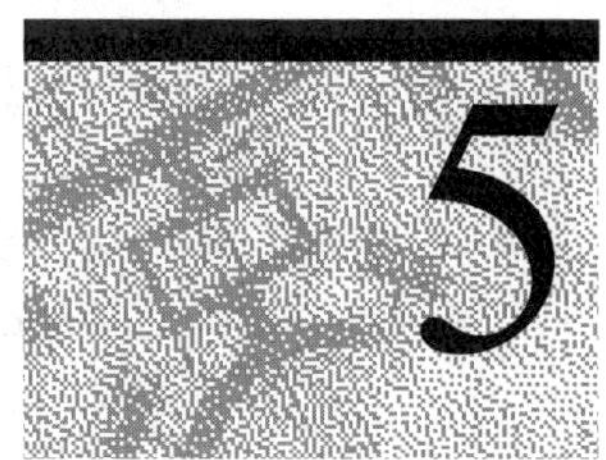

When you first look at Microsoft Windows NT 4.0, you'll notice the popular, functional interface introduced with Microsoft Windows 95. But, beneath that pretty face is the robust, preemptive multitasking, 32-bit operating system Microsoft designed for high-end users. This version was founded upon the same design principles as previous versions, and it maintains their most important advances.

Windows NT 4.0 continues to be compatible with many other operating systems, file systems, and networks. It runs on both complex instruction set computers (CISC) and reduced instruction set computers (RISC). Windows NT also supports high-performance computing by providing kernel support for symmetric multiprocessing.

The major architectural change in this version of Windows NT is the move of the Window Manager, Graphics Device Interface (GDI), and higher-level device drivers from the Win32 environment subsystem into the Windows NT Executive as an executive service. The first section of this chapter describes that change.

Other changes include:

- Support for Distributed Component Object Model (DCOM) applications. For more information on DCOM see "Distributed Applications and Windows NT" in Chapter 1 of the *Windows NT 4.0 Server Networking Guide* and "Sharing DCOM Applications" in Chapter 4 of *Windows NT 4.0 Concepts and Planning*.
- Support for DirectDraw™, DirectSound™, and DirectPlay™, components of DirectX™, the Windows 95 high-performance interface for games and other interface intensive applications. For more information, see "DirectX" later in this chapter.

This chapter provides an overview of the architecture. Other chapters in this book provide details about particular components such as the Windows NT security model, integrated networking features and connectivity options, Windows NT file systems, and the printing system.

What's Changed for Windows NT 4.0

In this release of Windows NT, the Window Manager (USER) and Graphics Device Interface (GDI) have been moved from the Win32 subsystem to the Windows NT Executive. Win32 user-mode device drivers, including graphics display and printer drivers, have also been moved to the Executive. These changes are designed to simplify graphics handling, reduce memory requirements, and improve performance.

An illustration of the architecture of Windows NT 3.51 and an illustration of the architecture of Windows NT 4.0 appear on facing pages on the inside back cover of this book.

Graphics Handling: Before and After

Previous versions of Windows NT included the following elements:

- *Console*, which provides text window support, shutdown, and hard-error handling.
- *Window Manager* (USER), which controls window displays, manages screen output, collects input from keyboard, mouse and other devices, and passes user messages to applications.
- *Graphics Device Interface* (GDI), a library of APIs for graphics output devices. It includes functions for line, text and figure drawing and graphics manipulation. The Window Manager calls these APIs, but user-mode applications can call them directly.
- *Graphics Device Drivers*, which collect and format data for hardware-dependent drivers in the Executive. The graphics display drivers, printer drivers, multimedia drivers, and video display drivers were part of the Win32 subsystem and ran in user mode. These drivers then call kernel-mode drivers in the Executive which interact with the hardware.
- *Miscellaneous environment functions*, special functions for 32-bit Windows applications, like those for creating and deleting processes.

The following figures show how the contents of the Win32 subsystem have changed from Windows NT 3.51 to Windows NT 4.0.

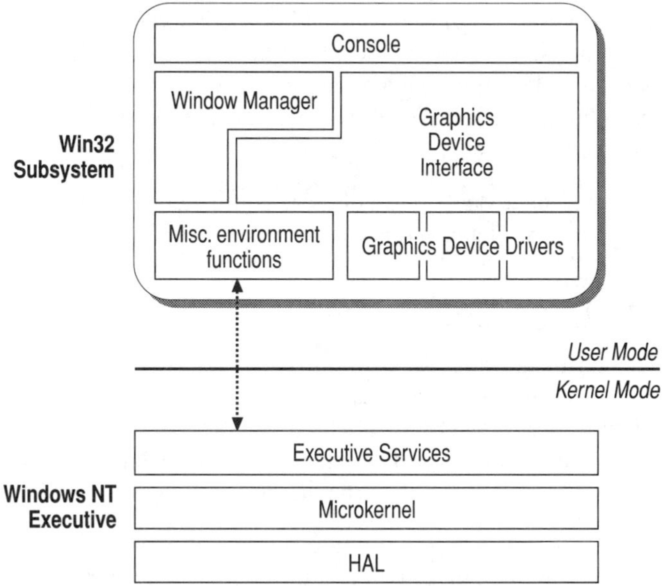

Figure 5.1 Contents of the Win32 Subsystem under Windows NT 3.51

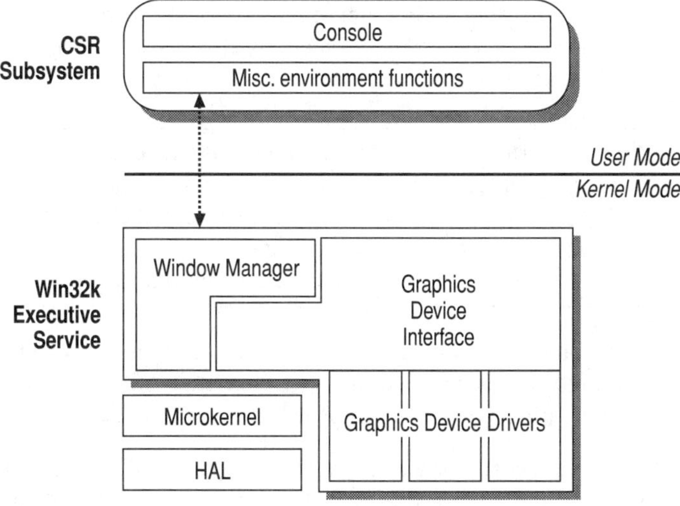

Figure 5.2 Contents of the Win32 Subsystem under Windows NT 4.0

In Windows NT 4.0, the Window Manager, GDI, and Win32 Graphics Device Drivers have been incorporated into the Windows NT Executive. The user-mode portions of Window Manger and GDI, Gdi32.dll and User32.dll, remain in user mode, along with the Console and miscellaneous environment functions. They run in the process created by the Client Server Runtime Subsystem, Csrss.exe, which once included all graphics functions in Win32. The server side functions of GDI and Window Manager, previously known as Winsrv.dll, have been incorporated into the Executive as Win32k.sys.

For a complete description of these components, see the section on the Windows NT Executive, later in this chapter.

Kernel Mode and User Mode

The most significant aspect of this change is that graphics services, which used to run in user mode like applications, now run in kernel mode like most of the operating system. The idea behind kernel mode and its alternative, user mode, is to separate applications from the operating system. Applications run in user mode; operating systems run in kernel mode.

Kernel mode is a highly privileged mode of operation where the code has direct access to all memory, including the address spaces of all user-mode processes and applications, and to hardware. Processes running in kernel mode have access to advanced CPU features for I/O and memory management. However, operating system memory is strictly protected and this protection is enforced by the processor. Applications cannot directly access hardware or the memory of any kernel-mode service. Kernel mode is also known as *supervisor mode*, *protected mode*, and *Ring 0*.

Note In earlier documentation, the terms kernel and microkernel were used interchangeably. In this document, *kernel* refers to a highly privileged mode of processing. The *Microkernel* is a component of the core operating system that provides basic operating system functions, like thread dispatching, interrupt handling, and multiprocessor synchronization.

Applications run in user mode. They have access only to their own address space and must use established interfaces to obtain other system services. This protects the operating system and improves its performance.

Environment subsystems, like those supporting Win32, POSIX, and OS/2, and integral subsystems, like Security, run in user mode but have protected address spaces. Each subsystem is a separate process and the operating system protects its memory from other subsystems and applications.

Communication between Processes

The logical boundary that separates user-mode and kernel-mode processes is designed to make the system robust by preventing direct access to hardware and protecting the core operating system from bugs and unauthorized access by user-mode processes. A failing application will not interfere with the operating system or its support of other applications.

To cross this boundary, user-mode processes must use well-documented application program interfaces (APIs) to switch their threads from user mode to kernel mode. Such a conversion is called a *kernel-mode transition*. Kernel-mode threads can use Executive services but must be switched back to user mode to return control to the application.

Accessing an environment subsystem involves several kernel/user mode transitions and consumes substantial memory and processor time. This is an example of a graphics call in previous versions of Windows NT. It demonstrates that interprocess communication can be quite complex, even when optimized:

- The application uses an API to make a graphics call to a user-mode dynamic link library. The component that implements the call makes a kernel-mode trap call to the Executive to switch its thread and copy its call parameters from its user mode stack to its kernel mode stack. Then, the processor's stack register is switched to point to kernel mode. Now the thread can run in the Executive.
- Applications communicate with protected subsystems by using local procedure calls (LPC), an application-independent method of communication between components on the same computer. After the thread is switched to kernel mode, the Microkernel schedules the LPC for delivery.
- Using Fast LPC, an optimized communication method, the Microkernel recognizes that the call from the application involves a thread in the environment subsystem. It considers the calling application thread and the receiving subsystem thread to be paired. The receiving thread can now use the unexpired time from the sending thread.
- The graphics call parameters are passed to the receiving subsystem thread. The receiving thread switches back to user mode to fulfill the graphics request.
- The subsystem completes its task and then returns control to the waiting calling thread in the application by the same method.
- The calling thread (from the DLL) is switched back to user mode before returning control to the application.

Microsoft operating-system engineers also used the concept of a *shared memory window* to speed up communication. Data is placed in a temporary shared memory window administered by the Process Manager in the Executive. This lets the application see into the subsystem's memory and share data without using LPCs. However, because the application thread must still run in the Executive, kernel/user mode transitions and thread switches are still required.

Why Change?

When Windows NT was first designed, the Win32 environment subsystem was designed as a peer to the environment subsystems supporting applications in MS-DOS, POSIX, and OS/2. However, applications and other subsystems needed to use the graphics, windowing, and messaging functions in the Win32 subsystem. To avoid duplicating these functions, the Win32 subsystem was used as a server for graphics functions to all subsystems.

This design worked respectably for Windows NT 3.5 and 3.51, but it underestimated the volume and frequency of graphics calls. Having functions as basic as messaging and window control in a separate process generated substantial memory overhead from client/server message passing, data gathering, and managing multiple threads. It also required multiple context switches, which consume CPU cycles as well as memory. The volume of graphics support calls per second degraded the performance of the system. It was clear that a redesign of this facet in Windows NT 4.0 could reclaim these wasted system resources and improve performance.

Evaluating the Change

Several features of the Windows NT operating system simplified this change from user mode to kernel mode:

- The modularity and extensibility of Windows NT Executive made it possible to add new components without disrupting existing ones.
- Application program interfaces are linked dynamically at run time, so code within the functions could be changed without recompiling all applications that used them. Also, no function calls or returns were changed, so these revisions of the Windows NT 4.0 architecture should be transparent to applications and users. Only user-mode printer and display drivers must be rewritten to run in kernel mode.
- Shifting the graphics functions into the Executive also simplified the operating system code and the process applications use to access Executive services. When an application calls a USER or GDI function now, the entry point executes a single kernel-mode trap call to switch the thread to kernel mode, eliminating the need for shared memory buffers and paired threads. After the thread transition is complete, application threads can run in the Executive and Microkernel code directly without further kernel-mode transitions or context switches. The savings is especially apparent in repeated, resource-intensive activities, such as high-frequency and high-bandwidth interactions with video hardware.

Although the new architecture eliminates many thread and process transitions, the kernel-mode transitions still take time and memory. Accordingly, GDI *batching* and *caching* have been retained to offset the effect. With batching, graphics calls are saved until a certain number (the default is ten) accumulate in a queue, and then the whole queue is sent to GDI in a single transition. With caching, read-only properties and data structures are stored near the application after they are retrieved, allowing subsequent retrieval to be nearly instantaneous.

Pure vs. Modified Microkernel Architecture

Along with the benefits comes a cost: Windows NT 4.0 is moving farther away from *pure microkernel architecture*.

Pure microkernel systems satisfy two criteria: They are modular, and they keep the number of the components running in kernel mode to a minimum. The ideal is to have only the hardware-manipulating segments of the operating system and the Microkernel running in kernel mode. The remaining operating system functions would run in user mode.

But the appeal of pure microkernel systems pales upon examination of their costs: They are inherently slow and inefficient, with every function requiring several process and thread transitions, memory buffers, and context switches.

Windows NT is completely modular. Each function is managed by just one component of the operating system. The rest of the operating system and all applications access that function through the responsible component using well-defined, secure interfaces. Data is encapsulated and hidden and there are no alternative routes to it. Modules can be upgraded, removed, and replaced without rewriting the entire system or its standard APIs.

However, Windows NT has always had a *modified* microkernel architecture: Its high-performance subsystems run in kernel mode where they interact with the hardware and each other without thread and process transitions. The Windows NT I/O Manager, Object Manager, Process Manager, Virtual Memory Manager, Security Reference Monitor, and Local Procedure Call facilities have always been part of the Windows NT Executive. Even segments of the graphics handling system, such as video ports, class drivers, and file systems drivers, have always run in kernel mode. So, the movement of USER, GDI, and graphics device drivers to the Executive simply completes this trend.

Performance and Memory

Making USER and GDI into Executive service components decreases their size and improves graphics performance. It eliminates shared memory buffers, reduces code size and complexity, and reduces thread transitions and context switches. For example, accessing GDI from the Win32 server on an Intel Pentium 90 takes at least 70 microseconds while accessing it in kernel mode takes 4 to 5 microseconds. When users are waiting for complex screen changes, these difference are noticeable. Graphics-dependent applications like Microsoft PowerPoint® run 15 to 20% faster on Windows NT 4.0.

Windows NT 4.0 is also much more efficient in its use of memory. It is estimated to save from 256K on machines running single applications to 1MB for users who have several applications running simultaneously. Some of this savings comes from simplifying the code needed to access graphics functions, but most comes from eliminating the 64K shared memory window used to optimize graphics performance in earlier versions of Windows NT.

These marked improvements allow us to incorporate new functionality, like the Windows 95 interface, with no net loss in performance or increase in memory requirements. Overall, the memory use and performance of Windows NT 4.0, should be very close to that of Windows NT 3.51.

Windows NT Design Goals

Windows NT 4.0 adheres to the design goals established for all versions of Windows NT and extends them.

Compatibility

C*ompatibility* is apparent in the integration of the popular Windows 95 interface, continued support for the FAT file system, for MS-DOS, OS/2, Windows 3.*x* and POSIX applications and for a wide variety of devices and networks.

Scalability and Portability

Portability means that Windows NT runs on both CISC and RISC processors. CISC includes computers running with Intel 486 or higher processors. RISC includes computers with MIPS R4000or Digital Alpha AXP, or PowerPC processors.

Scalability means that Windows NT 4.0 takes full advantage of symmetric multiprocessing hardware. It allows the Microkernel to execute on any processor and allows the processors to run any thread. It does this, in part, by allowing the Microkernel to preempt lower priority threads and requiring all code to be reentrant, even in the Executive.

Incorporating Win32 graphics functions into the Executive significantly improves the scalability of Windows NT because graphics calls no longer involve context switches. Context switching requires systemwide spinlocks which limit the efficacy of multiple processors. The simple kernel mode thread transitions now involved in graphics calls do not require spinlocks.

In addition, although the Window Manager and GDI now run in kernel mode, these threads are all still scheduled and preemptible and all code is reentrant. In fact, only Microkernel code which, technically, does not run on a thread, is not preemptible.

Also, the threads of the GDI still run asynchronously; that is, they do not wait for the threads of other applications and do not require application threads to wait for them. On multiprocessor computers, multiple threads can run in Window Manager and the GDI simultaneously. GDI synchronizes with applications only when they need access to the same device. This allows the threads of the GDI, and of the applications that call its functions, to run on any available processor.

Windows NT 4.0 applications now use a single thread to get graphics services from the Executive. Previous versions required two paired threads; one in the application and one in the Win32 subsystem. Ironically, Windows NT 4.0 is not losing the efficiency of running parallel threads simultaneously, just because it never had it. Even on symmetric multiprocessing systems, almost all calls to Win32 run synchronously. Each thread each waits for the other to finish before proceeding. However, even this single-threaded system runs more efficiently on multiprocessor systems than the double-threaded model because costly context switches are eliminated. Also, less memory is required when graphics services run in the context of a single thread, instead of paired thread stacks.

Security

Windows NT has a uniform security architecture designed to provide a safe environment to run mission-critical applications as judged by government security standards. Windows 3.5 has been evaluated by the United States National Computer Security Center as meeting the requirements of C2 level security. Windows NT 4.0 with networking is currently undergoing this evaluation.

Windows NT 3.51 is being evaluated in the UK and Germany for a F-C2 / E3 security rating. Windows NT 4.0 will be subject to the same standards.

The Windows NT 4.0 architectural changes do not affect the integral security subsystem or the Security Reference Monitor in the Executive. They are not expected to affect the U.S. or European security evaluations of Windows NT 4.0.

For more information about Windows NT Workstation security, see Chapter 6, "Windows NT Security." For more information about the C2 Evaluation of Windows NT, see the *Windows NT Administrator's Security Guide*. (It is available from Microsoft. Refer to Part #236-074-495.)

Distributed Processing

Distributed processing means that Windows NT is designed with networking built into the base operating system. Windows NT also allows for connectivity to a variety of host environments through its support of multiple transport protocols and high-level client-server facilities including named pipes, remote procedure calls (RPCs), and Windows Sockets.

Reliability and Robustness

Reliability and robustness mean that the architecture must protect the operating system and its applications from damage. In Windows NT 4.0, as in earlier versions, applications run in their own processes and cannot read or write outside of their own address space. The operating system data is isolated from applications. Applications interact with the kernel indirectly using well-defined user-mode APIs. Each call requires a kernel mode thread transition that is managed by the Windows NT Executive.

Kernel-mode operations are now more vulnerable to failures in the graphic user interface. As a user mode process, the graphics subsystems could not bring down the operating system but, as components of the Windows NT Executive, they can. This is mainly an issue for servers and peer-to-peer workstations. If a single workstation interface no longer responds to the user, it hardly matters that the operating system is still up and running. In fact, the USER and GDI are so critical that Windows NT has always been designed to shut down if they fail.

A more serious concern is that the USER, GDI, and device drivers can potentially overwrite the data structures of core operating system components. However, this threat is not new. Hardware drivers, like video ports, network card drivers, and hard disk drivers, have always run in kernel-mode. Microsoft offers technical assistance to manufacturers to ensure that their drivers are reliable.

Localization

Localization means that Windows NT is offered in many countries around the world, in local languages, and that it supports the International Organization for Standardization (ISO) Unicode standard.

Extensibility

Extensibility refers to the modular design of Windows NT, which, as described in the next section, allows Microsoft to add new modules to all levels of the operating system. As the industry advances, new features can be added without compromising the stability of the operating system. The new Windows NT 4.0 architecture demonstrates that modules can be moved within the operating system without disturbing existing components.

Windows NT Architectural Modules

Windows NT has a *modular* architecture, meaning that it comprises separate and distinct components, each having sole responsibility for its functions. This chapter introduces the modules in Windows NT 4.0 and then provides a detailed description of each, from the lowest level, nearest to the hardware, to the highest, nearest to the user applications.

Windows NT 4.0 architecture is divided into two main sections: *user mode* and *kernel mode*:

- Kernel mode is a highly privileged mode of operation in which the code has direct access to all hardware and all memory, including the address spaces of all user-mode processes. The part of Windows NT 4.0 running in kernel mode is called the *Windows NT Executive*. It includes the Hardware Abstraction Layer (HAL), the Microkernel, and the Windows NT Executive Service modules.
- User mode is a less privileged processor mode with no direct access to hardware. Code running in user mode acts directly only in its own address space. It uses well-defined operating system application program interfaces (APIs) to request system services. The environment and integral subsystems run in user mode.

Figure 5.3 shows the new Windows NT 4.0 architecture.

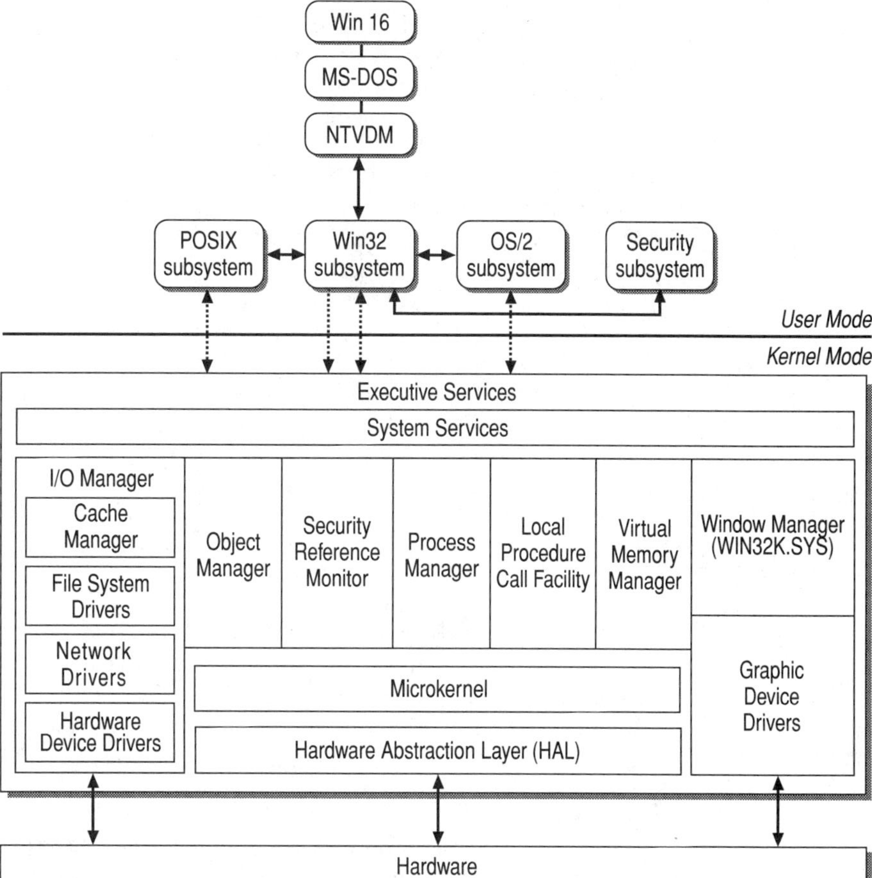

Figure 5.3 Windows NT 4.0 Modular Architecture

Note In earlier documentation, the terms kernel and microkernel were used interchangeably. In this document, *kernel* refers to the entire Windows NT Executive. The *Microkernel* is a component of the Windows NT Executive. *Kernel mode* refers to a highly privileged processing mode.

Hardware Abstraction Layer

The Hardware Abstraction Layer (HAL) is a kernel-mode library of hardware-manipulating routines provided by Microsoft or by the hardware manufacturer. It lies at the lowest level of the Windows NT Executive between the hardware and the rest of the operating system.

This software layer hides, or *abstracts*, the characteristics of the platform behind standard entry points so that all platforms and architectures look alike to the operating system. It enables the same operating system to run on different platforms with different processors. For example, it allows Windows NT to run on single or multiprocessor computers and enables higher-level device drivers, such as graphics display drivers, to format data for different kind of monitors.

A HAL is installed during setup. Different processor configurations often use different HAL drivers. The HAL routines are called by other components of the Windows NT Executive, including the Microkernel, and by higher-level device drivers.

Microkernel

Working very closely with the HAL is the *Microkernel*, the heart of Windows NT. The Microkernel schedules threads, and handles interrupts and exceptions. If a computer has multiple processors, it synchronizes activity among the processors to optimize performance. The Microkernel can run simultaneously on all processors in a multiprocessor configuration.

The role of the Microkernel is to keep the processors as busy and productive as possible. To do so, the Microkernel schedules or *dispatches* threads for the processor in order of priority. It enforces the processor scheduling policy implemented by the Windows NT Executive. The Microkernel also interrupts or *preempts* threads of lower priority in favor of higher-priority threads. It can force *context switches*, directing the processor to drop one task and pick up another. Therefore, code operating in this system must be *reentrant*, that is, able to be interrupted and resume unharmed and be shared by different threads executing different lines of the same code on different processors.

Although the Microkernel dispatches and preempts threads of application and operating system code, the Microkernel's own code does not, technically, run in threads. Hence, it is the only part of the operating system that is not preemptible or pageable. With few exceptions, the remainder of threads running in Windows NT 4.0, including those in the Executive, are preemptible and fully reentrant for maximum efficiency.

The Microkernel also synchronizes the activities of the Windows NT Executive Services, such as the I/O Manager and the Process Manager. The Executive components also rely on the Microkernel for higher levels of abstraction, called *Microkernel objects*, some of which are exported within user-level application programming interface (API) calls.

Scheduling and Priorities

The Microkernel schedules ready threads for processor time based upon their *dynamic priority*, a number from 1 to 31 which represents the importance of the task. The highest priority thread always runs on the processor, even if this requires that a lower-priority thread be interrupted. In Windows NT, priorities are organized in a hierarchy. Each level of the priority hierarchy establishes a range within which the lower level priorities can vary:

- The base priority class of a process establishes a range for the base priority of the process and of its threads. In Windows NT 4.0, the base priority classes are Idle, Normal, High, and Real-Time, each representing a numeric range of base priorities that sometimes overlap at the extremes. The base priority class is set in the application code. The operating system does not change the base priority class, but it does vary the base priority within the class to improve the response of processes to the user.
- The base priority of a process varies within the range established by its base priority class. When a user interacts with a process (the process window is at the top of the window stack), Windows NT boosts the base priority of the process to maximize its response.
- The base priority of a thread is a function of the base priority of the process in which it runs. Except for Idle and Real-Time threads, the base priority of a thread varies only within +/–2 from the base priority of its process.
- The dynamic priority of a thread is a function of its base priority. Windows NT continually adjusts the dynamic priority of threads within the range established by its base priority. This helps to optimize the system's response to users and to balance the needs of system services and other lower priority processes to run, however briefly.

Tip You can change the base priority class of a process while it is running by using Task Manager and other tools. These changes are effective only as long as the process runs. When it is restarted, it reverts to its original base priority class. You can also adjust the amount by which the base priority foreground processes (those the user is interacting with) is boosted by using the Control Panel systems applet Performance tab. (Right-click My Computer, select Properties, then select the Performance tab.) For more information, see "Measuring and Tuning Priorities" in Chapter 13, "Detecting Processor Bottlenecks."

Most applications started by users run at Normal priority. Table 5.1 lists the Windows NT thread priority classes and priorities. The higher the base number, the higher the priority.

Table 5.1 Thread Priorities in Windows NT

Base	Priority class	Thread priority
31	Real-time	Time critical
26	Real-time	Highest
25	Real-time	Above normal
24	Real-time	Normal
23	Real-time	Below normal
22	Real-time	Lowest
16	Real-time	Idle
15	Idle, Normal, or High	Time critical
15	High	Highest
14	High	Above normal
13	High	Normal
12	High	Below normal
11	High	Lowest
10	Normal	Highest
9	Normal	Above normal
8	Normal	Normal
7	Normal	Below normal
6	Normal	Lowest
6	Idle	Highest
5	Idle	Above Normal
4	Idle	Normal
3	Idle	Below normal
2	Idle	Lowest
1	Idle, Normal, or High	Idle

Several tools can help you monitor process and thread priority: two are Performance Monitor and Task Manager, which are built into Windows NT 4.0. See Part 3, "Optimizing Windows NT Workstation," for more information.

Symmetric Multiprocessing

The Windows NT Microkernel takes maximum advantage of multiprocessor configurations by implementing symmetric multiprocessing (SMP) and soft affinity.

Symmetric multiprocessing allows the threads of any process, including the operating system, to run on any available processor. Furthermore, the threads of a single process can run on different processors at the same time.

The Windows NT Microkernel allows processors to share memory and assigns ready threads to the next available processor or processors. This assures that no processor is ever idle or is executing a lower priority thread when a higher priority thread is ready to run. Allowing the operating system to run on multiple processors has significant advantages, especially when it is running processor-intensive applications. Server processes can now respond to more than one client at a time.

The Windows NT Microkernel also uses *soft affinity* in assigning threads to processors: If all other factors are equal, it tries to run the thread on the processor it last ran on. This helps reuse data still in the processor's memory caches from the previous execution of the thread. Applications can restrict threads to run only on certain processors (this is called *hard affinity*), but this is rare. In addition, Task Manager, a tool built into Windows NT 4.0 Workstation and Server, lets you determine which processor runs a process.

Microkernel Objects

The Microkernel manages two types of objects:

- *Dispatcher objects* have a signal state (signaled or nonsignaled) and control the dispatching and synchronization of system operations. Dispatcher objects include events, mutants, mutexes, semaphores, threads, and timers.
- *Control objects* are used to control the operation of the Microkernel but do not affect dispatching. Control objects include asynchronous procedure calls, interrupts, processes, and profiles.

Note The terms *mutex* and *mutant* are often confused. In the Windows NT Executive, mutexes are used only in kernel mode. Mutants are used in the Win32 subsystem to implement Win32 API mutexes. For example, the access control object used in the Win32 API, Create Mutex(), is actually a mutant.

Table 5.2 describes how the Executive uses each type of dispatcher object.

Table 5.2 Dispatcher Objects

Object type	Description
Event	Event objects record the occurrence of system and application events and synchronize events with other actions. They enable threads to stop executing until an anticipated event, like an asynchronous file operation, occurs then resume.
Mutant	Mutants control access to code to make sure that only one thread is executing a line of code at a time. Mutants are generally used in user-mode but can also be used in kernel mode.
Mutex	Mutexes also control access to code to make sure that only one thread is executing a line of code at a time. Unlike mutants, mutexes can be used only in kernel mode.
Semaphore	Semaphores are like traffic signals that let through only as many threads as a resource can support. If a resource is fully occupied, the semaphore signals that it is full. When the resource becomes available again, the semaphore signal changes to let more threads in. Semaphores make it possible for resources to be shared. If semaphore objects are named when they are created, they, too, can be shared by multiple processes.
Thread	Threads are the parts of a process that execute program code. The Microkernel schedules threads to run on processors. The process in which the thread runs determines the virtual address space mapping for the thread and accumulates its run time. A process can have one or many threads. Multiple threads are required for parallel processing, in which different threads of a process run simultaneously on different processors in a single address space.
Timer	Timers record the passage of time and end operations for which time has expired.
Section	Sections represent areas of memory that can be viewed as a contiguous sequence of addresses.

Table 5.3 describes how the Executive uses each type of control object.

Table 5.3 Control Objects

Object type	Description
Asynchronous Procedure Call	Used to break into the execution of a specified thread and to cause a procedure to be called in a specified processor mode.
Interrupt	Used to connect an interrupt source to an interrupt service routine by means of an entry in an Interrupt Dispatch Table (IDT). Each processor has an IDT that is used to dispatch interrupts that occur on that processor.
Process	Used to represent the virtual address space and control information necessary for the execution of a set of thread objects. A process object contains a pointer to an address map, a list of ready threads containing thread objects while the process is not in the balance set, a list of threads that belong to the process, the total accumulated time for all threads executing within the process, a base priority, and a default thread affinity. A process object must be initialized before any thread objects that specify the process as their parent can be initialized.
Profile	Used to measure the distribution of run time within a block of code. Both user and system code can be profiled.

The third and most intricate module that runs in kernel mode is the Executive. The next several sections describe the functions of the Executive and its components.

Windows NT Executive Services

The Windows NT Executive Services consist of a set of common services available to all components of the operating system. Each group of services is managed by one of these separate components of the Executive:

- I/O Manager
- Object Manager
- Security Reference Monitor (which, along with the Logon and Security protected subsystems, makes up the Windows NT security model)
- Process Manager
- Local Procedure Call Facility
- Virtual Memory Manager
- Window Manager
- Graphics Device Interface
- Graphics Device Drivers

The thin top layer of the Executive is called the *System Services*. The System Services shown in Figure 5.1 (and on the inside back cover of this book) are the interface between user-mode environment subsystems and kernel mode. The following sections describe the role of each Executive component.

I/O Manager

The I/O Manager manages all input and output for the operating system. A large part of the I/O Manager's role is to manage communications between drivers. The I/O Manager supports all file system drivers, hardware device drivers, and network drivers and provides an appropriate environment for each them. The I/O manager includes a formal, uniform interface that all types of drivers can call. This enables the I/O Manager to communicate with all drivers in the same way, without any knowledge of how the devices they control actually work.

The Windows NT I/O model uses a layered architecture that allows separate drivers to implement each logically distinct layer of I/O processing. For example, drivers in the lowest layer manipulate the computer's physical devices. Other drivers are then layered on top of the device drivers. These higher-level drivers do not know any details about the physical devices. With the help of the I/O Manager, higher-level drivers simply pass logical I/O requests down to the device drivers, which access the physical devices on their behalf. The Windows NT installable file systems and network redirectors are examples of high-level drivers that work in this way.

This scheme allows easy replacement of file system drivers and device drivers. It allows multiple file systems and devices to be active at the same time while being addressed through a formal interface.

Asynchronous I/O

Drivers communicate with each other using data structures called *I/O Request Packets* (IRPs). The drivers pass I/O request packets to the I/O Manager which delivers them to the target drivers using the drivers' standard services.

Windows NT 4.0 uses *asynchronous I/O* whenever possible to optimize application performance. When an application initiates an I/O operation, the application can continue processing while the I/O request is fulfilled. This differs from *synchronous I/O*, in which an application must stop processing until an I/O operation is complete.

Asynchronous I/O is efficient. Because most I/O devices are much slower than processors, an application can do a lot of work while the I/O operation is in progress. However, the application now needs to determine when I/O operations are complete. Some applications dedicate a wait thread to watch for the I/O. Others include an application procedure call (APC) that the I/O manager calls when the asynchronous I/O operation is complete. Other applications use synchronization objects, such as an event or the file handle, that the I/O system sets to the signaled state when the I/O operation is complete.

Look-Aside Lists

Windows NT 4.0 Workstation and Server now use Look-Aside Lists to help manage the amount of the nonpaged pool memory used by I/O Request Packets (IRPs). Look-Aside Lists replace the I/O zone used as the IRP memory management strategy for in Windows NT 3.51 and earlier versions. However, zones, which preallocate a fixed amount of physical memory, are still supported and used in other Windows NT drivers.

Look-Aside Lists keep track of the current number of entries freed from the nonpaged pool and an allowed maximum number of them. Space for the entries is allocated as needed from the Look-Aside List and counted against the maximum. If processes needs more than the maximum number of entries, space for them is allocated from the nonpaged pool, but the space is returned to the pool when the memory is released, not to the Look-Aside List. The maximum number of entries is based on the amount of physical memory in the system and whether it is a workstation or a server. For a given amount of physical memory, the maximum number of entries for servers is higher.

I/O Queuing

The I/O Manager processes requests from the I/O queue in order of priority, not in the order received. When an environment subsystem issues an asynchronous I/O request, the I/O Manager returns to the environment subsystem immediately after putting the request in a queue, without waiting for the device driver to complete its operations. Meanwhile, a separate I/O Manager thread administers the queue. When each I/O request is finished, the I/O Manager notifies the process that requested the I/O.

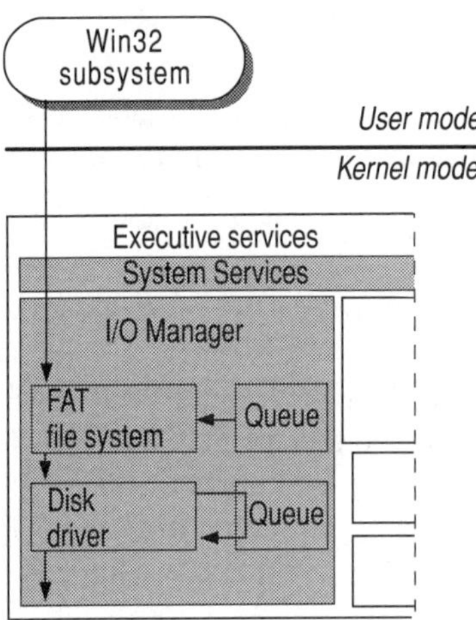

Figure 5.4 I/O Queueing

Cache Manager

The I/O architecture includes a single *Cache Manager* that handles caching for the entire I/O system. *Caching* is a method used by a file system to improve performance. Instead of reading and writing directly to the disk, frequently used files are temporarily stored in a cache in memory, and reads and writes to those files are performed in memory.Cache Manager uses a file-mapping model that is closely integrated with Windows NT Virtual Memory Manager. Cache Manager provides caching services to all file systems and network components under the control of the I/O Manager. Cache Manager can dynamically increase and decrease the size of the cache as the amount of available physical memory varies. When a process opens a file that already resides in the cache, Cache Manager simply copies data from the cache to the process's virtual address space, and vice versa, as reads and writes are performed.

Cache Manager offers services such as *lazy write* and *lazy commit*, which can improve overall file system performance. Lazy write lets you record changes in the file structure cache, which is quicker than recording them on disk. Then later, when demand on the processors is low, Cache Manager writes the changes to the disk. Lazy commit is similar to lazy write: Instead of immediately marking a transaction as successfully completed, the system caches the committed information and later writes it to the file system log as a background process.

File System Drivers

The I/O Manager routes communication to file system drivers. Windows NT 4.0 enables multiple NTFS (Windows NT File System) and FAT (File Allocation Table) systems to coexist in different logical partitions of the same physical device.

Note Windows NT 4.0 does not support High Performance File System (HPFS), the file system designed for OS/2 1.*x* operating systems. Support for this file system ends with this release.

The I/O Manager treats file system drivers as just another device driver, routing messages for certain volumes to the appropriate software driver for that device adapter. When the I/O Manager cannot determine the file system for a volume, it forwards messages to the RAW default file system, which attempts to interpret requests and determine the appropriate low-level device driver before logging an error.

NTFS, the file system designed for Windows NT, supports many features, including file system security, Unicode, recoverability, long filenames, and POSIX. FAT, which is a simpler file system, supports long filenames, but not file system security. FAT is supported for backward compatibility with MS-DOS and Windows 3.*x*.

Windows NT 4.0 also supports Compact Disc Filing System (CDFS), an ISO9660-compliant file system for CD-ROM devices.

The Windows NT I/O architecture not only supports traditional file systems but has implemented its network redirector and server as file system drivers. The I/O Manager sees no difference between accessing files stored on a remote networked computer and accessing those stored locally on a hard disk. In addition, redirectors and servers can be loaded and unloaded dynamically, just like any other driver, and multiple redirectors and servers can coexist on the same computer.

For more information about supported file systems, see Chapter 18, "Choosing a File System." For more information about supported redirectors and servers, see Chapter 1, "Windows NT Networking Architecture," in the *Windows NT Server Networking Guide*.

Hardware Device Drivers

Hardware device drivers are also components of the I/O architecture. Windows NT-compatible hardware device drivers—such as mouse drivers and disk drivers—are written in the C, C++, or Assembler programming language, are 32-bit addressable, and can be used with multiprocessor computers.

Device drivers access the hardware registers of the peripheral devices through entry points in Windows NT Executive dynamic link libraries. A set of these routines exists for every platform that Windows NT supports; because the routine names are the same for all platforms, the source code of Windows NT device drivers is portable across different processor types.

Designers of device drivers are encouraged to create separate drivers for different devices, rather than monolithic drivers, and the design of I/O Manager makes it easy to do so. This allows more flexibility to customize device configurations on the computer and to layer device drivers and other drivers.

For example, the Intel 8042 processor is an interface device: the keyboard and mouse communicate with the i8042 driver as well as with their own respective drivers. Three separate drivers are used—for the i8042, for the keyboard, and for the mouse—rather than one large monolithic driver. This makes it easier to change one component (exchanging the mouse for a different pointing device, for example).

Network Drivers

A third type of driver implemented as a component in the I/O architecture is the *network device driver*. Windows NT includes integrated networking capabilities and support for distributed applications. Networking is supported by a series of network drivers.

Redirectors and servers are implemented as file system drivers and run at or below a provider interface layer where NetBIOS and Windows Sockets reside.

Transport protocol drivers communicate with redirectors and servers through a layer called the Transport Driver Interface (TDI). Windows NT includes a number of transports that communicate with the redirector:

- Transmission Control Protocol/Internet Protocol (TCP/IP), a popular routable protocol for wide-area networks.
- NetBEUI, which is compatible with existing LAN Manager, LAN Server, and MS-Net installations.
- NWLink, an implementation of IPX/SPX, which provides connectivity with Novell NetWare.
- Data Link Control (DLC), which provides an interface for access to mainframes and network-attached printers.

Note DLC, unlike the other protocols in Windows NT (NetBEUI, NWLink IPX/SPX, TCP/IP), is not designed to be a primary protocol for use between personal computers. DLC only provides applications with direct access to the data link layer, and thus is not used by the Windows NT redirector.

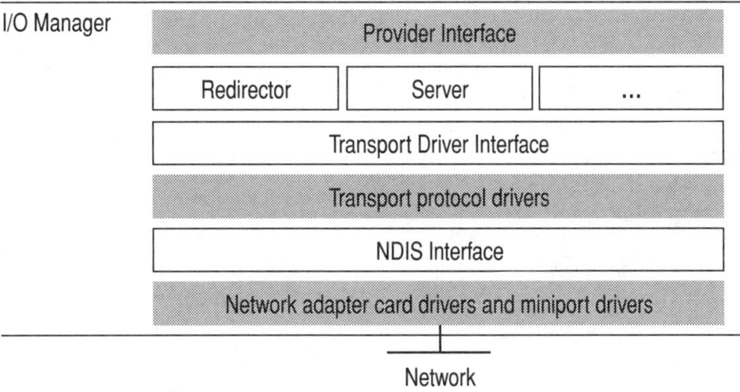

Figure 5.5 Networking Components in Windows NT

At the bottom of the networking architecture is the network adapter card device driver. Windows NT currently supports device drivers written to the *Network Device Interface Specification* (NDIS) version 3.0. NDIS allows for a flexible environment of data exchange between transport protocols and network adapters. NDIS 3.0 allows a single computer to have several network adapter cards installed in it. In turn, each network adapter card can support multiple transport protocols for access to multiple types of network servers.

For more information about network device drivers, see Chapter 1, "Windows NT Networking Architecture," in the *Windows NT Server Networking Guide*.

Object Manager

Object Manager is the part of the Windows NT Executive that provides uniform rules for retaining, naming, and setting the security of objects. *Objects* are software components that consist of a data type, attributes, and a set of operations the object performs.

Like other Windows NT components, the Object Manager is extensible so that new object types can be defined as technology grows and changes.

Object Manager also creates object handles. An *object handle* consists of access control information and a pointer to the object. Processes use object handles to manipulate Windows NT objects.

In addition, the Object Manager tracks the creation and use of objects and manages the global *namespace* for Windows NT. The namespace includes all named objects in the local computer environment. The object namespace is organized like a hierarchical file system, with directory names in a path separated by a backslash (\). Some of the objects that can have names include

- Directory objects
- Object type objects
- Symbolic link objects
- Semaphore and event objects
- Process and thread objects
- Section and segment objects
- Port objects
- File objects

Windows NT Security Model

In a multitasking operating system such as Windows NT, applications share a variety of system resources including the computer's memory, I/O devices, files, and system processor(s). Windows NT includes a set of security components that ensure that applications cannot access these resources without authorization. Together, these components—the Security Reference Monitor component, the Logon Process, and the Security protected subsystems—form the *Windows NT security model.*

The Security Reference Monitor is responsible for enforcing the access-validation and audit-generation policy defined by the local Security subsystem. It provides services to both kernel and user mode for validating access to objects, checking user privileges, and generating audit messages. The Reference Monitor, like other parts of the Executive, runs in kernel mode.

The user-mode Logon Process and Security protected subsystems are the other two components of the Windows NT security model. Because it affects the entire Windows NT operating system, the Security subsystem is known as an *integral subsystem* rather than an environment subsystem. (Environment subsystems are discussed later in this chapter.)

The Windows NT Kernel and Executive are based on an object-oriented model that allows for a consistent and uniform view of security, right down to the fundamental entities that make up the base operating system. This means that Windows NT uses the same routines for access validation and audit checks for all protected objects. That is, whether someone is trying to access a file on the disk or a process in memory, there is one component in the system that is required to perform access checks, regardless of the object type.

The Windows NT Logon Process provides for mandatory logon to identify users. Each user must have an account and must supply a password to access that account. Before users can access any resource on a Windows NT computer, they must logon through the Logon Process so that the Security subsystem can authenticate their username and password. After successful authentication, whenever a user tries to access a protected object, the Security Reference Monitor runs an access-validation routine against the user's security information to ensure the user has permission to access the object.

The security model also provides for discretionary access control so that the owner of a resource can specify which users or groups can access resources and what types of access they're allowed (such as read, write, and delete).

Resource protection is another feature provided by the security model. Tasks can access each others' resources, such as memory, only through specific sharing mechanisms. This feature helps enforce object hiding.

Windows NT also provides for auditing so that administrators can keep an audit trail of which users perform what actions.

By providing these features, the Windows NT security model prevents applications from gaining unauthorized access to the resources of other applications or the operating system either intentionally or unintentionally.

For more information about Windows NT Workstation security, see Part II, Chapter 6, "Windows NT Security." For more information about the C2 Evaluation of Windows NT, see the *Windows NT Administrator's Security Guide*. (It is available from Microsoft. Refer to Part #236-074-495.)

In addition to the protected subsystems, Logon Process and Security, Windows NT includes a number of other user-mode components called *environment subsystems*. The next section describes each of them.

Process Manager

The *Process Manager* is the operating system component that creates and deletes processes and tracks process objects and thread objects. It also provides a standard set of services for creating and using threads and processes in a particular subsystem environment.

Beyond that, the Process Manager does little to dictate rules about threads and processes. Instead, the Windows NT design allows for robust environment subsystems that can define specific rules about threads and processes. For example, the Process Manager does not impose any hierarchy or grouping rules for processes, nor does it enforce any parent/child relationships.

A *process* is an application program or modular part of a program. The operating system sees a process as an address space, a set of objects, and a set of threads that run in the context of the process. The *process object* specifies the virtual address space mapping for the thread and accumulates thread run time.

A process object:

- Includes a pointer to an address map.
- Maintains a list of ready threads when the process is not in the balance set.
- Maintains a list of threads that belong to the process.
- Keeps track of the time accumulated by all threads executing in the process.
- Records the process's base priority and default thread affinity.

A process object must be initialized before any thread objects that list that process as their parent can be initialized.

A *thread* is most the basic schedulable entity in the system. It has its own set of registers, its own kernel stack, a thread environment block, and user stack in the address space of its process.

The Windows NT Process Manager works with the Security Reference Monitor and the Virtual Memory Manager to provide interprocess protection. Each process is assigned a *security access token*, called the primary token of the process. This token is used by Windows NT access-validation routines when threads in the process reference protected objects. For more information about how Windows NT uses security access tokens, see Chapter 6, "Windows NT Security."

Local Procedure Call Facility

Applications and environment subsystems have a client-server relationship. That is, the client (an application) makes calls to the environment server (a subsystem) to satisfy a request for some type of system services. To allow for a client-server relationship between applications and environment subsystems, Windows NT provides a communication mechanism between them. The Executive implements a message-passing facility called a *Local Procedure Call* (LPC) facility. It works very much like the Remote Procedure Call (RPC) facility used for networked processing, but it is optimized for two processes running on the same computer.

For more information on RPCs, see Chapter 1, "Windows NT Networking Architecture," in the *Windows NT Server Networking Guide.*

Applications communicate with environment subsystems by using the LPC facility. The message-passing process is hidden from the client applications by function *stubs,* nonexecutable placeholders used by calls from the server environment. The stubs are kept in dynamic-link libraries (DLLs).

When an application makes an application program interface (API) call to an environment subsystem, the stub in the client application packages the parameters for the call and sends them to a server subsystem process which implements the call. The LPC facility allows the stub procedure to pass the data to the server process and wait for a response.

From the application's perspective, the function in the DLL satisfied the call. The application does not know that the work was actually performed by another subsystem or process or that a message was sent on its behalf.

Virtual Memory Manager

The *Virtual Memory Manager* maps virtual addresses in the process's address space to physical pages in the computer's memory.

It hides the physical organization of memory from the process's threads to ensure that the thread can access its own memory but not the memory of other processes. Therefore, as illustrated by Figure 5.6, a thread's view of its process's virtual memory is much simpler than the real arrangement of pages in physical memory.

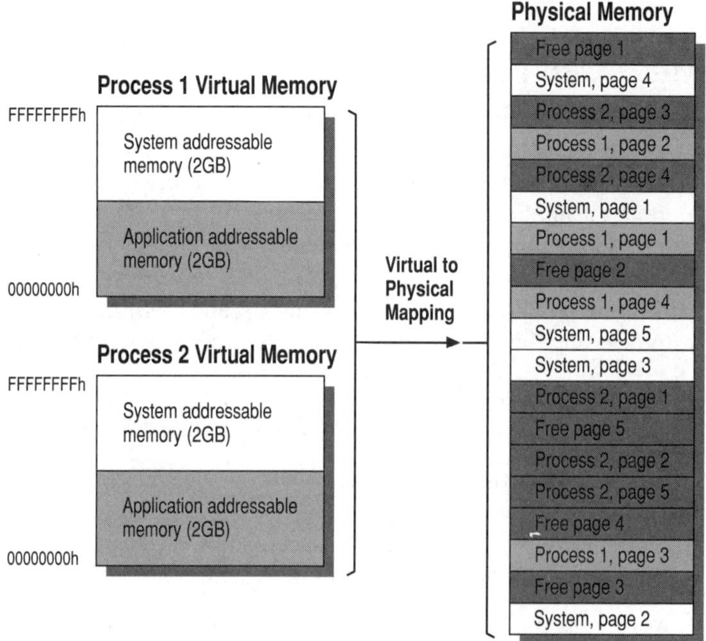

Figure 5.6 Mapping Virtual Memory to Physical Memory

Windows NT Workstation has a demand-paged virtual memory system based on a flat, linear address space with 32-bit addresses.

Virtual memory allows the operating system to allocate more than the actual physical memory of the computer. It does this by using disk space as an extension of memory and by swapping code between physical memory and disk as it is needed. The virtual memory is mapped to addresses in physical memory.

The Virtual Memory Manager allocates memory in two phases for efficiency: reserving it, then committing it. *Committed memory* is part of the paging file, the disk file used to write pages to physical memory. *Reserved memory* is held until needed, then committed. The act of reserving memory maintains a contiguous virtual address space for a process, which is then consumed as needed.

Linear addressing, in which memory addresses begin at 0 and continue in 1-byte increments to the extent of physical memory, replaces segmented memory schemes where each address begins with a segment number. Because virtual memory is limited only by the number of unique addresses, 32-bit addressing allows four billion bytes (4 gigabytes) of address space.

Demand paging is a method by which data is moved in pages from physical memory to a temporary paging file on disk. As the data is needed by a process, it is paged back into physical memory.

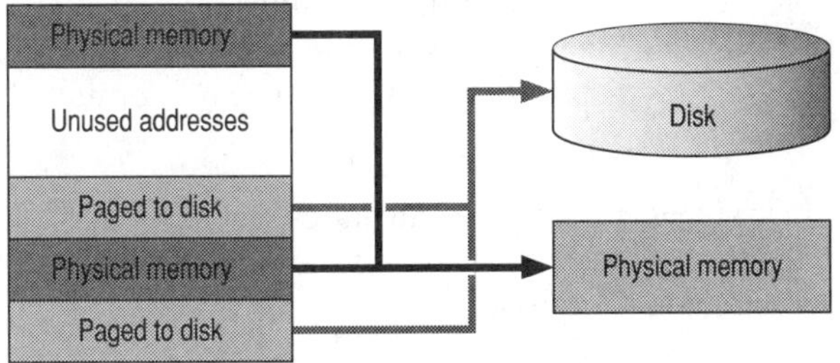

Figure 5.7 Conceptual View of Virtual Memory

The Virtual Memory Manager allocates to each process a unique protected set of virtual addresses available to the process's threads. Each process has a separate address space, so a thread in one process cannot view or modify the memory of another process without authorization. This address space appears to be 4 gigabytes (GB) in size, with 2 GB reserved for program storage and 2 GB reserved for system storage.

Note Windows NT versions prior to 3.51 included some 16-bit data structures that limited processes to 256 MB (64K pages) of virtual memory. These have been converted to 32-bit data structures, so 2 GB of virtual memory is available to all processes.

Window Manager

Window Manager is the part of the Windows NT Executive that creates the familiar screen interface. It is also responsible for processes, like messaging, that use windows functions without ever affecting the user interface.

The Window Manager (USER) and Graphics Device Interface (GDI) functions are implemented by a single component in the Windows NT Executive: Win32k.sys, known as Winsrv.dll in previous releases of Windows NT.

Applications call the standard USER functions to create windows and buttons on the display. Window Manager communicates these requests to GDI, which passes them to the graphics display drivers where they are formatted for the display device.

The Window Manager notifies applications when changes occur in the user's interaction with the interface, such as movement or resizing of windows, cursor movement, and icon selection.

Prior to Windows NT 4.0, the Window Manager was the USER component of the Win32 subsystem and ran in a protected process in user mode. With this release, they were moved into the Windows NT Executive to run in kernel mode. This change was designed to speed up graphics calls and reduce the memory requirements of interprocess communication.

Graphics Device Interface

The Graphics Device Interface (GDI), also called the *graphics engine*, consists of functions in Win32k.sys that display graphics on the computer monitor and printers. It is implemented by the same component as Window Manager.

GDI provides a set of standard functions that let applications communicate with graphics devices, including displays and printers, without knowing anything about the devices. GDI functions mediate between applications and graphics devices such as display drivers and printer drivers.

GDI interprets application requests for graphic output and sends them to graphics display drivers *en route* to the hardware. It includes functions for advanced line, text and figure drawing, and graphics manipulation. GDI provides a standard interface for applications to use varying graphics output devices. This enables application code to be independent of the hardware devices and their drivers.

GDI is also the display driver's connection to the operating system and to the applications it supports. GDI passes API requests to the graphics device drivers, and graphics devices drivers can request services from GDI.

GDI tailors its messages to the capabilities of the device, often dividing the request into manageable parts. For example, some devices can understand directions to draw an ellipse; others require GDI to interpret the command as a series of pixels placed at certain coordinates.

Prior to Windows NT 4.0, GDI was part of the Win32 subsystem and ran in a protected process in user mode. With this release, it was moved into the Windows NT Executive to run in kernel mode. This change was designed to speed up graphics calls and reduce the memory requirements of interprocess communication.

Graphics Device Drivers

Graphics device drivers are dynamic link libraries of functions that let GDI communicate with graphic output hardware devices such as monitors, printers, and fax machines. Display drivers and printer drivers are the most common graphics device drivers. The following section describes display drivers in detail. For more information about printer drivers, see Chapter 7, "Printing."

Display Drivers

Display drivers draw text and graphics on the display and retrieve information about the display device (such as color resolution, screen size and screen resolution). They are specific to a hardware device or group of devices and are sometimes provided by hardware vendors. Windows NT 4.0 Workstation and Server include graphics device drivers for most common devices.

Display drivers are higher-level drivers which reside between the Graphics Device Interface (GDI) and lower-level drivers which control the hardware. They receive application requests from GDI and call GDI functions to help fulfill requests, or break them down into simpler tasks that the hardware device can handle.

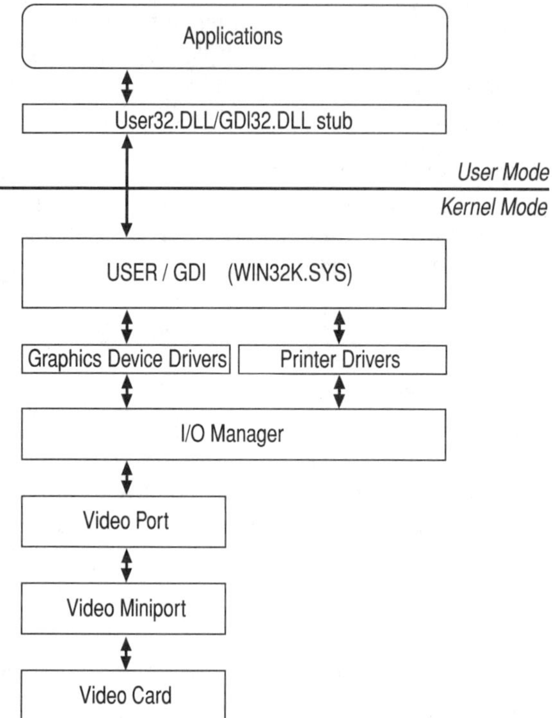

Display drivers depend on lower-level drivers. They are paired with video miniports, which are hardware-manipulating drivers provided by the display driver vendor. Windows NT provides a video port and a library of common functions to simplify the tasks of the display driver and video miniport. It also ships with several display drivers and their miniports.

The miniport carries out user and application requests to configure the hardware for a specific video mode. It also enables the graphics device drivers to communicate directly with the hardware. For example, when a miniport sets up registers and memory frame buffers for a hardware device, it also sends the display driver pointers to the buffers so that the GDI and the driver can write directly to the device's memory.

Prior to Windows NT 4.0, display drivers and printer drivers were part of the Win32 subsystem and ran in user mode. They are now part of the Windows NT Executive running in kernel mode. As a result, display drivers written for previous versions of Windows NT will not run on Windows NT 4.0, and new kernel-mode display drivers written for Windows NT 4.0 are not backward compatible. However, video miniports, which have always run in kernel mode, do not need to be revised to comply with the new architecture.

Environment Subsystems

Windows NT is designed to allow different types of applications to run seamlessly on the same graphical desktop. It runs applications written for existing operating systems and APIs such as MS-DOS, OS/2 1.*x*, and Windows 3.*x*, POSIX and Win32.

Windows NT supports a variety of applications through the use of *environment subsystems*, which are Windows NT processes that emulate different operating system environments.

This chapter has described how the Windows NT Executive provides generic services that all environment subsystems can call to perform basic operating system functions. The subsystems build on the Executive's services to produce environments that meet the specific needs of their client applications.

Each subsystem runs as a separate user-mode process, with each subsystem protected from errors in the others: Failure in one won't cause another subsystem or the Executive to be disabled. Applications are also user-mode processes, so they can't hinder the subsystems or Executive.

Windows NT provides the following protected environments subsystems and Virtual DOS Machines (VDMs):

- MS-DOS NTVDM
- Win16 NTVDMs
- OS/2 subsystem
- POSIX subsystem
- Win32 subsystem

Each environment is optional and is loaded only when its services are needed by a client application.

MS-DOS Environment

MS-DOS-based applications run on Windows NT 4.0 in a process called an *NT Virtual DOS Machine* (NTVDM). NTVDM is a 32-bit Windows application that simulates an Intel 486 computer running MS-DOS.

Each MS-DOS application runs in a separate NTDVM process, although all are named Ntvdm.exe by default. An unlimited number of NTVDM processes can be run. Each runs in its own address space. This protects the applications from each other and protects the rest of the operating system from the NTVDMs.

Note You can change the name of the process in which MS-DOS applications run by editing the configuration registry. For details, see "Monitoring MS-DOS Applications" in Chapter 9, "The Art of Performance Monitoring."

When Windows NT is running on an Intel 486 or higher processor, a processor mode called *Virtual-86* mode is available. This mode allows direct execution of most instructions in an MS-DOS-based application. A few instructions (such as I/O instructions) must be emulated in order to communicate with the hardware. On RISC processors, NTVDM emulates all Intel 486 instructions in addition to providing a virtual hardware environment.

An NTVDM running a MS-DOS application consists of three threads: an application thread on which the MS-DOS application runs, a *heartbeat* thread which simulates the timer interrupts to the MS-DOS application, and a console thread which handles console I/O for the application.

To run MS-DOS-based applications, the NTVDM creates a virtual computer including support for:

- Intel *x*86 instructions, provided by the Instruction Execution Unit
- Read-only memory basic input and output (ROM BIOS) interrupt services, provided by the MS-DOS emulation module
- MS-DOS Interrupt 21 services, provided by the MS-DOS emulation module
- Virtual hardware for devices, such as the screen and keyboard, provided by Virtual Device Drivers

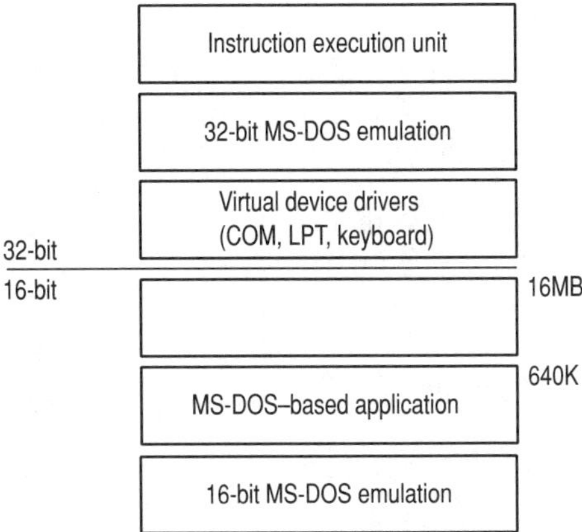

Figure 5.8 Structure of an MS-DOS NTVDM

On Intel 486-based computers, character-based applications can run either in a window or in a full screen. Graphic applications can run only in full screen. If an application in a window changes its video mode, it is automatically switched to full screen. On RISC-based computers, character-based and graphic applications run only in a window.

Windows 16-bit Environment

16-bit Windows applications also run in an NTVDM. An Intel 486 emulator in Windows NT enables16-bit Windows applications to run on RISC computers, too.

Windows NT 4.0 runs 16-bit Windows applications as separate threads in a single NTVDM process with a shared address space. This differs from MS-DOS applications which each run in a separate NTVDM process. The Win16 NTVDM is also known as *WOW* (for Win16-on-Win32). The Win16 NTVDM can also run 16-bit applications On RISC processors, NTVDM emulates all Intel *x*86 instructions in addition to providing a virtual hardware environment.

The Win16 NTVDM is a multithreaded process wherein each of the threads is a different 16-bit Windows application. This single process is multitasking—that is, on a multiprocessor computer, one of the 16-bit processes in the NTVDM can run at the same time as threads of other processes. However, only one 16-bit Windows application thread in an NTVDM can run at a time; all other threads of that NTVDM process are blocked. If a Win16 NTVDM thread is preempted (interrupted by a higher priority thread), the Microkernel always resumes with the thread that was preempted.

Every Win16 NTVDM includes two system threads: a Wowexec.exe thread which starts Win16 applications, and a *heartbeat* thread which simulates timer interrupts to the application. In addition, there is a thread for each Win16 application running in the process.

Windows NT 4.0 includes an option to run a 16-bit Windows application in its own separate NTVDM process with its own address space. This allows 16-bit Windows applications to be fully preemptible and multitasking. For more information, see "Optimizing 16-bit Windows Applications" in Chapter 9, "The Art of Performance Monitoring."

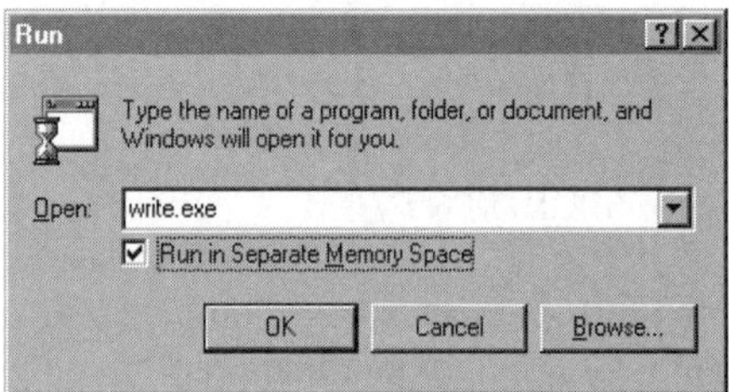

The Windows NT 4.0 NTVDM provides stubs for Windows 3.1 dynamic-link libraries and drivers, and it automatically handles translation of 16-bit Windows APIs and messages.

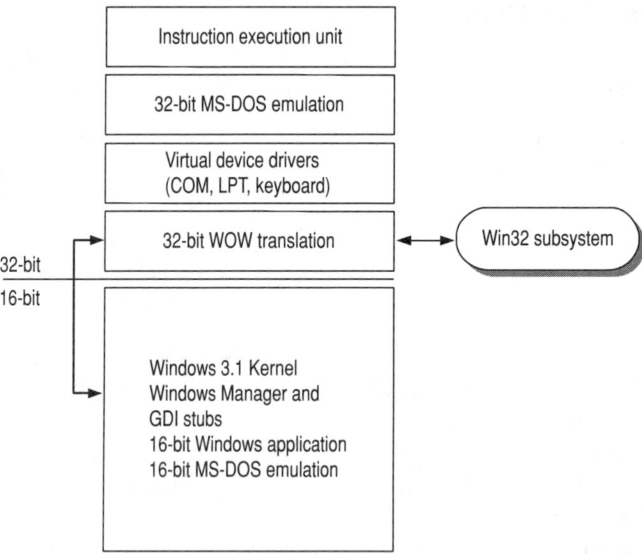

Figure 5.9 Structure of the Win16 VDM

For more information about using Windows 3.*x* applications on Windows NT, see Chapter 27, "Windows Compatibility and Migration."

OS/2 Subsystem

The OS/2 subsystem supports OS/2 1.*x* character-based applications on *x*86-based computers. Although this subsystem isn't supported on RISC computers, OS/2 real-mode applications can run on a RISC computer in the MS-DOS environment. Bound applications (those designed to run under either OS/2 or MS-DOS) will always run in the OS/2 subsystem if one is available.

Note Windows NT 4.0 does not support HPFS, the file system designed for OS/2 1.*x* operating systems. Support for this file system ends with this release.

For more information about using OS/2 1.*x* applications on Windows NT, see Chapter 28, "OS/2 Compatibility."

POSIX Subsystem

The Windows NT POSIX subsystem is designed to run POSIX applications and meets the requirements of POSIX.1.

POSIX (Portable Operating System Interface for Computing Environments) is a set of standards being drafted by the Institute of Electrical and Electronic Engineers (IEEE). It defines various aspects of an operating system, including topics such as programming interface, security, networking, and graphical interface. So far, only one of these standards, POSIX.1 (also called IEEE Standard 1003.1-1990), has made the transition from draft to final form and gained a base of customer acceptance.

POSIX.1 defines C-language API calls between applications and the operating system. It is an API based on ideas drawn from the UNIX file system and process model. Because POSIX.1 addresses only API-level issues, most applications written to the POSIX.1 API must rely on non-POSIX operating system extensions to provide services such as security and networking.

POSIX applications need certain file-system functionality, such as support for case-sensitive filenames and support for files with multiple names (or *hard links*). The new file system, NTFS, supports these POSIX requirements. Any POSIX application requiring access to file system resources must have access to an NTFS partition. POSIX applications that do not access file system resources can run on any supported file system.

For more information about using POSIX applications on Windows NT, see Chapter 29, "POSIX Compatibility."

Win32 Subsystem

Win32 is the native environment subsystem of Windows NT. Prior to Windows NT 4.0, this subsystem included graphics, windowing, and messaging support and the graphics device drivers. These functions have been moved into the Windows NT Executive as executive services running in user mode. For more information about this change, see "What's Changed for Windows NT 4.0," earlier in this chapter.

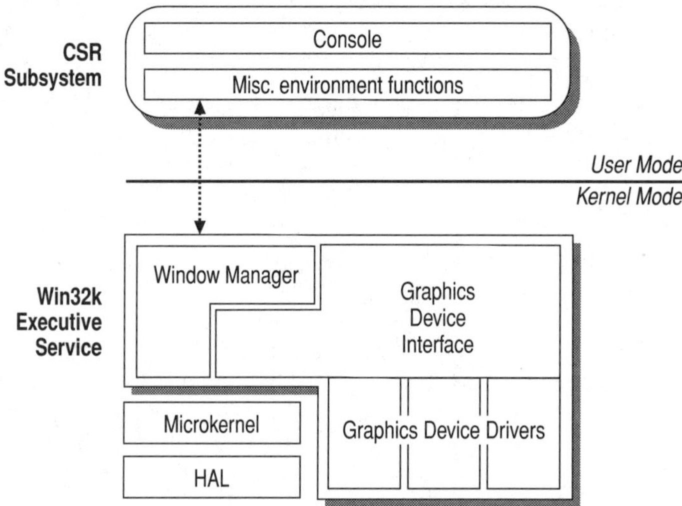

The remaining Win32 user-mode functions, known as the *Console and miscellaneous environment functions* support 32-bit Windows applications:

- The *Console* provides text window support, shutdown, and hard-error handling.
- *Miscellaneous environment functions* consist of specialized functions for 32-bit Windows applications, like creating and deleting processes.

Application Types on Various Hardware Platforms

Windows NT 4.0 runs on computers with Intel 486 or higher processors, MIPS, PowerPC, and Digital Alpha AXP processors. The following table shows how Windows NT supports applications of various types on these different hardware platforms.

Table 5.4 Application Compatibility

Processor	Win32	MS-DOS and Windows 3.*x*	POSIX	OS/2 1.*x*
Intel 486 and Pentium	Source-compatible	Runs application in a VDM	Source-compatible	16-bit character-based only
PowerPC	Source-compatible	Runs application in Intel 486 emulation	Source-compatible	Not available; can run real-mode applications in MS-DOS subsystem
Digital Alpha AXP	Source-compatible	Runs application in Intel 486 emulation	Source-compatible	Not available; can run real-mode applications in MS-DOS subsystem
MIPS R4000	Source-compatible	Runs application in Intel 486 emulation	Source-compatible	Not available; can run real-mode applications in MS-DOS subsystem

DirectX

Introduced with Windows 95, DirectX is a high-performance application program interface that hides hardware and operating system characteristics from the application. DirectX is designed to provide high-speed, real-time response to the user interface.

Windows NT 4.0 now includes three DirectX components: DirectDraw, DirectSound, and DirectPlay for Windows NT 4.0 let you run games and other applications designed for DirectX on Windows 95 on Windows NT 4.0 Workstation and Server.

DirectX for Windows NT 4.0 supports the application entry points called by programs designed for DirectX in Windows 95. The functions are implemented differently in Windows NT than in Windows 95, but they allow you to run the DirectX-based programs on a Windows NT 4.0 workstation or server without changes.

The goal for incorporating DirectX in Windows NT was to provide the best possible graphics performance without compromising the robustness of the system. For example, in Windows NT, DirectX functions never communicate directly with hardware; all graphics functions are mediated by the GDI.

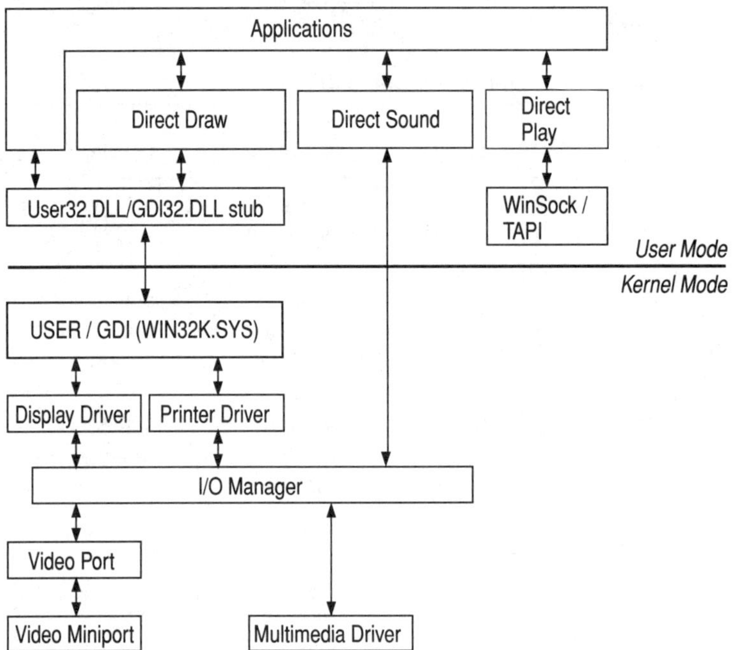

DirectDraw

DirectDraw for Windows NT 4.0 supports a 32-bit application program interface for accelerated drawing. DirectDraw also can emulate functions by breaking them down into simpler tasks for the hardware, much as GDI does for its clients.

Unlike DirectX for Windows 95, DirectDraw for Windows NT does not communicate directly with the driver or with any hardware. All DirectDraw functions are implemented in Windows NT 4.0 but are mediated by the GDI.

DirectSound

For Windows NT 4.0, DirectSound provides all application entry points for DirectX sound functions. However these functions are emulated and are not in accelerated form.

DirectPlay

DirectPlay is a DirectX DLL that simplifies communications between computers, allowing DirectX programs to be run over the network, using a modem, even modem-to-modem. The communications method is hidden from the application and optimized to have minimal effect on the real-time performance of the interface.

DirectPlay for Windows NT 4.0 supports TCP/IP and Novell IPX network protocols on a local area network as well as point-to-point modem connections using TAPI, the Windows Telephony API.

CHAPTER 6

Windows NT Security

Computer security refers to the protection of all components—hardware, software, and stored data—of a computer or a group of computers from damage, theft, or unauthorized use. A computer security plan that is well thought out, implemented, and monitored makes authorized computer use easy and unauthorized use or accidental damage difficult or impossible.

Microsoft included security as part of the initial design specifications for Windows NT, and it is pervasive in the operating system. The security model includes components to control who accesses which objects (such as files and shared printers), which actions an individual can take on an object, and which events are audited.

This chapter provides an overview of both the security features and the Windows NT security model itself. It describes the components that make up the model, and explains how Windows NT tracks each user and each securable object. It shows how Windows NT validates access requests and how it audits activities performed on protected objects.

This chapter also describes three levels of security—minimal, standard, and high-level—with recommendations for both assessing your needs and for implementing the most appropriate security measures for your organization. It concludes with a section describing C2 security.

Windows NT Security Features

A number of features make it easy to customize permissions in Windows NT. Introduced briefly in this section, these features are described in detail in the documentation for Windows NT Workstation and Windows NT Server. Become familiar with theses features so that you can plan and implement the security configuration you desire.

Caution No operating system can provide *physical* security for your computers. External media drives (floppy disk, CD-ROM, and so on) provide the physical means for anyone to bypass Windows NT and gain access to your files. For information on physical security, see the "Physical Security Considerations" section in "High-Level Security" later in this chapter.

User Accounts

Windows NT security is based on the concept of *user accounts*. You can create an unlimited number of accounts, grouping them as appropriate. You then permit or restrict their access to any computer resource. User accounts are described in detail in Chapter 2 "Working with User and Group Accounts" in *Microsoft Windows NT Server Concepts and Planning*. For procedural information, see Help.

Passwords

In Chapter 2, "Working with User and Group Accounts" in *Microsoft Windows NT Server Concepts and Planning,* you'll also find a description of the password enforcement options, such as minimum password length, minimum and maximum password age, password "uniqueness" (how often a password can be reused), and controls over whether a user can—or must—change his or her password. For procedural information, see Help

File and Directory Protection

A range of file protections can be set on a per-file or per-directory basis. The protections can be on a per-user or per-group basis. This feature is described in Chapter 4, "Managing Shared Resources and Resource Security," in *Microsoft Windows NT Server Concepts and Planning*. Specific files to protect are described later in this chapter, in the section "Protecting Files and Directories" under "High-Level Security." For procedural information, see Help.

Registry Protection

Because the Registry is the repository of all system configuration information, it is important to protect it from unauthorized changes. At the same time, individuals and programs that need to access or alter information in the Registry must be allowed to do so. Part V, "Windows NT Registry," describes the Registry and the Registry Editor, including information on protecting keys in the Registry. Specific keys to protect are described later in this book, in the "Protecting the Registry" sections under "Standard Security" and "High-Level Software Security Considerations." For procedural information, see Help.

Printer Protection

You can prevent specific users from printing to a system printer for all or part of the day. This feature is described in Chapter 4, "Managing Shared Resources and Resource Security," in *Microsoft Windows NT Server Concepts and Planning*. For procedural information, see Help.

Auditing

Auditing is built into Windows NT. This allows you to track which user account was used to attempt what kind of access to files or other objects. Auditing also can be used to track logon attempts, system shutdowns or restarts, and similar events. Auditing is described in Chapter 9 "Monitoring Events" of *Microsoft Windows NT Server Concepts and Planning*. For procedural information, see Help.

Monitoring Performance

The Windows NT Performance Monitor not only helps administrators fine-tune performance, but it can also warn of approaching problems. Performance Monitor can also help you spot the activity of a virus (by spotting performance degradation) or an attempted break-in (by tracking logon attempts). Performance Monitor can be set to send an alert to one or more administrators when certain events occur. For more information, see Chapter 8, "Monitoring Performance," in *Microsoft Windows NT Server Concepts and Planning*. For procedural information, see Help.

For a thorough discussion of performance monitoring in Windows NT, see Part III, "Optimizing Windows NT Workstation" in this book.

The Security Model

Chapter 5, "Windows NT 4.0 Workstation Architecture," describes the overall architecture of Windows NT. As shown in Figure 6.1, the Windows NT security model includes the following components:

- *Logon processes*, which accept logon requests from users. These include the initial interactive logon, which displays the initial logon dialog box to the user, and remote logon processes, which allow access by remote users to a Windows NT server process.
- *Local Security Authority*, which ensures that the user has permission to access the system.

  This component is the center of the Windows NT security subsystem. It generates access tokens (described later in this chapter), manages the local security policy, and provides interactive user authentication services. The Local Security Authority also controls audit policy and logs the audit messages generated by the Security Reference Monitor.
- *Security Account Manager (SAM)*, which maintains the user accounts database. This database contains information for all user and group accounts. SAM provides user validation services, which are used by the Local Security Authority. SAM is also known as the Directory database.
- *Security Reference Monitor*, which checks to see if the user has permission to access an object and perform whatever action the user is attempting. This component enforces the access validation and audit generation policy defined by the Local Security Authority. It provides services to both kernel and user mode to ensure the users and processes attempting access to an object have the necessary permissions. This component also generates audit messages when appropriate.

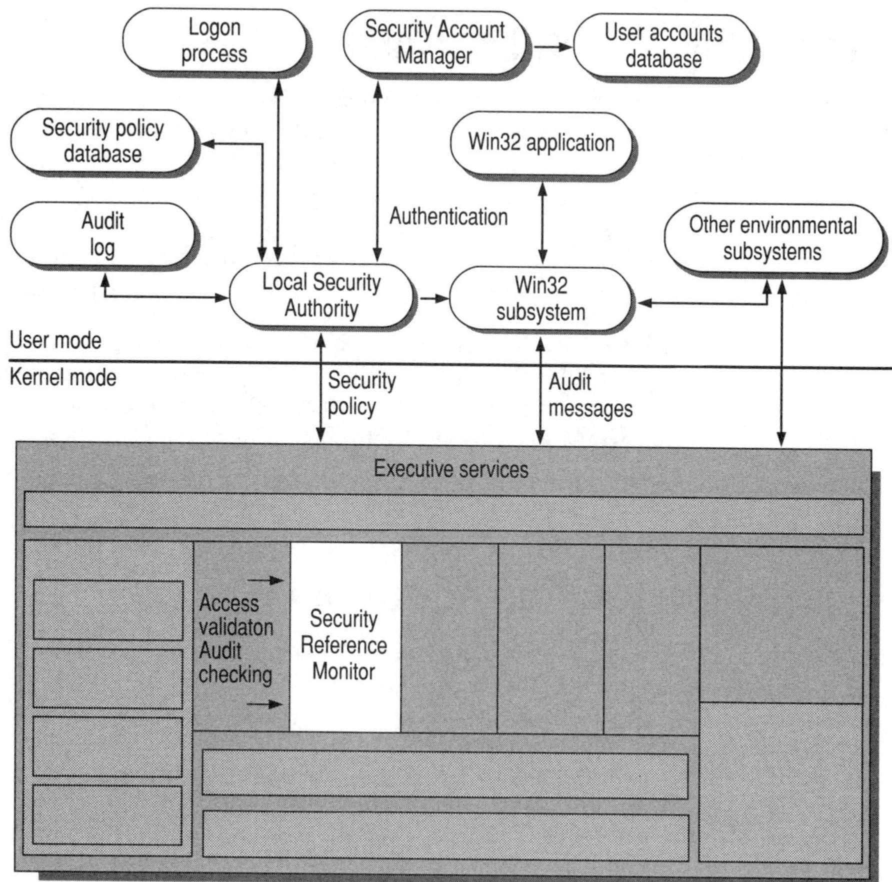

Figure 6.1 Windows NT Security Components

Together, these components are known as the *security subsystem.* (Note that because it affects the entire Windows NT operating system, this is considered an *integral subsystem* rather than an *environmental subsystem.*)

The Windows NT security model is designed for C2-level security as defined by the U.S. Department of Defense. For more information about C2-level security, see "C2 Security" later in this chapter.

Users, Objects, and Permissions

The key objective of the Windows NT security model is to regulate access to objects. The security model maintains security information for each user, group, and object. It can identify access attempts that are made directly by a user, and it can identify access attempts that are made indirectly by a program or other process running on a user's behalf. Windows NT also tracks and controls access to objects that users can see in the user interface (such as files and printers) and objects that users cannot see (such as processes and named pipes).

An administrator assigns *permissions* to users and groups to grant or deny access to particular objects. The ability to assign permissions at the discretion of the owner (or other person authorized to change permissions) is called *discretionary access control*. For more information, see Chapter 4, "Managing Shared Resources and Resource Security," in *Microsoft Windows NT Server Concepts and Planning*. For procedural information, see Help.

Security Information about Users

Users are identified to the system by a unique *security ID* (SID). Security IDs are unique, and there is no possibility of having two identical security IDs.

For example, suppose Sally, who has a Windows NT account, leaves her job at a company but later returns to a different job at the same company. When Sally leaves, the administrator deletes her account, and Windows NT no longer accepts her security ID as valid. When Sally returns, the administrator creates a new account, and Windows NT generates a new security ID for that account. The new security ID does not match the old one, so nothing from the old account is transferred to the new account.

When a user logs on, Windows NT creates a *security access token*. This includes a security ID for the user, security IDs for the groups to which the user belongs, plus other information such as the user's name and the groups to which that user belongs. In addition, every process that runs on behalf of this user will have a copy of his or her access token. For example, when Sally starts Notepad, the Notepad process receives a copy of Sally's access token.

Figure 6.2 illustrates the contents of an access token.

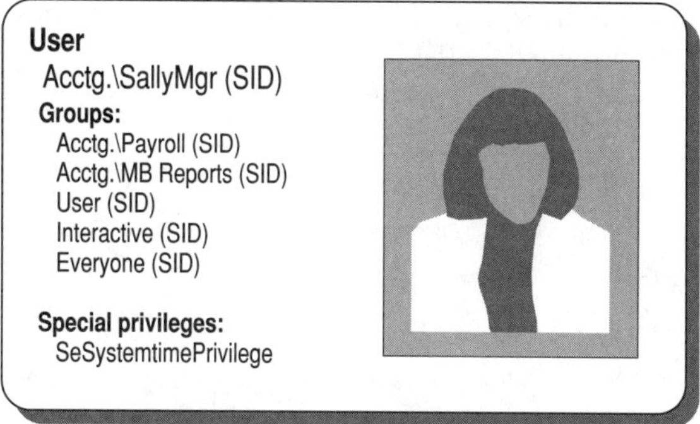

Figure 6.2 Access Token Contents

Windows NT refers to the security IDs within a user's access token when he or she tries to access an object. The security IDs are compared with the list of access permissions for the object to ensure that the user has sufficient permission to access the object.

How Windows NT Creates an Access Token

Before a user can do anything on a Windows NT system, he or she must log on to the system by supplying a username and password. Windows NT uses the username for identification and password for validation. The following procedure illustrates the interactive logon process for Windows NT.

The initial logon process for Windows NT is *interactive*, meaning that the user must type information at the keyboard in response to a dialog box the operating system displays on the screen. Windows NT grants or denies access based upon the information provided by the user.

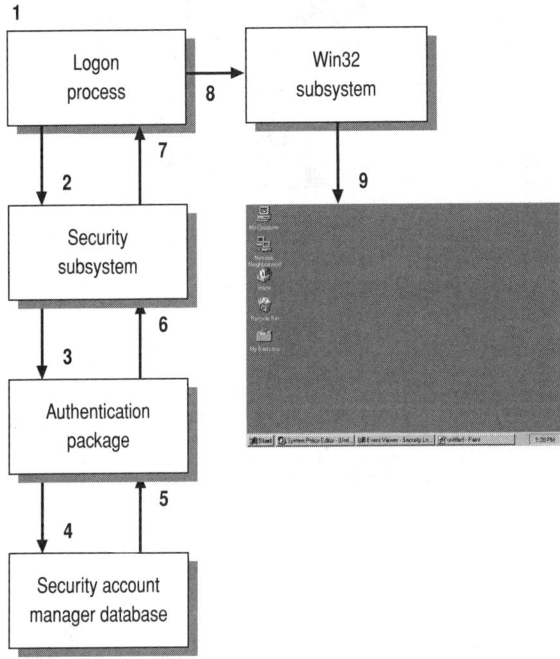

Figure 6.3 Windows NT Validation Process

The following list details the steps included in the interactive logon and validation process, as illustrated in Figure 6.3:

1. The user presses CTRL+ALT+DEL to gain the attention of Windows NT. This key combination before logon protects against Trojan Horse-type programs that impersonate the operating system and trick users into disclosing their username and password.
2. When the user provides a username and a password, the logon process calls the Local Security Authority.

3. The Local Security Authority runs the appropriate authentication package.

Note Windows NT can support multiple authentication packages that are implemented as DLLs. This flexibility gives third-party software vendors the opportunity to integrate their own custom authentication packages with Windows NT. For example, a network vendor might augment the standard Windows NT authentication package by adding one that allows users to log onto Windows NT and the vendor's network simultaneously.

---

4. The authentication package checks the user accounts database to see if the account is local. If it is, the username and password are verified against those held in the user accounts database. If it is not, the requested logon is forwarded to an alternate authentication package.
5. When the account is validated, the SAM (which owns the user accounts database) returns the user's security ID and the security IDs of any global groups to which the user belongs.
6. The authentication package creates a logon session and then passes the logon session and the security IDs associated with the user to the Local Security Authority.
7. If the logon is rejected, the logon session is deleted, and an error is returned to the logon process.

   Otherwise, an access token is created, containing the user's security ID and the security IDs of Everyone and other groups. It also contains user rights (described in the next section) assigned to the collected security IDs. This access token is returned to the logon process with a Success status.
8. The logon session calls the Win32 subsystem to create a process and attach the access token to the process, thus creating a *subject* for the user account. (Subjects are described in the section called "Subjects and Impersonation," later in this chapter.)
9. For an interactive Windows NT session, the Win32 subsystem starts the desktop for the user.

After the validation process, a user's shell process (that is, the process in which the desktop is started for the user) is given an access token. The information in this access token is reflected by anything the user does, or by any process that runs on the user's behalf.

User Rights

Typically, access to an object is determined by comparing the user and group memberships in the user's access token with permissions for the object. However, some activities performed by users are not associated with a particular object.

For example, you might want certain individuals to be able to create regular backups for the server. These people should be able to do their job without regard to permissions that have been set on those files. In cases like this, an administrator could assign specific *user rights* (sometimes called privileges) to give users or groups access to services that normal discretionary access control does not provide. (You can use the following dialog box—from the User Manager tool—to assign user rights.)

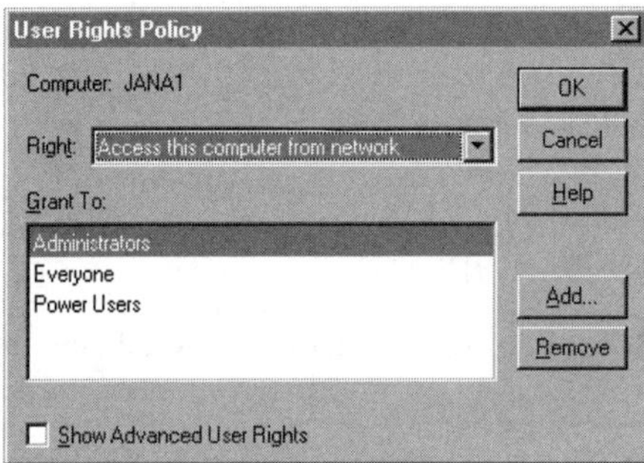

Backing up files and directories, shutting down the computer, logging on interactively, and changing the system times are all examples of user rights defined by Windows NT.

Note In the current release of Windows NT, the set of user rights is defined by the system and cannot be changed. Future versions of Windows NT might allow software developers to define new user rights appropriate to their application.

For more information about permissions and user rights, see "High-Level Software Security Considerations" in the "High-Level Security" section later in this chapter. Also, see Chapter 4, "Managing Shared Resources and Resource Security," in *Microsoft Windows NT Server Concepts and Planning*. For procedural information, see Help.

Subjects and Impersonation

One objective of the Windows NT security model is to ensure that the programs a user runs don't have greater access to objects than the user does.

A *subject* is the combination of the user's access token plus the program acting on the user's behalf. Windows NT uses subjects to track and manage permissions for the programs each user runs.

When a program or process runs on the user's behalf, it is said to be running in the *security context* of that user. The security context controls what access the subject has to objects or system services. To accommodate the client-server model of Windows NT, two classes of subjects exist within the Windows NT security architecture:

- A *simple subject* is a process that was assigned a security context when the corresponding user logged on. It is not acting in the capacity of a protected server, which might have other subjects as clients.
- A *server subject* is a process implemented as a protected server (such as the Win32 subsystem), and it does have other subjects as clients. In this role, a server subject typically has the security context of those clients available for use when acting on their behalf.

In general, when a subject calls an object service through a protected subsystem, the subject's token is used within the service to determine who made the call and to decide whether the caller has sufficient access authority to perform the requested action.

Windows NT allows one process to take on the security attributes of another through a technique called *impersonation*. For example, a server process typically impersonates a client process to complete a task involving objects to which the server does not normally have access.

In the scenario shown in Figure 6.4, a client is accessing an object on a Windows NT server.

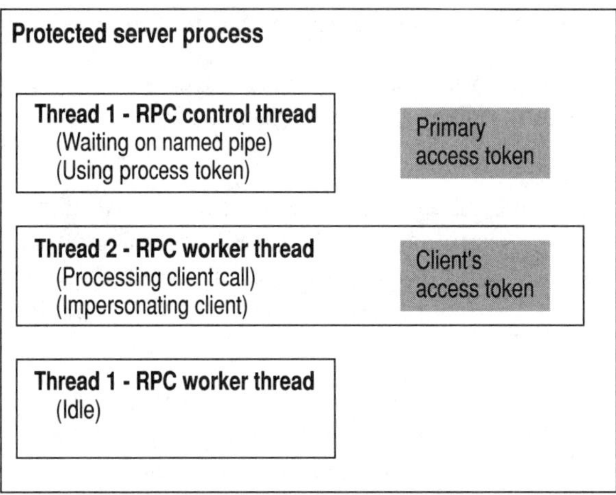

Figure 6.4 Server Subject Security Context

The first thread in the process is a *control thread.* It is waiting to receive remote procedure calls (RPCs) by means of a named pipe. This thread is not impersonating another process, so any access validation to which Thread 1 is subjected will be carried out against the process's primary token.

The second thread in the process is currently handling a call from a client. This thread handles the client's call by temporarily using the client's access token to run with that client's access permissions (that is, the client's security context). While impersonating the client, any access validation to which Thread 2 is subjected is carried out in the security context of the client.

The third thread in this scenario is an idle worker thread that is not impersonating any other process.

The following illustration shows an audited event in which impersonation was used. (Use the Event Viewer to see this type of information for your system.) Here, information for both the primary user and client user is recorded in the security log.

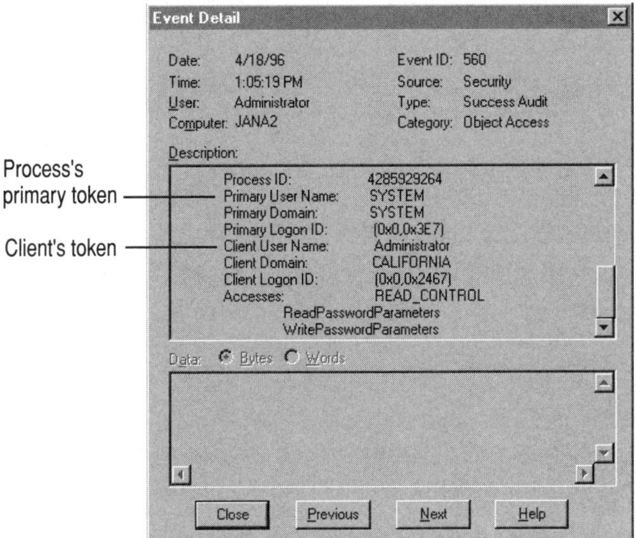

Security Information about Objects

All named (and some unnamed) objects in Windows NT can be secured. The security attributes for an object are described by a *security descriptor*. An object's security descriptor includes the following parts (as shown in Figure 6.5):

- An *owner security ID*, which indicates the user or group who owns the object. The owner of an object can change the access permissions for the object.
- A *group security ID*, which is used only by the POSIX subsystem and ignored by the rest of Windows NT.
- A discretionary *access control list* (ACL), which identifies which users and groups are granted or denied which access permissions. Discretionary ACLs are controlled by the owner of the object. (These are described later, in "Access Control Lists and Access Control Entries.")

- A *system ACL*, which controls which auditing messages the system will generate. (For more information about auditing objects, see "Auditing Security Events," later in this chapter.) System ACLs are controlled by the security administrators.

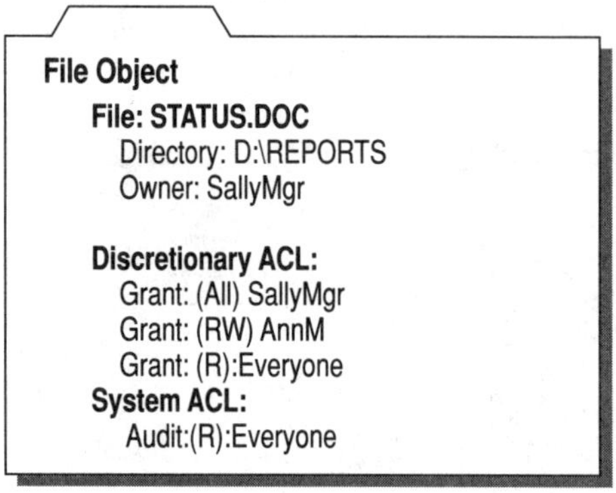

File Object

File: STATUS.DOC
Directory: D:\REPORTS
Owner: SallyMgr

Discretionary ACL:
Grant: (All) SallyMgr
Grant: (RW) AnnM
Grant: (R):Everyone
System ACL:
Audit:(R):Everyone

Figure 6.5 Security Descriptor for a File Object

Types of Objects

The type of permissions that can be granted or denied for an object are dictated by the object's type. For example, you can specify permissions like Manage Documents and Print for a printer queue, and for a directory you can specify Read, Write, Execute, and so on.

Another quality that affects the permissions of an object is whether that object is a container object or a noncontainer object. A *container object* is one that logically contains other objects; *noncontainer* objects do not contain other objects. For example, a directory is a container object that logically contains files and other directories. Files are noncontainer objects. This distinction between container and noncontainer objects is important because objects within a container object can inherit certain permissions from the parent container. For more information, see "Access Control Inheritance," later in this chapter.

Note NTFS supports the inheritance of ACLs from directory objects to file objects that are created within the directory. For more information about NTFS, see Chapter 17, "Disk and File System Basics" and Chapter 18, "Choosing a File System."

Access Control Lists and Access Control Entries

Each ACL is made up of *access control entries* (ACEs), which specify access or auditing permissions to that object for one user or group. There are three ACE types—two for discretionary access control and one for system security.

The discretionary ACEs are AccessAllowed and AccessDenied. Respectively, these explicitly grant and deny access to a user or group of users. The first AccessDenied ACE denies the user access to the resource, and no further processing of ACEs occurs.

Note There is an important distinction between a discretionary ACL that is empty (one that has no ACEs in it) and an object without any discretionary ACL. In the case of an empty discretionary ACL, no accesses are explicitly granted, so access is implicitly denied. For an object that has no ACL at all, there is no protection assigned to the object, so any access request is granted.

SystemAudit is a system security ACE which is used to keep a log of security events (such as who accesses which files) and to generate and log security audit messages.

Access Masks

Each ACE includes an *access mask*, which defines all possible actions for a particular object type. Permissions are granted or denied based on this access mask.

One way to think of an access mask is as a sort of menu from which granted and denied permissions are selected:

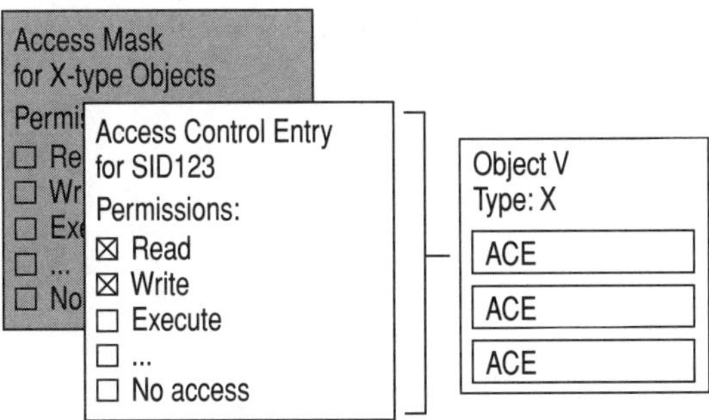

Figure 6.6 Access Control Mask

Specific types include access options that apply specifically to this object type. Each object type can have up to 16 specific access types. Collectively, the specific access types for a particular object type are called the *specific access mask*. (These are defined when the object type is defined.) For example, Windows NT files have the following specific access types:

ReadData	WriteEA (Extended Attribute)
WriteData	Execute
AppendData	ReadAttributes
ReadEA (Extended Attribute)	WriteAttributes

Standard types apply to all objects and consist of these access permissions:

- SYNCHRONIZE, which is used to synchronize access and to allow a process to wait for an object to enter the signaled state
- WRITE_OWNER, which is used to assign write owner
- WRITE_DAC, which is used to grant or deny write access to the discretionary ACL
- READ_CONTROL, which is used to grant or deny read access to the security descriptor and owner
- DELETE, which is used to grant or deny delete access

Generic types are broad types of access whose exact implementation is determined by the application defining an object. These rights are used when protecting an object. For example, an application that defines a voice-annotation object might define specific access rights by using VOICE_PLAY and VOICE_EDIT for playing and editing the object. It might set up a generic mapping structure in which GENERIC_EXECUTE maps to VOICE_PLAY and GENERIC_WRITE maps to both VOICE_PLAY and VOICE_EDIT.

The following table shows the generic types that are mapped from specific and standard types:

Generic type	Mapped from these specific and standard types
FILE_GENERIC_READ	STANDARD_RIGHTS_READ FILE_READ_DATA FILE_READ_ATTRIBUTES FILE_READ_EA SYNCHRONIZE
FILE_GENERIC_WRITE	STANDARD_RIGHTS_WRITE FILE_WRITE_DATA FILE_WRITE_ATTRIBUTES FILE_WRITE_EA FILE_APPEND_DATA SYNCHRONIZE
FILE_GENERIC_EXECUTE	STANDARD_RIGHTS_EXECUTE FILE_READ_ATTRIBUTES FILE_EXECUTE SYNCHRONIZE

Specific and standard types appear in the details of the security log. Generic types do not appear in the security log. Instead, the corresponding specific and standard types are listed.

Access Control Inheritance

Objects can be classified as either container objects or noncontainer objects. Container objects (such as directories) can logically contain other objects; noncontainer objects (such as files) cannot.

By default, when you create new objects within a container object, the new objects inherit permissions from the *parent* object. For example, in the following dialog box, D:\REPORTS\ANNM inherited permissions from its parent directory, D:\REPORTS.

In the case of files and directories, when you change permissions on a directory, those changes affect that directory and its files but do not automatically apply to existing subdirectories and their contents. They do, however, if you check the **Replace Permissions On Existing Files** check box. You can apply the changed permissions to existing subdirectories and their files by selecting the **Replace Permissions On Subdirectories** check box.

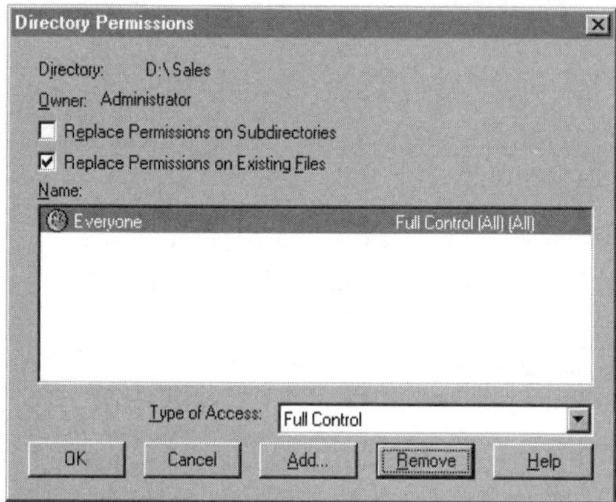

Access Validation

When a user tries to access an object, Windows NT compares security information in the user's access token with the security information in the object's security descriptor, as shown in Figure 6.7:

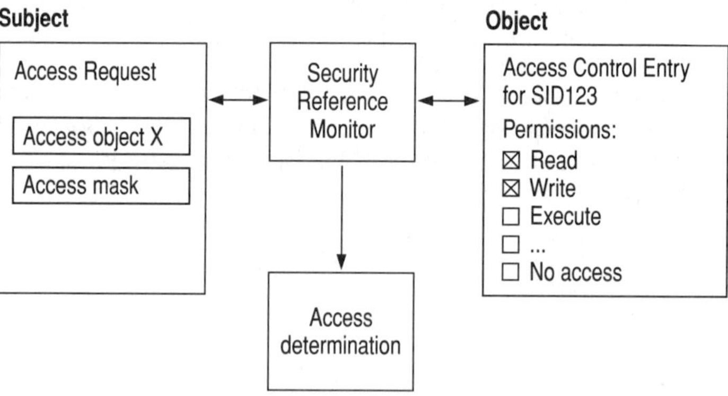

Figure 6.7 Access Validation

A *desired access mask* for the subject is created based on what type of access the user is attempting. This desired access mask, usually created by a program that the user is running, is compared with the object's ACL. (All generic access types in the ACL are mapped to standard and specific access types.)

Each ACE in the ACL is evaluated in this way:

1. The security ID in the ACE is compared with the set of security IDs in the user's access token. If a match is not found, the ACE is skipped.

   Further processing is based upon the type of the ACE. AccessDenied ACEs are ordered (and therefore processed) before AccessAllowed ACEs.
2. If access is denied, the system checks to see if the original desired access mask contained only a ReadControl and/or WRITE_DAC. If so, the system also checks to see if the requester is the owner of the object. In this case, access is granted.
3. For an AccessDenied ACE, the accesses in the ACE access mask are compared with the desired access mask. If there are any accesses in both masks, further processing is not necessary, and access is denied. Otherwise, processing continues with the next requested ACE.
4. For an AccessAllowed ACE, the accesses in the ACE are compared with those listed in the desired access mask. If all accesses in the desired access mask are matched by the ACE, no further processing is necessary, and access is granted. Otherwise, processing continues with the next ACE.
5. At the end of the ACL, if the contents of desired access mask are still not completely matched, access is implicitly denied.

Four examples of this access validation process are described next.

Example 1: Requesting Read and Write Access

A user whose user ID is FredMgr tries to open and change a file G:\File1.txt. The file has the discretionary ACL as shown in the next figure. The FredMgr access token indicates that he is a member of the groups Users, Mgrs, and Everyone.

Note The order in which permissions are listed by the **File Permissions** dialog box doesn't necessarily reflect the order in which ACEs are processed by Windows NT. It is important to note, however, that the Permissions Editor (controlled by means of this dialog box) orders all AccessDenied ACEs first so that they are the first to be processed within each ACL.

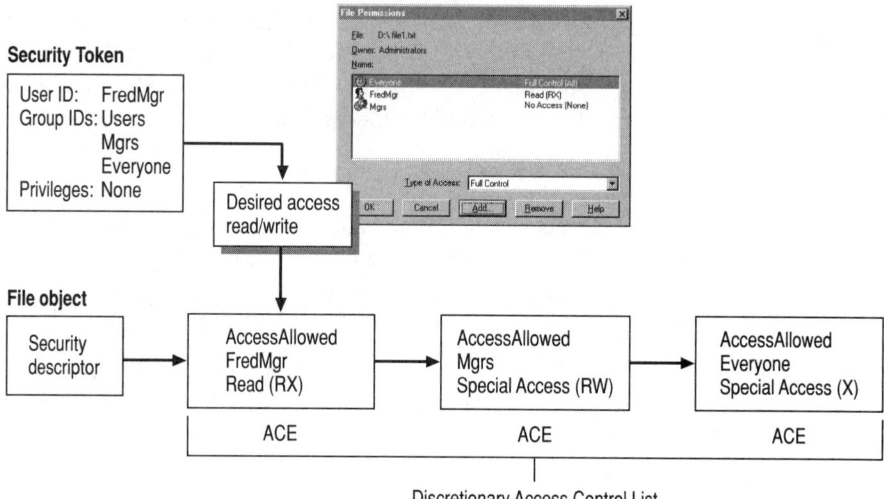

In this example, Windows NT evaluates the ACL by comparing the desired access mask with each ACE and processes the desired mask as follows:

1. Windows NT reads FredMgr's desired access mask to see that he is trying to gain Read and Write access.
2. Windows NT reads the AccessAllowed ACE for FredMgr and finds a match to the Read permission requested in the desired access mask.
3. Windows NT reads the AccessAllowed ACE for Mgrs and finds a match to the Write permission requested in desired access mask.

At this point, processing of the ACL stops even though there is another ACE in the ACL. Processing stops, and access is granted because Windows NT found matches for everything in the desired access mask.

Example 2: When Access Is Denied

In this example, FredMgr wants Read and Write access to the file whose discretionary ACL is shown next. FredMgr is a member of the Users and Mgrs groups.

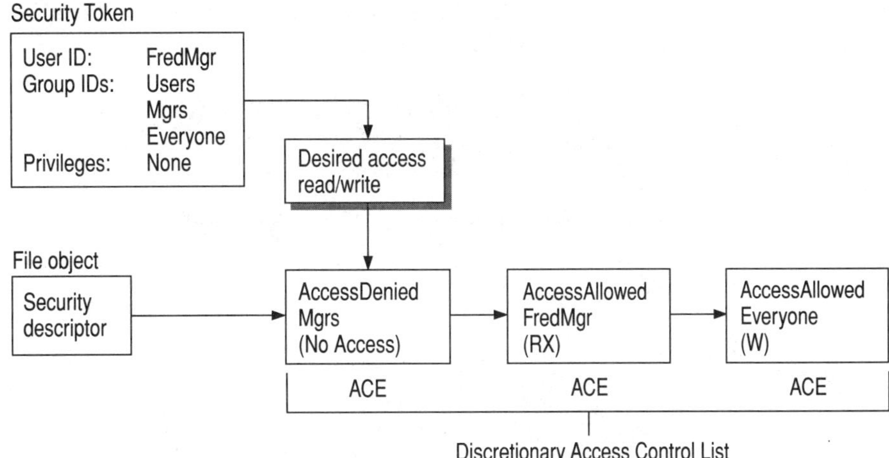

In Example 2, the ACL is evaluated as follows:

1. Windows NT reads FredMgr's desired access mask to see that he is trying to gain Read and Write access.
2. Windows NT reads the AccessDenied ACE, which denies all access (No Access) to Mgrs.

At this point, processing of the ACL stops even though there are other ACEs in the ACL that grant permissions to FredMgr.

Example 3: Requesting Read and Write Access as Object Owner

In this example, FredMgr is denied access to a file, but because he is the owner of the file he can change permissions so that he does have access. Windows NT knows by reading FredMgr's access token that he is a member of the Mgrs group. Processing of the ACL will stop as soon as Windows NT sees that NoAccess (None) is assigned to the Mgrs group, even though the other two ACEs allow Read, Write, and Execute access for FredMgr.

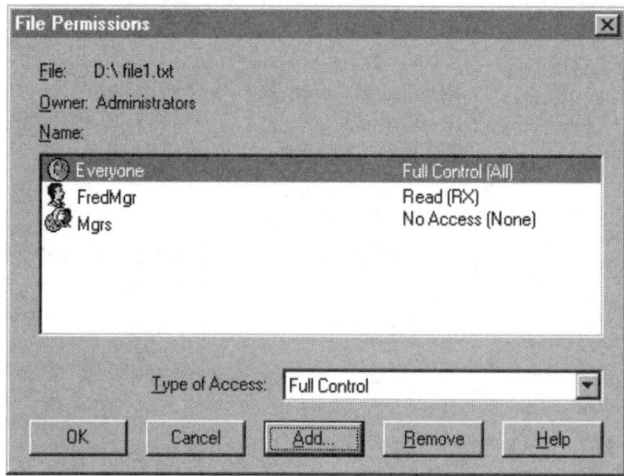

However, after failing to gain access by means of the discretionary ACL, Windows NT notices that FredMgr is the owner of the object. Because of this, he is granted ReadControl and WRITE_DAC automatically. Because this is all the access he is asking for, his request is granted.

If FredMgr had asked for any other access in addition to ReadControl and WRITE_DAC, the request would be denied even though Fred is the object's owner. In this case, FredMgr receives the following message:

```
G:\FILE2.TXT
You do not have permission to open this file.
See the owner of the file or an administrator to obtain permission.
```

In this case, because FredMgr is the owner, he can change his own permissions to grant himself appropriate access to the file.

Example 4: When a Custom Application Assigns Permissions

Important The three preceding examples demonstrate discretionary access control for file and directory permissions that are applied using the Windows NT Permissions Editor, either directly or by inheritance. If your organization develops its own custom application that sets and changes permissions on files and directories, it needs to order ACEs in the same way that Windows NT Permissions Editor orders them, or the Windows NT Permissions Editor won't be able to handle the ACL.

The user BobMgr wants Read and Write access to the file object that has the discretionary ACL shown next. The access token for BobMgr indicates that he is a member of the groups Users, JnrMgrs, and Everyone.

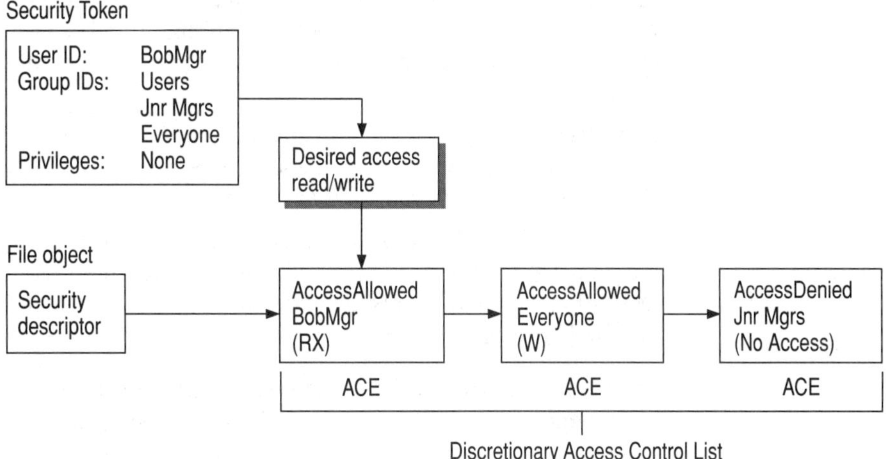

In this example, a custom application has been used to update the ACL for a file, thus confusing the usual order in which the ACEs for this file are processed. Normally, all AccessDenied ACEs are processed first.

Windows NT evaluates this ACL as follows:

1. Windows NT reads BobMgr's desired access mask to see that he is trying to gain Read and Write access.
2. Windows NT reads the AccessAllowed ACE for BobMgr and finds a match to the Read permission requested in the desired access mask.
3. Windows NT reads the AccessAllowed ACE for Everyone and finds a match to the Write permission requested in the desired access mask.

BobMgr is granted Read and Write access to the file object, even though the third ACE explicitly denies JnrMgrs access to the file object.

If the Windows NT Permissions property sheet had been used to apply the same permissions to the file object, the AccessDenied ACE for JnrMgrs would have been evaluated first in the ACL, and BobMgr would have been denied access to the file.

Auditing Security Events

Windows NT includes auditing features you can use to collect information about how your system is being used. These features also allow you to monitor events related to system security, to identify any security breaches, and to determine the extent and location of any damage. The level of audited events is adjustable to suit the needs of your organization. Some organizations need little auditing information, whereas others would be willing to trade some performance and disk space for detailed information they could use to analyze their system.

Note Remember that when you enable auditing, there is a small performance overhead for each audit check the system performs.

Windows NT can track events related to the operating system itself and to individual applications. Each application can define its own auditable events. Definitions of these events are added to the Registry when the application is installed on your Windows NT computer.

Audit events are identified to the system by the event source module name (which corresponds to a specific event type in the Registry) and an event ID.

In addition to listing events by event ID, the security log in Event Viewer lists them by category. The following categories of events are displayed in the Security Log. (Those in parentheses are found in the **Audit Policy** dialog box of User Manager.)

Category	Meaning
Account Management (User and Group Management)	These events describe high-level changes to the user accounts database, such as User Created or Group Membership Change. Potentially, a more detailed, object-level audit is also performed (see Object Access events).
Detailed Tracking (Process Tracking)	These events provide detailed subject-tracking information. This includes information such as program activation, handle duplication, and indirect object access.
Logon/Logoff (Logon and Logoff)	These events describe a single logon or logoff attempt, whether successful or unsuccessful. Included in each logon description is an indication of what type of logon was requested or performed (that is, interactive, network, or service).
Object Access (File and Object Access)	These events describe both successful and unsuccessful accesses to protected objects.
Policy Change (Security Policy Changes)	These events describe high-level changes to the security policy database, such as assignment of privileges or logon capabilities. Potentially, a more detailed, object-level audit is also performed (see Object Access events).
Privilege Use (Use of User Rights)	These events describe both successful and unsuccessful attempts to use privileges. It also includes information about when some special privileges are assigned. These special privileges are audited only at assignment time, not at time of use.
System Event (System)	These events indicate something affecting the security of the entire system or audit log occurred.

See "Security Event Examples" later in this chapter for examples of most of these event categories.

Audit Determination

Windows NT has an audit determination process similar to its access determination process, described earlier in this chapter. After access determination, Windows NT evaluates the following information for possible auditing:

- The subject attempting the access (that is, the set of identifiers representing the subject)
- The desired accesses with all generic access types mapped to standard and specific access types
- The final determination of whether access is granted or denied
- The audit ACL associated with the target object

Each ACE in the audit ACL is evaluated as follows:

1. Windows NT checks to see if the type is SystemAudit. If not, the ACE is skipped.
2. Windows NT compares the identifier in the ACE to the set of identifiers representing the subject. If no match is found, the ACE is skipped.
3. The desired accesses are compared to the access mask specified in the ACE.
4. If none of the accesses specified in the ACE's mask were requested, the ACE is skipped. The SUCCESSFUL_ACCESS_ACE_FLAG and FAILED_ACCESS_ACE_FLAG flags of the ACE are compared to the final determination of whether access was granted or denied.
5. If access was granted but the SUCCESSFUL_ACCESS_ACE_FLAG flag is not set, or if access was denied but the FAILED_ACCESS_ACE_FLAG flag is not set, the ACE is skipped.

If Windows NT performs all of these steps successfully, an audit message is generated.

The following scenario illustrates this process. In this scenario, a system access ACL is being evaluated. Here, Write access to the file object is granted, and the SUCCESSFUL_ACCESS_ACE_FLAG is set in each ACE.

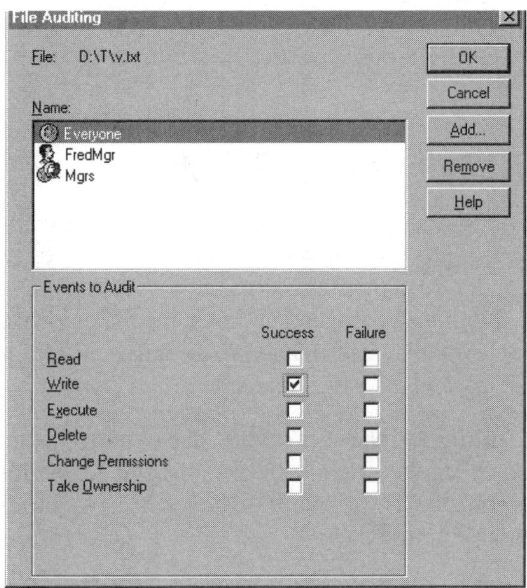

In this example, Windows NT evaluates the ACL by comparing the desired access mask with each ACE and processes the desired mask as follows:

1. Windows NT evaluates an ACE for SnrMgrs (of which FredMgr is a member). However, when the desired access is compared to the access mask of the ACE, no match is found, and the ACE is skipped.
2. Windows NT evaluates the ACE for FredMgr and finds a match.
3. Windows NT checks access flags and finds the SUCCESSFUL_ACCESS_ACE_FLAG is set. Processing stops, and an audit message is generated.

Managing the Security Log

One of the regular tasks of network administration is examining the security log to track significant events and monitor system usage and clearing the log as necessary. It is recommended that you routinely archive the log before clearing it. You can specify the maximum size for the security log and what happens when that size is reached.

Process IDs and Handle IDs of Audit Events

One of the most important aspects of security is determining who is actually behind operations of security interest, such as file writes or security policy change. Although a thread that requests access to a resource is identified by the user ID, the thread might be impersonating someone else. In this case, it would be misleading to log events by user ID and might not be useful in finding the perpetrator in the case of a security breach.

Windows NT auditing and the security log use two levels of subject identification: the user ID (also called the primary ID) and the impersonation ID (also called the client ID), as applicable. These two IDs show security administrators who are performing auditable actions.

In some cases, however, a security administrator wants to see what is happening with each process. To meet this need, auditing information also includes a subject's process ID.

When process tracking is enabled (through the **Audit Policy** dialog box of User Manager), audit messages are generated each time a new process is created. This information can be correlated with specific audit messages to see not only which user account is being used to perform auditable actions, but also which program was run.

Many audit events also include a handle ID, enabling the event to be associated with future events. For example, when a file is opened, the audit information indicates the handle ID assigned to the file. When the handle is closed, another audit event with the same handle ID is generated. With this information, you can determine exactly how long the file remained open.

The following list shows some of the information from the security access token that Windows NT uses for auditing:

- The security ID of the user account used to log on
- The group security IDs and corresponding attributes of groups to which the user is assigned membership
- The names of the privileges assigned to and used by the user, and their corresponding attributes
- Authentication ID, assigned when the user logs on

Security Event Examples

As described earlier, you can track several categories of security events. This section provides examples for most of these categories. This set of examples does not constitute a strategy for using the auditing capabilities of Windows NT; it merely serves as an introduction to show how to turn on auditing and to help you interpret these events when you enable auditing for your Windows NT system.

Example 1: Tracking File and Object Access

In this example, a user opens, modifies, saves, and closes a text file. Each of these actions generates an audit event. You must be logged on as an administrator, and make sure to enable auditing for file and object access in User Manager.

1. Create a .txt file using Notepad (it need not contain any text).
2. In Windows NT Explorer or in My computer, right-click on the .txt file icon, select Properties, and then click the Security tab.
3. Click Permissions, click Add, and then click Show Users.
4. Click to select the user, click Add to add the selected user to the list, and then click **OK**.
5. Give the user Full Control, and then click **OK**.
6. Click Auditing, click Add, and then click Show Users.
7. Click to select the user, click Add to add the selected user to the list, and then click **OK**.
8. Select the **Read Success**, **Read Failure**, **Write Success**, and **Write Failure** check boxes.
9. Click **OK** in both dialog boxes.
10. Have the user double-click the .txt file, write data to the file, save it, and then close the file.

This results in audit events, as shown in the following illustration:

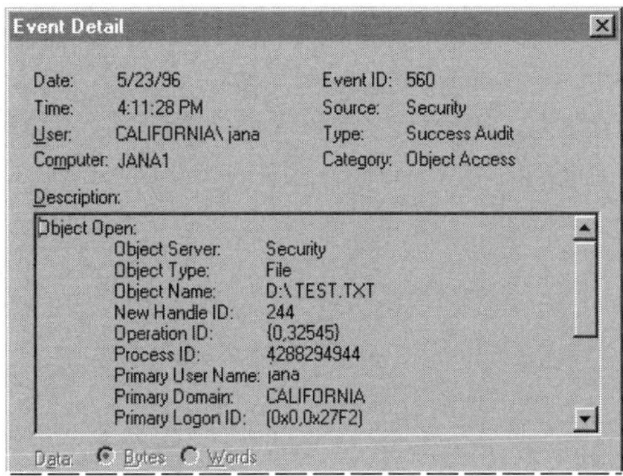

From this view of the security log, you get a quick summary of security-related events that occurred. Double-click the first event to examine the details. (For example, details of this first event are shown in the Event Detail box.)

The data that needs to be interpreted is listed in the Description list box. The following table summarizes the audited events for this example, in the order they occurred:

Table 6.1 Security Events for File Access Example

Event ID and description	Analysis
Event 560: Object Open Event 561: Handle Allocated Event 562: Handle Closed	In this sequence of events, Windows NT is doing some internal checks, such as checking to see if the file exists and checking to see that there is no sharing violation.
Event 592: A New Process Has Been Created Event 560: Object Open Event 561: Handle Allocated Event 562: Handle Closed	In this series of events, a new process is created for Notepad.exe. This process opens the .txt file for reading. Next, the process allocates, then closes, a handle to the file. Note that from the security log it is clear that Notepad does not keep an open handle to the file; it simply keeps a copy of the file in memory.
Event 560: Object Open Event 561: Handle Allocated Event 562: Handle Closed	The process opens the file for reading and writing, and since the event is a successful audit, new data is written to the file. Next, the handle is allocated for the open file, then closed.
Event 593: A Process Has Exited	This event indicates that the process, whose process ID relates to Notepad.exe, has ended.

Example 2: Use of User Rights

In this example, auditing is enabled by using User Manager to enable auditing for Success and Failure of Use of User Rights.

Use of User Rights generates audit events when a process initiates an operation that requires special privilege. For example, in order to set the system time, a user first must be given the user right to "Change The System Time" in User Manager.

For more information about User Rights see "User Rights" in the "High-Level Security" section later in this chapter.

When the user tries to change the system time, only one event is generated, as shown in the following illustration:

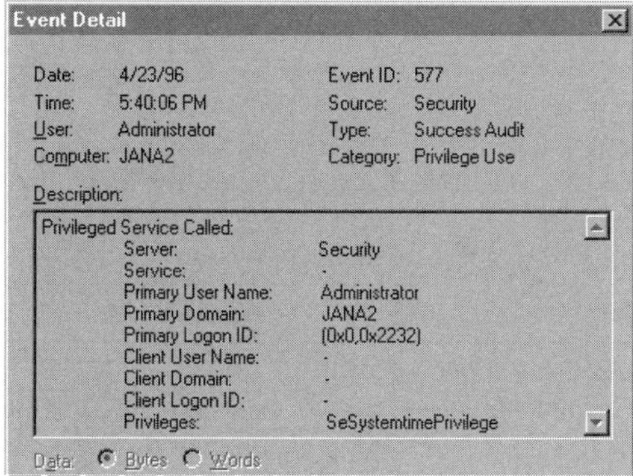

This event indicates that a privileged service was called and that a server component named *Kernel* has called an audit check on the primary username of the user. The audit type is a Success Audit, meaning that the user successfully exercised the right to use the SeSystemtimePrivilege (that is, the right to change the system time).

Example 3: User and Group Management

In this example, a new user account is added to the user accounts database. Auditing is enabled in User Manager by specifying both Success and Failure of User and Group Management. This generates four audit events, as shown in the following illustration:

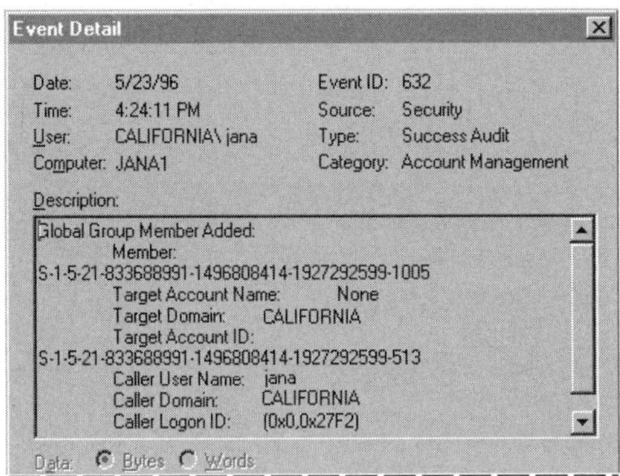

Table 6.2 Security Events for Added User Account

Event ID and description	Analysis
Event 632: Global Group Member Added Event 624: User Account Created	A new security ID (member) is created and added to the group represented by the target account ID. This is a default global group Domain Users. At this point, the security ID does not have a username allocated to it.
Event 642: User Account Changed	This event indicates that the account name of the security ID represented by the Target Account ID has been changed to the new user's.
Event 636: Local Group Member Added	This event indicates that the account represented by the new user's security ID is created. The new user is added to the local group represented by the security ID under Target Account ID (Users).

Example 4: Restart, Shutdown and System

In this example, auditing is enabled in User Manager for both Success and Failure of Restart, Shutdown and System.

In this example, seven events were generated. Note, however, that the number of events generated is related to the number of trusted systems that you start when the system is restarted. This number might vary if you replicate this scenario on your own Windows NT computer.

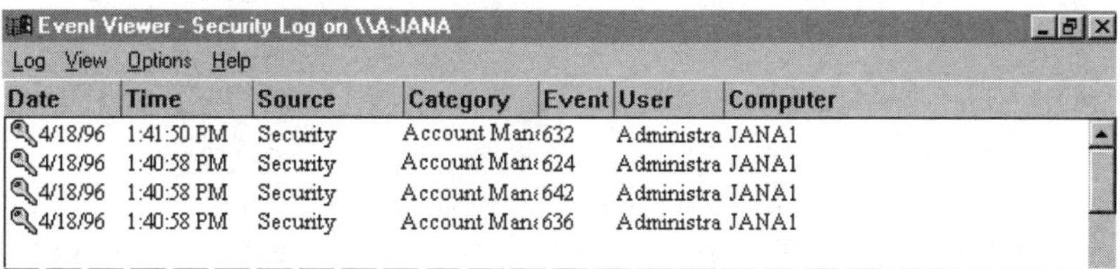

Table 6.3 Security Events for System Startup

Event ID and description	Analysis
Event 512: Windows NT is starting up.	Identifies the date and time the system started.

Event 514: Authentication package loaded	The description of this event says
	`An authentication package has been loaded by the Local Security Authority. This authentication package will be used to authenticate logon attempts.`
	`Authentication Package Name: msv 1_0`
	This is the standard authentication package shipped with Windows NT.

Events 515: Trusted logon process	The description for each of these events says `A trusted logon process has registered with the Local Security Authority. This logon process will be trusted to submit logon requests.` The logon process name is listed for each of these events, as follows: Winlogon Service Control Manager LAN Manager Workstation Service LAN Manager Server LAN Manager Redirector Each of these events is a successful audit in the category of system event. These events indicate that the respective logon processes have registered with the Local Security Authority and are now trusted to submit logon requests.

Establishing Computer Security

This section deals with the following topics on Windows NT security:

- Levels of security
- Off-the-shelf versus custom software
- Windows NT security features
- Performance monitoring

Levels of Security

Windows NT allows you to establish a full range of levels of security, from no security at all to the C2 level of security required by many government agencies. In this chapter we describe three levels of security—minimal, standard, and high-level—and the options used to provide each level. These levels are arbitrary, and you will probably want to create your own "level" by blending characteristics of the levels presented here.

Why not have maximum security at all times? One reason is that the limits you set on access to computer resources make it a little harder for people to work with the protected resources. Another is that it is extra work to set up and maintain the protections you want. For example, if only users who are members of the HR user group are allowed to access employee records, and a new person is hired to do that job, then someone needs to set up an account for the new hire and add that account to the HR group. If the new account is created but not added to HR, the new hire cannot access the employee records and therefore cannot perform his or her job.

If the security is too tight, users will try to circumvent security in order to get work done. For example, if you set the password policy so that passwords are hard to remember, users will write them down to avoid being locked out. If some users are blocked from files they need to use, their colleagues might share their own passwords in order to promote the flow of work.

The first step in establishing security is to make an accurate assessment of your needs. Then choose the elements of security that you want, and implement them. Make sure your users know what they need to do to maintain security, and why it is important. Finally, monitor your system and make adjustments as needed.

Off-the-Shelf vs. Custom Software

If you are using software made especially for your installation, or if you are using shareware that you aren't sure you can trust, and you want to maintain fairly high security, you might want to look at Appendix B, "Security In a Software Development Environment." This provides information on settings and calls that can support—or circumvent—security settings.

Minimal Security

You might not be concerned with security if the computer is not used to store or access sensitive data or if it is in a very secure location. For example, if the computer is in the home office of a sole proprietor of a business, or if it is used as a test machine in the locked lab of a software development company, then security precautions might be unnecessarily cumbersome. Windows NT allows you to make the system fully accessible, with no protections at all, if that is what your setup requires.

Physical Security Considerations

Take the precautions you would with any piece of valuable equipment to protect against casual theft. This step can include locking the room the computer is in when no one is there to keep an eye on it, or using a locked cable to attach the unit to a wall. You might also want to establish procedures for moving or repairing the computer so that the computer or its components cannot be taken under false pretenses.

Use a surge protector or power conditioner to protect the computer and its peripherals from power spikes. Also, perform regular disk scans and defragmentation to isolate bad sectors and to maintain the highest possible disk performance.

Minimal Software Security Considerations

For minimal security, none of the Windows NT security features are used. In fact, you can allow automatic logon to the Administrator account (or any other user account) by following the directions in Chapter 25 "Configuration Management and the Registry." This allows anyone with physical access to the computer to turn it on and immediately have full access to the computer's resources.

By default, access is limited to certain files. For minimal security, give the Everyone group full access to all files.

You should still take precautions against viruses, because they can disable programs you want to use or use the minimally secure computer as a vector to infect other computer systems.

Standard Security

Most often, computers are used to store sensitive and/or valuable data. This data could be anything from financial data to personnel files to personal correspondence. Also, you might need to protect against accidental or deliberate changes to the way the computer is set up. But the computer's users need to be able to do their work, with minimal barriers to the resources they need.

Physical Security Considerations

As with minimal security, the computer should be protected as any valuable equipment would be. Generally, this involves keeping the computer in a building that is locked to unauthorized users, as most homes and offices are. In some instances you might want to use a cable and lock to secure the computer to its location. If the computer has a physical lock, you can lock it and keep the key in a safe place for additional security. However, if the key is lost or inaccessible, an authorized user might be unable to work on the computer.

Standard Software Security Considerations

A secure system requires effort from both the system administrators, who maintain certain software settings, and the everyday users, who must cultivate habits such as logging off at the end of the day and memorizing (rather than writing down) their passwords.

Displaying a Legal Notice Before Logon

Windows NT can display a message box with the caption and text of your choice before a user logs on. Many organizations use this message box to display a warning message that notifies potential users that they can be held legally liable if they attempt to use the computer without having been properly authorized to do so. The absence of such a notice could be construed as an invitation, without restriction, to enter and browse the system.

The logon notice can also be used in settings (such as an information kiosk) where users might require instruction on how to supply a username and password for the appropriate account.

To display a legal notice, use the Registry Editor to create or assign the following Registry key values on the workstation to be protected:

Hive:	HKEY_LOCAL_MACHINE\SOFTWARE
Key:	\Microsoft\Windows NT\Current Version\Winlogon
Name:	LegalNoticeCaption
Type:	REG_SZ
Value:	Whatever you want for the title of the message box

Hive:	HKEY_LOCAL_MACHINE\SOFTWARE
Key:	Microsoft\Windows NT\Current Version\Winlogon
Name:	LegalNoticeText
Type:	REG_SZ
Value:	Whatever you want for the text of the message box

The changes take effect the next time the computer is started. You might want to update the Emergency Repair Disk to reflect these changes.

Examples

Welcome to the XYZ Information Kiosk

Log on using account name Guest and password XYZCorp.

Authorized Users Only

Only individuals currently assigned an account on this computer by XYZCorp may access data on this computer. All information stored on this computer is the property of XYZCorp and is subject to all the protections accorded intellectual property.

User Accounts and Groups

With standard security, a user account (username) and password should be required in order to use the computer. You can establish, delete, or disable user accounts with User Manager, which is in the Administrative Tools program group. User Manager also allows you to set password policies and organize user accounts into Groups.

Note Changes to the Windows NT computer user rights policy take effect when the user next logs on.

Administrative Accounts versus User Accounts

Use separate accounts for administrative activity and general user activity. Individuals who do administrative work on the computer should each have two user accounts on the system: one for administrative tasks, and one for general activity. To avoid accidental changes to protected resources, the account with the least privilege that can do the task at hand should be used. For example, viruses can do much more damage if activated from an account with Administrator privileges.

It is a good idea to rename the built-in Administrator account to something less obvious. This powerful account is the one account that can never be locked out due to repeated failed logon attempts, and consequently is attractive to hackers who try to break in by repeatedly guessing passwords. By renaming the account, you force hackers to guess the account name as well as the password.

The Guest Account

Limited access can be permitted for casual users through the built-in Guest account. If the computer is for public use, the Guest account can be used for public logons. Prohibit Guest from Writing or Deleting any files, directories, or Registry keys (with the possible exception of a directory where information can be left).

In a standard security configuration, a computer that allows Guest access can also be used by other users for files that they don't want accessible to the general public. These users can log on with their own user names and access files in directories on which they have set the appropriate permissions. They will want to be especially careful to log off or lock the workstation before they leave it. The Guest account is discussed in Chapter 2 "Working with User and Group Accounts" in *Microsoft Windows NT Server Concepts and Planning*. For procedural information, see Help.

Logging On

All users should *always* press CTRL+ALT+DEL before logging on. Programs designed to collect account passwords can appear as a logon screen that is there waiting for you. By pressing CTRL+ALT+DEL you can foil these programs and get the secure logon screen provided by Windows NT.

Logging Off or Locking the Workstation

Users should either log off or lock the workstation if they will be away from the computer for any length of time. Logging off allows other users to log on (if they know the password to an account); locking the workstation does not. The workstation can be set to lock automatically if it is not used for a set period of time by using any 32-bit screen saver with the Password Protected option. For information about setting up screen savers, see Help.

Passwords

Anyone who knows a username and the associated password can log on as that user. Users should take care to keep their passwords secret. Here are a few tips:

- Change passwords frequently, and avoid reusing passwords.
- Avoid using easily guessed words and words that appear in the dictionary. A phrase or a combination of letters and numbers works well.
- Don't write a password down—choose one that is easy for you to remember.

Protecting Files and Directories

The NTFS file system provides more security features than the FAT system and should be used whenever security is a concern. The only reason to use FAT is for the boot partition of an ARC-compliant RISC system. A system partition using FAT can be secured in its entirety using the **Secure System Partition** command on the **Partition** menu of the Disk Administrator utility.

With NTFS, you can assign a variety of protections to files and directories, specifying which groups or individual accounts can access these resources in which ways. By using the inherited permissions feature and by assigning permissions to groups rather than to individual accounts, you can simplify the chore of maintaining appropriate protections. For more information, see Chapter 4, "Managing Shared Resources and Resource Security" in *Microsoft Windows NT Server Concepts and Planning*. For procedural information, see Help.

In particular, make sure that users know that if they move rather than copy a file to a different directory on the same volume, it continues to have the protections it had before it was moved. If they copy the file, it inherits the protections (either more or less restrictive) from the directory it is copied to.

For example, a user might copy a sensitive document to a directory that is accessible to people who should not be allowed to read the document, thinking that the protections assigned to the document in its old location would still apply. In this case the protections should be set on the document as soon as it is copied, or else it should be first moved to the new directory, then copied back to the original directory.

On the other hand, if a file that was created in a protected directory is being placed in a shared directory so that other users can read it, it should be copied to the new directory; or if it is moved to the new directory, the protections on the file should be promptly changed so that other users can read the file.

When permissions are changed on a file or directory, the new permissions apply any time the file or directory is subsequently opened. Users who already have the file or directory open when you change the permissions are still allowed access according to the permissions that were in effect when they opened the file or directory.

Backups

Regular backups protect your data from hardware failures and honest mistakes, as well as from viruses and other malicious mischief. The Windows NT Backup utility is described in Chapter 6, "Backing Up and Restoring Network Files" in *Microsoft Windows NT Server Concepts and Planning.* For procedural information, see Help

Obviously, files must be read to be backed up, and they must be written to be restored. Backup privileges should be limited to Administrators and Backup operators—people to whom you are comfortable giving read and write access on all files.

Protecting the Registry

All the initialization and configuration information used by Windows NT is stored in the Registry. Normally, the keys in the Registry are changed indirectly, through the administrative tools such as the Control Panel. This method is recommended. The Registry can also be altered directly, with the Registry Editor; some keys can be altered in no other way.

The Registry Editor should be used only by individuals who thoroughly understand the tool, the Registry itself, and the effects of changes to various keys in the Registry. Mistakes made in the Registry Editor could render part or all of the system unusable.

Remote access to the Windows NT registry is supported by the Registry Editor. To restrict network access to the registry, use the Registry Editor to create the following registry key:

Hive:	HKEY_LOCAL_MACHINE
Key:	\CurrentcontrolSet\Control\SecurePipeServers
Name:	\winreg
Type	REG_DWORD
Value:	1

The security permissions set on this key define which users or groups can connect to the system for remote registry access. The default Windows NT Workstation installation does not define this key and does not restrict remote access to the registry. Windows NT Server permits only Administrators remote access to the registry.

The Backup utility included with Windows NT allows you to back up the Registry as well as files and directories.

Auditing

Auditing can inform you of actions that could pose a security risk and also identify the user accounts from which audited actions were taken. Note that auditing only tells you what user accounts were used for the audited events. If passwords are adequately protected, this in turn indicates which user attempted the audited events. However, if a password has been stolen or if actions were taken while a user was logged on but away from the computer, the action could have been initiated by someone other than the person to whom the user account is assigned.

When you establish an audit policy you'll need to weigh the cost (in disk space and CPU cycles) of the various auditing options against the advantages of these options. You'll want to at least audit failed logon attempts, attempts to access sensitive data, and changes to security settings. Here are some common security threats and the type of auditing that can help track them:

Threat	Action
Hacker-type break-in using random passwords	Enable failure auditing for logon and logoff events.
Break-in using stolen password	Enable success auditing for logon and logoff events. The log entries will not distinguish between the real users and the phony ones. What you are looking for here is unusual activity on user accounts, such as logons at odd hours or on days when you would not expect any activity.
Misuse of administrative privileges by authorized users	Enable success auditing for use of user rights; for user and group management, for security policy changes; and for restart, shutdown, and system events. (Note: Because of the high volume of events that would be recorded, Windows NT does not normally audit the use of the Backup Files And Directories and the Restore Files And Directories rights. Appendix B, "Security In a Software Development Environment," explains how to enable auditing of the use of these rights.)
Virus outbreak	Enable success and failure write access auditing for program files such as files with .exe and .dll extensions. Enable success and failure process tracking auditing. Run suspect programs and examine the security log for unexpected attempts to modify program files or creation of unexpected processes. Note that these auditing settings generate a large number of event records during routine system use. You should use them only when you are actively monitoring the system log.
Improper access to sensitive files	Enable success and failure auditing for file- and object-access events, and then use File Manager to enable success and failure auditing of read and write access by suspect users or groups for sensitive files.
Improper access to printers	Enable success and failure auditing for file- and object-access events, and then use Print Manager to enable success and failure auditing of print access by suspect users or groups for the printers.

High-Level Security

Standard security precautions are sufficient for most installations. However, additional precautions are available for computers that contain sensitive data, or that are at high risk for data theft or the accidental or malicious disruption of the system.

Physical Security Considerations

The physical security considerations described for minimal and standard security configurations also apply here. In addition, you might want to examine the physical link provided by your computer network, and in some cases use controls built in to certain hardware platforms to restrict who can turn on the computer.

Networks and Security

When you put a computer on a network, you add an access route to the computer, and you'll want that route to be secure. User validation and protections on files and other objects are sufficient for standard-level security, but for high-level security you'll need to make sure the network itself is secure, or in some cases isolate the computer completely.

The two risks from network connections are other network users and unauthorized network taps. If everyone on the network has the security clearance needed to access your secure computer, you will probably prefer to include the computer in the network to make it easier for these people to access data on the computer.

If the network is entirely contained in a secure building, the risk of unauthorized taps is minimized or eliminated. If the cabling must pass through unsecured areas, use optical fiber links rather than twisted pair to foil attempts to tap the wire and collect transmitted data.

If your installation needs access to the Internet, be aware of the security issues involved in providing access to—and from—the Internet community. Chapter 2, "Server Security on the Internet," in the *Windows NT Server Internet Guide* contains information on using network topology to provide security.

Controlling Access to the Computer

No computer will ever be completely secure if people other the than authorized user can physically access it. For maximum security on a computer that is not physically secure (locked safely away), follow all or some of the following security measures:

- If the computer has a floppy disk drive, set the Boot.ini time-out to 0. This disables the floppy disk drive on startup. If the computer doesn't require a floppy disk drive, remove it.
- The CPU should have a case that cannot be opened without a key. The key should be stored safely away from the computer.
- The entire hard disk should be NTFS.
- If the computer doesn't require network access, remove the network card.

Controlling Access to the Power Switch

You might choose to keep unauthorized users away from the power or reset switches on the computer, particularly if your computer's rights policy denies them the right to shut down the computer. The most secure computers (other than those in locked and guarded rooms) expose only the computer's keyboard, monitor, mouse, and (when appropriate) printer to users. The CPU and removable media drives can be locked away where only specifically authorized personnel can access them.

On many hardware platforms, the system can be protected using a *power-on password.* A power-on password prevents unauthorized personnel from starting an operating system other than Windows NT, which would compromise system security. Power-on passwords are a function of the computer hardware, not the operating system software. Therefore the procedure for setting up the power-on password depends on the type of computer and is available in the vendor's documentation supplied with the system.

High-Level Software Security Considerations

Some high-security options can be implemented only by using the Registry Editor. The Registry Editor should be used only by administrators who are familiar with the material in Part V of this book.

User Rights

There are several user rights that administrators of high-security installations should be aware of and possibly audit. Of these, you might want to change the default permissions on two rights, as follows:

User Right	Groups assigned this right by default	Recommended change
Log on locally. Allows a user to log on at the computer, from the computer's keyboard.	Administrators, Backup Operators, Everyone, Guests, Power Users, and Users	Deny Everyone and Guests this right.
Shut down the system. (SeShutdownPrivilege) Allows a user to shut down Windows NT.	Administrators, Backup Operators, Everyone, Power Users, and Users	Deny Everyone and Users this right.

The rights in the following table generally require no changes to the default settings, even in the most highly secure installations.

Right	Allows	Initially assigned to
Access this computer from the network	A user to connect over the network to the computer.	Administrators, Everyone, Power Users
Act as part of the operating system (SeTcbPrivilege)	A process to perform as a secure, trusted part of the operating system. Some subsystems are granted this right.	(None)
Add workstations to the domain (SeMachineAccountPrivilege)	Nothing. This right has no effect on computers running Windows NT.	(None)
Back up files and directories (SeBackupPrivilege)	A user to back up files and directories. This right supersedes file and directory permissions.	Administrators, Backup Operators
Bypass traverse checking (SeChangeNotifyPrivilege)	A user to change directories and access files and subdirectories even if the user has no permission to access parent directories.	Everyone

Right	Allows	Initially assigned to
Change the system time (SeSystemTimePrivilege)	A user to set the time for the internal clock of the computer.	Administrators, Power Users
Create a pagefile (SeCreatePagefilePrivilege)	Nothing. This right has no effect in current versions of Windows NT.	Administrators
Create a token object (SeCreateTokenPrivilege)	A process to create access tokens. Only the Local Security Authority can do this.	(None)
Create permanent shared objects (SeCreatePermanentPrivilege)	A user to create special permanent objects, such as \\Device, that are used within Windows NT.	(None)
Debug programs (SeDebugPrivilege)	A user to debug various low-level objects such as threads.	Administrators
Force shutdown from a remote system (SeRemoteShutdownPrivilege)	Nothing. This right has no effect in current versions of Windows NT.	Administrators, Power Users
Generate security audits (SeAuditPrivilege)	A process to generate security audit log entries.	(None)
Increase quotas (SeIncreaseQuotaPrivilege)	Nothing. This right has no effect in current versions of Windows NT.	(None)
Increase scheduling priority (SeIncreaseBasePriorityPrivilege)	A user to boost the execution priority of a process.	Administrators, Power Users
Load and unload device drivers (SeLoadDriverPrivilege)	A user to install and remove device drivers.	Administrators
Lock pages in memory (SeLockMemoryPrivilege)	A user to lock pages in memory so they cannot be paged out to a backing store such as Pagefile.sys.	(None)
Log on as a batch job	Nothing. This right has no effect in current versions of Windows NT.	(None)
Log on as a service	A process to register with the system as a service.	(None)
Log on locally	A user to log on at the computer, from the computer's keyboard.	Administrators, Backup Operators, Guests, Power Users, Users

Right	Allows	Initially assigned to
Manage auditing and security *log* (SeSecurityPrivilege)	A user to specify what types of resource access (such as file access) are to be audited, and to view and clear the security log. Note that this right does not allow a user to set system auditing policy using the Audit command in the Policy menu of User Manager. Also, members of the Administrators group always have the ability to view and clear the security log.	Administrators
Modify firmware environment variables (SeSystemEnvironmentPrivilege)	A user to modify system environment variables stored in nonvolatile RAM on systems that support this type of configuration.	Administrators
Profile single process (SeProfSingleProcess)	A user to perform profiling (performance sampling) on a process.	Administrators, Power Users
Profile system performance (SeSystemProfilePrivilege)	A user to perform profiling (performance sampling) on the system.	Administrators
Replace a process-level token (SeAssignPrimaryTokenPrivilege)	A user to modify a process's security access token. This is a powerful right used only by the system.	(None)
Restore files and directories (SeRestorePrivilege)	A user to restore backed-up files and directories. This right supersedes file and directory permissions.	Administrators, Backup Operators
Shut down the system (SeShutdownPrivilege)	A user to shut down Windows NT.	Administrators, Backup Operators, Power Users, Users
Take ownership of files or other objects (SeTakeOwnershipPrivilege)	A user to take ownership of files, directories, printers, and other objects on the computer. This right supersedes permissions protecting objects.	Administrators

Protecting Files and Directories

Among the files and directories to be protected are those that make up the operating system software itself. The standard set of permissions on system files and directories provide a reasonable degree of security without interfering with the computer's usability. For high-level security installations, however, you might want to set directory permissions to all subdirectories and existing files, as shown in the following list, immediately after Windows NT is installed. Be sure to apply permissions to parent directories before applying permissions to subdirectories.

Directory	Permissions
\WINNT35	Administrators: Full Control CREATOR OWNER: Full Control Everyone: Read SYSTEM: Full Control
\WINNT35\REPAIR	Administrators: Full Control
\WINNT35\SYSTEM	Administrators: Full Control CREATOR OWNER: Full Control Everyone: Read SYSTEM: Full Control
\WINNT35\SYSTEM32	Administrators: Full Control CREATOR OWNER: Full Control Everyone: Read SYSTEM: Full Control
\WINNT35\SYSTEM32\CONFIG	Administrators: Full Control CREATOR OWNER: Full Control Everyone: List SYSTEM: Full Control
\WINNT35\SYSTEM32\DHCP	(Delete this directory)
\WINNT35\SYSTEM32\DRIVERS	Administrators: Full Control CREATOR OWNER: Full Control Everyone: Read SYSTEM: Full Control
\WINNT35\SYSTEM32\RAS	(Delete this directory)
\WINNT35\SYSTEM32\OS2	(Delete this directory)
\WINNT35\SYSTEM32\SPOOL	Administrators: Full Control CREATOR OWNER: Full Control Everyone: Read Power Users: Change SYSTEM: Full Control
\WINNT35\SYSTEM32\WINS	(Delete this directory)

Several critical operating system files exist in the root directory of the system partition on Intel 80486 and Pentium-based systems. In high-security installations you might want to assign the following permissions to these files:

File	C2-Level Permissions
\Boot.ini, \Ntdetect.com, \Ntldr	Administrators: Full Control SYSTEM: Full Control
\Autoexec.bat, \Config.sys	Everybody: Read Administrators: Full Control SYSTEM: Full Control

To view these files in File Manager, choose the **By File Type** command from the **View** menu, then select the **Show Hidden/System Files** check box in the **By File Type** dialog box.

Protecting the Registry

In addition to the considerations for standard security, the administrator of a high-security installation might want to set protections on certain keys in the Registry.

By default, protections are set on the various components of the Registry that allow work to be done while providing standard-level security. For high-level security, you might want to assign access rights to specific Registry keys. This should be done with caution, because programs that the users require to do their jobs often need to access certain keys on the users' behalf. For more information, see Chapter 24, "Registry Editor and Registry Administration."

In particular, you might want to change the protections of the following keys so that the group Everyone is only allowed QueryValue, Enumerate Subkeys, Notify, and Read Control accesses.

In the HKEY_LOCAL_MACHINE on Local Machine dialog:

\Software\Microsoft\RPC (and its subkeys)

\Software\Microsoft\Windows NT\CurrentVersion

And under the \Software\Microsoft\Windows NT\CurrentVersion\ subtree:

Profile List

AeDebug

Compatibility

Drivers

Embedding

Fonts

FontSubstitutes

GRE_Initialize

MCI

FontSubstitutes

GRE_Initialize

MCI

MCI Extensions

Port (and all subkeys)

WOW (and all subkeys)

Windows3.1MigrationStatus (and all subkeys)

In the HKEY_CLASSES_ROOT on Local Machine dialog:

\HKEY_CLASSES_ROOT (and all subkeys)

Remote access to the Windows NT registry is supported by the Registry Editor. To restrict network access to the registry, use the Registry Editor to create the following registry key:

Hive:	HKEY_LOCAL_MACHINE
Key:	\CurrentcontrolSet\Control\SecurePipeServers
Name:	\winreg
Type	REG_DWORD
Value:	1

The security permissions set on this key define which users or groups can connect to the system for remote registry access. The default Windows NT Workstation installation does not define this key and does not restrict remote access to the registry. Windows NT Server permits only Administrators remote access to the registry.

The Schedule Service (AT Command)

The Schedule service (also known as the **AT** command) is used to schedule tasks to run automatically at a preset time. Because the scheduled task is run in the context run by the Schedule service (typically the operating system's context), this service should not be used in a highly secure environment.

By default, only Administrators can submit **AT** commands. To allow System Operators to also submit **AT** commands, use the Registry Editor to create or assign the following Registry key value:

Hive:	HKEY_LOCAL_MACHINE\SYSTEM
Key:	\CurrentControlSet\Control\Lsa
Name:	Submit Control
Type:	REG_DWORD
Value:	1

There is no way to allow anyone else to submit **AT** commands. The changes will take effect the next time the computer is started. You might want to update the Emergency Repair Disk to reflect these changes.

Hiding the Last Username

By default, Windows NT places the username of the last user to log on the computer in the Username text box of the **Logon** dialog box. This makes it more convenient for the most frequent user to log on. To help keep usernames secret, you can prevent Windows NT from displaying the username from the last logon. This is especially important if a computer that is generally accessible is being used for the (renamed) built-in Administrator account.

To prevent display of a username in the Logon dialog box, use the Registry Editor to create or assign the following Registry key value:

Hive:	HKEY_LOCAL_MACHINE\SOFTWARE
Key:	\Microsoft\Windows NT\Current Version\Winlogon
Name:	DontDisplayLastUserName
Type:	REG_SZ
Value:	1

Restricting the Boot Process

Most personal computers today can start a number of different operating systems. For example, even if you normally start Windows NT from the C: drive, someone could select another version of Windows on another drive, including a floppy drive or CD-ROM drive. If this happens, security precautions you have taken within your normal version of Windows NT might be circumvented.

In general, you should install only those operating systems that you want to be used on the computer you are setting up. For a highly secure system, this will probably mean installing one version of Windows NT. However, you must still protect the CPU physically to ensure that no other operating system is loaded. Depending on your circumstances, you might choose to remove the floppy drive or drives. In some computers you can disable booting from the floppy drive by setting switches or jumpers inside the CPU. If you use hardware settings to disable booting from the floppy drive, you might want to lock the computer case (if possible) or lock the machine in a cabinet with a hole in the front to provide access to the floppy drive. If the CPU is in a locked area away from the keyboard and monitor, drives cannot be added or hardware settings changed for the purpose of starting from another operating system.

Allowing Only Logged-On Users to Shut Down the Computer

Normally, you can shut down a computer running Windows NT Workstation without logging on by choosing Shutdown in the **Logon** dialog box. This is appropriate where the computer's operational switches can be accessed by users; otherwise, they might tend to turn off the computer's power or reset it without properly shutting down Windows NT Workstation. However, you can remove this feature if the CPU is locked away. (This step is not required for Windows NT Server, because it is configured this way by default.)

To require users to log on before shutting down the computer, use the Registry Editor to create or assign the following Registry key value:

Hive:	HKEY_LOCAL_MACHINE\SOFTWARE
Key:	\Microsoft\Windows NT\Current Version\Winlogon
Name:	ShutdownWithoutLogon
Type:	REG_SZ
Value:	0

The changes will take effect the next time the computer is started. You might want to update the Emergency Repair Disk to reflect these changes.

Controlling Access to Removable Media

By default, Windows NT allows any program to access files on floppy disks and CDs. In a highly secure, multi-user environment, you might want to allow only the person interactively logged on to access those devices. This allows the interactive user to write sensitive information to these drives, confident that no other user or program can see or modify that data.

When operating in this mode, the floppy disks and/or CDs on your system are allocated to a user as part of the interactive logon process. These devices are automatically freed for general use or for reallocation when that user logs off. Because of this, it is important to remove sensitive data from the floppy or CD-ROM drives before logging off.

Note Windows NT allows all users access to the tape drive, and therefore any user can read and write the contents of any tape in the drive. In general this is not a concern, because only one user is interactively logged on at a time. However, in some rare instances, a program started by a user can continue running after the user logs off. When another user logs on and puts a tape in the tape drive, this program can secretly transfer sensitive data from the tape. If this is a concern, restart the computer before using the tape drive.

▶ **To allocate floppy drives during logon**

- Use the Registry Editor to create or assign the following Registry key value:

Hive:	HKEY_LOCAL_MACHINE\SOFTWARE
Key:	\Microsoft\WindowsNT\CurrentVersion\Winlogon
Name:	AllocateFloppies
Type:	REG_SZ
Value:	1

If the value does not exist, or is set to any other value, then floppy devices will be available for shared use by all processes on the system.

This value will take effect at the next logon. If a user is already logged on when this value is set, it will have no effect for that logon session. The user must log off and log on again to cause the device(s) to be allocated.

▶ **To allocate CD-ROMs during logon**

- Use the Registry Editor to create or assign the following Registry key value:

Hive:	HKEY_LOCAL_MACHINE\SOFTWARE
Key:	\Microsoft\WindowsNT\CurrentVersion\Winlogon
Name:	AllocateCDRoms
Type:	REG_SZ
Value:	1

If the value does not exist, or is set to any other value, then CD-ROM devices will be available for shared use by all processes on the system.

This value will take effect at the next logon. If a user is already logged on when this value is set, it will have no effect for that logon session. The user must log off and log on again to cause the device(s) to be allocated.

C2 Security

The National Computer Security Center (NCSC) is the United States government agency responsible for performing software product security evaluations. These evaluations are carried out against a set of requirements outlined in the NCSC publication *Department of Defense Trusted Computer System Evaluation Criteria*, which is commonly referred to as the "Orange Book."

Windows NT has been successfully evaluated by the NCSC at the C2 security level as defined in the Orange Book, which covers the base operating system.

In addition, Windows NT is currently under evaluation for its networking component of a secure system in compliance to the NCSC's "Red Book." The Red Book is an interpretation of the Orange Book as applies to network security.

Some of the most important requirements of C2-level security are the following:

- The owner of a resource (such as a file) must be able to control access to the resource.
- The operating system must protect objects so that they are not randomly reused by other processes. For example, the system protects memory so that its contents cannot be read after it is freed by a process. In addition, when a file is deleted, users must not be able to access the data from that file.
- Each user must identify himself or herself by typing a unique logon name and password before being allowed access to the system. The system must be able to use this unique identification to track the activities of the user.

- System administrators must be able to audit security-related events. Access to this audit data must be limited to authorized administrators.
- The system must protect itself from external interference or tampering, such as modification of the running system or of system files stored on disk.

Evaluation vs. Certification

The NCSC evaluation process does a good job of ensuring that Windows NT can properly enforce your security policy, but it does not dictate what your security policy must be. There are many features of Windows NT that need to be considered when determining how to use the computer within your specific environment. What level of auditing will you require? How should your files be protected to ensure that only the right people can access them? What applications should you allow people to run? Should you use a network? If so, what level of physical isolation of the actual network cable is needed?

To address the environmental aspects of a computing environment, the NCSC has produced a document called *Introduction to Certification and Accreditation*. In this document, "certification" is described as a plan to use computer systems in a specific environment, and "accreditation" is the evaluation of that plan by administrative authorities. It is this certification plan, and the subsequent accreditation procedure, that balances the sensitivity of the data being protected against the environmental risks present in the way the computing systems are used. For example, a certification plan for a university computing lab might require that computers be configured to prevent starting from a floppy disk, to minimize the risk of infection by virus or Trojan Horse programs. In a top-secret Defense Department development lab, it might be necessary to have a fiber-optic LAN to prevent generation of electronic emissions. A good certification plan covers all aspects of security, from backup/recovery mechanisms to the Marine guards standing at the front door of your building.

Additional C2 Evaluation Information

If you need to set up a C2-certifiable system, see Chapter 2, "Microsoft Report on C2 Evaluation of Windows NT." That chapter lists the hardware configurations in which Windows NT has been evaluated. Chapter 2 also specifies the set of features that were implemented for C2 evaluation so that you can duplicate them if necessary for your own C2-certifiable system. These features are essentially those recommended for high-level security in this chapter.

For your C2 certification, you will need to choose the combination of security features described in this chapter, in Chapter 2 of *Windows NT Server Networking Guide*, and in the Windows NT documentation that fits your particular combination of resources, personnel, work flow, and perceived risks. You might also want to study Appendix B, "Security in a Software Development Environment," especially if you are using custom or in-house software. This appendix also provides information on managing and interpreting the security log and technical details on special-case auditing (for example, auditing base objects).

Setting Up a C2-compliant System

To make it easier to set up a C2-compliant system, the C2Config application has been created and included in the *Windows NT 4.0 Resource Kit*. C2config.exe lets you choose from the settings used in evaluating Windows NT for C2 security, and implement the settings you want to use in your installation. For details, see the online Help included with the application.

CHAPTER 7

Printing

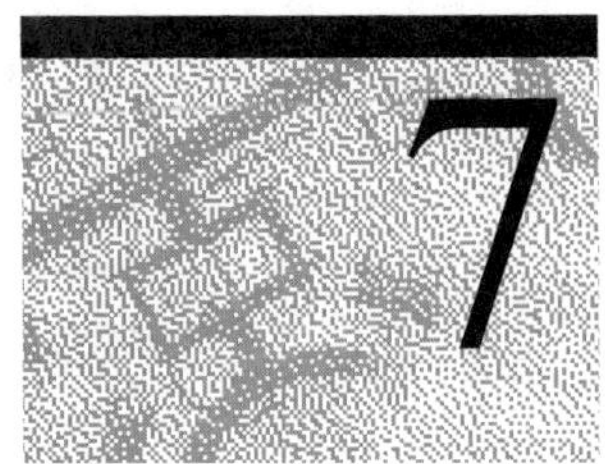

The primary focus of this chapter is on local printing from the Windows NT Workstation itself. But you can also provide printing to as many as 10 peer-to-peer connections with the Windows NT Workstation functioning as the print server.

This chapter begins with a glossary of terms used throughout the rest of the chapter. The glossary is followed by an overview of the Windows NT printing process and the flow of control. After you have a clear picture of the printing process and are comfortable with the terms, you can move on to read in-depth descriptions of each component of the printing architecture based on the network protocols and operating systems of your networked computers. The chapter concludes with sections on print security, troubleshooting, and some common questions and answers.

For additional information about printing with Windows NT 4.0 Workstation, refer to the following documentation.

Documentation Source	Descriptions
Microsoft Knowledge Base	An effective and consistent resource for troubleshooting printing problems.
Microsoft Technet	Microsoft White Papers, TechEd, and other articles are available on the Microsoft Technet CD.
Support Fundamentals for Windows NT, Chapter 13, "Printing with Windows NT"	A Microsoft Press® self-paced training manual.

Glossary of Printing Terms

A *print device* is the actual hardware device that produces printed output—what you call a "printer" in casual conversation.

Print-device resolution is measured in *dots per inch* (DPI). The higher the DPI, the finer the resolution.

A *printer*, or *logical printer*, is the software interface between the operating system and print device. The printer determines how the document gets to the printing devices (for example, by means of a local port or to a remote print share) and to other parameters of the printing process. A single printer can send print jobs to multiple print devices, and multiple printers can send jobs to a single print device. For more detail about printers and print devices, see "Planning How Users Access Printers" in *Microsoft Windows NT Server: Concepts and Planning Guide.* In the NetWare and OS/2 environments, this software interface is called a *queue*.

In Windows NT terminology, a *queue* is a group of documents waiting to be printed.

Print jobs are source code that contain both data and commands for print processing.

Print jobs are classified into *data types* based on what modifications, if any, the spooler must make to the job so that it prints correctly. For example, one data type requires no modifications, whereas another data type requires the addition of a form feed to the end of the job.

The print *spooler* is a collection of dynamic-link libraries (DLLs) that receives, processes, schedules, and distributes print jobs.

Spooling is only one of the processes performed by the spooler. Spooling is the process of writing the contents of a print job to a file on disk. This file is called a *spool file*. In the event of power loss during printing, the spool file prevents loss of data, ensuring that the print job can resume after power is restored. *Despooling* is the process of reading the contents from a spool file and sending those contents to a print device.

Rendering means creating a print job. An application calls the graphics device interface (GDI). GDI takes the document information sent by the application, calls the printer driver associated with the target print device, and creates a print job in the printer language of the print device. The print device has "firmware" that interprets the submitted printer language and creates a bitmap for each page.

A *print server* is the computer that connects one or more print devices to the network and shares them with other networked computers. A print server can also be a special hardware device that connects a print device to the network with a net tap on one side and a parallel or serial port on the other side.

This chapter presumes that the print server is a Windows NT 4.0 Workstation.

A *downlevel server* is a print server running a Windows product that is not Windows NT 4.0—for example, Windows for Workgroups or Windows NT 3.*x*.

Creating a printer means connecting to the print device, either over the network or over a serial or parallel port, naming the printer, and installing the printer driver. To create a printer, run the Add Printer wizard, and click the Local printer option. You'll be asked to install the printer driver, specify a port, and give the printer a name.

Connecting to a printer means connecting to the share on the computer that created the printer. To connect to a printer, run the Add Printer wizard, and click the Network printer option. You won't be required to install the printer driver. Only Windows NT and Windows 95 clients can "connect to" a printer shared out by a Windows NT 4.0 print server. Other print clients must "create" the printer shared by the Windows NT print server.

A *print client* is the computer that creates the print job sent to a Windows NT print server. The client can be a remote client sending the print job to the print server over a LAN. Or the client can be on the print server itself—a local client. This chapter presumes that most printing done with Windows NT Workstation is local.

A *client application* is any application that creates a print job. The client application can be local (on the print server) or it can be on a client computer on the network.

Network-interface printers are print devices connected directly to the network by means of their own network cards.

Print server services are software modules on the print server that receive print jobs and determine if the spooler should alter them. Different print server services support print jobs from various clients.

Printer drivers are software programs that enable applications to communicate fully and properly with print devices. Each print device can require unique codes and commnds to make available its special features, such as two-sided printing or custom paper sizes.

Anything described as *local* means that it exists on the same computer.

Overview of the Printing Process

This section provides a general overview of printing at a Windows NT Workstation. Although the primary focus of this chapter is on local printing from the Windows NT Workstation itself, you can also provide printing to as many as 10 peer-to-peer connections with the Windows NT Workstation functioning as the print server. For more information about network printing using a Windows NT 4.0 Workstation as a print server, see "Network Printing Using Windows NT Workstation" later in this chapter.

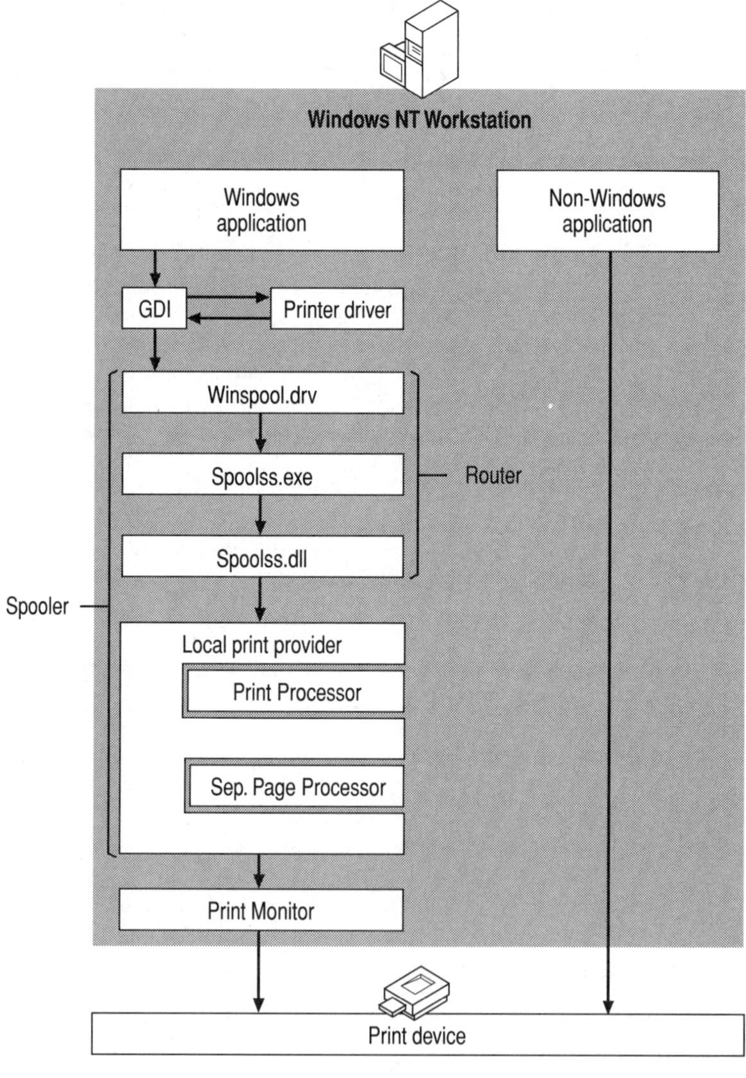

1. The user at the Windows NT Workstation chooses to print a document.

   For the Windows NT Workstation or for a client running any Windows operating system and printing from a Windows application, the application calls the graphics device interface (GDI). GDI calls the printer driver associated with the target print device. Using the document information from the application and the print device information from the printer driver, GDI renders the print job in the printer language of the print device.

2. The print job gets passed to the spooler.

   The client side of the spooler (Winspool.drv) makes a remote procedure call (RPC) to the server side of the spooler (Spoolss.exe), which makes a direct application programming interface (API) call to the router (Spoolss.dll). The router passes the print job to the local print provider (Localspl.dll), which spools it (writes it to disk).

3. The print job is altered, if necessary, to print correctly.

   The local print provider (Localspl.dll) polls the print processors. When a print processor recognizes the job's data type, that print processor receives the print job and alters it (or not) according to its data type to ensure that the job prints correctly.

4. Control of the print job passes to the separator page processor, which adds a separator page, if specified, to the front of the job.

5. The job is despooled to the print monitor.

   If the print device is bi-directional, the monitor is a language monitor, which handles bi-directional communication with the printer and then passes the job to the port monitor.

   If the print device is not bi-directional, the job goes directly to the port monitor, which transmits the print job to the print device or to another server over a specific communications channel.

6. The print device receives the print job, translates it into a bitmap, and prints it onto paper or another medium.

Print Jobs

Print jobs are not simply data: They are source code that contains both data and the commands for processing the data. The client application (along with the graphics engine and the printer driver) creates print jobs. For example, Microsoft Word 7.0 combines data objects such as text, fonts, and graphics with information from a printer driver to create source code for a document—the print job.

Data Types

Because each type of print client (for example, UNIX clients and Windows NT clients) creates print jobs a little differently, a variety of print server services are required to receive and prepare the jobs. Some print server services assign print jobs a *data type*, which tells the spooler whether and how to modify the print job in order to print correctly. Some services leave the data type blank (in which case the default data type in the **Print Processor** dialog box on the print server is assigned).

If you create a printer, the default data type is EMF (if the printer is a PCL printer) or RAW (if the printer is PostScript). To change the default data type, use the following procedure:

▶ **To change the default data type for a printer you have created**

1. Click Start, and then click Settings.
2. Click Printers.
3. Click to select the printer for which you want to change the data type.
4. Click Properties on the **File** menu.
5. Click the General tab.
6. Click the **Print Processor** button
7. In the Default Datatype list, click the data type.
8. Click **OK** in each dialog box.

The following sections describe the different data types.

EMF

Print jobs from Windows NT clients are enhanced metafiles (EMF). Instead of the RAW printer data being generated by the printer driver, EMF information is generated by the Graphical Device Interface (GDI) before spooling. After the EMF is created, control is returned to the user, and the EMF is interpreted in the background on a 32-bit printing subsystem spooler thread and sent to the printer driver.

EMF files are more portable than RAW files. An EMF file can be printed on any print device, whereas a RAW file can be printed on only one print device model. In addition, the set of EMF files that represent all pages in a print job are typically smaller than a RAW file that contains the same print job.

The first portion of the print job's rendering is done on the client computer. The last portion is rendered on the print server. This is especially helpful when the print job is a very large file, because the client application is not tied up for the entire rendering time. This data type also ensures that fonts specified on the client computer are the same ones used by the print server.

RAW

The RAW data type tells the spooler not to alter the job at all—that the print job is ready to print as is. Most jobs from non-Windows NT Windows clients are the RAW data type.

RAW [FF Appended]

This data type tells the spooler to assume the job is from an application that does not append a form-feed character (0x0C) to the end of each job. Without a trailing form-feed, the last page of the job does not print when sent to a PCL print device. The spooler appends a form-feed character to the end of the print job but makes no other alterations. None of the print server services supplied with Windows NT assign this data type, but you can set the default data type in the **Print Processor** dialog box to this type so that it affects jobs from Windows Network clients.

RAW [FF Auto]

This data type is similar to the RAW [FF Appended] data type, but RAW [FF Auto] tells the spooler to check for a form-feed character at the end of the job. It does not add a form feed if one is already present, and it makes no other alterations. None of the print server services supplied with Windows NT assign this data type, but you can set the default data type in the **Print Processor** dialog box to this type so that it affects jobs from Windows network clients.

TEXT

The TEXT data type tells the spooler that the job consists of ANSI text. The spooler uses the current print device driver to create a new print job that prints the text of the original job using the print device's factory default font, form, orientation, and resolution listed in the **Document Properties** dialog box. This is useful when the print job consists of simple text, and the target print device (for example, a PostScript printer) cannot interpret simple text jobs.

Text files consist of numeric values from 0 to 255, where each value is mapped to a particular character or symbol. Several character-mapping schemes (character sets) are in common use, and text files contain no indication of which character set to use when displaying or printing the file. The TEXT data type assumes the ANSI character set, so it might print some characters incorrectly if the application that created the job does not use the ANSI character set. Most character sets are identical for the values 0 through 127, so this problem usually affects extended characters (those with values from 128 through 255).

The following table shows five examples in which common character sets use different numbers to represent the same character. The PC-850 character set is commonly used by MS-DOS-based applications in Europe; ANSI is used by Windows-based applications; PC-437 is commonly used by MS-DOS-based applications in the United States; Roman-8 is the default PCL character set.

Table 7.1 Character Sets

Character	PC-850	ANSI	PC-437	Roman-8
Lowercase C Cedilla	135	231	135	181
Lowercase AE Diphthong	145	230	145	215
Lowercase N Tilde	164	241	164	183
Lowercase Eth	208	240	-	228
Lowercase Eszet	225	223	225	222

PSCRIPT1

This data type indicates that the print job consists of PostScript code from a Macintosh client and that the target printer is a non-PostScript print device. The spooler interprets the PostScript code and creates a bitmap of the page. GDI32 and the printer driver can convert the bitmap into the language of the target print device.

Print Devices

Print devices are the machines we call "printers." They produce hardcopy output by interpreting the printer language and creating a bitmap for each page.

Print devices have their own input and output channels; jobs can be directed to input channels such as parallel or serial cables or network adapters. Output can be produced on different media, including paper, film, or fabric.

Print devices have their own internal processors which can be proprietary or general-purpose (such as the Motorola 680*xx*-series chips in Apple LaserWriter devices). Incoming data is stored in the print-device RAM, which can range from a few bytes to a hundred megabytes. Each print device has software stored in ROM, called "firmware," which interprets the programming language of a print job's source code. Examples of programming languages are PostScript, PCL, and HP-GL/2.

Printer Drivers

Printer drivers are the software that enables an application to communicate with the variety of available print devices, regardless of the device type, model, or programming language interpreter.

In general, printer drivers are composed of three files that work together as a printer-driver unit:

- A printer graphics driver. This file renders device driver interface (DDI) commands from the graphics engine to commands that a print device can understand. Each graphics driver renders a different printer language. For example, a Pscript.dll renders PostScript printer language.
- A printer interface driver. This file provides the user interface you see when you configure a printer.
- A characterization data file. This file provides information about the configuration capabilities of a specific make and model of print device, including what resolutions it is capable of, whether it can print on both sides of the page, and what paper sizes it can accept.

These three files work as a unit. For example, when you set up and configure a new printer, the interface driver queries the characterization data file and then displays the available choices. Then, when you print, the graphics driver queries the interface driver about your selections so that it can create the proper printer commands.

Printer drivers are generally not binary-compatible across hardware-processor platforms. Consequently, printer drivers must be installed on the Windows NT print server for each Windows NT and Windows 95 client hardware platform. For example, when *x*86-based clients running Windows NT Workstation are served for printing by a Digital Alpha AXP–based Windows NT Server, you must install *x*86 printer drivers on the Alpha AXP–based print server.

The Windows NT and Windows 95 print client first attempts to use a local printer driver. If none is available, the Windows NT print server downloads the printer driver to the client computer's hard drive. The print client then uses its copy to create the print job.

In previous versions of Windows NT, printer drivers ran in user mode. With Windows NT 4.0, printer drivers run in kernel mode, thus reducing memory requirements and improving performance. For more information about user and kernel modes, see Chapter 5, "Windows NT 4.0 Workstation Architecture."

Note Print clients running Windows NT 4.0 won't be able to use printer drivers downloaded from a print server running an earlier version of Windows NT. You'll need to make sure that the client computer has the 4.0 printer drivers, or better yet, use Windows NT 4.0 on your print servers. A print server running Windows NT 4.0 can supply earlier version printer drivers to downlevel print clients, if necessary.

Platform-specific printer drivers are available with Windows NT 4.0 Workstation for the following:

- Intel *x*86-based computers running Windows NT 4.0, 3.5, or 3.51 and Windows 95
- MIPS RISC-based computers running Windows NT 4.0, 3.5, or 3.51 and Windows 95
- Digital Alpha AXP-based computers running Windows NT 4.0, 3.5, or 3.51 and Windows 95
- PowerPC running Windows NT 4.0, or 3.51 and Windows 95

Print devices can be classified as either raster, PostScript, or plotter. To support these three classes of print devices, Windows NT provides the following generic printer drivers:

- Universal printer driver
- PostScript printer driver
- HP-GL/2 plotter driver

Universal Printer Driver

The Universal printer driver (Unidriver) is sometimes referred to as the *raster driver* because it supports raster graphics printing. The Unidriver can carry out requests on most types of printers. Each print device vendor provides a device-specific minidriver (called a *characterization file*) that works with the Unidriver to communicate with its print devices.

This driver includes support for 24-bit color, scaleable TrueType fonts, device fonts, compression-run length encoding (RLE), and Tag Image File Format (TIFF) version 4.0. It also includes mechanisms that provide for smaller, more efficient bitmaps. These mechanisms include ignoring whitespace and supporting *rules*. (Hewlett-Packard LaserJet and compatible print devices use rules to print repeating elements on a page—such as bullets in a list—by repeating the information from a single bit of source code.)

The Universal printer driver consists of the following component files:

- Rasdd.dll is the printer graphics driver for printer languages based on raster (bitmap) images, including PCL, and most dot matrix printer languages.
- Rasddui.dll is the printer interface driver.
- Raster minidriver is the characterization data file. The filename for this component depends on the print device or printer family. Check the documentation that accompanies your print device.

The Windows NT Universal driver is a generic, text only (TTY) driver. It prints only text, and it prints it in the native font of the print device, regardless of any formatting in the original document.

PostScript Printer Driver

The Windows NT PostScript driver uses Adobe version 4.2-compatible PostScript printer description (.ppd) files. (Windows NT does not use the .wpd or .mpd files used by Windows 3.1). This driver supports key features, including binary transfer compression from Level II, resolution, and paper source.

The component files of the Windows NT PostScript printer driver are as follows:

- Pscript.dll is the printer graphics driver
- Pscriptui.dll is the printer interface driver
- *x*.ppd is the PostScript printer description (PPD) characterization data file

---

Note PPD files are the only printer driver files that are generally binary-compatible across processors and platforms.

HP-GL/2 Plotter Printer Driver

The Windows NT plotter driver supports a variety of plotters that use the HP-GL/2 language, but does not support HP-GL. The output from the Windows NT plotter driver requires a plotting device that can process all of the enhancements built into the HP-GL/2 language.

The Windows NT plotter driver consists of the following component files:

- Plotter.dll is the printer graphics driver.
- Plotui.dll is the printer interface driver.
- *x*.pcd is the characterization data file.

Establishing Printers

With Windows NT 4.0 you can establish printers with the Add Printer wizard or by using Point and Print.

Windows NT 4.0 provides the Printers folder to manage printing. Within it, the Add Printer wizard simplifies the task of establishing printers. You can open the Printers folder in the following ways:

- Click Start, point to Settings, and then click Printers.
- In My Computer, double-click the Printers Folder.
- In Control Panel, double-click the Printers icon.

▶ **To establish a printer with the Add Printer wizard**

- In the Printers folder, double-click the Add Printer icon.

  The Add Printer wizard leads you through the process of setting up and configuring a printer. The only differences between establishing a network printer and a local printer are as follows:

  - If you are establishing a local printer, you must install a printer driver. This action "creates" the printer on your computer.
  - If you are establishing a network printer, you must specify the path to the network printer or browse to find its network location. This action "connects to" the printer on the network print server.

▶ **To establish a printer using Point and Print**

1. Open the Printers folder.
2. Double-click **Network Neighborhood**.
3. Click the print server.
4. Drag the printer icon to your Printers folder.

   This action "connects to" the printer on the print server.

Creating vs. Connecting to a Printer

The method used to establish a printer on a client computer dictates the configuration of the client computer in relation to the printer. The following table details the various methods.

Connection Method	Windows NT Sending Software	Required Network Protocols	Windows NT Receiving Software
Connect to network printer in Add Printer wizard	Spoolss.exe	TCP/IP, NetBEUI, NWLink	Spoolss.dll
Create local printer in Add Printer wizard and Print To options for a UNC device.	Windows NT Workstation Service (NetBIOS redirector)	TCP/IP, NetBEUI, NWLink	Windows NT Server service
Create local printer and Print To options for an LPR port	LPR (Lpr.exe) Port Print Monitor	TCP/IP	TCP/IP (LPD) Print Service
Create local printer using Chooser and Print To options for an AppleTalk device	AppleTalk Print Monitor	AppleTalk	Services For Macintosh

Notice that only Windows NT and Windows 95 client computers can actually "connect to" a network printer served by a Windows NT print server. When a Windows NT or Windows 95 print client initiates a print request, the required printer driver is downloaded from the Windows NT print server if it is not already on the client's hard disk. All other client computers must "create" the printer—that is, they must install the printer driver directly on their hard disks, specify a port, name the printer, and so on.

Windows NT and Windows 95 print clients can also create a remote printer served by a Windows NT print server. Each method has advantages and disadvantages. Connecting to a remote printer is easier and faster than creating one. If the Windows NT client has connected to a printer, the print job doesn't spool on the client machine, so no spool options are available. (Windows 95 clients always spool locally and again remotely.) The "connected" client also cannot queue print jobs locally. Creating a printer gives the user more control, but that control is not always needed.

Specifying Virtual Printer Memory

You can change the amount of virtual memory that your PostScript printer has available for storing fonts. The PostScript driver uses a default setting recommended by the printer manufacturer for virtual memory.

To determine the right value, copy the Testps.txt file (supplied with the Windows NT Resource Kit) to the printer, and use the recommended virtual memory value printed on the resulting page.

► **To change your PostScript printer's virtual memory**

1. Click Start, point to Settings, and then click Printers.
2. Click to select the printer.
3. Click **Properties** on the **File** menu.
4. Click the Device Settings tab.
5. Double-click Available PostScript memory.
6. Type the value from Testps.txt in the Change Settings box.
7. Click **OK**.

Print Clients

Print clients, whether local (on the print server) or remote (on the network) send print jobs to a Windows NT print server. The print server services receive print jobs from remote clients as input/output (IO) requests that must be directed to the appropriate system process.

This chapter focuses on printing locally on the Windows NT Workstation and from Windows NT network clients. But, it also includes information about other network clients.

The following can all be print clients:

- Windows NT Workstation local clients
- Windows NT network clients
- Windows 95 network clients
- 16-bit Windows network clients
- MS-DOS network clients
- UNIX clients

Windows print clients receive printer alerts confirming successful prints or indicating errors. If a client doesn't want to receive printer alerts, you can disable them by adding the following entry to the [Network] section of the System.ini file:

```
SendPrintMessages=no
```

Note Disabling WinPopup does not disable printer alerts.

Windows NT Local Client

Windows-based applications and MS-DOS-based applications print in different ways and follow different rules. Windows-based applications send print jobs to printers added in the Printers folder. They typically use the printer drivers associated with those printers. However, some high-end desktop publishing or CAD applications have their own internal program copy of printer drivers.

In contrast, MS-DOS-based applications are unaware of the printers added in the Printers folder. They print to ports instead of to printers. This can cause problems. Whereas you could add several dozen printers in the Printers folder, most MS-DOS-based applications are limited to ports like LPT1–LPT3 and COM1–COM2. Windows NT accommodates MS-DOS-based applications in the following ways:

- If the port is controlled by the network redirector (for example, when a **net use** command redirects output to a shared resource), the redirector determines where the job goes.
- If the port is not controlled by a network redirector, but a printer prints to that port, the job is submitted to that printer, and that printer's spooling options take effect.
- If the port is not controlled by a network redirector, and no printer prints to that port, the job goes directly to the port device driver and prints (presuming, of course, that a print device is connected to that port).

EXAMPLE

Assume you are interactively logged on to a print server, and that there are two printers in the Printers folder and two print devices. The server is named \\PSERVER1, the printer named HPV prints to an LPT2 port supplied by a separate IO card, and the printer named HPIIISI prints to the FILE port. Both HPV and HPIIISI are shared on PSERVER1 over the network. There are print devices connected to both LPT1 and LPT2. You open a command prompt and type the following command:

```
NET USE LPT3: \\PSERVER1\HPIIISI.
```

When you copy a file to each of LPT1, LPT2, and LPT3, the following results:

COPY TEST.TXT LPT1:

NTVDM checks with the redirector and finds that the redirector is not managing LPT1. It checks with the spooler and finds that neither of the defined printers prints to LPT1, so the job goes to the parallel port device driver.

COPY TEST.TXT LPT2:

NTVDM checks with the redirector and finds that the redirector is not managing LPT2. It finds that the printer HPV is printing to LPT2. NTVDM submits the job to HPV and that printer's spooling options take effect as the job is printed on LPT2.

COPY TEST.TXT LPT3:

NTVDM checks with the redirector and finds that the redirector is managing LPT3, so the redirector takes control. The redirector is set so that data sent to LPT3 is actually sent to the print share \\PSERVER1\HPIIISI. It sends the job to that share and once it arrives, HPIIISI's spooling options take effect. Although you usually use the **net use** command to assign a local port to a remote shared resource, it is perfectly legal to assign a local port to a local shared resource. This is often useful in testing and troubleshooting.

32-bit Windows Network Clients

Windows NT and Windows 95 network clients can send print jobs using any of the following network protocols:

- NetBEUI
- NWLink
- TCP/IP
- AppleTalk

Windows NT 4.0 print clients now use enhanced metafile (EMF) data type instead of RAW. EMF allows the print job to be spooled to the server and rendered at the server into the appropriate print format. Remote rendering significantly speeds up the client computer's return to task.

Windows NT and Windows 95 network clients need not worry about printer drivers, because if the client doesn't have a needed driver it is automatically installed on the client's hard disk from the Windows NT 4.0 server when the client begins its print operation. If, however, the client computer is running Windows NT 4.0 and the server is running an earlier version, the printer drivers won't work. A Windows NT 4.0 print server can supply earlier version of printer drivers where necessary, but a Windows NT 4.0 client cannot use earlier versions of printer driver.

Windows 95 print jobs always spool EMF locally and playback locally to generate RAW data type before being sent to the print server. The print server spools them again.

The Windows NT print server receives print jobs from Windows 95 clients through the Windows NT Server service.

16-bit Windows Network Clients

There is little difference between the different versions of the 16-bit Windows platforms. They all support printing from MS-DOS-based applications and from Windows-based applications by using the 16-bit printer driver installed on the computer. They typically send jobs to a Windows NT print server by using one of the following MS Network client redirectors:

- LAN Manager
- Microsoft Network Client 3.0 for Windows
- Windows for Workgroups built-in redirector

The MS-Network redirectors send jobs by using the following protocols:

- NetBEUI
- NWLink
- TCP/IP

The Windows NT print server receives the job through the Windows NT Server service, which typically does not alter the print job. 16-bit Windows clients might also run third-party software for sending jobs to other print servers, such as LPR software for sending print jobs to UNIX print servers. This software is often able to send jobs to Windows NT as well.

Network Printing Using Windows NT Workstation

There are essentially two ways to implement printing using Windows NT Workstation as the print server:

- Workgroup printing
- Server printing

Workgroup Printing

With Workgroup printing, the assumption is that the printer or printers are connected directly to the network, and that each user on the LAN creates the printer on his or her own computer and does not share it. Each user then sets his or her own printer driver settings and each computer must have the printer driver installed.

The disadvantage to this configuration is that you can't be sure that, for example, the paper tray you've designated as letter-sized actually contains letter-sized paper unless you physically go check it right before you print. Someone may have designated that tray as legal-sized paper and recently replaced the letter-sized cartridge with a legal-sized cartridge.

Each computer also has its own printer queue displaying only those print jobs sent from that computer. This is a disadvantage for determining where your print job is in relation to all the print jobs (including those from other computers), and gives the user no feedback about when a particular print job might actually print.

Another disadvantage to this setup is that errors (such as paper jams or no paper in the tray) appear only on the queue for the current print job. No other computer gets the error message. If the user at the computer getting the error message has left for lunch, printing could be held up for some time.

Server Printing

The second way to set up printing is to have one Windows NT Workstation function as print server. One computer in the LAN creates the printer and shares it with other computers.

Windows NT Workstation can support a small (maximum 10 connections) local area network (LAN) for printing. Because it is not designed to provide server functions, Windows NT Workstation has the following limitations that you need to understand in order to get satisfactory network printing performance.

1. Services for Macintosh and File and Print Services for NetWare are not available with Windows NT Workstation. Consequently, Macintosh computers and NetWare network clients can't print to a print device served by a Windows NT Workstation.
2. Spooling is given a lower priority on Windows NT 4.0 Workstation than on Windows NT 4.0 Server. This means that a Windows NT Workstation functioning as a print server will print somewhat slower than a Windows NT Server. Also, if the print server is also used as someone's work machine, that person may find his or her applications running a little sluggishly while someone is printing.
3. You are limited to 10 connections, and they must be within the same LAN.

In this scenario, printer driver settings are controlled by the print server computer. A single queue appears on every computer connected to the printer, letting each user see where his or her print job is in relation to others waiting to print. Error messages, therefore, appear on everyone's computer, so that anyone can know to refill the paper tray, clear the paper jam, or plug the printer back in. This method also allows you to have a single administrative log if you audit your printing events.

Print Server Services

Print server services are the software on the Windows NT print server that receive print jobs from specific types of network clients, determine whether the spooler should alter them, and then send them to the spooler by calling the spooler application program interfaces (API).

Each print server service uses different programmatic logic and makes different assumptions about print jobs from its supported print clients. These differences are detailed in the sections describing each service.

Windows NT Workstation provides the following print server services:

- Windows NT Server Service
- TCP/IP Print Server Service, known as Line Printer Daemon (LPD)

Client applications on the Windows NT Workstation print server itself use these additional software modules:

- Windows NT Virtual DOS Machine (NTVDM)
- Graphical Device Interface 32-Bit (GDI32)

The following table lists each print server service and the type of print client processed by the service.

Table 7.2 Windows NT Print Server Services

Service	Registry Name	Supported Clients
Windows NT Server service	Srv.sys	MS Network clients using NetBIOS redirectors on MS-DOS, Windows, Windows for Workgroups, or Windows NT computers.
TCP/IP Print service	Lpdsvc.sys	LPR (line printer) clients on UNIX or Windows NT computers where the TCP/IP protocol is used.

Windows NT Server Service

The Windows NT Server service receives jobs from applications and computers that are using the MS Network client and NetBIOS redirectors. This includes print clients using any of the following:

- Windows NT

  The Windows NT Server service only receives jobs from Windows NT clients if the client has created the printer in his or her own machine. If the client has connected to the printer, the print job goes directly to the server's spooler. For more information about creating versus connecting to a printer, see "Creating vs. Connecting to a Printer" earlier in this chapter.
- LAN Manager
- MS Network Client (often used on clients running MS-DOS alone or MS-DOS with Windows Versions 3.0, 3.1 or 3.11)
- Windows For Workgroups
- Windows 95

The Windows NT Server service does not set the data-type value when it submits the print job to the spooler. Instead, the spooler uses the default data type specified in the **Print Processor** dialog box on the print server. You can change the default data type. For more information, see "Data Types" earlier in this chapter.

Note If you select EMFor PSCRIPT1, the print spooler ignores this data and, instead uses the RAW data type to process print jobs. Detailed information on print spooler processing of data types is provided later in this chapter in the "Print Processor" section.

TCP/IP Print Service (LPD)

The TCP/IP Print service is generally referred to as LPD, which stands for *line printer daemon* (or "service"). LPD receives print jobs from line printer remote (LPR) clients. LPR clients are often on UNIX systems, but LPR software exists for most operating systems, including Windows NT.

LPR is one of the network protocols in the TCP/IP protocol suite. It was originally developed as a standard for transmitting print jobs between computers running Berkeley UNIX. The LPR standard is published as Request For Comment (RFC) 1179. Previous versions of Windows NT supported TCP/IP printing as documented in RFC 1179, which describes an existing print server protocol widely used on the Internet for communicating between line printer daemons but does not specify an Internet standard. Different implementations support different options.

Windows NT 4.0 has added enhancements to support the most popular and requested options. Windows NT now supports multiple data files per control file, and when used in "print through" mode as an intermediate spooler, it correctly passes the hostname parameter through the Windows printing subsystem. Windows NT 3.5*x* sent all TCP/IP print jobs from Windows NT computers from TCP ports 721 through 731. If enough jobs were sent in quick succession the ports could become a bottleneck causing a delay. For Windows NT 4.0 LPR print jobs are sourced from any available reserved port between 512 and 1023.

The LPR protocol does not pass detailed error status information back to the LPR client. If anything goes wrong, from severe problems (such as the server being too busy to process requests) to print-device problems (such as running out of paper), the LPR protocol reports the same error condition.

LPD receives jobs from LPR clients and submits them to the spooler. LPR clients always send a "control file" (actually, a data structure within the print job) containing administrative information with each print job. LPD assigns a data type based on the control commands in that control file.

If the client sends the **f**, **o**, or **p** control command, the LPD assigns the TEXT data type to the print job—which tells the spooler to edit the job to make sure it prints. If the client sends the **l** control command, the LPD assigns the RAW data type to the print job—which tells the spooler the print job needs no editing to print correctly. For more detail about data types, see "Data Types" earlier in this chapter.

Control commands are documented in the LPR specification, Request For Comment (RFC) 1179, sections 7.17 through 7.29. For detailed information about RFC 1179, refer to the Windows NT Knowledge Base article, "Text of RFC1179 Standard for Windows NT TCP/IP Printing," reference number Q124734.

Note Notice that all the control commands defined in RFC 1179 are case sensitive. Notice also that many printer languages, including PCL, rely heavily on the ESC control character, which the **f** control command causes to be filtered from the print job. Do not use the **f** control command when sending print jobs that contain printer commands.

Because LPD assigns a data type explicitly, the default data type found in the **Print Processor** dialog box has no effect on print jobs received by LPD. To change the behavior of LPD, you must reconfigure the LPR client application to send a different control command with the print job. To reconfigure a LPR client application, consult the documentation for the application.

Windows NT Virtual DOS Machine (NTVDM)

MS-DOS-based applications run in a special Win32-based component referred to as a Windows NT virtual DOS machine (NTVDM). The NTVDM component translates MS-DOS operating system calls into calls used by the WIN32 subsystem.

If you print from a locally-run MS-DOS-based application or from a Windows NT command-line utility that sends data to a printer port, NTVDM receives the job. What happens next depends on whether the Windows NT redirector or the spooler manages the port:

- First, NTVDM queries the redirector to find out whether it is managing the target port. This would be the case if someone had issued a NET USE LPT1:\\SERVER\SHARE command. If so, the redirector takes control of the print job, and none of the spooler options affect the job.
- If the redirector is not managing the port, and someone has assigned a printer to that port using the Add Printer wizard, the job goes to that printer. In this case, the default data type of the print server and its spooling options are in effect.

- If neither the redirector nor printers are managing the port, the job goes to the port device driver unaltered. Naturally, this presumes a print device is physically connected to the port. If not, you'll get an error message.

For example, suppose one printer prints to COM1, and none of the printers print to LPT1 (but a print device is connected to LPT1). Also, suppose that you issue a **net use** command to redirect output from LPT2 to a network print share. If an MS-DOS-based application prints to LPT2, the job is sent to the network print share. If the application prints to COM1, NTVDM submits the job to the printer that prints to COM1, and that printer's default data type is used. If the application prints to LPT1, NTVDM submits the job directly to the parallel port device driver, and no print job alteration occurs.

Windows NT Graphical Device Interface (GDI32) for 16-bit Applications

On a Windows NT computer, Windows 3.*x*-based (16 bit) applications are supported by a Graphical Device Interface 32 (GDI32) engine. The GDI32 engine translates print and display application programming interface (API) calls to 32-bit WIN32 services.

The GDI32 graphics engine (Gdi32.dll) is the printing component that provides What You See Is What You Get (WYSIWYG) support across devices. The graphics engine communicates with Windows-based applications through the Windows Graphics Device Interface (GDI) and with printer drivers through the Device Driver Interface (DDI).

When a Windows-based application creates a print job, it describes the output it wants in a series of GDI commands. The GDI32 graphics engine is the component that translates these GDI commands into the DDI commands understood by components such as printer drivers and print processors.

The GDI32 graphics engine queries the printer driver to identify the capabilities of the print device, including supported fonts. Using this information, the GDI32 graphics engine uses other DDI commands to specify the positioning of each character in the document by the print device. The GDI32 graphics engine also uses DDI commands to define how the print device should draw and fill graphics and how to manipulate and print bitmaps.

The GDI32 graphics engine provides services to the printer driver, including compatibility with the environment subsystem (for example, MS-DOS or OS/2) and performance optimization, caching, client-server communications, and ANSI-to-Unicode conversion.

The GDI32 graphics engine calls the printer driver and provides information about the type of print device needed and the data type used. In response, the printer driver provides the graphics engine with the fully qualified path name for the print device and printer-setting information. This information is passed to the spooler.

Print Spooler

The preceding sections described network print clients, print server services, print jobs, data types, and print devices. These are entities at the beginning and end of the printing process. The following sections describe the Windows NT print spooler components and the processing that takes place on a Windows NT print server after the print job is created and before the print job reaches the print device.

The following figure shows the main spooler components used to process jobs on a Windows NT print server. Each component uses the services of the component directly below it.

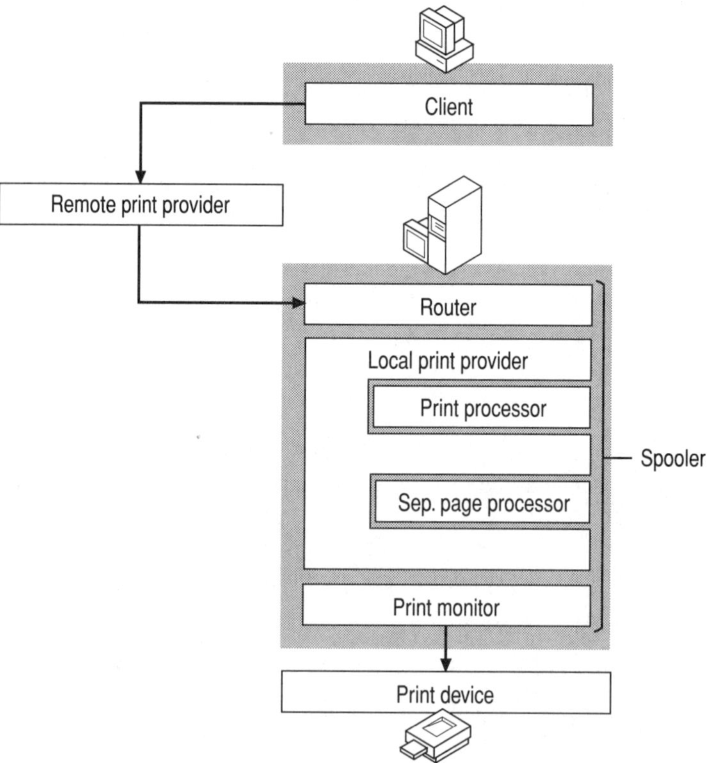

Figure 7.1 Print Spooler Components

As shown in the figure, the components below the client and above the print device are collectively called the *spooler*. The spooler is a series of 32-bit virtual device drivers and DLLs consolidated into a single architecture. It provides smooth background printing by using background thread processing. This means that the spooler passes data to the printer only when the printer is ready to receive more information. In Windows NT, the spooler components are implemented as a service that you can stop and restart from the Services icon on the Control Panel or from the command line by using the **net stop spooler** and **net start spooler** commands.

Important If you stop the spooler service, you will not be able to print until you start it again.

The spooler components reside on both the Windows NT print server and on the Windows NT client computer. Client computers running a different operating system might have different components, and they might interact differently with the Windows NT print server's spooler components. The following table lists the components of the Windows NT spooler:

Table 7.3 Print Spooler Components

Spooler Component	Desciption
Router	Winspool.drv, Spoolss.exe, Spoolss.dll.
Local Print Provider	Localspl.dll
Remote Print Providers	Win32sp.dll for Windows print servers.
	Nwprovau.dll for NetWare print servers.
Print Processors	Winprint.dll
	Sfmpsprt.dll
Print Monitors	Localmon.dll
	Hpmon.dll
	Lprmon.dll
	Sfmmon.dll
	Decpsmon.dll
	Lexmon.dll
	Nwmon.dll
	Pjlmon.dll

Each spooler component is described in more detail in the following sections.

Router

When a Windows NT application has a print job it wants to send to the printer, it communicates with the client side of the spooler (Winspool.drv). This file makes an RPC to the server side of the spooler (Spoolss.exe), which makes a direct API call to the router (Spoolss.dll—which is also on the server side of the spooler).

The router passes control of the print job to the appropriate print provider. In the case of local printing, the local print provider takes the print job. If the print is going to a server on the network, the router passes the print job to the appropriate remote print provider—the Windows remote print provider or the Novell NetWare print provider.

Do not confuse the software router component of the Windows NT spooler with the physical hardware router used in networks.

Remote Print Providers

When a client computer connects to a remote printer and sends a print job to it, the router polls each of the remote print providers on the client computer. The router passes control of the print job to the first remote print provider that recognizes the printer name.

Windows NT supplies the following remote print providers:

- Windows Network print provider (Win32spl.dll) transfers jobs to Windows Network print servers (such as print servers running Windows NT or Windows for Workgroups).
- Novell NetWare print provider (Nwprovau.dll) transfers jobs to Novell NetWare print servers.

Note Neither of these remote print providers performs spooling.

Windows Network Print Provider

If the local copy of the Windows network print provider, Win32spl.dll, recognizes the printer name, it performs additional processing based on the type of print server to which the job is going. If the print server is running Windows NT, Win32spl.dll makes remote procedure calls to the router (Spoolss.dll) on the print server. The router receives the print job over the network and passes it to the local print provider as if one of its own local clients had submitted it.

If the remote print server is a downlevel server, Win32spl.dll sends a message to the Windows NT NetBIOS redirector. The redirector forwards the job over the network to the downlevel server.

The functions provided by the Windows network print provider are illustrated in the following figure.

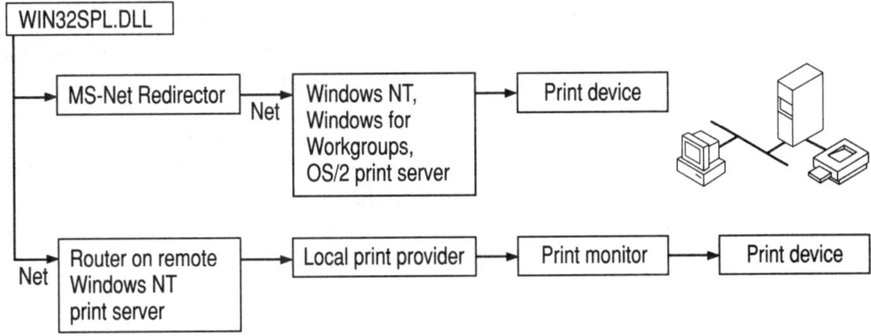

Figure 7.2 The Windows Network Print Provider (Win32spl.dll)

Novell NetWare Remote Print Provider

If the NetWare print provider (Nwprovau.dll) recognizes the printer name when polled by the router, it takes control of the print job. The NetWare print provider sends a message to the NetWare workstation service (Nwwks.dll), which in turn passes control to the NetWare redirector. The NetWare redirector transmits the print job over the network to the NetWare print server.

Note To send print jobs over Windows NT to a NetWare print server, you must install Gateway Services for NetWare. To receive print jobs from NetWare print clients, you must install File and Print Services for NetWare.

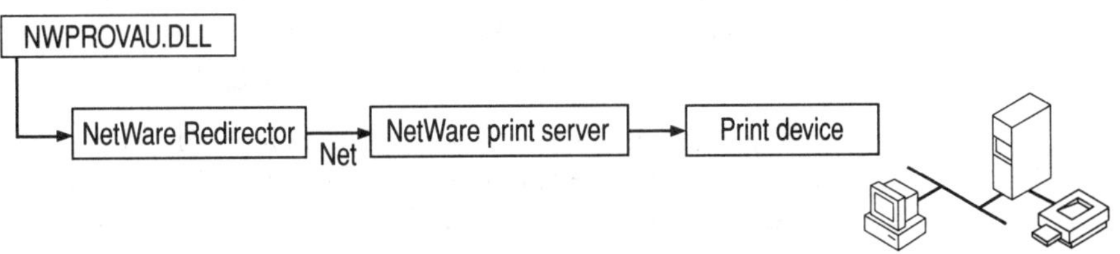

Figure 7.3 The NetWare Print Provider (Nwprovau.dll)

Local Print Provider (Localspl.dll)

The *local print provider* writes the print job contents to a spool (.spl) file and tracks administrative information (such as user name, document name, and data type) in a shadow (.shd) file. By default, both files are written to *%systemroot%*\system32\spool\printers.

If, however, the hard drive partition containing Windows NT Server doesn't have sufficient disk space to accommodate the spool files, you can change the location of spool files by changing the server properties.

► **To change the location of spool files**

1. Create a new spool file directory.
2. Click Start, and then point to Settings.
3. Click **Printers**.
4. Click **Server Properties** on the **File** menu.
5. Click the Advanced tab.
6. In the Spool Folder box, type the path for the new spool file directory.
7. Click **OK**.

Note You must create a directory for the new spool file location. If you attempt to spool directly to the root (C:\ or D:\, for example) the spool file will revert to the default spool directory.

Spooling a print job to a file protects the print job by saving it on disk. Should the print server suffer a power failure or other serious event before printing all jobs in the queue, the spool and shadow files on the server's hard disk preserve each job and prevent any loss of data once processing resumes.

By default, spool and shadow files are deleted after the job prints. However, you can enable spooler event logging to get valuable information about printer traffic, hard disk space, and other printing maintenance issues.

► **To enable spooler event logging**

1. In the Printers folder, click the printer to select it.
2. Click **Server Properties** on the **File** menu.
3. Click the Advanced tab.
4. Click Enable spooler event logging to add a check mark.
5. Click **OK**.

Next, LOCALSPL polls the installed print processors (such as Winprint.dll and Sfmpsprt.dll) to see if one of them recognizes the job's data type set. If the data type is not set, the Winprint.dll print processor receives the job and uses the default data-type set **Print Processor** dialog box on the print server.

You can set a new default location or override the default location on a printer-by-printer basis by manually editing the Registry. However, before doing so, read the "Spool File Security" section later in this chapter.

Enhanced Metafile (EMF) Spool Files

Enhanced metafiles (EMF) are one type of spool file used by the default Windows NT print spooler. EMF spool files are used to reduce the time between the initiation of a print request and when control is returned back to the operating system. This is done by storing only the GDI function calls that produce the graphic object the application wants printed. The much more time-consuming execution of function calls can then be carried out later, in the background, when the spool file is played back.

The way EMF spool files are encoded also provides the advantage of printer device-independence. In other words, a picture measuring 2 inches by 4 inches on a VGA display and stored in an EMF maintains those original dimensions whether it is printed on a 300 dpi laser printer or on a 75 dpi dot matrix printer.

RAW Spool Files

If the print job's data type is RAW, the spool file's data type is RAW. These files are device-dependent. The spooled data is destined and formatted for a particular device and does not need to be printable on a different device. An example of a RAW spool file is an encapsulated PostScript (EPS) file, which is formatted to be understood by the PostScript printer for which it is destined, but which is just RAW data to the Windows NT spooler.

Print Processor

The print processor is the component that make necessary alterations to print jobs, based on the data type of the print job. The print processor (Winprint.dll) works in conjunction with a printer driver to despool the spooled print jobs during print spool file playback.

A print device vendor might develop a custom print processors if

- The vendor develops its own printer driver, or
- The vendor supports a data type different from those supported by the Microsoft print processor.

Additional print processors may be supplied by third-party software vendors to support custom data types.

Print Monitors

Windows NT 4.0 supports two kinds of print monitors: *language monitors* and *port monitors*.

A language monitor is necessary to support bi-directional print devices. A bi-directional print device supports two-way communication between the print device and the spooler running on its print server. The language monitor allows the spooler to configure and monitor the status of a bi-directional printer. A language monitor can also add data (such as printer control information) to the print stream. When you create a printer, you install a printer driver. If a language monitor is associated with that printer driver, all data that flows from the printer driver to the print device goes through the language monitor before it goes through the port monitor and out to the printer.

Two-way communication between computer and print device allows a system administrator to configure the printer and to monitor printer status. The spooler running on the computer can request configuration and status information from the printer, and the printer can send unsolicited status information to the computer (such as the fact that the paper tray is empty). A common language is necessary for the two devices to understand each other.

The language monitor supplied with Windows NT 4.0 uses Printer Job Language. If a print-device vendor uses a printer language other than PJL, that vendor can develop a language monitor for it. A vendor might also develop a language monitor to add data, such as printer-specific control information, to the print stream going to a single directional printer.

Port monitors control the I/O port to which the physical print device is connected. The local print monitor executable (Localmon.dll) supplied by Microsoft controls parallel and serial I/O ports that may have a print device connected to them. Print devices connected to different types of I/O ports such as SCSI or Ethernet ports on a network card or adapter, are controlled by vendor-developed port monitors.

The print monitors supplied with Windows NT are described in the following sections.

- Local print monitor (Localmon.dll)
- Hewlett Packard Network Port print monitor (Hpmon.dll)
- Line Printer (LPR) Port print monitor (Lprmon.dll)
- Macintosh print monitor (Sfmmon.dll)
- Digital Network Port print monitor (Decpsmon.dll)
- LexMark Mark Vision print monitor (Lexmon.dll)
- NetWare Print Monitor (Nwmon.dll)
- PJL Language Monitor (Pjlmon.dll)

The Ports tab of the **Printer Properties** dialog box lists the default Windows NT ports.

By default, the list includes only standard ports controlled by the local print monitor, Localmon.dll. When you want to print over other communications channels (to a network-attached printer, for example), you must create a new port.

To create a new port

1. Click the **Start** button, and then point to Settings.
2. Click **Printers**.
3. Click **Add New Port**.
4. Click to select the port monitor that controls the type of communications channel you want to use.
5. Insert the disk or type the network path to the port monitor files.
6. Click **OK** in each dialog box.

Print monitors often depend on other software components and appear in this list only when you have installed the components they require. For example, the Hewlett-Packard Network print monitor transmits print jobs by using the DLC network protocol. This monitor appears in the list only if you have installed the DLC protocol.

Each monitor displays its own user interface, which you use to create a new port and configure a printer to use it. To reconfigure the new port (if the monitor allows reconfiguration), click the **Configure Port** button on the Ports tab of the **Printer Properties** dialog box.

When you read about each print monitor in the following sections, remember that each is associated with a data communications channel, not with the print device at the other end of that channel. In most cases, the port monitor is unaware of the make or model of the print device it is communicating with, nor does it need this information. Also, although different port monitors might use the same network protocol, this does not make them interchangeable. For example, both the Digital Network Port print monitor and the LPR Port print monitor use the TCP/IP protocol, but they send data over that protocol in very different ways.

Local Print Monitor (Localmon.dll)

The local print monitor, Localmon.dll, sends print jobs to local devices. These include familiar ports like LPT1 and COM1. Use of the less familiar FILE and Other ports are described below.

The FILE port appears in the default port list on the Ports tab of the **Printer Properties** dialog box. When you send jobs to a printer that uses this port, the local print monitor prompts you for the name of a file in which the print job should be stored.

If you select Other from the list of ports in the Print To box on the **Printer Properties** dialog box, and select the **Local Port** option, the local print monitor prompts you to enter a port name. Some possibilities include:

- An explicit filename, such as C:\dir\filename. All jobs sent to this port are written to the named file. Each new job overwrites the last one.
- The name of a print share, such as \\server\printer. Jobs sent to this port are transferred over the network to the named share by the network redirector. This can be useful if you need to send jobs to a network print server, but you want the job to spool locally as well as on the print server.
- The NULL port. Use this port to test whether network clients are able to send jobs. Simply pause the printer set to use this port, send a job from a network client, look at the printer in Print Manager to confirm that it arrived, and resume the printer. Jobs sent to NULL are simply deleted from the system without wasting paper or delaying real print jobs.

Hewlett-Packard Network Port Print Monitor (Hpmon.dll)

The Hewlett-Packard Network print monitor, Hpmon.dll, sends print jobs to HP JetDirect adapters. This includes both the network adapters commonly installed in print devices (such as the LaserJet 4 Si) and the JetDirect device (which connects a parallel print device to the network).

Although many JetDirect devices can communicate over several different network protocols, including DLC, IPX, TCP/IP, and AppleTalk, Hpmon.dll is specific to DLC; you must load the DLC protocol to use this print monitor.

The DLC protocol is bridgeable, but not routable. This means that if a Windows NT print server is on one physical subnet and a JetDirect device is on another physical subnet, the server can send jobs to the JetDirect if the two subnets are joined by a bridge but cannot send jobs if the two subnets are joined by a router.

The DLC protocol can be bound to multiple network adapters, but the HP print monitor software can only manage printers over one network adapter, and it must be either adapter 0 or adapter 1. If your Windows NT computer has multiple network adapters, make sure all the HP JetDirect-equipped printers are on the same physical subnet.

When you install, reinstall, or upgrade Windows NT, it assigns a number to each network adapter in your computer. The adapter with the lowest I/O base address is assigned the number 0; the adapter with the next lowest I/O base address is assigned the number 1, and so on. If you later add another network adapter, it is assigned the next unused number, regardless of its I/O base address. Later, if you upgrade or reinstall Windows NT, each adapter is again assigned a number based on its I/O base address. If the third adapter has a lower I/O base address than either of the other two, then the numbering changes. In this case, HPMON looks for JetDirect cards through the wrong network adapter on the server.

▶ **To correct adapter numbering after an upgrade**

1. Click Start, point to Settings, and then click Control Panel.
2. Double-click the Network icon.
3. Click the Adapters tab.
4. Remove each adapter that has an incorrect number.
5. Add the adapters back in the order that corresponds with their I/O addresses (the lowest address getting the lowest number).
6. Click OK.

   You'll need to restart the computer before the changes take effect.

You can configure ports managed by Hpmon.dll as either *job-based* or *continuous connection*. The setting affects all ports at once:

- With job-based connection, a print server connects to the JetDirect adapter, sends a print job, and disconnects when the job is finished printing. This enables other print servers to connect and print.
- With continuous connection, a print server connects to the JetDirect adapter and maintains the connection until either the print server or the adapter is rebooted, preventing other servers from connecting. The main advantage of continuous connection is that all users are validated by the Windows NT security model, and every print job access can be audited.

  For more information about auditing printing, see the *Windows NT 4.0 Workstation Online Resource Guide.*

Note If you configure two Windows NT print servers to send jobs to the same JetDirect device, configure both servers for job-based connections. If you configure one of the print servers for continuous connection, it prevents the job-based server from connecting to the print device.

Line Printer Port Monitor (Lprmon.dll/Lpr.exe)

Windows NT supplies a command line utility (Lpr.exe) and the LPR Port print monitor (Lprmon.dll). Both act as clients sending print jobs to an LPD service running on another computer. As mentioned previously, Windows NT also supplies an LPD service, the TCP/IP Print service, which receives print jobs sent by LPR clients, including UNIX computers and other Windows NT computers using the TCP/IP protocol.

To send print jobs, the LPR clients needs the network address of the LPD print server and the name that the LPD service associates with its print device. LPR sends print jobs to LPD along with instruction on how to process the job and the name of the print device.

When you add an LPR port while connecting to the LPR print server, you'll be asked in a dialog box to supply information identifying the print server (host) and the name of the printer. You can supply either the IP address or the host name of the server. The server can be one of the following:

- UNIX computer
- Windows NT computer
- Windows for Workgroups computer with a third-party LPD
- network adapter, such as an HP JetDirect or Emulex NetJet

For example, let's say you're connecting to a printer named LABLASER on a UNIX computer whose IP address is 11.22.33.44, and whose name (defined in the hosts file on your Windows NT computer) is UNIXBOX. You can enter either "UNIXBOX" or "11.22.33.44" (without the quotation marks) in the Name Or Address Of Host Providing LPD box. You would enter LABLASER in the Name Of Printer On That Machine box.

To obtain the IP address of a network adapter, check the adapter's documentation. Some adapters provide a character-based application that you can access either by network connection or by directly connecting to the adapter by means of a serial-to-serial port cable.

If the server is a UNIX computer, and you don't know a valid name for the printer, you can often find it by looking at the /etc/printcap file on the UNIX computer. Each entry corresponds to a print queue ("printer" in Windows NT terminology) on the UNIX computer. Fields in these entries are separated by ":" characters, and for readability an entry can be broken over several lines by ending a line with a "\" character and beginning the next line with a space or tab character. The first field of each entry lists valid names for the queue, separated by "|" characters.

Continuing the LABLASER example, we might find entries like the following in the printcap file on the computer named UNIXBOX:

```
lp|lablaser|The_Lab_Printer:\
:lp=/dev/ttya:br#9600:\
:lf=/usr/spool/lpd/lablaser-err:\
:sd=/usr/spool/lpd/lablaser:
```

The first line in this example defines a print queue with three valid names: lp, lablaser, and The_Lab_Printer. You can use any of these names in the second field of the **LPR Port** dialog box previously shown.

Note This example is provided for illustrative purposes only. The UNIX system documentation is your best source of detailed information on your system's printcap file. Also note that the term "queue" is the UNIX term. Its Windows NT equivalent is "printer."

When the LPR Port print monitor receives the LPD server's network address and the proper queue name, it can send print jobs and processing instructions.

The LPR Port print monitor sends the **l** command by default, whereas the command line Lpr.exe utility sends the **f** command by default. With the Lpr.exe utility, use the **-o** command if you want to override the default on a job-by-job basis. To change the default command for a particular printer controlled by the LPR Port print monitor, you must modify a Registry parameter. Use the Registry Editor (Regedt32.exe) to find the following key:

```
HKEY_LOCAL_MACHINE\SYSTEM\CurrentControlSet\Control\Print\Monitors\
   LPRPort\Ports\<portname>\<IP Address or Host name>:<printer name>
```

In this key, add a value named PrintSwitch with type REG_SZ, and enter the control command you want to use. For instance, enter the letter "f" (without the quotation marks) if you want to use the **f** command by default.

Some UNIX computers do not follow the control commands alone when deciding how to process a print job. For instance, if you send an ASCII text file with an **l** command (which tells the spooler not to alter the print job) to a PostScript printer, it does not print correctly. Consequently, many UNIX systems have added software that converts scans jobs that arrive with the **l** command. If the scanner finds PostScript commands, the job goes directly to the printer. If no PostScript is found, the added software adds the PostScript code so that the job prints correctly.

If you send PostScript jobs from a Windows NT computer using LPR, and the printer controlled by the UNIX server prints the PostScript code instead of interpreting it, the UNIX server might have a scanner that does not recognize the output from the Windows NT PostScript driver as valid PostScript code. If this happens, you might need to reconfigure Windows NT to use the **o** control command by default.

If the client sends the **f**, **o**, or **p** control command, the Windows NT TCP/IP Print service assigns the TEXT data type to the print job—which tells the spooler to edit the job to make sure it prints. If the client sends the **l** control command, the Windows NT TCP/IP Print service assigns the RAW data type to the print job—which tells the spooler the print job needs no editing to print correctly. For more detail about data types, see "Data Types" earlier in this chapter.

Control commands are documented in the LPR specification, Request For Comment (RFC)1179, sections 7.17 through 7.29. For detailed information about RFC 1179, refer to the Windows NT Knowledge Base article, "Text of RFC 1179 Standard for Windows NT TCP/IP Printing," reference number Q124734.

LPD-compliant print devices must supply one or more names for each of their print queues, even though these devices often have only one possible destination for the print jobs they receive. Each print-device manufacturer chooses naming conventions independently. Some, like the HP JetDirect adapter, accept any string as a legal print queue name. In comparison, the Emulex NetJet adapter accepts only two strings, and these are case sensitive, and default to TEXT and PASSTHRU. These strings are configurable. To find the names supported by any specific adapter, check its documentation, or contact the vendor's technical support group.

Remember that the local print provider spools print jobs, and that it despools them to the print monitors. In Windows NT, after LPRMON receives a job from the local print provider, it spools it a second time as a temporary file in the SYSTEM32 subdirectory. LPR must include an accurate byte count in the control file, and it cannot get that byte count from the local print provider. Instead, it respools the data to a temp file, finds the size of that temp file, and sends that size in the control file to the LPD server.

The most common problem people encounter when printing from UNIX systems to a Windows NT print server is that their print jobs are processed as TEXT data type instead of RAW data type, as they would be on a UNIX system. This happens because the UNIX systems almost always send the **f** control command, expecting that the control command isn't too important, because the TCP/IP (LPD) server parses the job to identify what data type to use and how to alter the job. However, Windows NT relies on the control command to determine the data type. As a result, the LPD service on Windows NT assigns the TEXT data type to most jobs.

To correct this problem, reconfigure the LPR client to send the **l** control command so the LPD will assign the RAW data type.

Macintosh Port Monitor (Sfmmon.dll)

The Macintosh port monitor, Sfmmon.dll, transmits jobs over a network using the AppleTalk protocol to network-attached print devices, such as the Apple LaserWriter family. It also lets you send jobs to AppleTalk spoolers, regardless of the print device that the spooler is attached to.

This monitor is available on both Windows NT Workstation and Windows NT Server computers and enables any Windows NT–based computer to send local print jobs to AppleTalk print devices. However, only Windows NT Server has a Macintosh print server component, so only a Windows NT Server computer can receive print jobs from Macintosh clients.

Some print devices process non-PostScript print jobs incorrectly if they receive those jobs over AppleTalk. Also, some print devices process PostScript jobs incorrectly if those jobs contain binary data and arrive over any protocol other than AppleTalk. These problems result from restrictions in those print devices; they do not indicate that the Windows NT print server is transmitting the jobs incorrectly.

Digital Network Port Monitor (Decpsmon.dll)

The Digital Network Port print monitor, Decpsmon.dll, sends print jobs to Digital Equipment Corporation's Digital PrintServer print devices and to other Digital Equipment Corporation print devices (such as the DEClaser 5100 and the DECcolorwriter 1000).

Windows NT supplies the TCP/IP network protocol, but does not supply the DECnetprotocol. If you want to use DECnet, you must contact Digital Equipment Corporation to obtain it.

LexMark Mark VisionPrint Monitor (Lexmon.dll)

LexMark's Mark Vision print monitor (Lexmon.dll) sends print jobs to LexMark MarkNet print devices (such as the MarkNetXL) and to network adapters (such as the MarkNetXLe). This print monitor uses any of the following protocols:

- DLC
- TCP/IP
- IPX

NetWare Print Monitor (Nwmon.dll)

NetWare's print monitor (Nwmon.dll) sends print jobs to Pserver print devices. Pserver is a print-device standard developed by Novell.

In most situations, the print server drives the trnsport process of delivering the print job over the port. In the case of a Pserver print device, Nwmon.dll manages the communication between the device and the server. The Pserver "grabs" the print job from a passive print queue.

PJL Monitor (Pjlmon.dll)

The PJL Language Monitor, which Windows NT 4.0 supplies, "speaks" printer job language (PJL). Any bi-directional print device that uses PJL can use PJL Language Monitor. For example, PJL is the language that implements all the bi-directional communication between an HP LaserJet 5Si (a bi-directional print device) and its print server.

Bi-directional Printing

Bi-directional communication allows applications to query the print device directly to determine its capabilities. It also provides the benefit of configuring printer driver settings on the server without user intervention. The printer driver can automatically determine how much memory the printer has, what printer fonts are available, and so on.

Bi-directional print devices can send unsolicited messages to Windows NT and to applications. For example, the print device might send an "out of paper" or "printer offline" message. Bi-directional communication enables much more detailed status reporting on a wider variety of information, such as low toner, paper jams, maintenance needs, and so on.

To take advantage of bi-directional printing, you must have the following:

- A bi-directional print device.
- An IEEE 1284-compliant cable (a cable that has "1284" printed on it).
- A correctly configured port. (Some parallel ports are set to IBM AT-compatible mode by default; in this case, you need to set the port to IBM PS/2 mode.)

Printer Properties

Printer properties include everything about a printer from what port you use to what security features you want to implement.

▶ **To set or change printer properties**

1. Click Start, and then point to Settings.
2. Click Printers.
3. In the Printers window, click the printer to select it.
4. Click **Properties** on the **File** menu.
5. On the Printer Properties sheet, click the tab you want.

   The tabs are described in the following table.
6. Click **OK**.

Tab	Description
General tab	Displays general information about the printer, such as its physical location, a descriptive comment, and the printer driver installed. You can also add or customize a separator page, select a vendor-supplied print processor, and print a test page.
Ports tab	Displays the computer's physical ports. You can also add, configure, and delete virtual ports.
Job Scheduling tab	Displays the times the printer is available, its priority level, and spooling options.
Sharing tab	Displays the share status and share name.
Security tab	**Permissions** button lets you set the level of access for different types of users. **Auditing** button lets you set up printing users and events to be tracked. **Ownership** button displays printer owner.
Device Settings tab	Displays everything from paper tray sizes to font substitutions table for that printer. Use it to download soft fonts, install font cartridges, increase printer virtual memory, etc.

Separator Page Files

Separator pages—also called burst pages, header pages, or banner pages—print before each print job. They typically identify the computer that created the job, the time it was created, and so on. The local print provider contains an interpreter that reads commands from a separator page file to produce separator pages.

By default, separator page files are stored in the *%systemroot%*\system32 directory. To use a separator page file, click the **Separator Page** button on the General tab of the printer's Printer Properties sheet. Either type the name of the Separator Page file, or browse through the directories and select a file. Windows NT provides four separator page files; you can use them as is, or modify them to create your own custom separator page files.

The following table lists the separator page files included with Windows NT.

Filename	Purpose	Compatible with
Sysprint.sep	Prints a page before each document	PostScript
Pcl.sep	Switches dual-language HP printer to PCL printing	PCL
Pscript.sep	Switches dual-language HP printer to PostScript printing	PostScript

To create a custom separator page file, copy and rename one of the supplied files, and then edit it. The following table provides the escape codes you can use. The separator file interpreter replaces these escape codes with appropriate data, which is sent to the printer.

Escape code	Function
\	The first line of the separator file must contain only this character. The separator file interpreter considers this the separator file command delimiter. This table assumes that character is a \ character.
\N	Prints the user name of the person who submitted the job.
\I	Prints the job number.
\D	Prints the date the job was printed. The representation of the time is the same as the Time Format in the International section on the Control Panel.
\L*xxx*	Prints all the characters (*xxx*) following it until another escape code is encountered.
\Fpathname	Prints the contents of the file specified by path name, starting on an empty line. The contents of this file are copied directly to the printer without processing.
\H*nn*	Sets a printer-specific control sequence, where *nn* is a hexadecimal ASCII code sent directly to the printer. To determine the specific numbers, see your printer manual.
\W*nn*	Sets the width of the separator page. The default width is 80 characters; the maximum width is 256. Any printable characters beyond this width are truncated.
\B\S	Prints text in single-width block characters until \U is encountered.
\E	Ejects a page from the printer. Use this code to start a new separator page or to end the separator page file. If you get an extra blank separator page when you print, remove this code from your separator page file.
n	Skips *n* number of lines (from 0 through 9). Skipping 0 lines simply moves priting to the next line.
\B\M	Prints text in double-width block characters until \U is encountered.
\U	Turns off block character printing.

Print Security

You can limit the access that users have to your network printers and spool file directory by using Windows NT security. You can provide additional security by forwarding print jobs to other print servers.

Printer Security

To specify security attributes on a printer-by-printer basis, use the Security tab in the **Printer Properties** dialog box. The most efficient way to establish security attributes is to assign permission levels to different user groups. For example, you could give all nonadministrative users in a department the Print level of permission and all managers Full Control permission.

The following table summarizes printer security permissions.

Table 7.4 Printer Security - User Permissions

Type of permission	Level of access
Full Control	Enables complete access and administrative control.
Manage Documents	Enables a person to change the status of any print job submitted by any user. Does not permit control of the printer status.
Print	Allows user to send print jobs to the printer and to control pause, resume, or delete for his or her own jobs.
No Access	Explicitly denies access to a specific printer.

The installation-default printer permissions are different for Windows NT Server and Windows NT Workstation computers. By default, the following print permissions are assigned on a Windows NT Workstation computer:

- Full Control permission for the Administrator
- Manage Documents permission for the Creator Owner group
- Print permission for all users

▶ **To change security permissions**

1. Click Start, and then point to Settings.
2. Click Printers.
3. Click to select the printer whose settings you want to change.
4. Click **Properties** on the **File** menu.
5. Click the Security tab.
6. Click Permissions.
7. Click to select the group whose permission you want to change, and then select the permission level from the Type Of Access dropdown list.

   To add a group, click the **Add** button. To remove a group, select it, and then click the **Remove** button.
8. Click **OK** in each dialog box.

Spool File Security

To implement spool file security, change the default spool directory to an NTFS partition and directory where write permission is limited on a user-by-user basis.

When a print job prints locally, the local print provider spools the job to disk during processing. By default, the Everyone group has Change permission in the default spool directory. This allows all user print jobs write access to the default spooler directory.

A print job that cannot be spooled to disk during processing does not print. If the spool directory location is changed, all users who need to print must have Change permission for the new spool directory.

As described in the section "Local Print Provider," the spool file (SPL_) and the shadow file (SHD) are written to the default spooler directory:
%Winnt\System32\Spool\Printers

For instructions on changing the default spool file directory, see "Local Print Provider" earlier in this chapter.

▶ To override the default location for one specific printer

1. Start the Registry Editor (Regedt32.exe).
2. Find the following key:

```
HKEY_LOCAL_MACHINE\SYSTEM\CurrentControlSet\Control\
Print\Printers
```

3. Find the key for the printer:

```
HKEY_LOCAL_MACHINE\SYSTEM\CurrentControlSet\Control\
Print\<Printername>
```

4. Add a new SpoolDirectory setting, and as its value provide the path to the spool directory that this printer should use.

Note You must create a directory for the new spool file location. If you attempt to spool directly to the root (C:\ or D:\, for example) the spool file will revert to the default spool directory.

The change in the Registry takes effect after you stop and restart the Spooler service.

Registry Security

Most printing-related Registry settings reside in the following subkey

```
HKEY_LOCAL_MACHINE\SYSTEM\CurrentControlSet\Control\Print
```

An administrator can use the Registry Editor to assign read-only access to these subkeys. Users with read-only access cannot add or configure printers, because the read-only access does not allow changes of these subkeys.

Windows-based applications also use the following subkey in the Registry to find information about available printers.

```
HKEY_CURRENT_USER\Software\Microsoft\WindowsNT\
CurrentVersion\PrinterPorts
```

Users with read-only access to this subkey cannot add new printers that are recognized by Windows-based applications.

Forwarding Jobs

To forward a print job to a different Windows NT print server, a Windows NT print server uses a null session. By default, the null session is disabled, preventing job forwarding. To enable job forwarding and null-session support, manually edit the following Registry subkey:

```
\HKEY_LOCAL_MACHINE\SYSTEM\CurrentControlSet\Services\
LanmanServer\Parameters
```

In this subkey is a value named NullSessionShares. Add a new line containing the share name for the printer. This change does not take effect until you stop and restart the Spooler service.

Troubleshooting Printing Problems

Troubleshooting Windows NT printing problems can be a challenge because of the number of variables involved in printing and the number of different clients and print devices that Windows NT supports.

Windows NT has a modular printing architecture, with a module for each major task (such as receiving jobs from network clients). By adding new modules you can easily add functionality (such as support for a new type of network client). This modularity gives Windows NT a great deal of flexibility, making it able to support a wide variety of client operating systems, applications, data objects, network configurations, spooling options, and print devices. That flexibility comes at a cost, however, because each additional configuration adds its own possible points of failure.

Successful troubleshooting depends on your ability to quickly rule in or rule out general categories of points of failure. The modularity makes this fairly easy: Network printing, for example, consists of seven processes that always occur in the same order. By testing one of the processes, you can determine whether the problem is occurring in that process, before it, or after it.

The following are the seven basic processes involved in a network printing job:

1. An administrator creates a print share on the print server.
2. A client system connects to that share.
3. The client system creates a print job.
4. The client system sends the print job to the print share on the print server.
5. The print server receives, spools, and sometimes modifies the print job.
6. The print server sends the job to the print device.
7. The print device interprets the job and produces hardcopy output.

The basic strategy for troubleshooting printing problems is to use problem symptoms to identify the process, or processes, that are creating the problems. If you still cannot correct the problem after you've located it, your technical support engineer will be much better able to help you correct it if you have first isolated the process where the problem exists.

▶ **To troubleshoot printing problems**

1. Identify which of the seven processes is failing:
   - Analyze symptoms to identify the most likely process.
   - Reconfigure that process.
   - Retest with the new configuration.
   - If the problem changes with the new configuration, you probably have the right process. Otherwise, you probably picked the wrong process.
2. Look for documented explanations or solutions from the following sources:
   - Product hardcopy documentation
   - Product online Help documentation
   - Microsoft Product Support Knowledge Base
3. If possible, reconfigure the process to avoid the problem in the short term.
4. Implement long term solutions.

To help you implement this strategy, this section presents the seven basic printing processes and gives the following information about each process:

- A basic description of what the process involves
- A list of variables that can affect the process
- Symptoms that would suggest a problem in this process
- Tests to prove or disprove the suspicion

Printer Definition and Configuration

A print server administrator can use the Add Printer wizard to:

- Create a local printer
- Connect to a remote printer

Both procedures install and configure a printer driver. Creating a printer gives more control over driver configuration than connecting to a printer, and the administrator can create new printer ports by entering values in the **Print To** field on the Printer Properties sheet. The administrator can also define form-to-tray mapping, security, and spooler options.

The problem is likely in this process if...

- You cannot launch the Add Printer wizard, or you cannot browse printers in the Add Printer wizard.
- You cannot create a new local printer or a new local printer port.
- The port name and port do not show up or are intermittent.
- The problem is specific to one printer or to a subset of the printers.
- You can create another printer (with the same driver, port, and configuration options, but a different name) and the problem does not occur with that new printer.
- You cannot install a particular printer driver, or the driver for that printer doesn't exist.
- You cannot share a printer.
- You cannot establish security on printers.
- You have problems with forms, separators, pages, fonts, halftones, or printer options.
- You can delete the printer, stop and restart the spooler, recreate the printer with the same name and configuration, and the problem no longer occurs.

Client Computer Connects to a Shared Printer

A printer is established on a print client computer.

The problem is likely in this process if...

- You have problems with forms, separators, pages, fonts, halftones or printer options.
- You can connect to another shared printer, on the same print server, and the problem goes away.
- You cannot connect to a remote printer.
- You cannot browse printers in the Add Printer wizard.

Client Application Creates a Print Job

A user on a client system runs an application that composes text and/or graphics to create a print job. The application may interact with a printer driver to create output in a printer language such as PCL, PostScript, or HP-GL/2.

The problem is likely in this process if...

- The error in one particular print job is not reproducible.
- You create a simple test document and print it to a file. Transfer that file to a different client system, and print it to a different printer on a different print server, and there it continues to fail.
- What you see on the screen is not the output that you get.
- The problem is limited to one particular user or the users in a specific group; one particular client operating system; a particular vendor's printer driver (or a particular version of the printer driver); a particular font or fonts from a particular vendor; certain extended ASCII characters; a particular graphic object, a particular graphic file format (such as EPS, BMP, or TIF); jobs created by a particular application or version of that application; color or shading; incorrect resolution (dots per inch); or the print job is missing line feeds or form feeds.
- A different driver works fine.

If the problem persists when you send a simple textprint job from several clients' systems, the problem is likely caused by another printing process.

Client Sends Job to Spooler

The user on the client system sends the job over the network to the print server. The client system's application software or operating system sends the job to the client's transport protocol, to the network adapter, over the network hardware, to the transport software on the print server, and finally to the appropriate print server service on the print server. The print server service (Windows NT Server, Services for Macintosh, or TCP/IP Print) assigns a data type to the print job and submits the print job to the spooler, or leaves it blank.

The problem is likely in this process if the problem is limited to...

- One particular client redirector (one vendor's software, or one version of that software).
- One particular network transport (for example, TCP/IP, NWLink, NetBEUI).
- One particular make or model of network adapter, or one firmware level.
- One particular intermediate system for example, one specific router, bridge, hub, or gateway.

- One particular kind of intermediate system, for example, all jobs from clients on the other side of any router, bridge, or gateway.
- One particular kind of client, for example MS Network or LPR clients.

The problem is also likely in this process if...

- The print job is not started until the application is exited.
- Pages come out incomplete.
- The print server has run out of disk space.

Suspect a problem elsewhere if...

- The print job prints fine on another printer of the same make, model, or version.
- You send a print job to the spooler in a different way and the problem does not go away.

Print Server Spooler Processes Print Job

The spooler receives the job from the print server service. If the printer was established by selecting the **Network Printer** option in the Add printer wizard, the remote print provider sends the job to the print server. Otherwise, the job goes to the local print provider.

Unless otherwise configured, the local print provider spools the job to disk and checks the data type assigned by the print server service. The data type (for example, RAW or PSCRIPT1) determines which print processor receives the job. The data type also effects whether the print processor alters the job or not, and if so, how it alters the job. If the spooler is configured to append a separator file, it does so before sending the job to the print monitor for delivery to the print device.

The problem is likely in this process if...

- Page size, font, or character set is wrong because of incorrect data type (UNIX).
- Disk space is limited.
- You get extra form feeds or no form feed.
- Changing the default data type affects the problem with MS-Network.
- The job gets stuck in the printer.
- The problem is specific to one type of client.
- The problem occurs only when the printer was established using the Add Printer wizard.

Print Server Spooler Sends Job to Print Device

The print monitor receives the job and interacts with local hardware drivers and transport drivers to send the job to its destination. The components in this process are:

- Print monitors, LOCALMON, redirector, LPRMON, DECMON, HPMON, NWMON, or LEXMON
- Transport protocols (either TCP/IP, NWLink, NetBEUI)
- Network hardware (routers, bridges)

The problem is likely in this process if it is limited to...

- All print devices accessed by a particular print monitor.
- All print devices on one segment of the LAN.
- One make/model/version of a particular print device.
- One parallel/serial cable.

The problem is also likely in this process if...

- Sending the same job to the same device by means of a different communication channel by using a different protocol, serial, or parallel port produces a successful print.
- Trying different parallel or serial cable produces a successful print.

Print Device Interprets Job

The final processing at this point is completed by the print device. The print device receives the print job from a hardware port. The print device interpreter interprets the job and produces hardcopy output.

The problem is likely in this process if...

- The problem is specific to a specific print device, or a print device that is a variation of the same model, make, or revision.
- Sending same print job to another print device of same make, model, and revision produces a successful print.

Questions and Answers

This section presents specific questions and answers about Server Printing.

Does the Windows NT print server support UNIX clients running LPSSCHED?

No, it does not support UNIX computers running LPSSCHED. UNIX client computers must have an LPD program installed when used with a Windows NT print server.

How can platform-specific printer drivers be installed for a print client on a hardware platform different than the Windows NT print server?

Microsoft places all new or updated printer drivers onto its electronic services for public download.

Also, a platform-specific printer driver is likely available on another computer in the network.

► **To install platform-specific printer drivers from another computer in the network**

1. Log on the client computer using an user account that has Full Control permission.
2. Double-click Network Neighborhood.
3. Double-click the print server.
4. Click to select a printer.
5. Click Properties on the File menu.
6. Type the location of the printer driver in the **Printer Properties** dialog box. The printer driver is installed on the print server where it is available to any client computer with the same hardware platform, that is connected to the Windows NT print server.
7. Click **OK**.

What kind of problems occur when a print job has been assigned an incorrect data type?

Typical problems that occur when there is some error in the data type assignment and consequent job alteration of a print job include the following:

- LPR client print jobs include PCL or PostScript code, include incorrectly printed extended characters, or print in the print device's default font.
- Extra page prints after a Microsoft Network client print job.
- Microsoft Network client print jobs include PCL or PostScript code, include incorrectly printed extended characters, or print in the print device's default font.

How many printers can be supported by a Windows NT print server?

The limitation on the number of printers that can be attached to Windows NT print server is dependent on whether the print server is a Windows NT Workstation computer or a Windows NT Server computer. Windows NT Workstation and Windows NT Server have been optimized for different roles in the network:

Windows NT Workstation is limited to 10 connections from other computers and should be used as a print server in small-network situations.

Windows NT Server has been optimized as a print, file, and application server.

CHAPTER 8

Fonts

This chapter examines technical issues related to fonts, focusing on TrueType, the font technology available in Windows NT. This chapter also presents details about using printer fonts with specific types of printers and about using Adobe Type 1 fonts.

About Typography in Windows NT

A *typeface* is a set of characters that share common characteristics (such as stroke width and the presence or absence of serifs). For example, Arial and Courier are both typefaces. Frequently, both the typeface and its name are copyrighted and/or trademarked by the typeface designer or manufacturer.

In Windows NT, a *font* is the name of a typeface, excluding attributes such as bold or italic. This general definition is more widely used than the traditional definition associated with traditional typography. For example, MS Serif is a font in Windows NT.

In Windows NT, a *font family* refers to a group of typefaces with similar characteristics. The families that Windows NT recognizes for font installation and mapping are Roman, Swiss, Modern, Script, and Decorative. For example, the sans serif typefaces Arial, Arial Bold, Arial Bold Italic, Arial Italic, Small Fonts, and MS Sans Serif are all part of the Swiss font family.

For printing and display in a computer system, each raster or vector font has its own character set according to the ASCII, ANSI, or original equipment manufacturer (OEM) standard or to another industry standard that defines what character is represented by a specific keystroke or combination of keystrokes. Most TrueType fonts shipped with Windows NT support multiple character sets. For more information about raster, vector, and TrueType fonts, see "About Windows NT Fonts" later in this chapter.

The following basic terms are used in Windows NT to define the appearance of a font in an application:

- *Font style* refers to specific characteristics of the font. The four characteristics you can define for fonts in Windows NT are italic, bold, bold italic, and roman. (Roman is often referred to as Normal or Regular in font dialog boxes).
- *Font size* refers to the vertical point size of a font, where a point is about 1/72 of an inch. Typical sizes for text are 10-point and 12-point.
- *Font effects* refers to attributes such as underlining, strikeout, and color that can be applied to text in many applications.

The following terms are also used to describe fonts and typefaces:

- *Spacing* can be either fixed or proportional. In a *fixed font*, such as Courier, every character occupies the same amount of horizontal space, like typewritten characters. In *a proportional font*, such as Arial or Times New Roman, character width varies.
- *Pitch* refers to the amount of horizontal space used for each character of fixed-width fonts. This is often specified in characters-per-inch (CPI), where 10-pitch equals 12-point, 12-pitch equals 10-point, and 15-pitch equals 8-point type. (Some fonts use other equivalencies.)
- *Serif* and *sans serif* describe specific characteristics of a typeface. Serif fonts, such as Times New Roman or Courier, have projections that extend from the upper and lower strokes of the letters. Sans serif fonts, such as Arial and MS Sans Serif, do not have serifs.
- *Slant* refers to the angle of a font's characters, which can be italic or roman (no slant).
- *Weight* refers to the heaviness of the stroke for a specific font, such as Light, Regular, Book, Demi, Bold, Heavy, Black, and Extra Bold.
- *Width* refers to whether the standard typeface has been extended or compressed horizontally. The common variations are Condensed, Normal, or Expanded.
- *X-height* refers to the vertical height of lowercase characters, such as "a" and "c," and the lower portion of lowercase characters, such as "h" and "k."

About Windows NT Fonts

Windows NT provides three basic font technologies. The differences between them reflect the way that the *glyph* (or symbol) for each character is stored in the respective font-resource file.

- *Raster fonts* are stored in files as bitmaps and are rendered as an array of dots for display on the screen and printing on paper. Raster fonts cannot be cleanly scaled or rotated.
- *Vector fonts* are outline fonts and are rendered from a mathematical model, where each character is defined as a set of lines drawn between points. Vector fonts can be scaled to any size or aspect ratio.
- *TrueType fonts* are outline fonts and are rendered from line and curve commands as well as a collection of hints. Windows uses the line and curve commands to define the outline of a character or symbol. Windows uses the hints to adjust the length of the lines and shapes of the curves when scaling or rotating the character. TrueType fonts can be scaled and rotated.

Note Windows NT also supports Adobe Type 1 fonts native on PostScript printers and via conversion to TrueType for screen and non-PostScript devices. However, no Adobe Type 1 fonts are included with Windows NT.

In addition, Windows NT fonts are described according to the output device:

- *Screen fonts* are font descriptions that Windows NT uses to represent characters on display devices. (TrueType fonts act as both screen and printer fonts.)
- *Printer fonts* are the font descriptions used by the printer to create a font. Windows NT–based applications can use three kinds of printer fonts: device fonts, downloadable soft fonts, and printable screen fonts, as described in "Printer Fonts and Windows NT," later in this chapter.

Because the bitmaps for each glyph in a raster font are designed for a specific resolution of device, raster fonts are generally considered to be device dependent. Vector fonts, on the other hand, are not device dependent, because each glyph is stored as a collection of scalable lines. However, vector fonts are generally drawn more slowly than raster or TrueType fonts. TrueType fonts provide both relatively fast drawing speed and true device independence. By using the hints associated with a glyph, a developer can scale the characters from a TrueType font up or down and still maintain their original shape.

As previously mentioned, the glyphs for a font are stored in a font-resource file. A font-resource file is actually a Windows library that contains only data—no code. For raster and vector fonts, this data is divided into two parts: a header describing the font's metrics and the glyph data. A font-resource file for a raster or vector font is identified by the .fon filename extension.

In 16-bit Windows TrueType fonts had two files for each font: The first file contains a relatively short header and the second contains the actual font data. The first file is identified by a .fot extension and the second is identified by a .ttf extension. Windows NT 4.0 still supports this for backwards compatibility, but doesn't require the .fot file. AddFontResource can be called from applications directly for a .ttf file.

As shown in the following illustration, you can identify the different fonts in Windows NT–based applications by the icons associated with the font name.

The next sections describe raster, vector, TrueType, and Adobe Type 1 fonts. Later sections in this chapter discuss screen fonts and printer fonts used by Windows NT.

Windows NT Raster Fonts

Raster fonts are bitmaps supplied in different sizes for specific video display resolutions. The Windows NT fonts MS Serif, MS Sans Serif, Courier, System, and Terminal are raster fonts.

A raster font file contains data that describes the style and all the characters of a typeface for a specific display device. Windows NT provides several raster font sizes for various display devices. For example, MS Serif comes in point sizes 8, 10, 12, and 14 for video graphics array (VGA) and 8514 display devices.

Windows NT can scale raster fonts, but if you try to scale them too far from their original size or style, they become jagged. Bold, italic, underline, and strikeout styles can also be generated from a standard raster font.

The following table lists the raster fonts included with Windows NT. You can install additional raster font sets. For instructions, see "Installing Fonts" later in this chapter.

Table 8.1 Windows NT Raster Fonts

Font	Filename	Character set
Courier	COUR*x*.FON	ANSI
MS Sans Serif	SSERIF*x*.FON	ANSI
MS Serif	SERIF*x*.FON	ANSI
Small	SMALL*x*.FON	ANSI
Symbol	SYMBOL*x*.FON	Symbol

Raster Font Sizes

The raster font sets for different display resolutions are distinguished by a letter suffix on the font name (represented as *x* in the previous table). To see the files that Windows NT installs for a given display or printer, add the appropriate letter (displayed in the following table) that identifies the resolution of the raster font filename. For example, the resource file for MS Serif fonts for VGA is named Serife.fon.

Table 8.2 Raster Font Sizes

Font set and output device	Horizontal resolution	Vertical resolution	Aspect ratio H:V
E = VGA display	96 dpi	96 dpi	1:1
F = 8514 display	120 dpi	120 dpi	1:1

Printing Raster Fonts on Your Printer

Raster fonts can be printed if their resolution and aspect ratio are close to what your printer requires. If you do not see raster fonts for your printer in a **Fonts** dialog box, check your printer's horizontal and vertical resolution, and compare it with the preceding table. If there is a close match, double-click the Fonts icon in Control Panel, and make sure the appropriate font set is installed. If there is no close match, you cannot print the Windows NT raster fonts on your printer.

Some applications, such as Microsoft Excel for Windows and Microsoft Paintbrush, work around this problem by sending documents to the printer in the form of bitmaps. By using bitmaps, the application can ensure that what prints closely matches what you see on the screen. Other applications, such as desktop publishing packages, allow you to choose only printable fonts.

In general, applications are written so that you can choose either displayable fonts or printable fonts. It is up to the developer of the application to decide which type of font you can choose.

You might be able to print raster fonts in a different resolution if the other resolution has an aspect ratio that matches your printer. Some printer drivers cannot print raster fonts, regardless of the aspect ratio.

Substituting Fonts Installed by Windows 3.*x*

In Windows NT, MS Serif and MS Sans Serif replace the identical raster fonts Tms Rmn and Helv that were installed by Windows 3.0 or earlier versions. Windows NT matches MS Serif to Tms Rmn and MS Sans Serif to Helv using the information stored in the FontSubstitutes key in the Registry:

```
HKEY_LOCAL_MACHINE\SOFTWARE\Microsoft\Windows NT
    \CurrentVersion\FontSubstitutes
```

You will still see the Tms Rmn and Helv typeface names in a **Fonts** dialog box if, for example, your Hewlett-Packard Printer Control Language (HPPCL) printer uses the Microsoft 1Z font cartridge.

Selecting a Readable Screen Font

The raster font named Small Font was designed for readable screen display of small fonts. For sizes under 6 points, Small Font is a better choice than any TrueType font for screen display, because it's easier to read.

Windows NT Vector Fonts

Vector fonts are sets of lines drawn between points, like a pen plotter drawing a set of characters. Vector fonts can be scaled to virtually any size, but generally they do not look as good as raster fonts in the sizes that raster fonts are specifically designed for.

Vector fonts are stored in Windows NT as collections of Graphical Device Interface (GDI) calls and are time-consuming to generate. But these fonts are useful for plotters and other devices where bitmap characters can't be used. Before TrueType, vector fonts were also used in some applications to create large characters or characters that were rotated or distorted from the baseline.

Some Windows NT–based applications automatically use vector fonts at larger sizes. Some applications allow you to specify at what point size you want to use vector fonts. For example, the Vector Above setting in Adobe PageMaker specifies the point size at which PageMaker will switch to vector fonts.

The Windows NT fonts Roman, Modern, and Script are vector fonts. Although the vector fonts use the ANSI character set, they are marked internally as an OEM character set. These fonts are sometimes referred to as *plotter fonts* because, unlike most other fonts, they can be used on plotters. For more information about the different character sets, see "Character Sets" later in this chapter.

Note Third-party, non-TrueType scalable font products that were supported by Windows 3.1 are not supported by Windows NT. These products include Adobe Type Manager (ATM), Bitstream Facelift, and Atech Publisher's PowerPak.

TrueType and Windows NT

Windows NT includes support for TrueType, an outline font technology. Instead of being composed of bitmaps (such as raster fonts) or lines (such as vector fonts), TrueType fonts are *glyph shapes* that are described by their outlines. A glyph outline consists of a series of contours. A simple glyph might have only one contour. More complex glyphs can have two or more contours. Figure 8.1 shows three glyphs with one, two, and three contours respectively.

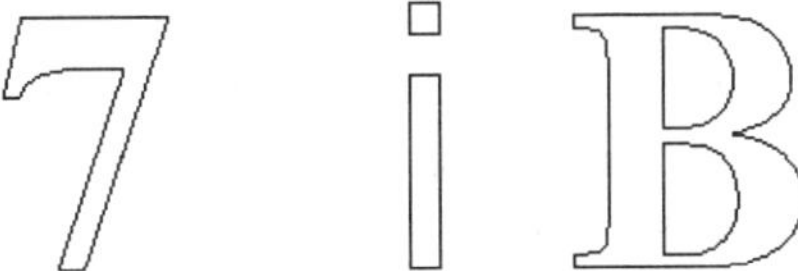

Figure 8.1 TrueType Glyphs

Note Windows NT supports all TrueType fonts that are supported by Windows 3.1.

TrueType fonts have many benefits over other kinds of Windows NT fonts:

- What you see is really what you get, because Windows NT can use the same font for both screen and printer. You don't have to think about whether you have a specific point size for a particular printer or for your display.
- You can scale and rotate TrueType fonts. TrueType fonts look good in all sizes and on all output devices that Windows NT supports.
- Your document will look the same when printed on different printers. And any printer that uses a Windows NT Universal driver can print TrueType fonts.
- Your document will look the same as you move it across platforms. For example, the text you format in Microsoft Word for Windows will look the same if you open the document in Microsoft Word for the Macintosh.

- Each TrueType typeface requires only a .ttf file to create fonts in all point sizes at all resolutions for all output devices. (Many raster font products include one font size per file. The raster fonts included with Windows NT are included within a single file.)
- TrueType fonts are integrated with the operating environment. For this reason, all Windows NT–based applications can use TrueType fonts in the same way they use other Windows NT raster fonts.

The TrueType fonts installed with Windows NT are Arial, Courier New, Lucida Console, Times New Roman, Symbol, and Wingdings in regular, bold, bold italic, and italic.

Note Windows NT 4.0 supports and ships on CD a set of Far East TrueType fonts. Users can install to view or print Far East documents and Web pages. The fonts are not installed by default.

How TrueType Works

TrueType fonts are stored as a collection of points and *hints* that define the character outlines. Hints are algorithms that distort the scaled font outlines to improve how the bitmaps look at specific resolutions and sizes. When a Windows NT application requests a font, TrueType uses the outline and the hints to render a bitmap in the size requested.

For each Windows NT session, the first time you select a TrueType font size, a bitmap is rendered for display or printing. Windows NT stores the rendered bitmaps in a font cache. Each subsequent time the font is used during that Windows NT session, display or printing performance improve.

The Windows NT Universal printer driver, PostScript printer driver, and plotter driver all support TrueType fonts. Any printer that works with these printer drivers will support TrueType fonts automatically. For more information about these printer drivers, see Chapter 7, "Printing."

Using TrueType Fonts in Windows NT–based Applications

TrueType fonts give you a broad range of fonts to use with your application. In many applications, TrueType fonts appear in the **Fonts** dialog box with a TT logo beside the typeface name. Typefaces that are device fonts have a printer icon beside their names in the list.

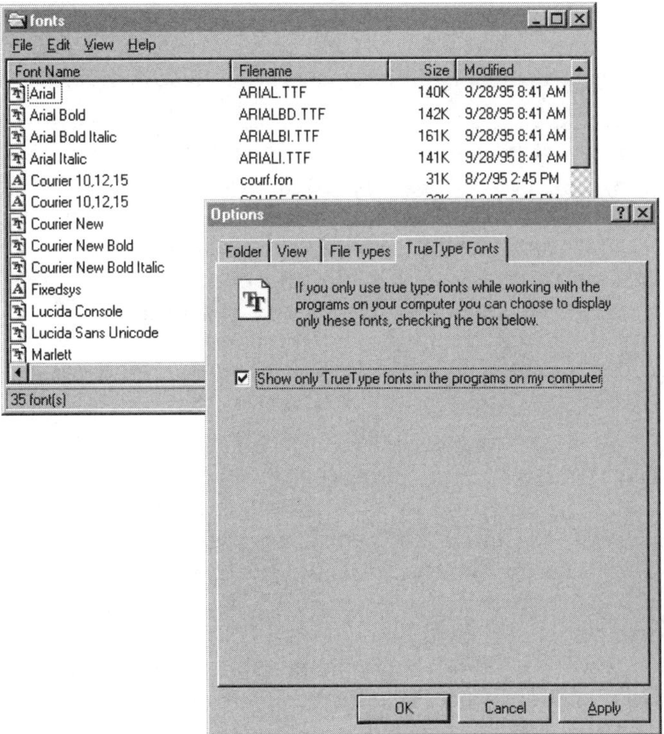

With TrueType fonts, you can specify any desired size; you're not limited to a list of raster or vector font sizes.

To make your life easier, you can specify that you want to use only TrueType fonts in the applications on your computer. This will ensure that type styles in your documents will print on any dot-matrix, HPPCL, or PostScript printer and that your documents can easily be moved to other platforms.

▶ **To specify that you want to use only TrueType fonts**

1. Double-click the Fonts folder in the Control Panel window to display the **Fonts** dialog box.
2. Click **Options** on the **View** menu.
3. Click the TrueType Fonts tab.

4. Check the Show Only TrueType Fonts In The Programs On My Computer box to add a check mark.
5. Click **OK**.

Windows NT does not automatically change fonts in documents that were produced with earlier font technologies. To update old documents to use TrueType fonts, you must update them manually. You might also contact your application vendor to see if there are new utilities available that will assist automatic upgrading of documents to use TrueType fonts.

Note TrueType fonts use a different character spacing (called *ABC widths*) from the spacing used for raster fonts. Applications that use this spacing will be able to space characters more accurately, especially for bold and italic text. However, because of this change in spacing, text can sometimes be adversely affected in applications written for Windows 3.0 or earlier versions. For example, the end of a highlighted text line might look odd on screen.

Using Adobe Type 1 Fonts

Adobe Type 1 fonts are the font technology native to PostScript printers. Like TrueType fonts, Type 1 fonts contain instructions to generate outlines of characters; the outlines are scaleable and rotatable. Type 1 fonts are a popular font technology in the desktop publishing industry. These fonts are designed to be downloaded to a PostScript printer, which can interpret their instructions and thereby produce hardcopy output. Although you can print Type 1 fonts, you cannot directly view them on screen. For this reason, Adobe created an application called Adobe Type Manager (ATM), which reads Type 1 font files and creates equivalent raster screen fonts for several platforms.

Windows NT supports Type 1 fonts in two ways: It lets you install Type 1 fonts for use on your PostScript printer, and it provides a font converter that achieves the same goal as ATM by reading Type 1 fonts and creating equivalent TrueType fonts for viewing on screen.

The Windows NT 4.0 Type 1 font converter achieves a high level of compatibility with ATM 2.5. If you format a document using Type 1 fonts on a computer running Windows for Workgroups 3.11 and ATM 2.5, and then load the same document under Windows NT 4.0 with the same set of Type 1 fonts converted to TrueType fonts, you will see the same character spacing and line breaks and the same output on your printer.

With the Type 1 installation process, you have the following options:

- **Convert Type 1 Font to TrueType** If you select this option, Windows NT will read the font outline instructions that make up the Type 1 font, convert them into TrueType, and write this equivalent TrueType font to your hard disk.
- **Install Type 1 Font Files for use on a PostScript printer**. If you select this option, Windows NT can send the Type 1 font to a PostScript printer. If you choose this option as well as the option described in the preceding paragraph, Windows NT will use the converted TrueType font for screen display and download the Type 1 font when you print.
- **Copy Type 1 Font Files to Windows Directory**. If you choose to install the Type 1 font for use on a PostScript printer, this option lets you copy it to the local computer's *systemroot*\SYSTEM directory.

Legal Issues Regarding TrueType Fonts

There are several legal issues to be aware of when converting TrueType fonts:

- With Windows NT 4.0, you can legally convert Type 1 fonts to TrueType fonts only if the third-party font vendor grants permission.

  Windows NT contains a database of the copyright strings that third-party vendors embed within their fonts. If you try to convert a Type 1 font and the font converter does not find a recognized third-party vendor's copyright string in the font, it warns that you might not have permission to convert this font. You are then advised to contact the third-party vendor to obtain permission to convert the Type 1 font.

  Although none of the third-party vendors that Microsoft contacted refused to allow conversion of their fonts, some vendors did not respond to the request. Those third-party vendors are not listed in the copyright string database, and their fonts will always produce a warning message.

  Note The copyright strings that third-party vendors embed within their fonts were never meant to be machine-readable. For this reason, the copyright strings in different fonts from the same vendor sometimes contain different punctuation marks or extra space characters, and so on. Most of these variations are represented in the copyright string database, but they can sometimes cause the font converter to reject a font, even though the third-party vendor has given its permission to convert it.

- The converted TrueType font is bound by the copyright restrictions that apply to the original Type 1 font. For example, if your Type 1 license does not permit you to use the Type 1 font on more than one computer at a time, then you are not permitted to use the converted TrueType font on more than one computer at a time.
- Converted TrueType fonts are only licensed for Windows NT 4.0. It is a copyright violation to copy converted fonts to other platforms, including Windows NT 3.*x*, Windows 95, or Windows For Workgroups 3.11.

In addition to the legal restrictions, there is a practical reason for not copying converted TrueType fonts to other platforms: Converted fonts are tuned to use features of the Windows NT 4.0 TrueType rasterizer that don't exist on other platforms' TrueType rasterizers. So, using converted fonts on other platforms will produce poor results. This is not a bug; it is an incentive to avoid illegal font copying.

Note All TrueType fonts behave the same way under Windows NT whether they were originally created as TrueType or were converted from Type 1 fonts.

Disk Space, Memory Use, and Speed

Fonts are resource intensive. Windows NT has been tested to load up to several thousand TrueType fonts at once. The more fonts used in a document, the more you can expect performance to be affected.

Installing Fonts

In Windows NT, fonts can be installed on your system in several ways.

Windows NT installs TrueType fonts and its screen fonts automatically during system installation. When you specify a printer and other options in the **Printer Properties** dialog box, Windows NT includes information about font cartridges and built-in fonts for your printer.

▶ **To install additional TrueType fonts or Adobe Type 1 fonts for Postscript printers**

1. Click Start, point to Settings, and then click Control Panel.
2. Double-click the Fonts icon.
3. Click **Install New Font** on the **File** menu.
4. Insert the disk containing the fonts, or locate the fonts on the network.
5. Select the fonts you want to install, or click **Select All**.
6. **Click OK**.

▶ **To install third-party soft fonts on your hard disk**

- Use the utility supplied by the third-party font vendor.

For information about installing font cards or cartidges, see "Font Cartridges" later in this chapter.

Information About Installed Fonts

Information about the fonts installed on your system are kept in the Windows NT Registry. As shown in the following illustration, most of the information about installed fonts is kept in the HKEY_LOCAL_MACHINE\SOFTWARE\Microsoft\Windows NT\Current Version\Fonts key.

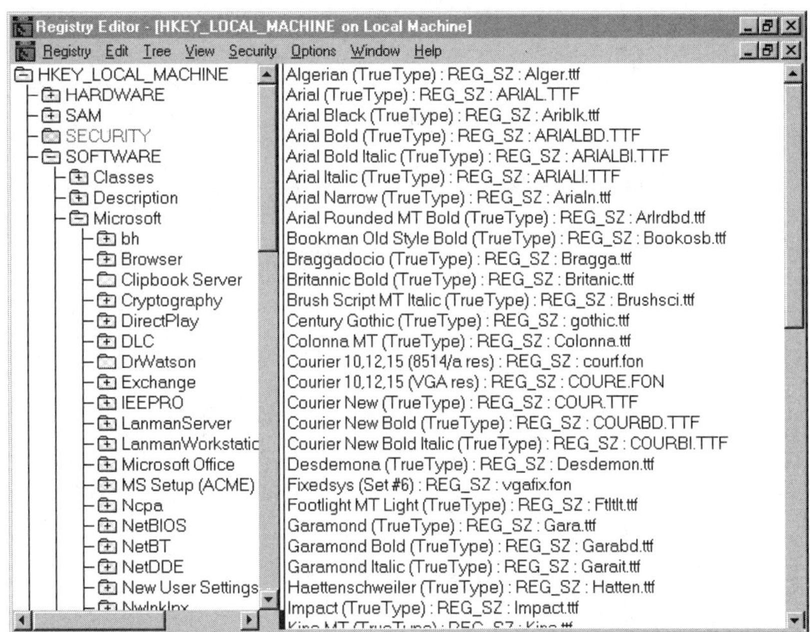

For more information, see Part V "Windows NT Registry".

If you installed Windows NT on a computer that previously had Windows 3.*x* installed, the Registry will include entries showing you where to find that information previously found in the **[Fonts]** and **[FontSubstitutes]** sections of the Win.ini file. For example, to find information that used to be in the **[Fonts]** section of the Win.ini file, look in the following location in the Registry:

```
HKEY_LOCAL_MACHINE\SOFTWARE\Microsoft\Windows NT\CurrentVersion\Fonts
```

How Windows NT Matches Fonts

When an application requests characters to print or display, Windows NT must find the appropriate font to use from among the fonts installed on your system. Finding the font can be complex because, for example, your document might contain fonts that aren't available on the current printer, or multiple fonts with the same name might be installed on your system.

To be sure you get the desired characters, see your printer documentation for the character set supported by the printer. Then see the online Help for Character Map for instructions on entering codes from the keyboard for special characters.

The basic rules that Windows NT uses for locating a font are as follows:

- If the font is a TrueType font, TrueType renders the character, and the result is sent to the display or to the printer.
- If the font is not a TrueType font, Windows NT uses the font-mapping table to determine the most appropriate device font to use.

When Windows NT uses the font mapping table to match screen fonts to printer fonts, the characteristics used to find the closest match are—in descending order of importance—character set, typeface name, variable versus fixed pitch, family, height, width, weight, slant, underline, and strikeout.

The following table shows which types of Windows NT fonts can be printed on different kinds of printers.

Table 8.3 Windows NT Printable Fonts

Printer type	Device fonts	Raster fonts	Vector fonts	TrueType fonts
Dot Matrix	Yes	Yes	Yes	Yes
HPPCL	Yes	No	Yes	Yes
PostScript	Yes	No	Yes	Yes
Plotter	Yes	No	Yes	Yes

The following table lists the character sets installed with Windows NT.

Table 8.4 Windows NT Character Sets

Font	Font type, spacing, and default sizes
Arial Bold Italic	TrueType, proportional, scalable
Arial Bold	TrueType, proportional, scalable
Arial Italic	TrueType, proportional, scalable
Arial	TrueType, proportional, scalable
Courier New Bold Italic	TrueType, fixed, scalable
Courier New Bold	TrueType, fixed, scalable
Courier New Italic	TrueType, fixed, scalable
Courier New	TrueType, fixed, scalable
Courier	Raster, fixed, 10,12,15
Lucida Console	TrueType, fixed, scalable
Lucida Console Bold	TrueType, fixed, scalable
Lucida Console Italic	TrueType, fixed, scalable
Lucida Console Bold Italic	TrueTrype, fixed, scalable
Modern	Vector, proportional, scalable
MS Sans Serif	Raster, proportional, 8, 10, 12, 14, 18, 24
MS Serif	Raster, proportional, 6, 7, 8, 10, 12, 14, 18, 24
Roman	Vector, proportional, scalable
Script	Vector, proportional, scalable
Small	Raster, proportional, 2, 3, 4,5, 6, 7
Symbol**	Raster, proportional, 8, 10, 12, 14, 18, 24
Symbol**	TrueType, proportional, scalable
System	Raster, proportional, display-dependent size
Terminal*	Raster, fixed, display-dependent size
Times New Roman Bold Italic	TrueType, proportional, scalable
Times New Roman Bold	TrueType, proportional, scalable
Times New Roman Italic	TrueType, proportional, scalable
Times New Roman	TrueType, proportional, scalable
Wingdings	TrueType, proportional, scalable

* OEM character set, rather than ANSI character set

** Symbol character set, rather than ANSI character set

You can also use the Windows NT Character Map to select and insert special characters in your document.

When you insert special characters in a document to print, the character you see on the screen might not be correct because it is displayed using the Windows ANSI portion of the Unicode character set and the best matching screen font for the current printer font. However, the printed document will contain the correct character. Conversely, if you type an ANSI character that appears on screen but is not supported in your printer fonts, some other character will be printed instead.

Screen Fonts and Windows NT

Windows NT uses special raster fonts as the system screen font for menus, window captions, messages, and other text. A set of system, fixed, and OEM terminal fonts is included with Windows NT to match your system's display capabilities (that is, for VGA or 8514 video displays). The default system screen font in Windows NT is System, a proportionally-spaced raster font.

The installed system screen fonts are listed in the following Registry keys:

```
HKEY_LOCAL_MACHINE\SOFTWARE\Microsoft\Windows NT
    \CurrentVersion\Fonts
HKEY_LOCAL_MACHINE\SOFTWARE\Microsoft\Windows NT
    \CurrentVersion\GRE_Initialize
```

By default, code page 437 (U.S.) fonts are installed using the Ega40woa.fon, Ega80woa.fon, and Dosapp.fon files. Other screen font files are included for international language support; they are identified by the code page number appended to the filename.

Windows NT supplies small and large font variations for several display drivers. The major difference between the small and large font variations is the system font set that the Setup program installs. The VGA-resolution system (small) fonts are VGAOEM, VGAFIX, and VGASYS. The 8514-resolution system (large) fonts are 8514OEM, 8514FIX, and 8514SYS.

Printer Fonts and Windows NT

A *printer font* is any font that can be produced on your printer. There are basically three kinds of printer fonts:

- *Device fonts* actually reside in the hardware of your printer. They can be built into the printer itself or can be provided by a font cartridge or font card.
- *Printable screen fonts* are Windows NT screen fonts that can be translated for output to the printer (including TrueType).
- *Downloadable soft fonts* are fonts that reside on your hard disk and are sent to the printer when needed. (Only the characters needed for the particular document are downloaded, not the whole font set.)

Not all printers can use all three types of printer fonts. For example, HPPCL printers cannot print Windows NT screen fonts.

The Windows NT Universal printer driver takes advantage of TrueType fonts and offers other improvements over older dot-matrix and HPPCL printer drivers. The Windows NT Universal printer driver is used instead of specific dot-matrix or HPPCL printer drivers.

Dot-Matrix Printer Fonts

Dot-matrix printers support device fonts and printable screen fonts. Usually, a dot-matrix printer includes only a limited range of internal device fonts. Typically, fixed-spacing fonts are supplied in a variety of characters-per-inch (CPI) sizes and are conventionally named "*typeface xx*CPI," where *typeface* is the typeface name and *xx* is the number of characters per inch. Distinguishing a device font on a dot matrix printer is usually as easy as checking for the CPI designation at the end of the font name, such as Courier 10 CPI.

Through the Universal printer driver, dot-matrix printers can also support TrueType. When you use TrueType fonts on a dot-matrix printer, Windows NT sends a rasterized graphics image to the printer.

Dot-matrix printers do not provide landscape device fonts, but vector and TrueType screen fonts can be printed in any resolution or orientation. Dot-matrix device fonts are faster but less flexible than screen fonts.

Dot-matrix printers are typically distinguished as either 9-pin or 24-pin printers (but not limited to these):

- 9-pin dot-matrix printers such as the Epson 9-pin and IBM Proprinter series usually print in a 1.67:1 aspect ratio. The Windows NT Epson 9-pin driver supports resolutions of 120x72 (1.67:1 aspect ratio), 120x144 (1:1.2), and 240x144 (1.67:1).
- 24-pin dot-matrix printers such as the Epson 24-pin and IBM Proprinter 24 series can print in 120x180 resolution (1:1.5 aspect ratio), 180x180 (1:1), and 360x180 (2:1). Some others, such as the NEC 24-pin, provide a 360x360 resolution. The 180x180 resolution is usually best for printing raster screen fonts. In 180x180 resolution, these printers can print 1:1 aspect ratio screen fonts, such as the E set (96x96 dpi) and the F set (120x120 dpi). E set fonts will be available at about 50 percent, and F set fonts at 75 percent of normal point sizes. A true 180x180 dpi screen font set is available by special order from Epson of America.

Some 24-pin dot-matrix printers, such as the Epson and NEC printers, also support font cards or cartridges. You can use these fonts if the Windows NT driver for that printer supports them. To use a font card or cartridge, see "Font Cartridges" later in this chapter.

HPPCL Printer Fonts

Printers that use the Hewlett-Packard Printer Control Language (HPPCL) can print several different types of fonts. HPPCL printers can use font cartridges, downloadable soft fonts, vector screen fonts, and TrueType fonts.

HPPCL printers cannot print Windows NT raster screen fonts.

When you use TrueType fonts on an HPPCL printer, TrueType performs all the font rendering in the computer and downloads bitmaps of the fonts to the printer. (Windows NT downloads these bitmaps only if the printer has enough memory.) TrueType downloads only the specific characters needed in a document, not the entire font.

Note If you use an HP LaserJet-compatible printer, be sure to specify accurately in the printer driver the amount of memory installed in your printer. This is important because the Windows NT HPPCL minidriver tracks the available memory in your printer. You might receive an out-of-printer-memory error or other errors if the memory is specified incorrectly.

Font Cartridges

Hewlett-Packard LaserJet-compatible font cartridges are supplied by numerous manufacturers, including Hewlett-Packard, Pacific Data Products, and IQ Engineering. Some cartridge vendors also produce custom font cartridges to your specifications.

Windows NT treats font cartridges as device fonts because they are always with the printer. Font cartridges can be selected on the Device Settings tab of the **Printer Properties** dialog box. The HPPCL minidriver available with Windows NT can support all HP font cartridges.

If you want to add a font cartridge that came out after the printer driver was written, you might need a printer cartridge metrics (.pcm) file. A .pcm file tells Windows NT the characteristics of the new font, and you install it the same way as soft fonts. For instructions, see "Downloadable Fonts" later in this chapter. After a .pcm file is installed, a new entry appears on the Device Settings tab of the **Printer Properties** dialog box.

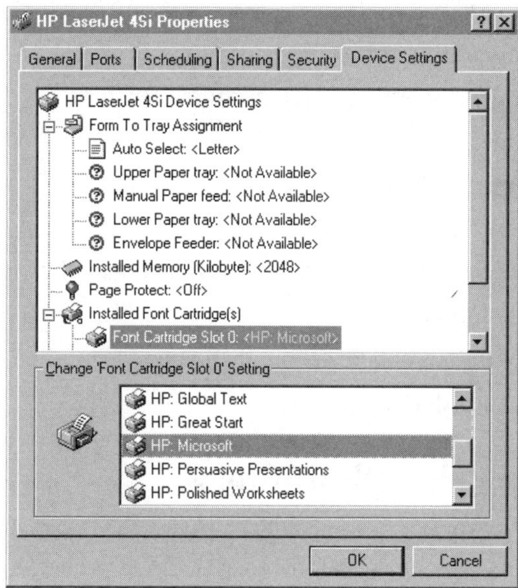

For new HP cartridges, contact Hewlett-Packard or other cartridge vendor for the appropriate .PCM file.

▶ To use fonts from a card or cartridge

1. Click Start, point to Settings, and then click Printers.
2. Click the printer to select it.
3. Click **Properties** on the **File** menu.
4. Click the Device Settings tab.
5. Click to select Installed Font Cartridges.
6. Click the card or cartidge to select it.
7. Click **OK**.

Downloadable Fonts

You can get HP LaserJet–compatible downloadable soft fonts from a number of sources, including Hewlett-Packard, Bitstream, SoftCraft, and CompuGraphics. Some downloadable font utilities also generate raster screen fonts for Windows NT. If an exact screen font match is not available, Windows NT uses one of its own screen fonts.

▶ **To install downloadable soft fonts**

1. Click Start, point to Settings, and then click Printers.
2. Click the printer to select it.
3. Click **Properties** on the **File** menu.
4. Click the Device Settings tab.
5. Scroll, if necessary, to display Soft Fonts, and then click it to select it.
6. Click the **Soft Fonts** button.
7. Type the path to the fonts disk, and then click Open.
8. Click **OK** in each dialog box.

Font Limitations for Older HPPCL Printers

Some older model HPPCL printers have a limit of 16 fonts per page. If you send a page that contains more than 16 fonts to an HPPCL printer, a warning message appears.

An Error 20 message might appear on the front panel of the HPPCL printer when printing a document that contains soft fonts. This also indicates that you tried to download more fonts than the printer's memory can hold. You can recover from this error by pressing the **Continue** button on the printer control panel. The soft font that caused the error is not downloaded and will not print.

To avoid this error, reduce the number of fonts that you try to download, or add more memory to your printer. Also make sure you have not downloaded any permanent soft fonts that are taking up memory in the printer.

Printer Fonts for HP Printers

The TrueType fonts shipped with Windows NT print on all printers. You can add other fonts described in the following sections.

HP LaserJet Printer Fonts

In Windows NT, all HPPCL (LaserJet) printers are supported by the Hppcl.dll or Hppcl5ms.dll minidrivers. Additional LaserJet III scalable outline fonts are available from Hewlett-Packard as cartridges or downloadable soft fonts. With the HPPCL drivers in Windows NT, downloadable outline fonts can be installed with the Font Installer.

HP DeskJet Printer Fonts

The HP DeskJet Printers are ink-jet printers. The Windows NT driver for the Hewlett-Packard DeskJet printer family supports Windows NT vector screen fonts, DeskJet internal fonts, soft fonts, and TrueType. DeskJet printers can print at resolutions of 75, 150, 300, and 600 dpi. Without font cartridges, the DeskJet includes only the built-in Courier and LinePrinter fonts. You can add font cartridges. For instructions, see "Font Cartridges" earlier in this chapter. At this time, font cartridges for DeskJet printers are available only from Hewlett-Packard.

DeskJet soft fonts are installed with the Font Installer. To use downloadable fonts on the DeskJet printers, you must install either HP22707A or HP22707B RAM cartridges. If you install more than one cartridge, be sure to specify the total amount of RAM required when setting printer memory. For more information about setting printer memory, see "Specifying Virtual Printer Memory" later in this chapter.

DeskJet internal, downloadable, and cartridge fonts will not work in landscape orientation. This is a hardware, not a driver, limitation. For landscape mode, print with Windows NT vector screen fonts such as Modern or Roman.

HP PaintJet Printer Fonts

The HP PaintJet is a color ink-jet printer. The Hewlett-Packard PaintJet driver in Windows NT composes a full page at a time in 180x180 dpi resolution and outputs each page to the PaintJet as a large bitmap. This produces the highest possible quality of output but results in large spool files. For improved printing speed, you can select the **Print Directly To The Printer** option on the Scheduling tab of the **Printer Properties** dialog box. This option prevents the creation of spool files.

Note Be aware that in the event of a disruption during printing, a spool file enables you to resume printing with no loss of data. Without spooling, you'll need to resend the document to the printer.

The PaintJet driver supports the printing of PaintJet internal fonts, Windows NT raster and vector screen fonts, PaintJet soft fonts, and TrueType. The same considerations apply for printing raster screen fonts on the PaintJet as for using the 24-pin dot matrix printers in 180x180 dpi resolution (see "Dot Matrix Printer Fonts," earlier in this chapter). PaintJet soft fonts are not downloadable fonts. They are used internally by the driver, which places them as necessary into the full-page bitmap during page composition. The font itself is never sent to the printer.

You can install PaintJet soft fonts, which have a .pjf filename extension, the same as downloadable soft fonts. For instructions, see "Downloadable Fonts" earlier in this chapter. Windows NT supports PaintJet soft fonts for Courier 10-CPI and Letter Gothic 12-CPI and 18-CPI. Additional soft fonts can be obtained from Hewlett-Packard. Scalable PaintJet soft fonts are also available from Hewlett-Packard in the HP Color PrintKit.

PostScript Printer Fonts

Adobe Type 1 PostScript fonts are scalable outlines that can be printed at any size. PostScript outline fonts can also be rotated to any angle and can be printed in both portrait and landscape modes. However, font size limits are often imposed by applications. A common PostScript font size limit in an application is 127 points.

Most PostScript printers include either the standard Apple LaserWriter Plus set of 35 scalable fonts or the earlier Apple LaserWriter set of 17 fonts.

Type 1 fonts are installed in the Fonts icon in Control Panel. When you install the font, Windows NT gives you the option of creating an equivalent TrueType font for use as a screen font.

PostScript printers can print Windows NT raster screen fonts, vector screen fonts, TrueType fonts, or Type 1 fonts.

LaserWriter Plus Typefaces

The LaserWriter Plus standard font set includes 11 typefaces, including the following 8, which are available in roman, bold, italic, and bold italic:

- AvantGarde Gothic
- Helvetica
- ITC Bookman
- Palatino
- Courier
- Helvetica Narrow
- New Century Schoolbook
- Times

The other three typefaces are Symbol, Zapf Chancery, and Zapf Dingbats. The Symbol typeface contains mathematical and scientific symbols; Zapf Chancery is a calligraphic font; and Zapf Dingbats contains decorative bullet characters and embellishments. These typefaces are available only in roman style.

PostScript Printers and TrueType

TrueType fonts are treated as downloaded fonts by the PostScript driver. When you use TrueType fonts on a PostScript printer, scaling and hints are always performed in the computer. Scan conversion can be done in the computer or in the printer, depending on the point size. At smaller point sizes, TrueType performs scan conversion in the computer; at larger point sizes, scan conversion is done in the printer.

Substituting PostScript Fonts

You can map a TrueType font to a PostScript font by editing the *Font Substitution Table*. This is helpful to view TrueType as a screen font and to get PostScript for the printout font. This will increase printing speed, but the results on the display might not be exactly the same as the printed output.

Alternatively, you can edit the Font Substitution Table to download TrueType fonts as soft fonts to the printer so that the printed output matches the screen display. In this case, the selected TrueType fonts will be sent to the printer as soft fonts. Repeat these steps until you have selected printer fonts to use in place of all the TrueType fonts in your document.

The changes you make in the Font Substitution Table affect only the fonts that are printed. The fonts that appear on the screen will not change; the original TrueType fonts are still used to display TrueType text in your document.

To edit the Font Substitution Table

1. Click Start, point to Settings, and then click Printers.
2. Click to select the printer.
3. Click **Properties** on the **File** menu.
4. Click the Device Settings tab.
5. Double-click Font Substitution Table.
6. Click to select the TrueType font from the Font Substitution Table.
7. Click to select the substitution font, or click Download as Soft Font from the Change Setting list.
8. Click **OK**.

PostScript Downloadable Outline Fonts

PostScript printers also accept downloadable outline fonts, which can be scaled to any size and printed in both portrait and landscape orientations. Downloadable PostScript fonts are available from several suppliers, including Adobe, Agfa, Bitstream, and Monotype.

Although PostScript downloadable outlines can be scaled to any size, Windows NT raster screen fonts cannot. If you specify a PostScript font size that does not have a corresponding screen font, Windows NT substitutes another screen font. This results in a little loss in display quality but no loss in print quality.

Specifying Virtual Printer Memory

You can change the amount of virtual memory that your PostScript printer has available for storing fonts. The PostScript driver uses a default setting recommended by the printer manufacturer for virtual memory.

To determine the right value, copy the Testps.txt file (supplied with the Windows NT Resource Kit) to the printer, and use the recommended virtual memory value printed on the resulting page.

To change your PostScript printer's virtual memory

1. Click Start, point to Settings, and then click Printers.
2. Click to select the printer.
3. Click **Properties** on the **File** menu.
4. Click the Device Settings tab.
5. Double-click Available PostScript memory.
6. Type the value from Testps.txt in the Change Settings box.
7. Click **OK**.

Embedding Fonts

Embedding a font is the technique of bundling a document and the fonts it contains into a file for transmission to another computer. Embedding a font guarantees that a font specified in a transmitted file will be present on the computer receiving the file. Not all fonts can be moved from computer to computer, however, because most fonts are licensed to only one computer at a time. In Windows, only TrueType fonts can be embedded.

Applications should embed a font in a document only when requested by a user. An application cannot be distributed along with documents that contain embedded fonts, nor can an application itself contain an embedded font. Whenever an application distributes a font, in any format, the proprietary rights of the owner of the font must be acknowledged.

It might be a violation of a font vendor's proprietary rights or user license agreement to embed fonts where embedding is not permitted or to fail to observe the following guidelines on embedding fonts. A font's license might allow only read-write permission for a font to be installed and used on the destination computer. Or the license might allow read-only permission. Read-only permission allows a document to be viewed and printed (but not modified) by the destination computer; documents with read-only embedded fonts are themselves read-only. Read-only embedded fonts may not be unbundled from the document and installed on the destination computer.

Character Sets

Most TrueType fonts shipped with Windows NT 4.0 suport multiple Windows character sets used in various countries or regions. Some (such as Europe and the United States) are single-byte sets, and others (such as Asia) are double-byte sets. This enables the Windows NT user to switch language keyboards and type in different alphabets, including Roman, Cyrillic, Arabic, and Far East Asian alphabets. The following is a list of the character sets supported by Windows NT 4.0:

- ANSI_CHARSET
- DEFAULT_CHARSET
- SYMBOL_CHARSET
- SHIFTJIS_CHARSET
- HANGEUL_CHARSET
- GB2312_CHARSET
- CHINESEBIG5_CHARSET
- OEM_CHARSET

- JOHAB_CHARSET
- GREEK_CHARSET
- TURKISH_CHARSET
- VIETNAMESE_CHARSET
- THAI_CHARSET
- EASTEUROPE_CHARSET
- RUSSIAN_CHARSET

A character set contains punctuation marks, numerals, uppercase and lowercase letters, and all other printable characters. Each element of a character set is identified by a number.

Most character sets used in Windows are supersets of the U.S. ASCII character set, which defines characters for the 96 numeric values from 32 through 127. There are five major groups of character sets:

- Windows
- Unicode
- OEM (original equipment manufacturer)
- Symbol
- Vendor-specific

Windows Character Set

The Windows character set is the most commonly used character set in Windows programming. It is essentially equivalent to the ANSI character set. The blank character is the first character in the Windows character set. It has a hexadecimal value of 0x20 (decimal 32). The last character in the Windows character set has a hexadecimal value of 0xFF (decimal 255).

Many fonts specify a default character. Whenever a request is made for a character that is not in the font, Windows provides this default character. Many fonts using the Windows character set specify the period (.) as the default character. TrueType fonts typically use an open box as the default character.

Fonts use a break character called a *quad* to separate words and justify text. Most fonts using the Windows character set specify that the blank character will serve as the break character.

Unicode Character Set

The Windows ANSI character uses 8 bits to represent each character; therefore, the maximum number of characters that can be expressed using 8 bits is 256 (2^8). This is usually sufficient for Western languages, including the diacritical marks used in French, German, Spanish, and other languages. However, Eastern languages employ thousands of separate characters which cannot be encoded by using a single-byte coding scheme. With the proliferation of computer commerce, double-byte coding schemes were developed so that characters could be represented in 8-bit, 16-bit, 24-bit, or 32-bit sequences. This requires complicated passing algorithms; even so, using different code sets could yield entirely different results on two different computers.

To address the problem of multiple coding schemes, the *Unicode* standard for data representation was developed. A 16-bit character coding scheme, Unicode can represent 65,536 (2^16) characters, which is enough to include all languages in computer commerce today, as well as punctuation marks, mathematical symbols, and room for future expansion. Unicode establishes a unique code for every character to ensure that character translation is always accurate.

OEM Character Set

The OEM character set is typically used in full-screen MS-DOS sessions for screen display. Characters 32 through 127 are usually the same in the OEM, U.S. ASCII, and Windows character sets. The other characters in the OEM character set (0 through 31 and 128 through 255) correspond to the characters that can be displayed in a full-screen MS-DOS session. These characters are generally different from the Windows characters.

Symbol Character Set

The Symbol character set contains special characters typically used to represent mathematical and scientific formulas.

Vendor-Specific Character Sets

Many printers and other output devices provide fonts based on character sets that differ from the Windows and OEM sets—for example, the Extended Binary Coded Decimal Interchange Code (EBCDIC) character set. To use one of these character sets, the printer driver translates from the Windows character set to the vendor-specific character set.

Questions and Answers About Fonts

This section answers some common questions about using fonts with Windows NT.

- I printed the same document with TrueType fonts from two different computers to the same PostScript printer. The two printouts are different. Why?

  TrueType font substitution is different on the two computers. Reconfigure font substitution on one of the computers.

- My document looks fine on the screen but prints with a different font. Why?

  This can happen for one of two reasons: Either you specified the wrong printer model during setup, or the downloadable font did not download to the print device. Check the General tab of the **Printer Properties** dialog box to see that the printer driver you are using matches the print device. Then click the Device Settings tab, and check the amount of memory for your printer. Make sure the amount shown accurately reflects the amount of memory for your print device. If there is too little memory, the print device might be unable to download fonts.

- My document prints OK, but it looks funny on the screen. Why?

  There is no direct displayable equivalent of a device font that you are using.

- I can't select a font that I know is provided by a cartridge installed in the printer. Why?

  Select the printer in the Printers folder, and then click **Properties** on the **File** menu. Click the Device Settings tab to make sure that the printer properties lists the correct cartridge.

PART III

Optimizing Windows NT Workstation

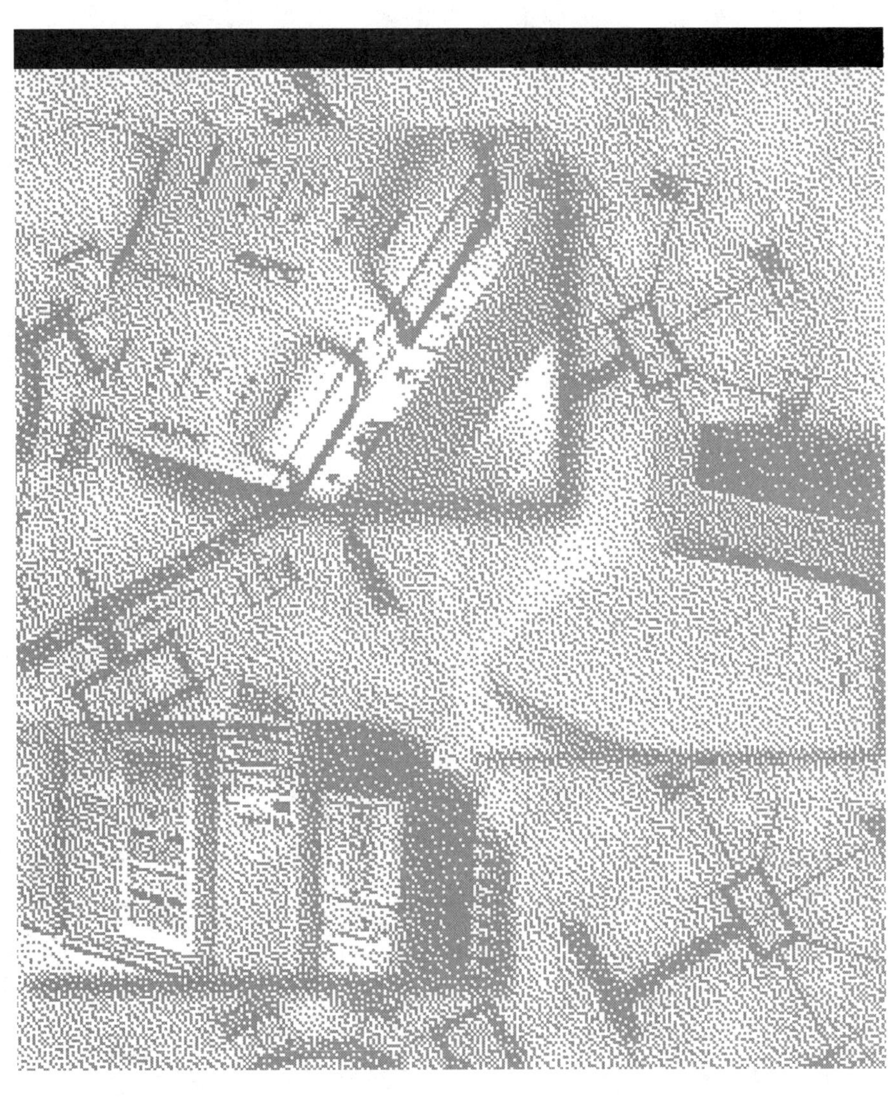

CHAPTER 9

The Art of Performance Monitoring

Detecting the source of a performance problem is not always a straightforward task. Sometimes it requires that you try different tools, running each in several ways, examining computer performance, and repeating the tests in a rigorous, scientific manner.

Problems can appear intermittently or be camouflaged by some greater or lesser matter. The following graph is an example of what you might see.

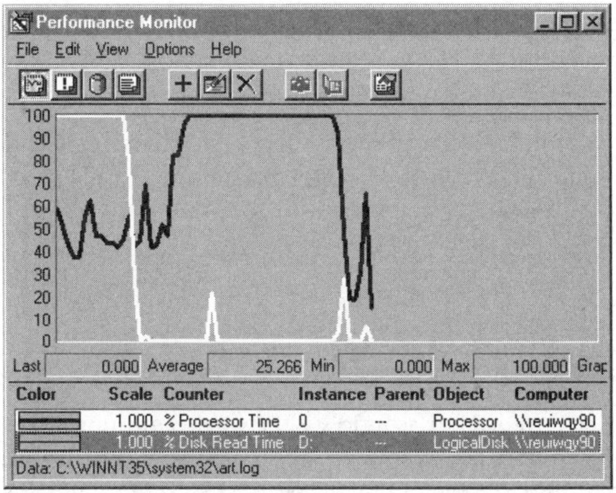

This is a Performance Monitor graph of processor and disk use over a 61-second interval. The white line represents disk activity; the black line represents processor activity. If you viewed just the first half of the interval, you would conclude that you have a *disk bottleneck*; the second half might lead you to believe you have a *processor bottleneck*. When the data is logged over time, you find that the processor is actually the problem—but you'd never know it from a one-minute glance.

This part of the Windows NT 4.0 Workstation Resource Guide is designed to help you tune and optimize Windows NT 4.0 Workstation. The remainder of the chapter includes some history and important information about Windows NT Workstation that affect how you monitor it.

The Resource Guide and Other Resources

The following materials might be of interest as well:

- Chapter 5 of this book, "Windows NT 4.0 Workstation Architecture," explains the organization of the Windows NT Workstation operating system. It is good background for understanding scheduling of processes, thread priorities, and changes in the architecture of the graphics subsystem that you'll be monitoring.
- Chapter 17 of this book, "Disk and File System Basics," provides the hardware background for the chapter on detecting disk bottlenecks.
- The Win32 Software Development Kit describes how to monitor and optimize your own applications and how to create extensible counters for Performance Monitor.
- The Windows NT Server Networking Guide describes the architecture of the Windows NT 4.0 Server and network and includes some information about network bottlenecks and capacity planning.
- The Windows NT Server Concepts and Planning Guide includes a clear and concise overview of performance monitoring with lots of useful tips and examples.

Optimizing Windows NT 4.0 Workstation

An original design goal of Windows NT was to eliminate the many parameters that characterized earlier systems. Adaptive algorithms were incorporated in Windows NT so that correct values are determined by the system as it runs. The 32-bit address space removed many limitations on memory and the need for users to manually adjust parameters to partition memory.

Windows NT has fundamentally changed how computers will be managed in the future. The task of optimizing Windows NT is not the art of manually adjusting many conflicting parameters. Optimizing Windows NT is a process of determining what hardware resource is experiencing the greatest demand and then adjusting the operation to relieve that demand.

Windows NT did not achieve the goal of automatic tuning in every case. A few parameters remain, mainly because it is not possible to know precisely how every computer is used. Default values for all parameters are set for a broad range of normal system use, and they rarely need to be altered. But special circumstances sometimes call for changes. In this book we will be sure to mention the few tuning parameters that remain in Windows NT and indicate when it is appropriate to change them from their default values.

Defining Bottlenecks

A *bottleneck* is a condition in which the limitations in one component prevent the whole system from operating faster. The device with the lowest maximum throughput is the most likely to become a bottleneck if it is in demand. Making any other device faster can never yield more throughput; it can only result in lower utilization of the faster device.

Even if all other components are infinitely fast, a bottleneck holds the system at a stall until it is cleared.

Although a foolproof bottleneck alarm and a direct bottleneck counter are not available, you can combine several different indicators to look for bottlenecks. The primary indicator is an extended high rate of use on one hardware resource and resulting low rates of use on related components. It is accompanied by sustained queues for one or more services, and slow response time.

Bottlenecks, Utilization, and Queues

The best bottleneck alarm is system response time, as perceived by the user. Users' perceptions are affected by their expectations and the kind of work they do. An accurate bottleneck alarm would be designed to reflect these same expectations and requirements. You need not demand the same throughput on a system supporting word processing as you do on one madly calculating routes to Jupiter. Even if your processors, disks, and memory are running at near capacity, if they are not developing the queues that degrade their response time, you do not have a problem (although you might want to plan more capacity for the future).

Although 100% utilization of a resource is a clear warning, it is neither a necessary nor sufficient condition for a bottleneck. You can have bottlenecks on devices with utilization well below 100% and you can, at least in theory, have a device perking along at nearly 100% utilization with no signs that it is a bottleneck. That is, the device is not preventing any other resource from getting its work done, nothing is waiting for it, and even if it were infinitely fast, things would not happen any sooner.

A bottleneck is determined by the number of requests for service, the arrival pattern of the requests, and the amount of time requested. If these factors are perfectly synchronized, no queues develop. But if they are random or unpredictable, queues develop at much lower utilization rates.

For example, suppose a process had ten threads, each of which used exactly 0.999 seconds of processor time once every ten seconds. If each request arrived exactly one second after the previous one in perfect sequence, the processor would be 99.9% busy, but there would be no queue, no interference between the threads and, technically, no bottleneck.

Admittedly, this is a highly idealized situation, but it is easy to see how any disruption in the pattern would quickly create a large queue. According to queuing theory, if the arrival pattern of requests and the duration of requested services are random or unpredictable, a device that is 66% utilized will produce a queue of two items. Even worse, if, instead of being random, requests for service are either very short or very long, queues can form at even lower utilization. That is, fewer requests for service produce even longer queues.

Monitoring Basics

These chapters introduce several tools to help you monitor hardware and software performance. Many tasks require switching between or combining tools. But no matter which tools you choose, some basic concepts are common to all of them. This section describes those commonalties and describes how to monitor

- System objects
- System processes
- 16-bit Windows applications
- MS-DOS applications

These topics are an introduction to the larger topics of using Performance Monitor, Task Manager, and the other Windows NT Resource Kit 4.0 CD tools to optimize Windows NT.

System Objects

Windows NT sees the active components running on the system as objects with characteristic properties. Some, such as processes and threads, are familiar; others, such as mutexes and semaphores, are less well known. For more information on Windows NT 4.0 objects, see "Microkernel Objects" in Chapter 5, "Windows NT 4.0 Workstation Architecture."

System object counts are important because each object takes up space in the operating system's nonpaged memory. Some just perform quick housekeeping and bookkeeping functions at background priority and rarely become a bottleneck. However, too many threads and processes can degrade performance on all functions, resulting in a bottleneck in processor or memory use.

Several performance monitoring tools let you keep track of the number of objects in your system:

- In Process Explode, the Objects box at the top of the first column displays counts for all system objects including events, sections, mutexes, and semaphores, as well as processes and threads.
- In Task Manager, select the Performance tab. The total number of active handles, threads, and processes for the system appear in the Totals box.
- In Performance Monitor, select the Object performance object, then select the counter for the type of object you want to track.. These include counters for operating system objects.

System Processes

Processes, which include both user applications and Windows NT services, can become bottlenecks. While investigating processor, disk, or memory use, chart use by process, and then start and stop the processes to see how your system responds.

Performance Monitor and Task Manager both show counts of running processes, including user programs and Windows NT services:

- Task Manager is useful for short term monitoring. It lets you stop and restart applications and system services.
- Performance Monitor includes more detailed counters and lets you log process data over time in chart or report format, set alerts on each process's use of resources, and monitor processes on remote computers.

Many of the tools on the Windows NT Resource Kit 4.0 CD also monitor processes in detail, including Process Viewer (PViewer.exe) and Process Monitor (PMon.exe). For more information, see Chapter 11, "Performance Monitoring Tools," and Rktools.hlp.

Note The Services Control Panel also displays Windows NT services and lets you start and stop them. The Services Control Panel shows all Windows NT services, regardless of the process in which they run. However, it lists services by service name whereas Performance Monitor and Task Manager display the names of executable files.

For a list of the default services and a description of each, see Windows NT Help in the Services Control Panel. Click Start, click Help, and type **Default Services**.

Task Manager

In Task Manager, select the Processes tab. It displays a table of active processes. From the **View** menu, click **Select Columns** to add additional measures of the processor time, memory use, process priority, handle and thread counts, and the process ID.

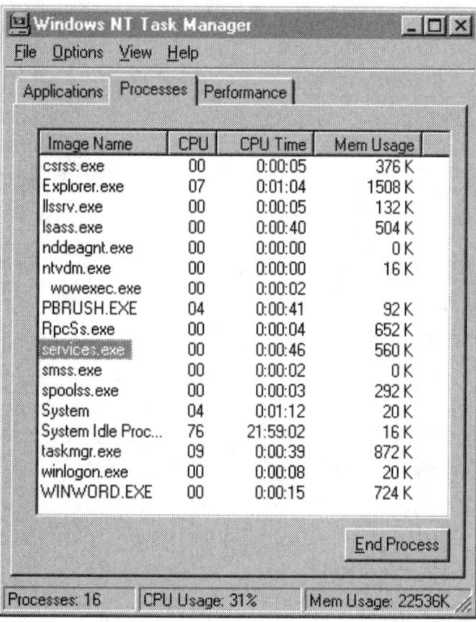

Performance Monitor

In Performance Monitor, select the Process object from the **Add To** dialog box. All active applications and services appear in the Instances box.

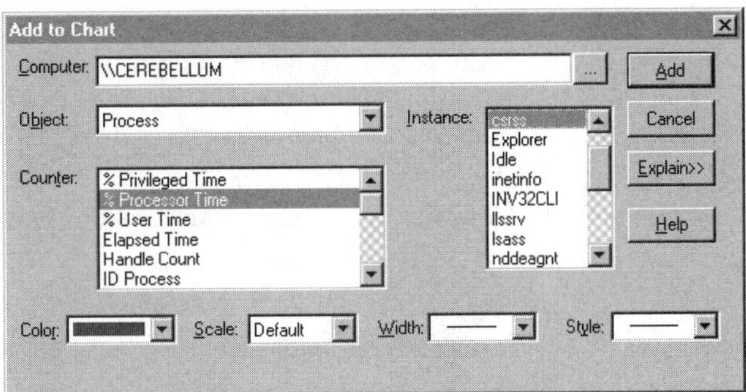

The following table lists processes commonly running on Windows NT 4.0 Servers and Workstations without a network connection. It shows them as they appear in Performance Monitor and in Task Manager.

Note Process Explode (Pview.exe), Process Viewer (Pviewer.exe), and Process Monitor (Pmon.exe) all display important counts of system processes. Although the information from these tools is instantaneous and cannot be logged or collected, the tools require almost no setup, so they are very valuable for a quick look.

Process name	Function
_Total	The sum of active processes, including idle. (Performance Monitor only.)
csrss	Client Server Runtime Subsystem, provides text window support, shutdown, and hard-error handling to the Windows NT environment subsystems. **Note:** Client Server Runtime Subsystem changed substantially with Windows NT 4.0. For more information, see "What's Changed for Windows NT 4.0" in Chapter 5, "Windows NT 4.0 Workstation Architecture."
Explorer	Windows NT Explorer, a segment of the user interface which lets users open documents and applications from a hierarchical display.
Idle (System Idle Process)	A process that runs to occupy the processors when they are not executing other threads. Idle has one thread per processor. For more information, see "The Idle Process" in Chapter 13, "Detecting Processor Bottlenecks."

Process name	Function
Llssrv	License Logging Service, the service that logs the licensing data for License Manager in Windows NT Server and the Licensing option in Control Panel on both Windows NT Server and Workstation.
Lsass	Local Security Administration Subsystem, the process running the Local Security Authority component of the Windows NT Security Subsystem. This process handles aspects of security administration on the local computer, including access and permissions. The Net Logon service shares this process.
Nddeagnt	Network DDE Agent, handles requests for network DDE services.
Ntvdm	NT Virtual DOS Machine, which simulates a 16-bit environment for MS-DOS and 16-bit Windows applications.
Perfmon	Performance Monitor executable.
RpcSs	Remote Procedure Call (RPC subsystem) which includes the RPC service and RPC locator.
Services	This process is shared by the Windows NT Services Control Manager, which starts all services, and a group of Windows NT 32-bit services, including Alerter, Clipbook Server, Computer Browser, Event Viewer, Messenger, Server and Workstation, and Plug and Play.
Smss	Session Manager Subsystem.
spoolss	Spooler Subsystem controls despooling of printer data from disk to printer.
System	Contains system threads that handle lazy writing by the file system cache, virtual memory modified page writing, working set trimming, and similar system functions.
taskmgr	Task Manager executable.
winlogon	Logon process executable. It manages logon and logoff of users and remote Performance Monitor data requests.

No matter what tool you choose, the processes that appear depend upon whether the computer is a server or workstation, and upon the services installed on the computer, including network services. User applications, including the executables for Performance Monitor and Task Manager, appear only when they are running.

Also, a process instance might not be visible for every active service. Performance Monitor and Task Manager display an instance for each executable process running on the system. Many services share a process to conserve system resources, so these appear together as one instance.

For example, many Windows NT 32-bit services, including Alerter, Clipbook Server, and Event Viewer, share the Services.exe process with the Windows NT Services Control Manager, a general process that starts all system services. Net Logon shares the Lsass.exe process with other security services.

It is difficult to monitor these services separately, although you can experiment in associating a service with threads in the process. The SC utility, in the Computer Configuration subdirectory on the Resource Kit CD, displays useful service configuration information, including the name of the process in which the service runs. For more information on SC, see Rktools.hlp.

Optimizing 16-bit Windows Applications

In Windows NT 4.0 Workstation and Server, by default, all active 16-bit Windows applications run as separate threads in a single multithreaded process called *NT Virtual DOS Machine* (NTVDM). The NTVDM process simulates a 16-bit Windows environment complete with all of the DLLs called by 16-bit Windows applications.

This configuration poses two challenges for running 16-bit applications:

- It prevents 16-bit applications from running simultaneously, which might impede their performance.
- It makes monitoring a bit trickier.

As a result, Windows NT 4.0 includes an option to run a 16-bit application in its own separate NTVDM process with its own address space.

You can monitor 16-bit Windows applications by identifying them by their Thread ID while they are running, or by running each application in a separate address space.

In addition to the 16-bit applications, each NTVDM process includes a *heartbeat thread* that interrupts every 55 milliseconds to simulate a processor timer-tic, and the Wowexec.exe thread, which helps to create 16-bit tasks and to handle the delivery of the 16-bit interrupt. You will see the heartbeat and Wowexec threads when monitoring 16-bit applications.

Win16 Application Performance

The NTVDM process is *multitasking*: A thread in the process (in this case, a 16-bit Windows application) can run at the same time as threads of other processes if the computer has more than one processor. It is also *preemptible*: Threads can be interrupted and resumed to allow virtual multitasking on a single-processor computer.

However, only one 16-bit Windows application thread in an NTVDM can run at one time and, if an application thread is preempted, the NTVDM always resumes with the same thread. This limits the performance of multiple 16-bit applications running in the same NTVDM process, although this limitation becomes an issue only when the processor is very busy.

Monitoring Win16 Applications

Almost all performance monitoring tools can monitor 16-bit applications on Windows NT 4.0 Server and Workstation. However, because they run in the same process, the trick to monitoring more than one 16-bit application is to distinguish among the threads of the NTVDM process.

To monitor one 16-bit application, simply select the NTVDM process in Performance Monitor, Task Manager, Process Explode, Process Viewer, Process Monitor, or another tool. If you have multiple 16-bit processes running in NTVDM, you can distinguish them by their thread IDs in all tools except Process Monitor. You might have to start and stop the 16-bit process to determine which thread ID is associated with which 16-bit process.

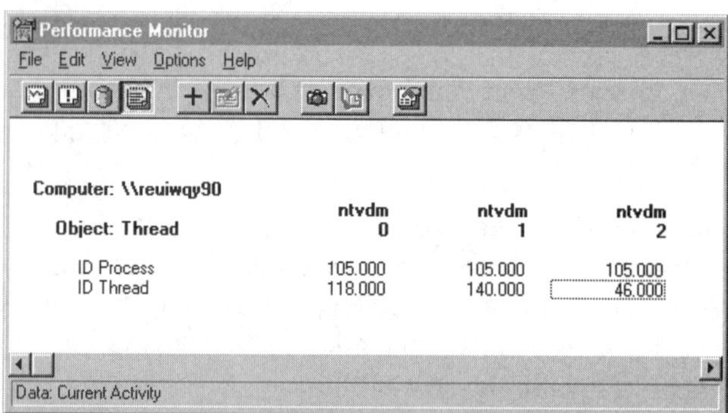

This figure is a Performance Monitor report on an a single NTVDM process (Process ID 105) with three threads. One of the threads is the heartbeat thread (Thread #0, Thread ID 118), one is the Wowexec thread (Thread #1, Thread ID 140), one is a 16-bit application, Write.exe (Thread #2, Thread ID 46).

Performance Monitor identifies threads by the process name and a thread number. The thread numbers are ordinal numbers (beginning with 0) that represent the order in which the threads started. The thread number of a running thread changes when a thread with a lower number stops; all threads with higher number move up in order to close the gap. For example, if thread 1 stopped, thread 2 becomes thread 1. Therefore, thread numbers are not reliable indicators of thread identity.

Performance Monitor can monitor the Process ID and Thread ID of a thread. The Process ID is the ID of the process in which the thread runs. Thread ID is the ID of the thread. Unlike thread number, it is assigned when the thread starts and remains with it until the thread stops.

The Process and Thread IDs are just ordinal numbers that are associated with the process or thread only for a single run. On subsequent runs, they just as likely to be assigned a different ID. However, you can use the ID to track them during execution.

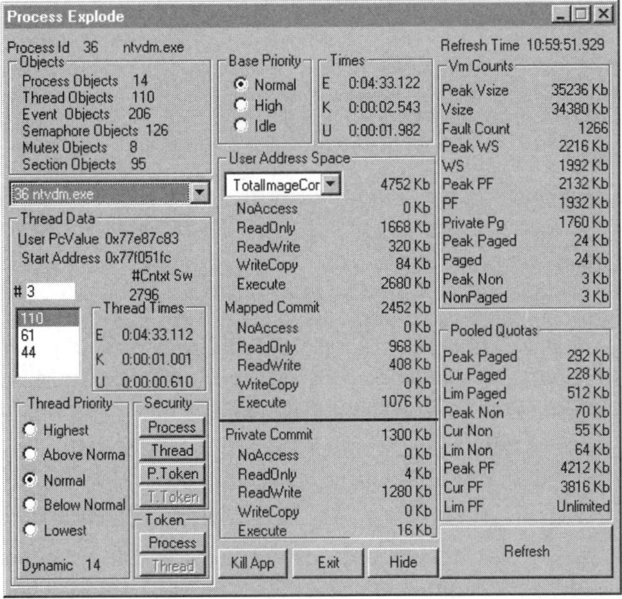

This figure shows Process Explode monitoring a 16-bit Windows application running in a single process (Ntvdm.exe). The three threads displayed in the Thread ID box (midway down the first column) represent the heartbeat thread, the Wowexec thread, and the thread of the 16-bit Windows application.

To see information about the thread in Process Explode, click on the Thread ID of the thread in the Thread ID box.

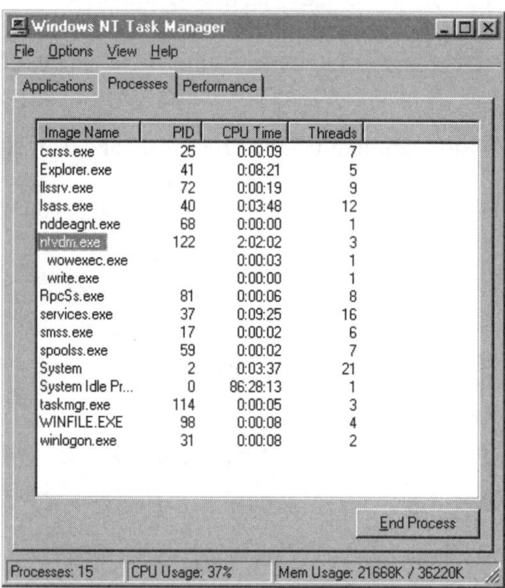

Task Manager makes it easy to identify 16-bit applications, because it displays the names of the executable files indented below the NTVDM process name. To monitor 16-bit processes in Task Manager, click the Processes tab, and from the **Options** menu click **Show 16-bit Tasks**.

In this example, you can see the Wowexec and Write threads. The heartbeat thread is not an executable and does not appear in Task Manager. However, the Thread Count column on the far right shows that all three threads are running in the NTVDM process.

Running Win16 Applications in a Separate Process

Windows NT 4.0 lets you opt to run a 16-bit Windows application in separate, unshared NTVDM process with its own memory space. This eliminates competition between NTVDM threads in a single process, making the 16-bit application thread fully multitasking and preemptible. It also simplifies monitoring.

▶ **To run a 16-bit application in its own address space, you can do any of the following:**

1. Click **Start**, then click **Run**. When you enter the name of the 16-bit process, the **Run in a Separate Memory Space** option is enabled. Click the option and click **OK**.

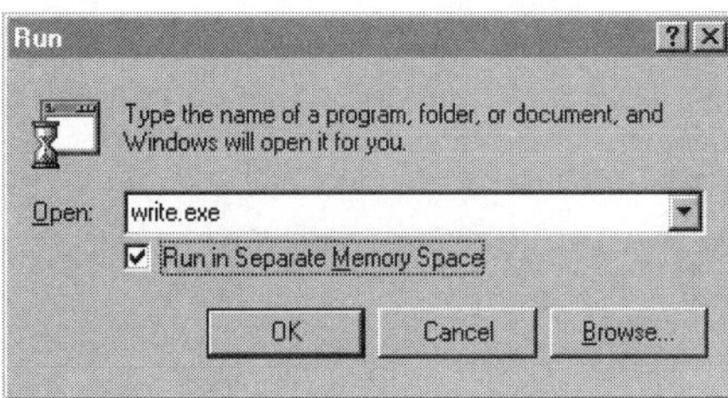

2. From the command line, type

```
start /separate processname
```

You can also type:

```
start /shared processname
```

to run in the shared NTVDM process.

3. Create a shortcut to the process: Click the right mouse button on the shortcut, then click Properties. Click the Shortcut tab, then click the **Run in Separate Memory Space** option.

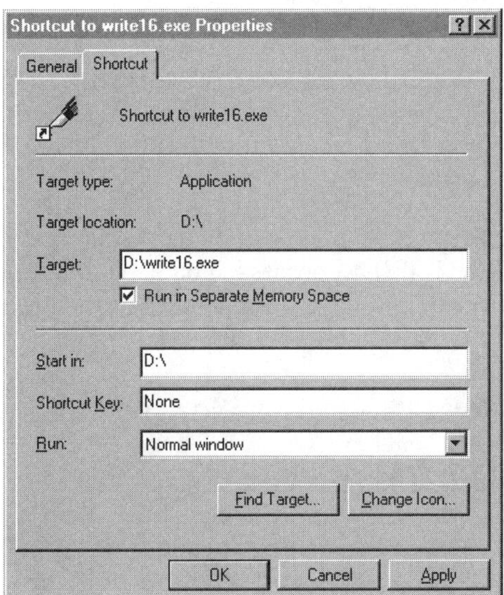

Tip Create two shortcuts to each of your 16-bit processes: One to run it in a separate memory space and one to run it in the shared memory space.

In Task Manager and Performance Monitor, two instances of the NTVDM process appear in the Process object Instances box. You can use their process IDs to distinguish between them.

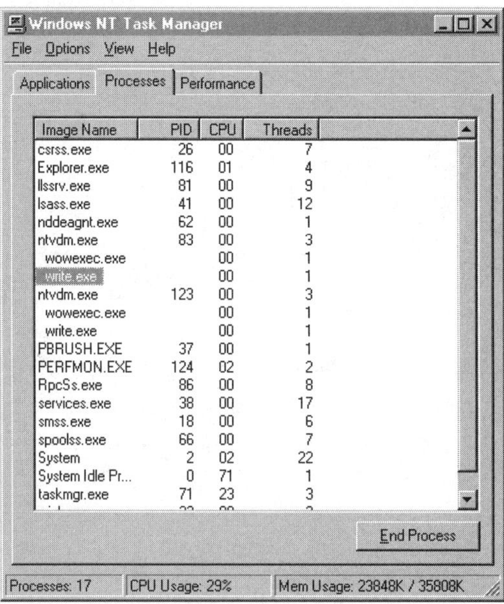

This example shows Task Manager monitoring two copies of 16-bit Write, each in its own NTVDM process.

When a 16-bit process runs in its own memory space, Performance Monitor shows two instances of the NTVDM process. You need to use process IDs to distinguish between them. (You might have to stop and start the processes to make the distinction.)

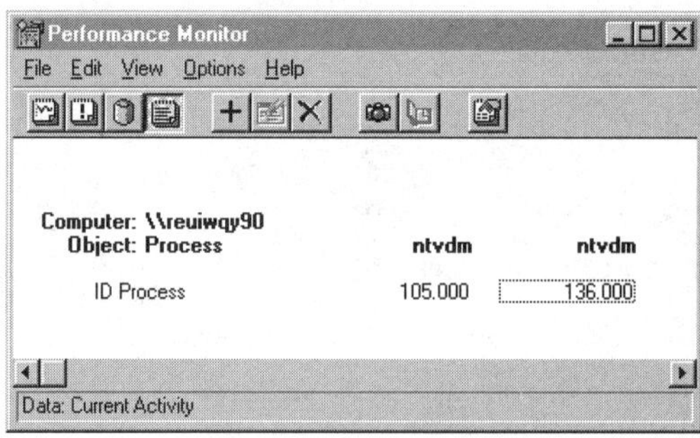

Monitoring MS-DOS Applications

In Windows NT 4.0, each MS-DOS application runs in its own NTVDM process, eliminating some of the problems encountered in Win16 applications. Unfortunately, all of the NTVDM processes are called Ndvdm.exe by default, but you can change that.

▶ To create a new process name for an NTVDM

1. Copy Ntvdm.exe to a file with a different name.
2. Edit the Registry by using a Registry editor. Regedt32.exe and Regedit.exe are installed when you install Windows NT.

Subtree	HKEY_LOCAL_MACHINE
Key	\System\CurrentControlSet\Control\WOW
Name	cmdline
Type	REG_DWORD
Values	%SystemRoot%\system32\ntvdm.exe

3. Double-click the **cmdline** value entry to change **ntvdm.exe** to the name of your copy of Ntvdm.exe. When you start an MS-DOS application, it will run in a process with that name.

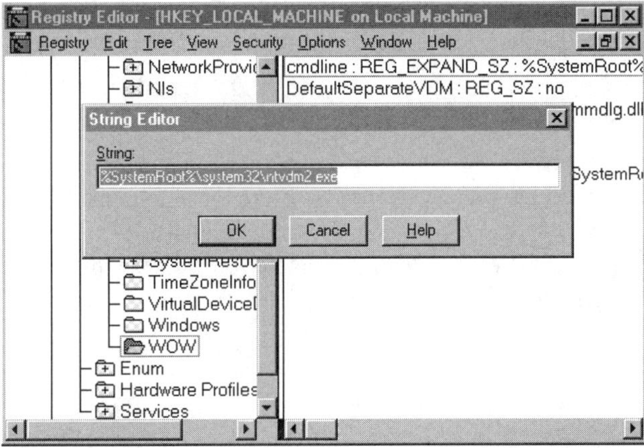

Tip You do not have to restart the computer for the registry change to take effect. Thus, you can change the registry between starting different DOS applications and have each start in a uniquely named process. It is also prudent to set it back to Ntvdm.exe when you are finished.

Unfortunately, this doesn't work with 16-bit Windows applications, so you need to distinguish those by thread or by process ID.

The Cost of Performance Monitoring

Performance monitoring tools are quite sophisticated, but they are plagued by the problem common to all experimental tools: Using them changes their results. Performance tools are just applications and, as such, they occupy the processor, use memory and disk space, and tax the graphics subsystem of the Windows NT Executive. Make sure to measure the effects of these tools, and subtract them from your data.

Note Performance Monitor for Windows NT 4.0 has lower overhead than previous versions, due almost entirely to changes in the Windows NT 4.0 architecture. Most of Performance Monitor overhead is consumed by its graphic displays, which are now more efficient, not by data collection.

Response Probe, a monitoring tool included on the CD, has no apparent overhead. It monitors its own toll on the system and subtracts it before displaying its results.

- To monitor Performance Monitor, include the Perfmon.exe process and its threads in your logs and charts and subtract them from your data.
- To determine how much disk space is consumed by Performance Monitor, log updates by doing a series of manual updates and watching the change in the log file size on the status bar in Log view.
- To measure the cost of monitoring particular objects, record the change in file size while adding and deleting those objects from a chart.
- If the cost of monitoring is too high, lengthen the Performance Monitor Update Interval to at least 15 seconds. Change the Task Manager Update Speed to Low.
- After you have collected baseline logging data, use Alerts to warn you of discrepancies. Alerts have the least overhead of any Performance Monitoring method. You can also log data over the network if you're studying disk performance.

CHAPTER 10

About Performance Monitor

Performance Monitor is a Windows NT 4.0 Administrative Tool for monitoring the performance of Windows NT workstations and servers. It uses a series of counters to track data, such as the number of processes waiting for disk time, the number of network packets transmitted per second, and the percentage of processor utilization. You can watch this data in real time, log it for future study, use it in charts and reports, and set alerts to warn you when a threshold value is exceeded.

What's New in Performance Monitor

With Performance Monitor for Windows NT 4.0, several new features, new counters and a new counter type have been added. This section is intended for people familiar with Performance Monitor for Windows NT 3.51 and who just need an update.

The _Total Instance

Performance Monitor for Windows NT 4.0 has a new instance, _Total, for counters in the Process, Thread, Paging File, Physical Disk, and Logical Disk objects. _Total is the sum of counter values for all instances of the object. The _Total counters are useful for screening and are easier to read than a chart of all instances.

However, the _Total instance does not make sense for some counters. For example, the total of Process ID or Thread ID, has no meaning. In these cases, Performance Monitor displays a zero for the _Total instance.

You can change the name of the _Total instance by editing the configuration registry entry, TotalInstanceName.

Subtree	HKEY_LOCAL_MACHINE
Key	\Software\Microsoft\WindowsNT\CurrentVersion\Perflib
Name	TotalInstanceName
Type	REG_SZ
Values	*InstanceName* (_Total is the default.)

Monitoring Instances with the Same Name

Performance Monitor can now recognize and monitor instances of objects with the same name. If you start two copies of Microsoft Word, for example, both will appear in the instances box for the process object, and Performance Monitor can monitor both.

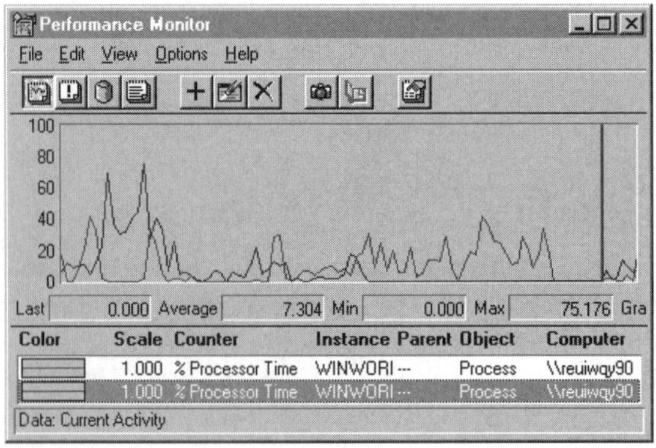

Note This does not apply to Alert view. You can only set an alert on the first instance of an object with the each name. All instances will appear in the Instances box for the counter, but only data collected from the first instance will trigger an alert.

Performance Monitor associates the name of a process with the first set of data it receives for that name. Any additional processes with the same name are associated with subsequent sets of data for that name.

This new ability to associate names and data might produce unreliable data when processes are stopped and new processes with the same name are started. A process might be associated with the wrong set of data.

If your data is suspect, chart Process: Process ID. If the Process ID changed during the course of the process, then data for more than once instance is combined. If you are working with logged data, you can use the Time Window to limit the data displayed to the part associated with a each Process ID. For more information, see "Monitoring Threads."

New Disk Counters

The Physical Disk and Logical Disk objects have a new set of counters designed for multidisk sets, like mirror and stripe sets and RAID (Redundant Array of Inexpensive Disk) systems.

The new disk counters, Avg. Disk Queue Length, Avg. Disk Read Queue Length, and Avg. Disk Write Queue Length use the same data as % Disk Time. However, they display the data as a decimal rather than a percentage, so it can exceed 100%. This is necessary for measuring multiple disks where total disk time often exceeds 100% of a single disk.

For more information on these counters, see "Monitoring Disk Sets" in Chapter 14, "Detecting Disk Bottlenecks."

Cache Counter Changes

This release brings a new cache counter, Cache: Read Aheads/sec and a redefinition of some original counters. For more information, see Chapter 15, "Detecting Cache Bottlenecks."

The Cache hit counters have been changed: They now measure the percentage of hits, regardless of the number of pages found. This better reflects the costs and benefits of cache hits and misses. The frequency of hits is much more important than the size of the hit.

The affected counters are:

- Cache: Copy Read Hits %
- Cache: Data Map Hits %
- Cache: MDL Read Hits %
- Cache: Pin Read Hits %

For more information, select each of these counters from the **Add to Chart** dialog box and click the Explain button.

Cache: Read Aheads/sec is a new Performance Monitor counter that counts read aheads in each second and averages the values over the last two timed intervals. A *read ahead* occurs when the Cache Manager detects that a file is read sequentially and moves larger blocks of sequential data into the cache. Read aheads are more efficient because more data is moved in each disk operation and fewer disk operations are required

Telephony Counters

Performance Monitor now includes a set of counters for monitoring telephone equipment attached to or associated with a computer, including telephones, telephone lines, and modems. Windows NT 4.0 Workstation and Server include a telephone device application program interface (TAPI) that allows Windows NT applications to communicate with telephone devices without regard to the characteristics of the device. The new Performance Monitor counters let you monitor devices that use TAPI.

The telephony counters are listed in Performance Monitor under the Telephony object. Counters include numbers of telephone devices, telephone lines, active lines, incoming and outgoing calls, and the number of applications using the telephone device.

DNS Names

Performance Monitor now includes support for long filenames of up to 260 characters. This lets you enter full Domain Name System pathnames in the Computer field for remote monitoring.

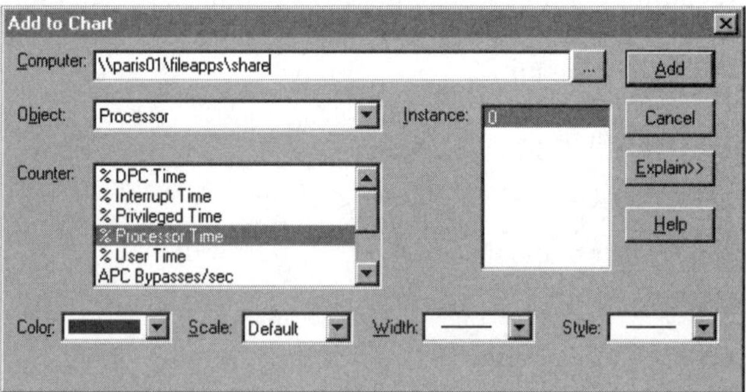

Unicode Characters

Performance Monitor will now display instances named in 16-bit per byte Unicode characters, including Kanji.

Warning Enabling Performance Monitor to read Unicode characters increases its overhead by approximately 0.65% on an Intel 486 processor.

To measure the overhead on your computer, log Process: %Processor Time for Perfmon.exe process for 3 minutes, then change the Registry to enable Unicode process names, repeat the test, and compare the results.

To enable Performance Monitor to read Unicode characters, edit the Registry by using a Registry Editor, such as Regedt32.exe. Add the CollectUnicodeProcessNames value entry, then set it to 1. Restart the computer to make it effective.

Subtree	HKEY_LOCAL_MACHINE
Key	\Software\Microsoft\WindowsNT\CurrentVersion\Perflib
Name	CollectUnicodeProcessNames
Type	REG_DWORD
Values	0 Get ANSI names from process header (8 bit only)
	1 Get Unicode process names from executable program file (16-bit)

New Counter Type

Difference counters display the change in value between the last two measurements. Performance Monitor can now interpret and display the positive differences reported by these counters, but it displays a zero if the difference is negative.

Performance Monitor does not include any Difference counters in its basic set, but other applications using Performance Monitor might, and you can create them for your applications. For information on writing performance counters, see the Win32 Software Development Kit.

New Troubleshooting Features

Four new troubleshooting options are available to Performance Monitor users:

- You can configure Performance Monitor to log an error to the Event Viewer application event log when it fails to retrieve data or gets unreadable or uninterpretable data. This is recommended for frequent users of Performance Monitor.
- You can configure the Performance Library to log its errors to the Event Viewer application event log and you can control the level of detail that it logs. Performance Library functions are the data source for Performance Monitor.
- You can also determine the extent to which Performance Library tests the data buffers of extensible counters. This is recommended for users and developers of extensible counters.
- With Windows NT 4.0, the Performance Library now times the Open procedure call of extensible counters and writes an error to the application event log when a time threshold is exceeded. This helps you identify counter problems that might otherwise prevent remote users from logging on to the computer.

For more information, see "Troubleshooting Features" later in this chapter.

Getting Started

Performance Monitor lets you:

- View data from multiple computers simultaneously.
- See how changes you make affect the computer.
- Change charts of current activity while viewing them.
- Export Performance Monitor data to spreadsheets or database programs, or use it as raw input for C programs.
- Trigger a program or procedure, or send notices when a threshold is exceeded.
- Log data about various objects from different computers over time. You can use these log files to record typical resource use, monitor a problem, or help in capacity planning.
- Combine selected sections of several log files into a long-term archive.
- Report on current activity or trends over time.
- Save different combinations of counter and option settings for quick starts and changes.

Performance Monitor is designed as a horizontal screening tool that shows a broad view of the computer's performance. In simpler cases, it might fully identify a problem. More often, you will use it to indicate which specialized tool, such as a profiler, a working set monitor, or a network analyzer to use next.

The next sections provide some tips for using Performance Monitor. For specific instructions, see Performance Monitor Help.

Starting and Setting Up Performance Monitor

You can start Performance Monitor from the **Administrative Tools** submenu on the **Start** menu or from the command line, but if you use it often, create a shortcut to it. You can also place it in your Startup folder to start when you boot or create a batch file to start one or many copies of Performance Monitor on different computers in your network.

When you use Performance Monitor, you select object counters and options to customize each of the four Performance Monitor views: Chart, Log, Report and Alert. You can save these counter and option settings to a file and design different settings files for all of your monitoring tasks.

Note Background startup activities and network traffic can interfere with testing. Unless you are testing how your computer starts Windows NT, wait until the computer settles before testing. Also, disconnect the computer from the network if you are not testing network activity. Network drivers might respond to network events even if they are not directed to your computer.

You can save settings for one view or save a group of view settings in a workspace. This table shows the file extensions associated with each view:

View	Settings File Extension
Alert	.pma
Chart	.pmc
Log	.pml
Report	.pmr
Workspace	.pmw

You can start Performance Monitor with a settings file or open the settings file after you start. If you don't specify a settings file, Performance Monitor looks for default chart file settings in \Winnt40\system32_Default.pmc. You can use only one settings file of each type at a time, but you can open multiple copies of Performance Monitor and use a different settings file or workspace with each.

You can also edit the settings file using the Setedit utility included on the CD-ROM with this book. For more information on Setedit, see Rktools.hlp.

When you start Performance Monitor from a batch file or from the command line, you can specify a one or more settings file listing the counters and options for each view. For example:

```
C:\> perfmon settings.pmc cachelog.pml
```

You can also specify a computer name in addition to, or instead of, a settings file. For example:

```
C:\> perfmon \\paris1
```

–Or–

```
C:\> perfmon settings.pmw \\issaquah
```

This computer will then appear as the default computer when you click the **Add To** command or **Add counter** button.

When you start Performance Monitor from a menu or shortcut, use the Performance Monitor **File** menu to open a setting file, or just drag the icon for a settings file from My Computer, Windows Explorer, or File Manager (Winfile.exe) onto the Performance Monitor icon or shortcut.

You can also create a shortcut to a settings file, or several shortcuts to settings files for different instances of Performance Monitor.

Objects and Instances

Performance Monitor measures the behavior of objects in your computer. The objects represent threads and processes, sections of shared memory, and physical devices. Performance Monitor collects data on activity, demand, and space used by the objects. Some objects always appear in Performance Monitor; others appear only if the service or process is running. Table 10.1 shows the objects that always appear when you run Windows NT 4.0 Server or Workstation.

Table 10.1 Windows NT Performance Monitor Objects

Object name	Description
Cache	The file system cache is an area of physical memory that holds recently used data.
Logical Disk	Disk partitions and other logical views of disk space
Memory	Random-access memory used to store code and data
Objects	Certain system software objects
Paging File	File used to back up virtual memory allocations
Physical Disk	Hardware disk unit (spindle or RAID device)
Process	Software object that represents a running program
Processor	Hardware unit that executes program instructions
Redirector	File system that diverts file requests to network servers
System	Counters that apply to all system hardware and software
Thread	The part of a process that uses the processor

Each *instance* of an object represents a component of the system. When the computer being monitored has more than one component of the same object type, Performance Monitor displays multiple instances of the object in the Instance box of the Add to Chart (View, Log, or Report) dialog box. It also displays the *_Total* instance, which represents a sum of the values for all instances of the object.

For example, if a computer has multiple physical disks, there will be multiple instances of the Physical Disk object in Add to Chart dialog box. This dialog box shows two instances of physical disks and a _Total instance. You can monitor the same or a different set of counters for each instance of an object.

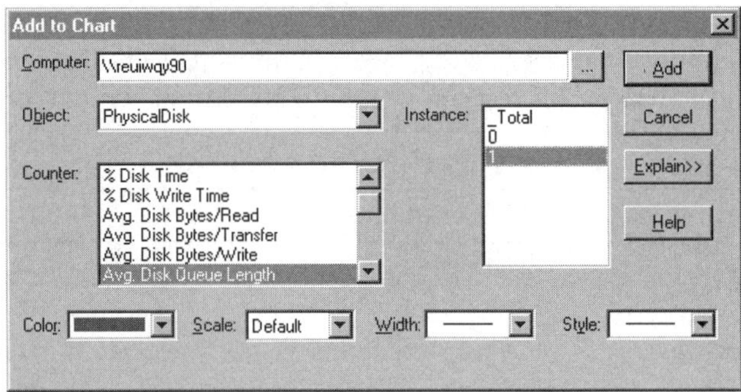

All counters for an object have the same instances. But, sometimes, the instances just don't make sense for a particular counter. For example, the totals of ordinal numbers, like _Total of Process: Process ID or Thread: Thread State, have no meaning. If you add them to you view, Performance Monitor displays the values as zeros.

Many of the instances you see are associated with Windows NT operating system processes. For more information about these processes, see "System Objects" and "System Processes" in Chapter 9, "The Art of Performance Monitoring."

Only 32-bit processes appear in the Instances box. Active 16-bit processes appear as threads running in a Windows NT Virtual DOS Machine (NTVDM) process. However, you can run each 16-bit application in a separate NTVDM process to make monitoring easier. For more information, see "Optimizing 16-bit Windows Applications," and "Monitoring MS-DOS Applications" in Chapter 9, "The Art of Performance Monitoring."

Note Only active instances appear in the Instances box. A process must be started before you can see it in Performance Monitor. If you are charting logged data, only processes that were active when you began logging appear in the Instances box.

To chart a process that started during logging, use the Time Window to move the beginning point to a time after the process was started. The process will then appear in the Instances box. Once you select it, you can expand the Time Window to include the whole log and the process will remain selected.

Some objects are parts of other objects or are dependent upon other objects. The instances of these related objects are shown in the Instances box in the following format:

```
Parent object = => Child object
```

where the child object is part of or is dependent upon the parent object. This makes it easier to identify the object.

For example, each logical partition of a disk is shown as the child of a parent physical disk.

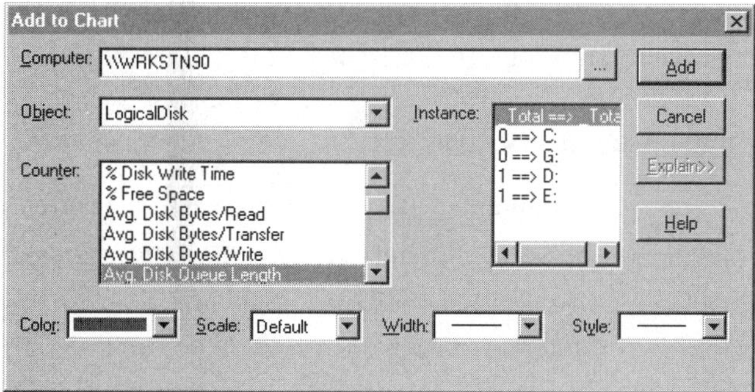

In this example, two physical disks, 0 and 1, are each divided into two logical disks. The instances box shows that logical disks C and G are partitions of physical disk 0, and logical disks D and E are partitions of physical disk 1.

Performance Monitor Counters

Performance Monitor does not really count anything. Its counters collect, average, and display data from internal counters by using the Windows NT Registry and the Performance Library DLLs. The internal counters are part of the computer hardware.

Performance Monitor collects data on various aspects of hardware and software performance, such as use, demand, and available space. You activate a Performance Monitor counter by adding it to a chart or report or by adding an object to a log. Performance Monitor begins collecting data immediately.

Note When you select a counter in any view, Performance Monitor collects data for all counters of that object, but displays only the one you select. This causes only minimal overhead, because most of Performance Monitor's overhead results from the display.

This book refers to counters by associating them with an object in the following format:

Object: *Counter*

For example, the % Processor Time counter of the Process object would appear as

Process: % Processor Time

to distinguish it from Processor: % Processor Time or Thread: % Processor Time.

Tip Click the **Explain** button in the **Add To** dialog box to display the definition for each counter. The **Explain** button works only when you are monitoring current activity, not logs.

There are three types of counters:

- *Instantaneous* counters display the most recent measurement

  For example, Process: Thread Count displays the number of threads found in the most recent measurement.

- *Averaging* counters, whose names include per second or percent, measure a value over time display the average of the last two measurements. When you start these counters, you must wait for the second measurement to be taken before any values are displayed.

  For example, Memory: Pages/sec, shows the average number of memory pages found in the last two reads during the second measured.

- *Difference* counters subtract the last measurement from the previous one and display the difference if it is positive. If it is negative, they display a zero.

  Performance Monitor does not include any difference counters in its basic set, but they might be included in other applications that use Performance Monitor, and you can write them yourself. For information on writing performance counters, see the Win32 Software Development Kit.

Some hardware and applications designed for Windows NT come with their own counters. Many of these *extensible* counters are installed automatically with the product, but some are installed separately. In addition, there are a few specialized counters on the Windows NT Resource Kit 4.0 CD that you can install. See your product documentation and Performance Monitor Help for detailed instructions on adding extensible counters.

Creating an Overview File

When you first start using Performance Monitor, the number of performance counters might seem overwhelming. It is not necessary to be familiar with all of the performance counters. Some are appropriate only for programmers writing Windows NT–based applications; others are useful for vendors who need to test hardware performance. Later chapters in this section recommend certain counters to diagnose problems on each component of your computer.

Begin by logging the Logical Disk, Memory, Process, Processor, System, and Thread objects. Run the log for at least a few days at an Update Interval of 60 seconds. Then, chart the results.

Create a chart settings file with counters that give you a broad view of your system. The default counters are a good starting point. When you open the Add To box, the Processor: % Processor Time counter is selected because this counter is used most often. Each object has a default counter which is highlighted when you select the object. These counters were selected as defaults because they are excellent indicators of the object's activity.

The following table shows the default counter for the most commonly monitored objects.

Object	Default Counter	Description
Cache	Data Map Hits %	How often requested data is found in the cache. This is an indicator of application I/O. A poor cache hit rate may indicate a memory shortage.
Logical Disk	Avg. Disk Queue Length	A measure of the activity of each logical partition of the disk. An Avg. Disk Queue Length of 1.0 indicates that the logical disk was busy for the entire sample time. Busy time includes all processing time for a disk I/O request, including driver time and time in the queue, so values for a single logical disk may exceed 1.0. Sustained high values over time indicated a possible disk bottleneck.

Object	Default Counter	Description
Memory	Pages/sec	The number of pages between main memory and the disk drives in each second. If this counter is consistently high, memory is in short supply. Sustained paging degrades performance.
Objects	Processes	An instantaneous count of the number of processes running. When charted with Processor: % Processor Time, it shows the effect on the processor of adding and removing processes.
Physical Disk	Avg. Disk Queue Length	A measure of the activity of the disk subsystem. It is the sum of Avg. Disk Queue Length for all logical partitions of the disk. This is a good measure of disk activity when measuring multiple physical disks in a disk set.
Process	% Processor Time	A measure of each process's use of the processor.
Processor	% Processor Time	A good indicator of the demand for and efficiency of a processor.
System	% Total Processor Time	Include this counter to monitor multiprocessor systems. It combines the average processor usage of all processors into a single counter.
Thread	% Processor Time	Threads are the components of a process that execute its code on the processor. This counter indicates which threads are getting processor time.

You should also include counters to monitor network throughput. The counters you choose depend upon your network protocol and whether the computer is primarily a client, a server, or both. NetBIOS: Bytes Total/sec for NWLink or Network Interface: Bytes Total/sec for TCPIP/SNMP are good overview counters.

If the computer is primarily a server, include Server: Bytes Total/sec to monitor network activity. You might also want to include Server: Context Blocks Queued/sec and System: Total Interrupts/sec.

You should also include a few alerts in the overview settings to notify you if Logical Disk: % Free Space, or Memory: Available Bytes falls below 20%, or if System: Processor Queue Length exceeds 3.

Save these counters in a workspace settings file, like Overview.pmw, so you can start them easily. They will provide a broad view of the performance of your computer.

Customizing Your Display

You can minimize the Performance Monitor display to keep it handy without cluttering up your work. This is a great way to monitor an application while using it or to watch several copies of Performance Monitor at once.

Use the **Options** menu to remove the Toolbar, Status Bar, Title Bar, Value Bar, Vertical Labels and Legend. Select the **Always on Top** option, and then shrink the window. Use hot keys to control the window, or double-click to display the title bar and menus.

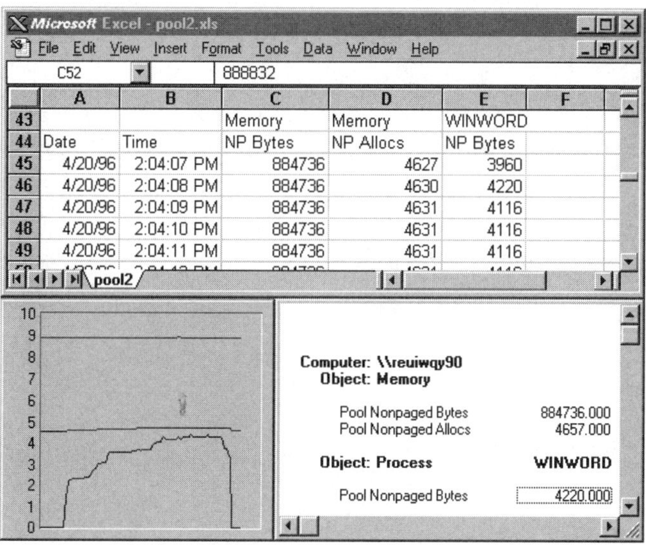

In this figure, two copies of Performance Monitor are running; one displaying a graph, the other, a report. The Excel spreadsheet displays data exported to it from Performance Monitor.

There are several reasons to start more than one copy of Performance Monitor:

- To monitor data from more than one computer
- To compare a current activity to logged activity
- To divide a busy chart into two or more readable charts
- To log data to two separate log files
- To peek at a running log file

Important Opening a log that is collecting data will stop the log and clear all counter settings. You can't peek at the log from chart or report view because the views share the same data source. Changing the Data From option affects all views, even the running log.

To peek at a running log, start a second copy of Performance Monitor, and set Data From to the running log. You can chart or report on all data logged until the time you open it. Newly collected data will not be added to your snapshot of the log file.

Although each copy has its own overhead, it might be worthwhile to get the data you need. You can also measure the overhead of the Performance Monitor process, Perfmon.exe, and subtract it from your results. You can also run Performance Monitor on a different workstation and chart the logfiles over a network.

The readability of charts is also improved by reducing the vertical maximum and/or increasing scale values. This will make small values easier to see.

Histograms, an alternative to the line charts, also simplify complex charts, especially ones with many instances of the same counter. Just click the **Histogram** button in Chart Options.

Running Performance Monitor

No matter which view you choose—Chart, Alert, Report, or Log—there are standard features built in to make Performance Monitor more flexible. From your computer, or another computer on the network running Network Monitor Agent, you can

- Use the Update Interval to determine how often performance is measured. There is a tradeoff between the precision of the data and Performance Monitor overhead.
- Use the PRINTSCREEN key to save a bitmapped image of the Performance Monitor screen. You can then print it or insert it in a document.
- Clear the display, delete a counter, or delete the full screen.
- Export the data in a tab delimited (.tsv) or comma delimited (.csv) text file to a spreadsheet or database program.

For specific instructions on these topics, see Performance Monitor Help.

Charting Current Activity

Customized charts that monitor the current performance of selected counters and instances are useful when:

- investigating why a computer or application is slow or inefficient.
- continuously monitoring systems to find intermittent performance problems.
- discovering why you need to increase capacity.

For specific instructions on using the chart view, opening an existing chart settings file, and creating a new blank chart, see the "Working with Charts" topic in Performance Monitor Help.

Adding Counters to a Chart

Different graphs require different settings. Creating charts to reflect these different requirements is a simple matter of selecting the computer to be monitored and adding the appropriate objects, counters, and instances. You can then save these selections under a filename for viewing whenever you want an update on their performance.

To enhance the readability of graphs, vary the scale of the displayed information and the color, width, and style of the line for each counter as you add it to the chart. You can also modify these properties after you add a selection.

The following table shows which options can be changed by editing the chart line:

Option	Description
Color	Use colors to distinguish lines in a graph from each other.
Scale	Change the scale at which the information is displayed. The numbers shown in the value bar are not scaled.
Width	Make the line thicker or thinner. Thick lines, however, cannot be styled. This is especially useful to distinguish a line in a graph when it will be printed or displayed in black and white.
Style	Make a graph line dashed or dotted. This only works on the thinnest lines.

You can change the scale of any displayed value to make it easier to see in a chart or to allow you to compare it with another value. The scale factor is applied to all currently selected counters. The factor displayed is multiplied by the counter value, and the product is charted. However, that the value bar continues to show the actual value, not the scaled value.

You can also change the vertical maximum on a graph to make very large or small values noticeable. This often reveals details of a curve that are hidden when the line is compressed on one axis.

Highlighting changes the line selected in a Performance Monitor chart legend to a thick white line for easy viewing. As you scroll through the legend the highlight moves with you. To toggle highlighting on and off, press CTRL+H.

For specific instructions on adding selections to a chart and saving chart selections in a settings file, see the "Adding Chart Selections" topic in Performance Monitor Help.

For specific instructions on changing how a selected counter is represented on the chart, see the "Changing Chart Selections" topic in Performance Monitor Help.

Using Chart Options

By using Chart Options you can customize your charts and change the method used for updating the chart values. Click Chart on the **Options** menu, or click the Options button on the toolbar to see the **Chart Options** dialog box. From here you can:

- Choose whether to display or hide horizontal and vertical grid lines, vertical labels, the value bar, and the legend and legend-information area.
- Change the vertical maximum value of the displayed graph labels and the time interval used for graphing the information from the counters. The chosen graph-time interval is reflected in the value bar, which also displays the last, average, minimum, and maximum values for the data visible on the chart.
- Change the display from a line graph to a histogram. This is useful for viewing the behavior of many instances of the same object.

For specific instructions on how to change chart options, see the "Changing the Chart Options" topic in Performance Monitor Help.

Setting Alerts on Current Activity

The *Alert* view enables you to continue working while Performance Monitor tracks events and notifies you as requested. Use it to create an alert log that monitors the current performance of selected counters and instances for objects on Windows NT.

With the alert log you can monitor several counters at the same time. When a counter exceeds a given value, the date and time of the event are recorded in the Alert view. One thousand events are recorded, after which the oldest event is discarded when the next new one is added. An event can also generate a network alert. When an event occurs, you can have a specified program run every time or just the first time that it occurs.

Note You cannot set alerts on two conditions of the same counter for the same instance. For example, you cannot set an alert to be triggered when Processor: %Processor Time on a single processor exceeds 90% and another to be triggered when it falls below 30%.

Also, you cannot set an alert on more than one instance of an object with the same name. For example, if you are running two processes with the same name, you can only set an alert for the first instance of the process. Both instances will appear in the Instances box, but only data collected from the first instance will trigger the alert.

For specific instructions on using the Alert view, opening an existing alert log settings file, and creating a new alert log file, see "Working with Alerts" in Performance Monitor Help.

Adding Counters in the Alert View

You can create alert logs to warn yourself about problems in different situations. You can then save these selections under a filename and reuse them when you want to see if the problems have been fixed.

Adding counters in Alert view is similar to adding counters in other views. However, when you set an alert, you specify under what conditions an alert is logged by choosing to have an alert logged if any counter is over or under a value you specify. You can also have Performance Monitor run a program either the first time or every time the alert is logged.

The alert condition applies to the value of the counter over the time interval you specify. The default time interval is 5 seconds. If you set an alert on Memory: Pages/sec > 50 using the default time interval, the average paging rate for a 5-second period has to exceed 50 per second before the alert is triggered.

Note When you configure Performance Monitor to run a program when an alert occurs, the program might not work properly or error messages might appear. This problem occurs because Performance Monitor passes the Alert condition, as a parameter, to the program. If a program run from Performance Monitor does not work properly, create a one line batch file that runs the program, and call the batch file from Performance Monitor.

When Performance Monitor is logging alerts, a list of your selections appears in the Alert Legend box at the bottom of the window, and Performance Monitor displays the resulting alerts in the Alert Log area.

If an alert occurs while you are not using the Alert view, an alert icon appears in the status bar showing the number of alerts that have occurred since you were last in the Alert view.

When a remote computer that is being monitored shuts down, an alert occurs and creates a comment in the alert log. Another alert occurs (with another corresponding comment) when that computer later reconnects.

For specific instructions on adding selections to an alert log and saving alert log selections in a settings file, see the "Adding Alert Selections" topic in Performance Monitor Help.

For specific instructions on how to change the way a selected counter is represented in the alert log, or to update alert log selections that have been saved in a settings file, see the "Changing Alert Selections" topic in Performance Monitor Help.

Using Alert Options

Choosing the **Alert** command on the **Options** menu enables you to specify not only the alert interval but the alert method, as well. Specify one or all of the following:

- Switch to the Alert view
- Log the event in the Event Viewer Application log
- Send a network alert message to yourself or someone else

Note To send a network alert message to yourself or to someone else, the Messenger Service must already be started and the net name must already be defined on the recipient's computer.

For specific instructions on how to change alert options, see the "Changing the Alert Options" topic in Performance Monitor Help. For more information on starting the Messenger Service or adding a net name, type **net start messenger /?** and **net name /?**.

Creating Reports

The *Report* view lets you display constantly changing counter and instance values for selected objects. Values appear in columns for each instance. You can adjust report intervals, print snapshots, and export data. Reports of averaged counters show the average value during the Time Window interval. Reports of instantaneous counters show the value at the end of the Time Window interval.

For specific instructions on using the Report view, opening an existing report settings file, or creating a new blank report file, see the "Working with Reports" topic in Performance Monitor Help.

Using Report Selections and Options

Creating reports using current activity can help you gain a better understanding of object behavior:

- Create a report on all the counters for a given object and then watch them change under various loads.
- Create reports to reflect the same information that you are charting or to monitor other specific situations. Then save these selections under a filename and reuse them when you need an update on the same information.

After you add selections to a report, your selections, listed by computer and object, appear in the report area, and Performance Monitor displays the changing values of your selections in the report.

For specific instructions on how to add objects, counters, and instances to a report or to save report selections in a settings file, see the "Adding to a Report" topic in Performance Monitor Help.

For specific instructions on how to change the reporting time interval, see the "Changing the Report" topic in Performance Monitor Help.

Logging Current Activity

Logging is recording information on the current activity of selected objects and computers for later viewing. You can also collect data from multiple systems into a single *log file*. Log files contain detailed data for detecting performance problems or other detailed analysis. For capacity planning, it lets you view trends over a long period, and append or relog files. You can chart, report, or export log file data to compare files or examine patterns.

Important Opening a log that is collecting data will stop the log and clear all counter settings. You can't peek at the log from chart or report view because the views share the same data source. Changing Data From affects all views, even the running log.

To peek at a running log, start a second copy of Performance Monitor, and set Data From to the running log. You can chart or report on all data logged until the time you open it. Newly collected data will not be added to your snapshot of the log file.

Setting Logging Options

Log view has a display area for listing objects and their corresponding computers you selected with the **Add To Log** command on the **Edit** menu. All counters and instances are logged for a selected object.

Choose the **Log** command on the **Options** menu to fill in or change the information shown in the gray boxes in the Log view, to start or stop logging, and to change the method used for updating the log values.

The Log view displays a list of objects and computers along with the current file size and the following items that you can specify in the **Log Options** dialog box:

- Complete path and name of the log file
- Log Interval in seconds, from 1 to 3600 seconds (1 hour)
- Status, either Collecting or Closed

After you start logging, a log symbol with the changing total file size appears on the right side of the status bar and remains there in all four views.

Notice also that when a remote computer from which you are logging data shuts down, a bookmark comment is added to the log file. Another bookmark comment is added when that computer later reconnects and logging starts again.

For specific instructions on how to change log options or start or stop logging, see the "Working with Information from Log Files" topic in Performance Monitor Help.

For specific instructions on adding selections for logging or saving your log selection settings, see the "Adding to a Log" topic in Performance Monitor Help.

Adding Bookmarks

Log files become more usable when you add *bookmarks* at various points while logging. With bookmarks you can highlight major points of interest or describe the circumstances under which the file was created and then easily return to these locations when you work with the log file. The **Bookmark** command becomes available when you start logging.

To add a bookmark, click **Bookmark** on the **Options** menu or click the **Bookmark** button on the toolbar.

Working with Input from Log Files

Log files can provide a wealth of information for troubleshooting or planning. Whereas charting, setting alerts, and creating reports on current activity provide instant feedback, working with log files enables you to track counters over a long period of time, allowing you examine information more thoroughly, and document system behavior.

The method of analyzing data is the same, whether the source is current activity or a log file. You can still chart, report and set alerts on data. In addition, you can relog the data at the same or at a shorter interval to compress it, and you can use the Time Window to view a selected portion of the logged data.

Appending and Relogging Log Files

You can append and relog log files in several ways:

- You can add data to an existing log file.
- You can relog the data to another log file or to an existing log file at a different rate.
- You can relog some or all objects in the log file at a longer time interval or change the start and stop times and relog only the data between them.

When you log current activity to an existing log file, the new data is just added to the end of the file. This lets you create a single archive file composed of multiple logs.

However, when you relog data, you can choose a new rate at which the data is collected and averaged. For example, if you collected data at a one-minute interval and relogged it at a five-minute interval, every fifth data point is collected, and the others are discarded. All minimum, maximums, and averages reflect the remaining data only and the new logfile uses only 1/5 of the disk space of the original file.

Note Data in a log must be in chronological order. If you are relogging to combine existing log files, be sure to relog them in chronological order.

To enable the **Relog File** button, enter a filename and select at least one counter to log. For specific instructions on how to relog an input log file, see the "Relogging Input Log Files" topic in Performance Monitor Help.

Troubleshooting Features

Windows NT 4.0 includes four new troubleshooting features that warn you when Performance Monitor, or its data source, Performance Library, collect uninterpretable data, or when extensible counters threaten the operating system or session.

Tip Extensible Counter List (Exctrlst.exe), a tool on the Windows NT Resource Kit 4.0 CD in the Performance Tools group (\PerfTool\CntrTool), lists the extensible counters installed on a computer. It can be used on the local or a remote computer. For more information, see Rktools.hlp.

- You can configure Performance Monitor to log warnings and errors to the Windows NT Event Viewer application event log when it fails to retrieve data or receives uninterpretable data. This is highly recommended for frequent users, because the event log is the only clear indicator that Performance Monitor has encountered bad data. Performance Monitor event logging is turned off by default.
- You can also configure the Windows NT *Performance Library*, the source of Performance Monitor data, to log its errors to the application event log and control the detail of events logged. The default is to log errors only, but if experience trouble with extensible counters, you might want to increase the logging level.
- You can determine how thoroughly Performance Library tests the data buffers returned by extensible counters, and adjust this value based on your estimation of the reliability of your counters. The default is maximum testing.
- Performance Library now times the Open procedure calls of extensible counters and writers an error to the Event Viewer application event log if the call exceeds a time threshold. You can increase the time threshold (the default is five seconds) to prevent unnecessary logging of normal delays, or shorten it to monitor the actual time of the calls.

This section explains each of these features. The troubleshooting features of Performance Monitor reveal the importance of its data source, the Windows NT Performance Library.

The Performance Library is dynamic link library of functions grouped by object. To collect counter data, Performance Monitor calls the Windows NT Registry which requests the data by using Performance Library functions. Performance Library functions request information from the Windows NT Executive, particularly from the Hardware Abstraction Layer (HAL), a platform-specific DLL. The Performance Library associates the system data with each performance object and returns data for each object to Performance Monitor.

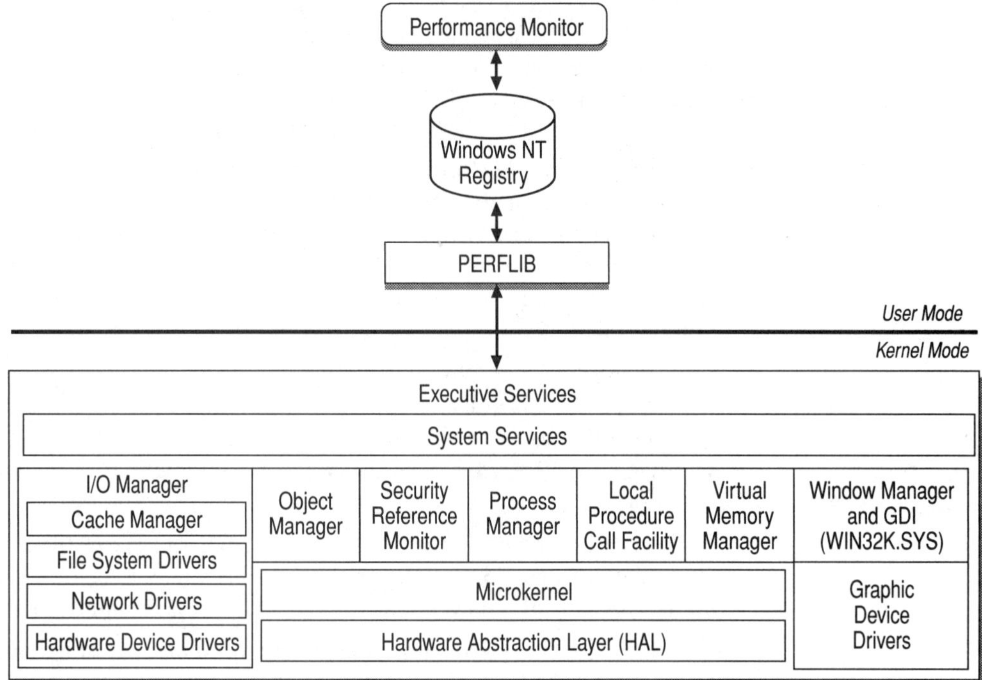

When Performance Library fails to retrieve data or encounters data errors or invalid data, these problems become apparent only in Performance Monitor.

Logging Performance Monitor Errors

When Performance Monitor fails to get data it requests, or when it receives uninterpretable data, it displays a zero as the counter value for that request. The data request might have failed because of a malfunction or simply because the computer or application it was monitoring had stopped. Data considered uninterpretable includes negative times, negative performance values, or percentages greater than 100.

Performance Monitor does not alert the user when it gets bad data or no data. However, you can configure Performance Monitor to log these incidents to the Event Viewer application event log as errors and warnings.

Note If Performance Monitor receives no data or bad data for the Processor: % Processor Time or the System: % Total Processor Time counters, it displays 100% as the counter value, not zero. Performance Monitor actually monitors the thread of the Idle process on each processor. It calculates the difference between 100% and the percentage of time the Idle threads ran. If a request for data on an Idle thread fails, Performance Monitor assumes it is zero and displays the difference, 100%, as the counter value.

Performance Monitor logs warnings and errors when it fails to retrieve data or receives bad data, and when connections to remote computers it is monitoring are lost and restored. Performance Monitor logging is either on or off; there are no intermediate or more detailed levels.

To log Performance Monitor errors and warnings to the Event Viewer application event log, use a Registry Editor, such as Regedt32.exe. Add the ReportEventsToEventLog value entry or change its value to 1, and then restart Performance Monitor.

Subtree	HKEY_CURRENT_USER
Key	\Software\Microsoft\PerfMon
Name	ReportEventsToEventLog
Type	REG_DWORD
Values	0, 1 (0 is the default)

After you have enabled Performance Monitor event logging and restarted the system, check the Event Viewer application event log routinely. You can use the Find or Filter Events options to display events with Source = PERFMON.

Many warnings and errors are attributable to normal and expected events such as processes or computers being stopped. Also, counters for threads are prone to uninterpretable values when the threads are stopped.

However, if Performance Monitor is logging negative time errors, there might be a problem with your HAL DLL. In the past, this has been encountered in some HALs for multiprocessor computers.

For more information on thread counters, see "Monitoring Processes and Threads."

Logging Performance Library Errors

Error events logged by the Performance Library often result from problems with extensible counters. These usually involve failures in loading or executing the functions in the DLLs for the counters.

By default, Performance Library logs errors in loading and executing extensible counters to the Event Viewer application event log, but it does not log warnings or informational messages. If you are monitoring an application using counters that did not come with Windows NT, or if you are having trouble loading or reading these counters, check the Event Viewer application log routinely. If you find errors, you can increase the logging level to show more detail.

Performance Library logging levels are:

Logging Level	Description
0	No logging.
1	Errors only. (This is the default.)
2	Errors and warnings.
3	Errors, warnings, information, and success/failure conditions.

To change the Performance Library logging level, use a Registry Editor, such as Regedt32.exe. Add the EventLogLevel value entry or change its value, and then restart Performance Monitor.

Subtree	HKEY_LOCAL_MACHINE
Key	\Software\Microsoft\WindowsNT\CurrentVersion\Performance Library
Name	EventLogLevel
Type	REG_DWORD
Values	0, 1, 2, 3

Note Changes to the Performance Library logging level take effect on the local computer when its copy of Performance Monitor is restarted. If remote computers are monitoring the system, then the local computer needs to be restarted or remote sessions need to be restarted to see the change.

Check the Application Event Log routinely. You can use the **Find** or **Filter Events** options to display events with Source = PERFLIB.

If you encounter errors with extensible counters, consult the provider.

Testing Extensible Counter Buffers

The functions in extensible counters might return inconsistent or unreadable data buffers to Performance Library. At a minimum, this could result in invalid counter values; at its worst, it could cause the operating system to stop. Thus, by default, Performance Library tests these data buffers thoroughly for errors and internal consistency. However, these tests have some overhead, so Windows NT lets you reduce the level of testing.

If you are not using extensible counters or if your extensible counters have been proven to be reliable, reducing the test level will reduce the processor load. If, however, you install a new product with performance counters, or if the system is being used to develop or test extensible counters, you can increase the test level.

Performance Library has three levels for testing the data buffers returned by functions of extensible counters. Note that **1** represents the highest level and **3** represents the lowest level.

Test level	Description
1	Thorough testing of buffer pointers and contents. (This is the default.)
2	Minimal testing of overall buffer length and pointers, but not of contents.
3	No testing.

To adjust the test level, use a Registry Editor, such as Regedt32.exe, to add or change the ExtCounterTestLevel value entry, and then restart Performance Monitor.

Subtree	HKEY_LOCAL_MACHINE
Key	\Software\Microsoft\WindowsNT\CurrentVersion\Perflib
Name	ExtCounterTestLevel
Type	REG_DWORD
Values	1, 2, 3

Check the Application Event Log routinely. You can use the Find or Filter Events options to display events with Source = PERFLIB.

If you encounter errors with extensible counters, consult the provider.

Timing Extensible Counters

Windows NT 4.0 Performance Library now times the Open procedure call of all extensible counters and writes an error to the Event Viewer application event log if the call time exceeds a threshold. The log entry helps you to identify counters that may be delaying or locking Performance Monitor during initialization. While the open call proceeds, local users cannot use Performance Monitor and remote users cannot log on to the affected computer. Usually this takes just a few milliseconds.

Tip Extensible Counter List (Exctrlst.exe), a tool on the Windows NT Resource Kit 4.0 CD in the Performance Tools group (\PerfTool\CntrTool), displays the names of the Open, Collect, and Close procedure calls of the extensible counters installed on a computer. For more information, see Rktools.hlp.

You can adjust the time threshold to allow more time for slower calls that are not in error. Only the Open calls of extensible counters are timed. Standard Performance Monitor counters and other calls to extensible counter functions are not affected.

To change the time threshold, use a Registry Editor, such as Regedt32, to add or change the OpenProcedureWaitTime value entry in the Registry, and then restart the computer.

Subtree	HKEY_LOCAL_MACHINE
Key	\Software\Microsoft\WindowsNT\CurrentVersion\Perflib
Name	OpenProcedureWaitTime
Type	REG_DWORD
Values	0 - 4 billion, in milliseconds. The default is 5000 milliseconds (5 seconds).

Remember to check the Event Viewer application event log for errors and to clear the log periodically to save space on the disk.

Mastering Performance Monitor

Work with Performance Monitor for a few days. Create a few workspace and settings files, and watch the counters. Soon you will have a better feel for your computer's performance and for Performance Monitor. Then, it is time to explore Performance Monitor's more advanced features.

One the best features is that you can run multiple copies of Performance Monitor on the same computer at the same time. Simply click the Performance Monitor icon, or your shortcut to it, again. Each time you click it, you get another copy of Performance Monitor:

- You can log data to only one log file with each copy of Performance Monitor, but you can chart or report on a single log file with multiple copies of Performance Monitor.
- You can have one copy measuring current activity, and another copy logging it.
- You can chart logged data in one copy and report on it in another.
- You can drag the icon for the same setting file to multiple copies of Performance Monitor.

This section describes the fine points of using Performance Monitor and will help you discover its range and its limitations.

Performance Monitor Limitations

As you use Performance Monitor and other monitoring tools, remember their limitations. Understanding the range and resolution of your tools is essential to accurate diagnosis.

Counter Limits

It is important to know just what your counters are counting. In each section of this book, we try to mention *how* the counters measure as well as *what* they measure. This information is important, especially when you are interpreting suspicious data or getting inconsistent results.

Update Interval

The Update Interval you select on the **Options** dialog box is designed to determine how often Performance Monitor measures counter values. However, Performance Monitor is just another application contending for processor time. On a busy computer, Performance Monitor might be competing with higher priority threads for access to the processor and might not be able to update the counters as frequently as you choose.

If Performance Monitor appears to be updating less frequently, chart the Process: % Processor Time or Process: Priority Base counters on all processes, including the Performance Monitor process, Perfmon.exe. Look for processes with high priorities or those getting a disproportionate share of processor time. These might be preventing Performance Monitor from updating at the rate you chose. Performance Monitor runs at a elevated base priority to make sure it can monitor under most circumstances, but it can get locked out like any other process. If necessary, you can use Task Manager to increase the base priority class of Perfmon.exe. For more information, see "Changing the Base Priority Class" in Chapter 11, "Performance Monitoring Tools."

Compound Problems

It is difficult to detect multiple bottlenecks in a system. You might spend several days testing and retesting to identify and eliminate a bottleneck, only to find that another appears in its place. Only thorough and patient testing of all elements can assure that you have found all of the problems.

It is not unusual to trace a performance problem to multiple sources. Poor response time on a workstation is most likely to result from memory and processor problems. Servers are more susceptible to disk and network problems.

Also, problems in one component might be the *result* of problems in another component, not the cause. For example, when memory is scarce, the system begins moving pages of code and data between disks and physical memory. The memory shortage is manifest in increased disk and processor use, but the problem is memory, not the processor or disk.

Lack of memory is by far the most common cause of serious performance problems in computer systems. If you suspect other problems, check Memory: Pages/sec to make sure a memory shortage is not appearing in another guise.

Monitoring Processes and Threads

Monitoring processes and threads is an essential part of tuning software performance and understanding how applications affect your hardware. However, some Performance Monitor counter values might be invalid if the threads or processes are stopping and starting while Performance Monitor is watching.

When processes with the same name start and stop, Performance Monitor sometimes mistakes them for a single process and combines the data for different processes into a single graph or report line. Threads are even more prone to mistaken identity and combination, because Performance Monitor knows them only by their thread number, a number which only indicates the order in which the threads started.

Fortunately, you can recognize and eliminate errant values from your data:

- Include the Process ID and Thread ID counters in graphs of your data. These are ordinal numbers assigned to processes and threads when they start, and which remain with them until they stop. If the line representing the ID is not straight, it means that data for more than one process is combined.
- When monitoring processes and threads, watch for spikes in the data. These spikes sometimes appear when Performance Monitor monitors the start of a process. They are an artifact of monitoring and do not represent valid values for the Performance Monitor counters.
- Always chart the data in a line graph first, even if you are preparing a report. Reports and histograms show last values and averages, which might hide a spike.
- Use the Performance Monitor Time Window to eliminate spikes from your data and to separate the data for different processes or threads from a single data line. For more details, see "The Time Window" later in this chapter.

Monitoring Processes

It is important to recognize when Performance Monitor has combined processes and to distinguish the values for each process from values for the others. Also, you must recognize and eliminate invalid data spikes which sometimes occur when you start a monitored process.

Data for the following graph was collected by starting Microsoft Word, stopping it, then starting it again. The thick line, representing Process ID, shows that the process ID changed (from 126 to 114). Because Process IDs do not change while a process is executing, this indicates that data from two different processes are represented in the same line. A graph of Process ID data is straight unless it represents data from more than one process.

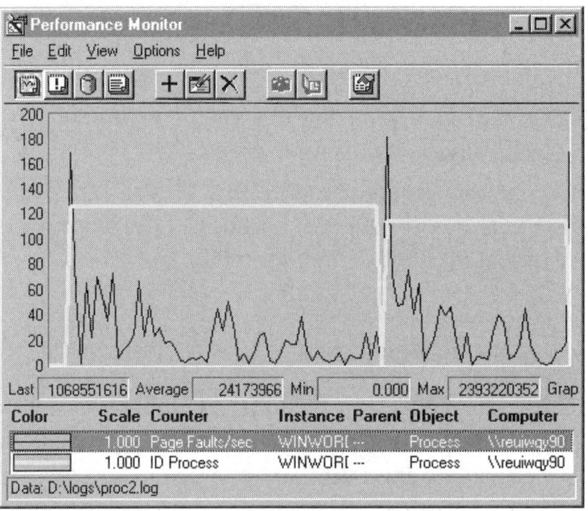

The thin line, representing page fault rates for the Microsoft Word process, Winword.exe, has two large spikes of unusually high values, as reflected in the status bar. These spikes don't represent page faults; they happen when processes with the same name stop and start.

Performance Monitor counters that measure rates/second or percentages actually display the change in value of an ever increasing internal counter associated with each object. When a process stops, the internal counter drops to zero and the change, as reported to Performance Monitor, is the absolute value of the largest long integer the computer's memory holds. Performance Monitor politely displays a zero.

However, when a new process starts, the difference between this huge number and the new thread value is displayed, causing the high value. The next value, the average of the last two, falls back to a more reasonable number.

The high values are not valid, nor are averages that include them. You can use the Performance Monitor Time Window, described later in this chapter, to exclude them from your sample. The remaining data is valid, but you might want to separate the data for the first process from data for the second process.

Monitoring Threads

Threads don't have names. They have thread numbers and Thread IDs. Performance Monitor collects and displays data on threads by process name and thread number. The thread number just indicates the order in which the threads started, beginning with 0. When a thread stops, the thread numbers of all of the threads behind it move up. For example, if a process has two threads, numbered 0 and 1, and thread 0 stops, thread 1 becomes thread 0. If Performance Monitor is watching, the counts for thread 0 now include data from both the old thread 0 and the new one.

Note Do not confuse the terms used to identify threads and processes. Here are some descriptions to help you distinguish among them.

- *Thread number* is an ordinal number assigned to threads in a process to show the order in which the thread started. A thread's thread number changes when threads with lower numbers stop, because the thread number of all later threads move up to fill in the gap.
- *Thread ID* is also an ordinal number which has no intrinsic association with a thread, but it remains with a started thread until it stops.
- *Process ID*, like Thread ID, is an ordinal number which has no intrinsic association with a process, but it is assigned to the process when it starts and remains with it until it stops. When the process starts again, it is just as likely to be assigned a different number.

That is what happened when data for this graph was collected.

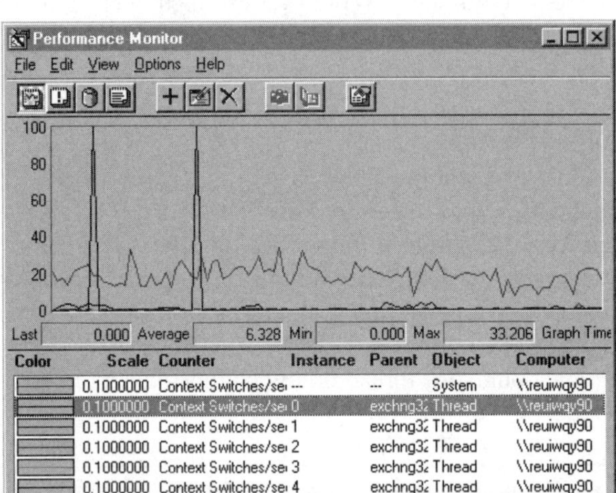

The spikes are a warning that the context switching rates shown for the threads might be invalid. This graph also includes the system-level counter for context switches, which runs at an average of about 200 context switches per second. Since the values in the spikes of Thread #4 are higher than system totals, it is clear that the high values represent threads starting and stopping, not context switches.

A graph of Thread ID confirms this guess. Thread ID, like Process ID (but unlike thread number), is assigned to the thread by the operating system and remains with it until it stops running.

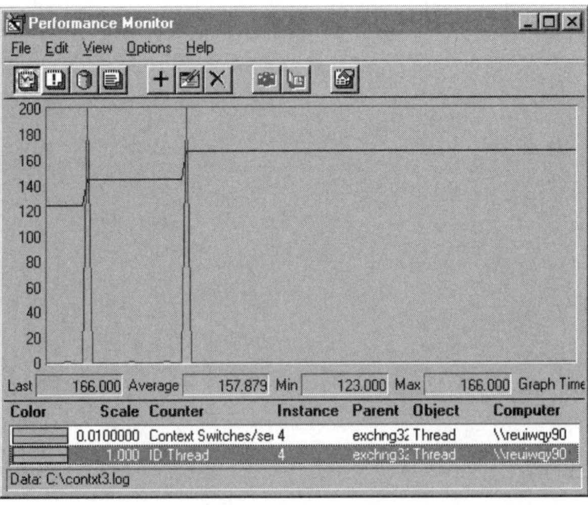

Each spike in the context switch graph coincides with a change in the thread ID. Thread 123 is the first thread identified to Performance Monitor as Thread #4. When it stops, data from Thread 143, which used to be Thread #5, is now collected as Thread 4. When Thread 143 stops, Thread 166, formerly Thread #5, now becomes thread #4.

These characteristic spikes are sufficient warning that some data is invalid, but they don't always appear. The following figure shows a different view of the same process.

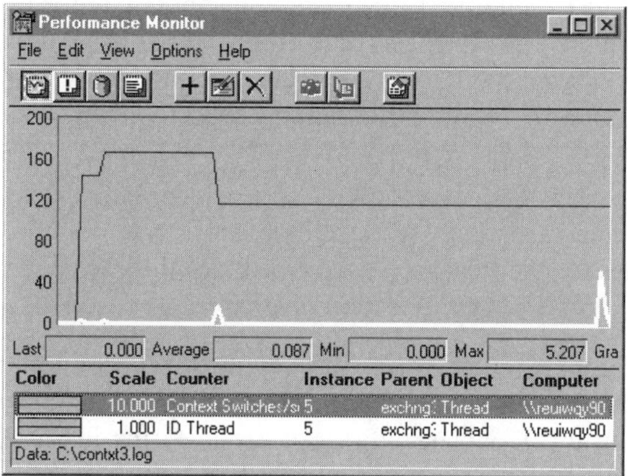

This is a graph of Thread ID and context switches for Thread #5 of the same process. In this case, the Thread IDs change, indicating that data from more than one thread is combined. However, there are no large spikes, even though the values are multiplied by 10, because none of the threads stopped while they were being monitored.

Each time the thread in Thread #4 stops, the fifth thread becomes Thread #4 and Thread #5 inherits a thread from Thread #6. The little peaks show the difference in the values of two running threads.

Although there are no spikes, data from this graph should still be distinguished by Thread ID and the data surrounding the thread transitions should be discarded. For more information on selecting data, see "The Time Window" later in this chapter.

Using Extensible Counters

Extensible counters are Performance Monitor counters that don't come with Windows NT. They come with other applications you run on Windows NT, or you can build them yourself with help from the Windows NT Software Developer's Kit. Extensible counters are usually installed when you install the product, but you might need to install them separately. For more information, consult the manuals that come with the product.

Tip Extensible Counter List (Exctrlst.exe), a tool on the Windows NT Resource Kit 4.0 CD in the Performance Tools group (\PerfTool\CntrTool), lists the extensible counters installed on a computer. It can be used on the local or a remote computer. For more information, see Rktools.hlp.

The Windows NT Resource Kit 4.0 CD provides some extensible counters that must be installed separately (for example, those that monitor Pentium processors). The help files for the Resource Kit CD, Rktools.hlp, explain how to install them, and the "Pentium Counters" section of Chapter 11 describes some common uses.

Regardless of their source, extensible counters must be monitored carefully. Damaged data buffers could damage the operating system. If you use extensible counters, consult "Troubleshooting Features," earlier in this chapter.

The Time Window

The *Time Window* lets you view selected portions of data from your log. When you change the Time Window interval, Performance Monitor recalculates all values, including minimum, maximum, and average values to match the selected time interval. The **Time Window** command on the **Edit** menu is activated when you are working with data from a log. It is available in all four views and the time selected applies to all views.

The Time Window is essential to viewing computers, processes, and threads that are started when the log is already in progress. When you graph data from a log, only those objects active when the log starts are visible. To see data on objects started later, you must advance the Time Window to a time when the object was active. After you select counters for the object, you can re-expand the Time Window to see the whole log.

The Time Window interface simplifies the process. When you click **Time Window** on the **Edit** menu, the Input Log File Timeframe dialog box appears. Unfortunately, it appears right on top of your graph. Move it to the side so you can see both the graph and the dialog box.

When you move the left and right slider tabs on the slider bar, gray vertical lines appear on the graph to show you which part of the data occurred at that time. You can click and drag the slider tabs with your mouse or use the arrow keys for more precise control.

The arrow keys work like this:

←	Moves begin time bar ←
Shift + ←	Moves end time bar ←
→	Moves end time bar →
Shift →	Moves begin time bar →

After you have the slider tabs set to a certain time interval, for example, one minute, you can click the space between the tabs and drag the one-minute interval across the graph.

Among its other functions, the Time Window lets you

- Limit your view of a log file to 100 points or less so no data is lost.
- Monitor objects that started during logging.
- Eliminate invalid data.
- Limit your charts and reports to specific events.
- Coordinate two copies of Performance Monitor so that they are reporting on the same data.

This section explains how to use the Time Window for precise control of Performance Monitor logs.

Recovering Lost Data Points

Charts and reports of log files are limited to 100 data points. If more data points are collected, the data is compressed to 100 points. For example, if 1000 data points are collected, Performance Monitor displays every 10th point. This loss of precision is most important when you are charting instantaneous counters.

You can narrow the Time Window to make all data points for that portion of the data visible, and then view the remainder of the data separately or in another copy of Performance Monitor.

Tip Set the slider bar tabs to 100 data points, then click the space on the slider bar between the tabs and drag the 100-point interval to surround the parts of the graph you want to examine in more detail.

The following figure shows the Time Window being adjusted on a chart of the instantaneous counter System: Processor Queue Length. More than 100 data points were recorded, so the data is compressed. The Time Window lines bracket the one section of the curve.

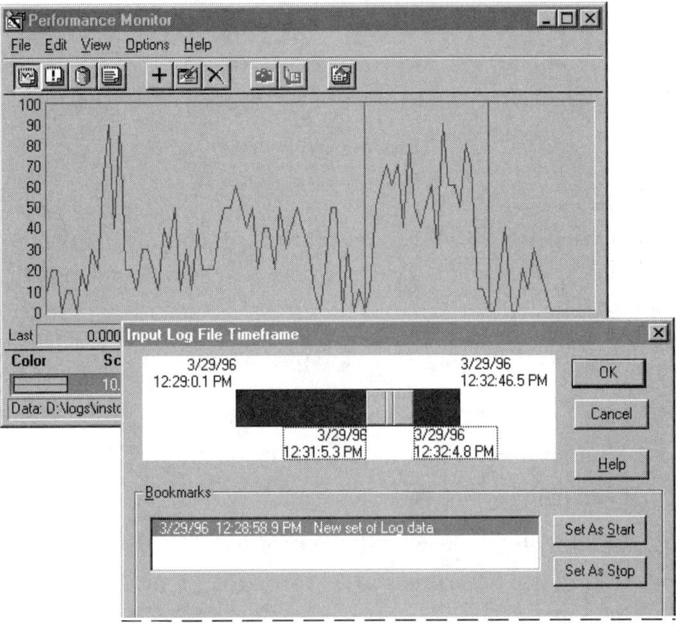

The following figure shows the graph that results when you narrow the Time Window to just a portion of the data. Here all of the data points in this part of the curve are visible, revealing more detail.

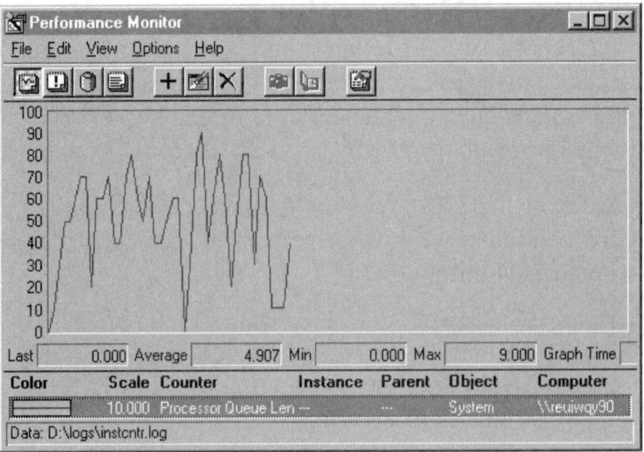

Monitoring Objects that Start During Logging

Only active objects appear in the Instances box of Performance Monitor counters. In logged data, objects that weren't active when the log started do not appear in the Instances box until the Time Window is adjusted. In order for the object to appear as an instance, you must adjust the Time Window interval to start after the object is started. After you have selected counters for the instance, you can expand the Time Window to show the whole log, and the instance remains monitored.

Note When monitoring threads that start and stop as the process proceeds, it is important to use the Time Window to search through the data for thread starts. Do not assume that all threads are apparent at the start of the process. After you have set at least one counter for each thread, you can expand the Time Window to show all of them.

For example, when you chart data from a log that includes the start of an process, the process does not appear in the Instances box if the Time Window interval begins before the process starts, even if the Time Window interval includes the start. When you adjust the Time Window interval to begin when the process is active, you can monitor it.

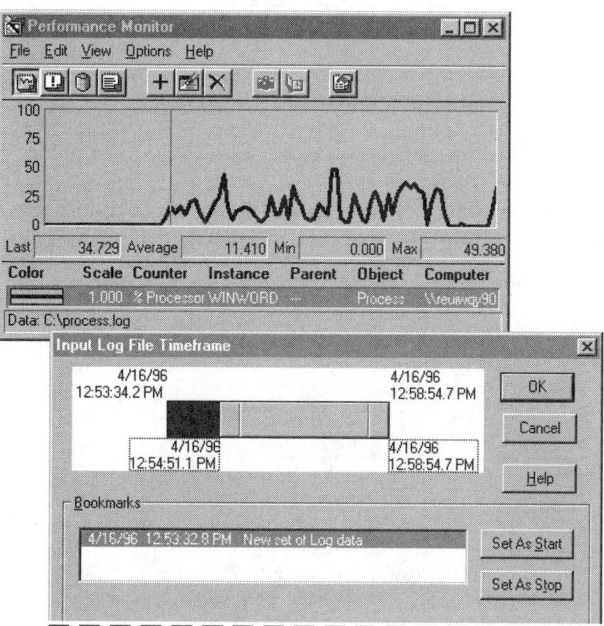

In this figure, the Time Window is adjusted to begin after the process starts so additional counters can be added. After the new counters are added, the Time Window can be expanded again.

Eliminating Invalid Data

You can use the Time Window to eliminate invalid or unwanted data from a sample. Simply set the Time Window interval to include only the data you want in your sample. All Performance Monitor statistics are recalculated to include only the data within the Time Window interval, including the data shown in averages, reports, and histograms.

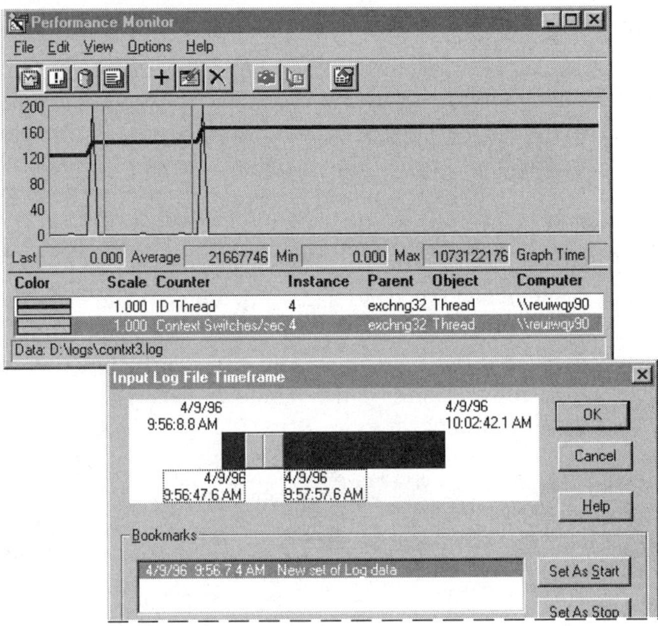

In this example, data is being limited to an interval during which a single thread is active. The resulting graph, below, shows that the data spikes that skewed the previous averages are eliminated.

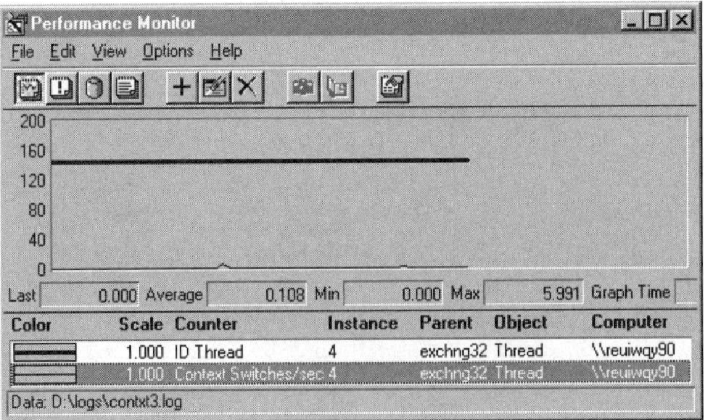

Precision Graphing

The Time Window lets you limit your reports to the most significant parts of the event. For example, when reporting on averages, it is vital to exclude startup and shutdown values which might skew the averages.

The following combined graph and report represent data logged before, during, and after a test. Notice the values shown in the report and then compare them to the values shown in the report section of the next figure.

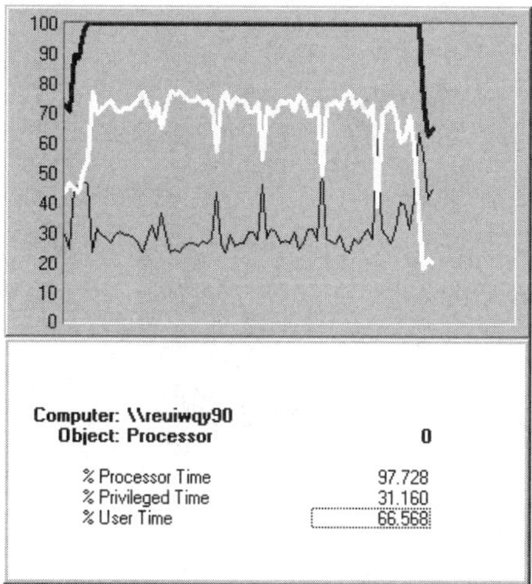

The following graph and report of the same event is limited to the test period. It was created by setting the Time Window to exclude the period before and after the test.

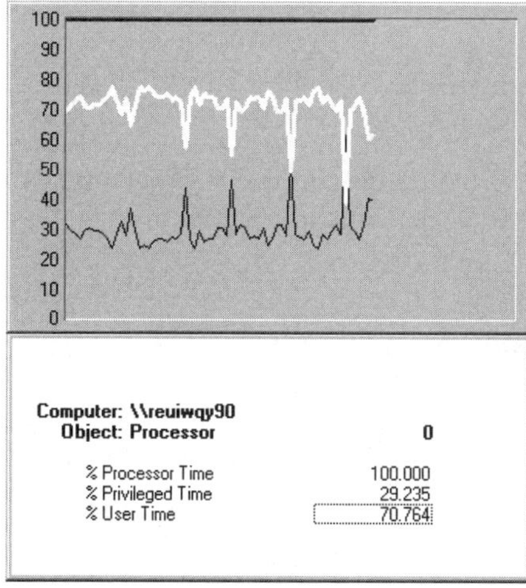

Coordinate Multiple Performance Monitors

The preceding figures were created by using two copies of Performance Monitor reading data from the same logfile. (To open a second copy of Performance Monitor, just double-click the Performance Monitor icon again.)

The Time Window helps to assure that the two copies are reporting on the same data. Arrange the windows on the screen so that they don't overlap. Click the **Time Window** menu option on each, then move the slider bars so that both copies reflect the same input data. Use the arrow keys for more precise control of the slider bar.

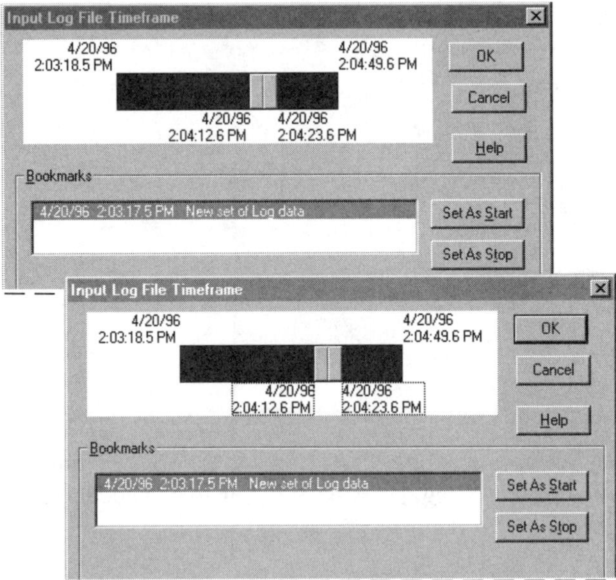

This figure shows the Input Log file Timeframe dialogs of two copies of Performance Monitor being coordinated.

Use the Time Window and other features of Performance Monitor to get the views you need and the precision you demand.

Hot Keys

The following list contains the hot keys for Performance Monitor functions:

Hot Key	Function
←AND→	Expand and contract the Time Window one data point at a time.
BACKSPACE or CTRL+H	Highlight current selection in legend.
CTRL+A	Switch to Alert view.
CTRL+B	Create bookmark.
CTRL+C	Switch to Chart view.
CTRL+E	Open Time Window.
CTRL+G	Display or hide legend.
CTRL+L	Switch to Log view.
CTRL+M	Display or hide menu and title bars.
CTRL+O	Open **Options** dialog box.
CTRL+P	Always on top.
CTRL+R	Switch to Report view.
CTRL+S	Display or hide status line.
CTRL+T	Display or hide toolbar.
CTRL+U	Manual update now.
CTRL+W	Save workspace.
F1	Help.
F12	Save settings As.
SHIFT+F12	Save settings.
CTRL+F12	Open file.
TAB or CTRL+I	Add counter to (Chart, Alert, Log, or Report).

Tips and Tricks

You might find the following Performance Monitor tips helpful. They are collected here for ease of reference.

- **Check memory first**

  Lack of memory is by far the most common cause of serious performance problems in computer systems. If you suspect other problems, check Memory: Pages/sec to make sure a memory shortage is not appearing in another guise.

- **Logging data**

  You can log data to only one log file with each copy of Performance Monitor. To log different objects to different files, open a second copy of Performance Monitor.

- **Peeking at a log file**

  Opening a log that is collecting data will stop the log and clear all counter settings. You can't peek at the log from chart or report view because the views share the same data source. Changing **data from** affects all views, even the running log.

  To peek at a running log, start a second copy of Performance Monitor, and set **data from** to the running log. You can chart or report on all data logged until the time you open it. Newly collected data will not be added to your snapshot of the log file.

- **Monitoring the start of a process - current activity**

  Processes and threads don't appear in Add to Chart as instances until they are started. To monitor the startup of a process or thread, start the process, select its instance in Add to Chart, and add whatever counters you will use to monitor the startup behavior. Now, stop the process. Its counters remain on the chart and Performance Monitor continues to look for it. Start the process again. Performance Monitor recognizes any application with the same name and begins monitoring immediately.

- **Monitoring the start of a process - logfile data**

  Processes and threads appear in the Instances box only if the Time Window includes the time the process was active. To monitor the logged activity of a process as it starts, move the Time Window to include the active phase of the process, add the instance, then expand the Time Window.

- **Delay in monitoring**

  When you add a counter to a chart, you will notice a slight delay before the chart begins to draw. The averaging counters need two data points for their first value. The chart should begin after the second data point is measured.

- **Responding to alerts**

  Do not start a command-line batch file from the **Alert** dialog box. (The > and < signs passed to the batch file will be interpreted improperly as a redirection of stdin and stdout.) Instead, create a one-line batch file that runs the program, and call the batch file from Performance Monitor.

- **Performance Monitor overhead**

  To determine how much disk space is consumed by each Performance Monitor log update interval, choose **Manual Update** from the log options. Take a series of snapshots and note the change in the log file size between each snapshot. The log file size is displayed on the status bar in Log view.

  Discard the first value (because it includes an index record that makes it larger than usual), and average the other values. Performance Monitor writes an index record with counter names on the first snapshot and then every 100th snapshot thereafter.

  You can also measure the cost of monitoring particular objects by recording the change in file size while adding and deleting those objects from a chart.

  You can also monitor the Performance Monitor process by using Task Manager, PMON or PViewer, and vice versa.

- **Finding missing data**

  Logged data is displayed over 100 data points, whether shown in a chart, histogram, or report format. If the log file contains fewer than 100 data points, all are displayed. However, if it contains more, the data is compressed to show 100 points. For example, if there are 1000 data points, every 10th point is displayed. To see missing data points, shrink the Time Window until all data is displayed.

  Exporting the data will also uncover the missing data points. When you export, Performance Monitor sends all data whether it appears in the graph or not.

- **Performance Monitor settings**

  The quickest way to open Performance Monitor with a settings file is to create a shortcut to the settings file and then double-click it.

  To change the settings quickly, drag the icon of a settings file to a running copy of Performance Monitor. Remember, though, if your settings file includes a log file, starting a second instance of Performance Monitor with the same settings will stop any active logging to that file by other Performance Monitor instances. Only one Performance Monitor can write to the log file at a time.

  You can also edit the settings file using the Setedit utility on the Windows NT Resource Kit CD-ROM.

- **Default settings file**

  If you don't start Performance Monitor with a settings file, it searches for the chart file, _Default.pmc. If it does not find it, it opens a blank Performance Monitor window. You can name your favorite settings file _Default.pmc, and it will load whenever you open a blank copy.

- **Monitoring disks**

  When testing disk performance, log Performance Monitor data to another disk or computer so that it does not interfere with the disk you are testing.

  When using Response Probe to test disk performance, set the FILEACCESSMODE parameter in the Thread Description file (*.scr) to UNBUFFERED. This tells the system to bypass the cache and go directly to disk. When using UNBUFFERED, remember that the number of bytes in RECORDSIZE must be a multiple of the disk sector size.

- **Interpreting zero values**

  Performance Monitor displays a value of zero when it fails to get data it requests and when it receives unreadable or meaningless data. It is hard to distinguish this error default value from actual values of zero. However, you can configure Performance Monitor to log errors to the Event Viewer application event log. For more information, see the section titled "Troubleshooting Performance Monitor."

- **Tiny footprint**

  You can minimize the Performance Monitor display to keep it handy without cluttering up your work. This is a great way to monitor an application while using it. Use the **Options** menu to remove the Toolbar, Status Bar, Vertical Labels and Legend, if you wish. Select the **Always on Top** option. Then shrink the window. Use hot keys to control the window, or double-click to display the title bar. You can save this setting and place it in your Startup group.

- **Controlling the Time Window**

  Use the left and right arrow keys to shrink and expand the Time Window in the Input Log Timeframe dialog. This lets you change the Time Window one data point at a time. The left arrow key controls the left button on the slider bar, and the right arrow key controls the right button. Press the arrow key alone to expand the time measured, or press SHIFT+arrow key to contract it.

Troubleshooting Performance Monitor

Here are the answers to some frequently asked questions, along with possible causes and suggested solutions.

Counter value is zero.

The counter for the same instance of the object already appears in the graph. When a duplicate counter is chosen, all data collected is displayed for the first copy.	You cannot have more than one copy of the same counter for the same instance of the same object. Delete one of copies.
The remote computer you are monitoring is offline.	No action required. Performance Monitor continues trying to monitor the instance and will find it when the computer is restarted.
The application or thread you are monitoring has stopped.	No action required. Performance Monitor continues trying to monitor the instance and will find it when the process or thread is restarted.
When an internal counter from which Performance Monitor collects data returns a negative or invalid value, Performance Monitor displays a zero.	Enable Performance Monitor event logging. Performance Monitor will then report any negative or invalid values to the Event Viewer application event log. For more information, see "Logging Performance Monitor Errors."

The counter value in my report is different than the value of the same counter in my graph.

You are reporting on an instantaneous counter value that decreases to zero at the end of the graph. Reports of instantaneous counters display the last value collected. Reports of averaged counters display the average of collected values.	In Log view, use the Time Window to change the end time on the graph to a more representative part of the curve. If you need to see more than just the end value in report form, export the graph to a spreadsheet.
Charts and reports of logged data sometimes collect different samples of the same data.	This sampling variance usually is less than 0.1, which is close to the resolution limit of the counters.
Averages of data for the Hit% counters on the Cache object are calculated differently in charts than in reports. Data for value bar in Chart view is calculated by averaging all changes during the test interval. The value displayed in Report view is the average of the difference between first and last counter values during the test interval.	

I had an application running while I was logging data, but when I graph data from the log, the application does not appear in the Instances box.

Applications that are not active when the log starts don't appear in the Instances box until you adjust the Time Window interval, even if the interval displayed includes the start time.

Use the Time Window to advance the beginning of the measured interval to a point when the application was active. Select at least one counter for the application. Now, use the Time Window to expand the interval so you can see all logged data. The application will continue to be monitored and all data will be accurate.

My log stopped when I tried to chart a different log.

The **Data From** option applies to all views. When you switch to Chart view and change the data source from current activity to a log file, the log no longer can collect data about current activity.

You can start a second copy of Performance Monitor and chart from a closed log file. However, you cannot chart a log file while it is collecting data.

All values for my disks are zero, but I know they are active.

The counters for the Physical and Logical Disk objects don't work until you install the Disk Performance Statistics Driver in your I/O Manager disk stack.

Use the Diskperf utility to install the Disk Performance Statistics Driver, then restart the computer and try again. For information about Diskperf, see "Enabling the Disk Counters" in Chapter 6, or see Performance Monitor Help.

I have several disks, but values are only shown for the first disk in the set.

When you ran Diskperf, you used the standard option, **diskperf -y**, which places the statistics collector above the fault tolerant driver, FTDISK. The statistics collector cannot see the different physical instances of the disk.

Run Diskperf using the **diskperf -ye** option, then restart the computer. This places the statistics collector below the fault tolerant driver so it can see physical disks before they are combined into a volume set.

How do I figure out which line represents which item in the graph?

Graphs can get busy. Use the highlight feature to help you.

Press the backspace key to highlight the graph line or bar corresponding to the counter selected in the legend. As you scroll through the legend, the highlight moves to the corresponding line or bar in the graph.

Where is Performance Monitor? I started it, but cannot find it.

Performance Monitor starts in the same condition it was in when you closed it. If you closed it while it was minimized, it comes up the same way. If your taskbar is hidden, it is hard to find it.

Point to the taskbar area to make it reappear, then click the Performance Monitor icon on the taskbar to start it.

Performance Monitor won't let me set an alert for an instance of a counter even though it appears in the Instances box.

You can set an alert only on the first instance of an object with a given name. If you have multiple instances with the same name, all instances will appear in the Instances box for the counter, but only data collected from the first instance will trigger an alert.

This applies only to alerts. You can chart, report, and log multiple instances with the same name.

I set two alerts, each for different values of the same counter for the same instance. Although both thresholds were exceeded, Performance Monitor reported alerts on only one.

You cannot set more than one alert on a counter for the same instance of an object. Data collected for that instance is compared only to the alert that was set first.

Explain button is grayed out.

Explanatory text is not available when you are working with data from a log file.

To see the Explanatory text for a counter, open a second copy of Performance Monitor with the Data From field set to current activity.

Start Log button is grayed out.

At least one object must be selected for logging to enable the Start Log button.

Select at least one object to be logged, and try again.

%Disk Read Time and %Disk Write Time don't sum to %Disk Time

All disk counters include time in the queue. When the queue gets long, the read and write time both include that time and don't sum to 100.

%Disk Read Time:_Total and %Disk Write Time_Total sum to more than 100% because you have more than one instance of the physical or logical disk.

The percentage counters are limited, by definition to 100% and cannot display higher values. Use the Avg. Disk Read Queue Length, Avg. Disk Write Queue Length, and Avg. Disk Queue Length counters instead. These report on the same data as the %Disk Time counters, but display the values in decimals that can exceed 1.0.

Why is there a _Total instance on the ID counters? What would a total ID Thread counter show?

Items in the Instances box are the same for all counters of an object.

When an instance has no meaning, as in the case of _Total for IDs, a zero value is displayed for the counter.

Process: Pool Nonpaged Bytes:_Total does not equal Memory: Pool Nonpaged Bytes

The Memory: Pool Nonpaged Bytes value comes from an internal counter that counts each byte. The Process: Pool Nonpaged Bytes counters are estimates from the Object Manager. The Object Manager counts accesses, not space, so its counts include requests to duplicate object handles as well as space for the object.

Ignore the static value of the counters and, instead, monitor any changes in the values.

Unfortunately, all tools use the same counters, so Performance Monitor, Task Manager, Process Explode, Process Viewer, and Process Monitor are limited to the same resolution.

Where is the Processor Queue Length Counter?

It is a System object counter. There is just one processor queue for all processors.

Counter values for instances of an object are greater than those for the total.	
The %Disk Time and %Processor Time counters are limited, by definition, to 100%. If you have multiple disks or processors, each could equal 100%, but the total counter cannot display the sum.	Monitor the physical instances separately. For disks, use the Avg. Disk Queue Length counters instead of the %Disk Time counters. These display the totals as decimal, not percentages, so they can exceed 1.0. For processors, use the System: %Total Processor Time counter. This averages the active time of each processor over all processors.
Values during spikes in the data are not included in the totals. Data spikes sometimes appear when threads and processes stop and start. They are artifacts of monitoring, not valid data.	Add the Process ID and Thread ID counters to your chart and use the Time Window to limit the data displayed a single instance of the process or thread. For details, see "Monitoring Processes and Threads" in this chapter.

CHAPTER 11

Performance Monitoring Tools

A collection of general purpose monitoring tools is available to augment and complement Performance Monitor. This chapter describes them.

Tool	Location
Task Manager	Integrated into Windows NT 4.0 Workstation and Server
Performance Data Log Service (PerfLog)	Resource Kit \PerfTool\MeasTool
Pentium Counters	Resource Kit \PerfTool\P5Ctrs
Process Monitor (PMON)	Resource Kit \PerfTool\MeasTool and \Computer Diagnostics
Process Explode (PView)	Resource Kit \PerfTool\MeasTool and \Computer Diagnostics
Process Viewer (PViewer)	Resource Kit \PerfTool\MeasTool and Computer Diagnostics
The SC Utility	Resource Kit \Computer Configuration
Data Logging Service	Resource Kit \PerfTool\MeasTool\ Datalog.exe and Monitor.exe
Microsoft Test	Microsoft product purchased separately
Response Probe	Resource Kit \PerfTool\Probe

This is not intended to be a complete list of performance monitoring tools. For more information about the tools on the Windows NT Resource Kit 4.0 CD, see the Alphabetical List of Tools in Rktools.hlp.

In addition to the general purpose tools described in this section, more specific tools are discussed throughout the book. They are listed here for reference only.

Tool	Description	Location	Chapter reference
Start	Starts a process and lets you set its properties, including priority, and whether it runs in a separate or shared memory space.	Included in Windows NT	Ch. 9, "The Art of Performance Monitoring" *Running Win16 Applications in a Separate Process* Ch. 13, "Detecting Processor Bottlenecks" *Measuring and Tuning Priorities*
Extensible Counter List	Lists installed Performance Monitor counters that did not come with Windows NT.	Resource Kit \PerfTool\CntrTool \Exctrlst.exe	Ch. 10, "About Performance Monitor" *Troubleshooting Features*
CreateFile	Creates a zero-filled file of a size you specify	Resource Kit \PerfTool\Probe \Creatfil.exe	Ch. 11, "Performance Monitoring Tools" *Creating Simulated Files*
Clearmem	Allocates all available memory, then releases it.	Resource Kit \PerfTool\MeasTool \Clearmem.exe	Ch. 12, "Detecting Memory Bottlenecks" *Determining the Minimum Working Set*
Page Fault Monitor (PFMON)	Produces a detailed report on all hard and soft page faults for a process	Resource Kit \PerfTool\MeasTool \Pfmon.exe	Ch. 12, "Detecting Memory Bottlenecks" *Examining Your Applications*
Working Set Tuner	Analyzes the patterns of function calls in your application code and recommends an organization that consumes the least possible physical memory.	Win32 Software Development Kit	Ch. 12, "Detecting Memory Bottlenecks" *Examining Your Applications*

Tool	Description	Location	Chapter reference
LeakyApp	Allocates all available memory to its process and retains it until it is stopped.	Resource Kit \PerfTool\MeasTool \leakyapp.exe	Ch. 12, "Detecting Memory Bottlenecks" *Examining Your Applications*
CPU Stress	Creates a single-threaded or multithreaded process using processor time. Users choose the number of threads and set the priorities of the process and its threads, the threads' activity level.	Resource Kit \Perftool\Meastool \CpuStres.exe	Ch. 13, "Detecting Processor Bottlenecks"
TotlProc	Installs a counter for measuring processor time on applications launched by the system interrupt.	Resource Kit \PerfTool\TotlProc \TotlProc.exe	Ch. 13, "Detecting Processor Bottlenecks" *Processor Sampling*
Performance Meter	Lists current statistics on the file system cache.	Resource Kit \PerfTool\MeasTool \Perfmtr.exe	Ch. 15, Detecting Cache Bottlenecks"

Note The tools on the Windows NT Resource Kit 4.0 CD are not supported. Whenever possible, use Performance Monitor and Task Manager, supported tools integrated into Windows NT.

Some tools are included in more than one category, so some duplication might occur. You can delete the duplicates.

Several of these tools are included on the Windows NT Resource Kit 4.0 CD. To install them, use the Setup program on the CD. To install all tools, use the Typical Installation mode in Setup. Use Custom Installation to install just one category of tools. Some Custom Installation categories, including Performance Tools, let you install the tools selectively. In Setup, click Performance Tools, then click Change Option to select a tool from the group.

The following figure shows the Custom/Complete dialog box of the Setup program configured so that only the performance tools are installed.

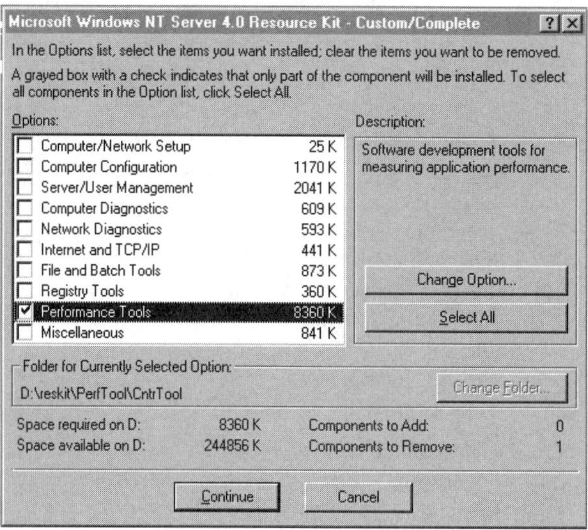

Task Manager

Task Manager is a new tool introduced with Windows NT 4.0 Server and Workstation. It lets you monitor active applications and processes on your computer, and start and stop them. Best of all, it has basic performance-monitoring capabilities and a friendly interface:

- It displays running applications and processes, including 16-bit processes.
- It displays the most commonly used performance measures for processes, including processor time, main memory size, virtual memory size, page faults, base priority and number of threads.
- It displays line graphs and instantaneous values of processor and memory use for the computer.
- It lets you set processor affinity for a process, change the base priority class of a process and activate a debugger, if you have one.

Task Manager gets its data from the same functions used by Performance Monitor. However, it calls these functions directly, bypassing the Performance Library and the registry. Thus, it cannot log data to a file and it cannot monitor remote computers. However, it is a useful tool for quick checks of basic counters and for training users to monitor their own computer.

Starting and Setting Up Task Manager

Task Manager is integrated into Windows NT 4.0 Workstation and Server and does not need to be installed separately. This section explains how to use Task Manager as a performance monitoring tool. For more general information, see Task Manager Help.

To start Task Manager, use any of these methods:

- Press CTRL+SHIFT+ESC.
- Use the right mouse button to click the Task Bar, then click Task Manager.
- Press CTRL+ALT+DELETE, then click Task Manager.

You can also start Task Manager from the command prompt or the **Run** command, and you can create a shortcut to Taskmgr.exe.

Task Manager has three tabs, but the status bar always displays the total number of processes, CPU use, and virtual memory use for the system. Note the following display possibilities:

- All Task Manager columns can be resized.
- Clicking a column sorts its entries in ascending or descending order.
- Double-clicking the window frame toggles the menu bar, tabs, and status bar on and off for a compact footprint. You can then resize the window as desired.
- Select **Always on Top** from the **Options** menu to keep the window in view as you switch between applications.
- Press CTRL+TAB to toggle between tabs.

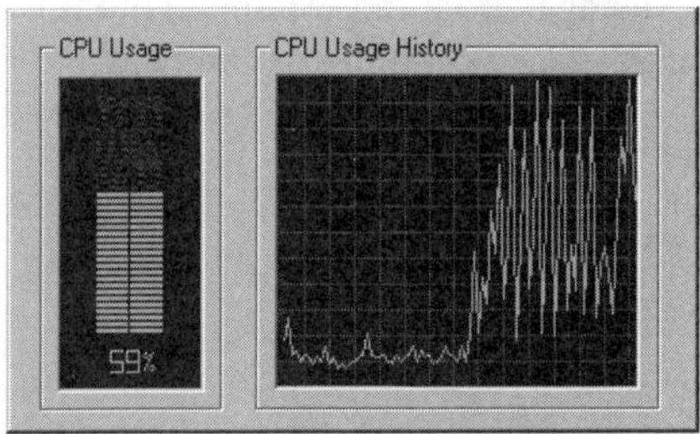

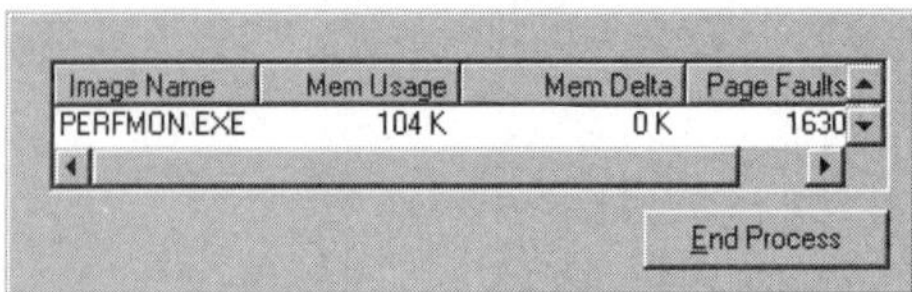

When Task Manager is running, an accurate miniature CPU usage gauge appears on the taskbar on the end opposite the **Start** button. When you touch it with the cursor, it displays the percentage of processor use in text format. The miniature gauge always matches the CPU Usage History chart on the Performance tab.

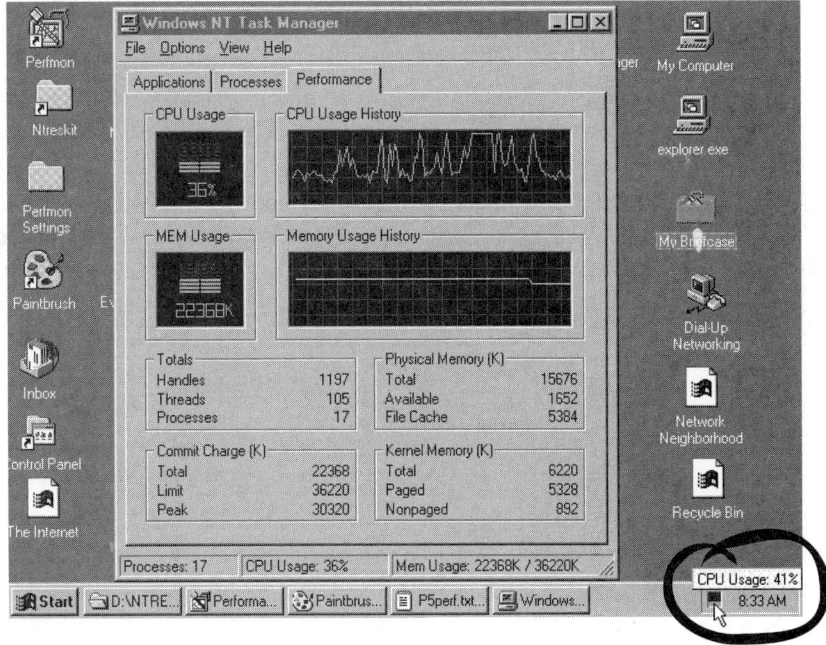

To make Task Manager the top window, double-click the gauge, or click the gauge with the right mouse button and select **Task Manager** from the menu that appears.

If you run Task Manager frequently and do not want to see its icon on your taskbar, click **Hide When Minimized** from the **Options** menu. To open a hidden Task Manager, click the Task Manager CPU gauge on the taskbar.

Monitoring Processes

Click the Task Manager Processes tab to see a list of running processes and measures of their performance. The Task Manager process table includes all processes that run in their own address space, including all applications and system services. From the **Options** menu, click **Show 16-bit Tasks** to include those in the display.

For a description of the most common system services that appear in the list, see "System Processes," in Chapter 9, "The Art of Performance Monitoring."

Note Task Manager displays its values in kilobytes, which are units of 1024 bytes. When comparing Performance Monitor and Task Manager values, multiply Task Manager values by 1024. For example, 108K bytes of memory usage for Explorer.exe, shown below, equals 110,592 bytes in Performance Monitor.

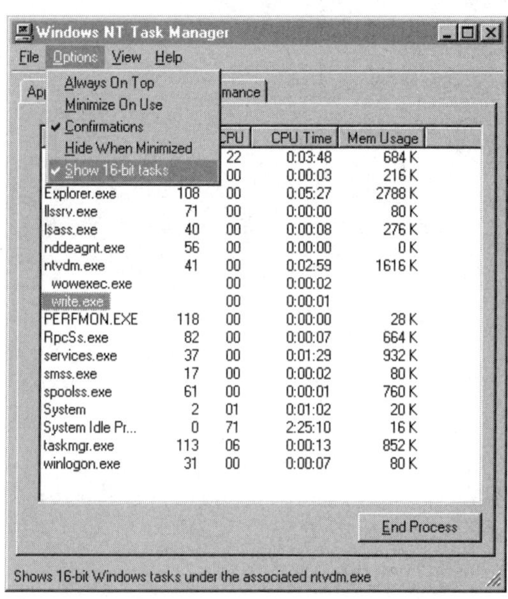

From the **View** menu, click **Select Columns** to add to or remove performance measures from the display. The following table briefly describes the measures and their Performance Monitor counterparts, if any.

Process Measure	Description	Performance Monitor Process counter
Image Name	Name of the process.	The process name in the Instances box.
PID (Process Identifier)	Numerical ID assigned to the process while it runs.	ID Process.
CPU Usage	The percentage of time the threads of the process used the processor since the last update.	%Processor Time.
CPU Time	The total processor time used by the process since it was started, in seconds.	None.
Memory Usage	The amount of main memory used by the process, in kilobytes.	Working Set.
Memory Usage Delta	The change in memory use since the last update, in kilobytes. Unlike Performance Monitor, Task Manager displays negative values.	None.
Page Faults	The number of times data had to be retrieved from disk for this process because it was not found in memory. This value is accumulated from the time the process is started.	None. Page faults/sec is the rate of page faults over time.
Page Faults Delta	The change in the number of page faults since the last update.	None.
Virtual Memory Size	Size of the process's share of the paging file, in kilobytes.	Page File Bytes.
Paged Pool	Amount of the paged pool (user memory) used by the process, in kilobytes. The paged pool is virtual memory available to be paged to disk. It includes all of user memory and a portion of system memory.	Pool Paged Bytes. (See note below.)

Process Measure	Description	Performance Monitor Process counter
Nonpaged Pool	Amount of the nonpaged pool (system memory) used by the process, in kilobytes. The nonpaged pool is operating system memory which is never paged to disk.	Pool Nonpaged Bytes. (See note below.)
Base Priority	The base priority of the process, which determines the order in which its threads are scheduled for the processor. The base priority is set by the process code, not the operating system. The operating system sets and changes the dynamic priorities of threads in the process within the range of the base. Use Task Manager to change the base priority of processes. See the next section for details.	Priority Base.
Handle Count	The number of object handles in the process's object table.	Handle Count.
Thread Count	The number of threads running in the process.	Thread Count.

Important The size of the paged and nonpaged memory pools, as shown on the Process tab, are not precise. These values are taken from internal counters which count duplicated object handles as well as space for the object. Also, they are rounded to page size, so if a process is using part of a page, its pool space is overestimated. However, they can be used to monitor *changes* in the size of the pool for a process.

The paged and nonpaged pool size for the whole system, shown on the Performance tab, are precise. Thus, the sum of values for each process might not match the count for the whole system.

Task Manager, Performance Monitor, Process Explode (Pview.exe), Process Monitor (Pmon.exe) and Process Viewer (Pviewer.exe) all use the same internal counters for monitoring the paged and nonpaged memory pools.

Changing the Base Priority Class

The *base priority class* of a process determines the range of dynamic or current priorities that the operating system can assign to the threads of that process. The base priority is usually set in the application code. You can use Task Manager to change the base priority class of a process. However, this change lasts only as long as the process runs. When the process is started again, it reverts to the original base priority class.

In a preemptible, multitasking operating system like Windows NT, the microkernel schedules threads for the processor in order of their priority and interrupts running threads if a higher priority thread appears.

You might want to increase the priority of a process, or decrease the priority of competing processes to improve their response.

Warning Changing the base priority class of a process to Real-Time can destabilize your system. A busy, Real-Time process can prevent other processes and system services from running.

To change the base priority class of a process, select the process name from the Task Manager Processes tab, click the highlighted name with the right mouse button, click Set Priority, and then select a new priority class from the Set Priority submenu.

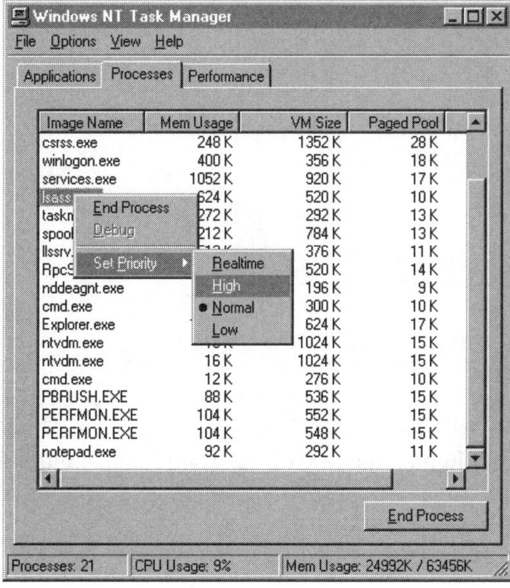

Selecting a Processor

You can use Task Manager to limit the execution of a process to one or more processors.

Note The Set Affinity option used for selecting a processor appears only on computers with more than one processor.

On multiprocessor computers, the Windows NT microkernel distributes thread-processing requests over all processors based on thread priority. Often, the threads of a single process are running on more than one processor. Windows NT uses *soft affinity* to distribute processor load. This means that when all other factors are equal, Windows NT reassigns threads to the same processor they ran on before. This takes best advantage of the processor cache. However, you can override this configuration and determine on which processors your processes run.

You might want to expedite a process by reserving a processor for it and rerouting all other processes to other processors.

To select processors for a process, click the process name in the Task Manager Processes tab, click the highlighted name with the right mouse button, click Set Affinity, and the select one or more processors from the list.

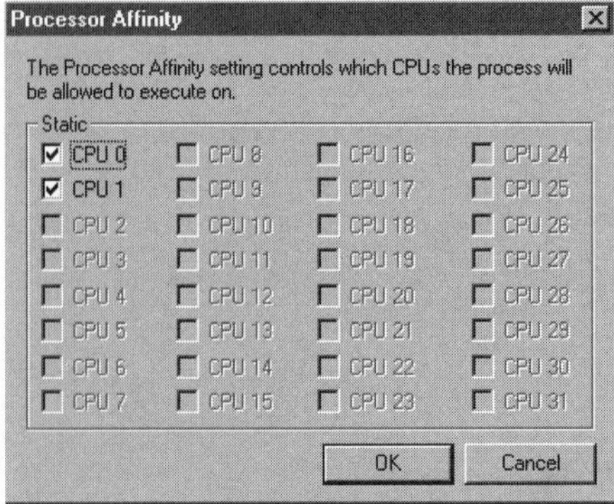

Starting your Debugger

If you have installed a debugger, you can activate the debugger on a process by using Task Manager. Click the process name in the Task Manager Processes tab. Then click the highlighted name with the right mouse button and click **Debug**.

Update Speed

You can control the rate at which Task Manager updates its counts. This will reduce Task Manager overhead, but might miss some data. You can force an update at any time by clicking **Refresh Now** on the **View** menu or by pressing F5.

Task Manager Update Speed options are:

High	Updates every half-second.
Normal	Updates once per second.
Low	Updates every four seconds.
Paused	Does not update automatically. Press F5 to update.

Monitoring the System

Click the Task Manager Performance Tab to see an dynamic overview of system performance, including a graph and numeric display of processor and memory usage.

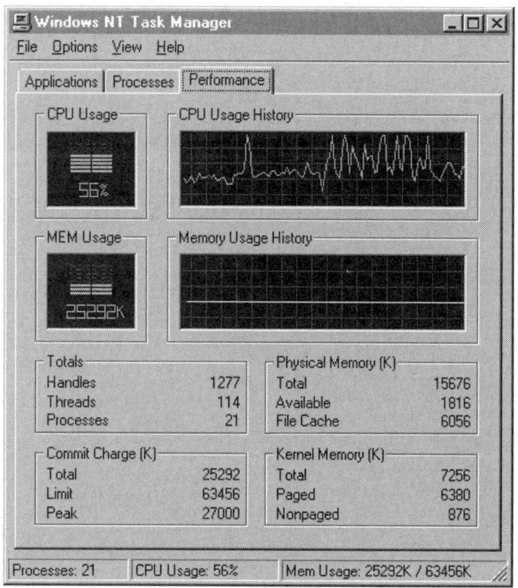

To graph the percentage of processor time in privileged or kernel mode, click **Show Kernel Times** on the **View** menu. This is a measure of the time applications are using operating system services. The remaining time, known as user mode, is spent running threads within the application code.

Users of multiple processor computers can click **CPU History** from the **View** menu and choose to graph the non-idle time of each processor in a single graph or in separate graphs.

The following table briefly describes the counts on the Performance tab and their Performance Monitor counterparts, if any.

Table 11.1 Relating Task Manager Counts to Performance Monitor Counters

Task Manager Counts	Description	Performance Monitor counters
CPU Usage	The percentage of time the processor is running a thread other than the Idle thread.	Processor: % Processor Time and System: % Total Processor Time
MEM Usage	The amount of virtual memory used, in kilobytes.	Memory: Committed bytes
Total Handles	The number of object handles in the tables of all processes.	Process: Handle Count: _Total
Total Threads	The number of running threads, including one Idle thread per processor.	Process: Thread Count: _Total
Total Processes	The number of active processes, including the Idle process.	Object: Processes is the same, but excludes the Idle process
Physical Memory: Total	Amount of physical, random access memory installed in the computer, in kilobytes.	None
Physical Memory: Available	Amount of physical memory available to processes, in kilobytes. It includes zeroed, free, and standby memory.	Memory: Available Bytes
Physical Memory: File Cache	Amount of physical memory released to the file cache on demand, in kilobytes.	Memory: Cache Bytes
Commit Charge: Total	Size of virtual memory in use by all processes, in kilobytes.	Memory: Committed Bytes

Table 11.1 Relating Task Manager Counts to Performance Monitor Counters *(Continued)*

Task Manager Counts	Description	Performance Monitor counters
Commit Charge: Limit	Amount of virtual memory, in kilobytes, that can be committed to all processes without enlarging the paging file.	Memory: Commit Limit
Commit Charge: Peak	The maximum amount of virtual memory used in the session, in kilobytes. The commit peak can exceed the commit limit if virtual memory is expanded.	None
Kernel Memory: Total	Sum of paged and non-paged kernel memory, in kilobytes. *Kernel* refers to memory available to operating system components running in highly privileged kernel mode.	None (Sum of Pool Paged Bytes and Pool Nonpaged Bytes)
Kernel Memory: Paged	Size of the paged pool allocated to the operating system, in kilobytes. The paged pool is an area of operating system memory that can be paged to disk as applications demand more memory.	Memory: Pool Paged Bytes
Kernel Memory: Nonpaged	Size of the nonpaged pool allocated to the operating system, in kilobytes. The nonpaged pool is the part of operating system memory that remains in physical memory as long as it is allocated.	Memory: Pool Nonpaged Bytes

Performance Data Log Service

Performance Data Log Service (PerfLog) is an new tool that logs data from performance counters to a tab-separated or comma-separated variable file. It lets you choose which performance counters you want to log, and it will start new log files automatically at intervals you select.

PerfLog is included on the Windows NT Resource Kit 4.0 CD in the Performance Tools group (\PerfTool\MeasTool\Perflog.exe).

PerfLog logs performance data to a comma-separated or tab-separated text file for later use as input to spreadsheets, databases, and other applications, as well as to Performance Monitor. Unlike Performance Monitor logs, which store data in a compact, multi-dimensional C-language data format, PerfLog logs can be used as direct input without reformatting.

PerfLog uses the same objects and counters as Performance Monitor, but it lets you select which counters you want to log for each instance of an object. You can also select the level of detail you need on an instance and let PerfLog select a set of counters for you.

For more information on PerfLog, see Rktools.hlp.

Pentium Counters

Intel Pentium and Pentium Pro processors have special counters that monitor the inner workings of the chip. You can see a graph of these counters by using Pperf, a tool on the Windows NT Resource Kit 4.0 CD. Better yet, you can set up the counters by using Pperf, and then use Performance Monitor to chart, log, report, or set alerts on them.

Tip The Pentium counters are extensible counters for Windows NT. You can confirm that the installation of these counters was successful and find useful information about them by using Extensible Counter List, a tool on the Windows NT 4.0 Workstation Resource Kit CD. Extensible Counter List is in the Performance Tools group in \PerfTool\Cntrtool\Exctrlst.exe. For more information, see Rktools.hlp.

▶ To use the counters

1. Install the P5Ctrs directory from the Windows NT Resource Kit 4.0 CD. It is in the Performance Tools group in \PerfTool\P5Ctrs.
2. Complete the installation of Pperf by loading new registry values, copying some files to different directories, and installing counter names and explain text for the Pentium counters in Performance Monitor. For instructions, see P5perf.txt, in the P5Ctrs subdirectory.
3. Use Pperf to activate the Pentium counters by selecting them and assigning them to registers. You activate two at a time. For instructions, see P5perf.txt, in the P5Ctrs subdirectory.

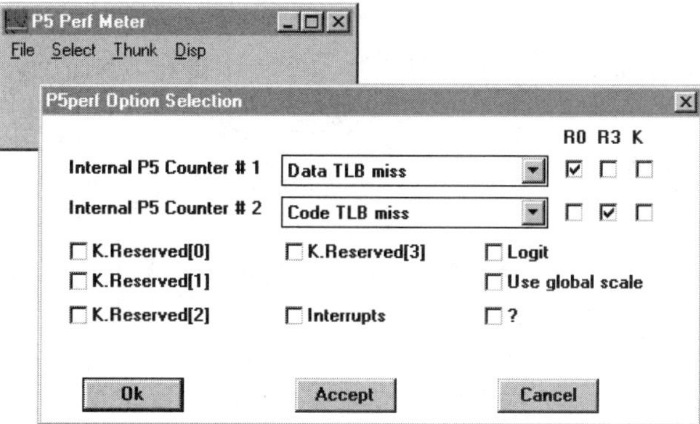

4. In Performance Monitor, select the Pentium object, then select one or both of the counters you activated with Pperf.

Note The Pentium object and the names of all Pentium counters appear in Performance Monitor when you complete the installation of Pperf. However, only the counters you activate by using Pperf will display valid values in Performance Monitor.

And, as you can with any Windows NT 4.0 application, you can create a shortcut to Pperf on your desktop.

Simple and Composite Counters

There are two types of Pentium counters: simple and composite. *Simple counters* require that one Pperf counter be activated for each Performance Monitor. C*omposite counters* require that two Pperf counters be activated for each Performance Monitor counter.

For example, to use the simple counter, FLOPs/sec, in Performance Monitor, FLOPs must be activated in Pperf. However, to use the composite counter % Data Cache Misses in Performance Monitor, both Data R/W and Data R/W Miss must be activated in Pperf.

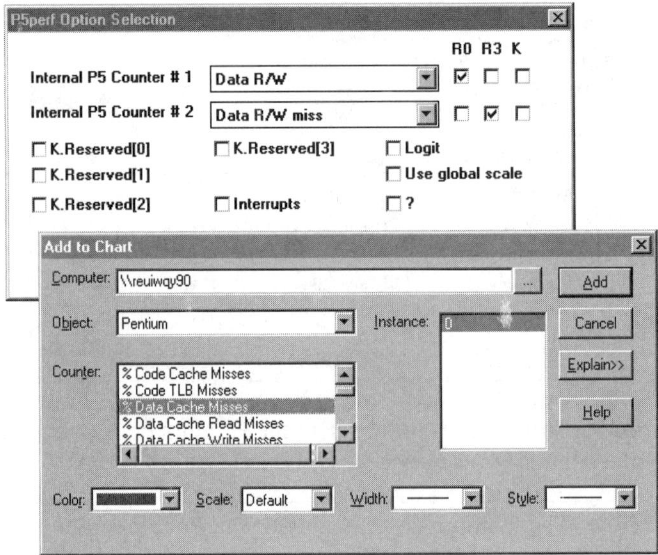

Counter Table

The following table associates the Pentium counters with the Pperf counters that activate them. Descriptions of the counters appear in the Explain text in Performance Monitor.

Pentium Counter (as seen in Performance Monitor)	Required Pperf Counters
% Branch Target Buffer Hit	Branches and BTB hits
% Branches	Instructions executed and Branches
% Code Cache Misses	Code Read and Code cache miss
% Code TLB Misses	Code Read and Code TLB miss
% Data Cache Misses	Data R/W and Data R/W miss
% Data Cache Read Misses	Data Read and Data Read miss
% Data Cache Write Misses	Data Write and Data Write miss
% Data Snoop Hits	Data cache snoops and Data cache snoop hits
% Data TLB Misses	Data R/W and Data TLB miss
% Segment Cache Hits	Segment cache accesses and Segment cache hits
% V-Pipe Instructions	Instructions executed and Instructions executed in vpipe
Bank Conflicts/sec	Bank conflicts
Branches Taken or BTB Hits/sec	Taken branch or BTB hits
Branches/sec	Branches
BTB Hits/sec	BTB hits
Bus Utilization (clks)/sec	Bus utilization (clks)
Code Cache Miss/sec	Code cache miss
Code Read/sec	Code Read
Code TLB Miss/sec	Code TLB miss
Data Cache Line WB/sec	Data Cache line WB
Data Cache Snoop Hits/sec	Data Cache snoop hits
Data Cache Snoops/sec	Data Cache snoops
Data R/W Miss/sec	Data R/W miss
Data Read Miss/sec	Data Read miss
Data Read/sec	Data Read
Data Reads & Writes/sec	Data R/W
Data TLB Miss/sec	Data TLB miss
Data Write Miss/sec	Data Write miss

Pentium Counter (as seen in Performance Monitor)	Required Pperf Counters
Data Write/sec	Data Write
Debug Register 0	Debug Register 0
Debug Register 1	Debug Register 1
Debug Register 2	Debug Register 2
Debug Register 3	Debug Register 3
FLOPs/sec	FLOPs
I/O R/W Cycle/sec	IO r/w cycle
Instructions Executed In vPipe/sec	Instructions executed in vpipe
Instructions Executed/sec	Instructions executed
Interrupts/sec	Interrupts
Locked Bus Cycle/sec	Locked bus cycle
Memory Accesses In Pipes/sec	Memory Accesses in pipes
Misaligned Data Refs/sec	Misaligned data refs
Non_Cached Memory Ref/sec	Non_cached memory ref
Pipe Stalled On Addr Gen (clks)/sec	Pipe stalled on addr gen (clks)
Pipe Stalled On Read (clks)/sec	Pipe stalled on read (clks)
Pipe Stalled On Writes (clks)/sec	Pipe stalled on writes (clks)
Pipeline Flushes/sec	Pipeline flushes
Segment Cache Accesses/sec	Segment cache accesses
Segment Cache Hits/sec	Segment cache hits
Segment Loads/sec	Segment loads
Stalled While EWBE#/sec	Stalled while EWBE#
Write Hit To M/E Line/sec	Write hit to M/E line

Process Monitor

Process Monitor (Pmon.exe) is a utility on the Windows NT Resource Kit 4.0 CD in \PerfTool\MeasTool and \Computer Diagnostics. It displays process statistics in text format in a command prompt window. The data is updated automatically every five seconds. Process Monitor requires no setup.

To start Process Monitor, at the command prompt, type **pmon**. To stop it, press Esc.

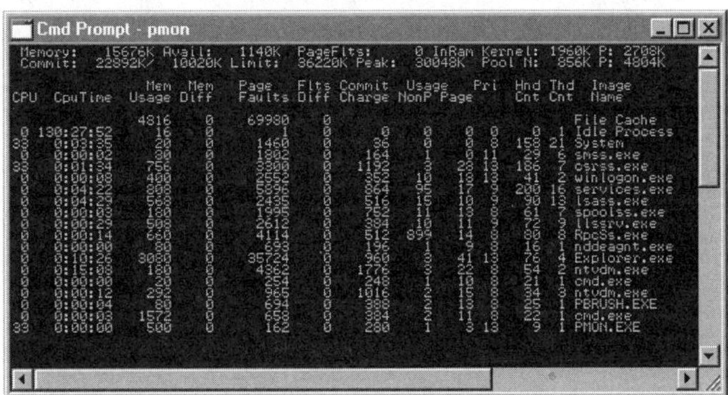

Process Explode

Process Explode (Pview.exe) is a utility on the Windows NT Resource Kit 4.0 CD in \PerfTool\MeasTool and \Computer Diagnostics. It provides a wealth of accurate and detailed information on many aspects of the system, processes, threads, and memory.

Much, but not all, of the information in Process Explode is also available in Performance Monitor, but Process Explode requires no setup. All of the information is provided in a single dialog box—a convenience once you are familiar with it and a mind-boggler until you are.

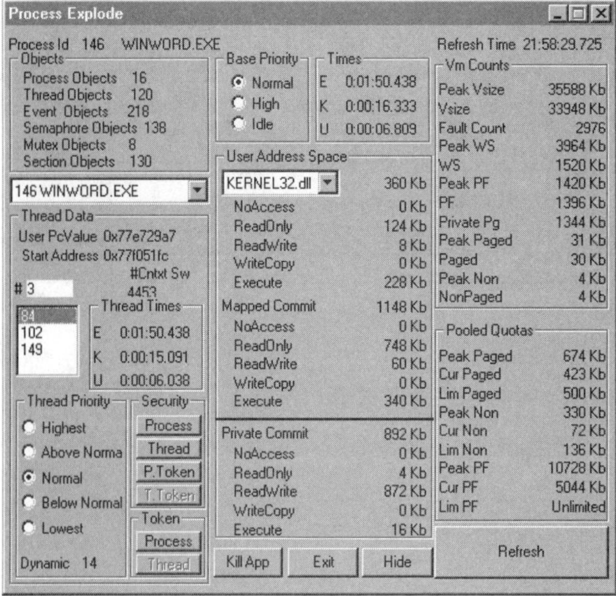

With Process Explode you can:

- See current counts of system objects.
- Change the base priority class of a process and see, but not change, the dynamic priority of its threads.
- Examine details of the process address space, with counters at the level of operating system kernel-mode DLLs.
- Examine detailed physical and virtual memory counts.
- Examine and change process, thread, and token permissions and some attributes of the security context in which a process runs.
- Stop running processes.

The Times box, at the top of the second column, shows the total elapsed time of the selected process since its start (E), as well as time elapsed in kernel mode (K) and user mode (U) processing. Thread times appear in a separate box halfway down the first column.

Process Explode is not updated automatically. Use the **Refresh** button in the lower right corner to update the data. The time of the last refresh is displayed in the upper right corner.

Note The **Hide** button, next to **Refresh**, makes the dialog box disappear, though the Pview.exe process continues to run. However, it places no icon on the Taskbar and it is unclear how to show it again once it is hidden.

Process and Thread Priority

Process Explode displays the base priority class of active processes and the dynamic priorities of active threads. You can use Process Explode to change the base priority class of processes.

Note You can see, but not change, the dynamic priorities of threads. The Process Explode Thread Priority box has clickable option buttons, but they are for display only; clicking them has no effect.

To display or change the base priority class of a process, select the process from the drop-down list in the first column. All process data in the dialog box changes to show the values for the process you selected. The base priority class of the process is displayed and can be changed in the Base Priority box at the top of the second column.

Process Explode displays three base priority classes: Idle, Normal, and High. Processes running at Real-Time priority appear in Process Explode as High. Process Explode does not let you set a process to Real-Time priority class.

To display the dynamic priority of a thread, select its process from the drop-down list in the first column. Then select the thread by its number from the list box halfway down the first column. All thread data in Process Explode changes to show values for that thread. The thread's dynamic priority is shown in the Thread Priority box at the bottom of the first column.

Process Viewer

Process Viewer (Pviewer.exe) is a utility on the Windows NT Resource Kit 4.0 CD in the Performance Tools group (\PerfTool\MeasTool). It displays information about processes on local and remote computers and is especially useful for investigating process memory use. It also lets you stop a running process and change the base priority class of the process.

Process Viewer is a subset of Process Explode, and its features work in the same way.

Note The select buttons in the Thread Priority box display the current dynamic priority of the thread. You cannot use them to change the thread priority.

It also lets you see the proportions of privileged and user processor time for each thread of the process.

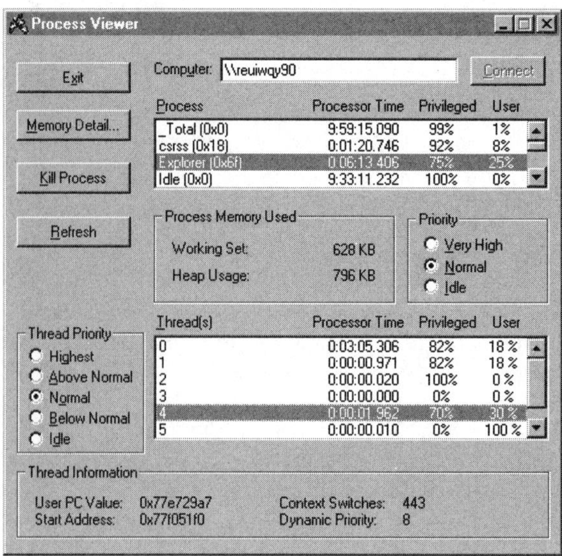

When you click a process in the process box, the whole dialog changes to show the values for that process.

To see memory detail, select a computer and a process, then click the **Memory Detail** button. The drop-down menu lets you display statistics for each item in the process address space. Note that Process Viewer is not automatically updated; use the **Refresh** button for manual updates.

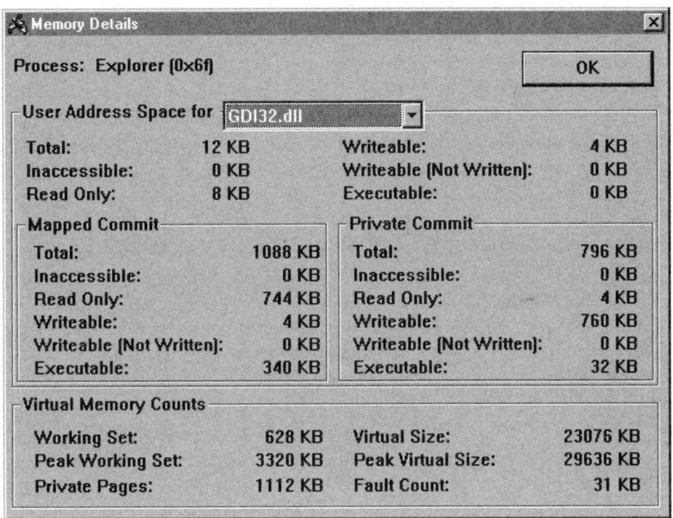

The SC Utility

The SC Utility is a command line interface for the service controller. It displays the configuration of the computer on which is it run. The SC Utility is on the Windows NT Resource Kit 4.0 CD in the Computer Configuration group. Run it from a command prompt window; it should not be started from the **Run** command on the **Start** menu.

At the command prompt, type **sc** to see a brief description of the commands. Among other things, SC lists all services and drivers on the system.

To see a listing of services, drivers, or both, type:

```
c:\> sc query
```

Or, for just services, type:

```
c:\> sc query type= service
```

Or, for just drivers, type:

```
c:\> sc query type= driver
```

For more detail on a driver or service, including the process in which it runs, type:

```
c:\> sc qc servicename
```

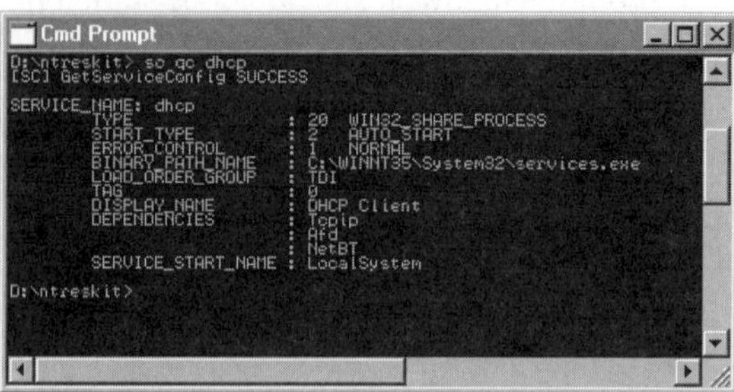

To find the display name, type:

```
c:\> sc getkeyname displayname
```

Data Logging Service

Data Logging Service is a Windows NT service that lets you log performance monitor data and alerts automatically as an unattended service. This is especially useful for logging data on a network of remote computers. The logs remain on the remote computer until you review them in Performance Monitor.

Two utilities are needed to set up Data Logging Service: Datalog.exe, the service executable, and Monitor.exe, which configures the settings file. These are included on the Windows NT Resource Kit 4.0 CD in \PerfTool\MeasTool. Instructions for using the utilities are in Rktools.hlp.

Microsoft Test

Microsoft Test is an application that lets you record a series of keystrokes and mouse movements into script files for later execution. These extended macros can then be used to manipulate any graphic user interface, including Performance Monitor.

Note Some older copies of Microsoft Test are intended for 16-bit applications. Be sure to use the 32-bit version for Performance Monitor.

Among other tasks, you can use Microsoft Test to

- Start and stop Performance Monitor at preset times, or run it on certain days of the week and change the update interval as the day progresses.
- Start multiple copies of Performance Monitor, with different settings files for each.
- Merge, relog, and batch Performance Monitor logs for long-term planning.

Response Probe

Response Probe is a utility that lets you design a simulated workload. It then uses that workload to test the performance of your hardware and software configuration. Repeated testing with a fixed, application-independent workload eliminates much of the uncertainty and doubt in performance testing. The response of your configuration is now the only independent variable in the test. When you change your configuration, you can be more confident that any changes in performance result from the new configuration.

Response Probe 2.3 is on the Windows NT Resource Kit 4.0 CD in the Performance Tools group in \PerfTool\Probe\Probe.exe. The Probe subdirectory also includes some useful sample script files and text files explaining how to use them. Response Probe 2.3 must be run from the Command Prompt window of the computer being tested. It cannot be run from the **Start** button.

This section describes Response Probe, tells you how to run it, how to interpret its output, and then explains how it really works.

What's New in Response Probe

Response Probe no longer requires that you create a simulated codepage file and enter its name in the Process Script File (*.scr). It now reads from a 1000-function internal codepage file in memory. You control the reading of the codepage function file by setting a mean and standard deviation for FUNCTION parameter in the Thread Description File (*.sct).

The *CodePageFileName* parameter has been eliminated from the Process Script file format. The CODEPAGE parameter in the Thread Description script file (*.sct) has been replaced by the FUNCTION parameter.

Note This feature was added to Response Probe 2.1 and later versions. Earlier versions of Response Probe still require the CodePageFileName and CODEPAGE parameters. To find the Response Probe version number, at the command prompt, type: **probe ?**

Using Response Probe

Response Probe is commonly used to

- Collect baseline performance statistics.
- Determine maximum throughput values.
- Model the behavior of an application or set of procedures.
- Systematically test the response of each component in your configuration to incremental changes in the workload.

The power of Response Probe is in the wide range of parameters you control and the range of values you can set for each parameter.

Response Probe tests are short and repeatable; that is, the same input will produce the same results every time. The tests can help you determine a range of expected responses for your system. Then, when you use Performance Monitor, you will be able to tell when counters are too high or too low because you know what is normal. Response Probe can help you predict how your equipment will handle workloads of various types, and determine how changes to your equipment have affected its capacity.

Workload Design

All Response Probe workloads have the same basic design. You customize a workload by setting parameters to describe its processes and threads, but you cannot alter the basic design. For more detailed information, see the section titled "How Response Probe Works," later in this chapter.

Response Probe workloads simulate a real user using a real computer. There are cycles of idle or think time, followed by some processing. The processing consists of file access followed by simulated computation that consumes processor cycles. This includes reading code page files and writing to data page files in memory. The following diagram shows a complete workload cycle:

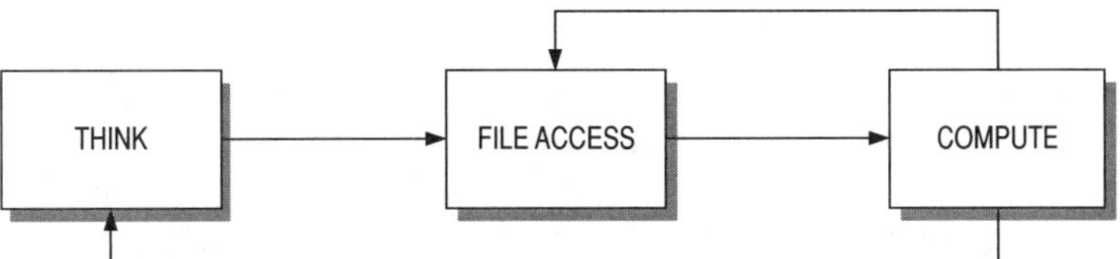

Response Probe simulates code pages and data pages. *Code pages* are pages of memory that contain the program's code. Response Probe's 1000-function internal code page file simulates a file of application program code from which instructions are read during a process. *Data pages* are memory pages that contain the data used by the program, including global program data, the stack, and heap allocations.

Understanding the Normal Distribution

You describe workloads to Response Probe, in part, by choosing a mean and standard deviation for several parameters that characterize threads in the workload. You choose a mean and standard deviation for

- Length of think times
- Number of processing cycles (file access and computing) between think times
- Length of computing times
- Position of records accessed from the workload file
- Position of pages accessed from the data page file
- Position of functions read from the code page file

The theory behind Response Probe is that real workloads are normally distributed; that is, the time spent thinking, accessing memory, reading and writing to files, finding a record in a file, computing, and other such tasks, are distributed on a standard bell-shaped curve. Alternatively, if the workloads were invariant or random, they would not simulate real use of real computers.

Note The actions of threads and processes are normally distributed, so they are not, technically, fixed. However, in repeated trials the same inputs will produce the same results.

In a bell-shaped curve, most activity is concentrated around the mean, decreasing with distance from the mean, and with the least frequency at both extremes. The standard deviation determines how much activity is concentrated near the mean and how often more distant values occur. By definition, 2/3 of all activity occurs within one standard deviation on either side of the mean, 95% is within two standard deviations, and 99% is within three standard deviations of the mean.

Usually, the midpoint is chosen as the mean, and one-third of the total (1/6 on either side of the mean) is chosen as the standard deviation.

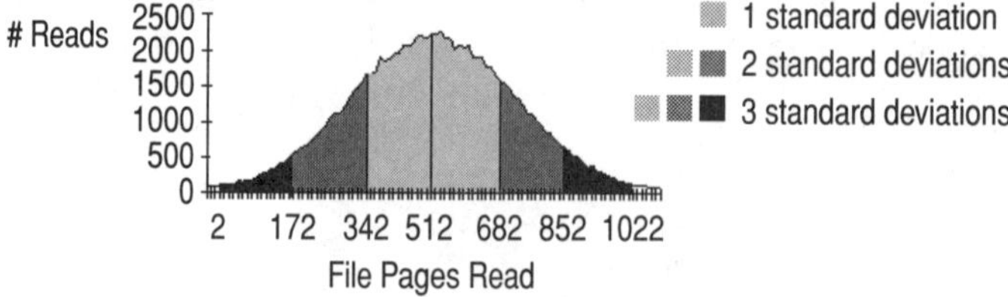

For example, in a 1024-page file, if page 512 is the mean and 170 pages is the standard deviation, then:

- 2/3 of reads will be from pages 342–682, (512-170 to 512+170).
- 95% will be from pages 172–852 (512 - (170 *2) to 512 + (170 * 2).
- 99% will be from pages 2–1022 (512 - (170 *3) to 512 + (170 * 3).

If, instead, the mean was 512 and the standard deviation was 256 (1/2 of 512), then 2/3 of reads will be from pages 256–768, and the remaining third would be equally distributed throughout the rest of the file. At the extremes, if the standard deviation is 0, page 512 is the only one read, and if the mean is equal to the standard deviation, reading is random, so all pages are equally likely to be read.

Customizing the Workload

You describe a workload to Response Probe by submitting script files and a simulated workload file. The name of the workload file is included in the script files.

Script Files

Script files are small, formatted text files you create with a text editor such as Notepad. The script files describe a simulated workload to Response Probe in terms of processes and their threads. There are three types of script files, and at least one of each type is required for each Response Probe run. Response Probe identifies the file type by its three-character file extension. You can assign any name to the files; simply add the correct file extension:

Tip You need not create the files from scratch. Use the sample files on the Windows NT Resource Kit 4.0 CD in the Probe subdirectory as a starting point.

- The Process script file (*.scr) is where you create each process in the workload. There is one Process script file for each Response Probe run.
- The Thread Definition file (*.scp) is where you create the threads that run in the processes.
- The Thread Description file (*.sct) describes the threads in each process. This is where you enter the means and standard deviations Response Probe uses to generate a normal distribution of work for each thread.

The files are closely related. Each process definition in the Process file includes the name of the file where threads for that process are defined. The definition of each thread includes the name of the file where the threads are described.

Process Script File

In the Process script file (*.scr), you create the processes that Response Probe runs. The file consists of one or more process lines, each of which creates, names, and specifies the attributes of one process.

Note Response Probe 2.0 and earlier required that you create a simulated code page file and enter its name in the Process Script file. Response Probe versions 2.1 and later include an internal 1000-function codepage file. They do not require, and will not accept, a *CodePageFileName* parameter.

By default, Response Probe tests run in a process called Probeprc.exe. You can change the process name to make it easier to distinguish among Response Probe tests in Performance Monitor. Although Performance Monitor 3.51 and later let you monitor multiple processes with the same name, changing the name makes later analysis easier.

To change the process name, copy Probeprc.exe to a file with a different name. Then, enter that name in the optional *ProcessName* field.

The REPEAT parameter creates separate processes with the same process name. In Performance Monitor, the Process object Instances box will show several instances of the same named process.

The format of each process line is

```
[REPEAT n] PROCESS ThreadDfFilename.scp DataSize [ProcessName
[PriorityClass]] [# Comments]
```

Item	Description
REPEAT *n*	Creates *n* instances of the process. Each repetition runs the same test with the same process name. This field is optional. The default is 1.
PROCESS	Required word that identifies the process statement.
ThreadDfFilename. scp	Name of the file that defines the threads for the process. When processes are repeated, all repetitions share the same Thread Definition file.
DataSize	Number of pages of virtual memory allocated to simulate data pages. For repeated processes, this number of pages will be allocated for each repetition. The minimum is 0. 10 is a commonly used value.
ProcessName	The name the process in which the test runs. You can change the process name to distinguish among Response Probe tests when analyzing them. To change the process name, copy Probeprc.exe to a file with the new process name. This field is optional, but is required if you choose a priority class.
PriorityClass	The base priority class of the process. Valid entries are I (idle = 4), N (normal = 8), H (high = 13), and R (realtime = 24). Enter only the first letter of the priority type. N is the default. This field is optional, but if you choose a priority class, you must also have a process name other than Probeprc.exe.
Comments	Comments can be included anywhere in the Process script file. Begin each line of comments with a # character.

For example, the following line runs one Response Probe test with a 500-page paging file in the PROBE06.EXE process at high priority:

```
PROCESS TestDisks.scp 500 Probe06.exe H
```

The following line runs three identical processes, each having the threads defined in A971012.scp. The processes share a 300-page paging file. All of the processes are called Probeprc.exe.

REPEAT 3 PROCESS A971012.scp 300

Thread Definition File

In the Thread Definition file (*.scp), you create the threads that run in the Response Probe processes. This file consists of one or more thread definitions. Each definition creates one thread and associates it with a thread description file.

The format of a thread definition is:

```
[REPEAT n] THREAD ThreadDescFile.SCT [ThreadPriorityAdjustment]
```

Item	Description
Repeat *n*	Creates *n* instances of the thread. Each instance is treated as a separate, though identical, thread. This field is optional. The default is 1.
THREAD	Required word that identifies the thread statement.
ThreadDescFile. SCT	Name of the file where the characteristics of the thread are described. If the thread is repeated, all repetitions will share the same Thread Description file.
ThreadPriority Adjustment	The amount by which the priority of the thread differs from the priority of the process. This field is optional. N is the default. Options are: (T)TimeCritical = +15, (H)Highest = +2, (A)AboveNormal = +1, (N)Normal = 0, (B)BelowNormal = -1, (L)Lowest = -2, and (I)Idle = -15. Enter only the first letter of the priority adjustment. You do not have to name threads to adjust their priority.

For example:

```
THREAD ThreadDesc.sct
```

–Or–

```
REPEAT 4  THREAD FastThread.sct I
```

You can also set a priority adjustment for the thread based upon the priority of the process. The actual priority of the thread will be the base priority of the process plus or minus the adjustment.

For example, if you set the priority of the process to Normal (8), and the thread adjustment to L (-2), the thread would run at priority 6.

Thread Description File

In the Thread Description file (*.sct), you set values for the parameters that describe each thread. The parameters may be listed in any order. The sample thread description files on the Windows NT Resource Kit 4.0 CD are a good starting point for creating your own thread description files.

Note In Response Probe versions 3.51 and later, the CODEPAGE parameter has been replaced by the FUNCTION parameter.

Thread Description files are arranged in a table. Each line is in the following format:

PARAMETER_NAME *Mean* *StandardDeviation* *Comments*

The following table describes the parameters. Optional parameters are shown in brackets [].

Parameter Name	Description	Valid Values for Mean	Values Often Used
THINKTIME	The mean and standard deviation of the idle time between processing, in milliseconds.	0 to trial time.	Mean = 0; Sdev = 0. or Mean = 100; Sdev = 30.
CYCLEREADS	The number of times FILEACTION and CPUTIME are executed between think times. Enter the mean and standard deviation.	Minimum is 1.	Mean = 0; Sdev = 30.
CPUTIME	The time spent in compute state. Enter the mean and standard deviation in milliseconds.	0 to trial time.	Mean = 0; Sdev = 0. or Mean = 100; Sdev = 30.
DATAPAGE	The position of the page to be written to in Response Probe's simulated data page file. Enter the mean and standard deviation of the page number.	0 to the data size specified in the Process script file (*.scr).	Use the midpoint as a mean and 1/6 as the standard deviation. In a 10-page file, use Mean=5, Sdev = 2.

Parameter Name	Description	Valid Values for Mean	Values Often Used
FUNCTION	The position of the function to be read from Response Probe's 1000-function internal code page file. Enter the mean and standard deviation of the function to be read.	1- 1000	Mean = 500; Sdev = 167.
FILEACCESS	The name of the workload file to be used in the test. This file can be created manually or by using the CREATFIL utility.		
FILESEEK	The position of the record to be accessed in a file. Enter the mean and standard deviation of the record number. This parameter is required for random file access and is ignored for sequential file access.	1 - #records in file. To find #records, filesize (bytes) / recordsize (bytes).	Use the midpoint as a mean and 1/6 as the standard deviation. In a 10-page file, use Mean=5, Sdev = 2.
[RECORDSIZE]	Size of each read from or write to the FILEACCESS workload file, in bytes. This parameter is optional. The default is 4096 bytes. If you change RECORDSIZE, the midpoint of the file will change, so remember to change FILESEEK to match it.	On buffered reads, 1 - filesize. On unbuffered reads, the minimum is one sector of the disk. Use the Windows NT Diagnostics Drive page to find the sector size for your disk.	Filesize/ Recordsize = #records. In a 20 MB file with 4096K reads, #records = 5000. Use: Mean = 2500; Sdev = 834.

Parameter Name	Description	Valid Values for Mean	Values Often Used
[FILEATTRIBUTE]	Enter RANDOM or SEQUENTIAL. This parameter is optional. RANDOM is the default. In random access, record numbers are chosen based on a normal distribution. For sequential mode, the record number from the last FILE ACCESS phase is used as a starting point. When the file system opens the file, it is told that the file is accessed sequentially. This maximizes read-ahead by the cache manager.		
[FILEACCESSMODE]	Specifies how files are accessed. This parameter is optional. BUFFER is the default. Valid values are BUFFER (use file system cache), UNBUFFER (no cache) or MAPPED (array in memory). If UNBUFFER is selected, RECORDSIZE must be a multiple of the disk sector size.		See Chapter 14, "Detecting Disk Bottlenecks," for more information.
[FILEACTION]	Specifies the pattern of reads and writes by using the letters R and W. For example, RWRRWWRRRWWW. This parameter is optional. The default is R (one read).		

Tip Type comments about each parameter after its specification. Any text on the parameter line after the standard deviation field is ignored. You might include a note on your rationale for that choice, list the units of measurement of the parameter, the date of the last change, your initials, or additional descriptions.

Another Tip Code pages are read and data pages are written once in each processor loop. To determine how many loops your processor generates per second, check the Relative Processor Speed field in the Response Probe output file, described later in this chapter.

Yet Another Tip In buffer mode, Response Probe simulates *fast reads* (reads that bypass the I/O Manager file system and go directly to the Cache Manager). When charting Response Probe tests with Performance Monitor, add the **Sync Fast Reads/sec** or **Async Fast Reads/sec** counters to see this activity.

Sample Thread Description Files

Here are some sample thread description files. There are more on the Windows NT Resource Kit 4.0 CD, and many have text files explaining how to use them.

This sample file tells Response Probe to do nothing and produces almost no response, because Response Probe calculates its own overhead and subtracts it from each cycle.

```
THINKTIME       0    0
CYCLEREADS      0    0
FILESEEK        0    0
CPUTIME         0    0
DATAPAGE        0    0
CODEPAGE        0    0
FILEACCESS      access.dat
```

The following example might be used to test disk performance. Response Probe is configured to read the same 4096-byte record in the ACCESS.DAT file 100 times without using the file system cache. Because the standard deviation for CYCLEREADS and FILESEEK is 0, the same record is read exactly 100 times in each cycle. The FILEACCESSMODE is set to UNBUFFER so the system bypasses the cache and goes directly to disk. (Remember, when using UNBUFFER, the RECORDSIZE must be a multiple of the disk sector size.)

The order of the parameters are changed and optional fields are included to make the test record more complete and easy to understand.

```
CYCLEREADS       100  0
FILEACCESS       access.dat
RECORDSIZE       4096
FILEACTION       R
FILEACCESSMODE   UNBUFFER
FILEATTRIBUTE    RANDOM
THINKTIME        0    0
FILESEEK         100  0
CPUTIME          0    0
DATAPAGE         0    0
FUNCTION         1    0
```

The following example simulates an application reading very small files directly from a 20 MB file on disk without using the file system cache. This sample test is on the Windows NT Resource Kit 4.0 CD in the Probe subdirectory. There are three variations, each reading slightly larger records. The files are called 512.sc*.

During this test, for each cycle, Response Probe is idle for an average of 1000 milliseconds, then does an average of 100 reads and writes randomly throughout the 40000-record (512-byte records in a 20 MB file) file. Then it computes for an average of 10 seconds, during which it write randomly throughout the 10-page datapage file and reads randomly throughout the 1000-function codepage file.

```
THINKTIME        1000 300
CPUTIME          10   3
CYCLEREADS       100  30
FILESEEK         20000 6667
DATAPAGE         5    2
FUNCTION         500  167
FILEACCESS       workfile.dat
FILEATTRIBUTE    RAN
FILEACCESSMODE   UNBUFFER
RECORDSIZE       512
FILEACTION       RW
```

The Workload File

The Process Script file includes the name of the *workload file*, a file that simulates data records that are read from and/or written to during the process. The content of this file is irrelevant, but its size is crucial. Performance often varies directly with the size of the file.

You enter the name of the workload file in the FILEACCESS parameter of the Thread Description file (.sct).

You can use real workload files, simulate them manually or use the Createfile utility, Creatfil.exe, to create them for you.

Creating Simulated Files

The Windows NT Resource Kit 4.0 CD includes CreateFile, a utility to create zero-filled files of a size you specify.

The CreateFile utility is installed when you do a typical installation or do a custom installation of Performance Tools. It is in \\RESKIT\PerfTool \Probe\creatfil.exe. It must be run from the Command Prompt Window; it cannot be run from the **Run** command on the **Start** button.

At the command prompt, type:

```
creatfil filename [filesize]
```

where *filename* is the name of the file it will create and *filesize* is the size of the file it will create, in units of 1024K bytes. The filesize is optional. The default is 1024K bytes.

For example, to create a 100K file called workfile.dat, type:

```
c:\ RESKIT\PERFTOOL\PROBE> creatfil workfile.dat 100
```

Creatfil produces a 1,048,576-byte file of zeros called workfile.dat.

Running Response Probe

After you have created the script files and working files, you are ready to execute the utility. Run it from a Command Prompt window.

1. Use a text editor such as Notepad to create one of each of the three types of Response Probe script files:
   - Process file (.scr)
   - Thread definition file (.scp)
   - Thread description file. (.sct)
2. At the command prompt, type:

   ```
   probe ProcessFileName.SCR TrialTime [OutputFileName]
   ```

Item	Description
ProcessFileName.scr	Name of the process script file.
TrialTime	Total trial time, in seconds.
OutputFileName.out	Name of the Response Probe output file. This field is optional. The default is *ProcessFileName*.out.

The value in the ***TrialTime*** parameter is important:

- It establishes the total time for the test. All threads stop when the time expires.
- It determines when Response Probe actually starts measuring performance.

  Response Probe does not begin measuring when the test begins; it waits for one-half of the trial time to pass before measuring any values. This is intended to allow time for all processes and threads to launch and to begin operating consistently. Then Response Probe can measure normal operation, not performance at startup time.
- Increasing the trial time produces more repeatable results.

  If the trial time is too short, Response Probe might begin measuring before all threads are launched and operating normally.

Interpreting the Output

Response Probe writes its results to a text output file. The default filename is the same as the Process script file name, but with the .out suffix. However, you can enter a different name as part of the command to run Response Probe.

The file begins with a header that includes copyright and version information, the date and time the test was run. The data lines appear below the header. One line of data is printed for each thread in the Response Probe test.

Response Probe times cycles, each of which consists of one think state, file access state, and compute state for the workload. The output values represent the time of workload cycles only. Response Probe computes and subtracts its own overhead from the values before displaying them.

The values in the output files are actual values, not necessarily those specified in the Thread Description file. Response Probe calculates values based on the means and standard deviations in the Thread Description file. When it calculates an uninterpretable value, such as a negative page number, it *folds* (recalculates) the number into one that makes sense. For more information, see "How Response Probe Works," later in this chapter.

The following figure is a sample output file. In an real file, the data line columns appear in a single row.

```
Multi-Processor Response Probe.
Copyright 1990-1993 Microsoft Corporation.
Version 2.1 (93.12.21)
Wed Mar 15 05:45:14 1997
Script File : 512.scr
Trial Time : 300 seconds
Stable interval : [50%..100%] of Trial Time == [150..300] (150 seconds)
Relative Processor Speed:    4.31
(All times are in milliseconds)


                          File      Rec      Total     Resp     Resp
  PID       TID           Mode      Size     Time      Time     Cnt
  ----      ----          -----     -----    -----     -----    -----
  138       131           R  U      512      303195    117847    5


                                             Think     Think    Reads
  Mean      Sdev          Min       Max      Mean      Sdev     Mean
  -----     -----         ----      ----     -----     -----    ------
  23569     8055          18860     37679    1000      300      100


  Reads    CPU      CPU      DataPg     DataPg     Func      Func
  Sdev     Mean     Sdev     Mean       Sdev       Mean      Sdev
  -----    ----     ----     -----      ------     -----     ------
   30      10       3        5          2          500       167
```

Item	Definition
Script File	The filename of the process script file (*.scr). The process file includes the name of thread definition file, and the thread definition file includes the name of the thread description file, so all Response Probe script files used in this test can be traced from this single entry.
Trial Time	This is the time limit you set for the test on the command line. The actual test time is shown in **Total Time** in the output table, below.

Item	Definition
Stable Interval	The time that elapsed before Response Probe started measuring. This is half of the value of the ***TrialTime*** parameter in the run command. Response Probe assumes that, by that time, all threads have launched and are processing, and increasing the time limit on the trial does not significantly change thread response times.
Relative Processor Speed	The number of times the compute loop must be executed to consume one millisecond of time on the processor. This is calibrated when Response Probe starts and is used to run the compute state for the time you chose.
PID	Process ID. Windows NT assigns an identifier to all processes. The IDs are assigned in the order that the processes start and do not imply any priority. This field is for identification only.
TID	Thread ID. Windows NT assigns an identifier to all threads in a process. The IDs are assigned in the order that the threads execute and do not imply any priority. This field is for identification only.
File mode	A combination of FILEATTRIBUTE and FILEACCESSMODE. Reports whether file access was random or sequential, and whether access was buffered, unbuffered, or mapped. This field should match the input in the Thread Definition file parameters.
Rec size	Size of the each read/write as specified in the RECORDSIZE parameter, in bytes. This field should match the input in the Thread Definition file RECORDSIZE parameter.
Total time	The actual elapsed time for the test. Compare this value to **Trial Time** in the output header.

Item	Definition
Resp time	Total elapsed time for all test cycles during the measured part of the test, that is, half of the trial time. Response Probe calculates its own time and subtracts it from the data.
Resp cnt	Number of cycles completed during the measured part of the test.
Mean	Average elapsed time of a cycle. This value should be the same in repeated trials with the same input. If it is not, lengthen the trial time of the test.
Sdev	The standard deviation of elapsed time of a cycle.
Min	The elapsed time of the quickest cycle.
Max	The elapsed time of the slowest cycle.
Think mean	Average elapsed time of the think states in the measured cycles.
Think Sdev	Standard deviation of the elapsed time of the think states in the measured cycles.
Reads mean	Average elapsed time of the file access states (reading and/or writing) in the measured cycles.
Reads Sdev	Standard deviation of the elapsed time of the file access states (reading and/or writing) in the measured cycles.
CPU mean	Average elapsed time of the compute states of the measured cycles.
CPU Sdev	Standard deviation of the elapsed time of the compute states of measured cycles.
DataPg mean	Average elapsed time of writes to Response Probe's internal data pages.
DataPg Sdev	Standard deviation of the elapsed time of writes to Response Probe's internal data pages.
Func mean	Average elapsed time of reads from Response Probe's 1000-function simulated codepage file.
Func Sdev	Standard deviation of the elapsed time of reads from Response Probe's 1000-function simulated codepage file.

How Response Probe Works

This section gives some basic details about the Response Probe methods, including the formula its uses to generate normally distributed values, and more details on the stages of the simulated workload.

Calculated Values

No two Response Probe tests are ever identical because Response Probe actions are random within the chosen mean and standard deviation. Nonetheless, tests using the same script files should produce similar values in repeated trials.

For each simulated action, such as using the processor or writing to a file, Response Probe calculates a value using this formula:

```
Value = Mean + (((Sum of 14 random numbers from 0 to 1) -7) * standard
deviation)
```

Fourteen random numbers are used to simulate a bell-shaped curve. Seven is subtracted to return the midpoint to the mean.

Folding

Sometimes, the actual standard deviation varies slightly from what you enter. This happens when Response Probe *folds* outlying values back toward the mean. While the difference is usually not significant, this folding might reduce the standard deviation slightly.

Response Probe folds values when a computed value has no meaning, such as negative time or record numbers greater than the file size.

If a computed value is negative, it is folded to use the absolute value. For example, if the computed value were -16, the folded value would be +16.

If a computed value is too high, Response Probe subtracts the difference between the computed value and the maximum value from the maximum value to fold the value.

```
Folded value = Maximum value - (Computed value - Maximum value)
```

For example, suppose a page number of 102 is computed for a 100-page file. The value is folded back toward the mean and the value used is 98:

```
100 - (102 - 100) = 98
```

Sometimes these strategies are combined. If a computed value for a 100-page file is 205, the folded value is 5:

```
100 - (205 - 100) = -5
|-5| = 5.
```

Relative Processor Speed

When Response Probe starts, it calibrates the number of cycles the processor can complete in one second. Then, when it needs to consume processor time, it knows how many cycles to consume. It calibrates at High priority.

Think State

The think state simulates a user thinking but not interacting with the computer. The Response Probe thread becomes idle during this state. The length of the think state is a normally distributed value based on the mean and standard deviation set in the THINKTIME parameter of the Thread Description file.

After the think state, Response Probe generates normally distributed value for the number of file access and compute states to execute before the next think state.

File Access State

During this state, Response Probe reads from and/or writes to the workload file specified in the FILEACCESS parameter of the Thread Description file. You choose whether records are accessed randomly or sequentially. If you choose random, Response Probe generates a normally distributed value to determine which records it accesses based on the values in the Thread Description file.

After the file is accessed, Response Probe generates a normally distributed value for the amount of processor time to consume.

Compute State

During this state, Response Probe consumes processor cycles for the time interval you specify. To occupy the processor, it simulates the reading of code pages by reading from a 1000-function internal file. It also simulates writing to data pages by writing to a section of virtual memory backed by the paging file written during computation. Functions and data pages are selected as normally distributed values based on the mean and standard deviation set in the CPUTIME parameter of the Thread Description File.

Troubleshooting Response Probe

Here are some solutions to the most common Response Probe problems. The format of this section is:

Error message or description	
Probable cause	Proposed solution

Response Probe error messages look like this:

```
***********************************
* FAILure-->Line=770File=g:\ntrk\source\probe\src\probe.c (pid=0x2A)
* RC=0x7FFFFF0D (Process exe is not found)
* StartProcesses() - FindExecutable failed for codepg.dat
* specified in testfunc.scr
***********************************
```

The error message is on the second and/or third lines, as shown above.

Please keep in mind that Response Probe is not an officially supported Microsoft product. As such, support is limited. Please read the documentation carefully.

Process.exe is not found	
You are using the codepage parameter in the Process script file (*.scr).	Response Probe version 2.1 and later uses a 1000-function internal file as its codepage file. Delete the codepage parameter from your Process script file (*.scr).

FindFirstFile failed for (filename)	
Response Probe cannot find the file specified in the FILEACCESS parameter of the thread description (*.sct) file.	Enter the name of a file for Response Probe to read from or write to. You can use a real file, use the 20 MB sample file of zeros on the CD, Workfile.dat, or use the CreateFile utility on the CD to create a zero-filled file of a different size.

Invalid probe data file argument	
You are using the CODEPAGE parameter in the thread description (*.sct) file.	Replace the CODEPAGE parameter from your Thread Description file (*.sct) with a FUNCTION parameter. Enter a mean and standard deviation for the 1000 function file.

InitializePrc() Virtual Alloc	
Response Probe can not run the test because it cannot allocate enough virtual memory.	Increase the size of your pagefile and try again. Use the System Control Panel Performance page to change the pagefile size.

Invalid Mean and/or Standard Deviation	
You have entered an invalid value for the mean or standard deviation of the FUNCTION parameter in the Thread Description (*.sct) file.	Valid values for the FUNCTION parameter range from 1 to 1000. 0 is not valid.

The output file has column headings but no data.	
There is an error in a script file.	Check that all of the parameters match the format statement. The run statement must include a Process script file (*.scr) name. The Process script file must include a thread definition (*.scp) file name, and the thread definition file must include a thread description (*.sct) file name.

CHAPTER 12

Detecting Memory Bottlenecks

Windows NT 4.0 has a virtual-memory system that combines physical memory, the file system cache, and disk into a flexible information storage and retrieval system. The system can store program code and data on disk until it is needed, and then move into physical memory. Code and data no longer in active use can be written back to disk. In this way, processes benefit from the combined space of memory and disk. But when a computer does not have enough memory, code and data must be written to and retrieved from the disk more frequently—a slow, resource-intensive process that can become a system bottleneck.

The best indicator of a memory bottleneck is a sustained, high rate of *hard page faults*. Hard page faults occur when the data a program needs is not found in its working set (the physical memory visible to the program) or elsewhere in physical memory, and must be retrieved from disk. Sustained hard page fault rates—over 5 per second—are a clear indicator of a memory bottleneck. To monitor hard fault rates and other indicators of memory performance, log the System, Memory, Logical Disk and Process objects for several days at an update interval of 60 seconds. Then use the following Performance Monitor counters, described in this chapter:

Object	Counter
Memory	Page Faults/sec
Memory	Page Reads/sec
Memory	Page Writes/sec
Memory	Pages Input/sec
Memory	Pages Output/sec
Memory	Available bytes
Memory	Nonpaged pool bytes
Process	Page Faults/sec
Process	Working set
Process	Private Bytes
Process	Page File Bytes

Windows NT 4.0 Workstation Memory Basics

Windows NT 4.0 has a flat, linear 32-bit memory. This means that each program can see 32 bits of address space or 4 gigabytes of virtual memory. The upper half of virtual memory is reserved for system code and data that is visible to the process only when it is running in privileged mode. The lower half is available to the program when it is running in user mode and to user-mode system services called by the program.

Note Windows NT versions prior to 3.51 included some 16-bit data structures that limited processes to 256 MB (64K pages) of virtual memory. These have been converted to 32-bit data structures, so 2 gigabytes of virtual memory is available to all processes.

Monitoring Windows 4.0 memory requires that you understand both the concepts used to discuss it and the Performance Monitor counters used to test it.

Terms and Concepts

The *Windows NT Virtual Memory Manager* controls how memory is allocated, reserved, committed, and paged. It includes sophisticated strategies for anticipating the code and data requirements of processes to minimizing disk access.

The code and data in physical memory are divided into units called *pages*. The size of a page varies with the processor platform. MIPS, Intel, and PowerPC platforms have 4096 bytes per page; DEC Alpha platforms have 8192 bytes per page.

The Virtual Memory Manager moves pages of code and data between disk and memory in a process called *paging*. Paging is essential to a virtual memory system, although excessive paging can monopolize processors and disks.

A *page fault* occurs when a program requests a page of code or data is not in its *working set* (the set of pages visible to the program in physical memory).

- A *hard page fault* occurs when the requested page must be retrieved from disk.
- A *soft page fault* occurs when then the requested page is found elsewhere in physical memory.

Soft page faults can be satisfied quickly and relatively easily by the Virtual Memory Manager, but hard faults cause paging, which can degrade performance.

Each page in memory is stored in a *page frame*. Before a page of code or data can be moved from disk into memory, the Virtual Memory Manager must find or create a free page frame or a frame filled with zeros. (Zero-filled pages are a requirement of the U.S. Government C2 security standard. Page frames must be filled with zeros to prevent the previous contents from being used by a new process.) To free a page frame, changes to a data page in the frame might need to be written to disk before the frame is reused. Code pages, which are typically not changed by a program, can be deleted.

When code or data paged into physical memory is used by a process, the system reserves space for that page on the *disk paging file*, Pagefile.sys, in case the page needs to be written back to disk. Pagefile.sys is a reserved block of disk space that is used to back up committed memory. It can be contiguous or fragmented. Because memory needs to be backed by the paging file, the size of the paging file limits the amount of data that can be stored in memory. By default, Pagefile.sys is set to the size of physical memory plus 12 MB, but you can change it. Increasing the size of the paging file often resolves virtual memory shortages.

In Windows NT 4.0 Workstation and Server, objects created and used by applications and the operating system are stored in *memory pools*. These pools are accessible only in privileged mode, the processing mode in which operating system components run, so application threads must be switched to privileged mode to see the objects stored in the pools.

- The *paged pool* holds objects that can be paged to disk.
- The *nonpaged pool* holds objects that never leave main memory, such as data structures used by interrupt routines or those which prevent multiprocessor conflicts within the operating system.

The initial size of the pools is based on the amount of physical memory available to Windows NT. Thereafter, the pool size is adjusted dynamically and varies widely, depending upon the applications and services that are running.

All virtual memory in Windows NT is either reserved, committed, or available:

- *Reserved memory* is a set of contiguous addresses that the Virtual Memory Manager sets aside for a process but does not count against the process's memory quota until it is used. When a process needs to write to memory, some of the reserved memory is committed to the process. If the process runs out of memory, available memory can be reserved and committed simultaneously.
- Memory is *committed* when the Virtual Memory Manager saves space for it in Pagefile.sys in case it needs to be written to disk. The amount of committed memory for a process is an indication of how much memory is it really using.

Committed memory is limited by the size of the paging file. The *commit limit* is the amount of memory that can be committed without expanding the paging file. If disk space is available, the paging file can expand, and the commit limit will be increased.

Memory that is neither reserved nor committed is *available.* Available memory includes free memory, zeroed memory (which is cleared and filled with zeros), and memory on the standby list, which has been removed from a process's working set but might be reclaimed.

Measuring Memory

There are many useful tools for measuring physical and virtual memory and memory use. Most provide current totals and peak values of memory counts for processes and threads from the time they were started.

About Windows NT

To see how much physical memory is available to Windows NT 4.0 Workstation, start Windows Explorer, and choose **About Windows NT** from the **Help** menu. Physical memory available to Windows is listed at the bottom.

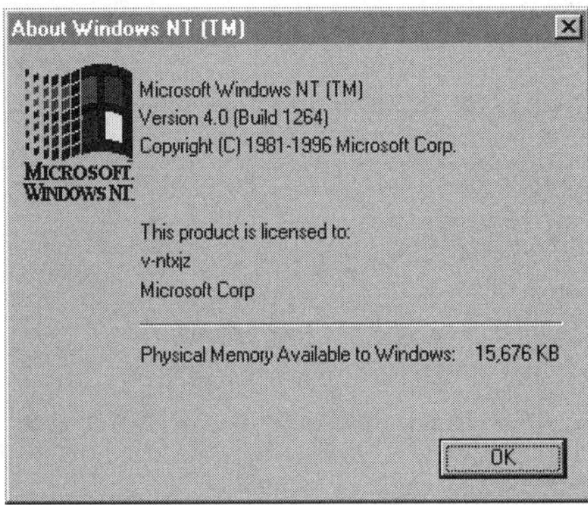

Task Manager

The Performance tab of Task Manager has a total physical memory field, memory usage counts, and a virtual memory graph. The Processes tab lists all processes running on the computer. From it, you can select columns to show Page Faults—a running total of page faults for the process since its start—and Page Faults Delta (PF Delta)—the change in page-fault totals between updates. Click the Page Faults or PF Delta column heading to sort processes by total page faults or by changes in page faults. The following figure shows the Task Manager Processes tab displaying the page-fault columns.

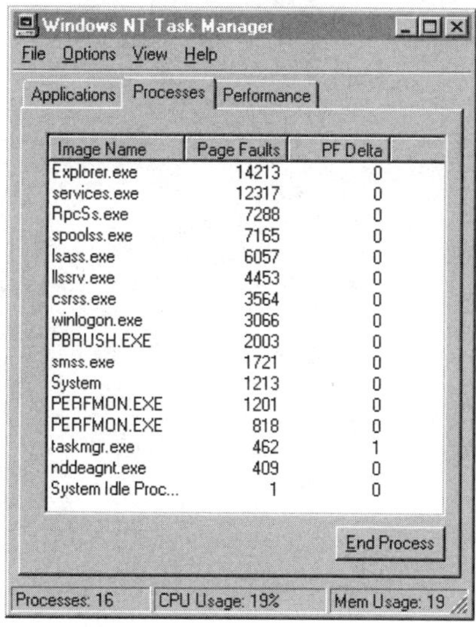

Resource Kit Utilities

Process Explode (Pview.exe) and Process Viewer (Pviewer.exe) show accurate and detailed current memory counts without any setup. Process Explode shows it all on one screen. In Process Viewer, click **Memory Detail** to see the counts for each segment of the process's address space.

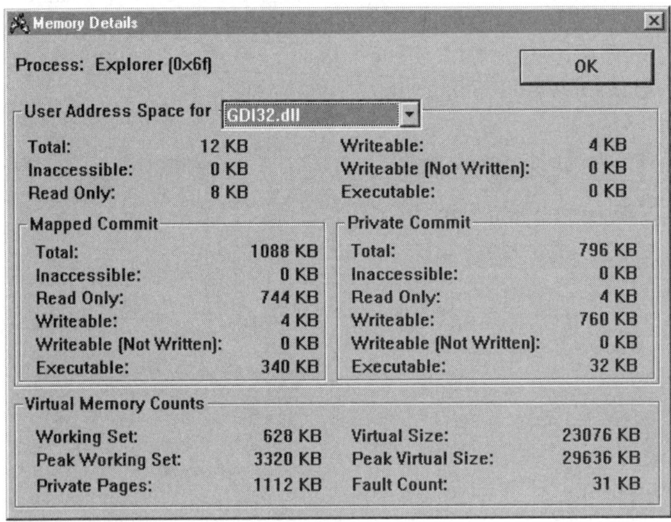

Page Fault Monitor (Pfmon.exe), a tool on the Windows NT Resource Kit 4.0 CD in the Performance Tools group (\Perftool\Meastool), produces a running list of hard and soft page faults generated by each function call in a running application. You can display the data, write it to a log file, or both.

You must run Page Fault Monitor from the command prompt window. Type **pfmon /?** to see a list of available switches. For more information, see Rktools.hlp.

Performance Monitor

Performance Monitor logs data over time and displays it in line graphs. This is, by far, the best presentation of data related to memory use. Page faults, page reads, and disk operations are not smooth, continuous increases; they are quick spikes in the data. Any totals or averaging hides the patterns.

The following figure is a Performance Monitor graph of Process: Page Faults/sec for several processes during their startup, when paging is high. The graph shows an increased page fault rate first for one application (the thin, gray line) and, later, for the other (the thick, black line). The white line represents page faults for the Services process which are interspersed throughout the sample interval.

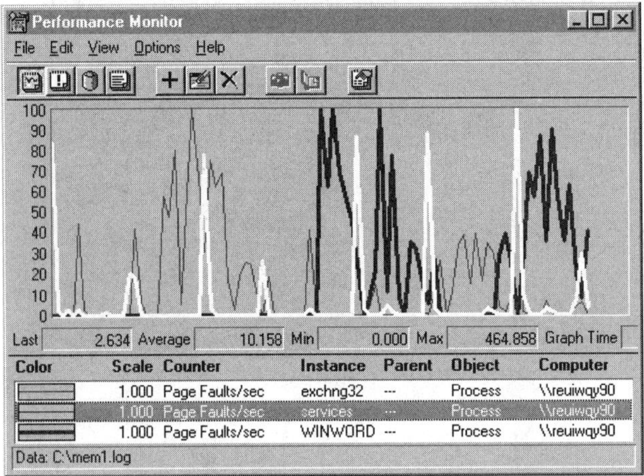

The following report shows the same data presented in a report of average values over the measured time.

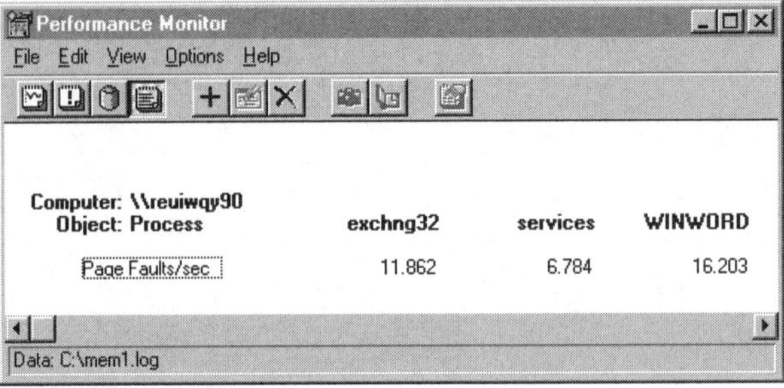

Although both provide useful information, the report does not reveal the patterns evident in the graph.

In addition to the monitoring tools, some simulation tools help you test the capacity of your memory. Clearmem, a utility on the Windows NT Resource Kit 4.0 CD, lets you measure the minimum working set for a process. It allocates all available memory, references it so it does not get paged out, then releases it. This forces the Virtual Memory Manager to trim the working sets of other processes to a minimum so that you can see how many pages your process is actually touching.

Memory Counters

The counters on the Performance Monitor memory object provide information on memory from different perspectives. The following table is a quick reference guide to the most commonly used memory counters.

Memory Counter	Description
Page Faults/sec	How often is data not found in a process's working set? This includes both hard page faults, which require disk I/O and soft page faults where pages are found elsewhere in memory. If requested code or data is repeatedly not found, the process's working set is probably too small because memory is limited.
Pages Input/sec	How many pages are being retrieved from disk to satisfy page faults? Compare with Page Faults/sec to see how many faults are satisfied by reading from disk, and how many come from somewhere else.
Pages Output/sec	How many pages are being written to disk to free up space in the working set for faulted pages? Pages must be written if they were changed by the process. A high rate indicates that most faulting is data pages and that memory is becoming scarce. If memory is available, changed pages are retained in a list in memory and written to disk in batches.
Pages/sec	Sum of Pages Input/sec and Pages Output/sec.
Page Reads/sec	How often is the system reading from disk because of page faults? How much is page faulting affecting the disk? The primary indicator of a memory shortage. Some page reads are expected, but a sustained rate of 5 pages per second or more indicates a memory shortage. Counts how often the disk is read, regardless of the number of pages per reads. The number of pages exceeds the number of reads when more than one page is read at a time.

Memory Counter	Description
Page Writes/sec	How often is the system writing to disk because of page faults? Counts how often the disk is written to, regardless of the number of pages written. The number of pages exceeds the number of writes when more than one page is written at a time. This counter is another good indicator of the effect of paging on the disk.
Available bytes	How much memory is left for processes to allocate? This is an instantaneous count, not an average.

Configuring Available Memory

You can reduce the amount of physical memory available to Windows NT on a computer with an Intel processor without changing its physical memory configuration. This lets you simulate and test the effects of low memory on your computer.

Use the MAXMEM parameter on the Boot.ini file to set the maximum physical memory available to Windows NT.

Note MAXMEM works only on Intel processor platforms. This information does not apply to RISC computers (DEC Alpha, MIPS, and PowerPC) which store their boot options in ARC firmware.

Intel computers store boot options in a Boot.ini file. Add the MAXMEM parameter to a boot option line in the Boot.ini file. You can create multiple boot option lines and choose from among the alternates at boot time.

Warning Do not set the memory on Windows NT 4.0 Workstation or Server below 8 MB. If you do, Windows NT might be unable to boot.

---

1. Open Boot.ini. Because this is a read-only file, you must change its properties before you can edit it. It looks something like this:

```
[boot loader]
timeout=30
default=multi(0)disk(0)rdisk(0)partition(1)\WINNT40
[operating systems]
multi(0)disk(0)rdisk(0)partition(1)\WINNT40="Windows NT Version 4.00"
c:\="MS-DOS"
```

2. Copy the boot option line under [operating systems] and paste it just below the existing one. Within the quotes, type some text that will identify this option to you when you see it on the screen during bootup. For example:

```
multi(0)disk(0)rdisk(0)partition(1)\WINNT40="Windows NT Version
    4.00,12Mb"
```

3. Following the quotes, type a space, then **/MAXMEM=*n*** where *n* is the amount of memory, in megabytes, you want to be available to Windows NT. Do not set this below 8 MB, or Windows NT might be unable to boot.

```
multi(0)disk(0)rdisk(0)partition(1)\WINNT40="Windows NT Version
    4.00,12Mb" /MAXMEM=12
```

4. You can create multiple boot option lines. Make sure the timeout parameter is long enough to let you choose from among them.
5. Reboot, choose the low memory option, then check About Windows NT or Task Manager to make sure the change was effective.

Memory Bottlenecks and Paging

The first step in investigating a memory problem is to measure paging. Although soft page faults (in which pages not in the process's working set are found elsewhere in physical memory) interrupt the processor, their effect is likely to be negligible.

If you suspect a memory shortage, chart the following Performance Monitor counters:

- Memory: Page Faults/sec
- Memory: Pages Input/sec
- Memory: Page Reads/sec

These counters indicate how often processes must look beyond their working sets to find the code or data they need. They also indicate how often these requests require paging from disk and how many pages are moved with each disk transfer.

Note The graphs for this section were produced on a 33-MHz 486 computer with only 10-12 MB of memory available to Windows NT 4.0 Workstation. Applications used in these examples will not cause memory bottlenecks when run with the recommended minimum of 16 MB of memory.

Compare the lines for Page Faults/sec and Pages Input/sec to determine the proportion of hard page faults (Pages input/sec) to all page faults (Page faults/sec). Both counters are measured in number of pages per second, so you can compare them without conversions. The lines intersect when the Virtual Memory Manager is reading from disk to satisfy a page fault. Space between the lines indicate soft page faults, which indicate that the missing page was found elsewhere in memory.

Pages input/sec is the number of pages read to satisfy a page fault, and Page Reads is the number of reads required to retrieve those pages. When the lines meet, the Virtual Memory Manager is moving one page per read operation. The space between the lines indicates that the Virtual Memory Manager is reading more than one page per operation. (You can calculate the amount of space by dividing Pages Input/sec by Page Reads/sec to find the number of pages per read operation. Space between the lines corresponds to a value greater than 1.)

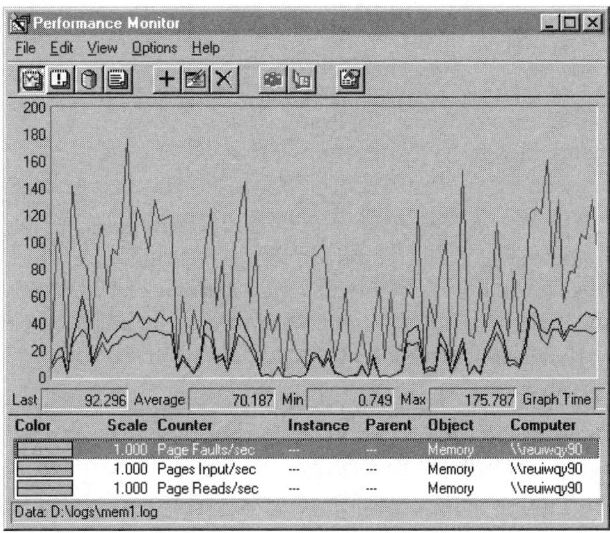

In this example, the total page fault rate, Page Faults/sec (the top line), averages 70 per second. Page faults can interrupt the processor, but only hard faults slow the system down significantly. The next line, Pages Input/sec, measures hard faults in the numbers of pages retrieved to satisfy the fault. In this example, the rate is 21.5 pages per second on average. Although hard faults represent only 31% of all pages faulted (21.5/70), 21.5 pages per second can produce enough disk activity to cause produce a disk bottleneck.

The area between the top two lines represents soft faults; that is, pages found elsewhere in memory, either in the file system cache, in transition to disk, in the working set of another process, or brought in from memory as zeros. In this case, there are many; approximately 69% of page faults are soft faults.

The bottom line, partially superimposed upon Pages Input/sec, is Page Reads/sec, the number of times the disk is read to satisfy a page fault. This is an important indicator of the type of paging that causes system bottlenecks. The average of 16 reads/sec is quite high. Although the line representing Pages Input/sec and Page Reads/sec are close to each other, at times they diverge, indicating multiple pages read during each read operation. On average, 21.5 pages/sec are read in 16 page reads/sec. This shows that the Virtual Memory Manager is reading about 1.3 pages during each read operation.

In this example, 69% of the pages faulted because they were not in the working set of the monitored process, were found elsewhere in memory, probably in the file system cache. Because it is much quicker to retrieve data from the cache than from disk, Windows NT uses all available physical memory as cache. However, the remaining 31% of faulted pages caused in average of 16 reads/sec from disk; enough to cause a disk bottleneck. The next step is to associate paging with disk use.

Paging and Disk Reads

The memory counters, Page Reads/sec and Pages Input/sec, are indirect indicators of disk activity due to paging. Use the counters on the Logical Disk object to show paging from the perspective of the disks.

Note To enable the physical or logical disks counters, you must first run the Diskperf utility. At the command prompt, type **diskperf -y**, then restart the computer. For fault tolerant disk configurations (FTDISK), type **diskperf -ye**, then restart the computer. For more information, see "Diskperf: Enabling the Disk Counters" in Chapter 14, "Detecting Disk Bottlenecks."

To investigate the effect of paging on your disks, add the following counters for the Logical Disk object to your memory charts and reports:

- % Disk Read Time: _Total
- Avg. Disk Read Queue Length: _Total
- Disk Reads/sec: _Total
- Avg. Disk Bytes/Read: _Total

The disk activity counters, % Disk Read Time and Avg. Disk Read Queue Length, indicate disk reading activity during periods of high paging, as measured by the memory counters. Because disk activity has many causes, the Disk Reads/sec counter is included. This lets you subtract the reads due to paging (Memory: Page Reads/sec), from all reads (Disk Reads/sec), to determine the proportion of read operations caused by paging.

The transfer rate (as represented by Avg. Disk Bytes/Read) multiplied by Disk Reads/sec yields the number of bytes read per second, another measure of disk activity.

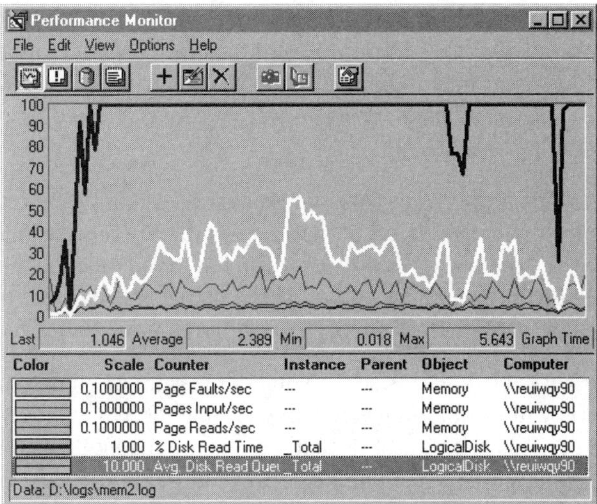

In this graph, the thick black line running at 100% for most of the test interval is % Disk Read Time: _Total As the following report shows, total disk read time for both disks actually exceeds 100%.

The white line, Avg. Disk Read Queue Length, shows that the high disk activity is producing a large queue to disk. The scale is multiplied by 10 so that you can see the line. The disk queue averages more than 2 and, at its maximum, exceeds 5. More than two items in the queue can affect performance.

The remaining lines, representing the memory counters, are scaled quite small so that they can fit in the graph. Their values are more evident in the following report.

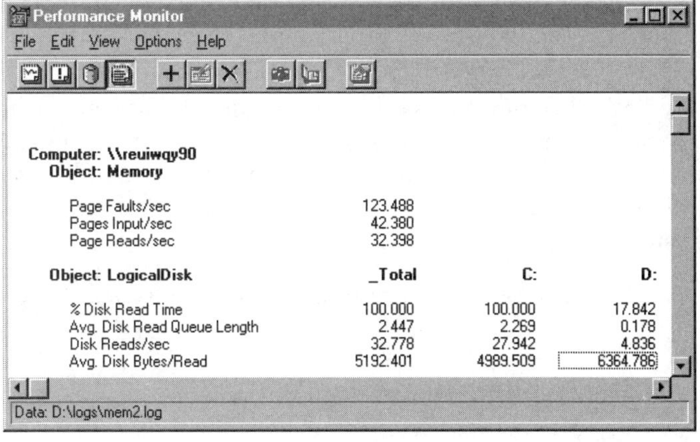

Although this report displays the same information as the graph, it shows average values for all counters. In this example, the average rate of page faults—123 per second—is extremely high. But the Pages Input/sec counter shows that, on average, only 42 of them, or 34%, were retrieved from disk. The rest of the pages are found in memory.

The 42 pages retrieved per second on average required 32 reads from the disk per second from the disk. Even though two-thirds of the page faults were satisfied by memory, the remaining one-third was enough to consume the disk and produce a large queue. In general, a high-performance disk is capable of 40 I/Os per second. This disk was quite close to its physical maximum.

Logical Disk: Disk Reads/sec: _Total, a measure of all disk reads, at 32.778 per second, is within sampling error range of the 32.398 average Memory: Page Reads/sec. This shows that virtually all of the reading was done to find faulted pages. This confirms that paging is cause of the bottleneck. If this pattern were to persist over time, it would indicate a memory shortage, not a disk problem.

Paging and Disk Writes

Paging causes many reads from the disk, but it also causes some writing to disk. When the Virtual Memory Manager locates a faulted page, if memory is available, it simply adds the retrieved pages to the working set of the process. When memory is scarce, it deletes a page of the current working set for every new page it brings in. If data on the page has changed, it must write the data to disk before it frees up the page frame. If many of the faulted pages are data pages with changes, the writing can be significant, and Performance Monitor can measure it.

Tip If your application's page faults are causing disk writes, they are probably faulting data pages, not code pages. Reorganizing your application's data structures and the way the program references them can reduce page faults.

To limit the writes to disk, the Virtual Memory Manager maintains a *modified page list*, a list of changed pages that need to be written to disk. Periodically, the *modified page writer,* a thread in the System process, writes some of the pages out to free up space. As free space becomes scarce, the modified page thread is activated more often.

To measure writes to disk resulting from paging, chart:

- Memory: Page Writes/sec
- Memory: Pages Output/sec
- Logical Disk: Disk Writes/sec
- Logical Disk: Disk Write Bytes/sec
- Logical Disk: Avg. Disk Write Queue Length

Memory: Page Writes/sec indicates how often changes to pages had to be written to back to disk to free up space in a working set.

Logical Disk: Disk Writes/sec represents all writing to disk, including writes not associated with paging, like writing the Performance Monitor log file, or updating system statistics. Comparing Disk Writes to Page Writes reveals the proportion of total disk writing that consists of writing pages from memory back to disk.

Comparing Memory: Pages Output/sec and Logical Disk: Disk Write Bytes/sec also indicates the proportion of disk writing activity that is directly related to paging, but it shows it in bytes, rather than time.

Pages output/sec is the number of pages written to disk to free up page frames.

Disk Write Bytes/sec is the number of bytes written to disk per second for all purposes.

To compare Pages Output/sec to Disk Write Bytes/sec, multiply the number of pages by the number of bytes per page. MIPS, Intel, and PowerPC processors have 4096 bytes per page; DEC Alpha processors have 8192 bytes per page.

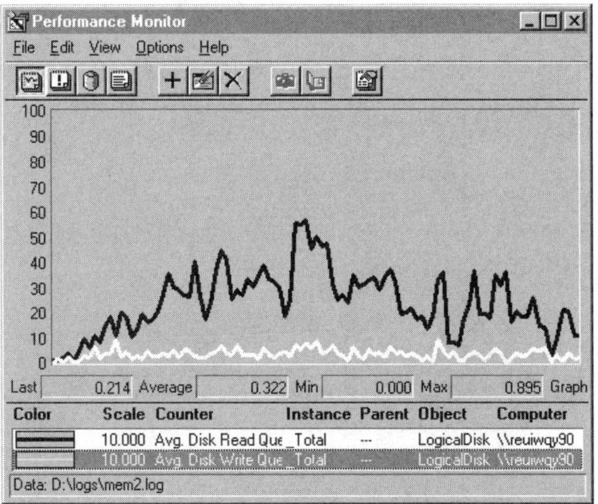

This graph compares disk read time with disk write time while the system is paging. The black line represents time reading from both physical disks on the system; the white line represents time writing. In this example, there was far more reading than writing, but the amount of writing is not insignificant.

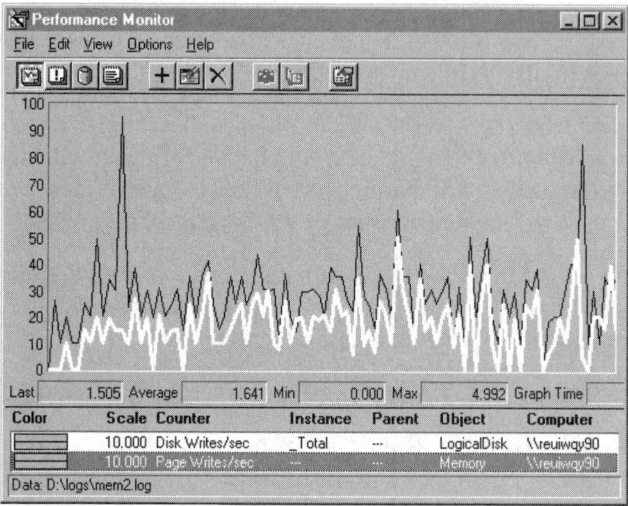

This graph of the same events shows how much of the writing time is attributable to paging. The thin black line represents all writes to disk per second; the heavy, white line represents disk-writes due to paging. The space between them represents disk-writes other than changed pages.

In this example, the curves are almost the same shape, but the there are twice as many disk writes as page writes. This indicates that the disk writes that did not consist of writing changed pages were related to writing them, such as writing the Performance Monitor log and writing system records.

The following report shows another measure of writing. The report includes counts of writing in pages as well as time.

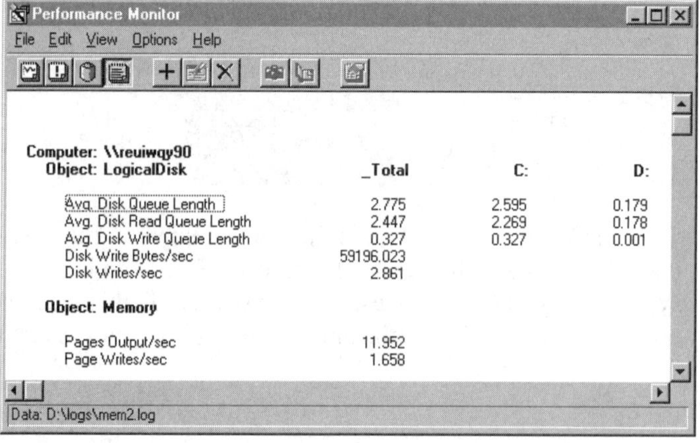

To compare the Disk Write Bytes/sec to Pages Output/sec, multiply the number of pages by the page size, in this case, 4096 bytes/page. In this example, 11.952 pages out of 14.452, or 82% of disk writing is directly attributable to paging.

The Paging File

It is useful to monitor the size of the paging file, Pagefile.sys, when investigating memory shortages. On systems that have relatively little excess memory, an increased demand for memory causes Windows NT to expand the paging file.

The paging file, Pagefile.sys, is a block of disk space reserved by the operating system to back up physical memory. When processes require more physical memory than is available, the Virtual Memory Manager frees up space in memory by writing less-frequently-referenced pages back to the paging file on disk. As demand for memory increases, the Virtual Memory Manager expands the paging file until it runs out of disk space or reaches the paging file reaches its maximum size.

Note Windows NT creates one paging file on the physical drive on which the operating system is installed. The default size is equal to physical memory plus 12 MB. You can change the size of the paging file, and you can create one additional paging files on each logical disk partition in your configuration.

Use the Control Panel System applet Performance tab. (Right-click My Computer, select Properties, then select the Performance tab.) The Virtual Memory box shows the current size of your paging files and lets you add new files or change the size of existing ones. To change the value, click the **Change** button to display the Virtual Memory window, and then click **Set**.

To observe the changing size of the paging file, chart Process: Page File Bytes for individual processes and Process: Page File Bytes: _Total, an instantaneous measure of total number of bytes in the paging file.

The data in the following graph was logged during a memory leak (when memory is allocated faster than it is freed). A testing tool, LeakyApp, was run to allocate as much memory as it could, and the thrashing at the end of the graph shows the system running out of virtual memory and repeatedly warning the user.

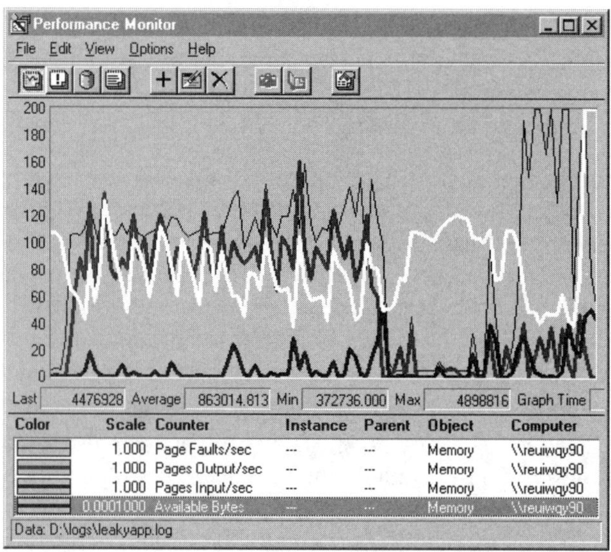

In this graph, the thin black line is Page Faults/sec. The next thick black line is Pages Output/sec. The thick white line is Available Bytes, and the thick black line at the bottom is Pages Input/sec.

The relatively low rate of pages input (those read from disk to satisfy page faults) and very high rate of pages output (those written back to disk to trim working sets and recover physical memory) reveals the strategy of the Virtual Memory Manager to conserve available bytes by writing pages from physical memory to the paging file. Even as physical memory is consumed by processes, the number of available bytes of memory rarely falls below 4 MB, though it might vary rapidly and considerably within its range. In this example, Available bytes never drops below 372,736 bytes, as indicated by the **Min** value on the value bar.

However, the paging file on disk (Pagefile.sys) fills up rapidly until it runs out of space on disk.

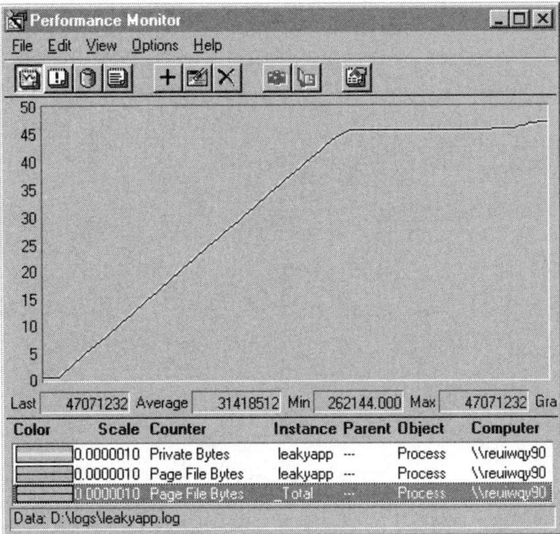

In this graph, the lines representing the private bytes LeakyApp allocated to itself, the size of the paging file used by LeakyApp, and the total number of used bytes in the paging file, are all superimposed upon each other. Although the values are not identical, they are quite similar.

The graph is evidence of the significant growth of the paging file during a memory shortage. The plateau on the graph indicates that the maximum size of the paging file was reached, and LeakyApp could no longer allocate additional memory.

To see the values of all data points of the Page File Bytes curve, export the data to a spreadsheet like Microsoft Excel. For details on exporting logged data, see "Exporting Data" in Performance Monitor Help.

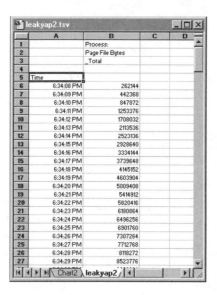

leakyap2.tsv

	A	B	C	D
1		Process:		
2		Page File Bytes		
3		_Total		
4				
5	Time			
6	6:34:08 PM	262144		
7	6:34:09 PM	442368		
8	6:34:10 PM	847872		
9	6:34:11 PM	1253376		
10	6:34:12 PM	1708032		
11	6:34:13 PM	2113536		
12	6:34:14 PM	2523136		
13	6:34:15 PM	2928640		
14	6:34:16 PM	3334144		
15	6:34:17 PM	3739648		
16	6:34:18 PM	4145152		
17	6:34:19 PM	4603904		
18	6:34:20 PM	5009408		
19	6:34:21 PM	5414912		
20	6:34:22 PM	5820416		
21	6:34:23 PM	6180864		
22	6:34:24 PM	6496256		
23	6:34:25 PM	6901760		
24	6:34:26 PM	7307264		
25	6:34:27 PM	7712768		
26	6:34:28 PM	8118272		
27	6:34:29 PM	8523776		

Chart2 leakyap2

Monitoring the Nonpaged Pool

The nonpaged pool is an area of kernel-mode operating system memory reserved for objects that cannot be paged to disk. The size of the nonpaged pool is adjusted by the Virtual Memory Manager based on the amount of physical memory in the computer and on the demand for pool space by applications and services. On workstations, the absolute size of the nonpaged pool is not relevant to performance monitoring. However *pool leaks*, which are characterized by continuous, unexplained growth in the nonpaged pool, are a concern. Pool leaks usually result from an application error. They can cause a memory shortage because space occupied by the pool is no longer available to other processes.

For more information about memory pools, see "Terms and Concepts" earlier in this chapter.

Note The size of the nonpaged pool usually is not a concern on workstations, but can be a factor on servers where the number of trusting account (user) domains depends on the size of the nonpaged pool. For more information, see "Number of Trusted Domains" in Windows NT Networking Guide, Chapter 2, "Network Security and Domain Planning."

Many performance monitoring tools monitor the paged and nonpaged memory pools. Process Explode (Pview.exe), Process Monitor (Pmon.exe) and Process Viewer (Pviewer.exe), tools included the Windows NT Resource Kit 4.0 CD, display the amount of space in the pools allocated to each process. Task Manager and Performance Monitor display the total size of each memory pool as well as the space allocated to each process. Although their display formats vary widely, all of the these tools collect their data from the same internal counters.

Important The internal counters that measure the size of the nonpaged pool for each process are not precise. The counter values are estimates which count duplicated object handles as well as space for the object. Also, because the process pool size counts are rounded to page size, pool space is overestimated when a process is using part of a page. Therefore, it is important to monitor *changes* in pool size for a process, not the absolute value. Total pool size counts are precise. Therefore, the sum of pool sizes for each process might not equal the value for the whole system.

In Task Manager, the current size of the nonpaged pool is listed in the Kernel Memory box on the Performance tab. On the Processes tab, you can add a column to monitor the size of the nonpaged pool allocated to each process. For more information, see "Task Manager" in Chapter 11, "Performance Monitoring Tools."

Performance Monitor lets you to log changes in pool size over time. Pool size changes slowly, so you might have to log for several hours or even days to catch a pool leak. Use these Performance Monitor counters to monitor the pool size:

- Memory: Pool Nonpaged Bytes
- Memory: Pool Nonpaged Allocations
- Process: Pool Nonpaged Bytes

The counters on the Memory object monitor the total size of the nonpaged pool and the number of allocations of pool space for the whole system. The counter on the Process object monitors nonpaged pool space allocated to each process.

To use Performance Monitor to monitor the nonpaged pool for leaks, follow these procedures:

- Record the size of the nonpaged pool when the system starts. Then log the Memory and Process objects for several days at a 60-second interval. You should be able to associate any increases in the size of the pool, as indicated by Nonpaged Pool Bytes, with the start of a process, as indicated by Process: % Processing Time. When processes are stopped, you should see a decrease in pool size.
- Set a Performance Monitor alarm to notify you when Nonpaged Pool Bytes increases by more than 10% from its value at system startup.

After the system is started, the nonpaged pool should increase in size only when a process is started. When the process ends, the nonpaged pool should return to its original size. Any other unexplained growth in the nonpaged pool is considered to be abnormal.

Pool leaks typically occur when an application creates objects, then fails to close their handles when it is done with them, or when an application repeatedly opens a file or other object unnecessarily. Each time the application attempts to open the object, more space is allocated for the same object in the nonpaged pool. The bytes allocated for the pool come from physical memory, and an unnecessarily large pool denies those bytes to the operating system and applications.

Windows NT dynamically adjusts the size of the paged and nonpaged memory pools for optimum performance. However, you can change the size of the paged and nonpaged pools on Windows NT Workstations and Servers by editing the Registry. Use Regedt32 or Regedit, tools installed with Windows NT, to edit the Registry. Editing the Registry might cause serious system problems that require reinstalling Windows NT. The values for this Registry entry are entered in bytes.

The registry parameters for paged and nonpaged pool are in:

Subtree	HKEY_LOCAL_MACHINE
Key	\System\CurrentControlSet\Control\SessionManager \MemoryManagerment
Name	NonPagedPoolSize PagedPoolSize
Type	REG_DWORD

Examining Your Applications

High, sustained paging rates indicate a memory shortage, but not its cause. You might have insufficient physical memory to support the operating system, applications, and network services. However, you might have an application that is using memory inefficiently or leaking memory—that is, allocating memory, but not releasing it.

When the hard page fault rate on your system rises, investigate the memory use of your applications by using the following counters:

- Process: Private Bytes
- Process: Working Set
- Process: Page Faults/sec
- Process: Page file Bytes

The first step is to distinguish between a general memory shortage that is affecting all applications and a memory shortage caused by a particular application. Chart Process: Page Faults/sec for all processes.

The following graph shows a general memory shortage that is causing page faults in many processes.

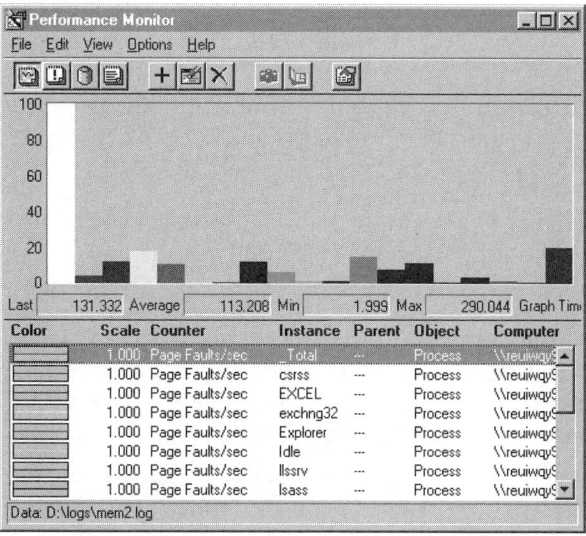

In this example, Memory: Page Faults/sec (the tall white bar) represents all page faults for the system. The other bars represent page faults for each application or service running on the system. This graph demonstrates that no single application is causing a memory shortage. In this case, the high paging rate is best resolved by adding more physical memory.

In contrast, the following graph shows a single application, LeakyApp, a test tool, causing a high rate of page faults.

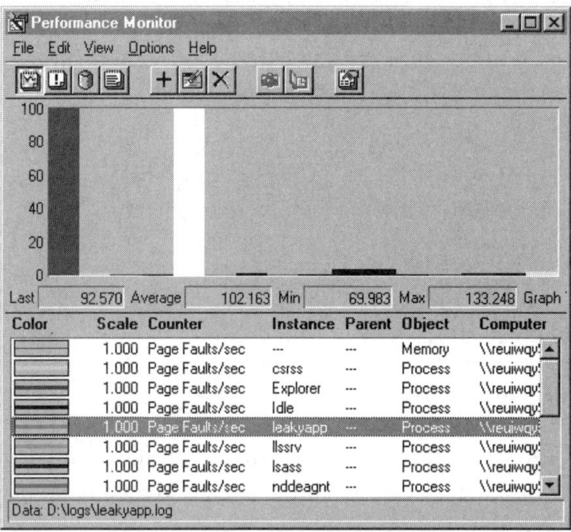

In this example, Memory: Page Faults/sec (the first tall bar) represents all page faults for the system. The tall white bar represents page faults for the test tool. The other bars, which are barely visible, represent the fault rates of other processes.

Although this memory shortage affects all system processes, it is attributable to a single application. Were it a real application instead of a test tool, a more thorough investigation would be in order. It would be prudent to consider replacing the application, moving it to another computer or, if it is your application, trying to improve it memory efficiency.

The standard performance monitoring tools are designed to determine that an application is using memory inefficiently, but not why. If you have an inefficient application, use the following tools for further diagnosis:

- Page Fault Monitor (Pfmon.exe), a utility on the Windows NT Resource Kit 4.0 CD in the Performance Tools group (\Perftool\Meastool), produces a running list of the hard and soft page faults generated by each function call in a running process. For more information, see Rktools.hlp.
- The Working Set Tuner analyzes the patterns of function calls in your application code and recommends a code organization that consumes the least possible physical memory. It requires some work from the developer, but has been demonstrated to improve memory efficiency by as much as 50%. The Working Set Tuner is part of the Win32 Software Development Kit.

The remainder of this section explains how to determine the effect of application memory use on your system.

Working Set

The *working set* of a process is the physical memory assigned to the process by the operating system. It contains the code and data pages recently referenced by the process. When a process needs code or data that is not in its working set, a page fault occurs, and the Virtual Memory Manager adds the new pages to the working set.

- When memory is plentiful, the Virtual Memory Manager leaves older pages in the working sets even when it adds new pages. This results in larger working sets.
- When memory becomes scarce, the Virtual Memory Manager recovers memory for the system by moving less recently referenced pages out of the working sets and by removing an older page for each new page added. Although trimming the working sets is necessary, it can cause more page faults.

One measure of application efficiency is how small its working set can get without causing a large number of page faults. In general, the more that data used in sequence is stored in sequence, the fewer pages the application needs and the smaller its working set can be.

To measure the working sets of processes, chart:

- Process: Working Set
- Process: Page Faults/sec
- Memory: Available Bytes

Working Set is an instantaneous counter that shows the current number of bytes in a process's working set. Process: Page Faults/sec is the rate of page faults for the process. The following graph demonstrates that the Virtual Memory Manager adjusts the size of a process's working set attempting to respond to a process's page fault rate by increasing its working set and then by trimming it.

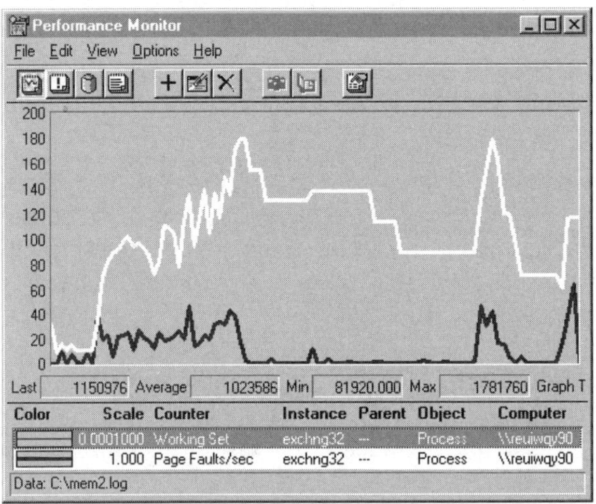

In this graph, the white line represents the working set of a process; the black line represents the page-fault rate for the process. Notice that the vertical maximum has been increased to 200 so that the working set curve fits in the graph. The similar shapes of these curves reflect their cause and effect relationship of the Virtual Memory Manager responding to the page faults.

In this example, the overall page-fault rate is quite high, averaging over 12 page faults/sec. As the page-fault rate rises, the Virtual Memory Manager adds pages to the working set of the process to reduce the rate of the page faults. About midway through the graph, as the page-fault rate drops to near zero—probably because the process has much of what it needs—the Virtual Memory Manager begins to trim the working set, but a resurgence of page faults drives the size of the working set back up.

Determining the Minimum Working Set

When you improve the organization of code and data references in your program, you:

- reduce its minimum working set.
- reduce the amount of physical memory it consumes.
- improve its use of the file system cache (as described in Chapter 7).

To demonstrate one aspect of this improvement, measure the minimum working set of an application before and after you tune it.

To see the actual minimum working set of a process, you must reduce available memory to its minimum. This compels the Virtual Memory Manager to trim all but currently active pages from a process's working set.

Clearmem, a utility on the Windows NT Resource Kit 4.0 CD in the Performance Tools group (\PerfTool\MeasTool), determines the size of your computer's physical memory, allocates enough data to fill it, then references the data as quickly as possible. It also accesses files to clear the cache. This reduces memory available to other processes to a minimum. Then, Clearmem releases the allocated memory to restore normal system functions.

▶ **To find the minimum working set for a process**

1. Start the process, then start a Performance Monitor log to measure the Process object once per second.
2. Run Clearmem, it usually runs for less than a minute.
3. Stop the log, change to Chart view, and in the **Options** menu, set **Data From** to the log file.
4. Use the Time Window to advance the beginning time to a point when Clearmem was running. (The Clearmem process does not appear in the **Add to Chart** dialog box unless the process is active at beginning time of the Time Window). Chart Process: % Processor Time for Clearmem to show the duration of the Clearmem process. Then, enlarge the Time Window so that the display begins just after Clearmem started running and ends just before Clearmem stopped running.
5. Chart Process: Working Set for the process you are testing.
6. Read the minimum working set size from the **Min** field on the value bar.

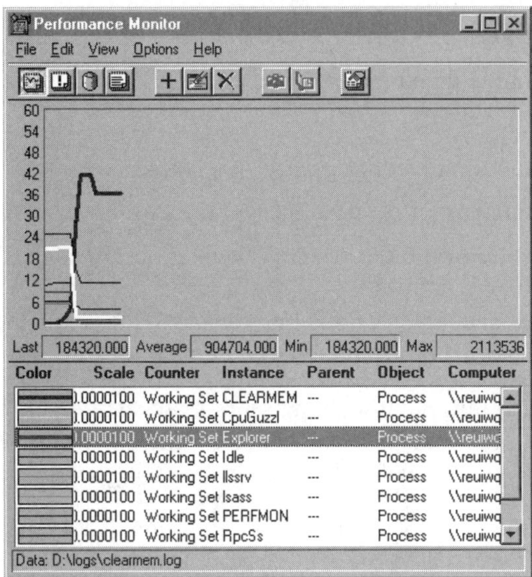

In this graph, the thick, black line is the working set of Clearmem, the memory-consuming test tool. As Clearmem increases its working set (as represented by the sharply increasing curve) the working sets of all other processes are trimmed until they contain only pages currently being used and those most recently accessed. The other lines in the graph represent the working sets of other processes. The value bar shows that the minimum working set for Explorer in this test is 184,320 bytes.

Available Bytes

Available bytes is a measure of free memory. The Virtual Memory Manager continually adjusts the space used in physical memory and on disk to maintain a minimum number of available bytes for the operating system and processes. When available bytes are plentiful, the Virtual Memory Manager lets the working sets of processes grow, or keeps them stable by removing an old page for each new page added. When available bytes are few, the Virtual Memory Manager must trim the working sets of processes to maintain the minimum required.

The following graph records the start of a process. It shows the relationship between page faults, the size of the working set of a process, and available bytes. When a process is faulting many pages, the Virtual Memory Manager increases the process's working set to slow the fault rate. The memory added to the working set is taken from available bytes, which shrinks accordingly. When available bytes falls close to the minimum tolerated by the system, the Virtual Memory Manager trims the working sets to recover some available bytes. The smaller working set makes page faults more likely, requiring the Virtual Memory Manager adjustment cycle to begin again.

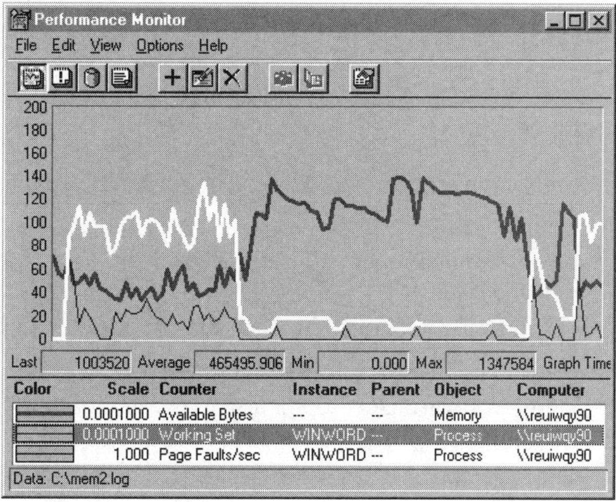

In this graph, which records the start of the Microsoft Word process, Winword.exe, the thick black line is Available Bytes, the white line is Working Set, and the thin black line is Page Faults/sec. The vertical maximum has been increased to 200 to accommodate the high values.

This example demonstrates the close association between the number of page faults and the increase in the working set. Note the inverse relationship between the size of the process's working set and available bytes for the system.

For the first third of the graph, the Virtual Memory Manager responds to page faults by dramatically increasing the size of the working set. Then, to recover available bytes, the working set is trimmed; thereafter, the Virtual Memory Manager responds to page faults by moving in just needed pages and by removing pages not recently referenced to keep the size of the working set to a minimum. At the end of the graph, an increase in the page fault rate drives the size of the working set back up.

Resolving a Memory Bottleneck

Although more memory is the easy solution to a memory bottleneck, it is not always the right solution.

- Monitor your applications and replace or correct those that leak memory or use it inefficiently.
- Localize your application's data references. Page Fault Monitor (Pfmon.exe), a tool on the Windows NT Resource Kit 4.0 CD, produces a running list of hard and soft page faults generated by each function call in a process.
- Localize your application's code references. The Working Set Tuner, included in the Win32 Software Development Kit, recommends an optimal organization of code functions to localize code page access.
- Increase the size of the paging file. In general, the bigger you can make it, the better it is. You can also have multiple paging files, though you can have only one on each logical drive. To change the size of the paging file, use the Control Panel System applet Performance tab. (Right-click My Computer, select Properties, then select the Performance tab.) The Virtual Memory box shows the current size of your paging files and lets you add new files or change the size of existing ones.
- Check the available space on your hard drives. If you have added memory, increase the size of your paging files. The paging file might need to expand to map the additional memory. If the space is not available, it might produce the symptoms of a memory bottleneck.
- Increase the size of your secondary memory cache, especially if you have just added memory. When you add memory, the secondary cache must map the larger memory space.

  The amount of secondary cache a system supports depends upon the design of the motherboard. Many motherboards support several secondary cache configurations (from 64K–512K or 256K–1 MB). Increasing cache size usually requires removing the existing static ram (SRAM) chips, replacing them with new SRAM chips, and changing some jumpers. Doing so would be helpful anytime you have a working set larger than your current secondary cache.
- Remove unnecessary protocols and drivers. Even idle protocols use space in the paged and nonpaged memory pools.

If all else fails, add memory. After struggling with a memory bottleneck and its grueling effects, you will find the improved response of the entire system well worth the investment.

CHAPTER 13

Detecting Processor Bottlenecks

The symptoms of a processor bottleneck are not difficult to recognize:

- Processor: %Processor Time often exceeds 90%.
- System: Processor Queue Length is often greater than 2.
- On multiprocessor systems, System: % Total Processor Time often exceeds 50%.

But these symptoms do not always indicate a processor problem. And even when the processor is the problem, adding extra processors does not always solve it. In this chapter, you will learn to use Performance Monitor to analyze such symptoms, determine the likely cause of processor bottlenecks, and implement effective solutions.

Note Before upgrading or adding processors, verify that the processor is the source of problem. Memory shortages, by far the most common bottleneck, often masquerade as high processor use. For more information see Chapter 12, "Detecting Memory Bottlenecks."

For more information on monitoring processor use on multiprocessor computers, see Chapter 16, "Monitoring Multiprocessor Computers."

Use the following counters to measure different aspects of processor use.

Object	Counter
System	% Total Processor Time
System	Processor Queue Length
Processor	% Processor Time
Process	% Processor Time
Process	% User Time
Process	% Privileged Time
Process	Priority Base
Thread	Thread State
Thread	Priority Base
Thread	Priority Current
Thread	Context Switches/Sec
Thread	% User Time
Thread	% Privileged Time

It is also useful to log Memory: Pages/sec, Logical Disk: % Disk Time and an activity count for your network to rule out problems in these components.

Measuring Processor Use

To investigate a processor bottleneck, log the System, Processor, Process, Thread, Logical Disk, and Memory counters for at least several days at an update interval of 60 seconds. Include a network counter if you suspect that network traffic might be interrupting the processor too frequently. The longer you can log, the more accurate your results will be. Processor use might be a problem only at certain times of the day, week or month, and you are likely to see these patterns if you log for a longer duration.

You can use At.exe or Microsoft Test to start and stop Performance Monitor at critical times and batch the logs for later examination.

- At.exe is included in Windows NT workstation and server. For instructions, open a command prompt window and, at the command line, type **at /?**.
- Microsoft Test is purchased separately. It is described in Chapter 11, "Performance Monitoring Tools."

You can also use CPU Stress to measure the response of your configuration to high processor use and to simulate processor bottlenecks. CPU Stress is a testing tool included on the Windows NT Resource Kit 4.0 CD in the Performance Tools group in \Perftool\Meastool\CpuStres.exe. For more information, see Rktools.hlp.

Performance Monitor includes some direct and some indirect indicators of processor use, for both single- and multiple-processor computers. This section discusses some characteristics of the measurements that you need to know to correctly interpret the values.

The Idle Process

Processors never rest. Once powered up, they must always be executing some thread of instructions. When not executing the thread of an active user or system process, they execute a thread of a process called *Idle*.

The Idle process has one thread per processor. It has such a low base priority that it runs only when nothing else is scheduled to run. This process does nothing but occupy the processors until a real thread is ready to use them. On a quiet machine, when you would expect processor use to be very low, the Idle process will be using most of the processor time.

Performance Monitor and Task Manager both use the Idle thread to indicate that the processor is not busy. Processor: % Processor Time, System: % Total Processor Time, and Task Manager's CPU Usage and CPU Usage History all measure the Idle thread and display processor busy time as the difference between the total time and the time spent running the Idle thread. Performance Monitor's Process: % Processor Time for the _Total instance even includes time processing the Idle thread.

To measure the Idle thread, use the Process: %Processor Time counter for the Idle process, or use the Processes tab on Task Manager.

Processor Sampling

Performance Monitor samples—rather than times—threads. Sampling uses far fewer resources, especially on Intel 486 and earlier processors which have a software timer on a separate chip. Consequently, processor time, process time, and thread time counters might underestimate or overestimate activity on your system.

The following graph demonstrates this sampling error.

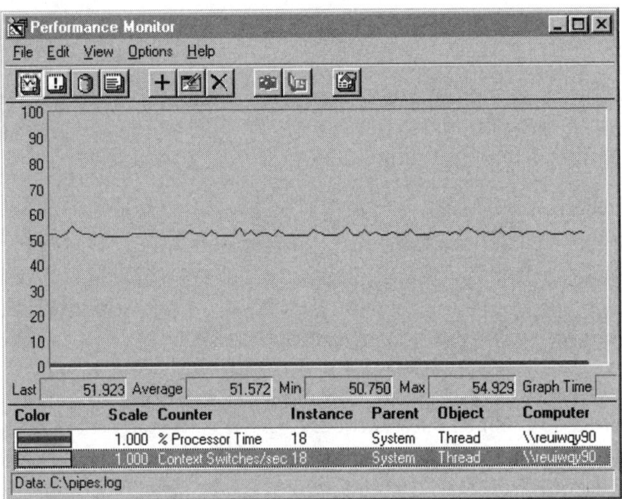

In this example, the context switch rate reveals that the processor is being switched from running the System 18 thread to running other threads about 50 times each second. However, the thread's total processor time (the thick line at the bottom) appears to be 0. This contradictory data results from sampling error: the thread ran so briefly between context switches that Performance Monitor missed it.

This sampling error is most evident on processes—such as Performance Monitor—that are launched by the processor interrupt. *TotlProc*, a utility on Windows NT Resource Kit 4.0 CD, installs an extensible Performance Monitor counter designed to measure processor time on interrupt-launched applications more accurately. TotlProc is in the Performance Tools group in \PerfTool\TotlProc. For more details, see Rktools.hlp.

Warning TotlProc is not compatible with the processor time counters on other tools. While TotlProc is running, Performance Monitor and Task Manager processor time counters always display 100%.

Understanding the Processor Counters

It is important to understand the components of the primary processor activity counters, and to distinguish them from each other.

Counter	Description
System: % Total Processor Time	For what proportion of the sample interval were all processors busy? A measure of activity on all processors. In a multiprocessor computer, this is equal to the sum of Processor: % Processor Time on all processors divided by the number of processors. On single-processor computers, it is equal to Processor: % Processor time, although the values may vary due to different sampling time.
System: Processor Queue Length	How many threads are ready, but have to wait for a processor? This is an instantaneous count, not an average, so it is best viewed in charts, rather than reports. Unlike disk queue counters, it counts only waiting threads, not those being serviced. The queue length counter is on the System object because there is a single queue even when there are multiple processors on the computer.
Processor: % Processor Time	For what proportion of the sample interval was each processor busy? This counter measures the percentage of time the thread of the Idle process is running, subtracts it from 100%, and displays the difference. This counter is equivalent to Task Manager's CPU Usage counter.
Processor: % User Time Processor: % Privileged Time	How often were all processors executing threads running in user mode and in privileged mode? Threads running in user mode are probably running in their own application code. Threads running in privileged mode are using operating system services. The user time and privileged time counters on the System and Processor objects do not always sum to 100%. They are measures of non-Idle time, so they sum to the total of non-idle time. For example, if the processor was running the Idle thread for 85% of the time, the sum of Processor: % User Time and Processor: % Privileged Time would be 15%.

Counter	Description
Process: % Processor Time	For what proportion of the sample interval was the processor running the threads of this process? This counter sums the processor time of each thread of the process over the sample interval.
Process: % Processor Time: _Total	For what proportion of the sample interval was the processor processing? This counter sums the time all threads are running on the processor, including the thread of the Idle process on each processor, which runs to occupy the processor when no other threads are scheduled. The value of Process: % Processor Time: _Total is 100% except when the processor is interrupted. (100% processor time = Process: % Processor Time: Total + Processor: % Interrupt Time + Processor: % DPC Time) This counter differs significantly from Processor: % Processor Time, which excludes Idle.
Process: % User Time Process: % Privileged Time	How often are the threads of the process running in its own application code (or the code of another user-mode process)? How often are the threads of the process running in operating system code? Process: % User Time and Process: % Privileged Time sum to Process: % Processor Time.
Process: Priority Base	What is the base priority of the process? How likely is it that this process will be able to execute if the processor gets busy? The base priority of the process establishes a range within which the dynamic priorities of its threads vary. The system schedules ready threads for the processor in order of their dynamic priority.
Thread: Thread State	What is the processor status of this thread? An instantaneous indicator of the dispatcher thread state, which represents the current status of the thread with regard to the processor. Threads in the Ready state (1) are in the processor queue. In Performance Monitor, the threads of the Performance Monitor process, Perfmon.exe always appear to be running. . Other threads that are getting processor time are those recorded as switching from Ready (1) to Waiting (5). A table of Windows NT thread states appears in “Thread State” later in this chapter.

Counter	Description
Thread: Priority Base	What is the base priority of the thread? The base priority of a thread is determined by the base priority of the process in which it runs. Except for Idle and Real-time threads, the base priority of a thread varies only +/-2 from the base priority of its process.
Thread: Priority Current	What is the current dynamic priority of this thread? How likely is it that the thread will get processor time? The Windows NT Microkernel schedules threads for the processor in order of their priority. The system adjusts the dynamic priority of threads within the range of the base priority of the process to optimize the response of processes interacting with the user.
Thread: % Privileged Time	How often are the threads in the process running in their own application code (or the code of another user-mode process)? How often are the threads of the process running in operating system code? Process: % User Time and Process: % Privileged Time sum to Process: % Processor Time.

Recognizing a Processor Bottleneck

Bottlenecks occur only when the processor is so busy that it cannot respond to requests for time. These situations are indicated, in part, by high rates of processor activity, but mainly by long, sustained queues and poor application response. If you do not have a long queue, you have a busy processor, but not a problem.

If you notice sustained high processor use and persistent, long queues:

- Rule out a *memory bottleneck*. These are much more common than processor bottlenecks, especially or workstations and small point-to-point networks. For more information, see Chapter 12, "Detecting Memory Bottlenecks."
- Identify the processes using processor time. Determine if a single process or multiple processes are active during a bottleneck.
- Examine the processor-intensive processes in detail. Determine how many threads run in the process and watch the patterns of thread activity during a bottleneck. If you develop or maintain these processes, you can write counters to monitor thread activity at a lower level.
- Consider the priority at which the process and its threads run. You may be able to eliminate a bottleneck merely by adjusting the base priority of the process or the current priorities of its threads.
- Choose a solution and test it, then log the general activity of your system, using counters like those in the Overview settings file described in Chapter 10, "About Performance Monitor."

Processor Queue Length

The System: Processor Queue Length counter shows how many threads are contending for the processor. Threads are considered to be in the queue if they are in the Ready thread state, but not running. (Thread states are discussed in more detail later in this section.) Processor Queue Length is part of the System object, not the Processor object, because there is a single queue even when there is more than one processor.

Tip Start a Performance Monitor alert on System: Processor Queue Length. Set it to report an alert if the queue is over 2 and to log the alerts to the Event Viewer application event log. Review the alert panel and the logs frequently for patterns of activity that produce long queues.

Note In Windows NT versions 3.5 and earlier, the Processor Queue Length counter did not work until a thread counter was added to the chart, log, or report. This was fixed in version 3.51 and is no longer necessary.

The clearest symptom of a processor bottleneck is a sustained or recurring queue of more than 2 threads. Although queues are most likely to develop when the processor is very busy, they can develop when utilization is well below 90%, and as low as 60–70%. The following graph shows a sustained processor queue with utilization ranging from 50–90%:

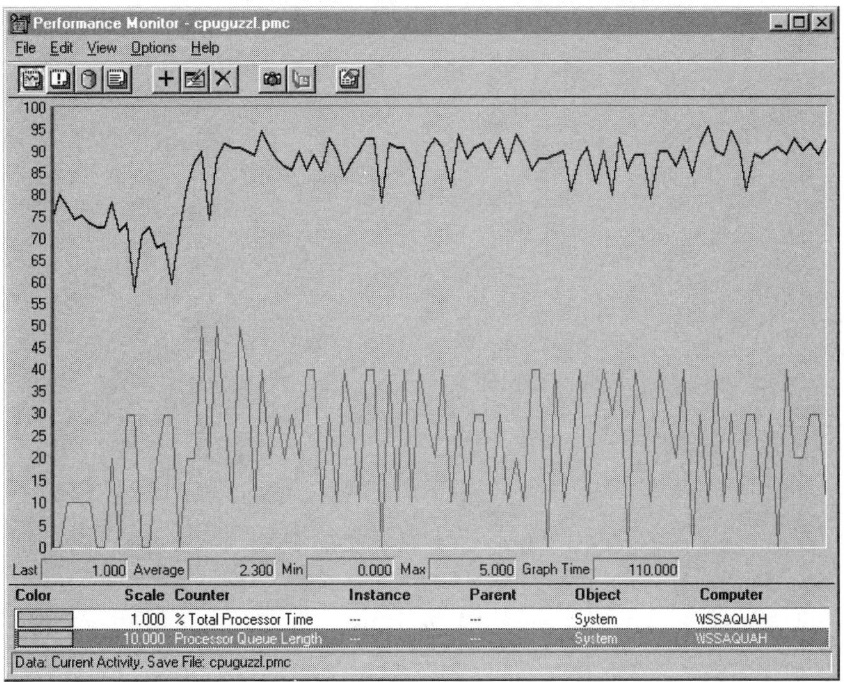

In this graph, the black line at the top represents System: %Total Processor Time. The gray line is System: Processor Queue Length. Queues are more likely to develop at lower processor use rates when the requests for processor time arrive in clusters or are random.

The following graph shows a sustained processor queue accompanied by processor use at or near 100%.

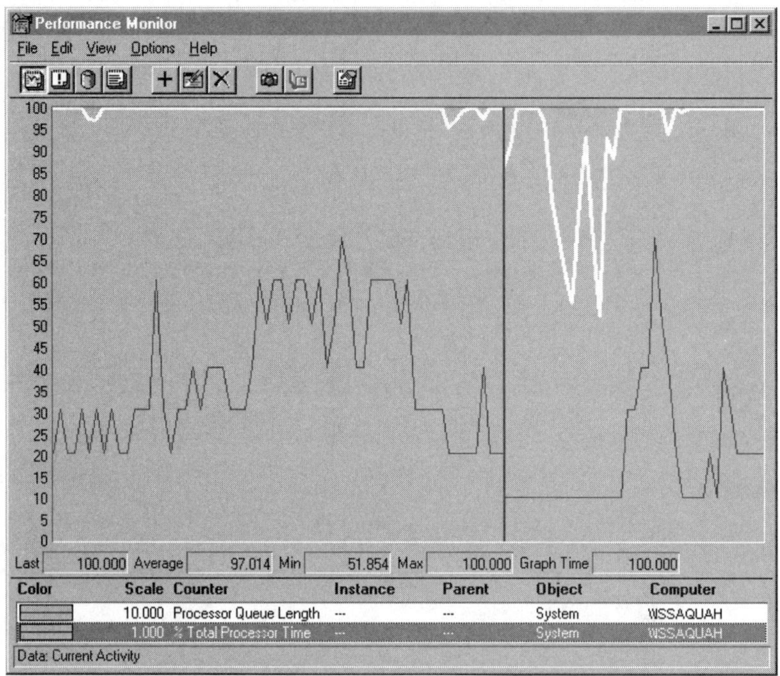

In this example, the queue length averages about 4 with a maximum of 7, and it never falls below 2. Note that the Processor Queue Length counter scale is multiplied by 10 to make the values easier to see. (The same effect could be achieved by reducing the vertical maximum to 10.)

If your system charts look like this, log over a longer period of time. This use pattern might be limited to a certain time of day. If so, you might be able to eliminate this bottleneck by changing the load balance between computers. However, if sustained queues appears frequently, more investigation is warranted.

The following figure uses the queue length counter to confirm a bottleneck. It shows that when a processor is already at 100% utilization, starting another process does not accomplish more work.

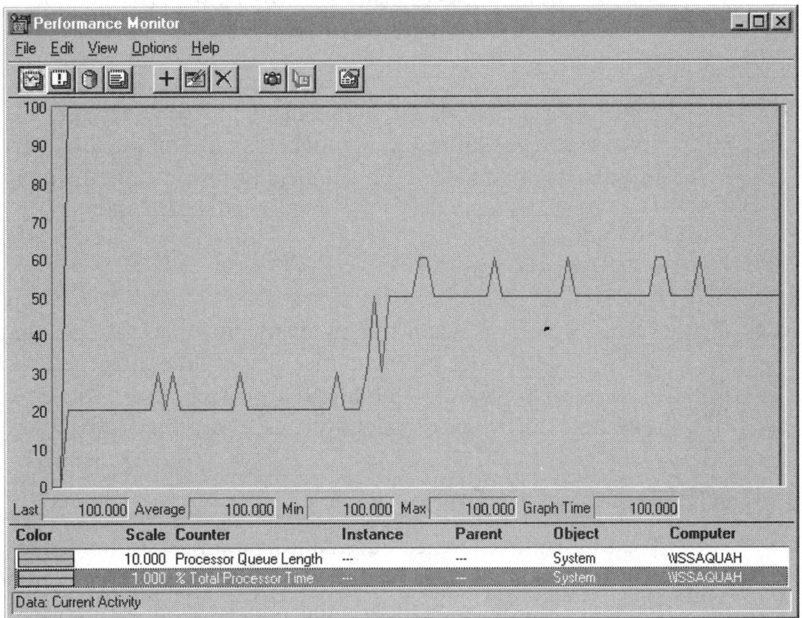

In this example, the dark line running across the top of the graph is System: % Total Processor Time. The gray line below it is System: Processor Queue Length. Midway through the sample interval, a process with three threads was started. The graph illustrates that the queue increased by three threads. Some of the threads of the added process might be in the queue, or they might be running, having displaced the threads of a lower priority process. Nonetheless, because the processor was already at maximum capacity, no more work is accomplished.

Processes in a Bottleneck

After you have recognized a processor bottleneck, the next step is to determine whether a single process is monopolizing the processor or whether the processor is consumed by running many processes.

Graphs of Processor: % Processor Time during single and multiple-process bottlenecks are nearly indistinguishable. Queue length is not much help either, because it tells you more about what is not running than what is. Moreover, queue length is an indicator of the numbers of threads, not the numbers of processes. The threads of a single, multithreaded process contending with each other and with other processes will produce as long a queue as the threads of several single-threaded processes.

The only clear indicator of how many processes are causing the bottleneck is a log of the processor use by each process over time. Log the Process object, then chart Process: % Processor Time for all processes except Idle and _Total. This will reveal how many (and which) processes are very active during the bottleneck.

Single-process Bottlenecks

The following figure, captured during a processor bottleneck, is a histogram of a processor bottleneck caused by a single process. This example was produced by running CPU Stress, a tool on the Windows NT Resource Kit 4.0 CD.

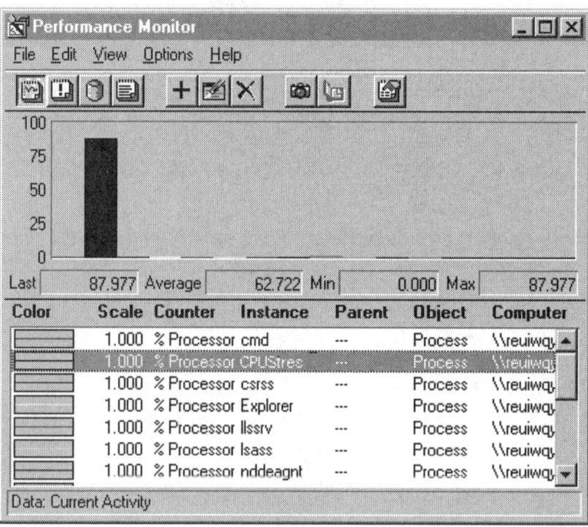

This histogram shows that a single process (represented by the tall, black bar) is highly active during a bottleneck; its threads are running for more than 80% of the sample interval. If this pattern persists and a long queue develops, it is reasonable to suspect that the application running in the process is causing the bottleneck.

Note that a highly active process is a problem only if a queue is developing because other processes are ready to run, but are shut out by the active process.

Note Histograms are useful for simplifying graphs with multiple counters. However, they display only instantaneous values, so they are recommended only when you are charting current activity and watching the graphs as they change. When you are reviewing data logged over time, line graphs are much more informative.

If you suspect that an application is causing a processor bottleneck:

- Stop using the application for a few days or move it to a different computer. Then, log processor use again. If the problem disappears, it is likely to have been caused by the application. If processor use continues to be a bottleneck even without the application, repeat the procedure, carefully monitoring the processes that are active when queues are longest.
- If you have traced the bottleneck to a single application, you might consider replacing it. If it is your application, you can examine its threads in detail or change its base priority. These options are described in the next sections.
- You can also use Performance Monitor to tune an inefficient application. The Win32 Software Development Kit includes tools and methods for optimizing applications, including instructions for building extensible counters to monitor the inner workings of your application.
- As a temporary solution, you can change the base priority of the active application or of an application that is being prevented from running. You can also change the relative priority of foreground to background applications. These solutions, discussed in detail in "Examining Priority" later in this chapter, might help you get your urgent work done while you search for a long-term solution.
- As a last resort, upgrade the processor or add additional processors. Multithreaded applications can run on multiple processors, relieving the load. However, single-threaded applications will not benefit; they must be resolved by replacing the processor with a faster one.

Multiple-process Bottlenecks

In a bottleneck caused by a multiple processes, no single process stands out above all others. When multiple processes are involved, several might be active, each using a smaller proportion of processor cycles. Multiprocess bottlenecks usually result when the processor cannot handle the process load. They do not usually indicate a problem with an application.

The following figure shows a histogram of processor time for many active processes.

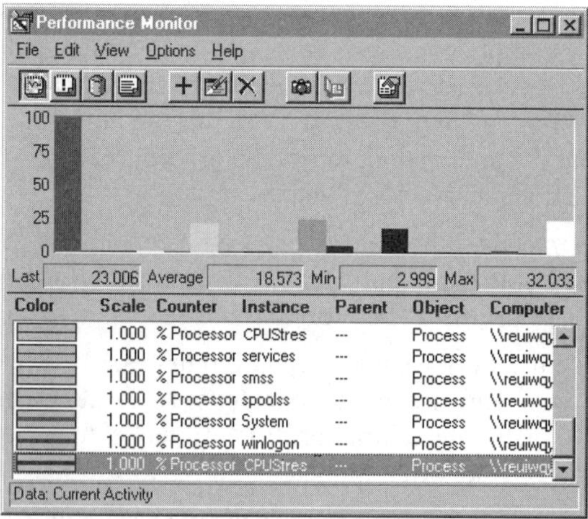

This example was produced by using four copies of a simulation tool, CPU Stress, which consumes processor cycles at a priority and activity level you specify.

In this example, the highest bar on the far left is System: % Total Processor Time. At least four other processes (represented by bars reaching about 20% processor time) are consuming the processor while sharing it nearly equally. Although each process is only using 10–20% of the processor, the result is the same as a single process using 100% of processor time.

The following figure shows Processor: Processor Queue length during this bottleneck.

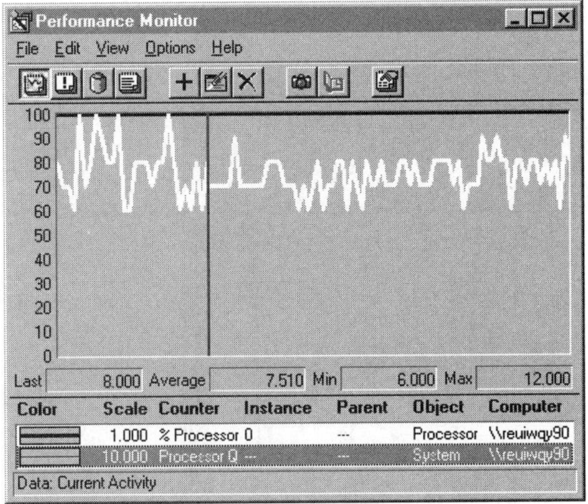

In the graph, Processor: % Processor Time (the black line running across the top of the graph) remains at 100% during the sample interval. System: Processor Queue Length (the white line) reveals a long queue. The value bar shows that the queue length varies between 6 threads and 12 threads, and averages over 7.5 threads.

The following figure shows Task Manager during the same bottleneck. It shows that four copies of CPU Stress are each using about one-fifth of the time of the single processor on the computer. (Task Manager displays current values, so you need to watch the display to see changes in processor use for each process.)

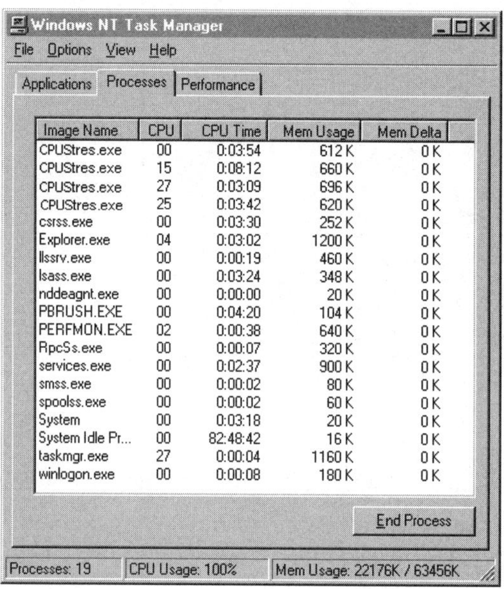

Although a faster processor might help this situation somewhat, multiple-process bottlenecks are best resolved by adding another processor. Multithreaded processes, including multithreaded Windows NT services, benefit the most from additional processors because their threads can run simultaneously on multiple processors. Even after adding another processor, it is prudent to continue testing with different priorities and processor loads to resolve this more complex situation.

Threads in a Bottleneck

After you have determined which process or processes are causing the bottleneck, it is time to think about threads. Threads are the components of a process that run on the processor. They are the objects that are waiting in the queue, running in user mode or operating system code, and being switched on to and off of the processor.

Understanding thread behavior is essential to understanding how processes use the processor. However, unless you are developing or maintaining an application, or have access to the person who is, there is little you can do about thread behavior.

Warning Performance Monitor counter values for threads are subject to error when threads are stopping and starting. Faulty values sometimes appear as large spikes in the data. For details, see "Monitoring Threads" in Chapter 10, "About Performance Monitor."

To study threads during a bottleneck, log the System, Processor, Process, and Thread objects for several days at an update interval of 60 seconds.

Note When logging the Thread object, you must also log the Process object. If you do not, the process names will not appear in the Instances box for the Thread object and threads will be difficult to identify.

Single vs. Multiple Threads in a Bottleneck

Sometimes a single thread in a process can cause a processor bottleneck, making the whole process and the processor function poorly. Bottlenecks caused by multiple threads in a single process, single threads in multiple processes, and multiple threads in multiple processes are essentially the same: Too many threads are contending for the processor at the same time. However, because these situations are resolved quite differently, it is worth distinguishing among them.

The following figure shows a graph of processor time and queue length during a bottleneck caused by a single, multithreaded process. The line running across the top is processor time. The white line is queue length.

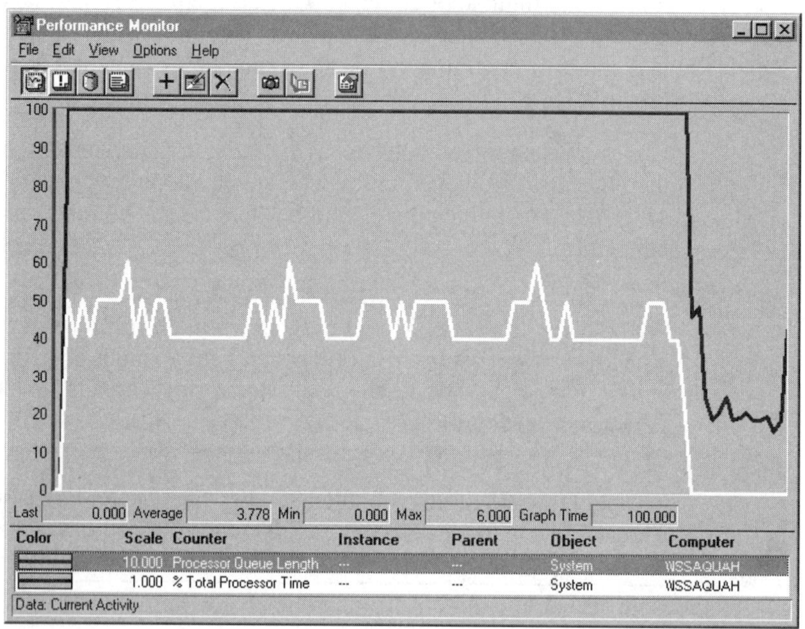

The queue is quite long, running between 4 and 5 ready threads with periodic peaks of 6 threads. The EKG-like pattern is just an artifact of the application. These large values might trick you into thinking multiple processes are at work. The clue that the queue is populated by many threads of just one process comes at the end of the graph when the process is stopped, and the queue length drops to 0.

Uncovering Multiple Threads

The best way to determine how many processes produced the threads in the queue is to chart the processor time used by each process.

The following figure is a histogram of Processor: % Processor Time for all processes running when the queue in the previous graph was measured:

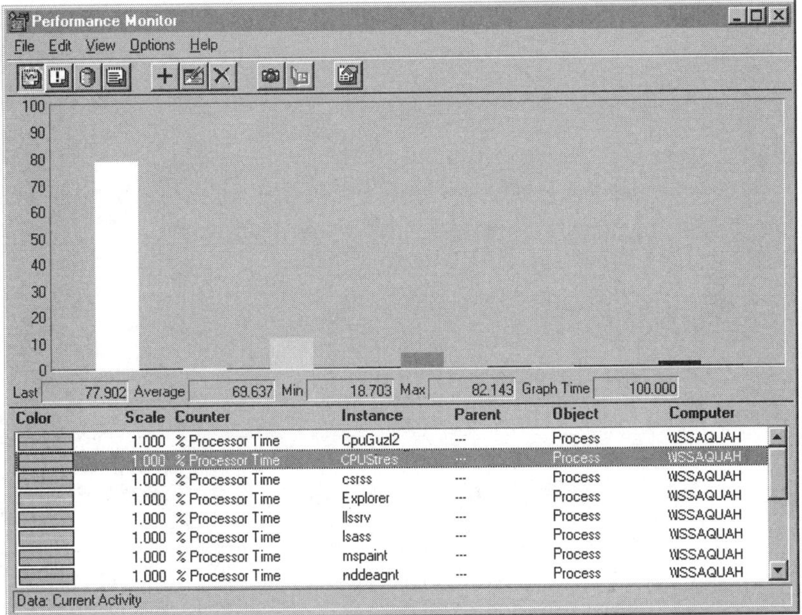

Despite the large queue, this chart makes it evident that a single process, represented by the tall, white bar, is using much more than its share of the processor—nearly 80% on average. If multiple processes were at work, no single bar would be so tall and there would be multiple bars at nearly the same height.

Charting the Threads

The Thread object also has a %Processor Time counter. It is most useful after you have determined that one or two processes are accounting for most of a processor's time.

The following figure is a histogram of Thread: % Processor Time for all threads running during the bottleneck.

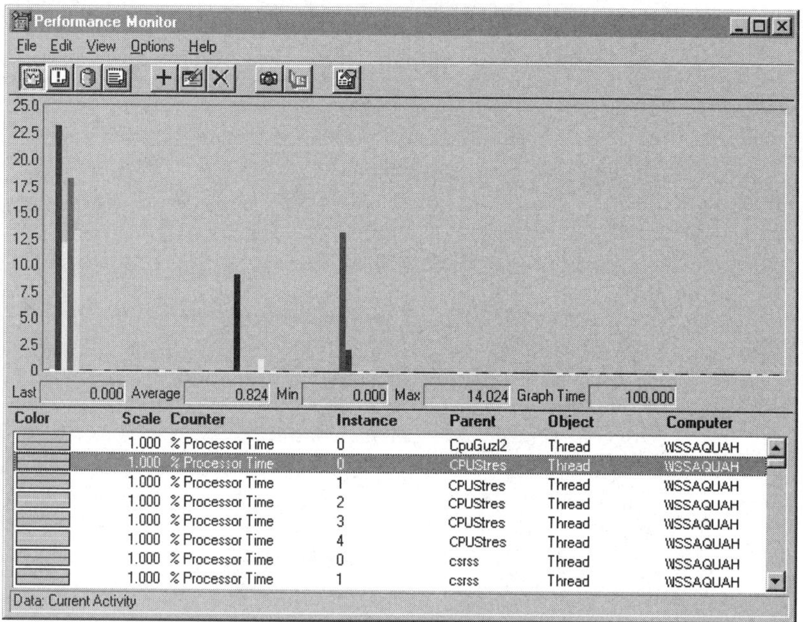

Each bar of the histogram represents the processor time of a single thread. Threads are identified by process name and thread number and, in this graph, the threads of each process are listed in sequence. (The order in which the threads appear on the graph depends on the order in which you add them to your chart.) The thread number represents the order in which the threads started, and it can change even as the thread runs.

This graph shows that the four threads of the five threads of the CPU Stress process (at the far left) are dominating the pattern of processor use, although a few other threads are getting some processor time.

If your graphs look like these, you might consider adding another processor. A bottleneck caused by one or more multithreaded applications is a prime candidate for a multiprocessor computer. Instead, you might choose to replace the application that is consuming the processor time, or measure, tune, and rewrite it. The next sections assumes you have taken the latter path and demonstrates a more detailed investigation of thread behavior.

Thread State

A long processor queue is a warning that a bottleneck, however brief, might be developing. The Thread: Thread State counter lets you examine which threads are in the queue and how long they remain before being serviced.

By definition, all of the threads in the processor queue are Ready, but are waiting for a processor to become available. *Ready* is a dispatcher thread state, one of eight states that signal when a thread is prepared to be dispatched to the processor.

The following table lists the thread states for threads in Windows NT.

Thread state	Definition
0	Initialized. The thread is recognized as an object by the microkernel.
1	Ready. The thread is prepared to run on the next free processor.
2	Running. The thread is executing.
3	Standby. The thread is assigned to a processor and about to run. Only one thread can be in Standby state at a time.
4	Terminated. The thread is finished executing.
5	Waiting. The thread is not ready for the processor. When it is ready, it will have to be rescheduled.
6	Transition. The thread is ready but waiting for resources other than the processor to become available.
7	The thread state is unknown.

To determine which threads are contending for the processor, chart the thread states of all threads in the system. The following figure shows such a chart. The vertical maximum is reduced to 10 to show the values which range from 0 through 7.

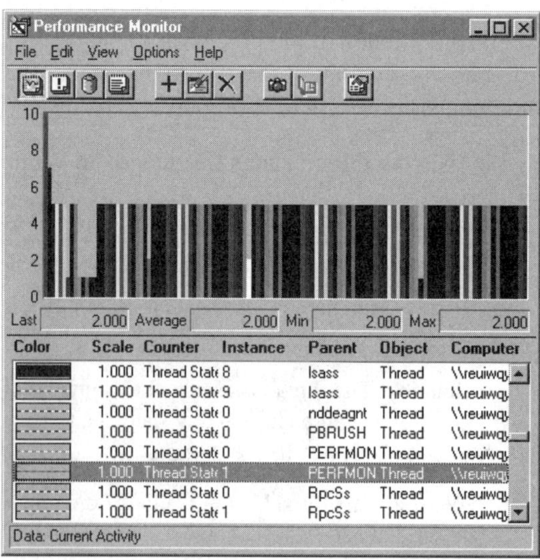

The first, tallest bar is System: % Total Processor Time, is 100%, scaled to 0.1 to fit in the chart. The next bar is System: Processor Queue Length, which is 7. The remaining bars represent the thread states of threads in active processes.

The thread that is running on the processor, that is, at Thread State 2, is PERFMON Thread 1, a thread of the Performance Monitor executable. (It is represented by the white bar in middle of the graph.) In fact, a Performance Monitor thread always appears as the running thread when it captures data; if it were not, it could not be capturing the data. This is an inescapable artifact of the tool.

Therefore, in Thread State charts or graphs, you need to assume that the processes getting processor time are those bouncing from Ready and in the queue (1) to Waiting (5). In this example, the bars at Ready (1) are the first few on the left, representing the processor-guzzling simulation tool, a System thread, two Services threads, and an RPC subsystem thread. (As you scroll through a running Performance Monitor graph, the thread state value appears in the value bar.)

The pattern of thread state activity is better seen in a line graph. Although it is much busier, it reveals the patterns of processor use by each thread.

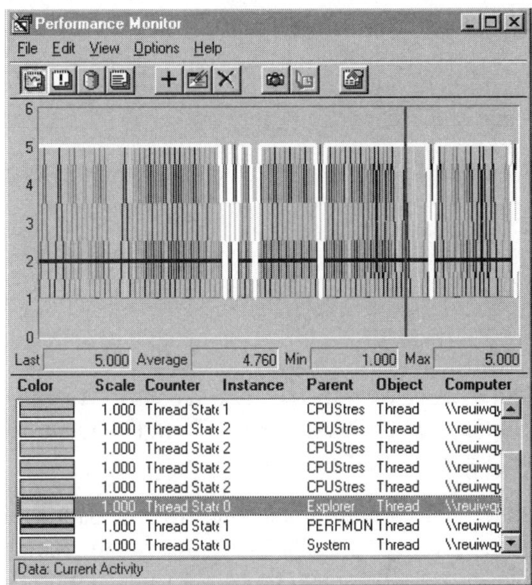

To create a graph like this one, chart all running threads, then delete threads that are never ready and set the vertical maximum to 6. This is a bit hard to read in still life, but the patterns for each thread become more apparent when you highlight the selected line by pressing the BACKSPACE key.

The black line that always appears to be running (at thread state 2) is PERFMON. The lines with the most activity are those of CPU Stress, the simulation tool. The white line is a thread of the Explorer process.

Although busy, this graph highlights which threads are in the queue and reveals their scheduling patterns. On logged data, you can use the Time Window to limit a thread state graph to selected data points, so you can measure the elapsed time a thread spent in each thread state. Summing the time in the ready state in each second sampled will tell you how long, on average, the threads are waiting in the queue. This information is quite useful when tuning thread behavior.

Context Switches

A *context switch* is when the microkernel switches the processor from one thread to another. Therefore, context switches are an indirect indicator of threads getting processor time. A careful examination of context switch data reveals the patterns of processor use for a thread and indicates how efficiently it shares the processor with other threads of the process or other processes.

Performance Monitor has context switch counters on the System and Thread objects:

- System: Context Switches/sec counts all context switches.
- Thread: Context Switches/sec is incremented when the thread gets or loses the attention of the processor.

Both rates are an average over the last two seconds. System: Context Switches/sec and Thread: Context Switches/sec: _Total should be identical or within the range of experimental error.

Care must be taken in interpreting the data. An application that is really monopolizing the processor actually lowers the rate of context switches because it does not let other process get much processor time. A high rate of context switching means that the processor is being shared, if only briefly.

The following figure is a histogram of Context Switches/sec for all running threads.

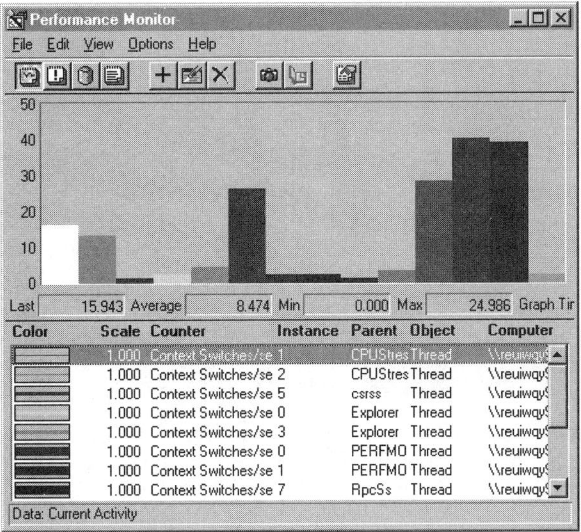

This histogram shows which threads are getting at least *some* processor time during a bottleneck. The large bars on the right side of the graph are system threads being moved onto and off of the processor during a bottleneck. The bottleneck is caused by the process represented by the first bar on the left. The process in the middle is Performance Monitor, which runs at a high priority to ensure that it gets some processor time.

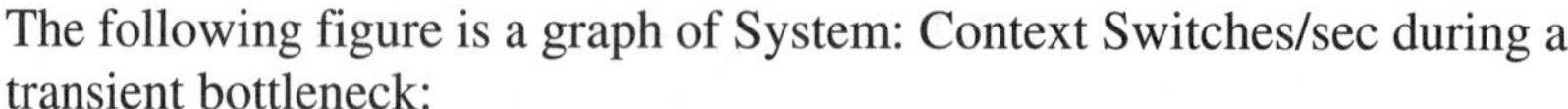

The following figure is a graph of System: Context Switches/sec during a transient bottleneck:

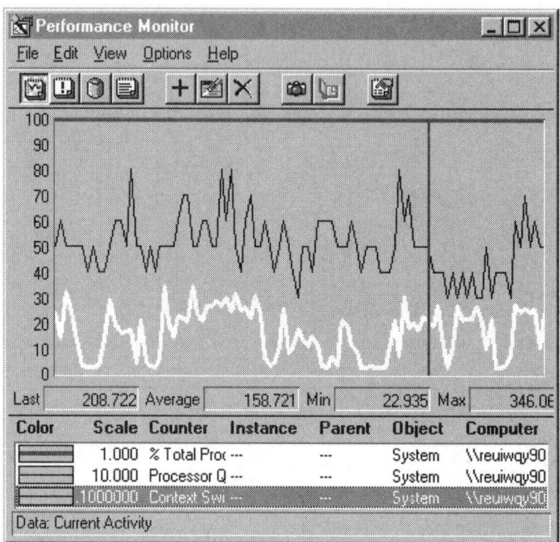

In this graph, System: % Total Processor time (the thick line running along the top of the graph) remains at 100% during the sample interval. System: Processor Queue Length (the thin line, scaled by a factor of 10), shows that the queue varies from 4 to 8, with a mean near 5. System: Context Switches (the white line), reveals an average of about 150 switches per second, a moderate rate. A much higher rate of context switches (near 500 per second) might indicate a problem with a network card or device driver.

User Mode and Privileged Mode

Another aspect of thread behavior is whether it is running in user mode or privileged mode:

- *User mode* is the processing mode in which applications run. Threads running in user mode are running in their own application code or the code of another user mode process, such as an environment subsystem. Processes running in user mode cannot access hardware directly and must call operating system functions to switch their threads to privileged mode to use operating system services.
- *Privileged* or *kernel mode* is the processing mode that allows code to have direct access to all hardware and memory in the system. The Windows NT Executive runs in privileged mode. Application threads must be switched to privileged mode to run in operating system code. Applications call privileged-mode operating system services for essential functions such as drawing windows, receiving information about user keyboard and mouse input, and checking security.

For more information about user mode and kernel mode, see "Windows NT 4.0 Workstation Architecture," earlier in this book.

You can determine the percentage of time that threads of a process are running in user and privileged mode. Process Viewer (Pviewer.exe), a tool on the Windows NT Resource Kit 4.0 CD in the Performance Tools group, displays the proportion of user and privileged time for each running process and, separately, for each thread in the process. It can monitor local and remote computers and requires no setup. For more information about Process Viewer, see Chapter 11, "Performance Monitoring Tools," and Rktools.hlp.

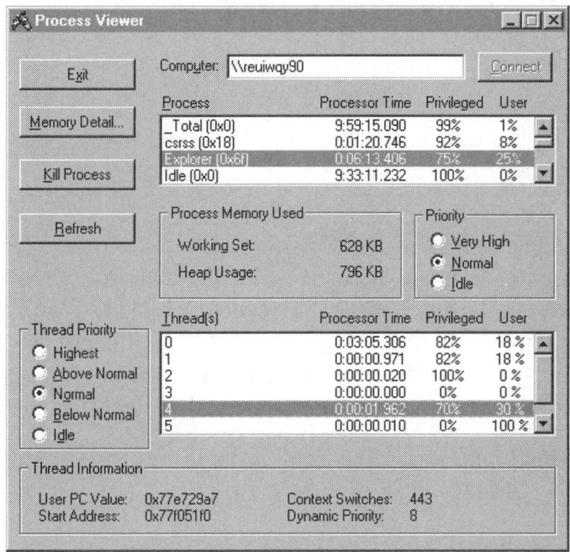

Performance Monitor has % Privileged Time and % User Time counters on the System, Processor, Process, and Thread objects. These counters are described in "Understanding the Processor Counters" earlier in this chapter.

In the user time and privileged time counters, Performance Monitor displays the proportion of total processor time that the process is spending in user or privileged mode. While Process Viewer values sum to 100%, Performance Monitor values sum to their percentage of processor time.

The following figure is a Performance Monitor report on the proportion of user and privileged time for three processes.

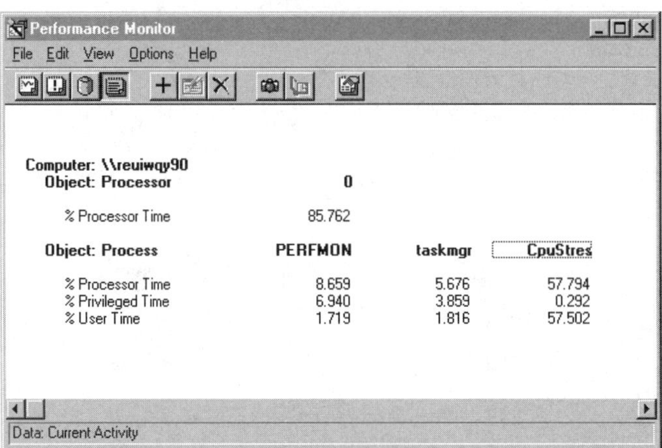

In this example, Perfmon, the Performance Monitor process is running mainly (80%) in privileged mode, perhaps collecting data from the Performance Library which resides in the Windows NT Executive. Taskmgr, the Task Manager process is also running mainly in privileged mode (70%), though this proportion varies significantly as the process runs. In contrast, CpuStres, the process for the CPU Stress test tool, runs entirely in user mode all of the time.

The following graph shows the proportion of user and privileged time for each thread of the Task Manager process.

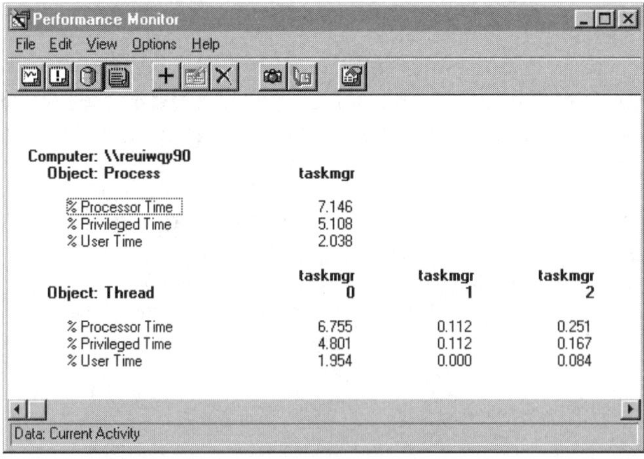

Examining Priority

Thread priority dictates the order in which threads run on the processor and, when the processor is busy, determines which threads get to run at all. The Windows NT Microkernel always schedules the highest priority ready thread to run, even if it requires interrupting a lower priority thread. This ensures that processors are always doing the highest priority task.

Examining process and thread priority is part of tuning your application and your hardware and software configuration for maximum efficiency. Windows NT adjusts thread priorities to optimize processes, but you can monitor process and thread priority, change the base priorities of processes, and change the relative priority of foreground and background applications.

Tip For more information about process and thread priority, including a table of all process and thread priorities, see "Scheduling and Priorities" in Chapter 5, "Windows NT 4.0 Workstation Architecture."

In Windows NT, priorities are organized into a hierarchy. Each level of the priority hierarchy limits the range within which the lower levels can vary. Priorities are associated with a number from 1 to 31. The priority classes are associated with a range of numbers which sometimes overlap at the extremes.

- The *base priority class* of a process establishes a range within which the base priority of the process can vary. Processes are assigned to one of the four *base priority* classes, (Idle, Normal, High, and Real-time). The base priority class is set in application code and is not changed by the operating system.
- The *base priority of a process* varies within its base priority class. Windows NT adjust the base priority of processes to optimize the response of processes to the user. In Performance Monitor, use Process: Priority Base to monitor this value.
- The *base priority of a thread* varies within the base priority of its process. Except for Idle and Read-time threads, the base priority of a thread varies only within +/- 2 of the base priority of its process. In Performance Monitor, use Thread: Priority Base to monitor this value.
- The *dynamic priority of a thread* determines its order in processor scheduling. Windows NT continually adjusts the dynamic priorities of threads to optimize performance within the range established by the base priority. The dynamic priority of a thread can equal or exceed its base priority, but it never falls below it.

Windows NT has several strategies for optimizing application performance by adjusting process and thread priority:

- *Foreground boost.* Windows NT boosts the base priority of the process whose window is at the top of the window stack. This is known as the foreground process. It is intended to maximize the response of the process with which the user is interacting.
- *Priority inversion.* Windows NT randomly boosts the priority of lower-priority threads that would not otherwise be able to run. This is designed, in part, to prevent a lower-priority thread from monopolizing a shared resource. The lower priority thread runs long enough to free the shared resource for use by higher-priority threads.
- *Dynamic priority boost.* When a thread has been waiting for a resource or for an I/O operation to complete, Windows NT boosts its priority as soon as the thread becomes ready. The amount of the boost depends upon what the thread was waiting for, but it is usually enough to assure that the thread runs soon thereafter, if not immediately. For example, the dynamic priority of thread waiting for disk I/O is increased by 1 when the disk I/O is complete. The dynamic priority of a thread waiting for keyboard input is increased by 5 when it is ready.

  Also, if a window receives input from a timer or input device, Windows NT boosts the priorities of all threads in the process that owns the window. For example, this boost allows a thread to change the mouse pointer when the mouse moves over its window.

Measuring and Tuning Priorities

Windows NT and the Windows NT Resource Kit 4.0 CD include several tools for monitoring the base priority of processes and threads and the dynamic priority of threads. You can set the base priority of processes and threads in the application code. Some Windows NT tools and Resource Kit tools let you change the base priority of a process as it runs, but the change lasts only until the process stops.

Warning Changing priorities may destabilize the system. Increase the priority of a process may prevent other processes, including system services, from running. Decreasing the priority of a process may prevent it from running, not just allow to run less frequently.

Tip When you start processes from a command prompt window by using the **Start** command, you can specify a base priority for the process for that run. To see all of the start options, type **Start /?** at the command prompt.

Using Performance Monitor

Performance Monitor lets you watch and record—but not change—the base and dynamic priorities of threads and processes. Performance Monitor has priority counters on the Process and Thread objects:

- Process: Priority Base
- Thread: Priority Base
- Thread: Priority Current

Because these counters are instantaneous and display whole number values, averages and the _Total instance are meaningless, and are displayed as zero.

The following figure is a graph of the base priorities of several processes. It shows the relative priority of the running applications. The Idle process (the white line at the bottom of the graph) runs at a priority of Idle (0) so it never interrupts another process.

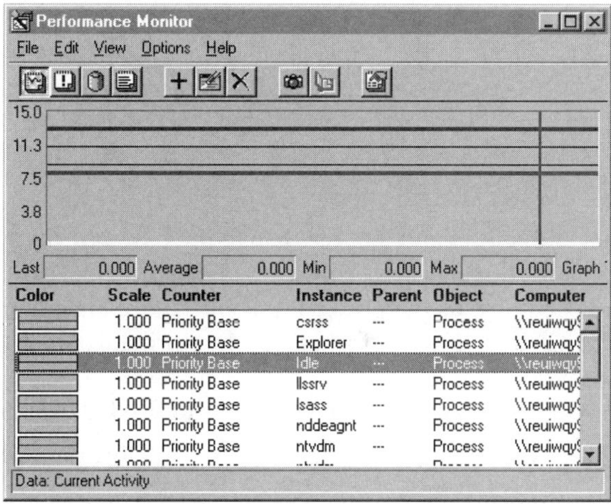

The following figure is a graph of the dynamic priority of the single thread in the Paintbrush applet, Pbrush.exe, as it changes in response to user actions. The base priority of the thread (the gray line) is 8 (foreground Normal). During this period of foreground use, the dynamic priority of the thread (the black line) is 14, but drops to 8 when other processes need to run.

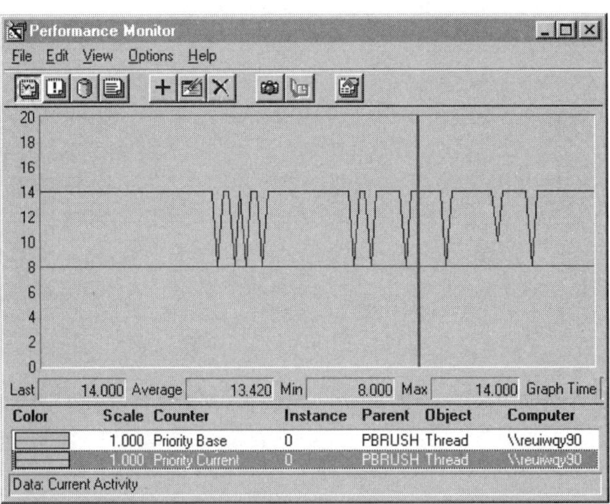

Using Task Manager

Task Manager displays and let you change the base priority of a process, but it does not monitor threads. Base priorities changed with Task Manager are effective only as long as the process runs. For more information, see "Task Manager" in Chapter 11, "Performance Monitoring Tools."

▶ **To display the base priorities of processes in Task Manager**

1. Open Task Manager (CTRL+SHIFT+ ESC), and click the **Processes** tab.
2. From the **View** menu, click **Select Columns**.
3. Select **Base Priority**.

▶ **To change the base priority of a process**

1. Click the Processes tab.
2. Click a process name with the right mouse button. A menu appears.
3. Click **Set Priority**, then click a new base priority to change it.

The change is effective at the next Task Manager update; you need not restart the process.

Using Process Viewer

Process Viewer (Pviewer.exe), a tool on the Windows NT Resource Kit 4.0 CD in the Performance Tools group (\PerfTool\MeasTool), lets you monitor process and thread priority and change the base priority class of a process. For more information, see "Process Viewer" in Chapter 11, "Performance Monitoring Tools" and Rktoools.hlp.

Note Process Explode (Pview.exe), also on the Windows NT Resource Kit 4.0 CD, is a superset of the functions of Process Viewer. Although the interface is different, both utilities get their information from the same source and you can change the base priority class by using either tool. For more information, see "Process Explode" in Chapter 11, "Performance Monitoring Tools."

To display the base priority of a process, open Process Viewer and select the computer you want to monitor.

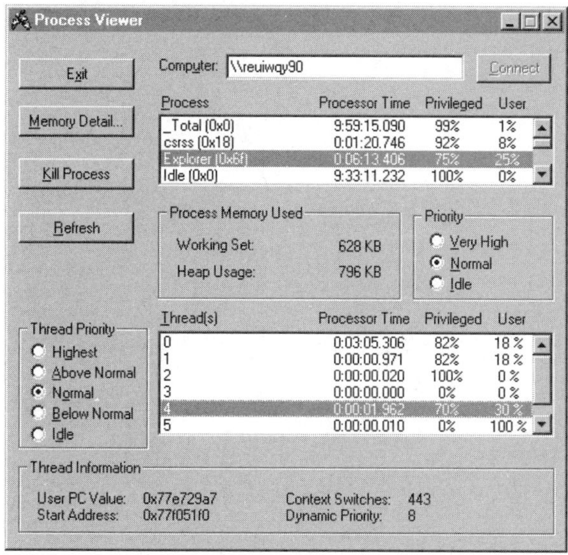

▶ **To display or change the base priority of a process**

1. In the Process box, click the line representing the process. All data in the dialog box changes to show the values for that process. The base priority of the process appears in the Priority box (under the Process box.).
2. To change the priority of the process for this run, click a button in the Priority box. The three priority classes listed—Idle, Normal, and Very High—are associated with the priority classes Idle, Normal, and High, respectively. You cannot change a process to the Real-time priority class.

To display the dynamic priority of a thread

1. In the Process box, click the line representing the process.
2. From the Thread box (near the bottom), select the line representing the thread. All thread data changes to show values for that thread. The Thread Priority box (to the left of the thread box) displays the thread's dynamic priority in radio buttons, but the buttons do not work: You cannot change the dynamic priority of a thread by using Process Viewer.

Tuning Foreground and Background Priorities

When a user interacts with an application, the application moves to the *foreground* and the operating system *boosts* (increases) the base priority of the process to improve its response to the user. The application returns to *background* priority—and loses the boost—when the user interacts with a different process.

You can change the amount of boost given to foreground applications and, in so doing, change the relative priority of foreground to background applications. Reducing the boost improve the response of background process when they are not getting enough processor time.

▶ To change the priority of foreground application

1. Double-click the Control Panel System applet and select the Performance tab. The Application Performance box shows the current setting for the boost.
2. Drag the arrow to set the boost. The default is Maximum (a priority boost of 2) but you can change it to 1 or to None (0), the setting at which foreground processes have no advantage over background processes. For example, most applications run at Normal priority (7) and are boosted to Foreground Normal priority (9) when the user moves the application window to the top of the window stack.

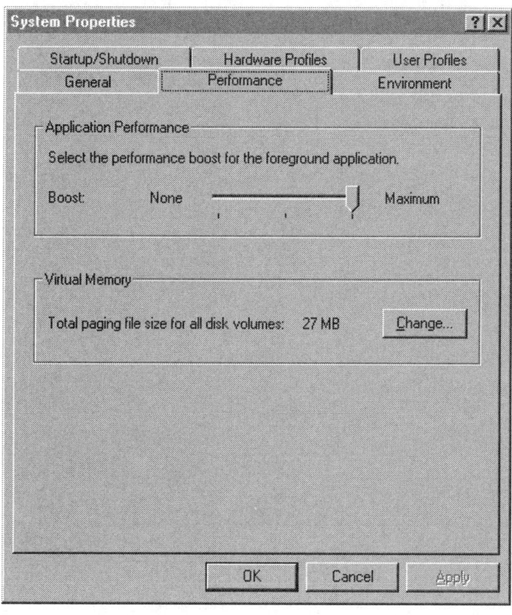

Priority Bottlenecks

When a processor has excess capacity, process and thread priority do not affect performance significantly. All threads run when ready, regardless of their priority. However, when the processor is busy, lower priority applications and services might not get the processor time they need.

The following graph shows threads of different priorities contending for processor time. It demonstrates the changing distribution of processor time among processes of different priorities as demand for processor time increases. (This test was conducted by using CPU Stress, a tool on the Windows NT Resource Kit 4.0 CD that lets you set the priorities and activity levels of a process and its threads.)

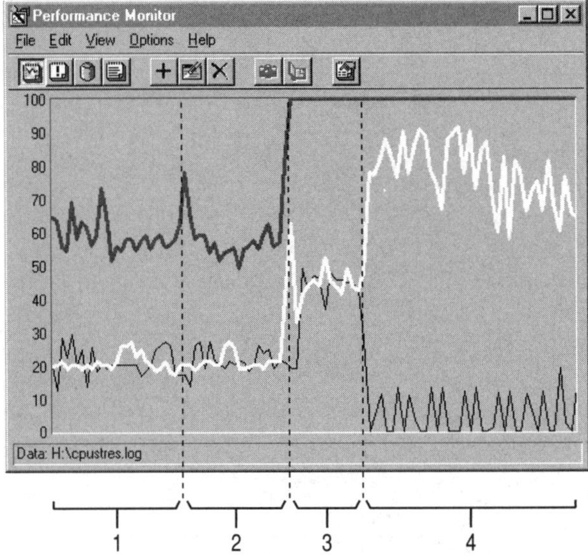

This graph shows two threads of the same process running on a single-processor computer. Lines have been added to show each of the four parts of the test. The thick, gray line is System: % Total Processor Time. The white line represents processor time for Thread 1; the white line represents processor time for Thread 2.

The test conditions and results are represented in the following table:

Object	Part 1	Part 2	Part 3	Part 4
Processor: % Processor Time	58.8	54.1	100	100
Thread 1				
Priority	Normal (8)	Above normal (9)	Normal (8)	Above normal (9)
Thread: %Processor Time	20.6	21.5	44.2	76.5
Thread 2				
Priority	Normal (8)	Normal (8)	Normal (8)	Normal (8.5) Varies from 8 - 14
Thread: %Processor Time	20.9	20.8	45.0	5.6

This test demonstrates that when the processor has extra capacity, increasing the priority of one thread has little effect on the processor time allotted to each of the competing threads. (The small variation is not statistically significant.) However, when the processor is at its busiest, increasing the priority one of the threads, even by one priority level, causes the higher priority thread to get the vast majority of processor time (an average of 76.5%).

In fact, in Part 4, when all processor time is consumed, Thread 2 might not have been scheduled at all were it not for Windows NT's priority inversion strategy. *Priority inversion* is when the Microkernel randomly boosts the priorities of ready threads running in Idle, Normal and High priority processes so that they can execute. (It does not boost the threads of Real-Time processes.) Windows NT uses priority inversion to give processor time to lower priority ready threads which would not otherwise be able to run.

The effect of priority inversion is shown in the following graph. This graph was created by using the Time Window to limit the data to Part 4 of the test. The current priority values were scaled by 10 to make them visible on the graph and the vertical maximum of the graph was increased to 150.

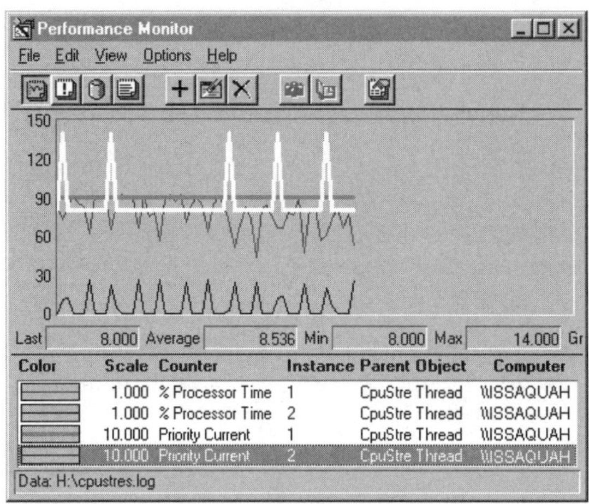

This graph compares priority with processor time during Part 4 of the test. The current priority of Thread 1 (the thick, black line) remains at 9 throughout the sample interval, and its processor time averages 76.5%. Although the priority of Thread 2 (the white line) was set to 8 by CPU Stress, it is repeatedly boosted to 14 in order to enable it to be scheduled. Despite the boost, it ran for an average of only 5.6% of the sample interval.

Eliminating a Processor Bottleneck

If you determine that you do have a processor bottleneck, consider some of these proposed solutions:

- Rule out a memory bottleneck that might be consuming the processor. Memory bottlenecks are far more common and severely degrade processor performance. For more information, see Chapter 12, "Detecting Memory Bottlenecks."
- Replace the application or try to fix it by using the performance optimizing tools in the Win32 Software Development Kit. Screen savers are notorious for monopolizing the processor, so monitor your screen saver executable.

- Upgrade your network or disk adapter cards. 8-bit cards use more processor time than 16-bit or 32-bit cards. The number of bits is the amount of data moved to memory from the adapter on each transfer, so 32-bit cards are the most efficient.

  Look for cards that use bus-mastering direct memory access (DMA), not programmed I/O to move their data. Programmed I/O relies on processor instructions. In bus-mastering DMA, the disk controller managers the I/O bus and uses the DMA controller to manage DMA operation. This frees the processor for other uses.

- Increase the processor clock speed. Clock doubler and tripler processors multiply the processor clock speed while leaving the rest of the memory and I/O bus speeds alone. This will improve application response, but typically by less than the multiplier because applications do more than just use the processor.

- Increase the size of your secondary memory cache, especially if you have just added memory. When you add memory, the secondary cache must map the larger memory space, usually resulting in lower cache hit rates and more processor work retrieving data from the disk or network. Processor-bound programs are especially vulnerable because they are scattered more widely throughout memory after new memory is added.

  The amount of secondary cache a system supports depends upon the design of the motherboard. Many motherboards support several secondary cache configurations (from 64K–512K or 256K–1MB). Increasing cache size usually requires removing the existing static ram (SRAM) chips, replacing them with new SRAM chips, and changing some jumpers. This is helpful when you have a working set that is larger than your current secondary cache.

- Upgrade to a faster processor or add another processor. The general rule is that a faster processor effectively improves performance when a single-threaded process is consuming the processor. Additional processors are recommended when you are running multiple processes or multithreaded processes.

Addendum: Architectural Changes and Processor Use

The Windows NT 4.0 Workstation and Server architecture has changed substantially from previous versions. To those monitoring performance, the most obvious change is in the behavior of Csrss.exe. This section describes how the architectural changes are likely to influence the performance of your Windows NT workstation.

For a complete discussion of the architectural changes, and the old and new components of Csrss.exe, see Chapter 5, "Windows NT 4.0 Workstation Architecture."

In prior versions of Windows NT, Csrss.exe (the process for the Client Server Runtime Subsystem) included all of the graphic display and messaging functions of the Win32 environment subsystem, including the Console, Window Manager (User), the Graphics Device Interface (GDI), the user-mode graphics device drivers, and miscellaneous environment functions to support 32-bit Windows applications. With Windows NT 4.0, the User, GDI, and graphics device drivers have been moved into the Windows NT Executive. Csrss.exe now represents just the Console and miscellaneous functions that remain in the Win32 environment subsystem.

The Win32 environment subsystem runs in a special protected process in user-mode, the processor mode used by application. In Windows NT 3.51 and earlier, calls to User and GDI required the use of special fast LPCs, 64-bit shared memory windows, and multiple user and kernel mode thread transitions to communicate with the process.

Moving User, GDI, and the graphics device drivers into the Windows NT Executive, and having them run in privileged mode, eliminates these complex transitions and improves performance and memory use. Windows NT applications must still call the User32 and GDI32 functions, but now these are calls to the Windows NT Executive which requires just one kernel-mode thread transition.

Measuring the Change

These architectural changes are manifest in several different ways but are most evident when you monitor the behavior of graphics-intensive applications.

The following figure is a graph of a Windows NT 3.0 running GDIDemo, a graphics demonstration tool in the Win32 Software Development Kit. All features of the tool were used simultaneously to generate the most graphics activity.

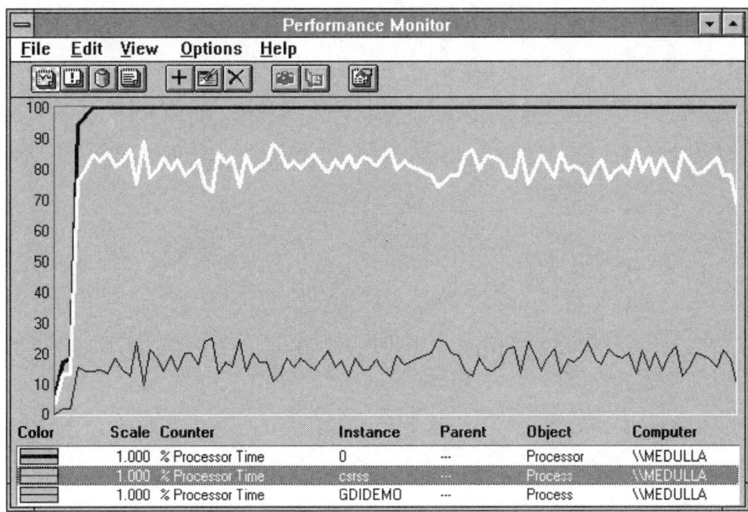

In this example, the processor is 100% busy and is spending most of its time running Csrss.exe. The following figure shows the same program running on Windows NT 4.0.

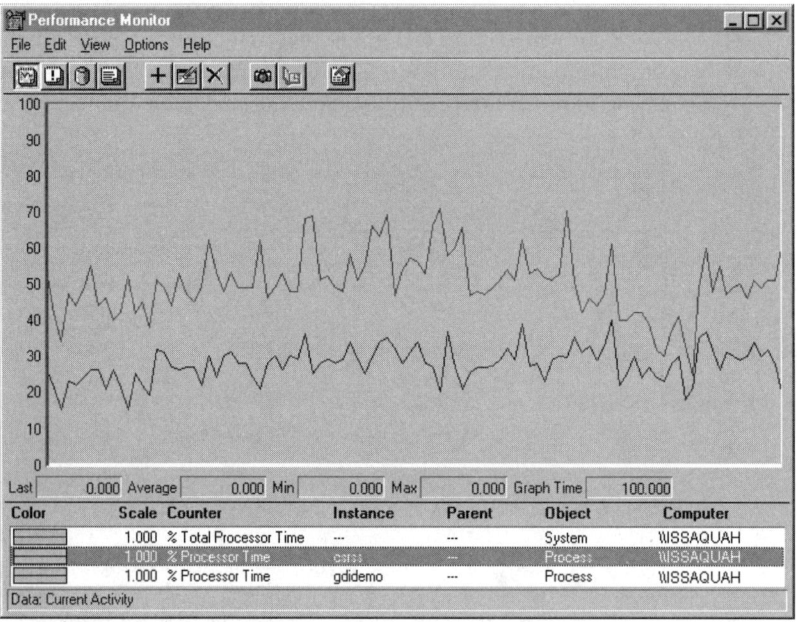

There are significant differences between the performance evidenced in the graphs.

Processor Time:

- The Windows NT 3.51 graph shows that the GDIDemo test used 100% of processor time. (System: % Total Processor Time is the thick, black line is running along the top of the graph.)
- The Windows NT 4.0 graph shows that the GDIDemo test used an average of 50% of processor time. (System: % Total Processor Time is the gray line)

  Some of this might be attributable to the new architecture, but it probably results from improvement in processor technology. The Windows NT 3.51 graph was captured on a computer with a 386 processor; the Windows NT 4.0 was captured on a computer with a 486 processor.

Process Time:

- In the Windows NT 3.51 graph, Process: % Processor Time for GDIDemo (the thin, black line) runs between 10 and 20% while Process: % Processor Time for CSRSS (the white line) averages between 75% and 85%. This indicates that in order to run GDIDemo, the processor was spending 10–20% of its time running in GDIDemo code and the remainder running in CSRSS code on behalf of GDIDemo.
- In the Windows NT 4.0 graph, Process: % Processor Time for GDIDemo (the thin, black line) runs between 25 and 35% while Process: % Processor Time for CSRSS (the white line) runs at nearly 0%. The processor may have been running some system code on behalf of GDIDemo, but it was not in CSRSS.

  The following graph of the Windows NT 4.0 test is the same as the previous one, but includes counters for privileged and user time and interrupts.

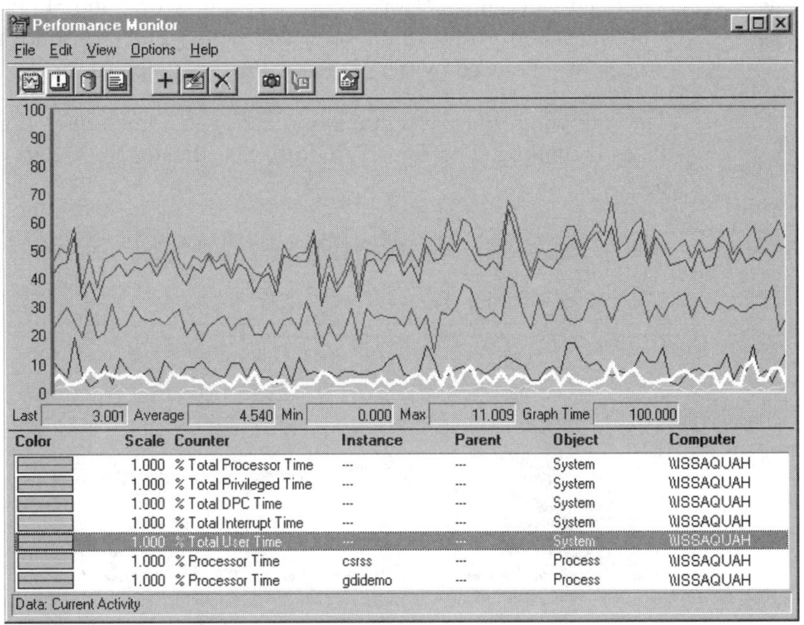

From top to bottom, the lines represent:

- System: % Total Processor Time
- System: % Total Privileged Time
- Process: % Processor Time: GDIDemo

- System: % Total DPC Time
- System: % Total User Time
- System: % Total Interrupt Time
- Process: % Processor Time: CSRSS

This data demonstrates that in Windows NT 4.0, GDIDemo graphics processing time is spent running in privileged mode code in the Windows NT Executive. In previous versions of Windows NT, graphics processing was part of CSRSS and ran mainly in user mode.

Measuring 3D Pipes

The 3D Pipes screensaver that comes with Windows NT Server and Workstation is entertaining, but it consumes substantial processor time. If you leave your computer while it is performing background work, and 3D Pipes is activated, your work must compete with the screensaver for processor time. You can measure the processor time used by the 3D Pipes process, Sspipes.scr.

The following figure is a graph of data logged on an Intel 486 processor while 3D Pipes is running. The Time Window was adjusted to 96 data points, so all data points are shown.

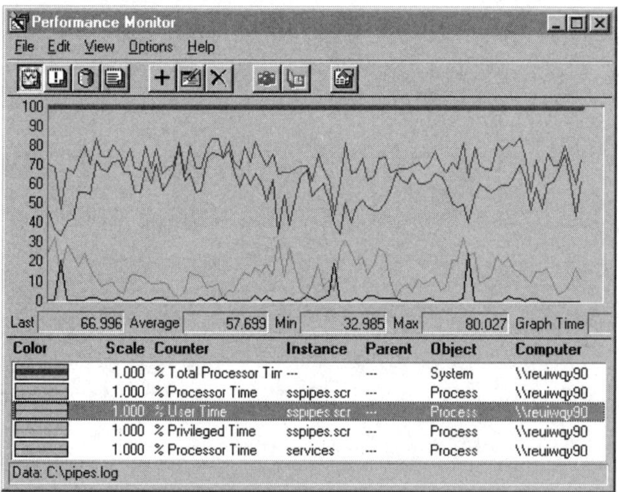

In this graph, the lines, from top to bottom, follow their order in the legend. System: % Total Processor Time (the thick line at the top) is 100% throughout the sample interval. The screensaver process, Sspipes.scr, is using more than 70% of that time. Although 3D Pipes is a graphics program, it runs almost entirely in user mode (82.4% = 57.7% user mode /70% Process: % Processor time) because it is using OpenGL application services instead of operating system services.

Context switching, the rate at which the processor is switched from one thread to another, is an indicator of which threads are getting processor time. In previous version of Windows NT, it was an indirect indicator of communication between the graphics subsystem and the Win32 subsystem. Each time an application needed a graphics service, its thread was switched back and forth several times between user mode and kernel mode to access the protected Win32 subsystem. Each thread transition generated a context switch. In the new architecture, each graphics call requires a single thread transition from user to kernel mode, and back. This design generates far fewer context switches.

The following report demonstrates the effect.

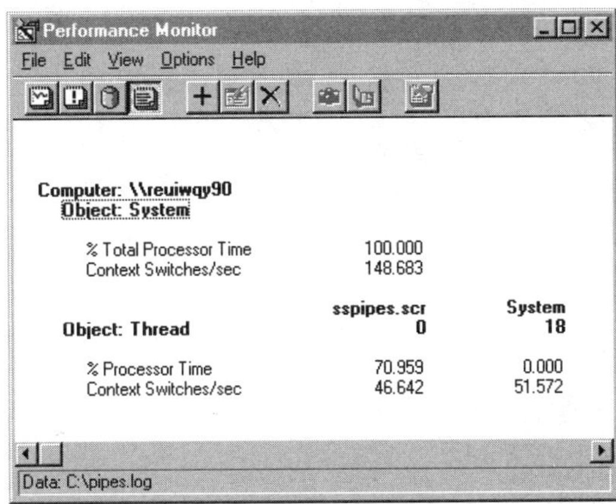

Running graphics-intensive programs like GDIDemo in Windows NT 3.0 generated a sustained average of 1500 context switches per second, with more than 650 context switches per second each attributable to GDIDemo and CSRSS. Running 3D Pipes in Windows NT 4.0, System: Context Switches/sec totaled 148, just 48 more than idle. Although processor use is very high for the screensaver, processor time is consumed by elements other than context switching.

CHAPTER 14

Detecting Disk Bottlenecks

Disk space is a recurring problem. No matter how large a hard disk you buy, your software seems to consume it. But disk bottlenecks pertain to time, not space. When the disk becomes the limiting factor in your workstation, it is because the components involved in reading from and writing to the disk cannot keep pace with rest of the system.

The parts of the disk that create a time bottleneck are less familiar than the megabytes or gigabytes of space. They include the I/O bus, the device bus, the disk controller, and the head stack assembly. Each of these components contributes to and, in turn, limits the performance of the disk configuration.

Performance Monitor measures different aspects of physical and logical disk performance. This chapter examines logical and physical disk performance, shows how to spot and eliminate disk bottlenecks, and describes some special strategies for tuning disk sets.

Tip "Disk and File System Basics," Chapter 17 of this book, provides a comprehensive introduction to the state-of-the-art disk terminology and technology. It is a useful foundation for the information in this chapter.

Prepare to monitor your disk configuration by logging the System, Logical Disk, and Memory objects for several days at an update interval of 60 seconds. If you suspect that slow disk response is periodic, for example, if it is exaggerated by downloads on certain days or certain times of day, log those times separately or place bookmarks in your general log.

Warning Performance Monitor will not monitor disk activity until you run Diskperf and restart the computer. For more information, see "Diskperf: Enabling the Disk Counters," later in this chapter.

Use the following Performance Monitor counters to measure the performance of physical and logical disks.

Object	Counter
Logical Disk/Physical Disk	% Disk Time
Logical Disk/Physical Disk	Avg. Disk Queue Length
Logical Disk/Physical Disk	Current Disk Queue Length
	(Known in previous versions as Disk Queue Length)
Logical Disk/Physical Disk	Avg. Disk sec / Transfer
Logical Disk/Physical Disk	Disk Bytes / sec
Logical Disk/Physical Disk	Avg. Disk Bytes / Transfer
Logical Disk/Physical Disk	Disk Transfers / sec
Logical Disk/Physical Disk	% Free Space
Logical Disk/Physical Disk	Free Megabytes

Disk Testing Tips

The following tips will help you test your disk configuration:

- Get to know your applications and test tools. To perform a complete analysis, you must log data over time while running a variety test tools and programs.

  For example, the following reports show two test tools running the same test on the same disk on the same computer. The Performance Monitor reports of their results are superimposed to make it easier to compare the values.

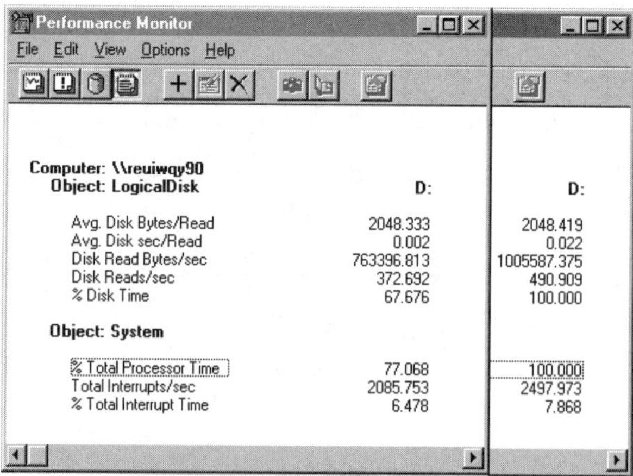

It appears that the disk was much more efficient on the second trial. The throughput rate, as measured by Disk Read Bytes/sec, increased from 763,397 in the first test to 1,005,587 in the second test, an improvement of almost one third! However, the disk performance did not change: The applications simply issued their reads at different rates during the interval.

- When testing disk performance, log Performance Monitor data to another physical disk or computer so that it does not interfere with the disk you are testing. If you cannot do this, log to another logical partition on the drive, or measure Performance Monitor overhead during an idle period and subtract it from your data.
- If you are writing your own tools to test disk performance, include the the FILE_FLAG_NO_BUFFERING parameter in the open call for your test files. This instructs the Virtual Memory Manager to bypass the cache and go directly to disk.
- When using Response Probe to test disk performance, set the FILEACCESSMODE parameter in the Thread Description file (*.sct) to UNBUFFER. This tells the system to bypass the cache and go directly to disk. When using UNBUFFER, remember that the number of bytes in RECORDSIZE parameter must be a multiple of the disk sector size.

  For more information, see "Response Probe" in Chapter 11, "Performance Monitoring Tools." To find your disk sector size, use Windows NT Diagnostics in the Administrative Tools group. Click the Drives tab, then double-click the drive number to see drive properties.
- Reading from and writing to compressed subdirectories on NTFS partitions always involves the cache and is optimized by the cache manager. Such tests are more a test of cache performance than disk performance. When testing disks with NTFS partitions, always read from or write to an uncompressed subdirectory.
- Read the following section on understanding the Performance Monitor disk counters. The time you invest in learning the tools will be repaid when it comes to analyzing the data.

Diskperf: Enabling the Disk Counters

To use the Performance Monitor physical and logical disk counters, you must first run the Diskperf utility included in Window NT. Once you run Diskperf and restart the computer, Performance Monitor can collect disk data. Otherwise, Performance Monitor displays zeros for all counter values for the disks.

Diskperf installs the Disk Performance Statistics Driver that collects data for Performance Monitor and a high-precision timer that times each disk transfer. The timer and the driver are omitted by default to avoid their overhead when you are not monitoring disk performance. This overhead has been measured at less than 1% on a 33-MHz 486 processor.

Note By default, Diskperf installs the Disk Performance Statistics Driver above the fault tolerant driver, Ftdisk.sys, in the I/O Manager's disk driver stack. To monitor the physical disks in disk configurations which include Ftdisk, use the **diskperf -ye** option. To determine if Ftdisk is started in your configuration, use the Devices Control Panel.

You must be a member of the Administrator's local group on a computer to run Diskperf on it. Run Diskperf from a command prompt window. At the command prompt, type one of the following, then restart the computer: The counters remain enabled, even when you reboot, until you remove them by using the **diskperf -n** option.

```
c:\> diskperf -y
```

This enables the counters on a standard disk configuration.

To run diskperf on a remote computer, type one of the commands in the following table, followed by the computer name, then restart the computer. For example:

```
diskperf -y \\ComputerName
```

Command	Description
diskperf	Tells whether disk counters are enabled or disabled.
diskperf -y	Enables the disk counters.
diskperf -ye	Enables disk counters on mirror and stripe sets and other noncontiguous partition sets. This option installs the performance statistics driver below the fault tolerant driver (Ftdisk) in the I/O stack.
diskperf -n	Disables the disk counters.

Diskperf -ye for Ftdisk Configurations

The **diskperf -ye** option is for disk configurations that use the fault tolerant disk driver, Ftdisk. This includes mirror sets, stripe sets with or without parity, and other combinations of noncontiguous physical disk space into a single logical disk.

Tip To determine if your configuration uses Ftdisk, find Ftdisk on the Devices Control Panel. Ftdisk will be marked as *Started* if it is used in the disk configuration.

Diskperf -ye places the Disk Performance Statistics Driver below the fault tolerant driver in the disk driver stack. In this position, the Disk Performance Statistics Driver can see physical instances of a disk before they are logically combined by Ftdisk. This lets Performance Monitor collect data on each physical disk in a disk set.

Hardware RAID configurations do not use Ftdisk. The physical disks are combined in the disk controller hardware, which is always below the Disk Performance Statistics Driver. Performance monitoring tools always see the drive set as a single physical disk. It does not matter whether you use **diskperf -y** or **diskperf -ye**.

At the command prompt, type **diskperf -ye**, then restart the computer. This installs or moves the Disk Performance Statistics Driver below the fault tolerant driver and installs a high-performance timer.

Note If you have already enabled disk collection using the default **diskperf -y** option, you can change it by typing **diskperf -ye** and restarting the computer.

The following figure shows the positioning of the Disk Performance Statistics Driver in the **diskperf -y** (default) and **diskperf -ye** (optional) configurations.

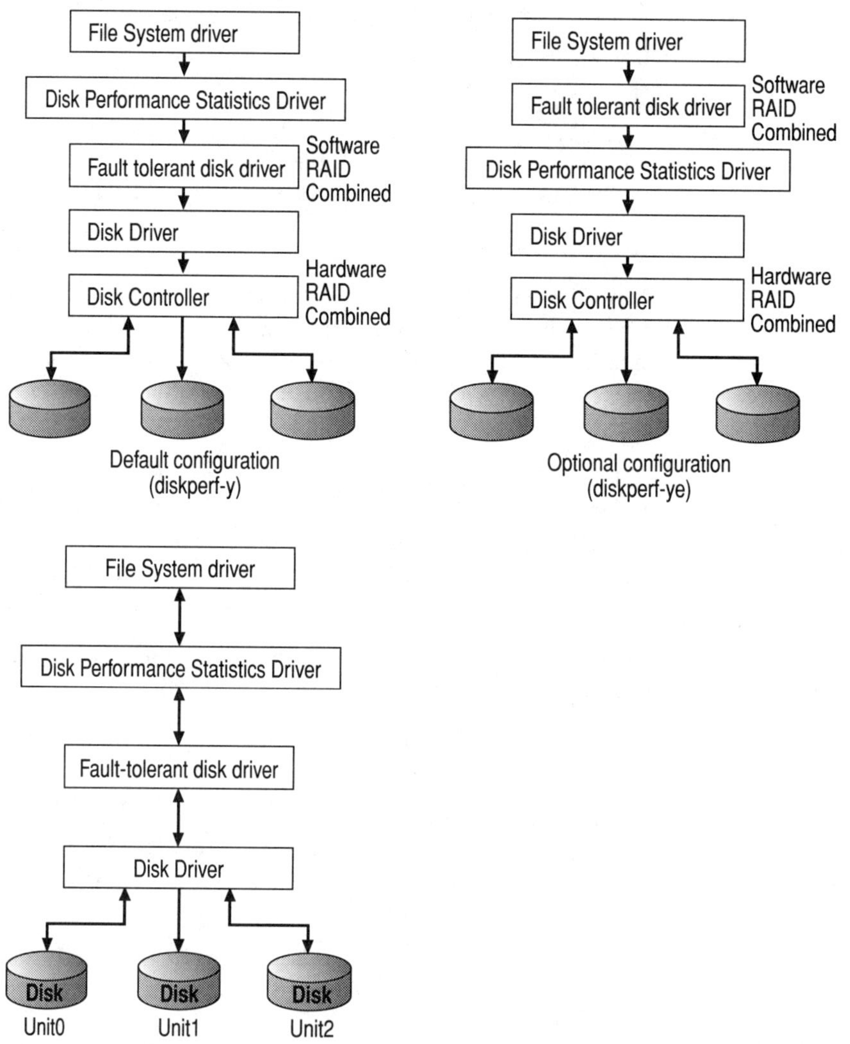

By using the optional configuration on software RAID, the physical disks in a software RAID set appear as separate physical instances in Performance Monitor and on other monitoring tools on Windows NT.

The Performance Monitor Disk Counters

Performance Monitor has many useful counters for measuring disk activity. This section

- Summarizes the most commonly used disk counters and describes how to use them.
- Explains some of the discrepancies you might see when you collect data on your disks, and describes how to prevent them.
- Introduces Performance Monitor's newest disk counters.

Understanding the Disk Counters

The following list describes the most commonly used logical disk counters in simple terms. (To see the complete list, scroll through the Physical Disk and Logical Disk counters listed in Performance Monitor and read the explanatory text for each counter.)

Logical Disk and Physical Disk counters	Description
% Disk Time	How often is the disk busy? If it is busy almost all of the time, and there is a large queue, the disk might be a bottleneck. This value is displayed as a percentage and is capped at 100%.
Avg. Disk Queue Length	How often is disk busy? If it is busy almost all of the time, and there is a large queue, the disk might be a bottleneck. This counter displays %Disk Time as a decimal with no defined maximum. (A %Disk Time of 100% equals an Avg. Disk Queue Length of 1.0.) This counter is recommended for disk sets where the combined activity of the disks can exceed 100% of a single disk.
Current Disk Queue Length (Known in previous versions as Disk Queue Length)	Are disk requests waiting? If more than two request are waiting over time, the disk may be a bottleneck. Unlike the other queue measures, this one measures requests, not time. It includes the request being serviced as well those waiting and is an instantaneous value, not an average.

Logical Disk and Physical Disk counters	Description
Avg. Disk sec / Transfer	How fast is data being moved (in seconds)? This counter measures the average time of each data transfer, regardless of the number of bytes read or written. It shows the total time of the read or write, from the moment it leaves the Disk Performance Statistics Driver to the moment it is complete. Avg. Disk sec / Read is usually in multiples of the time it takes for one rotation of the disk. Any variation usually represents time for driver processing or time in the queue. For example, on a 3600 rpm disk, the actual Avg. Disk sec/Read would be in multiples of 16 milliseconds.
Disk Bytes / sec	How fast is data being moved (in bytes)? This is the primary measure of disk throughput.
Avg. Disk Bytes / Transfer	How much data is being moved on each transfer? This counter measures throughput, an indication of disk efficiency. The disk is efficient if it is transferring large amounts of data relatively quickly (Avg. Disk sec/Transfer). This is the counter to watch when measuring maximum throughput.
Disk Transfers / sec	How fast are data requests being serviced? This measures the number of read and writes completed per second, regardless of how much data they involve. Transfers/sec is not the inverse of sec/Transfer. Transfers/sec counts the number of completed I/O requests in each second. Sec/Transfer times the transfer from its inception to completion.

Troubleshooting the Disk Activity Counters

Sometimes, the disk activity counters just do not add up. %Disk Read Time or %Disk Write Time might sum to more than 100% even on a single disk, and %Disk Time, which represents their sum, is still 100%. Even worse, on a disk set, the set looks 100% busy even when some disks are idle.

Even the fanciest disk cannot be more than 100% busy, but it can look that way to Performance Monitor. Several factors can cause this discrepancy and they are sometimes all happening at once:

- The Disk Performance Statistics Driver, which collects disk measurements for Performance Monitor, can exaggerate disk time. It does not actually time the disk, it times I/O requests. It assumes that, as long as a request is in process, the disk is busy. It also counts all processing time—including time in the disk driver stack and in the queue—as part of reading or writing time. Then it sums all busy time for all requests and divides it by the elapsed time of the sample interval. When more than one request is in process at a time, the total processing time is greater than the time of the sample interval, and the disk looks more than 100% busy.
- When Performance Monitor combines data for more than one component of a disk or disk set, it often just sums the values; it does not recalculate them in proportion to the whole component. Therefore, a sum can exceed 100%, even when some of the instances are idle.

  For example, the %Disk Time counter just displays the sum of %Disk Read Time and %Disk Write Time. The value is not recalculated as a percentage of all time for the disk.

  Similarly, the _Total instance of many counters is just a sum of the values for all physical or logical disks. The value is not recalculated as a percentage of time for all disks. For example, if one disk is 100% busy and another is idle, the _Total displays 100% busy, not 50% busy.

  Note When calculating the _Total instance for the Avg. Disk Bytes/Transfer, Avg. Disk sec/Transfer, and %Free Space counters, Performance Monitor recalculates the sums as a percentage for each disk.

  Also, the Physical Disk counters are sums of the values for the logical disk. If any logical disk is 100% busy, it looks like all partitions are 100% busy.
- Finally, the percentage counters are limited, by definition, to a maximum of 100%. When a value exceeds 100%, Performance Monitor still displays 100%. This is especially inconvenient when measuring values that are sums, which are even more likely to exceed 100%.

Now that you understand how the disk counters work, you can use them more effectively.

- Monitor individual instances in as much detail as you can see them. Whenever practical, avoid summed values and the _Total instance. When you need to use them, remember that they are sums.
- Use the new Performance Monitor disk activity counters, Avg. Disk Queue Length, Avg. Disk Read Queue Length, Avg. Disk Write Queue Length. They use the same data as the % Disk Time counters, so the busy time values can be exaggerated. However, they report these values in decimals that have no defined maximum, so they can display values above 100% accurately. For more information, see "New Disk Activity Counters," later in this chapter.
- If your disk configuration includes Ftdisk, use the **Diskperf -ye** option on the Diskperf utility. This installs the Disk Performance Statistics Driver low enough in the disk driver stack that it can see individual physical disks before they are logically combined. If you use **Diskperf -y,** statistics for all physical disks are summed as though they were one disk.
- If all else fails, factor in the discrepancy when you interpret the values.

  For example, if the disks in a five-disk set were busy 30%, 33%, 38%, 0%, and 0% of the time respectively, the Avg. Disk Queue Length would be 1.01. Remember that this means that about 20% of disk set capacity is used, not 101%.

New Disk Activity Counters

Performance Monitor for Windows NT 4.0 includes new counters for monitoring disk activity:

- Avg. Disk Queue Length
- Avg. Disk Read Queue Length
- Avg. Disk Write Queue Length

These counters tell how often the disk is busy during the sample interval. Despite their name, they do not count items in a queue. They use the same data as the %Disk Time counters, but they report the result in decimals, rather than percentages. This allows them to report values greater than 100%.

For example, if %Disk Read Time is 96%, then Avg. Disk Read Queue Length is 0.96.

The advantage of these counters is their ability to display values that exceed 100%.

For example, if %Disk Read Time is 90% and %Disk Write Time is 30%, %Disk Time cannot report the sum because it cannot exceed 100%. In this case, %Disk Time is 100% and Avg. Disk Queue Length is 1.2.

Still, you need to be cautious when interpreting these values, especially those that are sums. In a 3-disk set, if one disk is reading for 66% of the sample interval, another is reading for 70% of the interval, and the third is idle, the Avg. Disk Read Queue Length, would be 1.36. This does not mean that the set is 136% busy; it means that it is at about 45% (1.36/3) capacity.

Monitoring Application Efficiency

It is not easy to measure disk use by applications, though it is important. To measure how efficiently your application is using the disks, chart the memory and cache counters.

Applications rarely read or write directly to disk. The file system first maps application code and data into the file system cache and copies it from the cache into the working set of the application. When the application creates or changes data, the data is mapped into the cache and then written back to disk in batches. The exceptions are when an application requests a single write-through to disk or tells the file system not to use the cache at all for a file, usually because it is doing its own buffering.

Fortunately, the same design characteristic that improves an application's use of cache and memory also reduces its transfers from the disk. This characteristic is *locality of reference*, that is, having a program's references to the same data execute in sequence or close in time. When references are localized, the data the program needs is more likely to be in its working set, or certainly in the cache, and is less likely to be paged out when needed. Also, when a program reads sequentially, the Cache Manager does *read aheads*, that is, it recognizes the data request pattern and reads in larger blocks of data on each transfer.

If your application is causing a lot of paging, run it under controlled circumstances while logging Cache: Copy Read Hits %, Cache: Read Ahead/sec, Memory: Pages Input/sec, Memory: Pages Output/sec. Then try reorganizing or redesigning your data structures and repeat the test.

Also, use the file operation counters on the System object.

The relevant system counters are

- System: File Data Operation/sec
- System: File Read Operations/sec
- System: File Read Bytes/sec
- System: File Write Operations/sec
- System: File Write Bytes/sec

These count file control and data operations for the whole system. Unlike the disk counters, the count read and write requests from the file system to devices and count time in the cache.

Recognizing Disk Bottlenecks

Disk bottlenecks appear as sustained rates of disk activity above 85% of a sample interval and as persistent disk queues greater than 2 per disk, while paging, as measured by Memory: Page Reads/sec and Memory: Page Writes/sec, remains at less than 5 per second, on average.

High use, by itself, is a sign of demand, not a problem. In general, a high-performance disk is capable of about 40 I/O operations per second. However, nearly constant use and lengthy queues are a cause for concern. When response is poor; when you hear the disk clicking, and you see its light flashing, chart Logical Disk: Avg. Disk Queue Length and Memory: Pages/sec for all logical partitions on your workstation.

Note Sustained high disk use and persistent long queues typically are symptoms of a memory shortage, not a disk bottleneck. When physical memory is scarce, the system starts writing the contents of memory to disk and reading in smaller chunks more frequently. The less memory you have, the more the disk is used. Rule out a memory bottleneck before investing any money in disk technology. For more information, see the following section.

Disk Bottlenecks and Memory

The first step in diagnosing a disk bottleneck is distinguishing it from a memory bottleneck. Sustained paging, a symptom of a memory shortage, can look like a disk bottleneck.

Paging—moving pages of code and data between memory and disk—is a necessary part of the virtual memory system. Paging is expected, especially when the system or a process is starting. However, excessive paging that consumes the disk is a symptom of a memory shortage. The solution is to add memory, not disks.

To measure paging, chart the following counters:

- Memory: Page Reads/sec
- Memory: Page Writes/sec
- Memory: Pages input/sec
- Memory: Pages output/sec

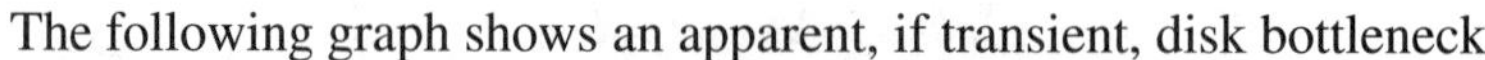

The following graph shows an apparent, if transient, disk bottleneck.

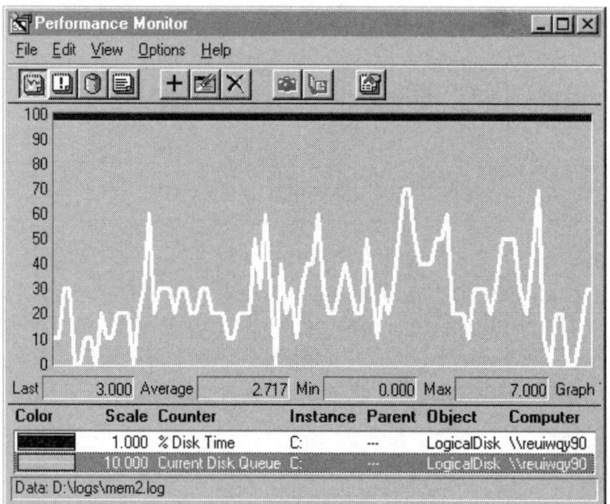

In this example, the thick black stripe on the top is % Disk Time, at a sustained rate of 100%. The white line is Current Disk Queue Length, an instantaneous count of the items in the disk queue. There are up to 7 items in the queue to disk in this sample, and the average is nearly 3. It looks like a faster disk is needed.

However, the following graph reveals at least one element contributing to the queue.

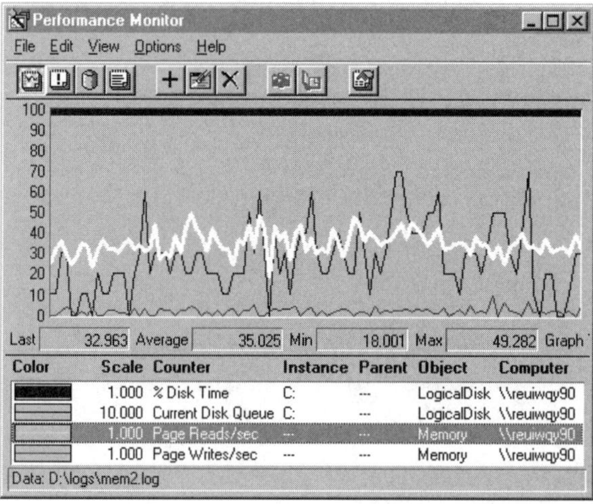

This graph is the same as the previous one, except for the addition of Memory: Page Reads/sec (the white line) and Memory: Page Writes/sec (the thin line at the bottom of the graph). Current Disk Queue is now the thin, black line behind Page Reads/sec. The memory counters show how many times the disk was accessed to retrieve pages that were not found in memory or to write pages to free up memory for new data coming in from disk.

The average of 37 disk accesses per second—including 35 Page Reads/sec (as shown in the value bar) and nearly 2 Page Writes/sec—is probably the maximum for this older technology disk.

If this pattern persists beyond the startup of the system or a process, you have a memory bottleneck, not a disk bottleneck. However, before you add memory, make sure that the memory bottleneck is not caused by an inefficient application. For more information, see Chapter 12, "Detecting Memory Bottlenecks."

Interrupts and Disk Use

Just as a memory shortage can look like a disk problem, a disk bottleneck can look like a processor problem. This happens when the rate of interrupts caused by disk activity consume the processor. Although different disk components use different strategies for transferring data to and from the disk, they all use the processor to some extent. You can measure the effect of the disk on the processor by charting

- Processor: Interrupts/sec
- Processor: %Interrupt Time
- System: Total Interrupts/sec
- System: % Total Interrupt Time

There is a lot of activity other than disk operations that produce processor interrupts, even on a relatively idle system. To determine the number of processor interrupts attributable to disk activity, you need to subtract from your measurements those attributable to other causes. On an Intel 486 or later processor, the processor clock interrupts every 10 milliseconds, or 100 times per second. Network interrupts can produce 200–1000 interrupts/sec. Also, hardware errors, like failing drivers, can produce thousands of interrupts.

The following report shows an example of interrupts during a maximum throughput test on a controller that uses *programmed I/O*, a disk transfer method that uses the processor to tell the drive what sectors to read. The computer was disconnected from the network during the test.

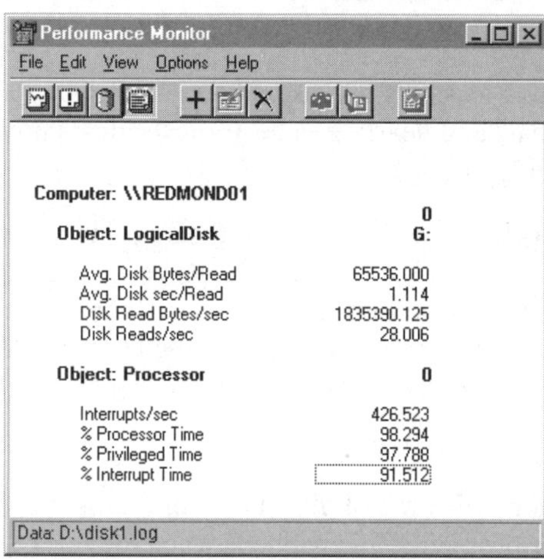

In this example, there were an average of 426.5 interrupts per second. Subtracting 100 per second for the system clock leaves 326.5 from the disk activity, or 76.5% of interrupts. The processor was 98.3% busy on average, and 97.8% of it was in privileged mode, where interrupts are serviced. On average, 91.5% of processor time was consumed by interrupts. Since the disk was responsible for 76.5% of interrupts, it is likely to have generated about 70% of processor use (76.5% of 91.5%). This is substantial and, if sustained, could slow the whole system.

Measuring Disk Efficiency

Each component of your disk assembly (the adapter bus, the device bus and cable, the disk controller, and the disk or disk cabinet) has a rate of maximum and expected throughput. The total configuration is limited to the maximum throughput of the slowest component, so it is important to find that value for your system. The booklets provided by the component manufacturer usually list maximum and expected transfer rates and throughput for each component.

The final components in your disk configuration are the applications that issue the I/O requests. They determine how the physical disks are used. In general, reading or writing a few large records is more efficient than reading or writing many small ones. This curve levels off when the disk is moving such large blocks of data that each transfer is slower, though its total throughput is quite high. Unfortunately, it is not always easy to control this factor. However, if your system is being used to transfer many small units of data, this inefficiency may help to explain, though not resolve, high disk use.

In this section, we will show you how to test the efficiency of your disk configuration at reading and writing and at sequential versus random transfers. We will also share some strategies for testing the maximum throughput of your disk, and point you to some files on the Windows NT Resource Kit 4.0 CD for testing disk throughput.

Reading and Writing

Some disks and disk configurations perform better when reading than when writing. You can compare the reading and writing capabilities of your disks by reading from a physical disk and then writing to the same physical disk.

To measure reading from and writing to disk, log the Logical and Physical Disk objects in Performance Monitor, then chart the following counters:

Reading	Writing
Avg. Disk Bytes/Read	Avg. Disk Bytes/Write
Avg. Disk sec/Read	Avg. Disk sec/Write
Disk Read Bytes/sec	Disk Write Bytes/sec
Disk Reads/sec	Disk Writes/sec

On standard disk configurations, you will find little difference in the time it takes to read from or write to disk. However, on disk configurations with parity, such as hardware RAID 5 and stripe sets with parity, reading is quicker than writing. When you read, you read only the data; when you write, you read, modify, and write the parity, as well as the data.

Mirror sets also are usually quicker at reading than writing. When writing, a mirror set writes all of the data twice. When reading, it reads simultaneously from all disks in the set. Magneto-optical devices (MOs), known to most of us as Read/Write CDs, also are quicker at reading than writing. When writing, they use one rotation of the disk just to burn a starting mark and then wait for the next rotation to begin writing.

Measuring Disk Reading

The following graph shows a test of disk-reading performance. A test tool is set to read 64K records sequentially from a 60-MB file on a SCSI drive. The reads are unbuffered, so the disk can be tested directly without testing the program's or system's cache efficiency. Performance Monitor is logging every two seconds.

Note The test tool used in this example submits all of its I/O requests simultaneously. This exaggerates the disk time and Avg. Disk sec/Transfer counters. If the tool submitted its requests one at a time, the throughput might be the same, but the values of counters that time requests would be much lower. It is important to understand your applications and test tools and factor their I/O methods into your analysis.

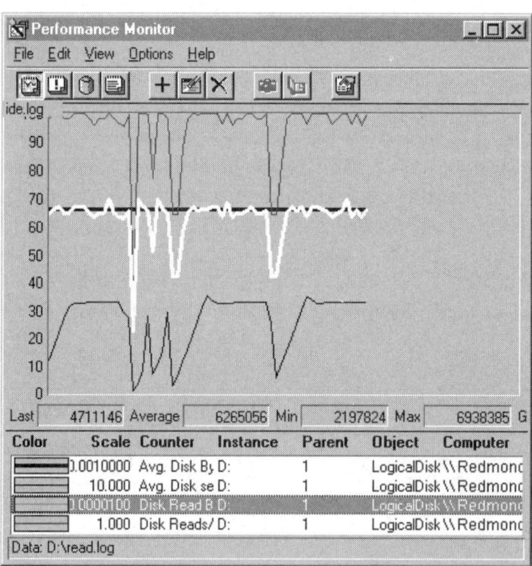

In this graph, the top line is Disk Reads/sec. The thick, black, straight line running right at 64K is Avg. Disk Bytes/Read. The white line is Disk Read Bytes/sec, and the lower thin, black line is Avg. Disk sec/Read. The scale of the counters has been adjusted to fit all of the lines on the graph, and the Time Window eliminates the starting and ending values from the averages.

In this example, the program is reading the 64K records from Logical Drive D and writing the Performance Monitor log to Logical Drive E on the same physical disk. The drive is doing just less than 100 reads and reading more than 6.2 MB per second. At the points where the heavy black and white lines meet, the drive is reading 100 bytes per second. Note that reading 6.2 MB/sec is reading a byte every 0.00000016 of a second. That is fast enough to avoid a bottleneck under almost any circumstances.

However, Avg. Disk sec/Read is varying between 0.05 and 3.6 second per read, instead of the 16 milliseconds that would be consistent with the rest of the data (1 second/64K bytes). As noted above, the value of Avg. Disk sec/Read tells us more about the test tool and the Performance Monitor counters than about the disk. However, you might see something like this, so it is worth understanding.

Avg. Disk sec/Read times each request from submission to completion. If this consisted entirely of disk time, it would be in multiples of 16 milliseconds, the time it takes for one rotation of this 3600 RPM disk. The remaining time counted consists of time in the queue, time spent moving across the I/O bus, and time in transit. Since the test tool submits all of I/O operations to the device at once, at a rate of 6.2 MB per second, the requests take 3 seconds, on average.

Measuring Writing while Reading

There are some noticeable dips in the curves of all three graphs. If Performance Monitor were logging more frequently, you could see that the disk stops reading briefly so that it can write to the log and update file system directories. It then resumes reading. Disks are almost always busy with more than one process, and the total capacity of the disks is spread across all processes. Although the competing process just happens to be Performance Monitor, it could be any other process.

The following graph shows the effect of writing on the efficiency of the reads.

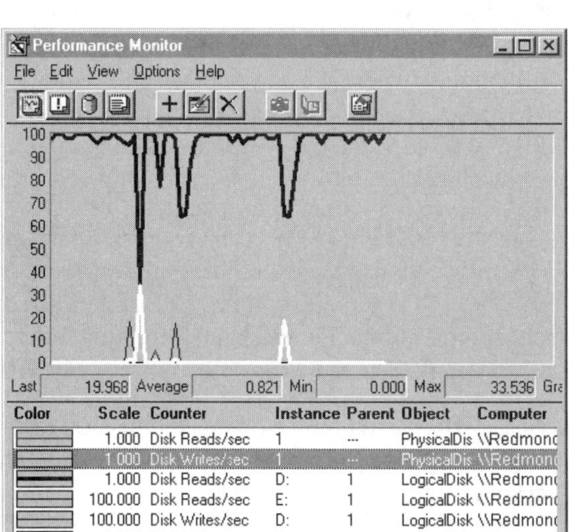

In this graph, several lines are superimposed, because the values are nearly the same. The thick, black line is Physical Disk: Disk Reads/sec and Logical Disk: Disk Reads/sec for Drive D; the thick, white line is Physical Disk: Disk Writes/sec and Logical Disk: Disk Writes/sec for Drive E. The thin, black blips at the bottom of the graph are Disk Reads/sec on Drive E and Disk Writes/sec on Drive D, both magnified 100 times to make them visible.

Although Disk Writes/sec on Drive D are negligible, fewer than 0.05 per second, on average, Performance Monitor is writing its log to Drive E, the other logical partition on the physical disk. This accounts for the writing on Physical Drive 1. Although the logical partitions are separate, the disk has a single head stack assembly that needs to stop reading, however briefly, while it writes. The effect is minimal here, but it is important to remember that logical drives share a physical disk, especially because most disk bottlenecks are in shared physical components.

The report on this graph shows the average values, but averages obscure the real activity, which happens in fits and starts. The following figure shows an Excel spreadsheet to which the values of writing to Drive D have been exported.

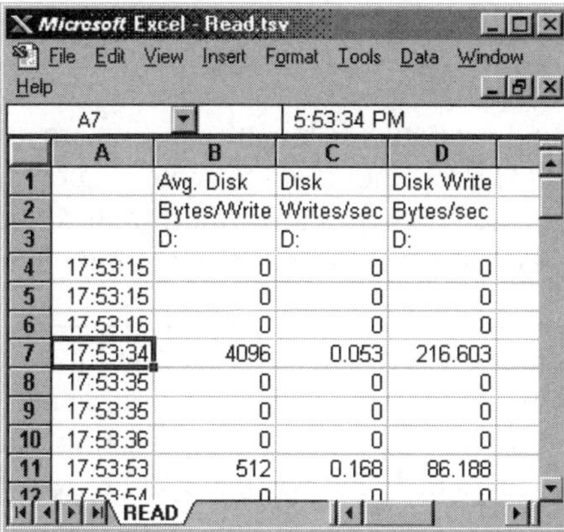

Microsoft Excel - Read.tsv

File Edit View Insert Format Tools Data Window Help

A7 | 5:53:34 PM

	A	B	C	D
1		Avg. Disk	Disk	Disk Write
2		Bytes/Write	Writes/sec	Bytes/sec
3		D:	D:	D:
4	17:53:15	0	0	0
5	17:53:15	0	0	0
6	17:53:16	0	0	0
7	17:53:34	4096	0.053	216.603
8	17:53:35	0	0	0
9	17:53:35	0	0	0
10	17:53:36	0	0	0
11	17:53:53	512	0.168	86.188

READ

Drive D is also writing, just to update file system directory information. It writes a page (4096 bytes), then a sector (512K bytes)—the smallest possible transfer on this disk. You can multiply column B, Disk Bytes/Write by column C, Disk Writes/sec, to get column D, Disk Write Bytes/sec. Although the transfer rates are not stellar here, we are reading very small records and have an even smaller sample.

The spreadsheet for Drive E follows.

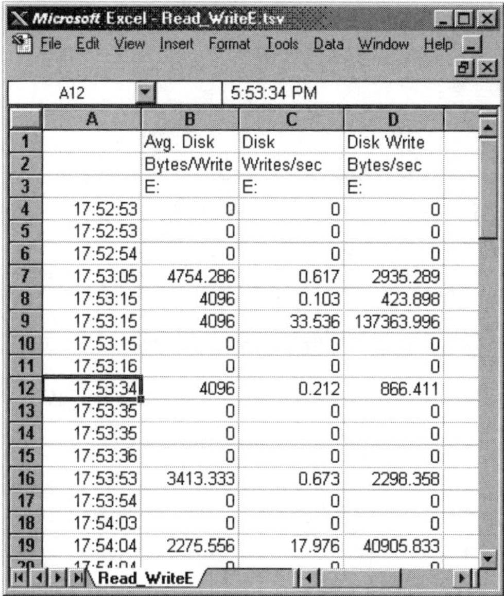

Microsoft Excel - Read_WriteE.tsv

File Edit View Insert Format Tools Data Window Help

A12 | 5:53:34 PM

	A	B	C	D
1		Avg. Disk	Disk	Disk Write
2		Bytes/Write	Writes/sec	Bytes/sec
3		E:	E:	E:
4	17:52:53	0	0	0
5	17:52:53	0	0	0
6	17:52:54	0	0	0
7	17:53:05	4754.286	0.617	2935.289
8	17:53:15	4096	0.103	423.898
9	17:53:15	4096	33.536	137363.996
10	17:53:15	0	0	0
11	17:53:16	0	0	0
12	17:53:34	4096	0.212	866.411
13	17:53:35	0	0	0
14	17:53:35	0	0	0
15	17:53:36	0	0	0
16	17:53:53	3413.333	0.673	2298.358
17	17:53:54	0	0	0
18	17:54:03	0	0	0
19	17:54:04	2275.556	17.976	40905.833

Read_WriteE

This shows the wide variation of writes in this small sample. In general, Drive E is writing about a page at a time, but the transfer rate varies widely, from less than a page per second, up to 33.5 pages per second. However, this small amount of writing is enough to account for the dips in the main reading data.

Measuring Disk Writing

The graphs of writing to this simple disk configuration are almost the same as those of reading from it. The test tool is set to write sequential 64K records to a 60 MB file on a SCSI drive. The writes are unbuffered, so they bypass the cache and go directly to disk. Performance Monitor is logging once per second.

Note Disks cannot distinguish between writing a file for the first time and updating an existing file. Recognizing and writing only changes to a file would require much more memory than is practical. The writing tests in this chapter consist of writing new data to disk, but writing changes to data would produce the same results.

The following figure shows the reading and writing measures side by side. The top graph measures reading; the bottom, writing.

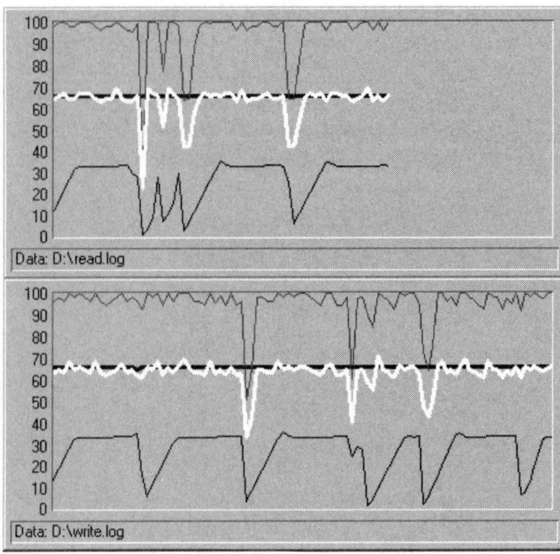

In these graphs, the lines (from top to bottom of each graph) represent

Reading (top graph)	Writing (bottom graph)
Disk Reads/sec	Disk Writes/sec
Avg. Disk Bytes/Read (thick, black line)	Avg. Disk Bytes/Write (thick, black line)
Disk Read Bytes/sec (white line)	Disk Write Bytes/sec (white line)
Avg. Disk sec/Read (thin, black line)	Avg. Disk sec/Write (thin, black line)

The actual values are almost identical or vary only within experimental error. The dips in the values represent the time the disk spent writing the Performance Monitor log to the other logical drive.

If you have enough disks, you can eliminate the variation caused by Performance Monitor logging. The following graph shows the test tool writing sequential 64K records to a 40 MB file. Because Performance Monitor is logging to a different physical drive, the logging does not interfere with the writing test.

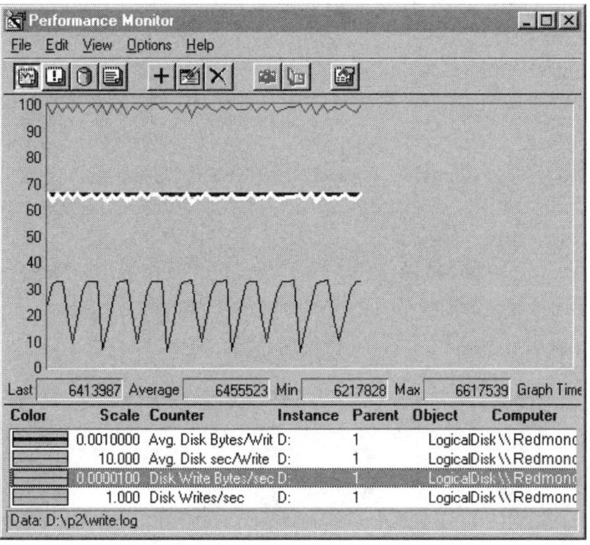

As expected, the dips in the graph are eliminated. The overall transfer rate is also somewhat improved, although writing a log does not have that much overhead. Whenever possible, isolate your tests on a single physical drive. Also, if you have a high-priority task, or an I/O intensive application, designating a separate physical drive for the task will improve overall disk performance.

Random vs. Sequential Reading

It is much quicker to read records in sequence than to read them from different parts of the disk, and it is slowest to read randomly throughout the disk. The difference is in the number of required *seeks*, operations to find the data and position the disk head on it. Moving the disk head, a mechanical device, takes more time than any other part of the I/O process. The rest of the process consists of moving data electronically across circuits. However slow, it is thousands of times faster than moving the head.

The operating system, disk driver, adapter and controller technology all aim to reduce seek operations. More intelligent systems batch and sequence their I/O requests in the order that they appear on the disk. Still, the more times the head is repositioned, the slower the disk reads.

Tip Even when an application is reading records in the order in which they appear in the file, if the file is fragmented throughout the disk or disks, the I/O will not be sequential. If the disk-transfer rate on a sequential or mostly sequential read operation deteriorates over time, run a defragmentation utility on the disk and test again.

The following figure compares random to sequential reading to show how random reading affects disk performance. In the top report, the disk is reading 64K records randomly throughout a 40 MB file. Performance Monitor is writing its log to a different physical drive. In the bottom report, the same disk is reading 64K records in sequence from a 60 MB file, with Performance Monitor logging to a different logical partition on the same drive.

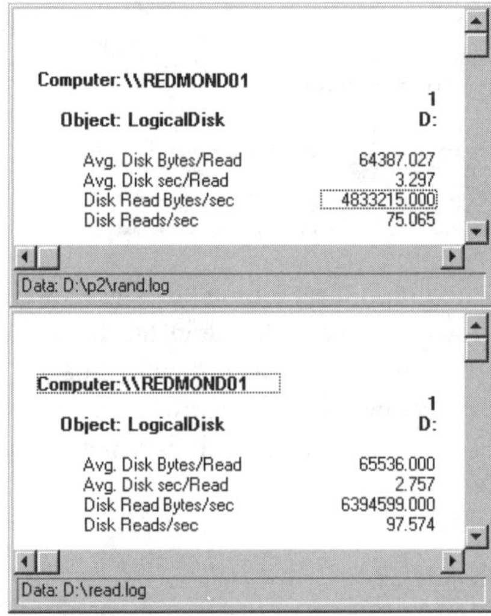

The difference is quite dramatic. The same disk configuration, reading the same size records, is 32% more efficient when the records read are sequential rather than random. The number of bytes transferred fell from 6.39 MB/sec to 4.83 MB/sec because the disk could only sustain 75 reads/sec, compared to 97.6 reads/sec for sequential records. Queue time, as measured by Avg. Disk sec/Read, was also 1/3 higher in the random reading test.

The following figure shows the graphs of the two tests so you can see the differences in the shape of the curves. The top graph represents random reading; the bottom represents sequential reading.

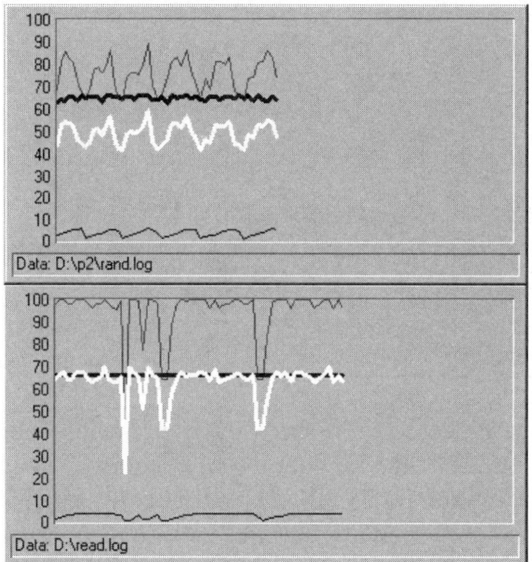

In both graphs, the top line is Disk Reads/sec, the thick, black line is Avg. Disk Bytes/Read, the white line is Disk Read Bytes/sec, and the thin, black line near the bottom is Avg. Disk sec/Read. The time window was adjusted on both graphs to eliminate startup and shutdown values, and the counter values were scaled to get them on the chart. The counter scales are the same on both charts.

Also, Disk Reads/sec and Disk Read Bytes/sec are scaled so that their lines meet when the disk is reading an average of 100 bytes/sec, the norm for this disk configuration reading sequential records of a constant size. Space between the lines indicates that the disk is reading more or less than 100 bytes/sec. This is where the 1/3 efficiency gain in sequential reads is most pronounced.

The sequential test graph is less regular because the log is being written to the same drive. Nonetheless, the transfer rate curve is straighter on the sequential test, showing that the disk is spending more time reading. The attractive pattern on the random graph appears because the disk assembly must stop reading and seek between each read. Had it been able to measure at a much higher resolution, it would show the transfer rate dropping to zero and then spiking back to 100 reads/sec.

To examine the cause of the pattern in the random test, add Processor: %Processor Time to the graph. If you have a multiprocessor computer, substitute System: %Total Processor Time.

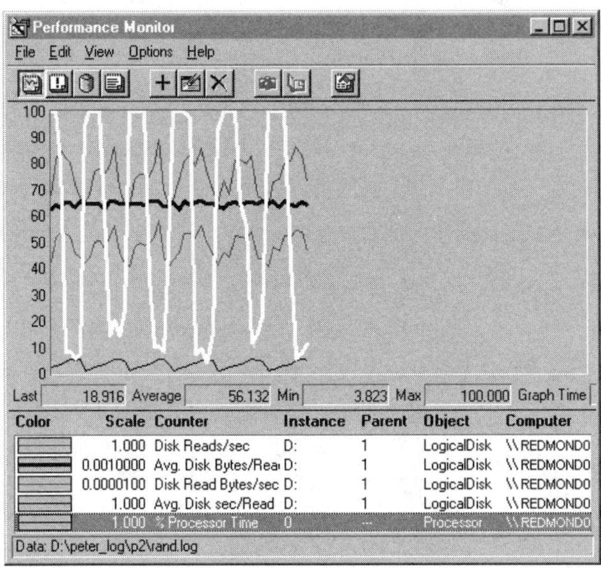

In this example, the Processor: % Processor Time is the white line superimposed upon the previous graph of the random test. The processor time follows the same pattern as the transfer rate, but is offset by about half of the read time. The processor, which is not particularly busy otherwise, is consumed for short periods while it locates the drive sector for the read operation. Once the sector is found, the read can begin, and the processor can resume its other threads until the read is complete, when it is again interrupted by the next seek request.

Although it is often impractical to read records sequentially in a real application, these tests demonstrate how much more efficient the same disk can be when reading sequentially. The following methods can improve disk efficiency:

- Run a defragmentation utility on the disk. It might be doing extra seeking because a file has become fragmented.
- If you have multiple logical or physical disks, move all of the files for your busiest application to a single logical partition or drive to minimize movement of the disk head.
- Examine your applications. Try to reorganize the code references and data structures so reading is more localized, if not sequential.

If your disk is used to read data from many different files in different locations, it cannot be as efficient as it might otherwise be. Adjust the expected values for the disk based upon the work it is expected to do.

Random vs. Sequential Writing

Seek operations affect writing to disk as well as reading from it. Use the following counters to measure and compare the effects of writing sequential records to writing randomly throughout the disk:

- Logical Disk: Avg. Disk Bytes/Write
- Logical Disk: Avg. Disk sec/Write
- Logical Disk: Disk Write Bytes/sec
- Logical Disk: Disk Writes/sec

Remember to defragment your disk before testing. If your disk is nearly full, the remaining free space is likely to be fragmented, and the disk must seek to find each sector of free space. The efficiencies won by writing sequential records will be lost in the added seek time.

The following figure compares random to sequential writing on the same disk. In the top graph, the disk is writing 64K records randomly throughout a 60 MB file. In the bottom graph, the same disk is writing the same size records to the same size file, but is writing sequentially. In both cases, Performance Monitor is logging to a different partition on the same physical disk.

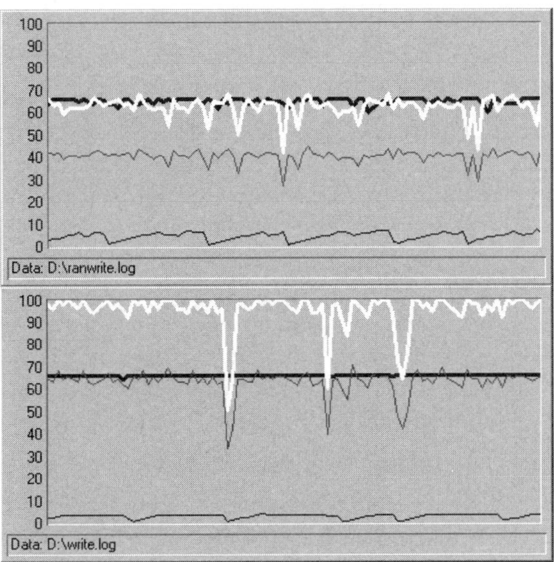

In both graphs, the white line is Disk Writes/sec, the thick, black line is Avg. Disk Bytes/Write, the gray line is Disk Write Bytes/sec, and the thin, black line near the bottom is Avg. Disk sec/Write.

The pattern of seek and read that was evident on the graph of random reading does not appear in this graph of random writing. In fact, the shapes of the random and sequential writing counter curves are quite similar, but their values are very different. Disk Writes/sec and Disk Write Bytes/sec are both 50% higher on the sequential writing test, an even greater effect than on the reading test.

The following comparison of reports makes this more evident. The top report is of the random writing test; the bottom report is of the sequential writing test.

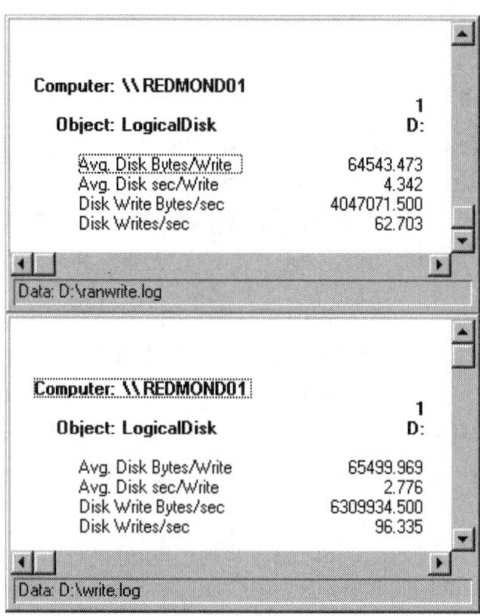

When writing throughout the disk, the transfer rate, as measured by Disk Writes/sec, drops from 96.335/sec to 62.703/sec on average. Disk Write Bytes/sec drops also by one-third, from 6.3 MB/sec to 4.0 MB on average.

Reading Smaller vs. Larger Records

All other things being equal, it is quicker and more efficient to read a few large records than many small ones. Although this seems obvious, it is vital to disk performance. If your applications are efficient in their I/O strategy, in localizing data access, and in minimizing repeated I/O requests, the application, the disk, and the computer will function more efficiently.

You can test how your computer responds to reading and writing in smaller and larger units. The Windows NT Resource Kit 4.0 CD includes Diskmax, a Response Probe test of maximum throughput which reads 64K records and Minread, a Response Probe test for reading in 512-byte records. The tests are on the Windows NT Resource Kit 4.0 CD in the Performance Tools group in the \Probe subdirectory. Instructions for running the tests are in Diskmax.txt and Minread.txt.

Note The Minread tests use 512-byte records as the minimum record size because unbuffered reads must be done in sectors, and 512-bytes is a common disk sector size. If your disk has a different sector size, substitute that value for 512 in the RECORDSIZE parameter of the Minread.sct file.

To find the sector size of your disk, use Windows NT Diagnostics in the Administrative Tools group. Select the Drives tab, double-click the drive letter to open the Properties page, then select the General tab. Sector size is listed along with other useful information.

The following figure displays the extremes. It compares the results of the Minread and Diskmax tests run on the same drive of the same computer. Performance Monitor was writing its log to a different physical drive. Both tests show Response Probe doing unbuffered reads of sequential records from a 20 MB file.

The figure was created by superimposing two Performance Monitor reports of the same counters. The data in the first column shows Response Probe reading 512-byte records. The data in the second column shows Response Probe reading 64K records. Avg. Disk Bytes/Read, the size of each read from the disk, is set by the test. The other values vary with the efficiency of the system.

Computer: \\reuiwqy90		
Object: LogicalDisk	D:	D:
Avg. Disk Bytes/Read	513.021	65379.152
Avg. Disk sec/Read	0.001	0.041
Disk Read Bytes/sec	336006.500	1529675.125
Disk Reads/sec	654.957	23.397
% Disk Time	50.081	95.749
Object: System		
% Total Processor Time	79.144	78.759
Total Interrupts/sec	1124.466	3651.517
% Total Interrupt Time	6.028	7.477

Data: C:\WINNT35\system32\minread.log

In this example, larger reads improved throughput substantially, but the transfer rate dropped as more of the disk time was consumed. While reading smaller records, the disk was only busy 50% of the time, so it could have been shared with another process. It managed 655 reads per second on average, at a quick 0.001 seconds per read. Reading the larger records, the disk was almost 96% busy, reading only 23.4 times/sec at 0.041 seconds per read.

Total throughput was much better for larger records. Disk Read Bytes/sec was 336K bytes per second on average for the small records and 1.5 MB/sec for the large records.

Interrupts/sec at 1124.466 were close to the expected 1 per sector for this disk, as shown in the following table. Note that although interrupts were high, they amounted to a small proportion of disk time. Some of the interrupts might not have been serviced.

	Interrupts on small records	Interrupts on larger records
Total interrupts/sec	1124	3651.5
System clock interrupts/sec	(100)	(100)
Network interrupts/sec	(300)	(300)
Subtotal	724	3251.5
Bytes/sec	335006.5	1529675
Bytes/interrupt	462.7	470.45

In this system, 100 interrupts per second are generated by the processor clock and about 300 interrupts per second are generated by the network. Thus, 724 interrupts per second can be attributed to disk activity while reading smaller records or about 1 interrupt for every 463 bytes (336006.5 / 724) on average. For larger records, 3252 interrupts per second are likely to be caused by disk activity or 1 interrupt for every 470 bytes (1529675.125 / 3252).

One important value, elapsed time, is not shown in the report, but can be calculated, at least roughly, from values that are shown. To read a 20 MB file in 512-byte chunks would take 40,000 reads. At about 655 disk reads per second, that would take longer than minute. ((20,048,000 / 512) / 655 = 61 seconds). To read the same file in larger records, even at the slower rate would take only just over 13 seconds (((20,480,000 / 65536) / 23.4) = 13.34).

This test of the extremes of record size performance used sequential reading with no memory access. To test within and beyond this range, copy and edit the Diskmax and Minread files.

- To test random reads, change the word 'SEQUENTIAL' to 'RANDOM' in the Diskmax.sct or Minread.sct file, and set midrange values for the FILESEEK parameter. For a 20 MB file reading 64K records, set the FILESEEK mean to 156 and the standard deviation to 52. For a 20 MB file reading 512-byte records, set the mean to 20000 and the standard deviation to 6667.
- To test writing at different file sizes, change the last R in the file to a W, or add a W to read and write in the same test.
- To vary the record size, change the RECORDSIZE parameter to a different multiple of the sector size. Remember to change the FILESEEK parameter to the new midpoint if you are doing random file access.

For more information on Response Probe, see "Response Probe" in Chapter 11, "Performance Monitoring Tools."

Reading Records of Increasing Size

Another interesting test is to read records of gradually increasing size. You can see how the system responds to the change in requirements.

In this test, a test tool was set up to do unbuffered, sequential reads from a 40 MB file. It did three reads each of 2K, 8K, 64K, 256K, 1024K, 4096K and 8192K records with a 5-second interval between cluster of three reads.

Note The Windows NT Resource Kit 4.0 CD includes all the files you need to use Response Probe to test the performance of your disk while reading records of increasing size. The Sizeread test is controlled by an MS-DOS batch file which runs a series of Response Probe tests. To run Sizeread, use Setup to install the Performance Tools group from the CD. The test files are in the Probe subdirectory. Instructions for running the test are in Sizeread.txt.

The following graphs show the data. The first two graphs show values for the smaller records, 2K, 8K, and 64K. Values for the larger files appear to stop at 100, but actually go off of the top of the graph. The last graph in this section shows values for the larger records, 256K, 1024K, 4096K, and 8192K. In these graphs, values for the smaller record sizes run along the bottom of the graph. Throughout the test, Performance Monitor was logging to a different physical drive.

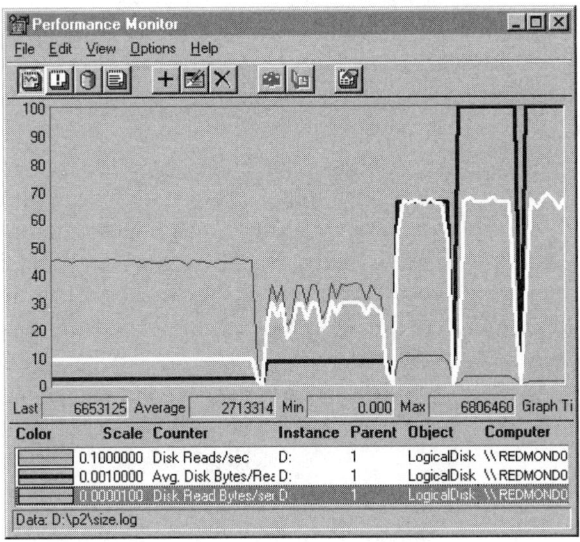

In this graph, the gray line is Disk Reads/sec, the black line is Avg. Disk Bytes/Read, and the white line is Disk Read Bytes/sec. As the record size (Avg. Disk Bytes/Read) increases, the throughput (Disk Read Bytes/sec) increases and the transfer rate (Disk Reads/sec) falls because it takes fewer reads to move the same amount data. At 8K, the reading performance wobbles as the system runs short of memory, then recovers. Above 64K, the values are greater than 100 and go beyond the top of the graph.

The following graph shows the affect of the disk activity on the processor.

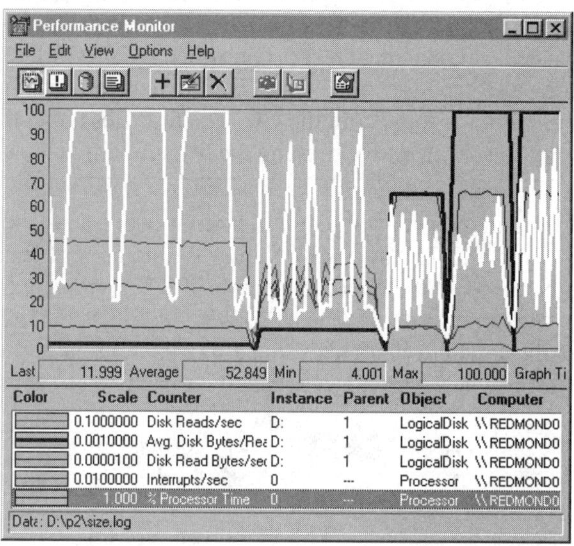

In this graph, Processor: % Processor Time (the white line) is added to the graph, along with Interrupts/sec. The processor time curve shows that the processor is used more frequently as throughput increases, but the amount of processor time decreases as the record size increases. This value is characteristic of the architecture of this disk, which interrupts for each read, not for each sector. On disks that interrupt at each sector, the pattern would be quite different.

The patterns seem to fall apart at record sizes greater than 64K bytes. The processor use begins to increase, and throughput rate hits a plateau and remains there.

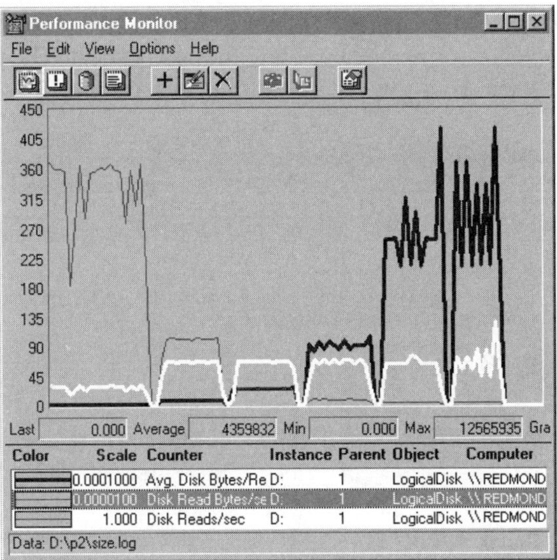

This graph is designed to show the larger values. The counters are scaled quite small, and the vertical maximum on the graph is increased to 450. The thick, black line (Avg. Disk Bytes/Read) represents the record size. The white line is the throughput, in Disk Read Bytes/sec. The gray line is transfer rate, in Disk Reads/sec.

The scales are so small that the first few record size variations just appear as close to zero. The first noticeable bump is 64K, the next is the attempt at 256K, then 1024K, 4096K and 8192K. The disk adapter cannot handle the higher disk sizes, so the actual values are closer to 252K, 900K, then 6.5M for both 4096K and 8192K.

What is clear from this otherwise busy graph, is that maximum throughput is reached at 64K and does not increase any further with record size, although the transfer rate continues to fall as the buses are loaded with larger and larger records.

The actual values are best shown on this Excel spreadsheet. It was prepared by using a single copy of Performance Monitor with a graph of Avg. Disk Bytes/Read in Chart view, and a report of the Logical Disk and Processor counters was created in Report view. In Chart view, the Time Window was adjusted to limit the values to a single record size segment, then the values were read from report view and entered into the spreadsheet. The procedure was repeated for each record size segment of the chart.

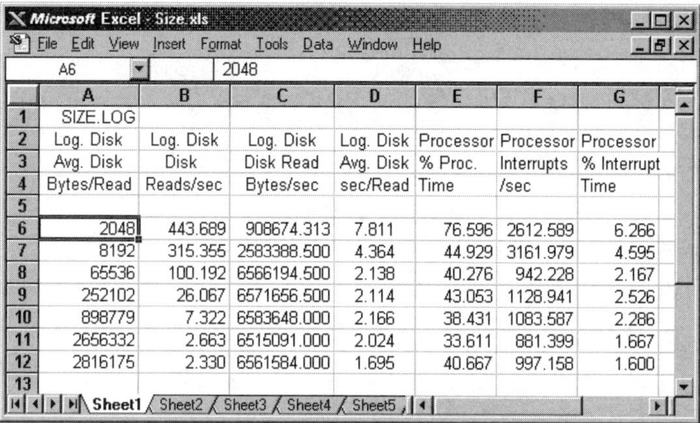

Microsoft Excel - Size.xls

	A	B	C	D	E	F	G
1	SIZE.LOG						
2	Log. Disk	Log. Disk	Log. Disk	Log. Disk	Processor	Processor	Processor
3	Avg. Disk	Disk	Disk Read	Avg. Disk	% Proc.	Interrupts	% Interrupt
4	Bytes/Read	Reads/sec	Bytes/sec	sec/Read	Time	/sec	Time
5							
6	2048	443.689	908674.313	7.811	76.596	2612.589	6.266
7	8192	315.355	2583388.500	4.364	44.929	3161.979	4.595
8	65536	100.192	6566194.500	2.138	40.276	942.228	2.167
9	252102	26.067	6571656.500	2.114	43.053	1128.941	2.526
10	898779	7.322	6583648.000	2.166	38.431	1083.587	2.286
11	2656332	2.663	6515091.000	2.024	33.611	881.399	1.667
12	2816175	2.330	6561584.000	1.695	40.667	997.158	1.600
13							

This spreadsheet reveals the I/O strategy of this system. When transferring data blocks greater than 64K, it breaks the transfers into 64K chunks. Above 64K, the transfer rate drops sharply, and throughput sticks at 6.5 MB. The buffer size appears to be at its maximum at an average record size of 2.8 MB, although the largest record transferred was 4.194 MB. (To determine the largest record size, use the time window to limit the graph to the single highest value on the chart, then read the **Max** value from the value bar.)

Processor use and interrupts also appear to level off at 64K. The remaining variation is just as likely to be due to sampling. It is beyond the resolution of this tool.

This is just an example of what you can test. Remember to use different applications and test tools and combine all results in your analysis. Save the data to show long term trends in disk performance, especially if your workload changes or memory or disks are upgraded.

Comparing Disks

Use the same testing methods to compare the performance of different disks. Disk components vary in architecture and design philosophy, and they use different protocols. As expected, performance varies widely and is usually correlated with the price of the components. Most workstations will perform adequately with the most moderately priced disk components. However, if you have a disk bottleneck, you might want to evaluate different disk components.

The following figure compares the reading performance of two very different disk configurations side by side. As you might expect, the graph on the right represents the more expensive disk. That disk uses direct memory access (DMA), a method of transferring data to disk that minimizes the use of the processor. The graph on the left represents the performance of a more traditional disk design which uses programmed I/O, a disk transfer method that uses the processor to determine which disk sectors are read.

The disks were both reading 64K records from a 40 MB file on an otherwise idle computer. Performance Monitor was writing its log to a different physical drive.

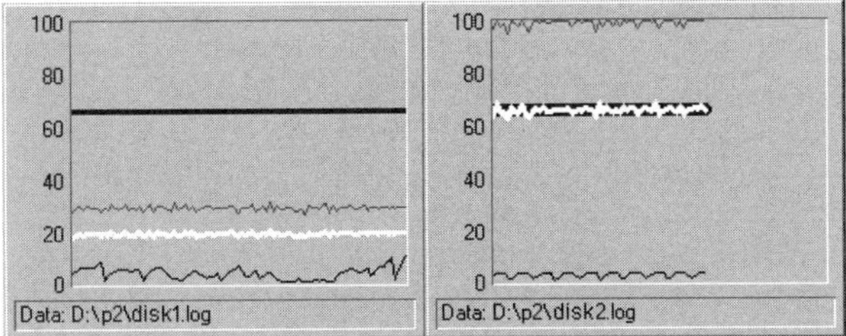

In both graphs, the heavy black line is Avg. Disk Bytes/Read, the gray line is Disk Read Bytes/sec, the white line is Disk Reads/sec, and the thin, black line near the bottom is Avg. Disk sec/Read. Because the lines do not curve much, they can be shrunk to show them side by side without losing too much detail.

In summary, the gray and white lines, representing Disk Read Bytes/sec and Disk Reads/sec, respectively, are much lower in the first graph than in the second. On the same task and the same computer, throughput on the disk that is represented by the graph on the right is 3.4 times higher than throughput on the disk represented by the graph on the left.

Because the lines are nearly straight, the averages shown in the following comparative reports are likely to represent disk performance accurately.

Computer: \\REDMOND01	0	1
Object: LogicalDisk	C:	D:
Avg. Disk Bytes/Read	65536.000	65536.000
Avg. Disk sec/Read	3.796	2.427
Disk Read Bytes/sec	1879557.875	6524845.000
Disk Reads/sec	28.680	99.561
Object: Processor	0	0
% Processor Time	99.858	53.443
% Interrupt Time	93.542	2.426

To produce a report like this one, superimpose two copies of Performance Monitor reports on the same counters for different disks. (You can also export the data to a spreadsheet, but this method is quicker.)

The reports are evidence of significant performance differences between the disks. In this example, Drive C uses programmed I/O; Drive D uses DMA. While reading from the C drive, the processor was nearly 100% busy, but because it was reading only 28.7 times per second, the throughput was just 1.88 MB/sec. When the same test was run on the D drive, the processor was only 53% busy, and it was reading nearly 100 times per second, for a total throughput of 6.5 MB/sec.

The difference in the strategies is revealed in the % Interrupt Time, which was 93.5% on the C drive and only 2% on the D drive. The C drive configuration uses the processor for disk access. The processor is interrupted between each 512-byte sector read. This amounts to 128 interrupts for each 65536-byte record read. The C drive is reading an average of 187955.875 bytes/sec, so the processor is being interrupted 3671 times each second. That is enough to consume all processor time.

In contrast, the more advanced D drive configuration interrupts the processor five times to set up the read operation, but does not issue any further interrupts for the remainder of the read. This strategy obviously benefits even more from larger records, whereas the C drive strategy produces ever more interrupts as the record size grows.

This test is just an example of the kinds of tests you can use to compare disk configurations. A complete test would use the same methods to test reading, writing, reading and writing randomly and sequentially, and reading and writing records of different sizes. A vital test, one to measure maximum throughput on your disk, is explained in the following section.

Testing Maximum Disk Throughput

Disk configurations vary widely between design technologies and manufacturers. If disk performance is important to your system, it is wise to assemble and test different disk components. A maximum throughput test will tell you one of the limits of your system.

The Windows NT Resource Kit 4.0 CD includes all the files you need to use Response Probe to test maximum throughput on your disks. Use Setup to install the Performance Tools group from the CD. The test files are in the Probe subdirectory. Instructions for running the test are in Diskmax.txt.

Warning Response Probe, like other Windows NT Resource Kit 4.0 CD tools, is not an officially supported tool. Be aware of this when using Response Probe and other tools on the CD.

To test how fast the disk can go, give it the best possible circumstances: Have it read large (but not excessively large) records sequentially from a large file. In this test, Response Probe reads 64K records sequentially from a 20 MB file of zeros. The reads are not buffered by the cache, there is no datapage access, and the same codepage function is read repeatedly to minimize the effect of codepage access.

While Response Probe is running, use Performance Monitor to log the System and Logical Disk objects once per second. Then chart the following counters:

- System: % Total Processor Time
- System: % Total Interrupts or Total Interrupts/sec
- Logical Disk: Avg. Disk Read Queue Length
- Logical Disk: Avg. Disk Bytes/Read
- Logical Disk: Avg. Disk sec/Read
- Logical Disk: Disk Read Bytes/sec
- Logical Disk: Disk Reads/sec

Disk Read Bytes/sec is the essential throughput measurement; the other counters are included to help to in interpreting its value.

The following report of Response Probe activity was generated by using the Diskmax test files on the CD.

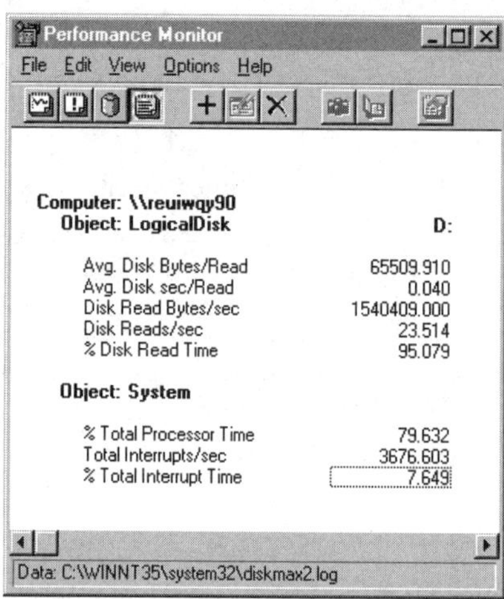

In this example, the maximum throughput, as measured by Disk Read Bytes/sec is 1.54 MB, which is quite good for this disk configuration, although higher throughput is expected from more advanced disk technologies. The disk was reading 23.5 of the 64K records per second and each read took 0.04 seconds on average.

Total interrupts for this activity, 3676 per second, seem excessive, but the processor was busy only 79% of the time, and the interrupts generated only 7.65% of that activity.

Run the Diskmax test on your disk configuration. When you have run it a few times, test the response of your disk configuration to changes in the test. For example, increase the size of the workload file to 60 or even 100 MB. Increase the record size, too. After you determine the maximum throughput for your disk, you can adjust the load on your disk so it does not become a bottleneck.

Monitoring Disk Sets

Two heads are better than one. In fact, when it comes to disks, the more heads the better, if you can keep them all busy. Because each physical disk typically has its own head stack assembly, and the heads work simultaneously, performance on disk sets can be significantly better on than single disks. However, some disk configurations are designed for data security, with performance as a secondary concern.

The Windows NT 4.0 Workstation Disk Administrator supports many different disk configurations, including *volume sets*, which are logical combinations of multiple physical disks. Performance Monitor and other monitoring tools can be set up to measure and help you tune performance on volume sets.

Note Whenever you combine noncontiguous physical disk space into a logical partition, the Disk Administrator adds Ftdisk.sys, a fault tolerant driver, to your disk driver stack and starts the FTDISK service. To see if FTDISK is started in your computer, check the Devices Control Panel.

There are three main strategies for combining physical disks. The terms introduced here are used throughout this section:

Term	Description
RAID (Redundant Array of Inexpensive Disks)	A standard technology for combining multiple physical disks into one or more logical disks.
Hardware RAID	Separate physical disks combined into one or more logical disks by the disk controller or disk storage cabinet hardware.
Software RAID	Noncontiguous disk space combined into one or more logical partitions by the fault tolerant software disk driver, FTDISK. This includes separate physical disks or noncontiguous space on a single physical disk.
Stripe sets	Associated free space on up to 32 different physical disks. When you write to a stripe set, some of the data is written to each of the physical disks in the set. Stripe sets are a type of software RAID that use FTDISK.
Mirror sets	Associated free space of the same size on two physical disks. When you write to a mirror set, the same data is written to each of the disks. This creates a real-time backup of the data. Mirror sets are supported only on Windows NT Server.
Stripe sets with parity	Associated free space on three or more disks. When you write, the file data and the parity data are distributed across all disks. Stripe sets with parity sets are supported only on Windows NT Server.

Testing Considerations

The counters used for single disks can also be used on disk sets. However, two issues are of particular concern for disk sets:

- On Hardware RAID sets, where physical disks are combined into a single logical unit by the disk controller, Performance Monitor cannot see the instances of physical disks. It combines the values for all disks as though the disk activity occurred sequentially, rather than simultaneously.
- The % Disk Time counters cannot display the sum of multiple disk activity if it exceeds 100%. The potential maximum disk activity for a RAID cabinet is 100% multiplied by the number of disks in the set.
- On software RAID, where Performance Monitor can see instances of the disks, it displays simple sums of values; it does not divide the sum by the number of disks.

Use the new disk counters. Avg. Disk Queue Length, Avg. Disk Read Queue Length, and Avg. Disk Write Queue Length display disk activity as a decimal, not a percentage, so that it can display values over 1.0 (100%). Then, remember to recalculate the values over the whole disk configuration. For more information, see "New Disk Activity Counters" earlier in this chapter.

Reading from Stripe Sets

Windows NT Workstation supports most hardware RAID configurations and stripe sets without parity. Testing the performance of these volume sets is much like testing single disk. The Response Probe tests used to measure single disks can also be run on any disk in a stripe set and on the virtual volume that hardware RAID exposes to Windows NT.

To test your volume sets, use the following counters:

- System: % Total Processor Time
- System: % Total Interrupts or Total Interrupts/sec
- Physical Disk: Avg. Disk Read Queue Length
- Physical Disk: Avg. Disk Bytes/Read
- Physical Disk: Avg. Disk sec/Read
- Physical Disk: Disk Read Bytes/sec
- Physical Disk: Disk Reads/sec

Note The equivalent counters for measuring writing (for example, Avg. Disk Write Bytes/sec) are used to test the performance of volume sets while writing to disk. The values for reading and writing in our tests were so similar that showing the writing test added little value. However, you can use the same methods to test writing to disk on your volume sets.

These reading tests were run on a stripe set of four physical disks. Disks 0, 1, and 2 are on a single disk adapter, and Disk 3 is on a separate adapter. Performance Monitor is logging to Disk 3. In each test, the test tool is doing unbuffered, sequential reads of 64K records from a 60 MB file on a FAT partition. The test begins with reading only from Disk 0. Another physical disk was added with each iteration of the test to end with 4 stripes. During the test, Performance Monitor was logging data to Stripe_read.log, which is included on the Windows NT Resource Kit 4.0 CD.

Tip The logs recorded during these tests are included on the Windows NT Resource Kit 4.0 CD in the Performance Tools group. The logs are Stripe_read.log (sequential reading), Stripe_rand.log (random reading), and Stripe_write.log (sequential writing). Use Performance Monitor to chart the logs and follow along with the discussion that follows. The logs include data for the Processor, Logical Disk, and Physical Disk objects, so you can add more counters than those shown here.

The following graph shows an overview of the test, and the disk time contributed by each disk to the total effort. In the first segment of the graph there is one disk, the second, two disks; the third, three disks; and the fourth, four disks.

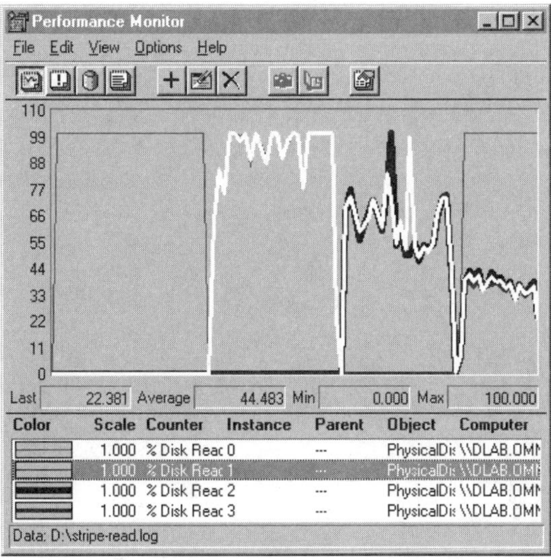

The graph consists of Physical Disk: % Disk Read Time for all disks in the stripe set. The thin gray line represents Disk 0, the white line is Disk 1, the heavy black line is Disk 2, and the heavy gray line is Disk 3. The striping strategy apportions the workload rather equally in this case, so the lines are superimposed upon each other. This graph is designed to show that, as new disks were added to the test, each disk needed to contribute a smaller portion of its time to the task.

The following table shows the average values of Avg. Disk Read Queue Length, a measure of disk time in decimals, for each disk during each segment of the test.

# Stripes	Avg. Disk Read Queue Length			
	Disk 0	**Disk 1**	**Disk 2**	**Disk 3**
1	58.673	0	0	0
2	1.047	1.054	0	0
3	0.603	0.639	0.645	0.000
4	1.562	0.366	0.377	0.355

This table shows how the FTDISK, the Windows NT fault tolerant disk driver, distributes the workload among the stripes in the set, so each disk requires less time. The exception is Disk 0 which has a disproportionate share of the activity during the last stage of the test.

The following graph shows the effect of their combined efforts in the total work achieved by the stripe set.

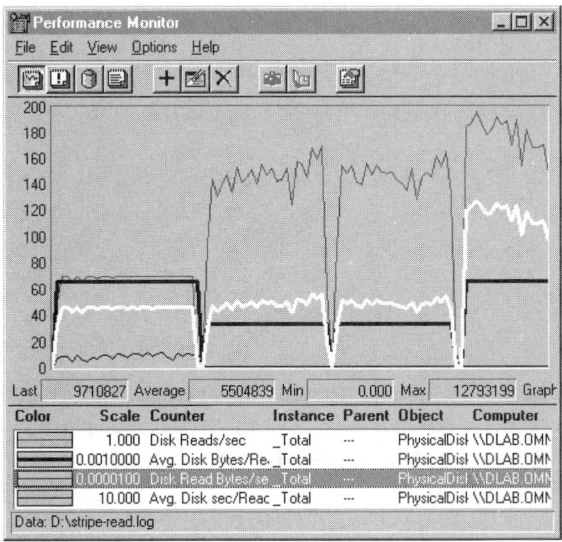

In this graph, the gray line is Disk Reads/sec: Total, the heavy black line is Avg. Disk Bytes/Read: Total, the white line is Disk Read Bytes/sec: Total and the thin, black line at the bottom is Avg. Disk sec/Read: Total. The vertical maximum on the graph is increased to 200 to include all values.

The following figure shows the average values for each segment of the test.

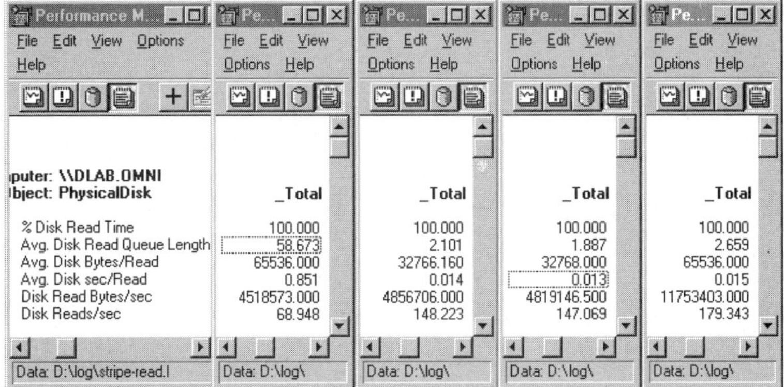

Tip To produce a figure like this, open four copies of Performance Monitor and chart the counters you want to see for all available instances. The first copy is used just to show the counter names. Use the time window to set each copy of Performance Monitor to a different time segment of the test. Then, you can scroll each copy to the instance you want to examine in that time segment. In this example, the Total instance is shown for all time segments.

The graph and reports show that the transfer rate (Disk Reads/Sec: Total) is most affected by adding stripes to the set. It increases from an average of 69 reads/sec on a single disk to an average of 179 reads per second with four stripes. Throughput (Disk Read Bytes/Sec: Total) increases from an average of 4.5 MB per second to 11.75 MB/sec with four stripes.

Note that there is almost no change in the values upon adding the third stripe, Disk 2, to the set. The total transfer rate increases significantly with the addition of the second disk, but not at all with the third disk. Throughput, which is 4.5 MB with one disk, inches up to an average of 4.8 MB, then stays there until the fourth disk is added.

We cannot measure it directly, but it appears that this plateau is caused by a bottleneck on the disk adapter shared by Disks 0, 1, and 2. Although each of the physical disks has a separate head stack assembly, they still share the adapter. Shared resource contention is one of the limits of scalability. Multiple computers share the network, multiple processors share memory, multiple threads share processors, and multiple disks share adapters and buses. Fortunately, we can measure it and plan for future equipment needs.

The following graph shows how each disk is affected when stripes are added to the set. While the totals go up, each disk does less work. Potentially, it has time available for other work.

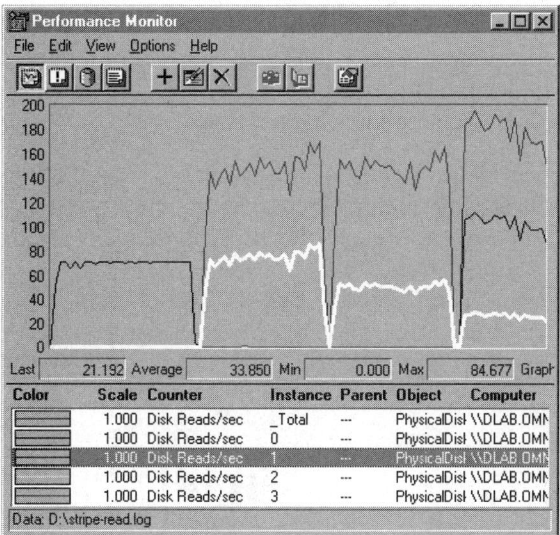

This is a graph of the transfer rate, as measured by Disk Reads/sec. The gray line is Disk Reads/Sec: Total, the black line is Disk Reads/sec: Disk 0, and the white line is Disk Reads/sec: Disk 1. The lines for Disks 2 and 3 run along the bottom of the graph until they are added, and then they are superimposed on the line for Disk 1.

The average values are:

#Stripes	**Disk Reads/sec**				
	Disk 0	**Disk 1**	**Disk 2**	**Disk 3**	**Total**
1	68.948	0.000	0.000	0.000	68.948
2	74.107	74.107	0.000	0.010	148.223
3	49.020	49.020	49.020	0.000	147.069
4	102.487	25.619	25.619	25.619	179.343

These averages are a fairly good representation of the strategy of the stripe set controller as it distributes the workload equally among the stripes in the set. Each disk does less work, and the total achieved increases two and half times. Note that the transfer rate did not increase fourfold; the difference is likely to be related to sharing of resources.

The cause of the exceptional values of Disk 0, which appear in every test, are not entirely clear. They probably result from updates to the File Allocation Table. The tests were run on a FAT partition which was striped across all participating drives. In each case, the File Allocation Table is likely to be written to the first disk, Disk 0. Because the File Allocation Table is contiguous and sequential, Disk 0 can perform at maximum capacity. It appears that distributing the load to the other disks let Disk 0 double its productivity in the last sample interval. More research will be required to determine what happened.

The next graph shows that the same pattern holds for throughput. As more stripes are added, the total throughput increases, and the work is distributed across all four disks. This data also shows the disproportionate workload on Disk 0.

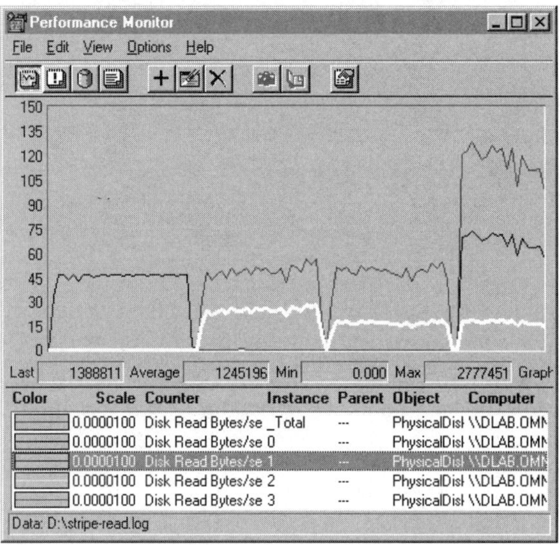

This is a graph of disk throughput, as measured by Disk Read Bytes/sec. The gray line is Disk Read Bytes/sec: Total, the black line is Disk Read Bytes/sec: Disk 0, the white line is Disk Read Bytes/Sec: Disk 1. Again, the lines for Disks 2 and 3 run along the bottom of the graph until they are added, and then they are superimposed on the line for Disk 1.

This table shows the average throughput, in megabytes, for each disk as the test progresses.

#Stripes	Disk Read Bytes/sec				
	Disk 0	Disk 1	Disk 2	Disk 3	Total
1	4.52	0.00	0.00	0.00	4.52
2	2.43	2.43	0.00	0.000039	4.86
3	1.61	1.61	1.61	0.00	4.82
4	6.72	1.68	1.68	1.68	11.75

The pattern, quite reasonably, is very similar to that for the transfer rate. The workload is distributed evenly and the total throughput rate achieved increases by 2.6%. Disk 0 is still doing a disproportionate share of the work (57%), which probably consists of its share of the read operations plus updating the FAT table.

Random Reading from Stripe Sets

Reading and writing randomly throughout a disk is about the most laborious process required of disks. The constant seek activity consumes the disk and the processor. These issues were discussed in detail in the earlier section, "Random vs. Sequential Reading." This section describes how to test the effect of random reading on your volume set.

Note As in the previous section, the relative values for reads and writes are nearly indistinguishable, so data for writing is not shown here. You can, however, use the same methods to explore random writing performance on your disks.

As before, these reading tests were run on a stripe set of four physical disks. Disks 0, 1, and 2 are on a single disk adapter, and Disk 3 is on a separate adapter. Also, Performance Monitor is logging to Disk 3. In each test, the test tool is doing random, unbuffered reads of 64K records from a 60 MB file. The test begins reading only from Disk 0, and adds a disk with each iteration of the test to end with four stripes.

During the test, Performance Monitor was logging to Stripe_rand.log. This log is included on the Windows NT Resource Kit 4.0 CD, so you can follow along and chart additional counters.

Stripes sets are know for their seeking efficiency. They are created by associating free space in multiple physical disks. Code and data written to the stripe set is distributed evenly across all disks. Because each disk in the set has its own head stack assembly, the heads on each disk in the set can seek simultaneously. Some performance loss is expected when the disk is reading randomly, but it should not be as pronounced as on single disks or on unassociated disk configurations.

This following graph shows an overview of random reading performance for the disk set.

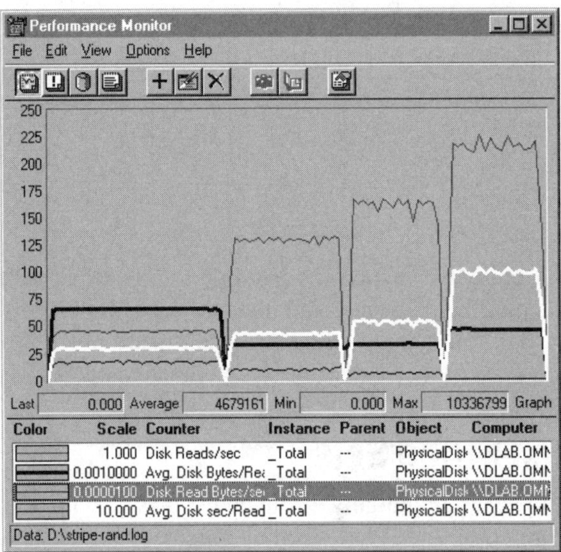

In this graph, the gray line is Disk Reads/Sec: Total, the thick, black line is Avg. Disk Bytes/Read: Total, the white line is Disk Read Bytes/Sec: Total and the thin, black line is Avg. Disk sec/Read: Total. The vertical maximum as been increased to 250 to incorporate all values.

The trend is much like that for sequential reads. As more stripes are added, the transfer rate (Disk Reads/sec) and throughput (Disk Read Bytes/sec) increase, and the queue (Avg. Disk sec/Read) diminishes.

The following figure compares the performance graphs of random and sequential reading by stripe sets. The graph on the left is sequential reading; the graph on the right is random reading. Both graphs in the figure show values for the _Total instance, representing all physical disks in the stripe set.

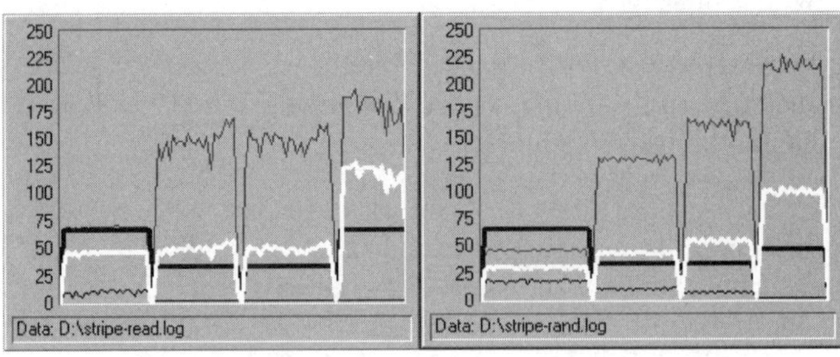

In both graphs, the gray line is Disk Reads/sec: Total, the thick, black line is Avg. Disk Bytes/Read: Total, the white line is Disk Read Bytes/Sec: Total and the thin, black line is Avg. Disk sec/Read: Total. The vertical maximum on both graphs has been set to 250 to incorporate all values.

This figure shows that although the patterns are similar, the values are slightly different. The transfer rate (Disk Reads/sec: Total) increases to more than 215 reads/sec in the random test. Throughput (Disk Read Bytes/sec: Total — the white line) runs lower on the random graph through almost every stage of the test.

The following tables compare the average values for sequential and random reading on the stripe set. To find these values, open a copy of Performance Monitor for each sample interval on the graph. Then use the time window to limit each one to a single sample interval, and display the disk reading counters in a report. These values were taken from four of such reports.

# Stripes	Total Disk Read Bytes/sec (in MB) Sequential	Total Disk Read Bytes/sec (in MB) Random	% Change
1	4.52	2.95	53.2%
2	4.86	4.23	15%
3	4.82	5.31	-9%
4	11.75	9.91	18.5%

# Stripes	Total Disk Reads/sec (in MB) Sequential	Total Disk Reads/sec (in MB) Random	% Change
1	68.948	45.024	53%
2	148.223	128.669	15%
3	147.069	161.310	-8.8%
4	179.343	215.760	-17%

Note that the performance lost by reading randomly diminishes significantly as disks are added. On a single disk, throughput on random is 53% lower than on sequential reading. The difference drops to 15% with two disks and, on four disks, throughput is 17% greater on random reading than on sequential reading.

The affect on individual disks in the set follows the patterns evidenced by the sequential reads. The following graph shows the effect of adding disks to the set on the transfer rate of each disk.

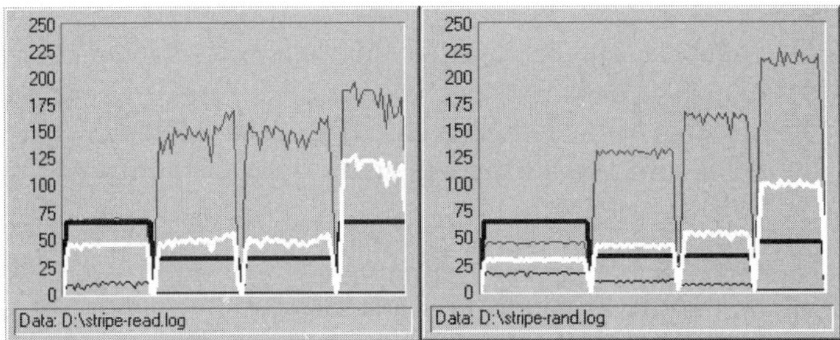

Physical Disk: Disk Reads/sec is charted for the _Total instance and for Disks 0 through 3. The gray line is the _Total, the black line is Disk 0, the white line is Disk 1. The lines representing Disks 2 and 3 run along the bottom of the graph until they are added to the test. Then they are superimposed upon the line for Disk 1.

The pattern continues. The transfer rate of the disk set increases with each disk added, but the work is distributed evenly to all disks in the set. The proportion of transfers for each disk declines accordingly.

The average values are shown in the following table.

#Stripes	**Disk Reads/sec**				
	Disk 0	**Disk 1**	**Disk 2**	**Disk 3**	**Total**
1	45.024	0.000	0.000	0.000	45.024
2	64.379	64.290	0.000	0.010	128.669
3	54.449	53.289	53.572	0.000	161.310
4	86.646	43.504	42.905	42.705	215.760

As observed in the sequential reads, the increased workload is distributed equally among all disks. There appears to be slightly more variation in the values, but it is too small to measure accurately without a much larger sample pool. Again, the transfer rate on Disk 0 increases significantly when the fourth disk is added. It is probably doing its share of the reading and also updating the FAT table.

The following graph shows the throughput values for random reading on a stripe set. The chart shows Disk Read Bytes/sec for all disks in the stripe set.

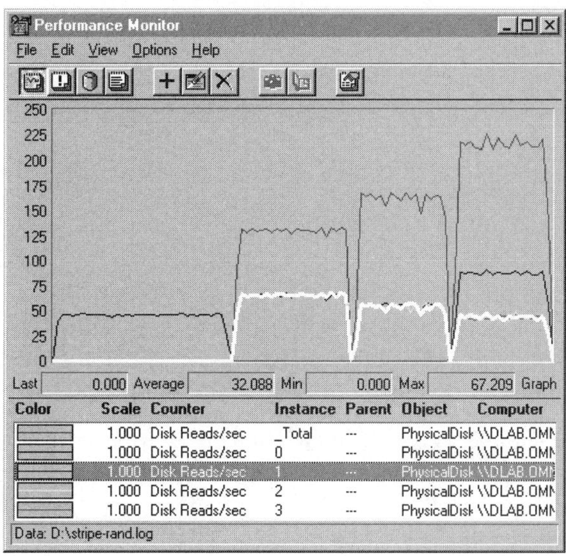

In this graph, the gray line is the _Total instance for all disks, which increases as more disks are added to the stripe set. The heavy, black line is Disk 0, and the white line is Disk 1. The lines representing Disks 2 and 3 run along the bottom of the graph until they are added to the test. Then, they are superimposed upon the line for Disk 1.

This table shows the average values.

#Stripes	**Disk Read Bytes/sec (in MB)**				
	Disk 0	**Disk 1**	**Disk 2**	**Disk 3**	**Total**
1	2.95	0.00	0.00	0.00	2.95
2	2.09	2.15	0.00	0.00	4.23
3	1.79	1.76	1.76	0.00	5.31
4	5.68	1.45	1.45	1.4	9.91

As disks are added, total throughput for the disk set increases 3.36 times, from 2.95 MB/sec to 9.91 MB/sec, compared to a 2.6 times increase for sequential reading. FTDISK is clearly taking advantage of the stripe set.

It is clear from this data that stripe sets are a very efficient means of disk transfer, and that the difference is especially apparent on very seek-intensive tasks such as random reading.

Although it is not shown in these graphs, processor use remained at 100% for the duration of the sequential and random reading and writing tests on stripe sets. The improved productivity has a cost in processor time.

Resolving a Disk Bottleneck

The obvious that the solution to a disk bottleneck is to add another disk. That is an appropriate solution if you are out of space. However, if your disk is too slow, the addition of a new disk might not be the cheapest or most effective solution. Disk systems have many parts, and any one could be the limiting factor in your disk configuration.

- Rule out a memory shortage. When memory is scarce, the Windows NT Virtual Memory Manager writes more pages to disk, resulting in increased disk activity. Because memory is the most common bottleneck on workstations, this is the first place to look.
- Consider upgrading your disk controller card. If you have a card that does transfers in units of 8 or 16 bits, your transfer rate will be improved by switching to a 32-bit controller. Also, choose a bus-mastering controller instead of one that does programmed I/O.
- Consider the architecture of the system I/O bus. The I/O bus and disk controller determine the maximum transfer rate of your disk configuration. After you select an architecture, you can then choose from the range of components, including disk adapters, device buses, and disk controllers that use that architecture. The performance of I/O buses varies widely from 16-bit buses that transfer less than 30 MB per second to 32-bit buses that transfer as much as 100 MB per second. However, the slowest component limits the maximum transfer rate. Even if you have the fastest I/O bus, a slow disk controller can become a bottleneck.
- Upgrade the device bus, the cable-and-pin connector that plugs into the disk. Some device buses transfer 8-bits at a time, but more advanced ones transfer twice as much, 16-bits at a time. There are no 32-bit designs. The transfer size is limited by the number of pins, each of which corresponds to a wire in the cable. For each additional pin, the cable must be shorter to avoid turbulence between the wires. Using current technology, 32-bit designs would not allow enough cable to be practical.

  Standard device buses support parallel transmission, that is, communication in one direction at a time. Serial buses allow simultaneous transmission across several paths in different directions. The performance of serial buses is, in theory, up to four times better than parallel buses.

- Upgrade your disk adapter to one that uses bus-mastering direct memory access (DMA) instead of programmed I/O. Programmed I/O uses the processor to set up disk transfers. In bus-mastering DMA, the disk controller managers the I/O bus and uses the DMA controller to manage DMA operation. This frees the processor for other uses.
- Finally, if you have decided that you must have another physical disk, consider placing one of more or your disks on a separate I/O bus. The benefit of multiple disks is reduced significantly when they need to share a crowded bus. One lesson of scaling—whether it is multiple computers, processors, or disks—is that if they have to share a scarce resource, their performance will be limited by the resource, not by their own performance potential.

CHAPTER 15

Detecting Cache Bottlenecks

The *Windows NT file system cache* is an area of memory into which the I/O system maps recently used data from disk. When processes need to read from or write to the files mapped in the cache, the I/O Manager copies the data from or to the cache as if it were an array in memory — without buffering or calling the file system. Because memory access is quicker than file operations, the cache provides an important performance boost to the processes.

Because the cache is just a part of physical memory, it is never really a bottleneck (although memory can be). However, when there is not enough memory to create an effective cache, the file system must retrieve more data from disk. This shortage of cache space is known as a *cache bottleneck.*

The size of the Windows NT file system cache is continually adjusted by the Virtual Memory Manager based upon the size of physical memory and the demand for memory space. In many operating systems, administrators can tune the cache size, but the Windows NT cache is designed to be self-tuning; you cannot change the cache size. For more information about the Cache Manager and the Virtual Memory Manager, see Chapter 5, "Windows NT 4.0 Workstation Architecture."

Note Cache bottlenecks are rare on workstations. More often the cache is monitored as an indication of application I/O, since almost all application file system activity is mediated by the cache.

Cache bottlenecks are mainly a server problem: Workstations rarely generate enough traffic to pressure the cache. However, complex programs such as CAD/CAM applications and large databases that access large blocks of multiple files and benefit from the cache will suffer when the cache is too small. Also, cache bottlenecks only affect applications that use the cache effectively, for example, by using data in the same sequence in which it is stored, so data requested is likely to be in the cache.

To monitor the cache, log the Memory, Cache, and Logical Disk objects for several days at a 60-second update interval, then chart the following counters:

Object	Counter
Memory	Cache Bytes
Memory	Cache Faults/sec
Memory	Page Fault/sec
Cache	Copy Reads/sec
Cache	Data Flushes/sec
Cache	Copy Read Hits%
Cache	Lazy Write Pages/sec
Cache	Lazy Write Flushes/sec
Cache	Read Aheads/sec
Logical Disk	Disk Reads/sec
Logical Disk	Pages Input/sec

The Windows NT File System Cache

Cache is a French word for a place to hide necessities or valuables. In computer terminology, a cache is an additional storage area close to the component that uses it. Caches are designed to save time: In general, the closer the data is, the quicker you can get to it.

Windows NT 4.0 supports several cache architectures: caches on processor chips, caches on the motherboard, caches on physical disks, and caches in physical memory. This chapter describes the *file system cache*, a cache in physical memory through which data files pass on their way to and from disk or other peripheral devices.

The file system cache is designed to minimize the need for disk operations. When an application requests data from a file, the file system first searches the cache:

- If the data is found in the cache, the Virtual Memory Manager copies it into the application's buffer and performs no disk I/O.
- If the data is not in the cache, the Virtual Memory Manager searches elsewhere in memory. As a last resort, it looks on the disk.

When determining what to cache, the Windows NT Virtual Memory Manager tries to anticipate the application's future requests for code and data, as well as its immediate needs. It might map an entire file into the cache, if space permits. This increases the likelihood that data requested will be found there.

The file system cache actually consists of a series of section objects created and indexed by the Windows NT Cache Manager. When the Virtual Memory Manager needs space in the cache, the Cache Manager creates a new section object. The files are then mapped—not copied—into the file system cache, so they do not need to be backed up in the paging file. This frees the paging file for other code and data.

Cache Hits and Misses

The simplest way to judge the effectiveness of the cache is to examine the percentage of cache *hits*, that is, how often data sought in the cache is found there. Cache *misses,* however, are even more important. When data is not found in the cache, or elsewhere in memory, the file system must make a time-consuming search of the disk. An application with a miss rate of 10% (a hit rate of 90%) requires twice as much disk I/O as an application with a miss rate of 5%.

Also, especially on a workstation, you must keep cache rates in perspective. On a system where cache reads are minimal, the hit-and-miss rates are not a significant performance factor. However, when running I/O-intensive applications such as databases, the cache hit-and-miss rates are an important performance measure of the computer and the application.

Cache Flushing

Pages are removed from the cache by *flushing*, that is, any changes are written back to disk, and the page is deleted. Two threads in the system process—the lazy writer thread and the mapped page writer thread—periodically flush unused pages to disk. The cache is also flushed when Virtual Memory Manager needs to shrink the cache because of memory constraints.

Applications can also request that a page copied from the cache be written back to disk. With *write-through caching*, the disk file is updated immediately; with *write-back caching* (the default), the Virtual Memory Manager waits until a batch of modifications has accumulated and writes them together.

Locality of Reference

Applications use memory most efficiently when they reference data in the same sequence or a sequence similar to the order in which the data is stored on disk. This is called *locality of reference*. When an application needs data, the data page or file is mapped into the cache. When an application's references to the same data, data on same page, or in the same the file, are localized, the data they seek is more likely to be found in the cache.

The nature of the application often dictates the sequence of data references. At other times, factors such as usability become more important in determining sequence. But by localizing references whenever possible, you can improve cache efficiency, minimize the size of process's working set, and improve application performance.

In general, *sequential reads*, which allow the Cache Manager to predict the application's data needs and to read larger blocks of data into the cache, are most efficient. Reads from the same page or file are almost as efficient. Reads of files dispersed throughout the disk are less efficient and *random reads* are least efficient.

You can monitor the efficiency of your application's use of the cache by watching the cache counters for copy reads, read aheads, data flushes and lazy writes. Read Aheads usually indicate that an application is reading sequentially, although some application reading patterns may fool the system's prediction logic. When data references are localized, a smaller number of pages are changed, so the lazy writes and data flushes decrease.

Copy read hits (when data sought in the cache is found there) in the 80-90% range are excellent. In general, Data flushes/sec are best kept below 20 per second, but this varies widely with the workload.

Unbuffered I/O

The file system cache is used, by default, whenever a disk is accessed. However, applications can request that its files not be cached by using the FILE_FLAG_NO_BUFFERING parameter in its call to open a file. This is called *unbuffered I/O*. Applications that use unbuffered I/O are typically database applications (such as SQL Server) that manage their own cache buffers. Unbuffered I/O requests must be issued in multiples of the disk sector size.

Cache Monitoring Utilities

In addition to Performance Monitor, several tools and utilities let you monitor the file system cache.

Task Manager

Task Manager displays the size of the file system cache on the Performance Tab in the Physical Memory box..

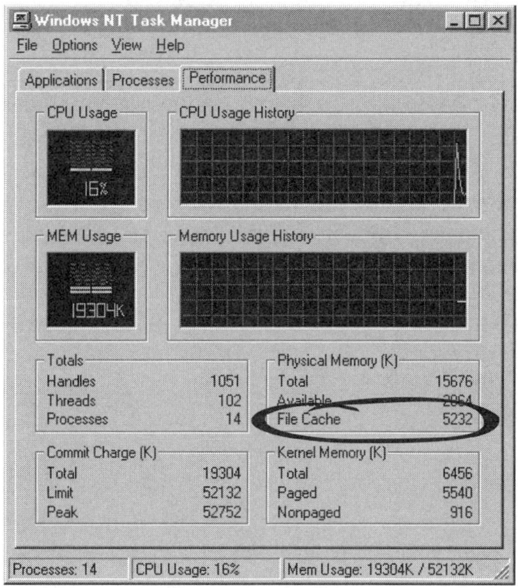

Performance Meter

Performance Meter (Perfmtr.exe), a tool on the Windows NT Resource Kit 4.0 CD in the Performance Tools group, lists current statistics on the file system cache. It is run at the command prompt. Start Performance Meter, then type **r** for Cache Manager reads and write statistics. Type **q** to quit.

Response Probe

Response Probe, a tool on the Windows NT Resource Kit 4.0 CD, lets you design a workload and test it on your system. When your workload includes file I/O, you can choose whether the files accessed use the cache or are unbuffered. In this way, you can measure the effect of the cache strategy on your application or test file operations directly. For more information, see "Response Probe" in Chapter 11, "Performance Monitoring Tools."

Clearmem

Clearmem, another tool on the Windows NT Resource Kit 4.0 CD, allocates and references all available memory, consuming any inactive pages in the working sets of all processes (including the cache). It clears the cache of all file data, letting you begin your test with an empty cache.

Understanding the Cache Counters

The following Performance Monitor Cache and Memory counters are used to measure cache performance and are described in this chapter.

Important The Hit% counters are best displayed in Chart view. Hits often appear in short bursts that are not visible in reports. Also, the average displayed for Hit% on the status bar in Chart view might not match the average displayed in Report view because they are calculated differently. In Chart view, the Hit% is an average of all changes in the counter during the test interval; in Report view, it is the average of the difference between the first and last counts during the test interval.

Counter	Description
Memory: Cache Bytes	How big is the cache? The Virtual Memory Manager regulates the size of the cache, which varies with the amount of physical memory and the demand for memory by other processes.
Memory: Cache Faults/sec	How many pages sought in the cache are not there and must be found elsewhere in memory or on the disk? This counts numbers of pages, so it can be compared with other page measures, like Page Faults/sec and Pages Input/sec.
Copy Reads/sec	How often does the file system look in the cache for data requested by applications? This is a count of all copy read calls to the cache, including hits and misses. Copy reads are the usual method by which file data found in the cache is copied into an application's memory buffers.

Counter	Description
Copy Read Hits %	How often do applications find what they need in the cache? Any value over 80% is excellent. Compare with Copy Reads/sec to see how many hits you are really getting. A small percentage of many calls might represent more hits than a higher percentage of an insignificant number of calls. This is the percentage of copy read calls satisfied by reads from the cache out of all read calls. Performance Monitor displays the value calculated for the last time interval, not an average. It also counts numbers of reads, regardless of amount of data reads.
Read Aheads/sec	How often can the Cache Manager read ahead in a file? Read aheads are a very efficient strategy in most cases. Sequential reading from a file lets the Cache Manager predict the pattern and read even larger blocks of data into the cache on each I/O.
Data Maps/sec	How often are file systems reading their directories? This counts read-only access to file system directories, the File Allocation Table in the FAT file system, and the Master File Table in NTFS. If this count is high, the Cache Manager might be occupied with directory operations. This is not a measure of cache use by applications.
Fast Reads	How often are applications able to go directly to the cache and bypass the file system? A value over 50% is excellent. The alternative is to send an I/O request to the file system.
Data Flushes/sec	How often is cache data being written back to disk? This counts application requests to flush data from the cache. It is an indirect indicator of the volume and frequency of application data changes.
Data Flush Pages/sec	How much data is the application changing? This counter measures data flushes in numbers of pages rather than number of disk accesses. Counts the number of modified pages in the cache that are written back to disk. This includes pages written by the System process when many changed pages have accumulated, pages flushed so the cache can be trimmed, and disk writes caused by an application write-through request.

Counter	Description
Lazy Write Flushes/sec	How much data is an application changing? How much memory is available to the cache? Lazy write flushes are a subset of data flushes. The Lazy Writer Thread in the system process periodically writes changed pages from the modified page list back to disk and flushes them from the cache. This thread is activated more often when memory needs to be released for other uses. This counter counts number of write and flush operations, regardless of the amount of data written.
Lazy Write Pages/sec	How much data is an application changing? How much memory is available to the cache? Lazy Write Pages are a subset of Data Flush Pages. Counts the numbers of pages written back to disk by a periodic system thread. Lazy writes are an asynchronous file operation that allows the application to update and continue without waiting for the I/O to be completed.

Recognizing Cache Bottlenecks

The file system cache is a part of memory. It can be thought of as the working set of the file system. When memory becomes scarce and working sets are trimmed, the cache is trimmed as well. If the cache grows too small, cache-sensitive processes will be slowed by disk operations.

To monitor cache size, use the following counters:

- Memory: Cache Bytes
- Memory: Available Bytes

Tip You can test the effect of a memory and cache shortage on your workstation without changing the physical memory in your computer. Use the MAXMEM parameter in the boot configuration to limit the amount of physical memory available to Windows NT. For more information, see "Configuring Available Memory" in Chapter 12, "Detecting Memory Bottlenecks."

The following graph shows that a memory shortage causes the cache to be trimmed, along with the working sets of processes, and other objects that compete with the cache for space in memory. The memory shortage was produced by running LeakyApp, a test tool that consumes memory.

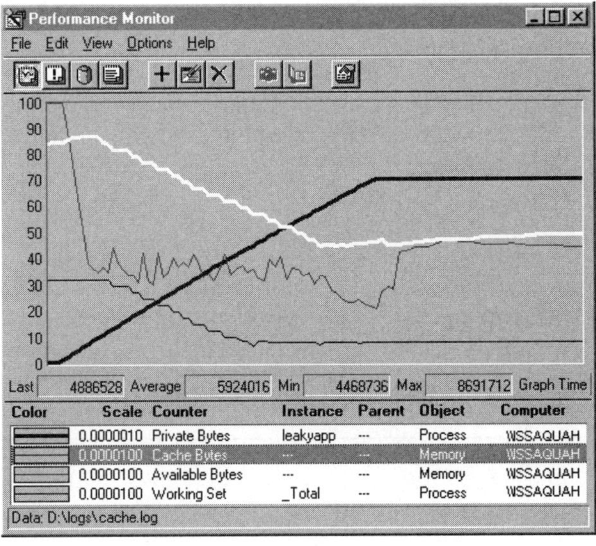

In this graph, the thick black line represents Process: Private Bytes for LeakyApp. (Note that it has been scaled to 0.000001 to fit on the graph.) At the plateau in this curve, it held 70.4 MB of memory. The white line represents Memory: Cache Bytes. The gray line is Memory: Available Bytes, and the thin black line is Process: Working Set.

In this example, run on a workstation with 32 MB of physical memory, the memory consumption by LeakyApp affects all memory, but not to the same degree. Available Bytes drops sharply then recovers somewhat, apparently because pages were trimmed from the working sets of processes. Cache size falls steadily until all available bytes are consumed, and then it levels off. In addition, page faults—not shown on this already busy graph—increase steadily as working sets and cache are squeezed.

The effect of a smaller cache on applications and file operations depends upon how often and how effectively applications use the cache.

Applications and Cache Bottlenecks

Applications that use the cache effectively are hurt most during a cache shortage. A relatively small cache, under 5 MB in a system with 16 MB of physical memory, is likely to become a bottleneck for the applications that use it.

However, normal rates of reads, hits, and flushes vary widely with the nature of the application and how it is structured. Thus, you must establish cache-use benchmarks for each application. Only then can you determine the effect of a cache bottleneck on the application.

To monitor the effect of a cache bottleneck on an application, log the Cache and Memory objects over time, then chart the following counters:

- Cache: Copy Reads/sec
- Cache: Copy Read Hits%

Tip To test your application with different size caches, add the MAXMEM parameter in the Boot.ini file. This lets you change the amount of memory available to Windows NT without affecting the physical memory in your computer.

A cache bottleneck appears in an application as a steady decrease in Copy Read Hits while Copy Reads/sec are relatively stable. There are no recommended levels for these counters, but running an application over time in an otherwise idle system with ample memory will demonstrate normal rates for the application. It will also let you compare how effectively different applications use the cache. When you run the same applications on a system where memory is scarce, you will see this rate drop if the cache is a bottleneck. In general, a hit rate of over 80% is considered to be excellent. A 10% decrease in normal hit rates is cause for concern and probably indicates a memory shortage.

The following graph shows a comparison of copy reads and copy hits for several instances of a compiler. Compilers are relatively efficient users of the cache because their data (application code) is often read and processed sequentially. During the short time-interval represented here, the cache size varied from 6.3 MB to 7.3 MB.

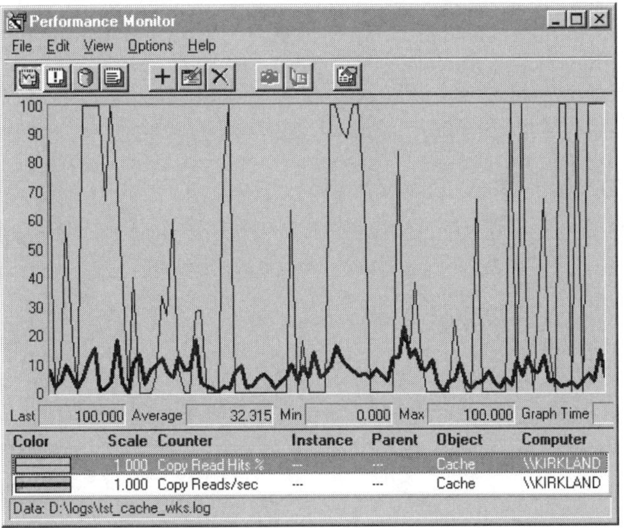

In this example, the thicker line is Copy Reads/sec and the thin line is Copy Read Hits %. The Copy Reads/sec, averaging 6 per second, are a moderate amount, and the Copy Read Hits %, at an average of 32%, are also moderate. This indicates that, on average, fewer than 2 reads/sec are satisfied by data found in the cache. The remainder are counted as page faults and sought elsewhere in memory or on disk.

It is important to put some of these rates in perspective. When copy reads are low (around 5 per second), a 90% average hit rate means that the data for 4.5 reads was found in the cache. However, when reads are at 50 per second, a 40% hit rate means that data for 20 reads was found in the cache.

Accumulating data like this while varying the amount of memory will help you determine the effect of cache size on your application.

Page Faults and Cache Bottlenecks

When memory is scarce, more data must remain on the disk. Accordingly, page faults are more likely. Similarly, when the cache is trimmed, cache hit rates drop and cache faults increase. Cache faults are a subset of all page faults.

Note The operating system sees the cache as the file system's working set, its dedicated area of physical memory. When data is not found in the cache, the system counts it as a *page fault*, just as it would when data was not found in the working set of a process.

To monitor the effect of cache bottlenecks on disk, use the following counters:

- Memory: Cache Faults/sec
- Memory: Page Faults/sec
- Memory: Page Reads/sec
- Logical Disk: Disk Reads/sec

The following graph shows the proportion of page faults that can be traced to the cache. Cache Faults/sec includes data sought by the file system for mapping as well as misses in copy reads for applications. Because both the Cache Faults/sec and Page Faults/sec counters are measured in numbers of pages, they can be compared without conversions.

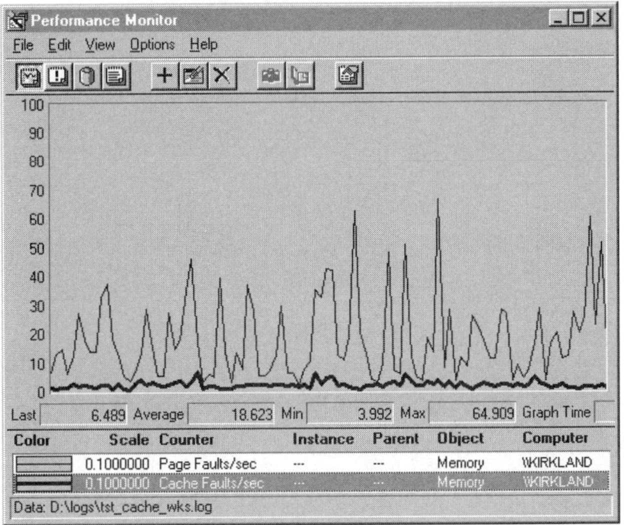

In this example, the thin black line represents all faulted pages; the thick black line represents pages faulted from the cache. Places where the curves meet indicate that nearly all page faults are cache faults. Space between the curves indicates faults from the working sets of processes. In this example, on average, only 10% of the relatively high rate of page faults happen in the cache.

The important page faults, however, are those that require disk reads to find the faulted pages. But the memory counters that measure disk operations due to paging make no distinction between the number of reads or pages read due to cache faults and those caused by all faults.

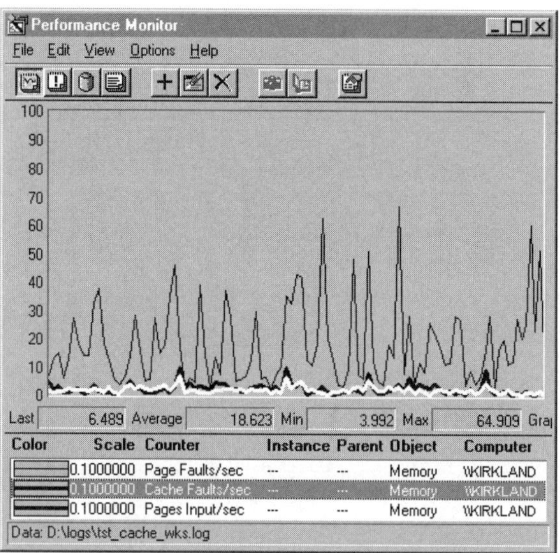

This graph and the report that follows show that most faulted pages are soft faults. Of the average of 182 pages faulted per second, only 21.586—less than 12%—are hard faults. It is even more difficult to attribute any of the pages input due to faults to the cache.

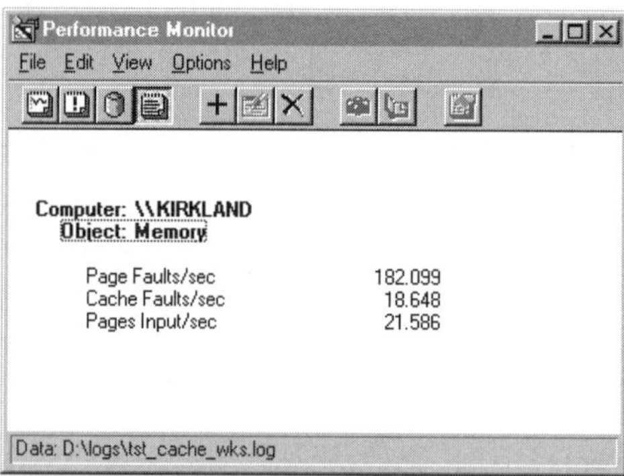

Applications and the Cache

Cache bottlenecks on workstations are uncommon. More often, the Performance Monitor cache counter values are used as indicators of application behavior. Although some large database applications, such as the Microsoft SQL Server, bypass the cache and do their own caching, most use the file system cache.

Data requested by an application is first mapped into the cache and then copied from there. Data changed by applications is written from the cache to disk by the Lazy Writer system thread or by a write-through call from the application. Thus, watching the cache is like watching your application I/O.

Remember, however, that if an application uses the cache infrequently, cache activity will have an insignificant effect on the system, the disks, and on memory.

Reading from the Cache

There are four types of application reads:

- In *copy reads*, data mapped in the cache is copied into memory so it can be read. An application's first read from a file usually is a copy read.
- Subsequent reads are usually *fast reads*, in which an application or other process calls the cache directly rather than calling the file system.
- With *pin reads*, data is mapped into the cache just to be changed and is then written back to disk. It is *pinned* in the cache; that is, it is held at the same address and is not pageable. This prevents page faults.
- With *read aheads*, the Virtual Memory Manager recognizes that the application is reading a file sequentially and, predicting its read pattern, begins to map larger blocks of data into the cache. Read aheads are usually efficient and are a sign that data references are localized. However, some application read patterns might fool the prediction logic of the Virtual Memory Manager and do read aheads when smaller reads might be more efficient. Only the application designer knows for sure!

The following graph shows the frequency of different kinds of cache reads during the run of a compiler. The intersecting curves are difficult to interpret, so a second copy of Performance Monitor—a report set to the same Time Window as the graph—is appended.

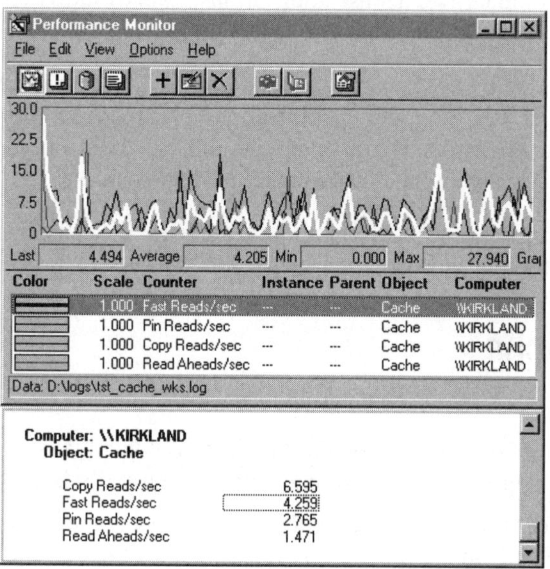

In this example, copy reads are more frequent than fast reads. This pattern of many first reads and fewer subsequent reads indicates that the application is probably reading from many small files. The rate of read aheads is also low, which is another indication that the application is skipping from file to file. When more fast reads than copy reads occur, the application is reading several times from the same file. The rate of read aheads should increase as well.

Writing to the Cache

Although most of this chapter has described using the cache to prevent repeated file operations for reading, it is important to note that applications can also write to data pages in the cache, though not directly. When applications write data to files in their memory buffers that have been copied from the cache, the changes are copied back to the cache. The application continues processing without waiting for the data to be written back to disk.

The system does not count copies or writes to cache directly, but these changes appear in Performance Monitor as data flushes and lazy writes when they are flushed. Cache pages are flushed to free up cache space in several different ways:

- The application issues a write-through request, instructing the Cache Manager to write the change back to disk immediately.
- The Lazy Writer thread in the system process writes pages back to disk. It writes more pages in each disk operation when the cache needs to be trimmed to recover space in memory.
- The Mapped Page Writer thread in the system process writes pages on the mapped page list back to disk. The Mapped Page List for the cache is like the Modified Page List for the paging file. This thread is activated when the number of pages on the mapped page list exceeds a memory threshold.

To measure the rate at which changed pages mapped into the cache are written to disk, use the following counters:

- Cache: Data Flushes/sec
- Cache: Data Flush Pages/sec
- Cache: Lazy Write Flushes/sec
- Cache: Lazy Write Pages/sec

In general, lazy writes reflect the amount of memory available in the cache. Lazy writes are a subset of all data flushes, which include write through request from applications and write-back requests by the mapped page writer thread.

The following display was made with three copies of Performance Monitor all charting from the same log file with the same time window.

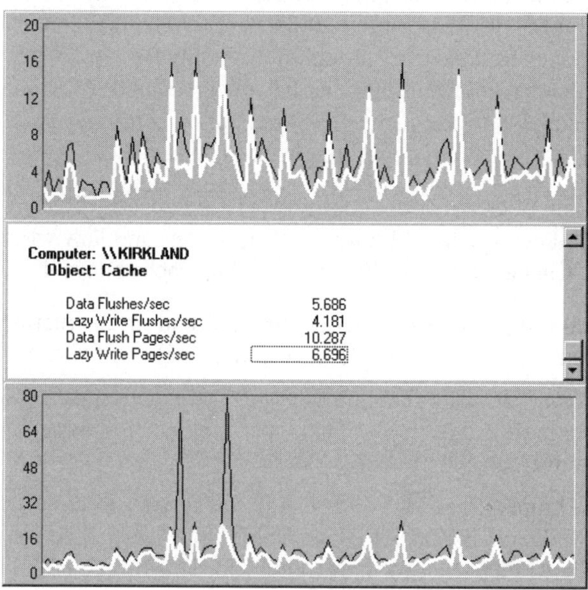

The top graph shows the ratio of Lazy Write Flushes/sec (the white line) to all data flushes, as represented by Data Flushes/sec (the black line). The space between the lines indicates mapped page writer flushes and application write-through requests. In this example, as the report shows, on average, 73.5% of the data flushes were lazy writes, but lazy writes accounted for only 60% of the pages flushed.

The bottom graph shows the relationship between Data Flush Pages/sec (the black line) and Data Flushes/sec (the white line). The points where the curves meet indicate that data is being flushed one page at a time. Space between the curves indicates that multiple pages are written. The report shows that the lazy writer flushed 1.6 pages per write on average compared to 1.8 pages for all flushes. These small numbers indicate that the system is reading from many small files. Lazy writes often average 15-16 pages of data.

The spikes in the data probably result from an application closing a file and the lazy writer writing all of the data back to disk. To see just how many pages went back to disk, narrow the time window to a single data point, and add the same counters to a report.

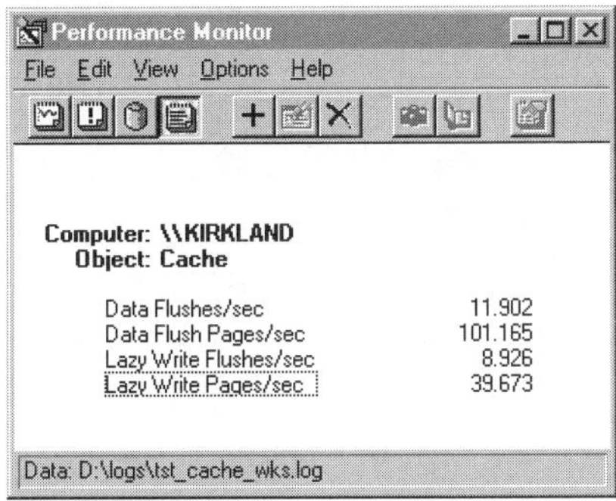

This report on the second spike shows that in that second (averaged for the last two data points), about 101 pages were written back to disk, nearly 40% of which were lazy writes.

Tuning the Cache

This is going to be a short section, because there is not much you can do to tune the Windows NT file system cache. The tuning mechanisms are built into the Virtual Memory Manager to save you time for more important things. Nonetheless, there are a few things you can do to make the most of the cache:

- Localize your application's data references. This will improve its cache performance and minimize its working set so it uses less space in memory.
- If you are running Windows NT Server, you can direct the Virtual Memory Manager to give the cache higher priority for space than the working sets of processes. In the Control Panel, double-click the Network icon. On the Services tab, double-click Server. To favor the cache, click Maximize Throughput for File Sharing. To favor working sets click, Maximize Throughput for Network Applications.
- Change the way work is distributed among workstations. Try dedicating a single computer to memory-intensive applications such as CAD/CAM and large database processors.
- Add memory. When memory is scarce, the cache is squeezed and cannot do its job. After the new memory is installed, the Virtual Memory Manager takes care of expanding the cache to use the new memory.

CHAPTER 16

Monitoring Multiple Processor Computers

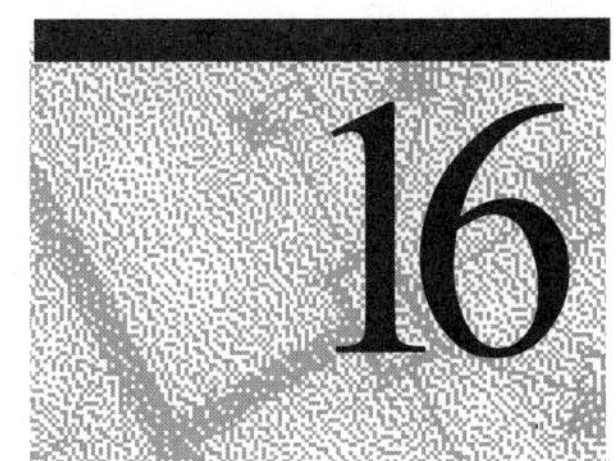

In an ideal world, five processors would do five times the work of one processor. But we live in a world of contention for shared resources, of disk and memory bottlenecks, single-threaded applications, multithreaded applications that require synchronous processing, and poorly coordinated processors. In our world, five processors can be five times as much work for the systems administrator!

Fortunately, Windows NT 4.0 is designed to make the most of multiprocessor configurations. Multiple processors enable multiple threads to execute simultaneously, with different threads of the same process running on each processor. The Windows NT 4.0 microkernel implements *symmetric multiprocessing* (SMP), wherein any processes—including those of the operating system—can run on any available processor, and the threads of a single process can run on different processors at the same time.

The most common bottlenecks on multiprocessor systems arise when all processors contend for the same operating system or hardware resource. If this resource is in short supply, the system cannot benefit from the additional processors.

Shared memory is the Achilles' Heel of multiprocessor systems: Although it enables the threads of a single process to be executed on different processors, it makes multiprocessor systems highly vulnerable to memory shortages, to the design of the cache controller, and to differences in cache management strategies.

Understanding the Multiple Processor Counters

Some Performance Monitor counters were designed for single processor systems and might not be entirely accurate for multiprocessor systems.

For example, on a multiprocessor computer, a process can (and often does) use more than the equivalent of 100% processor time on one processor. Although it is limited to 100% of any single processor, its threads can use several processors, totaling more than 100%. However, the Process: % Processor Time counter never displays more than 100%. To determine how much total processor time a process is getting, chart the Thread: % Processor Time counter for each of the process's threads.

Use the following counters to monitor multiple processor computers.

Counter	Use
System: %Total Processor Time	A measure of processor activity for all processors in the computer. This counter sums average non-idle time of all processors during the sample interval and divides it by the number of processors. For example, if all processors are busy for half of the sample interval, on average, it displays 50%. It also displays 50% if half of the processors are busy for the entire interval, and the others are idle.
System: Processor Queue Length	The length of the processor queue. There is a single queue, even when there are many processors.
Processor: % Processor Time	A measure of the processor time of each processor.
Process: % Processor Time	The sum of processor time on each processor for all threads of the process.
Thread: % Processor Time	The amount of processor time for a thread.

Charting Multiple Processor Activity

Logging and charting are similar for both multiple processor systems and single-processor systems. And because the graphs can get crowded and complex, its best to log the System, Processor, Process, and Thread objects, and then chart them one at a time. If you need to compare charts, start several copies of Performance Monitor and have them all chart or report on data from the same log file.

When monitoring a complex occurrence, a comparison of graphs can be more useful than a single graph.

- A chart of System: % Total Processor Time shows the overall performance of the system. This curve flattens into a horizontal line in a multiprocessor bottleneck.
- A chart of Processor: % Processor Time for each processor shows patterns of processor use. You can determine each processor's start time, as well as its utilization. Use bookmarks when you start processes to see the effect they have on the processors. The sum of Processor: % Processor Time for each processor is System: % Total Processor Time.
- A chart or histogram of Process: % Processor Time for all active processes reveals processor use by operating system services and network support, not to mention Performance Monitor.
- A Thread: % Processor Time chart is essential for diagnosing the processor problems. Although the operating system executes processes, the threads send instructions to the processors. Also, Thread: % Processor Time is a better indicator of processor use than Process: % Processor Time, because the latter has a maximum value of 100%.

  Compare a Thread: % Processor Time chart with a Processor: % Processor Time chart. You can match the threads to their processors because their curves have similar shapes and values. You can also determine which threads are doing background work and which are contending for the foreground.

  A chart of Thread: % Processor Time for all threads on a busy system is likely to be confusing, so chart the threads of each process separately, either one at a time, or with different copies of Performance Monitor reading the same log file.

You can also test each of your processors independently or in different combinations with single and multithreaded applications. Add Process: Thread Count to a Performance Monitor report to see how many threads are in each active process. Edit the Boot.ini file in your root directory to change the number and combination of active processors.

Task Manager, a new administrative tool, lets you determine which processes run on which processors of a multiprocessor computer. On the Task Manager Processes tab, click a process with the right mouse button, then select Set Affinity. The process you selected will run only on the processors selected on the panel. This is a great testing tool.

Resource Contention

The following figures use histograms of the Process: % Processor Time counter to compare two active processes running on one processor to the same processes running on two processors.

The first graph shows the processes running on a single processor computer. Each process is getting about half of the processing time. All other processes are nearly idle.

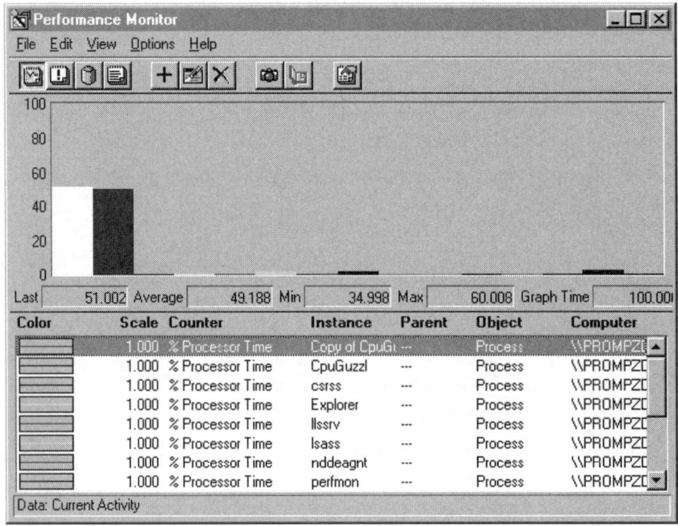

The following figure shows the same processes running on a computer with two processors.

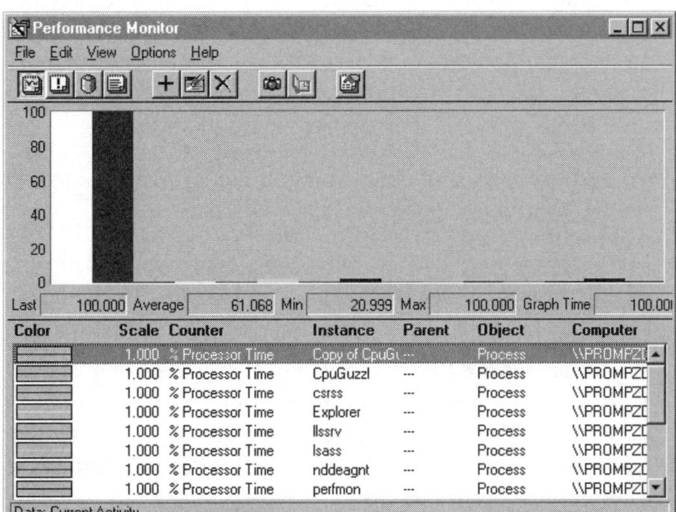

On the multiprocessor computer, each process is using 100% of a processor, and the system is doing twice the work. The processor time is the same as for a single process with a single processor all to itself.

However, to achieve this performance, the processes had to be entirely independent; the only thing they shared was their code. Each processor had a copy of the code in its primary and secondary memory caches, so the processes did not even have to share physical memory or any common system resources. This is the ideal, simulated by CpuStress, a test tool designed for the purpose.

Cache Coherency

In the previous case, several processes were competing for the same resource. But resource contention occurs even among multiple threads of a single process. Threads within a process share and contend for the same address space and frequently are writing to the same memory location. Although this is a minor problem for single-processor configurations, it can become a bottleneck in multiprocessor systems.

Unfortunately, you cannot see cache and memory contention directly with Performance Monitor because these conflicts occur at hardware level (where no counters exist). You can, however, get indirect evidence based on response time and total throughput: The processors simply *appear* to be busy.

In multiprocessor systems, shared memory must be kept consistent: that is, the values of memory cells in the caches of each processor must be kept the same. This is known as *cache coherency*. The responsibility for maintaining cache coherency in multiprocessor systems falls to the cache controller hardware. When a memory cell is written, if the cache controller finds that the memory cell is in use in the cache of any other processors, it invalidates or overwrites those cells with the new data and then updates main memory.

Two frequently used update strategies are known as *write-through caching* and *write-back caching*:

- In *write-through caching*, the cache controller updates main memory immediately so that other caches can get the updated data from memory.
- In *write-back caching*, the cache controller does not update main memory until it needs to reuse the memory cell. If another cache needs the data before it is written to main memory (which is more likely with more threads), the cache controller must obtain the data from the cache of the other processor. That processor's cache must listen in on bus requests and respond before main memory recognize the call.

Write-back caching usually causes fewer writes to main memory and reduces contention on the memory bus, but as the number of threads grows and the likelihood that they will need shared data increases, it actually causes more traffic and resource contention.

Resource sharing and contention is much more common than isolated processing. Although ample processors exist for the workload, they must share the single pool of virtual memory and contend for disk access. There is no easy solution to this problem. However, it demonstrates the limits of even the most sophisticated hardware. In this situation, the traditional solutions to a bottleneck—adding more processors, disk space, or memory—cannot overcome the limitations imposed by an application's dependence on a single subsystem.

PART IV

Reliability and Recoverability

CHAPTER 17

Disk and File System Basics

This chapter describes the organization, contents, and purpose of the information on hard disks. It contains information on the following topics:

- Disk basics.
- Volumes, partitions, volume sets, and stripe sets.
- File systems supported by Windows NT.
- Creating and formatting partitions.
- Master Boot Record.
- Partition Boot Sector.
- Using hard disks with more than 1024 cylinders.
- Using removable disks and floppy disks.

About Disks and Disk Organization

This section describes the physical structure of hard disks and floppy disks, and presents an overview of ways to logically organize areas on your disks.

Both hard disks and floppy disks work similar to an old-fashioned record player, with the record turning on the turntable and a needle playing the music. They are also similar to VCRs and stereo cassettes in that disks, cassette players, and VCRs all use a read/write head to access the information that is stored on the magnetic media.

Hard or fixed disks store information on a revolving platter of metal or glass coated with a magnetic material. The disk typically consists of several physical platters on a common spindle. This platter is similar to the record on a record player, except information is usually stored on both sides of a disk platter.

As the disk rotates, a transducer element called the head reads or writes binary data on the magnetic media. There are many methods for encoding data on the disk, such as modified frequency modulation (MFM) and run length limited (RLL). The disk controller logic determines the method used and the density of data on the disk.

Some high-end disks have as many as one head per track. Therefore, no time is lost physically moving the heads to a track in order to read information. These disks are more expensive and are normally found only on minicomputers or mainframes.

Current state-of-the-art disks do not have platters and heads, but use nonvolatile RAM (NVRAM) instead. The controller microcode organizes the memory into logical cylinders, heads, tracks, and sectors to provide a consistent interface to the operating system. Access times for these disks are measured in nanoseconds rather than the milliseconds for more conventional disks.

Hardware Terminology

Each disk consists of platters, rings on each side of each platter called tracks, and sections within each track called sectors. A sector is the smallest physical storage unit on a disk, almost always 512 bytes in size.

Figure 17.1 illustrates a hard disk with two platters. The remainder of this section describes the terms used on the figure.

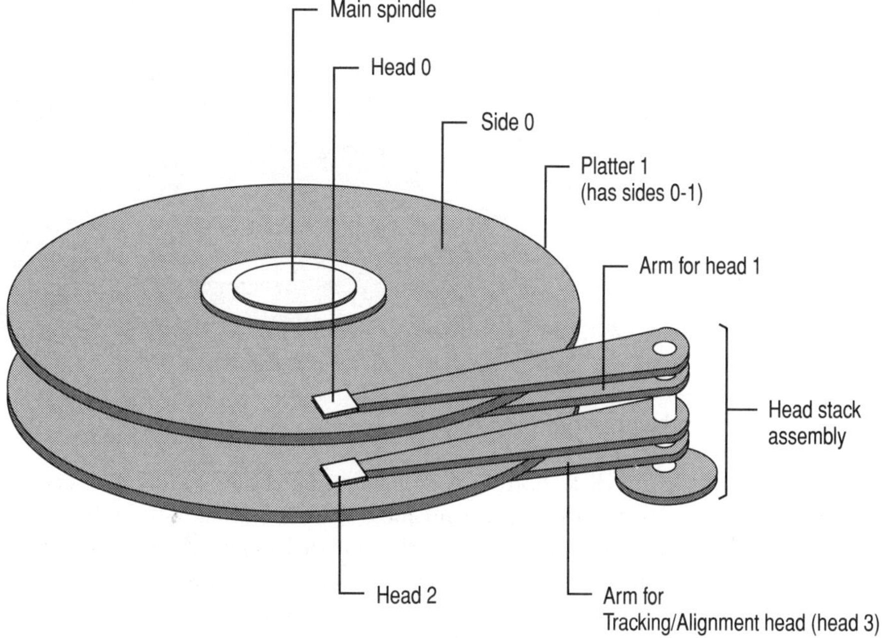

Figure 17.1 Illustration of a hard disk

The cylinder/head/sector notation scheme described in this section is slowly being eliminated. All new disks use some kind of translation factor to make their actual hardware layout appear as something else, mostly to work with MS-DOS and Windows 95.

Tracks and Cylinders

On hard disks, the data are stored on the disk in thin, concentric bands called tracks. There can be more than a thousand tracks on a 3½ inch hard disk. Tracks are a logical rather than physical structure, and are established when the disk is low-level formatted. Track numbers start at 0, and track 0 is the outermost track of the disk. The highest numbered track is next to the spindle. If the disk geometry is being translated, the highest numbered track would typically be 1023. Figure 17.2 shows track 0, a track in the middle of the disk, and track 1023.

A cylinder consists of the set of tracks that are at the same head position on the disk. In Figure 17.2, cylinder 0 is the four tracks at the outermost edge of the sides of the platters. If the disk has 1024 cylinders (which would be numbered 0-1023), cylinder 1023 consists of all of the tracks at the innermost edge of each side.

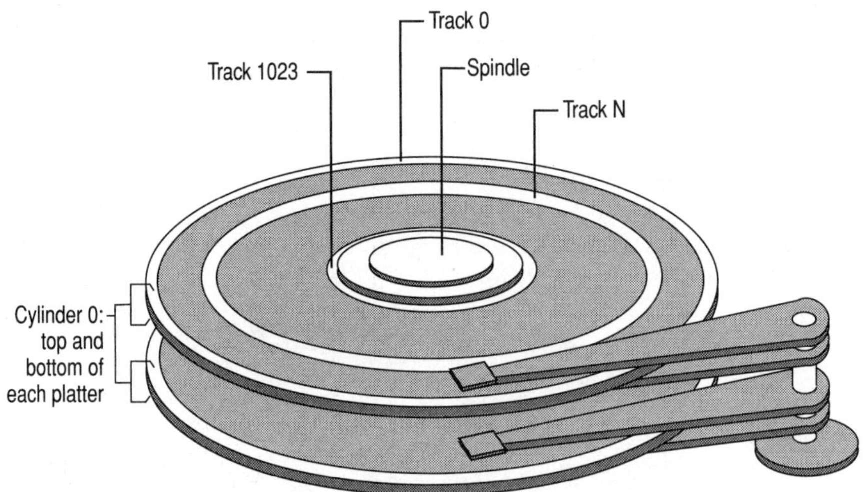

Figure 17.2 Tracks

Most disks used in personal computers today rotate at a constant angular velocity. The tracks near the outside of the disk are less densely populated with data than the tracks near the center of the disk. Thus, a fixed amount of data can be read in a constant period of time, even though the speed of the disk surface is faster on the tracks located further away from the center of the disk.

Modern disks reserve one side of one platter for track positioning information, which is written to the disk at the factory during disk assembly. It is not available to the operating system. The disk controller uses this information to fine tune the head locations when the heads move to another location on the disk. When a side contains the track position information, that side cannot be used for data. Thus, a disk assembly containing two platters has three sides that are available for data.

Heads and Sides

A head is a small transducer that can be positioned over a disk track by using a solenoid or servomotor. The head can change the properties of the magnetic media as it rotates underneath.

A specific area can be switched to either magnetic north or south, which corresponds to a binary state of 0 or 1. This series of binary information is the data stream the disk controller passes to and receives from the operating system.

There is one head for each side of each platter. The heads are normally attached to a common head-movement mechanism, so that the heads all move in unison. The heads are always positioned at the same logical track on each side of each platter.

Because disk tracks are concentric bands, the heads must move to the track that contains the data to be accessed. The moving of the heads from the current track to the track that contains the next data is called seeking. The heads are moved over the surface of the disk in small increments called steps. Each step corresponds to one track.

Sectors and Clusters

Each track is divided into sections called sectors. A sector is the smallest physcial storage unit on the disk. The data size of a sector is always a power of two, and is almost always 512 bytes.

Each track has the same number of sectors, which means that the sectors are packed much closer together on tracks near the center of the disk. Figure 17.3, presented later in this section, shows sectors on a track. You can see that sectors closer to the spindle are closer together than those on the outside edge of the disk. The disk controller uses the sector identification information stored in the area immediately before the data in the sector to determine where the sector itself begins.

Note On Multiple Zone Recording (MZR) disks, the number of sectors on each track is not the same across the entire disk, but the hardware makes the number appear to be the same. For more information, see the section titled "Multiple Zone Recording," presented later in this chapter.

The Windows NT file systems allocate storage in clusters, where a cluster is one or more contiguous sectors. Windows NT bases the cluster size on the size of the partition.

As a file is written to the disk, the file system allocates the appropriate number of clusters to store the file's data. For example, if each cluster is 512 bytes and the file is 800 bytes, two clusters are allocated for the file. Later, if you update the file to, for example, twice its size (1600 bytes), another two clusters are allocated.

If contiguous clusters (clusters that are next to each other on the disk) are not available, the data are written elsewhere on the disk, and the file is considered to be fragmented. Fragmentation is a problem when the file system must search several different locations to find all the pieces of the file you want to read. The search causes a delay before the file is retrieved. A larger cluster size reduces the potential for fragmentation, but increases the likelihood that clusters will have unused space.

Using clusters larger than one sector reduces fragmentation, and reduces the amount of disk space needed to store the information about the used and unused areas on the disk. Because the FAT file system can use only 16 bits for the cluster number, using clusters enables FAT volumes to be larger than 65,535 sectors. There is more information about the FAT file system presented later in this chapter, and in Chapter 18, "Choosing a File System."

Figure 17.3 shows a sector on one track and the grouping of four sectors into a cluster.

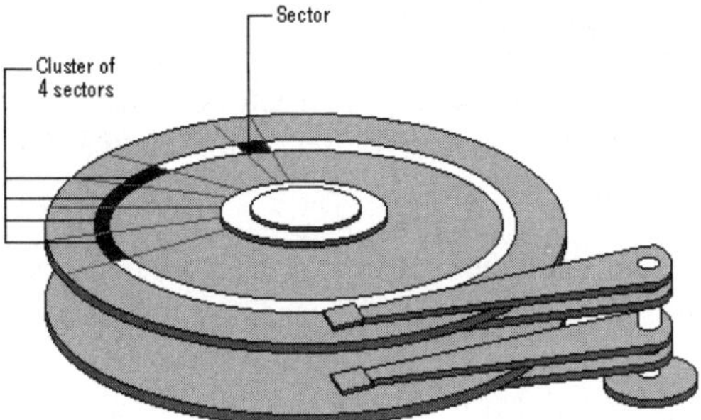

Figure 17.3 Sectors and clusters

Translation

Translation is the conversion of physical disk geometry (the number of cylinders on the disk, number of heads per cylinder, and sectors per track) to a logical configuration that is compatible with the operating system.

Since sector translation works between the disk itself and the system BIOS or firmware, the operating system is unaware of the actual characteristics of the disk. The disk could become inaccessible if the parameters used to set up the disk are lost, which can happen if the CMOS (described later in this section) or nonvolatile RAM (NVRAM) is corrupted or modified. In this case, the controller might translate to a configuration that adds up to the same total amount of disk space, but the operating system is not able to read data from the new arrangement. The disk has to be reformatted.

Many state-of-the-art disks now have a feature called Translation Mode. The disk controller queries the system BIOS (x86-based computers) or firmware (RISC-based computers) to determine the logical parameters the computer needs. If the number of cylinders, heads, and sectors per track the computer needs is within the range supported by the disk, the controller automatically configures itself to match those parameters. If the system BIOS or firmware does not support translation, the disk configures itself to its largest possible size, which is typically around 500 MB.

For example, all SCSI disks use some kind of translation, and many SCSI disks support hot swapping of sectors to fix bad sectors. This means that a SCSI disk maintains a set of unused sectors at the end of a disk. When a used sector goes bad, it is remapped to an unused sector and the data are written to the new sector. Windows NT uses absolute sector notation (also called logical sector notation, or LSN) for accessing disks. The translation of the sector number to the physical sector on the disk is handled by low-level disk device drivers and the hardware.

The translation is especially important when there are more than 1024 physical cylinders on the disk. The section titled "Using Hard Disks With More Than 1024 Cylinders (x86-based Computers)," presented later in this chapter, contains more details.

Multiple Zone Recording (MZR)

Some modern disks use MZR to solve the problem of wasted space on the outer tracks of the disk. The controller provides a layer of abstraction in disguising the physical layout of the sectors. The controller presents the disk to the system BIOS and the operating system as if each track had the same number of sectors per track.

MZR disks alter the operating frequency of the disk electronics, based on disk zones. Each zone is a contiguous group of cylinders. Using different frequencies means that each zone can have a different number of sectors per track. Since the zone frequency corresponds to the different data densities in each zone, the effect is to maintain a constant data density across the whole disk.

All this technology takes place entirely at the hardware level. The computer's operating system still sees the disk in the conventional logical layout of cylinders, heads, and sectors, where there is a constant number of sectors per cylinder.

When you format an MZR disk, you need to use the same parameters for sector size, tracks per cylinder, and sectors per track for all partitions.

CMOS (x86-based Computers)

The Complementary Metal Oxide Semiconductor (CMOS) chip in the computer stores information about the devices connected to the computer. When you install or change a non-SCSI disk in your computer, you need to use the BIOS setup program provided on your computer to update the information in the CMOS. (SCSI disks have their own configuration program, typically provided by the manufacturer.)

It is possible for the CMOS battery to run down if you do not turn your computer on for a long time. And the CMOS chip sometimes fails. See Chapter 21, "Troubleshooting Startup and Disk Problems," for information about identifying CMOS problems.

Logical Organization: Partitions, Volumes, Volume Set, and Stripe Sets

The Master Boot Record on each hard disk contains an area called the Partition Table that the computer uses to determine how to access the disk. It has room for four entries, called partitions, that you create to make it easier to organize information. A partition must be completely contained on one physical disk.

Use Disk Administrator to create and format partitions. The next figure is a Disk Administrator screen shot for a computer with a single disk.

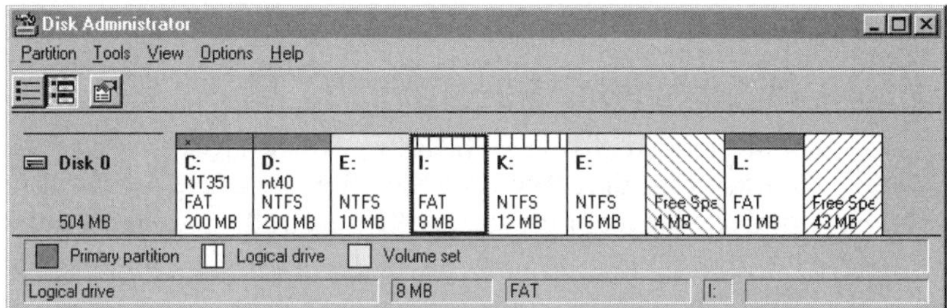

Figure 17.4 Disk Administrator screen shot of primary partitions and an extended partition

Disk Administrator screen shows you the layout of each of your disks, including:

- The size of each disk.
- The size, label, and file system used for each partition on the disk.
- The size and location of free space.

The remainder of this section describes partitions, and explains what you see in the Figure 17.4.

There are two types of partitions in the Master Boot Record, primary and extended. A primary partition is one into which you can install the files needed to load an operating system. A primary partition is formatted for a particular file system and is assigned a drive letter. Having multiple primary partitions enables you to install and start operating systems that do not use the same file system, such as Windows NT and UNIX. There are three primary partitions in Figure 17.4: C, D, and L.

You can have one extended partition on a hard disk. An extended partition is effectively a logical disk. Unlike a primary partition, you do not format the extended partition, nor does it get assigned a drive letter. Instead, you can create one or more logical drives within the extended partition, and each logical drive is assigned a drive letter. You format each logical drive for a particular file system.

An extended partition is a method for avoiding the four-partition limit and configuring a hard disk into more than four logical areas. An extended partition entry looks much like an entry for a primary partition in the Master Boot Record, except that it points to space on the disk that can contain one or more logical drives. The important information about an extended partition is how much of the disk it takes up and where it starts.

Note In this chapter, and other chapters in the "Reliability and Recoverability" part of this book, the term logical drive means a contiguous area in an extended partition, which is assigned a drive letter.

There is an extended partition in Figure 17.4, but it is not as obvious as the primary partitions. The extended partition consists of all the disk area between primary partitions D and L. If there are logical drives on a disk, then you have an extended partition on that disk. If you have free space for which the diagonal lines look like the ones for the 4 MB of free space to the left of L, then you have an extended partition on the disk.

Figure 17.4 shows an important point. The unpartitioned space at the end of the disk (to the right of primary partition L) cannot be used. You can have only three primary partitions and one extended partition on a hard disk, or four primary partitions. This disk already has the maximum for each of these types.

Note The distinction between the two areas of free space is that the one to the left of L is free space within an extended partition, while the free space on the right of L, which has a different background pattern, is not a part of any partition.

If you have more than one primary partition or logical drive on the same disk, you can format them for different file systems. However, the format program will use the same sector size, number of tracks per cylinder, and number of sectors per track for each partition or logical drive. The cluster size can be different for each one.

The system partition is the partition on a disk that contains the hardware-specific files used in loading and initializing the operating system. Only a primary partition can be used as a system partition. Some programs, such as Disk Administrator and the MS-DOS-based program Fdisk, use the term active partition to refer to the same thing. This book uses the term system partition unless it is specifically describing dialog boxes or menus that use the term active or active partition.

The boot partition is also used in starting the operating system. It contains the operating system files and other support files needed by the operating system. Both a primary partition and a logical drive in an extended partition can be used as a boot partition. The system partition and the boot partition can be the same partition, or they can even be on different disks. Chapter 19, "What Happens When You Start Your Computer," contains more information about the system and boot partitions.

Note To summarize, you can have as many as four primary partitions on a hard disk. If you have an extended partition on the disk, you can have up to three primary partitions. If the disk does not contain the system partition, you do not need to create any primary partitions. You can use the entire hard disk as an extended partition, and create as many logical drives within it as you want to have.

Windows NT requires that the system partition be a primary partition.

Some computers create an EISA configuration partition as the first primary partition on the hard disk. On these computers, you can only have three other primary partitions on the disk, or two primary partitions and one extended partition.

You create a volume set by combining multiple areas of free space on one or more hard disks into a single logical disk. When you create a volume set, Windows NT uses the HKEY_LOCAL_MACHINE\SYSTEM\DISK Registry subkey to access the areas on the disk(s) that are part of the volume set.

A volume set can be made from:

- Free space on multiple disks.
- Multiple areas of free space on one disk.
- Multiple areas of free space on multiple disks.

You use Disk Administrator to create and extend volume sets. See Disk Administrator Help for information about creating volume sets.

Each volume set can include up to 32 areas of free space from one or more physical disks. When creating a volume set, the free space can be an unallocated area within an extended partition, or an unpartitioned area elsewhere on the disk. Figure 17.4 shows a volume set E, which is made up of two areas in the extended partition on disk 0. Figure 17.4 also shows the two different types of free space. The free space between drives E and L is unallocated space in an extended partition. The free space at the right side of the screen shot is unpartitioned space.

You cannot use volume sets to avoid the limit of four Partition Table entries for a disk. For example, the Disk Administrator screen shot in Figure 17.4 shows three primary partitions (drives C, D, and L) and one extended partition. The free space between the second part of volume set E and the primary partition L is part of the extended partition. It can be used to create one or more logical drives in the extended partition. However, the free space to the right of primary partition L is wasted disk space, because there are already three primary partitions and an extended partition.

You can tell whether free space is unallocated space in an extended partition or is unpartitioned space, because the diagonal lines go in different directions for the two types of free space.

A stripe set is composed of unpartitioned areas on from 2 to 32 disks. You use Disk Administrator to create stripe sets. The amount of space used on each disk will be equal to the smallest unpartitioned space that you selected on the disks. Like volume sets, Windows NT must use the Registry subkey HKEY_LOCAL_MACHINE\SYSTEM\DISK to know how to access the disks.

Volume is the general term that refers to all of the following entities that you can create and use on a computer running Windows NT Workstation.

- Primary partition.
- Logical drive in an extended partition.
- Volume set.
- Stripe set.

A volume has a single drive letter assigned to it, and is formatted for use by a file system.

Which Programs to Use to Create and Format Volumes

This section provides information about how to create and format volumes. You can create and format a volume in one of the following ways:

- During Windows NT Setup, you can:
  - Create and format a new primary partition into which to install Windows NT, provided you have enough unpartitioned disk space for the Windows NT installation (approximately 150 MB for Windows NT Workstation on a RISC-based computer).
  - Format an existing, unformatted volume into which to install Windows NT.
  - When you choose to install Windows NT in an existing FAT primary partition or logical drive, you can convert the volume from the FAT file system to the NTFS file system. Converting preserves the data on the volume.

- If you have Windows NT installed on your computer, you can use Disk Administrator to create and format the volume. You can also use Disk Administrator to reformat an existing volume that is already formatted for the FAT file system or the NTFS file system. Reformatting a volume erases all information about which files used to be on the volume. You can reformat the volume as FAT or NTFS, regardless of what file system it is currently formatted for. For information about Disk Administrator procedures, see the Disk Administrator Help.
- If you want to specify special options during the format, such as a different cluster size, you can run the Format program from the command prompt. To see the options for the Format program, enter **format /?** at the command prompt.
- When running Windows NT, you can use the Convert program to convert an existing FAT volume to an NTFS volume, which preserves the data on the volume. For information about using the Convert program, see Chapter 22, "Disk, File System, and Backup Utilities."
- When you have started MS-DOS, you can use the **fdisk** command to create a primary partition or logical drive, and use the **format** command to format the volume for the FAT file system. See MS-DOS Help for information about these commands.
- On Alpha AXP–based computers and MIPS-based computers, you can use the Arcinst program to create and format volumes.

Note Converting a volume from the FAT file system to the NTFS file system can take a long time, depending on the amount of fragmentation and size of the FAT volume. For example, converting a 1 GB volume can take up to several hours. The conversion process has to read all of the files to build the information that NTFS needs to have about the data on the volume. When using the Convert program or converting the volume in Windows NT Setup, no status information is displayed to indicate that the conversion is proceeding. Although it looks like the conversion process is hung, it might just be taking a long time. For a large volume, it might be a good idea to run the file system conversion process overnight.

It might be faster to back up the data on the FAT volume to tape or a remote computer, reformat the volume as NTFS, and then restore the data.

If you create a single primary partition that occupies the entire disk, you cannot change the way your disk is organized without deleting the primary partition (which deletes all of the information in it) and creating new, smaller primary partitions or an extended partition. You have to back up the information that you need to save to a backup tape or a disk on a remote computer, reinstall Windows NT, and restore the data to the new volumes that you have created.

If there is no unpartitioned space left on your disk, the **Create** and **Create Extended** options on the Disk Administrator **Partition** menu are not available.

When you use Disk Administrator to create volumes, you have to write the changes to the Partition Table before you can format the volume. You can write the changes by using one of these methods:

- Click **Commit Changes Now** on the **Partition** menu. You can now click the volume, click the **Tools** menu, and click **Format**.
- Exiting Disk Administrator. If you have made changes to your disk configuration, Disk Administrator displays a dialog box that asks whether you want to save changes. Click **Yes**. You can now restart Disk Administrator, click the volume, click the **Tools** menu, and click **Format**.

If you have created a volume but not formatted it, Disk Administrator displays the volume as unformatted. You cannot access the volume in either My Computer or Windows NT Explorer until it has been formatted.

You cannot see an NTFS volume when you are running any operating system other than Windows NT. This means that your drive letters will probably be different when you are running Windows NT and other operating systems. For example, if you have two FAT volumes (C and E), and an NTFS volume (D), and you start MS-DOS, the second FAT volume will be labeled D. Because MS-DOS does not recognize the NTFS volume, the drive letter that was assigned to the NTFS volume when running Windows NT is used for the second FAT volume when running MS-DOS.

In Disk Administrator, you cannot delete the Windows NT boot partition when you are running Windows NT. You can delete the Windows NT boot partition if it is not the same primary partition as the system partition and you start another operating system that does not use the Windows NT boot partition as its boot partition.

Formatting Hard Disks and Floppy Disks

Before you can use a hard disk or a floppy disk, you must format the disk.

There are three steps to formatting a hard disk:

- Low-level formatting the hard disk.
- Creating partitions or logical drives in an extended partition.
- Doing a logical formatting of the primary partitions or logical drives.

Formatting a floppy disk is much simpler than formatting a hard disk, because there are fewer steps. You cannot create partitions on a floppy disk, so there are only two steps:

- Low-level formatting the floppy disk.
- Logical formatting of the disk.

When you format a floppy disk, the format program performs both a low-level format and a logical format, so there is really only one step. However, the low-level format on a floppy disk is not as thorough as on a hard disk.

The rest of this section discusses low-level formatting, creating primary partitions or volumes, and logical formatting. See the section "Which Programs to Use to Create and Format Volumes," presented earlier in this chapter, for more details.

Low-level Formatting

Each disk vendor provides the low-level format program to use for the disk. Consult your disk documentation or contact the vendor to find out how to do low-level formatting.

Each low-level format program determines the correct sector size to use, the number of tracks, and the number of sectors per track. This format program selects sector size based upon the disk and the information about the sectors in its circuitry. The program for almost all disks used in the United States uses a sector size of 512 bytes. The program also writes error correction and sector identification information for each sector onto the disk.

SCSI disks should always be low-level formatted when put on a new controller. The reason for this is that the translation in use on the disk varies from controller to controller, and can even vary between two identical controllers based upon the controller settings.

On x86-based computers, you must enable the BIOS on the SCSI controller if your system partition in on a SCSI disk. Depending upon your disk configuration, you might need to turn off translation in the SCSI controller. Also make sure that the CMOS has no entries for SCSI disks. For more information about the SCSI controller, see Chapter 20, "Preparing for and Performing Recovery."

There are some older IDE disks that you should not low-level format, because the factory formatting puts information on the disk that a low-level format erases. However, newer IDE disks, and all enhanced IDE disks (also known as EIDE) need to be low-level formatted. You must configure an IDE or EIDE disk in the CMOS before you can use it on the computer. See your hardware documentation for information about changing information in the CMOS.

If you have created and formatted volumes on your hard disk, but are getting errors from Chkdsk or other disk scan utilities about bad sectors on your disk, the only way to permanently eliminate them is to do a low-level format. Low-level formatting maps around the bad sectors. However, a low-level format erases all data on the disk. Therefore, be sure to back up any data on the disk before you low-level format it. You then need to create volumes (primary partitions or logical drives in an extended partition), and logically format them before you can restore the data to the disk.

Caution Do not low-level format IDE hard disks unless the manufacturer's literature describes that you should do so.

Creating Partitions on the Disk

When you create primary partitions or an extended partition on a disk, you logically divide it into one or more areas that can be formatted for use by a file system. The first partition on the disk (whether it is a primary partition or an extended partition) always starts at the outside of the disk, at cylinder 0, head 0, and sector 1. Because partition boundaries are always cylinder boundaries, the smallest partition that you can create on a disk consists of all of the tracks on a single cylinder.

When you have Windows NT installed on your computer, you should use Disk Administrator to create partitions. However, if you are setting up a new computer, you might not have any operating system. But you still need to create and format a partition into which to install Windows NT.

On x86-based computers, if you have an MS-DOS bootable floppy disk with the Fdisk program on it, you can start your computer from the MS-DOS floppy disk and create partitions by using Fdisk. On RISC-based computers, you can use the Arcinst program on the Windows NT Workstation CD to create partitions. Windows NT Setup displays an option to create a partition to use for Windows NT, provided that there is enough unpartitioned space on a hard disk.

Note On x86-based computers, you might not be able to access all your hard disk when using **fdisk**. If you have a disk that is larger than 4 gigabyte (GB), MS-DOS cannot see the space beyond 4 GB. Depending on the geometry, this limitation could even be 1 GB, because MS-DOS cannot access volumes that go beyond cylinder 1023. If you have more than 2 SCSI disks, MS-DOS generally does not see any disks after the first two, unless you load a SCSI device driver.

When you create the first partition on a disk (either a primary partition or an extended partition), the program that you use creates the Master Boot Record and writes it to the first sector on the disk (cylinder 0, head 0, sector 1). The Master Boot Record contains the Partition Table, which has information about each partition defined on the disk. When you make any changes to volumes on the disk, such as creating, deleting, or formatting them, the program that you are using updates the Partition Table.

You can configure the entire disk as one primary partition, and logically format it for one file system. Or you can create more than one primary partition, and use different file systems on them. You can also create an extended partition, and create one or more logical drives within the extended partition.

For more information about partitions, logical drives, and extended partitions, see "Logical Organization: Partitions, Volumes, Volume Set, and Stripe Sets," presented earlier in this chapter. For more information about the Master Boot Record and Partition Table, see "Disk Sectors Critical to the Startup Process," presented later in this chapter.

Logical Formatting

Before you can write any data to the volume, you must do a logical format; that is, format it for use by a file system. Logical formatting writes information needed by the file system onto the disk. The information includes:

- Partition Boot Sector.
- Changing the System ID byte in the Partition Table (hard disk only).
- File system metadata, including information about available and unused space and location of files and folders.
- Damaged areas.

There is more information about each of these data in the remainder of this chapter.

When you have Windows NT installed on your computer, you should use Disk Administrator to format the partitions.

On x86-based computers, you can format primary partitions and logical drives for the FAT file system before you install any operating systems by starting the computer from a MS-DOS bootable floppy disk that has the Format program on it. You can use the Format program only for volumes that do not go beyond cylinder 1023.

On Alpha-based computers and MIPS-based computers, you can run the Arcinst program from the Windows NT Workstation CD to format the hard disk.

On both x86-based computers and RISC-based computers, you can create and format a primary partition to use for Windows NT during Setup, provided that there is enough unpartitioned space on a hard disk.

About File Systems

This section contains information about the two file systems that Windows NT supports:

- File Allocation Table (FAT). The computer can access files on a FAT primary partition or logical drive when it is running Windows NT, Windows 95, MS-DOS, or OS/2.
- Windows NT File System (NTFS). The computer must be running Windows NT to be able to access files on an NTFS volume.

With Windows NT, you can create and use long filenames as well as short filenames. Long and short filenames can be used on both NTFS or FAT volumes. A long filename can be up to 256 characters long. Short filenames are in the format xxxxxxxx.yyy, and are compatible with MS-DOS and OS/2.

Information about long and short filenames that is unique to each file system is described in the "Filenames on FAT Volumes" and "Filenames on NTFS Volumes" sections, presented later in this chapter. The section "Generating and Viewing Short Filenames," presented later in this chapter, contains general information about short filenames for both NTFS and FAT volumes.

The FAT File System

The FAT file system is a simple file system originally designed for small disks and simple folder structures. The FAT file system is named for its method of organization, the file allocation table, which resides at the beginning of the volume. To protect the volume, two copies of the table are kept, in case one becomes damaged. In addition, the file allocation tables and the root folder must be stored in a fixed location so that the files needed to start the system can be correctly located.

A volume formatted with the FAT file system is allocated in clusters. The default cluster size is determined by the size of the volume. For the FAT file system, the cluster number must fit in 16 bits and must be a power of two. The default cluster sizes are shown in the following table. You can specify a different cluster size if you format an FAT volume by using the **format** program from the command prompt. However, the size you specify cannot be less than that shown in the table.

Partition size	Sectors per cluster	Cluster size
0 MB - 32 MB	1	512 bytes
33 MB - 64 MB	2	1K
65 MB - 128 MB	4	2K
129 MB - 255 MB	8	4K
256 MB - 511 MB	16	8K
512 MB - 1023 MB	32	16K
1024 MB - 2047 MB	64	32K
2048 MB - 4095 MB	128	64K

The FAT file system is not recommended for volumes larger than 511 MB because of its overhead. You cannot use the FAT file system on volumes larger than 4 GB, regardless of the cluster size.

Note On volumes with the number of sectors less than 32680, the cluster sizes can be up to 8 sectors per cluster. The format program, whether you format the volume by using Disk Administrator or run **format** at the command prompt, creates a 12-bit FAT. Volumes less than 16 MB will usually be formatted for 12-bit FAT, but the exact size depends on the disk geometry. The disk geometry also determines the point at which a larger cluster size will be needed, because the number of clusters on the volume must fit into 16 bits. Therefore, you might have a 33 MB volume that still has only 1 sector per cluster.

Structure of a FAT Volume

Figure 17.5 illustrates how the FAT file system organizes a volume. See the section titled "Relative Sectors and Number of Sectors Fields," presented later in this chapter, for information about the area between the Partition Boot Sector and FAT1.

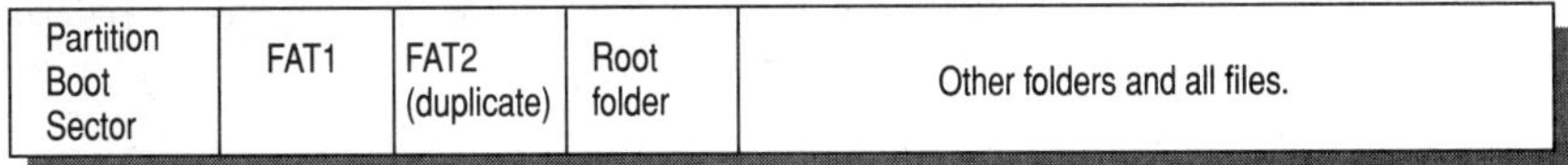

Figure 17.5 Organization of FAT volume

The file allocation table (areas FAT1 and FAT2 in Figure 17.5) contains the following types of information about each cluster on the volume:

- Unused
- Cluster in use by a file
- Bad cluster
- Last cluster in a file

The root folder contains an entry for each file and folder on the root. The only difference between the root folder and other folders is that the root folder is on a specified location on the disk and has a fixed size (512 entries for a hard disk, number of entries on a floppy disk depends on the size of the disk).

Folders have a 32-byte entry for each file and folder contained in the folder. The entry includes the following information:

- Name (eight-plus-three characters)
- Attribute byte (8 bits worth of information, described later in this section)
- Create time (24 bits)
- Create date (16 bits)
- Last access date (16 bits)
- Last modified time (16 bits)
- Last modified date (16 bits.)
- Starting cluster number in the file allocation table (16 bits)
- File size (32 bits)

There is no organization to the FAT folder structure, and files are given the first available location on the volume. The starting cluster number is the address of the first cluster used by the file. Each cluster contains a pointer to the next cluster in the file, or an indication (0xFFFF) that this cluster is the end of the file. These links and end of file indicators are shown in Figure 17.6.

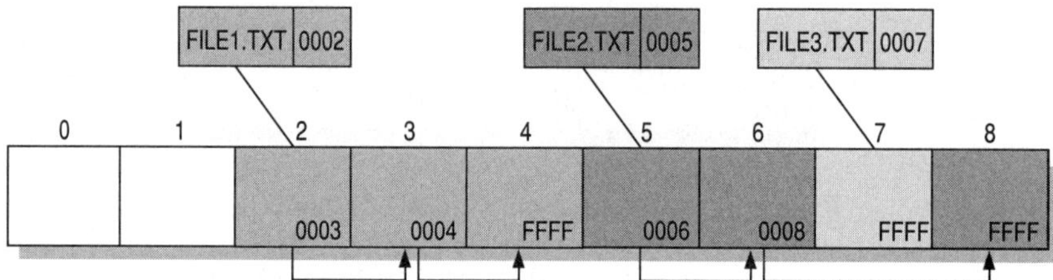

Figure 17.6 File Allocation Table

This illustration shows three files. The file File1.txt is a file that is large enough to use three clusters. A small file, File3.txt, fits completely in one cluster. The third file, File2.txt, is a fragmented file that also requires three clusters. In each case, the folder entry points to the first cluster of the file.

The information in the folder is used by all operating systems that support the FAT file system. In addition, Windows NT can store additional time stamps in a FAT folder entry. These time stamps show when the file was created or last accessed and are used principally by POSIX applications.

Because all entries in a folder are the same size, the attribute byte for each entry in a folder describes what kind of entry it is. One bit indicates that the entry is for a subfolder, while another bit marks the entry as a volume label. Normally, only the operating system controls the settings of these bits.

A FAT file has four attributes bits that can be turned on or off by the user—archive file, system file, hidden file, and read-only file.

Filenames on FAT Volumes

Beginning with Windows NT 3.5, files created or renamed on FAT volumes use the attribute bits to support long filenames in a way that does not interfere with how MS-DOS or OS/2 accesses the volume. Whenever a user creates a file with a long filename, Windows NT creates an eight-plus-three name for the file. In addition to this conventional entry, Windows NT creates one or more secondary folder entries for the file, one for each 13 characters in the long filename. Each of these secondary folder entries stores a corresponding part of the long filename in Unicode. Windows NT sets the volume, read-only, system, and hidden file attribute bits of the secondary folder entry to mark it as part of a long filename. MS-DOS and OS/2 generally ignore folder entries with all four of these attribute bits set, so these entries are effectively invisible to these operating systems. Instead, MS-DOS and OS/2 access the file by using the conventional eight-plus-three filename contained in the folder entry for the file.

Figure 17.7 shows all of the folder entries for the file Thequi~1.fox, which has a long name of The quick brown.fox. The long name is in Unicode, so each character in the name uses two bytes in the folder entry. The attribute field for the long name entries has the value 0x0F. The attribute field for the short name is 0x20.

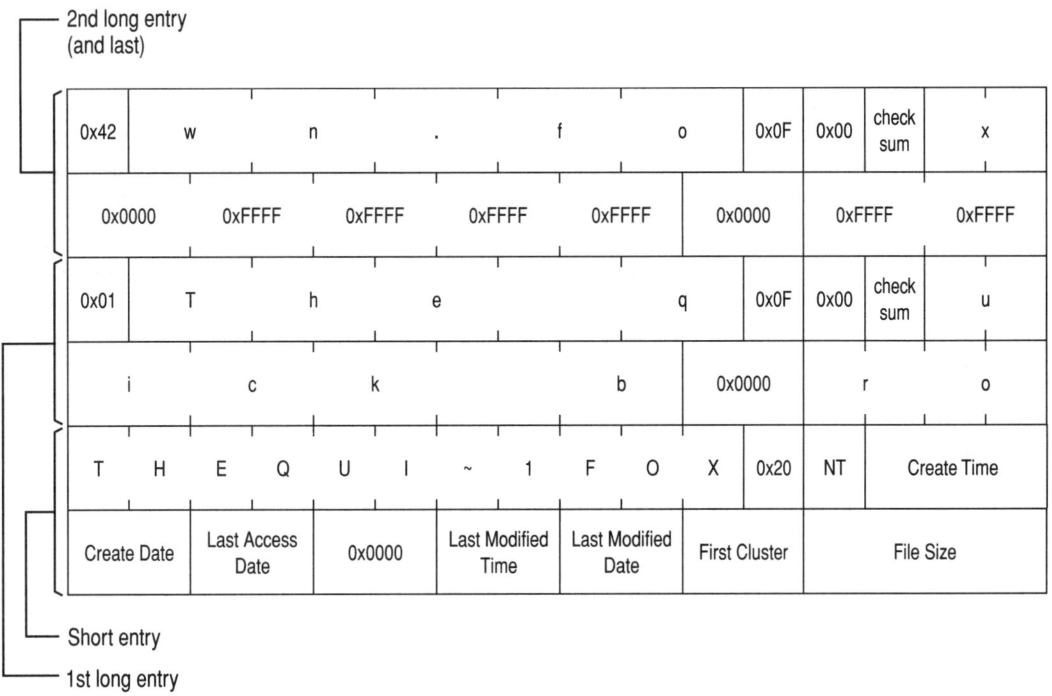

Figure 17.7 Long filename on a FAT volume

Note Windows NT and Windows 95 use the same algorithm to create long and short filenames. On computers that dual-boot these two operating systems, files that you create when running one of the operating systems can be accessed when running the other.

For information about how Windows NT creates the short filename, see "Generating and Viewing Short Filenames," presented later in this chapter.

By default, Windows NT versions 3.5 and higher support long filenames on FAT volumes. You can turn off creation of long filenames by setting the Win31FileSystem parameter in the following Registry entry to 1:

```
HKEY_LOCAL_MACHINE\System\CurrentControlSet\Control\FileSystem
```

Setting this value prevents Windows NT from creating new long filenames on all FAT volumes, but it does not affect existing long filenames.

Using the FAT File System with Windows NT

The FAT file system works the same in Windows NT as it does in MS-DOS, Windows 3.1*x*, and Windows 95. In fact, you can install Windows NT on an existing FAT primary partition or logical drive. When running Windows NT, you can move or copy files between FAT and NTFS volumes.

Note You cannot use Windows NT with any compression or partitioning software that requires disk drivers to be loaded by MS-DOS. Therefore, you cannot use MS-DOS 6.0 DoubleSpace® or MS-DOS 6.22 DiskSpace™ on a FAT primary partition or logical drive that you want to access when running Windows NT.

If you have a dual-boot configuration with Windows 95, you can create FAT partitions when running Windows 95 that you cannot use when running Windows NT. See the section "System ID Field," presented later in this chapter, for details.

The NTFS File System

The Windows NT file system (NTFS) provides a combination of performance, reliability, and compatibility not found in the FAT file system. It is designed to quickly perform standard file operations such as read, write, and search—and even advanced operations such as file-system recovery—on very large hard disks.

The NTFS file system includes security features required for file servers and high-end personal computers in a corporate environment. The NTFS file system also supports data access control and ownership privileges that are important for the integrity of critical data. While folders shared on a Windows NT computer are assigned particular permissions, NTFS files and folders can have permissions assigned whether they are shared or not. NTFS is the only file system on Windows NT that allows you to assign permissions to individual files. However, when you move or copy a file from an NTFS to a FAT volume, permissions and other attributes unique to the NTFS file system are lost.

The NTFS file system has a simple, yet very powerful design. Basically, everything on the volume is a file and everything in a file is an attribute, from the data attribute, to the security attribute, to the file name attribute. Every sector on an NTFS volume that is allocated belongs to some file. Even the file system metadata (information that describes the file system itself) is part of a file.

Structure of an NTFS Volume

Like the FAT file system, the NTFS file system uses clusters as the fundamental unit of disk allocation. In the NTFS file system, the default cluster size depends on the volume size. In Disk Administrator, you can specify a cluster size up to 4K. If you use the command prompt program **format** to format your NTFS volume, you can specify any cluster size shown in the next table.

The default cluster sizes for the NTFS file system are shown in the following table.

Partition size	Sectors per cluster	Cluster size
512 MB or less	1	512 bytes
513 MB - 1024 MB (1GB)	2	1K
1025 MB - 2048 MB (2GB)	4	2K
2049 MB - 4096 MB (4GB)	8	4K
4097 MB - 8192 MB (8GB)	16	8K
8193 MB - 16,384 MB (16GB)	32	16K
16,385 MB - 32,768 MB (32GB)	64	32K
> 32, 768 MB	128	64K

Note You cannot use NTFS compression when your cluster size is greater than 4K. See "NTFS Compression" in Chapter 18, "Choosing a File System," for more information.

Formatting a volume with the NTFS file system results in the creation of several system files and the Master File Table (MFT), which contains information about all the files and folders on the NTFS volume.

The first information on an NTFS volume is the Partition Boot Sector, which starts at sector 0 and can be up to 16 sectors long. It consists of two structures:

- The BIOS Parameter Block, which contains information on the volume layout and file system structures.
- Code that describes how to find and load the startup files for whatever operating system is being loaded. For Windows NT on x86-based computers, this code loads NTLDR.

The first file on an NTFS volume is the Master File Table (MFT). The next section of this chapter, "Master File Table (MFT) and the NTFS System Files," contains more information.

The following figure illustrates the layout of an NTFS volume when formatting has finished.

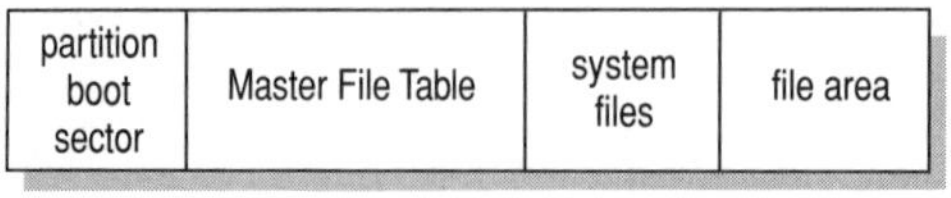

partition boot sector	Master File Table	system files	file area

Figure 17.8 NTFS volume layout

Master File Table (MFT) and NTFS System Files

When you format an NTFS volume, the format program creates a set of files that contains the metadata used to implement the file system structure. The NTFS file system reserves the first 16 records in the MFT for the information about these metadata files. The NTFS file system uses approximately 1 MB for the metadata files and the first 16 records in the MFT. The next table describes these records.

Table 17.1 NTFS System Files

System file	Filename	MFT record	Purpose of the file
Master File Table	$Mft	0	A list of all contents of the NTFS volume.
Master File Table2	$MftMirr	1	A mirror of the first three records of the MFT, used to guarantee access to the MFT in the case of a single-sector failure.
Log File	$LogFile	2	A list of transaction steps used for NTFS recoverability.
Volume	$Volume	3	The volume name, NTFS version, and other information about the volume.
Attribute Definition Table	$AttrDef	4	A table of attribute names, numbers, and descriptions.
Root Filename Index	$.	5	Root folder.
Cluster Bitmap	$Bitmap	6	A representation of the volume, showing which clusters are in use.
Partition Boot Sector	$Boot	7	The bootstrap for the volume, if this is a bootable volume.
Bad Cluster File	$BadClus	8	A location where all the bad clusters in the volume are located.
Quota Table	$Quota	9	Disk quota usage for each user on a volume. Currently unused.
Upcase Table	$Upcase	10	Used for converting lowercase characters to the matching Unicode uppercase characters.
		11-15	Reserved for future use.

The first record of the MFT describes the MFT itself, followed by the MFT mirror record. If the first MFT record is corrupted, the NTFS file system reads the second record to find the MFT mirror file, which is a copy of the first three records of the MFT. The locations of the data segments for both the MFT and the MFT mirror file are recorded in the Partition Boot Sector. A duplicate of the Partition Boot Sector is located at the end of the volume (Windows NT version 4.0) or the logical center of the volume (Windows NT version 3.51 and earlier).

The third record of the MFT is the log file, which the operating system uses to restore consistency to the NTFS file system in the event of a system crash. The log file size depends upon the volume size, and can be as large as 4 MB. The log file is discussed in more detail in the section titled "NTFS Recoverability" in Chapter 18, "Choosing a File System."

The MFT contains records that describe each file on an NTFS volume. The NTFS file system allocates space for each of the MFT records based upon the cluster size. The attributes of a file are written to the allocated space in the MFT. Small files and folders, such as the file illustrated in Figure 17.9, can be contained entirely within the MFT record.

Standard information	File or directory name	Security descriptor	Data or index	

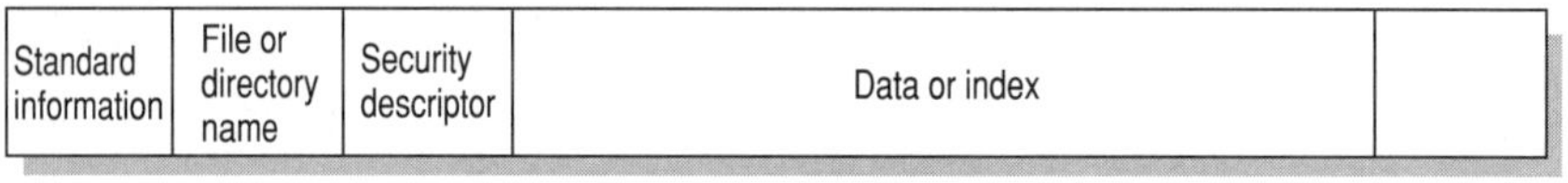

Figure 17.9 MFT Record for a Small File or Folder

Records for folders are contained within the MFT, just like records for files. All of the information for small folders reside entirely within the MFT record. Large folders are organized into B-trees, having records with pointers to external clusters containing folder entries that could not be contained within the MFT structure.

NTFS File Attributes

The NTFS file system views each file (or folder) as a set of file attributes. Elements such as the file's name, its security information, and even its data, are all file attributes. Each attribute is identified by an attribute type code and, optionally, an attribute name.

When a file's attributes can fit within the MFT file record, they are called resident attributes. For example, information such as filename and time stamp are always included in the MFT file record. When all of the information for a file is too large to fit in the MFT file record, some of its attributes are nonresident. The nonresident attributes are allocated one or more clusters of disk space elsewhere in the volume. NTFS creates the Attribute List attribute to describe the location of all of the attribute records.

Table 17.2 lists all of the file attributes currently defined by the NTFS file system. This list is extensible, meaning that other file attributes can be defined in the future.

Table 17.2 NTFS File Attribute Types

Attribute type	Description
Standard Information	Includes time stamps, link count, and so on.
Attribute List	Lists the location of all of the attribute records when they do not all fit in the MTF record.
Filename	A repeatable attribute for both long and short filenames. The long name of the file can be up to 255 Unicode characters. The short name is the MS-DOS-readable, eight-plus-three, case-insensitive name for this file. Additional names, or hard links, required by POSIX can also be included as additional filename attributes.
Security Descriptor	Shows information about who can access the file, who owns the file, and so on.
Data	Contains file data. NTFS allows multiple data attributes per file. Each file typically has one unnamed data attribute. In addition, a file can have one or more named data attributes, using a particular syntax.
Index Root	Used to implement folders.
Index Allocation	Used to implement folders.
Volume Information	Used only in the $Volume system file and includes information such as the version and name of the volume.
Bitmap	Provides a map representing records in use on the MFT or folder.
Extended Attribute Information	Used by file servers that are linked with OS/2 systems. This attribute type is not used by Windows NT.
Extended Attributes	Used by file servers that are linked with OS/2 systems. This attribute type is not used by Windows NT.

Filenames on NTFS Volumes

By default, Windows NT version 3.5 and later support MS-DOS-readable filenames on all NTFS volumes. To improve performance on volumes with many long, similar names, you can disable this feature by setting the NtfsDisable8dot3NameCreation parameter of the following Registry entry to 1:

```
HKEY_LOCAL_MACHINE\System\CurrentControlSet\Control\FileSystem
```

Windows NT does not generate short (eight-plus-three) filenames for files created by POSIX-based applications on an NTFS volume. This means that MS-DOS-based and Windows-based applications cannot view these filenames if they are not valid eight-plus-three filenames. If you want to use files that are created by a POSIX application with MS-DOS-based or Windows-based applications, be sure to use standard MS-DOS eight-plus-three naming conventions.

For general information about long and short filenames for both FAT and NTFS volumes, see the section "Generating and Viewing Short Filenames," presented later in this chapter.

Using MS-DOS-based Disk Programs

Do not use any third-party MS-DOS-based disk program to repair or defragment a FAT primary partition or logical drive used by Windows NT unless the disk program has been certified as being compatible with Windows NT version 3.5 or later. While instances of third-party utilities corrupting FAT volumes are relatively rare, some problems have occurred. Using non-Windows NT utilities is simply not worth the risk of losing an entire volume. Even the MS-DOS-based program Defrag might not work correctly if you have long filenames in the FAT volume.

You can use the Windows NT command prompt program Chkdsk to scan and repair FAT and NTFS volumes. This program incorporates all of the functionality of the MS-DOS-based Chkdsk and Scandisk utilities, including a surface scan. To do a surface scan, use **chkdsk /r**.

There is a Windows NT–based program available that can defragment both FAT and NTFS volumes. Microsoft has a directory that contains information about hardware and software products that are available for Windows NT, including defragmentation utilities. This directory is called InfoSource. For information about InfoSource, see http://www.microsoft.com/infosource.

Disk media verification can be done with the SCSI utilities that ship with most SCSI controllers. Consult the documentation accompanying your hardware or contact your hardware vendor for information on verification of disk media. It is always a good idea to do a complete backup of the disk before starting a procedure of this type.

Generating and Viewing Short Filenames

Filenames on Windows NT platforms can be up to 256 characters, and can contain spaces, multiple periods, and special characters that are illegal in MS-DOS filenames. These long filenames use the 16-bit Unicode character set. Windows NT makes it possible to access files with long names from other operating systems by automatically generating an MS-DOS-readable (eight-plus-three) name for each file. This way, files are accessible over a network by computers using the MS-DOS, Windows 3.1*x*, and OS/2 operating systems, as well as by computers using Windows NT and Windows 95 operating systems.

By creating eight-plus-three filenames for files, Windows NT also enables MS-DOS-based and Windows-based 3.*x* applications to recognize and load files that have long filenames. In addition, when an application saves a file on a computer running Windows NT, both the eight-plus-three filename and long filename are retained.

Note Use caution with MS-DOS-based or Windows 3.*x*-based applications when running under Windows NT. With these applications, if you save a file to a temporary file, delete the original file, and rename the temporary file to the original filename, the long filename is lost. Any unique permissions set on that file are also lost.

If the long name of a file or folder contains spaces, be sure to surround the name with quotation marks. For instance, if you have a program called DUMP DISK FILES that you want to run from the Start icon and you enter the name without quotation marks, you will get an error message that says "cannot find the program DUMP or one of its components."

You must also use quotation marks when a path typed at the command line includes spaces, as in the following example:

```
move "c:\This month's reports\*.*" "c:\Last month's reports"
```

Use wildcards such as * and ? carefully in conjunction with the **del** and **copy** command prompt commands. Windows NT searches both long and short filenames for matches to the wildcard combination you specify, which can cause extra files to be deleted or copied.

To copy or move files with case-sensitive long filenames, it is safest to select the files using a mouse in Windows NT Explorer and My Computer. That way, you can clearly identify which files you want to copy or move.

Because both the FAT file system and the NTFS file system use the Unicode character set for their names, there are several illegal characters that MS-DOS cannot read in any filename. To generate a short MS-DOS-readable filename for a file, Windows NT deletes all of these characters from the long filename and removes any spaces. Since an MS-DOS-readable filename can have only one period, Windows NT also removes all extra periods from the filename. Next, Windows NT truncates the filename, if necessary, to six characters and appends a tilde (~) and a number. For example, each nonduplicate filename is appended with **~1**. Duplicate filenames end with **~2**, **~3**, and so on. Filename extensions are truncated to three or fewer characters. Finally, when displaying filenames at the command line, Windows NT translates all characters in the filename and extension to uppercase.

When there are five or more files that would result in duplicate short filenames, Windows NT uses a slightly different method for creating short filenames. For the fifth and subsequent files, Windows NT:

- Uses only the first two letters of the long filename.
- Generates the next four letters of the short filename by mathematically manipulating the remaining letters of the long filename.
- Appends ~1 (or another number, if necessary, to avoid a duplicate filename) to the result.

This method provides substantially improved performance when Windows NT must create short filenames for a large number of files with similar long filenames. Windows NT uses this method to create short filenames for both FAT and NTFS volumes.

For example, these are the long and short filenames for six files that you create in the order test 1 through test 6.

Long filename	Short filename
This is test 1.txt	THISIS~1.TXT
This is test 2.txt	THISIS~2.TXT
This is test 3.txt	THISIS~3.TXT
This is test 4.txt	THISIS~4.TXT
This is test 5.txt	TH0FF9~1.TXT
This is test 6.txt	THFEF5~1.TXT

However, when you create the files in the order shown in this table, you get the following short filenames.

Long filename	Short filename
This is test 2.txt	THISIS~1.TXT
This is test 3.txt	THISIS~2.TXT
This is test 1.txt	THISIS~3.TXT
This is test 4.txt	THISIS~4.TXT
This is test 5.txt	TH0FF9~1.TXT
This is test 6.txt	THFEF5~1.TXT

Windows NT displays the long names for folders and files. You can use Windows NT Explorer and My Computer to see the short name by selecting the file or folder and selecting **Properties** on the **File** menu.

From the command line, to see both the long and short filenames for each file in the folder, type the following command:

```
dir /x
```

Tip To display both long and short filenames automatically when using the **dir** command, use the System option in Control Panel to set the **dircmd** variable to the value **/x**.

Disk Sectors Critical to the Startup Process

There are two sectors on every startup disk that are critical to starting the computer:

- Master Boot Record.
- Partition Boot Sector.

These sectors contain both executable code and the data required by the code. For more information about the startup process, see Chapter 19, "What Happens When You Start Your Computer." For a description of problems that you might encounter with these two sectors, see Chapter 21, "Troubleshooting Startup and Disk Problems."

Note Numbers larger than one byte are stored on x86-based computers in little endian format. For example, the sample value for the Relative Sector field in Table 17.3, 0x3F000000, is a little endian representation of 0x0000003F. The decimal equivalent of this little endian number is 63. Because most problems with the Master Boot Record and Partition Boot Sector occur on x86-based computers, the examples of these disk sectors are hexidecimal dumps from x86-based computers.

Master Boot Record

The Master Boot Record, created when you create the first partition on the hard disk, is probably the most important data structure on the disk. It is the first sector on every disk. The location is always track (cylinder) 0, side (head) 0, and sector 1.

The Master Boot Record contains the Partition Table for the disk and a small amount of executable code. On x86-based computers, the executable code examines the Partition Table, and identifies the system partition. The Master Boot Record then finds the system partition's starting location on the disk, and loads an copy of its Partition Boot Sector into memory. The Master Boot Record then transfers execution to executable code in the Partition Boot Sector.

Note Although there is a Master Boot Record on every hard disk, the executable code in the sector is used only if the disk is connected to an x86-based computer and the disk contains the system partition.

Figure 17.10 shows a hex dump of the sector containing the Master Boot Record. The figure shows the sector in two parts. The first part is the Master Boot Record, which occupies the first 446 bytes of the sector. The disk signature (FD 4E F2 14) is at the end of the Master Boot Record code. The second part is the Partition Table.

```
Physical Sector: Cyl 0, Side 0, Sector 1
 00000000: 00 33 C0 8E D0 BC 00 7C  - 8B F4 50 07 50 1F FB FC   .3.....|..P.P..
00000010: BF 00 06 B9 00 01 F2 A5  - EA 1D 06 00 00 BE BE 07   ................
00000020: B3 04 80 3C 80 74 0E 80  - 3C 00 75 1C 83 C6 10 FE   ...<.t..<.u.....
00000030: CB 75 EF CD 18 8B 14 8B  - 4C 02 8B EE 83 C6 10 FE   .u......L.......
00000040: CB 74 1A 80 3C 00 74 F4  - BE 8B 06 AC 3C 00 74 0B   .t..<.t.....<.t.
00000050: 56 BB 07 00 B4 0E CD 10  - 5E EB F0 EB FE BF 05 00   V.......^.......
00000060: BB 00 7C B8 01 02 57 CD  - 13 5F 73 0C 33 C0 CD 13   ..|...W.._s.3...
00000070: 4F 75 ED BE A3 06 EB D3  - BE C2 06 BF FE 7D 81 3D   Ou...........}.=
00000080: 55 AA 75 C7 8B F5 EA 00  - 7C 00 00 49 6E 76 61 6C   U.u.....|..Inval
00000090: 69 64 20 70 61 72 74 69  - 74 69 6F 6E 20 74 61 62   id partition tab
000000A0: 6C 65 00 45 72 72 6F 72  - 20 6C 6F 61 64 69 6E 67   le.Error loading
000000B0: 20 6F 70 65 72 61 74 69  - 6E 67 20 73 79 73 74 65    operating syste
000000C0: 6D 00 4D 69 73 73 69 6E  - 67 20 6F 70 65 72 61 74   m.Missing operat
000000D0: 69 6E 67 20 73 79 73 74  - 65 6D 00 00 80 45 14 15   ing system...E..
000000E0: 00 00 00 00 00 00 00 00  - 00 00 00 00 00 00 00 00   ................
000000F0: 00 00 00 00 00 00 00 00  - 00 00 00 00 00 00 00 00   ................
00000100: 00 00 00 00 00 00 00 00  - 00 00 00 00 00 00 00 00   ................
00000110: 00 00 00 00 00 00 00 00  - 00 00 00 00 00 00 00 00   ................
00000120: 00 00 00 00 00 00 00 00  - 00 00 00 00 00 00 00 00   ................
00000130: 00 00 00 00 00 00 00 00  - 00 00 00 00 00 00 00 00   ................
00000140: 00 00 00 00 00 00 00 00  - 00 00 00 00 00 00 00 00   ................
00000150: 00 00 00 00 00 00 00 00  - 00 00 00 00 00 00 00 00   ................
00000160: 00 00 00 00 00 00 00 00  - 00 00 00 00 00 00 00 00   ................
00000170: 00 00 00 00 00 00 00 00  - 00 00 00 00 00 00 00 00   ................
00000180: 00 00 00 00 00 00 00 00  - 00 00 00 00 00 00 00 00   ................
00000190: 00 00 00 00 00 00 00 00  - 00 00 00 00 00 00 00 00   ................
000001A0: 00 00 00 00 00 00 00 00  - 00 00 00 00 00 00 00 00   ................
000001B0: 00 00 00 00 00 00 00 00  - FD 4E F2 14 00 00         .........N......

                                                      80 01                  ..
000001C0: 01 00 06 0F 7F 96 3F 00  - 00 00 51 42 06 00 00 00   ....•.?...QB....
000001D0: 41 97 07 0F FF 2C 90 42  - 06 00 A0 3E 06 00 00 00   A....,.B...>....
000001E0: C1 2D 05 0F FF 92 30 81  - 0C 00 A0 91 01 00 00 00   .-....0.........
000001F0: C1 93 01 0F FF A6 D0 12  - 0E 00 C0 4E 00 00 55 AA   ...........N..U.
```

Figure 17.10 Hex Dump of the Master Boot Record for an x86-based computer

Disk Signature

The disk signature is a unique number at offset 0x1B8 that Windows NT uses as an index to store and retrieve information about the disk in the Registry subkey HKEY_LOCAL_MACHINE\SYSTEM\DISK.

The first time that you open Disk Administrator after formatting a hard disk, it displays this dialog box to inform you that no disk signature was found on the disk. You should select **Yes**, or Windows NT will not be able to access the disk.

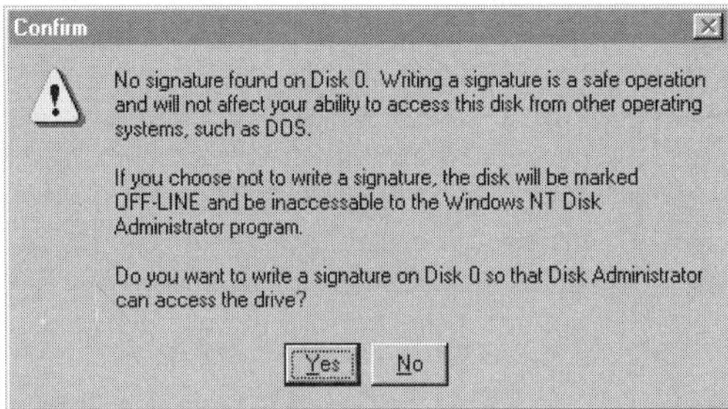

Viruses Can Infect the Master Boot Record

Many destructive viruses damage the Master Boot Record and make it impossible to start the computer from the hard disk. Because the code in the Master Boot Record executes before any operating system is started, no operating system can detect or recover from corruption of the Master Boot Record. You can use the DiskProbe program on *Windows NT Workstation Resource Kit* CD to display the Master Boot Record, and compare it to the Master Boot Record shown in Figure 17.10. There are also utilities on the Resource Kit that enable you to save and restore the Master Boot Record. See Chapter 21, "Troubleshooting Startup and Disk Problems," and Chapter 22, "Disk, File System, and Backup Utilities," for more information.

Partition Table

The information about primary partitions and an extended partition is contained in the Partition Table, a 64-byte data structure located in the same sector as the Master Boot Record (cylinder 0, head 0, sector 1). The Partition Table conforms to a standard layout that is independent of the operating system. Each Partition Table entry is 16 bytes long, making a maximum of four entries available. Each entry starts at a predetermined offset from the beginning of the sector, as follows:

- Partition 1 0x01BE (446)
- Partition 2 0x01CE (462)
- Partition 3 0x01DE (478)
- Partition 4 0x01EE (494)

The last two bytes in the sector are a signature word for the sector and are always 0x55AA.

The next figure is a printout of the Partition Table for the disk shown in Figure 17.4, presented earlier in this chapter. When there are fewer than four partitions, the remaining fields are all zeros.

```
                                                  80 01                  ..
000001C0: 01 00 06 0F 7F 96 3F 00 - 00 00 51 42 06 00 00 00    ....•.?...QB....
000001D0: 41 97 07 0F FF 2C 90 42 - 06 00 A0 3E 06 00 00 00    A.....,.B...>....
000001E0: C1 2D 05 0F FF 92 30 81 - 0C 00 A0 91 01 00 00 00    .-....0.........
000001F0: C1 93 01 0F FF A6 D0 12 - 0E 00 C0 4E 00 00 55 AA    ...........N..U.
```

Figure 17.11 Partition Table from an x86-based computer

The following table describes each entry in the Partition Table. The sample values correspond to the information for partition 1 in Figure 17.11.

Table 17.3 Partition Table Fields

Byte Offset	Field Length	Sample Value	Meaning
00	BYTE	0x80	Boot Indicator. Indicates whether the partition is the system partition. Legal values are: 00 = Do not use for booting. 80 = System partition.
01	BYTE	0x01	Starting Head.
02	6 bits	0x01	Starting Sector. Only bits 0-5 are used. Bits 6-7 are the upper two bits for the Starting Cylinder field.
03	10 bits	0x00	Starting Cylinder. This field contains the lower 8 bits of the cylinder value. Starting cylinder is thus a 10-bit number, with a maximum value of 1023.
04	BYTE	0x06	System ID. This byte defines the volume type. In Windows NT, it also indicates that a partition is part of a volume that requires the use of the HKEY_LOCAL_MACHINE\SYSTEM\DISK Registry subkey.
05	BYTE	0x0F	Ending Head.
06	6 bits	0x3F	Ending Sector. Only bits 0-5 are used. Bits 6-7 are the upper two bits for the Ending Cylinder field.
07	10 bits	0x196	Ending Cylinder. This field contains the lower 8 bits of the cylinder value. Ending cylinder is thus a 10-bit number, with a maximum value of 1023.
08	DWORD	3F 00 00 00	Relative Sector.
12	DWORD	51 42 06 00	Total Sectors.

The remainder of this section describes the uses of these fields. Definitions of the fields in the Partition Table is the same for primary partitions, extended partitions, and logical drives in extended partitions.

Boot Indicator Field

The Boot Indicator field indicates whether the volume is the system partition. On x-86-based computers, only one primary partition on the disk should have this field set. This field is used only on x86-based computers. On RISC-based computers, the NVRAM contains the information for finding the files to load.

On x86-based computers, it is possible to have different operating systems and different file systems on different volumes. For example, a computer could have MS-DOS on the first primary partition and Windows 95, UNIX, OS/2, or Windows NT on the second. You control which primary partition to use to start the computer by setting the Boot Indicator field for that partition in the Partition Table. For a description of how to set the field, see the section "Setting the System Partition (x86-based Computers)," in Chapter 19, "What Happens When You Start Your Computer."

System ID Field

For primary partitions and logical drives, the System ID field describes the file system used to format the volume. Windows NT uses this field to determine what file system device drivers to load during startup. It also identifies the extended partition, if there is one defined.

These are the values for the System ID field:

Value	Meaning
0x01	12-bit FAT primary partition or logical drive. The number of sectors in the volume is fewer than 32680.
0x04	16-bit FAT primary partition or logical drive. The number of sectors is between 32680 and 65535.
0x05	Extended partition. See section titled "Logical Drives and Extended Partitions," presented later in this chapter, for more information.
0x06	BIGDOS FAT primary partition or logical drive.
0x07	NTFS primary partition or logical drive.

Figure 17.11, presented earlier in this section, has examples of a BIGDOS FAT partition, an NTFS partition, an extended partition, and a 12-bit FAT partition.

If you install Windows NT on a computer that has Windows 95 preinstalled, the FAT partitions might be shown as unknown. If you want to be able to use these partitions when running Windows NT, your only option is to delete the partitions.

OEM versions of Windows 95 support the following four partition types for FAT file systems that Windows NT cannot recognize.

Value	Meaning
0x0B	Primary Fat32 partition, using interrupt 13 (INT 13) extensions.
0x0C	Extended Fat32 partition, using INT 13 extensions.
0x0E	Extended Fat16 partition, using INT 13 extensions.
0x0F	Primary Fat16 partition, using INT 13 extensions.

When you create a volume set or a stripe set, Disk Administrator sets the high bit of the System ID field for each primary partition or logical drive that is a member of the volume. For example, a FAT primary partition or logical drive that is a member of a volume set or a stripe set has a System ID value of 0x86. An NTFS primary partition or logical drive has a System ID value of 0x87. This bit indicates that Windows NT needs to use the HKEY_LOCAL_MACHINE\SYSTEM\DISK Registry subkey to determine how the members of the volume set or stripe set relate to each other. Volumes that have the high bit set can only be accessed by Windows NT.

When a primary partition or logical drive that is a member of a volume set or a stripe set has failed due to write errors or cannot be accessed, the second most significant bit is set. The System ID byte is set to C6 in the case of a FAT volume, or C7 in the case of an NTFS volume.

Note If you start up MS-DOS, it can only access primary partitions or logical drives that have a value of 0x01, 0x04, 0x05, or 0x06 for the System ID. However, you should be able to delete volumes that have the other values. If you use a MS-DOS-based low-level disk editor, you can read and write any sector, including ones that are in NTFS volumes.

On Windows NT Server, mirror sets and stripe sets with parity also require the use of the Registry subkey HKEY_LOCAL_MACHINE\SYSTEM\DISK to determine how to access the disks.

Starting and Ending Head, Sector, and Cylinder Fields

On x86-based computers, the Starting and Ending Head, Cylinder, and Sector fields on the startup disk are very important for starting up the computer. The code in the Master Boot Record uses these fields to find and load the Partition Boot Sector.

The Ending Cylinder field in the Partition Table is ten bits long, which limits the maximum number of cylinders that can be described in the Partition Table to 1024. The Starting and Ending Head fields are one byte long, which limits this field to the range 0 – 255. The Starting and Ending Sector field is 6 bits long, limiting its range to 0 – 63. However, sectors start counting at 1 (versus 0 for the other fields), so the maximum number of sectors per track is 63.

Since current hard disks are low-level formatted with the industry standard 512-byte sector size, the maximum capacity disk that can be described by the Partition Table can be calculated as follows:

```
MaxCapacity = (sector size) x (sectors per track) x (cylinders) x
(heads)
```

Substituting the maximum possible values yields:

```
512 x 63 x 1024 x 256 = 8,455,716,864 bytes or 7.8 GB
```

The maximum formatted capacity is slightly less than 8 GB.

However, the maximum cluster size that you can use for FAT volumes when running Windows NT is 64K, when using a 512 byte sector size. Therefore, the maximum size for a FAT volume is 4 GB.

If you have a dual-boot configuration with Windows 95 or MS-DOS, FAT volumes that might be accessed when using either of those operating systems are limited to 2 GB. In addition, Macintosh computers that are viewing volumes on a computer running Windows NT cannot see more than 2 GB. If you try to use a FAT volume larger than 2 GB when running MS-DOS or Windows 95, or access it from a Macintosh computer, you might get a message that there are 0 bytes available. The same limit applies to OS/2 system and boot partitions.

The maximum size of a FAT volume on a specific computer depends on the disk geometry, and the maximum values that can fit in the fields described in this section. The next table shows the typical size of a FAT volume when translation is enabled, and when it is disabled. The number of cylinders in both situations is 1024.

Translation mode	Number of heads	Sectors per track	Maximum size for system or boot partition
Disabled	64	32	1 GB
Enabled	255	63	4 GB

Note RISC-based computers do not have a limit on the size of the system or boot partitions.

If a primary partition or logical drive extends beyond cylinder 1023, all of these fields will contain the maximum values.

Relative Sectors and Number of Sectors Fields

For primary partitions, the Relative Sectors field represents the offset from the beginning of the disk to the beginning of the partition, counting by sectors. The Number of Sectors field represents the total number of sectors in the partition. For a description of these fields in extended partitions, see the section "Logical Drives and Extended Partitions," presented later in this chapter.

Windows NT uses these fields to access all partitions. When you format a partition when running Windows NT, it puts data into the Starting and Ending Cylinder, Head, and Sector fields only for backward compatibility with MS-DOS and Windows 95, and to maintain compatibility with the BIOS interrupt (INT) 13 for startup purposes.

See the section titled "Using Hard Disks With More Than 1024 Cylinders (x86-based Computers)," presented later in this chapter, for more information about the use of these fields.

Logical Drives and Extended Partitions

When more than four logical disks are required on a single physical disk, the first partition should be a primary partition. The second partition can be created as an extended partition, which can contain all the remaining unpartitioned space on the disk.

Note A primary partition is one that can be used as the system partition. If the disk does not contain a system partition, you can configure the entire disk as a single, extended partition.

Some computers create an EISA configuration partition as the first partition on the hard disk.

Windows NT detects an extended partition because the System ID byte in the Partition Table entry is set to 5. There can be only one extended partition on a hard disk.

Within the extended partition, you can create any number of logical drives. As a practical matter, the number of available drive letters is the limiting factor in the number of logical drives that you can define.

When you have an extended partition on the hard disk, the entry for that partition in the Partition Table (at the end of the Master Boot Record) points to the first disk sector in the extended partition. The first sector of each logical drive in an extended partition also has a Partition Table, which is the last 66 bytes of the sector. (The last two bytes of the sector are the end-of-sector marker.)

These are the entries in an extended Partition Table:

- The first entry is for the current logical drive.
- The second entry contains information about the next logical drive in the extended partition.
- Entries three and four are all zeroes.

This format repeats for every logical drive. The last logical drive has only its own partition entry listed. The entries for partitions 2-4 are all zeroes.

The Partition Table entry is the only information on the first side of the first cylinder of each logical drive in the extended partition. The entry for partition 1 in each Partition Table contains the starting address for data on the current logical drive. And the entry for partition 2 is the address of the sector that contains the Partition Table for the next logical drive.

The use of the Relative Sector and Total Sectors fields for logical drives in an extended partition is different than for primary partitions. For the partition 1 entry of each logical drive, the Relative Sectors field is the sector from the beginning of the logical drive that contains the Partition Boot Sector. The Total Sectors field is the number of sectors from the Partition Boot Sector to the end of the logical drive.

For the partition 2 entry, the Relative Sectors field is the offset from the beginning of the extended partition to the sector containing the Partition Table for the logical drive defined in the Partition 2 entry. The Total Sectors field is the total size of the logical drive defined in the Partition 2 entry.

Note If a logical drive is part of a volume set, the Partition Boot Sector is at the beginning of the first member of the volume set. Other members of the volume set have data where the Partition Boot Sector would normally be located.

This Disk Administrator screen shot shows a disk having an extended partition. The extended partition contains a volume set (drive E), two logical drives (drives I and K), and 4 MB of free space. This screen shot is identical to the one shown in Figure 17.4.

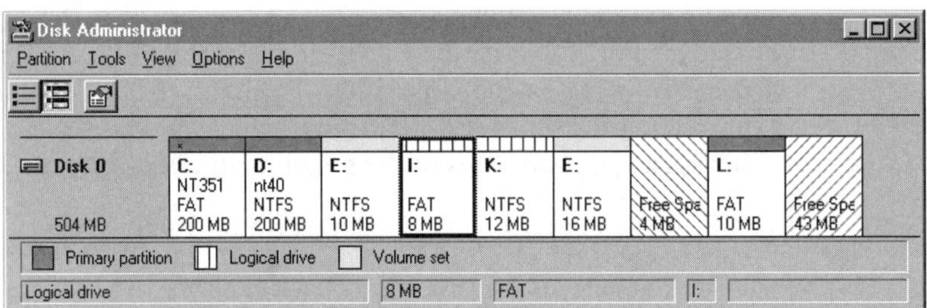

The following example is a printout from the DiskMap program of the information in the Master Boot Record (the section titled MBR) and the extended Partition Table entries (the sections titled EBR) for the disk configuration shown in the preceding Disk Administrator screen shot. For information about DiskMap, see Chapter 22, "Disk, File System, and Backup Utilities."

```
MBR:
          Starting                 Ending          System    Relative  Total
  Cylinder Head Sector  Cylinder Head Sector  ID        Sector    Sectors
*        0    1     1        406   15    63    0x06          63    410193
       407    0     1        812   15    63    0x07      410256    409248
       813    0     1        914   15    63    0x05      819504    102816
       915    0     1        934   15    63    0x01      922320     20160

EBR: (sector 819504)
          Starting                 Ending          System    Relative  Total
  Cylinder Head Sector  Cylinder Head Sector  ID        Sector    Sectors
       813    1     1        832   15    63    0x87          63     20097
       833    0     1        848   15    63    0x05       20160     16128

EBR: (sector 839664)
          Starting                 Ending          System    Relative  Total
  Cylinder Head Sector  Cylinder Head Sector  ID        Sector    Sectors
       833    1     1        848   15    63    0x01          63     16065
       849    0     1        872   15    63    0x05       36288     24192

EBR: (sector 855792)
          Starting                 Ending          System    Relative  Total
  Cylinder Head Sector  Cylinder Head Sector  ID        Sector    Sectors
       849    1     1        872   15    63    0x07          63     24129
       873    0     1        905   15    63    0x05       60480     33264

EBR: (sector 879984)
          Starting                 Ending          System    Relative  Total
  Cylinder Head Sector  Cylinder Head Sector  ID        Sector    Sectors
       873    1     1        905   15    63    0x87          63     33201
         0    0     0          0    0     0    0x00           0         0
```

Partition Boot Sector

The Partition Boot Sector contains information that the file system uses to access the volume. On x86-based computers, the Master Boot Record use the Partition Boot Sector on the system partition to load the operating system kernel files, or in the case of Windows NT, the boot loader.

The Windows NT Partition Boot Sector consists of:

- A jump instruction.
- The OEM name and version.
- A data structure called the BIOS Parameter Block.
- Another data structure called the extended BIOS Parameter Block.
- The bootstrap code.

The BIOS Parameter Block (bytes 11 through 35 of the Partition Boot Sector) describes physical parameters of the volume. The extended BIOS Parameter Block begins immediately after the BIOS Parameter Block. The length of this structure is different for FAT and NTFS volumes. The information in the BIOS Parameter Block and the extended BIOS Parameter Block is used by disk device drivers to read and configure volumes.

The Partition Boot Sector is the first 512-byte sector at the beginning of the volume. The sector always ends with 0x55AA, which is a sector signature word that marks the end of the sector.

FAT Partition Boot Sector

Table 17.4 describes the fields in the Partition Boot Sector for a volume formatted with the FAT file system. The sample values are the data in the corresponding fields in the hex dump in Figure 17.12, presented later in this section.

Table 17.4 Partition Boot Sector for FAT volumes

Byte Offset (in hex)	Field Length	Sample Value	Meaning
00	3 bytes	EB 3C 90	Jump instruction
03	8 bytes	MSDOS5.0	OEM Name in text
0B	25 bytes		BIOS Parameter Block
24	26 bytes		Extended BIOS Parameter Block
3E	448 bytes		Bootstrap code
1FE	2 bytes	0x55AA	End of sector marker

The following figure is a hex printout of the Partition Boot Sector for a FAT volume. The printout is formatted in three sections:

- Bytes 0 - 0x0A are the jump instruction and the OEM name.
- Bytes 0x0B - 0x3D are the BIOS Parameter Block and the Extended BIOS Parameter Block
- The rest of the printout is the bootstrap code and the end of sector marker.

```
Physical Sector: Cyl 0, Side 1, Sector 1
00000000: EB 3C 90 4D 53 44 4F 53  - 35 2E 30                   <.MS-DOS5.0

                                            00 02 08 01 00              .....
00000010: 02 00 02 00 00 F8 C9 00  - 3F 00 10 00 3F 00 00 00   ........?...?...
00000020: 51 42 06 00 80 00 29 CE  - 13 46 30 4E 4F 20 4E 41   QB....)..F0NO NA
00000030: 4D 45 20 20 20 20 46 41  - 54 31 36 20 20 20         ME    FAT16

                                                        33 C0                3.
00000040: 8E D0 BC 00 7C 68 C0 07  - 1F A0 10 00 F7 26 16 00   ....|h......&..
00000050: 03 06 0E 00 50 91 B8 20  - 00 F7 26 11 00 8B 1E 0B   ....P.. ..&.....
00000060: 00 03 C3 48 F7 F3 03 C8  - 89 0E 08 02 68 00 10 07   ...H........h...
00000070: 33 DB 8F 06 13 02 89 1E  - 15 02 0E E8 90 00 72 57   3.............rW
00000080: 33 DB 8B 0E 11 00 8B FB  - 51 B9 0B 00 BE DC 01 F3   3.......Q.......
00000090: A6 59 74 05 83 C3 20 E2  - ED E3 37 26 8B 57 1A 52   .Yt... ...7&.W.R
000000A0: B8 01 00 68 00 20 07 33  - DB 0E E8 48 00 72 28 5B   ...h. .3...H.r([
000000B0: 8D 36 0B 00 8D 3E 0B 02  - 1E 8F 45 02 C7 05 F5 00   .6...>....E.....
000000C0: 1E 8F 45 06 C7 45 04 0E  - 01 8A 16 24 00 EA 03 00   ..E..E.....$....
000000D0: 00 20 BE 86 01 EB 03 BE  - A2 01 E8 09 00 BE C1 01   . ..............
000000E0: E8 03 00 FB EB FE AC 0A  - C0 74 09 B4 0E BB 07 00   .........t......
000000F0: CD 10 EB F2 C3 50 4A 4A  - A0 0D 00 32 E4 F7 E2 03   .....PJJ...2....
00000100: 06 08 02 83 D2 00 A3 13  - 02 89 16 15 02 58 A2 07   .............X..
00000110: 02 A1 13 02 8B 16 15 02  - 03 06 1C 00 13 16 1E 00   ................
00000120: F7 36 18 00 FE C2 88 16  - 06 02 33 D2 F7 36 1A 00   .6........3..6..
00000130: 88 16 25 00 A3 04 02 A1  - 18 00 2A 06 06 02 40 3A   ..%.......*...@:
00000140: 06 07 02 76 05 A0 07 02  - 32 E4 50 B4 02 8B 0E 04   ...v....2.P.....
00000150: 02 C0 E5 06 0A 2E 06 02  - 86 E9 8B 16 24 00 CD 13   ............$...
00000160: 0F 83 05 00 83 C4 02 F9  - CB 58 28 06 07 02 76 11   .........X(...v.
00000170: 01 06 13 02 83 16 15 02  - 00 F7 26 0B 00 03 D8 EB   ..........&.....
00000180: 90 A2 07 02 F8 CB 42 4F  - 4F 54 3A 20 43 6F 75 6C   ......BOOT: Coul
00000190: 64 6E 27 74 20 66 69 6E  - 64 20 4E 54 4C 44 52 0D   dn't find NTLDR.
000001A0: 0A 00 42 4F 4F 54 3A 20  - 49 2F 4F 20 65 72 72 6F   ..BOOT: I/O erro
000001B0: 72 20 72 65 61 64 69 6E  - 67 20 64 69 73 6B 0D 0A   r reading disk..
000001C0: 00 50 6C 65 61 73 65 20  - 69 6E 73 65 72 74 20 61   .Please insert a
000001D0: 6E 6F 74 68 65 72 20 64  - 69 73 6B 00 4E 54 4C 44   nother disk.NTLD
000001E0: 52 20 20 20 20 20 20 00  - 00 00 00 00 00 00 00 00   R       ........
000001F0: 00 00 00 00 00 00 00 00  - 00 00 00 00 00 00 55 AA   ..............U.
```

Figure 17.12 Partition Boot Sector for a FAT volume on x86-based computer

Table 17.5 shows the layout of the BIOS Parameter Block and the extended BIOS Parameter Block. The sample values correspond to data in Figure17.10.

Table 17.5 BIOS Parameter Block and Extended BIOS Parameter Block Fields for FAT volumes

Byte Offset	Field Length	Value	Meaning
0x0B	WORD	0x0002	Bytes per Sector. The size of a hardware sector. For most disks in use in the United States, the value of this field is 512.
0x0D	BYTE	0x08	Sectors Per Cluster. The number of sectors in a cluster. The default cluster size for a volume depends on the volume size and the file system.
0x0E	WORD	0x0100	Reserved Sectors. The number of sectors from the Partition Boot Sector to the start of the first file allocation table, including the Partition Boot Sector. The minimum value is 1. If the value is greater than 1, it means that the bootstrap code is too long to fit completely in the Partition Boot Sector.
0x10	BYTE	0x02	Number of file allocation tables (FATs). The number of copies of the file allocation table on the volume. Typically, the value of this field is 2.
0x11	WORD	0x0002	Root Entries. The total number of file name entries that can be stored in the root folder of the volume. One entry is always used as a Volume Label. Files with long filenames use up multiple entries per file. Therefore, the largest number of files in the root folder is typically 511, but you will run out of entries sooner if you use long filenames.
0x13	WORD	0x0000	Small Sectors. The number of sectors on the volume if the number fits in 16 bits (65535). For volumes larger than 65536 sectors, this field has a value of 0 and the Large Sectors field is used instead.
0x15	BYTE	0xF8	Media Type. Provides information about the media being used. A value of 0xF8 indicates a hard disk.

Table 17.5 BIOS Parameter Block and Extended BIOS Parameter Block Fields for FAT volumes *(Continued)*

Byte Offset	Field Length	Value	Meaning
0x16	WORD	0xC900	Sectors per file allocation table (FAT). Number of sectors occupied by each of the file allocation tables on the volume. By using this information, together with the Number of FATs and Reserved Sectors, you can compute where the root folder begins. By using the number of entries in the root folder, you can also compute where the user data area of the volume begins.
0x18	WORD	0x3F00	Sectors per Track. The apparent disk geometry in use when the disk was low-level formatted.
0x1A	WORD	0x1000	Number of Heads. The apparent disk geometry in use when the disk was low-level formatted.
0x1C	DWORD	3F 00 00 00	Hidden Sectors. Same as the Relative Sector field in the Partition Table.
0x20	DWORD	51 42 06 00	Large Sectors. If the Small Sectors field is zero, this field contains the total number of sectors in the volume. If Small Sectors is nonzero, this field contains zero..
0x24	BYTE	0x80	Physical Disk Number. This is related to the BIOS physical disk number. Floppy drives are numbered starting with 0x00 for the A disk. Physical hard disks are numbered starting with 0x80. The value is typically 0x80 for hard disks, regardless of how many physical disk drives exist, because the value is only relevant if the device is the startup disk.
0x25	BYTE	0x00	Current Head. Not used by the FAT file system. Therefore, Windows NT uses this field to store two flags: ▪ The low order bit is a dirty flag, used to indicate that Windows NT should run the Chkdsk program against the volume when it starts. ▪ The second lowest bit indicates that a surface scan should also be run.
0x26	BYTE	0x29	Signature. Must be either 0x28 or 0x29 in order to be recognized by Windows NT.

Table 17.5 BIOS Parameter Block and Extended BIOS Parameter Block Fields for FAT volumes *(Continued)*

Byte Offset	Field Length	Value	Meaning
0x27	4 bytes	CE 13 46 30	Volume Serial Number. A unique number that is created when you format the volume.
0x2B	11 bytes	NO NAME	Volume Label. This field was used to store the volume label, but the volume label is now stored as special file in the root directory.
0x36	8 bytes	FAT16	System ID. Either FAT12 or FAT16, depending on the format of the disk.

For the Media Descriptor field, the following table lists some of the recognized media descriptor values and their associated media. A media descriptor value can be associated with more than one disk capacity.

Value	Capacity	Media Size and Type
F0	2.88 MB	3.5-inch, 2-sided, 36-sector
F0	1.44 MB	3.5-inch, 2-sided, 18-sector
F9	720 KB	3.5-inch, 2-sided, 9-sector
F9	1.2 MB	5.25-inch, 2-sided, 15-sector
FD	360 KB	5.25-inch, 2-sided, 9-sector
FF	320 KB	5.25-inch, 2-sided, 8-sector
FC	180 KB	5.25-inch, 1-sided, 9-sector
FE	160 KB	5.25-inch, 1-sided, 8-sector
F8	N/A	Fixed disk

NTFS Partition Boot Sector

Table 17.6 describes the fields in the Partition Boot Sector for a volume formatted with the NTFS file system. The sample values are the data in the corresponding fields in the hex dump in Figure 17.13, presented later in this section.

Table 17.6 Partition Boot Sector for NTFS volume

Byte Offset (in hex)	Field Length	Sample Value	Meaning
00	3 bytes	EB 5B 00	Jump instruction
03	8 bytes	NTFS	OEM Identifier
0B	25 bytes		BIOS Parameter Block
24	48 bytes		Extended BIOS Parameter Block
54	426 bytes		Bootstrap code
1FE	WORD	0x55AA	End of sector marker

Note The bootstrap code for an NTFS volume is longer than the 426 bytes shown here. When you format an NTFS volume, the format program allocates the first 16 sectors for the Partition Boot Sector and the bootstrap code.

The extra data fields after the BIOS Parameter Block form an extended BIOS Parameter Block for NTFS. The data in these fields enable the boot loader to find the Master File Table (MFT) during the startup process. In the NTFS file system, the MFT is not located in a predefined sector as is the case for the file allocation table on a FAT volume. Thus, the MFT can be moved if there is a bad sector in its normal location. However, if these data are corrupt, the MFT cannot be located and Windows NT assumes the volume has not been formatted.

The following figure is a hex dump of the Partition Boot Sector for an NTFS volume (formatted when running Windows NT 4.0). The printout is formatted in three sections:

- Bytes 0 - 0x0A are the jump instruction and the OEM name.
- Bytes 0x0B - 0x53 are the BIOS Parameter Block and the Extended BIOS Parameter Block
- The rest of the printout is the bootstrap code and the end of sector marker.

```
Physical Sector: Cyl 407, Side 0, Sector 1
00000000: EB 5B 90 4E 54 46 53 20  - 20 20 20                    .[.NTFS

                                            00 02 01 00 00                  .....
00000010: 00 00 00 00 00 F8 00 00  - 3F 00 10 00 90 42 06 00  ........?....B..
00000020: 00 00 00 00 80 00 80 00  - A0 3E 06 00 00 00 00 00  .........>......
00000030: 10 00 00 00 00 00 00 00  - 51 1F 03 00 00 00 00 00  ........Q.......
00000040: 02 00 00 00 04 00 00 00  - 5B 1F DD 2C 4F DD 2C A2  ........[.,O.,.
          00000050: 00 00 00 00                                         ....

                     00 00 00 00  - 00 00 00 00 00 FA 33 C0       ..........3.
00000060: 8E D0 BC 00 7C FB B8 C0  - 07 8E D8 C7 06 54 00 00  ....|........T..
00000070: 00 C7 06 56 00 00 00 C7  - 06 5B 00 10 00 B8 00 0D  ...V.....[......
00000080: 8E C0 2B DB E8 07 00 68  - 00 0D 68 56 02 CB 50 53  ..+....h..hV..PS
00000090: 51 52 06 66 A1 54 00 66  - 03 06 1C 00 66 33 D2 66  QR.f.T.f....f3.f
000000A0: 0F B7 0E 18 00 66 F7 F1  - FE C2 88 16 5A 00 66 8B  .....f......Z.f.
000000B0: D0 66 C1 EA 10 F7 36 1A  - 00 88 16 25 00 A3 58 00  .f....6....%..X.
000000C0: A1 18 00 2A 06 5A 00 40  - 3B 06 5B 00 76 03 A1 5B  ...*.Z.@;.[.v..[
000000D0: 00 50 B4 02 8B 16 58 00  - B1 06 D2 E6 0A 36 5A 00  .P....X......6Z.
000000E0: 8B CA 86 E9 8A 36 25 00  - B2 80 CD 13 58 72 2A 01  .....6%.....Xr*.
000000F0: 06 54 00 83 16 56 00 00  - 29 06 5B 00 76 0B C1 E0  .T...V..).[.v...
00000100: 05 8C C2 03 D0 8E C2 EB  - 8A 07 5A 59 5B 58 C3 BE  ..........ZY[X..
00000110: 59 01 EB 08 BE E3 01 EB  - 03 BE 39 01 E8 09 00 BE  Y.........9.....
00000120: AD 01 E8 03 00 FB EB FE  - AC 3C 00 74 09 B4 0E BB  .........<.t....
00000130: 07 00 CD 10 EB F2 C3 1D  - 00 41 20 64 69 73 6B 20  .........A disk
00000140: 72 65 61 64 20 65 72 72  - 6F 72 20 6F 63 63 75 72  read error occur
00000150: 72 65 64 2E 0D 0A 00 29  - 00 41 20 6B 65 72 6E 65  red....).A kerne
00000160: 6C 20 66 69 6C 65 20 69  - 73 20 6D 69 73 73 69 6E  l file is missin
00000170: 67 20 66 72 6F 6D 20 74  - 68 65 20 64 69 73 6B 2E  g from the disk.
00000180: 0D 0A 00 25 00 41 20 6B  - 65 72 6E 65 6C 20 66 69  ...%.A kernel fi
00000190: 6C 65 20 69 73 20 74 6F  - 6F 20 64 69 73 63 6F 6E  le is too discon
000001A0: 74 69 67 75 6F 75 73 2E  - 0D 0A 00 33 00 49 6E 73  tiguous....3.Ins
000001B0: 65 72 74 20 61 20 73 79  - 73 74 65 6D 20 64 69 73  ert a system dis
000001C0: 6B 65 74 74 65 20 61 6E  - 64 20 72 65 73 74 61 72  kette and restar
000001D0: 74 0D 0A 74 68 65 20 73  - 79 73 74 65 6D 2E 0D 0A  t..the system...
000001E0: 00 17 00 5C 4E 54 4C 44  - 52 20 69 73 20 63 6F 6D  ...\NTLDR is com
000001F0: 70 72 65 73 73 65 64 2E  - 0D 0A 00 00 00 00 55 AA  pressed.......U.
```

Figure 17.13 Partition Boot Sector for a NTFS volume on an x86-based computer

The next table describes the fields for the BIOS Parameter Block and the Extended BIOS Parameter Block. The fields starting at 0x0B, 0x0D, 0x15, 0x18, 0x1A, and 0x1C are the same as the corresponding fields for FAT volumes, as described in Table 17.5.

Table 17.7 BIOS Parameter Block and Extended BIOS Parameter Block Fields for NTFS volumes

Byte Offset	Field Length	Sample Value	Meaning
0x0B	WORD	0x0002	Bytes per Sector.
0x0D	BYTE	0x01	Sectors per Cluster.
0x0E	WORD	0x0000	Reserved sectors.
0x10	BYTE	0x00	Always 0.
0x11	WORD	0x0000	Always 0.
0x13	WORD	0x0000	Not used by NTFS.
0x15	BYTE	0xF8	Media Type.
0x16	WORD	0x0000	Always 0.
0x18	WORD	0x3F00	Sectors per Track.
0x1A	WORD	0x1000	Number of Heads.
0x1C	DWORD	90 42 06 00	Hidden Sectors.
0x20	DWORD	00 00 00 00	Not used by NTFS.
0x24	DWORD	80 00 80 00	Not used by NTFS.
0x28	LONGLONG	A0 3E 06 00 00 00 00 00	Total Sectors.
0x30	LCN	10 00 00 00 00 00 00 00	Logical cluster number for $MFT.
0x38	LCN	51 1F 03 00 00 00 00 00	Logical cluster number for $MFTMirr.
0x40	DWORD	02 00 00 00	Clusters per file record segment.
0x44	DWORD	04 00 00 00	Clusters per index block.
0x48	LONGLONG	5B 1F DD 2C 4F DD 2C A2	Volume Serial Number.
0x50	DWORD	00 00 00 00	Checksum.

For information about the Master File Table and the $MFT and $MFTMirr files, see "Master File Table (MFT) and NTFS System Files," presented earlier in this chapter.

Using Hard Disks With More Than 1024 Cylinders (x86-based Computers)

Windows NT can take advantage of hard disks with more than 1024 cylinders if you enable extended translation. Windows NT does not have a limit to the number of cylinders it can address, but the system and boot partitions are limited to 1024 cylinders by the system BIOS, which must use INT 13 to access the disk during startup. The section "Starting and Ending Head, Sector, and Cylinder Fields," presented earlier in this chapter, contains more information about the system and boot partitions.

The following error messages might appear when extended translation is not enabled on disks larger than 1024 cylinders, and the Master Boot Record is unable to locate the Partition Boot Sector:

- Error loading operating system.
- Missing operating system.

If you create your system and boot partitions in Windows NT Setup, you do not have to concern yourself with these details, because Setup will not create a partition that cannot be used to start Windows NT.

When Windows NT has completed startup, it does not use the values in the Starting and Ending Head, Sector, and Cylinder fields of the Partition Table. Instead, it uses the Relative Sectors and Number Of Sectors fields. These fields provide a full 32 bits to represent sectors, which results in volumes of up to 2^{32} sectors.

With a standard sector size of 512 bytes, the 32-bit fields used for the Relative Sectors and Number of Sectors result in a maximum possible volume size of:

512 bytes x 4,294,967,296 = 2,199,023,255,552 bytes, or 2 TB.

When creating partitions or logical drives on a disk, Windows NT writes the correct values to the Partition Table fields whenever possible. When the Ending Cylinder field for an entry in the Partition Table goes beyond cylinder 1023, Windows NT writes the maximum permitted values to these fields in the Partition Table. This prevents the system BIOS from calculating the Starting and Ending addresses based on erroneous data.

There are several Knowledge Base articles that discuss using large disks. Knowledge Base articles are included on the *Windows NT Workstation Resource Kit* CD.

SCSI Hard Disks

If your SCSI controller can be configured to perform translation, you can create a boot partition or system partition that is within the first 1 or 4 GB of the disk, depending upon the translation used by the controller. To create the largest possible system and boot partitions, enable translation and recreate the partitions on the disk. If translation was not already enabled, you will need to low-level format the hard disk before recreating the partitions. Check with your hardware manufacturer for specific advice and details.

Once Windows NT has been initialized, it uses its SCSI disk device drivers to directly interact with the disk without using the BIOS INT 13 interface. Therefore, the Starting and Ending Head, Sector, and Cylinder fields are not important after the computer has completed startup.

IDE and EIDE Hard Disks

The system and boot partitions on IDE hard disks are also limited to 1024 cylinders if the controller does not translate the disk address. Secondary disks that do not contain the system or boot partition might not be limited to 1024 cylinders, depending on the translation scheme used by the controller and disk.

IDE disks use a different data structure for representing the number of cylinders, number of heads, and number of sectors per track than the Partition Table and BIOS INT 13 interface. According to the IDE specifications, the maximum number of cylinders is 65536, the maximum number of heads is 16, and the maximum number of sectors per track is 255. The maximum size is 136.9 GB. Because the BIOS/IDE interface has been constrained to use the lowest common denominator, the result is a limit of about 504 MB for an IDE disk on an Intel-based ISA bus computer.

There are new controllers and disk device drivers that use an Enhanced Disk Parameter Table to translate between the logical sector layout internal to the IDE disk and the logical sector layout addressable by the BIOS INT 13 interface. These disk device drivers and devices can support larger disks. These disks and controllers are referred to as enhanced IDE, or EIDE, devices.

ESDI Hard Disks

ESDI disks are an older type that came before the IDE disks.

ESDI use the CHS (cylinder, head, sector) addressing and has a 1024 cylinder limitation. Some controller cards get around this limitation by implementing a translation scheme in the onboard controller BIOS.

The translation is totally transparent to Windows NT, and the standard disk device driver works without any change.

ESDI disks are capable of being low-level formatted with various values of sector per track, such as 53 or 63. Here are two examples:

```
1024 cylinders x 15 heads x 53 sectors per track x 512 bytes per sector
= 398 MB

1024 cylinders x 15 heads x 63 sectors per track x 512 bytes per sector
= 472 MB
```

Thus, using 63 sectors per track yields 74 MB more space. Windows NT is compatible with either geometry, and, depending on the disk or controller, can access cylinders beyond 1023. You can use Windows NT to create and format the disk space beyond cylinder 1023, but it cannot be accessed by MS-DOS. However, some controllers can remap the remaining cylinders beyond 1023 so that either MS-DOS or Windows NT can use the entire capacity. For example:

```
1632 cylinders x 15 heads x 53 sectors per track x 512 bytes per sector
= 634 MB
```

Microsoft has tested the ESDI controllers described in the following table.

Table 17.8 Using More Than 1024 Cylinders on ESDI Controllers

Controller	Achieving Maximum Capacity
Data Technology Corp. (DTC) Model 6282-24	The maximum MS-DOS geometry is 63 sectors per track and 1024 cylinders. Windows NT can access the cylinders beyond 1023. Do not perform a low-level format on the disk using Head Mapping mode.
Data Technology Corp. (DTC) Model 6290-24	The maximum MS-DOS geometry is 63 sectors per track and 1024 cylinders. Because this controller card does not have an on-board BIOS, Windows NT cannot access the cylinders beyond 1023.
Data Technology Corp. (DTC) Model 6290 SEZ (Dual SCSI/ESDI Controller)	The maximum MS-DOS geometry is 63 sectors per track and 1024 cylinders. Windows NT can access the cylinders beyond 1023.
Data Technology Corp. (DTC) Model 6295-24	The maximum MS-DOS geometry is 63 sectors per track and 1024 cylinders. This controller card does have an on-board BIOS, so Windows NT can access the cylinders beyond 1024. Do not perform a low-level format on the disk using Head Mapping mode.
Adaptec Model 2322D	Option 1. Disable disk translation and the on-board controller BIOS. In the CMOS, use a user-defined disk type with the actual disk parameters, such as Disk Type=48, Cylinders=1632, Heads=15, Sectors per Track=53. These parameters result in a 634 MB capacity. MS-DOS is limited to the first 1024 cylinders, which makes 398 MB available. Windows NT can access beyond cylinder 1023, yielding another 236 MB. Option 2. Both MS-DOS and Windows NT can access the entire disk. Set jumpers on the controller for Disk Splitting. Disable disk translation and the on-board controller BIOS. Set up the first physical disk in CMOS as Cylinders=1024, Heads=15, Sectors per Track=53. This gives a disk capacity of 398 MB. Set up the second disk (it appears as a physical disk) in the CMOS as Cylinders=606, Heads=15, sectors per track=53. This yields another 236 MB. Windows NT sees the disk as two physical disks.
UltraStor with PROM versions < nnnn-009	The maximum MS-DOS geometry is 63 sectors per track and 1024 cylinders. Windows NT can access the cylinders beyond 1023.
UltraStor with PROM versions >= nnnn-009	The maximum MS-DOS geometry is 63 sectors per track and 1024 cylinders. Both MS-DOS and Windows NT have access to the entire disk capacity.

Using Removable Disks and Floppy Disks

Most types of removable media can work with Window NT. Even though removable media are assigned a floppy disk icon in My Computer and Windows NT Explorer, they are not handled by the same part of the operating system. Floppy disks are handled by Floppy.sys. All SCSI-based removable media are handled through the normal SCSI disk device drivers. Most magneto-optical, Bernoulli, Syquest, and similar removable-media disks are treated like hard disks under Windows NT, and do not require special disk device drivers.

You can use My Computer or Windows NT Explorer to remove media while Windows NT is running. When pointing at the device, click the right mouse button. If the media can be ejected, the **Eject** command is available. If there is no **Eject** command in the menu, or the command is grayed, you cannot eject the media.

Note WORM and other types of "Write once" media are not supported in Windows NT.

There are several limitations that are unique to removable media in Windows NT.

- Removable media can only have a single primary partition. Extended partitions are not supported.
- Removable media devices cannot be used as part of a volume set or stripe set.
- It is not possible to format a floppy disk with the NTFS file system. The Windows NT operating system formats all floppy disks with the FAT file system, because the additional files required for the NTFS file system use too much space on a floppy disk.
- If you format a removable disk with the FAT file system, you can remove the disk while Windows NT is running.
- When you format any removable disk with the NTFS file system, or if the page file is located on removable media, you must force Windows NT to unmount the disk before you can remove it. This task is necessary because the removable disk could be used, and modified, on another system. If the NTFS disk was allowed to be remounted without being closed, it is possible that the NTFS information stored in memory would no longer be accurate.

  The steps that Windows NT needs to do to unmount a removable disk include:

  - Closing all open file handles, while ensuring that no new files are opened.
  - Flushing all data, including user data and file system metadata, to the disk.
  - Unregistering the disk, so that it is no longer possible to access it.

To unmount the disk, Windows NT has to insure that no program accesses the disk after NTFS has tried to flush the data, but before the disk is taken off line. Flushing works at shutdown, because shutdown terminates all processes that might want to write to the disk so there is nothing left running after the final flush.

CHAPTER 18

Choosing a File System

This chapter provides an overview of the capabilities and limitations of the FAT and NTFS file systems. Chapter 17, "Disk and File System Basics," describes the structure of FAT and NTFS volumes from the perspective of how each file system organizes the data on the disk. This chapter focuses on the user aspects of each file system.

You can use either or both of these file systems on a computer. Which one you choose for your computer, or for an individual volume on your computer, depends on such things as:

- How you expect to use the computer.
- The hardware platform.
- The size and number of hard disks.
- Security considerations.

NTFS provides several advantages when compared to FAT, which are described in this chapter. But, if you will be using another operating system in addition to Windows NT, you can access files on NTFS volumes only from Windows NT. You must use a file system other that NTFS for the system and boot partitions for the other operating systems.

For more information about file systems, especially NTFS, see *Inside the Windows NT File System*, by Helen Custer (Microsoft Press 1994, ISBN 1-55615-660-X), which documents the NTFS file system design.

Comparing FAT and NTFS File Systems

This section presents a high-level overview of why you might decide to use each of the file systems.

The FAT and NTFS file systems both support long filenames (up to 255 characters), so naming conventions do not matter when it comes to choosing the file system.

FAT File System Advantages

The FAT file system can be used with operating systems other than Windows NT, such as Windows 95, Windows for Workgroups, MS-DOS, and OS/2.

The FAT file system is best used on smaller volumes, because the FAT file system starts out with very little overhead. It works well up to about a 500 MB volume, but is very inefficient for volumes larger than 1 gigabyte (GB).

The FAT file system is a better choice than NTFS for volumes that are smaller than approximately 400-500 MB, because of the amount of disk space overhead involved in NTFS. This overhead is in the form of NTFS system files and the log file, which can use several percent of the total disk space on a small volume.

NTFS File System Advantages

The NTFS file system is best for use on volumes of about 400 MB or more, because performance does not degrade as much on larger NTFS volumes as compared to larger FAT volumes. However, if you want to use features that are available only on NTFS, such as file security or compression, you can use NTFS on smaller volumes.

There are several features that are provided only by the NTFS file system:

- You can assign permissions to individual files and folders, so you can specify who is allowed various kinds of access to a file or folder. The NTFS file system offers more permissions than the FAT file system, and you can set permissions for individual users or groups of users.
- The recoverability designed into the NTFS file system is such that a user should seldom have to run any disk repair program on an NTFS volume. In the event of a system crash, the NTFS file system uses its log file and checkpoint information to automatically restore the consistency of the file system.
- The B-tree structure of NTFS folders makes access to files on a large folder faster than access to files on a similar size folder on a FAT volume.
- You can compress individual files and folders on an NTFS volume. NTFS compression enables you to read and write the files while they are compressed, without having to first use a program to uncompress them.

There is more information about each of these features presented later in this chapter.

Which is Faster, FAT or NTFS?

There are no simple answers to this question.

For small folders, the FAT file system might provide faster access to files, because:

- The FAT structure is simpler.
- The FAT folder size is smaller for an equal number of files.
- FAT has no controls regarding whether a user can access a file or a folder Therefore, the system does not have to check permissions for an individual file or whether a specific user has access to the file or folder. However, Windows NT still has to determine if the file is read only, whether the file is on a FAT or NTFS volume, so the simpler controls for FAT volumes make little difference.

The NTFS file system uses a B-tree structure for all folders. This structure minimizes the number of disk accesses required to find a file, which makes access to the file faster than for a file on the FAT file system. In addition, if a folder is small enough to fit into the MFT record, you read the entire folder when you read its MFT record.

A FAT folder entry contains an index into the file allocation table, which identifies the cluster number for the first cluster of the folder. When you want to view a file, the FAT file system has to walk the folder structure to get to the file. For example, to start Disk Administrator, which is C:\Winnt40\System32\Windisk.exe, Windows NT finds the file on a FAT primary partition or logical drive by:

- Reading the root folder of the C drive and searching in it for Winnt40.
- Reading the starting cluster of Winnt40, and searching in that folder to find the System32 folder.
- Reading the starting cluster of System32, and searching in that folder to find Windisk.exe.
- Reading each of the clusters that contain parts of the file Windisk.exe.

In comparing performance on large folders having both long and short filenames, the speed of a FAT operation depends on the operation itself and the size of the folder. Creating files on a FAT folder might be faster. Opening a file might be faster on a FAT folder if the file is at the front of the folder. If the file does not exist, FAT has to search the entire folder to find this out. The search takes longer on FAT than on the B-tree structure used by the NTFS file system. Folder enumeration might be faster on a FAT folder. In mathematical terms, the average time to find a file on a FAT folder is a function of N/2, where N is the number of files. On an NTFS folder, the average time is a function of Log N. For small values of N, N/2 might actually be less than or equal to LogN. For larger values of N, LogN is less than N/2.

Several factors unique to the two file systems affect the speed with which Windows NT reads or writes a file.

- Fragmentation of the file — if a file is badly fragmented, NTFS usually requires fewer disk accesses than FAT to find all of the fragments.
- Cluster size — for both file systems, the default cluster size depends on the volume size, and is always a power of two. FAT addresses are 16 bits, and NTFS addresses are 64 bits. The default FAT cluster size is based upon the fact that the file allocation table can have at most 65,535 entries, so the cluster size is a direct function of the volume size divided by 65,535. Therefore, the default cluster size for FAT volume is almost always larger than the default cluster size for an NTFS volume of the same size. The larger cluster size for a FAT volume means that there might be less fragmentation in files on a FAT volume.
- Location of small files — with the NTFS file system, the entire file is contained within the MFT record. The maximum file size that fits in the MFT record depends upon the cluster size and the number of attributes for the file.

Maximum Sizes

The maximum file size and volume size for the FAT file system is 2^{32} bytes (4 GB). FAT can support a maximum of 65,535 clusters per volume.

The NTFS architecture is designed to use numbers up to 2^{64} bytes (16 exabytes, or 18,446,744,073,709,551,616 bytes). In theory, it is possible to have a volume 2^{64} bytes in size. Even if there were hardware available to supply a logical volume of that capacity, there are other limitations to the maximum size of a volume.

Partition Tables are limited by industry standards to 2^{32} sectors. (For more information about Partition Tables, see the sections titled "Partition Table" and "Using Hard Disks With More Than 1024 Cylinders (x86-based Computers)" in Chapter 17, "Disk and File System Basics."

The sector size is a function of hardware and industry standards, and is normally 512 bytes. While sector sizes might increase in the future, the current size puts a limit on a single volume of 2 terabytes (2^{32} * 512 bytes, or 2^{41} bytes).

Windows NT provides the capability to combine discontiguous disk areas when creating volume sets, and stripe sets, but these volumes have the same limitations. Even if there were physical disks with 2 terabyte (TB) capacity, they could not be combined to create larger volumes without increasing the physical sector size.

There is one case where you can combine disks that exceed the 2 TB limit. In Disk Administrator, there is an option to extend a volume set. You do this by selecting an existing primary partition, logical drive, or volume set that is already formatted as NTFS. You can then combine it with one or more areas of free space and select **Extend Volume Set** from the **Partition** menu. You end up with a larger NTFS volume set. However, if anything goes wrong with a volume set larger than 2 TB, you cannot just reformat it. You must again start with a smaller volume set (<=2 TB) and use the **Extend Volume Set** selection to extend the volume set to larger that 2 TB.

For the time being, 2 TB should be considered the practical limit for both physical and logical volumes using NTFS.

With the NTFS file system, you can have a maximum of 2^{32} clusters per file. This is an implementation limitation, not a file size restriction.

There is no specific limit to the number of files on an NTFS volume. However, you will not be able to create any new files when your volume is so full that Windows NT cannot allocate another entry in the MFT.

Which File System to Use on Which Volumes

This is a general recommendation for determining which file systems to use for which volumes:

- Use a small FAT primary partition (between 250 and 500 MB, depending on the total disk space and page file size) as the C drive. Use this partition for both your system and boot partition.
- Format the rest of your disk space as NTFS, and use the NTFS volumes for application programs and data. You might want to create more than one NTFS volume.

This arrangement gives you the following benefits:

- You have the recoverability of the NTFS file system for the most important information, your data. (You should always maintain your system and boot partitions by using backup tapes and creating an Emergency Repair Disk, as described in Chapter 20, "Preparing for and Performing Recovery").
- FAT is more efficient for smaller volumes and NTFS is more efficient for larger volumes.
- NTFS provides file and folder security for your application programs and data.
- If you have a startup failure on an x86-based computer, this means that you can start up the computer with an MS-DOS bootable floppy disk to troubleshoot and recover from the problem.

Here is some additional information to help you choose your file system(s):

- If the computer has only Windows NT installed, you can use just the NTFS file system.
- If you want to start another operating system on x86-based computers, such as Windows 95, Windows for Workgroups, MS-DOS, or OS/2, use the FAT file system for your system partition and the boot partition(s) for the other operating system(s). You can use the NTFS file system for your Windows NT boot partition and other volumes on the computer, as long as those volumes do not need to be accessed by an operating system other than Windows NT Workstation or Windows NT Server.

These additional guidelines might affect your decision as to which file system(s) to use on your computers:

- For an x86-based computer, when Windows NT starts up, it looks for certain files in the root folder of the hard disk that contains the system partition. This partition can be formatted with either the NTFS or FAT file system. This partition should be large enough to accommodate all the files you need to access under that file system.
- For a RISC-based computer, the system partition must be formatted with the FAT file system. You can use the NTFS file system on your boot partition, which needs to be large enough for all Windows NT system components. If you configure your partitions in this way, your system partition should be 5-10 MB, and your boot partition should be at least 150 MB, 250-500 MB to allow for growth.

- Because you must format your system partition with the FAT file system on RISC-based computers, you can use Disk Administrator to secure the system partition. This prevents anyone who does not have administrative privileges from accessing the system partition in spite of the fact that it is formatted as FAT. See online Help for the Disk Administrator for more information.

Note The system partition contains the Partition Boot Sector and other files needed to load the operating system, such as NTLDR (for x86-based computers) and OSLOADER (for RISC-based computers). The boot partition needs to include the folder with the operating system. The boot partition and the system partition can be a single partition with other folders in it.

Controlling Access to Files and Folders

On NTFS volumes, you can set permissions on files and folders that specify which groups and users have access to them, and what level of access is permitted. NTFS file and folder permissions apply both to users working at the computer where the file is stored and to users accessing the file over the network when the file is in a shared folder. With NTFS you can also set share permissions, which operate on shared folders in combination with file and folder permissions.

Note To preserve permissions when you copy or move files between NTFS folders, use the Scopy program on the *Windows NT Workstation Resource Kit* CD.

Although the NTFS file system provides access controls to individual files and folders, users can perform certain actions to files or folders even if permissions are set on a file or folder to prevent access to users.

For example, you have a folder (Dir1) containing a file (File1), and you grant Full Control to a user for the folder Dir1. If you specify that the user have No Access to File1, the user can still delete File1. This is because the user's Full Control rights in the folder allow the user to delete contents (or children) of the folder.

To prevent files from being deleted, you must set permissions on the file itself, and you must set permissions for the folder containing the file. Anyone who has Full Control in a folder can delete files from the folder.

Similarly, anyone who has List, Read, or greater permissions in a folder can view file properties on any file in the folder, even if they are prevented by file permissions from seeing the contents of the file.

With FAT volumes, you cannot set any permissions on the individual files and folders. The only security is share permissions that are set on the entire share, affect all files and folders on that share, and only function over the network. Once a folder is shared, you can protect the shared folder by specifying one set of share permissions that applies to users for all files and subfolders of the shared folder. Share permissions are set in very much the same way as file and folder permissions are set in NTFS. But because share permissions apply globally to all files and folders in the share, they are significantly less versatile than the file and folder permissions used for NTFS volumes.

Share permissions apply equally to NTFS and FAT volumes. They are enforced by Windows NT, not the individual file system.

POSIX Compliance

POSIX compliance permits UNIX programs to be ported to Windows NT. Windows NT is fully compliant with the Institute of Electrical and Electronic Engineers (IEEE) standard 1003.1, which is a standard for file naming and identification.

The following POSIX-compliant features are included in the NTFS file system:

- *Case-sensitive naming*. Under POSIX, README.TXT, Readme.txt, and readme.txt are all different files.
- *Hard links*. A file can be given more than one name. This allows two different filenames, which can be located in different folders, to point to the same data.
- *Additional time stamps*. These show when the file was last accessed or modified.

Caution You must use POSIX-based programs to manage filenames that differ only in case.

Using POSIX-based programs, you can create case-sensitive filenames, where two or more filenames can differ only in case (for example, annm.doc and AnnM.Doc).

While the Windows NT file systems support both case-preservation and case-sensitivity, you cannot use standard commands to manage filenames that differ only in case. (Standard commands include those used at the command-line—such as **copy**, **del**, and **move**—and their My Computer and Windows NT Explorer equivalents.) For example, if you type the following at the command prompt:

```
del AnnM.Doc
```

both annm.doc and AnnM.Doc are deleted.

For more information about POSIX, see Chapter 29, "POSIX Compatibility."

Features Unique to NTFS

This section describes NTFS functionality that is not supported by the FAT file system.

Multiple Data Streams

The NTFS file system supports multiple data streams. The stream name identifies a new data attribute on the file. Streams have separate opportunistic locks, file locks, allocation sizes, and file sizes, but sharing is per file.

The following is an example of an alternate stream:

```
myfile.dat:stream2
```

This feature permits related data to be managed as a single unit. For example, Macintosh computers use this type of structure to manage resource and data forks. Or, a company might create a program to keep a list of changes to the file in an alternate stream, thus keeping archive information with the current version of the file.

As another example, a library of files might exist where the files are defined as alternate streams, as in the following example:

```
library:file1
       :file2
       :file3
```

You could use a smart compiler to create a file structure like the following example:

```
program:source_file
       :doc_file
       :object_file
       :executable_file
```

You can use the Win32 API CreateFile to create an alternate data stream. Or, from the command prompt, you can enter commands such as:

```
echo text>program:source_file
more <program:source_file
```

Note Because the NTFS file system is not supported on floppy disks, when you copy an NTFS file to a floppy disk, data streams and other attributes not supported by the FAT file system are lost.

NTFS Compression

Windows NT supports compression on an individual file basis for NTFS volumes. Files that are compressed on an NTFS volume can be read and written without first being uncompressed by another program. Uncompression happens automatically during the read of the file. The file is compressed again when it is closed or explicitly saved.

Compressed files and folders have an attribute of C when viewed in My Computer or Windows NT Explorer. You can select an alternate color for compressed files and folders by:

- On the **View** menu, click **Options**.
- On the **View** tab, check **Display compressed files and folders with alternate color**.

Only the NTFS file system can read the compressed form of the data. When an program like Microsoft Word for Windows or an operating system command like **Copy** requests access to the file, the NTFS file system uncompresses the file before making it available. For example, if you copy a compressed file from a another Windows NT computer to a compressed folder on your hard disk, the file will be uncompressed, copied, and recompressed.

This compression algorithm is similar to that provided by the MS-DOS 6.0 DoubleSpace® and MS-DOS 6.22 DriveSpace® compression, with one important difference — the MS-DOS functionality compresses the entire primary partition or logical drive, while the NTFS file system enables the user to compress individual files and folders in the NTFS volume.

NTFS compression is not supported for cluster sizes larger than 4K, because

- Compression causes a performance degradation.
- The reason you use very large (>4K) clusters is to improve performance in some special cases.

Therefore, you should not use compression and large clusters at the same time. In other words, compression performs reasonably well on sizes up to 4K, but beyond that size, the savings in disk space is not worth the decrease in performance. When the cluster size is >4K on an NTFS volume, none of the NTFS compression functions are available.

For information about creating and formatting volumes, see "Which Programs to Use to Create and Format Volumes," in Chapter 17, "Disk and File System Basics."

Note Windows NT does not support DoubleSpace or DriveSpace compression.

Compressing and Uncompressing Folders and Files

Each file and folder on an NTFS volume has a compression state, which is either Compressed or Uncompressed. The compression state of a folder does not reflect the compression state of the files in that folder. For instance, a folder can have a compression state of Compressed, yet all of the files in that folder could be Uncompressed. Or some of the files in an Uncompressed folder could be Compressed.

You can set the compression state of folders, and compress or uncompress files by using My Computer, Windows NT Explorer, or a command-line program called Compact. When using My Computer or Windows NT Explorer, you can set the compression state of an NTFS folder without changing the compression state of existing files in that folder.

You can set My Computer and Windows NT Explorer to display compressed files and folders with a different color than uncompressed files and folders. On the **View** menu, click **Options**. On the **View** tab, check **Display compressed files and folders with alternate color**.

Note Compressing the page file does not accomplish much. Windows NT does not compress an open page file, so the user sees an error message box. When trying to compress a closed paging file, the file is compressed without warning (as with any other file). When you restart Windows NT, the page file automatically reverts to the uncompressed state. For information about the page file, look at topics for virtual or virtual memory in Windows NT Help.

Using My Computer or Windows NT Explorer

Each of these programs provide the same compression functionality on NTFS volumes. With My Computer or Windows NT Explorer, you can:

- Set the compression state of an NTFS folder to Compressed or Uncompressed.
- Specify whether to compress or uncompress all files in the folder when you change the state of the folder to Compressed or Uncompressed.
- Compress or uncompress individual files in the folder.

▶ **To set the compression state of the folder:**

1. Select the folder you want to compress or uncompress.
2. On the **File** menu, click **Properties** to display the **Properties** tab.
3. Select or clear the **Compressed** check box.

My Computer or Windows NT Explorer pop up a dialog box asking whether all the files and subfolders in the folder should be compressed or uncompressed. Existing files or subfolders in the NTFS folders retain their compression state unless you select **Yes** in this dialog box.

▶ **To work with individual files:**

1. Select the folder you want to compress or uncompress.
2. On the **File** menu, click **Properties** to display the **Properties** tab.
3. Select or clear the **Compressed** check box.

You can also use the **Properties** tab to view the compressed size and compression ratio of the selected file.

Using the Compact Program

The Compact program is the command line version of the compression functionality in My Computer or Windows NT Explorer. The Compact command displays and alters the compression of folders and files on NTFS volumes. It also displays the compression state of folders.

There are reasons why you would want to use this program instead of My Computer or Windows NT Explorer:

- You can use Compact in a batch script.
- If the system crashed when compression or uncompression was occurring, the file or folder is marked as Compressed or Uncompressed, even if the operation did not complete. You can use Compact to force the operation to complete.

Note Unlike My Computer or Windows NT Explorer, the Compact program does not prompt you on whether you want to compress or uncompress files and subfolders when you set the compression state of a folder. It automatically does the compression or uncompression of any files that are not already in the compression state you just set for the folder.

For more information about this program, type **compact /?** at the command prompt, or see "File System Utilities" in Chapter 22, "Disk, File System, and Backup Utilities."

Effects of Moving and Copying Files

When you replace an existing file in an NTFS folder, the file might retain its compression state regardless of the compression state of the folder and the compression state of the source file. Thus, if you copy a compressed NTFS file to a compressed NTFS folder, but it replaces an uncompressed file, the resulting file will probably be uncompressed.

For example, you have a file named Testthis in two folders, To and From. The To folder has a compression state of compressed, but the file To\Testthis is uncompressed. The From folder also has a compression state of compressed, and the file From\Testthis is compressed. When you use Windows NT Explorer to copy From\Testthis to To\Testthis, the file To\Testthis will be uncompressed.

Note The effects described in this section are generally true when using Microsoft programs. Third-party utilities might function differently.

Moving and Copying Files Within NTFS Volumes

On an NTFS volume, when you move a file or folder from one folder to another, the compression attribute, like any other attribute, is retained regardless of the compression of either the target or source folder. For example, if you move an uncompressed file to a compressed folder, the file remains uncompressed after the move.

However, if you copy a file from one folder to another, the compression attribute of the file is changed to that of the target folder. For example, if you copy a compressed file to an uncompressed folder, the file is automatically uncompressed when it is copied to the folder.

Moving and Copying Files Between NTFS Volumes

When you move or copy a file or folder from one NTFS volume to another NTFS volume, it inherits the compression attributes of the target folder.

Moving and Copying Files Between FAT and NTFS Volumes

Like files copied between NTFS folders, files moved or copied from a FAT folder to an NTFS folder always inherit the compression attribute of the target folder. Moving a file from a FAT folder to an NTFS folder causes a copy of the file, followed by a delete.

Since Windows NT supports compression only for NTFS files, any compressed NTFS files moved or copied to a FAT volume are automatically uncompressed. Similarly, compressed NTFS files copied or moved to a floppy disk are automatically uncompressed.

Adding Files to an Almost Full NTFS Volume

When adding files to an NTFS volume that is almost full, you can get unexpected error messages. The philosophy behind these errors is that the NTFS file system wants to make sure it has enough disk space to write the entire file if it cannot be compressed, regardless of the degree of compression in the file when it is opened. For instance, it is possible to get a read error when you are trying to open a compressed file.

If you copy files to a compressed NTFS folder that does not have enough room for all of the files in their uncompressed state, you might get an error that says "...there is not enough space on the disk" even though they will all fit when compressed. Because NTFS allocates space based upon the uncompressed size of the file, you can get this error even if the files are already compressed.

This situation occurs because compression is handled asynchronously, and Windows NT uses lazy write (see *Inside the Windows NT File System* for information about lazy writes). NTFS does not wait for the compression and write of one file to complete before it begins work on subsequent files, and the system does not get the unused space back from compression until after the buffer is compressed.

When you are running a program and save files to a compressed folder on a volume that is almost full, the save might or might not be successful — it depends on how much the file compresses, whether the beginning of the file compresses well, and numerous other factors.

If you cannot delete any files or do not have any files that you can compress, you can usually copy all of the files if you copy the largest and/or the ones that compress best first. You can also try copying them in smaller groups rather than all at one time.

Compression Algorithm

The book *Inside the Windows NT File System* provides a high-level description of NTFS compression.

Basically, the NTFS file system provides real-time access to a compressed file, uncompressing the file when it is opened and only compressing when it is closed.

When writing a compressed file, the system reserves disk space for the uncompressed size. The system gets back unused space as each individual compression buffer gets compressed.

Note Some programs do not allocate space before beginning the save, and only pop up an error message when they run out of disk space.

NTFS compression uses a 3-byte minimum search rather that the two-byte minimum used by DoubleSpace. This type of search enables a much faster compression and uncompression (roughly two times faster), while only sacrificing two percent compression for the average text file.

Each NTFS data stream contains information that indicates if any part of the stream is compressed. Individual compressed buffers are identified by "holes" following them in the information stored for that stream. If there is a hole, then the NTFS file system knows to uncompress the preceding buffer to fill the hole.

NTFS Compression Compared to Other Methods

Other compression utilities are available to compress files on computers running Windows NT. These utilities differ from NTFS compression in the following ways:

- They usually can be run only from the command line.
- Files cannot be opened when they are in a compressed state — the file must first be uncompressed by using the companion program to the one used to compress the file. When you close the file, it is saved in an uncompressed state, and you have to use a program to compress it.

The *Windows NT Workstation Resource Kit* includes a compress program and two expand utilities. The compress program can only be run from the command line. There are two versions of the expand program: one runs from the command line, and the other is a Windows NT–based program. For more information, see "File System Utilities" in Chapter 22, "Disk, File System, and Backup Utilities."

As described earlier, the DoubleSpace and DriveSpace compression features in MS-DOS cannot be used when running Windows NT.

NTFS Compression Issues

The only check for whether a user is allowed to change the compression state on a file is whether they have read or write permission. If they have write permission, they can change the compression state locally or across the network.

The two ways to measure the performance of NTFS data compression are size and speed.

You can tell how well compression works by comparing the uncompressed and compressed file and folder sizes. The earlier section of this chapter titled "Using My Computer or Windows NT Explorer" describes using the **Properties** tab to view the compressed size and compression ratio of a selected file. The section "File System Utilities" in Chapter 22, "Disk, File System, and Backup Utilities," describes using the DirUse program to see the compressed size of folders.

Using NTFS compression might cause performance degradation. One of the reasons this might happen is that, even when copied inside the same computer, a compressed NTFS file is uncompressed, copied, and then recompressed as a new file. Similarly, on network transfers, the file is uncompressed, which affects bandwidth as well as speed.

With data compression, the question is "How will it affect performance on a computer running Windows NT Workstation or Windows NT Server?"

The current implementation of NTFS compression is definitely oriented toward Windows NT Workstation. Compression on a computer running Windows NT Workstation does not seem to produce a substantial performance degradation. No one who has started using NTFS data compression at Microsoft has lodged any complaints about performance degradation.

A computer running Windows NT Server can be another story. Some normal production servers at Microsoft (source servers and binary release servers) have been converted to use NTFS data compression, without any complaints about performance. However, using a tough server benchmark, like NetBench, shows a performance degradation in excess of 50%. Read-only or read-mostly servers, or any lightly loaded servers, may not see a severe performance penalty. Heavily loaded servers with lots of write traffic are poor candidates for data compression, as shown by NetBench.

You really need to measure the effects of data compression in your own environment.

NTFS Recoverability

This section briefly discusses file system technology and describes how the NTFS file system implements data recoverability.

Until now, there were two types of file systems—careful-write file systems and lazy-write file systems. The NTFS file system introduces a third type—a recoverable file system.

A careful-write file system is designed around the idea that it is important to keep the volume structure consistent. Disk writes for each update are ordered so that if the system failed between two disk writes, the volume would be left in an understandable state, but with the possibility of an inconsistency. You seldom need to run utilities such as Chkdsk on a careful-write file system. An example of a careful-write file system is the FAT file system on MS-DOS.

The disadvantage of careful-write file systems is that serialized writes can be slow, because each disk write must be completed before the next disk write can begin.

A second kind of file system, such as the FAT file system on Windows NT and most UNIX file systems, is called a lazy-write file system. This type was designed to speed up disk accesses. A lazy-write file system uses an intelligent cache-management strategy and provides a way to recover data (such as the Chkdsk program) if there is an error when writing to the disk. All data are accessed via the file cache. While the user searches folders or reads files, data to be written to disk accumulates in the file cache. If the same data are modified several times, all those modifications are captured in the file cache. The result is that the file system needs to write to disk only once to update the data.

Chapter 5, "Windows NT 4.0 Workstation Architecture," and Chapter 15, "Detecting Cache Bottlenecks," contain more information about the file cache.

The disadvantage of a lazy-write file system is that, in the event of a disk crash, recovery is slower, because a program such as Chkdsk must then scan the disk to check that what should have been written to disk matches what was written.

NTFS is a third kind of file system—a recoverable file system. It combines the speed of a lazy-write file system with virtually instant recovery.

NTFS guarantees the consistency of the volume by using standard transaction logging and recovery techniques, although it does not guarantee the protection of user data. It includes a lazy-write technique plus a volume-recovery technique that takes typically only a second or two to insure the integrity of all NTFS volumes each time the computer is restarted. The transaction logging, which allows NTFS to recover quickly, requires a very small amount of overhead compared with careful-write file systems.

NTFS also uses a technique called bad-cluster remapping to minimize the effects of a bad sector on an NTFS volume. For more information, see the section "Cluster Remapping," presented later in this chapter.

It is possible for the Master Boot Record or Partition Boot Sector to be corrupted due to a disk error or system crash. When either of these sectors is corrupted, you might not be able to access any data on the volume. Recovery from errors with the Master Boot Record or the Partition Boot Sector are discussed in Chapter 20, "Preparing for and Performing Recovery."

Lazy Commit

Lazy commit is an important feature of NTFS. It allows NTFS to minimize the cost of logging to maintain high performance.

Lazy commit is similar to lazy write. Instead of using system resources to mark a transaction as successfully completed as soon as it is performed, the commitment information is cached and written to the log as a background process. If the power source or computer system should fail before the commit is logged, NTFS rechecks the transaction to see whether it was successfully completed. If NTFS cannot guarantee that the transaction was completed successfully, it backs out the transaction. No incomplete modifications to the volume are allowed.

Every few seconds, NTFS checks the cache to determine the status of the lazy writer and marks the status as a checkpoint in the log. If the system crashes subsequent to that checkpoint, the system backs up to that checkpoint for recovery. This method makes recovery faster by minimizing the number of queries that are required during recovery.

Transaction Logging and Recovery

NTFS considers an I/O operation to be a transaction, in the sense that it is an integral operation. Once a disk operation is started, all of its subcomponents must be completed. If the operation fails, there must be a way to rollback the I/O request to a previously known state.

To insure that an I/O operation can be completed or rolled back, NTFS uses the Log File Service to log all redo and undo information for the transaction. Redo is the information that NTFS uses to repeat the transaction, and undo enables NTFS to roll back the transaction that was incomplete or that had an error.

If a transaction completes successfully, the file update is committed. If the transaction is incomplete, NTFS ends or rolls back the transaction by following instructions in the undo information. If NTFS detects an error in the transaction, the transaction is also rolled back.

File system recovery is straightforward with NTFS. If the system crashes, NTFS performs three passes—an analysis pass, a redo pass, and an undo pass. During the analysis pass, NTFS determines exactly which clusters must now be updated, based on the information in the log file. The redo pass performs all transaction steps logged from the last checkpoint. The undo pass backs out any incomplete (uncommitted) transactions.

Effects of File and Disk Cache on Recoverability

The file cache is just an area of RAM that contains the data. When you write data to disk, Windows NT's lazy-write technique says that the data are written, when, in fact, they are still in RAM.

There can also be cache memory on the disk controller or on the disk itself. If you are running MS-DOS or Windows 3.1*x*, using the disk or controller caches can really help performance. The lazy-write technique in Windows NT improves performance to the point where you might not see much more improvement by using the cache on the disk or the controller.

This information should help you decide whether you want to enable the disk or controller cache:

- If disk performance is an issue, and specifically if the disk is being heavily written, turning on write caching is an option for improving performance, especially if it can be measured to improve the performance of the system.
- Controlling the write-back cache is a firmware function provided by the disk manufacturer. See the documentation supplied with the disk. You cannot configure the write cache from Windows NT.
- Write caching does not impact the reliability of the file system's own structures (metadata). NTFS instructs the disk device driver to insure that metadata writes get written through regardless of whether write caching is enabled or not. Non-metadata is written to the disk normally, so caching can occur for such data.
- Read caching in the disk has no impact on file system reliability.

Cluster Remapping

With transaction logging and recovery, NTFS guarantees that the volume structure will not be corrupted, so all files remain accessible after a system crash. However, user data can be lost because of a system crash or a bad sector.

The NTFS file system implements a recovery technique called cluster remapping. When Windows NT returns a bad sector error to the NTFS file system, NTFS dynamically replaces the cluster containing the bad sector and allocates a new cluster for the data. If the error occurred during a read, NTFS returns a read error to the calling program, and the data are lost. When the error occurs during a write, NTFS writes the data to the new cluster, and no data are lost.

NTFS puts the address of the cluster containing the bad sector in its Bad Cluster File so the bad sector will not be reused.

CHAPTER 19

What Happens When You Start Your Computer

This chapter describes what happens when you start a computer that has a Windows NT installed as one of the operating systems. In general, this chapter describes what happens at each step in the process when the computer successfully starts. Chapter 21, "Troubleshooting Startup and Disk Problems," discusses what you can do to isolate startup problems, and how to recover from them.

This chapter also describes dual-booting and triple-booting other operating systems, such as Windows 95 and MS-DOS. It provides information about the contents of the Boot.ini file on x86-based computers, and describes the firmware menus and how to use them on RISC-based computers.

Starting Windows NT

This section describes the steps involved in the successful startup of Windows NT, which are the following:

- Power On Self Test (POST) processing
- Initial startup process
- Boot loader process
- Selecting the operating system
- Detecting hardware
- Selecting a configuration
- Loading the Kernel
- Initializing the Kernel
- Logging on

The order and the processing is somewhat different, depending upon the hardware platform (x86-based computer or RISC-based computer).

The startup process begins when you:

- Power on the computer.
- Click **Shutdown and Restart** on the **Shutdown Computer** dialog box.
- Select **Shut Down** from the **Logon Information** dialog box.
- Select **Restart the computer** from the **Shut Down Windows** dialog box.

When you see the **Begin Logon** dialog box, with the text **Press Ctrl+Alt+Delete to log on**, your computer has completed the loading of Windows NT, and has completed much of the initialization. However, startup is complete only when a user can successfully log on at the **Begin Logon** dialog box.

Windows NT might not start up or operate correctly if any hardware components do not initialize correctly. Startup fails if any of the files required to start Windows NT are not present in the correct folder, or if one of the files has been corrupted. Table 19.1 describes the files that x86-based computers and RISC-based computers use to start Windows NT.

Table 19.1 Files required to start up Windows NT

x86-based file	Folder	RISC-based file	Folder
NTLDR	root of startup disk	Osloader.exe	\Os\<winnt>
Boot.ini	root of startup disk	no equivalent	
Bootsect.dos	root of startup disk	no equivalent	
Ntdetect.com	root of startup disk	no equivalent	
Ntbootdd.sys (SCSI only)	root of startup disk		
Ntoskrnl.exe	*%systemroot%*\ System32	Ntoskrnl.exe	*%systemroot%*\ System32
Hal.dll	*%systemroot%*\ System32	Hal.dll	\Os\<winnt>
no equivalent		*.pal files (Alpha-based computers)	\Os\<winnt>
SYSTEM key	*%systemroot%*\ System32\Config	SYSTEM key	*%systemroot%*\ System32\Config
device drivers	*%systemroot%*\ System32\Drivers	device drivers	*%systemroot%*\ System32\Drivers

Power On Self Test Processing

When you power on or restart a computer, it goes through its Power On Self Test (POST) routine, which determines:

- The amount of real memory.
- Whether the needed hardware components (such as the keyboard) are present.

Once the computer has run its POST routine, each adapter card with a BIOS runs its own POST routine. The computer and adapter card manufacturers determine what appears on the screen during the POST processing.

Initial Startup Process

The first sector on the hard disk is critical to the startup process. This sector contains the Master Boot Record and the Partition Table.

If the startup disk is a floppy disk, the first sector on the disk is the Partition Boot Sector.

For more information about the Master Boot Record, the system partition, and the Partition Boot Sector, see Chapter 17, "Disk and File System Basics."

Starting an x86-based Computer

After the POST on x86-based computers, the system BIOS attempts to locate the startup disk. If there is a floppy disk in drive A, the system BIOS uses drive A as the startup disk. If there is no disk in drive A, the system BIOS then checks the first hard disk that is powered up.

Note Some system BIOS versions enable the user to reconfigure the order in which it checks the floppy disks and hard disks for the startup disk.

When the hard disk is the startup disk, the system BIOS reads the Master Boot Record, and loads it into memory. The system BIOS then transfers execution to the Master Boot Record. The code in the Master Boot Record scans the Partition Table for the system partition. When the Master Boot Record finds the system partition, it loads sector 0 of the partition into memory, and executes it. Sector 0 on the system partition can be a utility or diagnostic program, or a Partition Boot Sector that contains startup code for an operating system. The Partition Boot Sector code starts the operating system in a manner defined by the operating system.

If there is no system partition on the first hard disk, the Master Boot Record displays errors such as the following:

- Invalid partition table
- Error loading operating system
- Missing operating system

The section "Setting the System Partition (x86-based Computers)," presented later in this chapter, describes identifying and changing the system partition.

The Master Boot Record is generally operating system independent. For example, on x86-based computers, you use the same Master Boot Record to start Windows NT, Windows 95, MS-DOS, and Windows 3.1x.

However, the Partition Boot Sector is dependent on both the operating system and the file system. On x86-based computers, the Windows NT Partition Boot Sector is responsible for:

- Understanding enough of the file system in use to find NTLDR in the root folder. On a FAT volume, the Partition Boot Sector is typically one sector long. On an NTFS volume, it can be up to 16 sectors long, with the extra sectors containing enough file system code to find NTLDR.
- Loading the boot loader, NTLDR, into memory.
- Starting execution of the boot loader.

On x86-based computers, the system partition must be on the first physical hard disk. The boot partition (the partition containing Windows NT operating system files) can be the same as the system partition, can be on a different partition on the same hard disk, or can even be on a different hard disk.

If the first hard disk does not contain the system partition that you want to use to start your computer, you need to power down the disk so that the system BIOS can access the correct disk.

For information about why you might want to use another hard disk as your startup disk, see Chapter 20, "Preparing for and Performing Recovery."

If there is a floppy disk in drive A, the system BIOS loads the first sector on the disk into memory. If the floppy is bootable, the first sector on the disk is the Partition Boot Sector. If the floppy disk is not bootable, you see errors such as:

```
Non-System disk or disk error
Replace and press any key when ready
```

Starting a RISC-based Computer

After a RISC-based computer completes the POST routine, the resident ROM firmware selects the startup disk by reading a boot precedence table from nonvolatile RAM (NVRAM). What the firmware does depends upon the platform (Alpha, PowerPC, or MIPS computer) and the information in the NVRAM. For example, to startup from the floppy disk, the NVRAM must define it as an alternate boot selection.

The NVRAM also defines the:

- Location for OSLOADER.
- Path to the boot partition.
- Folder that contains the operating system to start.

The system partition can be on any hard disk on RISC-based computers. You can use the **Boot selection** menu to set up or change the system partition. See "Manage Boot Selection Menu," presented later in this chapter, for more information about changing the firmware and NVRAM on RISC-based computers.

The system partition on a RISC-based computer must be formatted with the FAT file system. This is because the ARC standard requires that firmware have the following stub drivers built into it:

- SCSI miniport
- FAT file system

RISC-based computers go straight from the firmware into OSLOADER, which is the RISC-based computer's equivalent of NTLDR. Therefore, the firmware has to take over the functionality of the Partition Boot Sector, which means that the partition that has OSLOADER on it has to be FAT. Once OSLOADER loads, it has enough of the NTFS drivers built into it (just like NTLDR does) that it can access a %systemroot% folder on an NTFS partition.

Setting the System Partition (x86-based Computers)

On an x86-based computer, the system partition must contain the boot loader and other files that load the operating system. Windows NT Setup sets the partition into which it installs these files as the system partition, but there are situations in which you might want to use another.

When Windows NT is running, you can use Disk Administrator to set the system partition. You can also use the MS-DOS-based utility Fdisk to set the system partition. Only a primary partition can be used as a system partition. You cannot use a logical drive in the extended partition as a system partition. When you set a new system partition, both Disk Administrator and Fdisk clear the Boot Indicator field, if it was set for any other partition.

Note The Boot Indicator field in the Partition Table indicates whether a partition is the system partition.

▶ **To Use Disk Administrator to set the system partition**

1. Click a primary partition or logical drive on the hard disk.
2. Click the **Partition** menu. If the partition is the system partition, or is a logical drive in an extended partition, the **Mark Active** command is not available.
3. If the partition is not the system partition, and you want to set it as the system partition, click the **Mark Active** command. Disk Administrator displays the following message box:

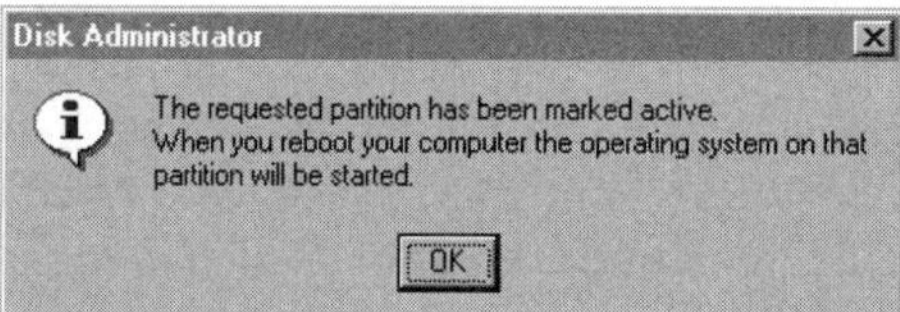

You cannot use Disk Administrator to set the system partition if you cannot start Windows NT. You can use the MS-DOS-based Fdisk utility to set the system partition, even if your entire disk is formatted with the NTFS file system.

▶ **To Use the Fdisk utility**

1. Start the computer under MS-DOS. If you do not have a system partition on your first hard disk, you must start MS-DOS from a floppy disk.
2. At the command prompt, type **fdisk**.
3. The **FDISK Options** menu has several choices. Type 2 to see the **Set Active Partition** screen. The system partition is identified by an **A** in the **Status** column.
4. Type the number of the partition that you want to set as the system partition. Press ESC to return to the **FDISK Options** menu, and press ESC again to exit Fdisk.

Boot Loader Process

The boot loader enables you to select the operating system that you want to start, and loads the operating system files from the boot partition. Boot loader processing is different on x86-based and RISC-based computers.

NTLDR Functions (x86-based Computer)

NTLDR controls the operating system selection process and hardware detection prior to the Windows NT Kernel initialization. NTLDR must be in the root folder of your startup disk, and also requires that the following files be located in the root folder:

- Ntdetect.com
- Boot.ini
- Bootsect.dos (if dual-booting)
- Ntbootdd.sys (if using the scsi() syntax in the Boot.ini file)

If the path name in the Boot.ini file for your system partition uses the scsi() syntax, the file Ntbootdd.sys must be in the root folder of the system partition. For more information about the scsi() syntax and Ntbootdd.sys, see Chapter 20, "Preparing for and Performing Recovery."

When NTLDR starts executing, it clears the screen and displays the boot loader message, which is:

```
OS Loader V4.0
```

NTLDR then performs the following steps:

- Switches the processor into the 32-bit flat memory mode. When x86-based computers first start, they are running in real mode, like an 8088 or 8086 CPU. Because NTLDR is mostly a 32-bit program, it must switch the processor to 32-bit flat memory mode before it can perform any other functions.
- Starts the appropriate minifile system. The code to access files on FAT and NTFS volumes is built into NTLDR. This code enables NTLDR to read, access, and copy files.
- Reads the Boot.ini file, and displays the operating system selections. This screen is referred to as the boot loader screen.
- Allows the user to select an operating system from the boot loader screen.
- If the user selects an operating system other than Windows NT, NTLDR loads Bootsect.dos and passes control to it. The other operating system then starts up as normal, because Bootsect.dos contains the Partition Boot Sector that was on the primary partition or logical drive before you installed Windows NT.
- If you select a Windows NT version, NTLDR executes Ntdetect.com to gather information about currently installed hardware.
- NTLDR presents you with the choice of starting the computer in the configuration in use when Windows NT was last shutdown (Default), or the Last Known Good configuration. You have this option only if you press the space bar when prompted, or you have more than one hardware profile. You have approximately five seconds to select this option.
- NTLDR loads and starts Ntoskrnl.exe. NTLDR passes the hardware information collected by Ntdetect.com to Ntoskrnl.exe.

OSLOADER Functions (RISC-based Computers)

On RISC-based computers, Osloader.exe performs all of the functions that are performed by the x86-based components NTLDR, Ntdetect.com, and Bootsect.dos.

The NVRAM contains environment variables that provide the functional equivalent of the Boot.ini file on x86-based computers.

Selecting the Operating System to Start

The boot loader displays the screen from which you select the operating system to start. The information on the screen is different for x86-based computers and RISC-based computers.

Boot Loader Screen (x86-based Computer)

NTLDR displays a menu from which you select the operating system to start. This screen is based upon the information in the Boot.ini file. The screen looks like this:

```
OS Loader V4.0

Please select the operating system to start:

     Windows NT Workstation Version 4.0
     Windows NT Workstation Version 4.0 (VGA mode)
     MS-DOS

Use ↑ and ↓ to move the highlight to your choice.
Press Enter to choose.

Seconds until highlighted choice will be started automatically: 29
```

If you do not select an entry before the counter reaches zero, NTLDR loads the operating system specified by the default parameter in the Boot.ini file. Windows NT Setup sets the default entry to the most recent copy of Windows NT that you installed. You can edit the Boot.ini file to change the default entry if you want to default to an operating system other than the most recently installed version of Windows NT.

For information about changing the Boot.ini file, see "Contents and Purpose of Boot.ini (x86-based Computers)," presented later in this chapter.

Boot Menu (RISC-based Computers)

The **Boot** menu contains the boot options. The first selection is always the default operating system, which is the most recently installed version of Windows NT unless you change the order of the boot selections.

To change the default operating system, or add or change boot selections , see the section titled "Manage Boot Selection Menu," presented later in this chapter.

This is a sample **Boot** menu from an Alpha-based computer:

```
ARC Multiboot Alpha AXP Version 3.5-11
Copyright (c) 1993 Microsoft Corporation
Copyright (c) 1993 Digital Equipment Corporation

Boot Menu:

    Boot Windows NT Workstation Version 4.0
    Boot an alternate operating system
    Run a program
    Supplementary menu. . .

Use the arrow keys to select, then press Enter.
Seconds until auto-boot. Select another option to override: 9
```

The first line on the **Boot** menu is highlighted. Pressing ENTER begins startup of the default operating system.

If you have included alternate boot selections in your NVRAM, you can select **Boot an alternate operating system**, which results in a screen like the following.

```
ARC Multiboot Alpha AXP Version 3.5-11
Copyright (c) 1993 Microsoft Corporation
Copyright (c) 1993 Digital Equipment Corporation

Boot Menu:

    Boot Windows NT Workstation 4.0 (Default)
    Boot Windows NT Workstation 3.51
    Boot SCO Unix v7.2

Use the arrow keys to select, then press Enter.
```

Detecting Hardware

On RISC-based computers, Osloader.exe obtains the hardware information from the firmware.

Ntdetect.com is the hardware detector for x86-based computers. It collects a list of currently installed components and returns this information to NTLDR.

On x86-based computers, Ntdetect.com executes after you select a Windows NT operating system on the boot loader screen (or the timer times out). When Ntdetect.com begins to execute, you see the following line on the screen:

```
NTDETECT V1.0 Checking Hardware . . .
```

Ntdetect.com detects the following components:

- Computer ID
- Bus/Adapter Type
- Video
- Keyboard
- Communication Ports
- Parallel Ports
- Floppy Disks
- Mouse/Pointing Device

Selecting a Configuration

When you have selected the version of Windows NT to start, and the boot loader has collected hardware information, you see the following screen:

```
OS Loader V4.0

Press spacebar now to invoke Hardware Profile/Last Known Good menu.
```

The boot loader waits a few seconds for you to press the SPACEBAR. If you do not press the SPACEBAR, and you have only one hardware profile, the boot loader loads Windows NT by using the Default control set. Otherwise, you see this screen:

```
    Hardware Profile/Configuration Recovery Menu

This menu allows you to select a hardware profile
to be used when Windows NT is started.

If your system is not starting correctly, then you may switch to a
previous system configuration, which may overcome startup problems.
IMPORTANT: System configuration changes made since the last successful
startup will be discarded.

    Original Configuration
    some other hardware profile

Use the up and down arrow keys to move the highlight
to the selection you want. Then press ENTER.
To switch to the Last Known Good Configuration, press 'L'.
To Exit this menu and restart your computer. press F3.

Seconds until highlighted choice will be started automatically: 5
```

The first hardware profile is highlighted. If you have created other hardware profiles, use the down arrow to select the one that you want to use. For more information about hardware profiles, use the **Find** tab in Windows NT Help and enter **profile**.

You can also select between the Last Known Good Configuration and the Default Configuration. Windows NT automatically uses the Default Configuration if you do not select the Last Known Good Configuration. When you use the Default Configuration, the boot loader uses the Registry information that Windows NT saved at the last shutdown.

If you switch to the Last Known Good Configuration by pressing L and ENTER, the boot loader uses the Registry information that it saved at the completion of the last successful startup to configure this startup.

See the sections "Loading the Kernel" and "Control Sets in the Registry," presented later in this chapter, for more information.

Loading the Kernel

When you press ENTER on the **Hardware Profile/Configuration Recovery** menu or the boot loader automatically makes the selection for you, the computer is in the Kernel load phase of Windows NT startup. You see several dots as the boot loader loads the Windows NT Kernel (Ntoskrnl.exe) and the hardware adaption layer (Hal.dll) into memory. It does not initialize these programs yet. Next, the boot loader loads the Registry key HKEY_LOCAL_MACHINE\SYSTEM from *%systemroot%*\System32\Config\System.

At this point, the boot loader creates the control set it will use to initialize the computer. The value in the HKEY_LOCAL_MACHINE\SYSTEM\Select subkey determines which control set in HKEY_LOCAL_MACHINE\SYSTEM to use. The loader uses the control set identified by the Default value, unless you are starting by using the Last Known Good Configuration. In this case, the value under LastKnownGood specifies the control set. Based on your selection and the value of the corresponding Select subkey, the loader determines which ControlSet00*x* to use. It sets the value of Current in the Select subkey to the number of the control set it will use.

See "Control Sets in the Registry," presented later in this chapter, for more information about the Select subkey and control sets.

At this time, the boot loader scans all of the services in the Registry subkey HKEY_LOCAL_MACHINE\SYSTEM\CurrentControlSet\Services for device drivers with a Start value of 0x0, which indicates that they should be loaded but not initialized. Device drivers with these values are typically low-level hardware device drivers, such as hard disk device drivers. The Group value for each device driver determines the order in which the boot loader loads them. The Registry subkey HKEY_LOCAL_MACHINE\SYSTEM\CurrentControlSet\Control\ServiceGroupOrder defines the loading order.

On x86-based computers, the loading of these device drivers into memory is done using BIOS INT 13 calls in real mode (or by Ntbootdd.sys).

On RISC-based computers, OSLOADER calls firmware primitives to find and load the critical files into memory.

The *Windows NT Workstation Resource Kit* CD contains more information about the Registry in the Help file Regentry.hlp. When you install the Resource Kit, double-clicking the Registry Help File icon opens the Regentry.hlp.

Initializing the Kernel

You know that the Kernel is initializing when the screen turns blue, and you see text similar to the following:

```
Microsoft (R) Windows NT (TM) Version 4.0 (Build 1345)
1 System Processor (16 MB Memory)
```

This means that Ntoskrnl.exe has successfully initialized and that control has passed to it.

The Kernel creates the HKEY_LOCAL_MACHINE\HARDWARE key by using the information that was passed from the boot loader. This key contains the hardware data that is computed at each system startup. The data include information about hardware components on the system board and about the interrupts hooked by specific hardware devices.

The Kernel creates the Clone control set by making a copy of the control set pointed to by the value of Current. The Clone control set is never modified, because it is intended to be an identical copy of the data used to configure the computer and should not reflect any changes made during the startup process.

Loading and Initializing Device Drivers

The Kernel now initializes the low-level device drivers that were loaded during the Kernel load phase. If an error occurs, the action taken is based on the HKEY_LOCAL_MACHINE\SYSTEM\CurrentControlSet\Services*DriverName*\ErrorControl value for the device driver that has a problem. See the section titled "ErrorControl Values," presented later in this chapter, for more information.

Ntoskrnl.exe now scans the Registry, this time for device drivers that have a HKEY_LOCAL_MACHINE\SYSTEM\CurrentControlSet\Services*DriverName*\Start value of 0x1. As in the Kernel load phase, the Group value for each device driver determines the order in which they are loaded. The Registry subkey HKEY_LOCAL_MACHINE\SYSTEM\CurrentControlSet\Control\ServiceGroupOrder defines the loading order.

Unlike the Kernel load phase, device drivers with a Start value of 0x01 are not loaded by using BIOS or firmware calls, but by using the device drivers loaded during the Kernel load phase and just initialized. The device drivers in this second group are initialized as soon as they are loaded. Error processing for the initialization of this group of device drivers is also based on the value of the ErrorControl data item for the device driver.

The section titled "Start Values," presented later in this chapter, contains more information about when components are loaded and started.

Loading Services

The Session Manager (Smss.exe) starts the higher-order subsystems and services for Windows NT. Information for the Session Manager is in HKEY_LOCAL_MACHINE\SYSTEM\CurrentControlSet\Control\Session Manager. Session Manager executes the instructions under the:

- BootExecute data item.
- Memory Management key.
- DOS Devices key.
- Subsystems key.

BootExecute Data Item

The BootExecute data item contains one or more commands that Session Manager runs before it loads any services. The default value for this item is Autochk.exe, which is the Windows NT version of Chkdsk.exe. The default setting is shown in this example:

```
BootExecute : REG_MULTI_SZ : autocheck autochk*
```

Session Manager can run more than one program. This example shows the item when the Convert utility will be run to convert the x volume from FAT to NTFS on the next system startup:

```
BootExecute : REG_MULTI_SZ : autocheck autochk* autoconv \DosDevices\x:
/FS:ntfs
```

After Session Manager runs the commands, the Kernel loads the other Registry keys from *%systemroot%*\System32\Config.

Memory Management Key

Next, the Session Manager creates the paging information required by the Virtual Memory Manager. The configuration information is located in these data items:

```
PagedPoolSize : REG_DWORD 0
NonPagedPoolSize : REG_DWORD 0
PagingFiles : REG_MULTI_SZ : c:\pagefile.sys 32
```

For information about the page file, use the **Index** tab in Windows NT Help, and enter virtual memory.

DOS Devices Key

Next, the Session Manager creates symbolic links. These links direct certain classes of commands to the correct component in the file system. The configuration information for these default items is located in:

```
PRN : REG_SZ : \DosDevices\LPT1
AUX : REG_SZ : \DosDevices\COM1
NUL : REG_SZ : \Device\Null
UNC : REG_SZ : \Device\Mup
PIPE : REG_SZ : \Device\NamedPipe
MAILSLOT : REG_SZ : \Device\MailSlot
```

SubSystems Key

Because of the messaging architecture of subsystems, the Windows subsystem (Win32) must be started. This subsystem controls all I/O and access to the video screen. The process name for this subsystem is CSRSS. The Windows subsystem starts the WinLogon process, which then starts several other vital subsystems.

The configuration information for required subsystems is defined by the value for Required in the Registry subkey HKEY_LOCAL_MACHINE\SYSTEM\CurrentControlSet\Control\Session Manager\SubSystems.

Logging on

The Windows subsystem automatically starts Winlogon.exe, and Winlogon.exe starts the Local Security Administration (Lsass.exe). You now see the **Begin Logon** dialog box, which contains the text **Press Ctrl+Alt+Delete to log on**. At this time, Windows NT might still be initializing network device drivers, but you can logon now.

Next the Service Controller (Screg.exe) executes, which makes a final pass through the Registry looking for services that are marked to load automatically. Auto-load services have a Start value of 0x2 in the subkeys HKEY_LOCAL_MACHINE\SYSTEM\CurrentControlSet\Services*DriverName*. The services that are loaded during this phase are loaded based on their dependencies, because they are loaded in parallel. The dependencies are described in the DependOnGroup and DependOnService entries in the subkey HKEY_LOCAL_MACHINE\SYSTEM\CurrentControlSet\Services*DriverName*.

Note Windows NT startup is not considered good until a user successfully logs on to the system. After a successful logon, the Clone control set is copied to the LastKnownGood control set.

Configuring the Computer for Dual-booting and Triple-booting

This section describes how to start up multiple operating systems and contains procedures for configuring your computer to do so.

Each operating system uses one or more file systems to organize data within volumes. Some operating systems can use the same file systems and some can not. For example, MS-DOS, Windows 95, and Windows NT can each use FAT volumes; Windows NT and Unix each use file systems that are unusable by the other. Operating systems that use the same file systems can share volumes, meaning that a user can access files on these volumes when running any of the operating systems.

Note Create an Emergency Repair Disk for your Windows NT installation by using the Repair Disk utility (Rdisk.exe) in the *%systemroot%*\System32 folder before you install other operating systems on the computer. You should also have a Windows NT startup floppy disk that you know works to start your computer. For more information about these disks, see Chapter 20, "Preparing for and Performing Recovery."

Using More Than One Windows Operating System

Windows 95, Windows 3.1, or Windows 3.11 can reside on the same computer as Windows NT. Windows NT can be installed in the same folder as Windows 3.1 or Windows 3.11 because Windows NT puts all of its important files in the system32 folder. Windows NT only uses the *%systemroot%* folder for legacy ini files that it maintains for 16-bit application programs and backwards compatibility. So, all of the Windows 3.1 or Windows 3.11 files will be either in the *%systemroot%* folder or in the *%systemroot%*\System folder. This organization allows the two operating systems to co-exist in the same folder.

You can also install Windows NT into a different folder. Windows 3.1 or Windows 3.11 still co-exist with Windows NT, but you do not get the option to migrate ini and program manager settings from Windows 3.1 or Windows 3.11.

If you install Windows 95 and Windows NT on the same disk, you must install them in different folders.

You can also install different versions of the Windows NT operating system on your hard disk, as long as you install them on different folders. If you are going to log into a domain, each instance of Windows NT must have a different computer name, which you specify during Windows NT Setup. You should ask your network administrator for the computer name to use before running Windows NT Setup.

When you install multiple Windows operating systems on the same computer, you need to install Windows-based application programs by using each operating system. For example, if you install both Windows 95 and Windows NT 4.0, you need to install application programs when you are running Windows NT 4.0 and when you are running Windows 95. If you have more than one version of Windows NT installed, you also need to install the application programs when running each version. To install Windows-based application programs when running Windows NT 4.0, you must log on with a user ID that has administrative privileges.

Dual-booting on x86-based Computers

When your system partition contains the Windows NT Partition Boot Sector, Windows NT supports dual-booting between one or more instances of Windows NT and one additional operating system. The additional operating systems that are currently supported are MS-DOS, Windows 95, and OS/2, versions 1.1 and 1.3. OS/2 versions 2.*x* might work, but are not supported.

You can also triple-boot Windows NT, Windows 95, and MS-DOS. You can install and start up other operating systems from your hard disk, but you need to change the system partition. For procedures to change the system partition, see "Setting the System Partition (x86-based Computers)," earlier in this chapter.

When you install a Windows NT operating system on an x86-based computer, Windows NT Setup copies the first sector of the system partition (the Partition Boot Sector) to a file named Bootsect.dos. It then replaces the Partition Boot Sector with its own Partition Boot Sector.

When you start your computer and the system partition contains the Windows NT Partition Boot Sector, the code in the Partition Boot Sector loads the Windows NT boot loader, NTLDR. The boot loader screen enables you to choose which Windows NT installation to start, or to start another operating system that is defined on the boot loader screen.

If you select an operating system other than Windows NT from the boot loader screen, NTLDR loads and starts the Bootsect.dos file. This functionality results in the other operating system starting as if NTLDR had not intervened. In the case of MS-DOS, the Bootsect.dos code looks for IO.sys; in the case of OS/2, the Bootsect.dos code looks for Os2ldr.exe.

Configuring for Windows NT and MS-DOS

You can dual-boot between Windows NT and MS-DOS on an x86-based computer.

Configuring your computer is easier if you install MS-DOS before you install Windows NT. If you decide to install MS-DOS after you have installed Windows NT, MS-DOS overwrites the Windows NT information in the Partition Boot Sector with its own information. You should have a current Emergency Repair Disk for the computer on which you are installing MS-DOS.

If you have already installed Windows NT and want to install MS-DOS, use one of the following procedures. After you install MS-DOS, you will need to replace the MS-DOS Partition Boot Sector with the Windows NT Partition Boot Sector.

▶ **To Install MS-DOS from floppy disks**

1. Boot from the A drive. The MS-DOS Setup program executes. Install MS-DOS following the instructions in the program.
2. When MS-DOS Setup completes, remove the floppy disk from the A drive.
3. Restore the Windows NT Partition Boot Sector by using the procedure described later in this section.
4. When you restart after replacing the Partition Boot Sector, you have a dual-boot computer.

▶ To Install MS-DOS from the network

1. Install MS-DOS from the network by executing Setup.exe.
2. When MS-DOS Setup completes, restore the Windows NT Partition Boot Sector by using the procedure described later in this section.
3. When you restart after the replacing the Partition Boot Sector, you have a dual-boot computer.

After you install MS-DOS, you need to replace the MS-DOS Partition Boot Sector with the Windows NT one. To be able to dual-boot MS-DOS, you also need to create the file Bootsect.dos. The next procedure does both of these things.

▶ To Restore the Windows NT Partition Boot Sector

1. Start up the computer from the Windows NT Setup disk 1. Follow the instructions to insert disk 2. When Windows NT Setup asks what you want to do, select the option to Repair by pressing the R key. Windows NT Setup displays the following options:

   ```
   [X]  Inspect registry files
   [X]  Inspect startup environment
   [X]  Verify Windows NT system files
   [X]  Inspect boot sector
   Continue (perform selected tasks)
   ```

2. Clear all selections except the last one, **Inspect boot sector**. Select **Continue (perform selected tasks)** and press ENTER.
3. Insert Setup Disk 3 when prompted.
4. You are prompted for the Emergency Repair Disk. Setup displays the following messages after it has finished processing the Emergency Repair Disk:

   ```
   Setup has completed repairs.
   If there is a floppy disk inserted in drive A:, remove it.
   Press ENTER to restart your computer.
   ```

When you restart the computer, you can select a Windows NT installation or MS-DOS from boot loader screen.

After you have installed MS-DOS and replaced the Partition Boot Sector, it is a good idea to make a MS-DOS bootable floppy disk. This floppy disk should include the MS-DOS files, as well as the Master Boot Record and Partition Boot Sector for each boot partition. See "MS-DOS Bootable Floppy Disk (x86-based Computers)" in Chapter 20, "Preparing for and Performing Recovery," for information about creating this disk.

Configuring for Windows NT and Windows 95

You can configure your computer to start either of these two operating systems. Currently, your installations are easier and less error-prone if you install Windows 95 first and then install Windows NT. This order is recommended because sometimes Windows 95 replaces a Windows NT Partition Boot Sector with its own Partition Boot Sector. A Windows 95 Partition Boot Sector causes a problem for NTFS volumes, because the Windows 95 Partition Boot Sector is for a FAT partition. Windows NT can no longer access the NTFS volume. If you install Windows 95 first, use the installation procedures provided with the Windows 95 CD-ROM.

If you want to be able to triple-boot Windows 95, Windows NT, and MS-DOS, you should install MS-DOS first, as described in "Configuring for Windows NT, Windows 95, and MS-DOS," presented later in this chapter.

If you have Windows NT installed, and want to be able to install and dual-boot Windows 95, you must configure Windows NT to dual-boot with MS-DOS. See "Configuring for Windows NT and MS-DOS," presented earlier in this chapter, for the procedures to install MS-DOS if you do not already have it installed. Then use the procedures described in "Configuring for Windows NT, Windows 95, and MS-DOS," presented later in this chapter.

Configuring for Windows NT, Windows 95, and MS-DOS

On an x86-based computer, you can configure your computer to triple-boot one of these three operating systems. You should install them in the following order:

- MS-DOS
- Windows 95
- Windows NT

Install each of these operating systems using their standard installation procedure. To start Windows NT, select the instance to start on the boot loader screen. You can also select Windows 95 from the boot loader screen.

To start MS-DOS, first select Windows 95 from the boot loader screen. Select ENTER on the screen, and press either the F4 or the F8 key. When you press F8, Windows 95 displays its **Startup** menu. **Select Previous version of MS-DOS** to start MS-DOS. Using the F4 key bypasses the Windows 95 **Startup** menu and starts MS-DOS directly.

Another way to be able to start all three of these operating systems is to configure your computer for a dual-boot of Windows NT and Windows 95, and start MS-DOS from an MS-DOS bootable floppy disk.

If you install Windows 95 in an existing Windows folder rather than doing a clean install, you need to edit Msdos.sys to enable Windows 95 to dual-boot MS-DOS. Do this by making the file visible, and then turning off the read only attribute. You can then change the file.

To Enable startup of MS-DOS **from Windows 95**

1. On the **View** menu of My Computer or Windows NT Explorer, click **Options**.
2. On the **Options** tab, select **Show all files**. Click **OK**.
3. Find Msdos.sys and click the filename.
4. On the **File** menu, click **Properties**.
5. In the **Attributes** box of the **General** tab, clear the **Read Only** and **Hidden** check boxes, and then click **OK**.
6. Using a text editor, such as Notepad, add the following line to the [Options] section of Msdos.sys:

   BootMulti=1

If you upgrade or reinstall Windows 95, Setup deletes any of these files that it finds in your MS-DOS folder and replaces them with the Windows 95 versions in the Windows95 folder and Windows95\Command folder:

Ansi.sys	Doskey.com	Keyb.com	Ramdrive.sys
Attrib.sys	Drvspace.bin	Keyboard.sys	Readme.txt
Chkdsk.exe	Drvspace.exe	Label.exe	Scandisk.exe
Choice.com	Drvspace.sys	Mem.exe	Scandisk.ini
Country.sys	Edit.com	Mode.com	Server.exe
Dblspace.bin	Edit.hlp	More.com	Share.exe
Dblspace.exe	Ega.cpi	Move.exe	Smartdrv.exe
Dblspace.sys	Emm386.exe	Mscdex.exe	Sort.exe
Debug.exe	Fc.exe	Msd.exe	Start.exe
Defrag.exe	Fdisk.exe	Networks.txt	Subst.exe
Deltree.exe	Find.exe	Nlsfunc.exe	Sys.com
Diskcopy.exe	Format.com	Os2.txt	Xcopy.exe
Display.sys	Help.com		

If you already have a dual-boot configuration of Windows NT and MS-DOS, you can install Windows 95 by using the following procedure. You should have a current Emergency Repair Disk for your Windows NT installation(s).

▶ **To Install Windows 95 on a Windows NT/**MS-DOS **dual-boot configuration**

1. Shut down Windows NT and restart your computer. Select **MS-DOS** from the boot loader screen.
2. Install Windows 95. Make sure you install Windows 95 to a separate folder, and not the Windows NT *%systemroot%* folder.

After you successfully install Windows 95 and restart the computer, the Windows NT boot loader screen should appear and you can choose between Windows NT and Windows 95. Windows 95 is the first entry on the screen. If you want to make Windows NT the default, see "Contents and Purpose of Boot.ini (x86-based Computers)," presented later in this chapter, for information about changing the order of the selections.

If the Windows NT boot loader screen does not appear, restore the Windows NT Partition Boot Sector by using the procedure in "Configuring for Windows NT and MS-DOS," presented earlier in this chapter.

Note If you do not install Windows 95 on the C drive, Windows 95 Setup creates a hidden, read only folder on your C drive that has the same name as the folder into which you are installing Windows 95.

Configuring for a Multi-boot With OS/2

If you want to install OS/2, this is the order in which you should install the operating systems:

- MS-DOS
- Windows 95
- Windows NT
- OS/2

This is the safest order in which to install all four operating systems. MS-DOS, Windows 95, and Windows NT all have to share a system partition (C:), but can be installed on their own individual partition. They can also be installed in the same partition, but Windows 95 and Windows NT must be installed in different folders. OS/2 requires its own primary partition on the first hard disk, and also requires a second, small primary partition for the BOOTLOADER.

If done correctly, the startup sequence will be:

1. The OS/2 bootloader loads, and you have the choice of starting from the OS/2 partition, or starting from the MS-DOS/Windows 95/Windows NT system partition.
2. When the Windows NT boot loader loads, you can select from one or more versions of Windows NT or Windows 95.
3. If you select Windows 95, you can press F8 and get the Windows 95 **Startup** menu, which allows you to start Windows 95, the Windows 95 command prompt only, or the previous version of MS-DOS.

The above sequence work if you install fewer than the four operating systems.

Dual-booting on RISC-based Computers

On RISC-based computers, you can install and dual-boot multiple versions of Windows NT, and you can also install and startup Unix. The Setup program for the operating system being installed updates the NVRAM with information for starting the operating system. The last operating system installed sets the NVRAM to have itself as the default operating system to start. See the section "Manage Boot Selection Menu," presented later in this chapter for information on changing the default operating system.

Control Sets in the Registry

A control set contains system configuration information, such as which device drivers and services to load and start. Control sets are stored in the Registry as subkeys of HKEY_LOCAL_MACHINE\SYSTEM. There can be several control sets, depending on how often you change system settings or have problems with the settings you choose. A typical installation of Windows NT contains these control set subkeys:

- Clone
- ControlSet001
- ControlSet002
- ControlSet003
- CurrentControlSet

The CurrentControlSet subkey is a pointer to one of the ControlSet00x keys. The Clone control set is a clone of the control set used to initialize the computer (either Default or LastKnownGood), and is created by the Kernel initialization process each time you start your computer. The Clone control set is not available after a user logs on.

In order to better understand how these control sets are used, you should know about the Registry subkey HKEY_LOCAL_MACHINE\SYSTEM\Select, which contains the following values:

- Current
- Default
- Failed
- LastKnownGood

Each of these values contain a REG_DWORD data type, which refers to a specific control set. For example, if the Current value is set to 0x1, then CurrentControlSet is pointing to ControlSet001. Similarly, if LastKnownGood is set to 0x2, then the Last Known Good control set is ControlSet002. The Default value is usually the same value as Current. Failed is the control set that was pointed to by Default when a user last started the computer by using the LastKnownGood control set.

The section titled "Selecting a Configuration," presented earlier in this chapter, describes initializing Windows NT by using either the Default configuration or the LastKnownGood configuration. When you select the Default configuration, the Kernel uses the value of Default to determine which control set to use.

There are only two times when the Kernel attempts to load the LastKnownGood configuration:

- The system is recovering from a severe or critical device driver loading error. For more information about this processing, see the section titled "ErrorControl Values," presented later in this chapter.
- You select the Last Known Good Configuration from the **Hardware Profile/Last Known Good** menu.

Starting by using the LastKnownGood control set provides a way to recover from problems such as:

- A device driver added to the system since the last startup is causing problems.
- User-modified value entries in the Registry prevent the computer from starting up.

The LastKnownGood option is useful only in cases of incorrect configurations. It does not solve problems caused by corrupted or missing device drivers or files.

Important If you select the Last Known Good Configuration, any configuration changes made during the last system boot are lost.

Once you have logged on, the CurrentControlSet is that one that is changed whenever you make changes to your configuration by using options in Control Panel. If you are manually editing a control set for some reason, the CurrentControlSet is the only one that you should change.

If you are not sure where to look under the CurrentControlSet for a particular key, you can use **Find Key** on the **View** menu of the Windows NT Registry Editor. Each control set contains two subkeys: Control and Services. Control contains miscellaneous system information, such as the size and location of the page file. Services contains device driver information, such as file system drivers, Kernel drivers, and status information for each.

Note There are two Registry Editor programs on the Windows NT Workstation product CD, Regedt32.exe and Regedit.exe. You can use either one to view the Registry.

Start Values

There is a Start value for each Services subkey in the Registry key HKEY_LOCAL_MACHINE\SYSTEM\<control set>\Services*DriverName*. It specifies the starting values for the device or service, as follows:

- 0x0 (Boot) = Loaded by boot loader (NTLDR or OSLOADER) before the Kernel is initialized. Disk device drivers are examples of device drivers that use this value.
- 0x1 (System) = Loaded by the I/O subsystem during Kernel initialization. The mouse device driver is an example of a device driver that uses this value.
- 0x2 (Auto load) = Loaded by Service Control Manager. To be loaded or started automatically for all startups, regardless of service type. The parallel port device driver is an example of a device driver with a value of auto load. The Alerter service is one of the services that uses this value.

- 0x3 (Load on demand) = Loaded by Service Control Manager only when explicitly instructed to do so. Available, regardless of type, but it is not be started until the user starts it (for example, by using the Devices option in Control Panel).
- 0x4 (Disabled) = Do not load. Windows NT sets device drivers to disabled when Service Control Manager should not load them, such as when the corresponding hardware is not installed. Having this value means that the device drivers are not loaded by Service Control Manager. File system drivers are the one exception to the Start value. They are loaded even if they have a start value of 4. If a device driver is accidentally disabled, reset this value by using the Services option in Control Panel.

Note You can view the Start value of device drivers by using the Devices option in Control Panel.

ErrorControl Values

These are the possible ErrorControl values in the Registry key HKEY_LOCAL_MACHINE\SYSTEM\<control set>\Services*DriverName*:

- Ignore (value 0x0) — If the device driver fails to load or initialize, startup continues with no warning message.
- Normal (value 0x1) — If the device driver or service fails to load or initialize, startup continues after displaying a warning message. Most device drivers and services have ErrorControl set to this value.
- Severe (value 0x2) — When the Kernel detects an error in this device driver or service, it switches to the LastKnownGood control set, and the startup process starts again. If the control set being used is already LastKnownGood, the error is ignored and processing continues.
- Critical (value 0x3) — The same procedure as Severe is used, with the exception that if the LastKnownGood control set is already being used, the startup process stops, and a failure error message is displayed.

Contents and Purpose of Boot.ini (x86-based Computers)

When you install Windows NT on an x86-based computer, Windows NT Setup puts the Boot.ini file at the root of the system partition. NTLDR uses information in the Boot.ini file to display the screen from which you select the operating system to start.

Here is a sample Boot.ini file:

```
[boot loader]
timeout=30
default=multi(0)disk(0)rdisk(0)partition(1)\WINNT
[operating systems]
multi(0)disk(0)rdisk(0)partition(1)\WINNT="Windows NT Workstation
Version 4.0"
multi(0)disk(0)rdisk(0)partition(1)\WINNT="Windows NT Workstation
Version 4.0 [VGA mode]" /basevideo /sos
C:\="Windows 95"
```

The Boot.ini file has two sections, [boot loader] and [operating system], which are described in the next two sections.

[boot loader] Section

This section contains the following information:

Parameter	Description
timeout	The number of seconds the user has to select an operating system from the boot loader screen before NTLDR loads the default operating system. If the value is 0, NTLDR immediately starts the default operating system without displaying the boot loader screen. You can also set this value to -1, in which case NTLDR waits forever for you to make a selection. You must edit the Boot.ini file to set the value to -1, because it is an illegal value for the System option in Control Panel.
default	The path to the default operating system.

[operating systems] Section

This section contains the list of available operating systems. Each entry includes the path to the boot partition for the operating system, the string to display in the boot loader screen, and optional parameters. There is an example of the use of this section of the Boot.ini file in the section titled "Boot Loader Screen (x86-based Computers)," presented earlier in this chapter.

The Boot.ini file supports starting of multiple versions of Windows NT operating systems, as well as starting one other operating system. The other operating systems that can be included in the Boot.ini file are Windows 95, MS-DOS, and OS/2. The section "Configuring the Computer for Dual-booting and Triple-booting," presented earlier in this chapter, contains more information about the other operating systems.

Boot.ini Switches

There are several switches that you can add to the end of the Windows NT entries in the [operating system] section of the Boot.ini file. They are not case sensitive. Chapter 21, "Troubleshooting Startup and Disk Problems," contains more information about many of these switches. For information about the debugger, see Chapter 39, "Windows NT Debugger."

Table 19.2 Boot.ini Switches

Switch	Description
/BASEVIDEO	The computer starts up using the standard VGA video driver. If you have installed a new video driver, but it is not working correctly, selecting the Windows NT entry with this switch enables you to start the computer so you can change to a different driver.
/BAUDRATE=nnnn	Specifies the baud rate to be used for debugging. If you do not set the baud rate, the default baud rate is 9600 if a modem is attached, and 19200 for a null-modem cable. This switch has a secondary effect of forcing the /DEBUG switch as well, whether or not use you use /DEBUG.
/CRASHDEBUG	The debugger is loaded when you start Windows NT, but remains inactive unless a Kernel error occurs. This mode is useful if you are experiencing random, unpredictable Kernel errors.
/DEBUG	The debugger is loaded when you start Windows NT, and can be activated at any time by a host debugger connected to the computer. This is the mode to use when you are debugging problems that are regularly reproducible.
/DEBUGPORT= com*x*	Specifies the com port to use for debugging, where *x* is the communications port that you want to use. Like /BAUDRATE, this switch will also force the /DEBUG mode.

Table 19.2 Boot.ini Switches *(Continued)*

Switch	Description
/MAXMEM:n	Specifies the maximum amount of RAM that Windows NT can use. This switch is useful if you suspect a memory chip is bad. See Chapter 21, "Troubleshooting Startup Disk Problems," for more information.
/NODEBUG	No debugging information is being used.
/NOSERIALMICE= [COM*x* | COM*x*,*y*,*z*...]	Disables serial mouse detection of the specified COM port(s). Use this switch if you have a component other than a mouse attached to a serial port during the startup sequence. If you use /NOSERIALMICE without specifying a COM port, serial mouse detection is disabled on all COM ports. See Chapter 20, "Preparing for and Performing Recovery," for more information.
/SOS	Displays the device driver names while they are being loaded. Use this switch if Windows NT will not start up and you think a device driver is missing. See Chapter 21, "Troubleshooting Startup Disk Problems," for more information.

Editing Boot.ini

When you install Windows NT, the Boot.ini file has the Read Only, System, and Hidden attributes set. You can edit the timeout and default parameters in the Boot.ini file by using the System option on Control Panel, regardless of the value of these attributes.

If you want to edit the Boot.ini file by using a text editor, you need to make the file visible before you can open it, and you need to turn off Read Only to be able to make changes to it. You can change the attributes by using My Computer, Windows NT Explorer, or the command prompt.

▶ **To change the attributes in My Computer or Windows NT Explorer**

1. On the **View** menu, click **Options**.
2. On the **Options** tab, select **Show all files**. Click **OK**.
3. Click the filename.
4. On the **File** menu, click **Properties**.
5. In the **Attributes** box of the **General** tab, clear the **Read Only**, **System**, and **Hidden** check boxes, and then click **OK**.

To change the attributes by using command prompt, enter:

```
attrib -s -h -r boot.ini
```

If you change the path to the Windows NT boot partition, make sure to edit both the default path and operating system path entries. If you change one but not the other, a new choice is added to the boot loader screen, with the default designator next to it.

Using a RISC-based Computer's Boot Menu

This section describes using the firmware menus on a RISC-based computer to change environment information in the NVRAM. There are three types of RISC-based computers: Alpha, MIPS, and PowerPC. The examples in this section are for an Alpha AXP–based computer, running firmware version 3.5-11. Menus for other versions of the firmware might be different. Menus and processing on MIPS-based computers and PPC-based computers are similar.

When you start an Alpha-based computer, you see the **Boot** menu, which looks like this:

```
ARC Multiboot Alpha AXP Version 3.5-11
Copyright (c) 1993 Microsoft Corporation
Copyright (c) 1993 Digital Equipment Corporation

Boot Menu:

    Boot Windows NT Workstation Version 4.0
    Boot an alternate operating system
    Run a program
    Supplementary menu. . .

Use the arrow keys to select, then press Enter.
```

The first two selections are described in the section titled "Boot Menu (RISC-based Computers)," presented earlier in this chapter. Information about those selections is not repeated here.

For more information about ARC path names, which are used in boot selections, see Chapter 20, "Preparing for and Performing Recovery."

Selecting Run a Program

When you select **Run a program**, you see the following screen:

```
ARC Multiboot Alpha AXP Version 3.5-11
Copyright (c) 1993 Microsoft Corporation
Copyright (c) 1993 Digital Equipment Corporation

    Program to run:
```

From this prompt, you can start any program that has been compiled for an Alpha-based computer. You must know the complete ARC path to the program, unless the NVRAM has the correct environment variables defined for devices. For example, if there are environment variables for the cd-rom drive (CD:) or the floppy disk (A:), you can use them instead.

For example, to start Windows NT Setup, where the CD is a default device on the computer, you can type the following:

```
Program to run: CD:\alpha\setupldr
```

When running a program stored on the hard disk, you must use the full ARC pathname and filename, such as the following:

```
Program to run: scsi(0)disk(0)rdisk()partition(1)\alpha\setupldr
```

If you try to use the MS-DOS syntax to run a program on the hard disk, you get an error message like the following:

```
Program to run:  C:\alpha\setupldr

Pathname is not defined
Press any key to continue...
```

Note The firmware routines can access only FAT partitions or CD-ROM drives. They cannot access NTFS partitions.

Running Arcinst

Arcinst.exe is an AXP native mode application program (requires no operating system) that performs the same functions as the MS-DOS-based utilities Fdisk and Format. You can use Arcinst to define and automatically format partitions. This application program is on the Windows NT product CD.

To start Arcinst, type in the following at the **Program to run** prompt:

```
Program to run:  cd:\alpha\arcinst
```

When the program starts, it displays the following menu:

```
Arc Installation Program Version 4.00
Copyright (c) 1995 Microsoft Corporation

     Configure Partitions
     Exit
```

Configure Partitions

If you select **Configure Partitions**, you see the following menu:

```
Arc Installation Program Version 4.00
Copyright (c) 1995 Microsoft Corporation

    Create Partition
    Delete Partition
    Make Existing Partition into System Partition
    Exit
```

Create Partition

Arcinst creates the first two partitions on a hard disk as physical partitions. The second partition is always an extended partition; any additional partitions are defined as logical drives within the extended partition. There are no user-defineable parameters for these options. Drive letters are not assigned, since the ARC specification for path names does not include them.

After creating any partition, the system automatically formats it as FAT. There is no option to skip formatting the new partition. This is a sample of the information you see when you select **Create Partition**:

```
Arc Installation Program Version 4.00
Copyright (c) 1995 Microsoft Corporation

Scsi bus 0, Identifier 3, Disk 0 (scsi(0)disk(3)rdisk(0))
Scsi bus 0, Identifier 0, Disk 0 (scsi(0)disk(0)rdisk(0))
```

When you select one of the disks, you see the following screen:

```
Enter size in MB (1-191):
```

The available size is the unpartitioned disk space remaining on the disk. When you enter the size, you see messages such as the following:

```
Partition successfully created.
Press any key to continue....

Formatting scsi(0)disk(0)rdisk(0)partition(3)
99 percent formatted
```

When formatting completes, you automatically return to the **Configure Partitions** menu.

If the disk that you select has no unpartitioned area, you see the following message:

```
Disk is full
Press any key to continue...
```

Delete Partition

You can delete any partition or logical drive, in any order. When you delete a volume, any data on that volume is no longer accessible. When you select **Delete Partition**, you see information such as this:

```
Arc Installation Program Version 4.00
Copyright (c) 1995 Microsoft Corporation

Scsi bus 0, Identifier 3, Disk 0 (scsi(0)disk(3)rdisk(0))
Scsi bus 0, Identifier 0, Disk 0 (scsi(0)disk(0)rdisk(0))
```

When you select one of the disks, you see a screen similar to this one:

```
1010 MB Fat Partition
```

Select a volume to delete. If the partition is the system partition, you get an error message like:

```
The selected partition is (or contains) a system partition
Are you sure you want to delete it (y/n)?
```

If the partition is not the system partition, you see a screen similar to:

```
509 MB Extended Partition also results in the deletion of:
    509 MB HPFS/NTFS Logical Volume
Are you sure you want to delete it (y/n)?
```

When you enter **y** to either of these preceding questions, you see the following screen:

```
Partition deleted successfully.
Press any key to continue.
```

When you press a key, you return to the **Configure Partitions** menu.

Make Existing Partition into System Partition

When you select this option, you see a screen similar to the following:

```
Arc Installation Program Version 4.00
Copyright (c) 1995 Microsoft Corporation

Scsi bus 0, Identifier 3, Disk 0 (scsi(0)disk(3)rdisk(0))
Scsi bus 0, Identifier 0, Disk 0 (scsi(0)disk(0)rdisk(0))
```

If the partition you select is already the system partition, you see the following screen:

```
Partition is already a system partition.
Press any key to continue...
```

Otherwise, you see information like the following:

```
      Partition 2 (200 MB HPFS/NTFS)
```

The system partition must be formatted as FAT. Selecting an NTFS partition results in this message:

```
System partitions must be formatted with the FAT filesystem.
Do you wish to format the chosen partition  (y/n)?
```

When you enter **y**, this message is displayed:

```
All existing data will be lost.  Are you sure (y/n)?
```

Entering **y** causes the partition to be formatted as FAT.

```
99% complete
Partition added successfully.
Press any key to continue...
```

You automatically return to the **Configure Partitions** menu.

Running the Repair Procedure

If your system files or Partition Boot Sector are corrupt, and you are unable to restart by using the Last Known Good Configuration, you can use the Repair process in Windows NT Setup to repair your system.

To repair a Windows NT installation, you need the configuration information on *%systemroot%*\Repair or the Emergency Repair Disk that you created when you installed Windows NT (or you created later by using the Repair Disk utility).

To start the Windows NT Setup program from the CD-ROM, select **Run a program** from the **Boot** menu and enter the following at the prompt:

```
Program to run: CD:\alpha\setupldr
```

Once **setupldr** starts, the procedures are the same as for an x86-based computer.

Selecting Supplementary Menu

When you select the **Supplementary menu** option from the **Boot** menu, the firmware displays this screen:

```
ARC Multiboot Alpha AXP Version 3.5-11
Copyright (c) 1993 Microsoft Corporation
Copyright (c) Digital Equipment Corporation

Supplementary menu:

    Install new firmware
    Install Windows NT from CD-ROM
    Set up the system...
    Display hardware configuration
    Boot menu...

Use the arrow keys to select, then press Enter.
```

Install New Firmware

Installing new firmware results in the following:

- All NVRAM settings, such as boot paths, definitions for CD: and A:, environment variables, and the default configuration, are deleted.
- EISA configuration information is cleared.

If you want to save the information that is currently in the NVRAM, you can use the **saveenv** and **restenv** utilities, which are available from Digital Equipment Corporation. Run these utilities from the **Run a program** menu to save your current NVRAM settings to a file on the disk, and then restore them.

▶ **To upgrade the firmware without wiping out all settings.**

1. Put the disk with the utilities in the floppy drive.
2. On the **Boot** menu, click **Run a program**, and enter **a:\saveenv**. You see the following message:

```
This saves the environment variables into the floppy
file fwenv.sav. Continue (Y,N)?
```

   When you click **Y**, you see these messages:

```
Opening eisa()disk()fdisk()fwenv.sav.
Saving the firmware environment variables.
Environment successfully saved! To restore them,
run the Restenv program.

Press any key to continue.
```

3. On the **Supplementary** menu, click **Install new firmware**, and follow these steps:

```
Searching floppy and CD-ROM for the firmware update tool...
```

   If the tool cannot be found or is corrupt, this message is displayed:

```
Error:  Bad device name/number or partition number, press any key to
continue
```

   If the firmware files are found, messages like these are displayed:

```
DECpc AXP 150 Flashfile Update Utility, revision 2.09
Copyright (c)1992, 1993 Microsoft Corporation
Copyright (c)1993 Digital Equipment Corporation

This will update your machine's firmware.

Press the "Y" key to continue with the update.
Hit any other key to abort.
```

   After selecting **Y**, you have choices such as the following:

```
Select location of update file.

Use the arrow keys to select, then press Enter.
Hit Escape to abort.

    Floppy #0\jensfw.bin
    CD-ROM\jensfw.bin
    Other location
    Exit
```

Select the floppy disk or CD-ROM, depending on the location of the firmware files. When you press ENTER, you should see:

```
Loading the update file...
Reading the update file...
```

followed by:

```
The update file is good!
The name of the firmware update is...:
```

The name depends on the firmware version.

```
Press the "Y" key to continue the update.
Hit any other key to abort.
```

When you select **Y**, you see:

```
Are you *really* sure?
Press the "Y" key to continue the update.
Hit any other key to abort.
```

When you select **Y** again, you should see information similar to:

```
Firmware ROM type:  0.
Updating these blocks:
   7 8 9 10 11

The update has succeeded.  Power-cycle the machine to see the
changes.

Press any key to continue...
```

The blocks that are updated depend on the firmware version being updated.

4. Do not restart the computer yet. On the **Supplementary** menu, click **Run a program**, and enter **a:\restenv**. You see the following messages:

```
Restenv version 4.31

This restores the environment variables from floppy
file fwenv.sav. Continue(Y,N)?
```

Enter **Y**, and you see the following messages:

```
Opening eisa()disk()fdisk()fwenv.sav.
Checking fwenv.sav type bye.
Reading the environment variables.

The environment variables have been restored
Power-cycle the machine after you return to the firmware

Press any key to continue
```

Press any key.

5. Restart your computer. You will get some error messages about the EISA configuration being out of date, which you can ignore for now.
6. Put the floppy disk with EISA configuration utility in the floppy drive.
7. On the **Supplementary** menu, click **Set up the system**.
8. On the **Setup** menu, click **Run EISA configuration utility from floppy**. All you should need to do when running this utility is press ENTER until you return to the **Setup** menu. The **Setup** menu is described later in this chapter.
9. On the **Setup** menu, click **Supplementary menu, and save changes**.
10. Restart the computer again. You should now be running with the new firmware.

Install Windows NT from CD-ROM

When you select **Install Windows NT from CD-ROM**, the firmware displays the message:

```
Loading Microsoft Windows NT Setup. . .
```

The next screen is the standard Windows NT Setup screen. The rest of the installation is identical to installing Windows NT on an X86-based computer.

You can also run the Repair procedure by selecting this option. When Windows NT Setup displays the **Welcome to Setup** screen, select R for repair. The rest of the repair procedure is identical to what happens on an x86-based computer.

Set Up the System (Setup Menu)

Selecting **Set up the system** takes you to the **Setup** menu, which enables you to change the configuration options for all operating systems, and the computer configurations options stored in the NVRAM. You can change the following types of information:

- Environment variables.
- Boot selection menus.

The following example shows the **Setup** menu. If you make changes to the computer configuration by making selections from the **Setup** menu, the additional selection:

```
Supplementary Menu, and save changes...
```

appears as the last line of the menu. Changes are not actually saved to the NVRAM until you make this selection. This example includes the additional line.

```
ARC Multiboot Alpha AXP Version 3.5-11      Tuesday, 2-20-96 2:53:19 PM
Copyright (c) 1993 Microsoft Corporation
Copyright (c) 1993 Digital Equipment Corporation

Setup menu:

    Set system time
    Set default environment variables
    Set default configuration
    Manage boot selection menu...
    Setup autoboot
    Machine specific setup...

    Edit environment variables
    Reset system to factory defaults

    Help
    Supplementary menu, and do not save changes...
    Supplementary menu, and save changes...

Use the arrow keys to select, then press Enter.
```

If any of the changes that you make by using the **Setup** menu result in inconsistent information in the NVRAM, the selection with the error is in yellow text. And the following message is displayed at the bottom of the screen, also in yellow text:

```
The yellow items should be done before booting Windows NT
```

Note The **Setup** menu on other versions of the Alpha-based computer firmware might have different entries. For example, you might have the entry **Run EISA configuration utility from floppy**.

Set System Time

To set the system date and time, select **Set system time** from the **Setup** menu. You can enter the following information:

```
                                        Tuesday, 2-20-1996  3:03:48 PM

Enter the new date (mm-dd-yy) :
Enter time (hh:mm:ss) :
```

When setting the time, you must enter the time in 24-hour format. For example, the time listed above should be entered as 15:03:48.

You automatically return to the **Setup** menu when you enter both fields.

Set Default Environment Variables

To set the defaults for booting, select **Set default environment variables** on the **Setup** menu. This example shows the user selecting the **SCSI Hard Disk** as the location of the default system partition.

```
                                        Tuesday, 2-20-1996  3:08:48 PM

Enter location of default system partition:

        Select media:
    SCSI Hard Disk
    Floppy Disk
    CD-ROM

        Enter SCSI bus number: 0
        Enter SCSI ID: 0
        Enter partition (must be FAT or NTFS): 1
```

Set Default Configuration

To set the default configuration, select **Set default configuration** on the **Setup** menu. The available selections depend upon your computer hardware.

```
                                        Tuesday, 2-20-1996  3:09:28 PM

Select monitor resolution:
    1280x1024
    1024x768
    800x600
    640x480

Select floppy drive capacity:
    5.25" 1.2MB
    3.5" 1.44MB
    3.5" 2.88MB

Is there a second floppy:
    Yes
    No

Select keyboard:
    U.S.101-key keyboard
    Japanese106-key keyboard
    French  102-key keyboard
    German  102-key keyboard
    Spanish 102-key keyboard
    Spanish variation
    Canadian French 102-key keyboard
    Swiss   102-key keyboard
    Italian 102-key keyboard
    Finnish/Swedish keyboard
    Norwegian keyboard
    Danish  102-key keyboard

Enter SCSI Host ID (0-7) for SCSI bus number :
```

After selecting the setting in each group, you are returned to the **Setup** menu.

Manage Boot Selection Menu

When you select **Manage boot selections menu** on the **Setup** menu, you can configure and manage the operating systems that appear on the **Boot** menu at startup. You can also configure custom startup folders and files if you have installed multiple copies of Windows NT.

The following choices are available on the **Boot selections** menu:

```
                                         Tuesday, 2-20-96 2:59:19 PM

ARC Multiboot Alpha AXP Version 3.5-11
Copyright (c) 1993 Microsoft Corporation
Copyright (c) 1993 Digital Equipment Corporation

Boot selections menu:

    Add a boot selection
    Change a boot selection
    Check boot selections
    Delete a boot selection
    Dump boot selections
    Rearrange boot selections
    Setup menu...

Use the arrow keys to select, then press Enter.
```

Add a Boot Selection

Select **Add a boot selection** on the **Boot selections** menu if:

- You have installed another operating system or more than one instance of Windows NT.
- You have configured your system partition or boot partition as a mirror set (Windows NT Server only).
- You want to create a boot selection for your Windows NT startup floppy disk. See Chapter 20, "Preparing for and Performing Recovery," for information about the Windows NT startup floppy disk.

When you make this selection, you can enter information similar to the following:

Note The right justified arrows (<----) in these examples indicate which selection was made, or the information that was entered.

```
                                        Tuesday, 2-20-96 3:09:19 PM

Select a system partition for this boot selection:
    SCSI Bus 0 Hard Disk 0 Partition 1
    New system partition

Enter location of system partition for this boot selection:
        Select Media:
    SCSI Hard Disk  <--------------------------------------------------
    Floppy Disk
    CD-ROM

        Enter SCSI bus number:  0                   <---------------------
        Enter SCSI ID:  2                           <---------------------
        Enter Partition (must be FAT or NTFS):  1 <---------------------

Enter the osloader folder and name: \os\winnt40\osloader.exe  <---------

Is the operating system in the same partition as the osloader:
    Yes
    No <----------------------------------------------------------------

Enter the location of os partition:
        Select Media:
    SCSI Hard Disk  <--------------------------------------------------
    Floppy Disk
    CD-ROM

        Enter SCSI bus number:  0 <------------------------------------
        Enter SCSI ID:  2         <------------------------------------
        Enter Partition:  2       <------------------------------------

Enter the operating system root folder:  \winnt         <--------------
Enter a name for this boot selection:  Boot Shadow Disk  <--------------

Do want to initialize the debugger at boot time:
         Yes
         No        <--------------------------------------------------
```

Change a Boot Selection

When you select **Change a boot selection** on the **Boot selections** menu, you can change environment variables for any of the boot selections that you have defined. This is a sample screen:

```
                                        Tuesday, 2-20-96 3:15:09 PM
Selection to edit:
    Boot Windows NT Workstation 4.0 (Default)
    Boot Windows NT Workstation 3.51
```

When you select one of the entries, you see a screen like this one:

```
                                        Tuesday, 2-20-96 3:17:19 PM

Use arrow keys to select a variable, ESC to exit:

    Name:

Environment variables for boot selection 1:
    LOADIDENTIFIER= Boot Windows NT Workstation 4.0
    SYSTEMPARTITION=scsi(0)disk(0)rdisk()partition(1)
    OSLOADER=scsi(0)disk(0)rdisk()partition(1)\os\winnt40\osloader.exe
    OSLOADPARTITION=scsi(0)disk(0)rdisk()partition(1)
    OSLOADFILENAME=\winnt
    OSLOADOPTIONS=nodebug
```

Use the arrow keys to select the environment variable to edit and press ENTER. The screen changes to have the heading **Value:** under **Name:**. For instance, if you select OSLOADOPTIONS and press ENTER, you see the following:

```
    Name: OSLOADOPTIONS
    Value: nodebug
```

Edit the value, and press ENTER when done. Press the ESCAPE key to exit this menu and return to the **Boot selections** menu.

Check Boot Selections

Under normal circumstances, when you select **Check boot selections** on the **Boot selections** menu, the screen briefly displays the various startup selections as they are checked for validity. If there is a problem, such as an invalid path or file, the following information is displayed:

```
                                        Tuesday, 2-20-96 3:25:11 PM

Problems were found with Windows NT Workstation 4.0... Choose an action:

    Ignore problems with this boot selection
    Delete this boot selection
    Change this boot selection
```

The error is displayed in yellow text below the options, such as the following:

```
OSLOADER cannot be found, value is:
    scsi(0)disk(0)rdisk(0)partition(1)\os\nt\xsloader.exe
```

The firmware only checks that the paths are valid and that the files or folders exist. It does not check file sizes, version numbers, dates, switches, or any other fields that might indicate consistency problems.

The firmware automatically returns you to the **Boot selections** menu.

Delete a Boot Selection

If you have deleted a Windows NT installation from your computer, you should select **Delete a boot selection** on the **Boot selections** menu to remove it from the NVRAM. This is the screen you see when you select this option:

```
                                          Tuesday, 2-20-96 3:25:09 PM


Selection to delete:
    Boot Windows NT Workstation 4.0 (Default)
    Boot Windows NT Workstation 3.51
```

Use the arrow keys to highlight the selection you want to delete, and press ENTER. There are no warnings or checks, and the selection is immediately deleted. Changes are not saved to NVRAM until you exit the **Setup** menu, however.

Dump Boot Selections

When you select **Dump boot selections** on the **Boot selections** menu, the NVRAM resets to no boot selections.

This is a sample screen:

```
LOADIDENTIFIER= Boot Windows NT Workstation 4.0;Boot Windows NT
Workstation 3.51
SYSTEMPARTITION=scsi(0)disk(0)rdisk(0)partition(1);
                scsi(0)disk(0)rdisk(0)partition(2);
OSLOADER=scsi(0)disk(0)rdisk(0)partition(1)\os\winnt40\osloader.exe;
         scsi(0)disk(0)rdisk(0)partition(2)\os\winnt351\osloader.exe;
OSLOADPARTITION=scsi(0)disk(0)rdisk(0)partition(1);
                scsi(0)disk(0)rdisk(0)partition(2);
OSLOADFILENAME=\winnt;\winnt
OSLOADOPTIONS=nodebug;sos debug baudrate:19200

  Press any key to continue...
```

Changes are not saved until you exit the **Setup** menu, and select **Supplementary Menu, and save changes**. If you save changes when exiting, the only ways to restore boot selections are to manually reenter the information or use the Emergency Repair disk.

Rearrange Boot Selections

The most common reason for rearranging the boot selections is because you have added a boot selection, which is automatically placed at the top of the list.

You see a screen like this one when you select **Rearrange boot selections** on the **Boot selections** menu:

```
                                         Tuesday, 2-20-96 4:01:03 PM

Pick selection to move to the top, ESC to exit:
    Boot Windows NT Workstation 4.0 (Default)
    Boot Windows NT Workstation 3.51
```

Use the arrow keys to highlight the selection you want to move to the top of the list, then press ENTER. You can do this repeatedly to rearrange the boot selection into any order you want.

As before, changes are not saved until you exit the **Setup** menu, and select **Supplementary Menu, and save changes**.

Setup menu

When you are finished with all of your changes on the **Boot Selections** menu, you can select **Setup menu** to return to the **Setup** menu.

Setup Autoboot

The **Setup autoboot** selection on the **Setup** menu enables you to set your computer to automatically start the default selection if you do not make a selection from the **Boot Loader** menu.

You see a screen like this one when you select this option on the **Setup** menu:

```
                                      Wednesday 2-21-1996  8:01:36  AM

Should the system autoboot:
    Yes
    No

Enter Countdown value (in seconds): 30
```

The **Enter Countdown value** prompt appears only if you select **Yes**. The countdown value provides the same functionality as the timeout value in the Boot.ini file on an x86-based computer.

Machine Specific Setup

When you select **Machine specific setup** on the **Setup** menu, you can set environment variables that are specific to the computer, such as:

```
                                          Wednesday 2-21-1996  11:01:36  AM

PCI Parity checking currently set to: Off

Set PCI Parity checking currently set to: On
Setup menu ...
```

Selecting one of the options sets the environment variable to the value specified. Selecting **Setup menu** returns you to that menu.

Edit Environment Variables

You can add, delete, or change information for the environment variables by selecting **Edit environment variables** on the **Setup** menu. The screen displays the variables that are defined, and their values, such as this example:

```
                                          Wednesday 2-21-1996  8:09:16 AM

Use the arrow keys to select a variable, ESC to exit:

    Name:


Environment variables:
    CONSOLEIN=multi()key()keyboard()console()
    CONSOLEOUT=multi()video()monitor()console()
    FWSEARCHPATH=scsi(0)disk(0)rdisk()partition(1)
    A:=multi(0)disk(0)fdisk(0)
    FLOPPY=2
    FLOPPY2=N
    KEYBOARDTYPE=0
    TIMEZONE=PST8PDT
```

You can add environment variables by typing in the name of the new variable at the **Name:** prompt and pressing ENTER. A prompt for **Value:** appears beneath the **Name:** prompt, and you enter the value.

For instance, to add the countdown variable:

```
Name:COUNTDOWN
Value: 20
```

To delete an environment variable, select it with the arrow keys, or type in the name at the **Name:** prompt. Then press ENTER at the **Value:** prompt. Environment variables with no string value are deleted from the NVRAM.

Reset System To Factory Defaults

Be careful when you select this option. When you execute this command, you might no longer be able to start the computer. Some reasons for the failure are:

- Windows NT might not have been pre-installed, so you would delete all references to Windows NT and all its environment variables.
- Windows NT could be on a different partition or folder than the factory default, so the path to Windows NT would not be correct.
- If you have changed hardware on the computer, you would get information only for the initial configuration.

Before you execute the command, write down all configuration information that you need to know, such as:

- Which partitions are defined.
- Which partitions are the system and boot partition.
- The environment variables for each boot selection, especially the paths to the boot selection.

This is a sample screen:

```
                                        Wednesday 2-21-1996  8:15:16 AM

This command will overwrite the environment, configuration,
and boot selections with new information.

Are you sure you want to do this?
    Yes
    No
```

Selecting **Yes** causes the default configuration information to be saved to NVRAM. Once you do this, there is no way to recover any previous configuration information. You have to rebuild all custom options and configuration parameters by using the firmware menus.

Help

This selection displays the system help screen.

```
                                  Wednesday 2-21-1996  8:26:11 AM

Do the following steps, in this order, to set up the system:

1. Set system time.
2. Set default environment variables.
3. Set default configuration.
4. Create at least one boot selection.
5. Setup autoboot.

-> A menu item with an arrow represents a section of the NVRAM with a
problem.  Select these items (in top to bottom order) to repair the
NVRAM before attempting to boot or install Windows NT.

"Reset system to factory defaults" does steps 2--5 for a typical system.

Home, End, Delete, and Backspace will help you edit strings.
The ESCape key returns from a menu and aborts a sequence.

The firmware automatically reboots if the configuration is changed.

Press any key to continue...
```

You return to the **Setup** menu when you press any key.

Exiting the Setup Menu

If you have made changes to the NVRAM by using the **Setup** menu, there are two ways to exit to the **Supplementary** menu:

```
Supplementary menu, and do not save changes...
Supplementary menu, and save changes...
```

If you choose to save the changes, they are saved to NVRAM. If you did not make any changes, the second option does not appear on the screen.

Display Hardware Configuration

Selecting **Display hardware configuration** on the **Supplementary** menu displays information about:

- Firmware.
- Processor.
- Video.
- Current environment variables for all devices on the system.
- EISA slots.

This is an example:

```
                                        Friday 2-23-1996    10:46:15 AM
Devices detected and supported by the firmware:

multi(0)video(0)monitor(0)
multi(0)key(0)keyboard(0)
multi(0)disk(0)fdisk(0)
multi(0)serial(0)
multi(0)serial(1)
scsi(0)disk(0)rdisk(0)
scsi(0)cdrom(4)fdisk(0)

Press any key to continue...
```

Selecting any key displays a list of supported hardware, such as the following:

```
                                    Friday 2-23-1996    10:46:55 AM
Alpha AXP Processor and System Information:

Processor ID        21066
Processor Revision  2
System Revision     1
Processor Speed     166.66Mhz
Physical Memory     32 MB
Backup Cache Size   256 KB

Press any key to continue...
```

When you press any key, the firmware displays the next set of information. When all hardware information has been displayed, selecting any key returns you to the **Supplementary** menu.

Boot Menu

When you select **Boot menu** on the **Supplementary** menu, the firmware returns you to the **Boot** menu.

CHAPTER 20

Preparing for and Performing Recovery

This chapter describes what you can do to:

- Reduce the possibility of problems.
- Recover from problems when they occur.

There is no way to make a computer running Windows NT failure proof. You can only make the computer more failure resistant. A memory module, cabling, or controller failure can corrupt data on any disk. In this event, the only option is to restore from a tape or a backup server that contains a copy of the data.

These are some things that you can do to make it easier to recover from problems:

- Develop plans and procedures for recovering from failures before you have one.
- Create and test floppy disks that enable you to restart the computer when you are having trouble starting from the system partition.
- Maintain software configuration information for your computers running Windows NT. At a minimum, keep track of the version of the operating system installed on each computer, including service packs and hotfixes.
- Record the hardware configuration of each computer running Windows NT, especially the disk configurations.

The topics covered in this chapter are:

- Maintaining configuration and other forms of information.
- Understanding ARC pathnames.
- Creating floppy disks to use to start the computer.
- Testing.
- Restoring disk information.
- Using an uninterruptible power supply

This chapter also describes using utilities on the *Windows NT Workstation Resource Kit* CD and the *Windows NT Workstation* CD to back up and restore critical data. Planning what utilities to use is as important as knowing how to use them. There is more information about these utilities in Chapter 22, "Disk, File System, and Backup Utilities."

These are some points to consider:

- Investigate the various utilities for doing a task, and decide which one(s) to use for which situations.
- When you have decided which utilities you want to use, prepare your floppy disks.
- Know how to use the utilities that you decide to use.
- Practice recovering from the common problems described in this chapter and in Chapter 21, "Troubleshooting Startup and Disk Problems."

Maintaining Configuration and Essential System Information

Hardware failures, power failures, and human errors can corrupt information that your computer needs to start Windows NT.

Recovery is easier if:

- You know the configuration of each computer and its history.
- You back up critical system files every time you make certain changes to your Windows NT configuration.

On computers running Windows NT Workstation, you can purchase disk subsystems that maintain redundant information on the disks. The redundant information is either parity information, or a complete, separate copy of the data. Having redundant information makes the disk subsystems fault tolerant, meaning that you can continue to access the data when one disk in a fault-tolerant configuration fails. This fault-tolerant technology is called RAID, for Redundant Array of Inexpensive Disks. A disk subsystem that implements fault tolerance using RAID technology is also called a RAID array.

For complete information about RAID, RAID terminology, and RAID arrays, see *The RAIDbook, A Source Book for Disk Array Technology*. The RAID Advisory Board in St. Peter, MN, publishes this book. The June 1995 edition is the basis for RAID information in this chapter.

Keeping a Log Book

You should have a log book for every computer, which contains information about the computer's configuration. Having current information makes it easier to rebuild your computer in the event of a serious system crash. This information also helps product support personnel to troubleshoot problems. The Registry contains information about your disk configuration in the subkeys HKEY_LOCAL_MACHINE\HARDWARE\DeviceMap\AtDisk and Scsi.

The type of information to keep includes:

- Computer type, model number, and serial number.
- Computer BIOS manufacturer and revision level (x86-based computers) or firmware revision level (RISC-based computers).
- CMOS information for x86-based computers.
- NVRAM information on RISC-based computers.
- Hardware configuration information, including IRQs, DMA addresses, I/O ports, and similar information. If the computer has an EISA bus, the EISA configuration and its associated CFG files should be backed up.
- SCSI controller model number, and the BIOS firmware revision level.
- Jumper settings for all peripheral devices.
- Complete map of the SCSI subsystem, including:
  - SCSI configuration information from the SCSI setup program.
  - Which devices are terminated and how they are terminated.
  - The SCSI ID and physical location on the chain of every SCSI device.
- Which versions of Windows NT are installed, and the partitions on which they are installed.
- Details of any device drivers or other system level software that did not come in the Windows NT retail package. This software would include such things as a Network File System (NFS) provider, network protocol, or network management software.
- Troubleshooting history for any system failures or Kernel STOP errors (blue screens). This information should include:
  - The time and date the problem occurred.
  - Any error messages, or events posted to the event log.
  - Any troubleshooting done and the outcome.
- Partition information, such as the size of the partitions and the file system used for each one. You can use the DiskMap program, described in Chapter 22, "Disk, File System, and Backup Utilities," to print a map of each of your disks by redirecting the output to a file or a printer.

Backing up the Registry

All of the Windows NT internal configuration information is stored in the Registry. It is critical to have up-to-date, reliable backups of this information. There are several ways to back up the all or part of the Registry, and you should have redundancy in this area.

If you have a backup device installed on your computer, you can include the Registry in normal backups. You have to specifically select this option in the Windows NT tape backup program Ntbackup.exe. Third-party Windows NT-compatible backup software might also require that you take specific action to back up the Registry. Be sure to test your Registry backup and restore procedures.

Note Windows NT Backup can only back up the Registry on the local system. You cannot use Windows NT Backup to back up a computer's Registry over the network.

After any change in the configuration of the operating system, including adding new software, you should use the Repair Disk program, Rdisk.exe, to update files in the *%systemroot%*\Repair folder, and create a new Emergency Repair Disk. For information about using the Repair Disk program, see "Creating an Emergency Repair Disk," presented later in this chapter. It is a good idea to make a copy of the Emergency Repair Disk and store it in a separate location, perhaps off site.

You can use the Windows NT Registry Editor, Regedt32.exe, to save and restore Registry keys.

The *Windows NT Workstation Resource Kit* CD contains utilities that enable you to back up and restore all or part of the Registry. For information about the Registry Backup (Regback.exe) and Registry Restore (Regrest.exe) utilities, see Rktools.hlp.

Saving the SYSTEM Key

The HKEY_LOCAL_MACHINE\SYSTEM key contains configuration information that Windows NT uses during startup. Even though this key is copied to the Emergency Repair Disk when you use the Repair Disk program, there are times that you might want to restore this key from another disk. For more information, see "Restoring the SYSTEM Key," presented later in this chapter.

You can save the SYSTEM key by using either Disk Administrator or the Windows NT Registry Editor (Regedt32.exe). The primary difference between these two methods is that the Disk Administrator always saves the key to a floppy disk, whereas you can specify any disk by using the Registry Editor.

Note The *%systemroot%*\System32\Config\System file is usually larger than the SYSTEM key saved by using Disk Administrator or Registry Editor. The smaller size results because the two programs compact the file before copying it to eliminate internal fragmentation and holes.

▶ **To use Disk Administrator to save the SYSTEM key**

1. On the **Partition** menu, click **Configuration**.
2. On the **Configuration** menu, click **Save**. A message is displayed describing what will be saved and where you should save it.
3. Insert any floppy disk with enough unused space to hold the configuration information (about 512K). Using the Windows NT startup floppy disk is highly recommended.
4. Click **OK** to write the data to the floppy disk.

▶ **To use Registry Editor to save the SYSTEM key**

1. Run Registry Editor (Regedt32.exe).
2. Click the HKEY_LOCAL_MACHINE\SYSTEM key. On the **Registry** menu, click **Save key**.
3. Enter the path to the file where you want to save the key.

Saving the DISK Subkey

The HKEY_LOCAL_MACHINE\SYSTEM\DISK subkey in the Registry contains configuration information about currently defined drive letters, volume sets, stripe sets, stripe sets with parity, and mirror sets, as well as CD-ROM mappings and drive mappings. Any time that you make changes to your disk configuration, Windows NT updates the DISK subkey. You should save this subkey whenever you make changes that affect it, such as:

- Creating or deleting a disk partition.
- Changing a drive letter.
- Creating or deleting a volume set or stripe set.

Having a backup is useful in situations when you do not want to restore the entire Registry or the entire SYSTEM key, such as the following:

- You want to move a volume set or stripe set to another computer because of a hardware failure.
- Configuration information about a set has been corrupted.
- You need to replace hardware.

For example, if you have changed a SCSI controller, restoring the entire SYSTEM key might make it difficult to start the computer. Restoring the DISK subkey enables you to have current disk configuration information without changing anything else in the Registry.

Note The DISK subkey does not exist the first time that you start Windows NT Workstation. Disk Administrator creates the subkey the first time that you run it.

▶ **To use the Registry Editor to save the DISK subkey**

1. Run Registry Editor (Regedt32.exe).
2. Click the HKEY_LOCAL_MACHINE\SYSTEM\DISK subkey. On the **Registry** menu, click **Save key**.
3. Enter the path to the file where you want to save the subkey.

Creating an Emergency Repair Disk

When you install Windows NT, Setup creates the Registry information in *%systemroot%*\System32\Config. For recovery purposes, Setup also creates a *%systemroot%*\Repair folder that contains the following files:

File Name	Contents
Autoexec.nt	Copy of *%systemroot%*\System32\Autoexec.nt, which is used to initialize the MS-DOS environment.
Config.NT	Copy of *%systemroot%*\System32\Config.nt, which is used to initialize the MS-DOS environment.
Default._	Registry key HKEY_USERS\DEFAULT, compressed.
Ntuser.da_	Compressed version of %systemroot%\Profiles\Default user\Ntuser.dat. The repair process uses Ntuser.da_ if this one needs to be repaired.
Sam._	Registry key HKEY_LOCAL_MACHINE\SAM, compressed.
Security._	Registry key HKEY_LOCAL_MACHINE\SECURITY, compressed.
Setup.log	Log of which files were installed, and cyclic redundancy check (CRC) information for use during the repair process. This file is Read Only, System, and Hidden, so it will not be visible unless you have configured My Computer or Windows NT Explorer to show all files.
Software._	Registry key HKEY_LOCAL_MACHINE\SOFTWARE, compressed.
System._	Registry key HKEY_LOCAL_MACHINE\SYSTEM, compressed.

During installation, Windows NT Setup asks whether you want to create an Emergency Repair Disk. You should choose **Yes**. When you create an Emergency Repair Disk during installation, or later by using the Repair Disk program (Rdisk.exe), the files are copied from *%systemroot%*\Repair to the floppy disk. You can also use the Emergency Repair Disk to repair a corrupt Partition Boot Sector for the system partition.

When you run the Repair Disk program, you can update the *%systemroot%*\Repair\Software and *%systemroot%*\Repair\System files with the current information in *%systemroot%*\System32\Config by using the Update Repair Info button.

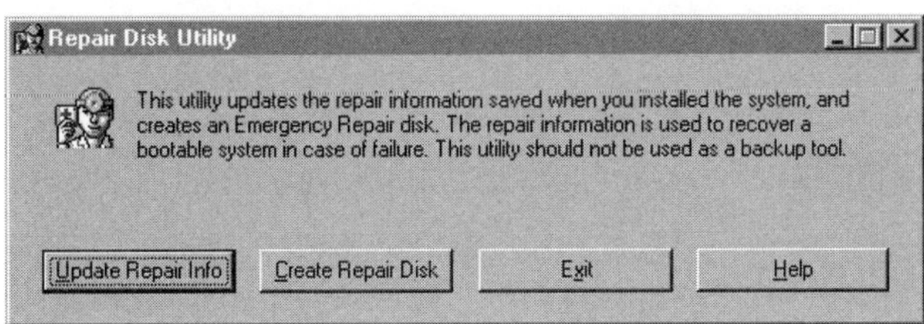

The Repair Disk program does not update the Default, Sam and Security files if you run the program from Windows NT Explorer or My Computer. To update all the files, you can run **rdisk** from the command prompt by entering:

```
rdisk /s
```

You can also update all of the files by clicking the Start button, clicking Run, and entering:

```
rdisk /s
```

Using the /s switch forces the Repair Disk program to update all of the Registry keys in the *%systemroot%*\Repair folder.

There are several points to consider about maintaining and using your Emergency Repair Disk:

- If you did not use the **/s** switch before you create the Emergency Repair Disk, and you use the Repair process to replace the SYSTEM Registry keys, all passwords in the system return to the passwords in effect at the time you last updated the Sam and Security files in *%systemroot%*\Repair. If you have more recently backed up these keys by using Windows NT Backup, Regback.exe, or Regedt32.exe, you can restore more current information.
- If you did not update the Emergency Repair Disk after using Disk Administrator to configure volume sets or stripe sets, it might be difficult or impossible to recover data on these volumes. When you create a volume set or a stripe set, Disk Administrator updates the DISK subkey in the Registry and sets the fault-tolerant bit on the System ID field of the Partition Table for each partition or logical drive in the set.
- You should make a copy of your current Emergency Repair Disk.
- If you convert your boot partition from the FAT file system to the NTFS file system on an x86-based computer, be sure to update your Emergency Repair Disk. The NTFS Partition Boot Sector must be on the Emergency Repair Disk, not the FAT Partition Boot Sector.
- The Emergency Repair Disk is not a replacement for backups.

For more information about creating an Emergency Repair Disk, see Help for the Repair Disk program. For more information about the *%systemroot%*\Repair and *%systemroot%*\System32\Config folders, and the Emergency Repair Disk, search the Knowledge Base. For information about the Knowledge Base, see Chapter 36, "General Troubleshooting."

Chapter 23, "Overview of the Windows NT Registry," contains more information about these keys and the *%systemroot%*\System32\Config folder.

Backing up the Master Boot Record and Partition Boot Sector

No operating system can protect itself from damage to these disk areas, which can be caused by viruses, faulty SCSI configurations, device driver problems, or power outages. You should back up the Master Boot Record on a disk every time you change partition information for primary partitions or an extended partition. You should back up a Partition Boot Sector when you format a volume, install Windows NT in the volume, or convert a volume from the FAT file system to the NTFS file system.

You can back up these disk sectors by using the Windows NT–based program, DiskProbe, or the MS-DOS-based program, DiskSave. Both of these utilities are on the *Windows NT Workstation Resource Kit* CD. The procedures for using DiskProbe and DiskSave are described in Chapter 22, "Disk, File System, and Backup Utilities."

If you have more than one hard disk, or more than one partition on a disk, you should back up every Master Boot Record and Partition Boot Sector. The Master Boot Record for the startup disk and the Partition Boot Sector for your system partition are the most critical. The ones for the other disks and volumes are not as critical to the startup process, but you might not be able to access files if the Master Boot Record for the disk or the Partition Boot Sector for the volume is not correct.

Chapter 21, "Troubleshooting Startup and Disk Problems," describes how to determine if you have a problem with one of these sectors.

Backing Up Data on Your Hard Disks

You should back up data on your hard disk(s) that are not available anywhere else. For example, you might not want to back up Windows-based application programs, because you can reinstall them. However, it might be faster to restore the application programs from a backup tape rather than reinstall them if you have to replace a disk.

You can use the Windows NT backup program, Ntbackup.exe, to back up the data to a cartridge tape. You can also back up to another computer, such as a file server or the disk on a computer that is shared by other users. If you back up to another computer, you should have your files included in the backup procedure for that computer.

Understanding ARC Pathnames

Advanced RISC Computing (ARC) naming conventions are a standard for identifying the location of a file or a program on a device such as a hard disk or a floppy disk. You must understand the ARC pathname conventions to be able to create paths to use to start the computer from the Windows NT startup floppy disk.

On x86-based computers, you use ARC pathnames to describe the location of the boot partition for each instance of Windows NT installed on the computer. On an x86-based computer, you can create alternate paths to the boot partition, as described in "Creating Alternate Boot Selections for an x86-based Computer," presented later in this chapter. The ARC path in the Boot.ini file appears in one of the following forms:

- multi(W)disk(X)rdisk(Y)partition(Z)\\%*systemroot*%
- scsi(W)disk(X)rdisk(Y)partition(Z)\\%*systemroot*%

On RISC-based computers, you use ARC pathnames to describe the location of:

- The folder containing Osloader.exe and Hal.dll.
- The full path to Osloader.exe.
- The path to the boot partition.
- Devices detected by the firmware, such as disks, keyboard, and video.

When you create a Windows NT startup floppy disk to use on a RISC-based computer, you need to modify the NVRAM to include the ARC path to the floppy disk. To create an entry for the Windows NT startup floppy disk, see the section titled "Creating Alternate Boot Selections for a RISC-based Computer," presented later in this chapter. On a RISC-based computer, only the scsi() syntax is used for hard disks. The boot selection has the following parts:

- SYSTEMPARTITION is the FAT partition that contains Osloader.exe and Hal.dll.
- OSLOADER is the path to the OSLOADER file itself.
- OSLOADPARTITION is the boot partition, which contains the Windows NT system files.
- OSLOADFILENAME is the name of the Windows NT folder in the boot partition, with no drive letter.
- OSLOADOPTIONS indicates any debugging options that should be set up when loading Windows NT.

This is an example of a boot selection for a RISC-based computer:

- LOADIDENTIFIER=Windows NT Workstation 4.0
- SYSTEMPARTITION=scsi(0)disk(0)rdisk(0)partition(1)
- OSLOADER=scsi(0)disk(0)rdisk(0)partition(1)\Os\Nt40\Osloader.exe
- OSLOADPARTITION=scsi(0)disk(0)rdisk(0)partition(2)
- OSLOADFILENAME=\Winnt
- OSLOADOPTIONS=nodebug

multi(W)disk(X)rdisk(Y)partition(Z)

This form of the ARC pathname, refered to as multi() in the rest of this chapter, is only used on x86-based computers. On Windows NT version 3.1, it was only valid for IDE, EIDE, and ESDI disks. In Windows NT version 3.5 and later it is valid for SCSI disks as well.

The multi() syntax indicates to Windows NT that it should rely on the system BIOS to load system files. This means that NTLDR, the boot loader for x86-based computers, will be using interrupt (INT) 13 BIOS calls to find and load Ntoskrnl.exe and any other files it needs to get the system running.

Note The term multi() syntax refers to the multi(W)disk(X)rdisk(Y)partition(Z) form of the ARC pathname.

The W, X, Y, and Z parameters have the following meaning:

W
: is the ordinal number of the controller, and should always be 0.

X
: is not used for multi(), and is always 0.

Y
: is the ordinal for the disk on the controller, and is always 0 or 1 for disks connected to the primary controller. The range is 0 through 3 for disks on a dual-channel EIDE controller.

Z
: is the partition number. All partitions receive a number except for type 5 (Extended) and type 0 (unused) partitions. These numbers start at 1, as opposed to all other entries, which start with 0.

Theoretically, the multi() syntax could be used to start Windows NT from any disk on the computer. However, this would require that all disks be correctly identified through the standard INT 13 interface. But support for this varies from controller to controller, and most system BIOS only identify a single controller through INT 13.

For a configuration with IDE or EIDE disks, the multi() syntax works for up to four disks on the primary and secondary channels of a dual-channel controller. In a SCSI-only configuration, the multi() syntax works for the first two disks on the first SCSI controller (the controller whose BIOS loads first). When your computer has both SCSI and IDE disks, the multi() syntax works only for the IDE disks on the first controller.

scsi(W)disk(X)rdisk(Y)partition(Z)

The scsi() syntax is used for both RISC-based and x86-based computers, and is used in all versions of Windows NT. Using the scsi() syntax indicates that Windows NT needs to load a SCSI device driver and use that driver to access the boot partition.

Note The term scsi() syntax refers to the scsi(W)disk(X)rdisk(Y)partition(Z) form of the ARC pathname.

On an x86-based computer, the device driver is Ntbootdd.sys, which can be found in the root of the system disk (usually C:). It is a copy of the device driver for the disk controller in use. On a RISC-based computer, the driver is built into the firmware, as required by the RISC standards, so no file is required.

The W, X, Y and Z parameters have the following meaning when using the scsi() syntax:

W
: is the ordinal number of the controller as identified by the Ntbootdd.sys driver.

X
: is the SCSI ID of the target disk.

Y
: is the SCSI logical unit number (LUN) of the disk that contains the boot partition. Y will almost always be 0.

Z
: is the partition number. All partitions receive a number except for type 5 (Extended) and type 0 (unused) partitions. These numbers start at 1, as opposed to all other entries, which start with 0.

When using scsi() syntax, the value of W depends upon Ntbootdd.SYS. Each SCSI device driver used in Windows NT has its own method of ordering controllers, although the controller order corresponds to the order that the BIOS on the controllers loads (if they are being loaded).

Additionally, if you have more than one SCSI controller, and they use different device drivers, you should only count the controllers that are controlled by Ntbootdd.sys when determining the value of the W parameter. For instance, if you have an Adaptec 2940 (which uses Aic78xx.sys) and an Adaptec 1542 (which uses Aha154x.sys), W will always be 0. What changes is the Ntbootdd.sys file:

- If you are loading Windows NT from a disk on the Adaptec 2940, Ntbootdd.sys will be a copy of Aic78xx.sys.
- If you are loading Windows NT from a disk on the Adaptec 1542, Ntbootdd.sys will be a copy of Aha154x.sys.

Example ARC Pathnames

This section contains examples that you can use as a model. The first two examples are for ARC paths on x86-based computers. The last example is the boot entry on a DEC Alpha AXP 150 computer, and should be good for all RISC-based computers with similar disk configurations.

More Than One SCSI Controller on an x86-based Computer

This example for an x86-based computer has the following disks and controllers:

- Two Adaptec 2940s, each with two 1 GB hard disks at ID 0 and ID 1.
- One Adaptec 1542, with two 1 GB hard disks at ID 0 and ID 4.

Each hard disk has a single, 1 GB primary partition. Partitions 1 and 2 are on the first 2940, partitions 3 and 4 are on the second 2940, and partitions 5 and 6 are on the 1542. These are the ARC paths that you would have in the Boot.ini file if each partition had a copy of Windows NT installed in a folder named Winnt:

- Partition 1: multi(0)disk(0)rdisk(0)partition(1)\Winnt
- Partition 2: multi(0)disk(0)rdisk(1)partition(1)\Winnt
- Partition 3: scsi(1)disk(0)rdisk(0)partition(1)\Winnt
- Partition 4: scsi(1)disk(1)rdisk(0)partition(1)\Winnt
- Partition 5: scsi(0)disk(0)rdisk(0)partition(1)\Winnt
- Partition 6: scsi(0)disk(4)rdisk(0)partition(1)\Winnt

For partitions 3 and 4, Ntbootdd.sys is a copy of Aic78xx.sys. For partitions 5 and 6, Ntbootdd.sys is a copy of Aha154x.sys. For partitions 1 and 2, you could also use the following paths:

- Partition 1: scsi(0)disk(0)rdisk(0)partition(1)\Winnt
- Partition 1: scsi(0)disk(1)rdisk(0)partition(1)\Winnt

provided that you had an Ntbootdd.sys file that was a copy of Aic78xx.sys. However, Windows NT Setup always use the multi() syntax for the first two SCSI disks.

Both EIDE and SCSI Controllers on an x86-based Computer

This example is for an x86-based computer with the following disks and controllers:

- A dual-channel EIDE controller with three 1 GB disks, two on the primary channel and one on the secondary channel.
- An Adaptec 2940 controller with a single 4 GB hard disk at ID 3.

The three EIDE disks each have a single 1 GB partition. Partitions 1 and 2 are on the primary channel of the EIDE controller, and partition 3 is on the secondary channel.

The SCSI disk has four 1 GB partitions. Partitions 4, 5, 6 and 7 are on the SCSI disk. Each partition would have the following ARC paths in the Boot.ini file, assuming that each partition has Windows NT installed in the Winnt folder:

- Partition 1: multi(0)disk(0)rdisk(0)partition(1)\Winnt
- Partition 2: multi(0)disk(0)rdisk(1)partition(1)\Winnt
- Partition 3: multi(0)disk(0)rdisk(2)partition(1)\Winnt
- Partition 4: scsi(0)disk(3)rdisk(0)partition(1)\Winnt
- Partition 5: scsi(0)disk(3)rdisk(0)partition(2)\Winnt
- Partition 6: scsi(0)disk(3)rdisk(0)partition(3)\Winnt
- Partition 7: scsi(0)disk(3)rdisk(0)partition(4)\Winnt

Loading Windows NT from partitions 4 through 7 requires that the Ntbootdd.sys file be a copy of Aic78xx.sys.

Boot Selection on a DEC Alpha AXP 150

On a RISC-based computer, all boot paths are defined in the NVRAM. When creating a new boot selection for a RISC-based computer, the firmware menus prompt you for the information to enter. There is an example for defining a boot selection in the section titled "Creating Alternate Boot Selections for a RISC-based Computer," presented later in this chapter.

The following example is a boot selection on a DEC Alpha AXP 150. The computer has a single hard disk at ID 0, which has a 4 MB system partition and a 396 MB boot partition. Windows NT is installed on the boot partition in a folder named Winnt and the OSLOADER folder is also named Winnt, although it is on the system partition. The boot selection has the following values:

- LOADIDENTIFIER=Windows NT Workstation 4.0
- SYSTEMPARTITION=scsi(0)disk(0)rdisk(1)partition(1)
- OSLOADER=scsi(0)disk(0)rdisk(1)partition(1)\Os\Winnt\Osloader.exe
- OSLOADPARTITION=scsi(0)disk(0)rdisk(1)partition(2)
- OSLOADFILENAME=\Winnt
- OSLOADOPTIONS=nodebug

Creating Floppy Disks for Starting Your Computer

For x86-based computers and RISC-based computers, you should create a floppy disk to use to start Windows NT if you cannot start up from the hard disk. For x86-based computers, you can also create a floppy disk that you can use to start MS-DOS if you cannot start Windows NT.

Creating each floppy disk requires two steps:

- Format the disk.
- Copy files to the disk.

After you create the Windows NT startup floppy disk or the MS-DOS bootable floppy disk, run a virus scan program to make sure the disk is not infected. Lock the floppy disk after you finish running the virus scan. (Most floppy disks have a tab on their back side that you slide down to lock the disk. You cannot write on a floppy disk when the tab is in the locked position.)

You should test each disk before you have to use it. You should also be familiar with using the programs that you copy to the floppy disks.

Depending on your disk configuration and whether you are using an x86-based computer or a RISC-based computer, you might also have to create alternate boot selections to your Windows NT startup floppy disk. For a description of the ARC pathname conventions that you need to use in boot selections, see "Understanding ARC Pathnames," presented earlier in this chapter.

Whenever possible, you should use an ARC path created by Windows NT Setup during an installation. When in doubt, install a copy of Windows NT onto the disk that you want to use for the boot partition, and then copy that ARC path, changing the partition number and folder name as necessary.

Windows NT Startup Floppy Disk

You must format your Windows NT startup floppy disk when you are running Windows NT. You can use My Computer to format the floppy disk, or enter **format a:** at the command prompt. Both of these utilities copy the Windows NT Partition Boot Sector, which is required to load the Windows NT boot loader, to the floppy disk. Windows NT Help describes the procedure for formatting a floppy disk by using My Computer.

You can use the Windows NT startup floppy disk to start Windows NT in the following circumstances:

- The Master Boot Record or Partition Boot Sector on the system partition has a problem.
- There are problems with the disk that contains the system partition and the boot partition is on another disk.
- You are reconfiguring hard disks and you want to be able to start Windows NT from the Windows NT startup floppy disk if you are having problems.

Note On x86-based computers, if the Partition Table in the Master Boot Record has been corrupted, especially if the information for the system partition or boot partition is all zeroes, you might not be able to start up by using the Windows NT startup floppy disk. If you have a current backup of the Master Boot Record, try starting MS-DOS from the MS-DOS bootable floppy disk, and use the DiskSave program to replace the Master Boot Record.

The files that you need to copy to the floppy disk normally have the Read Only, System, and Hidden attributes set. If the files have either the System or Hidden attribute set, they are not visible. You need to make the files visible before you can copy them.

▶ **To copy files to the Windows NT startup floppy disk**

1. Using My Computer or Windows NT Explorer, on the **View** menu, click **Options**.
2. On the **View** tab, select **Show all files**. Click **OK**.
3. Click the filename of the file to be copied.
4. On the **File** menu, click **Properties**.
5. In the **Attributes** box of the **General** tab, clear the **Read Only**, **System**, and **Hidden** check boxes, and click **OK**.

   Do steps 3, 4, and 5 for each file that you want to copy.
6. Select the files, and then copy them to the floppy disk.

Files to Copy for an x86-based Computer

Copy the following files from the root folder of your system partition to the floppy disk you just formatted:

- NTLDR — Windows NT boot loader program.
- Boot.ini — describes the location of the boot partitions, specified by using Advanced RISC Computing (ARC) naming conventions.
- Ntdetect.com — used for hardware detection.
- Bootsect.dos — if you want to be able to dual-boot another operating system when using the Windows NT startup floppy disk.
- Ntbootdd.sys — required only if you are using the scsi() syntax in the Boot.ini file. This file is not present in the root folder if you are using the multi() syntax.

The Ntbootdd.sys file is a renamed copy of the SCSI device driver used on your Windows NT computer. For example, if you are using the Adaptec 1542B SCSI controller, copy Aha154x.sys to the floppy disk, and then rename it to Ntbootdd.sys. If Windows NT Setup created an Ntbootdd.sys in your root folder, just copy that file.

You can find the device driver name by:

- Looking in the HKEY_LOCAL_MACHINE\HARDWARE\DeviceMap\Scsi Registry subkey.
- Double-clicking the SCSI Adapters option on Control Panel. In the **Devices** tab, click **Properties**. Click the **Driver** tab to see the driver filename.

Creating Alternate Boot Selections for an x86-based Computer

For Windows NT Workstation, you should not have to create alternate boot selections in your Boot.ini file. You might want to have other paths when you are reconfiguring disks. For instance, if you currently have a SCSI disk (with SCSI ID 0) and are adding an IDE disk to your configuration, the IDE disk must be the first one. If your SCSI disk has the BIOS enabled, and the boot partition is

```
multi(0)disk(0)rdisk(0)partition(1)\Winnt="Windows NT Workstation
Version 4.0"
```

you should disable the BIOS on the SCSI controller and add a second entry of:

```
scsi(0)disk(0)rdisk(0)partition(1)\Winnt="Windows NT Workstation Version
4.0 SCSI disk"
```

Note If you had translation enabled when you low-level formatted the SCSI disk, you will not be able to access the disk after you disable the BIOS on the controller.

This second entry enables you to start Windows NT from the SCSI disk to use Disk Administrator to partition and format the IDE disk.

You might also want to create alternate boot selections for debugging purposes. In this case, you can add other entries to the Boot.ini file and append switches to the pathname, such as:

```
multi(0)disk(0)rdisk(0)partition(1)\Winnt="Windows NT Workstation
Version 4.0" /sos /DEBUG
```

For more information about the switches, see:

- Chapter 19, "What Happens When You Start Your Computer."
- Chapter 21, "Troubleshooting Startup and Disk Problems."
- Chapter 39, "Windows NT Debugger."

The section "Understanding ARC Pathnames," presented earlier in this chapter, contains more information about the pathnames on the Boot.ini file.

Note The Boot.ini file has the Read Only attribute set by default. Remove this attribute before editing the file. Restoring the attribute is optional. Windows NT Setup sets the attribute to prevent accidental deletion.

Files to Copy for a RISC-based Computer

When you install Windows NT on a RISC-based computer, it creates a folder, such as \Os\Winnt40, that contains the Osloader.exe and Hal.dll files. On Alpha AXP–based computers, this folder also contains several files with the .pal extension. Some or all of these files might have the system, hidden, or read-only attributes set.

A Windows NT startup floppy disk for a RISC-based computer should have a folder tree identical to the RISC-based system partition. Therefore, you should create the \Os\Winnt40 folder on the floppy disk.

Copy the following files from the \Os\Winnt40 folder on your hard disk to the same folder on the floppy disk:

- Osloader.exe
- Hal.dll
- *.pal (AXP-based computers only)

Creating Alternate Boot Selections for a RISC-based Computer

RISC-based computers start from the system firmware. You should define a boot selection in the NVRAM that points to a Windows NT startup floppy disk. You only need to use the Windows NT startup floppy disk if there is a problem with the system partition (the partition with OSLOADER). If you do not create a path to the floppy disk ahead of time, and you cannot access the system partition, you will have to create a path to the Windows NT startup floppy disk to be able to start the computer.

For more information about firmware menus, see "Using a RISC-based Computer's Boot Menu" in Chapter 19, "What Happens When You Start Your Computer."

Note There are three types of RISC-based computers: Alpha, MIPS, and PowerPC. The examples in this section are for an Alpha AXP–based computer. The firmware menus that you use to get to the configuration options can be different for MIPS and PowerPC computers.

Creating a Path to the Windows NT Startup Floppy Disk

Once you have created the Windows NT startup floppy disk, you need to create the path to it by using the **Add a boot selection** menu. These are the steps to get to that menu:

1. Start the computer. You see the **Boot** menu.
2. On the **Boot** menu, click **Supplementary menu**.
3. On the **Supplementary** menu, click **Setup the system**.
4. On the **Setup** menu, click **Manage boot selection menu**.
5. On the **Boot selections** menu, click **Add a boot selection**.

The following example shows creating a path to the Windows NT startup floppy disk. Be sure that the path to the Osloader.exe on the Windows NT startup floppy disk matches the path to Osloader.exe on the hard disk.

Note The right justified arrows (<----) in these examples indicate which selection was made, or the information that was entered.

```
                                    Thursday, 03-07-96   11:18:43 AM

Select a system partition for this boot selection:
        SCSI Bus 0 Hard Disk 0 Partition 1
        New system partition  <-----------------------------------------

Enter location of system partition for this boot selection:
        Select Media:
    SCSI Hard Disk
    Floppy Disk  <--------------------------------------------------------
    CD-ROM

        Enter floppy drive number: 0  <-----------------------------------

Enter the osloader directory and name: \os\winnt40\osloader.exe <-------

Is the operating system in the same partition as the osloader:
        Yes
        No <---------------------------------------------------------------

Enter the location of os partition:
        Select Media:
    SCSI Hard Disk  <-----------------------------------------------------
    Floppy Disk
    CD-ROM

        Enter SCSI bus number: 0  <-----------------------------------
        Enter SCSI ID: 2          <-----------------------------------
        Enter Partition: 2        <-----------------------------------

Enter the operating system root directory: \winnt40          <----------
Enter a name for this boot selection: start from floppy disk  <---------
Do you want to initialize the debugger at boot time:
        Yes
        No  <--------------------------------------------------------------
```

Note The location of the operating system root folder and the values that you enter for the path to the partition on the SCSI disk depend on your system configuration. The SCSI bus number will usually be 0, but the SCSI ID can be anything from 0 to 6, although 2 is common.

After entering the data, you will be back at the **Boot selections** menu. Select **Setup menu**. On the **Setup** menu, select **Supplementary menu,** and **save changes**.

Using Alternate Boot Selections

When you have created alternate boot selections, you start an alternate one by selecting **Boot an alternate operating system** from the **Boot** menu. This example shows selecting the alternate operating system option.

```
ARC Multiboot Alpha AXP Version 3.5-11
Copyright (c) 1993 Microsoft Corporation
Copyright (c) 1993 Digital Equipment Corporation

Boot Menu:

    Boot Windows NT Server Version 4.0
    Boot an alternate operating system  <------------------------------
    Run a utility
    Supplementary menu. . .

Use the arrow keys to select, then press Enter.
Seconds until auto-boot. Select another option to override: 9
```

If you have added a boot selections for the Windows NT startup floppy disk, as described earlier in this section, and select **Boot an alternate operating system**, you would see a screen like the following.

```
ARC Multiboot Alpha AXP Version 3.5-11
Copyright (c) 1993 Microsoft Corporation
Copyright (c) 1993 Digital Equipment Corporation

Boot Menu:

    start from floppy disk
    Boot Windows NT Workstation 4.0 (Default)

Use the arrow keys to select, then press Enter.
```

Each time you create a new boot selection, it becomes the default selection. The preceding example shows the menu if you added a path to the Windows NT startup floppy disk after you had installed Windows NT Workstation 4.0. You should use the **Rearrange boot selections** menu to change the default boot selection back to the hard disk. See the section titled "Using a RISC-based Computer's Boot Menu ," in Chapter 19, "What Happens When You Start Your Computer," for information about managing boot selections.

MS-DOS Bootable Floppy Disk (x86-based Computers)

An MS-DOS bootable floppy disk is most useful if you have FAT partitions on your startup disk (the disk that contains the system partition that you use to start Windows NT).

Your MS-DOS bootable floppy disk contains the files that you need to start MS-DOS from the floppy disk. It also should contain utilities for examining the contents of disks, copying files, and creating and formatting partitions.

Note You must start the MS-DOS operating system to format the floppy disk that you will be using for your MS-DOS bootable floppy disk. Running **format** from the command prompt does not copy the correct Partition Boot Sector to the floppy disk.

▶ **To create an MS-DOS bootable floppy disk**

1. Start MS-DOS. Put a blank floppy disk in drive A. Type **format a: /s** and press ENTER. You must specify the **/s** switch to make the floppy disk bootable. This switch causes the format program to copy the file Command.com to the floppy disk.
2. Copy other MS-DOS-based utilities that you might want to use to the floppy disk. At a minimum, you should copy these files:
   - Attrib
   - Copy
   - Format
   - Fdisk
   - Mem
   - Sys.com
   - a text editor
   - DiskSave

Testing

Now that you have created floppy disks to use to start the computer, created an Emergency Repair Disk, and backed up the Master Boot Record and Partition Boot Sector, you should use the utilities and floppy disks to practice recovering from problems. Going through the recovery process will force you to be diligent about making backups (Emergency Repair Disk, Master Boot Record, Partition Boot Sector, and data). You will also have an idea as to how long doing each procedure should take.

You should have a computer that you can use to do the following:

- Look at Master Boot Records, Partition Tables, and Partition Boot Sectors.
- Find the backup Partition Boot Sector on an NTFS partition.
- Deliberately destroy and recover Master Boot Records and Partition Boot Sectors.
- Delete Windows NT system files and restore them by using the Emergency Repair Disk.

If you have multiple disks in your configuration or have more than one installation of Windows NT, you should thoroughly test using your Windows NT startup floppy disk to start the computer from each boot partition. This is especially critical on x86-based computers when you have a configuration that has both SCSI and IDE or EIDI disks. Sometimes, when the multi() syntax works to start from a SCSI hard disk, you must modify the Boot.ini file on the Windows NT startup floppy disk to use the scsi() syntax.

Restoring Disk Information

If you have backed up the Registry, Master Boot Records, and Partition Boot Sectors, as recommended earlier in this chapter, you can recover from many disk and startup problems without having to reinstall Windows NT. This section describes using the floppy disks and tools to restart your computer and restore information.

One important thing that you can learn from testing is the best recovery procedure to use in a particular situation. For example, there are several methods that you can use to replace a Partition Boot Sector. You also want to learn when to use the Windows NT startup floppy disk to restart your computer, and when you have to use the repair process and the Emergency Repair Disk to replace files in order to start.

Starting Up by Using the Windows NT Startup Floppy Disk

Using the Windows NT startup floppy disk enables you to start up Windows NT so that you can troubleshoot the problem, recover from the problem, or just get the computer running again. Being able to restart the computer also enables you to finish the work that you need to get done now, and troubleshoot the problem later.

In a way, the Windows NT startup floppy disk is a troubleshooting tool. If you cannot start the computer by using the hard disk, and you can start by using the Windows NT startup floppy disk, the problem is probably one of the following:

- There are problems with the disk that contains the system partition, and the boot partition is on another disk.
- Something is wrong with the system partition itself, the Partition Boot Sector for the system partition, or the files on the system partition that are needed to start Windows NT.
- On an x86-based computer, you are reconfiguring your disks, and your first hard disk does not have a system partition yet.

Using the Emergency Repair Disk

If your system files, Registry information, or Partition Boot Sector are corrupt, and you are unable to start Windows NT by using the Last Known Good control set, you can use the Repair process in Windows NT Setup to restore your system so you can start up.

To repair a Windows NT installation, Setup needs either the configuration information that is saved on the %systemroot%\Repair folder or the Emergency Repair Disk created when you installed the operating system (or you created later by using the Repair Disk program).

You cannot repair all disk problems by using the Emergency Repair Disk. Your Emergency Repair Disk needs to match the version of Windows NT that you have installed on your computer. It also needs to have current configuration information. If you have more than one installation of Windows NT on your computer, you should have an Emergency Repair Disk for each installation. You should never use an Emergency Repair Disk from another computer.

▶ **To use the Emergency Repair Disk**

1. Start the computer from the Windows NT Setup disk 1. Insert disk 2 when it is requested. When prompted, select the option to Repair by pressing the R key. Setup displays the following options:

   ```
   [X]  Inspect Registry files
   [X]  Inspect startup environment
   [X]  Verify Windows NT system files
   [X]  Inspect boot sector
        Continue (perform selected tasks)
   ```

   A description of each of the options follows this procedure.

2. Clear all selections that you do not want to use. Click **Continue (perform selected tasks)**.

3. After disk 3, you will be prompted for the Emergency Repair Disk. Follow the instructions.

   Setup displays the following messages after it has finished the repair process:

   ```
   Setup has completed repairs.
   If there is a floppy disk inserted in drive A:, remove it.
   Press ENTER to restart your computer.
   ```

Inspect Registry Files

The Repair process in Windows NT Setup is one of several ways that you can repair Registry keys. When you select **Inspect Registry files**, Setup provides you with a list of the Registry files that it can restore. It also warns you that restoring a Registry file can result in information being lost. These are the options:

```
[ ] SYSTEM (System Configuration)
[ ] SOFTWARE (Software Information)
[ ] DEFAULT (Default User Profile)
[ ] NTUSER.DAT (New User Profile)
[ ] SECURITY (Security Policy) and
    SAM (User Accounts Database)
    Continue (perform selected tasks)
```

Select the key(s) that you want to restore by entering an X between the brackets, such as:

```
[X] SYSTEM (System Information)
```

See "Creating an Emergency Repair Disk," presented earlier in this chapter, for information about how often to create the disk, and how to save the current keys.

Inspect Startup Environment

This option verifies that the Windows NT files in the system partition are the correct ones. If any of the files that are needed to start Windows NT are missing or corrupt, Repair replaces them from the *Windows NT Workstation* CD.

On x86-based computers, if Windows NT is not listed in the Boot.ini file, Repair adds a Windows NT option to the file. If there is no Boot.ini file, Repair creates one.

On a RISC-based computer, Repair inspects and repairs the startup information in the NVRAM.

Verify Windows NT System Files

This option uses a checksum to verify that each file in the installation is good and matches the file that was installed from the *Windows NT Workstation* CD. Repair uses the Setup.log file on the Emergency Repair Disk to determine what files were installed and their checksums. The repair process also verifies that files needed to start, such as NTLDR and Ntoskrnl.exe, are present and valid. To find out if one or more service packs need to be reinstalled, check Files.lst on each service pack. The *Windows NT Workstation* CD is required for this option.

When Repair determines that the file on the disk does not match what was installed, it displays a message that identifies the file and asks whether you want to replace it.

Inspect Boot Sector (x86-based Computers)

This option verifies that the Partition Boot Sector on the system partition still references NTLDR, and replaces it from the Emergency Repair Disk if it does not. The Repair process can only replace the Partition Boot Sector for the system partition on the first hard disk. The Repair process can also repair the Partition Boot Sector for the system partition on the startup disk.

If you have saved the Partition Boot Sector, you can also use the procedures described in "Replacing the Master Boot Record and the Partition Boot Sector," presented later in this chapter, to replace it.

Restoring Registry Information

There are several methods that you can use to restore Registry information.

- You can use the Repair process in Windows NT Setup, which requires the Emergency Repair Disk.
- If you have used Windows NT Backup or the *Windows NT Workstation Resource Kit* program Regback.exe to back up the Registry, you can restore the keys from the backup media.
- You can restore just the SYSTEM key or the DISK subkey by using the procedures described in this section.

Note *Windows NT* Setup and the Repair Disk program store Registry information on the Emergency Repair Disk in compressed format. If you decide to restore the key from the Emergency Repair Disk by using either Disk Administrator or the Registry Editor, you can uncompress the System._ file by using one of the expand utilities. See Chapter 22, "Disk, File System, and Backup Utilities."

Restoring the SYSTEM Key

You can use the procedures in this section to restore the SYSTEM key. Because the Emergency Repair Disk also contains this key, you would generally use these procedures only if:

- You do not have an Emergency Repair Disk.
- You cannot read the Emergency Repair Disk, or the information is not current.
- You had to reinstall Windows NT Workstation and want to have the most recent configuration information.

To use this procedure, you need to have saved the information, following the procedures in the section titled "Saving the SYSTEM Key," presented earlier in this chapter.

▶ **To use Disk Administrator to restore the SYSTEM key**

1. On the **Partition** menu, click **Configuration**.
2. On the **Configuration** menu, click **Restore**.

   A message warns you that this operation will overwrite your current disk configuration information with what was previously saved on the floppy disk. Also, any changes made during this session will be lost.
3. Insert the floppy disk containing the saved configuration information.
4. Click **OK**.

   Disk Administrator initiates a restart of your computer.

If you do not have a floppy disk that contains the current SYSTEM key, you can search for other Windows NT installations and restore the key from *systemroot*\System32\Config\System. In this case, the information might not match the configuration that you had been using.

▶ **To use Disk Administrator to search for and restore the SYSTEM key**

1. On the **Partition** menu, click **Configuration**.
2. On the **Configuration** menu, click **Search**.

   A message warns you that this operation will overwrite your current disk configuration information with the information from a different installation of Windows NT. Also, any changes made during this session will be lost.
3. Click **OK**.

   Disk Administrator scans your disk for other Windows NT installations, and displays a list of the installations.
4. Select an installation.
5. Click **OK**.

   Disk Administrator initiates a restart of your computer.

See Chapter 36, "General Troubleshooting," for details about troubleshooting problems by using the SYSTEM key.

Restoring the DISK Subkey

Both the Repair Disk program and Disk Administrator save the DISK subkey with the other information that they save. You would use this procedure only if you do not have current information on either of these media or you cannot read them. You might also want to use this procedure in special situations to restore just the DISK subkey, such as having to move a stripe set from one computer to another when the first computer has failed.

If you have previously saved the DISK subkey by using the Registry Editor (see the section titled "Backing up the Registry," earlier in this chapter), then you can restore it.

▶ **To restore the DISK subkey**

1. Select the Registry key HKEY_LOCAL_MACHINE\SYSTEM\DISK.
2. On the **Registry** menu, click **Restore**.
3. Enter the filename or click the path to the file.

   If you are restoring the key to a remote computer's Registry, the C drive designation that appears in the scroll list refers to the C drive on the remote computer.
4. Click **OK**.

Replacing the Master Boot Record and the Partition Boot Sector

For information about determining if you have a problem with either of these disk sectors, and procedures for displaying them, see Chapter 21, "Troubleshooting Startup and Disk Problems." For information about the utilities that you can use to save, replace, and edit these disk sectors, see Chapter 22, "Disk, File System, and Backup Utilities."

Caution Be careful when you use the low-level disk editors described in this section. If you replace the wrong sector, or change individual bytes to the wrong data, you can make your problems far worse. You could destroy information that is needed by Windows NT, and your only option would be to reformat the partition or the entire disk.

Replacing the Master Boot Record

There are two problems that can occur in the sector containing the Master Boot Record:

- The Master Boot Record might be corrupt.
- The Partition Tables can be damaged.

On many x86-based computers, the fastest and simplest way to replace the Master Boot Record is to use an MS-DOS bootable floppy disk with the MS-DOS-based program Fdisk on it.

Caution Do not use Fdisk to replace the Master Boot Record if you are using a:

- Third-party translation program.
- Dual-boot program that writes information in the area between the code and the Partition Table.
- Third-party partitioning program that writes information in the area between the code and the Partition Table.

If you do not know whether you are using a program like this, you should not use this method.

▶ **To replace the Master Boot Record**

1. Start the computer by using the MS-DOS bootable floppy disk. (You did run virus check and lock the floppy disk after you made it, didn't you?)
2. At the **A:** prompt, type **fdisk /mbr**.

   This command replaces the Master Boot Record without altering the Partition Tables at the end of the sector. There is no message or response.

If there is a *Windows NT* disk signature in the Master Boot Record, it is overwritten by the new Master Boot Record. Overwriting the disk signature is a problem only if the disk contains partitions or logical drives that are members of volume sets or stripe sets. You can safely overwrite the disk signature when the disk has no volume sets or stripe sets, because Disk Administrator writes a new disk signature the next time you run it.

Note The **fdisk /mbr** command requires MS-DOS 5.0 or later, and only works on the first hard disk on the computer.

If you have saved the Master Boot Record by using either DiskSave (x86-based computers only) or DiskProbe, you can use one of these utilities to replace the Master Boot Record. These utilities rewrite the entire sector, including the Partition Table. If you cannot start Windows NT from the hard disk, you can usually start the computer by using the Windows NT startup floppy disk if you want to use DiskProbe to replace the Master Boot Record.

If none of these methods are available to you, you can use a low-level disk editor to copy a good Master Boot Record from another disk to the startup disk (usually disk 0 on x86-based computers). Since the smallest disk write is a sector, when you copy the Master Boot Record from another disk, you are also copying the other disk's Partition Table, which is not valid for the current disk. Therefore, you must first write down the partition information in the Master Boot Record that you are going to replace, starting from 0x1BE. You have to manually reenter the Partition Table information in hex format into the newly copied sector.

If you can start Windows NT by using the Windows NT startup floppy disk, you can use DiskMap to print a map of the disk. When you have copied a Master Boot Record from another computer of the same type (for example, another computer made by the same manufacturer with the same models of disk controllers), use DiskProbe to enter the information for the Partition Table. For information about DiskMap and DiskProbe, see Chapter 22, "Disk, File System, and Backup Utilities."

After you have replaced the Master Boot Record, you should check that it is now correct. If the Master Boot Record is not correct after replacing it, there is either a hardware problem, such as incorrect SCSI termination, or (on x86-based computers) there is a virus in memory that is trapping INT 13 calls. You have to isolate and correct the problem that is corrupting the Master Boot Record.

Repairing the Partition Table

If you have not changed the Partition Table since you saved the Master Boot Record, replacing the Master Boot Record also replaces the Partition Table.

If you have made only minor changes to the Partition Table since you saved the Master Boot Record, you might be able to use the information on the backup to help you repair the Partition Table. For instance, if the only change you have made is to convert a partition from FAT to NTFS, just change the System ID byte from 06 to 07.

If your disk has more than one partition, and you did not save the Master Boot Record or write down the information, you might be able to reconstruct it. You can use DiskProbe to edit the Partition Table.

Note If you will have to completely rebuild your Partition Table, either because of corruption or you had to copy the Master Boot Record from another computer, it might be safer to completely rebuild your disk. In this case, you should back up all of your files to tape (or another computer), recreate and reformat the partitions on the hard disk, and restore the data. If the disk with the invalid Partition Table contains your system or your boot partition, you will probably have to use the Windows NT startup floppy disk to start your computer.

Replacing the Partition Boot Sector

There are several methods that you can use to replace the Partition Boot Sector.

If you have saved the Partition Boot Sector by using either the DiskProbe or the DiskSave program, you can replace the sector from the backup. This is the fastest way to replace the Partition Boot Sector.

For NTFS volumes, there is one other alternative. When you create or reformat an existing volume as an NTFS volume, the NTFS file system writes a duplicate of the Partition Boot Sector at the end of the volume (Windows NT version 4.0) or at the logical center of the volume (Windows NT 3.51 and earlier). You can use the Windows NT–based program DiskProbe to locate and copy this sector to the beginning of the volume. There are also third-party MS-DOS-based disk utilities that you can use to locate and copy this sector.

You might want to display the Partition Boot Sector to make sure it is now correct. Once you have copied the Partition Boot Sector to the first sector of the partition, you should be able to start Windows NT.

Restoring Windows NT Files on the System Partition

If any of the files that Windows NT installs on the system partition are missing or corrupt, you cannot start your computer. These are the files:

x86-based file	Folder	RISC-based file	Folder
NTLDR	root	Osloader.exe	\Os\Winnt40
Boot.ini	root	no equivalent	
Bootsect.dos	root	no equivalent	
Ntdetect.com	root	no equivalent	
Ntbootdd.sys (SCSI only)	root	no equivalent	
Hal.dll is in the boot partition		Hal.dll	\Os\Winnt40
no equivalent		*.pal files (Alpha-based computers)	\Os\Winnt40

You can restore any of these files by using the Repair process and the Emergency Repair Disk. However, because you copied these files to your Windows NT startup floppy disk when you created it, you can use that disk to restore them.

▶ **To use the Windows NT startup floppy disk to restore system files**

1. Start your computer by using the Windows NT startup floppy disk.
2. Replace individual files, or replace all of the files, by copying them from the Windows NT startup floppy disk to the corresponding location on your system partition.

Using an Uninterruptible Power Supply

An Uninterruptible Power Supply (UPS) supplies power to a computer system in the event of a power fluctuation or complete power loss. The UPS has electronics built in that constantly monitor line voltages. If the line voltage fluctuates above or below predefined limits, or fails entirely, the UPS supplies power to the computer system from built-in batteries. The UPS converts the relatively low Direct Current (DC) battery voltage into the Alternating Current (AC) voltage required by the computer system. The changeover to batteries must take place very rapidly or the computer can lose data.

Most UPS devices are one of the following types:

- Online UPS. You connect an online UPS between the main power and the computer to constantly supply your computer system with power. Connecting it to the main power keeps its battery charged. This method provides power conditioning, which means that it removes spikes, surges, sags, and noise.
- Standby UPS. This device is configured to provide either the main power or its own power source and to switch from one to the other as necessary. When the main power is available, the UPS device connects the main power directly to the computer and monitors the main power voltage level. When the main power fails or the voltage falls below an acceptable level, the UPS device switches the power fed to the computer from the main power to its own power.

UPS systems provide a hardware interface that can be connected to the computer. Using appropriate software, this interface enables an orderly handling of the power failure, including performing a system shutdown before the UPS batteries are depleted. Without such software, an orderly shutdown of the system is not possible without human intervention.

The most important consideration in selecting a UPS product is to use only hardware that is listed on the Windows NT 4.0 Hardware Compatibility List (HCL). Other items to consider are:

- Whether to use a UPS per computer or have larger capacity, centralized UPSs that protect multiple computers.
- What type of UPS you want (standby and online are the most common).
- The sizing for the UPS (how big the UPS needs to be to protect the load).
- How long it needs to keep running before automatic shutdown.

- Which features you want to have in your UPS, such as:
    - Continuous conditioning of the incoming power to provide clean, steady power.
    - A Simple Network Management Protocol (SNMP) card that you can plug into the UPS and use network management software to remotely monitor the UPS.
    - Software that logs UPS information to the event log, or produces statistics.
    - Software for testing the integrity and reliability of the UPS battery.

Windows NT has built-in UPS functionality that takes advantage of the special features that many UPS systems provide. These features ensure the integrity of data on the system and provide for an orderly shutdown of both the computer system and the UPS should a power failure last long enough that the UPS batteries become depleted. In addition, users connected to a computer running Windows NT Workstation can be notified that a shutdown will occur and new users are prevented from connecting to the computer. Finally, damage to the hardware from a sudden, uncontrolled shutdown can be prevented.

Some vendors also provide a user interface for configuring the UPS, which you can use instead of the one provided in Windows NT.

This section contains a general overview of the Windows NT UPS service and discusses configuring and using the UPS on a computer running Windows NT. To fully protect your network, you should also install UPSs on network devices such as routers, hubs, and bridges. For the best protection, install UPSs on the cables that connect your computer and modem, telephone, printer, and network equipment.

Configuring the UPS Service

Use the UPS option on Control Panel to configure the Windows NT UPS service. The following dialog box is displayed:

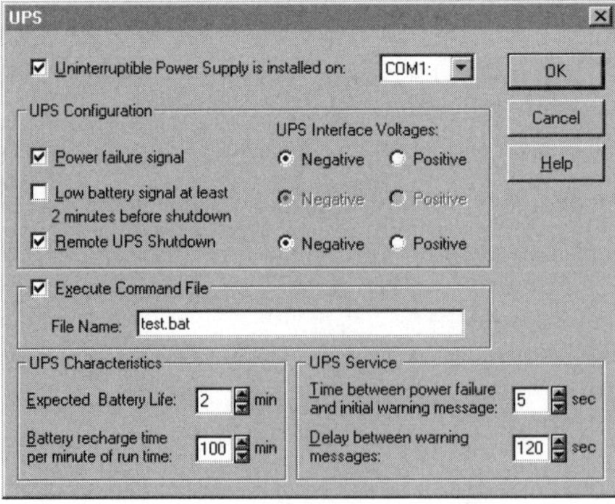

You need to specify the serial port that the UPS is installed on. The information that you enter in the other fields depends upon your specific UPS and how you want to use it.

When selecting the signals to use in the **UPS Configuration** group box, the interface voltages you specify are those that indicate an active state for the signal. In other words, if you select a negative interface voltage for the power failure signal, this means that the signal is normally positive and changes to negative when a power failure occurs.

If you want the UPS service to run a command file when a power failure occurs, select the **Execute Command File** check box and enter the name of the file. Windows NT terminates the command file if it does not complete its execution within 30 seconds. The command file should not contain a dialog box, since waiting for user input could exceed the 30 second requirement.

The command file must reside in your *%systemroot%*\system32 folder and have one of the following extensions:

- .exe
- .com
- .bat
- .cmd

If your UPS does not have a low battery signal, you need to set the fields in the **UPS Characteristics** group box. The documentation from your UPS vendor should specify the battery recharge rate.

At startup, the UPS service assumes that the battery has no charge. If the battery recharge rate is 100 minutes per minute of run time, the computer has to run for 100 minutes before Windows NT expects the battery to have one minute of life.

Signals Used by the UPS Service

Windows NT uses a serial (COM) port to connect to the UPS. Table 20.1 shows the signals that the Windows NT UPS service uses to communicate with the UPS, the associated pin numbers, and the function each signal provides to the UPS service. You need to know which of these signals your UPS supports so that you can configure the UPS service.

If you use a UPS service provided by your UPS vendor, the signals and their usage will probably be different than the signals that the Windows NT UPS service uses.

Table 20.1 UPS Serial Port Connections

RS-232 Signal	9 Pin Connector Pin #	25 Pin Connector Pin #	UPS Usage
CTS	8	5	Power failure
DCD	1	8	Low battery
DTR	4	20	UPS shutdown

In the **UPS Configuration** group box, check the boxes that correspond to the signals that your UPS supports. For each of these signals, the **UPS Interface Voltages** (negative or positive) indicates the voltage present when that event occurs.

Low Battery Signal

When the UPS battery begins to run low, the UPS uses this signal to notify the UPS service.

When fully charged, UPSs typically deliver from five to 20 minutes of DC power after AC power has failed. If your UPS can detect when the battery is running down, you should check the low battery signal box in the **UPS Configuration** group box.

If you do not check the low battery signal box, the UPS service uses the information in the **UPS Characteristics** group box to estimate how much time remains on the battery after a power failure.

Remote UPS Shutdown

You want to conserve the life of the UPS battery for as long as possible. The UPS service uses the UPS Shutdown signal to notify the UPS that Windows NT has completed its orderly shutdown and that the UPS can shut off power to the computer.

Power Failure Signal

The power failure signal is generated by the UPS to signal the UPS service that a power failure has occurred. The Windows NT processing that occurs when it receives this signal depends upon whether the UPS can send a low battery signal.

If the UPS can send a low battery signal:

- The Windows NT UPS service waits the amount of time specified in the **Time between power failure and initial warning message** field of the **UPS Service** group box. It then sends a message to all users connected to the computer running Windows NT telling them that a power failure has occurred. No more users can connect to the computer after the message is sent.
- If a signal is received from the UPS indicating that power has been restored before the low battery signal occurs, normal operations are resumed. Users are again allowed to connect to the computer.
- When the UPS signals a low battery condition, the file specified in the **Execute Command File** group box is executed. After execution of this file, Windows NT initiates shutdown.
- Once the shutdown is complete, the UPS service signals the UPS that battery power can be turned off if you have checked **Remote UPS Shutdown**.

If the UPS cannot send a low battery signal:

- The UPS service computes the expected battery life left by dividing the **Battery recharge time per minute of run time** (in the **UPS Characteristics** group box) into the amount of time that Windows NT has been running. If the result is less than two minutes, then the file specified in the **Execute Command File** group box is executed and allowed 30 seconds to complete. Windows NT then initiates a shutdown.
- If the expected battery life is greater than two minutes, the UPS service waits the amount of time specified in the **Time between power failure and initial warning message** field of the **UPS Service** group box. It then sends a message to all users connected to the computer running Windows NT telling them that a power failure has occurred. No more users can connect to the computer after the message is sent.
- If a signal is received from the UPS indicating that power has been restored while the expected battery life is still greater than two minutes, normal operation resumes. Users are again allowed to connect to the computer.
- When the calculated battery life reaches two minutes, the file specified in the **Execute Command File** group box is executed. After execution of this file, Windows NT initiates shutdown. If the program takes longer than 30 seconds to complete, Windows NT terminates it, and final shutdown take places.
- Once the shutdown is complete, the UPS service signals the UPS that battery power can be turned off if you have checked **Remote UPS Shutdown**.

Using the UPS Service

You should use the following Windows NT services in combination with the Windows NT UPS service:

- Alerter
- Messenger
- EventLog

The Alerter service sends alerts to selected users. The Messenger service sends messages to your local computer and to other users on the network who are running Windows NT. All detected power fluctuations and power failures are recorded in the event log, along with UPS service start failures and shutdown initiations.

If you want the UPS service to start each time you start your computer, you need to modify the startup information.

▶ **To start the UPS service automatically**

1. On Control Panel, double-click **Services**.
2. On the **Services** dialog box, click **UPS**, then click **Startup**.
3. On the UPS **Service** dialog box, select **Automatic**, and then click **OK**.

You might need to use the preceding procedure to set the other services to start automatically.

Testing the UPS

When the UPS service is started, it verifies the settings in the UPS dialog box by ensuring that the signal polarity on the CTS and DCD pins is opposite to that specified as the failure condition in the **UPS** dialog box. For example, if the **UPS** dialog box specifies that the UPS device supports a Power Failure Signal (CTS pin) with a positive signal, the UPS service checks to make sure that this pin is not already asserted positive (which would not happen unless you had started the system during a power failure).

This has some important implications. With an online UPS, the UPS device might shut itself off immediately if the configuration is incorrect. With a standby UPS, an incorrect configuration typically shuts the UPS device off as soon as a power failure is detected, effectively circumventing the purpose of the UPS. This is why it is important to configure and test your UPS device to ensure that it operates correctly.

On x86-based computers, there is one other reason that it is important to test your UPS. During startup, Windows NT sends a detection signal to each port in order to recognize hardware attached to that port. Some UPS units using serial monitoring implementations respond to the detection signal by turning off. If this happens, use the **/NoSerialMice** switch in the Boot.ini file to prevent the system from sending this signal to the COM port to which your UPS unit is connected.

You can use multiple /NoSerialMice switches. The format is:

```
/NoSerialMice=[COMx | COMx,COMy,COMz,...]
```

- If **/NoSerialMice** is specified without parameters, serial mouse detection is disabled on all the serial ports.
- If **/NoSerialMice=COM*x*** is specified, serial mouse detection is only disabled on COM*x*.
- If **/NoSerialMice=COM*x*,COM*y*,COM*z* ...** is specified, serial mouse detection is disabled on each of the specified ports.

To ensure that the computer is protected from power failures, you can test it by simulating a power failure (that is, by disconnecting the main power supply to the UPS device). Your computer and peripherals connected to the UPS device should remain operational, and messages should be displayed and events logged. Wait until the UPS battery reaches a low level to verify that a graceful shutdown occurs. Restore the main power to the UPS device, and check the event log to ensure that all actions were logged and that there were no errors.

Note Before you begin any UPS tests, make sure that your UPS has sufficient charge built up to run all of the devices connected to it for at least the duration of the test.

Simulating UPS Operation

The next figure shows a simple simulator that you can build to emulate the power failure and low battery signals from a UPS.

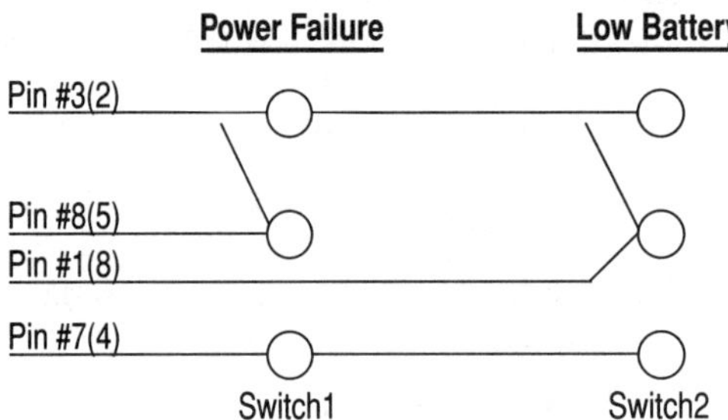

Figure 20.1 UPS Simulator

Note The pins numbers in the diagram are for a 9-pin serial port. For a 25-pin connector, use the pin numbers in parenthesis.

You can use two Single Pole Double Throw (SPDT) switches to construct the UPS simulator. To simulate normal operation, set both switches 1 and 2 to make contact with pin 7 (pin 4 on a 25-pin connector). Set both the **Power failure signal** and **Low battery signal at least 2 minutes before shutdown** to **Negative** in the **UPS** dialog box.

To simulate a power failure, move switch 1 to make contact with pin 3 (pin 2 on a 25-pin connector). Moving switch 2 to make contact with pin 3 simulates a low battery condition.

Simulating Power Failure and Low Battery Signals

To simulate the operation of a UPS with both a Power Failure and Low Battery signal, have both switches making contact with pin 7. Configure your UPS as shown in this dialog box:

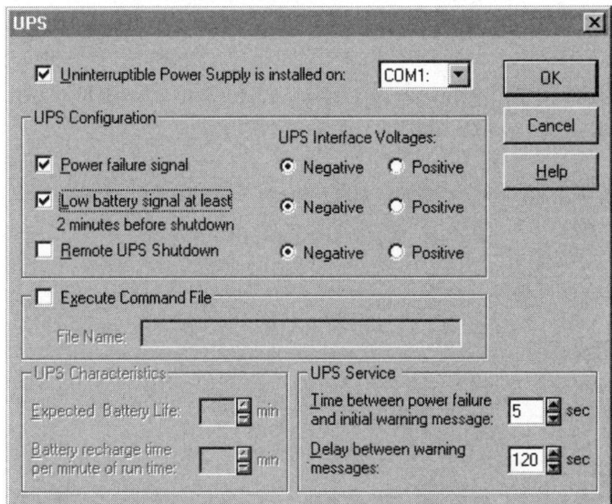

Flip switch 1 to simulate a Power Failure signal. After five seconds, the initial warning message should be displayed. Every 120 seconds, the warning message should be displayed again.

When you know that the Power Failure signal processing is working correctly, flip switch 2. If you have checked the **Execute Command File** check box and specified a filename, the file should begin execution immediately. If the file does not finish executing within 30 seconds, Windows NT should terminate it. Windows NT should perform an orderly shutdown after the file terminates or immediately after the Power Failure signal if no file is specified.

Simulating UPS With Power Failure Signal Only

To simulate the operation of a UPS with only a Power Failure signal, have both switches making contact with pin 7. For purposes of this test, you can set the values in the **UPS Characteristics** group box to make it seem that your computer does not have to run very long before the battery is fully charged. When you set the values this way, you have to make sure that your battery does have enough charge to be able to complete the tests. For instance, if you set the values as shown in this dialog box, and let your computer run for 20 minutes, the UPS service assumes that the battery is fully charged.

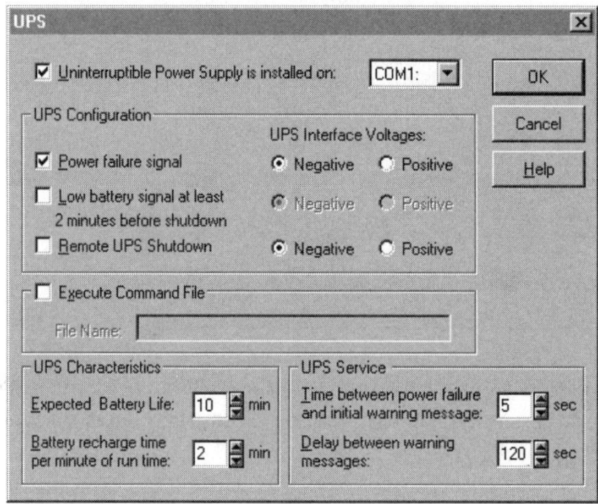

You can test two scenarios with this configuration:

- If you connect switch 1 to pin 3 within four minutes of starting the UPS service, the expected battery life is less than two minutes, and Windows NT should begin shutdown immediately.
- If you allow the computer to run for 20 minutes before you flip switch 1, the battery is assumed to be fully charged. When you flip switch 1, the warning message should be displayed after five seconds. Every 120 seconds, another warning message should be displayed. Shutdown should not begin until the expected battery life decreases to two minutes.

CHAPTER 21

Troubleshooting Startup and Disk Problems

This chapter discusses what you can do to find the cause of problems when your computer fails to complete startup. Failure to complete startup means that the computer stops or displays an error message before you can log on to Windows NT. This chapter also discusses causes of and recovery from disk problems.

There are several utilities that you can use to troubleshoot these kinds of problems. The *Windows NT Workstation Resource Kit* CD contains a Windows NT–based utility, DiskProbe, that you can use to examine and change information on individual disk sectors. Chapter 22, “Disk, File System, and Backup Utilities,” contains more information about DiskProbe and the MS-DOS-based utilities that you can use to read, write, and change information on disk sectors.

Other Sources of Information

There are several other sources of information for troubleshooting startup and disk problems:

- Chapter 23, "Overview of the Windows NT Registry," describes how to use information in the Registry for troubleshooting and configuration maintenance.
- Chapter 25, "Configuration Management and the Registry," provides problem solving techniques using the Registry.
- Chapter 36, "General Troubleshooting," contains details about Microsoft's sources for troubleshooting information and contains more details about troubleshooting hardware, software, and startup problems.
- Chapter 39, "Windows NT Debugger," describes the different kinds of Kernel STOP errors that you might see during startup. It also contains information about using the Windows NT Debugger.
- Windows NT online help contains a troubleshooting topic.
- The Microsoft Knowledge Base contains support information developed by Microsoft Product Support Specialists. The Windows NT Knowledge Base is included on the *Windows NT Workstation Resource Kit* CD. It is also included on the:
  - Microsoft Developer Network (MSDN) CD
  - TechNet CD
  - Microsoft Internet FTP host, ftp.microsoft.com
  - Technical Support and Services category on the Web page at http://www.microsoft.com/ntworkstation

Troubleshooting Startup Problems on x86-based Computers

There are several things that can prevent a computer from successfully completing startup. The first step in figuring out what may be causing a problem is to determine whether the problem is occurring before the operating system takes control. If you do not see the boot loader screen on an x86-based computer, the problem may be due to a hardware failure, the Master Boot Record, Partition Tables, or the Partition Boot Sector, which might be damaged.

There are several ways such damage can happen, including viruses. On x86-based computers, viruses use BIOS interrupt (INT) 13 calls to install themselves, so they are operating-system independent. Windows NT traps BIOS INT 13 calls while it is running, but cannot protect itself when the computer is started from an MS-DOS bootable floppy disk or is dual-booted by using MS-DOS. The Knowledge Base contains several articles about protecting your computer from viruses and recovering from problems with viruses.

If the problem occurs after selecting Windows NT from the boot loader screen, files that are needed by the operating system might be missing or corrupt.

If you have installed new hardware or new drivers, they could be causing the problem.

Problem Occurs Before the Boot Loader Starts

This section describes the problems that might occur between the time you turn the computer on until you see the boot loader screen.

Symptoms of problems in this group are:

- The computer hangs immediately after the Power On Self Test (POST).
- You do not see the boot loader screen.
- You receive messages such as:
  - Missing operating system.
  - A disk read error occurred.
  - Insert a system diskette and restart the system.
  - Invalid Partition Table.
  - Hard Disk Error.
  - Hard Disk Absent/Failed.

It is possible that you will not be able to start your computer to troubleshoot the problem. If all of your volumes are NTFS, using MS-DOS-based utilities will not do much good. If you have created a Windows NT startup floppy disk, as described in Chapter 20, "Preparing for and Performing Recovery," you can trying using that disk. If you cannot start the computer by using your Windows NT startup floppy disk, and repairing your system by using the Emergency Repair Disk does not fix the problem, you can try removing it from the computer and installing it as a second disk on another Windows NT computer. You can then use Windows NT–based utilities for troubleshooting.

Caution Moving disks between computers is not supported because of problems that can arise when the disk controllers on the two systems are incompatible or are configured differently. However, if your two computers are configured the same, you might be able to identify and correct the problem.

The problem could be one of the following:

- There is no system partition on the first hard disk.
- The Master Boot Record is corrupt.
- The Partition Boot Sector is corrupt.
- The Boot.ini file is missing.
- The Windows NT boot loader, NTLDR, is missing or corrupt.
- The Complementary Metal Oxide Semiconductor (CMOS) is corrupt, or the CMOS battery is run down.
- Hardware has malfunctioned.

Troubleshooting System Partition Problems

When you startup from the hard disk on x86-based computers, the system BIOS code identifies the startup disk (usually disk 0), and reads the Master Boot Record. The code in the Master Boot Record searches for a system partition on the hard disk. If it cannot find such a system partition, or cannot start Windows NT from it, the startup process stops. If you get an error message such as "Error loading operating system," then the Master Boot Record code found a system partition, but could not start the operating system.

It is possible that there is no system partition on the hard disk from which you want to startup the computer. You might also have the wrong partition identified as the system partition. You can use the MS-DOS-based utility Fdisk to look at the partition information. For information about other utilities that have similar functionality, see Chapter 22, "Disk, File System, and Backup Utilities."

Note The system partition is the primary partition on the startup disk (usually disk 0) that has the Boot Indicator field set to 0x80. It contains the files that are needed to load Windows NT, such as Boot.ini and NTLDR.

Fdisk refers to the system partition as the active partition.

▶ **To use Fdisk to check for and set the system partition**

1. Start MS-DOS, or start from an MS-DOS startup floppy disk that contains the Fdisk utility. Type **fdisk**.

   Fdisk displays the following message if there is no system partition on your first hard disk:

   ```
   WARNING!  No partitions are set active - disk 1 is not startable
   unless a partition is set active.
   ```

2. The FDISK Options screen has several choices. The cursor will be on "Enter choice." Type 2 (**Set Active partition**). Fdisk displays information about the partitions on the hard disk. One partition should have an **A** in the **Status** column, which indicates it is the (active) system partition.
3. If there is no system partition, or the wrong partition is set as the system partition, enter the number of the partition that contains the files to use when loading the operating system. Fdisk displays the message "Partition X made active," where X is the partition number you entered.
4. Press ESC to return to the **FDISK Options** screen, and press ESC again to exit Fdisk. You can now restart the computer. Be sure to remove the floppy disk.

Not all computers should be set to start from the first partition. For instance, you can configure multiple partitions and install different operating systems on each partition. Some computers have EISA configuration partitions, and normally start from the second physical partition. For example, many Compaq computers are configured this way. However, the system partition should always be on your first physical hard disk.

Troubleshooting Master Boot Record Problems

This section describes troubleshooting Master Boot Record problems. The section titled "Master Boot Record," in Chapter 17, "Disk and File System Basics," contains details about the Master Boot Record.

The functions of the Master Boot Record code are to:

- Read the Partition Table entries in the same sector.
- Determine the location of the Partition Boot Sector.
- Load and execute the code in the Partition Boot Sector.

If the executable code in the Master Boot Record does not do these functions, it displays one of these error messages:

- **Missing operating system.**
- **Invalid Partition Table.**

Note There is a Master Boot Record on each hard disk. However, only the Master Boot Record on the first hard disk is used in starting Windows NT.

Use DiskProbe or an MS-DOS-based utility to display the Master Boot Record. The example here shows what you should see at Cylinder 0, Side 0, Sector 1, which is the location for the Master Boot Record. This example shows the executable code in a Master Boot Record. This example might not match the code in the Master Boot Record on your computer, because some third-party boot and disk partitioning utilities modify the code in the Master Boot Record.

```
                                               Physical Sector: Cyl 0, Side 0, Sector 1
00000000: 00 33 C0 8E D0 BC 00 7C  - 8B F4 50 07 50 1F FB FC   .3.....|..P.P..
00000010: BF 00 06 B9 00 01 F2 A5  - EA 1D 06 00 00 BE BE 07   ................
00000020: B3 04 80 3C 80 74 0E 80  - 3C 00 75 1C 83 C6 10 FE   ...<.t..<.u.....
00000030: CB 75 EF CD 18 8B 14 8B  - 4C 02 8B EE 83 C6 10 FE   .u......L.......
00000040: CB 74 1A 80 3C 00 74 F4  - BE 8B 06 AC 3C 00 74 0B   .t..<.t.....<.t.
00000050: 56 BB 07 00 B4 0E CD 10  - 5E EB F0 EB FE BF 05 00   V.......^.......
00000060: BB 00 7C B8 01 02 57 CD  - 13 5F 73 0C 33 C0 CD 13   ..|...W.._s.3...
00000070: 4F 75 ED BE A3 06 EB D3  - BE C2 06 BF FE 7D 81 3D   Ou...........}.=
00000080: 55 AA 75 C7 8B F5 EA 00  - 7C 00 00 49 6E 76 61 6C   U.u.....|..Inval
00000090: 69 64 20 70 61 72 74 69  - 74 69 6F 6E 20 74 61 62   id partition tab
000000A0: 6C 65 00 45 72 72 6F 72  - 20 6C 6F 61 64 69 6E 67   le.Error loading
000000B0: 20 6F 70 65 72 61 74 69  - 6E 67 20 73 79 73 74 65    operating syste
000000C0: 6D 00 4D 69 73 73 69 6E  - 67 20 6F 70 65 72 61 74   m.Missing operat
000000D0: 69 6E 67 20 73 79 73 74  - 65 6D 00 00 80 45 14 15   ing system...E..
000000E0: 00 00 00 00 00 00 00 00  - 00 00 00 00 00 00 00 00   ................
000000F0: 00 00 00 00 00 00 00 00  - 00 00 00 00 00 00 00 00   ................
00000100: 00 00 00 00 00 00 00 00  - 00 00 00 00 00 00 00 00   ................
00000110: 00 00 00 00 00 00 00 00  - 00 00 00 00 00 00 00 00   ................
00000120: 00 00 00 00 00 00 00 00  - 00 00 00 00 00 00 00 00   ................
00000130: 00 00 00 00 00 00 00 00  - 00 00 00 00 00 00 00 00   ................
00000140: 00 00 00 00 00 00 00 00  - 00 00 00 00 00 00 00 00   ................
00000150: 00 00 00 00 00 00 00 00  - 00 00 00 00 00 00 00 00   ................
00000160: 00 00 00 00 00 00 00 00  - 00 00 00 00 00 00 00 00   ................
00000170: 00 00 00 00 00 00 00 00  - 00 00 00 00 00 00 00 00   ................
00000180: 00 00 00 00 00 00 00 00  - 00 00 00 00 00 00 00 00   ................
00000190: 00 00 00 00 00 00 00 00  - 00 00 00 00 00 00 00 00   ................
000001A0: 00 00 00 00 00 00 00 00  - 00 00 00 00 00 00 00 00   ................
000001B0: 00 00 00 00 00 00 00 00  - FD 4E F2 14 00 00 80 01   .........N......
000001C0: 01 00 06 0F 7F 96 3F 00  - 00 00 51 42 06 00 00 00   ....•.?...QB....
000001D0: 41 97 07 0F FF 2C 90 42  - 06 00 A0 3E 06 00 00 00   A....,.B...>....
000001E0: C1 2D 05 0F FF 92 30 81  - 0C 00 A0 91 01 00 00 00   .-....0.........
000001F0: C1 93 01 0F FF A6 D0 12  - 0E 00 C0 4E 00 00 55 AA   ..........N..U.
```

There are two things that you can check in the Master Boot Record:

- The error message text should be as shown in the example.
- There should be only zeroes between the text "Missing operating system" and location hex 1B8.

A disk signature might or might not be present starting at location 1B8. Having no disk signature does not necessarily indicate a problem.

▶ **To use DiskProbe to display the Master Boot Record**

1. Click the DiskProbe icon in the Resource Kit folder.
2. On the **Drives** menu, click **Physical Drive**. The **Available Physical Drives** are listed as PhysicalDrive*x*, where x=0 for the first hard disk. Double click the disk that contains the Master Boot Record used to start the computer. In the case of an x86-based computer, this disk is usually PhysicalDrive0.
3. In the **Handle 0** group box, click **Set Active**. Click **OK**.
4. On the **Sectors** menu, click **Read**. Set **Starting Sector** to 0 and **Number of Sectors** to 1. Click **Read**.

Troubleshooting Partition Boot Sector Problems

Several known viruses can cause problems with the Partition Boot Sector, even if the volume is formatted with the NTFS file system. Infection can occur by running an MS-DOS-based program from either a floppy disk or by starting up MS-DOS on a dual-boot computer. Most viruses use BIOS INT 13 calls to transfer themselves to an absolute sector on the disk. Windows NT cannot protect itself from this type of infection when it is not running.

In some cases, the damage to the Partition Boot Sector can cause the computer to stop after displaying a blue screen with the message STOP 0x0000007B INACCESSIBLE_BOOT_DEVICE. Another symptom of a Partition Boot Sector problem is that the computer stops before displaying any messages, and the screen remains black.

▶ **To use DiskProbe to display the Partition Boot Sector**

1. Use the DiskProbe procedure in "Troubleshooting Master Boot Record Problems," presented earlier in this chapter, to read the Master Boot Record, which contains the Partition Table.
2. On the **View** menu, click **Partition table**. In the **Partition table index** list box, double click the partition number whose Partition Boot Sector you want to read.
3. Click the **Go** button next to **Relative Sector**.
4. On the **View** menu, click **Bytes** to see a display of the Partition Boot Sector in hex. Otherwise, click **NTFS BootSector** or **FAT BootSector** to see a formatted display of the information.

Because the Partition Boot Sector contains several fields that are computer-specific, every byte in your Partition Boot Sector will not be identical to the information shown in the examples here. The following information should be the same:

- The first three bytes should be the jump instruction.
- The next 11 bytes should be the OEM header string.
- There should be error message text toward the end of the sector.

These examples show portions of the Partition Boot Sector that should be the same or contain similar text on all computers. The first example is for a FAT volume, the second one is for an NTFS volume formatted when running Windows NT 3.5, and the third one is for an NTFS volume formatted when running Windows NT 4.0.

```
00000000: EB 3C 90 4D 53 44 4F 53 - 35 2E 30 00 02 08 01 00   .<.MSDOS5.0.....
00000180: 90 A2 07 02 F8 CB 42 4F - 4F 54 3A 20 43 6F 75 6C   ......BOOT: Coul
00000190: 64 6E 27 74 20 66 69 6E - 64 20 4E 54 4C 44 52 0D   dn't find NTLDR.
000001A0: 0A 00 42 4F 4F 54 3A 20 - 49 2F 4F 20 65 72 72 6F   ..BOOT: I/O erro
000001B0: 72 20 72 65 61 64 69 6E - 67 20 64 69 73 6B 0D 0A   r reading disk..
000001C0: 00 50 6C 65 61 73 65 20 - 69 6E 73 65 72 74 20 61   .Please insert a
000001D0: 6E 6F 74 68 65 72 20 64 - 69 73 6B 00 4E 54 4C 44   nother disk.NTLD
000001E0: 52 20 20 20 20 20 20 00 - 00 00 00 00 00 00 00 00   R      .........
000001F0: 00 00 00 00 00 00 00 00 - 00 00 00 00 00 00 55 AA   ..............U.
```

```
00000000: EB 5B 00 4E 54 46 53 20 - 20 20 20 00 02 01 00 00   .[.NTFS    .....
00000130: F2 C3 1D 00 41 20 64 69 - 73 6B 20 72 65 61 64 20   ....A disk read
00000140: 65 72 72 6F 72 20 6F 63 - 63 75 72 72 65 64 2E 0D   error occurred..
00000150: 0A 00 29 00 41 20 6B 65 - 72 6E 65 6C 20 66 69 6C   ..).A kernel fil
00000160: 65 20 69 73 20 6D 69 73 - 73 69 6E 67 20 66 72 6F   e is missing fro
00000170: 6D 20 74 68 65 20 64 69 - 73 6B 2E 0D 0A 00 25 00   m the disk....%.
00000180: 41 20 6B 65 72 6E 65 6C - 20 66 69 6C 65 20 69 73   A kernel file is
00000190: 20 74 6F 6F 20 64 69 73 - 63 6F 6E 74 69 67 75 6F    too discontiguo
000001A0: 75 73 2E 0D 0A 00 33 00 - 49 6E 73 65 72 74 20 61   us....3.Insert a
000001B0: 20 73 79 73 74 65 6D 20 - 64 69 73 6B 65 74 74 65    system diskette
000001C0: 20 61 6E 64 20 72 65 73 - 74 61 72 74 0D 0A 74 68    and restart..th
000001D0: 65 20 73 79 73 74 65 6D - 2E 0D 0A 00 00 00 00 00   e system........
000001E0: 00 00 00 00 00 00 00 00 - 00 00 00 00 00 00 00 00   ................
000001F0: 00 00 00 00 00 00 00 00 - 00 00 00 00 00 00 55 AA   ..............U.
```

```
00000000: EB 5B 90 4E 54 46 53 20 - 20 20 20 00 02 01 00 00   .[.NTFS    .....
00000130: 07 00 CD 10 EB F2 C3 1D - 00 41 20 64 69 73 6B 20   .........A disk
00000140: 72 65 61 64 20 65 72 72 - 6F 72 20 6F 63 63 75 72   read error occur
00000150: 72 65 64 2E 0D 0A 00 29 - 00 41 20 6B 65 72 6E 65   red....).A kerne
00000160: 6C 20 66 69 6C 65 20 69 - 73 20 6D 69 73 73 69 6E   l file is missin
00000170: 67 20 66 72 6F 6D 20 74 - 68 65 20 64 69 73 6B 2E   g from the disk.
00000180: 0D 0A 00 25 00 41 20 6B - 65 72 6E 65 6C 20 66 69   ...%.A kernel fi
00000190: 6C 65 20 69 73 20 74 6F - 6F 20 64 69 73 63 6F 6E   le is too discon
000001A0: 74 69 67 75 6F 75 73 2E - 0D 0A 00 33 00 49 6E 73   tiguous....3.Ins
000001B0: 65 72 74 20 61 20 73 79 - 73 74 65 6D 20 64 69 73   ert a system dis
000001C0: 6B 65 74 74 65 20 61 6E - 64 20 72 65 73 74 61 72   kette and restar
000001D0: 74 0D 0A 74 68 65 20 73 - 79 73 74 65 6D 2E 0D 0A   t..the system...
000001E0: 00 17 00 5C 4E 54 4C 44 - 52 20 69 73 20 63 6F 6D   ...\NTLDR is com
000001F0: 70 72 65 73 73 65 64 2E - 0D 0A 00 00 00 00 55 AA   pressed.......U.
```

Although other corruption problems are possible, if any of the strings are incorrect or missing, you should assume the sector is corrupt.

Even if there is no obvious damage, the Partition Boot Sector might not be working correctly. One way to check for this problem is to change the name of NTLDR to anything else and restart Windows NT from the hard disk.

You should see this error message on a FAT primary partition:

```
Couldn't find NTLDR.
```

You should see this error message on an NTFS primary partition:

```
A kernel file is missing from the disk.
```

These errors indicate that the Partition Boot Sector is okay and that the problem is with a corrupt NTLDR file. In this case, see "Restoring Windows NT Files on the System Partition" in Chapter 20, "Preparing for and Performing Recovery," for information about replacing NTLDR.

If you do not get this error message, then the problem is probably a corrupt Partition Boot Sector. To replace the sector, see "Replacing the Partition Boot Sector," in Chapter 20, "Preparing for and Performing Recovery." Be sure to change the name back to NTLDR so that the Partition Boot Sector can find it again.

NTLDR usually has the Hidden, System, and Read Only attributes set. Because you cannot start Windows NT when the Partition Boot Sector on the boot partition is corrupt, you can start the MS-DOS operating system from the MS-DOS startup floppy disk to change the attributes. To change the attributes by using the MS-DOS attribute command, enter:

```
attrib -s -h -r ntldr
```

CMOS Problems

The CMOS typically stores information about the following:

- Time and date
- Floppy disks
- Video type
- Hard disks
- Memory installed

Each manufacturer and BIOS vendor can decide what a user should be able to configure, and what the standard configuration is. You can access the CMOS through either a utility or a keyboard sequence, depending on the manufacturer. You should write down or use a utility to print all of the CMOS information.

The computer uses the CMOS checksum to determine if any CMOS values have been changed other than by using the CMOS Setup program. If the checksum is not correct, the computer will not start.

Once the CMOS is correctly configured, CMOS problems are usually caused by one of the following:

- A weak battery, which can happen if the computer has not been powered on for a long time.
- The connection between the CMOS and the battery is loose or faulty.
- The CMOS has been damaged from static electric discharge.

All of these problems can result in information in the CMOS being set to zero or otherwise corrupt, thus halting the startup.

Hardware Problems

If a device fails to initialize during POST, there can be a problem with accessing it. If you have changed or added a device since the last startup, the problem might be with the new configuration.

If you have changed your disk configuration, you should check that:

- SCSI devices are terminated properly.
- The BIOS is enabled on only the first SCSI controller (if at all). See "Understanding ARC Pathnames" in Chapter 20, "Preparing For and Performing Recovery," for information about whether the controller BIOS should be enabled.
- There are no IRQ conflicts.

If you have not made any changes, check that:

- Controller cards are seated properly.
- Cables are properly connected.
- Disks are all powered up.

Chapter 36, "General Troubleshooting," discusses hardware problems. The Knowledge Base also contains information about troubleshooting these kinds of problems.

Problem Occurs After the Boot Loader Starts

This section describes troubleshooting problems that might occur from the time NTLDR starts executing through the time that you successfully log onto Windows NT. This phase of startup begins when you see the following message:

```
NTDETECT V1.0 Checking Hardware . . .
```

Using Checked Version of NTDETECT

On x86-based computers, NTDETECT detects installed hardware components.

There is a debug version of Ntdetect.com on the *Windows NT Workstation* product CD, called Ntdetect.chk. If Ntdetect.com fails to detect all of the hardware that you think it should find, you can use the debug version to help isolate the problem. A mouse or a disk controller are the components that typically cause problems.

To use the checked version:

- Rename Ntdetect.com to Ntdetect.bak in the root folder of your system partition.
- Copy Ntdetect.chk from Support\Debug\I386 to the root folder.
- Rename Ntdetect.chk to Ntdetect.com.

The utility Installd on the *Windows NT Workstation Resource Kit* CD performs the same functions.

Ntdetect.com has attributes of Hidden, System, and Read Only set when you install Windows NT. You need to clear these attributes to make the file visible. You can change the attributes by using **My Computer**, **Windows NT Explorer**, or the command prompt.

► **To change file attributes by using My Computer or Windows NT Explorer**

1. On the **View** menu, click **Options**.
2. On the **View** tab, select **Show all files**. Click **OK**.
3. Click the filename NTLDR at the root of the C drive.
4. On the **File** menu, click **Properties**.
5. In the **Attributes** box of the **General** tab, clear the **Read Only** and **Hidden** check boxes, and then click **OK**.

   To change the attributes by using the command prompt, enter:

   ```
   attrib -s -h -r ntldr
   ```

Shutdown Windows NT and restart the computer. When Ntdetect.chk executes, it displays information on the screen as it detects the hardware. This is a sample of the kind of information you might see:

```
Detecting System Component . . .
Reading BIOS date . . .
Done reading BIOS date (1/20/1994)
Detecting Bus/Adapter Component . . .
Collecting Disk Geometry . . .
Detecting Keyboard Component . . .
```

After it finishes displaying information about the components, press ENTER so Ntdetect.chk will continue. Ntdetect.chk next displays information about the current nodes for the controllers and peripherals. You need to press ENTER at the end of each screen of information.

When you have finished using Ntdetect.chk, you should rename Ntdetect.com to Ntdetect.chk and rename Ntdetect.bak to Ntdetect.com.

Using the /maxmem Switch

For x86-based computers, the Boot.ini file has a /maxmem switch that enables you to specify the maximum amount of RAM memory that Windows NT can use. You can use this switch to troubleshoot memory parity errors, mismatched SIMM speeds, and other memory-related problems. To use this switch, the memory must be contiguous. You should never specify a value less than 8 for Windows NT Workstation.

Note Windows NT Workstation can run in 8 MB RAM, although it will probably run quite slowly.

You include this switch at the end of the ARC path specified in the **[operating systems]** section of the Boot.ini file. This example restricts Windows NT Workstation to using only the first 12 MB RAM.

```
multi(0)disk(0)rdisk(0)partition(1)\winnt=Windows NT Workstation 4.0
/MAXMEM=12
```

Chapter 36, "General Troubleshooting," contains more information about troubleshooting memory problems.

Using the /sos Switch

You can add the /sos switch to the Boot.ini file to have NTLDR display the Kernel and device driver names while they are being loaded. Use this switch if Windows NT does not startup and you think a driver is missing or corrupted. See the section "Boot.ini Switches" in Chapter 19, "What Happens When You Start Your Computer," for information about changing Boot.ini switches.

These examples assume that you have installed Windows NT Workstation in the folder winnt40 on partition 2.

First, you should see this message:

```
multi(0)disk(0)rdisk(0)partition(2)\winnt40\System32\ntoskrnl.exe
```

And then this one:

```
Press spacebar now to invoke Hardware Profile/Last Known Good Menu
```

Regardless of whether you press the SPACEBAR, you should see these two messages:

```
multi(0)disk(0)rdisk(0)partition(2)\winnt40\System32\hal.dll
multi(0)disk(0)rdisk(0)partition(2)\winnt40\System32\config.sys
```

The **Hardware Profile/Last Known Good** menu displays at this time if you pressed the spacebar or you have more than one hardware profile. After NTLDR finishes processing the hardware profile information, it clears the screen and displays information such as:

```
multi(0)disk(0)rdisk(0)partition(2)\winnt40\System32\c_1252.nls
multi(0)disk(0)rdisk(0)partition(2)\winnt40\System32\c_437.nls
multi(0)disk(0)rdisk(0)partition(2)\winnt40\System32\n_intl.nls
multi(0)disk(0)rdisk(0)partition(2)\winnt40\FONTS\vgaoem.fon
multi(0)disk(0)rdisk(0)partition(2)\winnt40\System32\Drivers\Atdisk.sys
multi(0)disk(0)rdisk(0)partition(2)\winnt40\System32\Disk.sys
multi(0)disk(0)rdisk(0)partition(2)\winnt40\System32\CLASS2.SYS
multi(0)disk(0)rdisk(0)partition(2)\winnt40\System32\Diskperf.sys
multi(0)disk(0)rdisk(0)partition(2)\winnt40\System32\Ntfs.sys
```

Fatal System Error: 0x0000006B

In some cases on ESDI disks with more than 1024 cylinders, Windows NT Workstation appears to have been successfully installed. However, the first time that you attempt to start from the hard disk, NTLDR loads various files and then produces a Fatal System Error: 0x0000006B with the message that Phase 1 Process Initialization failed. Following this message is a hexadecimal dump and system lockup. If you experience this problem, read the section "ESDI Hard Disks" in Chapter 17, "Disk and File System Basics," for information about the ESDI controllers that Microsoft has tested.

Stop 0x0000007B — Inaccessible Boot Device

This Kernel STOP error means that Windows NT is unable to access the Partition Boot Sector or the required information is not found. A common cause of this error is a virus.

Another cause of the problem is incompatible Logical Block Addressing (LBA). The system BIOS is designed to allow access to fixed disks that use fewer than 1024 cylinders. Many modern disks, however, exceed 1024 cylinders. LBA is used to provide support for these disks. Such support is often built into the system BIOS. However, there are potential problems with LBA:

- If partitions were created and formatted with LBA disabled, and LBA is subsequently enabled, a STOP 0x0000007B can result. The partitions must be created and formatted while the LBA is enabled. In addition, changing LBA modes from one scheme to another can cause you to have to recreate and reformat the partitions.
- Some LBA schemes are not compatible with Windows NT. When in doubt, it is best to check with your vendor.

A corrupt Partition Boot Sector can also cause this problem, depending upon what part is corrupt. This problem is like a virus, except that the corruption is caused by such things as a defective disk or controller, or a bug in a program that somehow has corrupted the Partition Boot Sector.

MS-DOS Will Not Start

You might see one of the following error messages when you have configured your x86-based computer to dual-boot Windows NT and MS-DOS:

Non-System disk or disk error
Replace and press any key when ready

–Or–

Couldn't open boot sector file
multi(0)disk(0)rdisk(0)partition(1):\Bootsect.dos

These error messages occur because the Bootsect.dos file is missing or corrupt. Bootsect.dos is a hidden, system, read-only file that NTLDR uses to start the MS-DOS operating system.

Because Windows NT is able to load correctly and the Partition Boot Sector is not damaged, the Emergency Repair Disk might not detect a problem. To force the Emergency Repair Disk to rewrite Bootsect.dos, you should use the following procedure.

▶ **To replace Bootsect.dos**

1. Shut down and restart the system from an MS-DOS startup floppy disk that contains the MS-DOS program Sys.com. Type **sys c:** at the command prompt.

   You should receive a System Transferred message. Sys.com replaces the Partition Boot Sector, which loads NTLDR, with an MS-DOS Partition Boot Sector that loads Msdos.sys and Io.sys.

2. Start the computer from the Windows NT Setup disk 1. Insert disk 2 when it is requested. When prompted, select the option to **Repair** by entering **R**. Setup displays the following options:

   ```
   [X]  Inspect registry files
   [X]  Inspect startup environment
   [X]  Verify Windows NT system files
   [X]  Inspect boot sector
   Continue (perform selected tasks)
   ```

3. Clear all selections except **Inspect boot sector**. Select **Continue (perform selected tasks).**

4. After disk 3, you will be prompted for the Emergency Repair Disk. Setup displays the following messages after it has finished processing the Emergency Repair Disk:

   ```
   Setup has completed repairs.
   If there is a floppy disk inserted in drive A:, remove it.
   Press ENTER to restart your computer.
   ```

The Repair process replaces the Partition Boot Sector and creates Bootsect.dos so that the dual-boot configuration is restored.

Troubleshooting Startup Problems on RISC-based Computers

RISC-based computers generally have fewer problems at startup than x86-based computers. This is because they do not have problems with viruses destroying the Master Boot Record or the Partition Boot Sector. They also do not have problems with the disk configuration information in the computer not matching what the controller is using.

The startup problems common to RISC-based computers are:

- Missing or incorrect file(s). This problem is usually the result of a user deleting, moving, or renaming a file that is needed for startup. It is also possible that a device driver is not the correct version for the device.
- Incorrect firmware. Upgrading to a new version of Windows NT typically requires upgrading the firmware. The firmware upgrades are available through your RISC-based computer vendor.

On RISC-based computers, you can use the /sos switch to display the Kernel and device driver names while they are being loaded. Include this switch on the OSLOADOPTIONS variable in the NVRAM. See the section "Using the /sos Switch," presented earlier in this chapter, for a description of the output you see when using this switch. There is information about editing the firmware variables in the section titled "Using a RISC-based Computer's Boot Menu," in Chapter 19, "What Happens When You Start Your Computer."

Troubleshooting problems with RISC-based computers can be more difficult than troubleshooting problems with x86-based computers because there are few disk or hardware troubleshooting tools available outside of Windows NT. If you can startup Windows NT, which you might be able to do by using your Windows NT startup floppy disk, try using these utilities:

- The Windows NT Diagnostics in the Administrative Tools (common) program group, which enables you to look at hardware information.
- The DiskProbe utility on the *Windows NT Workstation Resource Kit* CD, which is a low-level disk editor that enables you to examine and change individual disk sectors.

On RISC-based computers, there are no recovery tools such as those available when you dual-boot MS-DOS on x86-based computers. If your startup problem is because of a problem with information on the hard disk, you might have to remove the disk from the RISC-based computer and install it as a second disk on an x86-based computer to troubleshoot the problem. When you use this approach, you can use a low-level disk editor to examine the information on the disk in the same way you would troubleshoot a problem with a disk on an x86-based computer. Although these kinds of problems do not occur very often, you might have to use this approach after a power failure or system crash.

Note On NTFS volumes, you need to use Windows NT–based utilities, such as DiskProbe, to examine information on the volume.

Troubleshooting Startup Problems Common to Both x86-based and RISC-based Computers

When starting your computer, Windows NT provides options for using alternative configurations. If you have changed hardware or device drivers since the last startup and Windows NT does not complete startup, try using one of the other options.

Troubleshooting by Using the Last Known Good Configuration

Windows NT provides two configurations in which you can start your computer:

- Default, the configuration that was saved when you shutdown the computer.
- Last Known Good, the configuration that was saved when you last logged on to your computer.

The configurations are stored as control sets in the Registry key HKEY_LOCAL_MACHINE\SYSTEM. If you made changes to your configuration when you were last logged on, such as adding drivers, changing services, or changing hardware, the two control sets will contain different information. As soon as you log on however, the information in these control sets will be the same. Therefore, if you are having problems with startup, and think the problems might be related to changes in your configuration, do not log on. Instead, shutdown the computer and restart it. Then, select **Last Known Good** from the **Hardware Profile/Last Known Good** menu to recover from the following types of problems:

- You install a new device driver, restart Windows NT, and the system stops responding. The Last Known Good control set enables you to startup because it does not contain any reference to the new, faulty driver.
- You install a new video driver and are able to restart the system. However, you cannot see anything, because the new video resolution is incompatible with your video adapter. Do not try to log on. If you have the option to shutdown the computer without logging on, do so. If that option is not available, you need to restart your computer by turning it off or using the reset button. Wait for all disk activity to stop before you initiate the restart, especially if the computer has FAT volumes.
- You accidentally disable a critical device driver (such as the Scsiport driver). Windows NT is not be able to start and automatically reverts to the Last Known Good control set.

Using the Last Known Good control set does not help in the following situations:

- Any problem that is not related to changes in control set information, such as information like user profiles and file permissions.
- After you logged on after making changes. Here, the Last Known Good control set has already been updated to include the changes.
- Switching between different hardware profiles, such as docked and undocked laptops. The Last Known Good control set is only a method to switch between configuration information in the Registry. Use Hardware Profiles for this.
- Startup failures caused by hardware failures or corrupted files.
- Copying a new driver over the top of an old one, and the old one is already active.

For more information about hardware profiles and control sets, see Chapter 19, "What Happens When You Start Your Computer." Chapter 36, "General Troubleshooting," contains more details about troubleshooting by using the Registry key HKEY_LOCAL_MACHINE.

Troubleshooting Video Problems

If your screen stays black or is skewed after a restart, either the video device is not resetting correctly during the restart or the video is sharing an IRQ.

Turn the power off and restart it. If the video works, you will probably need to turn the power off each time you restart Windows NT. This problem is video- and system-BIOS related.

If the video is still wrong after shutting the power down and restarting, check for IRQ and memory conflicts with other cards on your system. If you are using a PCI-based computer, make certain that the video is not using IRQs 2, 9, or 12.

If you have installed a new video driver, or changed the display type by using the Display option in Control Panel, you might have created an incompatibility between the driver and the video device. One way that you can tell you have a problem is if you get a black screen instead of the logon message when you restart Windows NT.

You can turn off your computer or use the reset button to restart your computer. Then select the Last Known Good configuration. This recovery method is described in "Troubleshooting by Using the Last Known Good Configuration," presented earlier in this chapter.

On x86-based computers, you have another way to recover. When you install Windows NT, it creates two paths to the Windows NT folder, such as:

```
scsi(0)disk(0)rdisk(0)partition(1)\WINNT="Windows NT Workstation Version
4.00"
scsi(0)disk(0)rdisk(0)partition(1)\WINNT="Windows NT Workstation Version
4.00 [VGA mode]" /basevideo
```

If you select the path with the VGA mode option, Windows NT starts up by using the standard VGA driver. You can then use the Display option to reconfigure your video device.

Note Windows NT version 4.0 requires new video and printer drivers. Windows NT version 3.51 drivers for these devices will not work correctly when you are running Windows NT version 4.0.

Troubleshooting Disk Problems That Occur After Logon

This section discusses problems that occur after you have successfully logged on.

Volume Is Displayed as Unknown

If you have created and formatted a volume with NTFS or FAT, but you can no longer access files on it and Disk Administrator displays the volume as Unknown, the Partition Boot Sector for the volume might be bad.

For NTFS volumes, there are two other possible causes for this error:

- Permissions for the volume have been changed.
- The Master File Table (MFT) is corrupt.

The Partition Boot Sector can be corrupted by viruses. Corruption problems can also occur if you have a dual-boot configuration with Windows 95 and you use the Windows 95 version of the Fdisk utility. To avoid problems with Fdisk, delete the Windows 95 version, make sure that you have the MS-DOS-based version, and run Fdisk only when you start MS-DOS.

To determine if a corrupt Partition Boot Sector is causing the problem, and for the description of the procedures to restore it, see “Replacing the Partition Boot Sector” in Chapter 20, “Preparing for and Performing Recovery.”

The permission problem occurs when you have done the following:

- Created a second volume.
- Removed the group Everyone from the Access Control List (ACL).
- Granted access to a specific user.

The single user has normal access, but when other users log on, or if Windows NT is reinstalled, Disk Administrator sees the drive as unknown.

To correct this problem, log on as an administrator and take ownership of all folders, or add the group Everyone back with full control (default).

If there is corruption in the MFT file, there is no general solution. If you suspect this kind of problem, you should contact your technical support personnel for assistance.

Extended Partition Problems

If a Partition Table that defines a logical drive within an extended partition becomes corrupt, Windows NT can no longer access that volume, or the volumes that follow it on the disk. Once the pointer to the next volume has been lost, Windows NT can no longer find out where the volumes start.

When an extended partition becomes corrupt, it might be possible to rebuild the information by using a sector editor or Partition Table editor.

For information about the organization of extended partitions, see "Logical Drives and Extended Partitions" in Chapter 17, "Disk and File System Basics." For information about ways to attempt to repair the extended partition, see the description of the DiskProbe utility in Chapter 22, "Disk, File System, and Backup Utilities."

CHAPTER 22

Disk, File System, and Backup Utilities

This chapter explains various disk utilities, file system utilities, and Backup utilities and how to use them. It shows where to obtain the utilities and other sources of related information.

Three chapters in this part of the *Windows NT Workstation Resource Guide* also identify situations in which you should use the utilities (described in this chapter) and contain more information about them:

- Chapter 17, "Disk and File System Basics."
- Chapter 20, "Preparing for and Performing Recovery."
- Chapter 21, "Troubleshooting Startup and Disk Problems."

The utilities described in this chapter are available from different sources.

The following utilities are on the *Windows NT Workstation* product CD. When you install Windows NT, they are installed in *%systemroot%*\System32. You must run all of these utilities from the command prompt. The Section column in the next table identifies the section in this chapter in which the utility is described.

Utility	Purpose	Section
AT	Run Windows NT backup at scheduled time.	Backup
Cacls	Display and modify Access Control Lists (ACLs) for NTFS files and folders.	File System
Compact	Display and change compression of NTFS files and folders.	File System
Convert	Convert volume from FAT to NTFS.	File System
Expand	Expand files that are compressed on the Windows NT Workstation product CD, the *Windows NT Workstation Resource Kit* CD, or that you compressed by using the Compress utility.	File System

The rest of the utilities described in this chapter are provided in the *Windows NT Workstation Resource Kit*. You can install the Resource Kit by double-clicking Setup.exe when you load the Resource Kit CD.

The Windows NT Resource Kit utilities are organized into subgroups, by functional area. Rktools.hlp contains info about each of the utilities on the resource kit. To find out which functional area contains which utilities, double-click Rktools.hlp, and double-click each Tools group on the Contents screen.

When you install the Windows NT Resource Kit, Setup creates a Resource Kit program group that has Rktools.hlp and Readme.txt in it. It also creates a program group within the Resource Kit program group for each subgroup that you install. You can install only those subgroups that you want by doing a custom install.

▶ To do a custom installation of the Resource Kit

1. Double-click Setup.exe at the root of the *Windows NT Workstation Resource Kit* CD.
2. Click the **Custom** button.
3. Check the group or groups that contain the utilities you want to install.

The following table contains information about each of the Resource Kit utilities described in this chapter. As in the previous table, the Section column identifies the section in this chapter in which the utility is described.

Utility	Type	Purpose	Subgroup	Section
Compress	Command prompt	Compress files and folders.	File	File System
DirUse	Command prompt	Display folder size information, including compression information for NTFS volumes.	File	File System
DiskMap	Command prompt	Display information about the disk and the contents of the Partition Table.	Disk/Fault Tolerance	Disk
DiskProbe	Windows NT –based	Low-level disk editor.	Disk/Fault Tolerance	Disk
DiskSave	MS-DOS-based	Save and restore Master Boot Record and Partition Boot Sector.	Disk/Fault Tolerance	Disk
Expndw32	Windows NT –based	Expand compressed files.	File	File System
FTEdit	Windows NT –based	Recover stripe sets and volume sets.	Disk/Fault Tolerance	Disk

Disk Utilities

DiskProbe, DiskSave, and FTEdit are low-level editors. When you use them, you are changing information on the disk without any checks as to whether the changes make sense. Each utility does display messages asking you to verify that you really want to change the information. However, you can easily make changes that have serious consequences, such as:

- You cannot start any operating system.
- A volume is no longer accessible.
- You have to recreate and reformat all of the partitions and logical drives.

Used carefully however, you can solve these same problems when they occur through human error, hardware problems, power outages, and similar events. It is a good idea to get familiar with using these utilities in a test situation before you need to use them for real. Testing is especially important if your configuration has volume sets, stripe sets, extended partitions, or extended volume sets.

DiskMap displays information layout of partitions and logical drives on your disk, and you cannot change information on the disk when using this utility.

Note You can save and restore Master Boot Records and Partition Boot Sectors by using both DiskProbe and DiskSave. Both utilities save these files in the same format, so they can be saved by using one utility and restored by using the other.

DiskMap — Display a Map of the Disk

This utility produces a report on the configuration of the disk that you specify. It provides information about the disk characteristics and a description for each partition and logical drive on the disk.

DiskMap can be run from the command prompt. The syntax is:

```
diskmap /d<drive#> [/h]
```

These are the options for DiskMap

Option	Description
/d<drive#>	Drive# is the physical disk for which you want a map.
/h	Indicates hexadecimal output. The default is decimal output.

Some fields in the DiskMap report are always hex or always decimal, regardless of whether you specify the **/h** option when you run the utility. These fields are shown in the next table. You can see the fields in the DiskMap sample report, shown later in this section.

Always hex	Always decimal
Signature	The MB portion of the DiskSize field
System ID	Partition number

As an example, Figure 22.1 is a Disk Administrator screen shot of a computer with one hard disk.

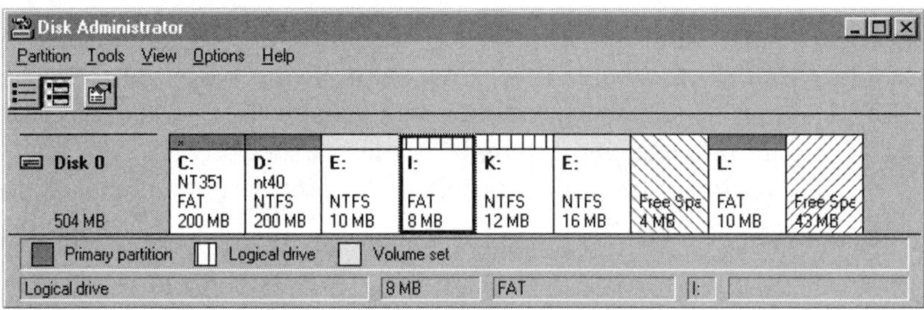

Figure 22.1 Disk Administrator screen shot

You get the following report for the disk configuration shown in Figure 22.1when you enter **diskmap /d0** at the command prompt:

```
Cylinders  HeadsPerCylinder SectorsPerHead BytesPerSector MediaType
     1023                16             63            512        12
TrackSize = 32256, CylinderSize = 516096, DiskSize = 527966208 (503MB)

Signature = 0x14f24efd
     StartingOffset    PartitionLength StartingSector PartitionNumber
*             32256          210018816             63               1
          210051072          209534976         410256               2
          472227840           10321920         922320               3
          419618304           10289664             63               4
          429940224            8225280             63               5
          438197760           12354048             63               6
          450584064           16998912             63               7

MBR:
          Starting                Ending         System    Relative  Total
  Cylinder Head Sector  Cylinder Head Sector    ID       Sector    Sectors
*        0    1      1       406   15     63    0x06           63   410193
       407    0      1       812   15     63    0x07       410256   409248
       813    0      1       914   15     63    0x05       819504   102816
       915    0      1       934   15     63    0x01       922320    20160
```

```
EBR: (sector 819504)
         Starting                 Ending       System    Relative  Total
  Cylinder Head Sector  Cylinder Head Sector   ID        Sector    Sectors
       813    1     1        832   15    63    0x87          63      20097
       833    0     1        848   15    63    0x05       20160      16128
         0    0     0          0    0     0    0x00           0          0
         0    0     0          0    0     0    0x00           0          0

EBR: (sector 839664)
         Starting                 Ending       System    Relative  Total
  Cylinder Head Sector  Cylinder Head Sector   ID        Sector    Sectors
       833    1     1        848   15    63    0x01          63      16065
       849    0     1        872   15    63    0x05       36288      24192
         0    0     0          0    0     0    0x00           0          0
         0    0     0          0    0     0    0x00           0          0

EBR: (sector 855792)
         Starting                 Ending       System    Relative  Total
  Cylinder Head Sector  Cylinder Head Sector   ID        Sector    Sectors
       849    1     1        872   15    63    0x07          63      24129
       873    0     1        905   15    63    0x05       60480      33264
         0    0     0          0    0     0    0x00           0          0
         0    0     0          0    0     0    0x00           0          0

EBR: (sector 879984)
         Starting                 Ending       System    Relative  Total
  Cylinder Head Sector  Cylinder Head Sector   ID        Sector    Sectors
       873    1     1        905   15    63    0x87          63      33201
         0    0     0          0    0     0    0x00           0          0
         0    0     0          0    0     0    0x00           0          0
         0    0     0          0    0     0    0x00           0          0
```

This utility is very useful for producing hardcopy reports for each disk, which should be kept with the other configuration information that you maintain for your computer. You can create a hardcopy by redirecting the output to a printer or to a file, which you can then print. This example creates a file:

```
diskmap /d0 >disk0map.txt
```

The first three lines of the output:

```
Cylinders  HeadsPerCylinder SectorsPerHead BytesPerSector MediaType
     1023                16             63            512        12
TrackSize = 32256, CylinderSize = 516096, DiskSize = 527966208 (503MB)
```

are information that DiskMap obtained by using IOCTL_DISK_GET_DRIVE_GEOMETRY. The information is the geometry of the disk as seen by Windows NT. The hardware might have different physical geometry, because translation can be performed either at the hardware or device driver layer. It is important to know what geometry Windows NT is using. You can use this information if you need to repair the Partition Table, which is described in the section entitled "Editing and Repairing the Partition Table," later in this chapter. The TrackSize, CylinderSize, and DiskSize values are bytes.

The second section of the output is information about the disk returned from IOCTL_DISK_GET_DRIVE_LAYOUT. Windows NT uses the signature to correlate information in the HKEY_LOCAL_MACHINE\SYSTEM\DISK Registry subkey with the appropriate physical disk when the disk contains volume sets or stripe sets. The StartingOffset and PartitionLength fields are the values for each of these data in bytes.

The MBR and EBR sections on the printout describe the contents of the Partition Table(s). The MBR section is for the Partition Table contained on the first sector of the disk. If there is no extended partition on the disk, there are no EBR sections. Otherwise, there is one EBR section for each logical drive in the extended partition. The fields in each of these sections are described in the "Partition Table" section in Chapter 17, "Disk and File System Basics."

Each partition that has an asterisk (*) at the left side is a system partition, which contains the files used to load an operating system such as Windows NT. On an x86-based computer, each disk can have a system partition, but there should only be one partition with the * on each disk. RISC-based computers can have more than one system partition on a disk.

The DiskMap utility has several possible error messages. Some messages are not serious, and you can easily correct them. Other messages usually are caused by some type of hardware problem or corruption of the data on the disk. This table describes the error messages that you might see. The *N* and *E* in the message indicate numbers.

Message	Meaning
BLOCKED: CreateFile() Failed /d*N* [Error *E*] Ensure that you have selected a valid drive number and that the selected drive is not locked by another process.	The attempt to open physical disk *N* failed. Either some other program, such as Disk Administrator or DiskProbe, has the drive open, or the value following /d is invalid (out of range or not a number).
Unable to get drive layout using IOCTL_DISK_GET_DRIVE_GEOMETRY. Error: [Error *E*]. This is a fatal error.	The call to DeviceIoControl() with the parameter IOCTL_DISK_GET_DRIVE_GEOMETRY failed. You would get this error if you removed the disk in a removable media device. Otherwise, it could indicate a hardware failure where a device that was available at startup is no longer available.
Unable to allocate memory	DiskMap tried to allocate memory for a temporary buffer and no memory was available. Try closing other programs.
Unable to get drive layout using IOCTL_DISK_GET_DRIVE_LAYOUT. Error: [Error *E*].	The call to DeviceIoControl() with the parameter IOCTL_DISK_GET_DRIVE_LAYOUT failed. In attempting to walk the Partition Table chain, some kind of error was encountered. This error indicates Partition Table corruption, hardware RAID array corruption, hardware failure, or a change in apparent disk geometry that makes portions of the volume inaccessible. More information about why the call failed might be available in other parts of the utility where it walks the chain manually.
Unable to read next EBR. Error: [Error *E*].	A call to ReadFile() failed. This is usually caused by an attempt to read past the end of the disk, as in the case where the pointer to the next EBR is not valid. It can also indicate a bad sector at the EBR location.

Message	Meaning
Next EBR failed to pass sanity check.	This message means that the Ending Head for each of the four Partition Table entries is not 0 or not equal to TracksPerCylinder-1, or that the last two bytes in the sector are not 0x55 0xAA. The problem is either an error in the chain of EBRs or this sector has been corrupted.
Detected partition corruption.	This message means that the value in the Relative Sector field for a Partition Table entry is not equal to the SectorsPerHead value.

In general, if the partition size and layout displayed by DiskMap looks about right and the utility does not display any error messages, then the Partition Tables are probably correct.

An example of where DiskMap can be very useful is when a Partition Table was written incorrectly and the last EBR referenced is past the end of the disk. Disk Administrator will not initialize in this situation, because it depends on the information from IOCTL_DISK_GET_DRIVE_LAYOUT, which would fail. DiskMap would also display an error about IOCTL_DISK_GET_DRIVE_LAYOUT, but would display the EBRs that it can read up to the point of failure. If you have a hardcopy of a map of the disk that had no errors, you can see where the two chains diverged. You can restore the original partition information by correcting the first EBR that has bad values by using a low-level disk editor such as DiskProbe. Typically, the rest of the original EBRs would not have been damaged by the bad EBR chain. Sometimes, though, it might be necessary to repair more than one EBR.

DiskProbe — a Low-level Disk Editor

This Windows NT–based utility enables you to save, restore, find, examine, and change data on the disk. DiskProbe gives an administrator access to every byte on the physical disk without regard to access privilege, and with it you can change any part of the disk. It is your responsibility to make sure that you have backups of the disk.

After starting DiskProbe, as shown in Figure 22.2, you use the **Drives** menu to open a physical disk or a logical drive.

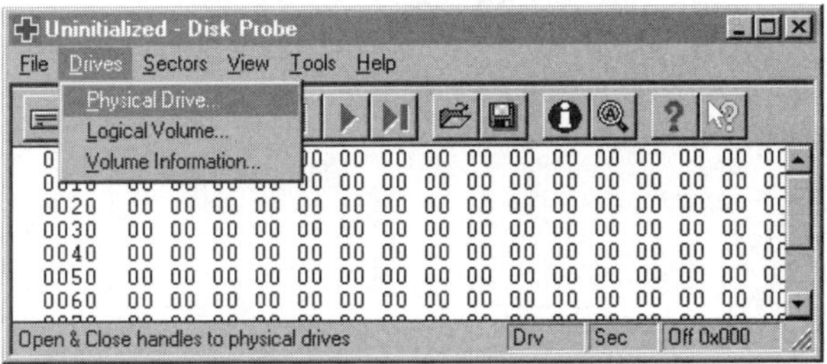

Figure 22.2 Opening a disk by using DiskProbe

Clicking **Physical Drive** on the **Drives** menu opens the entire physical disk. You can access any sector on the disk. When you read or write sectors, the sector number is the absolute sector from the beginning of the disk.

Clicking **Logical Volume** on the **Drives** menu opens the logical drive associated with a drive letter. Sector numbers are relative to the start of the logical drive, and you can only access sectors within the range of the logical drive. You cannot use DiskProbe to access a network drive.

When you have opened either a disk by clicking either **Physical Drive** or **Logical Volume**, you can get information about the characteristics of the disk by clicking **Volume Information** on the **Drives** menu. You get the same information regardless of how you opened the disk. This information is the same as what you see if you run the DiskMap utility for this disk. You can use this information if you need to repair the Partition Table. Here is an example:

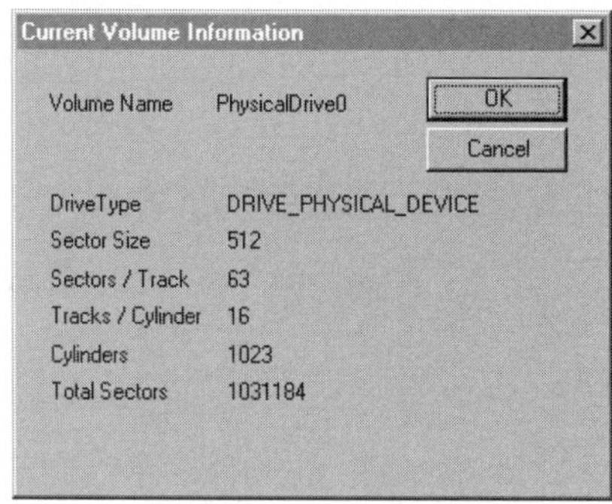

Whenever you use DiskProbe to read a sector, it displays the sector number of the first sector it read in the title bar. It also displays the sector number of the sector you are currently viewing in the status bar. This information is useful if you have read more than one sector.

When you are first using DiskProbe, or are looking at information in an extended partition, it is recommended that you write down the sector number for the start of each partition and logical drive. You should also write down the sector number of the Partition Boot Sector partition or logical drive. You can produce a hardcopy of the disk configuration by using the DiskMap utility, which is described earlier in this chapter.

If your disk has volume sets or an extended partition, remembering which partition or logical drive you are looking at can become difficult. You can always start over by reading sector 0, which reads the Partition Table for the disk.

Note In the DiskProbe utility, sectors are numbered starting from zero.

The location of some system information on NTFS volumes is different, depending on which version of Windows NT was used to format the volume. For example, Windows NT 4.0 writes a backup of the Partition Boot Sector for the volume at the end of the volume. Earlier versions of Windows NT put the backup at the center of the volume.

For more information about DiskProbe, see Dskprobe.hlp and Rktools.hlp on the *Windows NT Workstation Resource Kit* CD.

Comparing DiskProbe to Disk Administrator

Although DiskProbe and Disk Administrator both provide you with information about the organization of your hard disks, each utility has additional functionality. Disk Administrator enables you to configure and format your disks. DiskProbe enables you to save and change the data on the disk.

Disk Administrator shows you, for each disk, the size and organization of:

- Primary partitions
- Logical drives (single contiguous areas in an extended partition)
- Stripe sets
- Volume sets

When displaying information about stripe sets and volume sets, both DiskProbe and Disk Administrator read the HKEY_LOCAL_MACHINE\SYSTEM\DISK Registry subkey to determine which disks contain the members of the volumes.

When you view the Partition Table, DiskProbe enables you to determine the starting and ending location of primary partitions, logical drives, and volume sets.

DiskProbe simply displays the information that it finds in each Partition Table, it is up to you to understand how the individual entries in the Partition Table relate to what you have configured on your disks. If your configuration contains extended partitions, you might find it easier to understand the DiskProbe information if you print a screen shot of the Disk Administrator display (by pressing ALT+PRINT SCREEN, pasting the screen shot into Paint or a document, and then printing the picture or document). The section "Walking an Extended Partition," presented later in this chapter, contains an example of the Disk Administrator and DiskProbe information for an extended partition.

Note Because both DiskProbe and Disk Administrator can modify the Partition Table, and DiskProbe enables you to directly modify any sector on a disk, you should never have both of these utilities open at the same time. When you are using DiskProbe, you should also be very cautious about running any other programs. DiskProbe writes directly to the disk without using the file cache, the NTFS log file, or any file system device drivers.

Backing Up and Restoring the Master Boot Record

The Master Boot Record on the hard disk that you use to start your computer is the most important sector on the disk. The Master Boot Record on other disks is not as critical. However, if the partition information in the other Master Boot Records is not correct, you might not be able to access partitions on those disks.

For an example of a Master Boot Record, see Chapter 17, "Disk and File System Basics."

▶ To back up the Master Boot Record

1. In the Resource Kit folder, double-click the DiskProbe icon.
2. On the **Drives** menu, click **Physical Drive**. You will see the **Open Physical Drive** dialog box, which is shown in the following figure.

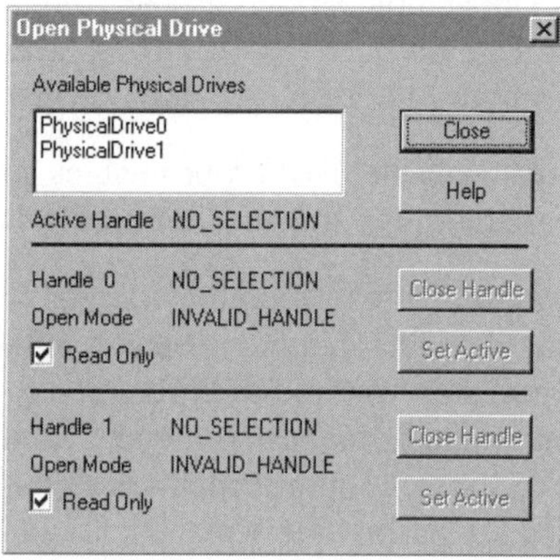

   The **Available Physical Drives** are listed as PhysicalDrive*n*, where n=0 for the first hard disk. Double-click the disk that contains the Master Boot Record you want to save. You should always save the Master Boot Record on the startup disk. In the case of an x86-based computer, the startup disk is usually PhysicalDrive0.

   When you have more than one disk, you should back up the Master Boot Record on each disk, since it contains the Partition Table for that disk.

3. In the **Handle 0** group box, click **Set Active**. Click **Close**.

4. On the **Sectors** menu, click **Read** to open the **Sector Range** dialog box, which is shown in the figure below. Set **Starting Sector** to 0 and **Number of Sectors** to 1. Click **Read**.

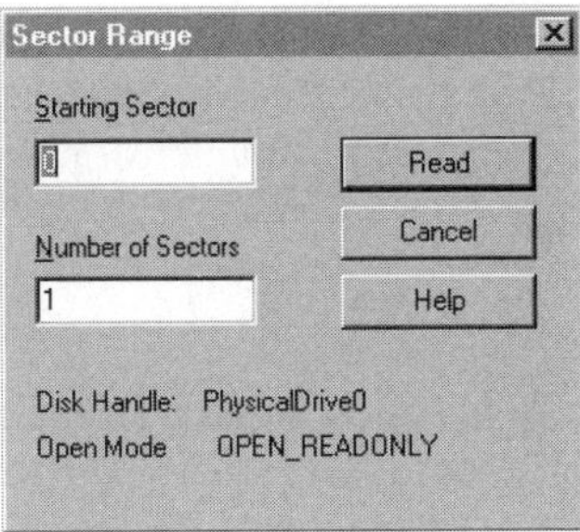

   Make sure that the sector you read looks like a Master Boot Record, as described in Chapter 17, "Disk and File System Basics."

5. On the **File** menu, click **Save As**. Enter the filename. Consider saving the file to the Emergency Repair Disk, the Windows NT startup floppy disk, or the MS-DOS bootable floppy disk. You can save it on more than one disk. If you have more than one disk whose Master Boot Record you are baking up, using a filename such as Mbrdiskn.dsk can help you remember which file corresponds to which disk.

▶ **To restore the Master Boot Record**

1. In the Resource Kit folder, double-click the DiskProbe icon.
2. On the **File** menu, click **Open**. Enter the filename and open the file. Verify that the file looks like a Master Boot Record and that it is 512 bytes. DiskProbe displays a message if the size of the file you open is not a multiple of 512.
3. On the **Drives** menu, click **Physical Drive**. The **Available Physical Drives** are listed as PhysicalDrive*n*, where n=0 for the first hard disk. Double-click the disk that contains the Master Boot Record you want to restore.
4. In the **Handle 0** group box, clear the **Read Only** check box, and click **Set Active**. Click **Close**.
5. On the **Sectors** menu, click **Write** to open the **Write Sector** dialog box. Set **Starting sector to write data** to 0. Click **Write it**.
6. DiskProbe displays a message box so you can verify the information.

Displaying and Using the Partition Table

The Master Boot Record is the first sector on each hard disk. The first step in troubleshooting Partition Table problems should be to read the Master Boot Record and look at the Partition Table. The description in this section applies to viewing the Partition Table in the Master Boot Record. See "Walking an Extended Partition," presented later in this chapter, for information about finding the Partition Table for an extended partition.

▶ **To display the Partition Table**

1. Read the Master Boot Record by using steps 1 through 4 in the procedure for backing up the Master Boot Record, given earlier in this chapter.
2. On the **View** menu, click **Partition Table** to see the information displayed in a user-friendly manner. You will see a screen like the following:

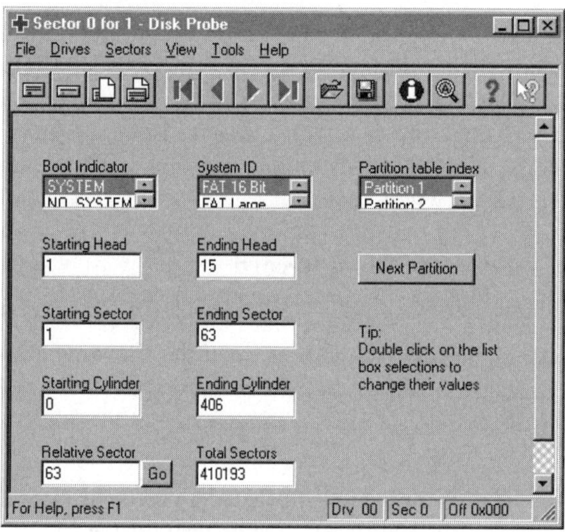

Figure 22.3 DiskProbe Partition Table view

DiskProbe makes it easy for you to look at the information for each partition. In the **Partition table index** list box, double-click the partition number for which you want to see the Partition Table entry.

Click the **Next Partition** button to see the information in the first sector of the next partition. For a primary partition, clicking the **Next Partition** button reads the Partition Boot Sector of the next partition. When the next partition is an extended partition, clicking **Next Partition** reads the Partition Table sector for the first logical drive in the extended partition.

For a primary partition, clicking the **Go** button next to the **Relative Sector** field reads the Partition Boot Sector for the current partition. When the **System ID** field is EXTENDED, clicking the **Go** button reads the Partition Table for the next logical drive in the extended partition.

If you make changes to the Partition Table, you must explicitly write the sector to disk by clicking **Write** on the **Sectors** menu.

When you are viewing the information for an extended partition in the Partition Table area of the Master Boot Record, the **Total Sectors** field is the total size of the extended partition, which is usually larger than the size of the first logical drive in the partition.

Walking an Extended Partition

If the disk has an extended partition, finding the information for each logical drive is more complicated than just looking at the Partition Table in the Master Boot Record, but DiskProbe does the work for you. "Logical Drives and Extended Partitions," within Chapter 17 describes the organization of an extended partition.

Information for the logical drives in an extended partition is basically chained from one logical drive to the next. The term *walking an extended partition* means that utilities like DiskProbe and DiskMap use the information defined for one logical drive in the chain to find the next logical drive in the chain. Knowing how to walk an extended partition is necessary if one of the links in the chain becomes corrupted, and you want to try to repair it.

The description in this section applies when you are viewing the Partition Table information in the first sector of each logical drive.

To help make the descriptions easier to understand, following is a screen shot from Disk Administrator, and the information from DiskProbe for the extended partition shown in the screen shot. The extended partition includes volume set E, logical drives I and K, and 4 MB of unused space between E and L. This example is the same disk configuration used in the section "DiskMap — Display a Map of the Disk," presented earlier in this chapter.

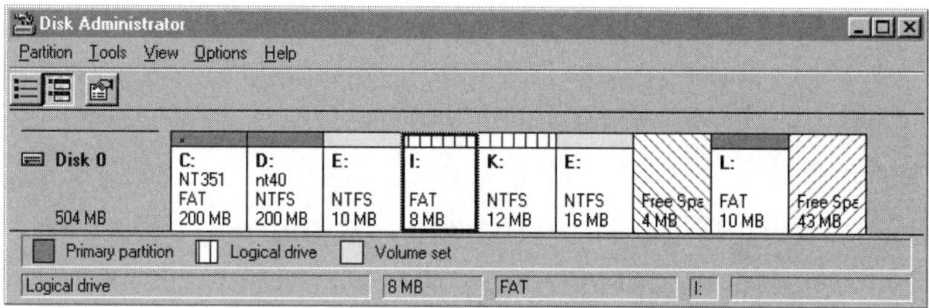

Note This example is for illustration purposes, and is not a good organization for the disk, because the free space at the end of the primary partition is unusable. This is because you can have only four partition table entries in the Master Boot Record. In this example, primary partitions C, D, and L each use one entry. The extended partition, which includes volume set E, logical drives I and K, and the free space between E and K, uses the other entry. Disk Administrator displays an error message if you try to use any of the area after drive L to create a partition or extend an NTFS logical drive.

The distinction between the two areas of free space is that the one on the left is free space within an extended partition, while the free space on the right, which has a different background pattern, is not a part of any partition.

To walk the extended partition in this example, start with the information for partition 3 in the Partition Table on relative sector 0. Partition 3 points you to the first logical drive in the extended partition. By following the links in the Partition Table entry for each logical drive, you can find the information for all of the logical drives.

The next table identifies which sectors contain information about the extended partition and the logical drives. The table also describes which buttons to click to walk the extended partition.

Relative sector	Contents
0	Partition 3 of the Master Boot Record contains an EXTENDED entry, which is the information about the first part of volume set E. Click **Go** when viewing partition 3 to read the Partition Table for the first part of volume set E.
819504	Partition 1 describes the first part of volume set E. Partition 2 is an EXTENDED entry with the information for logical drive I. Click **Next Partition** when viewing partition 1 to read the Partition Table for logical drive I.
839664	Partition 1 describes logical drive I, Partition 2 is an EXTENDED entry with the information for logical drive K. Click **Next Partition** when viewing partition 1 to read the Partition Table for logical drive K.
855792	Partition 1 describes logical drive K. Partition 2 is an EXTENDED entry with the information for the second part of volume set E. Click **Next Partition** when viewing partition 1 to read the Partition Table for the second part of volume set E.
879984	Partition 1 describes the second part of volume set E. Partition 2 is all zeroes (end of the extended partition).

The next table shows the information in Partition 3 of the Master Boot Record and each of the Partition 1 entries for the extended partition.

Field Name	Master Boot Record entry	First part of E (10 MB)	I (8 MB)	K (12MB)	Second part of E (16 MB)
System ID	EXTENDED	NTFS FT	FAT	NTFS	NTFS FT
Boot Indicator	NO_ SYSTEM	NO_ SYSTEM	NO_ SYSTEM	NO_ SYSTEM	NO_ SYSTEM
Start Head	1	1	1	1	1
End Head	15	15	15	15	15
Start Sector	1	1	1	1	1
End Sector	63	63	63	63	63
Start Cylinder	813	813	833	849	873
End Cylinder	914	832	848	872	905
Relative Sector	819504	63	63	63	63
Total Sectors	102816	20097	16065	24129	33201

When the **System ID** field for a Partition 2 in an extended partition contains the value EXTENDED, double-click Partition 1 in the **Partition table index** list box, and then click **Next Partition** to read the first sector of the next logical drive. The only information in the first sector of a logical drive is a Partition Table, which has two entries. The Partition 1 entry contains information about the current logical drive, and the Partition 2 entry is the information for the next logical drive in the extended partition. The **System ID** for each Partition 2 entry should be EXTENDED unless you are at the end of the extended partition.

The next screen shot shows the Partition Table entry for the first part of volume set E; the Partition Table is located at relative sector 819504.

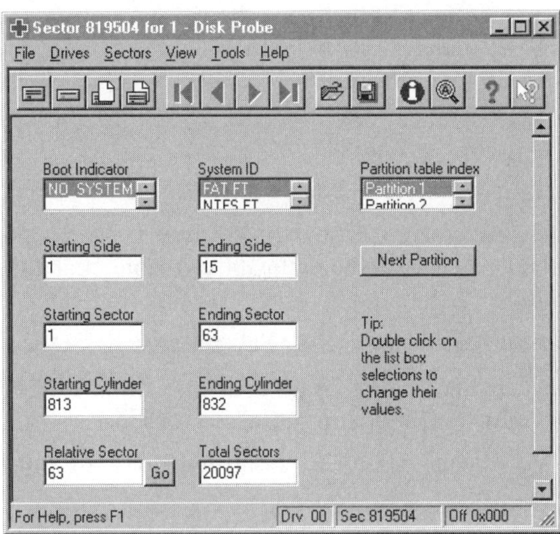

When the **System ID** field contains any value except EXTENDED or UNKNOWN, clicking the **Go** button next to the **Relative Sector** field reads the Partition Boot Sector for the logical drive.

To view the information for Partition 2 (the next logical volume), double-click Partition 2 or click **Next Partition** while viewing the information for Partition 1.

The **Relative Sector** field for each Partition 2 entry in an extended partition is the offset from the beginning of the extended partition, not the offset from the beginning of the Partition Table associated with the Partition 1 entry. Therefore, do not use the **Go** button to try to read the Partition Boot Sector for Partition 2.

Note Sometimes, the System ID byte for NTFS volume sets and stripe sets does not have the correct value. It should be 0x87, which DiskProbe displays as NTFS FT. Instead, it might be 0x86, which DiskProbe displays as FAT FT. Windows NT uses information in the Partition Boot Sector to determine which file system to use, so this incorrect value causes no problems, although it can be confusing to a person trying to understand the data on the disk. To be certain which file system is being used for a volume, look at the Partition Boot Sector.

Viewing the Partition Boot Sector

You can use DiskProbe to view the information in Partition Boot Sectors. You see a formatted view of the information in the BIOS Parameter Block and the Extended BIOS Parameter Block. For a description of these structures, see "Partition Boot Sector," in Chapter 17, "Disk and File System Basics."

▶ To view a Partition Boot Sector

1. In the Resource Kit folder, double-click the DiskProbe icon.
2. On the **Drives** menu, click **Logical Volume**. In the **Logical Volumes** list box of the Open Logical Volume dialog box, double-click the drive letter for the volume whose Partition Boot Sector you want to read.
3. In the **Handle 0** group box, click **Set Active**. Click **OK**.
4. On the **Sectors** menu, click **Read** to display the **Read Sectors** dialog box. Set **Starting Sector** to 0 and **Number of Sectors** to 1.
5. On the **View** menu, click **NTFS Bootsector** or **FAT Bootsector** to see the information.

The next screen shot shows the NTFS Bootsector view of primary partition D for the disk configuration shown in Figure 22.1.

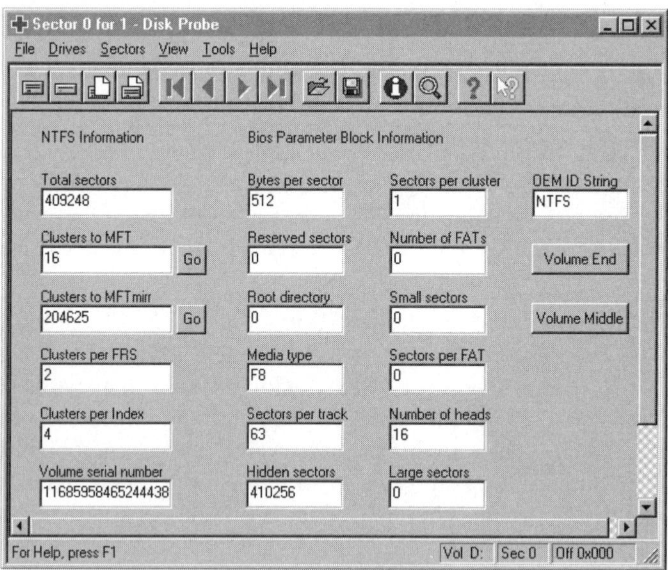

When viewing an NTFS Partition Boot Sector, there are **Go** buttons next to the fields **Clusters to MFT** and **Clusters to MFT mirr**. When you click one of these buttons, it reads the first sector of the MFT or the MFT mirror, respectively. For information about these structures, see "Master File Table (MFT) and NTFS System Files" in Chapter 17, "Disk and File System Basics."

Windows NT writes a backup of the NTFS Partition Boot Sector at the logical center of the volume (Windows NT version 3.51 and earlier) or the end of the volume (Windows NT 4.0). You can use the **Volume Middle** and **Volume End** buttons to read the backup Partition Boot Sector. However, there are some situations, when using Windows NT version 3.51 or earlier, where the backup Partition Boot Sector does not get written in the correct location:

- Converting a volume from FAT to NTFS does not put the backup Partition Boot Sector on the disk.
- Extending a volume set does not put the backup Partition Boot Sector on the disk.

View the sector you read to make sure it looks like an NTFS Partition Boot Sector, and that the information in it is accurate for the volume.

When viewing a FAT Partition Boot Sector, there is also a **Volume End** button, but there is no backup of the FAT Partition Boot Sector on the volume. If you are trying to find where volumes begin and end so you can repair a Partition Table, you can use the **Volume End** button for both FAT and NTFS primary partitions and logical drives to read what should be the sector immediately before the beginning of the next primary partition or logical drive.

Note If you are viewing a backup NTFS Partition Boot Sector, do not use the **Go**, **Volume End**, or **Volume Middle** buttons. These buttons read the correct sectors only when you are viewing the Partition Boot Sector at the beginning of the volume.

Backing Up and Restoring the Partition Boot Sector

The Partition Boot Sector contains information that the file system uses to access the volume. On x86-based computers, the Master Boot Record uses the Partition Boot Sector on the system partition to load the operating system kernel files, or in the case of Windows NT, the boot loader.

For examples of a Partition Boot Sector for a FAT and an NTFS volume, see Chapter 17, "Disk and File System Basics."

There are several procedures that you can use, depending on whether you are backing up or restoring the Partition Boot Sector for:

- A primary partition
- A logical drive, which is a single contiguous area in an extended partition
- Several Partition Boot Sectors in an extended partition
- A volume set
- A stripe set

You can open the disk to read the Partition Boot Sector by using either **Physical Drive** or **Logical Volume** on the **Drives** menu. When you use **Physical Drive**, you have to read the Partition Table to find the address of the Partition Boot Sector. When you use **Logical Volume**, you read the Partition Boot Sector by reading sector 0 of the logical drive. You cannot read the Master Boot Record when you use **Logical Volume**.

▶ **To back up a Partition Boot Sector for a primary partition by using Physical Drive**

1. Read the Partition Table and view it by using the procedure in "Displaying and Using the Partition Table," presented earlier in this section.
2. In the **Partition table index** list box, double-click the partition number for the Partition Boot Sector that you want to save. For instance, to save the Partition Boot Sector for the system partition, double-click the partition number that has the **Boot Indicator** set to **SYSTEM**.

3. To read the Partition Boot Sector, click the **Go** button next to the **Relative Sector** field. On the **View** menu, click **NTFS BootSector** or **FAT BootSector** to see the information displayed appropriately. Make sure that the sector you just read looks like a Partition Boot Sector, as described in Chapter 17, "Disk and File System Basics."
4. On the **File** menu, click **Save As**. Enter the filename. Consider saving the file to the Emergency Repair Disk, the Windows NT startup floppy disk, or the MS-DOS bootable floppy disk. You can save it to more than one disk. When you are saving a Partition Boot Sector, using a name such as PBS*ssssssss*DISK*n*.dsk, where *ssssssss* is the relative sector of the Partition Boot Sector and *n* is the disk number, can help you remember what the file contains.

▶ **To back up the Partition Boot Sector by using Logical Volume**

1. In the Resource Kit folder, double-click the DiskProbe icon.
2. On the **Drives** menu, click **Logical Volume**. In the **Logical Volumes** list box, double-click the drive letter for the volume whose Partition Boot Sector you want to save.
3. In the **Handle 0** group box, click **Set Active**. Close the dialog box.
4. On the **Sectors** menu, click **Read**. Set **Starting Sector** to 0 and **Number of Sectors** to 1. Make sure that the sector you read looks like a Partition Boot Sector, as described in Chapter 17, "Disk and File System Basics."
5. On the **File** menu, click **Save As**. Enter the filename. Consider saving the file to the Emergency Repair Disk, the Windows NT startup floppy disk, or the MS-DOS bootable floppy disk. You can save it to more than one disk. When you are saving a Partition Boot Sector in this manner, using a name such as PBS*d*DSK*n*.dsk, where *d* is the drive letter of the logical drive, and *n* is the disk number, can help you remember what the file contains. Using a name such as this assumes that you will not be changing drive letters.

▶ **To back up the Partition Boot Sectors in an extended partition by using Physical Drive**

1. Read the Partition Table and view it by using the procedure in "Displaying and Using the Partition Table," presented earlier in this section.
2. In the **Partition table index** list box, double-click the partition number for the extended partition, and then click **Go**. Doing this reads the first Partition Table entry in the extended partition.

3. You can walk the extended partition to find the logical drive whose Partition Boot Sector you want to back up. When you walk the extended partition, view the information for Partition 1 and click **Go** to read the Partition Boot Sector. You can use the **Search** function on the **Tools** menu to find each Partition Boot Sector. See "Finding a Partition Boot Sector," presented later in this chapter, for information about finding these disk sectors.

   You can also print a map of the disk by using the DiskMap utility, which provides you with the address of the Partition Table entry for each logical drive. You can then use DiskProbe to read the first sector of the logical drive whose Partition Boot Sector you want to back up, and use the **Go** button to read the Partition Boot Sector.

   Once you have read a Partition Boot Sector, on the **View** menu, click **NTFS BootSector** or **FAT BootSector** to see the information displayed appropriately. Make sure that the sector you just read looks like a Partition Boot Sector, as described in Chapter 17, "Disk and File System Basics."

4. On the **File** menu, click **Save As**. Enter the filename. Consider saving the file to the Emergency Repair Disk, the Windows NT startup floppy disk, or the MS-DOS bootable floppy disk. When you are saving a Partition Boot Sector, using a name such as PBS*ssssssss*DISK*n*.dsk, where *ssssssss* is the relative sector of the Partition Boot Sector and *n* is the disk number, can help you remember what all of the files contain.

▶ **To restore the Partition Boot Sector for a primary partition by using Physical Drive**

1. In the Resource Kit folder, double-click the DiskProbe icon.
2. On the **Drives** menu, click **Physical Drive**. In the **Available Physical Drives** group box, the disks are listed as PhysicalDrive*n*, where n=0 for the first hard disk. Double-click the disk that contains the Partition Boot Sector that you want to replace.
3. In the **Handle 0** group box, clear the **Read Only** check box, click **Set Active,** and click **Close**.
4. If you know the address of the sector you need to write, skip to step 6. To use DiskProbe to compute the sector, first read the Partition Table and view it by using the procedure in "Displaying and Using the Partition Table," presented earlier in this section. Figure 22-3 shows the DiskProbe Partition Table view.
5. In the **Partition table index** list box, double-click the partition number for the Partition Boot Sector that you want to replace. For example, to view information about the Partition Boot Sector for the system partition, double-click the partition number that has the **Boot Indicator** set to **SYSTEM**.

   The **Relative Sector** field contains the sector number for the Partition Boot Sector. Write down this number.

6. On the **File** menu, click **Open**, and enter the filename of the file that contains the Partition Boot Sector. Open the file. Verify that it looks like a Partition Boot Sector.
7. On the **Sectors** menu, click **Write** to display the **Write Sector** dialog box. In the **Starting sector to write data**, enter the sector number from step 5 (or that you already know is the correct sector). Click the option button for the disk to which you want to write the sector. Click **Write it**.

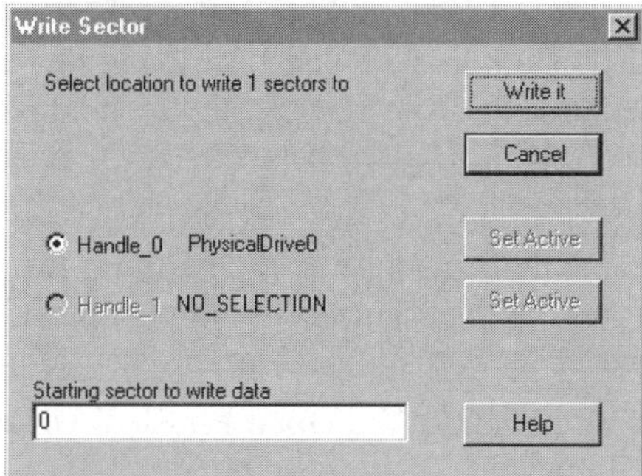

8. DiskProbe displays a message box so you can verify the information.

▶ **To restore the Partition Boot Sector by using Logical Volume**

1. In the Resource Kit folder, double-click the DiskProbe icon.
2. On the **Drives** menu, click **Logical Volume**. In the **Logical Volumes** list box of the **Open Logical Volume** dialog box, double-click the logical drive whose Partition Boot Sector you want to restore.
3. In the **Handle 0** group box, clear **Read Only,** click **Set Active**, and click **Close**.
4. On the **File** menu, click **Open**, and enter the filename of the file that contains the Partition Boot Sector. Open the file. Verify that it looks like a Partition Boot Sector and is 512 bytes. DiskProbe displays an error if the file size is not a multiple of 512.
5. On the **Sectors** menu, click **Write** to display the **Write Sector** dialog box. In the **Starting sector to write data**, enter 0 for the **Starting sector to write data**. Click **Write it**.
6. DiskProbe displays a message box so you can verify the information.

▶ **To restore the Partition Boot Sector in an extended partition by using Physical Drive**

1. If you know the address of the Partition Boot Sector that you want to restore (which you would know if the sector number is part of the filename), follow the procedure for restoring the Partition Boot Sector (given earlier in this chapter) for a primary partition, skipping steps 4 and 5. You are done.

   If you do not know the address, you can find it by walking the extended partition. Follow steps 1 through 3 in the procedure for backing up the Partition Boot Sector for an extended partition (given earlier in this chapter). Even though the Partition Boot Sector that you read is the one you want to replace, when you read it, DiskProbe displays its relative sector number. Write down this number.

   You can also calculate the address of the Partition Boot Sector by using a DiskMap output for the disk. The sector number for a Partition Boot Sector is the address of the EBR for the logical drive + the Relative Sector value.

2. In the **Handle 0** group box of the **Open Physical Drive** dialog box, be sure that **Read Only** is cleared.
3. On the **File** menu, click **Open**, and enter the filename of the file that contains the Partition Boot Sector. Open the file. Verify that it looks like a Partition Boot Sector.
4. On the **Sectors** menu, click **Write** to display the **Write Sector** dialog box. In the **Starting sector to write data**, enter the sector number that you found in step 1. Click the option button for the disk to which you want to write the sector. Click **Write it**.
5. DiskProbe displays a message box so you can verify the information.

If you formatted an NTFS volume when running Windows NT version 4.0, a backup of the Partition Boot Sector for NTFS volume is located at the end of the volume. Earlier versions of Windows NT put the backup at the center of the volume. If you did not make a backup of the Partition Boot Sector, you can find the backup sector and copy it to the first sector of the volume.

▶ **To restore the backup NTFS Partition Boot Sector**

1. In the Resource Kit folder, double-click the DiskProbe icon.
2. "Finding a Partition Boot Sector," presented later in this chapter, describes different methods for finding the Partition Boot Sector. When you find a Partition Boot Sector within the boundaries of an NTFS volume, make sure that the data are reasonable for the volume. If you have deleted volumes, or extended an NTFS volume set, there might be old, invalid, Partition Boot Sectors on the disk. Save the backup to a disk.
3. Close any handles that you opened to find the backup.
4. On the **Drives** menu, click **Logical Volume**. Click the **Close Handle** button for any drives or logical volumes that are currently open. In the **Logical Volumes** list box of the **Open Logical Volume** dialog box, double-click the logical drive whose Partition Boot Sector you want to restore.
5. In the **Handle 0** group box, clear **Read Only** and click **Set Active**. Click **OK**.
6. On the **File** menu, click **Open**, and enter the name of the file you copied to disk in step 2. Open the file.
7. On the **Sectors** menu, click **Write** to display the **Write Sector** dialog box. Since you are going to be writing to relative sector 0, make sure that the active handle is a drive letter, not PhysicalDrive*n*. Enter 0 for the **Starting sector to write data**. Click **Write it**.
8. DiskProbe displays a message box so you can verify the information.

Finding a Partition Boot Sector

This section discusses some approaches for finding primary partitions and logical drives on your disk in order to repair the Partition Table, which is discussed in "Editing and Repairing the Partition Table," presented later in this chapter.

When you are looking for Partition Boot Sectors in order to repair the Partition Table, you know that some information is wrong or missing. Therefore, you need to verify that the information you use to find a Partition Boot Sector, or a Partition Table in an extended partition, is accurate. For example, if you use the Number of Sectors field for one primary partition to calculate the location of the Partition Boot Sector for the next partition, make sure that there is a valid Partition Boot Sector at that sector.

The easiest way to find the start of a primary partition is to find the Partition Boot Sector for the partition. For an extended partition, subtract the sectors per track from the address of the Partition Boot Sector to find the Partition Table entry for the logical drive.

The Partition Boot Sector for the first partition on your hard disk is always the first sector on head 1 of cylinder 0. Because disks typically have 32 or 63 sectors per track, you can usually find the Partition Boot Sector for the first partition at either relative sector 32 or relative sector 63. You can get the sectors-per-track information by clicking **Volume Information** on the **Drives** menu.

If you think that the relative sector field for a primary partition or logical drive is correct, you can read the sector by clicking **Go** when you are viewing its information to see if the sector looks like a Partition Boot Sector.

There is also a **Total Sectors** field on the Partition Table view. If you think this field is accurate, you can use this value to calculate the start of the next primary partition or logical drive.

The FAT and NTFS Partition Boot Sectors each have a field that contains the total number of sectors. If you already know or have found the start of a primary partition or logical drive, you can add the number of sectors to the starting sector to find the start of the next partition or logical drive. For an NTFS Partition Boot Sector, on the **View** menu, click **NTFS BootSector**. The **Total sectors** field contains the value you want. For a FAT volume, on the **View** menu, click **FAT Bootsector**. If the size of the primary partition or logical drive fits in 16 bits, the **Small sectors** field contains the size. Otherwise, the size is in the **Large sectors** field.

You can also use DiskProbe to search for Partition Boot Sectors. As you find each one, write down its location, and use the Partition Table view in DiskProbe to enter the information.

There are three situations in which you can find a Partition Boot Sector that is not at the beginning of a volume. You need to know about these other Partition Boot Sectors so you do not use the information about where these Partition Boot Sectors are located to repair the Partition Table.

- If you formatted an NTFS volume, or converted a volume from FAT to NTFS when running Windows NT version 4.0, the NTFS volume has a backup of its Partition Boot Sector at the end of the volume. Earlier versions of Windows NT put the backup at the middle of the volume when you formatted it, but did not create a backup when you converted the volume.
- When you extend an NTFS volume set, Windows NT version 4.0 puts a new copy of the Partition Boot Sector in the middle of the extended volume set. It does not remove the old copy of the Partition Boot Sector. If you extend a volume set when running Windows NT version 3.51, it does not remove the old copy of the Partition Boot Sector either, nor does it write a new one.
- There can be old, invalid Partition Boot Sectors on the disk if you have deleted volumes.

▶ To search for Partition Boot Sectors

1. In the Resource Kit folder, double-click the DiskProbe icon.
2. On the **Drives** menu, click **Physical Drive**. The **Available Physical Drives** in the **Open Physical Drive** dialog box are listed as PhysicalDrive*n*, where *n*=0 for the first hard disk. Double-click the disk that you want to open, click **Set Active**, and click **Close**.
3. On the **Tools** menu, click **Search**. The information that you search for depends upon whether you want to find a FAT or an NTFS Partition Boot Sector. If you check the **Search at offset** check box and specify an **Offset in hex** at which to search for a specific value, the search runs much faster than searching each entire sector. You can search the entire disk if you do not change the default values in the **First sector to search** and **Last sector to search** fields.

   This is an example of a search for an NTFS Partition Boot Sector.

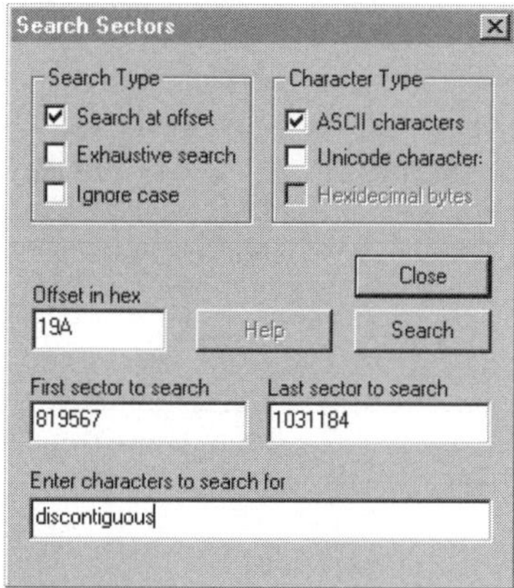

Note The contents of the Partition Boot Sector for an NTFS volume are slightly different, depending on whether you formatted the volume when running Windows NT version 4.0 or earlier versions of Windows NT. If you specify a value in the **Offset in hex** field, you might need to search at a different offset depending on the data you are searching for, and which version of Windows NT you used to format the volume. For example, the string "discontinguous" starts at location 19A when you use Windows NT version 4.0 to format the volume. But discontinguous is at hex location 195 if you formatted the volume when running Windows NT version 3.5. The string "NTFS" starts at offset 3 regardless of the version of Windows NT that you used to format the volume. If you do not know which version of Windows NT was used to format a volume, search for NTFS. Note that DiskProbe will find matches in sectors that are not Partition Boot Sectors.

---

4. If DiskProbe finds a match, it displays the address of the sector, as the following shows:

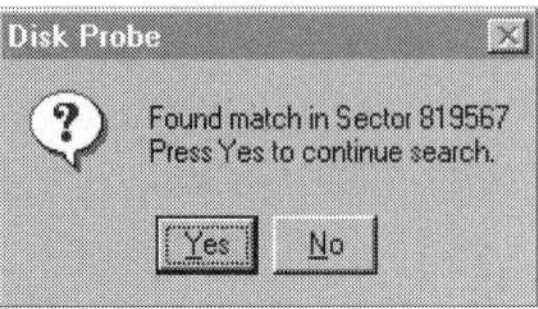

Be sure to verify that each sector DiskProbe finds is really a Partition Boot Sector. The **View** menu enables you to look at the data as bytes or formatted as an NTFS or a FAT Partition Boot Sector.

Editing and Repairing the Partition Table

You can use DiskProbe to display and change your Partition Table. Repairing a damaged Partition Table is risky, and should never be attempted by a user not familiar with the procedure. If all of the partitions on the disk are primary partitions, the repair process is much simpler than if you have an extended partition, volume sets, or stripe sets.

If the wrong partition is set as the system partition, or you do not have a system partition on the disk, you can use DiskProbe to set the Boot Indicator field for the correct partition.

Note The system partition is always a primary partition.

▶ **To change or set the Boot Indicator field**

1. View the Partition Table by using the procedure described in "Displaying and Using the Partition Table," presented earlier in this chapter.
2. Double-click each partition number in the **Partition table index** list box to determine which one is the system partition, or that none is set as the system partition. The partition that has the **Boot Indicator** field set to SYSTEM is the system partition.
3. To clear the **Boot Indicator** field for a partition, double-click its partition number, double-click **NOSYSTEM** in the **Boot Indicator** list box.
4. To set the system partition, double-click its partition number, and double-click **SYSTEM** in the **Boot Indicator** list box.
5. Make sure that the disk is in read/write mode. On the **Drives** menu, click **Physical Drive** to see the **Open Physical Drive** dialog box. Clear the **Read Only** check box, if it is checked. Click **Close**.
6. On the **Sectors** menu, click **Write**, and enter 0 in **Starting sector to write to**. Click **Write it**.
7. DiskProbe displays a message box so you can verify the information.

When you create a volume set or stripe set, Windows NT sets the FT bit of the System ID byte in the Partition Table. This bit indicates that Windows NT needs to use the Registry subkey HKEY_LOCAL_MACHINE\SYSTEM\DISK to know how to find all of the members of the volume. Because volume sets and stripe sets cannot be accessed without the DISK subkey, they can only be accessed by Windows NT. In a dual-boot configuration, the other operating system cannot use a partition with the FT bit set.

In general, you should use Disk Administrator, and not DiskProbe, to change the value of this field. You might want to set or clear the FT flag to test a recovery procedure, but be sure to have a backup of the Registry and the data on the partition before you do so.

▶ **To clear the Fault Tolerant (FT) flag for a primary partition**

1. View the Partition Table by using the procedure described in "Displaying and Using the Partition Table," presented earlier in this chapter.
2. Double-click the partition number in the **Partition table index** list box for which you want to change the value of the FT flag.
3. If you want to remove the FT flag from a FAT partition, you need to figure out whether the partition should be FAT 12 bit, FAT 16 bit, or FAT Large. See the section titled "System ID Field," in Chapter 17, "Disk and File System Basics," for information about the types of FAT partitions. Double-click either **FAT 12 bit**, **FAT 16 bit**, or **FAT Large** in the System ID field.
4. If you want to remove the FT flag from a NTFS partition, double-click **NTFS** in the System ID field.
5. Make sure that the disk is in read/write mode. On the **Drives** menu, click **Physical Drive** to see the Open Physical drives dialog box. Clear the **Read Only** check box, if it is checked. Click **Close**.
6. On the **Sectors** menu, click **Write**, and enter 0 in **Starting sector to write to**. Click **Write it**.
7. DiskProbe displays a message box so you can verify the information.

When you have found the Partition Boot Sectors, you can calculate all of the information for the Partition Table entries. If you do not know the values for the number of heads, number of sectors per track, or number of cylinders for the disk, open a handle by clicking either **Physical Drive** or **Logical Volume** on the **Drives** menu, and then click **Volume Information** on the **Drives** menu.

If none of the information in your Partition Table is correct, you might be safer to try to do a complete backup of the volumes. It might even be faster to backup and restore the data instead of repairing the Partition Table. You can then recreate the volumes, reformat your hard disk, and restore all of the data.

Note If a primary partition or logical drive extends beyond cylinder 1023, set the Starting and Ending Sector, Head, and Cylinder fields to the maximum values. Maximum values indicate to Windows NT that it needs to use the information in the Partition Boot Sector to know how to access the volume. Remember that your system and boot partitions should not go beyond cylinder 1023 if you have set up your computer to dual-boot MS-DOS or Windows 95.

▶ **Repairing the Partition Table**

1. For primary partitions, view the Partition Table by using the procedure described in "Displaying and Using the Partition Table," presented earlier in this section. For an extended partition, the section "Walking an Extended Partition," presented earlier in this chapter, describes finding the Partition Table entry for each logical drive.
2. Double-click the partition number for which you want to change information. Enter the new values.
3. Make sure that the disk is in read/write mode. On the **Drives** menu, click **Physical Drive** to see the **Open Physical Drive** dialog box. Clear the **Read Only** check box, if it is checked. Click **Close**.
4. On the **Sectors** menu, click **Write**, and enter the sector number of the Partition Table that you read in step 1. If you are changing information for primary partitions, the sector number is 0. Click **Write it**.
5. DiskProbe displays a message box so you can verify the information.

DiskSave — Back Up and Restore Critical Disk Sectors

DiskSave is an MS-DOS-based utility that enables you to save the Master Boot Record (MBR) and Partition Boot Sector (PBS) as binary files. You must start MS-DOS to run this utility. It will not run from the command prompt.

You should save these files to your Windows NT startup floppy disk or your MS-DOS bootable floppy disk. If your computer fails to start because it has a problem using the MBR or PBS, you can restore them and try the startup again.

This tool also enables you to turn off the FT bit in the System ID field of the system partition. This bit should never be set on Windows NT Workstation, because the system partition on Windows NT Workstation cannot be a volume set or stripe set.

The Master Boot Record contains code that the system BIOS on x86-based computers uses to read the Partition Table and find the Partition Boot Sector of the system partition. This sector also contains the partition table. If this sector becomes damaged, the computer cannot find or start the operating system.

The Partition Boot Sector contains code that loads the operating system kernel or a boot loader. A corrupt Partition Boot Sector can also cause startup failures.

Note If either of the sectors that you restore does not match the configuration of your computer, you can make your problems worse. Always be sure to save the Master Boot Record and the Partition Boot Sector whenever you make changes that affect them.

These are the DiskSave functions:

- F2, back up the Master Boot Record. This function saves cylinder 0, head 0, sector 1 of the startup disk to the filename that you enter. You need to save a new copy of this record any time that you create or delete a partition, or change the file system used on a partition.
- F3, restore the Master Boot Record. This function copies the file that you specify to cylinder 0, head 0, sector 1 of the startup disk. Restoring this sector also replaces the Partition Table. There are no checks to determine if the sector is a valid Master Boot Record.
- F4, backup the Partition Boot Sector. This function saves the first sector of the system partition on disk 0 to the filename specified.
- F5, restore the Partition Boot Sector. This function replaces the first sector of the system partition with the contents of the specified file. There are no checks to determine if the sector is a valid Partition Boot Sector.
- F6, turn off the FT bit for the system partition on disk 0. This function does not apply to Windows NT Workstation.

When DiskSave makes calls to the system BIOS, it checks the status of each call. The normal return value is zero. Originally, a nonzero value indicated an error, and the error codes were documented. Currently, there are system BIOSs that return nonzero values, which are not documented. These nonzero values do not seem to be errors. So far, all of these nonzero values that are not errors have occurred when using IDE disks.

If the value is non-zero, DiskSave displays a message at the bottom of the screen. If you see a message about a system BIOS call returning a nonzero value, it would be a good idea to check whether the function worked correctly. One way to check is to start Windows NT, and use the Windows NT–based utility DiskProbe to compare the sector that you tried to save or restore with a copy of the data. For example, if you see a message about a nonzero return code when you select F4 to save the Partition Boot Sector, finish saving the sector to a file. Then, using DiskProbe, read the Partition Boot Sector from disk, and compare the contents to the file that you just saved.

▶ **To use DiskSave to back up the Master Boot Record or Partition Boot Sector**

1. Start MS-DOS. Enter **disksave** at the command prompt. You now have the following options:
   - F2 — Backup the Master Boot Record
   - F3 — Restore Master Boot Record
   - F4 — Backup the Boot Sector
   - F5 — Restore Boot Sector
   - F6 — Disable FT on the Boot Drive
2. Press F2 to save the Master Boot Record and F4 to save the Partition Boot Sector. You need to enter the full name for the file, including the path. For example, to save the Master Boot Record to a folder on your C drive, use a name such as C:\Backup\Mbrdisk0.dsk. If you copy it to a floppy disk, the path should be similar to A:\Mbrdisk0.dsk.

Note DiskSave only saves the Master Boot Record on disk 0 and the Partition Boot Sector for the system partition on disk 0.

▶ To use DiskSave to replace the Master Boot Record or Partition Boot Sector

1. Start MS-DOS. Enter **disksave** at the command prompt. You have the following options:
   - F2 — Backup the Master Boot Record
   - F3 — Restore Master Boot Record
   - F4 — Backup the Boot Sector
   - F5 — Restore Boot Sector
   - F6 — Disable FT on the Boot Drive

2. Press F3 to replace the Master Boot Record and F5 to replace the Partition Boot Sector. You need to enter the full name for the file, including the path. For example, if you have saved the Master Boot Record on your Emergency Repair Disk or the Windows NT startup floppy disk, the path might be A:\Mbrdsk0.dsk.

Note DiskSave only restores the Master Boot Record on disk 0 and the Partition Boot Sector for the system partition on disk 0.

FTEdit — Recovering Volume Sets and Stripe Sets

The FTEdit utility on the *Windows NT Workstation Resource Kit* CD aids in the recovery of stripe sets, volume sets, stripe sets with parity, and mirror sets. Stripe sets with parity and mirror sets are available for Windows NT Server only, but are discussed here for completeness. For more information about using FTEdit, see Ftedit.hlp on the *Windows NT Workstation Resource Kit* CD.

Because stripe sets and volume sets are not fault tolerant, if one of the disks in a stripe set or volume set fails, the entire volume is no longer usable. And all the primary partitions or logical drives that are members of the volume are marked as orphans. In Disk Administrator, the members of the volume are displayed as Unknown.

All data about the configuration of volume sets and stripe sets are contained in the Registry subkey HKEY_LOCAL_MACHINE\SYSTEM\DISK. This disk configuration information is stored in binary format, so it is not practical to edit it manually. When the Registry information is corrupt or missing, and no backups are available, you can use FTEdit to build the Registry information and allow the operating system to read the volumes.

For example, if the disk containing the boot partition becomes unusable, or the computer fails, you might want to move the disks containing stripe sets and volume sets to another computer. Alternatively, you might decide to reinstall the operating system on a new disk. In either case, the operating system does not have any information about the volumes.

The operating system has information about which disks are members of volumes, but it cannot distinguish between a stripe set, a stripe set with parity, a volume set, or a mirror set without the Registry information. In this situation, when the volumes are displayed in Disk Administrator, the file system might be displayed as Unknown, and there will be no drive letter assigned to the volumes. This is to prevent writing to the volume, which could corrupt it.

When using FTEdit to rebuild the DISK Registry subkey, you need to know the order in which the unused areas on the disks were combined to create the volume. The following scenario shows why order is important.

A previous user created a volume set by combining unpartitioned areas on three disks in this order:

- 2 MB on disk 2
- 3 MB on disk 0
- 4 MB on disk 1

When someone creates a volume set, the Partition Boot Sector is the first sector on the first area selected. Data are written to the areas in the order in which they are combined. Thus, if someone created a 6 MB file on this volume set, the file would occupy the following areas:

- 2 MB on disk 2
- 3 MB on disk 0
- 1 MB on disk 1

Now you need to use FTEdit to rebuild the volume set. You select the disks in the order disk 0, disk 1, and then disk 2. Windows NT will not be able to find the Partition Boot Sector for the volume set, because the first sector of the volume set that you rebuilt is on disk 0, which contains only data. The Partition Boot Sector is actually on disk 2, but that disk area is at the end of the volume set you created. Your attempt to rebuild the volume set has failed, because you did not know the order in which to combine the disk areas.

The remainder of this section describes using FTEdit to build Registry information for a stripe set that has been moved from another computer. (Disks 1, 2, and 3 are the disks that have been moved.) Each disk is 519 MB and has one primary partition. Both computers are running Windows NT Workstation version 4.0.

▶ To rebuild a stripe set

1. Open Disk Administrator, so that you can update the disk configuration information. Disk Administrator needs to store the disk signature and other basic disk information before the disks can be recognized.
2. Open FTEdit. The following dialog box is displayed.

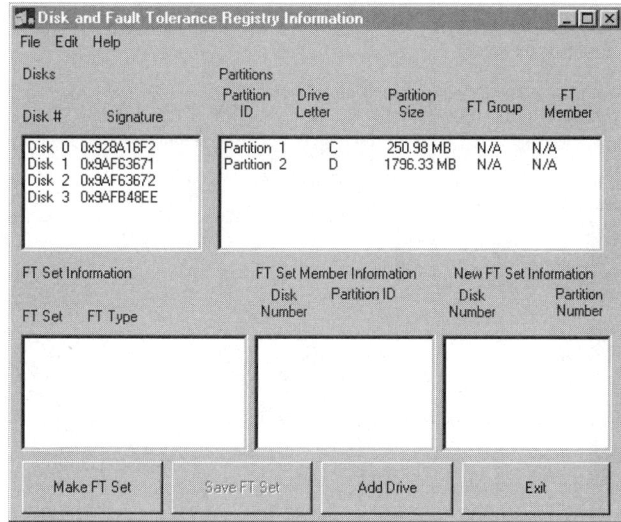

Figure 22.4 Using FTEdit to recover a stripe set

The **Disks** group box identifies all of the disks connected to the computer. The **Partitions** group box contains information about the disk currently selected, or the first disk if none is selected. Disk 0 is two gigabytes, and contains two partitions.

3. On the **Edit** menu, click **Create FT Set**. In the **FT Set Type** dialog box, click the option button for the type of volume you are building. In this example, click **Stripe Set**.

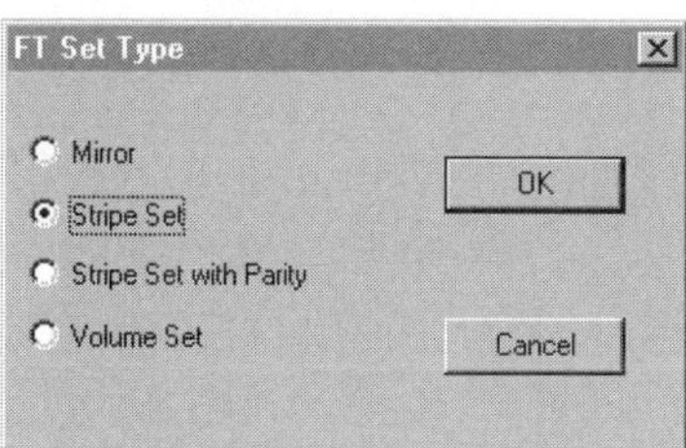

4. In the **Disks** list box, select the first disk that will be a member of the stripe set. Available partitions are displayed in the **Partitions** list box on the right.

   Double-click the partition from each disk that will make up the stripe set with parity. The disk and partition information will be displayed in the list box on the lower right. The title of this list box reflects the type of volume being built. For this example, the title is **Stripe Set Information**. The next screen shot shows the dialog box after double-clicking partition 1 on each of Disk 1, Disk 2, and Disk 3.

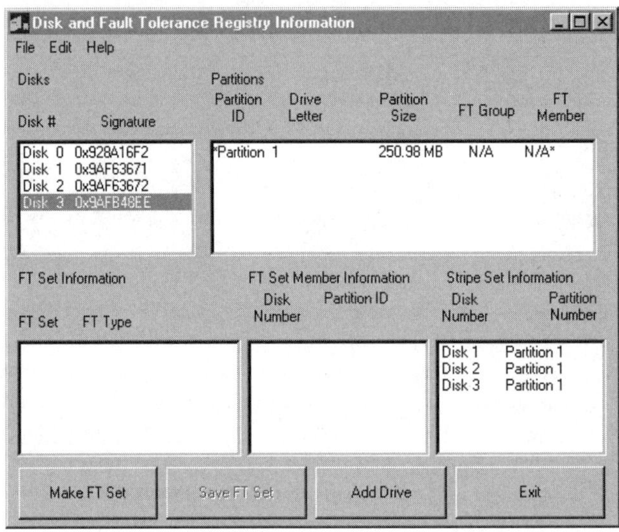

5. Click the **Save FT Set** button. The information is transferred to the **FT Set Member Information** list box. Check to make sure the information is correct. FTEdit should look like the following illustration:

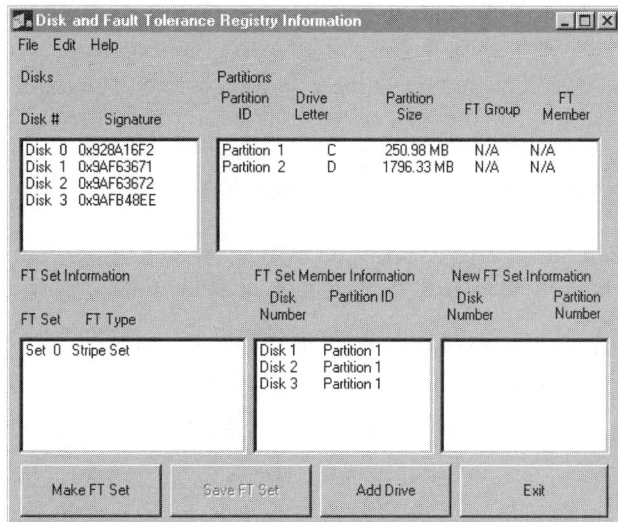

The **Partitions** list box shows the information for Disk 0. The disks that are used in creating the new volume are those listed in the **FT Set Member Information** list box.

6. On the **Edit** menu, click **Save Changes to System**. The following message box is displayed:

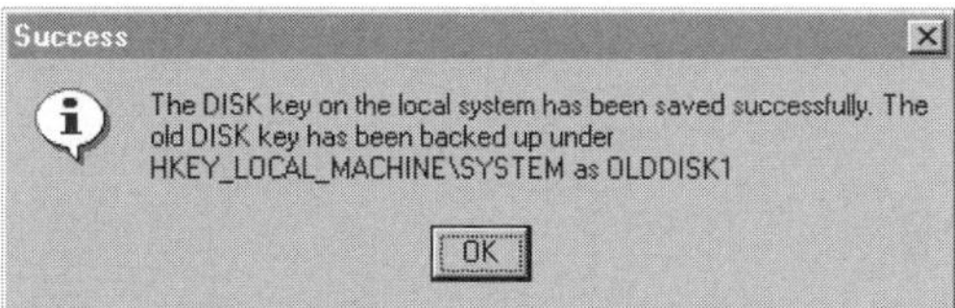

7. Exit FTEdit, close any open programs, and restart the system. You need to do this to get the new information loaded into the Registry.

8. Open Disk Administrator.

   Click one of the partitions in the stripe set. If the status bar has a message like **Stripe set #N [INITIALIZING],** the computer on which you were previously using the stripe set did not finish shutdown. Wait for Disk Administrator to finish the initialization. If the volume was functional before the disks were moved, and the correct information was entered in FTEdit, the data on the volume should be intact.

9. From the Disk Administrator **Tools** menu, click **Drive Letter**. In the **Assign Drive Letter** dialog box, click **Assign drive letter**, and then choose a drive letter for the new volume.

   The volume is now accessible from Windows NT Explorer, My Computer, and by the rest of the operating system.

10. After confirming that the volume is correctly configured and is accessible, be sure to add this new configuration information to the records that you keep for this computer.

    You might want to back up the volume at this time.

These same steps can be used to recover volume sets. To successfully use FTEdit to build Registry information, you must know the following information:

- Which disks contain stripe sets and volume sets.
- Which partitions belong to the stripe sets and volume sets.
- The order in which the partitions were combined into the stripe sets or volume sets.

If your configuration involves multiple stripe sets and volume sets on several different disks, you might face a very difficult job remembering which primary partitions and logical drives belong to which volumes. For this reason, it is a good idea to keep the disk configuration simple, and to keep recovery information as up-to-date as possible.

Note FTEdit edits the binary information in the Registry. It cannot recover damaged or corrupt data on the disk.

File System Utilities

The utilities described in this section are available on either the Windows NT Workstation product CD, or the *Windows NT Workstation Resource Kit* CD. This table shows which ones are on which CD.

Utility	Location
Cacls	product CD
Compact	product CD
Compress	resource kit CD
Convert	product CD
Diruse	resource kit CD
Expand	product CD
Expndw32	resource kit CD

Cacls: Changes ACLs of NTFS Files and Folders

You can use the Cacls utility to display or modify access control lists (ACL) of files or folders. A description of the command options follows the syntax. This is the format of the command:

```
CACLS <filename|folder> [/t] [/e] [/c] [/g user:perm] [/r user [...]]
[/p user:perm [...]] [/d user [...]]
```

Option	Description
filename or *folder name*	Displays ACLs.
/t	Changes ACLs of specified files in the current folder and all subfolders.
/e	Edit ACL instead of replacing it.
/c	Continue on access denied errors.
/g user:perm	Grant specified user access rights, where perm can be: R Read C Change (write) F Full control
/r user	Revoke specified user's access rights (only valid with /e).
/p user:perm	Replace specified user's access rights, where perm can be: N None R Read C Change (write) F Full control
/d user	Deny access to the specified user.

Wildcards can be used to specify more than one file in a command. You can specify more than one user in a command also.

If you already have permissions set for multiple users on a folder or file and do not use the /e option, all user permissions are removed except for the user and permissions specified on the command line. You should use the following syntax when modifying user permissions to include read, change, and full control respectively:

```
cacls <filename|folder> /e /r <username>
cacls <filename|folder> /e /g <username>:<permission>
cacls <filename|folder> /e /p <username>:<permission>
```

The Cacls utility does not provide a **/y** option that answers automatically with Y for Yes to the **ARE YOU SURE? Y/N** prompt. However, you can use the **echo** command to pipe the character Y as input to the prompt when you are running **cacls** in a batch file. Use the following syntax to automatically answer Y:

```
echo y| cacls <filename|folder> /g <username>:<permission>
```

Note Do not enter a space between the y and the pipe symbol (|). If you do, Cacls fails to make the permission change.

Compact: Compresses and Uncompresses NTFS Files and Folders

The Compact utility is the command line version of the compression functionality in My Computer or Windows NT Explorer. The Compact utility displays and alters the compression of folders and files on NTFS volumes. It also displays the compression state of folders. For more information about this utility, type **compact /?** at the command prompt. The table following describes the options.

The format of the command is:

```
compact [/c] [/u] [/s[:folder]] [/a] [/i] [/f] [/q] [filename [...]]
```

Option	Description
none	Displays the compression state of the current folder.
/c	Compresses the specified folder or file.
/u	Uncompresses the specified folder or file.
/s[:*folder*]	Specifies that the requested action (compress or uncompress) be applied to all subfolders of the specified folder, or to the current folder if none is specified.
/i	Ignores errors.
/f	Forces compression or uncompression of the specified folder or file.
/a	Displays files with the hidden or system attribute.
/q	Reports only the most essential information.
filename	Specifies a pattern, file, or folder. You can use multiple filenames and wild cards.

There are reasons why you would want to use this utility instead of My Computer or Windows NT Explorer:

- You can use Compact in a batch script. Using the **/i** option enables you to skip files that cannot be opened when you are running in batch mode, such as when a file is already in use by another program.
- If the system crashed when compression or uncompression was occurring, the file or folder is marked as Compressed or Uncompressed, even if the operation did not complete. You can force the operation to complete by using the Compact utility with the **/f** option (with either the **/c** or **/u**).

Note The Compact utility automatically compresses or uncompresses all of the files and subfolders when you change the compression state of a folder. It does not ask whether you want to change the compression state of the files or subfolders in it.

Compress: Compresses Files or Folders

This command line utility can be used to compress one or more files. You cannot open a file that has been compressed by using this utility. You have to expand it by using Expand or Expndw32 first.

To use this utility, type **compress** with the appropriate options at the command line:

compress [**-r**] [**-d**] *source* [*destination*]

Option	Description
-r	Renames compressed files.
-d	Updates compressed files only if out of date.
source	Specifies the source file. The "*" and "?" wildcards can be used.
destination	Specifies the destination file or path. The destination can be a folder. If source specifies multiple files and the **-r** option is not specified, then *destination* must be a folder.

Note You should not use this utility to compress files or folders on NTFS volumes. Instead, compress NTFS files and folders by using the Compact utility or by setting or clearing the **Compressed** attribute in My Computer or Windows NT Explorer. See Chapter 18, "Choosing a File System," for information about using My Computer or Windows NT Explorer.

Convert: Converts a Volume From FAT to NTFS

You can use the Convert utility to convert a volume from the FAT file system to the NTFS file system. This utility performs the conversion within the existing volume. You do not need to back up and restore the files when you use this utility.

You cannot convert the Windows NT boot partition while you are running Windows NT. Therefore, the Convert utility gives you the choice of converting the partition the next time you start Windows NT. When you convert the partition this way, Windows NT restarts twice to complete the conversion process.

To use this utility, type **convert** with the appropriate options (explained in the table following the syntax) at the command line:

convert *drive*: **/FS:NTFS [/v]**

Option	Description
drive	Logical drive that you want to convert.
/FS	You must specify that you want to convert to the NTFS file system.
/v	Run the utility in verbose mode.

DirUse: Provides Information About Usage of Disk Space

You can use the DirUse utility on the *Windows NT Workstation Resource Kit* CD to obtain disk space usage per folder. For more information about DirUse, type **diruse /?** at the command line, or see the Windows NT Resource Kit Tools Help for information about this utility.

This utility is useful to get the actual usage of space for compressed files and folders in NTFS volumes.

The format of the command is:

diruse [**/s** | **/v**] [**/q:#**] [**/m** | **/k** | **/b**] [**/a**] [**/l**] [**/d**] [**/o**] [**/c**] [**/,**] [**/***] [*dirs*]

The option of interest for compressed folders and files is **/c**, which causes the display of compressed file or folder size instead of apparent size. For example, if your D drive is an NTFS volume, type **diruse /s /m /c d:** at the command prompt to get the disk space actually used (in MB) and number of files in each of the folders. To see compression information for an individual file, you can use My Computer or Windows NT Explorer, select the file, and select **Properties** from the **File** menu.

Expand and Expndw32: Expand Compressed Files

You can use two utilities to expand one or more compressed files from your Windows NT CD, or a file that you compressed by using **compress**.

You can use Expndw32, the Windows NT–based expand utility, in one of these ways:

- If you have installed the *Windows NT Workstation Resource Kit*, you can double-click the Expand Files icon in the File Tools program group.
- From My Computer or Windows NT Explorer, open the Expndw32.exe file. If you have installed the *Windows NT Workstation Resource Kit*, this utility is in the folder into which you installed the *Windows NT Workstation Resource Kit*. On the *Windows NT Workstation Resource Kit* CD, use the version that corresponds to the hardware platform that you are using.

For help while you are using the utility, choose the **Help** button or press F1.

The MS-DOS-based expand utility runs from the command line. Type the **expand** command with the appropriate options, as shown in the table:

expand [**-r**] *source* [*destination*]

Option	Description
-r	Renames expanded files.
source	Specifies the source file. The "*" and "?" wildcards can be used.
destination	Specifies the destination file or path. The destination can be a folder. If source specifies multiple files and the **-r** option is not specified, then *destination* must be a folder.

Backup Utilities

AT: Enables You to Schedule Windows NT Backup

The Windows NT Backup utility, Ntbackup.exe, does not include functionality for schedule unattended backups. However, by using the Schedule service with the command line capabilities of Ntbackup, you can set up unattended backups.

The following procedure shows how to use the Schedule service and Ntbackup to schedule an unattended backup of the entire C drive of a computer with an installed tape device. With minor modifications, these steps could also allow for scheduling unattended backups from a computer on a network to a computer with an installed tape device or other configurations.

▶ **To schedule unattended backup**

1. Start the Schedule service on the computer with the tape device already installed. This can be done by using the Services option in Control Panel, clicking **Schedule**, and clicking **Start**. Alternatively, you can configure the Schedule service to start every time Windows NT starts by clicking **Startup** and setting the **Startup Type** to **Automatic**.
2. Using any text editor, such as Notepad, create a command file such as Mybackup.cmd to perform the commands to backup the files.

   This example:

   ```
   ntbackup backup c: /D "My Backup Files" /B /L "c:\backup.log"
   ```

   does the following:

   - Backs up all files on the C drive.
   - Replaces any files currently on the tape.
   - Labels the backup set "My Backup Files."
   - Backs up the local registry.
   - Logs all backup information to C:\Backup.log.
3. Using the AT command, schedule the command file (Mybackup.cmd) to run when desired. The following AT command schedules Mybackup.cmd to execute at 11:00 P.M. every Monday, Wednesday, and Friday:

   ```
   AT 23:00 /every:M,W,F MYBACKUP.CMD
   ```

When there is no tape in the drive and you use the AT command without the interactive switch to run Windows NT Backup, the backup encounters an error or is unable to accept the command line. As a result, Windows NT Backup stops responding. You cannot run Windows NT Backup again until you restart Windows NT.

Use the /INTERACTIVE switch with the AT command to open the interactive desktop. This way, if any errors occur, you will be able to correct them and continue, or quit Windows NT Backup.

For information about AT options, type **AT /?** at a command prompt or search the online Command Reference for AT. For additional information on available Ntbackup options, use the **Help** menu when running Ntbackup.exe.

PART V

Windows NT Registry

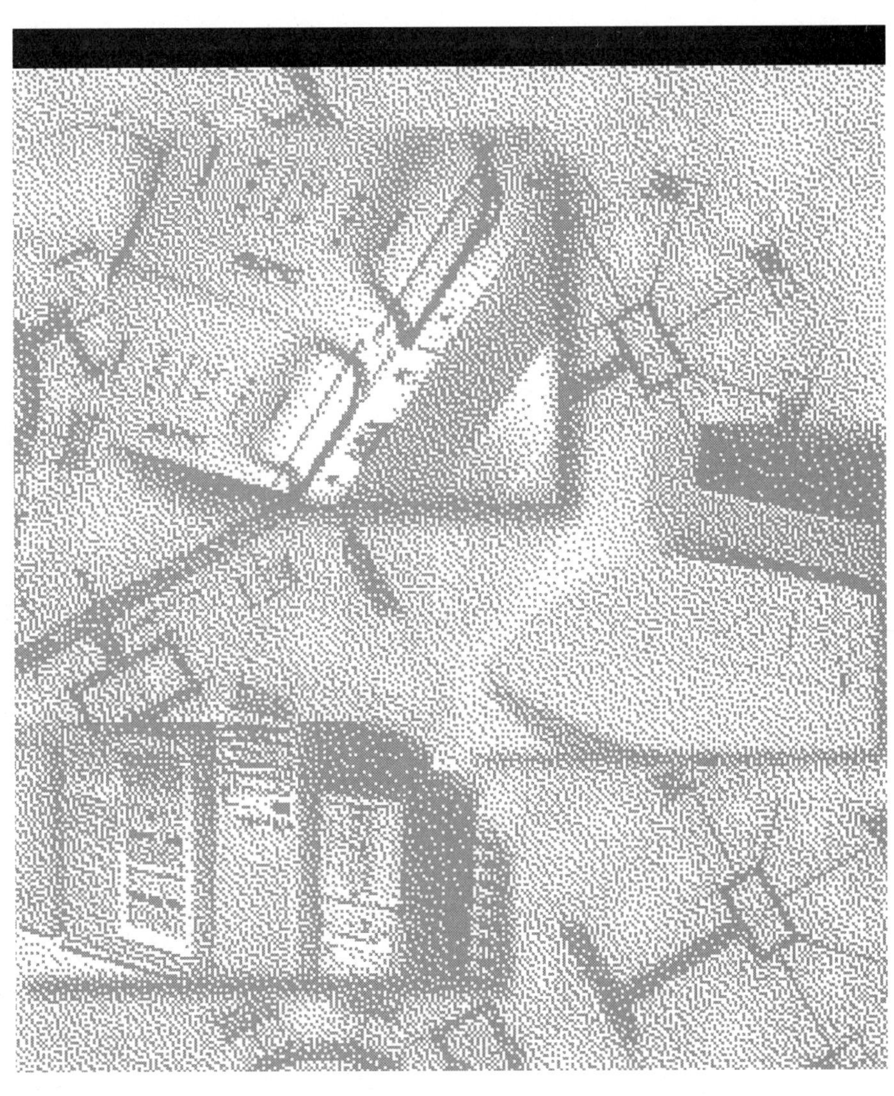

CHAPTER 23

Overview of the Windows NT Registry

System administrators must meet an enormous challenge in managing hardware, operating systems, and applications on personal computers. In Windows NT, the Registry helps simplify support by providing a secure, unified database that stores configuration data in a hierarchical form. By using the Registry and administrative tools in Windows NT, system administrators can provide local or remote support.

Chapters 23–26 of the *Windows NT Workstation Resource Guide* describe the Registry and show how to use the information in the Registry for troubleshooting and configuration maintenance.

- This chapter presents background information about the structure and contents of the Registry.
- Chapter 24, "Registry Editors and Registry Administration," provides details about the tools for viewing and editing Registry entries.
- Chapter 25, "Configuration Management and the Registry," provides specific problem-solving techniques that use the Registry.
- Chapter 26, "Initialization Files and the Registry," describes how Windows NT uses files such as Win.ini and Config.sys and how this information is mapped to the Registry.

In addition, Regentry.hlp, an online Help file on the *Windows NT Workstation Resource Kit* CD, lists the Registry values used for tuning and troubleshooting workstations and servers, system components, the network, and the user environment.

Caution Wherever possible, use the administrative tools such as Control Panel and User Manager to make configuration changes, rather than editing the Registry. It is safer to use the administrative tools because these tools are designed to store values properly in the Registry. If you make errors while changing values with a Registry editor, you will not be warned, because the Registry editor applications do not recognize and cannot correct errors in syntax or other semantics.

Editing the Registry directly can cause errors in loading hardware and software and prevent users from being able to log on to the computer.

Getting Started with the Registry Editors

To get the most out of the material in this chapter, run a Registry editing tool so that you can see the contents of the Registry for your computer.

Windows NT 4.0 includes two tools for viewing and editing the Registry, both called Registry Editor. The traditional tool, **Regedt32.exe**, is documented more thoroughly in these chapters. The new tool, **Regedit.exe**, has a Windows NT Explorer interface. It has many of the same functions as **Regedt32** and an expanded search capability. Both tools are installed automatically when you install Windows NT on any computer.

Figure 23.1 shows the Windows NT Registry as seen by **Regedit**:

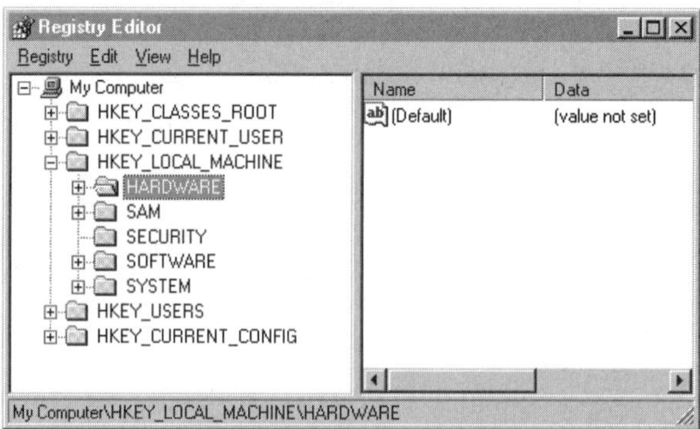

Figure 23.1 The Registry as viewed by Regedit

▶ **To run a Registry editor**

1. Start **Regedt32.exe** or **Regedit.exe** from Windows NT Explorer, or click **Run** on the **Start** menu.

   –Or–

   Type **regedt32** or **regedit** at the command prompt, and press ENTER.

2. From the **Options** menu in **Regedt32**, click **Read Only Mode**.

   This enables the **Regedt32** read-only mode, which protects the Registry contents from unintentional changes while you explore its structure and become familiar with the entries.

3. Click any folder icon to display the contents of that key.

In **Regedit**, click **Find** on the **Edit** menu to search for keys and subkeys, value entries, and values. In **Regedt32**, click **Find Key** on the **View** menu to search for a key or subkey. However, you cannot search for value entries or values by using the **Find Key** command in **Regedt32**.

For more information about **Regedt32** and **Regedit**, click **Help Topics** on the **Help** menu of either application.

For details about security and backup measures to take with the Registry and other issues, see Chapter 24, "Registry Editors and Registry Administration."

Figure 23.2 shows the Windows NT Registry as seen by **Regedt32**.

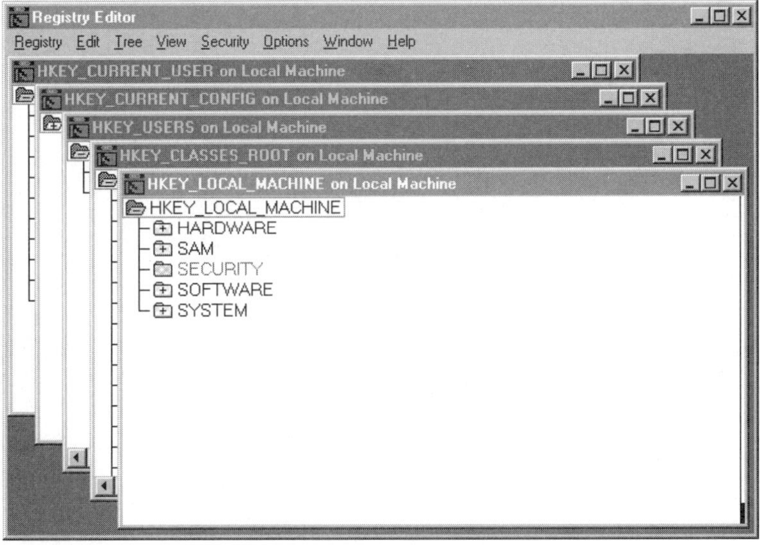

Figure 23.2 The Windows NT Registry as viewed by Regedt32

The Registry is a database, and Registry Editor displays the five subtrees used to access the contents of the database. The hierarchical structure that appears in Registry Editor looks similar to the hierarchical directory structures in Windows NT Explorer. The information in this chapter helps you understand where specific kinds of information can be found in the Registry and where you should or should not make changes.

In this chapter, the Registry keys are described in the same order as the order in which they appear in the Registry Editor windows. The information on Registry keys in this chapter focuses on those parts of the Registry that a system administrator is most likely to need to view or to change. Some information is provided merely to explain what is stored in certain keys.

The content or location of an individual Registry key on your computer might differ from what is described in these chapters. The Registry configuration depends on the services and software installed, on whether the computer is running Windows NT Workstation or Windows NT Server, and on other factors. However, you can use the general organization described in this chapter to help you understand how to navigate in Registry Editor.

Note Registry entries that system administrators most commonly examine or edit are found under HKEY_LOCAL_MACHINE\System\CurrentControlSet, described later in this chapter. Specific entries are defined in Regentry.hlp, a Help file included on the *Windows NT Workstation Resource Kit* CD.

How Windows NT Components Use the Registry

Under versions of Windows for MS-DOS, starting the system, connecting to the network, and running applications involves multiple configuration files with some form of synchronization between them. Under Windows NT, the operating system stores and checks the configuration information at only one location—the Registry. Figure 23.3 shows how data is handled by the Windows NT Registry.

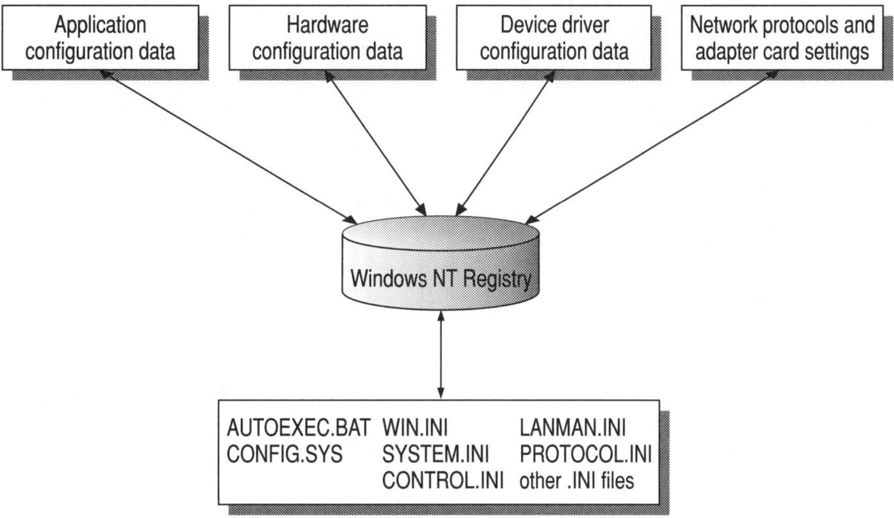

Figure 23.3 Data in the Windows NT Registry

Figure 23.4 shows how Windows NT components and applications use the Registry. The explanations in the list that follows provide details.

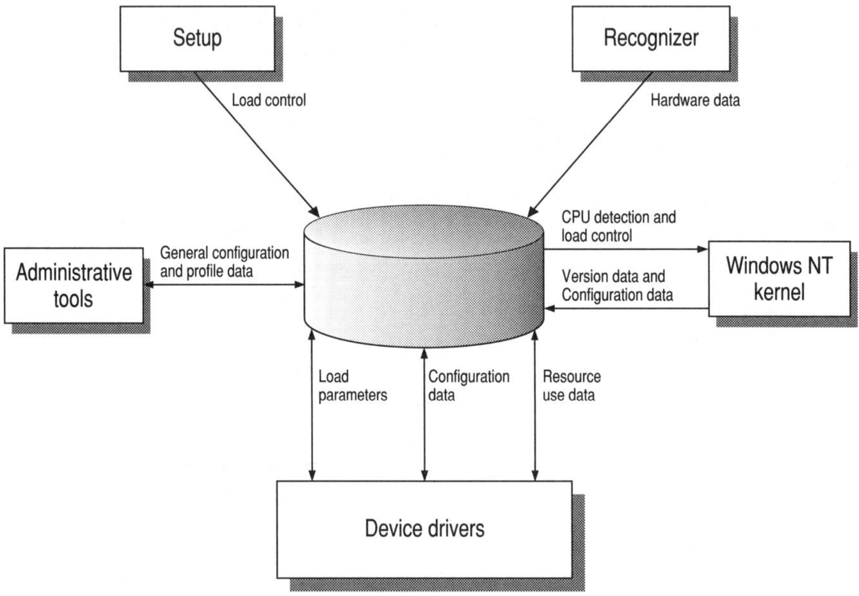

Figure 23.4 How Registry information is used by Windows NT

- *Setup.* Whenever you run the Windows NT Setup program or other setup programs for applications or hardware, the Setup program adds new configuration data to the Registry. For example, new information is added when you install a new SCSI adapter or change the settings for your video display. Setup also reads information from the Registry to determine whether prerequisite components have been installed.
- *Recognizer.* Each time you start a computer running Windows NT, the Hardware Recognizer places in the Registry a list of the installed hardware it detects. The Hardware Recognizer is a program that runs as part of the Windows NT startup sequence. On computers with Intel processors, hardware detection is done by **Ntdetect.com** and the Windows NT Kernel (**Ntoskrnl.exe**). On Reduced Instruction Set Computers (RISC), the hardware information is extracted from the ARC (Advanced RISC Computing) firmware.
- *Windows NT Kernel.* During system startup, the Windows NT Kernel extracts information from the Registry, such as which device drivers to load and their load order. The **Ntoskrnl.exe** program also passes information about itself (such as its version number) to the Registry.

- *Device drivers.* Device drivers send and receive load parameters and configuration data from the Registry. This data is similar to what you might find on the DEVICE= lines in the Config.sys file under MS-DOS. A device driver must report system resources that it uses, such as hardware interrupts and direct memory access (DMA) channels, so the system can add this information to the Registry. Applications and device drivers can read this Registry information to provide users with smart installation and configuration programs.
- *Administrative tools.* The administrative tools in Windows NT, such as those provided in Control Panel and in the Administrative Tools (common) folder, can be used to modify configuration data. The Registry editors are helpful for viewing and occasionally making detailed changes to the system configuration. You can also use Windows NT Diagnostics and the System Policy Editor to view configuration information stored in the Registry and to modify certain Registry keys.

For details, see Chapter 24, "Registry Editors and Registry Administration."

The Registry is analogous to the .ini files used under Windows for MS-DOS, with each key in the Registry similar to a bracketed heading in an .ini file, and entries under the heading similar to values in the Registry. However, Registry keys can contain subkeys; .ini files do not support nested headings. Registry values can also consist of executable code, rather than the simple strings representing values in .ini files. And individual preferences for multiple users of the same computer can be stored in the Registry, which is not possible with .ini files.

Although these chapters focus on using Registry entries instead of using .ini files, some applications (particularly 16-bit Windows-based applications) continue to use .ini files. Windows NT supports .ini files solely for compatibility with those applications and with related tools, such as setup programs. The files Autoexec.bat and Config.sys also still exist in some form to provide compatibility with applications created for MS-DOS and Windows 3.*x*.

For details about how Windows NT uses such files in conjunction with the Registry, see Chapter 26, "Initialization Files and the Registry."

Registry Structure

This section describes the hierarchical organization of the Registry and defines the overall structure of subtrees, keys, and subkeys. Following this section, details are provided about specific Registry keys.

The Registry Hierarchy

The Registry is structured as a set of subtrees of keys that contain per-computer and per-user databases. The per-computer information includes information about hardware and software installed on the computer. The per-user information includes the information in user profiles, such as desktop settings, individual preferences for certain software, and personal printer and network settings. In versions of Windows for MS-DOS, per-computer information was saved in the Win.ini and System.ini files, but it was not possible to save separate information for individual users.

In the Windows NT Registry, each individual key can contain data items called *value entries* and can also contain additional *subkeys.* In the Registry structure, keys are analogous to directories, and the value entries are analogous to files.

Figure 23.5 shows the subtrees of the Windows NT Registry.

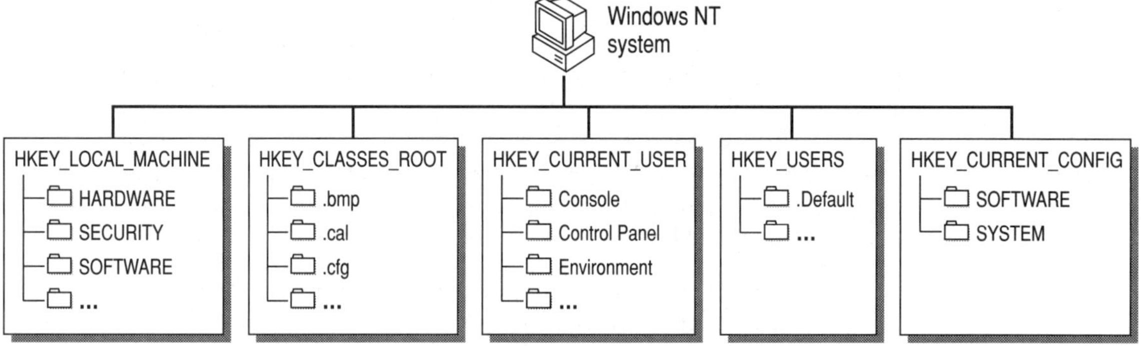

Figure 23.5 The subtrees of the Windows NT Registry

Each of these subtrees is described in detail later in this chapter. Each of the root key names begins with "HKEY_" to indicate to software developers that this is a *handle* that can be used by a program. A handle is a value used to uniquely identify a resource so that a program can access it.

Table 23.1 identifies and defines these subtrees.

Table 23.1 Registry Subtrees

Root key name	Description
HKEY_LOCAL_MACHINE	Contains information about the local computer system, including hardware and operating system data such as bus type, system memory, device drivers, and startup control data.
HKEY_CLASSES_ROOT	Contains the associations between applications and file types (by filename extension). It also contains object linking and embedding (OLE) Registry information associated with COM objects, and file-class association data (equivalent to the Registry in Windows for MS-DOS). The entries in this subtree are the same as in HKEY_LOCAL_MACHINE\Software\Classes. For detailed information on HKEY_CLASSES_ROOT, see the *OLE Programmer's Reference* in the Windows NT 4.0 Software Developer's Kit.
HKEY_CURRENT_CONFIG	Contains configuration data for the current hardware profile. Hardware profiles are sets of changes to the standard configuration of services and devices established by data in the Software and System keys under HKEY_LOCAL_MACHINE. Only the changes appear in HKEY_CURRENT_CONFIG. The entries in this subtree also appear in: HKEY_LOCAL_MACHINE\System \CurrentControlSet\HardwareProfiles\Current.
HKEY_CURRENT_USER	Contains the user profile for the user who is logged on, including environment variables, desktop settings, network connections, printers, and application preferences.
HKEY_USERS	Contains all actively loaded user profiles, including HKEY_CURRENT_USER, and the default profile. Users who are accessing a server remotely do not have profiles under this key on the server; their profiles are loaded into the Registry on their own computers.

Value Entries in the Registry Keys

Registry data is maintained as value entries under the Registry keys. As shown in Figure 23.6, Registry Editor displays data in two panes. The value entries in the right pane are associated with the selected key in the left pane. Click the folders and double-click the entries to see their contents.

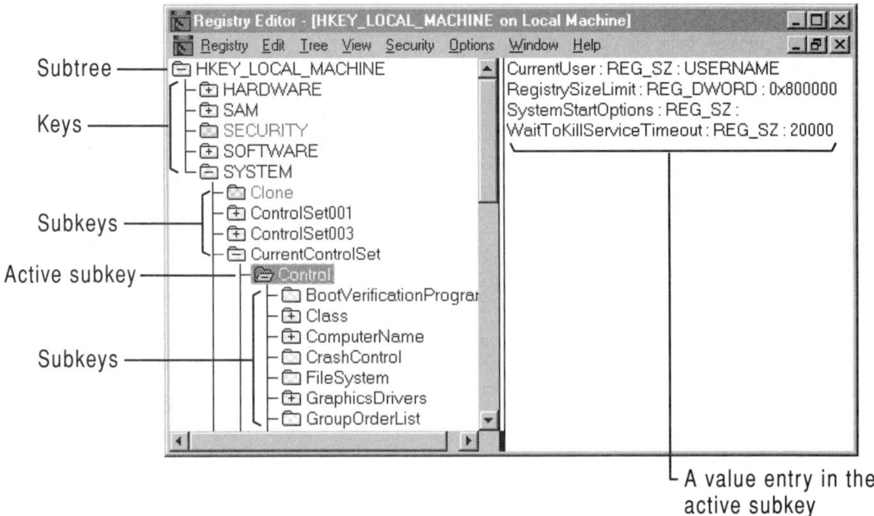

Figure 23.6 Terms used to describe items in the Registry Editor window

A value entry has three parts: the name of the value, the data type of the value, and the value itself, which can be data of any length. The three parts of value entries always appear in the following order:

Name / Data type / Value

RegistrySizeLimit REG_DWORD 0x800000

A value entry cannot be larger than about 1 MB. Values from 0 to 0x7fffffff are reserved for definition by the system, and applications are encouraged to use these types. Values from 0x80000000 to 0xffffffff are reserved for use by applications.

Table 23.2 lists the data types defined and used by the system.

Table 23.2 Data Types for Registry Entries

Data type	Description
REG_BINARY	Raw binary data. Most hardware component information is stored as binary data, and can be displayed in Registry Editor in hexadecimal format, or displayed by the Windows NT Diagnostics program (**Winmsdp.exe**) in an easy-to-read format. For example: `Component Information : REG_BINARY : 00 00 00...`
REG_DWORD	Data represented by a number that is 4 bytes long. Many parameters for device drivers and services are of this type and can be displayed in Registry Editor in binary, hex, or decimal format. For example, entries for service error controls are of this type: `ErrorControl : REG_DWORD : 0x1`
REG_EXPAND_SZ	An expandable data string, which is text that contains a variable to be replaced when called by an application. For example, for the following value, the string *%Systemroot%* will be replaced by the actual location of the directory containing the Windows NT system files: `File : REG_EXPAND_SZ : %Systemroot%\file.exe`
REG_MULTI_SZ	A multiple string. Values that contain lists or multiple values in human-readable text are usually of this type. Entries are separated by NULL characters. For example, the following value entry specifies the binding rules for a network transport: `Bindable : REG_MULTI_SZ : dlcDriver dlcDriver non non 50`
REG_SZ	A sequence of characters representing human-readable text. For example, a component's description is usually of this type: `DisplayName : REG_SZ : Messenger`

Hives and Files

The Registry is divided into parts called *hives*. A hive is a discrete body of keys, subkeys, and values rooted at the top of the Registry hierarchy. Hives are distinguished from other groups of keys in that they are permanent components of the Registry; they are not created dynamically when the system starts and deleted when it stops. Thus, HKEY_LOCAL_MACHINE\Hardware, which is built dynamically by the Hardware Recognizer when Windows NT starts, is not a hive.

Data in the hives is supported by files in the *Systemroot*\System32\Config and *Systemroot*\Profiles*Username* subdirectories. Figure 23.7 shows the relationship between the hives and their supporting files.

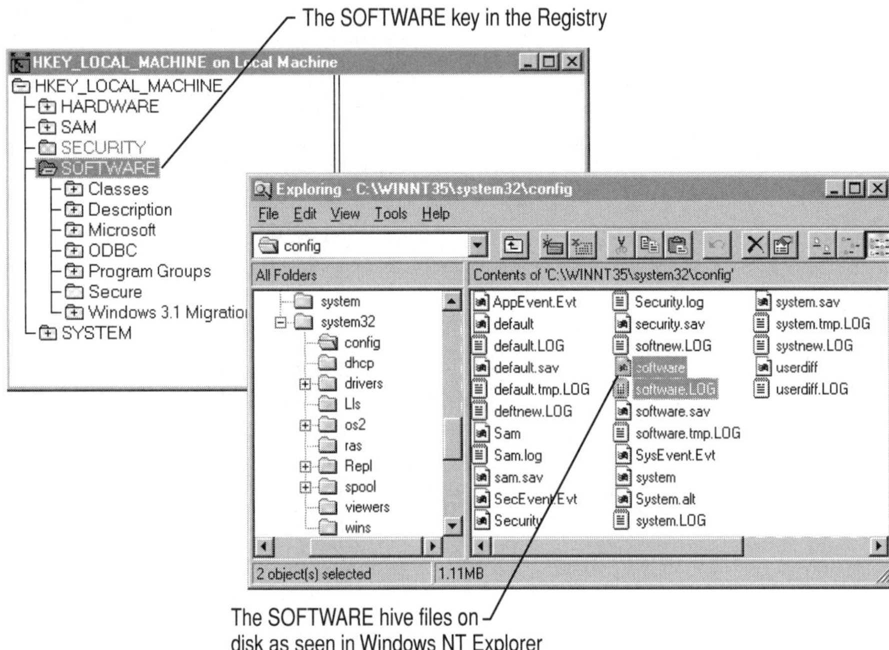

Figure 23.7 Hives and files in the Windows NT Registry

Each hive in the Windows NT Registry is associated with a set of standard files. Table 23.3 lists the standard hives for a computer running Windows NT.

Table 23.3 Standard Hive Files

Registry hive	Filenames
HKEY_LOCAL_MACHINE\SAM	Sam, Sam.log, Sam.sav
HKEY_LOCAL_MACHINE\Security	Security, Security.log, Security.sav
HKEY_LOCAL_MACHINE\Software	Software, Software.log, Software.sav
HKEY_LOCAL_MACHINE\System	System, System.alt, System.log, System.sav
HKEY_CURRENT_CONFIG	System, System.alt, System.log, System.sav
HKEY_USERS\.DEFAULT	Default, Default.log, Default.sav
(Not associated with a hive)	Userdiff, Userdiff.log
HKEY_CURRENT_USER	Ntuser.dat, Ntuser.dat.log

By default, the supporting files for all hives except HKEY_CURRENT_USER are in *Systemroot*\System32\Config.

The HKEY_CURRENT_USER support files are stored in all subdirectories of *Systemroot*\Profiles, except for the All Users subdirectory. The Ntuser.dat files store user profiles; the Ntuser.dat.log files track changes to Ntuser.dat.

The Ntuser and Userdiff files are new to Windows NT 4.0:

- The Ntuser.dat file, which stores the user profile, replaces the *usernamexxx* and *adminxxx* files in previous versions of Windows NT.
- The Ntuser.dat file in *Systemroot*\Profiles\DefaultUser replaces the Userdef file in previous versions of Windows NT. This profile is used to create the HKEY_CURRENT_USER hive when a new user logs on to Windows NT for the first time.
- The Userdiff files, which are only in *Systemroot*\System32\Config, are not associated with any hive. They are used to upgrade existing user profiles from previous versions of Windows NT to Windows NT 4.0. The user profiles are upgraded the first time the user logs on to Windows NT 4.0.

Four types of files are associated with hives. Table 23.4 describes each file type by its filename extension.

Table 23.4 File Types and Filename Extensions

File type	Description
No filename extension	Contains a copy of the hive.
.alt	Contains a backup copy of the critical HKEY_LOCAL_MACHINE\System hive. Only the System key has an .alt file.
.log	Contains a transaction log of changes to the keys and value entries in the hive.
.sav	Contains copies of the hive files as they looked at the end of the text mode stage in Setup. There are .sav files for Software, SAM, Security, System, and .Default. A new feature of Windows NT 4.0 backs up the contents of the hives during setup. Setup has two stages: text mode and graphics mode. The hive is copied to a .sav file after the text-mode stage of setup to protect it from errors that might occur if the graphics-mode stage of setup fails. If setup fails during the graphics-mode stage, only the graphics-mode stage is repeated when the computer is restarted; the .sav file is used to rebuild the hives.

The next section discusses features that, along with the supporting files, help to preserve the integrity of the Windows NT Registry.

Atomicity and Hive Recovery in the Registry

The Registry ensures *atomicity* of individual actions. This means that any change made to a value (to set, delete, or save) either works or does not work: The result will not be a corrupted combination of the old and new configuration even if the system stops unexpectedly because of power failure, hardware failure, or software problems. For example, if an application sets a value for an entry and the system shuts down while this change is being made, when the system restarts, the entry will have either the old value or the new value, but not a meaningless combination of both values. In addition, the size and time data for the key containing the affected entry will be accurate whether the value was changed or not changed.

Flushing Data

In Windows NT, data is written to the Registry only when a *flush* occurs, which happens after changed data ages past a few seconds, or when an application intentionally flushes the data to the hard disk.

The system performs the following flush process for all hives (except for the System hive):

1. All changed data is written to the hive's .log file along with a map of where it is in the hive, and then a flush is performed on the .log file. All changed data has now been written in the .log file.
2. The first sector of the hive file is marked to indicate that the file is in transition.
3. The changed data is written to the hive file.
4. The hive file is marked as completed.

Note If the system shuts down between steps 2 and 4, when the hive is next loaded at startup (unless it is a profile hive that is loaded at logon), the system sees the mark left in step 2, and proceeds to recover the hive using the changes contained in the .log file. That is, the .log files are not used if the hive is not in transition. If the hive is in transition, it cannot be loaded without the .log file.

A different flush process is used for the System hive because it is an important element during system startup and is used too early during startup to be recovered as described in the previous flush process.

The System.alt file contains a copy of the data contained in the System file. During the flush process, changes are marked, written, and then marked as done. Then the same flush process is followed for the System.alt file. If there is a power failure, hardware failure, or software problems at any point during the process, either the System or System.alt file contains the correct information.

The System.alt file is similar to a .log file except that at load time, rather than having to reapply the logged changes, the system just switches to System.alt. The System.alt file is not needed unless the System hive is in transition.

User Profile Hives

Each time a new user logs on to a computer, a new hive is created for that user with a separate file for the user profile. The system administrator can copy a user profile file to a different directory and view, repair, or copy entries to another computer by using Registry Editor. For specific information on this feature, see Chapter 25, "Configuration Management and the Registry." For information about the hive for the default profile, see "HKEY_USERS" later in this chapter.

Registry Size Limit

Registry data is stored in the paged pool, an area of physical memory used for system data that can be written to disk when not in use. The **RegistrySizeLimit** value establishes the maximum amount of paged pool space (and disk paging file space) that can be consumed by Registry data from all applications. It is designed to prevent the Registry from consuming space needed by processes.

The **RegistrySizeLimit** value establishes a maximum size for the Registry. It does not allocate space in the paged pool, nor does it assure that the space will be available if needed.

By default, **RegistrySizeLimit** is set to 25 percent of the size of the paged pool. When the paged pool size changes, either because it is adjusted by Windows NT or because an administrator changes it, the value of **RegistrySizeLimit** changes, too. (Typically, the paged pool is set at 32 MB, so the **RegistrySizeLimit** value is 8 MB.)

The system ensures that the minimum value for **RegistrySizeLimit** is 4 MB, and the maximum is approximately 80 percent of the **PagedPoolSize** value. Thus, the paged pool is limited to a maximum size of 128 MB, and the **RegistrySizeLimit** value cannot exceed 102 MB (80 percent of 128 MB).

To view or change the value of **RegistrySizeLimit**, edit the entry under the following subkey:

HKEY_LOCAL_MACHINE\System\CurrentControlSet\Control

RegistrySizeLimit must have a type of REG_DWORD and a data length of 4 bytes, or it will be ignored. The **RegistrySizeLimit** value is approximate.

To view or change the size of the paged pool, use the **PagedPoolSize** value entry under the following subkey:

HKEY_LOCAL_MACHINE\System\CurrentControlSet\Control
\Session Manager\Memory Management

The space controlled by **RegistrySizeLimit** includes the hive space, as well as some of the Registry's run-time structures. Other Registry run-time structures are protected by their own size limits or by other means.

To ensure that a user can always start the system and edit the Registry, the Registry is not subject to the value set in **RegistrySizeLimit** until after the first successful loading of a hive (that is, the loading of a user profile). For more details about **RegistrySizeLimit**, see Regentry.hlp, the Registry Help file on the *Windows NT Workstation Resource Kit* CD.

HKEY_LOCAL_MACHINE

HKEY_LOCAL_MACHINE contains the configuration data for the local computer. The information in this database is used by applications, device drivers, and the Windows NT system to determine configuration data for the local computer, regardless of which user is logged on and what software is in use.

HKEY_LOCAL_MACHINE contains five keys, as listed briefly in Table 23.5. The rest of this section describes these keys.

Note You can read information in any of these keys, but you can add or change information only in the Software and System keys.

Table 23.5 Keys in HKEY_LOCAL_MACHINE

Key name	Contents
Hardware	The database that describes the physical hardware in the computer, the way device drivers use that hardware, and mappings and related data that link kernel-mode drivers with user-mode code. All data in this key is recreated each time the system is started. ▪ The Description subkey describes the actual computer hardware. ▪ The DeviceMap subkey contains miscellaneous data in formats specific to particular classes of drivers. ▪ The ResourceMap subkey describes which device drivers claim which hardware resources. The Windows NT Diagnostics program (Winmsdp.exe) can report on its contents in an easy-to-read form.
SAM	The directory services database of security information for user and group accounts, and for the domains in Windows NT Server. (SAM is the Security Account Manager, now known as the directory services database.)

Table 23.5 Keys in HKEY_LOCAL_MACHINE *(continued)*

Key name	Contents
Security	The database that contains the local security policy, such as specific user rights. This key is used only by the Windows NT security subsystem.
Software	The per-computer software database. This key contains data about software installed on the local computer, along with various items of miscellaneous configuration data.
System	The database that controls system startup, device driver loading, Windows NT services, and operating system behavior.

By convention, if similar data exists under HKEY_CURRENT_USER and under HKEY_LOCAL_MACHINE, the data in HKEY_CURRENT_USER takes precedence. However, values in this key can also extend (rather than replace) data in HKEY_LOCAL_MACHINE. Also, some items (such as device driver loading entries) are meaningless if they occur outside of HKEY_LOCAL_MACHINE.

HKEY_LOCAL_MACHINE\Hardware Key

The HKEY_LOCAL_MACHINE\Hardware key contains the hardware data in the Registry that is computed at system startup. This includes information about hardware components on the system board and about the interrupts hooked by specific hardware devices.

The Hardware key contains distinct and important sets of data in three subkeys—Description, DeviceMap, and ResourceMap. These keys are described in the following sections.

All information in HKEY_LOCAL_MACHINE\Hardware is *volatile*, which means that the settings are computed each time the system is started and then discarded when the system stops. Applications and device drivers use this subtree to read information about the system components, store data directly into the DeviceMap subkey, and store data indirectly into the ResourceMap subkey.

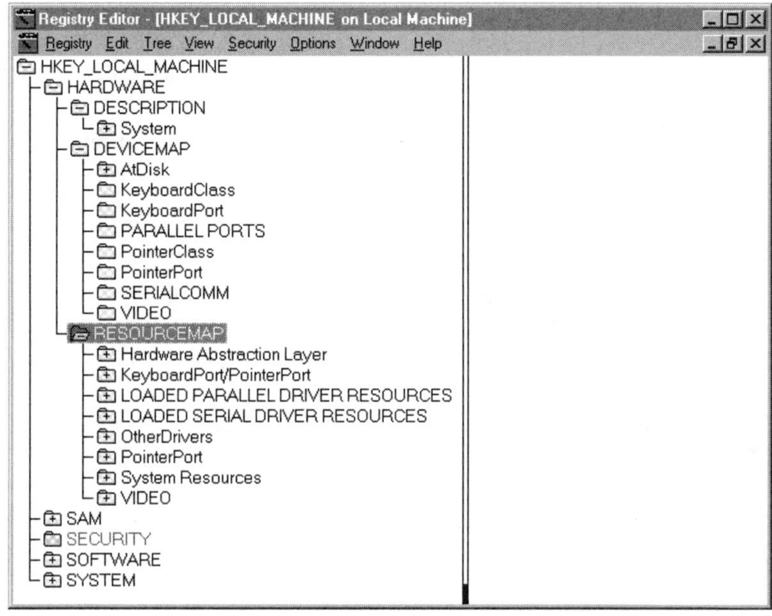

Tip Do not try to edit the data in HKEY_LOCAL_MACHINE\Hardware; much of the information appears in binary format, making it difficult to decipher.

To view data about a computer's hardware in an easy-to-read format, run Windows NT Diagnostics, click the **Services** tab, and then click the **Devices** button (in the lower right corner of the tab). Windows NT Diagnostics extracts the information from the Registry and renders it in a more readable format.

Description Subkey

The Description subkey under HKEY_LOCAL_MACHINE\Hardware displays information from the hardware database built by the firmware, the Hardware Recognizer (**Ntdetect.com**), and the Windows NT Executive, which manages the interface between the Kernel and the environment subsystems:

- On RISC-based computers, this hardware database is a copy of the ARC configuration database in the firmware.
- On a computer with an Intel processor platform, this database consists of the data found by **Ntdetect.com** and **Ntoskernel.exe**.
- On computers that are not PC-compatible, the manufacturer provides its own Hardware Recognizer.

The Hardware Recognizer for Intel-based computers detects the following items:

Bus/adapter type	Video adapter
Keyboard	Floating-point coprocessor
SCSI adapters	Mouse
Communication ports	Floppy drives
Machine ID	Parallel ports

Note Network adapter cards are not detected as part of startup; they are detected either during Windows NT Setup or when you install a new network adapter. To install a network adapter, in Control Panel, double-click **Network**, click the **Adapters** tab, then click **Add**. For details, see "Network Settings in the Registry," later in this chapter.

The key HKEY_LOCAL_MACHINE\Hardware\Description\System *MultifunctionAdapter* contains several other subkeys, each corresponding to specific bus controllers on the local computer. Each of these subkeys describes a class (or type) of controller, including controllers for disk drives, display, keyboard, parallel ports, pointing devices, serial ports, and SCSI devices. The subkey's path describes the type of component. The numbering for hardware components is zero-based, which means that, for example, the first (or only) disk controller appears under the 0 subkey.

The name of the *MultifunctionAdapter* subkey depends on the bus type. For example, for ISA and MCA buses the subkey name appears as MultifunctionAdapter. For EISA buses, the subkey name is EisaAdapter, and for TurboChannel buses, the subkey name is TcAdapter. Figure 23.8 shows a MultifunctionAdapter subkey.

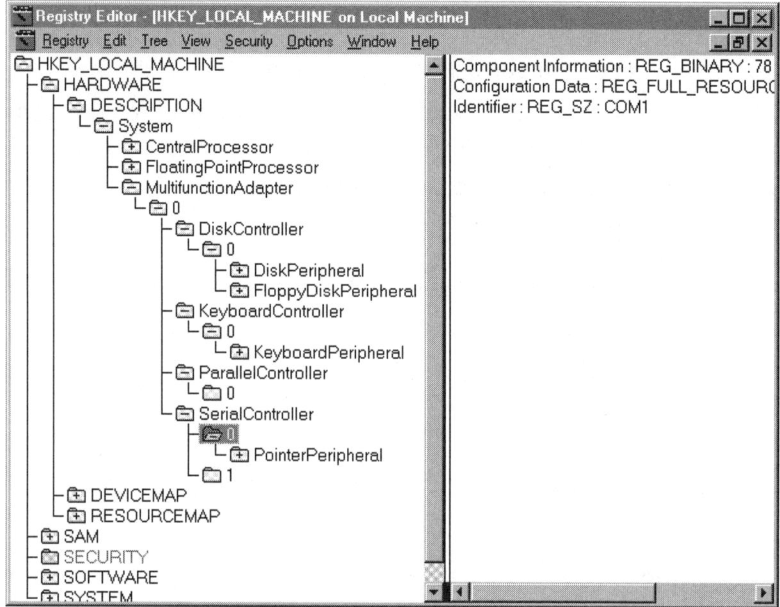

Figure 23.8 A MultifunctionAdapter subkey for an ISA or MCA bus

For each detected hardware component, the optional **Component Information** and **Configuration Data** value entries store version and configuration data in binary format. The **Identifier** entry contains the name of a component, if specified. For details on these value entries, see Regentry.hlp, a Help file on the *Windows NT Workstation Resource Kit* CD.

DeviceMap Subkey

In the HKEY_LOCAL_MACHINE\Hardware\DeviceMap*Device* key, each *Device* subkey contains one or more values to specify the location in the Registry for specific driver information for that kind of component.

Figure 23.9 shows an example of the DeviceMap subkey and the value entry for a selected device name.

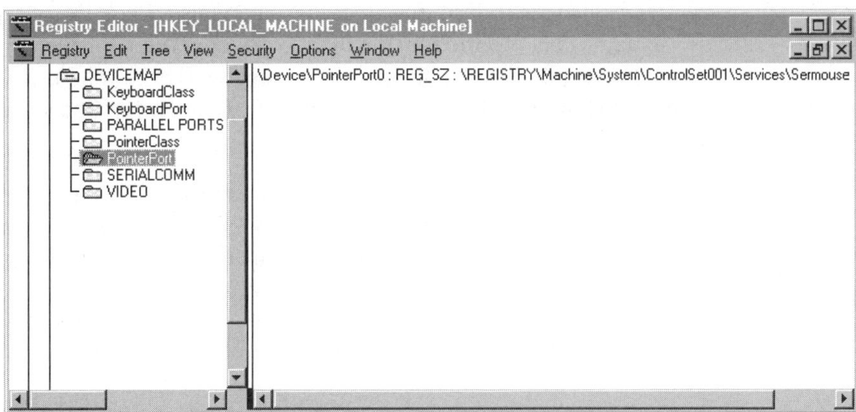

Figure 23.9 A DeviceMap subkey showing the value entry for a serial mouse device

The value for each *Device* subkey describes an actual port name or the path for a *Service* subkey in HKEY_LOCAL_MACHINE\System\ControlSet*nnn*\Services, which contains information about a device driver. That *Service* subkey contains the information a system administrator might need for troubleshooting and is also the information presented about the device by Windows NT Diagnostics.

Figure 23.10 shows DeviceMap entries for a computer that has multiple SCSI adapters.

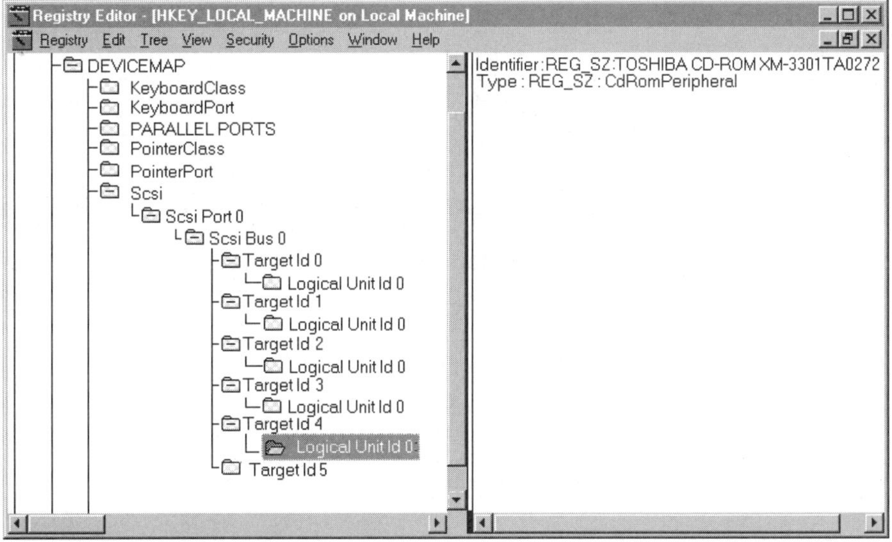

Figure 23.10 A DeviceMap subkey with value entries for multiple SCSI adapters

ResourceMap Subkey

The ResourceMap subkey under HKEY_LOCAL_MACHINE\Hardware maps device drivers to resources that the drivers use. Each ResourceMap subkey contains data reported by the device driver about its use of I/O ports, I/O memory addresses, interrupts, direct memory access (DMA) channels, and so on. The data in the ResourceMap subkey is volatile, meaning that the subkey is recreated each time you start Windows NT.

Under the ResourceMap subkey, there are *DeviceClass* subkeys for the general class (or type) of devices. Each of these subkeys contains one or more *DriverName* subkeys with information about a specific driver. For example, in Figure 23.11, Sermouse is the *DriverName* subkey under the PointerPort *DeviceClass* subkey. (The driver names in these subkeys match the services listed in HKEY_LOCAL_MACHINE\System\CurrentControlSet\Services.)

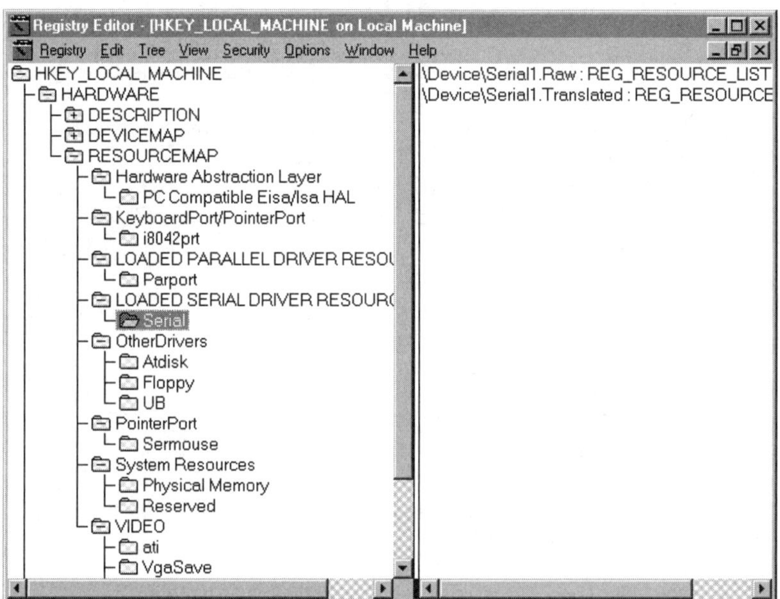

Figure 23.11 A DeviceMap subkey showing the value entry for a device

OwnerMap Subkey

The OwnerMap subkey under HKEY_LOCAL_MACHINE\Hardware appears in the Registry only when certain types of device bus, such as a PCI device bus, are installed on the computer. The OwnerMap subkey contains operating system data to associate drivers of a specified type with devices of the same type on each installed bus. This subkey is new to Windows NT 4.0. Figure 23.12 shows a typical configuration of OwnerMap.

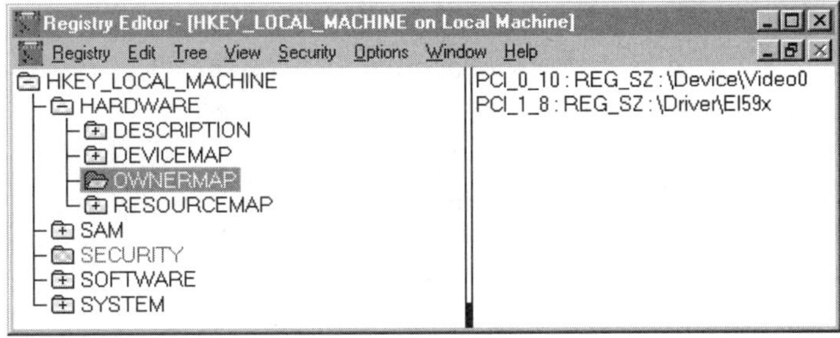

Figure 23.12 The OwnerMap subkey

HKEY_LOCAL_MACHINE\SAM Key

The HKEY_LOCAL_MACHINE\SAM key contains the user and group account information in the directory services database (formerly known as the Security Account Manager, or SAM) for the local computer. For a computer that is running Windows NT Server, this key also contains security information for the domain. This information appears in User Manager. Also, on computers with NTFS partitions, you can view and edit security information for a file in Windows NT Explorer. (From the **File** menu, click **Properties**, then click the **Security** tab. Click **Permissions** to modify user and group permissions in the directory services database.)

This key is mapped to HKEY_LOCAL_MACHINE\Security\SAM, so changes made in one Registry key also appear in the other.

Caution Do not edit the value entries in this subkey by using Registry Editor. The values are in binary format. Errors in this database may prevent users from being able to log on to the computer.

System administrators should use User Manager (Windows NT Workstation) or User Manager for Domains (Windows NT Server) to add or remove users, to change information about accounts, or to change security information for the local computer or for the domain.

HKEY_LOCAL_MACHINE\Security Key

The HKEY_LOCAL_MACHINE\Security key contains security information for the local computer, including user rights, password policy, and the membership of local groups, as set in User Manager.

The subkey HKEY_LOCAL_MACHINE\Security\SAM is mapped to HKEY_LOCAL_MACHINE\SAM, so changes made in one automatically appear in the other.

If you want to change global group membership or other security-related items, use User Manager or User Manager for Domains.

Caution The information in this database is in binary format and should not be changed by using Registry Editor. Errors in this database may prevent users from being able to log on to the computer.

HKEY_LOCAL_MACHINE\Software Key

The HKEY_LOCAL_MACHINE\Software key contains specific configuration information about software on the local computer. The entries under this key, which applies to any user of the computer, show which software is installed on the computer.

HKEY_LOCAL_MACHINE\Software\Classes contains data to associate applications with file types (by filename extension). It also includes Registry information associated with COM objects. The data under the Classes subkey is also reflected in HKEY_CLASSES_ROOT.

Figure 23.13 shows how the HKEY_LOCAL_MACHINE\Software subkey appears on one machine.

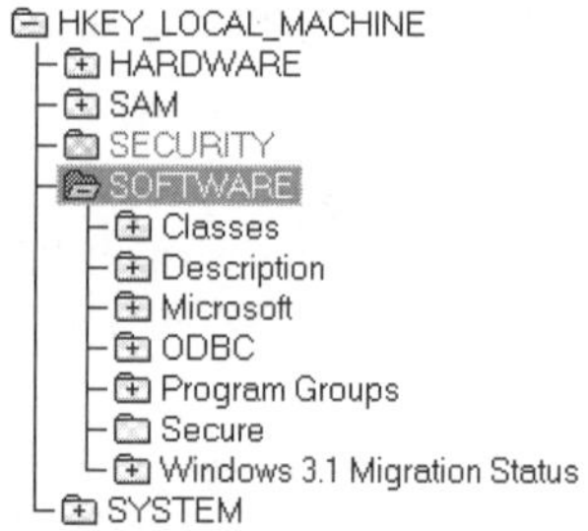

Figure 23.13 The HKEY_LOCAL_MACHINE\Software subkey

The HKEY_LOCAL_MACHINE\Software subtree contains several subkeys. The Classes, Program Groups, and Secure subkeys are described here, plus general information about the various *Description* subkeys that can appear in a Registry.

Classes Subkey

The Classes subkey contains two types of subkeys:

- *Filename-extension subkeys* associate applications with file types by their filename extension. These subkeys contain information you add by using the **File Types** tab in Windows NT Explorer, information added during installation of Windows-based applications, and information about applications installed by Windows NT.

  Figure 23.14 shows where data is stored to associate .avi files with an application.

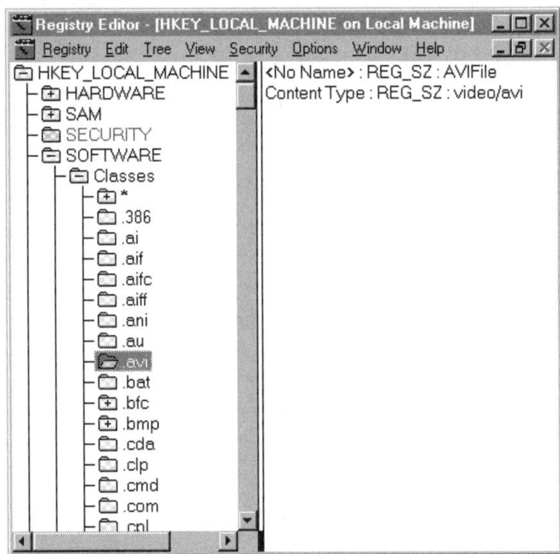

Figure 23.14 Filename-association subkeys in the Classes subkey

- *Class-definition subkeys* contain Registry information associated with Component Object Model (COM) objects. The data in these subkeys specifies the shell and OLE (COM) properties of an object. If an application supports dynamic data exchange (DDE), the Shell subkey can contain Open and Print subkeys that define DDE commands for opening and printing files, similar to the information stored in the Registry database under versions of Windows for MS-DOS.

Figure 23.15 shows the shell properties of **Regfile.exe**, the executable file for **Regedit**. In this example, the service (or friendly) name of **Regedit** is specified.

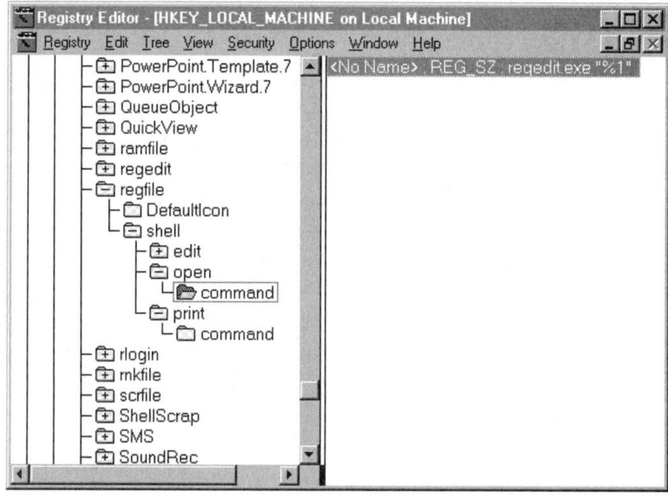

Figure 23.15 Shell properties for Regfile.exe in the Classes subkey

---

Important The COM information in the Registry must be created by the COM application. Do not change this information by using Registry Editor. To change the association between a file type and an application, click **Options** on the **View** menu in Windows NT Explorer, then use the **File Types** tab in the **Options** dialog box.

Description Subkeys

The HKEY_LOCAL_MACHINE\Software*Description* subkeys contain the names and version numbers of the software installed on the local computer. (Information about the configuration of these applications is stored on a per-user basis under HKEY_CURRENT_USER.)

During installation, applications record this information in the following form:

HKEY_LOCAL_MACHINE\Software\Description
*CompanyName**ProductName**Version*

Figure 23.16 shows some entries under the subkey for Microsoft (a *CompanyName*), which contains entries for the service software installed on the computer:

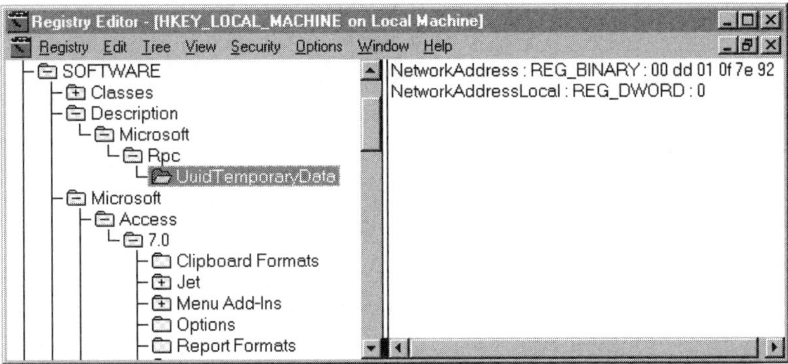

Figure 23.16 Description subkey entries

Note The information in each subkey is added by the related application. Do not edit entries in these subkeys unless directed to do so by your application vendor.

Microsoft Subkey

The HKEY_LOCAL_MACHINE\Software\Microsoft subkey contains configuration settings for Microsoft software installed on the computer.

The Windows NT\CurrentVersion subkey is of particular interest. This subkey contains information about software that supports services built into Windows NT, as well as data about the version and type of the current release (multiprocessor versus uniprocessor). For example, it is possible to run a Windows NT uniprocessor kernel on a multiprocessor computer, but you do not get any multiprocessor benefits by doing so. To find out which kernel type is running on a computer, see the data in the Registry under the Windows NT\CurrentVersion subkey.

Program Groups Subkey

The Program Groups subkey under HKEY_LOCAL_MACHINE\Software is redefined in Windows NT 4.0. In previous versions of Windows NT, it contained a list of the program groups used by all users of the local computer. In Windows NT 4.0, program groups have been replaced by the Windows NT Explorer directory structure. Now, this subkey is used only to record—as a yes/no, 0x1/0x0 value—whether all former program groups have been converted to the new directory structure.

The **ConvertedToLinks** value entry indicates whether the program groups were converted. A value of 1 (0x1) indicates that the conversion is complete.

When Windows NT 4.0 is installed on a computer that has never run Windows NT, there are no subkeys under the Program Groups subkey. However, upgraded versions can still contain binary data for common program groups that appear as Program Groups subkeys.

Secure Subkey

The Secure subkey provides a convenient place for applications to store configuration information that should be changed only by an administrator.

Windows 3.1 Migration Status Subkey

The Windows 3.1 Migration Status subkey contains data if the computer has been upgraded from Windows 3.*x* to Windows NT 4.0. The values in this subkey indicate whether .ini and Reg.dat files have migrated successfully to the Windows NT 4.0 format. If this subkey is deleted, Windows NT again attempts to migrate the files when the system is restarted.

There is also a Windows 3.1 Migration Status subkey under HKEY_CURRENT_USER. It tracks the migration of Program Group (.grp) files to the Windows NT Explorer format.

For more information about Windows 3.*x* migration, see Part 6, Chapter 27, "Windows Compatibility and Migration," in this book.

HKEY_LOCAL_MACHINE\System Key

All startup-related data that must be stored (rather than computed during startup) is saved in the System hive. A complete copy of the data is also stored in the System.alt file. The data in HKEY_LOCAL_MACHINE\System—which is the System hive—is organized into control sets that contain a complete set of parameters for devices and services as described in this section. You might occasionally need to change entries in the CurrentControlSet subkey, as described in Chapter 25, "Configuration Management and the Registry."

Figure 23.17 shows the structure of this subtree.

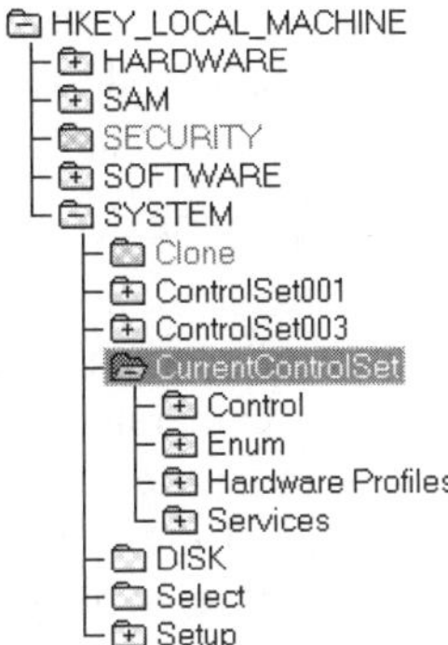

Figure 23.17 The HKEY_LOCAL_MACHINE\System key

The following sections describe the HKEY_LOCAL_MACHINE\System subkeys.

ControlSet*nnn*, Select, and CurrentControlSet Subkeys

The Registry, particularly data in the System hive, is essential to starting the system. To help ensure that the system can always be started, a kind of backup version is kept, which allows you to undo any configuration changes that did not have the intended effect. This section describes how it works.

Figure 23.18 shows the structure of subkeys under the HKEY_LOCAL_MACHINE\System key.

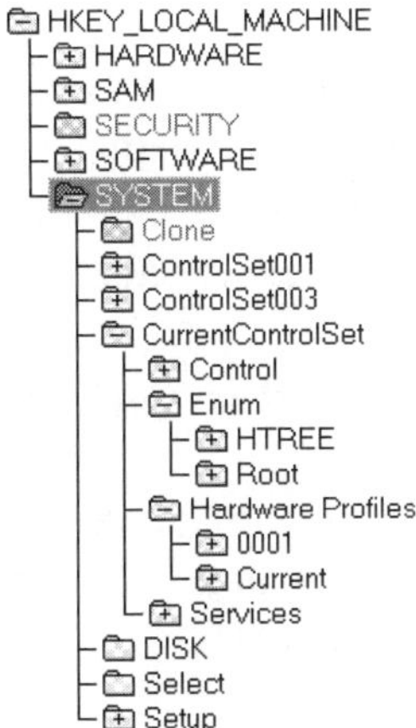

Figure 23.18 Subkeys under HKEY_LOCAL_MACHINE\System

All of the data required to control startup is gathered into subkeys called control sets in the Registry. Each control set has four subkeys:

- The *Control* subkey contains configuration data used to control the system, such as the computer's network name and the subsystems to start.
- The *Enum* subkey contains hardware configuration data for devices and drivers loaded by Windows NT.
- The *Hardware Profiles* subkey contains configuration data for drivers and devices specific to a hardware profile. Users can create multiple hardware profiles for each control set. Data appears under the Hardware Profiles subkey only when it differs from the standard settings for drivers and devices. The current hardware profile in the CurrentControlSet subkey also appears in HKEY_CURRENT_CONFIG.
- The *Services* subkey contains a list of drivers, file systems, user-mode service programs, and virtual hardware keys. Its data controls which services are loaded and their load order. The data in the Services subkey also controls how the services call each other.

Multiple control sets are saved as subkeys of HKEY_LOCAL_MACHINE \System under names such as ControlSet001 and ControlSet003. Although as many as four control sets (numbered 000–003) can appear, there are usually two sets. This is similar to having multiple sets of Config.sys files under MS-DOS—a current file and a backup copy known to start the system correctly. However, all of the work of creating and maintaining backups is done automatically by the system.

The Select subkey consists of four value entries that describe how the control sets are used:

- **Default** specifies the number of the control set (for example, 001 = ControlSet001) that the system will use at next startup, barring an error or manual invocation of the LastKnownGood control set by the user.
- **Current** specifies the number of the control set actually used to start the system this time.
- **LastKnownGood** specifies the number of the control set that is a clean copy of the last control set that actually worked.
- **Failed** specifies the control set that was replaced if the LastKnownGood control set was used to start the system this time. You can examine this control set to learn why the replacement was required.

The Clone subkey contains the last control set used to start the system. If the start was successful ("good"), the contents of the Clone become the LastKnownGood control set.

The CurrentControlSet subkey is not the root of an actual control set; rather, it is a symbolic link to the control set indicated by the value of **Current**. It is there so that constant paths can be used to refer to subkeys in the currently used control set, even though the name of that control set may change.

These multiple control sets are used to allow an escape from various problems. Each time the system starts, the control set used to start is saved (under HKEY_LOCAL_MACHINE\System\Clone). If the startup is declared to be "good," the LastKnownGood control set is discarded, and the Clone subkey is copied to replace it. An administrator can change the requirements for a startup to be classified as "good," but a startup is typically declared to be "good" if no severe or critical errors occurred while starting the services and if at least one user logged on successfully.

The LastKnownGood configuration is used when the user chooses LastKnownGood from the **Hardware Profile/Configuration Recovery** menu during startup or if startup fails (is not "good"). When this happens, a new control set is created by copying the LastKnownGood control set and the values of the entries in HKEY_LOCAL_MACHINE\System\Select are changed to point to different control sets:

- The control set identified as **Default** is identified as **Failed.**
- The control set identified as **LastKnownGood** is identified as **Default**.

User profile data is stored elsewhere and is therefore unaffected.

Tip When you start Windows NT, you can choose which control set the system uses. At the Boot Loader command prompt, select Windows NT, then press the SPACEBAR. The **Hardware Profile/Configuration Recovery** menu appears. Follow the instructions on the screen to select the control set or LastKnownGood configuration from the menu.

To find out whether Default or LastKnownGood was used, see the values in the Select subkey.

To modify the information stored in these subkeys, use the Devices, Network, Server, and Services options in Control Panel, or use Server Manager.

To modify the configuration by using Registry Editor, make changes under the CurrentControlSet subkey.

The Control and Services subkeys found in each control set are described in the following sections.

Control Subkey for All Control Sets

The Control subkey contains startup parameters for the system, including information about the subsystems to load, computer-dependent environment variables, the size and location of the paging files, and so on. Figure 23.19 shows the typical Control subkeys, and Table 23.6 describes the contents of some typical subkeys.

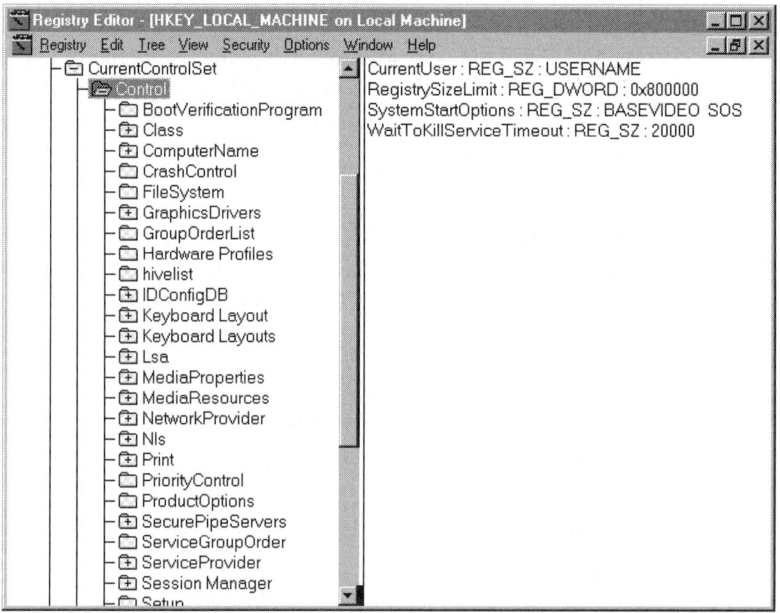

Figure 23.19 A typical configuration of the Control subkey for a control set

Table 23.6 Typical Subkeys of \CurrentControlSet\Control for All Control Sets

Subkey	Contents
BootVerificationProgram	A value that can be set to define a nonstandard mechanism to declare system startup as "good," as described in Chapter 25, "Configuration Management and the Registry."
ComputerName	The names of the default and active computers, stored in two subkeys, ComputerName and ActiveComputerName. To set the computer name, use the Network option in Control Panel.
GroupOrderList	Specifies the order in which to load services for all groups that have one, used in combination with Tags. ServiceGroupOrder specifies the order for loading groups.
ServiceGroupOrder	Specifies the order in which to load various groups of services. Order within groups is specified by using Tags and GroupOrderList.

Table 23.6 Typical Subkeys of \CurrentControlSet\Control for All Control Sets *(continued)*

Subkey	Contents
HiveList	The location of the files that contain Registry information. This value should be maintained only by the system.
Keyboard Layout	The DLLs for the keyboard language used as the default layout, plus a subkey named DosKeybCodes that lists the other available keyboard layouts. To set keyboard layout, use the **Input Locales** tab under the Keyboard option in Control Panel.
Lsa	The authentication package for the local security authority. This value should be maintained only by the system—errors can prevent anyone from being able to log on to the computer.
NetworkProvider	Can contain two subkeys, Active and Order, that specify the network provider and the order in which to load providers. Control settings for network providers by using the Network option in Control Panel.
Nls	Information on national language support in three subkeys: CodePage, Language, and OEMLocale. Set preferences about language and locale in Windows NT by using the Regional Settings option in Control Panel.
Print	Information about the current printers and printing environment, contained in several subkeys: ▪ Environments, which contains subkeys defining drivers and print processors for system environments such as Windows NT on Digital Alpha, Windows NT on MIPS R*x*4000, and Windows NT on Intel-based computers. ▪ Monitors, which can contain subkeys with data for specific network printing monitors. ▪ Printers, which can contain subkeys describing printer parameters for each installed printer. ▪ Providers, which can contain subkeys describing DLLs for network print services. To change printing parameters, click the **Start** button, point to **Settings**, then point to the **Printers** folder.
PriorityControl	The Win32 priority separation. Set this value *only* by using the System option in Control Panel.
ProductOptions	The product type, such as Windows NT. These values should be maintained only by the system.

Table 23.6 Typical Subkeys of \CurrentControlSet\Control for All Control Sets *(continued)*

Subkey	Contents
Session Manager	Global variables used by Session Manager and these subkeys: ▪ DOSDevices, which defines the MS-DOS devices AUX, MAILSLOT, NUL, PIPE, PRN, and UNC. ▪ Environment, which defines the **ComSpec**, **Path**, **Os2LibPath**, and **WinDir** variables. To set user environment variables, in Control Panel double-click **System**. To change or add to the computer's default path, or add default system environment variables, change the values in this subkey. For more details, see Regentry.hlp, a Registry Help file on the *Windows NT Workstation Resource Kit* CD. ▪ FileRenameOperations, which is used during startup to rename certain files so that they can be replaced. These values should be maintained only by the system. ▪ KnownDLLs, which defines the directories and filenames for the Session Manager DLLs. These values should be maintained only by the system. ▪ MemoryManagement, which defines paging options. Define the paging file by using the System option in Control Panel. ▪ SubSystems, which defines information for the Windows NT subsystems. These values should be maintained only by the system.
Setup	Hardware setup options. These values should be maintained only by the system. Users can make choices by running Windows NT Setup.
TimeZoneInformation	Values for time zone information. Set these values by using the Date/Time option in Control Panel.
VirtualDeviceDrivers	Virtual device drivers. These values should be maintained only by the system.
Windows	Paths for the Windows NT directory and system directory. These values should be maintained only by the system.
WOW	Options for 16-bit Windows-based applications running under Windows NT. These settings should be maintained only by the system.

Enum Subkey for All Control Sets

The Enum subkey contains configuration data for hardware devices, independent of the drivers they use.

This subkey, new with Windows NT 4.0, was one of several keys added to HKEY_LOCAL_MACHINE to enable Windows NT to access and control drivers and devices in ways similar to those used in Windows 95. (The methods are similar—but not the same, because the architecture of Windows NT differs from that of Windows 95.)

The changes reflected in these new keys prepare Windows NT to run the new generation of Plug and Play drivers and devices implemented in Windows 95. Plug and Play drivers are not included in Windows NT 4.0, but when the drivers become available, these changes will enable them to be implemented with fewer changes to the operating system.

Warning: Do not use a Registry editor to change the data in this key. Errors in this key can prevent Windows NT from detecting or operating hardware devices necessary to the operation of the computer. Windows NT protects this key from changes by all users, including administrators. Administrators can change the permissions on the key, but this is strongly discouraged. In your applications, use the standard Device Installer or Config Manager API to change data in the Enum subkeys.

By using the Device Installer or Config Manager API, you can enable applications to modify the data in Enum subkeys without including the path name of the Registry key in the application code. The Windows NT Registry has a different structure than the Registry in Windows 95. Because of this, if your application refers to this Registry key by path name, the application will not run on both Windows NT and Windows 95.

In general, the Enum subkey contains configuration data for devices. The subkeys under Enum represent a device hierarchy (or tree) that starts at a tree root (the top) and ends at the lowest branch with configuration data for a specific instance of a device, such as the keyboard on the local computer.

The Enum subkey itself is merely a container. It is not associated with any value entries. There are at least two subkeys immediately under Enum: Htree represents the hardware tree; the remaining keys represent *enumerators*, the means by which Windows NT learned about a device.

The Htree\Root\0 subkey is a reserved space in the Registry that represents the root (the top) of the hardware tree It contains the **AttachedComponents** value entry, which lists devices rooted at the top of the hardware tree.

Figure 23.20 shows the Htree\Root\0 subkey and its **AttachedComponents** value listing.

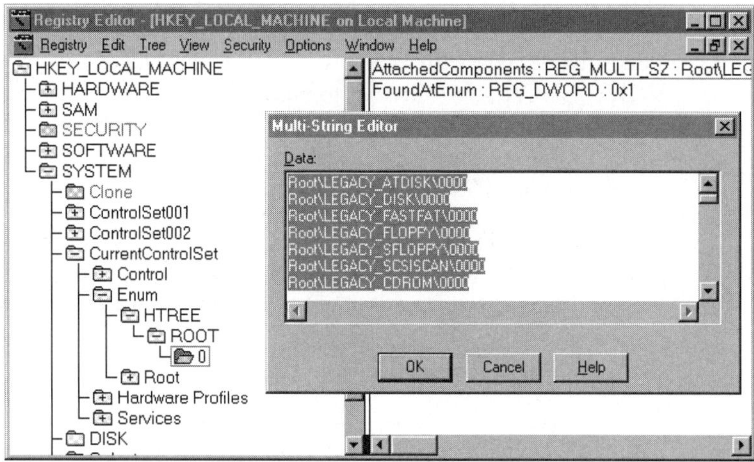

Figure 23.20 AttachedComponents value listing under Htree\Root\0

The remaining subkeys immediately under Enum represent enumerators and contain the subkeys of devices that have the same enumerator. For Plug and Play devices, the enumerator is the device bus on which the device runs, such as PCI or ISAPNP. A default enumerator, Root, is used for non–Plug and Play devices (known as *legacy* devices), which are enumerated by other parts of the system.

Figure 23.21 shows the Root enumerator of a typical computer running Windows NT.

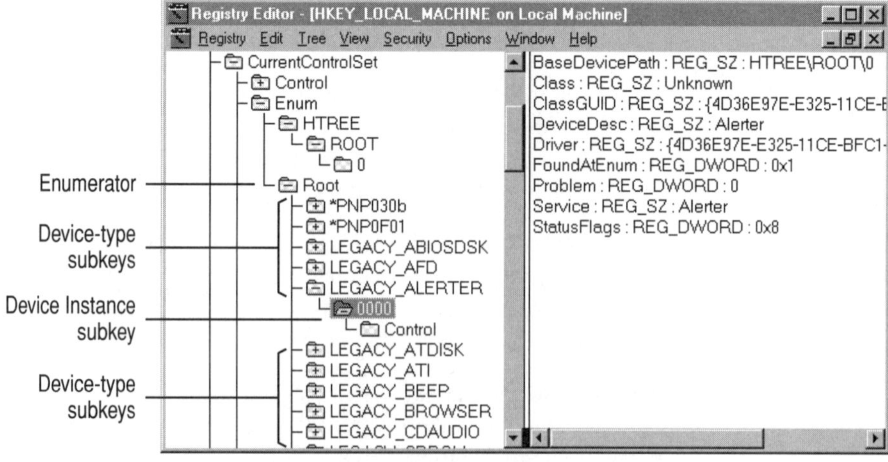

Figure 23.21 Typical contents of a Root enumerator subkey

Each enumerator subkey, such as Root, contains subkeys that represent device types or models. The device type subkeys, in turn, contain the subkeys that represent devices of that type. The device type subkeys for each enumerator vary depending on the devices installed on the computer.

The name of each device type subkey indicates whether it is a Plug and Play device or a legacy (non–Plug and Play) device.

- For Plug and Play devices and for all modems, the name of the device type subkey varies with the device. A modem is a special case because its driver, Modem.sys, includes some Plug and Play functionality. For example, on a computer with more than one modem, Windows NT can detect an individual instance of each modem even when all modems share the same driver.
- For most legacy devices, Windows NT builds a device-type ID of the form LEGACY_*DriverName*. This subkey contains data for all devices controlled by that driver.
- For legacy keyboards and mouse devices, the device type ID typically begins with *PNP followed by an alphanumeric string. The Windows NT drivers for keyboards and mouse devices have some limited Plug and Play functionality. For example, Windows NT accesses keyboards and mouse devices in some of the same ways as it accesses Plug and Play devices.

The subkeys under the device type are the device instance subkeys. These subkeys contain value entries that specify the configuration of a device. However, the device(s) to which the value entries apply depend on whether the device is a Plug and Play device or a legacy device.

- For Plug and Play devices (including modems), each device type subkey can contain multiple device instance subkeys. The name of each device instance subkey uniquely identifies a particular device to Windows NT, and the value entries in the subkey apply only to that device. Because of this, users and applications can configure each instance of a device individually.
- For legacy devices, there is only one key—0000—to represent all instances of devices on the computer that are controlled by the driver for which the subkey is named. The configuration data in this subkey applies to all of the devices; they cannot be configured separately by using Windows NT.

The value entries and subkeys under the device instance subkeys vary with the device and its driver. For more information, see Regentry.hlp, the Registry Help file on the *Windows NT Workstation Resource Kit* CD.

Services Subkey for All Control Sets

The Services subkey in each control set lists all device drivers, file system drivers, and Win32 service drivers that can be loaded by the Boot Loader, the I/O Manager, and the Service Control Manager. The Services subkey also contains subkeys that are static descriptions of hardware to which drivers can be attached. Table 23.7 describes some typical Services subkeys for a computer running Windows NT.

Entries that appear under the DeviceMap subkeys include values that refer to entries in the Services subkey in the control set. For example, for a serial mouse, the following entry might appear under the DeviceMap\PointerPort subkey in HKEY_LOCAL_MACHINE\Hardware:

```
\Device\PointerPort0 : \REGISTRY\Machine\System\ControlSet001
    \Services\Sermouse
```

A related Services subkey named Sermouse defines values for the serial mouse driver. Figure 23.22 shows a typical configuration of the Sermouse subkey.

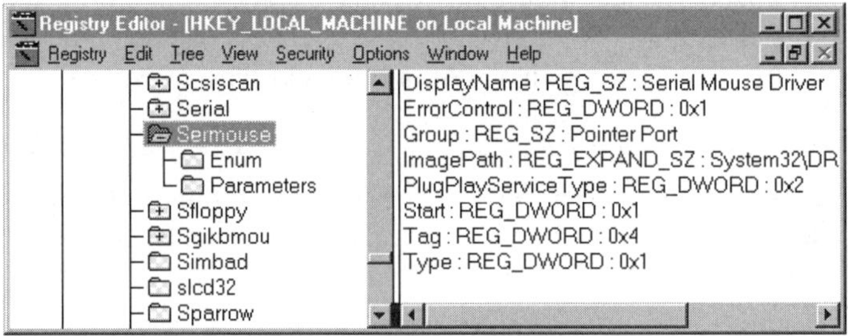

Figure 23.22 The Sermouse subkey

To view this information in a more readable format, use Windows NT Diagnostics or the Control Panel.

- To find detailed information about a driver, in Windows NT Diagnostics, click the **Services** tab, click the **Devices** button (in the lower right corner), then double-click the name of the device.
- To change startup settings and other parameters for a driver, in Control Panel double-click **Devices**.

For suggestions on using the information in Windows NT Diagnostics and the Control Panel for troubleshooting, see Chapter 25, "Configuration Management and the Registry."

Each subkey includes several standard (but optional) entries, as shown in Figure 23.23, where Alerter is the name of a Windows NT service.

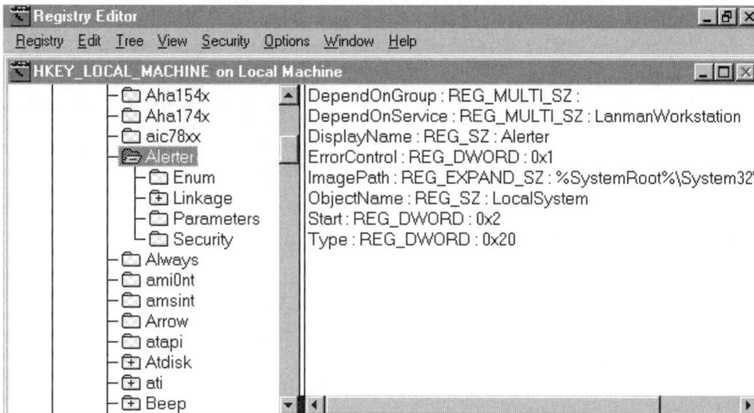

Figure 23.23 Subkey for the Alerter service under Services

The value entries that govern the behavior of a service include **ErrorControl**, **Group**, **DependOnGroup**, **DependOnService**, **ImagePath**, **ObjectName**, **Start**, **Tag**, and **Type**. For definitions of these value entries, see Regentry.hlp, the Registry Help file on the *Windows NT Workstation Resource Kit* CD.

The optional Linkage subkey specifies the binding options for the driver by using the **Bind** and **Export** values.

The **OtherDependencies** value that appears in the Linkage subkey for some services enables nodes to be loaded in an order related to other specific nodes with which they are closely associated. For example, the NBF transport depends on an NDIS driver. Therefore, to load the NBF protocol stack successfully, an NDIS network card driver must be loaded first. For details about loading order dependencies for network components, see "Dependency Handling for Network Components," later in this chapter.

The Parameters subkey (optional for some Services subkeys such as an adapter entry) contains a set of values to be passed to the driver. These values vary for each device driver. Figure 23.24 shows parameters for the serial mouse driver.

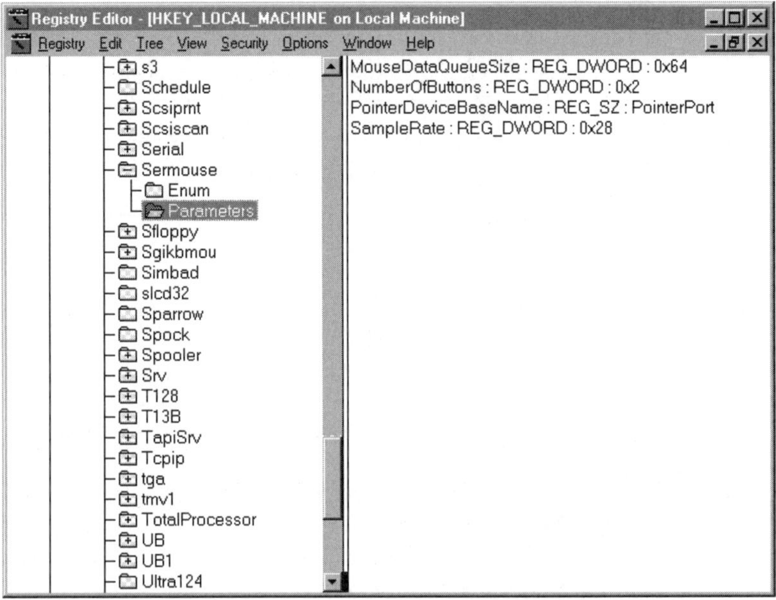

Figure 23.24 Parameters subkey for the serial mouse driver

Because the entries in the Services list are Registry keys, no assumptions can be made about their order in an enumeration, so services can explicitly specify load ordering by grouping services and drivers in order by type. For example, the SCSI port driver can be loaded before any of the miniport drivers. The ordering is specified under the \Control\ServiceGroupOrder subkey in a control set.

Settings for the drivers that appear under the Services subkeys can be changed by using the Devices, Network, or Services options in Control Panel or, for network services, User Manager for Domains in Windows NT. Specific parameters for drivers and services are described in online Help for the Registry.

Table 23.7 describes typical Services subkeys for a Windows NT–based computer.

Table 23.7 Descriptions of Typical Services Subkeys for a Windows NT–Based Computer

Service name	Description
Abiosdsk	Primary disk[1]
Aha*xxx*	Adaptec SCSI adapters[1]
Alerter	Alerter service for the workstation[3]
AtDisk	Primary disk driver for non-SCSI hard disks[1]
Ati	ATI video display[1]
Beep	Base sound driver[1]
Browser	Computer browser used by Workstation and Server services[3]
BusLogic	BusLogic SCSI adapter[1]
Busmouse	Bus mouse pointer[1]
Cdaudio	Filter[1]
Cdfs	SCSI CD-ROM file system driver[1]
Cirrus	Cirrus Logic video display[1]
ClipSrv	ClipBook (Network DDE service)[3]
Cpqarray	Compaq array driver (no additional Registry values)
Dell_DGX	Dell DGX video display[1]
Diskperf	Disk Performance Monitoring Statistics Driver[1]
DptScsi	DPT SCSI adapter[1]
Et4000	Tseng ET4000 video display[1]
EventLog	Event log service[3]
Fastfat	FAT file system driver[1]

1 Change settings for this driver by using the Devices option in Control Panel.

2 Change settings for this driver by using the Network option in Control Panel.

3 Change settings for this driver by using the Services option in Control Panel or by using Server Manager in Windows NT Services.

Table 23.7 Descriptions of Typical Services Subkeys for a Windows NT–Based Computer *(continued)*

Service name	Description
Fd16_700	Future Domain MCS 600/700, TMC-7000ex, 800-series SCSI adapters[1]
Floppy	Primary disk[1]
Ftdisk	Filter[1]
i8042pt	Keyboard driver[1]
Inport	Microsoft InPort Mouse pointer[1]
Jazzg*xxx*	Video display[1]
Jzvxl484	Video display[1]
Kbdclss	Keyboard class driver[1]
LanmanServer	Server service[3]
Lanman Workstation	Workstation service[3]
Messenger	Messenger service for workstation[3]
Mouclass	Mouse class driver[1]
Mup	Network[1]
Nbf	NetBEUI transport protocol[1, 2]
Ncr*xxx*	NCR SCSI controllers and adapters[1]
NetBIOS	NetBIOS transport interface[1, 2]
NetDDE et al.	Network DDE and Network DDE DSDM[3]
NetDetect	Network detection[1]
NetLogon	Network logon for workstation[3]
Ntfs	NTFS file system driver[1]
Null	Base driver for null port[1]
Oliscsi	Olivetti SCSI adapter[1]
Parallel	Parallel port[1]
Qv	Qvision video display driver[1]
RAS	Remote Access Service[3]
Rdr	Network redirector[1]

1 Change settings for this driver by using the Devices option in Control Panel.

2 Change settings for this driver by using the Network option in Control Panel.

3 Change settings for this driver by using the Services option in Control Panel or by using Server Manager in Windows NT Services.

Table 23.7 Descriptions of Typical Services Subkeys for a Windows NT–Based Computer*(continued)*

Service name	Description
Replicator	Directory replicator for workstation and server[3]
RPCLocator	Remote Procedure Call (RPC) locator (name service provider)[3]
RPCSS	Remote Procedure Call (RPC) service[3]
S3	S3 video display[1]
Schedule	Network schedule service[3]
Scsi*xxxx*	SCSI class devices, which do not add parameters to the Registry, including Scsicdrm, Scsidisk, Scsiflip, Scsiprnt, and Scsiscan
Serial	Serial port[1]
Sermouse	Serial mouse[1]
Sgikbmou	Silicon Graphics keyboard and mouse driver[1]
Sgirex	Silicon Graphics video display driver[1]
Simbad	Filter[1]
Sparrow	SCSI adapter[1]
Spock	SCSI adapter[1]
Srv	Network server[3]
T128, T13B	Trantor SCSI adapters[1]
Trident	Trident video display[1]
UB*xxx*	Ungermann-Bass NDIS drivers[1, 3]
Ultra*xxx*	UltraStore SCSI adapters[1]
UPS	Uninterruptible power supply (UPS)[3, 4]
V7vram	Video Seven VRAM video display[1]
Vga	VGA video display[1]
Videoprt	Video display[1]
Wd33c93	Maynard SCSI adapter[1]
Wdvga	Western Digital/Paradise video display[1]
Xga	IBM XGA video display[1]

1 Change settings for this driver by using the Devices option in Control Panel.

2 Change settings for this driver by using the Network option in Control Panel.

3 Change settings for this driver by using the Services option in Control Panel or by using Server Manager in Windows NT Services.

4 Change settings for this driver by using the UPS option in Control Panel.

Hardware Profiles Subkey for All Control Sets

The Hardware Profiles subkey in each control set contains the configuration data for all hardware profiles in a Windows NT–based system. This subkey is new to Windows NT 4.0.

A *hardware profile* is a set of changes to the standard configuration of devices and services (including drivers and Win32 services) loaded by Windows NT when the system starts. For example, a hardware profile can include an instruction to disable (that is, not load) a driver, or an instruction to Windows NT to not connect an undocked laptop computer to the network. Because of the instructions in this subkey, users can modify the service configuration for a particular use while preserving the standard configuration unchanged for more general uses.

Windows NT creates a default hardware profile (called Original Configuration). But users can create multiple hardware profiles and, when Windows NT starts, select from them the settings they want .

To create hardware profiles, use the System, Services, and Devices options in Control Panel. For more information on creating hardware profiles, double-click **System** in Control Panel, click the **Hardward Profiles** tab and open Help.

Figure 23.25 shows the Hardware Profiles subkey under CurrentControlSet.

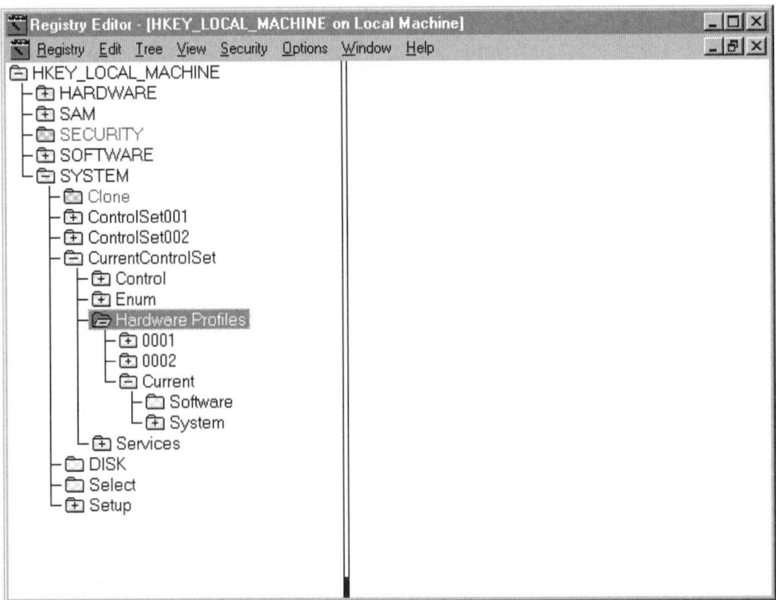

Figure 23.25 The Hardware Profiles subkey for CurrentControlSet

Each numbered subkey under Hardware Profiles contains the configuration data for one hardware profile on the system. If there is more than one hardware profile, the system identifies a subkey as current when the user chooses it during startup. The Current subkey is a symbolic link to one of the numbered subkeys.

The HKEY_CURRENT_CONFIG subtree is an alias pointing to the Hardware Profiles\Current subkey of CurrentControlSet; the contents of the Current subkey appear in the HKEY_CURRENT_CONFIG subtree.

Tip To determine which numbered subkey under Hardware Profiles represents the current hardware profile, see HKEY_LOCAL_MACHINE\System\CurrentControlSet \Control\IDConfigDB subkey. The value of **CurrentConfig** in the IDConfigDB subkey corresponds to the number of the subkey that contains the current hardware profile.

The data in each hardware profile subkey consists of profile-specific modifications to the standard service configuration. Only data that has been changed from the standard configuration is stored there, but organized in the same structure as the standard configuration. The standard configuration is defined by data stored throughout the Software and System subkeys of HKEY_LOCAL_MACHINE. Hence, the structure of a hardware profile is modeled on the structure of HKEY_LOCAL_MACHINE and can be thought of as a limited or condensed version of HKEY_LOCAL_MACHINE .

Figure 23.26 demonstrates the similar structures of HKEY_LOCAL_MACHINE and the subkeys under Hardware Profiles\0001.

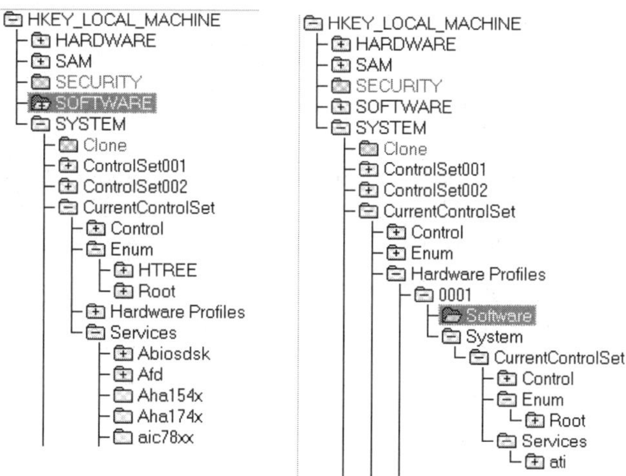

Figure 23.26 HKEY_LOCAL_MACHINE and Hardware Profiles\0001 subkeys

When a hardware profile specifies a change to a value entry in the Software or System subkeys of HKEY_LOCAL_MACHINE, the original value in the Software or System subkey is not changed; instead that change is stored in the analogous subkey of Hardware Profiles*Number*.

For example, if a user creates a hardware profile in which the Diskperf driver (which collects performance statistics for disks) is not loaded, the HKEY_LOCAL_MACHINE\System\CurrentControlSet\Enum\Root \LEGACY_DISPERF subkey is not changed. Instead, the change is stored in HKEY_LOCAL_MACHINE \System\CurrentControlSet\Hardware Profiles*Number*\System\CurrentControlSet\Enum\Root \LEGACY_DISPERF.

The subkeys of a hardware profile store the same kind of information as their counterparts in the Software and System subkeys of HKEY_LOCAL_MACHINE, but the hardware profile subkeys store *changes only*. This means that the driver, service, and device settings loaded when a hardware profile is chosen consist of those specified in the Software and System subkeys of HKEY_LOCAL_MACHINE, as modified by the data in the Software and System subkeys of the hardware profile.

For information about the subkeys of a hardware profile, see the descriptions of their analogs in the Software and System subkeys of HKEY_LOCAL_MACHINE. For information about the value entries in these subkeys, see Regentry.hlp, the Registry Help file on the *Windows NT Workstation Resource Kit* CD.

Setup Subkey

The Setup subkey under HKEY_LOCAL_MACHINE\System is used internally by Windows NT for the Setup program. Do not change these value entries. These settings should be maintained only by the system.

HKEY_CLASSES_ROOT

HKEY_CLASSES_ROOT contains information about file associations and data associated with COM objects. As shown in Figure 23.27, this is the same data as in the Classes subkey under HKEY_LOCAL_MACHINE\Software.

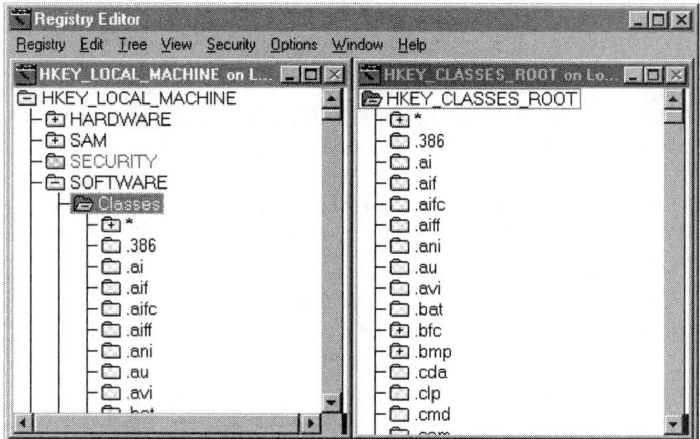

Figure 23.27 HKEY_CLASSES_ROOT and the HKEY_LOCAL_MACHINE \Software\Classes subkey

The sole purpose for HKEY_CLASSES_ROOT is to provide compatibility with the Windows 3.1 registration database.

HKEY_CLASSES_ROOT contains the data that associates file types (by filename extension) with the applications that support them. Do not change file associations by using Registry Editor. Instead, to change a file association, in Windows NT Explorer, from the **Options** menu, click **View**, then click the **File Types** tab.

For more information about HKEY_CLASSES_ROOT, see the *OLE Programmer's Reference* in the Windows NT 4.0 Software Developer's Kit.

HKEY_CURRENT_CONFIG

The HKEY_CURRENT_CONFIG subtree, new to Windows NT 4.0, contains configuration data for the hardware profile currently in use on the computer. This subtree is actually an alias pointing to HKEY_LOCAL_MACHINE\System \CurrentControlSet\Hardware Profiles\Current. The contents of the Hardware Profiles\Current subkey appear in this subtree.

HKEY_CURRENT_CONFIG was added to the Windows NT 4.0 Registry to be compatible with the HKEY_CURRENT_CONFIG subtree in the Windows 95 Registry. Because it was added to Windows NT, applications that use the HKEY_CURRENT_CONFIG subtree can run on both Windows 95 and Windows NT.

Warning: The Windows NT Registry has a different structure than the Windows 95 Registry. Hardware data is stored in different locations in the two registries. In your applications, use the standard Device Installer API or Config Manager API to change data in the Class and Enum subkeys of HKEY_CURRENT_CONFIG. If your application refers to these Registry keys by path, it will not run on both Windows NT and Windows 95.

Figure 23.28 displays the structure of HKEY_CURRENT_CONFIG and demonstrates that HKEY_CURRENT_CONFIG is just another way to view the contents of HKEY_LOCAL_MACHINE\System\CurrentControlSet \Hardware Profiles\Current.

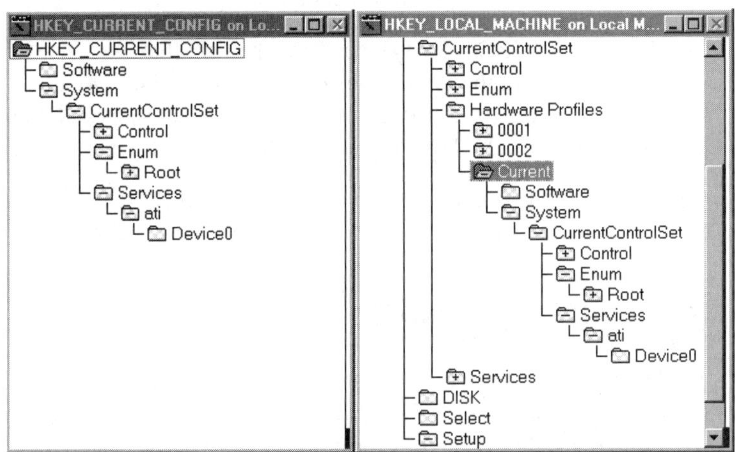

Figure 23.28 HKEY_CURRENT_CONFIG and the Hardware Profiles\Current subkey of HKEY_LOCAL_MACHINE

HKEY_CURRENT_CONFIG contains data that describes the current hardware profile.

A hardware profile is a set of changes to the standard configuration of devices and services (including drivers and Win32 services) loaded by Windows NT when the system starts. For example, a hardware profile can include an instruction to disable (that is, not load) a driver, or an instruction to Windows NT to not connect an undocked laptop computer to the network. Because of the instructions in this subkey, users can modify the service configuration for a particular use while preserving the standard configuration unchanged for more general uses.

The *current* hardware profile is the one used to start Windows NT. Users can create multiple hardware profiles and, when Windows NT starts, select from them the settings they want. To create hardware profiles, use the System, Services, and Device options in Control Panel. For more information on creating hardware profiles, double-click **System** in Control Panel, click the **Hardware Profiles** tab and open Help.

In the Registry, hardware profiles are stored in the Hardware Profiles subkey in all control sets under HKEY_LOCAL_MACHINE\System. The current hardware profile appears in the Current subkey under each Hardware Profiles subkey, and the subkey under CurrentControlSet appears in HKEY_CURRENT_CONFIG.

The data in HKEY_CURRENT_CONFIG consists of profile-specific modifications to the standard service configuration. This standard configuration is defined by data stored throughout the Software and System subkeys of HKEY_LOCAL_MACHINE. Hence, the structure of HKEY_CURRENT_CONFIG is modeled on the structure of HKEY_LOCAL_MACHINE and can be thought of as a limited or condensed version of HKEY_LOCAL_MACHINE.

When the current hardware profile specifies a change to a value entry in the Software or System subkeys of HKEY_LOCAL_MACHINE, the original value in the Software or System subkey is not changed; instead that change is stored in the analogous subkey of HKEY_CURRENT_CONFIG.

Note If you change a hardware profile by using a Registry editor, most drivers will be unable to read those changes. Use Control Panel to create and configure hardware profiles.

For example, if a user creates a hardware profile in which the Diskperf driver (which collects performance statistics for disks) is not loaded, the HKEY_LOCAL_MACHINE\System\CurrentControlSet\Enum\Root \LEGACY_DISPERF subkey is not changed. Instead, the change is stored in HKEY_LOCAL_MACHINE\System\CurrentControlSet\Hardware Profiles *Number*\System\CurrentControlSet\Enum\Root\LEGACY_DISPERF.

Figure 23.29 shows the subkeys in this example.

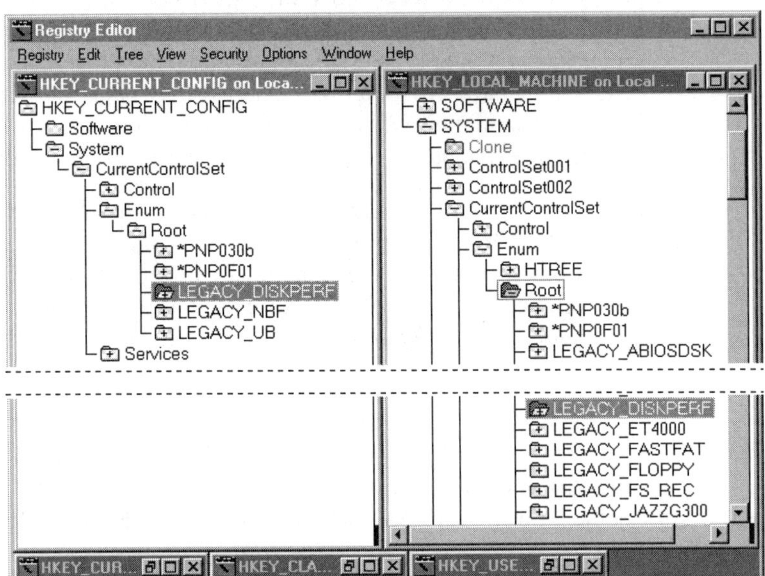

Figure 23.29 The Diskperf driver subkeys in HKEY_CURRENT_CONFIG and HKEY_LOCAL_MACHINE

For more information on the contents of HKEY_CURRENT_CONFIG, see "Hardware Profiles Subkey for All Control Sets" in "HKEY_LOCAL_MACHINE," earlier in this chapter.

HKEY_CURRENT_USER

HKEY_CURRENT_USER contains the database that describes the user profile for the user who is currently logged on to the local computer. A user profile contains information that defines the appearance and behavior of the individual user's desktop, network connections, and other environment settings. A user profile ensures that Windows NT looks and acts the same at any computer where that user logs on, if that person's profile is available at that computer or on the same domain in Windows NT Server.

HKEY_CURRENT_USER contains all the information necessary to set up a particular user environment on the computer. This includes information about settings such as application preferences, screen colors, and other personal preferences and security rights. Many of these settings are similar to the information that was stored in the Win.ini file under Windows for MS-DOS.

HKEY_CURRENT_USER includes the default subkeys described in Table 23.8. For details about the contents of subkeys in HKEY_CURRENT_USER, see Regentry.hlp, the Registry Help file on the *Windows NT Workstation Resource Kit* CD.

Table 23.8 Default Subkeys in HKEY_CURRENT_USER

Subkey	Contents
AppEvents	Subkeys that define application events, including the *sound scheme*, the set of relationships between user actions and the sound produced by the computer.
Console	Subkeys that define the options and window size for a console (the interface between the user-mode and character-mode applications). This includes settings for the Windows NT command prompt. These settings should be changed by using the commands in the **Control** menu of each non–Windows-based application. (The subkey for the command prompt does not appear unless the font or screen colors have been changed by the current user.)
Control Panel	Subkeys that correspond to parameters that can be changed by using the options in Control Panel. This includes information that was stored in the Win.ini and Control.ini files under Windows for MS-DOS.
Environment	Value entries that correspond to the current user's settings for environment variables. This includes information that was stored in the Autoexec.bat file under MS-DOS. Values should be set by using the System option in Control Panel.
Keyboard Layout	Subkeys that specify the language used for the current keyboard layout. To change the language associated with the keyboard, use the **Input Locales** tab under the Keyboard option in Control Panel.
Network	This key is no longer used. (In previous versions of Windows NT, it stored persistent connections. Persistent connections are now stored in HKEY_CURRENT_USER\Software\Microsoft\Windows NT \CurrentVersion\Network\Persistent Connections.)
Printers	Subkeys that describe the printers installed for the current user. To change printer values, click the **Start** button, point to **Settings**, then point to the **Printers** folder.
Software	Subkeys that describe the current user's configurable settings for installed software that the user can use. This information has the same structure as HKEY_LOCAL_MACHINE\Software. This information contains application-specific information that was stored in the Win.ini file or private initialization files under Windows for MS-DOS.

Table 23.8 Default Subkeys in HKEY_CURRENT_USER *(continued)*

Subkey	Contents
UNICODE Program Groups	This subkey is not used in Windows NT 4.0. If the computer was upgraded to Windows NT 4.0 from a previous version of Windows NT, this subkey might contain old subkeys in binary form. However, neither this subkey nor any subkeys it contains holds valid data used by Windows NT 4.0.
Windows 3.1 Migrations Status	This subkey contains data only if the computer has been upgraded from Windows 3.*x* to Windows NT 4.0. It contains the subkeys that indicate whether Program Group (.grp) and .ini files have been successfully converted to the Windows NT 4.0 format. If you delete this key, Windows NT tries to convert the files again when the system restarts. There is also a Windows 3.1 Migration Status subkey under HKEY_LOCAL_MACHINE\Software that tracks the conversion of .ini and Reg.dat files to the Windows NT format.

Whenever similar data exists in the HKEY_LOCAL_MACHINE subtree and the HKEY_CURRENT_USER subtree, the data in HKEY_CURRENT_USER takes precedence, as described earlier in "HKEY_LOCAL_MACHINE." The most significant example is environment variables, where variables defined for the user who is currently logged on take precedence over system variables. Use the System option in Control Panel to define system variables.

HKEY_CURRENT_USER is mapped to HKEY_USER*SID_#*, where *SID_#* is the Security ID string of the current user. The Windows NT logon process builds a user's personal profile environment based upon what it finds in HKEY_USER*SID_#*. If no such data is available, HKEY_CURRENT_USER is built from the data in *Systemroot*\Profiles\Default User\Ntuser.dat.

Note To find the name of the file that goes with a hive, see the HiveList subkey in HKEY_LOCAL_MACHINE\System\CurrentControlSet\Control. To find which hive file goes with a user profile (whether or not the user is logged on), see the ProfileList subkey under HKEY_LOCAL_MACHINE\Software\Microsoft\Windows NT \CurrentVersion. To locate a specific subkey quickly, you can use the **Find Key** command from the **View** menu in Registry Editor.

HKEY_USERS

HKEY_USERS contains all actively loaded user profiles. HKEY_USERS has at least two keys: .DEFAULT and the Security ID string for the user who is currently logged on. The information in the .DEFAULT subkey is used when no users are logged on to the computer (the CTRL+ALT+DELETE login prompt is displayed).

The .DEFAULT key contains the same subkeys as in HKEY_CURRENT_USER. These are described in Table 23.9. For details about the contents of subkeys in HKEY_USERS, see Regentry.hlp, the Registry Help file on the *Windows NT Workstation Resource Kit* CD.

To delete profiles from a computer, click **Delete User Profiles** on the **Options** menu in Windows NT Setup.

Network Settings in the Registry

When a network component is installed, information is added to the Registry. Each network component is represented in two distinct areas of the Registry:

- Software registration subkeys for the component's driver and adapter card under HKEY_LOCAL_MACHINE\Software
- Service registration keys for the component's driver and adapter under HKEY_LOCAL_MACHINE\System

The following sections describe the general organization and content of the software and service registration information for network components and then conclude with information about bindings for network components and dependency handling.

Note The information in this section is provided so that you can find entries in the Registry easily. Do not change settings for network adapters and supporting software by directly editing values in the Registry. Instead, use the **Adapters** tab under the Network option in Control Panel.

Network Component Types in the Registry

Table 23.9 describes the network component types.

Table 23.9 Network Component Types

Component type	Meaning
Adapter	A piece of hardware
Driver	A software component associated directly with a piece of hardware
Transport	A software component used by services
Service	A software component providing capability directly to user applications
Basic	A token used to represent a fundamental class name (that is, a class with no parent)

Each type of network component requires subkeys for both software and services. Therefore, the installation of a single network card usually results in the creation of four distinct subkeys in the Registry:

- The software registration subkey for the driver, found in HKEY_LOCAL_MACHINE\Software*Company**ProductName**Version.*

  For example, the path for the driver for an Etherlink adapter is HKEY_LOCAL_MACHINE\Software\Microsoft\Elinkii\CurrentVersion.
- The software registration subkey for the network adapter card, found in HKEY_LOCAL_MACHINE\Software\Microsoft\Windows NT \CurrentVersion\NetworkCards*Netcard#.*
- The service registration subkey for the driver, found in HKEY_LOCAL_MACHINE\System\CurrentControlSet\Services.
- The service registration subkey for the network adapter card, found in HKEY_LOCAL_MACHINE\System\CurrentControlSet\Services.

Software Registration Information for Network Components

Because installation of a network adapter card results in separate Registry entries for the driver and for the adapter, the Software key contains several subkeys to describe the network component. For each network component, a special subkey named NetRules is created in the appropriate driver or adapter registration subkeys. The NetRules subkey identifies the network component as part of the network ensemble.

For example, the standard software registration entry for the Etherlink II driver appears under the path HKEY_LOCAL_MACHINE\Software\Microsoft \Elinkii\CurrentVersion.

The standard entries for the driver might include the following values:

```
Description = 3Com Etherlink II Adapter Driver
InstallDate = 0x2a4e01c5
...
RefCount = 0x1
ServiceName = Elnkii
SoftwareType = driver
Title = 3Com Etherlink II Adapter Driver
```

And under the Etherlink II driver's related NetRules subkey, these value entries might appear:

```
bindable = elnkiiDriver elnkiiAdapter non exclusive
bindform = "ElnkIISys" yes no container
class = REG_MULTI_SZ "elnkiiDriver basic"
Infname = OEMNADE2.INF
InfOption = ELNKII
type = elnkiiSys ndisDriver elnkiiDriver
use = driver
```

The Etherlink adapter is described in a NetworkCards subkey under the path HKEY_LOCAL_MACHINE\Software\Microsoft\Windows NT\CurrentVersion \NetworkCards*Netcard#*.

The standard entries for the adapter might include these values:

```
Description = 3Com Etherlink II Adapter
InstallDate = 0x2a4e01c5
Manufacturer = Microsoft
ProductName = Elnkii
ServiceName = Elnkii02
Title = [01] 3Com Etherlink II Adapter
```

And these value entries might appear under the adapter's related NetRules subkey:

```
bindform = "Elnkii02" yes yes container
class = "elnkiiAdapter basic"
Infname = OEMNADE2.INF
InfOption = ELNKII
type = elnkii elnkiiAdapter
```

The value entries for the NetRules subkeys are defined in the online Help for the Registry. The information in the main entries for network adapters and drivers is maintained by the system and should not be changed by users.

Service Registration Information for Network Components

The HKEY_LOCAL_MACHINE\System\CurrentControlSet\Services subkey is the service registration area that contains the information used to load a network component into memory. These subkeys contain required information, such as the location of the executable file, the service type, and its start criterion.

Each network component's software registration information (as described in the previous section) contains an entry named **ServiceName**, whose value is the name of the service corresponding to the network component. This name acts as a symbolic link to the CurrentControlSet\Services parameters.

Some network components are actually sets of services, each of which has its own subkey in the Services subkey. There is usually a "main" service, with the other services listed as its dependencies.

For example, as shown in the previous section, the Etherlink driver's **ServiceName** value is Elnkii, and this name would appear as a Services subkey that defines the location of the driver file, dependencies, and other startup information. The Elnkii subkey in turn contains other subkeys that define the parameters and linkage rules for the driver.

The Etherlink adapter's **ServiceName** value is Elnkii02, which also appears as a Services subkey that defines linkage rules for bindings plus physical parameters of the network card, such as its I/O address and interrupt request (IRQ) number, as specified on the **Adapters** tab under the Network option in Control Panel.

The value entries for the subkeys describing adapters and drivers are defined in "Registry Entries for Network Adapter Cards" in the online Help for the Registry.

Bindings for Network Components

For the networking software in a computer to operate properly, several different pieces of software must be loaded, and their relationships with other components must be established. These relationships are often called *bindings*. To determine the complete set of optimal bindings among an ensemble of configured network components, the system checks the following information in the Registry:

- The set of network components to be configured
- The types of network components in this set
- The constraining parameters for the network components and their bindings
- The possible bindings that could occur
- The proper way to inform each network component about its bindings

During system startup, the CurrentControlSet\Services subkey is checked for binding information for each service. If any is found, a Linkage subkey is created, and values are stored. For example, these two strings might appear in a value entry under the CurrentControlSet\Services\LanmanWorkstation\Linkage subkey:

```
Bind = \Device\Nbf_Elnkii01  \Device\Nbf_Elnkii02
```

This entry describes the binding information used by the Windows NT Redirector when two separate network cards are present. Each network card's symbolic name is suffixed with a network card index number. This name is joined to the name of the transport through which the network card is accessed. The names are generated by the system according to the constraints defined by the network component's rules.

Bindings have a *usability* requirement that means the binding must terminate either at an adapter (that is, a physical device) or at a *logical endpoint*, which is simply a software component that manages all further interconnection information internally. This requirement avoids loading software components that can never be of actual use. For example, a user might have a running network and then choose to remove the adapter card. Without the usability restriction, the bindings still connect components and prepare them for loading even though the network is entirely unusable.

The following example uses Nbf.sys and Srv.sys in an ensemble with two Etherlink II network cards and an IBM Token Ring card. First, in the values in the CurrentControlSet\Services\Nbf\Linkage subkey are the following:

```
Bind=   "\Device\ElnkII1"
        "\Device\ElnkII2"
        "\Device\IbmTok1"
Export= "\Device\Nbf\ElnkII1"
        "\Device\Nbf\ElnkII2"
        "\Device\Nbf\IbmTok1"
Route=  "ElnkIISys ElnkII1"
        "ElnkIISys ElnkII2"
        "IbmtokSys IbmTok1"
```

Under the CurrentControlSet\Services\Srv\Linkage subkey, the following might appear:

```
Bind=    "\Device\Nbf\ElnkII1"
         "\Device\Nbf\ElnkII2"
         "\Device\Nbf\IbmTok1"
Export=   "\Device\Srv\Nbf\ElnkII1"
         "\Device\Srv\Nbf\ElnkII2"
         "\Device\Srv\Nbf\IbmTok1"
Route=   "Nbf ElnkIISys ElnkII1"
         "Nbf ElnkIISys ElnkII2"
         "Nbf IbmtokSys IbmTok1"
```

The names in the **Bind** and **Export** entries are based upon the object names defined in the component's NetRules subkey; these value entries can therefore be different from the actual names of the services, although in the previous example, for the sake of clarity, they are not. The names in the **Route** entry are the names of the Services subkeys comprising the full downward route through the bindings protocol.

When the system finishes computing the bindings for network components and the results are stored in the Registry, some network components might need to be informed of changes that occurred. For example, TCP/IP must prompt the user for an IP address for any network adapter that has been newly configured. If the NetRules subkey for a network component has a value entry named **Review** set to a nonzero value, the .inf file for the network component will be checked every time the bindings are changed.

Dependency Handling for Network Components

Services can be dependent upon other services or drivers, which can be dependent upon others, and so on. The system can establish these types of dependencies:

- Specific dependencies, which are represented by the names of the services upon which a service is dependent
- Group dependencies
- Static dependencies, which are required in all circumstances

Specific Dependencies

A specific dependency is simply the name of a necessary service. By default, the system generates explicit names for all dependent services discovered during bindings generation. Specific dependencies are marked in the Registry as a value of the **Use** entry under the component's NetRules subkey.

For example, assume the Workstation service is dependent upon NBF. NBF is connected to two adapter cards and so is dependent upon their drivers. The system marks NBF as dependent upon the two network card drivers and marks the Workstation service as dependent upon the network card drivers and NBF.

Group Dependencies

It often happens that a service should be loaded if any member of a set of dependencies successfully loads. In the previous example, the Workstation service fails to load if either of the network card drivers fails to initialize.

Groups are used to support this approach. Any service (driver, transport, or others) can identify itself as being a member of a service group. All Windows NT network card drivers, for example, are treated as members of the group NDIS.

Group dependencies are marked in the Registry as a value of the **Use** entry under the component's NetRules subkey. Groups are symbolic names listed in the CurrentControlSet\Control\GroupOrderList subkey.

Static Dependencies

A *static dependency* is a required service in all circumstances and is unrelated to how the system otherwise determines bindings.

When the system computes dependencies, it discards any previously listed dependencies. To guarantee that a service is always configured to be dependent upon another service, you can create the value entry **OtherDependencies** under the component's Linkage subkey. The **OtherDependencies** value is of type REG_MULTI_SZ, so it can contain the names of as many services as needed.

CHAPTER 24

Registry Editors and Registry Administration

Windows NT 4.0 includes two tools for viewing and editing the Registry, both called Registry Editor. The traditional tool, **Regedt32.exe**, is featured in this chapter. The new tool, **Regedit.exe**, written for Windows 95, has many of the same functions as **Regedt32** and uses the Windows NT Explorer interface. Both tools are installed automatically when you install Windows NT on any computer.

You can use either Registry editor to add, delete, or modify Registry entries. This chapter describes the Registry editors and how to use them, with an emphasis on protecting the Registry contents and using Registry editors to monitor and maintain the system configuration on remote computers.

The following topics are included in this chapter:

- Using Registry editors and Windows NT Diagnostics (**Winmsd.exe**)
- Viewing the Registry of a remote computer
- Editing Registry value entries
- Maintaining the Registry

It is recommended that, wherever possible, you make changes to the system configuration by using Control Panel or the applications in the Administrative Tools (Common) group.

Caution You can impair or disable Windows NT with incorrect changes or accidental deletions if you (or other users) use Registry Editor to change the system configuration. Wherever possible, you should use the Control Panel, Windows NT Diagnostics, and Administrative Tools in Windows NT to change the Registry. Registry Editor should be used only as a last resort.

To protect the system configuration, administrators can restrict users' access to the Registry, as described in "Maintaining Registry Security," later in this chapter.

Using Registry Editors and Windows NT Diagnostics

The Registry editors, **Regedt32** and **Regedit**, do not appear in any menus or as icons in any window. However, they are installed automatically when you install Windows NT.

▶ **To run a Registry editor**

1. Start **Regedt32.exe** or **Regedit.exe** from Windows NT Explorer.

   –Or–

   Click **Start**, point to **Run**, then type **Regedt32** or **Regedit** in the **Run** dialog box.

   –Or–

   Type **Regedt32** or **Regedit** at the command prompt, and press ENTER.
2. **Regedt32** has a read-only mode that protects the Registry contents from unintentional changes while you explore its structure and become familiar with the entries. From the **Options** menu in **Regedt32**, click **Read Only Mode**.
3. Click any folder icon to display the contents of that key.

Working in the Registry Editor Windows

You can use the mouse or commands to manipulate the windows and panes in a Registry editor. For example:

- Double-click a folder or key name to expand or collapse that entry. Or, use commands on the **View** and **Tree** menus to control the display of a selected key and its data.
- Use the mouse or the arrow keys to move the vertical split bar in each window to control the size of the left and right panes.
- From the **Window** menu, click **Tile** or **Cascade** to arrange the Registry Editor windows.

- From the **Options** menu in **Regedt32** click **Auto Refresh** to update the display continuously, or update it manually by clicking **Refresh All** or **Refresh Active** on the **View** menu. **Regedit** does not have an automatic refresh feature. To update the display when you are using **Regedit**, from the **View** menu, click **Refresh** or press F5.

Tip Turning off **Auto Refresh** in **Regedt32** improves its performance.

- To search for keys and subkeys, value entries, and values in **Regedit**, use the **Find** command on the **Edit** menu. You search for a key or subkey by using the **Find Key** command on the **View** menu in **Regedt32**, but you cannot search for value entries or values.

Table 24.1 shows some methods of using the keyboard to display data in each of the Registry Editor windows.

Table 24.1 Keyboard Actions for Viewing Registry Data

Procedure	Keyboard action
Expand one level of a selected Registry key.	Press ENTER.
Expand all of the levels of the predefined handle in the active Registry window.	Press CTRL + *.
Expand a branch of a selected Registry key.	Press the asterisk (*) key on the numeric keypad.
Collapse a branch of a selected Registry key.	Press ENTER or the minus (–) sign on the numeric keypad.

For more information about **Regedt32** and **Regedit**, click **Help Topics** on the **Help** menu of either application.

Using Windows NT Diagnostics to View System Configuration Data

You can also use the Windows NT Diagnostics tool to view configuration data in the Registry. Windows NT Diagnostics (**Winmsdp.exe**) is installed in the Administrative Tools (Common) group on the **Start** menu and in Windows NT Explorer in the *Systemroot*\System32 directory when you set up Windows NT.

When you want to browse for system information, Windows NT Diagnostics is the best tool to choose. Figure 24.1 shows the **Windows NT Diagnostics** dialog box.

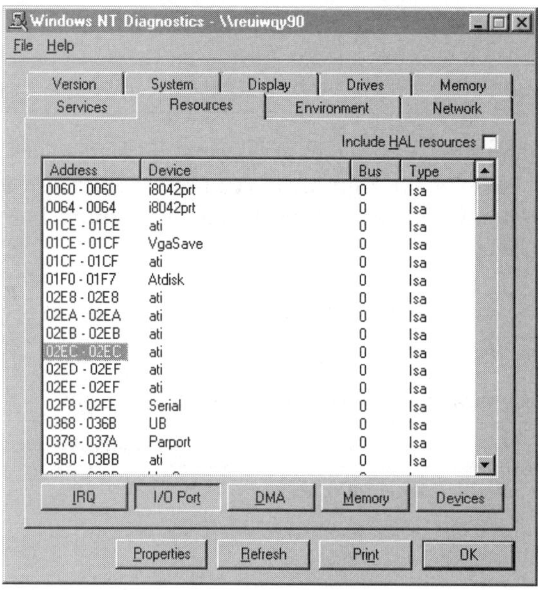

Figure 24.1 The Windows NT Diagnostics dialog box

In the **Windows NT Diagnostics** dialog box, click a tab to display data from the Registry in an easily readable format.

Tip You cannot edit value entries by using Windows NT Diagnostics, so the Registry contents are protected while you browse for information. However, you can select and copy any value if you want to paste information by using Registry Editor or a text editor.

Viewing the Registry of a Remote Computer

In the same way that you can use Event Viewer or User Manager to view details of another computer, you can use Registry Editor to view and change the contents of another computer's Registry if the Server service on the remote computer is running.

The ability to view a computer's configuration remotely means that the system administrator can examine a user's startup parameters, desktop configuration, and other parameters. So you, as the administrator, can provide troubleshooting or other support assistance over the telephone while you view settings on the other computer from your own workstation.

▶ **To view the Registry of a remote computer with Regedt32**

- From the **Registry** menu, click **Select Computer**, then type the name of the computer whose Registry you want to access, or double-click a name from the **Select Computer** list. If you are running Windows NT Server, the first name in this list represents the name of a domain. If no computer name appears after this domain name, double-click the domain name to view a list of the computers in that domain.

Note In **Regedt32**, **Auto Refresh** is not available when you are viewing the Registry from a remote computer. To update the display, use the **Refresh All** and **Refresh Active** commands on the **View** menu.

Two Registry windows appear in **Regedt32** for the remote computer, one for HKEY_USERS and one for HKEY_LOCAL_MACHINE. You can view or modify the information on keys for the remote computer if the access controls defined for the keys allow you to perform such operations. If you are logged on as a member of the Administrators group, you can perform actions on all keys.

To disconnect from the Registry of a remote computer by using **Regedt32**, from the **Registry** menu, click **Close** for each subtree window.

▶ **To view the Registry of a remote computer by using Regedit**

- From the **Registry** menu, click **Connect Network Registry**, then type the name of the computer whose Registry you want to access, or click **Browse** to select a computer name from the network list.

An icon representing the remote computer appears in the **Regedit** window. Click the plus sign (+) to view the contents of the Registry. To disconnect from the Registry of a remote computer by using **Regedit**, from the **Registry** menu, click **Disconnect Network Registry**, click the name of the computer from which you are disconnecting, then click **OK**.

Loading Hives from a Remote Computer

An alternative to viewing another computer's Registry remotely is to save copies of the other computer's Registry hives and then load them into **Regedt32** on your computer. You can use this method to view and change the keys and subkeys of the HKEY_LOCAL_MACHINE and HKEY_USERS hives of another computer's Registry. This enables you to investigate and repair the Registry values and value entries of a computer that is not configured properly or cannot connect to the network.

The subtrees of your computer's Registry are loaded automatically when you start the computer, and you can view its contents in a Registry editor. To view or change the contents of another computer's Registry, you must load a saved copy of all or part of its hive.

You might load the hive of another computer's Registry for the following reasons:

- To view or repair a hive on a computer that temporarily cannot run Windows NT. For details, see "Backing Up Registry Hives" and "Restoring Hives from Backup Files," later in this chapter.
- To view or repair the profiles of users who are not currently logged on to a computer. For details and examples, see "Managing User Profiles Through the Registry" in Chapter 25, "Configuration Management and the Registry."
- To view or repair a hive of a computer that is not connected to the network. Save a copy of its hive on a floppy disk, then load it into **Regedt32** on another computer.
- To create a custom version of the LastKnownGood control set and other startup controls. For details and examples, see "Making Sure the System Always Starts" in Chapter 25, "Configuration Management and the Registry."

Please note the following rules when loading a hive from another computer's Registry by using **Regedt32**:

- Before you can load a hive, you must save it as a file by using the **Save Key** command in **Regedt32** (described later in this chapter). You can also load another computer's system hive files—those that Windows NT creates for its own use—but only while Windows NT is not running on that computer. By default, the system's hive files are stored in *Systemroot*\System32\Config and *Systemroot*\Profiles.
- You can load only the keys and subkeys of HKEY_LOCAL_MACHINE and HKEY_USERS. Also, you can neither save nor load keys and subkeys that are *volatile*, that is, those that are created each time the system starts and deleted when the system stops. (You can save nonvolatile keys in volatile hives. For example, although the HKEY_LOCAL_MACHINE\Hardware key is volatile, you can save nonvolatile subkeys under that key.)

- To load or unload a hive, you must log on to the computer as Administrator or as a member of the Administrator group, and you must have Restore and Backup permissions.
- The **Load Hive** command is enabled only when the HKEY_USERS or HKEY_LOCAL_MACHINE subtree is selected in **Regedt32**. The **Unload Hive** command is enabled only when the root (highest key) of a loaded hive is selected.

Note Versions of Windows NT previous to version 4.0 did not allow you to load hive files that had filename extensions. This restriction does not apply to Windows NT 4.0.

If you are unable to connect to another computer over the network, you can load a hive file from a floppy disk.

▶ To load a hive file into Regedt32

1. In **Regedt32**, click the HKEY_LOCAL_MACHINE or HKEY_USERS subtree window.
2. From the **Registry** menu, click **Load Hive**.
   The **Load Hive** dialog box appears. This is a Windows NT Explorer dialog box that lists the drives of the local computer and represents all computers connected to the local computer.
3. Locate the saved hive file and double-click its entry.

Note When locating a hive file on a remote computer, use a path relative to the remote computer, not to the local computer. For example, if you are using your G: drive to connect to \\Text01\Public to save Hive.tst, enter **\\Text01\Public\Hive.tst**, not **G:\Hive.tst**. The G:\Hive.tst entry directs **Regedt32** to look for the file on the G: drive of the remote computer, not the G: drive of the local computer.

---

4. In the second **Load Hive** dialog box, type the name you want to use for the key where the hive will be loaded, then click **OK**.

   This names a new subkey in the selected subtree. You can specify any name that is not being used for another file or another key in the Registry.

Data from the loaded hive appears as a new subkey in the subtree selected when you loaded the hive file. A loaded hive remains in the system until you unload it.

The **Load Hive** command creates a new hive in the memory space of the Registry and uses the specified file as the backing hive file (*Filename*.log) for it. The specified file is held open, but nothing is copied to the file unless the information in a key or value entry is changed. Likewise, the **Unload Hive** command does not copy or create anything; it merely unloads a loaded hive.

▶ To unload a hive from Regedt32

- Select the root (top) key of the hive you want to unload. From the **Registry** menu, click **Unload Hive**.

  The connection is ended and the selected key is removed from **Regedt32**.

Note You cannot unload a hive that was loaded by the system. Also, you cannot unload a hive if an application has an open handle to any subkey in the hive. (A *handle* is a means for controlling access to objects in the system.) However, there is no way to detect whether an application has an open handle to a key.

If an attempt to use the **Unload Hive** command fails, close all applications not in immediate use and try again.

Saving and Restoring Keys

You can use **Regedt32** or **Regedit** to save all or part of a Registry subtree to a file. This file can then be used to restore that Registry or the Registry of another computer by replacing a damaged key with the contents of the file. If you save the key to a file by using **Regedt32**, you can also load the file into **Regedt32** on any computer to examine its contents or to edit it.

Regedt32 and **Regedit** save Registry keys in different formats and use different methods for restoring the Registry. Decide which tool you will use before beginning the process. You cannot save a key to a file with one tool and use the other tool to restore a Registry with that file.

- **Regedt32** saves Registry keys in a compressed format similar to that used by the system for its own hive files. You can load these files into **Regedt32** on any computer to examine or edit them. You can also use **Regedt32** to restore a damaged Registry key by replacing the damaged key with the contents of the saved file.
- **Regedit** saves Registry keys to a text file with a .reg filename extension. You cannot view or edit the contents of a .reg file from within **Regedit**, but you can view the file contents in any text editor, such as Notepad. (You should not edit a .reg file unless you know the format.) You can also use **Regedit** to replace Registry keys with the contents of a .reg file by importing the file into the Registry.

The remainder of this section describes how to save and restore Registry keys by using **Regedt32** and **Regedit**.

Using Regedt32 to Save and Restore Registry Keys

To save a Registry key and its subkeys to a hive file, use the **Save Key** command in **Regedt32**. You can then use the **Load Hive** command in **Regedt32** to view and edit the file and use the **Restore** command to replace a Registry key with the file contents.

Note Do not confuse the hive files you create by using the **Save Key** command with the hive files created by the system for its own use. The system hive file of a remote computer, usually stored in *Systemroot*\System32\Config and *Systemroot*\Profiles, can be loaded or restored only while Windows NT is not running on that computer.

Changes in the Registry are saved automatically, whether you make changes by using a Registry editor or by changing settings in applications. The **Save Key** command is used specifically to save portions of the Registry as a file on disk.

To use the **Save Key** command, you need Backup permissions, which you have if you are logged on as a member of the Administrators group.

You can use the **Save Key** command on any key. However, you cannot save volatile keys. A *volatile* key is one that is created when the system starts and deleted when it stops. Some volatile keys have nonvolatile subkeys that can be saved. For example, the HKEY_LOCAL_MACHINE\Hardware key is volatile, but you can save the nonvolatile subkeys under that key. To view the entire Hardware key for debugging, save it in a text file by using the **Save Subtree As** command on the **Registry** menu, as described later in this chapter.

▶ **To save a Registry key by using Regedt32**

1. Select the key that you want to save as a hive file on a disk.
2. From the **Registry** menu, click **Save Key**, then type a filename for the saved file in the **Save Key** dialog box.

Note When saving a hive file on a remote computer, use a path relative to the remote computer, not to the local computer. For example, if you are using your G: drive to connect to \\Text01\Public to save Hive.tst, enter **\\Text01\Public\Hive.tst**, not **G:\Hive.tst**. The G:\Hive.tst entry directs **Regedt32** to save the file on the G: drive of the remote computer, not the G: drive of the local computer.

The selected key is now saved as a file. When you use the **Load Hive** command, you can select the filename for any files that you saved by using the **Save Key** command.

For example, as part of system maintenance, you use the **Save Key** command to save a key as a file. When the key that you saved is ready to be returned to the system, you use the **Restore** command.

You can use the **Restore** command to make a hive file a part of the system configuration by loading the data from the hive file into an existing key. The contents of the file overwrite and replace the contents of the Registry key, except for the key name.

To use the **Restore** command, you need Restore permissions, which you have if you are logged on as a member of the Administrators group.

▶ **To restore a key by using Regedt32**

1. Select the key you want to restore from a hive file.
2. From the **Registry** menu, click **Restore**, then enter the name of the hive file from which data will be taken to overwrite the key.

Note When restoring a hive from a file on a remote computer, use a path relative to the remote computer, not to the local computer.

You cannot restore a key while the system is using it or any of its subkeys. For example, you cannot restore the SAM or Security keys because the system is always using these keys. The **Restore** command is used only for special conditions, such as to restore user profiles on a damaged system. To switch to a backup version of a hive, use **Regrest.exe**, a tool distributed on the *Windows NT Workstation Resource Kit* CD. For more information about **Regrest**, see Rktools.hlp, a Help file for tools on the *Windows NT Workstation Resource Kit* CD.

Using Regedit to Save Registry Keys

You can save Registry keys and their subkeys by using the **Export Registry** command in **Regedit**. This command saves a specific branch or the entire Registry in a text file with a .reg filename extension. Later, you can use the **Import Registry** command to rebuild a key or the entire Registry from an exported Registry file.

You can run **Regedit** from the **Regedit** window within Windows NT or from a command prompt. This section describes both methods.

To save a Registry key by using the Regedit window

1. From the **Registry** menu, click **Export Registry File.**
2. In the **Export Range** box of the **Export Registry File** dialog box, specify the part of the Registry you want to save.
   - Click **All** to save the entire Registry

     –Or–

   - Click **Selected Branch** to save a subtree, key, or subkey.

     The **Selected Branch** edit box displays the name of the Registry keys or subkeys that were selected when you clicked the command. You can save that key or type the name of any key over it. (**Regedit** saves the key you select and all of the subkeys and value entries it contains.)
3. Type a path and filename for the Registry file in the **File name** edit box, or navigate to a folder by using the Windows NT Explorer interface in the **Export Registry File** dialog box, then type a filename.

   Regedit appends the .reg filename extension to the filename you enter.
4. Click **Save** to return to **Regedit**.

To save a Registry key by using Regedit from a command prompt.

- Run **Regedit** from a command prompt to export Registry keys to .reg files. Use the following format:

  regedit /e *Filename*.reg [*Registry key*]

  The *Registry key* field is optional. The default is to export the entire Registry to a file.

Using Regedit to Restore Registry Keys

You can restore or replace a Registry key by importing a .reg file containing that key into the Registry. The contents of the Registry key are overwritten and replaced by the contents of the .reg file. If the Registry that is being restored is running on a computer that can still run Windows NT, use the **Regedit** window to restore the key. However, you can also run **Regedit** from the command prompt, if necessary.

This section describes the **Regedit** window interface method first, then the command prompt method.

Warning Use extreme caution in restoring keys. As with any Registry changes, an error can prevent Windows NT from loading and running, or prevent users from logging on to the system.

▶ **To restore a Registry key by using the Regedit window**

1. From the **Registry** menu, click **Import Registry File**.
2. Locate the .reg file you are using to restore the Registry key, then click **OK**.

▶ **To restore a Registry key by using Regedit from a command prompt**

- If the Registry is damaged or if the system no longer starts, run **Regedit** from a command prompt to diagnose and correct the problem. From the command line, use **Regedit** commands to export, import, or create a Registry.

You can also import Registry keys to .reg files from a command prompt. Use the following format:

regedit /i ***filename*.reg**

–Or–

regedit /c ***filename*.reg**

The **/i** (import) switch is used to import .reg files that contain a part of the Registry. The Registry keys (and their contents) saved in the .reg file overwrite only the analogous keys in the Registry. Please note that this command does not have a field to specify a Registry key. All of the Registry keys (and their subkeys and values) saved in the .reg file overwrite the analogous keys in the Registry. You cannot specify that only a subset of the keys be replaced.

The **/c** (complete) switch assumes that the .reg file contains a copy of an entire Registry. The contents of the .reg file overwrite all keys in the Registry.

Caution Use the **regedit /c** command with extreme care, and only when you are sure that the .reg file specified contains a complete image of the Registry. The **regedit /c** command replaces the entire contents of the Registry.

Editing Registry Value Entries

Within the Registry, you can alter the value entries for a selected key or assign new value entries to keys. This section describes how to find keys and how to add, edit, or delete keys and value entries.

Finding a Key in the Registry

A Registry key might be in a different place in the tree structure of your computer's Registry than where it is described in this chapter, depending on whether a computer is running Windows NT Workstation or Windows NT Server, and on other factors as well.

You can search for a specific key name in the Registry tree. Key names appear in the left pane of the Registry Editor window. The search begins from the currently selected key. A search beginning from a predefined key searches all its descendent keys.

Each search is local to the subtree where the search begins. That is, if you search in the HKEY_LOCAL_MACHINE subtree window, the search does not include keys found under any other subtree.

▶ **To search for a key by using Regedt32**

1. From the **View** menu, click **Find Key**.
2. In the **Find What** box of the **Find Key** dialog box, type the name of the key that you want to find.
   - If you want to restrict the scope of the search or define the search direction, select the **Match Whole Word Only** box, the **Match Case** option, or select **Up** or **Down** in the **Direction** box.
   - To see the next occurrence of the key name you specified, click **Find Next**.
3. Click **Find**.

Key names are not unique. To be sure you find the key you want, it is a good idea to search for additional occurrences of a specific key name.

Tip Some key names include spaces, underscores, or a continuous string (such as KeyboardPort/PointerPort). To ensure that you find the key you want, search for a portion of the name, and make sure that the **Match Whole Word Only** check box in the **Find** dialog box is cleared .

To find specific keys or value entries related to specific topics, you can also use Regentry.hlp, the Registry Help file on the *Windows NT Workstation Resource Kit* CD.

In **Regedt32**, you can search only for keys and subkeys of the Registry. **Regedit**, however, has an expanded search capability: you can search for value entries and values as well as keys and subkeys. In addition, you determine the level at which **Regedit** searches. This can expedite a search for a subkey by preventing **Regedit** from looking at every value entry.

▶ **To search for a key by using Regedit**

1. From the **Edit** menu, click **Find**.
2. In the **Find** dialog box, enter the name of the key, subkey, value entry, or value you want to find. Use the check boxes to limit or expand your search. Click **OK**.

3. To see the next occurrence of the entry, from the **Edit** menu, click **Find Next** or press F3.

Editing Values in the Registry

Each value entry in Registry Editor appears as a string that consists of three components, as shown in Figure 24.2.

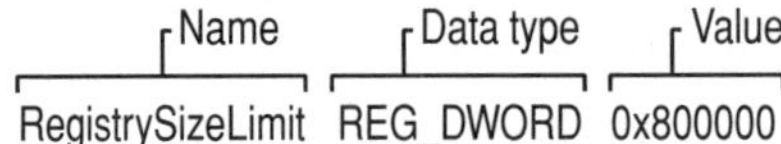

Figure 24.2 The three components of a value entry

The following rules govern the content of these three value entry components:

- The name of the value is a string of up to 16,000 Unicode characters (32K). This name can contain backslash (\) characters. The name itself can be null (that is, " ").
- The data type of the value is REG_BINARY, REG_DWORD, REG_EXPAND_SZ, REG_MULTI_SZ, or REG_SZ. Other data types can be defined by programs, but Registry Editor edits values of these types only. For more information about the value types, see "Value Entries for Registry Keys" in Chapter 23, "Overview of the Windows NT Registry."
- The value in a value entry can be data of a size up to 1 MB in any datatype except REG_DWORD, including arbitrary strings and raw binary data. However, to be efficient, values larger than 2048 bytes should be stored as files, with the filenames stored in the Registry.

The Registry preserves case as you type it for any entry but ignores case in evaluating the data. However, the data is defined by specific applications (or users), so applications that use the data might be case sensitive, depending on how the program that uses it treats the data.

▶ **To edit a value by using Regedt32 or Regedit**

1. In the right pane of the Registry Editor window, double-click the value entry.

   –Or–

   In **Regedt32**, from the **Edit** menu, click **String**, **Binary**, **DWORD**, or **Multi String** as appropriate for the selected value. In **Regedit**, from the **Edit** menu, click **Modify**.

2. Edit the value that appears in the related **Editor** dialog box, then click **OK**.

   The **Binary** and **DWORD** options in **Regedt32** let you select the base of the number system you use to edit your data. In the Binary editor, you can edit your data as binary (base 2) or hexadecimal (*hex*—base 16). In the DWORD editor, you can edit your data in binary, hex, or decimal (base 10). Hex is the default base for both editors. The right pane of the Registry Editor always displays these types of data in hex.

   Tip To view numbers in decimal format, double-click the value entry and select the **Decimal** format option. Cancel the dialog box when you finish checking the value.

Information stored in a nonvolatile key remains in the Registry until you delete it. Information stored in a volatile key is discarded when you shut down the system. However, volatile keys can contain nonvolatile subkeys and nonvolatile keys can contain volatile subkeys. For example, the HKEY_LOCAL_MACHINE\Hardware key is volatile, but many of its subkeys are nonvolatile.

Note As your Registry grows in size, eventually you might want to set a larger value for **RegistrySizeLimit**. For more information, see "Registry Size Limit" in Chapter 23, "Overview of the Windows NT Registry."

Adding a Key

You can add a key to store data in the Registry. For example, you can add a subkey under CurrentControlSet\Services to start a service process you have written or to install a device driver that does not have an installation program.

To do this, you must have Create Subkey access permission for the key under which you are adding a subkey, as described in "Assigning Access Rights to Registry Keys," later in this chapter.

▶ **To add a key to the Registry by using Regedt32**

1. Select the key or subkey under which you want the new key to appear.
2. From the **Edit** menu, click **Add Key** or press the INS key.
3. In the **Key Name** box of the **Add Key** dialog box, type the name that you want to assign to your key.

   The key name cannot contain a backslash (\), and it must be unique in relation to other subkeys at the same level in the hierarchy. That is, Key1 and Key2 can each have a subkey named Key3, but Key1 cannot have two subkeys named Key3.
4. Leave the **Class** box blank. This box is reserved for a future use.
5. Click **OK** to display the new key in the Registry Editor window.

▶ **To add a key to the Registry with Regedit**

1. Select the key or subkey under which you want the new key to appear.
2. From the **Edit** menu, click **New**, then click **Key**.
   A new folder appears under the selected key, with the name of the folder selected so that you can edit it.
3. Type a name for the key and press ENTER.

Adding a Value Entry to a Registry Key

You can use the Registry editors to assign a new value entry to a key or edit the value entry of an existing key. When you do this, the value that you add appears in the data pane of the selected Registry window.

To determine value entries you might add, see the tuning and troubleshooting information in Regentry.hlp, which is included in the *Windows NT Workstation Resource Kit* CD.

▶ **To add a value entry to a Registry key by using Regedt32**

1. Select the subkey to which you want to add a value entry.
2. From the **Edit** menu, click **Add Value**.

Tip To quickly open the **Add Value** dialog box, switch to the right pane by using the TAB key or the mouse, then press the INS key.

---

3. In the **Add Value** dialog box, type the name you want to assign to the new value entry.

4. In the **Data Type** box, select the type that you want to assign to the value entry.

   The data types are described in "Value Entries in the Registry Keys" in Chapter 23, "Overview of the Windows NT Registry."

5. Click OK, then type the value in the **String Editor** dialog box. Click **OK** again to display the new entry in the Registry Editor window.

▶ **To add a value entry to a Registry key by using Regedit**

1. Select the subkey to which you want to add a value entry.
2. From the **Edit** menu, click **New**, then click **String Value**, **Binary Value**, or **DWORD Value** depending upon the data type of the value you are adding.
3. The new value entry appears in the right panel with the name of the value entry selected so you can edit it.
4. Type a name for the value entry.
5. To edit the value, double-click the value entry, then edit the value in the **Value data** box of the *Datatype* **Editor** dialog box, then click **OK**.

Deleting a Key or a Value Entry

To remove selected keys or value entries from the Registry, you can use the **Delete** command from the **Edit** menu or you can press the DELETE key. However, you cannot delete any of the predefined subtrees or change the name of a key.

Caution There is no **Undo** command for deletions. Registry Editor prompts you to confirm the deletions if **Confirm On Delete** is selected from the **Options** menu. When you delete a key, the message does not include the name of the key you are deleting. Check your selection carefully before proceeding. To recover a subkey of HKEY_LOCAL_MACHINE\System\CurrentControlSet, restart the computer. Press the SPACEBAR immediately when you see the message **Press spacebar now to invoke Hardware Profile/Last Known Good Menu**.

In **Regedt32**, you can protect the Registry from accidental deletions by using the following methods:

- Protect data through read-only mode.

  From the **Options** menu, select **Read Only Mode**. When this option is selected, **Regedt32** does not save any changes. This protects the data from accidental changes.

- Protect data through confirmation.

  From the **Options** menu, select **Confirm On Delete**. When this option is selected, **Regedt32** prompts you to confirm deletion of any key or value.

Maintaining the Registry

Windows NT enforces access control on Registry files, so it is difficult for users to accidentally or intentionally damage or delete hives on a running system. While the system is running, hive files are reserved by the system for exclusive access on all file systems. If the Windows NT *Systemroot* is not on an NTFS volume, the Registry can be tampered with—specifically, users can remove keys for user profiles that are not currently loaded. With NTFS, such tampering can be prevented.

You should plan how to protect the Registry for each computer at your site that runs Windows NT. This section describes how to ensure that you will have working Registry files under most conditions.

For more details about how to ensure recoverability under all conditions, see "Making Sure the System Always Starts" in Chapter 25, "Configuration Management and the Registry."

Maintaining Registry Security

Do not allow a user to log on as a member of the Administrators group unless that individual has specific administrative duties.

You can also opt not to put **Regedt32.exe** on workstations, because you can easily administer any workstation from a remote computer. And you can place access controls on **Regedt32.exe** in Windows NT Explorer, which limits the rights of users to start this program.

This section describes the additional steps you can take to protect the Registry:

- Protect Registry files.
- Assign access rights to Registry keys.
- Audit Registry activities.

Protecting Registry Files for User Profiles

You can protect the user profiles in the Registry in the same way that you protect other files in Windows NT—by restricting access through Windows NT Explorer. If the files are stored on an NTFS volume, you can use the security features of Windows NT Explorer to assign permissions for the Registry files or Registry editors. From the **File** menu, click **Properties**, then click the **Security** tab. For details about using these commands, see the Windows NT Explorer Help.

Caution You should change permissions for user profiles only. The permissions for other Registry keys are maintained automatically by the system and should not be changed.

For information about safeguarding files with backups, see "Backing Up and Restoring Registry Hives," later in this chapter.

Assigning Access Rights to Registry Keys

To determine who has access to specific Registry data, set permissions on the Registry keys to specify the users and groups that can have access to that key. (This is sometimes called *changing ACLs*, in reference to the *access control lists* that govern who has access to data.) You can also add names to or remove names from the list of users or groups authorized to access the Registry keys.

You can assign access rights to Registry keys regardless of the type of file system on the partition where the Windows NT files are stored.

Caution Changing the permissions to limit access to a Registry key can have severe consequences. If, for example, you set No Access permissions on a key needed for configuration by the **Network** option in Control Panel, the application will fail.

At a minimum, give Administrators and the System full access to the key, thus ensuring that the system starts and that the Registry key can be repaired by an administrator.

If you change permissions on a Registry key, you should audit that key for failed access attempts. For details, see "Auditing Registry Activities," later in this chapter.

Because assigning permissions on specific keys can have serious consequences, you should reserve this action for keys that you add to accommodate custom applications or other custom settings. After you change permissions on a Registry key, be sure to turn on auditing in User Manager, and then test the system extensively through a variety of activities while logged on under different user and administrative accounts.

In **Regedt32**, the commands on the **Security** menu for assigning permission and ownership of keys work in the same way as similar commands for NTFS partitions in Windows NT Explorer for assigning access rights for files and directories. For details about these commands, see help for the Registry editor.

To assign permissions on a key

1. Make a backup copy of the Registry key before making changes.
2. Select the key for which you want to assign access permission. Then, from the **Security** menu, click **Permissions**.
3. In the **Registry Key Permissions** dialog box, assign an access level to the selected key by selecting an option in the **Type of Access** box as described in the following table, and then click **OK**.

Type of access	Meaning
Read	Allows users on the **Permissions** list to read the key's contents, but prevents changes from being saved.
Full Control	Allows users on the **Permissions** list to access, edit, or take ownership of the selected key.
Special Access	Allows users on the **Permissions** list some custom combination of access and edit permission for the selected key. For a description of the Special Access types, see "Auditing Registry Activities," later in this chapter.

4. Turn on auditing in User Manager (in Windows NT Workstation) or User Manager for Domains (in Windows NT Server), and then test the system extensively to ensure that the new access control does not interfere with system or application operations.

As a system administrator, you might need to take ownership of a key to protect access to that key. To take ownership of a Registry key, click **Owner** on the **Security** menu, then complete the **Ownership** dialog box. You add users or groups to the **Permissions** list by following the same procedure for managing lists of users and groups as you use throughout Windows NT.

You (or any user) can take ownership of any Registry key if you log on to the computer as a member of the Administrator group. However, if an Administrator takes ownership of a key without being assigned full control by its owner, the key cannot be given back to its original owner, and the event is audited.

Auditing Registry Activities

To audit Registry activities, you must complete these separate activities:

- Turn on auditing and set the audit policies in User Manager or User Manager for Domains for the activities you want to audit.
- Specify the groups and users whose activities you want to audit for selected keys by using the **Auditing** command in Registry Editor.
- View the Security log in Event Viewer for a selected computer to see the results of auditing.

For each of these activities, you must be logged on as a member of the Administrators group for the specific computer you are auditing. Auditing policies are set on a per-computer basis. Before you can audit activities in Registry keys, you must turn on security auditing for the computer.

▶ **To turn on auditing**

1. In User Manager or User Manager for Domains, from the **Policies** menu, click **Audit**. Select the **Audit These Events** option to turn on auditing.
2. Select **Success** and **Failure** options for each type of event to be audited, then click **OK**.

Note At a minimum, you should select the **Failure** option for **File And Object Access**. Selecting **Success** for many items can produce a large number of meaningless entries in the event log.

You can audit actions for a specific Registry key. For example, you can audit:

- Keys where you want to know about changes being made by users or applications.
- Keys you added that you want to test.

▶ To audit user actions for a selected Registry key

1. From the **Security** menu in Registry Editor, click **Auditing**, then complete the dialog box.

   This command in Registry Editor is similar to the **Auditing** command in Windows NT Explorer.

2. Select the **Success** or **Failure** option for the following activities:

Audit option	Audits events that attempt to
Query Value	Open a key with Query Value access.
Set Value	Open a key with Set Value access.
Create Subkey	Open a key with Create Value access.
Enumerate Subkeys	Open a key with Enumerate Subkeys access (that is, events that try to find the subkeys of a key).
Notify	Open a key with Notify access.
Create Link	Open a key with Create Link access.
Delete	Delete the key.
Write DAC	Determine who has access to the key.
Read Control	Find the owner of a key.

▶ To view the results of auditing

- Run Event Viewer, select the computer that you are interested in, then click **Security** on the **Log** menu.

Note If you change permissions for any Registry key, you should turn on Auditing in User Manager and specify the **Failure** auditing option for **File And Object Access**. Then, if any application is not working because of changes in permissions, you can check the Security event log for details.

Backing Up and Restoring Registry Hives

You might need to restore backed-up versions of Registry hives. This can occur, for example, when a new computer replaces an old one, when a disk controller or hard disk becomes corrupted, or when an electrical failure erases large parts of a disk. This section describes how to back up and restore Registry hives.

How this restoration is done depends on what hardware is available and what file system is in use. You can, of course, restore only what you have backed up.

Important Back up all important files, including system files, frequently and consistently.

Your regular backup routine should include using Disk Administrator to create an uncompressed backup of the System hive. (In Disk Administrator, from the **Partition** menu, click **Configuration**, then click **Save**.) Also, the Emergency Repair Disk includes a compressed version of the System hive. For details, see Disk Administrator Help, and Chapter 20 of this book, "Preparing for and Performing Recovery."

Backing Up Registry Hives

You can make a Registry hive backup in one of four ways:

- Use a tape drive and the Windows NT Backup program. To automatically include a copy of the local Registry files in the backup set, select the **Backup Local Registry** option in the **Backup Information** dialog box. This is the preferred method for creating backups if you have a tape drive.
- If you do not have a tape drive, use a utility that backs up the Registry, such as the Repair Disk Utility (**Rdisk.exe**), which is automatically installed when you install Windows NT. You can also use **Regback.exe**, a tool included on the *Windows NT Workstation Resource Kit* CD. For more information, see Repair Disk Utility Help or Rktools.hlp on the *Windows NT Workstation Resource Kit* CD.

- Use a different operating system to start the computer. Then copy all files in the *Systemroot*\System32\Config directory to a safe backup location. For example, use another instance of Windows NT if the Registry is stored on an NTFS partition, or use MS-DOS if the Registry is stored on a FAT partition.
- In **Regedt32**, use the **Save Key** command, which backs up Registry keys manually.

  For each key immediately below HKEY_LOCAL_MACHINE and HKEY_USERS, click the key, and then, from the **Registry** menu, click **Save Key**. Choose filenames that match the key names. For example, save the System key to \Backdir\System.

Note Volatile subkeys, that is, those created each time the system starts and deleted when it stops, cannot be saved. However, you can save the nonvolatile subkeys of volatile keys. For example, although the HKEY_LOCAL_MACHINE\Hardware key is volatile, you can save nonvolatile subkeys under that key.

Restoring Hives from Backup Files

If you have a good set of backup files, which you update regularly, you can restore Registry hives that are damaged or missing.

But you cannot use Registry Editor to fully restore hives, because you must use the **ReplaceKey** operation to restore active parts of the Registry. Registry Editor cannot perform this operation.

To restore a damaged system, you must first restore the basic operating system installation. To do this, you can use the Emergency Repair Disk to restore your system to its postinstallation status, or you can simply run Windows NT Setup again. If you rerun Setup, the system starts the computer but lacks changes made since you first set it up. You can recover most of those changes if you copy files from backups by using the Windows NT Backup program for tape backups or by copying from disk backups.

Tip To update the Emergency Repair Disk after making changes that affect the Registry, use the Repair Disk Utility (**Rdisk.exe**), a tool included in Windows NT. If you use the **rdisk** command alone (no switches), it backs up the System and Software hives only. If you use **rdisk /s**, it backs up the SAM and Security hives as well. However, if the system includes many user accounts, the file might be too large to fit on the single floppy disk required for the Emergency Repair Disk update process.

However, you cannot merely copy the backups of Registry hive files, because those files are protected while Windows NT is running. So, after the system and all of the additional files such as device drivers are restored, you must restore the Registry. You can do this in one of the following ways, depending on which backup mechanism you used:

- For tape backups, you can use Windows NT Restore to restore the Registry.
- Start the computer by using an alternative instance of the operating system (or using MS-DOS if the system files are on a FAT partition). Copy the files to the *Systemroot*\System32\Config directory. Then restart the computer by using the regular operating system.
- Use **Regrest.exe**, a tool included on the *Windows NT Workstation Resource Kit* CD. **Regrest** replaces the default files installed by Windows NT Setup with data from backup files, and saves the default files under other filenames. To see the restored Registry, restart the computer after running **Regrest**.

Compacting Registry Data

The memory used for the Registry is approximately equal to the size of a hive when it is loaded into memory. Hives vary in size on disk from 20K to more than 500K. The amount of space used depends chiefly on how many local user profiles are retained and how much information is stored in each profile.

You should remove unused or out-of-date user profiles from a computer by using the **Delete User Profiles** command in Windows NT Setup. (The Setup program protects you from deleting the profile for the currently logged on user.)

You can use the **Save Key** command to save a user hive, and then use the **Restore** command so you can use this smaller hive. How much space you gain depends on how much was stored in various user profiles.

This procedure is useful only for user profiles, not for the SAM, Security, Software, or System hives.

Viewing and Printing Registry Data as Text

You can examine the contents of a Registry key as text for troubleshooting. You can save a key as a text file, and you can print data from Registry Editor, including a key, its subkeys, and all of the value entries of all of its subkeys.

The **Save Subtree As** command on the **Registry** menu in **Regedt32** also works for the HKEY_LOCAL_MACHINE\Hardware key, which you cannot otherwise save in its entirety as a hive file.

▶ **To save a Registry key as a text file**

- In **Regedt32**, select the key you want to save as a text file. From the **Registry** menu, click **Save Subtree As**. Use the **Save As** dialog box to navigate to the subdirectory of your choice, type a filename, and then click **OK**.
- In **Regedit**, from the **Registry** menu, click **Print**, then click the **Print To File** check box, and click **OK**. In the **Print To File** dialog box, type a path and filename for the text file.

▶ **To print a Registry key**

- In **Regedt32**, select the key or subkey you want to print. Then, from the **Registry** menu, click **Print Subtree**. Printing begins immediately. (Print options must be set in advance by clicking **Printer Setup** on the **Registry** menu.)
- In **Regedit**, from the **Registry** menu, click **Print**. In the **Print** dialog box, select an option under **Print Range**. The **All** option prints the entire Registry. The **Selected branch** option prints a specified path in the Registry. (If you click a key or subkey before clicking **Print**, its path appears in the **Selected branch** box, but you can type a path as well.) Click **OK**.

Summary of Administrative Tools for the Registry

Table 24.2 summarizes the tools provided with Windows NT (in addition to Registry Editor and Windows NT Diagnostics) that you can use to administer the Registry.

Table 24.2 Tools in Windows NT for Registry Management

Tool	Description
Backup	Backs up Registry hives as part of a tape backup routine.
Emergency Repair Disk	Restores hives to the system.
Repair Disk Utility (**Rdisk.exe**)	Updates the Emergency Repair Disk with a current backup of Registry hives.
Windows NT Explorer	Applies access controls to Registry Editor and hive files on NTFS partitions.

Table 24.3 summarizes the tools on the *Windows NT Workstation Resource Kit* CD that you can use to administer the Registry. For details about these and other utilities provided with the *Windows NT Resource Kit*, see Rktools.hlp on the *Windows NT Workstation Resource Kit* CD.

Table 24.3 Tools on the Resource Kit CD

Tool	Description
Regback.exe	Creates backups of Registry files.
Regentry.hlp	Documents Windows NT Registry entries.
Regini.exe	Makes Registry changes by using script files.
Regrest.exe	Restores Registry hives.

CHAPTER 25

Configuration Management and the Registry

This chapter provides some examples of problem-solving tasks that involve changes made to the Registry by using Registry Editor. The topics in this chapter include the following:

- Solving users' environment problems by using the Registry
- Making sure the system always starts
- Changing driver and service configuration data

Caution Use extreme care if you follow any procedures described here for changing the Registry directly by using Registry Editor. Editing entries in the Registry is equivalent to editing raw sectors on a hard disk. You can easily make mistakes that prevent the computer from starting.

Wherever possible, use Control Panel, the tools in the Administrative Tools group, and Windows NT Explorer to change the system configuration.

Solving Users' Environment Problems by using the Registry

Using a Registry editor to view the contents of the Registry for a remote computer makes it easier for a system administrator to solve users' configuration problems.

Windows NT 4.0 includes two tools for viewing and editing the Registry, both called Registry Editor. The traditional tool, **Regedt32.exe**, is documented more thoroughly in these chapters. The new tool, **Regedit.exe**, has a Windows NT Explorer interface. It has many of the same functions as **Regedt32** and an expanded search capability. Both tools are installed automatically when you install Windows NT on any computer.

You can use a Registry editor on your computer to view and edit the Registry of a remote computer. Then you can browse Registry entries to identify problems. To view and edit the Registry of a remote computer:

- In **Regedt32**, from the **Registry** menu, click **Select Computer**, then type the name of the remote computer.
- In **Regedit**, from the **Registry** menu, click **Connect Network Registry**, then type the name of the remote computer.

You can also load a copy of a hive from another computer to view and change entries, as described in "Loading Hives from a Remote Computer" in Chapter 24, "Registry Editors and Registry Administration."

Registry Editor is most useful as a tool to find the source of problems, not to edit value entries. After you find the source of a problem, Control Panel or other tools can be more safely used to solve the problem.

For example, you can easily check the user's desktop settings by examining the values under the Console and Control Panel subkeys for the user. The Console subkeys define settings for the command prompt and other character-based applications. The Control Panel subkeys in the Registry define the appearance and behavior of items in the Windows NT desktop.

▶ **To view a user's desktop settings**

1. Use a Registry editor to view the Registry of the user's computer.
2. Under HKEY_USERS for the selected computer, double-click the subkey that represents the profile of the user. (The subkeys are named by the Security ID string (*SID_#*) of each user.)

Tip To determine which *SID_#* subkey is associated with a user, see the values for **ProfileImagePath** in the following Registry path:

HKEY_LOCAL_MACHINE\Software
  \Microsoft
    \Windows NT
      \CurrentVersion
        \ProfileList
          SID_#

Double-click the **ProfileImagePath** value entry. The value of **ProfileImagePath** is a binary representation of the directory name of the user's profile, which includes the user's name.

---

3. Double-click the Console subkey if the problem involves a character-based screen.

   –Or–

   Double-click the Control Panel subkey if the problem involves a Windows NT window.
4. Check values as described in the Help topic for User Preferences on the *Windows NT Workstation Resource Kit* CD.

For example, suppose a user complains that their screen turns black whenever they click the shortcut icon for a utility that runs in a command prompt window. You can select this computer in a Registry editor, and then select the following subkey:

HKEY_USERS
  SID_#
    \Console
      Name of shortcut

In this example, if the value of **ScreenColors** is 0, both the text and the screen background have been set to black, and this is the source of the user's problem. To fix this by selecting new colors, the user can double-click the shortcut icon, press ALT+SPACEBAR to display the **Control** menu, click **Properties**, then click the **Colors** tab.

Tip To change the colors or the bitmap that appear on the CTRL+ALT+DELETE logon screen, change the **Wallpaper** value entry under HKEY_USERS\.DEFAULT\Control Panel\Desktop. For example, if you want a bitmap of your company's logo on the logon screen, change the value of **Wallpaper** to specify the path and filename of the logo bitmap.

Making Sure the System Always Starts

This section discusses:

- Starting a system with configuration problems
- Reconstructing a system with damaged files
- Creating a custom startup verification program

The goal in all of these situations is to make sure a Windows NT system starts correctly each time you turn on the switch. Of course, you need to plan ahead for system safety by doing the following:

- Maintain a regular backup program, including backups of Registry hives, as described in "Maintaining the Registry" in Chapter 24, "Registry Editors and Registry Administration."
- Maintain a copy of the Emergency Repair Disk created when you installed Windows NT. Each Emergency Repair Disk works only for the computer where it was made. Use Repair Disk Utility (**Rdisk**), a tool installed with Windows NT, to update the Emergency Repair Disk with the current version of Registry hives. For more information, see Help for the Repair Disk Utility.
- Install a redundant copy of the operating system to make the system more robust, as described in Chapter 2, "Customizing Setup."

You can also rely on Windows NT to automatically recover from damages to startup data. Specifically, to protect the system from corrupted sectors in the System hive, Windows NT automatically creates a backup of the System hive—the System.alt file—which is stored in *Systemroot*\System32\Config. If any problems are encountered while reading the System hive during startup, such as damage to the file, the Boot Loader automatically switches to the System.alt file to continue startup. For more information about the System.alt file, see "Hives and Files" in Chapter 23, "Overview of the Windows NT Registry."

Starting a System with Configuration Problems

This section describes how to start a computer when hardware or software problems prevent normal system startup.

For a computer running Windows NT, the Registry includes several control sets. Each control set is a complete set of system parameters that define startup, system recovery, and driver load controls plus service parameters and other system configuration data. The control set that appears under the CurrentControlSet key is the one used to start the system for the current session. For details about control sets, see "HKEY_LOCAL_MACHINE\System Key" in Chapter 23, "Overview of the Windows NT Registry."

Whenever you start Windows NT, the Boot Loader automatically tries to boot by using the current control set described under the HKEY_LOCAL_MACHINE \System\Select subkey. If the system cannot start by using this control set (because of erroneous user changes or bad-sector errors on a file), the Boot Loader automatically tries the LastKnownGood control set, as defined in the Select subkey.

You can also switch to the Last Known Good configuration manually, bypassing the automatic process.

▶ **To manually switch to a previous system configuration**

1. Press ENTER to select Windows NT at the startup prompt, and then immediately press the SPACEBAR.
2. From the **Hardware Profile\Configuration Recovery** menu, click **Use Last Known Good Configuration**, press L, then press ENTER.

Note If you select the LastKnownGood option at startup, the system discards any configuration changes to the HKEY_LOCAL_MACHINE\System\CurrentControlSet subkey made since the computer's last successful startup.

During system startup, you can choose between the default and the LastKnownGood control set only. For information about how the LastKnownGood control set is selected and stored, see "HKEY_LOCAL_MACHINE\System Key" in Chapter 23, "Overview of the Windows NT Registry."

If you have created more than one hardware profile, you can also choose a hardware profile. A *hardware profile* is a set of changes to the standard configuration of services (including drivers and Win32 services) and devices loaded when Windows NT starts.

For more information on hardware profiles, double-click **System** in Control Panel, click the **Hardware Profiles** tab and open Help. See also "Hardware Profiles Subkey for All Control Sets" in Chapter 23, "Overview of the Windows NT Registry."

Reconstructing a System with Damaged Files

You might need to restore a user's system configuration and working environment if hardware fails or is being replaced, or if files have been damaged on the hard disk. You can use the Emergency Repair Disk created during Windows NT installation to restore the system files. However, you lose any changes that were made to the system after installation when you use the Emergency Repair Disk to repair files such as the Registry hives unless you updated hive files on the Emergency Repair Disk. To update the Emergency Repair Disk with a current copy of the Registry hive files, use Repair Disk Utility (**Rdisk.exe**), a tool installed with Windows NT.

You can use one of the following methods to reconstruct the system from backups (as described in "Backing Up and Restoring Registry Hives" in Chapter 24, "Registry Editors and Registry Administration"):

- Use Windows NT Restore to restore the Registry from tape backups.
- Start the computer by using another instance of the operating system (or by using MS-DOS for a FAT partition). Copy the backup files to the *Systemroot*\System32\Config and *Systemroot*\Profiles subdirectories.

  If you attempt to restore damaged SAM or Security hives, you must use this second method. You cannot replace these hives while Windows NT is running. This means that if your system files are on an NTFS volume, you must have another instance of Windows NT available on that system to be able to restore the SAM and Security hives. Or, you can use the Emergency Repair Disk to restore the default SAM and Security hives.
- Use **Regrest.exe**, a tool on the *Windows NT Workstation Resource Kit* CD. **Regrest** replaces the default files installed by Windows NT Setup with data from backup files, and saves the default files under other filenames.

Creating a Custom Startup Verification Program

System startup is usually declared "good" if the following two procedures are complete:

- All startup drivers are loaded.

  When a service fails to load during startup, its **ErrorControl** value is checked, as defined in the CurrentControlSet\Services*Servicename* subkeys. Whether the system startup process continues or halts depends on this value.
- At least one user successfully logs on to the computer by pressing CTRL+ALT+DELETE and supplying a valid user name, domain, and password.

This basic standard for verifying system startup suits the needs of most situations; however, your site might require additional steps before considering a computer to be successfully started and ready to participate in the network.

For example, you can redefine startup validation for a server no one normally logs on to, or for which you want system startup to be validated as successful only after a particular process has started.

Or, for a server running Microsoft SQL Server, you might want a system startup to be marked as good only after the server responds to a request. To do this, you can write a program that queries the SQL database and checks the response. If the response is not as expected, the program can call the **NotifyBootConfigStatus()** function with a value of FALSE, prompting the system to restart by using the LastKnownGood control set. Or, the program can direct the system to run without saving the current configuration as the LastKnownGood control set. Conversely, if SQL Server responds as expected, the program can call the **NotifyBootConfigStatus()** function with a value of TRUE, which prompts the system to save the current configuration as the LastKnownGood control.

You can run such a verification program from the command prompt. Or you can have the program run automatically during startup by specifying value entries under the BootVerificationProgram subkey in the Registry.

▶ To create a custom startup verification program

1. Change the value of **ReportBootOK** to 0 under the following Registry path:

   HKEY_LOCAL_MACHINE\Software
   \Microsoft
   \Windows NT
   \CurrentVersion
   \WinLogon

   The data type for **ReportBootOK** is REG_SZ. When the value of **ReportBootOK** is set to 0, it disables the automatic acceptance of startup after the first successful logon.

2. Create the executable program that you want to run as part of startup verification. Then specify its filename as a value for **ImagePath** in the BootVerificationProgram subkey under this Registry path:

   HKEY_LOCAL_MACHINE\System
   \CurrentControlSet
   \Control
   \BootVerificationProgram

   The data type for **ImagePath** must be REG_SZ or REG_EXPAND_SZ.

As another example, a computer setup for a turnkey application is a candidate for a custom startup verification routine: The computer does not usually interact directly with users and you therefore do not want a successful user logon to be part of the system startup.

If you want a good system startup to be accepted from a remote computer (either manually or automatically), you can use the **Bootvrfy.exe** program that is supplied with Windows NT. In this case, the remote computer accepts the system startup by starting the Bootvrfy service. You can also write your own verification service, which can reject the system startup and revert to the LastKnownGood control set to restart the computer.

▶ To verify system startup from a remote computer

1. For the local computer, add a BootVerification subkey under the following Registry path:

   HKEY_LOCAL_MACHINE\System
   \CurrentControlSet
   \Services

2. Add the following value entries under this new BootVerification key:

   ```
   Start : REG_DWORD : 0x00000003
   Type : REG_DWORD : 0x00000020
   ErrorControl : REG_DWORD : 0x00000001
   ImagePath : REG_EXPAND_SZ : bootvrfy.exe
   ObjectName : REG_SZ : LocalSystem
   ```

   For more information about these entries, see Regentry.hlp, the Registry Help file on the *Windows NT Workstation Resource Kit* CD.

3. Change the value of **ReportBootOK** to 0 under the following Registry path:

   HKEY_LOCAL_MACHINE\Software
   \Microsoft
   \Windows NT
   \CurrentVersion
   \WinLogon

4. Start the Bootvrfy service from a remote computer.

   This service tells the service controller on the local computer to save the current startup configuration as the LastKnownGood configuration, and then the service terminates itself.

Important You cannot use the Bootvrfy service in conjunction with settings in the BootVerificationProgram subkey. These are mutually exclusive methods.

You might also want a good system startup to depend on whether a specific service or driver loads. For example, for a server you can program the Boot Loader to choose the LastKnownGood control set if the Server service does not start on the computer.

▶ **To change system startup to depend on a service or driver**

1. Select the subkey for the service under the following Registry path:

   HKEY_LOCAL_MACHINE\System
   \CurrentControlSet
   \Services
   Servicename

   Servicename can be any service you want successful system startup to depend on.

2. Double-click the service's **ErrorControl** entry, then change its value to 0x2 (which specifies to switch to LastKnownGood if the service does not start).

   On rare occasions, you might want to change the **ErrorControl** value to 0x3 (which specifies to stop the attempted startup if the service does not start); however, this **ErrorControl** value is usually reserved for critical services such as file system drivers.

3. To put the new values into effect, close Registry Editor, shut down the system, and restart the computer.

4. If you do not get the intended effect, restart the computer and manually select the LastKnownGood control set as described in "Starting a System with Configuration Problems," earlier in this chapter. (All changes in the last session will be discarded.)

Customizing Windows NT Logon

You can change the Windows NT logon process in either of the following two ways:

- Create a custom logon message, especially for secure sites
- Allow automatic logon for a computer

During Windows NT logon, the first message that appears instructs the user to press CTRL+ALT+DELETE to log on. Then, when the **Welcome** dialog box appears, the user can type a user name, domain, and password.

You can define a custom message to display after the user presses CTRL+ALT+DELETE. For example, you can warn users that a particular computer is restricted to only certain users. Or, for all computers on the network, you can warn against unauthorized attempts to log on.

▶ To create a custom logon message

1. In Registry Editor, select the following subkey:

   HKEY_LOCAL_MACHINE\Software
   \Microsoft
   \Windows NT
   \CurrentVersion
   \Winlogon

2. Add a value entry named **LegalNoticeCaption** of type REG_SZ, and type text that will be the caption for the message.
3. Add a value entry named **LegalNoticeText** of type REG_SZ, and type text for the message.

If either **LegalNoticeCaption** or **LegalNoticeText** is defined in the Registry, a user cannot log on to the computer without acknowledging the message by clicking **OK**.

For a computer used as a print server and another special-use system, you might enable system startup without a user having to supply a user name or password. You can define automatic logon for a computer by adding some value entries in the Registry.

▶ To allow automatic logon for a computer

1. In Registry Editor, select the following subkey:

   HKEY_LOCAL_MACHINE\Software
   \Microsoft
   \Windows NT
   \CurrentVersion
   \Winlogon

2. Add a value entry named **AutoAdminLogon** of type REG_SZ, and specify a value of 1.
3. Add a value entry named **DefaultPassword** of type REG_SZ, and enter the password of the user who is listed under the value **DefaultUserName**.

Changing Driver and Service Configuration Data

The hardware detected on a computer is stored in the volatile HKEY_LOCAL_MACHINE\Hardware key. Because this key is destroyed each time the system stops and recreated each time the system starts, you cannot usefully edit hardware settings.

You can use Windows NT Diagnostics to view hardware data in an easy-to-read format. Based on this information, you can discover conflicts and their causes or determine how to set up new hardware before installing it. You can also get information about conflicts by looking at the System event log in the Event Viewer.

This section presents some suggestions for solving hardware and related driver problems by using Registry Editor.

To carry out some procedures described in this section, you need to follow the instructions for saving keys in "Saving and Restoring Keys" in Chapter 24, "Registry Editors and Registry Administration."

Recovering from an Unsuitable Video Display Choice

You can use the Windows NT Setup Display option in Control Panel to change the type of video driver, the color depth, or the resolution for a display adapter. If you make an unsuitable setting, one of the following two events occurs:

- The driver fails to recognize the card and, therefore, fails to load at system startup. By default, the system tries to load VGA in base mode as a kind of reserve. So, if your video setting fails, the computer starts in VGA and screen resolution is poor. However, you can use the Display option in Control Panel to try another setting. (This happens only on an Intel-based computer.)
- The driver recognizes the card and proceeds as though the parameters selected are acceptable. Because they are not acceptable (for example, you tried to use 1280x1024 resolution on a monitor that is only capable of 1024x768), you cannot see anything on your screen, although the system starts with no apparent trouble. (This always happens on a RISC-based computer when an inappropriate option is selected, but it can also occur on an Intel-based computer.)

If you cannot see anything on the screen after changing the display settings, do not attempt to log on. Instead, wait for the disk activity to stop, then use the power switch to restart the computer. When you restart, choose the VGA Mode version of Windows NT. If this does not work, follow the instructions in "Starting a System with Configuration Problems," earlier in this chapter. Then you can use the Display option in Control Panel to try another selection.

Changing Driver Loading Controls in the Registry

Under most circumstances, you should define the startup behavior of a device or a service by using the Devices option or the Services option in Control Panel, or by using Server Manager under Windows NT Server. Use these methods in specific cases where you cannot define behavior by using the other administrative tools.

You can change the basic value entries in the Registry to control driver loading for a specific driver. For example, you can change:

- At what point the driver is loaded or the service is started, including turning off driver loading during startup.
- The load order for a driver, a service, or a group during system startup.
- Error control for a driver or service, so that startup continues or halts depending on whether the item is initialized.
- Parameters that can be set for a driver or service.

▶ **To change the behavior of a driver or service**

1. Select the subkey for the driver or service in the following Registry path:

   HKEY_LOCAL_MACHINE\System
   \CurrentControlSet
   \Services
   DriverName

2. If you want to change how system startup proceeds if the driver is not loaded or the service is not started, change the value of **ErrorControl** as follows:

Value	Meaning
0x3	Critical. Fail the attempted system startup.
0x2	Severe. Switch to LastKnownGood or, if already using LastKnownGood, continue in case of error.
0x1	Normal. Continue startup if the driver fails to load, but display a message noting the failure.
0x0	Ignore.

3. If you want to change the dependencies for loading the service, specify new values for the **DependOnGroup, DependOnService**, or **Tag** value entry.

4. If you want to change when the service is started or the driver is loaded, change the **Start** value as follows:

Value	Start type	Meaning
0x0	Boot	Loaded by the Boot Loader.
0x1	System	Loaded at Kernel initialization.
0x2	Auto load	Loaded or started automatically at startup.
0x3	Load on demand	Available, but started only by the user.
0x4	Disabled	Do not start.

5. To put these values into effect, close Registry Editor, then shut down and restart the computer.

For details about **Start** and **ErrorControl** values, see their definitions in Regentry.hlp, the Registry Help file on the *Windows NT Workstation Resource Kit* CD.

Controlling Multiport Serial I/O Cards

The Microsoft serial driver can be used to control many *dumb* multiport serial cards. *Dumb* indicates that the control includes no on-board processor. Each port of a multiport board has a separate subkey under the CurrentControlSet\Services\Serial subkey in the Registry. In each of these subkeys, you must add values for **DosDevices**, **Interrupt**, **InterruptStatus**, **PortAddress**, and **PortIndex** because these are not detected by the Hardware Recognizer. (For descriptions and ranges for these values, see Regentry.hlp, the Registry help file on the *Windows NT Workstation Resource Kit* CD.

For example, if you have a four-port COMTROL Hostess 550 board configured to use address 0x500 with an interrupt of 0x2, the values in the Registry are:

Serial2 subkey:

```
PortAddress = REG_DWORD 0x500
Interrupt = REG_DWORD 2
DosDevices = REG_SZ COM3
InterruptStatus = REG_DWORD 0x507
PortIndex = REG_DWORD 1
```

Serial3 subkey:

```
PortAddress = REG_DWORD 0x508
Interrupt = REG_DWORD 2
DosDevices = REG_SZ COM4
InterruptStatus = REG_DWORD 0x507
PortIndex = REG_DWORD 2
```

Serial4 subkey:

```
PortAddress = REG_DWORD 0x510
Interrupt = REG_DWORD 2
DosDevices = REG_SZ COM5
InterruptStatus = REG_DWORD 0x507
PortIndex = REG_DWORD 3
```

Serial5 subkey:

```
PortAddress = REG_DWORD 0x518
Interrupt = REG_DWORD 2
DosDevices = REG_SZ COM6
InterruptStatus = REG_DWORD 0x507
PortIndex = REG_DWORD 4
```

Certain multiport boards, such as Digiboard non-MCA bus cards, use a different scheme to determine which port is interrupting. These boards should include the **Indexed** value entry in the configuration data for each port under its subkey in CurrentControlSet\Services\Serial. This entry indicates that the board uses an indexed interrupt notification scheme as opposed to a bitmapped method.

For example, if you have an eight-port Digiboard communications board configured to be at address 0x100 with an interrupt of 0x3, the values in the Registry are:

Serial2 subkey:

```
PortAddress = REG_DWORD 0x100
Interrupt = REG_DWORD 3
DosDevices = REG_SZ COM3
InterruptStatus = REG_DWORD 0x140
Indexed = REG_DWORD 1
PortIndex = REG_DWORD 1
```

Serial3 subkey:

```
PortAddress = REG_DWORD 0x108
Interrupt = REG_DWORD 3
DosDevices = REG_SZ COM4
InterruptStatus = REG_DWORD 0x140
Indexed = REG_DWORD 1
PortIndex = REG_DWORD 2
```

Serial4 subkey:

```
PortAddress = REG_DWORD 0x110
Interrupt = REG_DWORD 3
DosDevices = REG_SZ COM5
InterruptStatus = REG_DWORD 0x140
Indexed = REG_DWORD 1
PortIndex = REG_DWORD 3
```

Serial5 subkey:

```
PortAddress = REG_DWORD 0x118
Interrupt = REG_DWORD 3
DosDevices = REG_SZ COM6
InterruptStatus = REG_DWORD 0x140
Indexed = REG_DWORD 1
PortIndex = REG_DWORD 4
```

Serial6 subkey:

```
PortAddress = REG_DWORD 0x120
Interrupt = REG_DWORD 3
DosDevices = REG_SZ COM7
InterruptStatus = REG_DWORD 0x140
Indexed = REG_DWORD 1
PortIndex = REG_DWORD 5
```

Serial7 subkey:

```
PortAddress = REG_DWORD 0x128
Interrupt = REG_DWORD 3
DosDevices = REG_SZ COM8
InterruptStatus = REG_DWORD 0x140
Indexed = REG_DWORD 1
PortIndex = REG_DWORD 6
```

Serial8 subkey:

```
PortAddress = REG_DWORD 0x130
Interrupt = REG_DWORD 3
DosDevices = REG_SZ COM9
InterruptStatus = REG_DWORD 0x140
Indexed = REG_DWORD 1
PortIndex = REG_DWORD 7
```

Serial9 subkey:

```
PortAddress = REG_DWORD 0x138
Interrupt = REG_DWORD 3
DosDevices = REG_SZ COM10
InterruptStatus = REG_DWORD 0x140
Indexed = REG_DWORD 1
PortIndex = REG_DWORD 8
```

Deleting Serial Ports

You can configure communication ports as described in the previous section. You might also need to delete one or more COM ports. Communication ports should be deleted by using the Ports option in Control Panel.

▶ **To delete a COM port by using Control Panel**

- In Control Panel, double-click Ports. In the **Ports** dialog box, select the port you want to delete, then click **Delete**.

Sometimes, if you use Control Panel to delete a COM port that was created manually, the process leaves unwanted data in the Registry. If the deleted COM port is generating error events in the Event Log, you can remove the port directly from the Registry.

▶ **To delete a COM port by using a Registry editor**

1. In a Registry editor, locate the *Serialxxxxx* subkey for the port in the following Registry path:

   HKEY_LOCAL_MACHINE\System
     \CurrentControlSet
       \Services
         \Serial
           \Parameters

Tip To identify the *Serialxxxxx* subkey for the COM port, double-click the **DosDevices** value entry for a *Serialxxxxx* subkey. The value entry identifies the port by number, such as COM3.

---

2. Delete the *Serialxxxxx* subkey for the COM port. In **Regedt32** or **Regedit**, from the **Edit** menu, click **Delete**.

If the communication port is active and detected by the Hardware Recognizer, the port reappears in the Control Panel **Ports** list when the system is restarted. If you do not want a built-in serial port to be active in Windows NT, you must disable the hardware by using a tool such as the computer's CMOS setup program.

CHAPTER 26

Initialization Files and the Registry

Although the Registry replaces the initialization (.ini) files used in versions of Microsoft Windows created for MS-DOS, some .ini files still appear in the Windows NT system directory. Also, applications created for 16-bit Microsoft Windows must still be able to read and write .ini values that previously were stored in the Win.ini or System.ini file.

This chapter describes how .ini files and other configuration files are used under Windows NT and how these values are stored in the Registry. The following topics are discussed in this chapter:

- How Windows NT uses MS-DOS configuration files
- How .ini files are mapped to the Registry
- Microsoft OS/2 version 1.*x* entries in the Registry
- POSIX entries in the Registry

Related topics are discussed in documentation forWindows NT version 4.0:

- For details about the Shared32.ini file, see Appendix A of the Windows NT Server *Concepts and Planning*.
- For details about Registry entries for Microsoft Mail and Microsoft Schedule+ initialization values, see Regentry.hlp, the Registry Help file in the *Windows NT Workstation Resource Kit* CD.

How Windows NT Uses MS-DOS Configuration Files

During system startup, Windows NT adds any Path, Prompt, and Set commands from the C:\Autoexec.bat file to the Windows NT environment variables and then ignores the rest of the contents of C:\Autoexec.bat and C:\Config.sys. If these files are not present when you install Windows NT, the Setup program creates them. Setup also creates default Autoexec.nt and Config.nt files.

The path and other Windows NT environment information are stored under the following Registry key:

HKEY_LOCAL_MACHINE\System
\CurrentControlSet
\Control
\Session Manager
\Environment

When an MS-DOS-based application is started, Windows NT executes files specified in the application's program information file (PIF) or the Autoexec.nt and Config.nt files in the *Systemroot*\System32 directory. Any changes made in one of these files take effect as soon as the file is saved and a new MS-DOS-based application is started that uses that file. You do not need to restart your system after changing the .nt files. Windows NT uses these files as follows:

Files	Use in Windows NT
C:\Autoexec.bat	Path and environment variables are added to the Windows NT environment at system startup.
C:\Config.sys	Not used by Windows NT.
Autoexec.nt and Config.nt in *Systemroot*\System32	Used every time an MS-DOS-based application is run with _Default.pif. (Custom .nt files can be created and used when starting an application from another PIF.)

You can use any text editor to view the contents of the Autoexec.nt and Config.nt files.

Commands in the Autoexec.bat and Config.sys files for starting applications and initializing drivers are ignored in Windows NT.

- To run an application automatically when you start Windows NT, use the **Taskbar** option on the **Start** menu to place a shortcut to the application in the Taskbar Startup group. For more information, see *Windows NT Start Here.*
- To run a service or driver automatically, use the Services option in Control Panel: In Control Panel, double-click **Services**. Select a service from the list, then click the **Startup** button. In the **Startup type** field of the **Service** dialog box, click **Automatic**, then click **OK**. This setting is saved as the **Start** value in the service's subkey under HKEY_LOCAL_MACHINE\System\CurrentControlSet\Services in the Registry.

Windows NT Virtual MS-DOS Machines

In Windows NT, each MS-DOS-based application and 16-bit Windows-based applications run in a Windows NT virtual MS-DOS machine (NTVDM), a single-threaded process that supports 16-bit applications in a 32-bit environment. Windows NT includes the necessary virtual device drivers (VDDs) for the mouse, keyboard, printer, COM ports, and network support. The VDDs are loaded into every VDM based on values stored in the Registry. Information about VDDs is found in the following Registry path:

```
HKEY_LOCAL_MACHINE\System
  \CurrentControlSet
    \Control
      \VirtualDeviceDrivers
```

The system manages any changes to the VDD entries automatically when you add a device driver by using Windows NT Setup.

Windows for MS-DOS on Windows NT

In Windows NT, each application written for MS-DOS runs in its own NTVDM process.

Windows NT runs the application by using a NTVDM and VDDs. This process is called WOW, for Win16-on-Win32. Using a 16-bit NTVDM, Windows NT translates Windows 3.1–based application calls in Enhanced mode on all Intel-based and RISC-based computers.

Control parameters for WOW startup and for the WOW application environment are found under the following Registry path:

```
HKEY_LOCAL_MACHINE\System
  \CurrentControlSet
    \Control
      \WOW
```

The system maintains the settings in this key automatically. They should not require manual changes.

The environment settings equivalent to the System.ini file for Windows 3.*x* are found in this Registry path:

```
HKEY_LOCAL_MACHINE\Software
  \Microsoft
    \Windows NT
      \CurrentVersion
        \WOW
```

The WOW subkeys have the same names as headings in the System.ini file, and the values are the same as items contained in the old System.ini file. For details about these entries, see the online Help for the Registry.

How .ini Files Are Mapped to the Registry

If you install Windows NT as an upgrade to Windows 3.*x*, all of the settings in the initialization files are copied into the Registry, including settings in Control.ini, Progman.ini, System.ini, Win.ini, and Winfile.ini. You can see where the Windows initialization files are mapped in the Registry by viewing the subkeys and value entries under this path:

HKEY_LOCAL_MACHINE\Software
  \Microsoft
    \Windows NT
      \CurrentVersion
        \IniFileMapping

When you install an application created for 16-bit Windows, the application's setup program creates its own .ini file or creates entries for the Win.ini or System.ini file in the same way that it does for any version of Windows 3.*x*. These entries are not updated in the Registry because these applications do not have a way to access the Windows NT Registry. For this reason, basic System.ini, Win.ini, and Winfile.ini files appear in the *Systemroot* directory in Windows NT.

If a Windows-based application tries to write to Win.ini, System.ini, or any other section listed in the IniFileMapping key, and if the application uses the Windows NT Registry APIs, the information is stored in the Registry. If the application writes to other sections of the .ini file or tries to open the .ini file directly without using the Windows NT Registry APIs, the information is saved in an .ini file.

To find mapping information in the HKEY_LOCAL_MACHINE\Software key, the system searches for the filename extension of the initialization file. If it finds the filename extension, it looks under the mapped key for the name of the application associated with that file type and a variable name. If necessary, it continues to look for keys whose value entries are the variable names. If no mapping for either the application name or filename is found, the system looks for an .ini file to read and write its contents.

Tables 26.1 through 26.3 show where system settings are saved in the Registry in comparison to initialization files used with Windows 3.1 for MS-DOS.

In the entries in the IniFileMapping key and in Tables 26.1 through 26.3, the following symbols are used:

Symbol	Description
!	Forces all writes to go to both the Registry and to the .ini file on disk.
#	Causes the Registry value to be set to the value in the Windows 3.1 .ini file whenever a new user logs on for the first time after Setup, if Windows NT was installed on a computer that had Windows 3.1 already installed.
@	Prevents any reads from going to the .ini file on disk if the requested data is not found in the Registry.
USR	Stands for HKEY_CURRENT_USER, and the text after the prefix is relative to that subtree.
SYS	Stands for HKEY_LOCAL_MACHINE\Software, and the text after the prefix is relative to that key.

Win.ini Settings in the Registry

The information stored in the keys described in Table 26.1 is used by applications that expect to find this information in a Win.ini file.

Table 26.1 Registry Paths for Win.ini Sections

Win.ini section	Registry path	Description
[colors]	#USR\Control Panel\Colors[1]	Defines colors for the Windows display as set by using the Display option in Control Panel.
[compatibility]	#SYS...\Compatibility[3]	—
[desktop]	#USR\Control Panel\Desktop[1]	Specifies appearance of the desktop as set by using the Desktop option in Control Panel.
[embedding]	#SYS...\Embedding[3]	Lists the server objects used in OLE; created during software setup.
[extensions]	#USR...\Extensions[2]	Associates types of files with applications as set by using **Options** on the **View** menu of Windows NT Explorer.
[fonts] and **[fontSubstitutes]**	#SYS...\Fonts and \FontSubstitutes[3]	Describes the screen font files loaded by Windows as set by using the Fonts option in Control Panel.
[intl]	#USR\Control Panel\International[1]	Describes items for languages and locales as set by using the Regional Settings option in Control Panel.
[mci extensions]	SYS...\MCI Extensions[3]	Associates file types with Media Control Interface devices as set by using the Drivers option in Control Panel.

Table 26.1 Registry Paths for Win.ini Sections *(continued)*

Win.ini section	Registry path	Description
[network]	USR...\Network\Persistent Connections[2]; network printers in HKEY_LOCAL_MACHINE \System\Control\Print	Describes network printer port settings as set by using the Printers option in Control Panel and the persistent network connections as set by using Windows NT Explorer.
[ports]	SYS...\Ports[3]	Lists all available printer and communications ports as set by using the Ports option in Control Panel.
[printerPorts] and **[devices]**	SYS...\PrinterPorts and \Devices[3]	Lists active and inactive output devices to be accessed by Windows as set by using the Printers option in Control Panel.
[sounds]	#USR \Control Panel\Sounds[1]	Lists the sound files assigned to each system event as set by using the Sound option in Control Panel.
[TrueType]	#USR...\TrueType[2]	Describes options for using TrueType fonts as set using the Fonts option in Control Panel.
[Windows Help]	USR\Software \Microsoft\Windows Help[1]	Lists settings for the Help window as set by using the mouse or menus in any Help window.
[Winlogon]	#SYS...\Winlogon[3]	Specifies the Windows environment and user startup options as set by using the Desktop, Keyboard, and Mouse options in Control Panel.

1 Full path = HKEY_CURRENT_USER

2 Full path = HKEY_CURRENT_USER\Software\Microsoft\Windows NT\CurrentVersion

3 Full path = HKEY_LOCAL_MACHINE\Software\Microsoft\Windows NT\CurrentVersion

System.ini Settings in the Registry

Entries from a System.ini file in 16-bit Windows 3.*x* on the computer when you install Windows NT are preserved as entries under this key:

HKEY_LOCAL_MACHINE\Software
  \Microsoft\Windows NT
    \CurrentVersion
      \WOW

Table 26.2 describes where you can view or edit entries for similar purposes in Windows NT. These entries are used by applications that look for values in the System.ini file.

Table 26.2 Registry Paths for System.ini Sections

System.ini section	Registry path	Description
[boot] and **[boot.description]**	#SYS...\WOW\Boot and \Boot.description[3]; replaced by ...CurrentControlSet\Control	Lists drivers and Windows modules as set by using the System option in Control Panel.
[drivers]	Replaced by #SYS...\Drivers32[3]	Contains a list of aliases (or names) assigned to installable driver files as set by using the Drivers and Devices options in Control Panel.
[keyboard]	#SYS...\WOW\Keyboard[3]; #USR\Keyboard Layout[1]	Contains information about the keyboard as set by using the Regional Settings option in Control Panel or as dentified by the Hardware Recognizer.
[mci] and **[mci32]**	Replaced by #SYS...\MCI and \MCI32[3] and #SYS...\Drivers.desc[3]	Lists Media Control Interface (MCI) drivers as set by using the Drivers option in Control Panel.
[**NonWindows App**]	#SYS...\WOW\NonWindowsApp[3]	Contains information used by non-Windows–based applications as defined in PIFs for specific applications or in Config.nt.
[standard]	Standard in #SYS...\WOW[3]	Contains information used by 16-bit Windows 3.*x* in Standard and 386 enhanced mode. All memory management is handled automatically by Windows NT.

1 Full path = HKEY_CURRENT_USER

2 Full path = HKEY_CURRENT_USER\Software\Microsoft\Windows NT\CurrentVersion

3 Full path = HKEY_LOCAL_MACHINE\Software \Microsoft\Windows NT\CurrentVersion

Other Initialization File Settings in the Registry

Table 26.3 describes where you can view or edit Registry entries equivalent to Control.ini, Progman.ini, and Winfile.ini entries.

Table 26.3 Registry Paths for Other Initialization Files

.Ini file section	Registry path	Description
Control.ini **[Current]**, **[Color Schemes]**, **[Custom Colors]**	Color Schemes, Current, and Custom Colors subkeys in #USR \Control Panel[1]	Describes color schemes and custom colors as set by using the Colors option in Control Panel.
Control.ini **[Patterns]** and **[Screen Saver*]**	Patterns and Screen Saver.*x* subkeys in #USR\Control Panel[1]	Describes elements of desktop appearance and behavior as set by using the Desktop option in Control Panel.
Control.ini **[MMCPL]**, **[Drivers.Desc]**, **[Userinstallable.drivers]**	#USR\Control Panel\MMCPL[1]; #SYS...\Drivers.Desc and \Userinstallable.drivers[3]	Contains values for installable drivers and devices used for multimedia as set by using the Drivers option in Control Panel.
Progman.ini **[groups]**, **[restrictions]**, **[settings]**	Groups, Restrictions, and Settings subkeys in #USR...\Program Manager[2]	Describes window appearance, groups and the icons in the groups, and restrictions on Taskbar operations. Restrictions are set in User Manager for Domains.
Msmail32.ini	USR...\Mail[4]	Contains parameters that can be set for Microsoft Mail.
Schdpl32.ini	#USR...\Schedule+[5]	Contains parameters that can be set for Schedule+.
Winfile.ini **[settings]**	#USR...\File Manager[2]	Describes the appearance and behavior of items in File Manager as set by using the Windows NT Explorer.

[1] Full path = HKEY_CURRENT_USER

[2] Full path = HKEY_CURRENT_USER\Software\Microsoft\Windows NT\CurrentVersion

[3] Full path = HKEY_LOCAL_MACHINE\Software\Microsoft\Windows NT\CurrentVersion

[4] Full path = HKEY_LOCAL_MACHINE\Software\Microsoft\Microsoft Mail

[5] Full path = HKEY_LOCAL_MACHINE\Software\Microsoft\Schedule+

Microsoft OS/2 Version 1.*x* Entries in the Registry

The Microsoft OS/2 version 1.*x* subsystem starts whenever a user starts an OS/2 character-based application on an Intel-based computer. The Registry entries for the OS/2 subsystem are found under this key:

HKEY_LOCAL_MACHINE\System
  \CurrentControlSet
    \Control
      \Session Manager
        \SubSystems

The **OS2** entry in this subkey describes the path to the executable file used to start the OS/2 subsystem. The directory path for the OS/2 library is the **Os2LibPath** value defined under the Session Manager\Environment subkey.

When Windows NT is installed on a computer, if Setup finds a copy of Config.sys for OS/2, a copy is placed in the *Systemroot*\System32 directory. This information is used to configure the OS/2 subsystem whenever an OS/2 application is started. If a Config.sys file is not found, a substitute is created in the Registry, with the following values:

```
PROTSHELL=C:\os2\pmshell.exe c:\os2\os2.ini c:\os2\os2sys.ini
    %Systemroot%\system32\cmd.exe
SET COMSPEC=%Systemroot%\system32\cmd.exe
```

The OS/2 Config.sys information is stored in the following Registry entry:

HKEY_LOCAL_MACHINE\Software
  \Microsoft
    \OS/2 Subsystem for NT
      \Config.sys

The other subkeys under the OS/2 Subsystem key do not contain entries.

If you subsequently edit the C:\Config.sys file by using a text editor, the LIBPTH=, SET PATH=, and SET WINDIR= entries are appended to the end of the file from the Windows NT environment. Any changes made to the path or environment variables take effect after the system is shut down and restarted.

For details about managing this environment under Windows NT, see Appendix B, "Other Application Environments," in Windows NT Server *Concepts and Planning*.

You can disable an OS/2 subsystem in Windows NT and still run a bound application under a VDM. Many bound applications run better under a VDM than under the OS/2 subsystem.

▶ **To disable the OS/2 subsystem in Windows NT**

- In Registry Editor, change the value of **GlobalFlag** to 20100000 in the following Registry path:

  HKEY_LOCAL_MACHINE\System
    \CurrentControlSet
      \Control
        \SessionManager

You can also use **Forcedos.exe**, a utility supplied with Windows NT in the *Systemroot*\System32 subdirectory. This enables you to run a bound application under a VDM. To see how to use the **Forcedos** utility, type **forcedos /?** at the command prompt.

POSIX Entries in the Registry

The POSIX subsystem starts whenever a user starts a POSIX application. The Registry entries for the POSIX subsystem are found under this key:

HKEY_LOCAL_MACHINE\System
  \CurrentControlSet
    \Control
      \Session Manager
        \SubSystems

The **Posix** entry in this subkey describes the path to the executable file used to start the POSIX subsystem. The POSIX subsystem does not have any parameters or environmental variables that the user can set.

PART VI

Compatibility

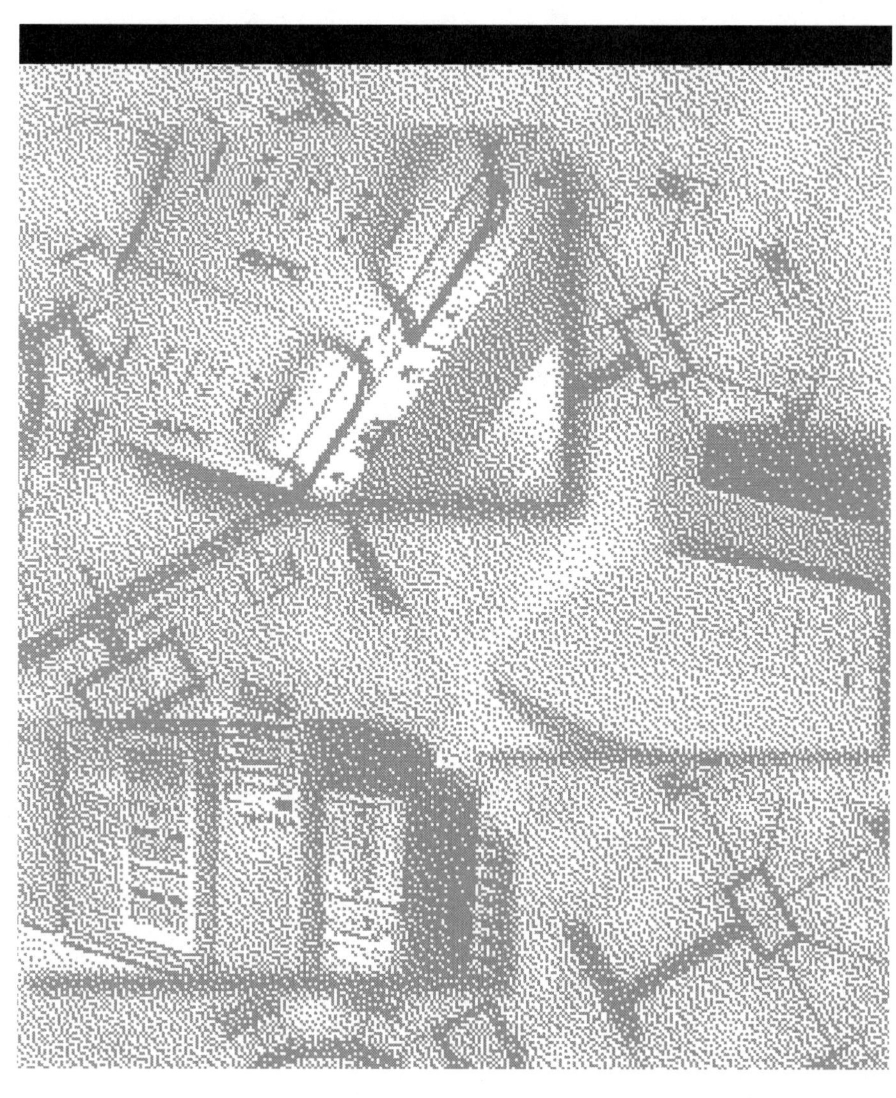

CHAPTER 27

Windows Compatibility and Migration

This chapter begins with a discussion of interoperating with Windows 3.*x*, and it describes what does and does not get migrated upon upgrading to Windows NT Workstation 4.0. After this comes a discussion of the compatibility of the 16-bit Windows subsystem with Windows 3.*x* applications and the restrictions on applications running under it. This chapter also explains in detail how the 16-bit Windows subsystem is implemented.

Next, the chapter describes compatibility with Windows NT 3.51.

Finally, this chapter presents a discussion of upgrading Windows 95 to Windows NT Workstation 4.0. Also included is an explanation of issues of compatibility, reliability, and security within a mixed operating system environment that includes Windows NT and Windows 95.

Compatibility with Windows 3.*x*

Windows NT provides a straightforward upgrade from any Windows 3.*x* operating system. The 16-bit Windows subsystem includes a layer that emulates MS-DOS, and a Win16-on-Win32 (WOW) layer that emulates the functionality of Windows 3.1 and 16-bit API stubs. Win16 applications can run in their own or in a shared memory space.

Interoperating with Windows 3.*x*

If a previous version of Windows (Windows 3.*x*, Windows for Workgroups) is installed on your computer, and you want to run your installed applications from both the previous version of Windows and from Windows NT, then install Windows NT in the same directory as the previous version of Windows. This allows Windows NT to configure the Windows environment based on the existing environment and allows Windows NT to support the features of currently installed applications.

Note For information about interoperating with Windows 95, see "Compatibility with Windows 95" later in this chapter.

When the first logon occurs on the newly-installed Windows NT computer, the system migrates Reg.dat and portions of the various .ini files from the previous version of Windows to the Registry in Windows NT. See the following section "What is Migrated at the First Logon" for a complete list. The status of each step in the migration is recorded in the Application Log, which can be viewed with Event Viewer. For more information about Event Viewer, see Chapter 9,"Monitoring Events," of *Microsoft Windows NT Server Concepts and Planning*

The first time new users log in, Windows NT presents a dialog box that lets them select the parts of the previous version of Windows to migrate into the Windows NT environment. The users can select whether to migrate the .ini files and/or the Program Manager .grp files to the Registry. If the users cancel the dialog box and would later like to migrate the files, they must delete the following keys from the Registry and then log off and log back into Windows NT:

```
HKEY_CURRENT_USER\Windows 3.1 Migration Status

HKEY_LOCAL_MACHINE\SOFTWARE\Windows 3.1 Migration Status
```

Refer to Part 5, "Windows NT Registry," for information on the Registry and its entries.

Note The per-user dialog box and migration option do not happen for the Administrator, Guest, and System user accounts.

If users choose to migrate the .ini files, then each time they log into Windows NT, the system reads the Win.ini file and the System.ini file and stores the information in the Registry. When the user logs off from Windows NT, the system updates the Win.ini file and the System.ini file with any changes made to the environment. This keeps the configuration of Windows NT and the previous version of Windows synchronized with each other.

If Windows NT is not installed in the same directory as the previous version of Windows, then configuration changes made under one version of Windows are not available to the other version. The same is true if you install Windows 3.*x* after installing Windows NT.

If you install an application under Windows 3.*x* after installing Windows NT, that application would not be available in Windows NT. You can reinstall the application under Windows NT (into the same directory into which it is installed under Windows3.*x*). Or, you can delete the two Windows 3.1 Migration Status registry keys mentioned earlier in this section, and then remigrate the settings by logging on again.

Regardless of where Windows NT is installed, changes made to the Desktop or to the arrangement of the Program Groups are not synchronized with the previous version of Windows.

Note Setup installs TrueType font and font header files in *%SystemRoot%*SYSTEM\FONTS. Be careful not to delete the TrueType files from this directory. These files are used by Windows NT 32-bit applications as well as 16-bit applications. For more information on the TrueType font and font header files included with Windows NT, refer to Chapter 8, "Fonts."

What Is Migrated at the First Logon

The following items are migrated to the Registry when the first logon occurs on a newly-installed Windows NT computer:

- All OLE information kept in the Windows 3.*x* registry (Reg.dat)
- The following sections and variables from the Win.ini file and stored in HKEY_CLASSES_ROOT:

  [Compatibility]

  [Embedding] (except SoundRec, Package, and PBrush)

  [Fonts]

  [FontSubstitutes]

  [Windows]
  DeviceNotSelectedTimeout
  Spooler
  TransmissionRetryTimeout

When Each User First Logs On

The following sections describe what is and what is not migrated when each user first logs on.

What Is Migrated

The following items are migrated the first time new users log in, if they select to migrate the .ini files and the .grp files. This per-user migration does not happen for the usernames Administrator, Guest, and System.

- The following sections and variables from the Win.ini file:

  [Windows]

  CursorBlinkRate

  BorderWidth

  ScreenSaveTimeOut

  ScreenSaveActive

  KeyboardSpeed

  KeyboardDelay

  Beep

  SwapMouseButtons

  DoubleClickSpeed

  DoubleClickHeight

  DoubleClickWidth

  MouseThreshold1

  MouseThreshold2

  MouseSpeed

  SnapToDefaultButton

  Spooler

  DeviceNotSelectedTimeout

  TransmissionRetryTimeout

- The following sections from the Control.ini file:

  [Color Schemes]

  [Current]

  [Custom Colors]

  [Patterns]

  [Screen Saver.Marquee]

  [Screen Saver.Mystify]

  [Screen Saver.Stars]

- The following section from the Winfile.ini file:

  [Settings]

- The entire Viewer.ini file.
- The entire Ntbackup.ini file.
- The entire Clock.ini file.
- The entire Schdpl32.ini file.
- The following section from the System.ini file:

  [Drivers]

What Is Not Migrated

- Persistent shares and users from Windows for Workgroups.
- Default domain and user ID from Windows for Workgroups or the Lanman.ini file.
- Per-user profiles maintained by the WINLOGIN add-on product for Windows for Workgroups.
- Any changes that users have made to their Accessories, Games, Main, and Startup groups in Windows 3.*x*. These groups are not migrated because their names match the names of 32-bit Windows NT Start menu groups.
- MS-DOS drive letters. If you have FAT partitions and HPFS or NTFS partitions on a computer that dual-boots MS-DOS and Windows NT, use Disk Administrator to assign drive letters to your non-FAT partitions. Begin with the first drive letter after the one that MS-DOS assigns to your last FAT partition. This ensures that the FAT partition drive letters are the same for both systems and that any migrated path names are valid.
- The options **Auto Arrange**, **Minimize on Run**, and **Save Settings on Exit** from the Progman.ini file.
- Font information for character-mode command windows.

- The Language and Keyboard settings in the International applications.
- The default screen saver (Scrnsave.exe) in the **[BOOT]** section of the System.ini file. 16-bit screen savers are ill-behaved under Windows NT.
- The **[Settings]** section from the Winfile.ini file.
- All 16-bit Windows 3.*x* Program Manager group files listed in the Progman.ini file. If a group name (contained in the group file, not the actual .grp filename) matches the name of a 32-bit Windows NT Personal or Common Start menu group, then that 16-bit group will not be migrated (for example, Accessories, Games, Main, and Startup). Each group is migrated "as is."
- The Country setting in the international applications.

Running Win16 Applications

The 16-bit Windows subsystem runs 16-bit Windows-based applications, which you can launch from My Computer, Windows NT Explorer, or from the command prompt. There are no user-visible distinctions between 16-bit and 32-bit Windows-based applications.

Restrictions on Win16 Applications

This section describes the few restrictions that apply to running applications under the 16-bit Windows subsystem:

- All MS-DOS functions except task-switching APIs (application programming interface functions) are supported.
- Block mode device drivers are not supported. (Block devices are not supported, so MS-DOS IOCTL APIs that deal with block devices and SETDPB functions are not supported.)
- Interrupt 10 function 1A returns 0; all other functions are passed to read-only memory (ROM).
- Interrupt 13 calls that deal with prohibited disk access are not supported.
- Interrupt 18 (ROM BASIC) generates a message that says ROM BASIC is not supported.
- Interrupt 19 will not reboot the computer, but will cleanly terminate the current virtual DOS machine (VDM).

- Interrupt 2F dealing with the DOSKEY program call outs (AX = 4800) is not supported.
- Microsoft CD-ROM Extensions (MSCDEX) functions 2, 3, 4, 5, 8, E, and F are not supported.
- The 16-bit Windows subsystem on an *x*86 computer supports Enhanced mode applications; it does not, however, support 16-bit VXDs (virtual device drivers). The subsystem on a non-*x*86 computer emulates the Intel 40486 instruction set, which lets the computer run Enhanced mode applications, such as Visual Basic®, on RISC computers.

Terminating the Subsystem

If an ill-behaved application locks up the 16-bit Windows subsystem, you can terminate the subsystem.

► **To terminate the 16-bit Windows subsystem**

1. Press CTRL+SHIFT+ESC to display Task Manager.
2. Click the **Applications** tab.
3. Click to select the application.
4. Click **End Task**.

If the application does not respond, an additional dialog box appears giving you the option to wait or to end the task.

Implementation of the Subsystem

The following sections describe the 16-bit Windows subsystem.

VDM Structure

The 16-bit Windows subsystem is implemented as a virtual MS-DOS machine (VDM) with a layer that emulates Windows 3.1 functionality. By default, 16-bit Windows-based applications run in a single VDM, a multithreaded Win32 process in which each application runs in its own thread. Windows NT preemptively multitasks the VDM with respect to other processes but cooperatively multitasks the Win16 apps with respect to each other.

Each Win16 and MS-DOS application can, however, run in its own private address space, thus protecting it from other Win16 programs. This allows Windows NT to preemptively multitask all operating system services and all applications.

▶ **To run each Win16 application in its own VDM**

1. Right-click the **Start** button.
2. Click Open.
3. Locate the Win16 application, and click to select it.
4. Click **Properties** on the **File** menu.
5. Click the **Shortcut** tab.
6. Select the **Run In Separate Memory Space** check box.
7. Click **OK**.

The following diagram shows the 16-bit Windows subsystem VDM. A description of each layer follows.

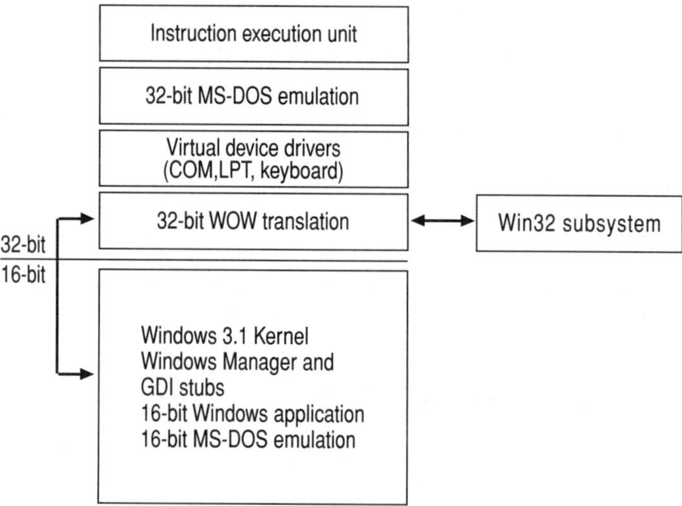

Figure 27.1 16-bit Windows Subsystem VDM

The 16-bit MS-DOS emulation layer contains all the information to emulate BIOS calls and tables. Some 16-bit Windows applications depend upon BIOS calls, because 16-bit Windows is built on top of MS-DOS.

The Windows 3.1 emulation layer provides the functionality of the Windows 3.1 kernel and 16-bit API stubs. A 16-bit application cannot call a 32-bit API routine. When an application calls a 16-bit API routine, that call is made to a stub routine, which in turn calls a 32-bit API routine. The 32-bit API routine performs the required action, and the result is transformed back into the format expected by the 16-bit API stub, which returns the result to the application. The transformation between 16-bit and 32-bit formats is known as *thunking* and is carried out by the 32-bit WOW translation layer. (WOW stands for Win16-on-Win32.)

16-bit Windows–based applications use the memory from 640K to 16 MB for their own purposes.

Windows NT does not support 16-bit device drivers that have unrestricted access to hardware (character-mode device drivers that do not depend on special hardware are supported). A secure and robust multitasking operating system cannot let user-level applications talk directly with the hardware because they could completely bypass security and crash the system. (There are exceptions to this, however; refer to "Restrictions on Win16 Applications," earlier in this chapter). The VDM contains a layer of virtual device drivers (VXDs) that allow the sharing of hardware and provide the necessary functionality in a way that is consistent with the design of Windows NT.

The 32-bit MS-DOS emulation layer is for the DOS Protect Mode Interface (DPMI) and 32-bit memory access. This layer replaces calls made to the MS-DOS-level functions for extended and expanded memory with Windows NT memory calls. Windows NT then makes the appropriate conversions so that the 16-bit application sees segmented memory as it normally would.

For Windows NT running on a non-*x*86 computer, the Instruction Execution Unit emulates the Intel 80486 instruction set, which lets the computer run the binary application.

On an *x*86 computer, the Instruction Execution Unit acts as a trap handler, capturing instructions that cause hardware traps and transferring control to the code that handles them. A VDM (such as the 16-bit Windows subsystem) on an *x*86 computer supports Enhanced mode applications; it does not, however, support 16-bit VXDs (virtual device drivers).

Input Queue

Under Windows NT, each application has its own input queue. This eliminates lockups due to programs halting the queue. Under Windows 3.*x*, all applications receive input from the same queue. As in Windows 3.*x*, the 16-bit Windows-based subsystem provides just one input queue. A 16-bit Windows application can lock up the subsystem by halting the queue. This does not affect any 32-bit applications running under Windows NT, as they each have their own input queue.

If, however, you run each Win16 application in its own VDM, each application is then treated by Windows NT as a Win32 application, and each has its own input queue.

Scheduling

Within a VDM, threads are scheduled cooperatively. Because Win16 applications running in a single VDM share memory, a single input queue, and are scheduled cooperatively, an ill-behaved application can cause the subsystem to lock up. This will not affect the rest of Windows NT, because Windows NT treats the VDM as a whole just like any other 32-bit application. Each VDM is scheduled preemptively along with all of the other 32-bit applications. Running each Win16 application in its own private address space causes it to be preemptively multitasked.

Files Used

The following are the principal files used by the 16-bit Windows subsystem:

File	Purpose
Ntvdm.exe	The main loader for a VDM.
Wowexec.exe	Provides the Windows 3.1 emulation for the VDM. The first time you launch an MS-DOS or Win16 application, the WOWEXEC program is loaded, making that VDM the 16-bit Windows subsystem.
Wow32.dll	Provides the DLL portion of the Windows 3.1 emulation layer. When you use the PViewer utility to look at running NTVDM processes, you can identify the one that is the 16-bit Windows subsystem by Wow32.dll being listed in its memory detail.
Autoexec.nt Config.nt	Used to boot the files necessary for running 16-bit Windows applications. The Autoexec.nt and Config.nt files are usually in the \SYSTEM32 directory, but you can change this location by using _Default.pif. Windows NT creates the Autoexec.nt file from the Autoexec.bat file and creates the Config.nt file from scratch. It writes comments to the Autoexec.bat and Config.sys files that describe the .NT versions. Refer to the *Windows NT System Guide* for more information.

Communication with Other Subsystems

An application running under the 16-bit Windows subsystem can communicate with applications in other subsystems (as well as with 32-bit applications running under Windows NT) through the usual mechanisms of OLE, Dynamic Data Exchange (DDE), and named pipes.

Compatibility with Windows NT 3.51

When you upgrade from Windows NT 3.51 to 4.0, your user profile is converted. However, because of the changes to the user interface between 3.51 and 4.0, some of the settings do not migrate. If you are working in a mixed environment that includes both 3.51 and 4.0, you will have a separate user profile for each version. Changes made to one will not be reflected in the other.

Compatibility with Windows 95

It would be impossible to satisfy the broad range of home and business computer needs, as well as technology constraints, with a single operating system. For example, "complete reliability" and "real-mode device driver support" are mutually exclusive features that cannot be built into a single operating system. In response to these challenges, Microsoft's strategy is to provide a family of operating systems. Using both Windows 95 and Windows NT in a single network environment, today's corporation gets the best of flexibility, reliability, compatibility, and security.

Upgrading from Windows 95 to Windows NT 4.0

Because of differences in their respective registries and in hardware device support, no automatic upgrade path from Windows 95 to Windows NT Workstation currently exists. An upgrade path is planned for the next release of Windows NT Workstation.

You can manually upgrade from Windows 95 to Windows NT by installing Windows NT in a separate directory. No system or application settings will be migrated, and you will need to reinstall each application after Windows NT is installed. You should then delete the Windows 95 directory, although this step is optional.

A dual boot (giving the user a choice of operating systems on startup) is not recommended and is not supported. Windows NT does not support all the device drivers that Windows 95 does. A few Windows 95 device drivers require direct access the hardware, such as sound cards, video, scanners, hard disk, and so on. In Windows NT, only the Hardware Abstraction Layer (HAL) of the microkernel has access to the hardware. Where the application vendor has not provided the necessary driver for Windows NT, those device drivers are not supported. Windows NT also does not support Virtual Device Drivers (VXDs), such as multimedia titles, games, and memory management applications.

Both Windows NT and Windows 95 support long filenames.

For more information about running a mixed environment including Windows NT and Windows 95 computers, see Chapter 4 "Planning for a Mixed Environment."

Registry Incompatibility

The registries in Windows NT and Windows 95 use different file formats and are structured differently, rendering the two incompatible for migrating system and application settings. For example, although both systems support roaming user profiles (desktop settings that follow users, by means of their user accounts, from computer to computer), users accessing both Windows 95 and Windows NT computers need two user profiles. Changes made to one will not affect the other. For more information, see Chapter 3, "Managing User Work Environments," in *Microsoft Windows NT 4.0 Server Concepts and Planning.*

System Reliability and Performance Comparison

Windows NT protects all of its operating system code by locating it in either kernel mode (or Ring 0 of the Intel protection model) or in protected subsystems in user mode (or Ring 3), each of which runs in its own address space. Thus, all Windows NT operating system code and data are protected from applications.

Applications, which run in user mode, have access only to their own address spaces. To communicate with system services, an application must utilize specific application programming interfaces (APIs) to convert their threads from user to kernel mode. In order for the application to regain control of the threads, they must be converted back to user mode. Thus, applications have no access to the memory of the subsystems and cannot interfere with the operating system or its support of other applications.

For more information about kernel and user mode, see "Kernel Mode and User Mode" in Chapter 5, "Windows NT 4.0 Workstation Architecture."

Windows 95 locates most of its operating system components in kernel mode, but its system services DLLs (GDI, GDI32, KERNEL, KERNEL32, USER, USER32) run in user mode for the purposes of enhanced performance as well as for backward compatibility with MS-DOS and Windows 3.*x* applications and device driver software, etc. An ill-behaved application can gain access to and write to operating system memory and crash the system. For more information about Windows 95 architecture, see *Windows 95 Resource Kit.*

Running Win16 and DOS Applications

Both Windows 95 and Windows NT run Win16 and DOS applications along with the Win32 applications developed to run on Win32 operating systems. The two systems handle Win16 applications differently, and generally Windows NT is the recommended operating system for computers that run both types of applications.

Windows 95 uses *cooperative multitasking* with Win16 applications. Cooperative multitasking allows an application to voluntarily pass CPU access to another application when the message input queue is empty. Because of this, a Win16 application that fails to check the queue can halt the system for all Win16 applications. Win32 applications that are running should not be affected because the Win16 apps are preemptively multitasked with respect to other processes.

Windows 95 runs Win16 applications as a single multithreaded process in a shared address space. Windows 95 system services DLLs (GDI, GDI32, KERNEL, KERNEL32, USER, USER32) are mapped into the address space of each process. These components, as mentioned earlier, run in user mode. This makes the operating system vulnerable to applications which might write to memory belonging to the operating system.

The system services DLLs in Windows 95 each have a Win32 and a Win16 component. The system is designed to use Win32 code wherever it improves performance without sacrificing application compatibility and uses Win16 code where Win32 code would increase memory requirements without improving performance. Consequently, in Windows 95 both Win16 and Win32 applications require some *thunking* (translation) between 16-bit and 32-bit threads.

Additionally, the Win16 code in Windows 95 is *nonreentrant*, whereas Win32 code is *reentrant*. Reentrant code can be interrupted and resume unharmed, and it can be shared by different threads executing different lines of the same code. The nonreentrant code in Windows 95 would be vulnerable to Win32 threads, except for a flag (called *Win16Mutex*) that prevent threads from accessing code another thread is using to execute. Consequently, performance of even Win32 applications is slower when Win16 applications are running.

Windows NT can run each Win16 and MS-DOS application in its own private address space within a Win32 application called a Virtual DOS Machine (VDM), thus protecting it from other Win16 programs. This allows Windows NT to preemptively multitask all operating system services and all applications. For a more detailed description of preemptive multitasking and scheduling, see Chapter 5, "Windows NT 4.0 Workstation Architecture."

DOS applications run well on both systems, running in separate VDMs, but in Windows 95—because some memory is available to all virtual machines—DOS applications can crash the system. In Windows NT, no operating system memory is available to processes outside of kernel mode.

For details about how Windows NT handles Win16 and MS-DOS applications, see "Implementation of the Subsystem" earlier in this chapter. For details about how Windows 95 handles Win16 applications, see the *Windows 95 Resource Kit.*

Security

Windows NT Workstation was designed with built-in security features. For example, the secure logon screen, invoked by pressing CTRL+ALT+DEL, prevents Trojan Horse programs from simulating an operating system's logon screen and capturing user names and passwords.

Windows 95 was also designed with built-in security, but its security is less restrictive. For example, Windows 95 lets you log in to the local computer without a user account. (To log into a Windows NT computer you must enter a user name and password that already exists on the machine.)

The Windows NT file system, NTFS, provides a range of file protections, which can be set on a per-file or per-directory basis, and user permissions that can be set on a per-user or per-group basis. In addition, NTFS enables an administrator to protect portions of the registry from intentional or inadvertent changes to system settings.

Windows 95 supports share-level and user-level security for peer resource sharing which are measurably less restrictive than the file-level user permissions in Windows NT. Share-level security requires that anyone wanting access to the share must supply the correct password. With user-level security, a request to access a shared resource is passed through a security provider (either a Windows NT Server or NetWare server, utilizing system policies) which grants or denies the request.

The two systems have a notable difference in user permissions:

- On Windows 95, if a user belongs to a group that has access to a resosurce, the user has access to the resource, even if the user belongs to another group that does not have access.
- On Windows NT 4.0, if a user belongs to a group that does not have access to a resource, the user does not have access, even if the user belongs to another group that does have access.

For most effective security, critical resources should always be shared from Windows NT computers.

Each user's Recycle bin on a Windows NT Workstation computer is secure, provided the bin is on an NTFS drive or partition. Windows 95 does not support NTFS.

For more information about security in Windows NT see Chapter 6, "Windows NT Security." For more information about security in Windows 95, see the *Windows 95 Resource Kit.*

Remote Administration

Windows NT provides powerful tools for remotely managing a mixed environment network. For a detailed description, see "Remote Administration" in Chapter 4, "Planning for a Mixed Environment."

Feature Comparison

Because of the difference in their missions, Windows NT and Windows 95 support different types of additional features. An organization that includes both operating systems gains the best that computing has to offer. The following sections compares these features.

DCOM support

COM (Component Object Model) is the basis of OLE. COM is the standard by which software components can make use of or be used by one another, integrating features among disparate applications. For example, a user can include an illustration created with one application in a document created with another application. By linking the illustration in the document to the illustration's source file, the document's illustration is updated as its source file is edited and the link between the two is updated.

Distributed Component Object Model is network OLE—that is, COM with a longer "wire." DCOM is a new technology built into Windows NT 4.0 Workstation that enables software components to work with each other across a network or across the Internet. It is a fast transport for distributed applications built with COM. Existing COM applications can use DCOM. They will require only minor modification to a system's configuration, but none to the application code itself. The programming model is identical to ActiveX technologies, so integration is seamless.

With DCOM, indirect connection (a client connecting to a server to connect to another server) is eliminated. After the pointer is established at the target server, DCOM allows the pointer to be given to the client enabling direct client/server communication.

DCOM eliminates the need for objects to implement the communication protocols for accessing remote objects. DCOM centrally handles the communication for all objects.

Windows 95 plans DCOM support in the near future but currently runs DCOM applications as COM applications.

Plug and Play

Windows 95 supports Plug and Play, and Windows 95 applications must be aware of on-the-fly configuration changes.

Windows NT does support static configuration changes, but it is not aware of on-the-fly configuration changes for this release.

File Compression

NTFS provides file compression as part of the user interface, whereas Windows 95 relies on a separate utility for compression. By right-clicking on a file within an NTFS partition and then clicking Properties, the user can select the **Compressed** check box on the General tab to reduce the size of the file by about 50 percent.

Multimedia APIs

Windows NT supports a series of direct application programming interfaces (APIs) to promote Windows as a platform for game developers and for multimedia-based training. These DirectX APIs—DirectDraw, DirectPlay, and DirectSound—give developers a standard set of services that make game development quicker and easier.

DirectX was introduced with Windows 95. The functions are implemented differently in Windows NT 4.0 than in Windows 95 due to the inaccessibility of the hardware on a Windows NT computer.

DirectDraw for Windows NT supports a 32-bit API for accelerated drawing. It allows an application to manipulate video memory easily and take advantage of the capabilities of different types of video hardware without becoming device-dependent. It enables digital video playback to take advantage of several types of hardware support that are included in advanced graphics adapters.

The Windows NT 4.0 implementation of DirectDraw does not communicate directly with the hardware. (This is in contrast to Windows 95 DirectDraw). All functions are mediated by GDI. DirectDraw can emulate functions by reducing them into simpler tasks, much as GDI does for its clients.

DirectSound utilizes accelerated sound hardware features without requiring the application to query the hardware or program specifically. DirectSound takes advantage of on-card memory, sound mixing (for example, the sound of the crowd mixed with the sound of the announcer mixed with the crack of the bat in a baseball-game application), hardware mixing, and hardware sound-buffer memory.

The DirectSound API provides direct control of audio hardware and is designed to enable 3-D audio support in games. Direct sound runs in emulation mode for Windows NT 4.0 Workstation. API calls are converted to the existing APIs at runtime.

Platform support

Windows 95 is designed for Intel ISA. It runs on *x*86, Pentium, and Pentium Pro computers. Windows NT supports Intel ISA, Alpha, R4X00, and PowerPC. Windows NT also supports multiprocessor environments with symmetric multiprocessing. Windows 95 supports single processor only.

C H A P T E R 2 8

OS/2 Compatibility

This chapter describes the OS/2 subsystem in Windows NT. It describes the types of applications that the subsystem currently supports, as well as those that it does not support. It describes the supported, unsupported, and partially supported OS/2 application programming interfaces (APIs). This chapter also describes how the OS/2 subsystem is implemented and the Win32 thunking mechanism.

Running Applications

The OS/2 subsystem allows OS/2 16-bit character-based applications to run directly with Windows NT with essentially no modification. You can launch a character-based or video I/O (VIO) application from the Windows NT command prompt, from My Computer, from the Windows NT Explorer, or indirectly from within a Win32 or OS/2 application. You can create a single batch file that can launch any combination of MS-DOS, Windows, or OS/2 programs. Windows NT recognizes an OS/2 application from information stored in the header of the executable file; it then calls the OS/2 subsystem to load the application.

If you never run an OS/2 application, the subsystem does not use any Windows NT resources. When you run an application, the OS2SRV process is loaded and continues to exist even after you have quit the application. To free up the minimal resources that the OS2SRV process uses, run the PViewer utility (which is provided with the *Windows NT Resource Kit*) and quit the OS2SRV process. If you later run another OS/2 application, the OS2SRV process is reloaded.

Supported Applications

You can run the following types of applications with the OS/2 subsystem:

- OS/2 1.*x* 16-bit applications on *x*86 computers only
- Character-based applications

Unsupported Applications

You cannot run the following types of applications with the OS/2 subsystem:

- OS/2 2.*x* applications.
- Presentation Manager (PM) applications (unless you install the Windows NT Add-On Subsystem for Presentation Manager, which can be ordered separately from Microsoft)
- Advanced video I/O (AVIO) applications (unless you install the Windows NT Add-On Subsystem for Presentation Manager)
- OS/2 applications on RISC-based computers.
- Applications that directly access hardware memory or I/O ports at Ring 2 or below.

  For example, applications that directly access video memory to manipulate text or graphics are not supported. Some OS/2 applications, which rely on the statement IOPL=YES in the Config.sys file to run Ring 2 code segment, will run nevertheless under the OS/2 subsystem as long as the privileged instructions they issue in those segments are CLI/STI instructions and not IN/OUT instructions. For more details, see "I/O Privilege Mechanism" later in this chapter.
- You cannot run custom device drivers (those not included with OS/2 itself). These must be rewritten to the Windows NT device driver interface.

If you want to run an OS/2 application that is not supported, you have the following choices:

- If this is a bound application (one that can run under both OS/2 and MS-DOS), you can try to run it with the MS-DOS subsystem. To do so, run the **forcedos** command from the command line:

  FORCEDOS [**/D** *directory*] *filename* [*parameters*]

  where */directory* is the current directory for the application to use, *filename* is the application to start, and *parameters* is the parameters to pass to the application.
- If this is not a bound application and you have the source code, you can recompile the source without the unsupported APIs, which are specified in the error message that is displayed when you try to run the application. If you do not have the source, contact the application's developer.

Partially Supported Applications

Video input/output (VIO) applications are partially supported. Some will work and some will not, depending on the API functions that the applications use. The robustness and security of Windows NT restrict access to physical hardware, which restricts the use of VIO physical buffer APIs, certain **DosDevIOCtl** functions, and I/O privilege level (IOPL). For more information, see the following section on APIs.

Note Presentation Manager and AVIO applications are supported by the Windows NT Add-on Subsystem for Presentation Manager, available from Microsoft.

APIs

A complete list of the APIs that are supported, unsupported, or partially supported is provided in the Os2api.txt file on the *Resource Kit* disk.

Supported APIs

APIs with the following prefixes are supported:

- **Dos** (except **DosDevIOCtl** and **DosDevIOCtl2**, which are partially supported)
- **Kbd** (except those that conflict with the security and robustness of Windows NT)
- **Mou** (except those that require Presentation Manager or AVIO)
- **Vio** (except those that conflict with the security of Windows NT by accessing the physical video hardware and those that require PM or AVIO)
- **WinQueryProfile** and **WinWriteProfile**
- **Net** (selected APIs based on their commercial use)

Unsupported APIs

APIs with the following prefixes are not supported:

- **Dev**
- **Gpi**
- **Kbd** (those that conflict with the security and robustness of Windows NT)
- **Mou** (those that require PM or AVIO)
- **Vio** (those that conflict with the security of Windows NT by accessing the physical video hardware and those that require PM or AVIO)
- **Win** (except **WinQueryProfile** and **WinWriteProfile** APIs)

Partially Supported APIs

The following APIs are partially supported:

- **DosDevIOCtl** and **DosDevIOCtl2**
- **VioGetConfig**
- **VioGetMode** and **VioSetMode**
- **VioGetState** and **VioSetState**

Note APIs with the **Mou** or **Vio** prefixes that require Presentation Manager (PM) or advanced video I/O (AVIO) are supported by the Windows NT Add-on Subsystem for Presentation Manager, available from Microsoft.

Implementation of the OS/2 Subsystem

This section describes how the OS/2 subsystem is implemented.

Memory Map of an OS/2 Application

The following is a map of memory usage while the OS/2 subsystem is running an application.

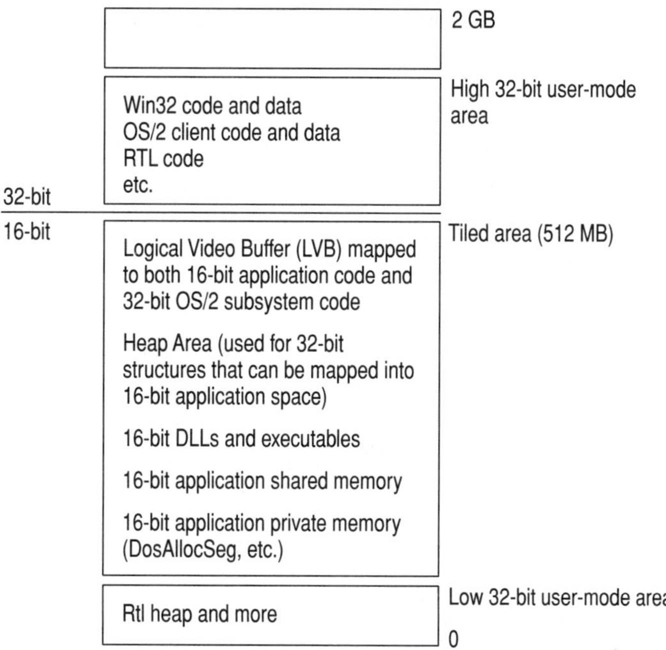

Figure 28.1 OS/2 Subsystem Memory Map

The *tiled area* is 512 MB of virtual address space that is reserved up-front and then committed or decommitted when 16-bit applications need segments. The OS/2 subsystem maintains a local descriptor table (LDT) for each process, with shared memory segments at the same LDT slot for all OS/2 processes.

Architecture Diagram

The OS/2 subsystem is implemented as a protected server; OS/2 applications communicate with the subsystem by using the local procedure call (LPC) message-passing facility. The subsystem and each application run in their own protected address spaces, which protects them from other processes running with Windows NT.

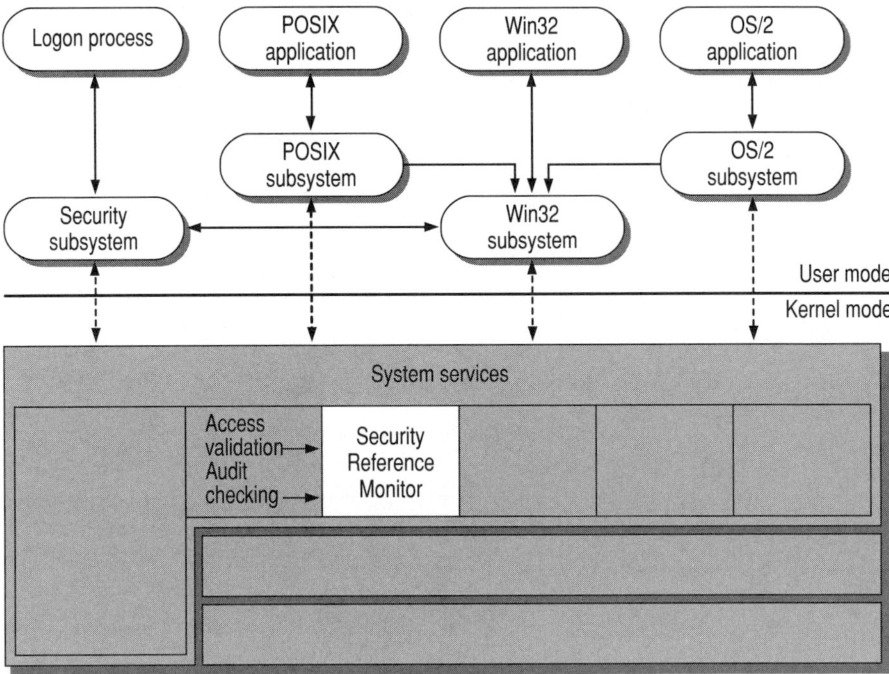

Figure 28.2 OS/2 Subsystem in Windows NT

In native OS/2, applications run in user mode (Ring 3) and communicate with the OS/2 kernel by using calls to the DLLs. Some application programs and DLLs contain I/O privilege segments and are allowed to perform I/O operations in Ring 2. The OS/2 subsystem will attempt to run such programs but those using the I/O privilege to perform IN/OUT instructions (to access some hardware device) violate the robustness features of Windows NT and thus will be terminated with a general protection fault. For more information, see "I/O Privilege Mechanism" later in this chapter.

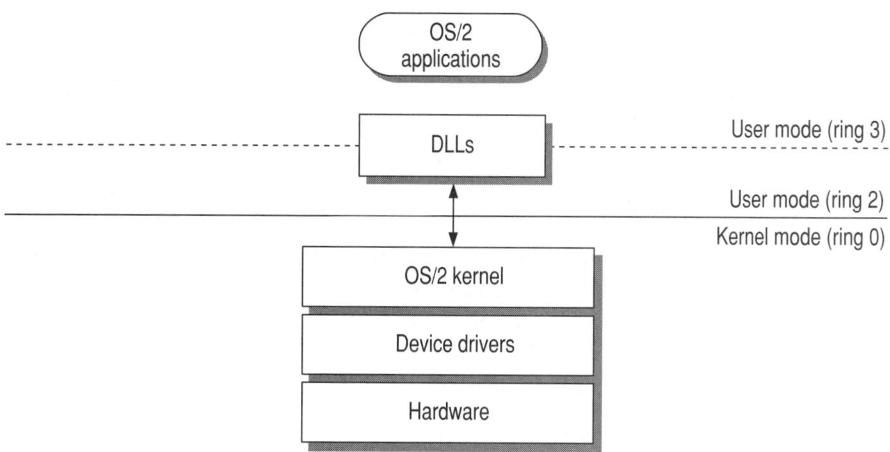

Figure 28.3 Native OS/2

Multitasking

Process

The OS/2 subsystem uses OS/2 semantics to maintain the various OS/2 objects. Examples of this include process IDs, the process tree, handles, local and global **infosegs**, thread-1 semantics, exit-list processing, signals, and semaphores. Windows NT objects are used only when they are relevant; they are then embedded inside OS/2 objects (for example, file handles).

The process tree records the descendent processes of a given process. The subsystem uses the process tree in all related operations, such as ending a program by pressing CTRL+C.

Thread

Every thread created by an OS/2 application is implemented with a Windows NT thread in the same process. The thread receives the priority and ID that are relevant in OS/2. The exact OS/2 semantics (such as contents of the register and the stack) are retained when the thread function starts.

Scheduler

The Windows NT scheduler handles the scheduling of OS/2 threads, with the OS/2 priorities 0–63 mapping to Windows NT variable priorities 0–15. (OS/2 priorities are changed only by the application; they are not changed by the scheduler). OS/2 threads never receive Windows NT real-time priorities 16–31.

VIO User Interface

The VIO user interface is partially supported. Applications cannot get direct control of the video hardware. The use of a logical video buffer, as opposed to a physical video buffer, is allowed. For specific information, see the lists of APIs earlier in this chapter.

Dynamic Linking

The OS/2 subsystem implements a full OS/2 loader, which loads DLLs, executables, and resources in exactly the same way as in OS/2. Static linking, load-time dynamic linking, and run-time dynamic linking all function as they do in OS/2.

Memory Management

Protection Model

The OS/2 subsystem implements the protection between OS/2 applications. It constructs their address spaces (both the flat address space and LDTs) and implements the same protection as exists in OS/2.

Some of the memory management limitations of OS/2 1.*x* are removed. The most important of these is the limit of 16 MB of physical RAM; the OS/2 subsystem uses the large memory capability of Windows NT. This translates into increased performance for applications that can use the additional memory, such as Microsoft's SQL Server. SQL Server asks for the physical memory available in the system at setup time. It then uses this number to determine the level of caching it will use. In OS/2, you cannot use more than 16 MB; however, in the OS/2 subsystem in Windows NT, you can use 32 MB (for example) and double your caching capability.

Segment Swapping

The OS/2 subsystem uses the Windows NT paging mechanism; no segment swapping is performed. Segment swapping is inferior to paging and exists in OS/2 only to support the 80286 processor, which is not supported for Windows NT.

Interprocess Communication

The OS/2 subsystem implements all OS/2 IPC mechanisms (semaphores, pipes, shared memory, queues, and signals).

Named Pipes

The OS/2 subsystem implements named pipes on top of the Windows NT named-pipe file system. These are supported transparently between Win32, MS-DOS, Win16, and OS/2 applications, both locally and remotely. Microsoft LAN Manager 2.*x* named pipe functionality is supported in its entirety.

Anonymous Pipes

Anonymous pipes, including inheritance, are fully supported. They are integrated into the OS/2 file handle space.

Shared Memory

The full functionality of OS/2 1.*x* shared memory, including Get and Give semantics, is implemented using Windows NT shared memory features. The discardable segments property is ignored. (It is invisible to the OS/2 application.)

Semaphores

The OS/2 subsystem supports the full range of OS/2 1.*x* semaphore APIs, including RAM semaphores in private and shared memory, system semaphores, and fast-safe RAM semaphores. Association of semaphores with timers and named pipes is fully supported. The OS/2 subsystem uses a combination of the Windows NT semaphore object and the Windows NT event object to implement an OS/2 semaphore.

Queues

OS/2 1.*x* queues are fully supported, using shared memory between OS/2 processes and OS/2 semaphores as required.

Signals

OS/2 signals are fully supported, using Windows NT APIs to manipulate thread context. The OS/2 subsystem controls the address space of OS/2 processes and uses it to manipulate the register content and the stack of thread 1 of the process to be signaled.

I/O Architecture

Device Drivers

Existing private OS/2 device drivers will not be supported in the OS/2 subsystem directly, but must be rewritten for the Windows NT device driver model. In this context, *private device driver* means a driver that a particular application requires but that is not included in the OS/2 operating system itself.

Examples of such drivers include those that provide custom support for security, fax, MIDI, or 3270 communication cards. Once an OS/2 device driver has been rewritten for the Windows NT model, however, an OS/2 application can communicate with that device driver using the same OS/2 API, **DosDevIoctl**; no changes will be required within the application itself. Additionally, support exists for the native device drivers included with Windows NT, such as the display, printer, disk, communications, keyboard, and mouse devices.

For example, suppose that a corporation has written a custom device driver to control a security card. The OS/2 device driver for this card uses an internal name, SECDEV, and an entry for this device driver appears in the Config.sys file. In OS/2, the operating system reads the Config.sys file and adds SECDEV to the device driver list. When an application calls the OS/2 API, **DosOpen**, this list is searched first. The OS/2 subsystem will read this file during initialization and add symbolic links that will allow the OS/2 application to call the Windows NT device driver from the subsystem. For information about how to set the Config.sys file for the OS/2 subsystem to load a Windows NT device driver, see "OS/2 Configuration" later in this chapter.

The OS/2 application code, as opposed to the device driver code, can still load and run in a binary-compatible manner because the device-specific parameters passed by **DosDevIoctl**(2) APIs are just PVOID buffers. Of course, the new Windows NT version of the ported device driver would have to be made compatible with the original by accepting the same set of parameters within the buffers. Other related OS/2 APIs, such as **DosOpen**, are supported compatibly, just as they are for supporting native Windows NT system device drivers such as the communications device, the keyboard, and the screen.

File System

The OS/2 subsystem supports long names and extended attributes but no longer supports HPFS. The subsystem does not utilize or expose recoverability and C2 security functions.

Network Connectivity

The OS/2 subsystem implements many LAN Manager APIs. It also implements NetBIOS (both version 2.*x* and version 3.0 functionality), named pipes, and mail slots.

The OS/2 subsystem maintains remote drives compatible with OS/2. With these, any OS/2 application can use redirected drives transparently with the file I/O APIs. Uniform naming convention (UNC) naming is supported as well. Redirected drives of various network operating systems can be used, provided that the related Win32 Windows NT device drivers (redirectors) have been installed.

I/O Privilege Mechanism

Under native OS/2, if the statement IOPL=YES is present in the Config.sys file, applications may include Ring 2 segments in which it is possible to execute CLI/STI instruction (disable-enable hardware interrupts), but not IN/OUT.

The OS/2 subsystem of Windows NT allows OS/2 applications to run Ring 2 code segments (no special statement required in the OS/2 C:\Config.sys) but with the following important restrictions:

- CLI/STI instructions will work.

  The OS/2 subsystem will suspend all the other OS/2 applications in the system and all the other threads in the OS/2 process issuing the CLI instructions, until an STI instruction follows. This emulation of CLI/STI instruction is much more costly in run-time overhead than on native OS/2 (where the CPU simply disables external interrupts, which would violate the Windows NT robustness design rules) and also much more costly than semaphore calls. Therefore, when it is possible to modify the OS/2 application, semaphore calls are the preferred way to implement critical sections.
- IN/OUT instructions are *not* supported.

  Such instructions will cause a general-protection fault and the application will be terminated.

Filters

Filters are supported and are integrated with Win32 and MS-DOS; that is, you can redirect input and output between OS/2, MS-DOS, and Win32 applications transparently.

Device Monitors

Device monitors are a feature that OS/2 provides in the device driver level, which violates Windows NT security if given across the system. Therefore, the OS/2 subsystem implements device monitors within an OS/2 session (an OS/2 application and all of its descendants). Within the session the implementation of device monitors is complete and compatible with OS/2. The vast majority of OS/2 applications use monitors within a session already.

Printing

Printing from the OS/2 subsystem is identical to base-level printing on OS/2. For example, you can connect to a remote printer by typing the following at the command prompt:

NET USE LPT1: *myprinter**pscript*

You can then use the dialog boxes within an application to set up a printer and print.

Security

The OS/2 subsystem is subject to the security measures imposed by Windows NT. OS/2 processes, among themselves, have only the security restrictions of OS/2 (no ACLs attached, and so on). OS/2 processes run under the logged-on user token, just as Win32 processes do.

Communication with Other Subsystems

Subsystems communicate by passing messages to one another. When an OS/2 application calls an API routine, for example, the OS/2 subsystem receives a message and implements it by calling Windows NT system services or by passing messages to other subsystems. When it is finished, the OS/2 subsystem sends a message containing the return values back to the application. The message passing and other activities of the subsystem are invisible to the user.

Communication between OS/2 and Windows NT processes can be accomplished by means of named pipes, mail slots, NetBIOS, files, and COM devices. The Win32 subsystem directs user input to an OS/2 application; it handles all screen I/O for OS/2 applications.

Calling 32-bit DLLs

The OS/2 subsystem provides a general mechanism to allow 16-bit OS/2 and PM applications to load and call any Win32 DLL. This feature could be extremely useful in the following cases:

- When you need to call from your OS/2 application some functionality available under Windows NT only as Win32 code.

  Without the ability to call Win32 DLLs, the alternative would be to split the application into an OS/2 application and a Win32 application, then communicate between them using, for example, named pipes. This would be much more complicated to implement and may not yield a good performance.
- When you want to port your OS/2 application to Win32 but would like to do so in stages, by porting only part of the application at first.

A small set of new APIs is provided. See "Win32 Thunking Mechanism" later in this chapter.

OS/2 Configuration

The OS/2 subsystem handles Os2.ini compatibly with OS/2. The WIN*xxx* APIs supported in this release of Windows NT are provided for this purpose. Startup.cmd is just a batch file.

When the OS/2 subsystem starts for the first time, it checks the Registry for OS/2 subsystem configuration information. If it doesn't find any, it looks for information in the original Config.sys file and adds the information to the Registry. If the original Config.sys file does not exist or is not an OS/2 configuration file, the subsystem adds the following default information to the Registry:

```
PROTSHELL=c:\os2\pmshell.exe c:\os2\os2.ini c:\os2\os2sys.ini
    %SystemRoot%\system32\cmd.exe
SET COMSPEC=%SystemRoot%\system32\cmd.exe
```

The subsystem updates the environment variable, **Os2LibPath**, with LIBPATH information found in the original Config.sys file. The updated **Os2LibPath** is <*systemroot*>\SYSTEM32\OS2\DLL concatenated with the list of directories specified in the LIBPATH line of the original Config.sys file.

The PATH information found in the original Config.sys file is not entered automatically into the default Windows NT path. To add the location of OS/2 applications, use the System applet in the Control Panel to add a PATH variable to the user environment variables. This information is appended automatically by Windows NT each time a user logs on to the system.

Windows NT supports the OS/2 configuration commands shown in the following table. If you use commands that are not supported, Windows NT ignores them.

Table 28.1 OS/2 Configuration Commands Supported by Windows NT

Command	Function
protshell	Specifies the command interpreter. Only the Windows NT command interpreter is supported.
devicename	Specifies a user-defined Windows NT device driver used by OS/2 applications.
libpath	Specifies the location of OS/2 16-bit dynamic-link libraries.
set	Sets environment variables.
country	Sets a country code that defines country-dependent information such as time, date, and currency conventions.
codepage	Specifies the code pages your system is prepared to use.
devinfo=KBD	Specifies the information the keyboard needs in order to use a particular code page.

The **libpath**, **set**, and **devicename** commands are processed as follows:

- The **libpath** command appends path information to the OS/2 library path in the Windows NT environment. At the command prompt, you can change the library path for OS/2 applications by using the **os2libpath** command.
- The following **set** commands are ignored:

set path	**set comspec**	**set video_devices**
set vio_ibmvga	**set vio_vga**	**set prompt**

- The **devicename** command specifies a device driver compatible with Windows NT for use with an OS/2 application. The syntax for the **devicename** command is as follows:

  DEVICENAME=*OS/2devicename* [[*path*][*NTdevicename*]]

  OS/2devicename is the logical name that OS/2 applications use to address the device. *Path* and *NTdevicename* specify the Windows NT device driver to which the OS/2 device name is mapped. If these are not specified, the device is mapped to \DEVICE*os/2devicename*.

Changing OS/2 Configuration Information

Although the OS/2 configuration information is stored in the Registry, you can edit that information just as you would edit an OS/2 Config.sys file. To edit the information, you must use an OS/2 text editor.

Note To change configuration information, you must be logged on as a member of the Administrators group.

▶ **To change configuration information**

1. While running Windows NT, start an OS/2 text editor in a window.
2. Open a file called C:\CONFIG.SYS.

   Windows NT retrieves the configuration information from the Registry and stores it in a temporary file that you can edit.
3. Edit the configuration information.
4. Save and close the file.
5. Quit the editor.

   Windows NT stores the new information in the registry.
6. Log off from Windows NT, and restart your computer.

File List

The main files that make up the OS/2 subsystem are listed in the following table. Many additional files, not listed here, are needed when running the Windows NT Add-On Subsystem for Presentation Manager, such as all the 16-bit PM DLLs (Pmwin.dll, Pmgre.dll etc.) and 16-bit EXEs (Pmshell.exe, Pmspool.exe, etc.).

Table 28.2 OS/2 Subsystem Files

File	Purpose
Os2srv.exe	This file is the subsystem server. It is invoked when you run the first OS/2 application, and it remains to serve new applications as they are run.
Os2.exe	This file is the client side of every OS/2 application. There is an instance of Os2.exe for each OS/2 application that is running.
Doscalls.dll[1]	This file contains the DOS*xxx* APIs. The other DLLs that are used in OS/2, such as KBDCALLS and VIOCALLS, are provided in memory by the OS/2 subsystem.
Netapi.dll[1]	This file contains the LM APIs.

[1] This file is located in the SYSTEM32\OS2\DLL or C:\OS2\DLL directories when running the Windows NT Add-On Subsystem for Presentation Manager.

Win32 Thunking Mechanism

As mentioned earlier in this document, the OS/2 subsystem provides a general mechanism to allow 16-bit OS/2 and PM applications to load and call any Win32 DLL. To take advantage of this feature, you typically need to complete the following tasks:

- Write a small Win32 DLL thunking layer that will be called by the 16-bit OS/2 application.

  This Win32 thunking layer will in turn call the real Win32 API, using the parameters passed by the 16-bit code. The need for such a thunking layer (rather than calling the real Win32 DLL directly from 16-bit) stems from the fact that the OS/2 subsystem thunking mechanism allows only for one generic pointer parameter. Most Win32 APIs require more parameters or of different type so that a small Win32 thunking layer is required to retrieve parameters via the parameter pointer. This parameter pointer points to application-defined data, which will typically be a structure with the parameters for the actual call to the real Win32 API.
- Change your 16-bit application to include calls to the Win32 thunking APIs described below.

The following 16-bit APIs are to be used by the OS/2 application code. (These APIs are defined in the same manner as OS/2 APIs. See the OS/2 1.2 *Programmer's Reference Manual.*)

```
USHORT pascal far Dos32LoadModule (
    PSZ DLLName,
    PULONG pDllHandle);
```

Purpose: Load a Win32 thunk DLL that will intermediate between an OS/2 application and Win32 APIs.

Returns: If NO_ERROR is returned, the value pointed to by **pDllHandle** is used for other Win32 thunk APIs as described below. It is invalid for usage with regular OS/2 APIs. If ERROR_MOD_NOT_FOUND is returned, the value pointed to by **pDLLHandle** is undefined.

```
USHORT pascal far Dos32GetProcAddr (
    ULONG DllHandle,
    PSZ pszProcName,
    PULONG pWin32Thunk);
```

Purpose: Get a cookie (flat pointer) to a routine in a Win32 thunk DLL, previously opened by **Dos32LoadModule**. For example, if the OS/2 application wants to call the **WinSocketFoo** API, it builds a Win32 intermediate DLL, named Mysock.dll, that exports **MyWinSocketFoo**. The application calls **Dos32LoadModule** with Mysock.dll and then **Dos32GetProcAddr** with **pszProcName** of value **MyWinSocketFoo**. If no error is returned, it can use the value pointed to by **pWin32Thunk** in a later call to **Dos32Dispatch**, for calling the **MyWinSocketFoo** routine, which in turn will call a real Win32 API (for example, **WinSocketFoo**).

Returns: NO_ERROR if the **pszProcName** is exported by the Win32 intermediate DLL which relates to **DllHandle**. If ERROR_PROC_NOT_FOUND or ERROR_INVALID_HANDLE is returned, the value pointed to by **pWin32Thunk** is undefined.

```
USHORT pascal far Dos32Dispatch (
    ULONG Win32Thunk,
    PVOID   pArguments,
    PULONG pRetCode);
```

Purpose: **Dos32Dispatch** calls the 32-bit thunk routine **Win32Thunk**, previously obtained by **Dos32GetProcAddr**. It returns the error code returned by **Win32Thunk** in **pRetCode**. It translates the **pArguments** 16:16 pointer to a flat pointer and passes it to the **Win32Thunk** call. The structure pointed to by **pArguments**, and the values of **pRetCode** are application specific and are not interpreted or modified by the OS/2 subsystem.

On the Win32 side, i.e. in the Win32 DLL, the Win32 thunk must be defined as follows:

```
ULONG MyWinSocketFoo (
    PVOID pFlatArg);
```

The return code from **MyWinSocketFoo** is application-defined and is copied by the OS/2 subsystem to **pRetCode**.

Returns: NO_ERROR if the **pFlatArg** argument is a valid pointer and no exception occurred in the call to it.

```
USHORT pascal far Dos32FreeModule (
    ULONG DllHandle);
```

Purpose: Unload a Win32 thunk DLL that intermediates between an OS/2 application and Win32 APIs.

Returns: NO_ERROR if **DllHandle** indeed corresponds to a Win32 DLL previously loaded by **Dos32LoadModule** (after the call, **DllHandle** is no longer valid). Otherwise, ERROR_INVALID_HANDLE is returned.

```
USHORT pascal far FarPtr2FlatPtr(
    ULONG FarPtr,
    PULONG pFlatPtr);
```

Purpose: Translates the segmented pointer FarPtr to a flat pointer pointed to by **pFlatPtr**.

Returns: NO_ERROR if **FarPtr** is a valid 16:16 pointer: in this case, upon completion of the call **pFlatPtr** contains a valid 32-bit flat pointer to be used by Win32 code. ERROR_INVALID_PARAMETER is returned if the 16:16 pointer is not valid: in this case the value pointed to by **pFlatPtr** is undefined.

```
USHORT pascal far FlatPtr2FarPtr(
    ULONG FlatPtr,
    PULONG pFarPtr);
```

Purpose: Translates the flat pointer **FlatPtr** to a far pointer which it stores into **pFarPtr**.

Returns: NO_ERROR if the 32-bit **FlatPtr** maps to a valid 16:16 pointer in the 16-bit application's context: in this case, upon completion of the call **pFarPtr** contains a valid 16:16 segmented pointer to be used by the 16-bit OS/2 code. Otherwise, i.e. if the 16:16 pointer is not a valid address in the 16-bit application's context, ERROR_INVALID_PARAMETER is returned and **pFarPtr** is undefined.

The following are the .h file and .def file that should be compiled and linked with the 16-bit OS/2 application:

The .H File

```
//
// Definition of WIN32 thunk APIs.
//

extern USHORT pascal far
Dos32LoadModule(PSZ DllName, PULONG pDllHandle);

extern USHORT pascal far
Dos32GetProcAddr(ULONG Handle, PSZ pszProcName, PULONG pWin32Thunk);

extern USHORT pascal far
Dos32Dispatch(ULONG Win32Thunk, PVOID pArguments, PULONG pRetCode);

extern USHORT pascal far
Dos32FreeModule(ULONG DllHandle);

extern USHORT pascal far
FarPtr2FlatPtr(ULONG FarPtr, PULONG pFlarPtr);

extern USHORT pascal far
FlatPtr2FarPtr(ULONG FlatPtr, PULONG pFarPtr);
```

The .DEF File

```
IMPORTS
   DOSCALLS.DOS32LOADMODULE
   DOSCALLS.DOS32GETPROCADDR
   DOSCALLS.DOS32DISPATCH
   DOSCALLS.DOS32FREEMODULE
   DOSCALLS.FARPTR2FLATPTR
   DOSCALLS.FLATPTR2FARPTR
```

CHAPTER 29

POSIX Compatibility

This chapter describes the Windows NT implementation of a POSIX subsystem. It includes information about the following topics:

- Definition of POSIX
- Conformance and compliance to POSIX.1
- Running applications
- Implementation of subsystem
- Windows NT POSIX files

Note This chapter is not intended to be a POSIX tutorial.

Definition of POSIX

POSIX, which stands for *Portable Operating System Interface* for computing environments, began as an effort by the IEEE community to promote the portability of applications across UNIX environments by developing a clear, consistent, and unambiguous set of standards. POSIX is not limited to the UNIX environment, however. It can be implemented on non-UNIX operating systems, as was done with the IEEE Std. 1003.1-1990 (POSIX.1) implementation on the VMS, MPE, and CTOS operating systems. POSIX actually consists of a set of standards that range from POSIX.1 to POSIX.12.

As the following table shows, most of these standards are still in the proposed state. This section deals with the Windows NT implementation of a POSIX subsystem to support the international ISO/IEC IS 9945-1:1990 standard (also called *POSIX.1*). POSIX.1 defines a C-language source-code-level application programming interface (API) to an operating system environment.

Table 29.1 Family of POSIX Standards

Standard	ISO Standard	Description
POSIX.0	No	A guide to POSIX Open Systems Environment. This is not a standard in the same sense as POSIX.1 or POSIX.2. It is more of an introduction and overview of the other standards.
POSIX.1	Yes	Systems application programming interface (API) [C language].
POSIX.2	No	Shell and tools (IEEE approved standard).
POSIX.3	No	Testing and verification.
POSIX.4	No	Real-time and threads.
POSIX.5	Yes	ADA language bindings to POSIX.1.
POSIX.6	No	System security.
POSIX.7	No	System administration.
POSIX.8	No	Networking A. Transparent file access B. Protocol-independent network interface C. Remote Procedure Calls (RPC) D. Open system interconnect protocol-dependent application interfaces
POSIX.9	Yes	FORTRAN language bindings to POSIX.1.
POSIX.10	No	Super-computing Application Environment Profile (AEP).
POSIX.11	No	Transaction Processing AEP.
POSIX.12	No	Graphical user interface.

POSIX Conformance

For a system to be given a certificate of POSIX.1 conformance, it must meet the following requirements:

- The system must support all interfaces as defined in the ISO/IEC 9945-1.
- The vendor must supply a *POSIX.1 Conformance Document* (PCD) with the vendor's implementation as specified in ISP/IEC 9945-1.
- The implementation must pass the appropriate *National Institute of Standards and Technology* (NIST) test suite.

Windows NT version 3.51 Workstation and Windows NT Server have been tested and certified using the official NIST PCTS for *Federal Information Processing Standard* (FIPS) 151-2, and NIST has validated the test results. Windows NT 4.0 will begin testing soon. Windows NT version 3.5 is in the process of being verified for POSIX.1 compliance and will also be submitted to NIST for FIPS 151-2 certification. FIPS 151-2 incorporates POSIX.1 as a reference standard and also requires a number of the optional features defined in POSIX.1 to promote application portability among conforming implementations. An implementation that conforms to FIPS 151-2 also conforms to POSIX.1. Note that conformance is specific to the manufacturer, hardware platform, and model number on which the implementation is tested.

POSIX.1 is a source-level standard; it does not provide any binary compatibility.

Application Compliance to POSIX.1

POSIX.1 has four categories of compliance, ranging from very strict to very loose. The various categories are described in this section.

The current release of Windows NT supports strictly conforming POSIX.1 applications and ISO/IEC conforming POSIX.1 applications. Windows NT supports the latter by virtue of the fact that only 110 of the 149 functions of standard C are part of POSIX.1, and standard C is itself an ISO standard (ISO/IEC 9899).

Strictly Conforming POSIX.1 Applications

A *strictly conforming POSIX.1 application* requires only the facilities described in the POSIX.1 standard and applicable language standards. This type of application accepts the following conditions:

- Any behavior described in ISO/IEC 9945-1 as unspecified or implementation-defined
- Symbolic constants
- Any value in the range permitted in ISO/IEC 9945-1

This is the strictest level of application conformance, and applications at this level should be able to move across implementations with just a recompilation. At this time, the only language interface that has been standardized for POSIX.1 is the C-language interface. (As shown in the figure below, a strictly conforming POSIX application can use 110 calls from the standard C libraries.)

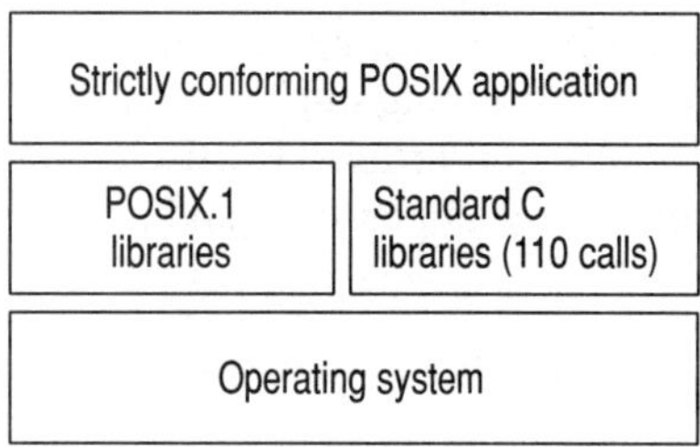

Figure 29.1 A Strictly Conforming POSIX Application

Applications Conforming to ISO/IEC and POSIX.1

An *ISO/IEC-conforming POSIX.1 application* is one that uses only the facilities described in ISO/IEC 9945-1 and approved conforming language bindings for the ISO or IEC standard. This type of application must include a statement of conformance that documents all options and limit dependencies, and all other ISO or IEC standards used.

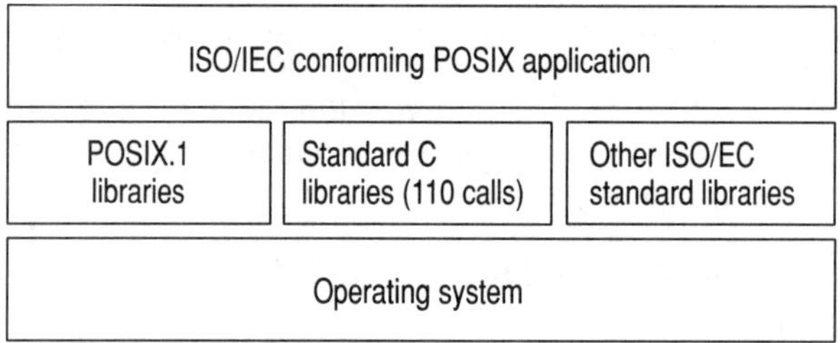

Figure 29.2 An ISO/IEC-conforming POSIX.1 Application

This level of conformance is not as strict as the previous one for two reasons: First, it allows a POSIX.1 application to make use of other ISO or IEC standards, such as GKS. Second, it allows POSIX.1 applications within this level to require options or limit values beyond the minimum. For example, such an application could require that the implementation support filenames of at least 16 characters. The POSIX.1 minimum is 14 characters.

Applications Conforming to POSIX.1 and <National Body>

A *<National Body> conforming POSIX.1 application* differs from an ISO/IEC-conforming POSIX.1 application in that this type of application may also use specific standards of a single ISO/IEC organization, such as ANSI or British Standards Institute (BSI). This type of application must include a statement of conformance that documents all options and limit dependencies, and all other *<National Body>* standards used.

For example, you could have a *<National Body>* conforming POSIX application that uses calls from a BSI-standard set of calls.

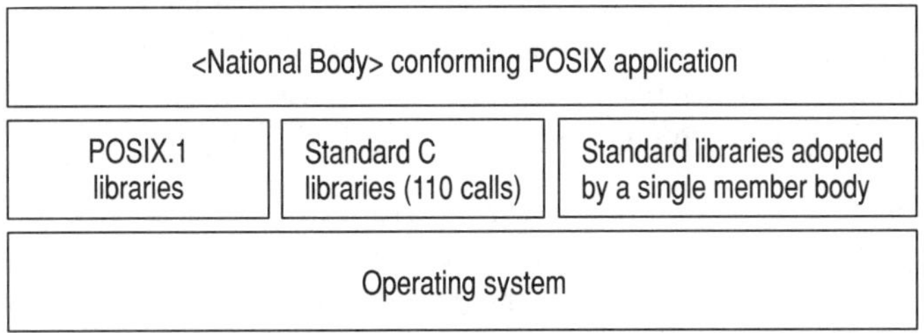

Figure 29.3 A National Body Conforming POSIX.1 Application

POSIX.1-Conformant Applications That Use Extensions

A *conforming POSIX.1 application using extensions* is an application that differs from a conforming POSIX.1 application only because it uses nonstandard facilities that are consistent with ISO/IEC 9945-1. Such an application must fully document its requirements for these extended facilities.

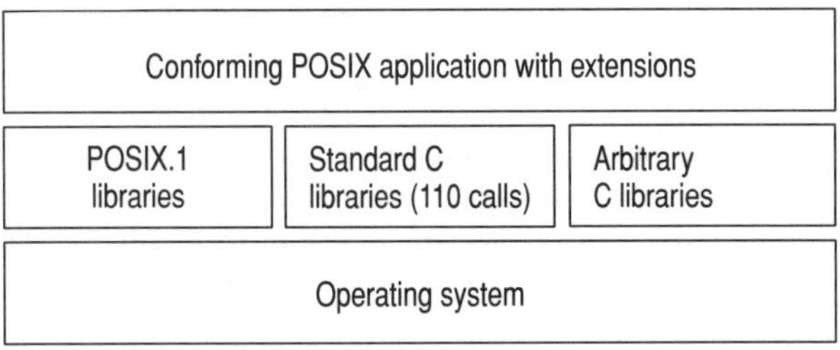

Figure 29.4 A Conforming POSIX.1 Application Using Extensions

This is the lowest level of conformance; almost any C program could satisfy this with the appropriate documentation.

Running Applications

POSIX applications can be started from a Windows NT console window (command prompt), My Computer, the Windows NT Explorer, or by invocation from within another POSIX application.

File Systems

POSIX requires a certain amount of functionality from the file system, such as the ability for a file to have more than one name (or *hard links*) and case-sensitive file naming. Neither FAT nor HPFS supports these features, which is another reason why a new file system was required for Windows NT. NTFS supports both hard links and case-sensitive naming. If you want to run in a POSIX-conforming environment, you need at least one NTFS disk partition on your computer.

You can run POSIX applications from any Windows NT file system. If the application does not need to access the file system, the application will run with no problems. However, if the application does require access to the file system, it might not behave correctly on a non-NTFS disk partition.

Bypass Traverse Checking

By default, when you install Windows NT for the first time, the user right *Bypass Traverse Checking* is granted to everyone. This right allows a user to change directories through a directory tree even if the user has no permission for those directories.

If you want to run in a POSIX-conforming environment, you must disable this privilege for your account by using the User Manager Administrative tool.

Note You must be an administrator to do this.

▶ **To disable the Bypass Traverse Checking right for an account**

1. Select the account in User Manager.
2. From the **Policies** menu, select **User Rights**.

   The **User Rights Policy** dialog box is displayed. Be sure the **Show Advanced User Rights** check box is selected.
3. Select the Bypass Traverse Checking right.
4. Click **Remove**.
5. Click **OK**.

Printing

The POSIX subsystem itself does not directly support printing, but Windows NT supports redirection and piping between subsystems. If your POSIX application writes to **stdout**, and if you have connected or redirected either your serial or parallel ports to a printer, you can redirect the output of a POSIX application to that printer. For example, the following sequence of commands will send to a network printer the output of a POSIX application that writes to **stdout**:

```
NET USE LPT1: \\MYSERVER\PRINTER
POSIXAPP.EXE > LPT1:
```

Network Access

The POSIX.1 specification does not have a requirement for access to remote file systems, but as with any of the other subsystems, the POSIX subsystem and POSIX applications have transparent access to any Win32 remotely connected file system.

Restrictions on POSIX Applications

With this release of Windows NT, POSIX applications have no direct access to any of the facilities and features of the Win32 subsystem, such as memory mapped files, networking, graphics, or dynamic data exchange.

Implementation of Subsystem

The POSIX subsystem is implemented in Windows NT as a protected server. POSIX applications communicate with the POSIX subsystem through a message-passing facility in the Executive known as a *Local Procedure Call* (LPC).

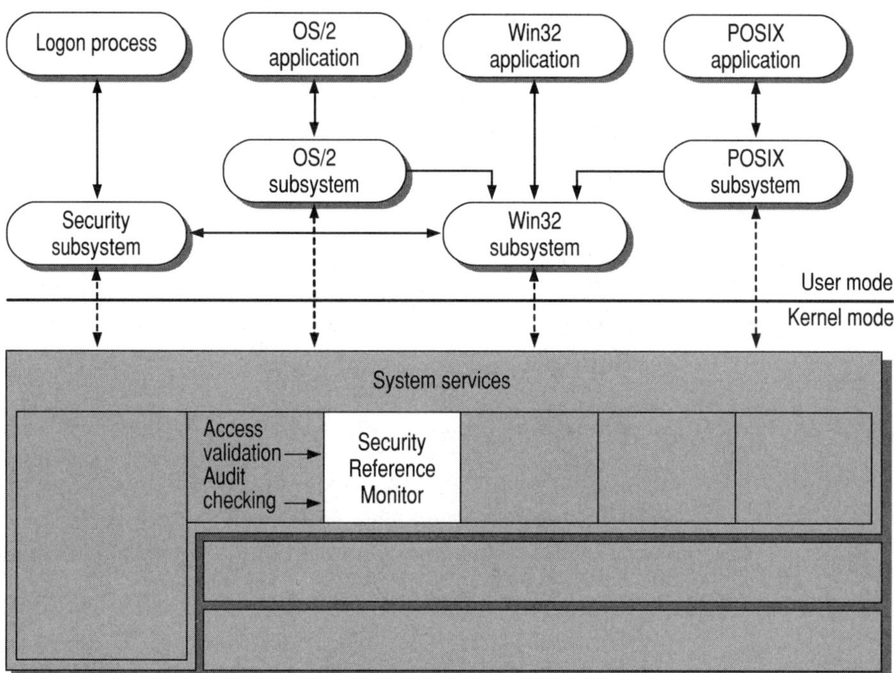

Figure 29.5 POSIX Subsystem in Windows NT

The POSIX subsystem and each POSIX application run in a protected address space that protects them from any other application that might be running on Windows NT. POSIX application are preemptively multitasked with respect to each other and with respect to other applications running in the system.

Files Used

The following table lists the principal files used by the POSIX subsystem, and the figure shows how they interact.

File	Purpose
Psxss.exe	The POSIX subsystem server
Posix.exe	The POSIX console session manager
Psxdll.dll	The POSIX dynamic link library

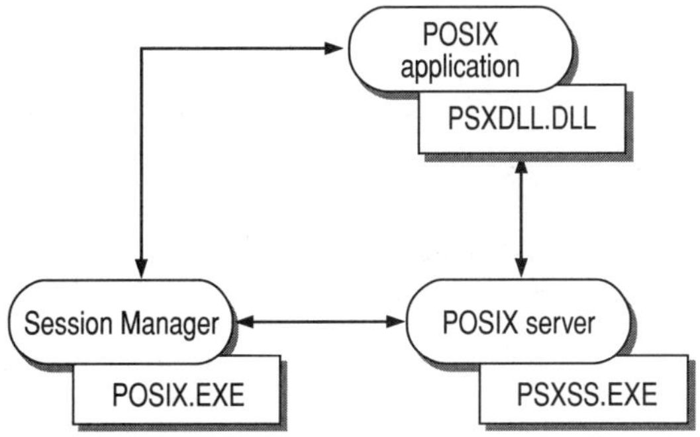

Figure 29.6 How POSIX Subsystem Files Interact

Communicating with Other Subsystems

Windows NT supports a common command processor that can run commands from any subsystem. In addition, Windows NT supports piped input and output between commands of different subsystems. For example, you could run the **ls** utility and pipe the results through the **more** command to the console:

```
ls -l | more
```

Further Information

For further information on the POSIX standards, contact the following resources:

- For information on POSIX.1 (ANSI/IEEE 1003.1-1990, ISO/IEC 9945-1:1990), contact:

  Publication Sales
  IEEE Service Center
  P.O. Box 1331445
  Hoes Lane

  Piscataway, NJ 08855-1331

- For information on other POSIX standards, contact:

  IEEE Computer Society
  Attention: Assistant Director/Standards
  1730 Massachusetts Avenue Northwest
  Washington, DC 20036

PART VII

Networking with Windows NT Workstation

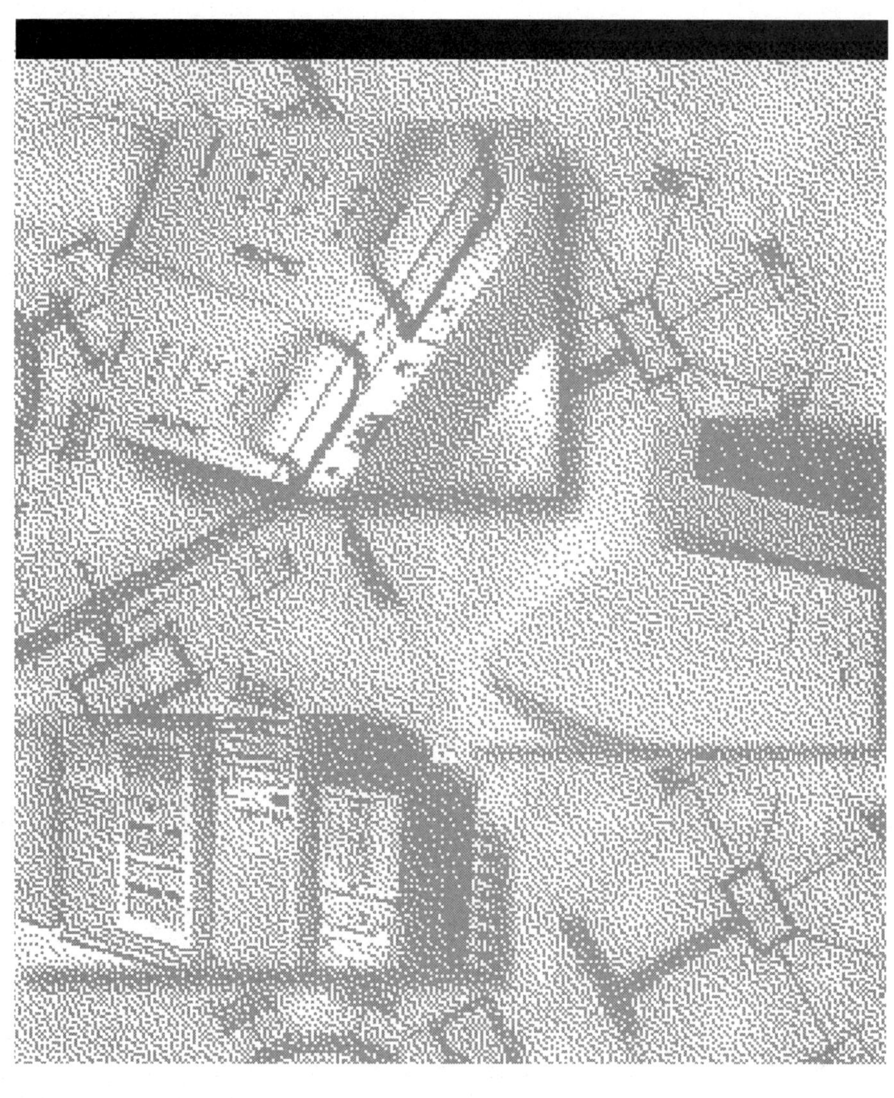

CHAPTER 30

Microsoft TCP/IP and Related Services for Windows NT

The Transmission Control Protocol/Internet Protocol (TCP/IP) suite is a standard set of networking protocols that govern how data passes between networked computers. With TCP/IP you can communicate with Windows NT platforms, with devices that use other Microsoft networking products, and with non-Microsoft systems (such as UNIX systems). TCP/IP is the primary protocol of the Internet and the World Wide Web. It is also the primary protocol for many private *internetworks*, which are networks that connect local area networks (LANs) together.

For procedural information about installing and configuring TCP/IP under Windows NT, see the online Help. For more detailed information about TCP/IP and its integration with Windows NT and other networking products, see the *Microsoft Windows NT Server Resource Kit Networking Guide*.

Benefits of Using TCP/IP

Microsoft TCP/IP for Windows NT Server and Windows NT Workstation offers the following advantages:

- A standard, routable networking protocol that is the most complete and accepted protocol available. All modern operating systems offer TCP/IP support, and most large networks rely on TCP/IP for much of their network traffic.
- A technology for connecting dissimilar systems. Many standard connectivity utilities are available to access and transfer data between dissimilar systems, including File Transfer Protocol (FTP) and Terminal Emulation Protocol (Telnet). Several of these standard utilities are included with Windows NT.
- The enabling technology necessary to connect Windows NT to the global Internet. TCP/IP, Point to Point Protocol (PPP), Point to Point Tunneling Protocol (PPTP), and Windows Sockets provide the foundation needed to connect and use Internet services.
- A robust, scaleable, cross-platform, client-server framework. Microsoft TCP/IP supports the Windows Sockets interface, which is a Windows-based implementation of the widely used Berkeley Sockets interface for network programming.

Core Technology and Third-party Add-ons

Microsoft TCP/IP is a full-featured implementation of the protocol suite and related services. It includes the following:

- Core TCP/IP protocols, including the Transmission Control Protocol (TCP), Internet Protocol (IP), User Datagram Protocol (UDP), Address Resolution Protocol (ARP), and Internet Control Message Protocol (ICMP). This suite of Internet protocols dictates how computers communicate and how networks are interconnected. Support is also provided for Point to Point Protocol (PPP), Point to Point Tunneling Protocol (PPTP), and Serial-Line IP (SLIP), which are protocols used for dial-up access to TCP/IP networks, including the Internet.
- Support for network programming interfaces such as Windows Sockets, remote procedure call (RPC), NetBIOS, and network dynamic data exchange (Network DDE).
- Basic TCP/IP connectivity utilities, including **finger**, **ftp**, **lpr**, **rcp**, **rexec**, **rsh**, **telnet**, and **tftp**. These utilities allow users running Windows NT to interact with and use resources on non-Microsoft hosts (such as those running UNIX).
- TCP/IP diagnostic tools, including **arp**, **hostname**, **ipconfig**, **lpq**, **nbtstat**, **netstat**, **ping**, **route**, and **tracert**. Use these utilities to detect and resolve TCP/IP networking problems.
- Services and related administrative tools, including the Internet Information Server for setting up Internet or Intranet Web sites, Dynamic Host Configuration Protocol (DHCP) service for automatically configuring TCP/IP on computers running Windows NT, Windows Internet Name Service (WINS) for dynamically registering and querying NetBIOS computer names on an internetwork, Domain Name System (DNS) Server service for registering and querying DNS domain names on an internetwork, and TCP/IP printing for accessing printers connected to computers running UNIX or connected directly to the network with a dedicated network adapter.
- Simple Network Management Protocol (SNMP) agent. This component allows a computer running Windows NT to be monitored remotely with management tools such as Sun® Net Manager or HP® Open View. Microsoft TCP/IP also includes SNMP support for DHCP and WINS servers.

- The server software for simple network protocols, including Character Generator, Daytime, Discard, Echo, and Quote of the Day. These protocols allow a computer running Windows NT to respond to requests from other systems that support these protocols.
- Path MTU Discovery, which provides the ability to determine the datagram size for all routers between Windows NT-based computers and any other systems on the WAN. Microsoft TCP/IP also supports the Internet Group Management Protocol (IGMP), which is used by workgroup software products.

Figure 30.1 shows the elements of Microsoft TCP/IP alongside the variety of additional applications and connectivity utilities provided by Microsoft and other third-party vendors.

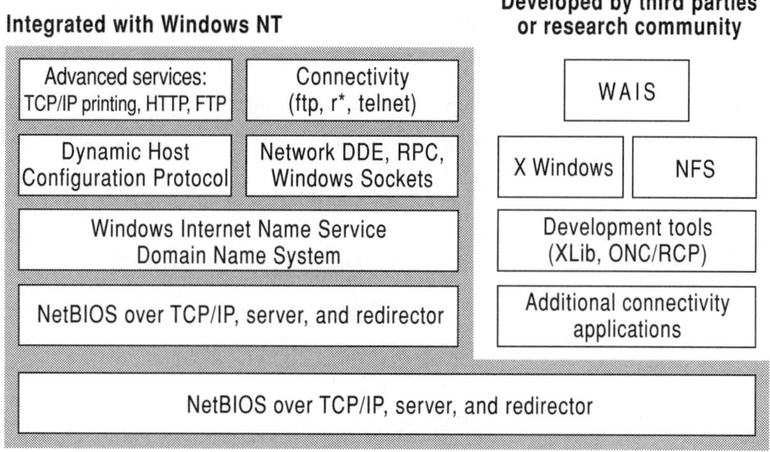

Figure 30.1 Microsoft TCP/IP Core Technology and Third-party Add-ons

Microsoft TCP/IP for Windows NT does not include a complete suite of TCP/IP connectivity utilities or server services (*daemons*). Many such applications and utilities—available in the public domain or from third-party vendors—are compatible with Microsoft TCP/IP.

Note For computers running Windows for Workgroups, you can install Microsoft TCP/IP-32. For computers running MS-DOS, you can install the Microsoft Network Client for MS-DOS. Both are available on the Windows NT Server compact disc. For installation information, see the Windows NT Server *Concepts and Planning* book.

Supported Standards

Requests for Comments (RFCs) are an evolving series of reports, proposals for protocols, and protocol standards used by the Internet community. TCP/IP standards are defined in RFCs published by the Internet Engineering Task Force (IETF) and other working groups. Table 30.1 lists the RFCs supported in this version of Microsoft TCP/IP (and Microsoft Remote Access Service).

Table 30.1 Requests for Comments (RFCs) Supported by Microsoft TCP/IP

RFC	Title
768	User Datagram Protocol (UDP)
783	Trivial File Transfer Protocol (TFTP)
791	Internet Protocol (IP)
792	Internet Control Message Protocol (ICMP)
793	Transmission Control Protocol (TCP)
816	Fault Isolation and Recovery
826	Address Resolution Protocol (ARP)
854	Telnet Protocol (TELNET)
862	Echo Protocol (ECHO)
863	Discard Protocol (DISCARD)
864	Character Generator Protocol (CHARGEN)
865	Quote of the Day Protocol (QUOTE)
867	Daytime Protocol (DAYTIME)
894	IP over Ethernet
919, 922	IP Broadcast Datagrams (broadcasting with subnets)
950	Internet Standard Subnetting Procedure
959	File Transfer Protocol (FTP)
1001, 1002	NetBIOS Service Protocols
1034, 1035	Domain Name System (DNS)
1042	IP over Token Ring
1055	Transmission of IP over Serial Lines (IP-SLIP)
1112	Internet Group Management Protocol (IGMP)
1122, 1123	Host Requirements (communications and applications)
1134	Point to Point Protocol (PPP)
1144	Compressing TCP/IP Headers for Low-Speed Serial Links
1157	Simple Network Management Protocol (SNMP)
1179	Line Printer Daemon Protocol

Table 30.1 Requests for Comments (RFCs) Supported by Microsoft TCP/IP *(continued)*

RFC	Title
1188	IP over FDDI
1191	Path MTU Discovery
1201	IP over ARCNET
1231	IEEE 802.5 Token Ring MIB (MIB-II)
1332	PPP Internet Protocol Control Protocol (IPCP)
1334	PPP Authentication Protocols
1518	An Architecture for IP Address Allocation with CIDR
1519	Classless Inter-Domain Routing (CIDR): An Address Assignment and Aggregation Strategy
1533	DHCP Options and BOOTP Vendor Extensions [1]
1534	Interoperation Between DHCP and BOOTP
1541	Dynamic Host Configuration Protocol (DHCP)
1542	Clarifications and Extensions for the Bootstrap Protocol [2]
1547	Requirements for Point to Point Protocol (PPP)
1548	Point to Point Protocol (PPP)
1549	PPP in High-level Data Link Control (HDLC) Framing
1552	PPP Internetwork Packet Exchange Control Protocol (IPXCP)
1553	IPX Header Compression
1570	Link Control Protocol (LCP) Extensions
Draft RFCs	NetBIOS Frame Control Protocol (NBFCP); PPP over ISDN; PPP over X.25; Compression Control Protocol

[1] The Microsoft DHCP server does not support BOOTP. BOOTP requests are silently ignored. However, a DHCP server and a BOOTP server can coexist.

[2] Windows NT Server can be configured to act as a BOOTP relay agent.

Note For details on retrieving RFCs by means of FTP or email, send an email message to "rfc-info@isi.edu" with the subject "getting rfcs" and the message body "help: ways_to_get_rfcs".

RFCs can be obtained by means of FTP from nis.nsf.net, nisc.jvnc.net, venera.isi.edu, wuarchive.wustl.edu, src.doc.ic.ac.uk, ftp.concert.net, ds.internic.net, or nic.ddn.mil.

Internetworking

This section summarizes how Microsoft TCP/IP works with Windows NT to provide enterprise internetworking solutions. For a more detailed discussion of these points, see the *Microsoft Windows NT Resource Kit Networking Guide*.

Using TCP/IP for Scalability

TCP/IP delivers a scalable internetworking technology widely supported by hardware and software vendors.

When TCP/IP is used as the enterprise-networking protocol, the Windows-based networking solutions from Microsoft can be used on an existing internetwork to provide client and server support for TCP/IP and connectivity utilities. These solutions include

- Microsoft Windows NT Workstation, with enhancements to support wide area networks (WAN), TCP/IP printing, FTP, Telnet, DHCP, WINS, and DNS client software, Windows Sockets, and extended LMHOSTS file.
- Microsoft Windows NT Server, with the same enhancements as Windows NT Workstation, plus Internet Information Server, DHCP Server, WINS Server, and DNS Server software.
- Microsoft Windows 95, with enhancements to support wide area networks (WAN), DHCP, WINS, and DNS client software, extended LMHOSTS file, and Windows Sockets.
- Microsoft TCP/IP-32 for Windows for Workgroups, with Windows Sockets support, can be used to provide access for Windows for Workgroups computers to Windows NT, LAN Manager, and other TCP/IP systems. Microsoft TCP/IP-32 includes DHCP, WINS and DNS client software.
- Microsoft LAN Manager—including both client and server support for Windows Sockets—and MS-DOS–based connectivity utilities. The Microsoft Network Client 2.0 software on the Windows NT Server compact disc includes new Microsoft TCP/IP support with DHCP and WINS clients.

As shown in Figure 30.2, the current version of TCP/IP for Windows NT also supports IP routing in systems with multiple network adapters attached to separate physical networks (*multihomed systems*).

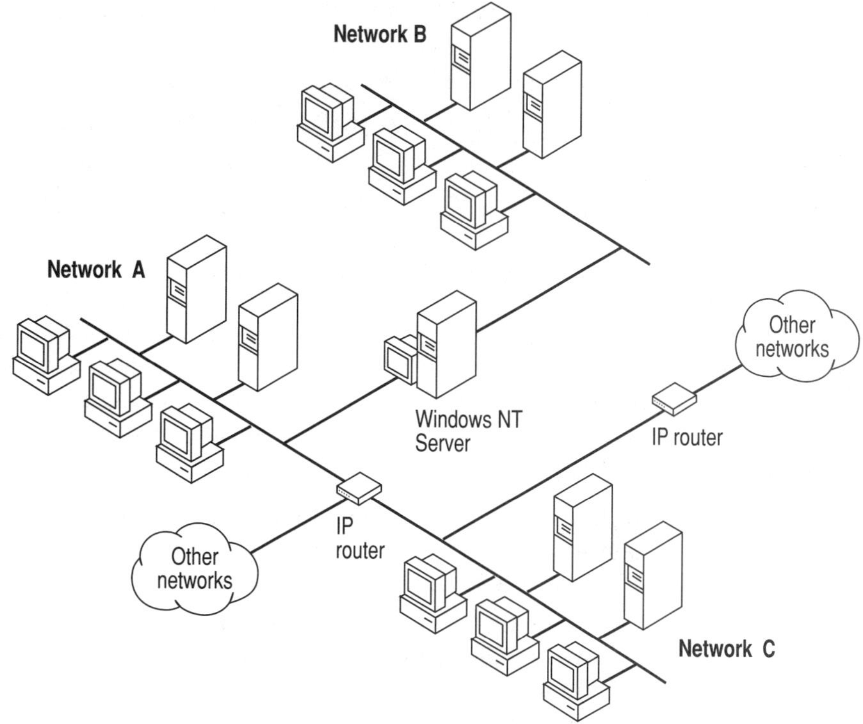

Figure 30.2 TCP/IP for Windows NT Supports IP Routing for Multihomed Systems

Using TCP/IP in Heterogeneous Networks

Because most modern operating systems support TCP/IP protocols, heterogeneous computers on an internetwork can use simple networking applications and utilities to share information. TCP/IP enables Windows NT to communicate with many non-Microsoft systems, including

- Internet hosts
- Apple Macintosh systems
- IBM mainframes
- UNIX systems
- Open VMS systems
- Printers with network adapters connected directly to the network

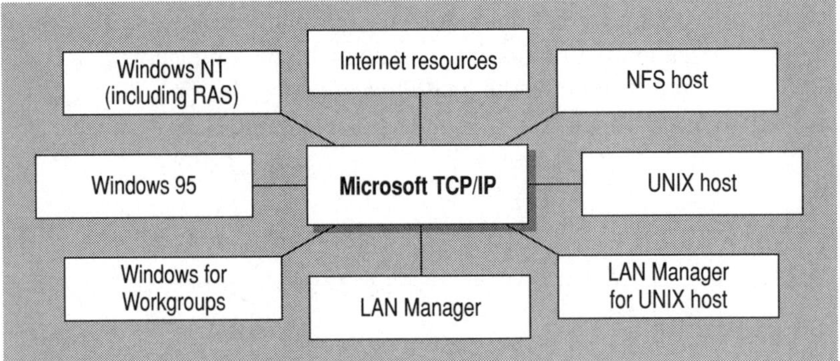

Figure 30.3 Microsoft TCP/IP Connectivity

As shown in Figure 30.3, Microsoft TCP/IP provides a framework for interoperable heterogeneous networking. The modular architecture of Windows NT networking with its transport-independent services contributes to the strength of this framework. For example, Windows NT supports the following transport protocols:

- IPX/SPX for use in NetWare environments, using the Microsoft NWLink transport. Besides providing interoperability with NetWare networks, IPX/SPX is a fast LAN transport for Windows-based networking as well.
- TCP/IP for internetworks based on IP technologies. TCP/IP is the preferred transport for internetworks and provides interoperability with UNIX and other TCP/IP-based networks.
- NetBEUI as the protocol for local area networking on smaller networks and compatibility with existing LAN Manager and IBM LAN Server networks.
- AppleTalk for connecting to and sharing resources with Macintosh systems.

Note Transport protocols (such as DECnet and OSI) from third-party vendors can also be used by Windows NT networking services.

Using TCP/IP with Third-Party Software

TCP/IP is a common denominator for heterogeneous networking, and Windows Sockets is a standard used by application developers. Together they provide a framework for cross-platform client-server development.

The Windows Sockets standard defines a networking API that developers use to create applications for the entire family of Microsoft Windows operating systems. Windows Sockets is an open standard that is part of the Microsoft Windows Open System Architecture (WOSA) initiative. It is a public specification based on Berkeley UNIX sockets, which means that UNIX applications can be quickly ported to Microsoft Windows and Windows NT. Windows Sockets provides a single standard programming interface supported by all major vendors implementing TCP/IP for Windows systems.

The Windows Sockets standard ensures compatibility with Windows-based TCP/IP utilities developed by many vendors. This includes third-party applications for X Windows, sophisticated terminal emulation software, NFS, electronic mail packages, and more. Because Windows NT offers compatibility with 16-bit Windows Sockets, applications created for Windows 3.*x* Windows Sockets run on Windows NT without modification or recompilation.

For example, third-party applications for X Windows provide strong connectivity solutions by means of X Windows servers, database servers, and terminal emulation. With such applications, a computer running Windows NT can work as an X Windows server while retaining compatibility with applications created for Windows NT, Windows 95, Windows 3.*x*, and MS-DOS on the same system. Other third-party software includes X Windows client libraries for Windows NT, which enable developers to write X Windows client applications on Windows NT that can be run and displayed remotely on X Windows servers.

The TCP/IP utilities for Windows NT use Windows Sockets, as do 32-bit TCP/IP applications developed by third parties. Windows NT also uses the Windows Sockets interface to support Services for Macintosh and IPX/SPX in NWLink. Under Windows NT, 16-bit Windows-based applications created under the Windows Sockets standard will run without modification or recompilation. Most TCP/IP users will use programs that comply with the Windows Sockets standard (such as **ftp** or **telnet**) or third-party applications.

The Windows Sockets standard allows a developer to create an application with a single common interface and a single executable that can run over many TCP/IP implementations. Windows Sockets is designed to:

- Provide a familiar networking API to developers using Windows NT, Windows 95, Windows for Workgroups, or UNIX.
- Offer binary compatibility between vendors for heterogeneous Windows-based TCP/IP stacks and utilities.
- Support both connection-oriented and connectionless protocols.

Typical Windows Sockets applications include graphic connectivity utilities, terminal emulation software, Simple Mail Transfer Protocol (SMTP) and electronic mail clients, network printing utilities, SQL client applications, and corporate client-server applications.

Specifications for Windows Sockets are available on numerous Internet sites such as www.microsoft.com, the Microsoft Network (MSN™), and CompuServe.

CHAPTER 31

Microsoft TCP/IP Architecture

TCP/IP protocols map to a four-layered conceptual model: Application, Transport, Internet, and Network Interface. This model is officially known as the TCP/IP Internet Protocol Suite but is often referred to as the TCP/IP protocol family. As shown in Figure 2.1, each layer in the TCP/IP model corresponds to one or more layers of the International Standards Organization (ISO) seven-layer Open Systems Interconnection (OSI) model.

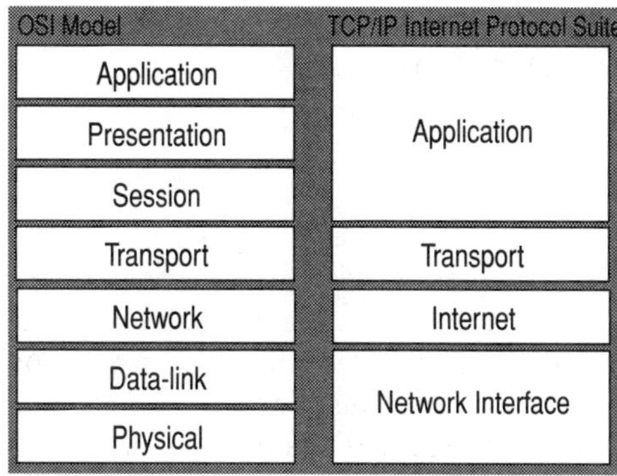

Figure 31.1 TCP/IP and the OSI Model

The TCP/IP Protocol Suite

Defined within the four layers of TCP/IP are protocols that dictate how computers connect and communicate. The most common of these protocols are Transmission Control Protocol (TCP), User Datagram Protocol (UDP), Internet Protocol (IP), Address Resolution Protocol (ARP), and Internet Control Message Protocol (ICMP). The following sections introduce these protocols, explain how they relate to Windows NT networking, and describe where and how TCP/IP configuration parameters are stored on Windows NT.

Transmission Control Protocol

The most common higher-level protocol in the suite is Transmission Control Protocol (TCP). It provides a reliable, connection-oriented packet delivery service on top of (or encapsulated within) IP. TCP guarantees the delivery of packets, ensures proper sequencing of the data, and provides a checksum feature that validates both the packet header and its data for accuracy. If the network either corrupts or loses a TCP packet during transmission, TCP is responsible for retransmitting the faulty packet. This reliability makes TCP the protocol of choice for session-based data transmission, client-server applications, and critical services, such as electronic mail.

This reliability has a price. TCP headers require additional bits to provide proper sequencing of information, as well as a mandatory checksum to ensure reliability of both the TCP packet header and the packet data. To guarantee successful data delivery, the protocol also requires that the recipient acknowledge successful receipt of data.

Such acknowledgments (ACKs) generate additional network traffic, diminishing the rate at which data passes in favor of reliability. To reduce the impact on performance, most hosts send an acknowledgment for every other segment or when a specified time interval has passed.

User Datagram Protocol

If reliability is not essential, User Datagram Protocol (UDP), a TCP complement, offers a connectionless datagram service that guarantees neither delivery nor correct sequencing of delivered packets (much like IP). Higher-level protocols or applications might provide reliability mechanisms in addition to UDP/IP. UDP data checksums are optional, providing a way to exchange data over highly reliable networks without unnecessarily consuming network resources or processing time. When UDP checksums are used, they validate the integrity of both the header and data. ACKs are not enforced by the UDP protocol; this is left to higher-level protocols.

UDP also supports sending data from a single sender to multiple receivers.

Internet Protocol

Internet Protocol (IP) provides packet delivery for all other protocols within the suite. It provides a best-effort, connectionless delivery system for computer data. That is, IP packets are not guaranteed to arrive at their destination, nor are they guaranteed to be received in the sequence in which they were sent. The protocol's checksum feature confirms only the IP header's integrity. Thus, responsibility for the data contained within the IP packet (and the sequencing) is assured only by using higher-level protocols.

Address Resolution Protocol

Not directly related to data transport, but important nonetheless, the Address Resolution Protocol (ARP) is one of the maintenance protocols that supports the TCP/IP suite and is usually invisible to users and applications.

If two systems are to communicate across a TCP/IP network, the system sending the packet must map the IP address of the final destination to the physical address of the final destination. IP acquires this physical address by broadcasting a special inquiry packet (an ARP request packet) containing the IP address of the destination system. All ARP-enabled systems on the local IP network detect these broadcast messages, and the system that owns the IP address in question replies by sending its physical address to the requester (in an ARP reply packet). The physical/IP address is then stored in the ARP cache of the requesting system for subsequent use.

Because the ARP reply can also be broadcast to the network, other systems on the network can use this information to update their own ARP caches. (Use the **arp** program to view the ARP tables.)

Internet Control Message Protocol

Internet Control Message Protocol (ICMP) is another of the maintenance protocols. It allows two systems on an IP network to share status and error information. This information can be used by higher-level protocols to recover from transmission problems or by network administrators to detect network trouble. Although ICMP packets are encapsulated within IP packets, they are not considered to be a higher-level protocol. (ICMP is required in every IP network implementation.)

The **ping** program uses the ICMP echo request and echo reply packets to determine whether a particular IP system on a network is functional. For this reason, the **ping** program is useful for diagnosing IP network or router failures.

TCP/IP and the Windows NT Network Architecture

The architecture of the Microsoft Windows NT operating system with integrated networking is protocol-independent. This architecture, illustrated in Figure 2.2, provides application, file, print, and other services over any network protocol that supports the transport driver interface (TDI). The protocols package network requests for applications in their respective formats and send the requests to the appropriate network adapter by means of the network device interface specification (NDIS) interface. NDIS allows multiple network protocols to reside over a wide variety of network adapters and media types.

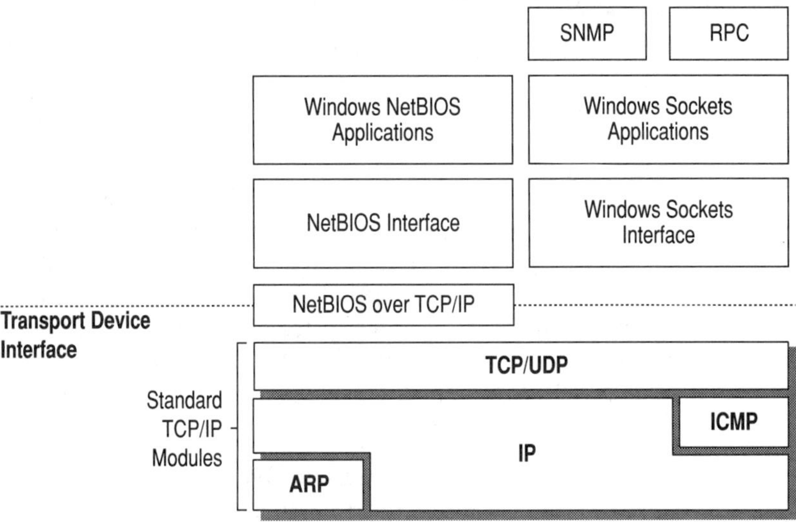

Figure 31.2 Architectural Model of Windows NT with TCP/IP

Under the Windows NT transport-independent architecture, TCP/IP is a suite of protocols that can be used to offer Windows-based networking capabilities. The TCP/IP protocols give Windows NT, Windows for Workgroups, and LAN Manager computers transparent access to each other and enable communication with non-Microsoft systems in the enterprise network.

TCP/IP and the Windows NT Configuration Database

TCP/IP configuration information is stored in the Windows NT Registry. The Registry, illustrated in Figure 31.3, is a hierarchical database that provides a central repository for hardware-specific information.

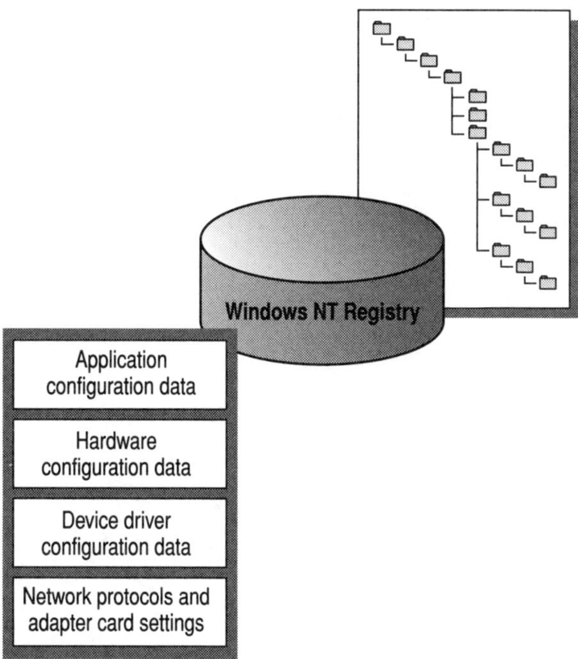

Figure 31.3 Conceptual View of the Windows NT Registry

In general, the TCP/IP-configuration parameters (such as IP address and computer name) are modified by means of the Windows NT Control Panel or the Administrative Tools (Common) folder. However, parameters that are not routinely changed, such as default Time To Live (TTL) and default Type Of Service (TOS), can be modified only by means of the Registry (with the Registry Editor).

Caution Incorrectly adjusting TCP/IP registry parameters may adversely affect system performance. For a description of these parameters, see the Regentry.hlp help file on the *Microsoft Windows NT Resource Kit* CD-ROM.

CHAPTER 32

Networking Name Resolution and Registration

Administration of Microsoft TCP/IP and related services splits roughly into two functional areas:

- *Client Configuration Options.* Every computer on a TCP/IP internetwork must be given a unique computer name and IP address. The IP address identifies both the computer and the subnetwork to which it is attached. When the computer is moved to a different subnetwork, the IP address must be changed to reflect the new subnetwork ID.
- *Name Resolution Services.* People use "friendly" names to connect to computers; programs use IP addresses. TCP/IP internetworks require a *name resolution service* that converts computer names to IP addresses and IP addresses to computer names.

This chapter is intended for the administrator of small peer-to-peer workstation subnet, or single workstation environments, that connect to Internet or TCP/IP network resources. This information in this chapter is required knowledge for the following chapter "Using LMHOSTS Files."

Understanding IP Addressing

To receive and deliver packets successfully between computers, TCP/IP requires that each computer be configured with three values provided by the network administrator: an IP-address, a subnet mask, and a default gateway (router).

Note Users running Windows NT on networks with Windows NT Server–based DHCP servers can take advantage of automatic system configuration and do not need to manually configure a computer with these TCP/IP values.

IP Addresses

Every device attached to a TCP/IP network is identified by a unique *IP address*. (If a computer has multiple network adapters, each adapter will have its own IP address.) This address is typically represented in dotted-decimal notation, that is, with the decimal value of each octet (eight bits, or one byte) of the address separated by a period. Here is a sample IP address:

```
138.57.7.27
```

Important Because IP addresses identify devices on a network, each device on the network must be assigned a unique IP address.

Network ID and Host ID

Although an IP address is a single value, it contains two pieces of information: the network ID and the host ID of your computer.

- The *network ID* identifies the systems that are located on the same physical network. All systems on the same physical network must have the same network ID, and the network ID must be unique to the internetwork.
- The *host ID* identifies a workstation, server, router, or other TCP/IP device within a network. The address for each device must be unique to the network ID.

A computer connected to a TCP/IP network uses the network ID and host ID to determine which packets it should receive or ignore and to determine the scope of its transmissions. (Only computers with the same network ID accept each other's IP-level broadcast messages.)

Note Networks that connect to the public Internet must obtain an official network ID from the *Internet Network Information Center* (InterNIC) to guarantee IP network ID uniqueness. For more information, visit the InterNIC home page on the Internet at: **http://www.internic.net/**

After receiving a network ID, the local network administrator must assign unique host IDs for computers within the local network. Although private networks not connected to the Internet can use their own network (intranet) identifier, obtaining a valid network ID from InterNIC allows a private network to connect to the Internet in the future without reassigning addresses.

The Internet community has defined address *classes* to accommodate networks of varying sizes. The address class can be discerned from the first octet of an IP-address. Table 32.1 summarizes the relationship between the first octet of a given address and its network ID and host ID fields. It also identifies the total number of network IDs and host IDs for each address class that participates in the Internet addressing scheme. This example uses w.x.y.z to designate the bytes of the IP address.

Table 32.1 IP Address Classes

Class	w values [1,2]	Network ID	Host ID	Available networks	Available hosts per network
A	1–126	w	x.y.z	126	16,777,214
B	128–191	w.x	y.z	16,384	65,534
C	192–223	w.x.y	z	2,097,151	254

1 Inclusive range for the first octet in the IP address.

2 The address 127 is reserved for loopback testing and interprocess communication on the local computer; it is not a valid network address. Addresses 224 and above are reserved for special protocols (Internet Group Management Protocol multicast and others) and cannot be used as host addresses.

Subnet Masks

Subnet masks are 32-bit values that allow the recipient of IP packets to distinguish the network ID portion of the IP address from the host ID. Subnet masks are created by assigning 1's to network ID bits and 0's to host ID bits. The 32-bit value is then converted to dotted-decimal notation, as shown in Table 32.2.

Table 32.2 Default Subnet Masks for Standard IP Address Classes

Address class	Bits for subnet mask	Subnet mask
Class A	11111111 00000000 00000000 00000000	255.0.0.0
Class B	11111111 11111111 00000000 00000000	255.255.0.0
Class C	11111111 11111111 11111111 00000000	255.255.255.0

For example, when the IP address is 138.57.7.27 and the subnet mask is 255.255.0.0, the network ID is 138.57 and the host ID is 7.27.

Because the class of a host is easily determined, configuring a host with a subnet mask might seem redundant. But subnet masks are also used to further segment an assigned network ID among several local networks. Sometimes only *portions* of an octet need to be segmented using only a few bits to specify subnet IDs.

Important To prevent addressing and routing problems, all computers on a logical network must use the same subnet mask and network ID.

IP Routing

The Internet and other TCP/IP networks are interconnected by *routers*, which are devices that pass IP packets from one network to another.

For each computer on an IP network, you can maintain a table with an entry for every other computer or network with which the local computer communicates. In general, this is not practical, and the default gateway (router) is used instead. (The default gateway is a computer connected to the local subnet and to other networks. It has knowledge of the network IDs for other networks in the internetwork and how to reach them. It is needed only for computers that are part of an internetwork.)

When IP prepares to send a packet, it inserts the local (source) IP address and the destination address of the packet in the IP header. It then examines the destination address, compares it to a locally maintained *route table*, and takes appropriate action based on what it finds. There are three possible actions:

- It can pass the packet up to a protocol layer above IP on the local host.
- It can be forwarded through one of the locally attached network adapters.
- It can be discarded.

The search for a match of the destination address in the route table proceeds from the specific to the general in the following order:

- The table is examined for an exact match (host route).
- The host portion is stripped from the destination address, and the table is examined for a match (subnet route).
- The subnet portion is stripped from the destination address, and the table is examined for a match (network route).
- The default gateway is used.
- If a default gateway has not been specified, the packet is discarded.

Because the default gateway contains information about the network IDs of the other networks in the internetwork, it can forward the packet to other routers until the packet is eventually delivered to a router connected to the specified destination. This process is known as *routing* and is illustrated in Figure 32.1.

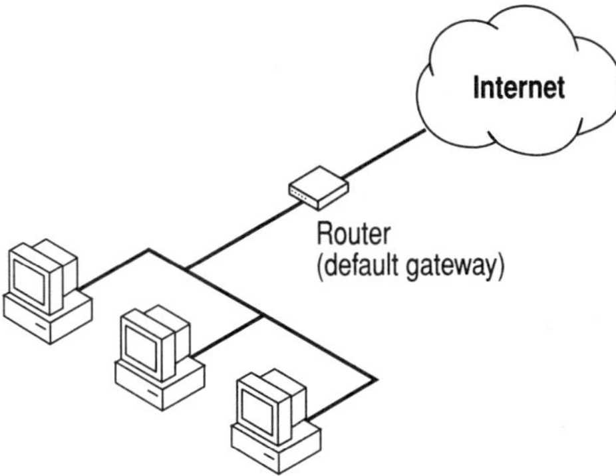

Figure 32.1 Routers (default gateway)

Note If the default gateway becomes unavailable, communication beyond the local subnet can be impaired. To prevent this, use the Network application in Control Panel to specify multiple default gateways, or use the **route** utility to manually add routes to the route table for heavily used systems or networks.

IP Addressing for RAS

Remote dial-in access to internetworks is provided by a built-in feature of Windows NT known as *Remote Access Service* (RAS). RAS is based on a client-server architecture in which a remote RAS-based client connects to a local RAS server. After the connection has been made, the client running RAS becomes a full-fledged host on the network, and the remote user can then use the same Windows-based tools as a local user to access resources such as files, printers, electronic mail, and databases.

As shown in Figure 32.2, RAS supports multiple protocols, two of which are TCP/IP over Point-to-Point Protocol (PPP), and Serial Line IP (SLIP). Such protocol support allows a client with a RAS connection to interoperate with the heterogeneous servers typically found on today's internetworks.

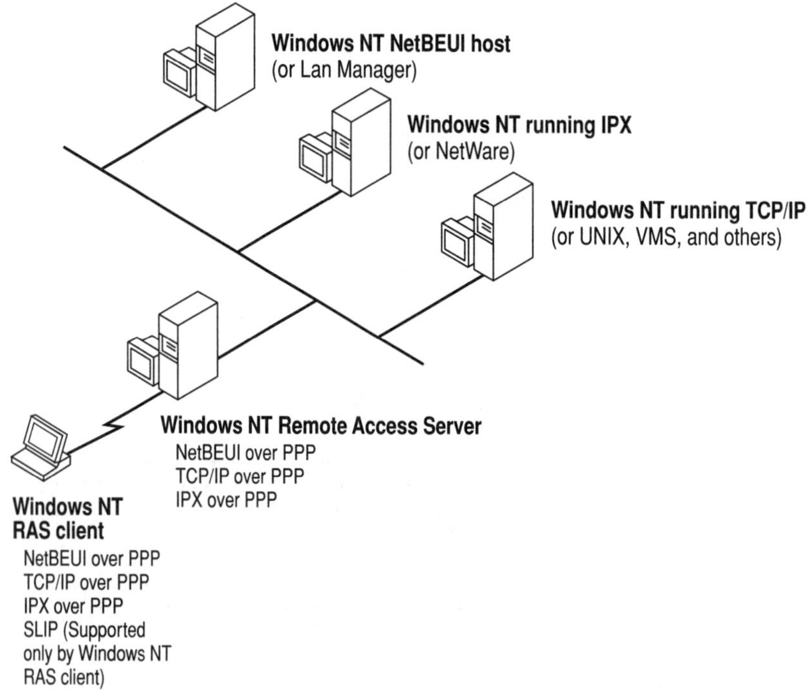

Figure 32.2 Network Access with RAS in Windows NT

Client configuration options are handled directly by the RAS server. The RAS server reserves a pool of IP addresses for static configuration during RAS installation. These addresses are automatically assigned to RAS clients who dial in using PPP. If the administrator sets up the RAS server to use a static pool of addresses, all clients dialing into a particular RAS server are assigned the same network ID as the RAS server, plus unique host IDs. Clients running RAS can use the same name resolution services as hosts connected directly to the internetwork.

Name Resolution Services

Windows NT with TCP/IP requires a unique IP address and computer name for each computer on the network. A mechanism must be available on a TCP/IP network to match computer names to IP addresses. These are called *name resolution services.*

Background

As networks have grown in complexity, so have these name resolution mechanisms increased in sophistication.

NetBIOS and DNS Computer Names

Windows NT networking components rely on a naming convention known as *NetBIOS*. In general, NetBIOS computer names consist of a single part.

In contrast, TCP/IP components rely on a naming convention know as the *Domain Name System* (DNS). DNS computer names consist of two parts: a *host name* and a *domain name*, which combined form the *fully qualified domain name* (FQDN).

Fortunately, NetBIOS computer names are compatible with DNS host names, making interoperation possible between the two. Windows NT combines the NetBIOS computer name with the DNS domain name to form the FQDN.

Note Under Windows NT, the DNS host name defaults to the same name as the NetBIOS computer name. You can change this if you need separate names.

Flat vs. Hierarchical Name Spaces

The original naming scheme for both NetBIOS and TCP/IP consisted of a *flat name space* where each computer was assigned a single-part name. (A single-part name consists of a short sequence of characters without any additional structure.) Flat name spaces worked well for simple networks with relatively few interconnected computers, but as network complexity increased, they rapidly become inadequate for the following reasons:

- Single-part names are derived from a finite set of identifiers. The potential for conflict increases with the number of computers interconnected.
- Administration of the name space rests with a central authority. Someone must ensure that each computer is assigned a unique name. Because there is no convenient way to segment a flat name space, control of name assignment must be centralized.
- All changes to the network must be approved by the central authority. Before a new computer is added to the network or an existing computer is moved to a different subnet, the change must be coordinated with the central authority. For a large network, this results in a significant administrative burden.

A hierarchical name space implemented as a multi-part naming scheme enables authority to be distributed and administration to be decentralized. A hierarchical name space can be viewed as an inverted tree with the branches and leaves pointing down. A central authority still manages the top of the tree, but below the top level the structure can be distributed into autonomous administrative units. Name uniqueness must still be enforced at the lowest administrative level, but this is a reasonable task for a well-segmented name space. The hierarchical structure of the name space guarantees name uniqueness above these lower levels.

Implementations of hierarchical naming schemes exist for both TCP/IP and NetBIOS: Domain Name System (DNS) for TCP/IP and NetBIOS Scope for NetBIOS.

Name Space Implementations

The first implementations of name spaces—both flat and hierarchical—relied on text files for mapping of computer name to IP address. Each computer on the internetwork had its name and IP address on a line in the file, and a copy of the file existed on each computer. This solution worked well for simple networks having relatively few interconnected computers. As networks grew in size and complexity, this method ran into scaling problems similar to those experienced with a flat name space.

Newer implementations have largely done away with the need for a mapping file on each machine; instead, server-based repositories store the necessary information. Mapping files still exist but are typically used in simple networks or as a safety feature in case the name servers are down.

The mapping files are

- HOSTS for DNS names
- LMHOSTS for NetBIOS names

Note When you install Windows NT, example HOSTS and LMHOSTS files are placed in the *systemroot*\System32\Drivers\Etc directory.

NetBIOS over TCP/IP (NetBT) Name Resolution

Name resolution services for Windows NT fall into two general categories. Each provides similar services for clients and can operate independently or in tandem. They are

- *NetBIOS over TCP/IP* (NetBT)
- *Domain Name System* (DNS)

NetBT is the session-layer network service that performs name-to-IP address mapping for name resolution. Under Windows NT, it is implemented through the broadcast name resolution and Windows Internet Name Service (WINS) (on those networks with WINS servers). The two most important aspects of the related naming activities are *registration* and *resolution*:

- Registration is the process used to register a unique name for each computer (node) on the network. A computer typically registers itself when it starts.
- Resolution is the process used to determine the specific address for a computer name.

Note RFCs 1001 and 1002 specify how NetBIOS should be implemented over TCP/IP and define the name resolution modes.

Defined within NetBT are modes that specify how network resources are identified and accessed. The most common NetBT modes are

- *b-node*, which uses broadcast messages to resolve names
- *p-node*, which uses point-to-point communications with a name server to resolve names
- *m-node*, which first uses b-node and then—if necessary—p-node to resolve names
- *h-node*, which first uses p-node for name queries and then b-node if the name service is unavailable or if the name is not registered in the database

The two most common node types for client computers running Windows NT are h-node and b-node. The default node type is b-node.

Note If the Windows NT Workstation computer can access a DHCP server or WINS server, the node type is assigned by the DHCP server. If the client computer is configured to use WINS, Windows NT defaults to h-node.

In Windows NT, the Netbt.sys module provides the NetBT functionality that supports name registration and resolution modes. NetBT uses b-node broadcast messages to resolve names. NetBT can also use LMHOSTS files and DNS for name resolution, depending on how TCP/IP is configured on a particular computer.

Note When WINS servers are in place on the network, NetBT resolves names on a client computer by communicating with the WINS server, before using LMHOSTS files.

Windows NT supports all NetBT modes described in the following sections. NetBT is also used with the LAN Manager 2.*x* Server message protocol.

B-Node

The b-node mode uses broadcast messages for name registration and resolution. For example, if a computer named NT_PC1 wants to communicate with a computer named NT_PC2, NT_PC1 sends a broadcast message that it is looking for NT_PC2, and then it waits a specified time for NT_PC2 to respond.

B-node has two major problems:

- In a large environment, it loads the network with broadcast messages.
- Typically, routers do not forward broadcast messages, so computers on opposite sides of a router never hear the requests.

P-Node

The p-node mode addresses the issues that b-node does not solve. In a p-node environment, computers neither create nor respond to broadcast messages. All computers register themselves with the WINS server, which is responsible for knowing computer names and addresses and for ensuring that no duplicate names exist on the network.

In this environment, when NT_PC1 wants to communicate with NT_PC2, it queries the WINS server for the address of NT_PC2. Upon receipt of the address, NT_PC1 goes directly to NT_PC2 without broadcasting. Because the name queries go directly to the WINS server, p-node avoids loading the network with broadcast messages. Because broadcast messages are not used, and because the address is received directly, computers can be on opposite sides of routers.

The most significant problems with p-node are the following:

- All computers must be configured to know the address of the WINS server.
- If the WINS server is down, computers that rely on it to resolve addresses cannot get to any other systems on the network.

M-Node

The m-node mode was created primarily to solve the problems associated with b-node and p-node. In an m-node environment, a computer first attempts registration and resolution using b-node. If that fails, it switches to p-node. Advantage are as follows:

- M-node can cross routers.
- Because b-node is always tried first, computers on the same side of a router continue to operate as usual if the WINS server is down.
- In theory, it should increase local area network (LAN) performance.

H-Node

The h-node mode solves the most significant problems associated with broadcast messages and with routed-environment operations. It is a combination of b-node and p-node that uses broadcast messages as a last effort. The h-node mode does more than change the order for using b-node and p-node: If the WINS server is down—making broadcast messages a necessity—the computer continues to poll the WINS server. When the WINS server can be reached again, the system returns to p-node. H-node can also be configured to use the LMHOSTS file after broadcast name resolution fails.

Because p-node is used first, no broadcast messages are generated if the WINS server is running, and computers can be on opposite sides of routers. If the WINS server is down, b-node is used, so computers on the same side of a router continue to operate as usual.

Other Combinations

Another variation, known as *modified b-node*, is also used in Microsoft networks so that messages can go across routers. Modified b-node does not use p-node mode or a WINS server. In this mode, b-node uses a list of computers and addresses stored in an LMHOSTS file. If a b-node attempt fails, the system looks in LMHOSTS to find a name and then uses the associated address to cross the router. However, each computer must have this list, which creates an administrative burden in maintaining and distributing the list. Both Windows for Workgroups 3.11 and LAN Manager 2.*x* used such a modified b-node system. Windows NT uses this method if WINS servers are not used on the network. In Windows NT, some extensions have been added to this file to make it easier to manage (as described in the "Using LMHOSTS Files" chapter in this book), but modified b-node is not an ideal solution.

Some sites might require both b-node and p-node modes. Although this configuration can work, administrators must exercise extreme caution, using it only for transition situations. Because p-node hosts disregard broadcast messages, and b-node hosts rely on broadcast messages for name resolution, the two hosts can potentially be configured with the same NetBIOS name, leading to unpredictable results. Also, if a computer configured to use b-node has a static mapping in the WINS database, a computer configured to use p-node cannot use the same computer name.

Computers running Windows NT can be configured as WINS proxy agents to help the transition to using WINS. Windows-based networking clients (WINS-enabled Windows NT, Windows 95, or Windows for Workgroups 3.11 computers) can use WINS directly. Non-WINS computers that are b-node compatible (as described in RFCs 1001 and 1002) can access WINS through *proxies.* A WINS proxy is a WINS-enabled computer that listens for name-query broadcast messages and then respond for names that are not on the local subnet. Proxies are p-node computers.

Figure 32.3 shows a small internetwork with two local area networks connected by a router. One of the subnets has a WINS name server, which can be used by clients on both subnets. The WINS proxy computer (which must be WINS by using TCP/IP Configuration), can access the WINS server directly. The name registration and resolution broadcasts from the non-WINS enabled computers are intercepted by the WINS proxy. Proxies intercept the broadcast messages and send them directly to the WINS server on the other subnet.

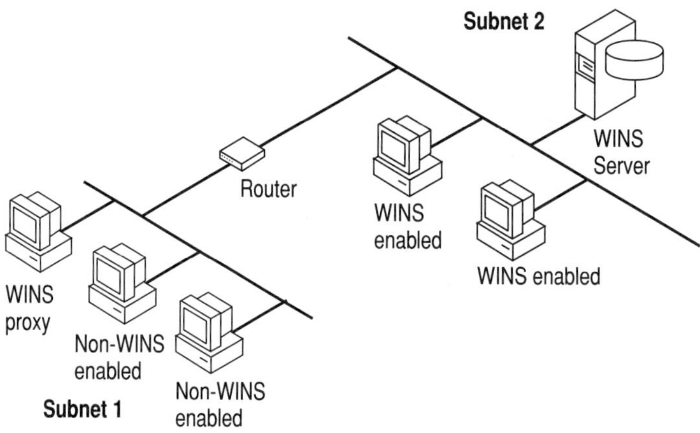

Figure 32.3 Routed Network with WINS Server

In a WINS and broadcast name resolution environment, a WINS-enabled client computer will behave differently than a non-WINS-enabled client computer. These differences will be apparent in the way these clients handle *resolution*, *registration*, *release*, and *renewal*.

Name Resolution

NetBIOS computer names are resolved using two basic methods, depending on whether WINS resolution is available and enabled on the client computer. Whatever name resolution method is used, the process is transparent to the user after the system is configured.

If WINS is not enabled on the client: The computer registers its name by sending *name registration request* packets (as broadcast messages) to the local subnet. To find a particular computer, the non-WINS computer sends *name query request* packets (as broadcast messages) on the local subnet. (This broadcast message cannot be passed on through IP routers.) If local name resolution fails, the local LMHOSTS file is consulted. These processes are followed whether the computer is a network server, a workstation, or other device.

If WINS is enabled on the client: The computer first queries the WINS server. If that fails, it sends name registration and query requests (as broadcast messages).

Name Registration

Name registration ensures that the NetBIOS computer name and IP address are unique for each device.

If WINS is not enabled on the client: For a non-WINS computer to register its name, a *name registration request* packet is broadcast to the local network, stating its NetBIOS computer name and IP address. Any device on the network that previously claimed that name challenges the name registration (with a *negative name registration response*), resulting in an error for the computer attempting to register the duplicate name. If the *name registration request* remains unchallenged for a specific time period, the requesting computer adopts that name and address.

After a non-WINS computer claims a name, it must challenge duplicate name registration attempts (with a *negative name registration response*) and respond positively to name queries issued on its registered name (with a *positive name query response*). The *positive name query response* contains the IP address of the computer so that the two systems can establish a session.

If WINS is enabled on the client: The name registration request is sent directly to the WINS server to be added to the database. A WINS server accepts or rejects a computer name registration depending on the current contents of its database:

- If the database contains a different address for that name, WINS challenges the current entry to determine whether that device still claims the name.
- If another device is using that name, WINS rejects the new name registration request.
- Otherwise, WINS accepts the entry and adds it to its local database together with a timestamp, an incremental unique version number, and other information.

Name Release

When a computer finishes using a particular name (such as when the Windows NT Workstation service or Server service is stopped), it no longer challenges other registration requests for the name. This is referred to as *releasing a name*.

If WINS is not enabled on the client: When a non-WINS computer releases a name, a broadcast is made to allow any systems on the network that might have cached the name to remove it. Upon receiving name query packets specifying the deleted name, computers simply ignore the request, allowing other computers on the network to acquire the released name.

For non-WINS computers to be accessible from other subnets, their names must be added as static entries to the WINS database or in the LMHOSTS file(s) on the remote system(s), because they will respond only to those name queries that originate on their local subnet.

If WINS is enabled on the client: Whenever a computer is shut down properly, it releases its name to the WINS server, which marks the related database entry as *released*. If the entry remains released for a certain period of time, the WINS server marks it as *extinct*, updates the version number, and notifies other WINS servers of the change.

- If a name is marked released at a WINS server, and a new registration arrives using that name but a different address, the WINS server can immediately give that name to the requesting client because it knows that the old client is no longer using that name. This might happen, for example, when a DHCP-enabled laptop changes subnets.
- If the computer released its name during an orderly shutdown, the WINS server does not challenge the name when the computer is reconnected. If an orderly shutdown did not occur, the name registration with a new address causes the WINS server to challenge the registration. The challenge fails and the registration succeeds, because the computer no longer has the old address.

Domain Name System Name Resolution

The Domain Name System (DNS) is a distributed database providing a hierarchical naming system for identifying hosts on the Internet. DNS was developed to solve the problems that arose when the number of hosts on the Internet grew dramatically in the early 1980s. DNS specifications are defined in RFCs 1034 and 1035. Although DNS might seem similar to WINS, there is a major difference: WINS is fully dynamic, whereas DNS requires static configuration for computer name-to-IP address mapping.

The Domain Name Space

The DNS database is a tree structure called the *domain name space.* Each domain (node in the tree structure) is named and can contain subdomains. The *domain name* identifies the domain's position in the database in relation to its parent domain. A period (.) separates each part of the names for the network nodes of the DNS domain. For example, the DNS domain name *csu.edu*, specifies the *csu* subdomain whose parent is the *edu* domain; *csu.com* specifies the *csu* subdomain whose parent is the *com* domain. Figure 32.4 illustrates the parent-child relationships of DNS domains.

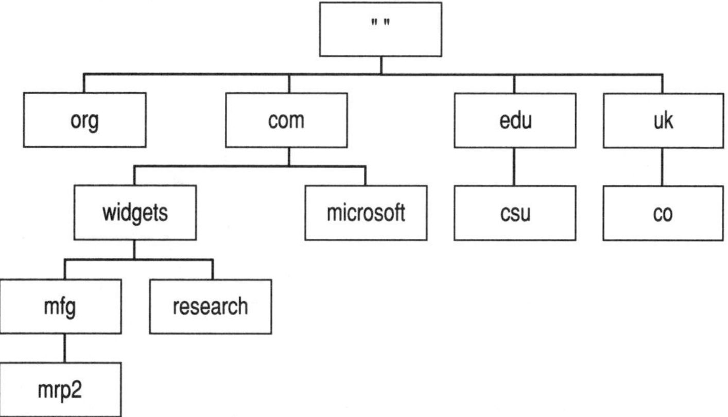

Figure 32.4 A Portion of the DNS Database

As shown in Figure 32.4, the root node of the DNS database is unnamed (null). It is referenced in DNS names with a trailing period (.). For example, in the name: "*research.widgets.com.*", it is the period after *com* that denotes the DNS root node.

Top-Level Domains

The root and top-level domains of the DNS database are managed by the InterNIC. The top-level domain names are divided into three main areas:

- *Organizational domains* (3-character names)
- *Geographical domains* (2-character country codes found in ISO 3166)
- The *in-addr.arpa. domain* (a special domain used for address-to-name mappings)

Organizational domain names were originally used in the United States, but as the Internet began to grow internationally, it became obvious that an organizational division was inadequate for a global entity. Geographical domain names were then introduced. Even though a **.us** country domain exists, domain names in the United States are still predominantly organizational. As shown in Table 32.3, there are currently seven organizational domains.

Table 32.3 The DNS Organizational Domains

DNS domain name abbreviation	Type of organization or institution
com	Commercial
edu	Educational
gov	Government
org	Noncommercial
net	Networking
mil	Military
int	International

Delegation

Responsibility for managing the DNS name space below the top level is delegated to other organizations by the InterNIC. These organizations further subdivide the name space and delegate responsibility down. This decentralized administrative model allows DNS to be autonomously managed at the levels that make the most sense for each organization involved.

Zones

The administrative unit for DNS is the *zone*. A zone is a subtree of the DNS database that is administered as a single separate entity. It can consist of a single domain or a domain with subdomains. The lower-level subdomains of a zone can also be split into separate zone(s). Figure 32.5 illustrates the relationship between DNS domains and zones.

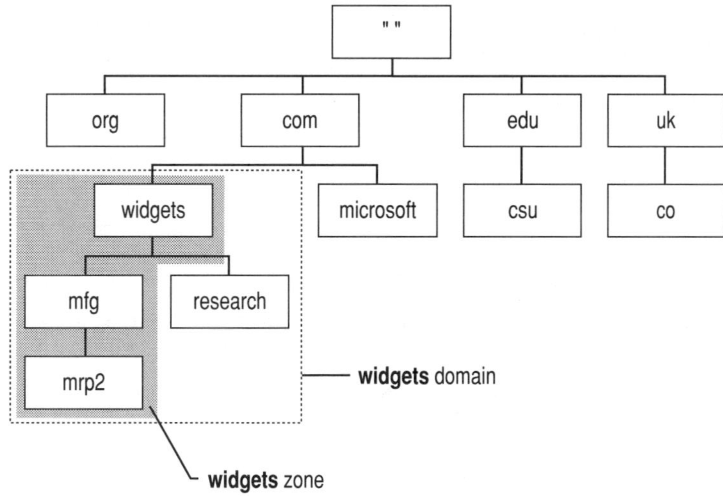

Figure 32.5 DNS Zones

Fully Qualified Domain Names

With the exception of the root, each node in the DNS database has a name (*label*) of up to 63 characters. Each subdomain must have a unique name within its parent domain. This ensures name uniqueness throughout the DNS name space. DNS domain names are formed by following the path from the bottom of the DNS tree to the root. The node names are concatenated, and a period (.) separates each part. Such names are known as *fully qualified domain names* (FQDN). Here is an example of one:

```
mrp2.widgets.mfg.universal.co.uk.
```

Note In practice, most DNS host entries appear no lower than the fifth level of the DNS tree, with three or four being more typical.

Name Resolution

The key task for DNS is to present friendly names for users and then resolve those names to IP addresses, as required by the internetwork. Name resolution is provided through DNS by the name servers, which interpret the information in a FQDN to find its specific address. As illustrated in Figure 32.6, the process begins when a resolver passes a query to its local name server. If the local name server does not have the data requested in the query, it queries other name servers on behalf of the resolver. In the worst-case scenario, the local name server starts at the top of the DNS tree with one of the *root name servers* and works its way down until the requested data is found.

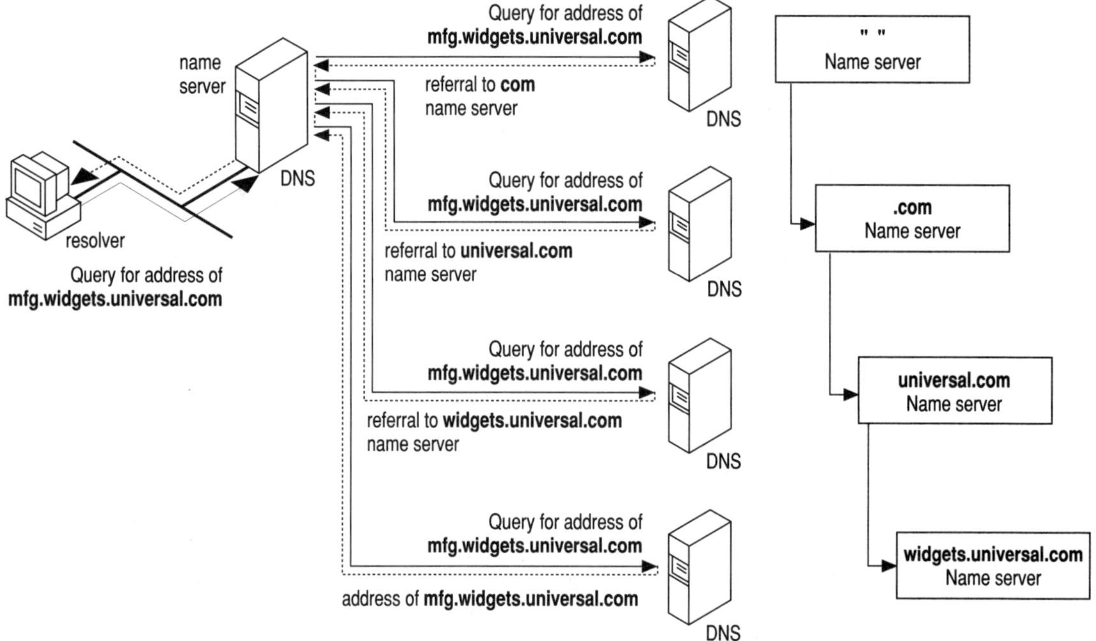

Figure 32.6 DNS Name Resolution

DNS name resolution consists of three key concepts: *recursion, iteration*, and *caching*.

- Recursion

  A resolver typically passes a *recursive resolution request* to its local name server. A recursive resolution request tells the name server that the resolver expects a complete answer to the query, not just a pointer to another name server. Recursive resolution effectively puts the workload onto the name server and allows the resolver to be small and simple.

- Iteration

  If the local name server cannot fully resolve the query, it enlists the aid of other DNS name servers throughout the DNS name space. A well-behaved local name server keeps the burden of processing on itself and passes only *iterative resolution* requests to other name servers. An iterative resolution request tells the name server that the requester expects the best answer the name server can provide without help from others. If the name server has the requested data, it returns it; otherwise it returns pointers to name servers that are more likely to have the answer. However, if a primary master name server is unable to resolve a request for data that should be in its zone, it returns an error to the requester.

- Caching

  As local name servers process recursive requests, they discover a lot of information about the DNS domain name space. To speed the performance of DNS and ease the burden on both the internetwork and the other name servers, local name servers temporarily keep this information in a local cache. Whenever a resolver request arrives, the local name server checks both its static information and the cache for an answer. Even if the answer is not cached, the identity of the name server for the zone might be, which reduces the number of iterative requests the name server has to process.

Note For more information about DNS see the *Networking Guide* for Microsoft Windows NT Server version 4.0 Resource Kit.

Name Resolution with Host Files

For computers located on remote subnets where WINS is not used, the HOSTS and LMHOSTS files provide mappings for names to IP addresses. This name-resolution method was used on internetworks before DNS and WINS were developed. The HOSTS file can be used as a local DNS equivalent; the LMHOSTS file can be used as a local WINS equivalent.

Note Sample versions of LMHOSTS and HOSTS files are added to the Windows NT *systemroot*\System32\drivers\Etc directory when you install Microsoft TCP/IP.

HOSTS

Microsoft TCP/IP can be configured to search HOSTS (the local host table file) for mappings of remote host names to IP addresses. The HOSTS file format is the same as the format for host tables in the 4.3 Berkeley Software Distribution (BSD) UNIX */etc/hosts* file. For example, the entry for a computer with an address of 192.102.73.6 and a host name of mfg1.widgets.com looks like this:

```
192.102.73.6     mfg1.widgets.com
```

You can create the file by using a text editor—for example, Notepad—to create, and change the HOSTS file because it is a simple text file. (An example of the HOSTS format is provided in the file named HOSTS.sam in the Windows NT *%systemroot%*\System32\Drivers\Etc directory. This is only an example file; do not use this file as the primary HOSTS file.)Edit the sample HOSTS file (created when you install TCP/IP) to include remote host names and IP addresses for each computer with which you will communicate.

LMHOSTS

The LMHOSTS file is a local text file that maps IP addresses to NetBIOS computer names. It contains entries for Windows-networking computers located outside the local subnet. The LMHOSTS file is read when WINS or broadcast name resolution fails; resolved entries are stored in a local cache for later access.

For example, the LMHOSTS table file entry for a computer with an address of 192.45.36.5 and a computer name of mrp2 looks like this:

```
192.45.36.5      mrp2
```

You can create the file by using a text editor—for example, Notepad—to create, and change the LMHOSTS file because it is a simple text file. (An example of the LMHOSTS format is provided in the file named LMHOSTS.sam in the Windows NT *%systemroot%*\System32\Drivers\Etc directory. This is only an example file; do not use this file as the primary LMHOSTS file.)Edit the sample LMHOSTS file (created when you install TCP/IP) to include remote NetBIOS names and IP addresses for each computer with which you will communicate.

The LMHOSTS file is typically used for small-scale networks that do not have servers. For more information about the LMHOSTS file, see "Using LMHOSTS Files" chapter in this book.

CHAPTER 33

Using LMHOSTS Files

Windows NT supports several different name resolution services to locate, communicate with, and connect to resources on the network. For example, a command to connect to an application server by using the server name must be resolved to an IP address in TCP/IP networks before the command can be successfully completed. This is referred to as *name resolution*.

If WINS servers are available on the network, the LMHOSTS file can be used to support the subnets that do not have a WINS server, and to provide a backup name resolution service in case the WINS server is not available. The LMHOSTS file provides a NetBIOS name resolution method that can be used for small networks that do not use a WINS server.

This chapter provides information about the following topics:

- Using LMHOSTS files to find remote computers and services
- Creating the LMHOSTS file
- Configuring TCP/IP to use LMHOSTS name resolution
- Maintaining the LMHOSTS file
- Troubleshooting the LMHOSTS file

Using the LMHOSTS File to Find Computers and Services

Windows NT versions 4.0 and 3.5*x* provide name resolution services for both NetBIOS computer names and Domain Name System (DNS) host names on TCP/IP networks. For an overview of all the Windows NT name resolution services for TCP/IP networks, refer to the chapter "Implementation Considerations" in the *Windows NT Server Networking Supplement*.

The LMHOSTS file is one method of name resolution for NetBIOS name resolution for TCP/IP networks. The other NetBIOS over TCP/IP (NetBT) name resolution methods that are used, depending on the computer's configuration, are:

- NetBIOS name cache
- IP subnet broadcasts
- WINS NetBIOS name server

Note NetBT is defined by RFCs 1001 and 1002. These RFCs define the different configurations—b-node, p-node, m-node, and h-node—that define how a computer attempts to resolve NetBIOS names to IP addresses.

By installation default, a Windows NT–based computer not configured as a WINS client or WINS server, is a *b-node* computer. A b-node computer is one that uses IP broadcasts for NetBIOS name resolution.

IP broadcast name resolution can provide dynamic name resolution. However, the disadvantages of broadcast name queries include increased network traffic and ineffectiveness in routed networks. Resources located outside the local subnet do not receive IP broadcast name query requests because, by definition, IP-level broadcasts are not passed to remote subnets by the router (default gateway) on the local subnet.

As an alternate method to IP broadcasts, Windows NT enables you to manually provide NetBIOS name and IP address mappings for remote computers by using the LMHOSTS file. Selected mappings from the LMHOSTS file are maintained in a limited cache of NetBIOS computer names and IP address mappings. This memory cache is initialized when a computer is started. When the computer needs to resolve a name, the cache is examined first and, if there is no match in the cache, Windows NT uses b-node IP broadcasts to try to find the NetBIOS computer. If the IP broadcast name query fails, the complete LMHOSTS file (not just the cache) is parsed to find the NetBIOS name and the corresponding IP address. This strategy enables the LMHOSTS file to contain a large number of mappings, without requiring a large chunk of static memory to maintain an infrequently used cache.

The LMHOSTS file can be used to map computer names and IP addresses for computers outside the local subnet (an advantage over the b-node broadcast method). You can use the LMHOSTS file to find remote computers for network file, print, and remote procedure services and for domain services such as logons, browsing, replication, and so on.

The Windows NT–based LMHOSTS method of name resolution is compatible with Microsoft LAN Manager 2.*x* TCP/IP LMHOSTS files.

Locating Remote Computers

Computer names can be resolved outside the local broadcast subnet if the remote computer name and IP address mappings are specified in the LMHOSTS file. For example, suppose your computer, named ClientA, is configured without the WINS client service, but you want to use TCP/IP to connect to a computer, named ServerB, that is located on another TCP/IP subnet. By default, your computer is a b-node computer that uses NetBIOS cache and IP broadcasts, and is enabled for LMHOSTS file lookup, by using an LMHOSTS file provided by your network administrator.

At system startup, the name cache on ClientA is preloaded only with entries from the LMHOSTS file, defined as preloaded by a special keyword, the #PRE keyword. For this example, ServerB is on a remote subnet outside of your local subnet IP broadcast area and is *not* one of the entries in preloaded cache. A strict b-node IP broadcast (as defined in RFCs 1001 and 1002) fails by timing out when no response is received. In this example, ClientA's IP broadcast to locate ServerB will time out, because ServerB is located on a remote subnet and does not receive ClientA's broadcast requests.

This example is summarized in the following steps:

1. ClientA enters a Windows NT command, such as a print file command, using the NetBIOS name of ServerB.
2. The NetBIOS name cache on ClientA is checked for the IP address that corresponds to the NetBIOS name of ServerB.
3. Because ServerB was not preloaded, its NetBIOS name is not found in the name cache, and ClientA broadcasts a name request with the NetBIOS name of ServerB.
4. Because ServerB is on a remote network, ClientA does not receive a reply to its name request broadcast because IP broadcasts are not routed to remote subnets. (If ServerB were on the local network, ClientA would receive a response to its broadcast and the response would contain the IP address of ServerB.)
5. Because the LMHOSTS method has been enabled on ClientA, Windows NT continues to attempt to resolve the NetBIOS name to an IP address. The LMHOSTS file in the *%systemroot%*\System32\Drivers\Etc directory is examined to find the NetBIOS name, ServerB, and its corresponding IP address. If the NetBIOS name is not found in the LMHOSTS file, and no other name resolution method is configured on ClientA, an error message appears.

Specifying Domain Controllers

The most common use of the LMHOSTS file is to locate remote servers for file and print services. But the LMHOSTS file can also be used to find domain controllers providing domain services on routed TCP/IP networks. Examples of such domain controller activities include domain controller pulses (used for account database synchronization), logon authentication, password changes, master browser list synchronization, and other domain management activities.

Windows NT primary domain controllers (PDCs) and backup domain controllers (BDCs) maintain the user account security database and manage other network-related services. Because large Windows NT domains can span multiple IP subnets, it is possible that routers could separate the domain controllers from one another or separate other computers in the domain from the domain controllers. In a network that does not use WINS servers, LMHOSTS name resolution can be used to allow client computers to connect to domain controllers located across routers on different subnets.

Using Centralized LMHOSTS Files

The primary LMHOSTS file on each computer is always located in the *%systemroot%*\System32\Drivers\Etc directory. With Microsoft TCP/IP, you can include other LMHOSTS files from local and remote computers.

Network administrators can manage the LMHOSTS files used by computers on the network by providing one or more global LMHOSTS files on a central server. Windows NT–based computers on the network can be configured to import the correct and up-to-date computer name-to-IP-address mappings.

Users can import the LMHOSTS file from remote computers on the network by using #INCLUDE statements in the LMHOSTS file or by selecting the **Import LMHOSTS...** option on the **WINS Address** tab of the **Microsoft TCP/IP Properties** page. See Figure 10.1 in the section "Configuring TCP/IP to Use LMHOSTS Name Resolution" later in this chapter.

Alternatively, an administrator can use the replicator service to distribute multiple copies of the global LMHOSTS file to multiple servers.

Note If network clients access a central LMHOSTS file, the computer on which the file is located must include the Registry parameter **NullSessionShares** for the LMHOSTS location. The **NullSessionShares** parameter is in the Registry key:

```
HKEY_LOCAL_MACHINE\SYSTEM\CurrentControlSet\Services\LanManServer\
Parameters
```

For detailed information on Registry parameters, see online Help.

Creating the LMHOSTS File

Before configuring a computer to use the LMHOSTS file, you must create the primary LMHOSTS file on each computer, name the file LMHOSTS, and save the file in the *%systemroot%*\System32\Drivers\Etc directory.

You can create the file by using a text editor—for example, Notepad—to create, and change the LMHOSTS file because it is a simple text file. (An example of the LMHOSTS format is provided in the file named LMHOSTS.sam in the Windows NT *%systemroot%*\System32\Drivers\Etc directory. This is only an example file; do not use this file as the primary LMHOSTS file.)

The following sections describe the different types of entries that can be created and edited in the LMHOSTS file.

Creating Entries in the LMHOSTS File

Use the following rules to create and to edit entries in the LMHOSTS file:

- Each entry must be on a separate line. The final entry in the file must be terminated by a carriage return.
- Enter the IP address in the first column, followed by the corresponding computer (NetBIOS) name.

> **Caution** You cannot add an LMHOSTS entry for a computer that is a DHCP client, because the IP addresses of DHCP clients change dynamically. To avoid problems, make sure that the computers whose names are entered in the LMHOSTS files are configured with static IP addresses.

- The address and the computer name must be separated by at least one space or tab.
- NetBIOS names can contain uppercase and lowercase characters and special characters. If a name is placed between double quotation marks, it is used exactly as entered. For example, `"AccountingPDC"` is a mixed-case name, and `"HumanRscSr      \0x03"` generates a name with a special character.

- Every NetBIOS name is 16 characters long. The user-definable portion of the NetBIOS name is the first 15 characters. The16th character is reserved to identify the network client service that registered the name. The most familiar example of a NetBIOS name is the computer name on any Windows-based computer. When the computer is started, the Microsoft Network Client services are started and register their names, which consist of the computer name plus a unique 16th character. For example, the name <computer_name[0x00]> is the Microsoft Workstation service; the name <computer_name[0x20]> is the Microsoft Server service. As you can see, the only difference between these two names is the 16th character. The 16th character makes it possible to uniquely identify each of the Network Client services running on the computer. For more information, see Appendix G, "NetBIOS Names."
- Entries in the LMHOSTS file can represent Windows NT Server computers, Windows NT Workstation computers, Windows 95 computers, LAN Manager servers, or Windows for Workgroups 3.11 computers running Microsoft TCP/IP. There is no need to distinguish between different platforms in LMHOSTS.
- The number sign (#) character is usually used to mark the start of a comment. However, it can also designate special keywords, as described in Table 10.1.

The keywords listed in the following table can be used in the LMHOSTS file for Windows NT–based computers. (LAN Manager 2.*x*, which also uses LMHOSTS for NetBT name resolution, treats these keywords as comments.)

Table 33.1 LMHOSTS Keywords

Keyword	Description
\0x*nn*	Support for nonprinting characters in NetBIOS names. Enclose the NetBIOS name in double quotation marks and use \0x*nn* notation to specify a hexadecimal value for the character. This enables custom applications that use special names to function properly in routed topologies. However, LAN Manager TCP/IP does not recognize the hexadecimal format, and so you surrender backward compatibility if you use this feature. Note that the hexadecimal notation applies only to one character in the name. The name should be padded with blanks so that the special character is last in the string (character 16).
#BEGIN_ALTERNATE	Used to group multiple #INCLUDE statements. Any single successful #INCLUDE statement causes the group to succeed.
#END_ALTERNATE	Used to mark the end of an #INCLUDE statement grouping.

Table 33.1 LMHOSTS Keywords *(continued)*

Keyword	Description
#DOM:<*domain*>	Part of the computer name-to-IP-address mapping entry that indicates that the IP address is a domain controller in the domain specified by <*domain*>. This keyword affects how the Browser and Logon services behave in routed TCP/IP environments. To preload a #DOM entry, you must *first* add the #PRE keyword to the line. #DOM groups are limited to 25 members.
#INCLUDE <*filename*>	Forces the system to seek the specified <*filename*> and parse it as if it were local. Specifying a Uniform Naming Convention (UNC) <*filename*> allows you to use a centralized LMHOSTS file on a server. If the server on which the specified <*filename*> exists is outside of the local broadcast subnet, you must add a preloaded entry for the server before adding the entry in the #INCLUDE section.
#MH	Part of the computer name-to-IP-address mapping entry that defines the entry as a unique name that can have more than one address. The maximum number of addresses that can be assigned to a unique name is 25. The number of entries is equal to the number of network cards in a multihomed computer.
#PRE	Part of the computer name-to-IP-address mapping entry that causes that entry to be preloaded into the name cache. (By default, entries are not preloaded into the name cache but are parsed only after WINS and name query broadcasts fail to resolve a name.) The #PRE keyword must be appended for entries that also appear in #INCLUDE statements; otherwise, the entry in the #INCLUDE statement is ignored.
#SG	Part of the computer name-to-IP-address mapping entry that associates that entry with a user-defined special (Internet) group specified by <*name*>. The #SG keyword defines Internet groups by using a NetBIOS name that has 0x20 in the 16TH byte. A special group is limited to 25 members.

The following example shows how all of these keywords are used:

```
102.54.94.102    "appname        \0x14"              #special app server
102.54.94.123    printsrv        #PRE                #source server
102.54.94.98     localsrv        #PRE
102.54.94.97     primary         #PRE #DOM:mydomain  #PDC for mydomain
```

```
#BEGIN_ALTERNATE
#INCLUDE \\localsrv\public\lmhosts        #adds LMHOSTS from this server
#INCLUDE \\primary\public\lmhosts         #adds LMHOSTS from this server
#END_ALTERNATE
```

In the preceding example:

- The servers named `printsrv`, `localsrv`, and `primary` are defined by using the #PRE keyword as entries to be preloaded into the NetBIOS cache at system startup.
- The servers named `localsrv` and `primary` are defined as preloaded and also identified in the #INCLUDE statements as the location of the centrally maintained LMHOSTS file.
- Note that the server named `"appname          \0x14"` contains a special character after the first 15 characters in its name (including the blanks), and so its name is enclosed in double quotation marks.

The following sections further explain the use of the keywords #PRE, #DOM, #INCLUDE, and #SG.

Adding Remote System Names by Using #PRE

Using #PRE entries improves access to the identified computers because name and IP address mappings are contained in the computer's cache memory. However, by default, Windows NT limits the preload name cache to 100 entries. (This limit affects only entries marked with the #PRE keyword.)

If you specify more than 100 #PRE entries, only the first 100 #PRE entries are preloaded into the computer's cache. Any additional #PRE entries are ignored at startup and are used only if name resolution by the cache and IP broadcast fails. Windows NT then parses the complete LMHOSTS file which contains all the entries, including the #PRE entries that exceeded the cache limit of 100.

You can change the default maximum allowed #PRE entries by adding a **MaxPreLoads** value entry to the Registry. This value entry must be added to the following Registry key:

```
HKEY_LOCAL_MACHINE\SYSTEM\CurrentControlSet\Services\Netbt\Parameters
```

For example, the LMHOSTS file could contain the following information:

```
102.54.94.91     accounting                 #accounting server
102.54.94.94     payroll                    #payroll server
102.54.94.97     stockquote        #PRE     #stock quote server
102.54.94.102    printqueue                 #print server in Bldg 7
```

In this example, the server named `stockquote` is preloaded into the name cache, because it is tagged with the #PRE keyword. The servers named `accounting`, `payroll`, and `printqueue` would be resolved only after the cache entries failed to match and after broadcast queries failed to locate them. After non-preloaded entries are resolved, their mappings are cached for a period of time for reuse.

Adding Domain Controllers by Using #DOM

The #DOM keyword can be used in LMHOSTS files to distinguish a Windows NT domain controller from other computers on the network. To use the #DOM tag, follow the name and IP address mapping in LMHOSTS with the #DOM keyword, a colon, and the domain in which the domain controller participates. For example:

```
102.54.94.97 primary     #PRE#DOM:mydomain    #The mydomain PDC
```

Using the #DOM keyword to designate domain controllers adds entries to a *domain name cache* that is used to contact available controllers for processing domain requests. When domain controller activity such as a logon request occurs, the request is sent to the domain group name. On the local subnet, the request is broadcast and is picked up by any local domain controllers. However, if you use the #DOM keyword to specify domain controllers in the LMHOSTS file, Microsoft TCP/IP uses datagrams to also forward the request to domain controllers located on remote subnets. Adding more domain controllers in the LMHOSTS file will help distribute the load on all the controllers.

The following list contains guidelines for mapping important members of the domain by using the #DOM keyword.

- It is recommended that the #DOM entries be pre-cached by using the #PRE keyword. Note that the #PRE keyword must precede the #DOM keyword.
- For each local LMHOSTS file on a Windows NT computer that is a member in a domain, there should be #DOM entries for all domain controllers in the domain that are located on remote subnets. This ensures that logon authentication, password changes, browsing, and so on, all work properly for the local domain. These are the necessary minimum entries.
- For local LMHOSTS files on all servers that can be backup domain controllers, there should be mappings for the primary domain controller's name and IP address, plus mappings for all other backup domain controllers. This ensures that promoting a backup to primary domain controller status does not affect the ability to offer all services to members of the domain.

- If trust relationships exist between domains, all domain controllers for all trusted domains should also be listed in the local LMHOSTS file.
- For domains that you want to browse from your local domain, the local LMHOSTS files should contain at least the name and IP address mapping for the primary domain controller in the remote domain. Again, backup domain controllers should also be included so that promotion to primary domain controller does not impair the ability to browse remote domains.

Names that appear with the #DOM keyword in the LMHOSTS file are placed in a special domain name list in NetBT. When a datagram is sent to this domain using the DOMAIN<1C> name, the name is resolved first by using WINS or IP broadcasts. The datagram is then sent to all the addresses contained in the list from LMHOSTS, and there is also a broadcast on the local subnet.

Adding User-Defined Special Groups by Using #SG

You can group resources such as printers, or computers that belong to groups on the intranet, for easy reference, browsing, or broadcasting, by using the #SG keyword to define a special group in the LMHOSTS file. Special groups are limited to a total of 25 members. (If you are using WINS, they can also be defined by using the WINS Manager.)

Specify the name just as you would a domain name except that the keyword portion of the entry is #SG. For example:

```
102.54.94.99 printsrvsg      #SG:mycompany    #Specialgroup of computers
```

The preceding example results in a special group being created. In some cases you may want to just specify the name of a special group without specifying an IP address. This can be done by giving the name of the group preceded by #SG. For example:

```
printsrvsg      #SG:mycompany    #Specialgroup of computers
```

Addresses entered by using the LMHOSTS file become permanent addresses in the special group and can be removed only by using the WINS Manager.

Adding Multihomed Devices by Using #MH

A multihomed device is a computer with multiple network interface cards (NICs). A multihomed device can be defined by a single, unique name with which multiple IP addresses are associated.

You can provide multihomed name-to-IP-address mappings in the LMHOSTS file by creating entries that are specified by using the keyword #MH. An #MH entry associates a single, unique NetBIOS computer name to an IP address. You can create multiple entries for the same NetBIOS computer name for each NIC in the multihomed device, up to a maximum of 25 different IP addresses for the same name.

The format of the LMHOSTS entry that is used to specify name-to-IP-address mappings for multihomed devices is the same as the other keyword entries. For example, the entries required to map name to IP address for a multihomed device with two NICs are:

```
102.54.94.91 accounting                 #accounting server NIC 1
102.54.94.91 accounting                 #accounting server NIC 2
```

Defining a Central LMHOST File by Using #INCLUDE

For small- to medium-sized networks with fewer than 20 domains, a single common LMHOSTS file usually satisfies all workstations and servers on the intranet. An administrator can:

- Use the Windows NT Replicator service to maintain synchronized local copies of the global LMHOSTS file.
- Use centralized LMHOSTS files, as described in this section.

Use the #BEGIN_ALTERNATE and #END_ALTERNATE keywords to provide a list of servers maintaining copies of the same LMHOSTS file. This is known as a *block inclusion*, which allows multiple servers to be searched for a valid copy of a specific file. The following example shows the use of the #INCLUDE and #_ALTERNATE keywords to include a local LMHOSTS file (in the C:\Private directory):

```
102.54.94.97primary         #PRE  #DOM:mydomain      #primary DC
102.54.94.99backupdc        #PRE  #DOM:mydomain      #backup DC
102.54.94.98localsvr        #PRE  #DOM:mydomain

#INCLUDE     c:\private\lmhosts                 #include a local lmhosts
```

```
#BEGIN_ALTERNATE
#INCLUDE     \\primary\public\lmhosts         #source for global file
#INCLUDE     \\backupdc\public\lmhosts        #backup source
#INCLUDE     \\localsvr\public\lmhosts        #backup source
#END_ALTERNATE
```

Important This feature should never be used to include a remote file from a redirected drive because the LMHOSTS file is shared between local users who have different profiles and different logon scripts. Even on single-user systems, redirected drive mappings can change between logon sessions.

In the preceding example, the servers `primary` and `backupdc` are located on remote subnets from the computer that owns the file. The local user has decided to include a list of preferred servers in a local LMHOSTS file located in the C:\Private directory. During name resolution, the Windows NT computer first includes this private file, then gets the global LMHOSTS file from one of three locations: `primary`, `backupdc`, or `localsvr`. All names of servers in the #INCLUDE statements must have their addresses preloaded using the #PRE keyword; otherwise, the #INCLUDE statement is ignored.

The block inclusion is satisfied if one of the three sources for the global LMHOSTS file is available and none of the other servers is used. If no server is available, or for some reason the LMHOSTS file or path is incorrect, an event is added to the event log to indicate that the block inclusion failed.

Configuring TCP/IP to Use LMHOSTS Name Resolution

By default, the LMHOSTS name resolution method is enabled when TCP/IP is installed on a computer. You can disable LMHOSTS name resolution by clearing the **Enable LMHOSTS Lookup** checkbox on the **WINS Address** tab of the **Microsoft TCP/IP Properties** page. It is recommended that you do not disable LMHOSTS name resolution because it provides a backup name service for WINS servers that are off-line or unavailable.

To use an LMHOSTS file from a remote computer or different directory on the local computer, click **Import LMHOSTS…** as illustrated in the following figure.

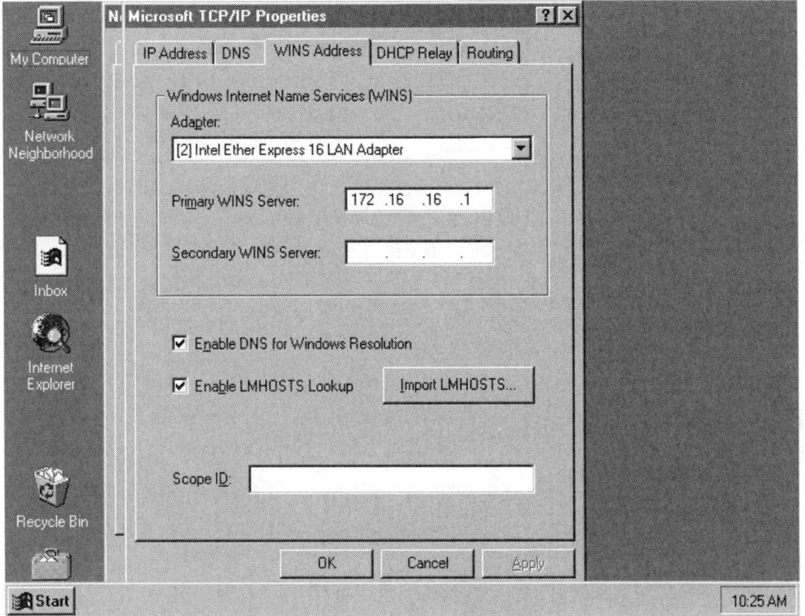

Figure 33.1 Configuring TCP/IP to Enable LMHOSTS Lookup

Maintaining the LMHOSTS File

When you use an LMHOSTS file, be sure to keep it up-to-date and organized. Use the following guidelines:

- Update the LMHOSTS file whenever a computer is changed or removed from the network.
- Because LMHOSTS files are searched one line at a time from the beginning, list remote computers in priority order, with the ones used most often at the top of the file, followed by remote systems listed in #INCLUDE statements.

- Use #PRE statements to preload into the local computer's name cache frequently accessed workstations and servers listed in the #INCLUDE statements. #PRE keyword entries should be entered at the end of the file, because these are preloaded into the cache at system startup time and are not accessed later. This increases the speed of searches for the entries used most often. Because each line is processed individually, any comment lines that you add will increase the parsing time.
- Use the **nbtstat** command to remove or correct preloaded entries that might have been typed incorrectly or any names cached by successful broadcast resolution. You can reprime the name cache by using the **nbtstat -R** command to purge and reload the name cache, reread the LMHOSTS file, and then insert entries tagged with the #PRE keyword. For more information about using the **nbtstat** command, see the Help topic "TCP/IP Procedures Help" or refer to Appendix A, "TCP/IP Utilities Reference."

Troubleshooting LMHOSTS Files

When using the LMHOSTS file, problems such as failure to locate a remote computer can occur because one or more of the following errors is present in the LMHOSTS file:

- The LMHOSTS file does not contain an entry for the remote server.
- The computer (NetBIOS) name in the LMHOSTS file is misspelled. (Note that LMHOSTS names are automatically converted to uppercase.)
- The IP address for a computer name in the LMHOSTS file is not valid.
- The required carriage return at the end of the last entry in the LMHOSTS file is missing.

CHAPTER 34

Managing User Work Environments

User work environments include the desktop items and settings, such as screen colors, mouse settings, window size and position, and network and printer connections.

You can use the following tools to manage user work environments on a Windows NT network:

- User profiles

  The user profile contains all user-definable settings for the work environment of a computer running Windows NT, including display settings and network connections. All user-specific settings are automatically saved into the Profiles folder within the system root folder (typically C:\winnt\profiles).

- System Policy Editor

  System policy enables you to control the user-definable settings in Windows NT and Windows 95 user profiles, as well as system configuration settings. You can use the System Policy Editor to change desktop settings and restrict what users can do from their desktops.

- Logon scripts

  A logon script is a batch file (.bat) or executable (.exe) file that runs whenever a user logs on at any type of workstation on the network. The script can contain operating system commands, such as commands to make network connections or start applications.

- Environment variables

  Environment variables specify the computer's search path, directory for temporary files, and other similar information.

User Profiles

On computers running Windows NT Workstation or Windows NT Server, user profiles automatically create and maintain the desktop settings for each user's work environment on the local computer. A user profile is created for each user when the user logs on to a computer for the first time.

User profiles provide several advantages to users:

- When users log on to their workstations, they receive the desktop settings as they existed when they logged off.
- Several users can use the same computer, and each receives a customized desktop when they log on.

If you have a computer running Windows NT Server on your network, user profiles can be stored on a server so that user profiles can follow users to any computer running the Windows NT version 4.0 platform on the network. These are called roaming user profiles. You can also assign mandatory user profiles to prevent users from changing any desktop settings.

For more information about roaming user profiles and mandatory user profiles, see Chapter 3, "Managing User Work Environments" in Windows NT Server version 4.0 *Concepts and Planning*.

Settings Saved in a User Profile

A user profile contains configuration preferences and options for each user: a snapshot of a user's desktop environment.

The following table describes the settings in a user profile.

Source	Parameters saved
Windows NT Explorer	All user-definable settings for Windows NT Explorer.
Taskbar	All personal program groups and their properties, all program items and their properties, and all Taskbar settings.
Printers Settings	Network printer connections.
Control Panel	All user-defined settings made in Control Panel.
Accessories	All user-specific application settings affecting the user's Windows NT environment, including Calculator, Clock, Notepad, Paint, and HyperTerminal, among others.
Windows NT–based applications	Any application written specifically for Windows can be designed so that it tracks application settings on a per-user basis. If this information exists, it is saved in the user profile.
Online Help bookmarks	Any bookmarks placed in the Windows NT Help system.

Structure of a User Profile

User profiles are comprised of the profile directory, a cached copy of the Windows NT Registry HKEY_CURRENT_USER subtree, and the common program groups, contained in the All Users folder.

User Profile Folders

Every user profile begins as a copy of Default User, a default user profile stored on each computer running Windows NT Workstation or Windows NT Server. The Default User profile folder, user profile folders for each user, and All User profile folders are located in the Profiles folder in the system root (usually C:\Winnt). The Default User folder and individual user profile folders contain an NTuser.dat file plus a directory of links to desktop items.

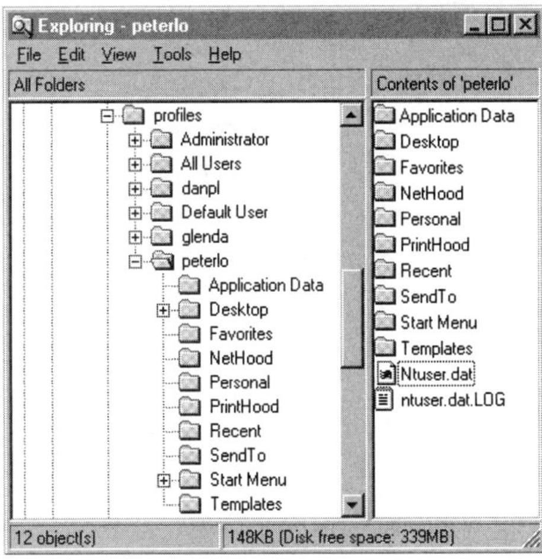

The user profiles folders contain links to various desktop items.

User profile folder	Contents
Application Data	Application-specific data. For example, a customer dictionary. Application vendors decide what data to store in the User Profile folder.
Desktop	Desktop items, including files and shortcuts.
Favorites	Shortcuts to program items and favorite locations.
NetHood	Shortcuts to Network Neighborhood items.
Personal	Shortcuts to program items.
PrintHood	Shortcuts to printer folder items
Recent	Shortcuts to the most recently used items.
SendTo	Shortcuts to document items.
Start Menu	Shortcuts to program items.
Templates	Shortcuts to template items.

Note The NetHood, PrintHood, Recent, and Templates folders are hidden and, by default, do not appear in Windows NT Explorer. To view these folders and their contents in Windows Explorer, click **Options** on the **View** menu, and then click **Show all files**.

NTuser.dat File

The NTuser.dat file is the registry portion of the user profile. NTuser.dat is a cached copy of the Windows NT Registry HKEY_CURRENT_USER subtree on the local computer. The registry is a database repository for information about the computer's configuration, including the hardware, installed software, environment settings, and other information. In the registry, the settings that determine the work environment for the user who is currently logged on to the computer are stored in HKEY_CURRENT_USER.

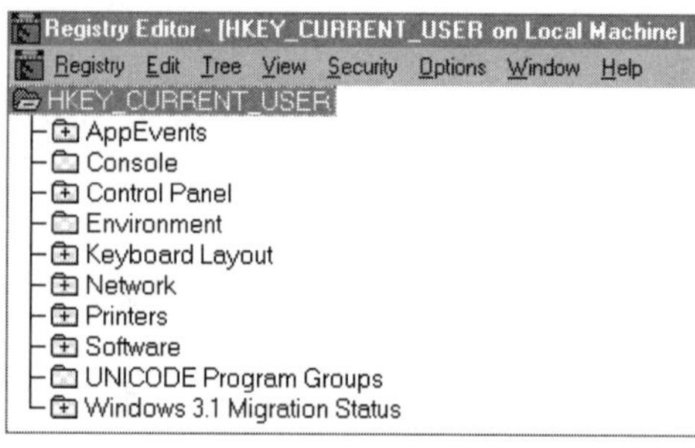

All Users Folder

Although they are not copied to user profile folders, the settings in the All Users folder are used with user profile folders to create the user profile.

The Windows NT platform supports two program group types:

- Common program groups are always available on a computer, no matter who is logged on. Only administrators can add, delete, and modify them.
- Personal program groups are private to the user who creates them.

Common program groups are stored in the All Users folder under the Profiles folder. The All Users folder also contains settings for the Desktop and **Start** menu.

On computers running Windows NT Workstation or Windows NT Server, only members of the Administrators group can create common program groups.

For information on adding new program groups, see "To add a new submenu to the Programs menu" in Windows NT Help.

How Local User Profiles Are Created

The local user profile is the user profile stored on the computer under the user name in the Profiles folder. When no preconfigured server-based (roaming) user profile exists for a user, the first time a user logs on to a computer, a user profile folder is created for the user name. The contents of Default User are then copied to the new user profile folder. The user profile, along with the common program group settings in the All Users folder, create the user's desktop. When the user logs off, any changes made to the default settings during the session are saved to the new user profile folder. The user profile in Default User remains unchanged.

If the user has a user account on the local workstation in addition to a domain user account or more than one domain user account, the local user profile is different for each account because different user profiles are generated for each user that logs on. When the user logs off, changed settings are saved to only one user profile, depending on which account the user logged on to.

When a user has a local user profile on a computer, the user profile folder contains the NTuser.dat file and a transaction log file named NTuser.dat.log. The log file is used to provide fault tolerance, allowing Windows NT to recover if a problem occurs while the NTuser.dat file is being updated.

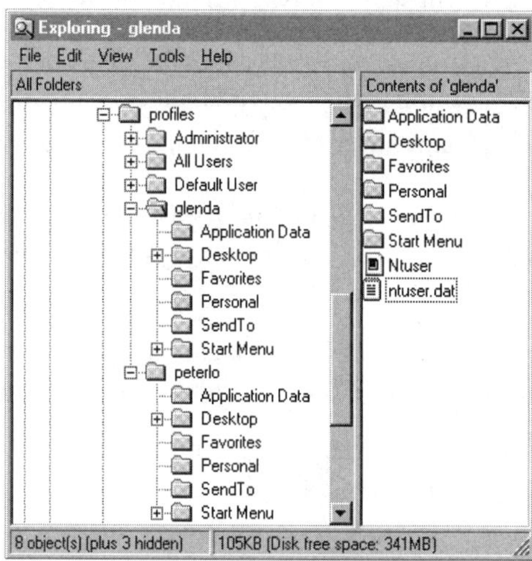

System Default Profile

When Windows NT is running on a computer that no user is logged on to, a dialog box appears, prompting you to press CTRL+ALT+DEL to log on. This dialog box and other aspects of the Windows NT environment at this point, such as the screen's background color and its use of wallpaper and screen savers, are controlled by the system default profile. The settings for this profile are stored in System32\config\default. The system default profile can be changed by using either Windows NT Registry Editor (Regedt32 or Regedit) to edit the Default key in HKEY_USERS.

For information about using Windows NT Registry Editor, see Part 5, "Windows NT Registry."

System Policy

On computers running Windows NT Workstation or Windows NT Server, the contents of the user profile are taken from the user portion of the Windows NT Registry. Another portion of the registry, the local computer portion, contains configuration settings that can be managed, along with user profiles, using System Policy Editor. With this tool, you create a system policy to control user work environments and actions, and to enforce system configuration for all computers running Windows NT Workstation and Windows NT Server.

With system policy, you can control some aspects of user work environments without enforcing the restrictions of a mandatory user profile. You can restrict what users can do from the desktop; such as restrict certain options in Control Panel, customize parts of the desktop, or configure network settings.

To enforce system policy on your network, you need at least one computer on your network running Windows NT Server, configured as a primary domain controller (PDC). For information on enforcing system policy on your network, see Chapter 3, "Managing User Work Environments" in Windows NT Server version 4.0 *Concepts and Planning*.

Using System Policy Editor to Edit the Registry

You can use the **Open Registry** command on the System Policy Editor **File** menu to make changes to the Windows NT Registry settings on the local computer. Using **Open Registry**, the changes you set in System Policy Editor are made immediately in the registry when you use **Save** on the **File** menu.

You can use the **Connect** command on the System Policy Editor **File** menu to make changes to the Windows NT Registry settings on a remote computer. This feature allows remote adjustment to computer registries. For example, a help desk technician can connect to a computer and correct settings that a user mistakenly changed.

Note System Policy Editor is designed to manage registry settings for the entire domain; direct changes to registry settings are not recommended unless a specific instance of user or computer incompatibility occurs.

Using Logon Scripts to Configure User Work Environments

A logon script runs automatically whenever a user logs on to a computer running either Windows NT Server or Windows NT Workstation. Although a logon script is typically a batch file (.bat or .cmd extension), any executable program (.exe extension) can also be used.

Logon scripts are optional. They can be used to configure user working environments by creating network connections and starting applications. Logon scripts are useful when you want to affect the user work environment without managing all aspects of it.

Note User profiles can restore network connections at logon that were established prior to logging off, but they cannot be used to create new network connections at logon.

To use Logon scripts, you need at least one computer on your network running Windows NT Server, configured as a primary domain controller (PDC). For information on enforcing system policy on your network, see Chapter 3, "Managing User Work Environments" in Windows NT Server version 4.0 *Concepts and Planning*.

Changing the System Environment Variables

Windows NT requires certain information to find programs, to allocate memory space for some programs to run, and to control various programs. This information—called the system and user environment variables—can be viewed using the System option in Control Panel in the **Environment Variables** tab. These environment variables are similar to those that can be set in the MS-DOS operating system, such as PATH and TEMP.

The system environment variables are defined by Windows NT Workstation and Windows NT Server and are the same no matter who is logged on at the computer. If you are logged on as a member of the Administrators group, you can add new variables or change the values.

The user environment variables can be different for each user of a particular computer. They include any environment variables you want to define or variables defined by your applications, such as the path where application files are located.

After you change any environment variables in the **Environment Variables** tab in the **System Properties** dialog box and click **OK**, Windows NT saves the new values in the registry so they are available automatically the next time you start your computer.

If any conflict exists between environment variables, Windows NT Workstation and Windows NT Server resolve the conflict in this way:

- System environment variables are set first.
- User environment variables defined in the **System** dialog box are set next and override system variables.
- Variables defined in Autoexec.bat are set last, but do not override system or environmental variables.

Note Path settings, unlike other environmental variables, are cumulative. The full path (what you see when you type **path** at the command prompt) is created by appending the path contained in Autoexec.bat to the paths defined in the System option in Control Panel.

CHAPTER 35

Using Windows NT Workstation on the Internet

This chapter introduces the components that enable a computer running Windows NT to access the Internet and explains how those components work together to let you use the Internet. This discussion focuses on using Windows NT Workstation as an Internet client. Peer Web Services is described in the final section.

This chapter covers these topics:

- Connecting to the Internet
- Security
- Using Peer Web Services

For general information about using the Internet, consult one of the many books available in your bookstore or library. Many resources about using the Internet are also available on the Internet itself.

Connecting to the Internet

Windows NT Workstation includes all the software you need to connect to and use the Internet. These components enable you to access the Internet:

- The Transmission Control Protocol/Internet Protocol (TCP/IP) network protocol in Windows NT version 4.0.

  The TCP/IP network protocol is used by virtually all computers on the Internet.
- Windows NT Workstation Dial-Up Networking.

  Dial-Up Networking is used to connect to an Internet service provider (ISP) or other online service over a modem and phone line or by using an Integrated Services Digital Network (ISDN) card and ISDN line.

You can install Dial-Up Networking and the TCP/IP protocol by using the Networks option in Control Panel. For more information, see "TCP/IP Internet Configuration" and "Dial-Up Networking Internet Configuration" in this chapter or the corresponding topics in online Help or the *Windows NT Server Networking Supplement.*

There are two methods used to connect clients to the Internet:

- By using Point to Point Protocol (PPP).
- By using Serial Line Internet Protocol (SLIP).

  The most popular and more robust method is PPP. The Microsoft Network (MSN) acts as a PPP provider, connecting users who have MSN accounts to the Internet. See the procedure in the next section for an example of how to connect to MSN.

In addition to the Windows NT Workstation software listed above, before you connect to the Internet, you need the following items:

- A modem and telephone line or ISDN card and ISDN line.
- An account with an Internet service provider .

  An Internet service provider is a company that gives remote users access to the Internet. ISPs now offer Internet access at reasonable rates in many places worldwide.
- Internet tools such as Internet Explorer, FTP, and Telnet.

  Internet Explorer, FTP, and Telnet are all Internet clients provided in Windows NT Workstation.

Procedural Overview

This section provides procedures for connecting to the Internet or MSN, then gives a technical overview of installing TCP/IP and Dial-Up Networking and configuring them for Internet access.

▶ **To connect to the Internet**

1. Secure your computer and disks.

   For information on how to do this, see "Security for Internet Clients," later in this chapter.
2. Install the TCP/IP network protocol.
3. Install and start Dial-Up Networking.
4. In the **Dial-Up Networking** dialog box, click **New**.

   If this is the first time you have used Dial-Up Networking, in the Dial-Up Networking wizard, select the check box to edit the phonebook directly, and click **Finish**.

5. On the **Basic** tab, type a name for your entry, for example, **Internet**.
6. Type the phone number to your ISP and select a modem to use.
7. On the **Server** tab, select the TCP/IP protocol.
8. Click **OK** and then click **Dial**.

You can use The Microsoft Network as your Internet provider only if you have already created an MSN account by using Windows 95. When you use MSN to connect to the Internet through Windows NT, proprietary online services such as e-mail or bulletin boards are not available.

▶ **To connect to MSN**

1. Secure your computer and disks.

   For information on how to do this, see "Security for Internet Clients," later in this chapter.
2. Install the TCP/IP network protocol.
3. Install and start Dial-Up Networking.
4. In the **Dial-Up Networking** dialog box, click **New**.

   If this is the first time you have used Dial-Up Networking, in the Dial-Up Networking wizard, select the checkbox to edit the phonebook directly, and click **Finish**.
5. On the **Basic** tab, type a name for your entry, for example, **MSN**.
6. Enter the phone number for the local MSN number that allows Internet access.
7. Select a modem and use the default modem configuration.
8. On the **Server** tab, in the **Dial-Up Server Type** box, select **PPP**.

   In the **Protocols** box, select only the **TCP/IP** protocol.

   Clear the **Enable PPP LCP Extensions** box.
9. On the **Security** tab, select the **Accept any authentication including clear text** check box and click **OK**.
10. Click **Dial**. In the **Authentication** dialog box, supply your MSN user name by typing **MSN/***username.*
11. Type your MSN password and click **OK**.

TCP/IP Internet Configuration

TCP/IP is the suite of network protocols used for all Internet traffic. The TCP/IP protocol included with Windows NT is fully compatible for use on the Internet.

You install TCP/IP by using the Network option in Control Panel. Once TCP/IP is installed, you might need to configure the following parameters to operate correctly on the Internet:

- **IP Address.** The IP address configuration you specify by using the Network option in Control Panel is for your intranet use and will be assigned to the network card in your computer. Usually you have only one network card and IP address for intranet use, although you can have multiple network card and IP addresses. You can obtain an additional IP address for your connection to the Internet that uses Dial-Up Networking. The Dial-Up Networking IP address is usually randomly assigned by your ISP on each connection, but you might need to enter a fixed IP address in the Dial-Up Networking entry for your ISP.
- **Default Gateway.** If you connect to an Internet server through Dial-Up Networking, the default gateway configured through Dial-Up Networking is used.
- **DNS.** If the Domain Name System (DNS) configuration on your computer is for use on your intranet only, to efficiently access the Internet you might need to add DNS server IP addresses in the Dial-Up Networking entry for your ISP.
- **HOSTS or LMHOSTS file.** You can improve efficiency of connections to frequently accessed servers on the Internet by adding entries to your HOSTS file. In some cases, you can connect to a computer on the Internet by using its NetBIOS name; NetBIOS names are mapped to IP addresses in the LMHOSTS file. Windows NT consults these local files for name resolution before consulting a DNS server on the Internet.

Dial-Up Networking Internet Configuration

Dial-Up Networking is used to connect to an Internet service provider (ISP) or other online service over a phone line or ISDN line. Windows NT Dial-Up Networking clients support the PPP protocol and the SLIP protocol. Most ISPs use these protocols, which enables Windows NT Workstation clients to connect to virtually all ISPs. Some ISPs support the Point-to-Point Tunneling Protocol (PPTP) and X.25 WAN protocols.

To connect to an ISP and use the Internet, you must configure Dial-Up Networking on your computer. Windows NT Dial-Up Networking steps you through the procedures to connect to the Internet.

To install Dial-Up Networking, double-click **Dial-Up Networking** in My Computer. Follow the instructions on-screen to complete Dial-Up Networking installation. For detailed instructions on installing Dial-Up Networking, see online Help.

Configuring Dial-Up Networking Entries for Internet Use

To call an Internet service provider, you must create an entry in Dial-Up Networking. The Windows NT Dial-Up Networking wizard steps you through creating the first entry. This section explains how to manually configure a Dial-Up Networking entry to work with an ISP.

Modifying an Entry

Double-click **Dial-Up Networking** in **My Computer**; or, click **Start**, point to **Programs**, point to **Accessories**, then click **Dial-Up Networking**. The first time Dial-Up Networking is started, the Dial-Up Networking wizard steps you through creating the first entry; otherwise, click **New**. Provide all the information requested by the Dial-Up Networking wizard. See the sections below for additional information about Internet configuration.

PPP or SLIP Settings

An Internet service provider must provide either PPP connections or SLIP connections to operate with Windows NT Dial-Up Networking.

▶ **To configure an entry for a PPP connection**

1. Double-click **Dial-Up Networking**. Select a Phonebook entry to dial. Click **More** and select **Edit entry and modem properties**.
2. On the **Server** tab, in the **Dial-up server type** box, select **PPP**.
3. The **TCP/IP** and **NetBEUI** check boxes are automatically selected. Clear the **IPX** check box if it is selected. The **Enable PPP LCP extensions** (RFC 1570) check box enables newer PPP features and should be cleared only if you are unable to establish a connection while this setting is enabled. The **Enable software compression** check box should be selected.
4. Click **TCP/IP Settings**.
5. If your Internet service provider has assigned an IP address for your use, enter that number in the **Specify an IP address** box. If no number was assigned or if you know the server assigns IP addresses, select the **Server assigned IP address** check box.
6. If your Internet service provider has assigned primary and secondary DNS and/or WINS server IP addresses for your use, enter those numbers in the **Specify name server addresses** box. If no numbers were assigned or if you know the server assigns name server addresses, select the **Server assigned name server addresses** check box.
7. Leave the **Use default gateway on remote network** and **Use IP header compression boxes** selected.

Depending on your Internet service provider, you might need to make some modifications to your security settings, as described in the next section.

▶ **To configure an entry for a SLIP connection**

1. Double-click **Dial-Up Networking**. Select a Phonebook entry to dial. Click **More** and select **Edit entry and modem properties**.
2. On the **Server** tab, in the **Dial-up server type** box, select **SLIP**.
3. The **TCP/IP** check box is automatically selected.
4. Click **TCP/IP Settings**.
5. Enter the IP address provided by your ISP in the **IP address** box.
6. Enter the primary and secondary DNS server IP addresses and the primary and secondary WINS server IP addresses in the **Name server addresses** box.
7. Leave the **Use default gateway on remote network** and **Force IP header compression** check boxes selected. Select a frame size in the **Frame size** box if indicated by your ISP, otherwise leave the default setting.

Depending on your Internet service provider, you might need to make some modifications to your security settings, as described in the next section.

Security Settings

When you connect to the Internet service provider, some form of logon or authentication occurs. Your Internet service provider should tell you the logon sequence for its servers. You use the **Script** tab to configure Dial-Up Networking for logging on to the Internet service provider.

▶ **To configure an entry for authentication on the remote server**

1. Click the **Dial-Up Networking** icon. Select a Phonebook entry to dial. Click **More** and select **Edit entry and modem properties**.
2. On the **Security** tab, select the authentication method specified by your Internet service provider.

   Many Internet service providers require a clear-text terminal logon. If in doubt, select the **Accept any authentication including clear text** check box.

   If you select **Accept any authentication including clear text**, you must also know the sequence of logon for your ISP, and any required commands.
3. If your Internet service provider has a well-defined logon sequence, you can create a script in the Switch.inf file that provides the required commands automatically at logon. You create and activate a script on the **Script** tab.
4. After you have selected the security and script settings, click **OK**. Click **OK** again to complete security configurations.

Modems and WAN Connections

Your connection to an ISP will probably be through a modem and telephone line, or through an ISDN card and ISDN line.

If you use a modem, the faster its speed, the faster you access pages on the Internet. Modems of 9600 bits per second (bps) or above are recommended. ISDN can provide speeds up to 128,000 bps.

Obtaining an Internet Account with a Service Provider

There are ISPs around the world. As with other online services or bulletin boards, you dial the service number and log on to the remote system. Once connected, you have access to the Internet and any other services, such as electronic mail, offered by the service provider. Fees usually apply for all commercial Internet services.

Internet Tools

Windows NT Workstation provides three standard tools for accessing Internet servers: Internet Explorer, FTP, and Telnet.

A multitude of other tools are available to access the information and services on the Internet. For example, you can use an Internet Relay Chat (IRC) client to participate in real-time discussions in "rooms" hosted on an IRC server. You can use the Inbox application on the Windows NT Desktop to send and receive electronic mail. Which tools you choose depend on the information you want and how it is stored on the Internet.

This section briefly describes some Internet tools and provides the process for installing them on a computer running Windows NT. For comprehensive discussions of the tools available for using the Internet, consult the Internet or your local library or bookstore.

History of Internet Tools

The Internet has been evolving since the early 1970s. Early servers on the Internet conformed to original Internet protocols, such as the File Transfer Protocol (FTP) or Virtual Terminal Protocol (VTP, now called Telnet). These protocols generally provide a way to copy files and/or issue commands or start programs through a character-based interface or, more recently, through a graphical user interface such as Windows or X Windows.

Internet technology has now grown beyond the simple file transfers on character-based FTP or Telnet servers. Newer servers on the Internet now have graphical interfaces and present information and services to Internet users by using hypertext documents. World Wide Web (WWW) servers now automatically provide formatted text, sounds, and animation to Internet users. You must use the proper browser (such as Internet Explorer) to use these Internet servers. Fortunately, Internet Explorer also supports the older standards, such as FTP, so you can use Internet Explorer to access multiple servers and data types.

Internet Explorer

Internet Explorer is a Web browser that allows you to connect to Web servers and view the information provided by that server. The servers transmit the files by using the Hypertext Transport Protocol (HTTP). The files are typically text files that have been formatted by using the Hypertext Markup Language (HTML). However, the Internet and Internet Explorer support viewing (or downloading) nearly any file type.

FTP

Windows NT Workstation provides an FTP command-line utility that enables you to connect to FTP servers and transfer files. Multiple variations of FTP clients are also available on the Internet or commercially. FTP has the advantage of allowing clients to upload files to a remote FTP server.

Telnet

Telnet is a graphical application that you use to log on to remote computers and issue commands as if you were at the computer's keyboard. By using Telnet, you can use the resources of remote computers to run programs and perform other functions.

Other Tools

Many other tools are available through the Internet or commercially. These tools include:

- IRC
- CUSEEME
- Gopher
- E-mail

The Windows NT TCP/IP protocol provides FTP and Telnet. These tools can be used to gather more Internet tools. Two popular FTP sites for obtaining public-domain Internet tools (and other Windows Sockets applications) are sunsite.unc.edu and ftp.cica.indiana.edu.

Once you have a connection to an Internet service provider, you can use the FTP program provided with Windows NT TCP/IP to connect to an FTP server and download files, including Internet tools. The same tool can exist for different operating systems or processors. Make sure you obtain the correct version of the tool.

The files are probably compressed by using the shareware program **Pkzip**. Use the shareware program **Pkunzip** to expand the .zip files on your local hard disk. The shareware compression tools are often available on local bulletin boards or FTP servers in an uncompressed format.

After you uncompress the files for a particular program, read any available Readme files for specific information about installing and configuring the program, and comply with those instructions. Most public domain software designed for Windows 95, Windows for Workgroups, or Windows 3.1 works on Windows NT without modification.

To add shortcuts for easy access to the new programs, see online Help. With shortcuts you can start the Internet tool from the Windows NT Workstation Desktop.

Security for Internet Clients

It is important to remember that the Internet, like other networks, provides two-way communication. When you are connected to the Internet, other computers can see your computer. By default, Windows NT Workstation security protects your computer from casual intrusion. However, while it is very unlikely that your computer will be attacked while you are browsing the Internet, it is still a good idea to configure your computer securely. Before you install and configure TCP/IP and Dial-Up Networking, you should review the security configuration of your computer.

If your computer is also connected to an in-house network (an intranet), it is especially important to prevent access to your intranet from the Internet. This section provides tips to help you secure your computer before connecting to the Internet.

Single Workstations

Review the security measures described in this section when configuring single computers running Windows NT Workstation.

Restrict User Rights Access

Review the User Rights policies in User Manager. You should remove the following groups from each user right. By default, the group Everyone is granted access to your computer from the network and the group Guests is permitted to log on locally. You should remove these default settings.

User Right	Remove Group
Access this computer from the network	Everyone
Log on locally	Guests

Eliminate the Server Service and Other Network Services

Disable any services not absolutely necessary on your computer by clearing them in the Services option in Control Panel. Specifically, you should disable the Server service; this prevents any access to your computer through this service.

The FTP Server service included with Windows NT versions 3.1 through 3.51 should also be disabled or configured to ensure adequate security.

You should review all other network services that you use, and remove or disable unused network services. The fewer services you run on your system, the less likely it is that a mistake in administration can occur and be exploited.

Eliminate Unnecessary Accounts and Use Good Passwords

You should remove all unnecessary user accounts. You should also remove any unnecessary accounts from the Administrator group. By limiting user accounts and the members of the Administrator group, you limit the number of users who might choose passwords that could expose your system.

Also, the password for the Administrator account should always be difficult to duplicate and should never be left empty.

Eliminate Shared Directories

Check the properties of shared directories available on your computer. Shared resources on your computer might be available to other remote computers, depending on your Internet service provider. Disable sharing or change the sharing properties of any resources you do not want remote computers to use. In the **Shared Directory Properties** dialog box, select the **Not Shared** check box to disable sharing of a resource, as shown in Figure 35.1.

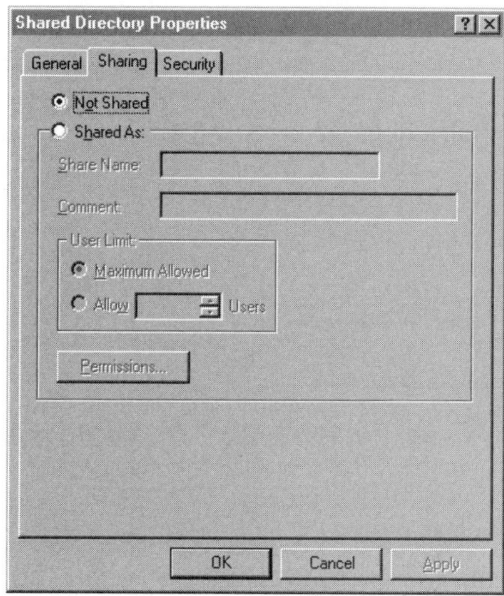

Figure 35.1 The Shared Directory Properties dialog box

Networked Workstations

Multihomed computers—computers that run Windows NT Workstation and are connected to an intranet, and that also have one or more additional connections to the Internet—should comply with the security measures above, plus these additional precautions.

Unbind Unnecessary Services from Your Internet Adapter Cards

You should unbind unnecessary services from network cards connected to the Internet.

▶ **To unbind services from network adapter cards**

1. Double-click **Network** in **Control Panel**.
2. On the **Bindings** tab, show the bindings for all services, then select the binding under the service and click **Disable**.

Figure 35.2 shows the **Bindings** tab of the **Network** dialog box.

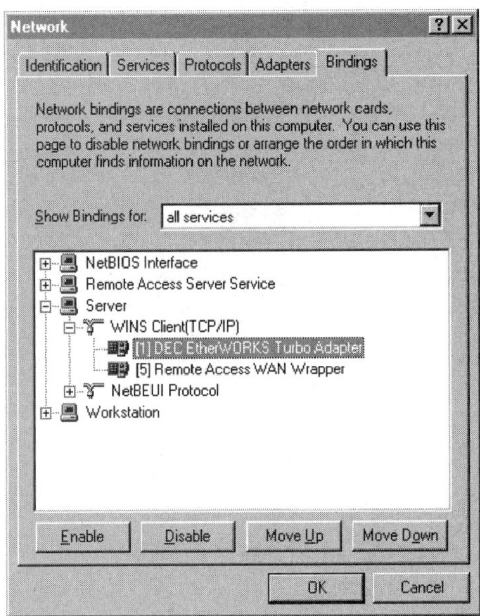

Figure 35.2 The Bindings tab of the Network dialog box

For example, you might use the Server service to copy new images and documents from computers in your internal network on an Intel EtherExpress 16 LAN Adapter. However, when you are connected to the Internet using Dial-Up Networking, Internet users also have direct access to your computer through the Server service through the Remote Access WAN Wrapper binding as shown in Figure 35.2.

The Remote Access WAN Wrapper binding under the Server service should be disabled to prevent attacks through the Server service.

Note You can use the Windows NT Server service over the Internet; however, you should fully understand the security implications and licensing issues. For more information about security and licensing, see *Windows NT Server Concepts and Planning*.

Disable Routing

You should disable routing when you configure the TCP/IP protocol. If routing is enabled, you run the risk of passing data from your intranet to the Internet.

To configure the TCP/IP protocol,

1. Double-click **Network** in Control Panel.
2. Click the **Protocols** tab, select **TCP/IP Protocol,** and click **Properties**.
3. On the **Routing** tab, clear the **Enable IP Forwarding** check box if it is selected.

Figure 35.3 shows the **Routing** tab with the **Enable IP Forwarding** check box cleared.

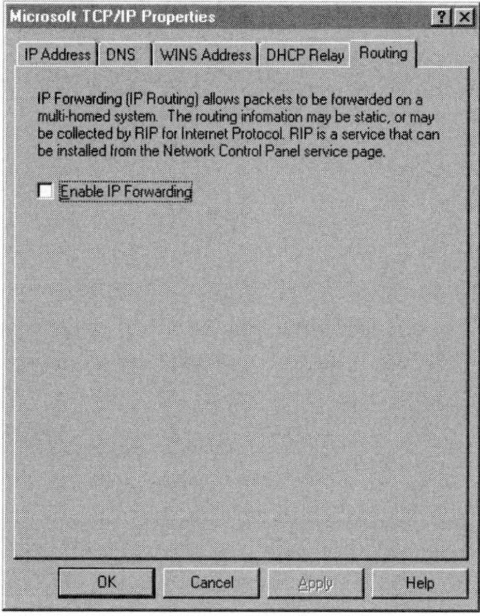

Figure 35.3 Disable routing by clearing the Enable IP Forwarding check box

Check Permissions on Network Shares

On a default installation, you do not need to change any network shares. However, note that Windows NT Workstation automatically creates special shares for administrative and system use. For example, the root of every directory is shared to the Administrators, Backup Operators, and Server Operators groups. The share uses the convention

*Computername**Driveletter*$

For example, a share may be called **\\maria2\c$**. You cannot change this default setting. For more information about the default shares, see your Windows NT documentation.

If you do run the Server service on your Internet adapter cards, and you have created network shares, you should permit access only to those users and groups that you want to use the files. Double-check the permissions set on the shares you have created on the system. It is also wise to double-check the permissions set on the files contained in the shares' directories to ensure that you have set them correctly. In general, you should remove the group Everyone.

Maintain Strict Account Policies

User Manager provides a way for the system administrator to specify how quickly account passwords expire (thus forcing users to regularly change passwords), and to set other policies, such as how many incorrect logon attempts are tolerated before a user is locked out. You should change the default settings. User Manager is used to set account policies. Pay particular attention to accounts with Administrator access. These steps help prevent exhaustive or random password attacks.

Peer Web Services

You can use Peer Web Services for Windows NT Workstation version 4.0 and Windows 95 to publish web pages on a small scale, such as your own home page on your company's network. You can also use Peer Web Services to develop and test content and applications for Windows NT Server Internet Information Server without requiring that you run the Windows NT Server operating system on the computer used to create the content.

Peer Web Services is a subset of Internet Information Server. Although limited in capability, this personal version is still suitable for Web application development. Peer Web Services supports all extensions and filters supported by Internet Information Server.

Table 35.1 compares Peer Web Services and Internet Information Server.

Table 35.1 Comparison of Peer Web Services and Internet Information Server

Feature	Peer Web Services	Internet Information Server
Operating system	Windows NT Workstation 4.0 and Windows 95	Windows NT Server 4.0
Version	2.0	2.0
Purpose	For low-volume personal publishing on a non-dedicated workstation in the corporate intranet—similar to peer-level file services	For publishing on the Internet or corporate intranet
Services	WWW, FTP, and Gopher	WWW, FTP, and Gopher
Control access via IP address	No	Yes
Virtual servers	No	Yes
Log to ODBC database	No	Yes
Limit network bandwidth	No	Yes
Internet Database Connector	Included	Included
SSL support	40-bit keys	40-bit and 128-bit keys (128-bit support available in U.S. and Canadian versions only)
HTML-based administration	Yes	Yes
HTTP version string	Microsoft-IIS-W/2.0 Microsoft-IIS-W95/2.0 (Windows 95)	Microsoft-IIS-S/2.0
TransmitFile()	Restricted to two concurrent **TransmitFile()** operations	Yes
Concurrent connect limit	No limit	No limit
Completion ports used	Yes	Yes
Remote IIS server discovery	No	Yes
File handle caching	No	Yes
CPU scaling for threads	No	Yes
Socket listen backlog	5	None

Except for the restrictions listed on the previous page, Peer Web Services is completely compatible with Internet Information Server.

For more information about using either of these Microsoft web servers, see the *Windows NT Server Internet Guide*.

PART VIII

Windows NT Workstation Troubleshooting

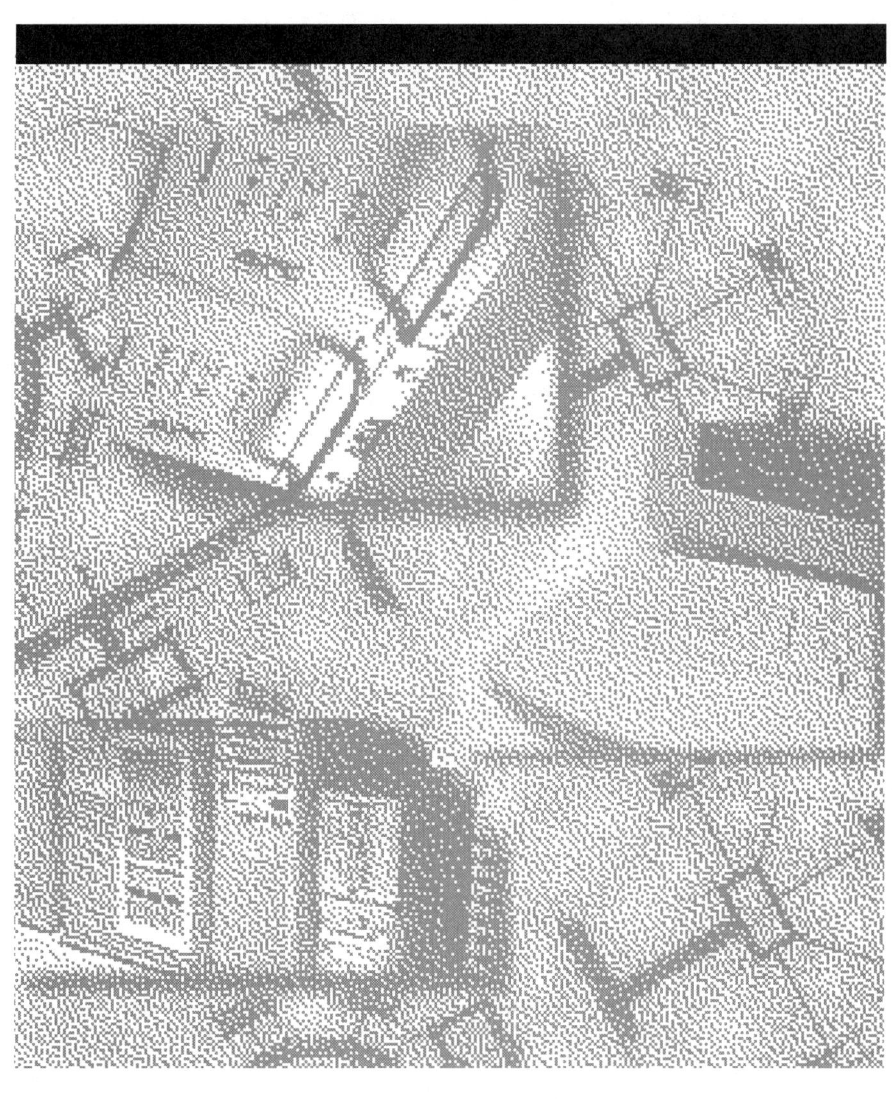

CHAPTER 36

General Troubleshooting

This chapter identifies tools that are available in Windows NT to help you troubleshoot problems. It contains information about troubleshooting hardware problems, and how to use information in the Registry to determine why services are not working correctly. It also contains an example of using information in the Registry for troubleshooting.

Careful record keeping is essential to successful troubleshooting. You should have records of your network layout, cabling, previous problems and their solutions, dates of installation of hardware and software, and so on, all readily accessible.

Many problems can be avoided with routine virus checks. Be sure to check for viruses before installing or upgrading Windows NT on a computer that is already in use.

This chapter identifies other chapters with troubleshooting help; methodology; provides an overview of Windows NT tools; describes hardware problem-solving; and explains how to identify which services or drivers are working.

Sources of Troubleshooting Information

In addition to the troubleshooting tools that are described in this chapter, there are several other sources of troubleshooting information:

- Chapter 23, "Overview of the Windows NT Registry," describes how to use information in the Registry for troubleshooting and configuration maintenance.
- Chapter 25, "Configuration Management and the Registry," provides problem solving techniques using the Registry.
- Chapter 21, "Troubleshooting Startup and Disk Problems," discusses what you can do to find the cause of problems when your computer fails to complete startup.

- Chapter 39, "Windows NT Debugger," describes the different types of STOP messages. It also contains information about using the Windows NT Debugger.
- The Messages database, included in this Resource Kit, is another source of troubleshooting information. Here, thousands of messages are documented, with the probable cause and recommended solution to each of them. In particular, the Kernel STOP errors that appear when the system fails (with a blue screen) are documented in the Messages database. Chapter 38, "Windows NT Executive Messages," discusses the various types of messages generated by the Windows Windows NT Executive, and categorizes them by their type and severity.
- Windows NT Help contains a troubleshooting topic.
- Appendix A in the *Windows NT Workstation Start Here* book describes how to overcome problems installing Windows NT 4.0 on x86-based computers.
- The *Windows NT Workstation Start Here* book describes Microsoft's AnswerPoint Information Services, which provide easy telephone access to the latest technical and support information for Microsoft products.
- The Microsoft Knowledge Base contains support information developed by Microsoft product support specialists. You can search for all Windows NT troubleshooting articles by specifying **winnt** and **tshoot** in the query. The Windows NT Knowledge Base is included on the *Windows NT Workstation Resource Kit CD*. It is also included in the:
  - Microsoft Developer Network (MSDN) CD.
  - TechNet CD.
  - Microsoft Internet FTP host, ftp.microsoft.com.
  - Technical Support and Services category on the Web page http://www.microsoft.com/ntworkstation.

Troubleshooting Methodology

This section discusses approaches for solving problems and presents an example of a troubleshooting scenario. There are three parts to this methodology:

- Isolating the problem.
- Identifying whether the action has ever worked properly on this computer, or works properly on another computer.
- Defining an action plan.

Isolating the Problem

First, try to isolate the problem. What, precisely, is not working correctly? Try to narrow down exactly what you expect to have happen versus what is happening.

For example, if your computer does not complete startup, you need to identify how far it gets, and write down any error messages. On an x86-based computer, if you get an error such as **Missing operating system** from the system BIOS when you start your computer, the problem is very different than if startup fails after the boot loader (NTLDR) starts. You know that the NTLDR has started when you see the message

```
NTDETECT V1.0 Checking Hardware . . .
```

Another way to isolate the problem is to figure out if there are related programs or functionality that works correctly on this computer. If so, what are the differences between what works and what does not work?

Identifying Whether It Works in Other Situations

Has what you are trying to do ever worked on this computer before? If so, something might have changed that affects it. Have you changed hardware or installed new software? Has somebody else been using the computer, and could that person have made changes you do not know about?

If this program or functionality has never worked on this computer, compare the setup and configuration on this computer with the same program on another computer to identify differences.

As an example, identical 624 MB IDE disks are installed on two different x86-based computers. On one computer, 609 MB are available after creating and formatting partitions. On the other computer, only 504 MB are available. If you look at the messages that the system BIOS displays when starting up the two computers, you may see that the computer with 609 MB has a newer BIOS than the other computer. You would need to upgrade one computer's system BIOS, or obtain a third-party translation utility that enables the computer to access the entire disk.

Defining an Action Plan

Try to identify all of the variables that could affect the problem. As you troubleshoot the problem, try to change only one of these variables at a time. Keep records of what you do and the effect of each action.

It is advantageous to develop your plan on paper. Decide what steps you want to take, and what you expect to do based on the results of each step. Then do the steps in order, and follow your plan.

If you see a result for which you have no plan:

- Go back to the isolation phase.
- Identify what happens in similar situations.
- Define another plan.

Troubleshooting Scenario

Here is a scenario that shows applying this approach to an actual problem. A user was trying to upgrade his home computer to a newer version of Windows NT 4.0 (before the final product was available). The user was about half finished with copying files from the CD to the hard disk when a message came up saying that a file could not be copied. This was how the user isolated the cause of his problem.

The user has successfully installed earlier versions of Windows NT version 4.0 on this computer. Since last upgrading Windows NT, the CD has been used to install another program, with no problems.

The user has changed nothing on the computer since the last upgrade, except installing the other program. That program should have no relationship to the problem. Other people can install the same version of Windows NT from CD on similar computers.

The user noticed that the CD-ROM drive made noises like it was spinning faster and then slower just before the error message.

These are the steps that were used to identify and recover from the problem.

Step 1. Check the event log to see if there are any errors logged. The CD-ROM drive was reporting bad blocks on the CD, so Windows NT knew that there were problems.

Step 2. Inspect the CD for dust or scratches. There were no obvious problems on the CD, and the user previously had no problems using the CD.

Step 3. Copy files from the CD manually rather than running Windows NT Setup. The file that caused the error copied fine, but other files on the CD could not be copied.

Step 4. Get another CD of the same build and try to install Windows NT from it. Perhaps there is a problem with the CD itself. Windows NT Setup failed on the same file on both CDs, and manually copying files fails on the same files.

Step 5. Install software from other CDs that have worked on this computer before. The user noted that some work, some do not. The ones that do not work have more data on them than ones that install successfully. Therefore, something must be wrong with accessing data on the later tracks of the CD. Data is recorded on CDs starting on the innermost track. CDs vary their spin rate when reading inner versus outer tracks. Something might be wrong with the motor synchronization spin rate.

Step 6. Look inside the CD-ROM drive for signs of dust or hair that might interfere with proper operation at one end of the read head's range of motion. A hair was found stuck to the read head.

Using Troubleshooting Tools

This section provides a brief overview of the troubleshooting tools that are available on the Windows NT Workstation product CD and the *Windows NT Workstation Resource Kit* CD.

Windows NT Tools

These tools are installed when you install Windows NT Workstation:

Tool	Purpose	For more information:
Event Viewer	Display the system, security, and application logs.	Chapter 37, "Monitoring Events," in this *Resource Guide*.
Performance Monitor	Measure your computer's efficiency, identify and troubleshoot possible problems, and plan for additional hardware needs.	Chapter 10, "About Performance Monitor," in this *Resource* Guide.
Task Manager	Monitor active applications and processes on your computer, and start and stop them.	Chapter 11, "Performance Monitoring Tools," in this *Resource Guide*.
Windows NT Diagnostics	Enables you to view hardware information in the Registry, such as currently loaded device drivers and IRQ values.	"Using the Windows NT Diagnostics Administrative Tool," presented later in this chapter.
Windows NT Hardware Detection Tool (NTHQ)	Identifies installed hardware and settings for diagnostic purposes.	"Using the Windows NT Hardware Detection Tool (NTHQ)," presented later in this chapter.

Windows NT Workstation Resource Kit Tools

The *Windows NT Workstation Resource Kit* contains many tools that can be used for troubleshooting. For information about all of the tools available in the *Windows NT Workstation Resource Kit*, refer to the online Resource Kit Tools Help (Rktools.hlp) and double click each of the tools groups from the Contents page.

Troubleshooting Hardware Problems

There are three Microsoft products that you can use to help troubleshoot hardware problems:

- Hardware Compatibility List (HCL)
- Windows NT Hardware Detection Tool (NTHQ)
- Windows NT Diagnostics Administrative Tool

Using the Hardware Compatibility List (HCL)

The most common cause of hardware problems is the use of hardware that is not listed on the Hardware Compatibility List (HCL). The HCL included in the *Windows NT Workstation Resource Kit* lists the hardware components that have been tested and have passed compatibility testing with Windows NT version 4.0. It is especially important for you to refer to the HCL if you plan to use any modems, tape backup units, and SCSI adapters.

The latest HCL is available on:

- The Web at http://www.microsoft.com/ntworkstation/
- Microsoft's FTP server at ftp://microsoft.com/bussys/winnt/winnt_docs/hcl

To avoid problems make sure that you are using a device make and model that is listed on the HCL. If several models from one manufacturer are included in the HCL, only those models are supported; a slightly different model might cause problems. Where special criteria are required for a model to be supported (for example, if a particular version of driver is required), this information is described as a footnote in the HCL. As additional hardware is tested, the HCL is updated. New device drivers and other system components are added to the HCL. The updated list and software are available through the electronic services listed at the end of the HCL.

Using the Windows NT Hardware Detection Tool (NTHQ)

NTHQ is an MS-DOS-based program. The next procedure describes how to run the program.

▶ **To run NTHQ**

1. When running Windows NT, insert a blank 3.5-inch floppy disk in the drive.
2. Run Makedisk.bat from the \Support\Hqtool directory on the Windows NT Workstation product CD.
3. Leave the floppy disk inserted, and shut down your computer.
4. When your computer restarts, you are running NTHQ.

The file Readme.txt on the floppy disk contains details about NTHQ. You can see the same information by clicking the Help button on the NTHQ screen.

These are the three ways that NTHQ is most often used:

- Print hardware information, save it to a file, and keep the report and file with the other configuration information for your computer. You can use the report when planning to change the configuration.
- If you are having problems installing Windows NT, you can start NTHQ from the floppy disk and use it for troubleshooting, The Readme.txt file contains troubleshooting tips for installation problems.
- If you cannot start Windows NT, or have installed new hardware and cannot access it, NTHQ might help you troubleshoot the problem. Because NTHQ enables you to view the hardware that it detects, you can find out if any devices are not being detected. For example, if you have not changed your configuration since the last time you produced an NTHQ report, run a new one and compare the results. If you find a difference, you might have a hardware problem.

Using the Windows NT Diagnostics Administrative Tool

You can use this program to display Registry information in an easily-readable format. Windows NT Diagnostics Administrative Tool enables you to:

- View information about the hardware connected to the computer.
- Identify device drivers and services that should be started when you start the computer.

▶ **To run Windows NT Diagnostics**

1. Click the **Start** button
2. Click **Programs**.
3. Click **Administrative Tools (Common).**
4. Double-click **Windows NT Diagnostics**.

The information that you can view is organized into nine tabs. The next screen shot shows the kind of information that you see when you click the **System** tab.

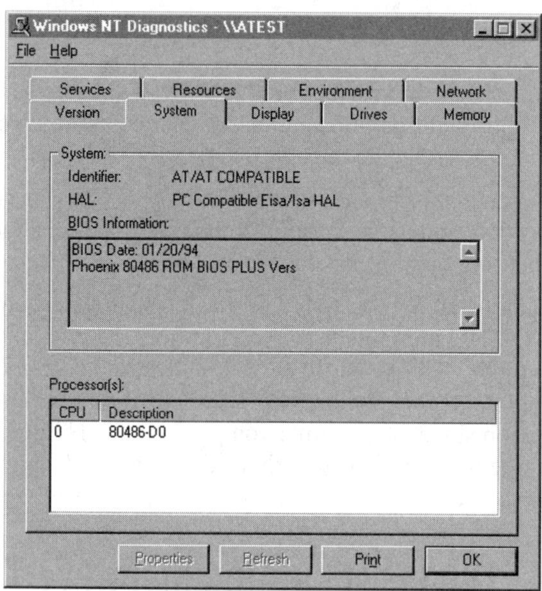

These are the tabs that you can select in Windows NT Diagnostics:

- **Version** shows operating system and hardware information, such as the number and type of processors.
- **System** displays more details about the computer, including the type of processor and the Hardware Abstraction Layer (HAL). The **System** tab is shown in the preceding screen shot.
- **Display** describes the video display and its driver.
- **Drives** displays information about the disks connected to the computer, the partitions on hard disks, and network shares.
- **Memory** displays physical memory and page file information.
- **Services** provides the status of all services and devices. It provides more information than is available by using the Services and Devices options in Control Panel.
- **Resources** displays information about IRQs, I/O ports, DMA channels, and memory addresses.
- **Environment** displays system and user environment settings.
- **Network** displays user and network information.

Other Approaches to Troubleshooting Hardware Problems

If your hardware components are listed on the HCL, and you are still having problems, check that the physical connections are secure.

If you are using a SCSI device, check its termination. Even if you are sure the termination is correct, and you are having problems that could be due to incorrect termination, open the computer case and check again. You should use active rather than passive terminators whenever possible.

Note Terminators are used to provide the correct impedance at the end of a cable. If the impedance is too high or too low, internal signal reflections can take place. These echoes represent noise on the cable, and can corrupt subsequent signals, which can result in degraded performance or data loss.

Passive terminators are resistors with the appropriate resistance value for the characteristic impedance of the cable. Active terminators are slightly more sophisticated electronics that are able to better maintain the correct impedance necessary to eliminate signal reflection.

Verify that the SCSI cables are not longer than they need to be. If a two-foot cable is long enough to connect the device to the controller, do not use a three-foot cable just because you have one available. The acceptable lengths vary depending on such factors as whether you are using basic SCSI, SCSI-2, wide SCSI, ultra-wide SCSI, differential SCSI; the quality of the termination; and the quality of the devices being used. Consult your hardware documentation for this information.

Check your hardware configuration. I/O and interrupt conflicts that went unnoticed under another operating system must be resolved when you switch to Windows NT. Likewise, you must pay much closer attention to CMOS and EISA configuration parameters when using Windows NT.

The Knowledge Base is a good source of information for hardware problems. There are several articles about memory problems, memory parity errors, SCSI problems, and other hardware information in the Knowledge Base.

If your computer crashes randomly and inconsistently, you might have memory problems. On x86-based computers, you can use the /maxmem switch in your Boot.ini file to troubleshoot memory problems. Chapter 21, "Troubleshooting Startup and Disk Problems," contains more information about the /maxmem switch and video problems.

Troubleshooting Using HKEY_LOCAL_MACHINE

Problems can often be traced to services, device drivers, or startup control data. The Registry key HKEY_LOCAL_MACHINE contains this configuration information, so it is a good place to look for information to solve these types of problems. You have two Registry editors that you can use to look at information in the Registry:

- Regedt32.exe has the most menu items, and more choices for the menu items. You can search for keys and subkeys in the Registry.
- Regedit.exe enables you to search for strings, values, keys, and subkeys. This feature is useful if you want to find a specific value or string.

Most of the examples in this section use the Regedt32.exe. You see the following screen when you run Regedt32.exe.

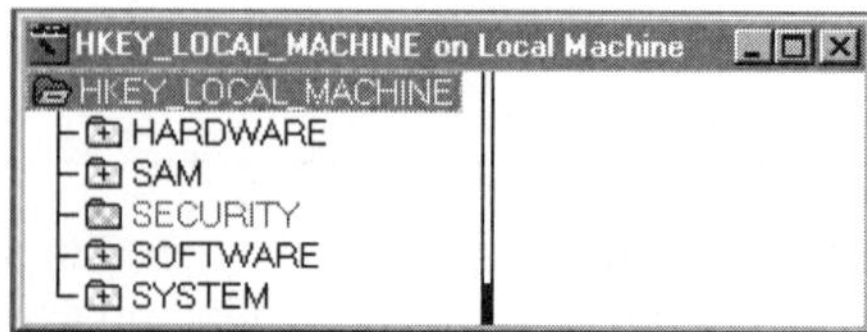

The following table briefly describes the Registry keys.

Key	Description
HARDWARE	Describes the physical hardware in the computer, the way device drivers use that hardware, and mappings and related data that link Kernel-mode drivers with various user-mode code.
SAM	Contains security information for user and group accounts.
SECURITY	Contains the local security policy, such as specific user rights.
SOFTWARE	Describes the per-computer software.
SYSTEM	Controls system startup, device driver loading, Windows NT services, and operating system behavior.

The HARDWARE and SYSTEM keys are the most useful for troubleshooting.

Note Do not change information in the Registry when you are using it for troubleshooting. Instead, use the options in Control Panel, such as Services, Devices, Network, and SCSI Adapters, to change Registry information.

The Registry information and examples in this section are for a Windows NT Workstation computer that uses the TCP/IP network protocol. It uses a DHCP server to get IP addresses. If your computer has a different configuration, or has third-party device drivers or services installed, the Registry will contain different information.

HKEY_LOCAL_MACHINE\HARDWARE

This key describes the physical hardware in the computer. Since the data in the HARDWARE key is stored in binary form, the best way to view the data is by using Windows NT Diagnostics, one of the programs in the Administrative Tools (Common) program group. See the section titled "Windows NT Diagnostics," presented earlier in this chapter, for more information about the program.

For more information about the HKEY_LOCAL_MACHINE\HARDWARE key, see Chapter 23, "Overview of the Windows NT Registry."

HKEY_LOCAL_MACHINE\SYSTEM

The HKEY_LOCAL_MACHINE\SYSTEM key contains information that controls system startup, device driver loading, Windows NT services, and operating system behavior. All startup-related data that must be stored (rather than computed during startup) is saved in the SYSTEM key. This screen shot shows the SYSTEM key and its subkeys.

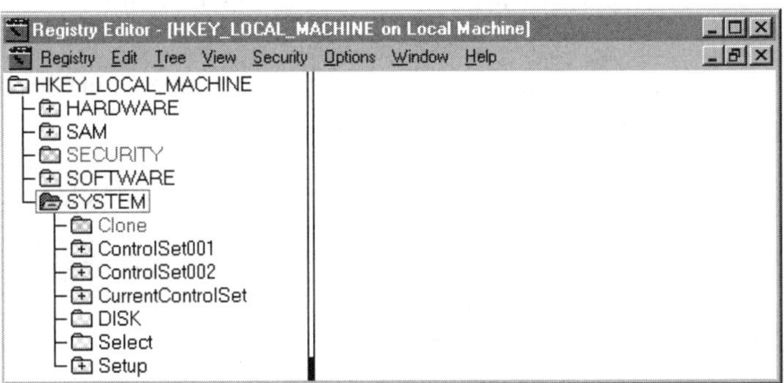

The most important troubleshooting information in the Registry key HKEY_LOCAL_MACHINE\SYSTEM are the control sets. A control set contains system configuration information, such as which device drivers and services to load and start. There are at least two control sets, and sometimes more, depending on how often you change system settings, or have problems with the settings you choose. The preceding screen shot shows the following control sets:

- Clone
- ControlSet001
- ControlSet002
- CurrentControlSet

The Registry subkey HKEY_LOCAL_MACHINE\SYSTEM\Select identifies how the control sets are used, and determines which control set is used at startup. This subkey contains the following value entries:

- Current. Identifies which control set is the CurrentControlSet. When you use Control Panel options or Registry Editor to change the Registry, you are changing information in the CurrentControlSet.
- Default. Identifies which control set will be used the next time you start Windows NT, unless you select Last Known Good Configuration. Default and Current typically contain the same control set number.
- Failed. The control set that was pointed to by Default when a user last started the computer by using the LastKnownGood control set.
- LastKnownGood. The control set that is a clean copy of the last control set that actually worked. After a successful logon, the Clone control set is copied to the LastKnownGood control set.

The next screen shot shows the value entries for the Select subkey.

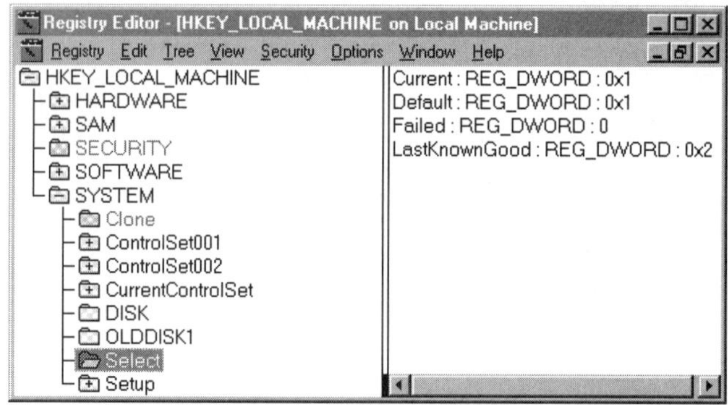

Note The Registry editors each display the Registry in a similar way. The window on the left contains the key and subkey names. The window on the right contains *value entries*. In the preceding screen shot, one value entry is Current : REG_DWORD : 0x1. In this example, Current is the *name*, REG_DWORD is the *data type*, and 0x1 is the *value*. These terms will be used in the rest of this section.

The values for the value entries in the Select subkey identify which control set is Current, Default, Failed, and LastKnownGood. For example, a value of 0x1 indicates that you should look at ControlSet001 to find the infromation.

In the preceding screen shot, Current and Default are both 0x1. Failed is 0, and LastKnownGood is 0x2.

Therefore, ControlSet001 is the Current and the Default control set. ControlSet001 will be the one modified if you make any changes by using options in Control Panel. ControlSet001 will be used for the Default control set the next time you start the computer.

ControlSet002 is the LastKnownGood control set. If you decide to use the Last Known Good control set to start the computer, Windows NT will use ControlSet002.

For more information about the use of the control sets, see:

- Chapter 19, "What Happens When You Start Your Computer"
- Chapter 21, "Troubleshooting Startup and Disk Problems"
- Chapter 25, "Configuration Management and the Registry"
- The online help file: Regentry.hlp on the *Windows NT Workstation Resource Kit* CD.

Finding Service and Device Dependencies

This section describes using information in the Control and Services subkeys to troubleshoot problems with your computer. The next screen shot shows the CurrentControlSet and its subkeys.

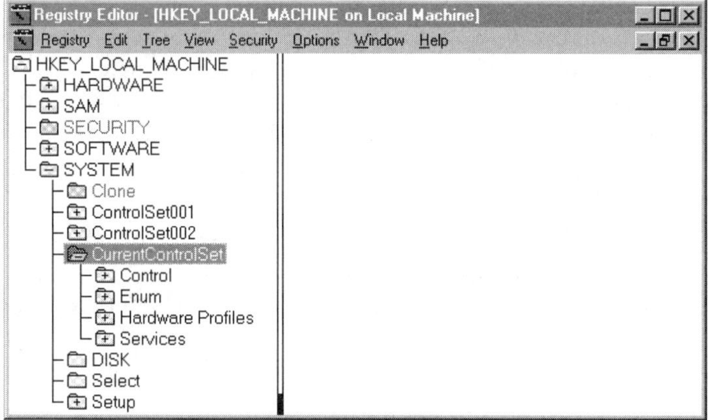

When you install Windows NT, it creates the Control and Services subkeys for each control set in HKEY_LOCAL_MACHINE\SYSTEM. Some information, such as which services are part of which group, and the order in which to load the groups, is the same for all Windows NT computers. Other information, such as which devices and services to load when you start your computer, is based on the hardware installed on your computer and the network software that you select for installation.

Each control set has four subkeys:

- Control—Contains startup data for Windows NT, including the maximum size of the Registry.
- Enum—Contains the Plug and Play hardware tree.
- Hardware Profiles—Enables you to define different configurations for your computer and select the one you want to use at startup.
- Services—Lists all Kernel device drivers, file system drivers, and Win32 service drivers that can be loaded by the boot loader, the I/O Manager, and the Service Control Manager. It also contains subkeys describing which drivers are attached to which hardware devices, as well as the services that are installed on the system.

ServiceGroupOrder Subkey

You can see the order in which device drivers should be loaded and initialized by viewing the Registry subkey HKEY_LOCAL_MACHINE\SYSTEM\CurrentControlSet\Control\ServiceGroupOrder.

Individual drivers that are members of a service group are loaded in the following order:

- System Bus Extender
- SCSI miniport
- Port
- Primary disk
- SCSI class
- SCSI CDROM class
- Filter
- Boot file system
- Base
- Pointer Port
- Keyboard Port
- Pointer Class
- Keyboard Class
- Video Init
- Video
- Video Save
- File system
- Event log
- Streams Drivers
- PNP_TDI
- NDIS
- TDI
- NetBIOSGroup
- SpoolerGroup
- NetDDEGroup
- Parallel arbitrator
- Extended base
- RemoteValidation
- PCI Configuration

"Service Groups," presented later in this chapter, lists drivers that are in each group.

Services Subkey

The Registry subkey HKEY_LOCAL_MACHINE\SYSTEM\CurrentControlSet \Services*Service name* controls how services are loaded. This section describes some of the value entries for this subkey, with an explanation of their values. The next screen shot shows the subkey HKEY_LOCAL_MACHINE\SYSTEM \CurrentControlSet\Services\LanmanWorkstation and its value entries.

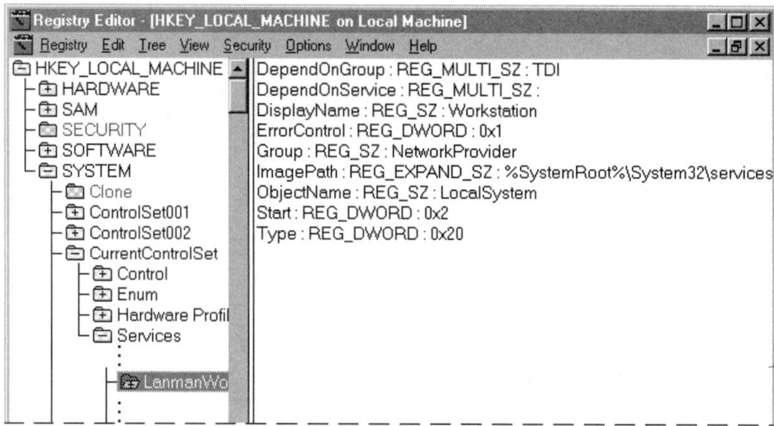

Figure 36.1 The Registry subkey HKEY_LOCAL_MACHINE\SYSTEM \CurrentControlSet\Services\LanmanWorkstation

DependOnGroup Value Entry

When a subkey has a value for the DependOnGroup value entry, at least one service from the group must be loaded before this service is loaded. This table shows services that have a value for DependOnGroup. The LanmanWorkstation service, shown in Figure 36.1, has a value for the DependOnGroup value entry.

Service	Depends on
Cdfs	SCSI CDROM Class
Cdrom	SCSI miniport
Disk	SCSI miniport
LanmanServer	TDI
LanmanWorkstation	TDI
LmHosts	Network Provider
NetBIOS	TDI
Parallel	Parallel arbitrator
Scsiprnt	SCSI miniport
Scsiscan	SCSI miniport
Sfloppy	SCSI miniport

DependOnService Value Entry

This value entry identifies specific services that must be loaded before this service is loaded. The "Troubleshooting Example," presented later in this chapter, shows how you can use information in the DependOnService value entry to determine which services need to be started.

This table lists the services on the example computer that have a value for DependOnServices.

Service	Depends on		
Alerter	LanmanWorkstation		
Browser	LanmanWorkstation	LanmanServer	LmHosts
ClipSrv	NetDDE		
DHCP	Afd	NetBT	TCP/IP
Messenger	LanmanWorkstation	NetBIOS	
NetBT	TCP/IP		
NetDDE	NetDDEDSDM		
NetLogon	LanmanWorkstation	LmHosts	
Parallel	Parport		
Replicator	LanmanServer	LanmanWorkstation	

By knowing the dependencies, you can troubleshoot a problem more effectively. For example, if you stop the Workstation service, the Alerter, Messenger, and Net Logon services are also stopped, because they are dependent upon the Workstation service. If an error occurs when you try to start the Workstation service, any of the files that are part of Workstation service could be missing or corrupt. This is also why, if you start one of the services that depend on Workstation service, the Service Control Manager will automatically start the Workstation service if it is not already running.

ErrorControl Value Entry

This value entry controls whether an error during the startup of this driver will cause the system to switch to the LastKnownGood control set. If the value is 0 (Ignore, no error is reported) or 1 (Normal, error reported), startup proceeds. If the value is 2 (Severe) or 3 (Critical), an error is reported and LastKnownGood control set will be used.

The ErrorControl value for LanmanWorkstation is 0x1, which indicates that if there was an error starting LanmanWorkstation, an error would be logged in the event log, but Windows NT would complete startup.

ImagePath Value Entry

This value entry identifies the path and file name of the driver. You can use My Computer or Windows NT Explorer to verify the existence of the named file. The ImagePath for LanmanWorkstation is %SystemRoot%\System32\Services.exe.

Start Value Entry

This value entry determines when services are loaded during system startup. If a service is not starting, you need to know when and how it should be starting. Then look for the services that should have been loaded prior to this service. The values are described as follows:

Value	Meaning	Description
0	Boot	Loaded by the boot loader (NTLDR or OSLOADER) during the startup sequence.
1	System	Loaded at Kernel initialization during the load sequence.
2	Auto Load	Loaded or started automatically at system startup.
3	Load On Demand	Driver is manually started by the user or another process.
4	Disabled	Driver is not to be started under any condition. If a driver is accidentally disabled, reset this value by using the Services option in Control Panel. File System drivers are the one exception to the Start value. They are loaded even if they have a start value of 4.

Type Value Entry

The Type value entry helps you know where the service fits in the architecture. These are its possible values:

Value	Description
0x1	Kernel device driver.
0x2	File System driver, which is also a Kernel device driver.
0x4	Set of arguments for an adapter.
0x10	A Win32 program that can be started by the Service Controller and that obeys the service control protocol. This type of Win32 service runs in a process by itself.
0x20	A Win32 service that can share a process with other Win32 services.

Many of the services that have a Type value of 0x20 are part of the Services.exe. For example, if your network protocol is TCP/IP, and you are configured to use a DHCP server to get IP addresses, these services that have a Type value of 0x20 are in the Services.exe:

- Alerter
- Browser
- DHCP
- EventLog
- LanmanServer
- LanmanWorkstation
- LmHosts
- Messenger
- NtLmSsp
- PlugPlay

These services are part of the Netdde.exe:

- NetDDE
- NetDDEdsdm

Service Groups

Many device drivers are arranged in groups to make startup easier. When device drivers and services are being loaded, Windows NT loads the groups in the order defined by ServiceGroupOrder. The next table shows which drivers are in each group.

Group name	Services		
BASE	Beep	KSecDD	Null
Boot Files System	Fastfat	Fs_Rec	
Event log	EventLog		
Extended Base	Modem Parallel	Scsiprnt	Serial
File System	Cdfs Msfs	Npfs	Ntfs
Filter	Cdaudio Changer	Diskperf Ftdisk	Simbad
Keyboard Class	Kbdclass		
Keyboard Port	i8042prt		
NDIS	EE16	NDIS	
NetBIOSGroup	NetBIOS		
NetDDEGroup	NetDDE		

Group name	Services		
Network	Mup	Rdr	Srv
NetworkProvider	LanmanWorkstation		
Parallel Arbitrator	Parport		
PCI Configuration	PCIDump		
PlugPlay	PlugPlay		
Pointer Class	Mouclass		
Pointer Port	Busmouse	Inport	Sermouse
Port	none		
PNP_TDI	NetBT	Tcpip	
Primary Disk	Abiosdsk Atdisk	Floppy	Sfloppy
RemoteValidation	NetLogon		
SCSI CDROM Class	Cdrom		
SCSI Class	Disk	Scsiscan	
SCSI Miniport	Aha154x Aha174x aic78xx Always ami0nt amsint Arrow atapi BusLogic Cpqarray dac960nt dce376nt	Delldsa DptScsi dtc329x Fd16_700 Fd7000ex Fd8xx mitsumi mkecr5xx Ncr53c9x Ncrc700 Ncrc710 ncrc810	Oliscsi Ql10wnt slcd32 Sparrow Spock T128 T13B tmv1 Ultra124 Ultra14f Ultra24f Wd33c93
SpoolerGroup	Spooler		
Streams Drivers	none		
System Bus Extender	Pcmcia		
TDI	Afd	DHCP	
Video	Ati Cirrus Dell_DGX Et400 Jazzg30 Jazzg364 Jzvxl484	mga mga_mil ncr77c22 psidisp qv s3 tga	v7vram VgaSave wd90c24a wdvga weitekp9 Xga
Video Init	VgaStart		
Video Save	VgaSave		

Troubleshooting Example

This section describes using information in the DependOnGroup and DependOnService value entries to find the cause of the following error message that you see after you log on.

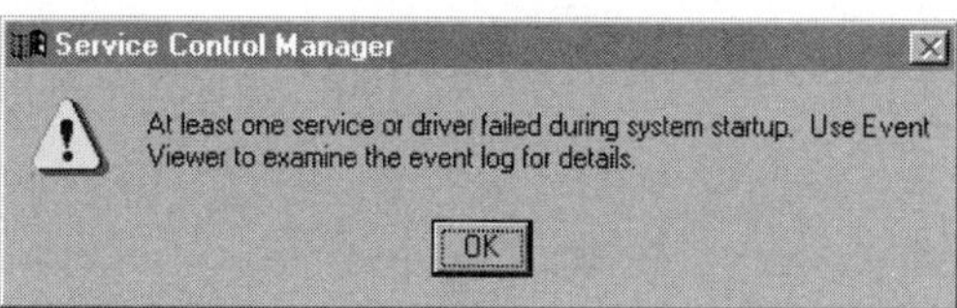

You can use the Event Viewer to see which services or drivers did not start.

To run Event Viewer

1. Click the **Start** button
2. Click **Programs**
3. Click **Administrative Tools (Common)**
4. Double-click **Event Viewer**
5. If the screen is displaying a log other than System Log, on the **Log** menu, click **System**

The event log shows the following entries.

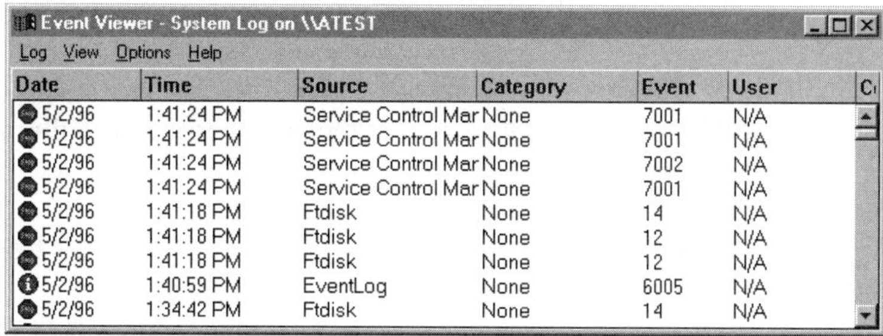

Date	Time	Source	Category	Event	User	C
5/2/96	1:41:24 PM	Service Control Mar	None	7001	N/A	
5/2/96	1:41:24 PM	Service Control Mar	None	7001	N/A	
5/2/96	1:41:24 PM	Service Control Mar	None	7002	N/A	
5/2/96	1:41:24 PM	Service Control Mar	None	7001	N/A	
5/2/96	1:41:18 PM	Ftdisk	None	14	N/A	
5/2/96	1:41:18 PM	Ftdisk	None	12	N/A	
5/2/96	1:41:18 PM	Ftdisk	None	12	N/A	
5/2/96	1:40:59 PM	EventLog	None	6005	N/A	
5/2/96	1:34:42 PM	Ftdisk	None	14	N/A	

Sometimes, as you can see by the preceding System Log screen shot, several events are logged at approximately the same time. In this example, the newest event is entered at the top. Usually, if you look at the oldest event, you will find the reason that all of the events are logged. In this example, the fourth entry from the top was the first one logged at 1:41:24. Double-clicking on it results in this event detail.

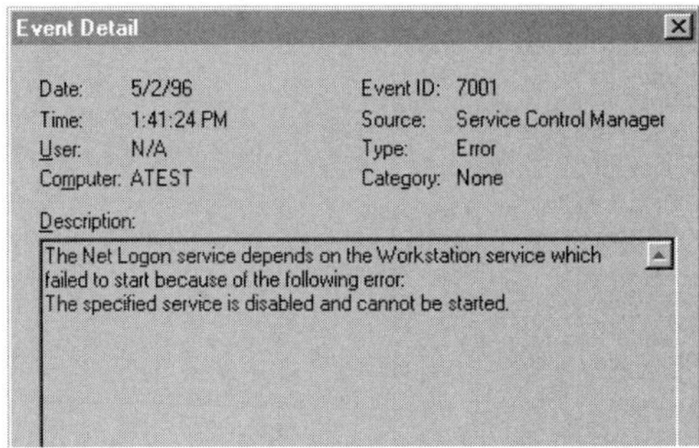

But when you look in the Registry there is no subkey HKEY_LOCAL_MACHINE\SYSTEM\CurrentControlSet\Services\Workstation. How do you find it? You have two methods that you can use.

You can use Regedit.exe to find the name anywhere in the control set.

To use Regedit.exe to find the Workstation service

1. Click the **Start** button.
2. Click **Run**, and enter Regedit.exe.
3. Double-click **HKEY_LOCAL_MACHINE**, double-click **SYSTEM**, double-click **CurrentControlSet**, and click **Services**.
4. On the **Edit** menu, click **Find**.
5. In the **Find what** box, enter **Workstation** and check the **Keys** and **Data** checkboxes. Clear **Match whole string** only.
6. Click **Find**.
7. If the match is not what you are looking for, on the **Edit** menu, click **Find Next** until you find the correct key.

If you think that the service name is part of the key name, you can use the Windows NT Registry Editor.

To use Regedt32.exe to find the Workstation service

1. Click the **Start** button.
2. Click **Run**, and enter Regedt32.exe.
3. Double-click **HKEY_LOCAL_MACHINE**, double-click **SYSTEM**, double-click **CurrentControlSet**, and click **Services**.
4. On the **View** menu, click **Find key**.
5. In the **Find what** box, enter **Workstation**. Clear **Match whole word only** and **Match case**.
6. Click **Find Next**.

Both Registry editors find a match on the subkey HKEY_LOCAL_MACHINE\SYSTEM\CurrentControlSet\Services\LanmanWorkstation. The DisplayName value entry contains the name that you see when you use the Services icon in Control Panel, or the Services tab in the Windows NT Diagnostics administrative tool, to view information about services.

Therefore, this subkey is the one you are searching for. Its Start value is 0x4, which means it is disabled. It should be set to 0x2, which indicates it would start automatically when you start Windows NT.

As it turns out, you specifically disabled the Workstation service by using the Services icon in Control Panel and setting the **Startup Type** to **Disabled**. The computer was restarted to see what happened.

But what about the other errors that are in the event log? If you double-click each of the first three entries, you find the following descriptions:

```
The Messenger service depends on the Workstation service which
failed to start because of the following error.
The specified service is disabled and cannot be started.

The Computer Browser service depends on the TCP/IP NetBIOS
Helper service which failed to start because of the following error.
The dependency group or service failed to start.

The TCP/IP NetBIOS Helper service depends on the NetworkProvider
group and no member of this group started.
```

Changing the LanmanWorkstation service to start automatically will solve the problem with the Messenger service failing to start.

The Computer Browser and TCP/IP NetBIOS errors are both the result of no member of the NetworkProvider group starting. How do you find what services are in the NetworkProvider group? Regedt32.exe does not have an option to search for data, so you can use the Regedit.exe to find the NetworkProvider group.

► To use Regedit.exe to find the NetworkProvider group

1. Click the **Start** button.
2. Click **Run**, and enter Regedit.exe.
3. Double-click **HKEY_LOCAL_MACHINE**, double-click **SYSTEM**, double-click **CurrentControlSet**, and click **Services**.
4. On the **Edit** menu, click **Find**.
5. In the **Find what** box, enter **NetworkProvider** and check the **Data** checkbox.
6. Click **Find Next**.

The only subkey that has a Group value of NetworkProvider is LanmanWorkstation. Changing LanmanWorkstation to start automatically will also solve these problems.

Identifying a Service or Driver That Does Not Start

Some services are configured to start automatically on Windows NT. The specific services depend on your computer configuration, and which network services and protocols you are using.

You can use the Services option on Control Panel to view which services should have started automatically and see which ones did start. For example, the next screen shot was taken when the Workstation service was disabled.

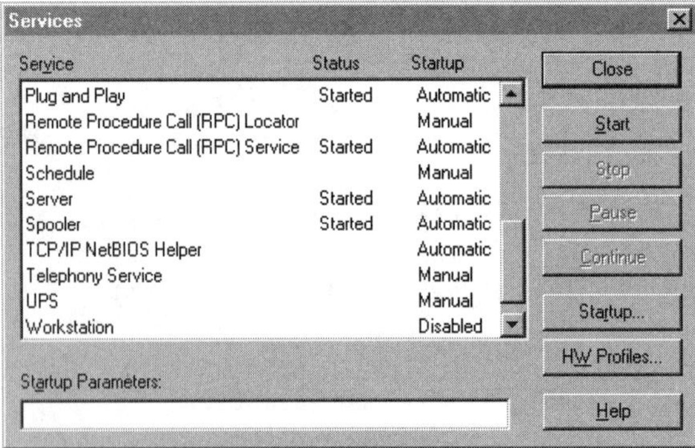

You can see that TCP/IP NetBIOS Helper is configured to start automatically, but it did not start. The section "Troubleshooting Example," presented earlier in this chapter, describes why it did not start.

Sometimes, if a file that is needed to load or run Windows NT becomes corrupt or is deleted, the system displays a message about a problem with the file. You might also get information logged in the event log. You can use the message or the information in the event log to find the problem.

But not all executables or dynamic link libraries report missing or corrupt files, and the symptoms can be unpredictable with a file missing. What do you do if there is no indication of an error, but you think some component did not start correctly?

You can check to see if all the Windows NT system files exist and appear to be uncorrupted. Symptoms of file corruption include a file being an unusual size (for example, zero bytes or larger than its original size), or having a date or time that does not match the Windows NT installation date or dates on service packs that you have installed. You can compare files in your *%systemroot%*\System32 folder and subfolders with files in these folders on another computer that has the same Windows NT version and service packs installed.

If you think that you might be having a problem with a Windows NT system file, you can run Windows NT Setup and repair the problem by using the **Verify Windows NT system files** option.

If you can log onto your computer, you can use the Drivers utility on the *Windows NT Workstation Resource Kit* CD to display information about the device drivers that were loaded. If you have previously printed the output from the Drivers utility (by redirecting the output to a printer or a file), you can compare the previous output with one that you produce when you think you might be having problems with drivers not loading. Another method of determining if there are drivers missing from the list is to run the Drivers utility on a similar computer and compare the results.

This is a description of the output from the Drivers utility. The most important field is ModuleName, which is the name of the component.

Column	Definition
ModuleName	The driver's file name.
Code	The non-paged code in the image.
Data	The initialized static data in the image.
Bss	The uninitialized static data in the image. This is data that is initialized to 0.
Paged	The size of the data that is paged.
Init	Data not needed after initialization.
LinkDate	The date that the driver was linked.

To get a hardcopy of the output from the Drivers utility, enter **drivers** >*filename* at the command prompt, and then print the file. The next example shows some of the output from a Drivers report.

```
ModuleName    Code    Data  Bss   Paged   Init          LinkDate
------------------------------------------------------------------------
ntoskrnl.exe  265472  39040    0  432128  76800 Mon Apr 15 16:28:07 1996
     hal.dll   19904   2272    0    8992  10784 Wed Apr 10 10:24:22 1996
  Atdisk.sys   12352     64    0       0  10368 Wed Apr 10 10:30:24 1996
    Disk.sys    2304      0    0    7648   1504 Wed Apr 10 10:31:18 1996
  CLASS2.SYS    6112      0    0    1472   1024 Thu Apr 11 09:21:58 1996
  Ftdisk.sys   22880     32    0    1504   2048 Fri Apr 12 12:00:30 1996
Diskperf.sys    2048      0    0       0    768 Wed Apr 10 10:30:17 1996
```

Troubleshooting Laptop Problems and Using Laptops

Windows NT version 4.0 provides a new feature that is especially useful for laptops: hardware profiles. You can have one hardware profile for running your laptop when it is in the docking station, and another one for the undocked situation. When you have more than one hardware profile defined, you select the one that you want to use during startup, from the **Hardware Profile/Configuration Recovery** menu.

The easiest way to set up the hardware profiles is to install Windows NT Workstation when your laptop is docked. Windows NT Setup installs the network software that you need to use your docking station, and creates a hardware profile called Original Configuration (Current). You can copy this hardware profile, and customize the new hardware profile.

▶ **To create a hardware profile for an undocked configuration**

1. Double-click the System option on Control Panel.
2. Click the **Hardware Profiles** tab.
3. If you do not already have a hardware profile for your undocked laptop, copy the Original Configuration (Original). Click **Original Configuration (Current).** Click **Copy**, and enter a name for the undocked configuration.
4. On the **Hardware Profiles** tab, click the profile for undocked, and click **Properties**.
5. On the **General** tab, check This is a portable computer, and click the **Radio** button for **The computer is undocked**.
6. Click the **Network** tab. Check **Network-disabled hardware profile**. Click **OK**.

You can also use the undocked hardware profile to set a different video resolution for your laptop. For example, your Original Configuration can have the video resolution set to 1024x768 to run on your monitor. And you can change your undocked configuration to use a resolution of 640x480, or 800x600, or whatever size is appropriate.

The next procedure assumes that you have already created a hardware profile for the undocked configuration, as described earlier in this section.

▶ To change the video resolution

1. Start your computer, and select the undocked hardware profile on the **Hardware Profile/Configuration Recovery** menu.
2. Double-click the Display option on Control Panel.
3. Click the **Settings** tab.
4. In the **Desktop Area** group box, move the slider bar until you see the resolution that you want to use.
5. Click **OK**. You can test the new size by clicking the **Test** button.
6. Click **OK** to exit the **Display Properties** dialog box.

Windows NT does not yet support the following on laptops:

- Power management. On most laptops, you can configure power management in the CMOS.
- Hot-swappable PC cards (formerly called PCMCIA). There is a PC Card option on Control Panel, but you cannot insert or remove cards while the laptop is running.

C H A P T E R 3 7

Monitoring Events

An event is any significant occurrence in the system (or in an application) that requires users to be notified. Some critical events, such as a full disk drive or an interrupted power supply, are noted in an on-screen message. Those events not requiring immediate attention are noted in an event log. Event logging starts automatically each time you start Windows NT Workstation. With an event log and a tool called Event Viewer, you can troubleshoot various hardware and software problems and monitor Windows NT Workstation security events. You can also archive logs in various file formats.

Overview

Windows NT Workstation records events in three kinds of logs:

- The system log contains events logged by the Windows NT Workstation system components. For example, the failure of a driver or other system component to load during startup is recorded in the system log. The event types logged by system components are predetermined by Windows NT Workstation.
- The security log can contain valid and invalid logon attempts as well as events related to resource use, such as creating, opening, or deleting files or other objects. For example, if you use User Manager to enable logon and logoff auditing, attempts to log on to the system are recorded in the security log.
- The application log contains events logged by applications. For example, a database program might record a file error in the application log. Application developers decide which events to monitor.

System and application logs can be viewed by all users; security logs are accessible only to system administrators.

> **Enabling Security Logging**
>
> By default, security logging is turned off. To enable security logging, run User Manager to set the Audit policy.

Note The *Windows NT Workstation Resource Kit* includes Crystal Reports Event Log Viewer, a full-featured report writer that provides an easy way to extract, view, save, and publish information from event logs in a variety of formats. For more information on Crystal Reports Event Log Viewer, see Readme.hlp in the \Crystal\Disk1 folder on the *Windows NT Workstation Resource Kit* 4.0 CD.

Interpreting an Event

Event logs consist of a header, a description of the event (based on the event type), and optionally, additional data. Most security log entries consist of the header and a description.

Event Viewer displays events from each log separately. Each line shows information about one event, including date, time, source, event type, category, Event ID, user account, and computer name.

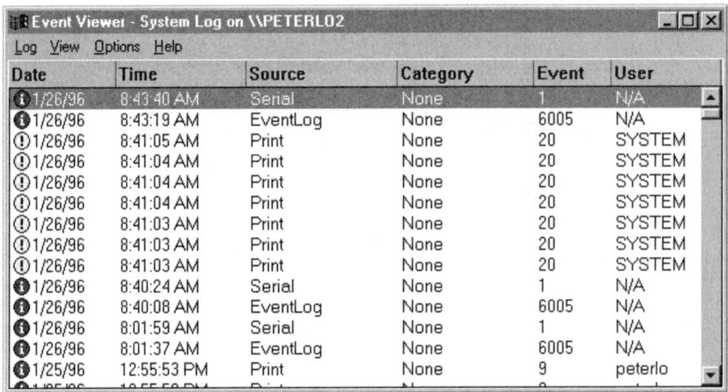

For more information about Windows NT Workstation events, see the Messages Database Help file on the *Windows NT Workstation Resource Kit* 4.0 CD.

The Event Header

The event header contains the following information.

Information	Meaning
Date	The date the event occurred.
Time	The (local) time the event occurred.
User	The username of the user on whose behalf the event occurred. This name is the client ID if the event was actually caused by a server process, or the primary ID if impersonation is not taking place. Where applicable, a security log entry contains both the primary and impersonation IDs. (Impersonation occurs when Windows NT Workstation allows one process to take on the security attributes of another.)
Computer	The name of the computer where the event occurred. The computer name is usually your own, unless you are viewing an event log on another Windows NT computer.
Event ID	A number identifying the particular event type. The first line of the description usually contains the name of the event type. For example, 6005 is the ID of the event that occurs when the Event log service is started. The first line of the description of such an event is "The Event log service was started." The Event ID and the Source can be used by product support representatives to troubleshoot system problems.
Source	The software that logged the event, which can be either an application name, such as "SQL Server," or a component of the system or of a large application, such as a driver name. For example, "Elnkii" indicates the EtherLink II driver.
Type	A classification of the event severity: Error, Information, or Warning in the system and application logs; Success Audit or Failure Audit in the security log. In Event Viewer's normal list view, these are represented by a symbol.
Category	A classification of the event by the event source. This information is primarily used in the security log. For example, for security audits, this corresponds to one of the event types for which success or failure auditing can be enabled in the **User Manager Audit Policy** dialog box.

Event Description

The format and contents of the event description vary, depending on the event type. The description is often the most useful piece of information, indicating what happened or the significance of the event.

Event Types

The symbol on the left side of the Event Viewer screen indicates the event type:

Symbol	Event Type	Meaning
	Error	Significant problems, such as a loss of data or loss of functions. For example, an Error event might be logged if a service was not loaded during Windows NT Workstation startup.
	Warning	Events that are not necessarily significant but that indicate possible future problems. For example, a Warning event might be logged when disk space is low.
	Information	Infrequent significant events that describe successful operations of major server services. For example, when a database program loads successfully, it might log an Information event.
	Success Audit	Audited security access attempts that were successful. For example, a user's successful attempt to log on to the system might be logged as a Success Audit event.
	Failure Audit	Audited security access attempts that failed. For example, if a user tried to access a network drive and failed, the attempt might be logged as a Failure Audit event.

Additional Data

The optional data field, if used, contains binary data, which can be displayed in bytes or words. This information is generated by the application that was the source of the event record. Because the data appears in hexadecimal format, its meaning can be interpreted only by a support technician familiar with the source application.

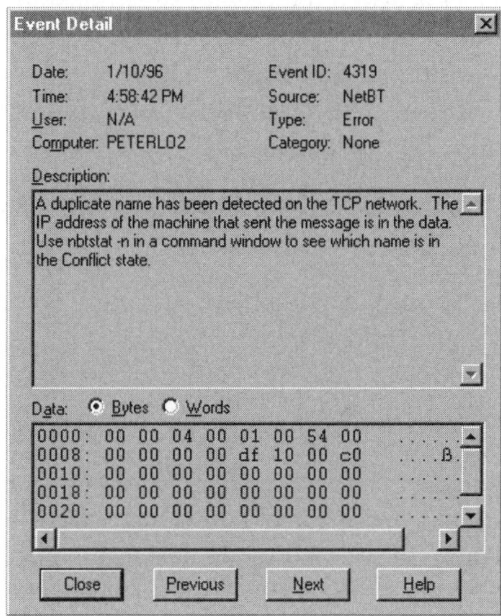

When viewing an error log on a LAN Manager 2.*x* server, only the date, time, source, and event ID are shown. When viewing an audit log on a LAN Manager 2.*x* server, only the date, time, category, user, and computer are shown.

Using Event Viewer

You determine which event log to view by switching between the system, security, and application logs. You can also use Event Viewer to view logs on other computers.

Selecting a Log

Use the **Log** menu to select a log for event viewing. Although the system log of the local computer appears the first time you start Event Viewer, you can choose to view the security or application log.

Selecting a Computer

When you first start Event Viewer, the events for the local computer appear.

To view events for another computer, click **Select Computer** on the **Log** menu. (It can be a computer running Windows NT Workstation or Windows NT Server, or a LAN Manager 2.*x* server.)

If the computer you select is across a link with slow transmission rates, select **Low Speed Connection**. If this option is selected, Windows NT Workstation does not list all the computers in the default domain, thereby minimizing network traffic across the link. (If slow transmission rates are commonplace, click **Low Speed Connection** on the **Options** menu.)

If you select a LAN Manager 2.*x* server for viewing, Event Viewer can display its error (system) log and its audit (security) log.

For information on how to select a computer for event viewing, see "Select Computer" in Event Viewer Help.

Refreshing the View

When you first open a log file, Event Viewer displays the current information for that log. This information is not updated automatically. To see the latest events and to remove overwritten entries, choose the **Refresh** command.

For more information, see "Refresh" in Event Viewer Help.

Changing the Font

You can change the font used in Event Viewer. Changing this font affects only the display of the list of events in the main Event Viewer window.

For more information, see "Changing the Font Selection" in Event Viewer Help.

Viewing Specific Logged Events

After you select a log to view in Event Viewer, you can:

- View descriptions and additional details that the event source logs.
- Sort events from oldest to newest or from newest to oldest.
- Filter events so that only events with specific characteristics are displayed.
- Search for events based on specific characteristics or event descriptions.

Viewing Details About Events

For many events, you can view more information than is displayed in Event Viewer by double-clicking the event.

The **Event Detail** dialog box shows a text description of the selected event and any available binary data for the selected event. This information is generated by the application that was the source of the event record. Because the data appears in hexadecimal format, its meaning can be interpreted only by a support technician familiar with the source application. Not all events generate such data. For more information, see "Viewing Event Details" in Event Viewer Help.

To control the types of security events that are audited, click **Audit** on the **Policies** menu in User Manager. To control the auditing of file and folders access, click **Auditing** on the **Security** tab in the **Windows NT Explorer Properties** dialog box.

Sorting Events

By default, Event Viewer lists events by date and time of occurrence from the newest event to the oldest. To change the order from oldest to newest, click **Oldest First** on the **View** menu. If the **Save Settings On Exit** command on the **Options** menu is checked when you quit, the current sort order is used the next time you start Event Viewer.

When a log is archived, the sort order affects the order in which event records are archived in a text format or comma-delimited text format file; sort order does not affect the order of event records archived in log file format. For more information, see "Using Archived Log Files" later in this chapter.

For information on how to specify the sort order, see "Sorting Events" in Event Viewer Help.

Filtering Events

By default, Event Viewer lists all events recorded in the selected log. To view a subset of events that have specific characteristics, click **Filter Events** on the **View** menu. When filtering is on, a check mark appears by the **Filter** command on the **View** menu and "(Filtered)" appears on the title bar. If **Save Settings On Exit** on the **Options** menu is checked when you quit Event Viewer, the filters remain in effect the next time you start Event Viewer.

Filtering has no effect on the actual contents of the log: It changes only the view. All events are logged continuously, whether the filter is active or not. If you archive a log from a filtered view, all records are saved, even if you select a text format or comma-delimited text format file. For more information on archiving, see "Using Event Viewer with Archived Log Files" later in this chapter.

The following table describes the options available in the **Filter** dialog box

Use	To filter for
View From	Events after a specific date and time. By default, this is the date of the first event in the log file.
View Through	Events up to and including a specific date and time. By default, this is the date of the last event in the log file.
Information[1]	Infrequent significant events that describe successful operations of major server services. For example, when a database program loads successfully, it might log an Information event.
Warning[1]	Events that are not necessarily significant but that indicate possible future problems. For example, a Warning event might be logged when disk space is low.
Error[1]	Significant problems, such as a loss of data or loss of functions. For example, an Error event might be logged if a service was not loaded during Windows NT Workstation startup.
Success Audit[1]	Audited security access attempts that were successful. For example, a user's successful attempt to log on to the system might be logged as a Success Audit event.
Failure Audit[1]	Audited security access attempts that failed. For example, if a user tried to access a network drive and failed, the attempt might be logged as a Failure Audit event.
Source[2]	A source for logging events, such as an application, a system component, or a driver.
Category[3]	A classification of events defined by the source. For example, the security event categories are Logon and Logoff, Policy Change, Privilege Use, System Event, Object Access, Detailed Tracking, and Account Management.
User[3]	A specific user that matches an actual user name. This field is not case sensitive.
Computer[3]	A specific computer that matches an actual computer name. This field is not case sensitive.
Event ID[2]	A specific number that corresponds to an actual event.

[1] This option is not available for LAN Manager 2.x servers.

[2] This option is not available for audit logs on LAN Manager 2.x servers.

[3] This option is not available for error logs on LAN Manager 2.x servers.

For information on how to filter for events and turn off filtering of events, see "Filtering Events" in Event Viewer Help.

For information on how to return to the default criteria, see "Reset to Default Settings" in Event Viewer Help.

Searching for Events

To search for events that match a specific type, source, or category, click **Find** on the **View** menu. Searches can be useful when you are viewing large logs: For example, you can search for all Warning events related to a specific application, or search for all Error events from all sources.

Your choices in the **Find** dialog box are in effect throughout the current session. If **Save Settings On Exit** on the Event Viewer **Options** menu is checked when you quit, the current filter settings are available the next time you start Event Viewer.

For more information, see "Searching for Events" in Event Viewer Help.

Setting Options for Logging Events

Logging starts automatically when you start the computer. Logging stops when an event log becomes full and cannot overwrite itself either because you have set it for manual clearing or because the first event in the log is not old enough.

Use the **Log Settings** command on the **Log** menu to define logging parameters for each kind of log. You can set the maximum size of the log and specify whether the events are overwritten or stored for a certain period of time.

The **Event Log Wrapping** option lets you define how events are retained in the log selected in the **Change Settings For** dialog box. (The default logging policy is to overwrite logs as needed, provided events are at least seven days old.) You can customize this policy for different logs.

The options include the following.

Use	To
Overwrite Events As Needed	Have new events continue to be written when the log is full. Each new event replaces the oldest event in the log. This option is a good choice for low-maintenance systems.
Overwrite Events Older Than [ ] days	Retain the log for the number of days you specify before overwriting events. The default is 7 days. This option is the best choice if you want to archive log files weekly. This strategy minimizes the chance of losing important log entries and at the same time keeps log sizes reasonable.
Do Not Overwrite Events	Clear the log manually rather than automatically. Select this option only if you cannot afford to miss an event, for example, for the security log at a site where security is extremely important.

Note When a log is full (when no more events can be logged), you can free the log by clearing it. Reducing the amount of time you keep an event also frees the log if it allows the next record to be overwritten.

For information on how to clear a log, see "Clearing All Events" in Event Viewer Help.

Although you can increase (to the capacity of the disk and memory) or decrease the maximum log size, each log file has an initial maximum size of 512K. Before decreasing a log's size, you must clear the log.

Using Event Logs to Troubleshoot Problems

Careful monitoring of event logs can help you predict and identify the sources of system problems. For example, if log warnings show that a disk driver can only read or write to a sector after several retries, the sector will likely go bad eventually. Logs can also confirm problems with application software: If an application crashes, an application event log can provide a record of activity leading up to the event.

The following are suggestions to help you use event logs to diagnose problems:

- Archive logs in log format. The binary data associated with an event is discarded if you archive data in text or comma-delimited format.
- If you suspect a hardware component is the origin of system problems, filter the system log to show only those events generated by the component.
- If a particular event seems related to system problems, try searching the event log to find other instances of the same event or to judge the frequency of an error.
- Note Event IDs. These numbers match a text description in a source message file. This number can be used by product-support representatives to understand what occurred in the system.

Monitoring Windows NT Security Events

You enable auditing from the **User Manager Auditing Policy** dialog box. Through auditing, you can track Windows NT Workstation security events. You can specify that an audit entry is to be written to the security event log whenever certain actions are performed or files are accessed. The audit entry shows the action performed, the user who performed it, and the date and time of the action. You can audit both successful and failed attempts at actions, so the audit trail can show who actually performed actions on the network and who tried to perform actions that are not permitted.

Events are not audited by default. If you have Administrator permission, you can specify what types of system events are audited through User Manager. The Audit policy determines the amount and type of security logging Windows NT Workstation performs. For file and object access, you can then specify which files and printer to monitor, which types of file and object access to monitor, and for which users or groups. For example, when **File and Object Access** auditing is enabled, you can use the **Security** tab in a file or folder's **Properties** dialog box (accessed through Windows NT Explorer) to specify which files are audited and what type of file access is audited for those files.

Note You can audit file and folder access on only Windows NT File System (NTFS) drives.

Because the security log is limited in size, select the events to be audited carefully, and consider the amount of disk space you are willing to devote to the security log. The maximum size of the security log is defined in Event Viewer.

Note When administering domains, the Audit policy applies to the security log of the primary and backup domain controllers in the domain because they share the same Audit policy. When administering a computer running Windows NT Workstation or a computer running Windows NT Server as a member server, this policy applies only to the security log of that computer.

The following table describes the types of events that can be audited.

Type of event	Description
Logon and Logoff	A user logged on or off or made a network connection.
File and Object Access	A user opened a directory or a file that is set for auditing in File Manager, or a user sent a print job to a printer that is set for auditing in Print Manager.
Use of User Rights	A user used a user right (except those rights related to logon and logoff).
User and Group Management	A user account or group was created, changed, or deleted. A user account was renamed, disabled, or enabled; or a password was set or changed.
Security Policy Changes	A change was made to the User Rights, Audit, or Trust Relationships policies.
Restart, Shutdown, and System	A user restarted or shut down the computer, or an event has occurred that affects system security or the security log.
Process Tracking	These events provided detailed tracking information for things like program activation, some forms of handle duplication, indirect object accesses, and process exit.

Auditing File and Folder Access

You can audit the access of files and folders on NTFS volumes to identify who took various types of actions with the files and folders and hold those users accountable for their actions.

To set auditing on a file or folder, use User Manager to enable auditing of File and Object Access, and then use Windows NT Explorer to specify which files to audit and which type of file access events to audit. To view audit entries, use the Event Viewer.

You can audit successful and failed attempts of the following types of directory and file access:

Types of directory access	Types of file access
Displaying names of files in the directory	Displaying the file's data
Displaying directory attributes	Displaying file attributes
Changing directory attributes	Displaying the file's owner and permissions
Creating subdirectories and files	Changing the file
Going to the directory's subdirectories	Changing file attributes
Displaying the directory's owner and permissions	Running the file
Deleting the directory	Deleting the file
Changing directory permissions	Changing the file's permissions
Changing directory ownership	Changing the file's ownership

To audit the following activities on a directory, select the events shown.

● Event audits action
○ Event does not audit action

	Read	Write	Execute	Delete	Change Permissions	Take Ownership
Displaying the file's data	●	○	○	○	○	○
Displaying attributes	●	○	●	○	○	○
Displaying the file's owner and permissions	●	●	●	○	○	○
Changing data	○	●	○	○	○	○
Changing attributes	○	●	○	○	○	○
Running the file	○	○	●	○	○	○
Deleting the file	○	○	○	●	○	○
Changing the file's permissions	○	○	○	○	●	○
Changing the file's ownership	○	○	○	○	○	●

To audit the following activities on a file, select the events shown.

● Event audits action
○ Event does not audit action

	Read	Write	Execute	Delete	Change Permissions	Take Ownership
Displaying filenames	●	○	○	○	○	○
Displaying attributes	●	○	●	○	○	○
Changing attributes	○	●	○	○	○	○
Creating subdirectories and files	○	●	○	○	○	○
Going to the directory's subdirectories	○	○	●	○	○	○
Displaying owner and permissions	●	●	●	○	○	○
Deleting the directory	○	○	○	●	○	○
Changing directory permissions	○	○	○	○	●	○
Changing directory ownership	○	○	○	○	○	●

Note To audit files and directories, you must be logged on as a member of the Administrators group.

Auditing Printer Access

By auditing a printer, you track its usage. For a particular printer, you can specify which groups or users and which actions to audit. You can audit both successful and failed actions.

Important To audit a printer, you must set the audit policy to audit file and object access.

To audit the following activities for a printer, select the events shown in the following table.

● Event audits action
○ Event does not audit action

	Print	Full Control	Delete	Change Permissions	Take Ownership
Printing documents	●	○	○	○	○
Changing job settings for documents	○	●	○	○	○
Pausing, restarting, moving, and deleting documents	○	●	○	○	○
Sharing a printer	○	●	○	○	○
Changing printer properties	○	●	○	○	○
Deleting a printer	○	○	●	○	○
Changing printer permissions	○	○	○	●	○
Taking ownership	○	○	○	○	●

Halting the Computer When the Security Log Is Full

If you have set the security log either to "Overwrite Events Older than *n* Days" or "Do Not Overwrite Events (Clear Log Manually)," you can prevent auditable activities while the log is full. No new audit records can be written. To do so, use the Registry Editor to create or assign the following registry key value:

Hive:	HKEY_LOCAL_MACHINE\SYSTEM
Key:	\CurrentControlSet\Control\Lsa
Name:	CrashOnAuditFail
Type:	REG_DWORD
Value:	1

The changes take effect the next time the computer is started. You can update the Emergency Repair Disk to reflect these changes.

If Windows NT Workstation halts as a result of a full security log, the system must be restarted and reconfigured to prevent auditable activities from occurring again while the log is full. After the system is restarted, only administrators can log on until the security log is cleared. For more information on recovering after Windows NT halts, see the "Recovering After Windows NT Halts Because it Cannot Generate an Audit Event Record" in Event Viewer Help.

Using Event Viewer with Archived Log Files

You can archive security logs so that you can monitor security events over a period of time. Or you can archive application logs so that you can track the Warning and Error events that occur for specific applications.

When you archive a log file, the entire log is saved, regardless of any filtering options specified in Event Viewer. If you changed the sort order in Event Viewer, event records are saved exactly as displayed if you archive the log in a text or comma-delimited text file.

Archiving a Log

When you archive an event log, you save it in one of three file formats:

- *Log file format*, which enables you to view the archived log again in Event Viewer.
- *Text file format*, which enables you to use the information in an application, such as a word processor.
- *Comma-delimited text file format*, which enables you to use the information in an application, such as a spreadsheet or a flat-file database.

The binary event data is saved if you archive a log in log file format, but it is discarded if you archive the log in text file format or in comma-delimited text file format. The event description is saved in all archived logs. When you archive a sorted log, the sort order affects the order in which event records are archived in a text file format or comma-delimited text file format. However, sort order does not affect the order of event records in a log archived in log file format. In either case, the sequence of data within each individual event record is record in the following order:

1. Date[1]	4. Type	7. User
2. Time	5. Category	8. Computer
3. Source	6. Event	9. Description

1 Depends on the sort order specified on the View menu.

Archival has no effect on the current contents of the active log. To clear the original log, you must click **Clear All Events** on the **Log** menu. To remove an archived log file, delete the file as you would other kinds of files.

For information on how to archive an event log, see "Archiving Event Logs" in Event Viewer Help.

Viewing a Log Archived in Log File Format

You can view an archived file in Event Viewer *only* if the log was saved in event log-file format. You cannot click the **Refresh** or **Clear All Events** commands to update the display or to clear an archived log.

Note If you do not specify the correct log type (application, security, or system), the Description displayed for the archived log in the **Event Detail** dialog box will not be correct.

For information on how to display an archived log in Event Viewer, see "Viewing a Log Archived in Log File Format" in Event Viewer Help.

Using Logs Archived in a Text Format

An event log saved in text- or comma-delimited text format can be opened in other applications. These applications can be used to filter, sort, and format the archived event records. You can also combine event records from two or more archived text files to create reports.

For example, you can copy lines of text from an archived log to include as supporting information in an electronic mail message. Or you can archive a security log in comma-delimited format so that you can place the information in a spreadsheet and produce a chart showing the archived information.

CHAPTER 38

Windows NT Executive Messages

There are three types of Windows NT Executive messages:

- Character-mode STOP messages
- Character-mode hardware-malfunction messages
- Windows-mode STATUS messages

For help with hardware-malfunction messages, first contact a technician within your own organization to run hardware diagnostics on your computer. If you then need to find help outside your organization, contact the hardware vendor for your specific brand of computer, adapter, or peripheral device.

Most users also need to ask for help with the STOP messages from a technical support person who has been trained to support Windows NT. For more information on what you can do to help that trained technician use the Windows NT debugger utilities, see Chapter 39, "Windows NT Debugger."

The Executive is the part of the Windows NT operating system that runs in Kernel mode. *Kernel mode* is a privileged processor mode in which a thread has access to system memory and to hardware. (*User mode* is a nonprivileged processor mode in which a thread can only access system resources by calling system services.) The Windows NT Executive provides process structure, thread scheduling, interprocess communication, memory management, object management, object security, interrupt processing, I/O capabilities, and networking.

The Windows NT Kernel is the part of the Windows NT Executive that manages the processor. It performs thread scheduling and dispatching, interrupt and exception handling, and multiprocessor synchronization. It also provides primitive objects to the Windows NT Executive, which uses them to create user-mode objects.

These messages were created to cover everything that could possibly happen, so you might never see some of them. For example, one of the STOP messages is "Unhandled Kernel exception." This message is displayed only after the Kernel exception dispatcher has exhausted its search of the Kernel call stack for exception-handling code. Similarly, a STATUS message announces the termination of a thread only after the Executive has searched the entire user call stack and the subsystem associated with the application for exception-handling code.

Character-mode Messages

Two types of character-mode messages occur when the Windows NT Kernel detects an inconsistent condition from which it cannot recover: STOP messages and hardware-malfunction messages. You can organize these messages into the following groups:

- STOP messages that can appear only during the relatively short Windows NT startup period, which is Phase 4 of the Windows NT boot sequence.
- STOP messages that can be traced to a software condition detected by the processor.
- Hardware-malfunction messages that can be traced to a hardware condition detected by the processor.
- All the rest of the STOP messages.

The STOP Message Screen

Character-mode STOP messages are always displayed on a full character-mode screen rather than in a Windows-mode message box. They are also uniquely identified by a hexadecimal number and a symbolic string, as in the following example:

```
*** STOP: 0x00000001
APC_INDEX_MISMATCH
```

The content of the symbolic string may suggest, to a trained technician, which part of the Kernel detected the condition that left no recourse but to stop. However, keep in mind that the cause may actually be in another part of the system.

Figure 38.1 is an example of a complete STOP message screen generated by the Windows NT Kernel.

```
Section 1:  Debug Port Status Indicators
DSR CTS SND
```

```
Section 2:  BugCheck Information
*** STOP:  0x0000000A (0x00000000,0x0000001A,0x00000000,0xFC873D6C)
IRQL_NOT_LESS_OR_EQUAL*** Address fc873d6c has base at fc870000 - i8042prt.SYS
CPUID:GenuineIntel 5.1.5 irql:1f   SYSVER 0Xf0000421
```

```
Section 3:  Driver Information
Dll Base  DateStmp - Name                    Dll Base  DateStmp - Name
80100000  2fc653bc - ntoskrnl.exe            80400000  2fb24f4a - hal.dll
80010000  2faae87f - ncrc810.sys             80013000  2faae8ca - SCSIPORT.SYS
8001b000  2faae8c5 - Scsidisk.sys            8029e000  2fc15d19 - Fastfat.sys
fc820000  2faae8af - Floppy.sys              fc830000  2fb16eef - Scsicdrm.SYS
fc840000  2faae8ff - FS_Rec.SYSfc850000   2faae8b7 - Null.SYS
fc860000  2faae8a1 - Beep.SYS                fc870000  31167860 - i8042prt.SYS
fc880000  2faae8b5 - Mouclass.SYS            fc890000  2faae8b4 - Kbdclass.SYS
fc8b0000  2faae88d - VIDEOPRT.SYS            fc8c0000  2fb67626 - ati.SYS
fc8a0000  2faae892 - vga.sys                 fc8e0000  2faae8fd - Msfs.SYS
fc8f0000  2faae8ec - npfs.SYS                fc900000  2faae91a - ndistapi.sys
fc910000  2fc4f4b2 - ntfs.SYS                fc980000  2fc12af6 - NDIS.SYS
fc970000  2faaee1e - asyncmac.sys            fc9a0000  2dd47963 - epront.sys
fc9b0000  2fb52712 - ndiswan.sys             fc9e0000  2faae945 - TDI.SYS
fc9c0000  2fae6a5f - nbf.sys                 fc9f0000  2faec8b1 - afd.sys
fca00000  2faaee1f - rasarp.sys              fca10000  2fbf9993 - streams.sys
fca30000  2fc1557b - tcpip.sys               fca50000  2e6ce2d3 - ubnb.sys
fca60000  2e64646c - mcsxns.sys              fca70000  2fc0daf7 - netbt.sys
```

```
Section 4:  Kernel Build Number and Stack Dump
Address    dword dump  Build [1057]                   - Name
8014004c fc873d6c fc873d6c ff05e051 00000000 ff05e04b 0000002f - i8042prt.SYS
8014007c 801400c4 801400c4 00000000 00000023 00000023 00000037 - ntoskrnl.exe
80140098 fc87258e fc87258e 801400e8 00000030 ff0d141c ff0d1598 - i8042prt.SYS
8014009c 801400e8 801400e8 00000030 ff0d141c ff0d1598 00000002 - ntoskrnl.exe
801400b0 801400f8 801400f8 00000000 fc873d6c 00000008 00010202 - ntoskrnl.exe
801400b8 fc873d6c fc873d6c 00000008 00010202 ff0ced88 ff0d1598 - i8042prt.SYS
801400e0 801400c4 801400c4 fca460f4 ffffffff fc874f78 fc870418 - ntoskrnl.exe
801400e4 fca460f4 fca460f4 ffffffff fc874f78 fc870418 ffffffff - tcpip.sys
801400ec fc874f78 fc874f78 fc870418 ffffffff 80140110 8013be2a - i8042prt.SYS
801400f0 fc870418 fc870418 ffffffff 80140110 8013be2a ff0ced88 - i8042prt.SYS
801400f8 80140110 80140110 8013be2a ff0ced88 ff0d1350 80137502 - ntoskrnl.exe
801400fc 8013be2a 8013be2a ff0ced88 ff0d1350 80137052 00000031 - ntoskrnl.exe
```

```
Section 5:  Debug Port Information
Kernel Debugger Using: COM2 (Port 0x2f8, Baud Rate 19200)
Beginning dump of physical memory
Physical memory dump complete.  Contact your system administrator or
technical support group.
```

Figure 38.1 STOP Message Screen

STOP Screen Sections

A Windows NT STOP screen contains five major sections, as shown in Figure 38.1. Whenever a STOP error occurs, you should examine at least the BugCheck Information section for analysis when troubleshooting the problem. The next most useful information is the filenames listed on the right side of the stack dump (Section 4).

Section 1: Debug Port Status Indicators

These indicators provide serial communication information, much like the indicators on a modem. This area shows DSR and CTS. Also, the text "SND" flashes to indicate that data is being sent to the COM port. The COM port being used is detailed in Section 5: Debug Port Information.

Section 2: BugCheck Information

This section contains the error code—up to four developer-defined parameters—and an interpretation of the error. In Figure 38.1, the error code is 0x0000000A. The error code can also be called a BugCheck code.

Under some conditions, the Kernel displays only the top line of the STOP message. This can occur if vital services needed for the display have been affected by the trap condition.

Section 3: Driver Information

This section lists driver information in three columns. The first two columns list the preferred load address (base address in memory) and the link time stamp (date created) for each loaded driver. The third column displays the names of all drivers loaded on the computer at the time the STOP message occurred. This information is important because many STOP messages contain in their parameter list the address of the instruction that caused the error. The date-stamp (seconds since 1970) can be converted to the common date/time format by using **Cvtime.exe**.

Section 4: Kernel Build Number and Stack Dump

This is the build number of the kernel, Ntoskrnl.exe (Build 1057 in Figure 38.1). The presence of service packs and third-party device drivers is not indicated because this is the base build number only.

The dump portion is a stack dump. Rather than showing the name of specific functions, it shows the range of addresses that pertain to the module that failed. A true stack trace requires the kernel debugger.

Sometimes, the top few lines can tell what component or driver caused the error. For example:

```
Section 4:  Kernel Build Number and Stack Dump
Address dword dump  Build [1057]                 - Name
8014004c fc873d6c fc873d6c ff05e051 00000000 ff05e04b 0000002f -
i8042prt.SYS  ←
8014007c 801400c4 801400c4 00000000 00000023 00000023 00000037 -
ntoskrnl.exe
80140098 fc87258e fc87258e 801400e8 00000030 ff0d141c ff0d1598 -
i8042prt.SYS
8014009c 801400e8 801400e8 00000030 ff0d141c ff0d1598 00000002 -
ntoskrnl.exe
```

The topmost routines on the stack do not always represent the failing code. The code for various kernel trap handlers might execute last as the error information is preserved. This depends on the particular trap error.

Section 5: Debug Port Information

This section provides confirmation of the communications parameters (COM port and baud rate) used by the Kernel debugger on the target computer, if enabled. It also confirms whether a dump file was created.

Key Screen Details to Examine

It is possible, in some cases, to determine the cause of a STOP screen by closely examining STOP screen data before rebooting. Under Windows NT 4.0, the screen divides into the five logical sections. (Processor Register Dump from Windows NT 3.1 is not included in current versions of Windows NT.)

The failing module can sometimes be identified by comparing the data in BugCheck Information with that in Driver Information and Stack Dump.

The Bugcheck Information shown is:

```
*** STOP:  0x0000000A (0x00000000,0x0000001A,0x00000000,0xFC873D6C)
```

```
IRQL_NOT_LESS_OR_EQUAL*** Address fc873d6c has base at fc870000 -
i8042prt.SYS
```

```
CPUID:GenuineIntel 5.1.5 irql:1f   SYSVER 0Xf0000421
```

Notice that the first four digits of the code address shown (0xFC873D6C) are FC87. This identifies the base, which is shown as FC870000. In this case the description specifies that the address is located in i8042prt.sys:

```
*** Address fc873d6c has base at fc870000 - i8042prt.SYS
```

If this description is not given, you can obtain it by searching Driver Information to find a match on the following line:

```
Section 3:  Driver Information

Dll Base  Date Stamp - Name                   Dll Base  Date Stamp - Name

fc860000  2faae8a1 - Beep.SYS                 fc870000  31167860 -
i8042prt.SYS
```

The 0xFC870000 base matches the i8042prt.sys driver (the keyboard driver). Also, the stack dump can sometimes identify the failing driver, as it does in this case:

```
Section 4:  Kernel Build Number and Stack Dump

Address  dword dump Build [1057]            - Name

8014004c fc873d6c fc873d6c ff05e051 00000000 ff05e04b 0000002f -
i8042prt.SYS  ←

8014007c 801400c4 801400c4 00000000 00000023 00000023 00000037 -
ntoskrnl.exe
```

Often, this points to kernel code 0x80140000 because a trap handler in the kernel processes the failure. The BugCheck data and stack trace in these cases points to the kernel trap handler code. You can always compare this address information to narrow the list of problem driver components. In this case, the i8042prt.sys driver is a candidate for close scrutiny. Be sure this driver is the most current version available. Also, it is important to write down the first four lines of trap information for future reference (in case another trap occurs) and to provide this information to your technical support person as part of the problem description details.

STOP Messages That Occur Only at Executive Initialization

One group of STOP messages comes up only during the relatively short Windows NT startup period, which is Phase 4 of the Windows NT boot sequence. Executive initialization is one step during Phase 4. That step can be further broken down into two phases: Phase 0 and Phase 1. During Phase 0 initialization, interrupts are disabled and only a few Executive components, such as the hardware abstraction layer (HAL), are initialized. During Phase 1 initialization, the system is fully operational, and the Windows NT subcomponents do a full initialization.

If you get one of the following Phase 0 initialization STOP messages, run the hardware diagnostics. If no hardware problems are found, reinstall Windows NT and try to initialize it again. If you get the same message again, contact a trained technician.

Table 38.1 Phase 0 Initialization STOP Messages

Message ID	Symbolic name
0x0031	PHASE0_INITIALIZATION_FAILED
0x005C	HAL_INITIALIZATION_FAILED
0x005D	HEAP_INITIALIZATION_FAILED
0x005E	OBJECT_INITIALIZATION_FAILED
0x005F	SECURITY_INITIALIZATION_FAILED
0x0060	PROCESS_INITIALIZATION_FAILED

If you get one of the following Phase 1 initialization STOP messages, reinstall Windows NT and try to initialize it again. If you still get the same message, contact a trained technician.

Table 38.2 Phase 1 Initialization STOP Messages

Message ID	Symbolic name
0x0032	PHASE1_INITIALIZATION_FAILED
0x0061	HAL1_INITIALIZATION_FAILED
0x0062	OBJECT1_INITIALIZATION_FAILED
0x0063	SECURITY1_INITIALIZATION_FAILED
0x0064	SYMBOLIC_INITIALIZATION_FAILED
0x0065	MEMORY1_INITIALIZATION_FAILED
0x0066	CACHE_INITIALIZATION_FAILED
0x0067	CONFIG_INITIALIZATION_FAILED
0x0068	FILE_INITIALIZATION_FAILED
0x0069	IO1_INITIALIZATION_FAILED
0x006A	LPC_INITIALIZATION_FAILED
0x006B	PROCESS1_INITIALIZATION_FAILED
0x006C	REFMON_INITIALIZATION_FAILED
0x006D	SESSION1_INITIALIZATION_FAILED
0x006E	SESSION2_INITIALIZATION_FAILED
0x006F	SESSION3_INITIALIZATION_FAILED
0x0070	SESSION4_INITIALIZATION_FAILED
0x0071	SESSION5_INITIALIZATION_FAILED

STOP Messages Caused by a Software Trap

Another group of STOP messages is caused by a software condition detected by the processor. This condition, called a software trap, happens when a processor detects a problem in an executing instruction from which the processor will not continue. For instance, a processor will not carry out an instruction that contains invalid operands.

When you get a STOP message that is caused by a software trap, follow the steps given in "Remaining STOP Messages," later in this chapter.

The following is an example of the first line of the STOP message that is displayed for all software traps:

```
*** STOP: 0x0000007F (0x0000000n, 00000000, 00000000, 00000000)
UNEXPECTED_KERNEL_MODE_TRAP
```

The first parameter (shown as 0x0000000*n* in the example) in the message parameter list indicates which of twelve possible traps has occurred. For instance, in the case of an instruction that contains invalid operands, the message appears as follows:

```
*** STOP: 0x0000007F (0x00000006, 00000000, 00000000, 00000000)
UNEXPECTED_KERNEL_MODE_TRAP
```

Table 38.3 shows the possible values and their meanings for that first parameter.

Table 38.3 Value of First Parameter in Software Trap STOP Messages

Parameter	Processor detected
0x00000000	An attempt to divide by zero.
0x00000001	A system-debugger call.
0x00000003	A debugger breakpoint.
0x00000004	An arithmetic operation overflow.
0x00000005	An array index that exceeds the array bounds.
0x00000006	Invalid operands in an instruction or an attempt to execute a protected-mode instruction while running in real mode.
0x00000007	A hardware coprocessor instruction, with no coprocessor present.
0x00000008	An error while processing an error (also known as a "double fault").
0x0000000A	A corrupted Task State Segment.
0x0000000B	An access to a memory segment that was not present.
0x0000000C	An access to memory beyond the limits of a stack.
0x0000000D	An exception not covered by some other exception—a protection fault that pertains to access violations for applications.

STOP Screens During Installation

When you attempt to install Windows NT on a new computer, an unsuccessful installation can result in a STOP screen. When a STOP screen appears, first check the compatibility of the computer and its peripheral hardware. To do this, refer to the latest Windows NT Hardware Compatibility List (HCL). Computers and associated hardware that appear in the HCL were tested to determine how well they work with Windows NT. These computers have gone through rigorous component and compatibility testing by Microsoft. The HCL is available in the Windows NT Resource Kit and is updated frequently with newly tested hardware.

If the hardware you are using is not included on the Windows NT HCL, contact the hardware manufacturer as a first-line resource for available information, newly tested hardware, and/or BIOS and firmware revisions. It may also help to reduce hardware components to a minimum to pinpoint installation conflicts.

STOP Screens After Installation

Even in a complex and robust operating system such as Windows NT, catastrophic problems sometimes cause the system to stop responding or trap (display a STOP screen). In Windows NT, a driver or file system can generate a kernel STOP message by introducing an unhandled error (exception) in the code or by performing some illegal operation.

Some problems can be resolved through troubleshooting procedures such as verifying instructions, reinstalling key components, and verifying file dates. Diagnostic tools—such as Winmsdp, Microsoft Network Monitor, Network General Sniffer, and Microsoft Resource Kit utilities—may help isolate and resolve issues.

Debugging is especially helpful when a specific message is displayed or when a problem repeats often. In these cases, it is possible to pinpoint the failing code in a driver or application by using a debugger. For debugging, it is important to capture the exact text of the message. Also, it is critically important to record the exact steps involved in repeating the failure. This information can help you isolate a complex problem and help to develop a viable workaround or a program replacement. For problems occurring within Windows NT code, contact the Microsoft Support Network to find out if a service pack is available to correct the problem.

Hardware-malfunction Messages

Hardware-malfunction messages are caused by a hardware condition detected by the processor. The first one or two lines of a hardware-malfunction message may differ depending on which company manufactured the computer. However, these lines always convey the same idea, as shown in the following example for an Intel-based computer:

```
Hardware malfunction.
Call your hardware vendor for support.
```

The additional lines in each manufacturer's message screen also differ in format and content. Therefore, before doing what the sample message recommends, contact a technician within your own organization to run hardware diagnostics on your computer. The information provided below the first two lines helps your technician decide which hardware diagnostics to run. For example, for Intel-based ISA bus computers, information is displayed that indicates whether this is a memory-parity error or a bus-data error. On Intel-based EISA computers, if the hardware problem is in an adapter, the adapter slot number on the system board is displayed.

If you still need to find help from outside your organization to interpret the information on the screen, contact the hardware vendor for your specific brand of computer, adapter, or peripheral device.

Remaining STOP Messages

A typical user cannot diagnose the cause of any of the remaining STOP messages. When you get one of these messages, first record the top few lines of the STOP message and then restart the computer. If the STOP message occurs again, you have four options for diagnosing the STOP condition, all of which should be handled by a trained technician at your own site:

- Diagnose the problem by using the information displayed in the STOP message and any pertinent information from the Microsoft Web site (www.microsoft.com), where Microsoft maintains an up-to-date list of causes for these STOP messages.
- Use the Windows NT debugger to get more information about the problem.

  If you use this option or the next one, be sure to switch Windows NT to debug mode before you restart your computer. For information on how to prepare your computer for debugging, see Chapter 39, "Windows NT Debugger."
- Contact your own or another technical support group for assistance in using the Windows NT debugger remotely.
- Contact your own or another technical support group to discuss the information in the STOP message. They might see a familiar pattern in the information.

The following list provides the ranges of unique hexadecimal numbers for the STOP messages that are least likely to appear. If you do see one, you will see it after Windows NT Executive startup is complete. These messages are not caused by hardware or software traps in a processor.

0x00000001 through 0x00000009

0x0000000B through 0x0000001D

0x0000001F through 0x00000030

0x00000033 through 0x0000005B

0x00000072 through 0x0000007B

Windows-mode STATUS Messages

The Executive displays a Windows-mode STATUS message box when it detects conditions within a process (such as an application) that you need to know about. STATUS messages can be divided into three types:

- System-information messages. All you can do is read the information in the message box and click **OK**. The Kernel continues to run the process or thread.
- Warning messages. Some advise you to take an action that enables the Kernel to keep running the process or thread. Others warn you that, although the process or thread continues to run, the results might not be correct.
- Application-termination messages. These warn you that the Kernel is about to terminate either a process or a thread.

System-information Messages

System-information messages from the Executive provide status information on conditions within a process that should be noted but that do not stop the application from running. All that you can do is read the information in these messages and click **OK**.

If one of the following messages appears frequently while you are working in the same application, contact either the supplier of the application or your system administrator to adjust the configuration of your Windows NT–based computer:

Expedited Data Received

Image Relocated

Invalid Current Directory

Local Session Key

Object Exists

Partial Data Received

Partial Expedited Data Received

Password Too Complex

Redundant Read

Redundant Write

Registry Recovery

Segment Load

Serial IOCTL Complete

Serial IOCTL Timeout

TDI Event Done

TDI Event Pending

Thread Suspended

Working Set Range Error

Warning Messages

Warning messages from the Executive provide status information on more serious conditions within a process that can stop the application or cause damage to your data. Some warning messages prompt you indirectly for a user action, as in the following example:

```
Out of Paper:  The printer is out of paper.
```

If one of the following messages appears frequently while you are working in the same application, contact either the supplier of the application or your system administrator to adjust the configuration of your Windows NT–based computer:

Alignment Fault
Breakpoint
Buffer Overflow
Device Busy
Device Offline
Device Power Is Off
End of Media
Filemark Found
Guard Page Exception
GUID Substitution
Handles Closed
Illegal EA
Inconsistent EA List
Invalid EA Flag
I/O Bus Reset
Kernel Debugger Awakened
Media Changed
No more EAs
No More Entries
No More Files
Non-Inheritable ACL
Out of Paper
Page Locked
Page Unlocked
Partial Copy
Single Step
Too Much Information
Verifying Disk

Application-termination Messages

Application-termination messages from the Executive appear when the Kernel is about to terminate either the process in which an application is running or the thread of an application. Some of these messages advise you to perform an action before restarting the application, as in the following example:

```
The application or DLL <filename> is not a valid Windows NT image.
Please check this against your installation disk.
```

In other cases, the user action is strongly implied. The following example implies that you should make sure that the dynamic-link library is in the path before you restart the application:

```
The dynamic-link library <filename> could not be found in the specific
path <path>
```

In yet other cases, you can only restart the application. If one of the messages listed in Table 38.4 reappears, contact the supplier of the application.

Table 38.4 Application-termination Messages

Message box title	Message text
Access Denied	A process has requested access to an object, but has not been granted those access rights.
Already Committed	The specified address range is already committed.
Application Error	The exception *name* (*number*) occurred in the application at location *address*.
Application Error	The application failed to initialize properly (*number*). Click **OK** to terminate the application.
Application Exit by CTRL+C	The application terminated as a result of pressing CTRL+C.
Bad CRC	A cyclic redundancy check (CRC) checksum error occurred.
Bad File	The attributes of the specified mapping file for a section of memory cannot be read.
Bad Image	The application or DLL *filename* is not a valid Windows NT image. Please check this against your installation disk.
Buffer Too Small	The buffer is too small to contain the entry. No information has been written to the buffer.
Cancel Timeout	The driver *name* failed to complete a canceled I/O request in the allotted time.
Cannot Continue	Windows NT cannot continue from this exception.
Conflicting Address Range	The specified address range conflicts with the address space.
Corrupted Disk	The file system structure on the disk is corrupted and unusable. Run the Chkdsk utility on the volume *name*.
Corrupted File	The file or directory *filename* is corrupted and unreadable. Run the Chkdsk utility.
Data Error	An error in reading or writing data occurred.
Data Late	A data late error occurred.
Data Not Accepted	The TDI client could not handle the data received during a transmission.
Data Overrun	A data overrun error occurred.
Device Timeout	The specified I/O operation on *name* was not completed before the time-out period expired.
DLL Initialization Failed	Initialization of the dynamic-link library *filename* failed. The process is terminating abnormally.
Drive Not Ready	The drive is not ready for use; its door may be open. Check drive *drive letter* and make sure that a disk is inserted and that the drive door is closed.

Table 38.4 Application-termination Messages *(Continued)*

Message box title	Message text
Entry Point Not Found	The procedure entry point *name* could not be located in the dynamic-link library *filename*.
EXCEPTION	A real-mode application issued a floating-point instruction and floating-point hardware is not present.
EXCEPTION	Array bounds exceeded.
EXCEPTION	Floating-point denormal operand.
EXCEPTION	Floating-point division by zero.
EXCEPTION	Floating-point inexact result.
EXCEPTION	Floating-point invalid operation.
EXCEPTION	Floating-point overflow.
EXCEPTION	Floating-point stack check.
EXCEPTION	Floating-point underflow.
EXCEPTION	Integer division by zero.
EXCEPTION	Integer overflow.
EXCEPTION	Privileged instruction.
EXCEPTION	Possible deadlock condition.
Fatal System Error	The *name* system process terminated unexpectedly with a status of *address*. The system has been shut down.
File Not Found	The file *filename* does not exist.
Floppy Disk Error	While accessing a floppy disk, the track address from the sector ID field was found to be different than the track address maintained by the controller.
Floppy Disk Error	While accessing a floppy disk, an ID address mark was not found.
Floppy Disk Error	The floppy disk controller reported an error that is not recognized by the floppy disk driver.
Floppy Disk Error	While accessing a floppy disk, the controller returned inconsistent results by way of its registers.
Hard Disk Error	While accessing the hard disk, a recalibrate operation failed, even after retries.
Hard Disk Error	While accessing the hard disk, a disk operation failed even after retries.
Hard Disk Error	While accessing the hard disk, a disk controller reset was needed, but even that failed.
Illegal Instruction	An attempt was made to execute an illegal instruction.
Incorrect Network Resource Type	The specified device type (LPT, for example) conflicts with the actual device type on the remote resource.

Table 38.4 Application-termination Messages *(Continued)*

Message box title	Message text
Incorrect Password to LAN Manager Server	You specified an incorrect password to a LAN Manager 2.*x* or MS-NET server.
Incorrect System Call Level	An invalid level was passed into the specified system call.
Incorrect Volume	The target file of a rename request is located on a different device than the source of the rename request.
Invalid Lock Sequence	An attempt was made to execute an invalid lock sequence.
Invalid Mapping	An attempt was made to create a view for a section that is bigger than the section.
Invalid Parameter	The specified information class is not a valid information class for the specified object.
Missing System File	The required system file *filename* is bad or missing.
Network Name Not Found	The specified share name cannot be found on the remote server.
Network Request Timeout	The session with a remote server has been disconnected because the time-out interval for a request has expired.
No Disk	There is no disk in the drive. Insert a disk into drive *drive letter*.
No Paging File Specified	No paging file was specified in the system configuration.
Not Enough Quota	Not enough virtual memory or paging file quota is available to complete the specified operation.
Not Implemented	The requested operation is not implemented.
Operation Failed	The requested operation was unsuccessful.
Ordinal Not Found	The ordinal *number* could not be located in the dynamic-link library *filename*.
Out of Virtual Memory	Your system is running low on virtual memory. Close some applications. To create an additional paging file or to increase the size of your current paging file: double-click **System** in Control Panel; then, on the **Performance** tab, click **Change** under **Virtual Memory**.
Path Not Found	The path *path* does not exist.
Privilege Failed	The I/O permissions for the process could not be changed.
Registry File Failure	The Registry cannot load the key (file) *name* or its log or alternative. It is corrupted, absent, or cannot be written to.
Section Too Large	The specified section is too big to map the file.
Sector Not Found	The specified sector does not exist.
Still Busy	The specified I/O request packet (IRP) cannot be disposed of because the I/O operation is not complete.

Table 38.4 Application-termination Messages *(Continued)*

Message box title	Message text
Registry Is Corrupted	The structure of one of the files that contains Registry data is corrupted, or the image of the file in memory is corrupted, or the file cannot be recovered because the alternative copy or log was absent or corrupted.
Unable to Create Paging File	The creation of the paging file *filename* failed (*number*). The requested size was *number*.
Unable To Locate DLL	The dynamic-link library *filename* cannot be found in the specified path *path*.
Unable to Retrieve Browser Server List	The list of servers for this workgroup is not currently available.
Unexpected Failure in DebugActiveProcess	An unexpected failure occurred while processing a DebugActiveProcess API request. Click **OK** to terminate the process, or click **Cancel** to ignore the error.
Unknown Disk Format	The disk in drive *drive letter* is not formatted properly. Check the disk, and reformat if necessary.
Write Protect Error	The disk cannot be written to because it is write protected. Remove the write protection from the volume *name* in drive *drive letter*.
Wrong Type	There is a mismatch between the type of object required by the requested operation and the type of object that is specified in the request.
Wrong Volume	The wrong volume is in the drive. Insert volume *name* into drive *drive letter*.

CHAPTER 39

Windows NT Debugger

This chapter first defines debugging terminology and provides an overview of debugging on Windows NT. Next, it describes setting up the computers for debugging. This chapter goes into how to create a memory dump file, the utilities that you can use to process the memory dump file, and interpreting the information in the memory dump file.

For Windows NT versions 3.51 and 4.0, **Windbg**, the utility used for reading memory dump files in earlier Windows NT releases, was replaced with a set of utilities that automatically read and interpret memory dump files. These new utilities simplify the process of dealing with kernel memory dump files and aid in sending memory dump files to support personnel for advanced analysis.

New material about the debugger and information about using the output from the **Dumpexam** utility is also included in this chapter.

Debugging Terms

This section defines some common terms and procedures you need when you debug kernel STOP errors.

Kernel STOP Error, Blue Screen, or Trap

When Windows NT encounters hardware problems, inconsistencies within data necessary for its operation, or other similar errors, the operating system processes the error based upon the information entered in the **Recovery** dialog box. For information about the **Recovery** dialog box, see "Creating a Memory Dump File," later in this chapter.

If the user did not select **Automatically reboot** in the **Recovery** dialog box, Windows NT displays a blue screen containing error information, then stops.

Knowledge Base articles and other Windows NT documentation sometimes refer to this type of error as *blue screen*, *kernel error*, or even *trap*. This chapter uses the term *kernel STOP error*. However, if the context specifically refers to Windows NT stopping with the blue screen displayed, the term *blue screen* is used instead. The term *trap* is used in this chapter to mean that the kernel has detected an error and might write a memory dump file as part of its processing of the error.

Symbols and Symbol Trees

Usually, when code is compiled, one of two versions of the executable file can be created: a debug (also known as *checked*) version, or a nondebug (also known as *free*) version. The checked version contains extra code that enables a developer to debug problems, but this means a larger and possibly slower executable file. The free version of the executable file is smaller and runs at a normal speed, but cannot be debugged.

Windows NT combines the speed and smaller size of free versions with the debugging capabilities of the checked versions. All executable files, drivers, dynamic-link libraries, and other program files in Windows NT are the free versions. However, each program file has a corresponding symbol file, which contains the debug code that is normally part of the checked file. These symbol files are on the Windows NT Server product CD, in the Support\Debug*Platform*\Symbols directories, where *Platform* is I386, Alpha, MIPS, or PowerPC. Within each Symbols directory, there is one directory for each type of file (such as .exe, .dll, and .sys). This structure is referred to as a *symbol tree*. Table 39.1 describes directories that exist in a standard symbol tree.

Table 39.1 Standard Symbol Tree Directories

Directory	Contains symbols for
ACM	Microsoft Audio Compression Manager files
COM	Executable files (.com)
CPL	Control Panel programs
DLL	Dynamic-link library files (.dll)
DRV	Driver files (.drv)
EXE	Executable files (.exe)
SCR	Screen-saver files
SYS	Driver files (.sys)

All of the utilities used to debug Windows NT or interpret memory dump files require a symbol tree containing the symbol files for the version of Windows NT you were running at the time of the kernel STOP error. With some utilities, you need the \Symbols directory to be on your hard drive, in the *Systemroot* directory.

With other utilities, you can specify the path to the \Symbols directory as a command-line option or in a dialog box.

Target Computer

The term *target computer* refers to the computer on which the kernel STOP error occurs. This computer is the one that needs to be debugged. It can be a computer located within a few feet of the computer on which you run the debugger, or it can be a computer that you dial in to by using a modem.

Host Computer

The term *host computer* refers to the computer on which you run the debugger. This computer should run a version of Windows NT that is at least as recent as the one on the target computer.

Debugging Overview

There are three approaches you can take to finding the cause of kernel STOP errors:

- Set up a remote debug session with the Microsoft Support Network. This process is needed if a memory dump file cannot be generated or if the target computer halts with a STOP screen. The connection process involves configuring your target computer for a connection (modem to modem) to a host computer located at Microsoft.
- Set up a local debug session with Microsoft Support Network by using a Remote Access Service (RAS) server. This process is needed if a memory dump file cannot be generated or if the target computer halts with a STOP screen. The connection process involves using a null modem cable to configure both your target computer and your host computer. The host is then networked to a RAS server and the debugging information is sent to Microsoft over an asynchronous connection. You can also analyze the debugging information at your host computer.
- Set up your target computer to write the contents of its RAM to a memory dump file when a kernel STOP error occurs. You can then use the dump analysis utilities to analyze the memory dump, or send the memory dump file to technical support personnel for their analysis.

Kernel Debuggers

The Windows NT kernel debuggers—**I386kd.exe**, **Alphakd.exe**, **Mipskd.exe**, and **Ppckd.exe**—are 32-bit executable files that are used on the host computer to debug the kernel on the target computer. Each host hardware platform has its own set of utilities, which are provided on the Windows NT product CD in the \Support\Debug directory.

The kernel debuggers can be used for either remote or local kernel debugging. If you use local kernel debugging, the host computer is located within a few feet of the target computer and the two computers communicate through a null modem serial cable. If you use remote kernel debugging, the host computer can be at any distance from the target computer because communication takes place through modems.

The host and target computers send debugging information back and forth through their communications ports. The ports on both computers must be configured to pass data at the same rate in bits per second (bps).

After a blue screen appears, record the important information in the message, then restart the computer. You might need to configure the target computer for local or remote debugging and reboot it a second time. You can then continue running Windows NT until the message is displayed again. After the blue screen is displayed the second time, call your technical support group and request assistance with the debugging. They can decide whether to debug the kernel STOP error locally or remotely and instruct you to configure your system appropriately.

Dump Analysis Utilities

To use the Windows NT dump analysis utilities, you must first configure your computer to write a memory dump file when it gets a kernel STOP error. Use the **Recovery** dialog box to configure the target computer to write the memory file, as described in the section "Creating a Memory Dump File" later in this chapter. This file preserves information about the state of the computer at the time of the kernel STOP error. The memory dump file can be used by the dump analysis utilities to troubleshoot the problem. If you use this option, you can run the dump analysis utilities on any Windows NT–based computer after you load the memory dump file, including the computer on which the kernel STOP error occurred.

This approach is usually the best for a computer running Windows NT Server because it minimizes the amount of time the server is unavailable. The default for a Windows NT Server–based computer is to automatically restart after writing an event to the system log, then alert administrators and dump system memory to the Memory.dmp file. Because of this, to preserve memory dump files, you rename the newest one each time a kernel STOP error occurs. You can then run the dump analysis utilities and send the information to your technical support group for processing.

Setting Up for Debugging

If you decide to use the kernel debugger to analyze the kernel STOP error, you need to set up the host and connect your host and target computers. To do this, you use either a null modem cable for a local debug session or a modem cable for a remote debug session. Before you can start debugging, you must complete several steps.

▶ **To prepare for debugging**

1. Set up the modem connection.
2. Configure the target system for debugging.
3. Set up a symbol tree on the host system.
4. Set up the debugger on the host system.
5. Start the debugger on the host system.

Note None of the procedures in this section are necessary if you use the **Recovery** dialog box to create a memory dump file. For information about that alternative, see "Creating a Memory Dump File," later in this chapter.

Setting Up a Remote Debugging Session on an Intel-based Computer

If you enable the kernel debugger on your target computer, it sends debugging information to a host computer for a remote user to analyze. A support engineer often requests this to help analyze a fatal error in Windows NT that cannot be diagnosed from the Memory.dmp file or if a Memory.dmp file is not produced.

The process of remote debugging occurs when two computers are connected by means of modems over a phone line. The target and the host computer can thus communicate by using a special debugging API and protocol.

The following figure shows the connection between the host and the target computer for a remote debugging session.

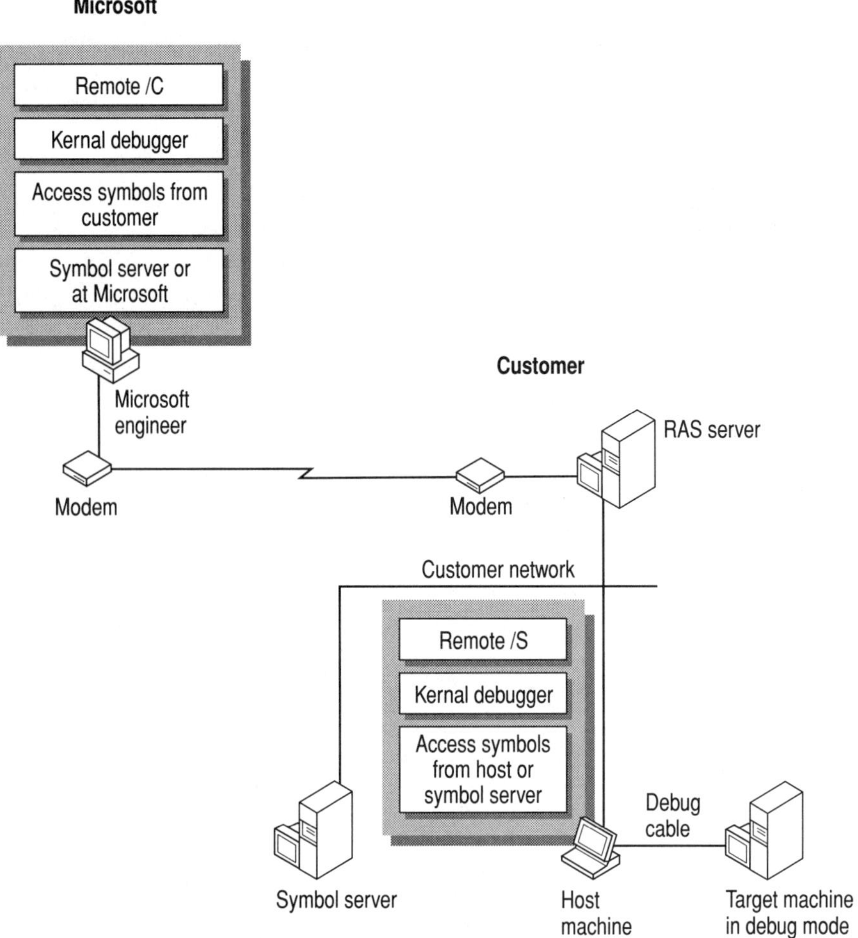

Figure 39.1 Remote Debugging

To configure a system for remote debugging, you change the boot options to set Windows NT to load the kernel debugger. On an x86-based platform, you do this by editing the Boot.ini file. On a RISC-based system (DEC Alpha, MIPS and PowerPC processors), you change the boot options in the firmware menu. You must also connect an external modem to the appropriate COM port on the target computer and connect an inbound phone line to the modem.

Booting the Target Machine

If the target computer stops at a blue screen every time you boot it, or does not keep running long enough for you to edit the Boot.ini file to enable the debugger, you can try these options:

- If your boot partition is FAT, you can start MS-DOS from a boot floppy disk and use the MS-DOS-based editor to edit Boot.ini.
- If your boot partition is NTFS (or HPFS, if you are running Windows NT version 3.1 or 3.5), you can install Windows NT on a different partition and boot from that partition. (You must use this method because you cannot access files on an NTFS or HPFS partition from MS-DOS.)
- If you previously created a Windows NT boot recovery disk for the workstation that has the problem, you can use this disk on another machine to edit the Boot.ini file, and then boot the target machine.

Setting Up the Modem on the Target Machine

To set up a remote debugger session, you must connect an external modem to the target machine and reconfigure the modem parameters to meet the requirements of the kernel debugger. To configure the modem, you must be able to run Terminal.exe or some other communications program. If you are unable to run these programs on the target machine, connect the modem to a computer that is close to the target machine. Make sure you can move the modem back to the target machine without losing power to the modem. An internal modem does not work because rebooting the system resets the configuration changes you have made to the modem.

The modem must be connected to a spare COM port and must be configured as shown in the following table:

Auto answer mode	On
Hardware compression	Disabled
Error detection	Disabled
Flow control	Disabled
Baud rate 9600 bps for x86-based system and 19200 bps for RISC-based system.	

Consult your modem documentation for the correct string values to send to the modem during the configuration process. The following table gives an example of how to configure a USRobotics modem for a remote debugging session.

Function	String Value
Set Back to Factory Defaults	AT&F
Disable Transmit Data Flow Control	AT&H0
Disable Receive Data Flow Control	AT&I0
Disable Data Compression	AT&K0
Disable Error Control	AT&M0
Auto Answer On	ATS0=1
Disable Reset Modem on Loss of DTR	AT&D0
Write to NVRAM	AT&W

▶ To configure the modem

1. Connect the modem to an unused COM port on the target machine or on another computer that is close enough to the target machine to connect by using a standard modem cable.

   Note If you connect the modem to a computer other than the target machine, make sure you can move the modem back to the target COM port without removing power from the modem.

2. Run Terminal.exe or some other communications program to configure the modem parameters.
3. Set the modem speed to 9600 bps. See your modem documentation to find out how to do this.
4. Turn off all hardware compression, flow control, and error detection.

   How to do this varies widely from modem to modem. See your modem documentation for the correct strings to send to the modem.
5. Enable auto-answer by sending the string ATS0=1 to your modem. Consult your modem documentation to verify that this will work with your modem.
6. If the modem was configured on a machine other than the target computer, move it to the target computer without removing the power from the modem.

Editing the Boot.ini File on the Target Machine

To configure a target system for a remote or local remote debugging, you edit the boot options in the Boot.ini file to tell Windows NT to load the kernel debugger.

Debugger Options

The following table lists the boot options that can be used to configure the system for debugging. These options are the same on Intel x86 and RISC platforms, but the slash (/) is not required when used on a RISC platform.

/Debug	Causes the kernel debugger to be loaded during boot and kept in memory at all times. This means that a support engineer can dial into the system being debugged and break into the debugger, even when the system is not suspended at a kernel STOP screen.
/Debugport	Specifies the serial port to be used by the kernel debugger. If no serial port is specified, the debugger will default to COM2 on Intel x86–based computers and to COM1 on RISC computers.
/Crashdebug	Causes the kernel debugger to be loaded during boot but swapped out to the pagefile after boot. As a result, a support engineer cannot break into the debugger unless Windows NT is suspended at a kernel STOP screen.
/Baudrate	Sets the speed that the kernel debugger will use in bits per second. The default rate is 19200 bps. A rate of 9600 bps is the normal rate for remote debugging over a modem.

When you use Debugport or Baudrate, you need not use Debug, as Windows NT assumes that the computer will load in Debug mode. You must use at least one of the options described in Table 39.1 to configure a computer for remote debugging. Otherwise, Windows NT does not load the debugger at all.

To set up the target computer on an Intel x86–based computer, edit the Boot.ini file by using a standard ASCII text editor and add the appropriate debugger options to the file. The Boot.ini file is located in the system root directory (usually the C drive) and has the Hidden, System, and Read-Only attributes set. These attributes must be changed.

To Change the Attributes of the Boot.ini File

1. Type the following at a command prompt:

   attrib -s -h -r c:\boot.ini

2. To restore the Read-Only, Hidden, and System attributes when you finish debugging the system, type the following at a command prompt:

   **attrib +h +r +s c:\boot.ini **

To Configure the Boot Options in the Boot.ini File

To configure the target computer for remote or local debugging, add the /Debug and /Baudrate options to the Boot.ini file. If you cannot use the default COM port (COM 2) for debugging, use **/Debugport=COM***x* where *x* is the COM port number. Use the MS-DOS-based Editor to edit the Boot.ini file.

1. At a command prompt, type:

   edit boot.ini

   The Boot.ini file appears in the MS-DOS Editor window. It looks similar to this:

   [boot loader]

   timeout=30

   default=multi(0)disk(0)rdisk(0)partition(1)\WINDOWS

   [operating systems]

   multi(0)disk(0)rdisk(0)partition(1)\WINDOWS="Windows NT Version 4.0"

   multi(0)disk(0)rdisk(0)partition(1)\WINDOWS="Windows NT Version 4.0"

   [VGA mode] /BASEVIDEO

   C:\="MS-DOS"

2. Select the startup option that you normally use and add the **/Debug** option at the end of the line.
3. To specify the communications port, add the option **/Debugport=com***x* where *x* is the communications port that you want to use.
4. Add the option **/Baudrate=9600**.

   This is the output if the Boot.ini file after it has been modified by steps 1-4:

   [boot loader]

   timeout=30

   default=multi(0)disk(0)rdisk(0)partition(1)\WINDOWS

   [operating systems]

   multi(0)disk(0)rdisk(0)partition(1)\WINDOWS="Windows NT Version 4.0" /debug /debugport=com1 /baudrate=9600

   multi(0)disk(0)rdisk(0)partition(1)\WINDOWS="Windows NT Version 4.0"

   [VGA mode] /BASEVIDEO

   C:\="MS-DOS"

5. Save the Boot.ini file and quit the text editor or the MS-DOS Editor.
6. Restart the computer to run under Windows NT.

Your technical support group can now call the modem to establish the remote debugging session.

Setting Up a Remote Debugging Session on a RISC-based Computer

To prepare a RISC-based computer for a remote or local kernel debugging session, you edit one line in a startup file. But you access that file in a different way. The procedure for all Alpha systems is the same. The options you use to configure the PowerPC-based system are the same as the options you select to configure the MIPS-based system. However, the path to the firmware menus may vary for MIPS-based and PowerPC-based systems.

On RISC-based computers, the default COM port is always COM1, and the default speed is always 19200 bps.

Before you begin the procedure to configure the target machine, make sure you set it up properly for communication. If you cannot run Terminal.exe or any other communications programs on the target machine, connect the modem to a computer that is near the target machine. Make sure that you can move the modem back to the target machine without removing the power to the modem.

All modem parameters are configured for a RISC-based computer in the same way as they are for an x86-based system with the exception of the modem speed. The default speed is always 19.2 kbps for a RISC-based system. For more information, see "Setting up the Modem on the Target Machine," earlier in this chapter.

After you have set up your computer for communication, restart the computer. The ARC System screen appears, displaying the main menu, from which you can select an action. Now you are ready to configure.

To configure the target machine

1. On a MIPS RISC–based system, select Run Setup to display the Setup menu, then select Manage Startup. A menu of boot options appears.

   On a Digital Alpha AXP RISC–system or a PowerPC RISC–based system, select the menu options listed in the following table to get to the Boot selections menu.

On Menu	Select
System Boot	Supplementary menu
Supplementary	Setup the system
Setup	Manage boot selections

2. On the Boot Selections menu, select Change a Boot Selection. A list of the operating systems that are installed on this computer appears.

3. From the list of operating systems, select the Windows NT operating system. If you have more than one version of Windows NT installed, select the version that you want to debug.

   A two-part screen appears with options for changing the current settings of the environment variables used to start the RISC-based computer. The environment variable that controls whether or not the RISC-based computer starts up in debug mode is the OSLOADOPTIONS variable.

4. Select the OSLOADOPTIONS variable from the list of environment variables.

   You edit the value of the OSLOADOPTIONS variable to control whether the RISC-based computer starts up in debug mode.

   After you select OSLOADOPTIONS, it appears in the Name box at the top of the screen.

5. Press ENTER to display the Value box.

6. Type the options that you want to add in the Value box separated by spaces. Press ENTER to save them and to turn on the debug mode.

   You can also add a value that explicitly sets the communications port, as in the following example:

   ```
   OSLOADOPTIONS debug debugport=com2
   ```

   If you do not specify the debug port, the default debug port is set to COM1. Because RISC-based computers allow only a default modem speed of 19.2 Kbps, you do not need to specify the baud rate.

7. Press ESC to stop editing.

8. Return to the ARC System screen by using the method for your system:

System	Procedure
MIPS RISC and PowerPC RISC	Select Return to Main Menu, then Exit.
Digital Alpha AXP	Select Supplementary Menu, save your changes, then select Boot Menu.

If this is the first time that you have debugged a Digital Alpha AXP RISC–based system, follow these steps after connecting the local host computer to the target:

- Shut down both computers.
- Restart the host (debugger) computer.
- Run Alphakd.exe on the local host.

- Restart the target (Digital Alpha AXP RISC–based) computer while Alphakd.exe is running on the host computer to set up configuration information on the target computer, and prepare it for either local or remote debugging.

Note After you complete steps 1-4, you can use either a local or a remote host to debug the target.

---

9. To run under Windows NT, restart the RISC-based computer.

   You may now contact your technical support group or a trained technician and have them call the modem to establish a remote debugging session.

Setting Up a Local Debugging Session on a Host Computer

You need a local debug session for debugging in cases where a user-mode .dll or a device driver is causing server crashes. In such a case, you use a user-mode debugger (such as NTSD) and you build the server symbols on the host computer.

You can also use this setup if your Remote Access Service (RAS) account allows a Microsoft Support engineer to dial into your network and debug the computer. This debug option overcomes many modem-related issues.

You use a local debug setup in cases where:

- You debug a user-mode component in Windows NT by using NTSD or CDB.
- A live remote debug does not work because of modem connection issues.
- Customer has worked with a senior ESS debug engineer and the situation warrants a local debug session.

To debug a Windows NT-based target computer by using a local host system, you need to:

- Connect the host and the target computers by using a null-modem serial cable.
- Set up a symbol tree on the local host computer to match the version of Windows NT that resides on the target computer. If you are using NTSD or CDB, you will need to set up a symbol tree on the target computer, in the directory %SYSTEMROOT%\Symbols.
- Set up the debugging files on the host computer.
- Start the debugger on the host.

Figure 39.2 shows the connection between the host and the target computer for a local debugging session. It also shows how to use your RAS account to connect to the Microsoft Support Network for help in analyzing the debug information.

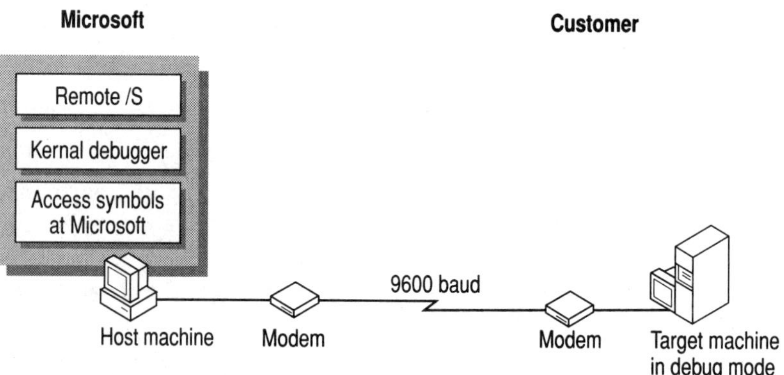

Figure 39.2 Local Debugging

Setting Up for Local Debugging

To set up for a local debugging session, you use a null-modem cable to connect the target and the host machines. For an x86-based system, the boot options in the Boot.ini file must be configured on the target machine to invoke the debugger and to set the data transfer rate between the target computer and the host computer. On a RISC-based system, the boot options are configured from a firmware menu.

For information on configuring the boot options for an x86-based system, see "Editing the Boot.ini File on a Target Machine," earlier in this chapter. For information on configuring a RISC-based system for a local debug session, see "Setting Up a Remote Debugging Session on a RISC-Based Computer," earlier in this chapter.

Be sure to start the host computer before restarting the target computer.

Setting Up a Null-Modem Connection

A modem is not used in a local debug session. Therefore, the procedure for setting up the null-modem cable is the same on both the host computer and target computer.

A standard, commercially available null-modem serial cable has this configuration:

- Transmit Data connected to Receive Data
- Receive Data connected to Transmit Data
- Ground connected to Ground

For 9-pin and 25-pin D-subminiature connectors (known as db9 and db25, respectively), the cable connects as follows:

- Pin 2 to pin 3
- Pin 3 to pin 2
- Pin 7 to pin 7

The debugger on the host does not depend on any control pins (such as Data Terminal Ready, Data Set Ready, Request To Send, or Clear To Send). However, you might need to put a jumper in the connectors on both ends of the cable from Data Terminal Ready to Data Set Ready and from Request To Send to Clear To Send, as follows:

Connector	Jumpers
db9	From pin 4 to pin 6 and from pin 7 to pin 8
Db25	From pin 20 to pin 6 and from pin 4 to pin 5

Connect the null-modem cable to an unused serial port on both the host computer and the target computer.

Setting Up the Symbol Tree on the Host

You set up the symbol tree on the host machine to match the version of Windows NT that you are running on the target computer.

The Windows NT Server and Windows NT Workstation product CDs come with symbol trees already created. They are in the Symbols directories on the CD under Support\Debug*platform*, where *platform* is I386, Alpha, MIPS, or PowerPC. The *platform* sprcification must match your target computer.

If you have not installed any service packs or hot fixes and do not have a multiprocessor system, you might need to specify only the path to the correct Symbols directory on the CD, or copy that directory to *Systemroot* and use this as the symbol path.

If you have installed service packs or hot fixes to Windows NT, or if you are using any HAL (Hardware Abstraction Layer) other than the standard, single-processor HAL, you must construct a symbol tree.

▶ To construct a symbol tree

1. Copy the correct tree from the Support directory on the CD to your hard drive.
2. Copy the symbols into this tree for the updates you have applied in the same order in which you applied the updates, so that the later versions overwrite the earlier versions.
3. If you are using kernel debuggers to debug a multiprocessor system, or a single-processor system that is using a special HAL, you must rename some of the symbol files. The rest of this section discusses what to rename and how to rename it.

   The kernel debuggers always load the files named Ntoskrnl.dbg for kernel symbols and Hal.dbg for HAL symbols. Therefore, you need to determine which kernel and HAL you are using, and rename the associated files to these filenames.

   If you have a multiprocessor computer, you only need to rename Ntkrnlmp.dbg to Ntoskrnl.dbg. These files are in the \Exe subdirectory of the symbol tree.

   If your computer uses a special HAL, there are a number of possibilities. Tables 39.2-39.5 list the possible HAL files for each hardware platform. These tables list the actual name of the .dll file as it exists on the product CD and the uncompressed size of the file in bytes. Each .dll file has a corresponding .dbg file, which is in the \Dll subdirectory of the symbol tree. Determine which HAL you are using, and rename the associated .dbg file to Hal.dbg. If you are not sure which HAL you are using, compare the file size in the table with the Hal.dll file on the target system. The Hal.dll file can be found in *Systemroot*\System32.

Table 39.2 HAL Files for I386 Systems

Filename	Uncompressed size (bytes)	Description
Hal.dll	52,768	Standard HAL for Intel systems
Hal486c.dll	51,712	HAL for 486 c Step processor
Halapic.dll	68,096	Uniprocessor version of Halmps.dl
Halast.dll	49,328	HAL for AST® SMP systems
Halcbus.dll	87,328	HAL for Cbus systems
Halcbusm.dll	85,376	

Table 39.2 HAL Files for I386 Systems *(Continued)*

Filename	Uncompressed size (bytes)	Description
Halmca.dll	49,696	HAL for MCA-based systems (PS/2® and others)
Halmps.dll	70,240	HAL for most Intel multiprocessor systems
Halmpsm.dll	69,184	
Halncr.dll	83,920	HAL for NCR® SMP computers
Haloli.dll	42,992	HAL for Olivetti® SMP computers
Halsp.dll	56,592	HAL for Compaq Systempro®
Halwyse7.dll	43,728	HAL for WYSE7 systems

Table 39.3 HAL Files for DEC Alpha Systems

Filename	Uncompressed size (bytes)	Description
Hal.dll	60,160	Standard HAL for DEC Alpha systems
Hal0jens.dll	60,160	Digital DECpc AXP 150 HAL
Halalcor.dll	69,120	Digital AlphaStation 600 Family
Halavant.dll	69,856	Digital AlphaStation 200/400 Family HAL
Haleb164.dll	84,768	
Haleb64p.dll	76,320	Digital AlphaPC64 HAL
Halflex.dll	89,472	
Halgammp.dll	82,560	Digital AlphaServer 2x00 5/xxx Family HAL
Halx3.dll	79,072	
Halmikas.dll	73,184	Digital AlphaServer 1000 Family Uniprocessor HAL
Halnonme.dll	68,320	Digital AXPpci 33 HAL
Halqs.dll	68,000	Digital Multia MultiClient Desktop HAL
Halrawmp.dll	93,280	
Halsabmp.dll	78,496	Digital AlphaServer 2x00 4/xxx Family HAL
Halxl.dll	81,568	

Table 39.4 HAL Files for MIPS Systems

Filename	Uncompressed size (bytes)	Description
Hal.dll	41,856	Standard HAL for MIPS
Halacr.dll	42,496	ACER HAL
Haldti.dll	66,240	DESKStation Evolution
Halduomp.dll	41,536	Microsoft-designed dual MP HAL
Halflex.dll	96,640	
Halfxs.dll	41,856	MTI with an R4000 or R4400
Halfxspc.dll	41,984	MTI with an R4600
Halnecmp.dll	47,040	NEC® dual MP
Halntp.dll	140,096	NeTpower FASTseries
Halr94a.dll	193,760	
Halr96b.dll	194,432	
Halr98mp.dll	108,608	NEC 4 processor MP
Halsni4x.dll	99,936	Siemens Nixdorf UP and MP
Halsnip.dll	116,864	
Haltyne.dll	65,888	DESKStation Tyne

Table 39.5 HAL files for PowerPC Systems

Filename	Uncompressed size (bytes)	Description
Halcaro.dll	234,240	HAL for IBM-6070
Haleagle.dll	211,232	HAL for Motorola PowerStack and Big Bend
Halfire.dll	292,384	Hal for Powerized_ES, Powerized_MX, and Powerized_MX MP
Halppc.dll	233,600	HAL for IBM-6015
Halps.dll	207,552	
Halvict.dll	244,896	
Halwood.dll	233,888	HAL for IBM-6020

In some cases, a HAL file might have been supplied by your computer manufacturer. If so, you need to obtain symbols for the file from the manufacturer, rename that symbol file to Hal.dbg, and place it in the \Dll subdirectory of the symbol tree. For example, Compaq provides updated HAL files for their Proliant™ systems. This also applies if you have drivers from third-party sources. Obtain symbols from your third-party vendor and put them in the appropriate directory.

Setting Up the Debugger Files on the Host

To set up the debugger on the host, first ensure that you have the correct files available. Copy these files from the Support\Debug*platform* directory to a debug directory on the hard drive, where *platform* matches the platform of the host computer.

Some files that you copy from the directory must match the platform of the target computer, as described in the following table. These files are necessary for kernel debugging.

File	Source List
*platform*Kd.exe*	Alphakd.exe
	I386kd.exe
	Mipskd.exe
	Ppckd.exe
Imagehlp.dll	
Kdext*platform*.dll*	Kdextalp.dll
	Kdextx86.dll
	Kdextmip.dll
	Kdextppc.dll

* *platform* matches the platform of the target computer

For instance, if your host computer is a 486 computer and the target computer is a MIPS RISC–based system, you copy the following files from the \Support\Debug\I386 directory:

- Mipskd.exe
- Imagehlp.dll
- Kdextmip.dll

Once you have set up the symbol tree and copied the necessary files to it, use a batch file or command line to set the following environment variables on the host:

Variable	Purpose
_NT_DEBUG_PORT	COM port being used on host for debugging.
_NT_DEBUG_BAUD_RATE	Max baud rate for debug port. On x86-based computers, maximum is 9600 or 19200 bps for modems, 19200 bps for null-modem serial cables. On RISC-based computers, rate is always 19200 bps.
_NT_SYMBOL_PATH	Path to symbols directory
_NT_LOG_FILE_OPEN	Optional, the name of the file to which to write a log of the debug session

After these environment variables have been set, you can start the host debugger.

Note Setting the _NT_LOG_FILE_OPEN variable does not always result in a log file being written. You can also create the log file from the debugger. The command format is:

.logopen pathname

You might also need to issue the **!reload** command to get this to work.

Starting the Debugger on the Host

You can start the host debugger from the command line or a batch file by using the name of the executable file as the command. Each debugger supports the following command-line options:

Option	Action
-b	Causes the debugger to stop execution on the target computer as soon as possible by causing a debug breakpoint (INT 3).
-c	Causes the debugger to request a resync on connect. Resynchronization ensures that the host and target computers are communicating in sequence.
-m	Causes the debugger to monitor modem control lines. The debugger is only active when the carrier detect (CD) line is active; otherwise, the debugger is in terminal mode, and all commands are sent to the modem.
-n	Causes symbols to be loaded immediately, rather than in a deferred mode.
-v	Indicates verbose mode; displays more information about such things as when symbols are loaded.
-x	Causes the debugger to break in when an exception first occurs, rather than letting the application or module that caused the exception deal with it.

The most commonly used options are **-v** (verbose) and **-m** (for modem debugging).

Generally, the best way to start the debugger is to create a batch file with the necessary commands to set the environment variables, followed by the command to start the correct kernel debugger.

Using the Remote Utility to Start the Debugger

If the host computer is connected to a network, you can use the **remote** utility, included in the *Windows NT Resource Kit*, to start the debugger. **Remote** is a server/client utility that provides remote network access by means of named pipes to applications that use STDIN and STDOUT for input and output. Users at other computers on the network can then connect to your host debugger session and either view the debugging information or enter commands themselves. The syntax for starting the server (host) end of the remote session is as follows:

remote /s "*command*" *Unique_Id* [**/f** *foreground_color*|**/b** *background_color*]

For example:

```
REMOTE /S "i386kd -v" debug
```

You end the server session by entering the @K command.

To interact with this session from some other computer, use the **remote /c** command. The syntax of this command is as follows:

remote /c *ServerName Unique_Id* [**/l** *lines_to_get*|**/f** *foreground_color*|**/b** *background_color*]

To exit from the remote session on a client and leave the debugger running on the host computer, enter the @Q command.

For example, if a session with the ID **debug** was started on the host computer \\Server1 by using the **remote /s** command, you can connect to it with the command

```
REMOTE /C server1 debug
```

For more information on using the **remote** command, see the Rktools.hlp file on the *Windows NT Resource Kit* CD.

Examples

Assume the following:

- Debugging needs to take place over a null-modem serial cable on COM2.
- The symbols are on a CD on the E drive.
- A log file called Debug.log is to be created in C:\Temp.

Note The log file holds a copy of everything you see on the debug screen during your debug session. All input from the person doing the debugging, and all output from the kernel debugger on the target system, is written to the log file.

A sample batch file for local debugging is:

```
REM Target computer is local
set _NT_DEBUG_PORT=com2
set _NT_DEBUG_BAUD_RATE=19200
set _NT_SYMBOL_PATH=e:\support\debug\i386\symbols
SET _NT_LOG_FILE_OPEN=c:\temp\debug.log
remote /s "i386kd -v" debug
```

The last line of the batch file uses the **remote** utility to start the host debugger. If you use this, users of Windows NT–based computers who are networked to the host computer (and who have a copy of the **remote** utility) can connect to the debug session by using the command:

remote /c *computername* **debug**

where *computername* is the name of the host computer.

To allow remote debugging, which requires the use of a modem, begin with the batch file in the previous example. Change the baud rate to 9600, and add the **-m** switch to the last line. The result is as follows:

```
REM Target computer is remote from the host
set _NT_DEBUG_PORT=com2
set _NT_DEBUG_BAUD_RATE=9600
set _NT_SYMBOL_PATH=e:\support\debug\i386\symbols
SET _NT_LOG_FILE_OPEN=c:\temp\debug.log
remote /s "i386kd -v -m" debug
```

You run the batch file from the directory that contains the debugger files.

When you start the debugger, one of two screens appears, depending upon whether you are doing local debugging or remote debugging.

When doing local debugging, the following screen appears:

```
**************************************
***********   REMOTE   ************
***********   SERVER   ************
**************************************
To Connect: Remote /C BANSIDHE debug

Microsoft(R) Windows NT Kernel Debugger
Version 3.51
(C) 1991-1995 Microsoft Corp.

Symbol search path is:
KD: waiting to connect...
```

At this screen, you can press CTRL+C to gain access to the target computer, if it is still running. If the target is currently stopped at a blue screen, you will probably gain access automatically. If you have any problems, press CTRL+R to force a resync between the host computer and the target computer.

If you are doing remote debugging, the same screen as shown for local debugging appears, with the following extra line:

```
KD: No carrier detect - in terminal mode
```

In this case, the debugger is in terminal mode, and you can issue any of the standard AT commands to your modem. Begin by sending commands to disable hardware compression, flow control, and error correction. These commands will vary from modem to modem, so consult your modem documentation. Once you connect to the target system and have a carrier detect (CD) signal, you are returned to the debugger.

Creating a Memory Dump File

If you do not want to or are unable to do local or remote debugging, you can configure Windows NT Server or Windows NT Workstation to write a memory dump file each time it generates a kernel STOP error. This file contains all the information needed by the **dumpexam** utility to troubleshoot the kernel STOP error, as if you were connected to a live computer experiencing the problem.

Using the memory dump file enables you to examine the error at any time, so you can immediately restart the computer that failed. Thus, your target computer can be available while you are using the debugger. The only drawback to this method is that you must have sufficient space on a hard disk partition for the resulting memory dump file, which will be as large as your RAM memory. Therefore, whenever a kernel STOP error occurs, a computer with 32 MB of RAM produces a 32-MB memory dump file. You must also have a page file on your system root drive that is at least as large as your RAM memory.

▶ **To configure Windows NT to save STOP information to a memory dump file**

1. In Control Panel, double-click System.
2. In the System Properties dialog box, click the Startup/Shutdown tab.
3. Under Recovery, select the Write debugging information to check box. Either accept the default path and filename (C:*systemroot*\Memory.dmp) or type a path in the text box.
4. If you want this memory dump file to overwrite any file of the same name, select the Overwrite any existing file check box. If you set the option to overwrite an existing file, rename or move the file so it does not get overwritten before you have time to process it. If you clear this check box, Windows NT will not write a memory dump file if there is already a file by that name.

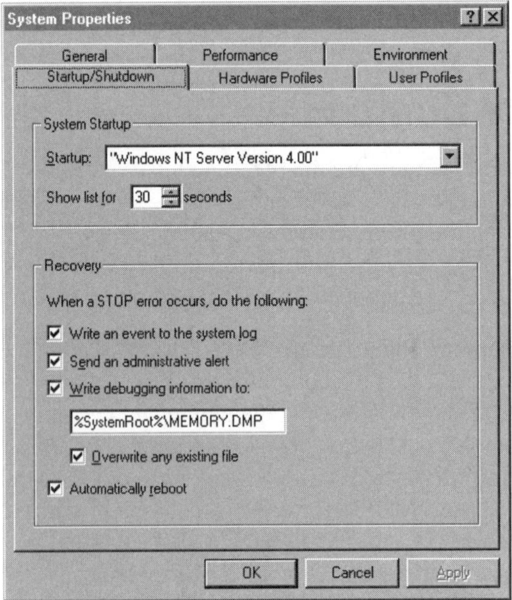

Using Utilities to Process Memory Dump Files

Included on the Windows NT Server and Windows NT Workstation version 3.51 CDs are three utilities for processing memory dump files: **dumpflop**, **dumpchk**, and **dumpexam**. All three utilities are on the product CDs in the Support\Debug*platform* directories, where *platform* is I386, Alpha, MIPS, or PowerPC.

The primary purpose of these utilities is to create files on floppy disks or a text file that you can send to technical support personnel for analysis.

Dumpflop

Dumpflop is a command-line utility that you can use to write a memory dump file in segments to floppy disks, so it can be sent to a support engineer. This is rarely the most efficient way to send a memory dump file, but it is sometimes the only way. **Dumpflop** compresses the information it writes to the floppy disks, so a 32 MB memory dump file can fit onto 10 floppy disks, rather than 20 or more. **Dumpflop** does not require access to symbols.

To store the crash dump onto floppy disks, use **dumpflop** with the following command-line syntax:

dumpflop *options CrashDumpFile Drive:*

To assemble a crash dump from floppy disks, use **dumpflop** with the following command-line syntax:

dumpflop *options Drive: CrashDumpFile*

In either case, **Options** can include:

Option	Action
-?	Displays the command syntax.
-p	Only prints the crash dump header on an assemble operation.
-v	Shows compression statistics.
-q	Formats the floppy disk, when necessary, before writing the memory dump file to the floppy disk. When reading the floppy disks to assemble the file, overwrites an existing memory dump file.

If executed with no parameters, **dumpflop** attempts to find a memory dump file in the *systemroot* directory (the default location for creating a memory dump file) and writes it to floppy disks on the A drive.

Dumpchk

Dumpchk is a command-line utility that you can use to verify that a memory dump file has been created correctly. **Dumpchk** does not require access to symbols.

Dumpchk has the following command-line syntax:

dumpchk *options CrashDumpFile*

The Options can include:

Option	Action
-?	Displays the command syntax.
-p	Prints the header only (with no validation).
-v	Specifies verbose mode.
-q	Performs a quick test.

Dumpchk displays some basic information from the memory dump file and then verifies all the virtual and physical addresses in the file. If any errors are found in the memory dump file, it reports them. The following is an example of the output of a **Dumpchk** command:

```
Filename . . . . . . .memory.dmp
Signature. . . . . . .PAGE
ValidDump. . . . . . .DUMP
MajorVersion . . . . .free system
MinorVersion . . . . .807
DirectoryTableBase . .0x00030000
PfnDataBase. . . . . .0xffb7e000
PsLoadedModuleList . .0x80196d40
PsActiveProcessHead. .0x80196c38
MachineImageType . . .i386
NumberProcessors . . .1
BugCheckCode . . . . .0xc000021a
BugCheckParameter1 . .0xe17b7b68
BugCheckParameter2 . .0xc0000005
BugCheckParameter3 . .0x00000000
BugCheckParameter4 . .0x00000000

ExceptionCode. . . . .0x80000003
ExceptionFlags . . . .0x00000001
ExceptionAddress . . .0x8015f015

NumberOfRuns . . . . .0x3
NumberOfPages. . . . .0x3f9e
Run #1

 BasePage . . . . . .0x1
 PageCount. . . . . .0x9e
Run #2

 BasePage . . . . . .0x100
 PageCount. . . . . .0xec0
Run #3

 BasePage . . . . . .0x1000
 PageCount. . . . . .0x3040

**************
```

```
**************--> Validating the integrity of the PsLoadedModuleList
**************

**************
**************--> Performing a complete check (^C to end)
**************
**************
**************--> Validating all physical addresses
**************
**************
**************--> Validating all virtual addresses
**************
```

In this example, the most important information (from a debugging standpoint) is the following:

```
MajorVersion . . . . .free system
MinorVersion . . . . .807
MachineImageType . . .i386
NumberProcessors . . .1
BugCheckCode . . . . .0xc000021a
BugCheckParameter1 . .0xe17b7b68
BugCheckParameter2 . .0xc0000005
BugCheckParameter3 . .0x00000000
BugCheckParameter4 . .0x00000000
```

This information can be used to determine what kernel STOP error occurred and what version of Windows NT was in use.

Dumpexam

Dumpexam is a command-line utility that examines a memory dump file, extracts information from it, and writes it to a text file. This text file can then be used by support personnel to determine the cause of the kernel STOP error. In many cases, the **dumpexam** analysis provides enough information for support personnel to determine the cause of the error without directly accessing the memory dump file.

Three files are required to run **dumpexam**, and they all must be in the same directory. You can find them on the Windows NT Server or Windows NT Workstation CD in the directory Support\Debug*platform*, where *platform* is I386, Alpha, MIPS, or PowerPC. The first two files are:

- Dumpexam.exe
- Imagehlp.dll

The third file is one of the following, depending on the type of computer on which the memory dump file was generated:

- Kdextx86.dll
- Kdextalp.dll
- Kdextmip.dll
- Kdextppc.dll

You can run **dumpexam** directly from the product CD with no parameters, if

- The computer on which the dump occurred was running Windows NT version 4.0.
- You have not applied any hot fixes or service packs on that computer.
- The memory dump file you want to examine is in the location specified in the Recovery dialog box.

Dumpexam creates a text file called Memory.txt, located in the same directory as the Memory.dmp file, that contains information extracted from the memory dump file.

You can also use **dumpexam** to examine memory dump files created on computers running earlier versions of Windows NT. However, you can run it only with Windows NT version 3.51 or 4.0. Therefore, if your memory dump file was created in an earlier version of Windows NT, you must move the memory dump file or access it over the network. In addition, you must replace the Kdext*.dll files listed above with copies from the version of Windows NT that was running on the computer on which the dump occurred. These files contain debug information specific to that version of Windows NT. You must also specify the path to the symbols for the operating system version that was running on that computer.

Syntax for Dumpexam

The syntax for **dumpexam** is:

dumpexam *options CrashDumpFile*

where options can include:

Option	Action
-?	Displays the command syntax.
-p	Prints the header only.
-v	Specifies verbose mode.
-f *filename*	Specifies the output filename and path.
-y *path*	Sets the symbol search path.

You need to specify the memory dump file path only if you have moved the memory dump file.

You need to specify the symbol search path (using the **-y** option) only if you are using an alternative symbol path. The symbol path for **dumpexam** can contain several directories, separated by semicolons(**;**). Because these directories are searched in the order in which they are listed, you list directories with the most recently installed hot fixes or service packs first.

Examples

In the first example, the memory dump file was created on a computer running Windows NT Workstation version 3.51, and no service packs were installed. The symbols are all in the directory C:\Symbols. The memory dump file is in the directory C:\Dump and is called Machine1.dmp. The command line reads as follows:

```
dumpexam -y c:\symbols c:\dump\machine1.dmp
```

The results of the exam will be in *Systemroot*\Memory.txt.

In the next example, the memory dump file was created on a DEC Alpha computer running Windows NT Server version 3.5, with Service Pack 2 installed. The Service Pack 2 symbols are in D:\Sp2\Symbols. The Windows NT Server 3.5 symbols are on the product CD, which is in the E drive. The memory dump file Memory.dmp is in D:\Temp. The output file is to be put in the same directory as the memory dump file. The command line reads as follows:

```
dumpexam -y d:\sp2\symbols;e:\support\debug\alpha -f d:\temp\memory.txt
d:\temp\memory.dmp
```

Using the Dumpexam Output File

Dumpexam reads a memory dump file, executes debugger commands on it, and writes the output in a text file, called Memory.txt, by default. The same debugger commands are executed on each memory dump file.

A full interpretation of the output requires knowledge of Windows NT kernel processes and the ability to read assembly language; however, there are some guidelines you can follow to get an idea of what the output means. This section first describes each part of the memory dump file output, giving sample output and a description. Then several common traps are discussed, along with guidelines on which sections of the Memory.txt file can help you determine what caused the kernel STOP error.

Because the primary purpose of the **dumpexam** utility is to create a text file to send to support personnel, the descriptions in this section do not provide complete details of the contents of the Memory.txt file.

The following sections of the Memory.txt file each occur once, as they include information that applies to the whole system. These sections are listed in the order in which they appear in Memory.txt.

Windows NT Crash Dump Analysis

The first section of output is Windows NT Crash Dump Analysis, which looks like the following:

```
*****************************************************************
**
** Windows NT Crash Dump Analysis
**
*****************************************************************
*
Filename . . . . . . .c:\temp\dumps\mac.dmp
Signature. . . . . . .PAGE
ValidDump. . . . . . .DUMP
MajorVersion . . . . .free system
MinorVersion . . . . .1057
DirectoryTableBase . .0x0006f005
PfnDataBase. . . . . .0x83fce000
PsLoadedModuleList . .0x800ee5c0
PsActiveProcessHead. .0x800ee590
MachineImageType . . .alpha
NumberProcessors . . .2
BugCheckCode . . . . .0x0000002e
BugCheckParameter1 . .0x00000000
BugCheckParameter2 . .0x00000000
BugCheckParameter3 . .0x00000000
BugCheckParameter4 . .0x00000000
ExceptionCode. . . . .0x80000003
ExceptionFlags . . . .0x00000001
ExceptionAddress . . .0x800bc140
```

Most of the information here is useful only for determining whether the memory dump file is corrupted. The following items are most important, especially if you did not record any information from the blue screen generated when the computer trapped:

Parameter	Meaning
BugCheckCode	This code lists the number of the stop that occurred. The stop code can be used by support personnel to determine what trap occurred. In the preceding example, the code was 0x0000002e, which is a DATA_BUS_ERROR.
BugCheckParameters	These are the four parameters that are normally included with each STOP code.

Symbol File Load Log

This section of the Memory.txt file includes any errors that were generated when the symbols were loaded. If no errors were generated, this section will be blank.

!drivers

The **!drivers** command is a debug command that you use to list information on all the device drivers loaded on the system. The information for the device drivers looks like this:

```
*****************************************************************
** !drivers
*****************************************************************
*
Loaded System Driver Summary

Base    Code Size     Data Size    Driver Name   Creation Time
80080000 f76c0 (989 kb) 1f100 (124 kb) ntoskrnl.exe Fri May 26 15:13:00 1995
80400000 d980 ( 54 kb) 4040 ( 16 kb)   hal.dll Tue May 16 16:50:34 1995
80654000 3f00 ( 15 kb) 1060 ( 4 kb) ncrc810.sys Fri May 05 20:07:04 1995
8065a000 a460 ( 41 kb) 1e80 ( 7 kb) SCSIPORT.SYS Fri May 05 20:08:05 1995
```

The following information can be determined from the above output:

Parameter	Meaning
Base	The starting address of the device driver code, in hexadecimal. When the code that causes a trap falls between the base address for a driver and the base address for the next driver in the list, then that driver is frequently the cause of the fault. For instance, the base for Ncrc810.sys is 0x80654000. Any address between that and 0x8065a000 belongs to this driver.
Code Size	The size in kilobytes of the driver code, in both hexadecimal and decimal.
Data Size	The amount of space in kilobytes allocated to the driver for data, in both hexadecimal and decimal.
Driver Name	The driver filename.
Creation Time	The link date of the driver. Do not confuse this with the file date of the driver, which can be set by external utilities. The link date is set by the compiler when a driver or executable file is compiled. It should be close to the file date, but it will not always be the same.

!locks

The **!locks** command is a debugger command that displays all locks held on resources by threads. A lock can be shared or exclusive, which means no other threads can access that resource. This information is useful when a deadlock occurs on a system, because a deadlock is caused when one nonexecuting thread holds an exclusive lock on a resource needed by an executing thread.

```
*****************************************************************
** !locks -p -v -d
*****************************************************************
*
**** DUMP OF ALL RESOURCE OBJECTS ****
KD: Scanning for held locks.................

Resource @ 0xffb6ed14  Shared 2 owning threads
   Threads: ffb3bb70-01
0012fb50: Unable to read ThreadCount for resource

Resource @ 0xffb6ecdc  Shared 2 owning threads
   Threads: ffb3bb70-02
0012fb50: Unable to read ThreadCount for resource
```

!memusage

The **!memusage** command gives a short description of the current memory use of the system. Then it gives a much longer listing of the memory usage summary. The output looks something like this:

```
*****************************************************************
** !memusage
*****************************************************************
*
loading PFN database..............................................

       Zeroed:  405 ( 3240 kb)
        Free:   0 (    0 kb)
      Standby:  3242 ( 25936 kb)
      Modified:  135 ( 1080 kb)
  ModifiedNoWrite:   0 (    0 kb)
    Active/Valid:  4410 ( 35280 kb)
     Transition:   0 (    0 kb)
      Unknown:   0 (    0 kb)
       TOTAL:  8192 ( 65536 kb)

Usage Summary in KiloBytes (Kb):
Control Valid Standby Dirty Shared Locked PageTables name
80975548   0    56    0    0    0    0 mapped_file(oemnxpip.inf)
80975248   0    16    0    0    0    0 mapped_file(oemnxpnb.inf)
8096aa68   0   160    0    0    0    0 mapped_file(SFMATALK.SY_)
80974f48   0   104    0    0    0    0 mapped_file(oemnxpsm.inf)
809758e8   0    96    0    0    0    0 mapped_file(utility.inf)
```

This section provides information for some memory leak issues, but it is more useful to refer to the **!vm** section for memory information for most common kernel STOP errors.

!vm

The **!vm** command lists the system's virtual memory usage. The output of **!vm** looks like this:

```
*****************************************************************
** !vm
*****************************************************************
*
*** Virtual Memory Usage ***
    Physical Memory:  32784  (131136 Kb)
    Available Pages:  27435  (109740 Kb)
    Modified Pages:    33  (  132 Kb)
    NonPagedPool Usage:  461  ( 1844 Kb)
    PagedPool 0 Usage:  1519  ( 6076 Kb)
    PagedPool 1 Usage:  125  (  500 Kb)
    PagedPool 2 Usage:  149  (  596 Kb)
```

```
PagedPool Usage:    1793  ( 7172 Kb)
    Shared Commit:    173  (  692 Kb)
    Process Commit:    254  ( 1016 Kb)
    PagedPool Commit:  1793  ( 7172 Kb)
    Driver Commit:    321  ( 1284 Kb)
    Committed pages:   4261  ( 17044 Kb)
    Commit limit:    80792  (323168 Kb)
```

All memory usage is listed in pages and in kilobytes. The most useful information in the **!vm** section for diagnosing problems is:

Parameter	Meaning
Physical Memory	The total physical memory in the system.
Available Pages	The number of pages of memory available on the system, both virtual and physical. If this is low, it might indicate a problem with a process allocating too much virtual memory.
NonPagedPool Usage	The amount of pages allocated to the nonpaged pool. The nonpaged pool is memory that cannot be swapped out to the pagefile, so it must always occupy physical memory. This number should rarely be larger than 10% of the total physical memory. If it is larger, this is usually an indication that there is a memory leak somewhere in the system.

!errlog

The debugger sometimes keeps track of kernel errors logged by the system when a problem occurs. The **!errlog** section contains a dump of this log. In most cases, the error log is empty. If it is not empty, you can sometimes use it to determine the component or process that caused the blue screen.

!irpzone full

An Interrupt Request Packet (IRP) is a data structure used by device drivers and other kernel mode modules to communicate information to each other. The **!irpzone full** command displays a list of all the pending IRPs on the system. The following information is displayed in this section:

```
*****************************************************************
** !irpzone full
*****************************************************************
*
Small Irp list
Irp is from zone and active with 1 stacks 1 is current
 No Mdl System buffer = fb564000 Thread fb5688a0: Irp stack trace.
 cmd flg cl Device  File   Completion-Context
> d  0 1 fb56a030 fb56cd48 00000000-00000000  pending
      \FileSystem\MacSrv
           Args: 00001000 00000000 00121020 00000000
```

```
Large Irp list
Irp is from zone and active with 4 stacks 5 is current
 No Mdl Thread fb4b6860: Irp is completed. Pending has been returned
 cmd flg cl Device  File   Completion-Context
  0   0 0 00000000 00000000 00000000-00000000

           Args: 00000000 00000000 00000000 00000000
  0   0 0 00000000 00000000 00000000-00000000

           Args: 00000000 00000000 00000000 00000000
  0   0 0 00000000 00000000 00000000-00000000

           Args: 00000000 00000000 00000000 00000000
  d   0 0 fb5e3020 00000000 f8a8c711-fb48df10
      \FileSystem\Ntfs SrvCompleteRfcbClose
           Args: 00000000 00000000 00000000 00000000
```

Each entry lists information about a different IRP and points to the driver that currently owns the IRP. This information can be useful when the trap analysis (which occurs later in the Memory.txt file) points to a problem with a corrupted or bad IRP. The IRP listing usually contains several entries in both the small and large IRP lists.

!process 0 0

This command lists all processes and their headers. The process header list will contain entries like the following:

```
****************************************************************
** !process 0 0
****************************************************************
*
**** NT ACTIVE PROCESS DUMP ****
PROCESS fb667a00 Cid: 0002  Peb: 00000000 ParentCid: 0000
  DirBase: 00030000 ObjectTable: e1000f88 TableSize: 112.
  Image: System

PROCESS fb5edde0 Cid: 0018  Peb: 7ffdf000 ParentCid: 0002
  DirBase: 01587000 ObjectTable: e11d59a8 TableSize: 48.
  Image: SMSS.EXE
```

The important information in the **!process 0 0** section is:

Parameter	Meaning
Process ID	The 8-character hexadecimal number after the word PROCESS is the process ID. This is used by the system to track the process. For the first process in the example, this is fb667a00.
Image	The name of the module that owns the process. In the above example, the first process is owned by System, the second by Smss.exe.

!process 0 7

This command also lists process information. But instead of just listing the process header, the **!process 0 7** command lists all information about the process, including all threads owned by each process. This is a very long listing because each system has a large number of processes and each process has one or more threads. In addition, if the stack from a thread is resident in kernel memory (as opposed to swapped to the page file), it is listed after the thread information. Most process and thread listings look like the following:

```
*****************************************************************
** !process 0 7
*****************************************************************
*
**** NT ACTIVE PROCESS DUMP ****

PROCESS fb667a00 Cid: 0002  Peb: 00000000 ParentCid: 0000
  DirBase: 00030000 ObjectTable: e1000f88 TableSize: 112.
  Image: System
  VadRoot fb666388 Clone 0 Private 4. Modified 9850. Locked 0.
  FB667BBC MutantState Signalled OwningThread 0
  Token                e10008f0
  ElapsedTime             15:06:36.0338
  UserTime              0:00:00.0000
  KernelTime             0:00:54.0818
  QuotaPoolUsage[PagedPool]     1480
Working Set Sizes (now,min,max) (3, 50, 345)
  PeakWorkingSetSize        118
  VirtualSize            1 Mb
  PeakVirtualSize          1 Mb
  PageFaultCount          992
  MemoryPriority          BACKGROUND
  BasePriority           8
  CommitCharge           8

    THREAD fb667780 Cid 2.1 Teb: 00000000 Win32Thread: 80144900 WAIT:
(WrFreePage) KernelMode Non-Alertable
    80144fc0 SynchronizationEvent
    Not impersonating
    Owning Process fb667a00
    WaitTime (seconds)   32278
    Context Switch Count  787
    UserTime          0:00:00.0000
    KernelTime         0:00:21.0821
    Start Address Phase1Initialization (0x801aab44)
    Initial Sp fb26f000 Current Sp fb26ed00
    Priority 0 BasePriority 0 PriorityDecrement 0 DecrementCount 0

    ChildEBP RetAddr Args to Child
    fb26ed18 80118efc c0502000 804044b0 00000000 KiSwapThread+0xb5
    fb26ed3c 801289d9 80144fc0 00000008 00000000
KeWaitForSingleObject+0x1c2
```

The following entries in the process information can be important:

Parameter	Meaning
UserTime	Lists the amount of time the process has been running in user mode. If the value for UserTime is exceptionally high, it might identify a process that is taking up all the resources and starving the system.
KernelTime	Lists the amount of time the process has been running in kernel mode. If the value for KernelTime is exceptionally high, it might identify a process that is taking up all the resources and starving the system.
Working Set Size	Lists the current, minimum, and maximum working set size for the process, in pages. An exceptionally large working set size can also be a sign of a process that is leaking memory or using too many system resources.
QuotaPoolUsage Entries	List the paged and nonpaged pool used by the process. On a system with a memory leak, looking for excessive nonpaged pool usage on all the processes can tell you which process has the memory leak.

In addition to the process list information, the thread information also contains a list of the resources on which the thread has locks. This information is listed right after the thread header. In this example, the thread has a lock on one resource, a SynchronizationEvent with an address of 80144fc0. By comparing this address to the list of locks shown in the **!locks** section, you can determine which threads have exclusive locks on resources.

Processor-specific Information in Memory.txt

The following sections in the Memory.txt file occur once for each processor on the system. In a four-processor system, these sections will be repeated for processors 0 through 3. In addition, some traps generate a few extra sections, such as STOP 0x0000001E.

Register Dump for Processor #*x*

A dump of the state of all registers at the time of the trap is included in this section. For an x86-based system, it appears as follows:

```
*****************************************************************
** Register Dump For Processor #0
*****************************************************************
*
eax=ffdff13c ebx=00000000 ecx=00000000 edx=fb5a7db4 esi=00000d31 edi=00000d31
eip=8013b446 esp=f88b6de4 ebp=f88b6df8 iopl=0     nv up di pl nz na pe nc
cs=0008 ss=0010 ds=0023 es=0023 fs=0030 gs=0000       efl=00000286
cr0=8001003b cr2=00000d31 cr3=00030000 dr0=00000000 dr1=00000000 dr2=00000000
dr3=00000000 dr6=ffff0ff0 dr7=00000400 cr4=00000000
gdtr=80036000  gdtl=03ff idtr=80036400  idtl=07ff tr=0028 ldtr=0000
```

For a RISC-based system, the register dump varies from processor type to processor type. The following example is from a DEC Alpha system:

```
v0=80006000   t0=00000000   t1=00000000   t2=800ef538
t3=00000008   t4=00000000   t5=800ec440   t6=00000000
t7=00000000   s0=c53f2000   s1=00000002   s2=00000001
s3=00000000   s4=00000001   s5=0018da83   fp=fc90f940
a0=00000002   a1=c53f2000   a2=c53f2000   a3=00000000
a4=00000000   a5=00000002   t8=800ed580   t9=80a4752c
t10=c53f2000  t11=80a4752c   ra=8009b0bc  t12=80a61ecc
at=a0000000   gp=800ed430   sp=fc90f890  zero=00000000
pcr=0000000008000000  softfpcr=0000000000000000    fir=800bf2fc
psr=0000000a
mode=0 ie=1 irql=2
```

In general, the register dump is valuable only if you are skilled in reading assembly language on the system you are debugging.

Stack Trace for Processor *x*

The next section includes a trace of the stack for that processor. The stack trace is important because it tells you what functions were called. You can use it to trace back from a trap to determine why it happened. Included right after each stack trace is a section of disassembled code from the area in memory around the last instruction in the stack. This information also looks different, depending on platform.

The first example is an excerpt from an x86-based computer on which a STOP 0x0000000A occurred:

```
*****************************************************************
** Stack Trace
*****************************************************************
*
ChildEBP RetAddr Args to Child
f88b6e00 f89805b0 fb55ea88 fb55e988 fb55ea88 KiTrap0E+0x252 (FPO: [0,0,0])
f88b6df8 fb4a71a0 fb4a6028 f89805b0 fb55ea88 NTSend+0x142

  8013B430: 8B 4D 64      mov     ecx,dword ptr [ebp+64h]
  8013B433: 83 E1 02      and     ecx,2
  8013B436: D1 E9        shr     ecx,1
  8013B438: 8B 75 68      mov     esi,dword ptr [ebp+68h]
  8013B43B: 56          push    esi
  8013B43C: 51          push    ecx
8013B43D: 50          push    eax
  8013B43E: 57          push    edi
  8013B43F: 6A 0A       push    0Ah
  8013B441: E8 00 C6 FD FF   call    KiTrap0E+24Eh
--->8013B446: F7 45 70 00 00 02 test    dword ptr [ebp+70h],offset
KiTrap0E+255h
      00
  8013B44D: 74 0D       je     KiTrap0E+268h
  8013B44F: 83 3D EC 05 14 80 cmp     dword ptr [KiTrap0E+25Dh],0
      00
  8013B456: 0F 85 29 FE FF FF jne     KiTrap0E+264h
  8013B45C: 83 3D 38 49 14 80 cmp     dword ptr [KiTrap0E+26Ah],0
      00
  8013B463: 0F 85 1C FE FF FF jne     KiTrap0E+271h
  8013B469: 83 3D C0 4D 14 80 cmp     dword ptr [KiTrap0E+277h],0
      00
  8013B470: 0F 85 0F FE FF FF jne     KiTrap0E+27Eh
  8013B476: B8 FF 00 00 00   mov     eax,offset KiTrap0E+283h
  8013B47B: EB AC       jmp     KiTrap0E+235h
  8013B47D: A1 52 F0 DF FF   mov     eax,[KiTrap0E+28Ah]
  8013B482: C6 05 52 F0 DF FF mov     byte ptr [KiTrap0E+290h],0
```

The arrow (--->) indicates the line in the assembly code at which the system trap occurred.

The most important information here is the stack trace at the top. This tells you in which part of the code the system trapped. Each line of a stack trace is a different instruction that has been pushed on the stack, with the first line being the last thing pushed on the stack. The following information is included in each line of an *x*86 stack trace:

Parameter	Meaning
ChildEBP	The base pointer. This is an address on the stack.
RetAddr	The return address. This is the address that the processor returns to when it finishes executing the current thread. This is also the address of the instruction on the next line of the stack.
Args to Child	The first three arguments passed to the function when it was called. These are usually pointers, but can also be other values.
Function name and offset	The final piece of information is a function name and an offset into that function that identifies the location, in code, whose address was pushed on the stack.

The next example is from a DEC Alpha system that experienced STOP 0x0000002E:

```
Callee-SP       Arguments to Callee      Call Site
fc8e4f90 80403e08 : 80ae1060 00000000 00000000 00000000
KeBugCheckEx+0x58
fc8e5290 800c3ce8 : 80ae1060 00000000 00000000 00000000
HalMachineCheck+0x198
fc8e52d0 800c33b8 : 80ae1060 00000000 00000000 00000000
KiMachineCheck+0x28
fc8e52e0 800c1c20 : 80ae1060 00000000 00000000 00000000
KiDispatchException+0x68
fc8e55e0 800c1bcc : 80ae1060 00000000 00000000 00000000
KiExceptionDispatch+0x50
fc8e5680 80409d4c : 80ae1060 00000000 00000000 00000000
KiGeneralException+0x4
fc8e5880 f7361344 : 80ae1060 00000000 00000000 00000000
READ_REGISTER_UCHAR+0x6c
fc8e5880 f71313c4 : 80ae1060 00000000 00000000 00000000
AtalkReceiveIndication+0x654
fc8e5930 f71361a4 : 80ae1060 00000000 00000000 00000000
EthFilterDprIndicateReceive+0x234
fc8e5990 f713218c : 80ae1060 00000000 00000000 00000000
MiniportSendLoopback+0xb14
fc8e5a30 f71308d8 : 80ae1060 00000000 00000000 00000000
MiniportSyncSend+0x20c
fc8e5a70 f73628c0 : 80ae1060 00000000 00000000 00000000 NdisMSend+0x158

  800BC12C: B21DF170 stl       a0,KeBugCheckEx+80x4(gp)
800BC130: 0000001C call_pal    rdpcr
  800BC134: A0000CA0 ldl       v0,KeBugCheckEx+80x4(v0)
```

```
  800BC138: 22000060 lda      a0,KeBugCheckEx+80x5(v0)
  800BC13C: D3406778 bsr      ra,RtlCaptureContext
--->800BC140: 0000001C call_pal   rdpcr
  800BC144: A0000CA0 ldl      v0,KeBugCheckEx+t0x5(v0)
  800BC148: 22000060 lda      a0,KeBugCheckEx+t0x6(v0)
  800BC14C: D34006DC bsr      ra,KiSaveProcessorControlState
  800BC150: 0000001C call_pal   rdpcr
  800BC154: 45299801 xor      s0,76,t0
  800BC158: 221E00D0 lda      a0,KeBugCheckEx+o0x7(sp)
  800BC15C: A0000CA0 ldl      v0,KeBugCheckEx+o0x7(v0)
  800BC160: 223F0230 mov      KeBugCheckEx+E0x78,a1
  800BC164: 22400060 lda      a2,KeBugCheckEx+o0x7(v0)
  800BC168: D340803D bsr      ra,OtsMove
  800BC16C: 47EB0402 mov      s2,t1
```

In an Alpha stack trace, the Callee-SP parameter serves the same purpose as the ChildEBP parameter in the *x*86 stack. The number right after the Callee-SP is the return address, and the next four numbers are the arguments that were pushed on the stack. The values for these are usually 0 because a RISC-based system uses special registers and does not pass arguments on the stack.

!process

A **!process** command without any parameters lists information on the process currently running on the active processor. Its output looks exactly the same as the output in the **!process 0 7** section, except that it is only for one process, and no thread information is listed.

!thread

A **!thread** command without any parameters behaves exactly as a **!process** command without any parameters, and lists the thread that is currently running. The thread output looks exactly the same as the output in the **!process 0 7** section.

Note There are three very similar versions of the same information so it is easier to find which thread(s) are currently executing. A **!process 0 7** command lists all process and thread information, which results in 10–15 pages of data just for the process and thread output. Picking out the process or thread that is currently running from this long list can be difficult.

Dump Analysis Heuristics for Bugcode

This section appears in a dump for the processor that actually caused the trap only. This section includes information specific to the STOP code and can be very important. The exact information presented in this section varies for different STOP codes, but it lists the address at which the STOP occurred and any more information that is available.

This is an example from STOP 0x0000000A:

```
*****************************************************************
** Dump Analysis Heuristics for Bugcode IRQL_NOT_LESS_OR_EQUAL
*****************************************************************
*
Invalid Address Referenced: 0x00000020
IRQL:            2
Access Type:        Write
Code Address:       0xfa6325a5
```

This example is from a STOP 0x0000001E:

```
*****************************************************************
** Dump Analysis Heuristics for Bugcode KMODE_EXCEPTION_NOT_HANDLED
*****************************************************************
*
Exception Code:       0xc0000005
Address of Exception:     0x801704a7
Parameter #0:       0x00000001
Parameter #1:       0x00000001
```

Common STOP Codes

By looking through the Memory.txt output of common STOP codes, you can sometimes identify the module or driver that caused the problem. Given this information, you might be able to determine whether a service pack or update to Windows NT will fix the problem. In many cases, you will still need to contact support personnel, but looking at the Memory.txt output gives you an idea about what is wrong.

STOP 0x0000000A IRQL_NOT_LESS_OR_EQUAL

STOP 0x0000000A indicates that a kernel mode process or driver attempted to access a memory address that it did not have permission to access. The most common cause of this error is a bad or corrupted pointer to an incorrect location in memory. A pointer is a variable used by a program to refer to a block of memory. If the variable has an incorrect value in it, then the program tries to access memory that it should not be using.

When this occurs in a user-mode application, it generates an access violation.

When it occurs in kernel mode, it generates a STOP 0x0000000A message. This trap can be caused by either hardware or software. Contact support personnel to determine the exact cause.

To determine the general cause of a STOP 0x0000000A message, look at the Stack Trace for Processor X section of the Memory.txt file. If you have a multiprocessor system, check the output for all processors and look for a stack trace that has a line similar to the following at the top of the stack:

```
ChildEBP RetAddr Args to Child
f88b6e00 f89805b0 fb55ea88 fb55e988 fb55ea88 KiTrap0E+0x252 (FPO:
[0,0,0])
```

This is the processor on which the trap occurred. After the stack trace section, additional information on the trap appears in the Dump Analysis Heuristics section. To determine the module that caused the trap, look at the line on the stack trace occurring immediately after the line in the preceding example. This line is usually the line of code that caused the trap. From this information, you can identify the module in which the trap occurred. For example, the top lines of the stack trace can read:

```
ChildEBP RetAddr Args to Child
fa679758 fa6325a5 fcdb0b58 fccd3770 02611e6c KiTrap0E+0x252
fa6797e0 fa63ae8e fcc37528 fa67992e fccd3770 FindNameOrQuery+0x141
fa679838 fa6444a5 fa679854 fa6a33d0 fa6798d0 NbtConnect+0x3ae
fa679860 fa630393 fccd3770 fcdb2e08 fa679900 NTConnect+0x2b
```

The first line of the stack trace contains the reference to KiTrap0E and the second line contains FindNameOrQuery+0x141, which means that the processor trap occurred in the function FindNameOrQuery.

STOP 0x0000001E KMODE_EXCEPTION_NOT_HANDLED

STOP 0x0000001E can also be caused by either hardware or software. It is caused by hardware more often than a STOP 0x0000000A is, but can be caused by software.

When looking at **dumpexam** output from STOP 0x0000001E, you see two stack trace listings for the processor on which the STOP occurred. The first listing is the stack after the trap occurred, which shows only the kernel calls made to handle the trap and does not include any information about what code caused the trap.

The second listing shows the stack just before the trap occurred. This is the listing you use for your analysis. The register dump for the processor is also duplicated, with the first dump showing the status of the registers after the trap and the second showing the state of the registers when the trap occurred. These two sets of information are separated by a section that looks like the following:

```
*****************************************************************
** !exr fca49c20
*****************************************************************
*
Exception Record @ FCA49C20:

  ExceptionCode: c0000005
 ExceptionFlags: 00000000
 Chained Record: 00000000
ExceptionAddress: 801704a7
NumberParameters: 00000002

  Parameter[0]: 00000001
  Parameter[1]: 00000001
```

This section includes the following information:

Parameter	Meaning
ExceptionCode	A status code that identifies what type of exception occurred. In this case, the code is c0000005, which indicates an access violation. To find out what a particular status code means, contact support personnel.
ExceptionAddress	The address of the instruction that caused the STOP.

The first stack trace from STOP 0x0000001E, the one that does not provide any useful information, looks like the following:

```
ChildEBP RetAddr Args to Child
fca49968 8013387e fca49990 801367ab fca49998
PspUnhandledExceptionInSystemThread+0x18 (FPO: [0,0,0])
fca49970 801367ab fca49998 00000000 fca49998 PspSystemThreadStartup+0x4a
(FPO: [0,0,0])
fca49f7c 8013e452 fca54bae 00000001 00000000 _except_handler3+0x47
00000000 00000000 00000000 00000000 00000000 KiThreadStartup+0x16
```

To determine where the trap occurred, ignore this stack and look at the second listing, after the **!exr** entry. The first line in this listing indicates the location in code that caused the trap.

With STOP 0x0000001E, it is also useful to compare the exception address listed in the **!exr** section to the list of device drivers in the **!drivers** section of the Memory.txt file. If the trap was caused by a specific driver, this address falls into the address range in the drivers list. If this is the case, it can indicate a problem either with the device that the driver controls or with the driver itself. Here is an example:

```
FramePtr RetAddr  Param1   Param2   Param3   Function Name
fa1bcda4 8010e244 fcff3940 00000000 00000220 NT!PsReturnPoolQuota+0xe
fa1bcdd4 80117085 fcbee668 fcddf648 fcbff020 NT!ExFreePool+0x16c
fa1bce24 8011c60b fcddf648 fa1bce58 fa1bce54 NT!IopCompleteRequest+0xbd
fa1bce5c 8013de15 00000000 00000000 00000000 NT!KiDeliverApc+0x83
fa1bce7c 8011a1ce 00000000 00000000 80179a01 NT!@KiSwapThread@0+0x15d
fa1bcea0 80179b3f fcc4bf60 00000006 80179a01 NT!KeWaitForSingleObject+0x1c2
fa1bcef0 80139b09 00000114 00000001 00000000 NT!NtWaitForSingleObject+0xaf
fa1bcef0 77f893eb 00000114 00000001 00000000 NT!KiSystemService+0xa9
00000000 00000000 00000000 00000000 00000000 NTDLL!ZwWaitForSingleObject+0xb
```

STOP 0x0000007F UNEXPECTED_KERNEL_MODE_TRAP

STOP 0x0000007F usually occurs in the processor itself and almost always indicates a hardware fault. There are several kinds of STOP 0x0000007F, which you can determine by the first parameter of the STOP code, found in the Windows NT Crash Dump Analysis section at the beginning of the Memory.txt file.

The following are common kernel mode traps:

First Parameter	Meaning
0x00000000	Divide by zero error
0x00000004	Arithmetic overflow
0x00000006	Invalid opcode
0x00000008	Double fault

A divide by zero error is caused when a DIV instruction is executed and the divisor is 0. This can be caused by problems which need to be investigated further, such as memory corruption, hardware problems, or software failures.

Here is an example of a divide by zero error:

```
ChildEBP RetAddr Args to Child
8019d778 8013cdcc fe483688 00000000 00000000 NT!_KiSystemFatalException+0xe
 (FPO: [0,0] TrapFrame @ 8019d778)
8019d7e8 fbb053be 0001440d 000004a9 000004a9 NT!_RtlEnlargedUnsignedDivide+0xc
 (FPO: [4,0,0])
8019d80c 8010f613 0001440d 000004a9 fe482bd0 bhnt!_BhStationQueryTimeout+0x44
 (FPO: [4,0,1])
8019d820 fb910aa6 fe50a000 fe44255a fe44254c NT!_KeSetTimer+0x8f
8019d85c fb9409b3 fe4820c8 fe44255a fe44254c
 NDIS!_EthFilterDprIndicateReceive+0x111
8019d894 fb94044a fe482b98 fe483688 ffdff401 netflx!NetFlexProcessEthRcv+0x85
8019d8ac fb910ba1 fe482aa8 fb910b30 00000001
 netflx!_NetFlexHandleInterrupt+0x4a
8019d8c4 80137c06 fe482bac fe482b98 00000000 NDIS!_NdisMDpc+0x71 (FPO: [EBP
 0xfb910b30] [4,0,4])
fb910b30 18247c8b 8b34778b 4e8d106f d015ff30 NT!_KiIdleLoop+0x5a
kd> !trap 8019d778
eax=0001440d ebx=00000003 ecx=8019d81c edx=000004a9 esi=fe4820c8 edi=fe46a188
eip=8013cdcc esp=8019d7ec ebp=8019d820 iopl=0     nv up ei pl zr na po nc
cs=0008 ss=0010 ds=0023 es=0023 fs=0030 gs=0000       efl=00010246
ErrCode = 00000000
8013cdcc f774240c     div   dword ptr [esp+0xc]
```

An arithmetic overflow error occurs when the result of a multiplication operation is larger than a 32-bit integer. This error can be caused by a software failure, but it is also frequently a hardware problem.

An invalid opcode error occurs when the processor attempts to execute an instruction that is not defined. This error is almost always caused by hardware memory corruption. If you receive this error, run memory diagnostics on your regular memory and both L1 and L2 cache memory.

A double fault trap occurs when two kernel-mode traps occur simultaneously and the processor is unable to handle them. This trap is almost always caused by hardware failure.

If a particular trap can be caused by either software or hardware, more analysis is required to determine which is the cause. If you suspect a hardware problem, try the following hardware troubleshooting steps:

1. Run diagnostic software to test the RAM in the computer. Replace any RAM reported to be bad. Also, make sure that all the RAM in the computer is the same speed.
2. Try removing or swapping controllers, cards, or other peripherals.
3. Try a different motherboard on the computer.

PART IX

Appendixes

A P P P E N D I X   A

Answer Files and UDFs

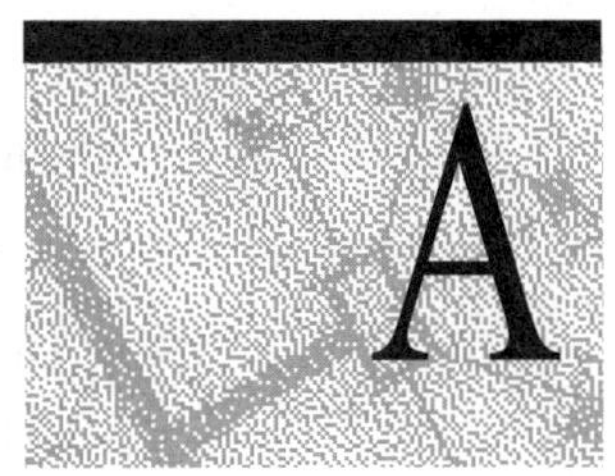

When Windows NT Workstation or Windows NT Server is installed using the **winnt /u:***answer_file* or **winnt32 /u:***answer_file* command, the options specified in the answer file (Unattend.txt) are applied to the installation. If the **/udf:***uniqueness_database_file* option is also specified on the **winnt** or **winnt32** command line, the entries in the specified uniqueness database file (UDF) are also applied, overriding entries in the answer file.

For information on editing and using answer files and UDFs, see Chapter 2, "Customizing Setup," of the *Windows NT Workstation 4.0 Resource Guide*. This Appendix describes the sections and keys used in these files. Additional entries may be listed in the sample Unattend.txt file on the product compact disc.

Sections in Answer Files and UDFs

Information in the answer file is divided into sections. Each section begins with the section name in square brackets, on a line by itself. Each section may contain one or more keys, with associated values. Each key is a character string, recognizable by the Setup program, that controls an element of the configuration to be installed. For example, there is a key to specify the computername, a key to specify whether the primary partition is converted to NTFS, and a key to specify the time zone for the computer.

The same sections and keys are used in the UDFs, provided they are used after text-mode setup. Information that the Setup program uses during text-mode setup can only be specified in the answer file, not in the UDF.

The sections are:

[Unattended]
The keys in this section define the behavior of the Setup program during text mode setup. This section can only be specified in the answer file, not in the UDF.

[OEMBootFiles]
To install onto x86 computers, OEM\OEMFILES\TXTSETUP.OEM and all files listed in it (HALs and drivers), must be listed in this section. This section can only be specified in the answer file, not in the UDF.

[MassStorageDrivers]
This section is used to specify SCSI drivers. This section can only be specified in the answer file, not in the UDF.

[KeyboardDrivers]
This section is used to specify keyboard drivers. This section can only be specified in the answer file, not in the UDF.

[PointingDeviceDrivers]
This section is used to specify pointing device drivers. This section can only be specified in the answer file, not in the UDF.

[OEM_Ads]
This section describes a banner, logo, and background bitmap to be displayed during GUI-mode setup.

[DisplayDrivers]
This section is used to specify display drivers.

[Display]
This section is used to specify settings for video display.

[DetectedMassStorage]
This section is used to specify mass storage devices that Setup is to recognize, even if they are not physically present on the system at the time you perform the installation. This section can only be specified in the answer file, not in the UDF.

[GuiUnattended]
: The keys in this section define the behavior of the Setup program during GUI mode setup.

[UserData]
: The keys in this section specify information associated with each user or computer.

[LicenseFilePrintData]
: This section pertains only to installations of Windows NT Server. It is used to supply information regarding the license agreement.

[Network]
: This section is used to specify settings used for networking, such as protocols and adapters. If this section is not present, support for networking will not be installed.

[Modem]
: This section header is used to identify whether a modem should be installed or not. It is used by RAS to install a modem if **DeviceType = Modem** is in the list of RAS parameters.

Some of the keys in these sections point to additional sections, which you must create and name. For example, to install protocols other than the defaults, you need to use the InstallProtocols key in the [Network] section to identify the name of the section in which the protocols are listed. You must also create and populate the section pointed to in the Install Protocols key.

Adding Specific Functionality to Your Customized Setup

The keys you can add to the answer file or UDF are listed in the remainder of this Appendix, grouped according to the kind of effect they produce.

Preferred Options in the Retail Product

These options affect the choices a user can make while installing the retail version of Windows NT Workstation.

Preserving Settings of Existing Windows NT Workstation Systems

By default, Setup installs Windows NT Workstation 4.0 with the retail default settings, except where different settings are specified in the answer file and the UDFs. As an option, you can have Setup upgrade existing installations of Windows NT Workstation, with the system settings intact.

To preserve existing settings when upgrading from an earlier version of Windows NT Workstation, add the following line to the [Unattended] section:

```
NtUpgrade = manual | yes | no | single
```

Where:

manual
: indicates that the user is to be prompted as to whether the existing installation is to be completely replaced, or upgraded with system settings intact. If the user chooses to replace the existing version, he or she will also be prompted to specify a directory in which to install Windows NT Workstation 4.0. If the user chooses to retain existing settings, the remainder of the settings in the answer file and in the UDF will be ignored.

yes
: indicates that the existing installation of Windows NT Workstation is to be upgraded with system settings intact. If **NtUpgrade = yes**, the remainder of the settings in the answer file and in the UDF will be ignored. If multiple installations are detected, the settings in first installation detected are used. On x86-based systems, the system that is listed first in the Boot.ini file is the first installation detected. On Alpha AXP–based, MIPS-based, and PowerPC-based systems, the first installation is the first one listed in the Startup Environment.

no
: indicates that the existing installation of Windows NT Workstation is to be completely replaced. The retail default settings will be used, except where keys in the answer file or UDF override them. This is the default option.

single
: indicates that if only one existing installation of Windows NT Workstation is detected, it is to be upgraded with system settings intact. If multiple previous installations are detected, the user must indicate which settings are to be retained.

This key can only be specified in the answer file, not in the UDF.

Preserving Settings of Existing Windows for Workgroups 3.1 or Windows 3.1 Systems

By default, Setup installs Windows NT Workstation 4.0 with the retail default settings, except where different settings are specified in the answer file and the UDFs. As an option, you can have Setup upgrade existing installations of Windows for Workgroups 3.1 or Windows 3.1, with the system settings intact.

To preserve existing settings when upgrading from either of these systems, add the following line to the [Unattended] section:

```
Win31Upgrade = yes | no
```

Where:

yes
: indicates that if an existing installation of Windows for Workgroups 3.1 or Windows 3.1 is detected, the existing settings are to be preserved.

no
: indicates that the existing installation of Windows NT Workstation is to be completely replaced. The retail default settings will be used, except where keys in the answer file or UDF override them. This is the default option.

If any other values are supplied for the Win31Upgrade key, the user will be prompted to specify whether the settings should be retained.

This key can only be specified in the answer file, not in the UDF.

Specifying the Directory in Which to Install Windows NT Workstation

You can specify the directory on the destination computer in which the files for Windows NT Workstation 4.0 are to reside. To do so, add the following line to the [Unattended] section:

```
TargetPath = manual | * | path
```

Where:

manual
  indicates that the user is to be prompted for a directory.

*
  indicates that the Setup program is to generate a unique directory name, and place the Windows NT Workstation 4.0 files in that directory. This is the default option.

path
  indicates the name of the directory in which the Windows NT Workstation 4.0 files are to be placed. If the directory does not exist, it will be created.

This key can only be specified in the answer file, not in the UDF.

Replacing OEM Files with Windows NT Workstation Product Files

You can choose whether to replace older files that Setup finds on the system with files from the retail product that have the same name. By default, these files are overwritten.

To specify whether to keep the older versions of such files, add the following line to the [Unattended] section:

```
OverwriteOemFilesOnUpgrade = yes | no
```

If any Windows NT file in the existing installation has been overwritten by another application, you must set *OverwriteOEMFilesOnUpgrade = yes.*

This key can only be specified in the answer file, not in the UDF.

Converting to NTFS

In general, partitions greater than 512 MB should be converted to NTFS. To specify whether to convert the primary partition to NTFS during installation, add the following line to the [Unattended] section:

```
FileSystem = ConvertNTFS | LeaveAlone
```

Specifying When to Configure Graphics Devices

By default, graphics devices are configured during Setup. However, you can specify that the graphics devices be configured the first time someone logs on to the new system. To specify when the graphics devices are to be configured, add the following line to the [Display] section:

```
ConfigureAtLogon = 0 | 1
```

If **ConfigureAtLogon = 1**, no specific video setting is made during setup. Instead, the user is prompted to select the screen resolution the first time the computer is started after setup.

If **ConfigureAtLogon = 0**, graphics configuration will be done during setup. If this option is selected, the following other preconfiguration values may be set, also in the [Display] section:

```
BitsPerPel = n
XResolution = number_of_pixels
YResolution = number_of_pixels
VRefresh = n
Flags = n
```

If an entry has a value of 0, or the entry is not present, the defaults will be applied.

Table A.1 Default Values for Video Settings

Key	Default Value
BitsPerPel	8 If this is not a valid value, the lowest valid value is used.
XResolution	640 If this is not a valid value, the lowest valid value is used.
YResolution	480 If this is not a valid value, the lowest valid value is used.
VRefresh	60 Hz If this is not a valid value, the lowest valid value is used.
Flags	Any that are available.

For example, if all of these keys are set to = 0, the video settings would be 640x480, 256 colors, 60 Hz (as long as that mode exists).

As another example, if BitsPerPel = 16 and all other values are set to 0, then the card will be configured in 640x480, 64 K colors, and 60 Hz (again, as long as that mode exists).

Normally, the user is prompted to test the video settings. For an unattended installation, you might want the settings to be stored without testing. To specify whether the settings should be stored without testing, add the following line to the [Display] section:

```
AutoConfirm = 0 | 1
```

If **AutoConfirm = 0**, or if it is not specified, the video settings specified elsewhere in the [Display] section are used, and the user must test the selected video mode in order to save the setting and continue with setup.

If **AutoConfirm = 1**, the settings are stored with no user intervention.

Additional Files and Applications

This section describes keys you can add to the answer file or UDF to add your own files or information to the retail version of Windows NT Workstation.

Displaying Your Company Information During Setup

To specify your own advertising or information during GUI Mode Setup, the following section must exist:

```
[OEM_Ads]
Banner = text
Logo = file_name[, n]
Bitmap = file_name[, n]
```

The value of the **Banner** key is the text string to be displayed as a banner in the upper left of the screen during GUI Mode Setup. The text must contain the substring "Windows NT Workstation" or "Windows NT Server" in order to be displayed. To create a multi-line banner, insert an asterisk (*) where a line break is to appear. If the **Banner** key is empty or does not contain the "Windows NT Workstation" or "Windows NT Server" substring, the Windows NT retail banner will be displayed.

The value of the **Logo** key is the filename of a bitmap to be displayed in the upper right corner of the screen during GUI Mode Setup. If your bitmap is referenced in a dynamic link library (DLL), you can specify the name of the DLL followed by the resource ID. The DLL must be in OEM\Oemfiles, and the resource ID must be supplied in base-10 format. If only a file name is specified, it must be the name of a .bmp file in OEM\Oemfiles that contains the bitmap.

If the **Logo** key is not specified, or its value is empty, or it specifies a non-existent bitmap, then the Windows NT retail bitmap will be displayed.

The value of the **Bitmap** key is the name of a bitmap that is to be tiled as a background during end-user setup.

If your bitmap is referenced in a dynamic link library (DLL), you can specify the name of the DLL followed by the resource ID. The DLL must be in OEM\Oemfiles, and the resource ID must be supplied in base-10 format. If only a file name is specified, it must be the name of a .bmp file in OEM\Oemfiles that contains the bitmap.

If the **Bitmap** key is not specified, or its value is empty, or it specifies a non-existent bitmap, then the Windows NT retail bitmap will be displayed.

For best results on VGA-based displays this bitmap should be exactly 640 x 480 pixels. On ARC computers (which do not necessarily use VGA mode during setup) other optimal sizes may be possible. If the bitmap is monochrome, it will be tinted blue when displayed (like the retail background bitmap, which is itself monochrome).

Running a Program Concurrently with Setup

To run a custom program concurrently with Setup, add the following line to the [GuiUnattended] section:

```
DetachedProgram = path\filename
```

where *path* and *filename* describe the location of the custom program. For example:

```
DetachedProgram = c:\mt32\mtrun.exe
```

To supply arguments to the custom program, add the following line to the [GuiUnattended] section:

```
Arguments = path\filename/argument
```

where *path\filename* indicates the path to the program and *argument* indicates the arguments you want to supply. For example:

```
Arguments = c:\mt32\script1.pcd/H
```

Using Files You Supply in the Subdirectories of OEM

To include files you have added to customize the application, the following line must be present in the [Unattended] section:

```
OemPreinstall = Yes
```

A **Yes** value indicates that Windows NT Setup might need to install some OEM-supplied files located in subdirectories of OEM.

The default value is **No**. The default is used when the **OemPreinstall** key is missing. The **No** value implies that Setup will perform a regular unattended installation.

This key can only be specified in the answer file, not in the UDF. The keys described in the following sections are used only if **OemPreinstall = Yes**.

Installing Display Drivers

To install display drivers, include the following section:

```
[DisplayDrivers]
driver_description = Retail | OEM
.
```

This section is optional. If the [DisplayDrivers] section is empty or absent, Setup will install all the Windows NT retail display drivers during Text Mode Setup. During GUI Mode Setup, any drivers that fail to initialize will be disabled.

The *driver_description* value identifies the driver to be installed. This value must match one of the strings defined in the right-hand side of the [Display] section of Txtsetup.sif (except for the string **"Standard VGA (640x480, 16 colors)"** or Txtsetup.oem (for an OEM-supplied driver).

This key can only be specified in the answer file, not in the UDF. This section is valid only if **OemPreinstall = Yes**.

Installing SCSI Drivers

To install SCSI drivers, include the following section:

```
[MassStorageDrivers]
driver_description = Retail | OEM
.
```

This section is optional. If the [MassStorageDrivers] section is empty or absent, Setup will attempt to detect and install all known miniport drivers.

The *driver_description* value identifies the driver to be installed. This value must match one of the strings defined in the [SCSI] section of Txtsetup.sif or Txtsetup.oem (for an OEM-supplied driver).

This key can only be specified in the answer file, not in the UDF. This section is valid only if **OemPreinstall = Yes**.

Installing Keyboard Drivers

To specify keyboard drivers to be installed, include the following section:

```
[KeyboardDrivers]
driver_description = Retail | OEM
.
```

This section is optional. If the [KeyboardDrivers] section is absent or empty, Setup will detect and install a keyboard driver from the retail Windows NT product.

The *driver_description* value identifies the driver to be installed. This string must match one of the strings defined in the [Keyboard] section of the Txtsetup.sif or Txtsetup.oem (for an OEM-supplied driver).

This key can only be specified in the answer file, not in the UDF. This section is valid only if **OemPreinstall = Yes**.

Installing Pointing Device Drivers

To install pointing device drivers, include the following section

```
[PointingDeviceDrivers]
driver_description = Retail | OEM
:
```

This section is optional. If the [PointingDeviceDrivers] section is absent or empty, Setup will detect and install a pointing device driver from the retail Windows NT product.

The *driver_description* value identifies the driver to be installed. This string must match one of the strings defined in the [Mouse] section of Txtsetup.sif or Txtsetup.oem (for an OEM-supplied driver).

This key can only be specified in the answer file, not in the UDF. This section is valid only if **OemPreinstall = Yes**.

Networking Options

If networking is to be installed, you must include a [Network] section. If this section header is missing, network installation will be skipped. If the section is present but empty, the user will be presented with various error messages.

Specifying Manual Installation of Network Components

If you want the network components to be installed interactively during an otherwise unattended installation, include the following line in the [Network] section:

```
Attend = Yes
```

For the installation of network components to proceed without user intervention, this key must be absent.

Detecting Network Adapters

To detect network adapter cards installed on a computer, the following must be specified under the [Network] section:

```
DetectAdapters = adapters_section[,adapters_section]. . .
```

The value for the **DetectAdapters** key is a user-defined section name. For example, you could name a section [DetectAdaptersData] and specify it in this key. Create this section, and add to it the following keys:

```
DetectCount = number_of_cards_to_detect
LimitTo = inf_option [, inf_option] . . .
inf_option = parameter_section
```

The **DetectCount** key specifies the number of detection attempts Setup should make. The default is 1. If more cards than the number specified in **DetectCount** are present, the additional cards will not be detected.

The **LimitTo** key specifies a list of cards; detection will be limited to cards in that list. If this key is not present, any detectable adapters will be installed. The values can be obtained from the network-adapter INF files.

Each *inf_option* listed in the **LimitTo** key can also be listed as a key. The value of these keys will be the parameter normally associated with a network adapter. The values listed here will override detected values.

To detect and install only the first network adapter card, use following line under the [Network] section:

```
DetectAdapters = ""
```

Note that there is no space between the beginning and end quotation marks.

If neither the DetectAdapters key nor the InstallAdapters key (described under "Installing Network Adapter" later in this appendix) is present, user participation will be required. If DetectAdapters is present but contains no value, then the first adapter is detected and installed. The DetectAdapters and InstallAdapters keys can both be present.

Example

```
[Network]
   InstallProtocols = SelectedProtocolsList

[SelectedProtocolsList]
   TC = TCPIPParameters
   ATALK = AppleTalkParameters
```

Installing Network Adapters

To install network adapters, the following key must be included in the [Network] section:

```
InstallAdapters = adapters_list_section[, adapters_list_section]. . .
```

The value for the **InstallAdapters** key is a user-defined section name. For example, you could name a section [InstallAdaptersList] and specify it in this key. All network adapters listed in the [InstallAdaptersList] section would then be installed. Create this section, and add to it a line for each adapter to be installed, using the following format:

```
inf_option = parameter_section[, oem_path]
```

If the **InstallAdapters** key and the **DetectAdapters** key are not present, user participation will be required.

Each *inf_option* key in this section defines the *inf_option* to be installed. The answers for the *inf_option* key are adapter-specific. If the adapter is an OEM-supplied card, the path can be specified.

Example

```
[Network]
   InstallAdapters = SelectedAdaptersList

[SelectedAdaptersList]
   NE2000 = NovelParameters
   ELNKII = 3ComParameters
   MSNETULTRA = MacrosoftNetUltraParameters, A:\
```

Note For network adapters, you must know and specify the necessary parameters for the cards you want to preinstall. To determine whether a card supports unattended setup, search for **stf_unattended** in the INFs for that card.

Installing Network Services

To install network services, the following keys should be specified under the [Network] section:

```
InstallServices = services_list_section[, services_list_section] . . .
```

All services listed will be installed. If the **InstallServices** key is absent, no extra services will be installed.

The value for the **InstallServices** key is a user-defined section name. Create the section named by the **InstallServices** key, and in it list the service to be installed, using the following syntax:

```
inf_option = parameter_section[, oem_path]
```

Each *inf_option* key in this section defines the options to be installed. The value for this key is a user-defined section name and the OEM source path, if necessary. Create the section named by the *inf_option* key, and in it list the parameters to be used.

Example

```
[Network]
   InstallServices = SelectedServicesList

[SelectedServicesList]
   SFM = ServicesForMacParameters
   WINS = WINServiceParameters
```

Installing Network Protocols

To detect network adapter cards installed on a computer, the following must be specified under the [Network] section:

```
InstallProtocols = protocol_list_section[, protocol_list_section] . . .
```

The value for the **InstallProtocols** key is a user-defined section name. For example, you could name a section [InstallProtocolsList] and specify it in this key. Create this section, and add to it a line for each protocol to be installed, using the following format:

```
inf_option = parameter_section[, oem_path]
```

The value on the left of the equals sign, *inf_option*, is the notation for the protocol, as it appears in the [Options] section of the INF file for that protocol. Protocol INFs have the filename Oemxp*xx*.inf, where *xx* refers to a particular protocol. The value on the right of the equals sign is a user-defined section name and the OEM source path, if necessary. Create the section named by the *inf_option* key, and in it list the parameters to be used for that protocol.

All protocols listed will be installed. If this key is not present, the default protocols will be installed and user participation might be required for Setup to continue.

Specifying the TCP/IP protocol is one case within the general topic of installing protocols, and is discussed in the section, "Installing TCP/IP."

Example

```
[Network]
   InstallProtocols = SelectedProtocolsList

[SelectedProtocolsList]
   TC = TCPIPParameters
   ATALK = AppleTalkParameters
```

Installing NetBEUI

To install NetBEUI, it must be specified in the "*protocol_list_section*" section specified by the **InstallProtocols** key described in the [Network] section. This is described under "Installing Network Protocols" earlier in this Appendix. In the *protocol_list_section*, include the following line:

```
NBF = NetBEUI_parameters_section
```

The section you specify as the value for NBF must exist, but is empty since NetBEUI does not require any parameters. For example, your answer file might include the following lines:

```
[Network]
   InstallProtocols = SelectedProtocolsList

[SelectedProtocolsList]
   NBF = NetBEUI_params
   TC = TCPIPParameters

[NetBEUI_params]

[TCPIPParameters]
   .
   .
   .
```

Installing TCP/IP

To install TCP/IP, it must be specified in the section specified by the **InstallProtocols** key described in the [Network] section. This is described under "Installing Network Protocols" earlier in this Appendix. Create a separate section for the parameters, and refer to it in the section specified by the **InstallProtocols** key

The supported TCP/IP parameters are as follows:

```
DHCP = Yes | No
ScopeID = scope_ID
```

If you have set DHCP = No, you must also provide the following parameters. For a discussion of these parameters see Chapter 7, "Using Microsoft DHCP Servers," in the *Windows NT Server Networking Guide*.

```
IPAddress = ddd.ddd.ddd.ddd
Subnet = ddd.ddd.ddd.ddd
Gateway = ddd.ddd.ddd.ddd
DNSServer = IPAddress, IPAddress, IPAddress
            ;Up to 3 IP addresses can be specified
WINSPrimary = IPAddress
WINSSecondary = IPAddress
DNSName = DNS_Domain_Name
```

Both TCP/IP and SNMP allow you to configure computers on a *site basis* and/or on a *computer-specific basis*. A site-based configuration configures each computer with identical parameters, whereas a computer-specific configuration allows a computer to have unique parameters. These two configurations can be mixed together. The generic or site-specific parameters are processed first. If computer-specific parameters exist, they are overlaid on the site-specific ones.

Example: TCP/IP without DHCP

```
[Network]
    InstallProtocols = SelectedProtocolsList

[SelectedProtocolsList]
TC = TCPIPParameters

[TCPIPParameters]

DHCP     = NO
IPAddress          = 192.9.1.1
Subnet       = 255.0.0.0
Gateway      = 111.1.1.1
DNSServer          = 192.9.1.7, 192.9.1.8, 192.9.1.9
WINSPrimary = 111.2.2.2
WINSSecondary    = 111.3.3.3
DNSName      = microsoft.com
ScopeID      = This_is_the_scope_id
```

Example: TCP/IP with DHCP, and adding DNS and WINS parameters

```
[Network]
    InstallProtocols = SelectedProtocolsList

[SelectedProtocolsList]
TC = TCPIPParameters

[TCPIPParameters]

DHCP     = YES
DNSServer        = 192.9.1.7, 192.9.1.8, 192.9.1.9
WINSPrimary = 111.2.2.2
DNSName      = microsoft.com
ScopeID      = This_is_the_scope_id
```

Installing the SNMP Service

To install the Simple Network Management Protocol (SNMP) service, it must be specified in the section that you create and that you specify in the **InstallServices** key. The **InstallServices** key is described under "Installing Network Services" earlier in this Appendix. On the line that specifies the protocol, you name the section (also created by you) that contains the parameters for the protocol. This is illustrated in the example at the end of this section.

The supported parameters are as follows:

```
Accept_CommunityName = Name1, Name2, Name3   ;maximum of 3 names
Send_Authentication = Yes | No
Any_Host = Yes | No
Limit_Host = host1, host2, host3             ;limit to 3 hosts
Community_Name = name
Traps = IPaddress | IPXaddress               ;maximum of 3 addresses
Contact_Name = name                          ;limit to 1 name
Location = location_name                     ;limit to 1 name
Service = Physical, Applications, Datalink, Internet, EndToEnd
    ; Any combination is valid
```

For a discussion of these parameters, see Chapter 11, "Using SNMP for Network Management," in the *Windows NT Server Networking Guide*.

If a parameter is an IP address, all four octets must be specified in dotted decimal notation only.

Both TCP/IP and SNMP allow you to configure computers on a site basis and/or on a computer-specific basis. A site-based configuration configures each computer with identical parameters, whereas a computer-specific configuration allows a computer to have unique parameters. These two configurations can be mixed together. The generic or site-specific parameters are processed first. If computer-specific parameters exist, they are overlaid on the site-specific ones.

Example

```
[Network]
    InstallServices = SelectedServicesList

[SelectedServicesList]
SNMP = SNMPParameters

[SNMPParameters]
    Accept_CommunityName= MicrosoftCommunity
    Send_Authentication = YES
    Any_Host           = NO
    Limit_Host           = HostSystem

    Community_Name       = MyCommunity
    Traps                = 1234567890AB, 192.001.001, 3456123456

    Contact_Name       = NT_Administration
    Location             = Building_26
    Service            = Physical, Datalink, Internet
```

Installing NWLNKIPX

To install NWLNKIPX, it must be specified in the "*protocol_list_section*" section specified by the **InstallProtocols** key described in the [Network] section. This is described under "Installing Network Protocols" earlier in this Appendix. In the *protocol_list_section*, include the following line:

```
NWLNKIPX = NetBEUI_parameters_section
```

The section you specify as the value for NWLNKIPX must exist, but is empty since NWLNKIPX does not require any parameters. For example, your answer file might include the following lines:

```
[Network]
   InstallProtocols = SelectedProtocolsList

[SelectedProtocolsList]
   NWLNKIPX = NWLNKIPX _params
   TC = TCPIPParameters

[NWLNKIPX _params]

[TCPIPParameters]
    .
    .
    .
```

Installing Client Service for NetWare (NWWKSTA Option)

To install Client Service for NetWare, it must be specified in the section specified by the **InstallServices** key (the **InstallServices** key is included in the [Network] section). To the section specified by the **InstallServices** key, add the following line:

```
NWWKSTA = NetWareClientParametersSection
```

You can assign any name for the *NetWareClientParametersSection*. Create a section with that name and specify the NetWare client parameters that you want to use in that section. The recognized parameters are as follows:

```
DefaultLocation = server_location
DefaultScriptOptions = 0 | 1 | 3
```

DefaultLocation identifies the default logon server for the NetWare client. The DefaultScriptOptions key specifies the default action to take with scripts, and can be assigned any of the following values:

0	Do not run a script
1	Run NW 3.x level scripts only
3	Run NW 3.x or NW 4.x scripts

Example

```
[Network]
InstallServices = SelectedServicesList

[SelectedServicesList]
NWWKSTA = ClientNetwareParameters

[ClientNetwareParameters]
DefaultLocation = NWServer
DefaultScriptOptions = 0
```

Installing Remote Access Service (RAS)

To install Remote Access Service (RAS), include the following line in the section you defined with the InstallServices key in the [Network] section:

```
RAS = RAS_parameters_section
```

where *RAS_parameters_section* is a section that you define and use to specify the following parameters:

```
PortSections        = MYCOM1, MYCOM2, MYCOM3-25
DialoutProtocols= TCP/IP | IPX | NETBEUI | ALL>
DialinProtocols     = TCP/IP | IPX | NETBEUI | ALL
NetBEUIClientAccess = Network | ThisComputer
```

```
TcpIpClientAccess    = Network | ThisComputer
UseDHCP          = YES | NO
StaticAddressBegin  = IP_address
StaticAddressEnd IP_address
ExcludeAddress      = IP_address1-IP_address2
ClientCanRequestIPAddress    = YES | NO
IpxClientAccess     = Network | ThisComputer
AutomaticNetworkNumbers = YES | NO
NetworkNumberFrom    = IPX_net_number
AssignSameNetworkNumber = YES | NO
ClientsCanRequestIpxNodeNumber  YES | NO
```

Defaults and restrictions are as follows:

PortSections	Any number of port section names
DialoutProtocols	ALL implies all installed protocols
DialinProtocols	ALL implies all installed protocols
NetBEUIClientAccess	Default is Network
TcpIpClientAccess	Default is Network
UseDHCP	Default is YES
StaticAddressBegin	Required if UseDHCP = NO
StaticAddressEnd	Required if UseDHCP = NO
ExcludeAddress	One or more ranges, comma separated. StaticAddressBegin and StaticAddressEnd should be specified.
ClientCanRequestIPAddress	Default is NO
IpxClientAccess	Default is Network
AutomaticNetworkNumbers	Default is YES
NetworkNumberFrom	1 to 0xFFFFFFFE; required if AutomaticNetworkNumbers is NO
AssignSameNetworkNumber	Default is YES
ClientsCanRequestIpxNodeNumber	Default is NO
DeviceType = Modem	

If you have specified a "*PortSection*" you must create the section, which can have the following keys:

```
PortName = COM1 | COM2 | COM3-COM25
DeviceType = Modem
DeviceName = device_name
PortUsage = DialOut | DialIn | DialInOut
```

Where:

PortName
: indicates the names of the ports to be configured in a particular port section.

DeviceType
: indicates the type of device RAS should install. For the current release of Windows NT Workstation, the only available device type is a modem. If **DeviceType = Modem**, the **InstallModem** key must be included in the [Modem] section.

DeviceName
: specifies the name of the device to be installed.

PortUsage
: defines the dialing properties for the ports being configured.

For a discussion of RAS features and parameters, see Chapter 5, "Understanding Remote Access Service," in the *Networking Supplement* included with the product documentation.

Example: RAS Using One Dialout Port

```
[Network]
   InstallServices = SelectedServicesList

[SelectedServicesList]
   RAS = RemoteAccessParameters

[RemoteAccessParameters]
   PortSections = MYCOM1
   DialoutProtocols = TCP/IP

[MYCOM1]
   PortName      = COM1
   DeviceType        = Modem
   DeviceName        = "Intel Fax Modem 144e"
   PortUsage     = DialOut
```

Example: RAS Using One Dialout, One Dialin and Four Dialin and Dialout Ports, With All Installed Protocols

This configuration uses default values for all protocols:

```
[Network]
   InstallServices = SelectedServicesList

[SelectedServicesList]
   RAS = RemoteAccessParameters
```

```
[RemoteAccessParameters]
   PortSections = Dialin, Dialout, Dialinout
   DialoutProtocols = ALL
   DialinProtocols  = ALL

[Dialin]
   PortName     = COM1
   DeviceType       = Modem
   DeviceName       = "USR Sportster V.34"
   PortUsage    = DialOut

[Dialout]
   PortName     = COM2
   DeviceType       = Modem
   DeviceName       = "USR Sportster V.34"
   PortUsage    = DialOut

[Dialinout]
   PortName     = COM3-COM6
   DeviceType       = Modem
   DeviceName       = "USR Sportster V.34"
   PortUsage    = DialInOut
```

Example: RAS 16 Dialin Ports, With TCP/IP and DHCP Enabled

```
[Network]
   InstallServices = SelectedServicesList

[SelectedServicesList]
   RAS = RemoteAccessParameters

[RemoteAccessParameters]
   PortSections          = InternetPorts
   DialoutProtocols          = TCP/IP
   DialinProtocols           = TCP/IP
   TcpIpClientAccess         = Network
   UseDHCP               = YES
   ClientCanRequestIPAddress     = NO

[InternetPorts]
   PortName              = COM3-COM17
   DeviceType                = Modem
   DeviceName                = "USR Sportster V.34"
   PortUsage             = DialIn
```

Example: RAS 16 Dialin Ports, With TCP/IP and Static IP Address Pool

```
[Network]
   InstallServices = SelectedServicesList

[SelectedServicesList]
   RAS = RemoteAccessParameters

[RemoteAccessParameters]
   PortSections          = InternetPorts
   DialoutProtocols          = TCP/IP
   DialinProtocols           = TCP/IP
TcpIpClientAccess            = Network
   UseDHCP               = NO
   StaticAddressBegin        = 101.16.1.1
   StaticAddressEnd          = 101.16.1.16
   ClientCanRequestIPAddress     = NO

[InternetPorts]
   PortName              = COM3-COM17
   DeviceType                = Modem
   DeviceName                = "USR Sportster V.34"
   PortUsage             = DialIn
```

Example: RAS 16 Dialin Ports, With IPX and Static IPX Address Pool

```
[Network]
   InstallServices = SelectedServicesList

[SelectedServicesList]
   RAS = RemoteAccessParameters

[RemoteAccessParameters]
   PortSections              = InternetPorts
   DialoutProtocols              = IPX
   DialinProtocols               = IPX
   IpxClientAccess               = Network
   AutomaticNetworkNumbers           = NO
   NetworkNumberFrom             = 0xa100
   AssignSameNetworkNumber       = NO
   ClientsCanRequestIpxNodeNumber    = NO

[InternetPorts]
   PortName                  = COM3-COM17
   DeviceType                    = Modem
   DeviceName                    = "USR Sportster V.34"
   PortUsage                 = DialIn
```

Hardware Support

This section describes keys you can add to specify what hardware is detected during setup, and what hardware support is installed.

Installing a Modem Driver for Use with RAS

If the RAS parameters include the line DeviceType = Modem, the following line must be included in the [Modem] section:

```
InstallModem = Modem _Parameter_Section
```

where *Modem_Parameter_Section* is a section that you create and give any name you choose. This section contains the parameters required to install the modem on a specified COM port. If the section is empty, RAS will detect modems on its preconfigured ports and install any modem it finds.

The [*Modem_Parameter_Section*] contains one line for each COM port on which a modem is to be installed, using the following syntax:

```
[Modem_Parameter_Section]
COMx = "description" [,Manufacturer, Provider]
```

Where:

COM*x*
: identifies the COM port on which the modem is to be installed (for example COM1, COM2…)

description
: must match a modem description in a Mdmxxxxx.inf file that corresponds to the modem to be installed. This string must be enclosed in quotes.

Manufacturer
: is an optional field that identifies the manufacturer of a particular modem when *description* is not unique to a particular manufacturer.

Provider
: is an optional field that identifies the provider of a particular modem when *description* is not unique to a particular manufacturer.

Using Hardware Detected by Setup

You can have the user confirm the hardware and mass storage devices detected by Setup, or you can specify that Setup proceed with the installation without seeking confirmation. Mass storage devices include any devices controlled by a SCSI mini port driver. For example, all CD-ROM drives, SCSI adapters, and hard drive controllers (except ATdisk, abiosdsk, and standard floppy disks) are mass storage devices.

To specify whether the user is to confirm the hardware detected, add the following line to the [Unattended] section:

```
ConfirmHardware = yes | no
```

Yes indicates that the user must confirm hardware and mass storage devices detected by the Setup program. **No** indicates that the Setup program should use hardware detected by the Setup program.

This key can only be specified in the answer file, not in the UDF.

Note If OEMPreinstall = yes, then the ConfirmHardware key is ignored.

Specifying Mass Storage Devices

When installing onto an x86-based computer, you can have Setup prepare the system for mass storage devices you specify, even if they are not physically present on the system at the time you perform the installation. To do so, add the section [DetectedMassStorage]. Copy the entries for the devices you want to specify from the [SCSI] section of the Txtsetup.sif file. This file is on the Setup boot floppy disks.

This section can only be specified in the answer file, not in the UDF.

If this section is present and contains entries, support for the specified devices will be included in the installation, as if the devices had actually been detected by Setup.

If this section is present and has no entries, the result is the same as if Setup detected no mass storage devices.

If this section is not present, Setup will attempt to detect the mass storage devices on the computer by loading all known miniport drivers.

Specifying a Keyboard Layout

To specify a keyboard layout, add the following line to the [Unattended] section:

```
KeyboardLayout = layout_description
```

This key is optional. If the **KeyboardLayout** key is not specified or is absent, Setup will detect and install a keyboard layout from the retail Windows NT Workstation product.

The *layout_description* value must match one of the strings in the [KeyboardLayout] section of Txtsetup.sif.

This key can only be specified in the answer file, not in the UDF.

Per-user Settings

For a completely unattended installation, you must specify user settings in either the answer file or the UDF.

Specifying User Data

If the user's full name, the organization name, the computer name, and a product ID for the copy of Windows NT Workstation are not provided to the Setup program, the user will be prompted for them. This information can be included in an answer file, but it is generally more effective to provide it in a UDF. Indeed, the UDF functionality is designed to allow you specify a variant of the basic configuration for each user, rather than create separate answer files, one for each user, with most of the information copied in each answer file.

The section and keys are the same, whether you specify the data in an answer file or UDF. In the [UserData] section, add the following lines:

```
FullName = "User's full name"
OrgName = "Organization name"
ComputerName = computername
ProductId = "123-456789012345"
```

The **ProductId** key specifies the Microsoft product identification number. This must be an authentic number that will be requested by Microsoft Product Support Services if you call for technical support. Note that you must include the hyphen in the product identification number. Note also that for the FullName, OrgName, and ProductId keys, the value must be enclosed in quotation marks.

Specifying a Time Zone

If no time zone is specified, the user will be prompted to select one. To specify a time zone, add the following line to the [GuiUnattended] section:

```
TimeZone = "time_zone"
```

Where *time_zone* is one of the following:

(GMT) Greenwich Mean Time; Dublin, Edinburgh, London

(GMT+01:00) Lisbon, Warsaw

(GMT+01:00) Paris, Madrid

(GMT+01:00) Berlin, Stockholm, Rome, Bern, Brussels, Vienna

(GMT+02:00) Eastern Europe

(GMT+01:00) Prague

(GMT+02:00) Athens, Helsinki, Istanbul

(GMT-03:00) Rio de Janeiro
(GMT-04:00) Atlantic Time (Canada)
(GMT-05:00) Eastern Time (US & Canada)
(GMT-06:00) Central Time (US & Canada)
(GMT-07:00) Mountain Time (US & Canada)
(GMT-08:00) Pacific Time (US & Canada); Tijuana
(GMT-09:00) Alaska
(GMT-10:00) Hawaii
(GMT-11:00) Midway Island, Samoa
(GMT+12:00) Wellington
(GMT+10:00) Brisbane, Melbourne, Sydney
(GMT+09:30) Adelaide
(GMT+09:00) Tokyo, Osaka, Sapporo, Seoul, Yakutsk
(GMT+08:00) Hong Kong, Perth, Singapore, Taipei
(GMT+07:00) Bangkok, Jakarta, Hanoi
(GMT+05:30) Bombay, Calcutta, Madras, New Delhi, Colombo
(GMT+04:00) Abu Dhabi, Muscat, Tbilisi, Kazan, Volgograd
(GMT+03:30) Tehran
(GMT+03:00) Baghdad, Kuwait, Nairobi, Riyadh
(GMT+02:00) Israel
(GMT-03:30) Newfoundland
(GMT-01:00) Azores, Cape Verde Is.
(GMT-02:00) Mid-Atlantic
(GMT) Monrovia, Casablanca
(GMT-03:00) Buenos Aires, Georgetown
(GMT-04:00) Caracas, La Paz
(GMT-05:00) Indiana (East)
(GMT-05:00) Bogota, Lima
(GMT-06:00) Saskatchewan
(GMT-06:00) Mexico City, Tegucigalpa
(GMT-07:00) Arizona
(GMT-12:00) Enewetak, Kwajalein
(GMT+12:00) Fiji, Kamchatka, Marshall Is.
(GMT+11:00) Magadan, Soloman Is., New Caledonia

(GMT+10:00) Hobart

(GMT+10:00) Guam, Port Moresby, Vladivostok

(GMT+09:30) Darwin

(GMT+08:00) Beijing, Chongqing, Urumqi

(GMT+06:00) Alma Ata, Dhaka

(GMT+05:00) Islamabad, Karachi, Sverdlovsk, Tashkent

(GMT+04:30) Kabul

(GMT+02:00) Cairo

(GMT+02:00) Harare, Pretoria

(GMT+03:00) Moscow, St. Petersburg

For example:

```
TimeZone = "(GMT-08:00) Pacific Time (US & Canada); Tijuana"
```

Joining a Workgroup or Domain

The computer can be part of either a workgroup or a domain. If the computer is a server, a third option, domain controller, is available. The key for establishing the computer as a domain controller is described under "Windows NT Server Settings," later in this appendix.

To join a workgroup, the following key must be specified under the [Network] section:

```
JoinWorkgroup = workgroup_name
```

The *workgroup_name* value specifies the workgroup the computer will participate in.

To join an existing domain, specify the following under the [Network] section:

```
JoinDomain = domain_name
```

The *domain_name* value specifies the domain to join.

In the lab, you might also want to define user credentials (for example, Administrator) and password required to create a computer account on the domain specified. In this case you would add the following under the [Network] section:

```
JoinDomain = domain_name
CreateComputerAccount = [user_name_with_creation_rights
    [, user_password]
```

The **CreateComputerAccount** key supplies the credentials and password to create the computer account. The user account specified in the **CreateComputerAccount** key must already exist in the specified domain.

The [Network] section must contain one of the keys **JoinWorkgroup**, **JoinDomain**, or **InstallDC**. The **InstallDC** key applies only to Windows NT Server, and is described under "Installing a Domain Controller."

Windows NT Server Settings

The following options apply only to installations of Windows NT Server:

Setting License Options

When installing Windows NT Server, you must specify whether the server is licensed in "per seat" or "per server" mode. If this is not specified in the answer file, Setup will prompt for the information.

To specify the license mode, add the following key to the [LicenseFilePrintData] section:

```
AutoMode = PerSeat | PerServer
```

If the AutoMode key is empty or missing, Setup prompts for the license mode.

PerSeat indicates that a client access license has been purchased for each computer that accesses the server.

PerServer indicates that client access licenses have been purchased for the server to allow a certain number of concurrent connections to the server. If AutoMode is set to PerServer, AutoUsers must also be specified, as follows:

```
AutoUsers = n
```

where *n* is the number of concurrent client connections that the server is licensed to support. This will be a number between 0 and 999999.

If **AutoMode = PerServer** and **AutoUsers** is missing or empty, Setup will prompt for the number of concurrent client connections that the server is licensed to support.

For information on the licensing modes, see Chapter 12, "Licensing and License Manager," in the *Concepts and Planning Guide* included with the Windows NT Server retail product. The chapter includes a worksheet to help you decide which licensing mode is best for your organization.

Installing a Domain Controller

When installing Windows NT Server, you can use the JoinWorkgroup or JoinDomain key in the [Network] section (as described under "Joining a Workgroup or Domain" earlier in this Appendix), or you can set the computer to be a domain controller. To establish the computer as a domain controller, add the following line to the [Network] section:

```
InstallDC = domain_name
```

If the specified domain does not exist, it will be created. This key is only valid if the server role has been set as a primary or backup domain controller and the **AdvServerType** key has been set accordingly.

If you are creating a backup domain controller (BDC), add the following line to the [Network] section to define the user credentials and password required to create a computer account on the domain specified:

```
CreateComputerAccount = [user_name_with_creation_rights
    [, user_password]
```

The [Network] section must contain one of the keys **JoinWorkgroup**, **JoinDomain**, or **InstallDC**.

Example: Creating a Backup Domain Controller for the Marketing Domain

```
[Network]
InstallDC = Marketing
CreateComputerAccount = Administrator, FishScale
```

A computer account is also created for this computer, using the Administrator account and supplying the password (FishScale) for the Administrator account.

Setting the Server Role

A computer running Windows NT Server can be a standalone server, a primary domain controller (PDC), or a backup domain controller (BDC). To specify which role the computer is to have in the network, add the following line to the [GuiUnattended] section:

```
AdvServerType = SERVERNT | LANMANNT | LANSECNT
```

Where:

SERVERNT
: indicates that the computer will be a standalone server.

LANMANNT
: indicates that the computer will serve as a primary domain controller (PDC).

LANSECNT
: indicates that the computer will be a backup domain controller (BDC).

Installing the Internet Information Server (NT Server Only)

To install Internet Server on a Windows NT Server, add the following line to the [Network] section. This key is only valid for Windows NT Server, and will be ignored when installing Windows NT Workstation.

```
InstallInternetServer = Internet_Server_Parameter_Section
[Internet_Server_Parameter_Section]
```

where *Internet_Server_Parameter_Section* is a section that you create, and that contains parameters for installing Internet Server.

Example

```
[Network]
InstallInternetServer = InternetServerParameters
[InternetServerParameters]
```

Create a section called [INETSTP], and add some or all of the following keys, depending on the features you want to install, to that section:

```
InstallINETSTP= 1 | 0
InstallFTP=1 | 0
InstallWWW=1 | 0
InstallGOPHER=1 | 0
InstallADMIN=1 | 0
InstallMOSAIC=1 | 0
InstallGATEWAY=1 | 0
InstallDNS=1 | 0
InstallHELP=1 | 0
InstallSMALLPROX=1 | 0
InstallCLIENTADMIN=1 | 0
WWWRoot=c:\wwwroot
FTPRoot=c:\ftproot
GopherRoot=c:\gophroot
InstallDir=c:\inetsrv
EmailName=email_address
UseGateway=1 | 0
GatewaysList=\\gateway1 \\gateway2
```

Where the possible values for a key are 1 or 0; 1 means "yes" and 0 means "no." The effects of these keys are shown in the following table:

InstallINETSTP=	Specifies whether Internet Services will be installed.
InstallFTP=	Specifies whether the FTP Service will be installed.
InstallWWW=	Specifies whether the WWW Service will be installed.
InstallGOPHER=	Specifies whether the Gopher Service will be installed.
InstallADMIN=	Specifies whether the Internet Administrator Manager will be installed.
InstallMOSAIC=	Specifies whether the Internet Explorer Browser will be installed.
InstallGATEWAY=	Specifies whether the Gateway Service will be installed.
InstallDNS=	Specifies whether the DNS Service will be installed.
InstallHELP=	Specifies whether the HELP Files will be installed. (Applies to Windows NT Workstation only.)
InstallSMALLPROX=	Specifies whether the Access Gateway Proxy will be installed. (Applies to Windows NT Workstation only.)
InstallCLIENTADMIN=	Specifies whether the client administrator tools will be installed. (Applies to Windows NT Workstation only.)
WWWRoot=c:*wwwroot*	Specifies the virtual root for the WWW service.
FTPRoot=c:*ftproot*	Specifies the virtual root for the FTP service.
GopherRoot=c:*gophroot*	Specifies the virtual root for the Gopher service.
InstallDir=c:*inetsrv*	Specifies the installation directory for all components of Internet Services.
EmailName=*email_name*	Specifies the Internet e-mail name of the user.
UseGateway=	Specifies whether a gateway is to be used.
GatewaysList=*gateway1* *gateway2*	Lists the gateways to be used (if UseGateway=1).

Using an Extended Partition for Text Mode Files

If you are installing Windows NT Workstation on a disk larger than 2 GB, you can cause Setup to extend the partition on which the temporary files are located into any available unpartitioned space that physically follows it on the disk. These temporary files must be installed on a primary partition. The space used must be limited to 1024 cylinders. Writing beyond cylinder 1024 will cause the installation to fail.

To control whether Setup extends the partition on which the temporary files are located, add the following line to the [Unattended] section:

```
ExtendOemPartition = 0 | 1
```

Where:

0
: specifies that the partition not be extended.

1
: specifies that the partition is to be extended. When the value is **1**, you must set **FileSystem = ConvertNTFS**.

Stopping Setup Before GUI Mode Begins

If **OEMPreinstall = Yes**, the Setup program stops at the end of text mode by default, rather than continuing into GUI mode. This gives you the ability to duplicate disks with the operating system and applications pre-installed. The first time a computer is started with the duplicated disk in place, the system boots into GUI mode. The user can then be prompted for information such as username, computername, and the Workgroup or Domain that the computer is to join.

You can specify whether Setup continues into GUI mode at the end of text mode by adding the following line to the [Unattended] section:

```
NoWaitAfterTextMode = 0 | 1
```

Where:

0
: specifies that Setup should stop at the end of text mode.

1
: specifies that Setup should automatically reboot into GUI mode at the end of text mode.

Sample Unattend.txt File

```
[Unattended]
    Method = express
    TargetPath = srv1231

[GuiUnattended]
    AdvServerType = SERVERNT
;    AdvServerType = LANMANNT (PDC) | LANSECNT (BDC) | SERVERNT
(STANDALONE)
    TimeZone = "(GMT-08:00) Pacific Time (US & Canada); Tijuana"

[UserData]
    FullName = "John L. Smith"
    OrgName = "Microsoft"
    ComputerName = JohnSm_1
    ProductId = "123456789012345"

[LicenseFilePrintData]
    AutoMode = PerSeat

[Network]
    DetectAdapters = DetectParams
;    InstallAdapters = AdaptersList
    InstallProtocols = ProtocolsList
;    InstallServices = ServicesList

;    JoinWorkgroup = OurWorkGroup

    JoinDomain = NTWKSTA
    CreateComputerAccount = JohnSm, FriedFrogs

; for a PDC install
;    InstallDC = Our_DOMAIN

; for a BDC install
;    InstallDC = Our_DOMAIN
;    CreateComputerAccount = Administrator, FishScale

[DetectParams]
    DetectCount = 1
    LimitTo = IEEPRO, ELNKII

[AdaptersList]
    IEEPRO = IntelEEProParams
    ELNKII = 3ComELIIParams
```

```
[ProtocolsList]
    TC = TCPIPParams
;    NBF = NetBEUIParams
;    NWLNKIPX = NWLinkIPXParams

[ServicesList]
    RAS = RemoteAccessParameters

[IntelEEProParams]
    Interrupt = 5
    IoChannelReady = 4
    Transceiver = 4
    IoAddress = 784

; irq = 5
; i/o = 0x310
; io channel = auto
; transceiver = auto

[3ComELIIParams]
    InterruptNumber = 2
    IOBaseAddress = 512
    Transceiver = 2
    MemoryMapped = 0

;    where Transceiver = 1 - External; 2 - On Board
;        MemoryMapped = 1 - ON; 0 - OFF

; Optional:
;   !AutoNetInterfaceType = 0 | 1 | 2 ...
;   !AutoNetBusNumber = 0 | 1 | ...

[RemoteAccessParameters]
PortSections= MYCOM1
    DialoutProtocols= TCP/IP

[MYCOM1]
    PortName    = COM1
    DeviceType      = Modem
    DeviceName      = "Intel Fax Modem 144e"
    PortUsage       = DialOut
```

APPENDIX B

Security in a Software Development Environment

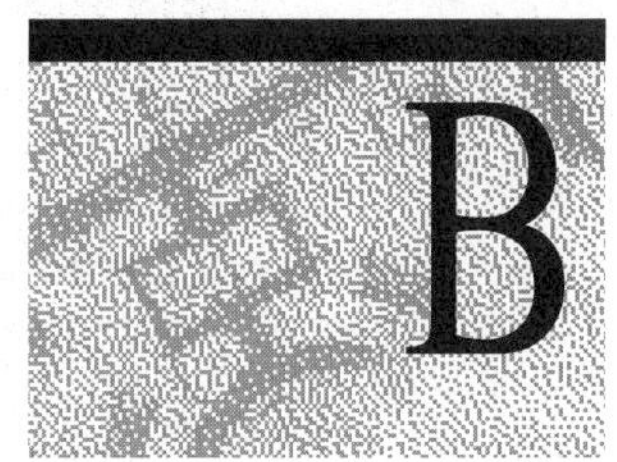

Windows NT provides a number of different "environment subsystems," such as the Windows subsystem, the POSIX subsystem, and the OS/2 subsystem. Each of these subsystems presents a set of application programming interfaces (APIs). These subsystems are built using an underlying set of programming interfaces and mechanisms that are primarily used only in the development of the operating system and operating system components (such as device drivers and environment subsystems). These underlying mechanisms are not designed to be used in the development of applications, such as word processors or database server packages, and so generally are of little interest to a security administrator. However, this is not always the case, and in some circumstances these mechanisms are of vital interest to security administrators.

A typical shrink-wrapped product from a reputable manufacturer uses only the programming features explicitly provided for application development. However, what do you really know about a shareware program downloaded from a public network server? It might try to take advantage of some of the mechanisms in Windows NT that are not intended to be used by application programmers — either for beneficial uses, or maybe to introduce a Trojan Horse or virus program into your system. This might also be true if you purchase software from a company more interested in exploiting every bell and whistle, rather than producing quality products using published interfaces and mechanisms. Even your own developers, if your company does its own in-house software development, could use these mechanisms in their programs. As you can see, there are situations where understanding some of these underlying mechanisms and being able to monitor their use is vitally important.

This document helps you to understand some of Windows NT's underlying and internal APIs and mechanisms. It also provides information that can be used by a security administrator to monitor these mechanisms and to interpret the log files generated as a result of this monitoring. This information is, necessarily, quite technical in nature, being roughly equivalent to programmer documentation. In fact, the information in this document might also prove to be useful background for anyone wishing to write some automated security monitoring tools.

User Rights

The following rights can be assigned to user accounts through the Windows NT Win32 application programming interface. Security event log entries that record the assignment and use of privileges refer to the privileges using the name shown in parentheses.

Create a token object (SeCreateTokenPrivilege)
: This right allows a process to create access tokens. Only the Local Security Authority can do this. By default, no account has this privilege. Use of this right is not auditable. For C2 certification, it is recommended that it not be assigned to any user.

Debug programs (SeDebugPrivilege)
: This right allows a user to debug various low-level objects such as threads. By default, the Administrators account has this privilege. Use of this right is not auditable. For C2 certification, it is recommended that it not be assigned to any user, including system administrators.

Generate security audits (SeAuditPrivilege)
: This right allows a process to generate security audit log entries. By default, no account has this privilege. Use of this right is not auditable. For C2 certification, it is recommended that it not be assigned to any user.

Audit Record Format

The format and contents of the audit event records are based on the design of Event Viewer. Event Viewer uses information from the Registry to locate message files and to determine how to present the information in an event record.

Event Viewer expects a number of *event source modules* to be defined as part of the security audit log information in the Registry. At least one event source module must be provided by each product that generates audit event records. For example, if a mail product is installed, that product's installation procedure needs to add its event source module information to the security log information in the Registry. A special event source module shipped with Windows NT contains default information, so that information does not have to be replicated in other event source modules.

The information defined for event source modules includes:

- Event Message File. This file contains the displayable strings for each audit event record. It includes parameter substitution markers to be replaced at viewing time with Unicode strings logged in the event record.

  Only the event source module shipped with Windows NT should define an event message file. This single event message file serves as the default for other event source modules.
- Category Message File. Categories are discussed in "Elements of an Event Record," later in this document. Only the security event source module shipped with Windows NT should define a category message file. This single category message file serves as the default for other event source modules. In Windows NT version 3.51, this file is not actually used for auditing.
- Parameter Message File. The parameter message file is used to provide object type-specific access names. Each security event source module should (but does not have to) provide a parameter message file. If object type-specific access names are not provided by an event source module, then default names will be used (such as "Specific Access Bit 0").

When Event Viewer is asked to display an audit record, it uses the event source module name and event ID from the record to retrieve a message string for that event. This string can include parameter substitution markers and other format characters that are interpreted and acted upon by a call to FormatMessage(). For example, the string for a successful logon audit might look like:

```
Successful Logon: \n\t\tUser Name:\t%1 \n\t\tDomain:\t%2
```

Notice that this message string includes two parameter substitution markers (%1 and %2). These parameter strings are obtained from the event record. So, if Administrator logged on to a computer named ACCTG, an event record containing those two strings would be recorded. The corresponding event record in Event Viewer would look like this:

```
Successful Logon:
        User Name:  Administrator
        Domain: ACCTG
```

Before Event Viewer formats the entire message string, it must format the individual parameter strings received in the event record. In the preceding example, the parameter strings needed no formatting. In the case of an audit generated when a file is opened for WRITE_DATA and WRITE_DAC, however, the event message might be:

```
Object Open:\n\t\tObject Type:\t%1\n\t\tObject
Name:\t%2\n\t\tAccesses:\t%3
```

and parameter strings received in the audit record might be:

- Parameter string 1: "File"
- Parameter string 2: "C:\accounting\payroll\hours_worked.dat"
- Parameter string 3: "%%972\n\t\t\t%%1032"

The "%%" directive tells Event Viewer to look up and substitute the message specified by the number following the directive from the parameter message file for the event source module. Assuming message numbers 972 and 1032 in the message file are "Write DAC" and "Write Data" respectively, the third string will be changed to:

```
Write DAC\n\t\t\tWrite Data
```

This would cause the resultant display by Event Viewer to look like:

```
Object Open:
        Object Type:File
        Object Name:C:\accounting\payroll\hours_worked.dat
        Accesses:   Write Dac
                    Write Data
```

(This example is for illustrative purposes only and does not correspond to an actual event-record type.)

Tight Security for Shared Objects

As shipped and installed, Windows NT is configured to provide a high degree of ease of use. In some cases, this ease of use can be seen as a security threat. This is particularly true of "denial of service" attacks, in which a user is able to deny others the use of various parts of the system. There are a number of components of the underlying mechanisms of Windows NT that may be affected in this manner by anyone with the programming knowledge to locate and manipulate them.

A highly security-conscious system administrator might choose to trade this ease of use for added security. It is impossible to enumerate all the ways in which this tradeoff might be seen or experienced by each user or application. However, you can expect that the biggest area of impact will be for users that redefine system-wide resource attributes, such as the attributes of COM1: or of printers. In general, by tightening base security, you must accept that these shared resources will be administered only by system administrators.

To strongly protect shared objects, use the Registry Editor to create or assign the following Registry key value:

Hive:	HKEY_LOCAL_MACHINE\SYSTEM
Key:	\CurrentControlSet\Control\Session Manager
Name:	ProtectionMode
Type:	REG_DWORD
Value:	1

If this value does not exist, or is set to anything other than one (1), then standard protection is applied to these objects.

The changes take effect the next time the computer is started. You might want to update the Emergency Repair Disk to reflect these changes.

Auditing

This section describes special cases of auditing that might be of interest to administrators of high-level security installations.

Auditing Backup and Restore Activities

When files are being backed up, Windows NT checks to ensure that the user performing the backup has the Back Up Files and Directories special right each time the backup program attempts to copy a file to the backup media. In the same way, Windows NT checks for the Restore Files and Directories right for each file that is being restored from backup media. Obviously, if Windows NT were to record an audit event each time those rights were invoked, thousands of events would be recorded during a routine backup. Because this would flood the security log with event records that most often would be of little value for maintaining system security, Windows NT does not normally record audit events for the use of these rights, even when success auditing of Use of User Rights is enabled in the system user rights policy.

To audit the use of these rights, use the Registry Editor to create or assign the following Registry key value:

Hive:	HKEY_LOCAL_MACHINE\System
Key:	\CurrentControlSet\Control\Lsa
Name:	FullPrivilegeAuditing
Type:	REG_BINARY
Value:	1

The changes take effect the next time the computer is started. You might want to update the Emergency Repair Disk to reflect these changes.

Note The *use* of the following rights is never audited, even when the FullPrivilegeAuditing Registry entry is set to 1. However, the *assignment* of these rights, during logon, is audited.

- Bypass traverse checking (SeChangeNotify)
- Generate security audits (SeAuditPrivilege)
- Create a token object (SeCreateTokenPrivilege)
- Debug programs (SeDebugPrivilege)
- Create a new security context for a new logon (AssignPrimaryToken)

Managing Auditing of Particular Objects

In addition to letting you audit system-wide events (such as users logging on), Windows NT gives you the ability to record such events as whether a specific user fails to open a given object (such as a file or printer) for a particular type of access.

Note Only files and directories in NTFS partitions can be audited, and it is only access that is auditable, not intent. In other words, the audit log records will show that a particular user opened a specific file or directory; it will not tell you what the user's intent was. Copying a file, reading a file, or viewing a file's attributes all write the same set of audit records to the log.

To be able to audit object access in this way, you must first use the Audit Policy dialog of User Manager to enable auditing of file and object access events. You can enable auditing of success or failure events, or both. This establishes the global object-access auditing policy for the system. The global policy determines whether object-specific auditing will occur at all; to record access events for a particular object, you must also specify the type of auditing to be performed for that object. File Manager lets you set up auditing for files and directories, Print Manager lets you configure auditing for printers, and Registry Editor lets you specify auditing for Registry entries.

In a sense, object-access auditing works like a building's electrical system. You can turn on and off switches for lamps throughout the building, but if the master circuit breaker is off, no lamps will actually turn on. On the other hand, if the master circuit breaker is on, then only those lamps whose switches are in the on position will light up.

Because the security log is limited in size, and because a large number of routine audit records can make it difficult to find records that suggest a security problem, you should carefully consider how you will audit object access. Generating too many audit records might require you to review and clear the security log more often than is practical. On the other hand, judicious use of object-access auditing can be invaluable in helping you identify areas where your security policy should be tightened or even where a security breach has been attempted successfully or unsuccessfully.

For example, if you use permissions to control users' access to sensitive files and directories, you should enable auditing of those users' access to those files and directories to ensure that the permissions are working as expected.

If a directory has a list of users whose access to the directory is to be audited, a new file added to the directory will inherit the auditing list from the directory. You can ensure that Windows NT Workstation will record access to new files by making sure the new files are placed in directories with auditing lists.

Note Only new files and directories inherit auditing lists from the directory in which they are created. To ensure that access to existing files will be audited, be sure to select both Replace Auditing On Subdirectories and Replace Auditing On Existing Files in the Directory Auditing dialog box when creating a directory auditing list.

For procedures for managing access auditing for files and directories, see the "File Manager" chapter in the Windows NT Workstation or Windows NT Server *System Guide*. For procedures for managing access auditing for printers, see the "Print Manager" chapter in the Windows NT Workstation or Windows NT Server *System Guide*. For information about auditing access to Registry keys, see the online Help for Registry Editor and Part IV, "Windows NT Registry," in the *Windows NT Resource Guide*.

Base Object Auditing

In addition to Files, Registry Keys, and Printers, Windows NT has a number of objects that are not generally visible to or known by a typical user. Application programmers or people writing I/O device drivers might have learned about these objects in software development or device driver development kits. Normal interactive users, however, have no direct ability to affect these objects except as intended by Windows NT.

Generally speaking, these objects are used by Windows NT in a manner that makes auditing their use not very interesting. In fact, doing so can introduce so many audit entries into the security log that locating real security problems becomes considerably more difficult.

However, in some situations, it might be desirable to audit accesses to base objects. For example, where custom applications are being developed, the "users" are not just the people that interactively log on, but also the programmers who are developing applications. These programmers might be able to directly access the base objects.

Note It is only access that is auditable, not intent. In other words, the audit log records will show that a particular user opened an object; it will not tell you what the user's intent was.

To audit the use of base objects, first set your system's audit policy to audit successful and/or failed object accesses, and then use the Registry Editor to create or assign the following Registry key value:

Hive:	HKEY_LOCAL_MACHINE\SYSTEM
Key:	\CurrentControlSet\Control\Lsa
Name:	AuditBaseObjects
Type:	REG_DWORD
Value:	1

The changes take effect the next time the computer is started. You might want to update the Emergency Repair Disk to reflect these changes.

Accesses to shared base objects appear in the security log as Object Access events, like those for Files, Registry Keys, and Printers, but with different object type names and access names. For a full description of each of the base object types and their access types, refer to the Microsoft Software Developer's Network (MSDN). To receive MSDN level 2, call 800-759-5474.

When the Security Log Is Full

If you have set the security log either to "Overwrite Events Older than *n* Days" or "Do Not Overwrite Events (Clear Log Manually)", you might want to enable CrashOnAuditFail. The CrashOnAuditFail registry entry directs the operating system to crash (shutdown abnormally and display a blue screen) when the audit log is full. This assures that no auditable activities, including security violations, occur while the system is unable to log them. To enable CrashOnAuditFail, use the Registry Editor to create the following Registry key value:

Hive:	HKEY_LOCAL_MACHINE\SYSTEM
Key:	\CurrentControlSet\Control\Lsa
Name:	CrashOnAuditFail
Type:	REG_DWORD
Values:	1 Crash if the audit log is full.
	2 (This value is set by the operating system just before it crashes due a full audit log. While the value is 2, only the administrator can log on to the computer. This value confirms the cause of the crash. To reset, change this value back to 1.)

The changes take effect the next time the computer is started. You might want to update the Emergency Repair Disk to reflect these changes. Note that there is no 0 value for this key. To disable CrashOnAuditFail, delete the key from the registry.

If Windows NT halts as a result of the security log becoming full, the system must be restarted and reconfigured to restore it to high-level security. When Windows NT restarts, the Security log is full and so no auditable actions are recorded until the Security log is cleared.

► **To recover when Windows NT halts because it cannot generate an audit event record**

1. Restart the computer and log on using an account in the Administrators group.
2. Use Event Viewer to clear all events from the Security log, archiving the currently logged events. For details, see the "Event Viewer" chapter in the Windows NT Workstation or Windows NT Server *System Guide*.
3. Use the Registry Editor to change the value of **CrashOnAuditFail**, to **1**, under HKEY_LOCAL_MACHINE\SYSTEM\CurrentControlSet\Control\Lsa (as described earlier in this section).
4. Exit, and then restart the computer.

Interpreting the Security Log

When you view the security log, you can use filters to specify criteria for the records you want to view. For example, you can choose to view events recorded by a particular source within a range of dates.

If you need a more complex analysis of the information in the security log, you can save the security log in one of two text formats. The information can then be imported into an analysis tool (such as a spreadsheet). See the "Event Viewer" chapter in the Windows NT Workstation or Windows NT Server *System Guide* for more information about using security log data archived in a text format.

Elements of an Event Record

All event-log records, regardless of type, consist of a header containing standard information, a description that varies depending on the event type, and (optionally) additional data. Most security log entries consist of the header and a description.

The event-record header contains the following information:

Date	The date the event occurred.
Time	The (local) time the event occurred.
User	The username of the user on whose behalf the event occurred. This is the client ID if the event was actually caused by a server process, or the primary ID if impersonation is not taking place. Where applicable, a security log entry contains both the primary and impersonation IDs.
Computer	The name of the computer where the event occurred. (Event Viewer can be used to view event logs on other Windows NT computers on a network.)
Event ID	A unique number identifying the particular event type. The first line of the description usually contains the name of the event type. For example, 562 is the ID of the event that occurs when a new object handle is created, and so the first line of the description of such an event is "Handle Allocated."
Source	The name of the system component that actually recorded the event in the security log. Usually, this is Security, indicating that it is the result of Windows NT security auditing. Applications can also define their own auditable events that can be recorded in the security log.
Type	Either Success Audit or Failure Audit, indicating whether the audit is a record of a successful or failed attempt. In Event Viewer's normal list view, these are represented by a key or a lock, respectively.
Category	A classification of the event by the event source. For security audits, this corresponds to one of the event types for which success or failure auditing can be enabled in the User Manager Audit Policy dialog.

The format and contents of the description that appears with these items vary with the event category. The various event categories are discussed later, under "Audit Categories."

Identifying the User Behind the Action

The security log identifies the user account that caused each recorded event to happen. In some cases, more than one account is actually involved because of the client-server design of Windows NT. This design makes it possible for one process (called a server process) to perform actions on behalf of another process (called the client process).

When the server process is acting on behalf of the client, Windows NT security treats it as though it were the client process. The server process is not allowed to access objects that are off limits to the client.

Also, the audit records for events performed by a server impersonating a client identify the "user" that "owns" the server process as the primary user (typically identified as SYSTEM), and the user responsible for starting the client process as the client user. When there is no impersonation taking place, the primary user is the actual user who started the process that caused the audited event to occur. Most often, this is the user who is actually logged on to the computer, although sometimes it can be SYSTEM.

Process IDs

Primary IDs and impersonation IDs provide enough information for many security administrators because they show who is performing auditable actions. However, in some cases, an operator might want to see what is going on at a process-by-process level of detail. If detailed tracking auditing is enabled, the security log shows when a new process is created (such as when an application program begins execution). Each process is assigned its own, globally unique process ID, which is included in all records of events caused by that process, to the point at which the process ends.

This information can be correlated with specific audit event records to see which user account is being used to perform auditable actions and which program was being run. Process IDs are included in audit event records regardless of whether process-level tracking is enabled. However, process IDs are useful only if process-level tracking is enabled.

Note Because of the way impersonation works, it is impossible to know what the process ID of a client is at audit time. In fact, a single access token can actually be used by several processes simultaneously. For this reason, process IDs can only be displayed by audits generated by the Kernel.

Handle IDs

When a particular operation consists of multiple actions, Windows NT assigns an *operation ID* to each so you can properly associate the separate actions with the operation. This operation ID is unique only to the process performing the operation. Furthermore, to help you track how a process accesses a particular object, each object is identified by a *handle ID*. Typically a new handle is allocated immediately after a file is opened, and then closed when the file is closed. If the handle ID refers to a Kernel object, the handle ID is unique only to the process to which the handle belongs. If the handle ID refers to an object managed by a protected server, the handle ID is unique across all processes.

The handle ID enables the audit to be associated with future audits. For example, when a file is opened the audit information indicates the handle ID assigned. When that handle is closed another audit event record is generated which also includes the handle ID. This allows you to determine the entire span of time the file was open, which can be useful when attempting to assess damage following a security breach.

There are two types of handle IDs, often called Kernel object handle IDs and protected server object handle IDs. Handle IDs to Kernel objects are unique only to the process to which the handle belongs. As a result, two processes can have a handle with an ID of 35, for example; they are distinguished by the process ID associated with them. Handle IDs to protected servers on the other hand, come from a single ID space and are unique across all processes.

Audit Event Record Contents and Meaning

This section describes the contents and meaning of each audit event record.

Common Event Record Data

Audit event records include header information that is present in all event records. The following list describes this common information.

- The time the event was generated.
- The SID of the subject that caused the event to be generated. If possible, Event Viewer translates this SID to an account name for display. The SID is the impersonation ID if the subject is impersonating a client, or the primary ID if the subject is not impersonating.
- The name of the system component or module that submitted the event. For security audits this is always Security.
- The module-specific ID of the specific event.
- The event type, either Success Audit or Failure Audit.
- The event category, used to group related events such as logon audits, object access audits, and policy change audits.

When an event is displayed in detail, this information is displayed at the top of that window. The following is an example of how this information is displayed:

```
Date:        8/12/96          Event ID:   172
Time:        10:32:11 AM      Source:     Security
User:        Administrator    Type:       Failure Audit
Computer:    ACCTG            Category:   Logon/Logoff
```

Audit Categories

Audit event records are divided into auditing *categories*. These categories are displayed by Event Viewer and allow a user to visually distinguish or automatically filter audit events of interest. These audit categories are listed in the following table, and discussed in detail in the Audit Categories Help file (Auditcat.hlp).

Category	Description
System Event	Events in this category indicate that something affecting the security of the entire system or of the audit log has occurred.
Logon/Logoff	Events in this category describe a single successful or unsuccessful logon or logoff. Included in each logon description is an indication of what type of logon was requested/performed (for example, interactive, network, or service).
Object Access	Events in this category describe both successful and unsuccessful accesses to protected objects.
Privilege Use	Events in this category describe both successful and unsuccessful attempts to use privileges. The Privilege Use category also covers a special case of informing when some special privileges are assigned. These special privileges are only audited when they are assigned, not when they are used.
Account Management	Events in this category describe high-level changes to the security account database, such as the creation of a user account or a change in group membership. There can also be a finer granularity of auditing performed at the object level under the Object Access category.
Policy Change	Events in this category describe high-level changes in security policy, such as the assignment of privileges or changes in the audit policy. There can also be a finer granularity of auditing performed at the object level under the Object Access category.
Detailed Tracking	Events in this category provide detailed subject tracking information, such as program activation, some forms of handle duplication and indirect object accesses, and process exit.

APPENDIX C

Port Reference for Microsoft TCP/IP

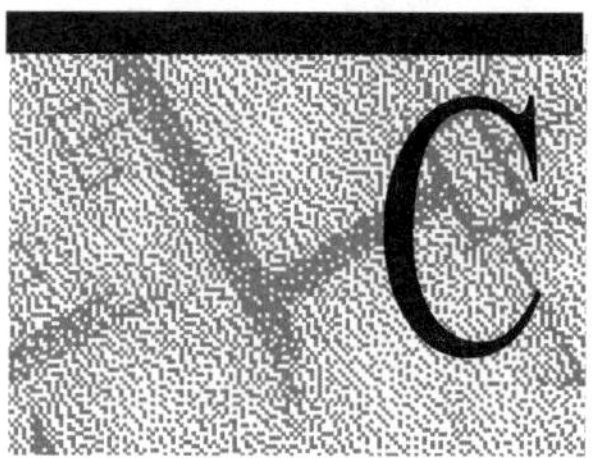

In TCP/IP, a *port* is the mechanism that allows a computer to simultaneously support multiple communication sessions with computers and programs on the network. A port is basically a refinement of an IP address; a computer that receives a packet from the network can further refine the destination of the packet by using a unique port number that is determined when the connection is established. A number of "well known" ports have reserved numbers that correspond to predetermined functions.

This appendix describes the Windows NT Server and Windows NT Workstation default port assignments for TCP/IP and User Datagram Protocol (UDP). The Services file controls port assignments used by Windows NT Server and Windows NT Workstation. The Services file is located in the \systemroot\Winnt\System32\Drivers\Etc\Services directory.

Port Assignments for Well-known Ports

Well-known services are defined by RFC 1060. The relationship between the well-known services and the well-known ports is described in this excerpt from RFC 1340 (J. Reynolds and J. Postal, July 1992):

> The well-known ports are controlled and assigned by the Internet Assigned Numbers Authority (IANA), and on most systems can only be used by system (or root) processes or by programs executed by privileged users.
>
> Ports are used in TCP to name the ends of logical connections that carry long term conversations. For the purpose of providing services to unknown callers, a service contact port is defined. This list specifies the port used by the server process as its contact port. The contact port is sometimes called the "well - known port."

UDP ports are not the same as TCP ports, though to the extent possible, TCP and UDP may use the same port assignments. The UDP specification is defined in RFC 768.

The assigned ports use a small portion of the possible port numbers. For many years, the assigned ports were in the range 0–255. Recently, the range for assigned ports managed by the IANA has been expanded to the range 0–1023.

The following table describes both TCP and UDP port assignments for well-known ports.

Table C.1 Port Assignments for Well-known Ports

Decimal	Keyword	Description
0/tcp, udp		Reserved
1/tcp, udp	tcpmux	TCP Port Service Multiplexer
2/tcp, udp	compressnet	Management Utility
3/tcp, udp	compressnet	Compression Process
4/tcp, udp		Unassigned
5/tcp, udp	rje	Remote Job Entry
6/tcp, udp		Unassigned
7/tcp, udp	echo	Echo
8/tcp, udp		Unassigned
9/tcp, udp	discard	Discard; alias=sink null
10/tcp, udp		Unassigned
11/udp	systat	Active Users; alias=users
12/tcp, udp		Unassigned
13/tcp, udp	daytime	Daytime
14/tcp, udp		Unassigned
15/tcp, udp		Unassigned [was netstat]
16/tcp, udp		Unassigned
17/tcp, udp	qotd	Quote of the Day; alias=quote
18/tcp, udp	msp	Message Send Protocol
19/tcp, udp	chargen	Character Generator; alias=ttytst source
20/tcp, udp	ftp-data	File Transfer [Default Data]
21/tcp, udp	ftp	File Transfer [Control], connection dialog
22/tcp, udp		Unassigned
23/tcp, udp	telnet	Telnet
24/tcp, udp		Any private mail system
25/tcp, udp	smtp	Simple Mail Transfer; alias=mail

Table C.1 Port Assignments for Well-known Ports *(continued)*

Decimal	Keyword	Description
26/tcp, udp		Unassigned
27/tcp, udp	nsw-fe	NSW User System FE
28/tcp, udp		Unassigned
29/tcp, udp	msg-icp	MSG ICP
30/tcp, udp		Unassigned
31/tcp, udp	msg-auth	MSG Authentication
32/tcp, udp		Unassigned
33/tcp, udp	dsp	Display Support Protocol
34/tcp, udp		Unassigned
35/tcp, udp		Any private printer server
36/tcp, udp		Unassigned
37/tcp, udp	time	Time; alias=timeserver
38/tcp, udp		Unassigned
39/tcp, udp	rlp	Resource Location Protocol; alias=resource
40/tcp, udp		Unassigned
41/tcp, udp	graphics	Graphics
42/tcp, udp	nameserver	Host Name Server; alias=nameserver
43/tcp, udp	nicname	Who Is; alias=nicname
44/tcp, udp	mpm-flags	MPM FLAGS Protocol
45/tcp, udp	mpm	Message Processing Module
46/tcp, udp	mpm-snd	MPM [default send]
47/tcp, udp	ni-ftp	NI FTP
48/tcp, udp		Unassigned
49/tcp, udp	login	Login Host Protocol
50/tcp, udp	re-mail-ck	Remote Mail Checking Protocol
51/tcp, udp	la-maint	IMP Logical Address Maintenance
52/tcp, udp	xns-time	XNS Time Protocol
53/tcp, udp	domain	Domain Name Server
54/tcp, udp	xns-ch	XNS Clearinghouse
55/tcp, udp	isi-gl	ISI Graphics Language
56/tcp, udp	xns-auth	XNS Authentication
57/tcp, udp		Any private terminal access
58/tcp, udp	xns-mail	XNS Mail
59/tcp, udp		Any private file service

Table C.1 Port Assignments for Well-known Ports *(continued)*

Decimal	Keyword	Description
60/tcp, udp		Unassigned
61/tcp, udp	ni-mail	NI MAIL
62/tcp, udp	acas	ACA Services
63/tcp, udp	via-ftp	VIA Systems - FTP
64/tcp, udp	covia	Communications Integrator (CI)
65/tcp, udp	tacacs-ds	TACACS-Database Service
66/tcp, udp	sql*net	Oracle SQL*NET
67/tcp, udp	bootpc	DHCP/BOOTP Protocol Server
68/tcp, udp	bootpc	DHCP/BOOTP Protocol Server
69/ udp	tftp	Trivial File Transfer
70/tcp, udp	gopher	Gopher
71/tcp, udp	netrjs-1	Remote Job Service
72/tcp, udp	netrjs-2	Remote Job Service
73/tcp, udp	netrjs-3	Remote Job Service
74/tcp, udp	netrjs-4	Remote Job Service
75/udp		Any private dial out service
76/tcp, udp		Unassigned
77/tcp, udp		Any private RJE service
78/tcp, udp	vettcp	Vettcp
79/tcp, udp	finger	Finger
80/tcp, udp	www	World Wide Web HTTP
81/tcp, udp	hosts2-ns	HOSTS2 Name Server
82/tcp, udp	xfer	XFER Utility
83/tcp, udp	mit-ml-dev	MIT ML Device
84/tcp, udp	ctf	Common Trace Facility
85/tcp, udp	mit-ml-dev	MIT ML Device
86/tcp, udp	mfcobol	Micro Focus Cobol
87/tcp, udp		Any private terminal link; alias=ttylink
88/tcp, udp	kerberos	Kerberos
89/tcp	su-mit-tg	SU/MIT Telnet Gateway
89/udp	su-mit-tg	SU/MIT Telnet Gateway
90/tcp, udp		DNSIX Security Attribute Token Map
91/tcp, udp	mit-dov	MIT Dover Spooler
92/tcp, udp	npp	Network Printing Protocol

Table C.1 Port Assignments for Well-known Ports *(continued)*

Decimal	Keyword	Description
93/tcp, udp	dcp	Device Control Protocol
94/tcp, udp	objcall	Tivoli Object Dispatcher
95/tcp, udp	supdup	SUPDUP
96/tcp, udp	dixie	DIXIE Protocol Specification
97/tcp, udp	swift-rvf	Swift Remote Virtual File Protocol
98/tcp, udp	tacnews	TAC News
99/tcp, udp	metagram	Metagram Relay
100/tcp	newacct	[unauthorized use]
101/tcp, udp	hostname	NIC Host Name Server; alias=hostname
102/tcp, udp	iso-tsap	ISO-TSAP
103/tcp, udp	gppitnp	Genesis Point-to-Point Trans Net; alias=webster
104/tcp, udp	acr-nema	ACR-NEMA Digital Imag. & Comm. 300
105/tcp, udp	csnet-ns	Mailbox Name Nameserver
106/tcp, udp	3com-tsmux	3COM-TSMUX
107/tcp, udp	rtelnet	Remote Telnet Service
108/tcp, udp	snagas	SNA Gateway Access Server
109/tcp, udp	pop2	Post Office Protocol - Version 2; alias=postoffice
110/tcp, udp	pop3	Post Office Protocol - Version 3; alias=postoffice
111/tcp, udp	sunrpc	SUN Remote Procedure Call
112/tcp, udp	mcidas	McIDAS Data Transmission Protocol
113/tcp, udp	auth	Authentication Service; alias=authentication
114/tcp, udp	audionews	Audio News Multicast
115/tcp, udp	sftp	Simple File Transfer Protocol
116/tcp, udp	ansanotify	ANSA REX Notify
117/tcp, udp	uucp-path	UUCP Path Service
118/tcp, udp	sqlserv	SQL Services
119/tcp, udp	nntp	Network News Transfer Protocol; alias=usenet
120/tcp, udp	cfdptkt	CFDPTKT
121/tcp, udp	erpc	Encore Expedited Remote Pro.Call
122/tcp, udp	smakynet	SMAKYNET
123/tcp, udp	ntp	Network Time Protocol; alias=ntpd ntp
124/tcp, udp	ansatrader	ANSA REX Trader
125/tcp, udp	locus-map	Locus PC-Interface Net Map Server
126/tcp, udp	unitary	Unisys Unitary Login

Table C.1 Port Assignments for Well-known Ports *(continued)*

Decimal	Keyword	Description
127/tcp, udp	locus-con	Locus PC-Interface Conn Server
128/tcp, udp	gss-xlicen	GSS X License Verification
129/tcp, udp	pwdgen	Password Generator Protocol
130/tcp, udp	cisco-fna	Cisco FNATIVE
131/tcp, udp	cisco-tna	Cisco TNATIVE
132/tcp, udp	cisco-sys	Cisco SYSMAINT
133/tcp, udp	statsrv	Statistics Service
134/tcp, udp	ingres-net	INGRES-NET Service
135/tcp, udp	loc-srv	Location Service
136/tcp, udp	profile	PROFILE Naming System
137/tcp, udp	netbios-ns	NetBIOS Name Service
138/tcp, udp	netbios-dgm	NetBIOS Datagram Service
139/tcp, udp	netbios-ssn	NetBIOS Session Service
140/tcp, udp	emfis-data	EMFIS Data Service
141/tcp, udp	emfis-cntl	EMFIS Control Service
142/tcp, udp	bl-idm	Britton-Lee IDM
143/tcp, udp	imap2	Interim Mail Access Protocol v2
144/tcp, udp	news	NewS; alias=news
145/tcp, udp	uaac	UAAC Protocol
146/tcp, udp	iso-ip0	ISO-IP0
147/tcp, udp	iso-ip	ISO-IP
148/tcp, udp	cronus	CRONUS-SUPPORT
149/tcp, udp	aed-512	AED 512 Emulation Service
150/tcp, udp	sql-net	SQL-NET
151/tcp, udp	hems	HEMS
152/tcp, udp	bftp	Background File Transfer Program
153/tcp, udp	sgmp	SGMP; alias=sgmp
154/tcp, udp	netsc-prod	Netscape
155/tcp, udp	netsc-dev	Netscape
156/tcp, udp	sqlsrv	SQL Service
157/tcp, udp	knet-cmp	KNET/VM Command/Message Protocol
158/tcp, udp	pcmail-srv	PCMail Server; alias=repository
159/tcp, udp	nss-routing	NSS-Routing

Table C.1 Port Assignments for Well-known Ports *(continued)*

Decimal	Keyword	Description
160/tcp, udp	sgmp-traps	SGMP-TRAPS
161/tcp, udp	snmp	SNMP; alias=snmp
162/tcp, udp	snmptrap	SNMPTRAP
163/tcp, udp	cmip-man	CMIP/TCP Manager
164/tcp, udp	cmip-agent	CMIP/TCP Agent
165/tcp, udp	xns-courier	Xerox
166/tcp, udp	s-net	Sirius Systems
167/tcp, udp	namp	NAMP
168/tcp, udp	rsvd	RSVD
169/tcp, udp	send	SEND
170/tcp, udp	print-srv	Network PostScript
171/tcp, udp	multiplex	Network Innovations Multiplex
172/tcp, udp	cl/1	Network Innovations CL/1
173/tcp, udp	xyplex-mux	Xyplex
174/tcp, udp	mailq	MAILQ
175/tcp, udp	vmnet	VMNET
176/tcp, udp	genrad-mux	GENRAD-MUX
177/tcp, udp	xdmcp	X Display Manager Control Protocol
178/tcp, udp	nextstep	NextStep Window Server
179/tcp, udp	bgp	Border Gateway Protocol
180/tcp, udp	ris	Intergraph
181/tcp, udp	unify	Unify
182/tcp, udp	audit	Unisys Audit SITP
183/tcp, udp	ocbinder	OCBinder
184/tcp, udp	ocserver	OCServer
185/tcp, udp	remote-kis	Remote-KIS
186/tcp, udp	kis	KIS Protocol
187/tcp, udp	aci	Application Communication Interface
188/tcp, udp	mumps	Plus Five's MUMPS
189/tcp, udp	qft	Queued File Transport
190/tcp, udp	gacp	Gateway Access Control Protocol
191/tcp, udp	prospero	Prospero
192/tcp, udp	osu-nms	OSU Network Monitoring System

Table C.1 Port Assignments for Well-known Ports *(continued)*

Decimal	Keyword	Description
193/tcp, udp	srmp	Spider Remote Monitoring Protocol
194/tcp, udp	irc	Internet Relay Chat Protocol
195/tcp, udp	dn6-nlm-aud	DNSIX Network Level Module Audit
196/tcp, udp	dn6-smm-red	DNSIX Session Mgt Module Audit Redir
197/tcp, udp	dls	Directory Location Service
198/tcp, udp	dls-mon	Directory Location Service Monitor
199/tcp, udp	smux	SMUX
200/tcp, udp	src	IBM System Resource Controller
201/tcp, udp	at-rtmp	AppleTalk Routing Maintenance
202/tcp, udp	at-nbp	AppleTalk Name Binding
203/tcp, udp	at-3	AppleTalk Unused
204/tcp, udp	at-echo	AppleTalk Echo
205/tcp, udp	at-5	AppleTalk Unused
206/tcp, udp	at-zis	AppleTalk Zone Information
207/tcp, udp	at-7	AppleTalk Unused
208/tcp, udp	at-8	AppleTalk Unused
209/tcp, udp	tam	Trivial Authenticated Mail Protocol
210/tcp, udp	z39.50	ANSI Z39.50
211/tcp, udp	914c/g	Texas Instruments 914C/G Terminal
212/tcp, udp	anet	ATEXSSTR
213/tcp, udp	ipx	IPX
214/tcp, udp	vmpwscs	VM PWSCS
215/tcp, udp	softpc	Insignia Solutions
216/tcp, udp	atls	Access Technology License Server
217/tcp, udp	dbase	dBASE UNIX
218/tcp, udp	mpp	Netix Message Posting Protocol
219/tcp, udp	uarps	Unisys ARPs
220/tcp, udp	imap3	Interactive Mail Access Protocol v3
221/tcp, udp	fln-spx	Berkeley rlogind with SPX auth
222/tcp, udp	fsh-spx	Berkeley rshd with SPX auth
223/tcp, udp	cdc	Certificate Distribution Center
224-241		Reserved
243/tcp, udp	sur-meas	Survey Measurement
245/tcp, udp	link	LINK

Table C.1 Port Assignments for Well-known Ports *(continued)*

Decimal	Keyword	Description
246/tcp, udp	dsp3270	Display Systems Protocol
247-255		Reserved
345/tcp, udp	pawserv	Perf Analysis Workbench
346/tcp, udp	zserv	Zebra server
347/tcp, udp	fatserv	Fatmen Server
371/tcp, udp	clearcase	Clearcase
372/tcp, udp	ulistserv	UNIX Listserv
373/tcp, udp	legent-1	Legent Corporation
374/tcp, udp	legent-2	Legent Corporation
512/tcp	print	Windows NT Server and Windows NT Workstation version 4.0 can send LPD client print jobs from any available reserved port between 512 and 1023. See also description for ports 721 to 731.
512/udp	biff	Used by mail system to notify users of new mail received; currently receives messages only from processes on the same computer; alias=comsat
513/tcp	login	Remote logon like telnet; automatic authentication performed, based on privileged port numbers and distributed databases that identify "authentication domains"
513/udp	who	Maintains databases showing who is logged on to the computers on a local net and the load average of the computer; alias=whod
514/tcp	cmd	Like exec, but automatic authentication is performed as for logon server
514/udp	syslog	
515/tcp, udp	printer	Spooler; alias=spooler. The print server LPD service will listen on tcp port 515 for incoming connections.
517/tcp, udp	talk	Like tenex link, but across computers; unfortunately, does not use link protocol (this is actually just a rendezvous port from which a TCP connection is established)
518/tcp, udp	ntalk	
519/tcp, udp	utime	Unixtime
520/tcp	efs	Extended file name server
520/udp	router	Local routing process (on site); uses variant of Xerox NS routing information protocol;alias=router routed

Table C.1 Port Assignments for Well-known Ports *(continued)*

Decimal	Keyword	Description
525/tcp, udp	timed	Timeserver
526/tcp, udp	tempo	Newdate
530/tcp, udp	courier	RPC
531/tcp	conference	Chat
531/udp	rvd-control	MIT disk
532/tcp, udp	netnews	Readnews
533/tcp, udp	netwall	For emergency broadcasts
540/tcp, udp	uucp	Uucpd
543/tcp, udp	klogin	
544/tcp, udp	kshell	Krcmd; alias=cmd
550/tcp, udp	new-rwho	New-who
555/tcp, udp	dsf	
556/tcp, udp	remotefs	Rfs server; alias=rfs_server rfs
560/tcp, udp	rmonitor	Rmonitord
561/tcp, udp	monitor	
562/tcp, udp	chshell	Chcmd
564/tcp, udp	9pfs	Plan 9 file service
565/tcp, udp	whoami	Whoami
570/tcp, udp	meter	Demon
571/tcp, udp	meter	Udemon
600/tcp, udp	ipcserver	Sun IPC server
607/tcp, udp	nqs	Nqs
666/tcp, udp	mdqs	
704/tcp, udp	elcsd	Errlog copy/server daemon
721-731/tcp	printer	Under Windows NT 3.5*x*, all TCP/IP print jobs *sent* from a Windows NT computer were sourced from TCP ports 721 through 731. This is changed for Windows NT Server and Windows NT Workstation version 4.0, which sources LPD client print jobs from any available reserved port between 512 and 1023.
740/tcp, udp	netcp	NETscout Control Protocol
741/tcp, udp	netgw	NetGW
742/tcp, udp	netrcs	Network based Rev. Cont. Sys.
744/tcp, udp	flexlm	Flexible License Manager

Table C.1 Port Assignments for Well-known Ports *(continued)*

Decimal	Keyword	Description
747/tcp, udp	fujitsu-dev	Fujitsu Device Control
748/tcp, udp	ris-cm	Russell Info Sci Calendar Manager
749/tcp, udp	kerberos-adm	Kerberos administration
750/tcp	rfile	Kerberos authentication; alias=kdc
750/udp	loadav	
751/tcp, udp	pump	Kerberos authentication
752/tcp, udp	qrh	Kerberos password server
753/tcp, udp	rrh	Kerberos userreg server
754/tcp, udp	tell	Send; Kerberos slave propagation
758/tcp, udp	nlogin	
759/tcp, udp	con	
760/tcp, udp	ns	
761/tcp, udp	rxe	
762/tcp, udp	quotad	
763/tcp, udp	cycleserv	
764/tcp, udp	omserv	
765/tcp, udp	webster	
767/tcp, udp	phonebook	Phone
769/tcp, udp	vid	
770/tcp, udp	cadlock	
771/tcp, udp	rtip	
772/tcp, udp	cycleserv2	
773/tcp	submit	
773/udp	notify	
774/tcp	rpasswd	
774/udp	acmaint_dbd	
775/tcp	entomb	
775/udp	acmaint_transd	
776/tcp, udp	wpages	
780/tcp, udp	wpgs	
781/tcp, udp	hp-collector	HP performance data collector

Table C.1 Port Assignments for Well-known Ports *(continued)*

Decimal	Keyword	Description
782/tcp, udp	hp-managed-node	HP performance data managed node
783/tcp, udp	hp-alarm-mgr	HP performance data alarm manager
800/tcp, udp	mdbs_daemon	
801/tcp, udp	device	
888/tcp	erlogin	Logon and environment passing
996/tcp, udp	xtreelic	XTREE License Server
997/tcp, udp	maitrd	
998/tcp	busboy	
998/udp	puparp	
999/tcp	garcon	
999/udp	applix	Applix ac
999/tcp, udp	puprouter	
1000/tcp	cadlock	
1000/udp	ock	

Port Assignments for Registered Ports

The registered ports are not controlled by the IANA and on most systems can be used by user processes or programs. Registered ports between 1024 and 5000 are also referred to as the *ephemeral* ports. Although the IANA cannot control uses of these ports, it does register or list uses of these ports as a convenience to the TCP/IP community. To the extent possible, these same port assignments are used with UDP. The registered ports are in the range 1024–65535.

This list specifies the port used by the Windows NT Server and Windows NT Workstation server process as its contact port for services and third-party software.

Note Programs that use Remote Procedure Call (RPC) to communicate can *randomly* select a registered port above 1024.

Table C.2 Port Assignments for Registered Ports

Decimal	Keyword	Description
1024		Reserved
1025/tcp, udp	blackjack	Network blackjack
1109/tcp	kpop	Pop with Kerberos
1167/udp	phone	
1248/tcp, udp	hermes	
1347/tcp, udp	bbn-mmc	Multimedia conferencing
1348/tcp, udp	bbn-mmx	Multimedia conferencing
1349/tcp, udp	sbook	Registration Network Protocol
1350/tcp, udp	editbench	Registration Network Protocol
1351/tcp, udp	equationbuilder	Digital Tool Works (MIT)
1352/tcp, udp	lotusnote	Lotus Note
1512/tcp, udp	WINS	Reserved for future use for Microsoft Windows Internet Name Service
1524/tcp, udp	ingreslock	Ingres
1525/tcp, udp	orasrv	Oracle
1525/tcp, udp	prospero-np	Prospero nonprivileged
1527/tcp, udp	tlisrv	Oracle
1529/tcp, udp	coauthor	Oracle
1600/tcp, udp	issd	
1650/tcp, udp	nkd	
1666/udp	maze	
2000/tcp, udp	callbook	
2001/tcp	dc	
2001/udp	wizard	Curry
2002/tcp, udp	globe	
2004/tcp	mailbox	
2004/udp	emce	CCWS mm conf
2005/tcp	berknet	
2005/udp	oracle	
2006/tcp	invokator	
2006/udp	raid-cc	RAID
2007/tcp	dectalk	
2007/udp	raid-am	

Table C.2 Port Assignments for Registered Ports *(continued)*

Decimal	Keyword	Description
2008/tcp	conf	
2008/udp	terminaldb	
2009/tcp	news	
2009/udp	whosockami	
2010/tcp	search	
2010/udp	pipe_server	
2011/tcp	raid-cc	RAID
2011/udp	servserv	
2012/tcp	ttyinfo	
2012/udp	raid-ac	
2013/tcp	raid-am	
2013/udp	raid-cd	
2014/tcp	troff	
2014/udp	raid-sf	
2015/tcp	cypress	
2015/udp	raid-cs	
2016/tcp, udp	bootserver	
2017/tcp	cypress-stat	
2017/udp	bootclient	
2018/tcp	terminaldb	
2018/udp	rellpack	
2019/tcp	whosockami	
2019/udp	about	
2020/tcp, udp	xinupageserver	
2021/tcp	servexec	
2021/udp	xinuexpansion1	
2022/tcp	down	
2022/udp	xinuexpansion2	
2023/tcp, udp	xinuexpansion3	
2024/tcp, udp	xinuexpansion4	
2025/tcp	ellpack	
2025/udp	xribs	
2026/tcp, udp	scrabble	

Table C.2 Port Assignments for Registered Ports *(continued)*

Decimal	Keyword	Description
2027/tcp, udp	shadowserver	
2028/tcp, udp	submitserver	
2030/tcp, udp	device2	
2032/tcp, udp	blackboard	
2033/tcp, udp	glogger	
2034/tcp, udp	scoremgr	
2035/tcp, udp	imsldoc	
2038/tcp, udp	objectmanager	
2040/tcp, udp	lam	
2041/tcp, udp	interbase	
2042/tcp, udp	isis	
2043/tcp, udp	isis-bcast	
2044/tcp, udp	rimsl	
2045/tcp, udp	cdfunc	
2046/tcp, udp	sdfunc	
2047/tcp, udp	dls	
2048/tcp, udp	dls-monitor	
2049/tcp, udp	shilp	Sun NFS
2053/tcp	knetd	Kerberos de-multiplexer
2105/tcp	eklogin	Kerberos encrypted rlogon
2784/tcp, udp	www-dev	World Wide Web - development
3049/tcp, udp	NSWS	
4672/tcp, udp	rfa	Remote file access server
5000/tcp, udp	commplex-main	
5001/tcp, udp	commplex-link	
5002/tcp, udp	rfe	Radio Free Ethernet
5145/tcp, udp	rmonitor_secure	
5236/tcp, udp	padl2sim	
5555/tcp	rmt	Rmtd
5556/tcp	mtb	Mtbd (mtb backup)
6111/tcp, udp	sub-process	HP SoftBench Sub-Process Control
6558/tcp, udp	xdsxdm	
7000/tcp, udp	afs3-fileserver	File server itself

Table C.2 Port Assignments for Registered Ports *(continued)*

Decimal	Keyword	Description
7001/tcp, udp	afs3-callback	Callbacks to cache managers
7002/tcp, udp	afs3-prserver	Users and groups database
7003/tcp, udp	afs3-vlserver	Volume location database
7004/tcp, udp	afs3-kaserver	AFS/Kerberos authentication service
7005/tcp, udp	afs3-volser	Volume management server
7006/tcp, udp	afs3-errors	Error interpretation service
7007/tcp, udp	afs3-bos	Basic overseer process
7008/tcp, udp	afs3-update	Server-to-server updater
7009/tcp, udp	afs3-rmtsys	Remote cache manager service
9535/tcp, udp	man	Remote man server
9536/tcp	w	
9537/tcp	mantst	Remote man server, testing
10000/tcp	bnews	
10000/udp	rscs0	
10001/tcp	queue	
10001/udp	rscs1	
10002/tcp	poker	
10002/udp	rscs2	
10003/tcp	gateway	
10003/udp	rscs3	
10004/tcp	remp	
10004/udp	rscs4	
10005/udp	rscs5	
10006/udp	rscs6	
10007/udp	rscs7	
10008/udp	rscs8	
10009/udp	rscs9	
10010/udp	rscsa	
10011/udp	rscsb	
10012/tcp	qmaster	
10012/udp	qmaster	
17007/tcp, udp	isode-dua	

Glossary

A

access permission A rule associated with an object (usually a directory, file, or printer) to regulate which users can have access to the object and in what manner. *See also* user right.

access privileges Permissions set by Macintosh users that allow them to view and make changes to folders on a server. By setting access privileges (called permissions when set on the computer running Windows NT Server) you control which Macintoshes can use folders in a volume. Services for Macintosh translates access privileges set by Macintosh users to the equivalent Windows NT permissions.

account *See* user account; group account.

account lockout A Windows NT Server security feature that locks a user account if a number of failed logon attempts occur within a specified amount of time, based on account policy lockout settings. (Locked accounts cannot log on.)

account policy Controls the way passwords must be used by all user accounts of a domain, or of an individual computer. Specifics include minimum password length, how often a user must change his or her password, and how often users can reuse old passwords. Account policy can be set for all user accounts in a domain when administering a domain, and for all user accounts of a single workstation or member server when administering a computer.

ACK Short for acknowledgment. The transmission control protocol (TCP) requires that the recipient of data packets acknowledge successful receipt of data. Such acknowledgments (ACKs) generate additional network traffic, diminishing the rate at which data passes in favor of reliability. To reduce the impact on performance, most hosts send an acknowledgment for every other segment or when a specified time interval has passed.

Active The window or icon that you are currently using or that is currently selected. Windows NT always applies the next keystroke or command you choose to the active window. If a window is active, its title bar changes color to differentiate it from other windows. If an icon is active, its label changes color. Windows or icons on the desktop that are not selected are inactive.

adapter card *See* network card.

address When using Network Monitor, an address refers to a hexadecimal number that identifies a computer uniquely on the network.

address classes Predefined groupings of Internet addresses, with each class defining networks of a certain size. The range of numbers that can be assigned for the first octet in the IP address is based on the address class. Class A networks (values 1-126) are the largest, with over 16 million hosts per network. Class B networks (128-191) have up to 65,534 hosts per network, and Class C networks (192-223) can have up to 254 hosts per network. *See also* octet.

address pairs Refers to the two specific computers between which you want to monitor traffic using Network Monitor. Up to four specific address pairs can be monitored simultaneously to capture frames from particular computers on your network. *See also* frame.

address resolution protocol (ARP) A protocol in the TCP/IP suite that provides IP address-to-MAC address resolution for IP packets. *See also* media access control (MAC); IP address; packet.

administrative account An account that is a member of the Administrators local group of a computer or domain.

administrative alerts Administrative alerts relate to server and resource use and warn about problems in areas such as security and access, user sessions, server shutdown due to power loss (when UPS is available), directory replication, and printing. When a computer generates an administrative alert, a message is sent to a predefined list of users and computers. *See also* Alerter service; UPS.

administrator A person responsible for setting up and managing domain controllers or local computers and their user and group accounts, assigning passwords and permissions, and helping users with networking issues. To use administrative tools such as User Manager or User Manager for Domains, an administrator must be logged on as a member of the Administrators local group of the computer or domain, respectively.

Administrator privilege One of three privilege levels you can assign to a Windows NT user account. Every user account has one of the three privilege levels (Administrator, Guest, and User). *See also* administrator; User privilege and Guest privilege.

agent In SNMP, agent information consists of comments about the user, the physical location of the computer, and the types of service to report based on the computer's configuration. *See also* SNMP.

Alerter service Notifies selected users and computers of administrative alerts that occur on a computer. Used by the Server and other services. Requires the Messenger service. *See also* administrative alerts; Messenger service.

API Acronym for application programming interface, a set of routines that an application programmer uses to request and carry out lower-level services performed by a computer's operating system. These maintenance chores are performed by the computer's operating system, and an API provides the program with a means of communicating with the system, telling it which system-level task to perform and when.

AppleShare Client software that is shipped with all Macintoshes and with Apple Computer's server software. With Services for Macintosh, Macintoshes use their native AppleShare client software to connect to computers running Windows NT Server that have Services for Macintosh.

AppleTalk Apple Computer's network architecture and network protocols. A network that has Macintosh clients and a computer running Windows NT Server with Services for Macintosh functions as an AppleTalk network.

AppleTalk Filing Protocol The presentation layer protocol that manages access of remote files in an AppleTalk network.

AppleTalk Phase 2 The extended AppleTalk internet model designed by Apple Computer, which supports multiple zones within a network and extended addressing capacity.

AppleTalk Protocol The set of network protocols on which AppleTalk network architecture is based. Setting up Services for Macintosh installs its AppleTalk Protocol stack on a computer running Windows NT Server so that Macintosh clients can connect to it.

AppleTalk Transport The layer of AppleTalk Phase 2 protocols that deliver data to its destination on the network.

application A computer program used for a particular kind of work, such as word processing. This term is often used interchangeably with "program."

application log The application log contains specific events logged by applications. Applications developers decide which events to monitor (for example, a database program might record a file error in the application log). Use Event Viewer to view the application log.

application window The main window for an application, which contains the application's menu bar and work area. An application window may contain multiple document windows.

ARC Acronym for Advanced RISC Computing. ARC names are a generic method of identifying devices within the ARC environment. *See also* RISC.

archive bit Backup programs use the archive bit to mark the files after backing them up, if a normal or incremental backup is performed. *See also* backup types.

ARP Acronym for Address Resolution Protocol, one of the network maintenance protocols that is a member the TCP/IP suite (not directly related to data transport). *See also* TCP/IP.

ARP reply packet All ARP-enabled systems on the local IP network detect ARP request packets, and the system that owns the IP address in question replies by sending its physical address to the requester in an ARP reply packet. The physical/IP address is then stored in the ARP cache of the requesting system for subsequent use. *See also* ARP; ARP request packet; IP; MAC address.

ARP request packet If two systems are to communicate across a TCP/IP network, the system sending the packet must map the IP address of the final destination to the physical address of the final destination. This physical address is also referred to as a MAC address, a unique 48-bit number assigned to the network interface card by the manufacturer. IP acquires this physical address by broadcasting a special inquiry packet (an ARP request packet) containing the IP address of the destination system. *See also* ARP; IP; MAC; MAC address.

AS/400 A type of IBM minicomputer.

ASCII file Also called a text file, a text-only file, or an ASCII text file, refers to a file in the universally recognized text format called ASCII (American Standard Code for Information Interchange). An ASCII file contains characters, spaces, punctuation, carriage returns, and sometimes tabs and an end-of-file marker, but it contains no formatting information. This generic format is useful for transferring files between programs that could not otherwise understand each other's documents. *See also* text file.

associate To identify a filename extension as "belonging" to a certain application, so that when you open any file with that extension, the application starts automatically.

attributes Information that indicates whether a file is a read-only, hidden, system, or compressed file, and whether the file has been changed since a backup copy of it was made.

auditing Tracking activities of users by recording selected types of events in the security log of a server or a workstation.

audit policy For the servers of a domain or for an individual computer, defines the type of security events that will be logged.

authentication Validation of a user's logon information. When a user logs on to an account on a computer running Windows NT Workstation, the authentication is performed by that workstation. When a user logs on to an account on a Windows NT Server domain, authentication may be performed by any server of that domain. *See also* server; trust relationship.

B

Backup Domain Controller (BDC)
In a Windows NT Server domain, a computer running Windows NT Server that receives a copy of the domain's directory database, which contains all account and security policy information for the domain. The copy is synchronized periodically and automatically with the master copy on the primary domain controller (PDC). BDCs also authenticate user logons and can be promoted to function as PDCs as needed. Multiple BDCs can exist on a domain. *See also* member server; Primary Domain Controller.

backup set A collection of files from one drive that is backed up during a single backup operation.

backup set catalog At the end of each backup set, Windows NT Backup stores a summary of file and/or directory information in a backup set catalog. Catalog information includes the number of tapes in a set of tapes as well as the date they were created and the dates of each file in the catalog. Catalogs are created for each backup set and are stored on the last tape in the set. *See also* backup set.

backup set map At the end of each tape used for backup, a backup set map maintains the exact tape location of the backup set's data and catalog.

backup types:

copy backup Copies all selected files, but does not mark each file as having been backed up. Copying is useful if you want to back up files between normal and incremental backups, because copying will not invalidate these other backup operations.

daily backup Copies all selected files that have been modified the day the daily backup is performed.

differential backup Copies those files created or changed since the last normal (or incremental) backup. It does not mark files as having been backed up.

incremental backup Backs up only those files created or changed since the last normal (or incremental) backup. It marks files as having been backed up.

normal backup Copies all selected files and marks each as having been backed up. Normal backups give you the ability to restore files quickly because files on the last tape are the most current.

bandwidth In communications, the difference between the highest and lowest frequencies in a given range. For example, a telephone line accommodates a bandwidth of 3000 Hz, the difference between the lowest (300Hz) and highest (3300 Hz) frequencies it can carry. In computer networks, greater bandwidth indicates faster data-transfer capability and is expressed in bits per second (bps).

batch program An ASCII file (unformatted text file) that contains one or more Windows NT commands. A batch program's filename has a .cmd or .bat extension. When you type the filename at the command prompt, the commands are processed sequentially.

batch queue facility A program that effects a logon without user input, used for delayed logons.

BDC *See* Backup Domain Controller.

binary A base-2 number system, in which values are expressed as combinations of two digits, 0 and 1.

binary-file transfer A method of transferring binary files from Windows NT HyperTerminal to a remote computer. Binary files consist of ASCII characters plus the extended ASCII character set. These files are not converted or translated during the transfer process. *See also* ASCII file.

binding A process that establishes the communication channel between a protocol driver (such as TCP/IP) and a network card. *See also* network card; TCP/IP.

bookmarks A Windows NT feature which enables you to highlight major points of interest at various points in a Performance Monitor log file and then return to them easily when you work with that log file later on during performance monitoring. Bookmarks are also used in other applications such as Microsoft Word.

boot loader Defines the information needed for system startup, such as the location for the operating system's files. Windows NT automatically creates the correct configuration and checks this information whenever you start your system.

boot partition The volume, formatted for either an NTFS or FAT file system, that has the Windows NT operating system and its support files. The boot partition can be (but does not have to be) the same as the system partition. *See also* partition; File Allocation Table; NTFS.

BOOTP *See* Bootstrap protocol.

Bootstrap protocol (BOOTP) A TCP/IP network protocol, defined by RFC 951 and RFC 1542, used to configure systems. DHCP is an extension of BOOTP. *See also* DHCP.

bps An abbreviation for bits per second, a measure of the speed at which a device, such as a modem, can transfer data.

branch A segment of the directory tree, representing a directory (or folder) and any subdirectories (or folders within folders) it contains.

bridge Connects multiple networks, subnets, or rings into one large logical network. A bridge maintains a table of node addresses and based on this, forwards packets to a specific subnet, reducing traffic on other subnets. In a bridged network, there can be only one path to any destination (otherwise packets would circle the network, causing network storms). A bridge is more sophisticated than a repeater, but not as sophisticated as a router. *See also* packet; repeaters; router; subnet.

broadcast datagrams An IP datagram sent to all hosts on the subnet. *See also* datagram; Internet Protocol (IP); subnet.

broadcast message A network message sent from a single computer that is distributed to all other devices on the same segment of the network as the sending computer.

Broadcast name resolution A mechanism defined in RFC 1001/1002 that uses broadcasts to resolve names to IP addresses through a process of registration, resolution, and name release. *See also* broadcast datagrams; IP address.

brouter Combines elements of the bridge and the router. Usually, a brouter acts as a router for one transport protocol (such as TCP/IP), sending packets of that format along detailed routes to their destinations. The brouter also acts as a bridge for all other types of packets (such as IPX), just passing them on, as long as they are not local to the LAN segment from which they originated. *See also* bridge; packet; router.

browse To view available network resources by looking through lists of folders, files, user accounts, groups, domains, or computers. Browsing allows users on a Windows NT network to see what domains and computers are accessible from their local computer. *See also* Windows NT browser system.

browse list A list kept by the master browser of all of the servers and domains on the network. This list is available to any workstation on the network requesting it. *See also* browse.

browse master *See* master browser; Windows NT browser system.

buffer A reserved portion of memory in which data is temporarily held pending an opportunity to complete its transfer to or from a storage device or another location in memory. Some devices, such as printers or the adapters supporting them, commonly have their own buffers. *See also* memory.

built-in groups Are default groups provided with Windows NT Workstation and Windows NT Server which have been granted useful collections of rights and built-in abilities. In most cases, a built-in group provides all the capabilities needed by a particular user. For example, if a domain user account belongs to the built-in Administrators group, logging on with that account gives a user administrative capabilities over the domain and the servers of the domain. To provide a needed set of capabilities to a user account, assign it to the appropriate built-in group. *See also* groups, User Manager, User Manager for Domains.

C

cache A special memory subsystem that stores the contents of frequently accessed RAM locations and the addresses where these data items are stored. In Windows NT, for example, user profiles have a locally cached copy of part of the registry.

caching In DNS name resolution, caching refers to a local cache where information about the DNS domain name space is kept. Whenever a resolver request arrives, the local name server checks both its static information and the cache for the name to IP address mapping. *See also* DNS; IP address; mapping.

capture The process by which Network Monitor copies frames. (A frame is information that has been divided into smaller pieces by the network software prior to transmission.) *See also* frame.

capture buffer Refers to a reserved, resizable storage area in memory where Network Monitor copies all frames it detects from the network. When the capture buffer overflows, each new frame replaces the oldest frame in the buffer.

capture filter Functions like a database query to single out a subset of frames to be monitored in Network Monitor. You can filter on the basis of source and destination addresses, protocols, protocol properties, or by specifying a pattern offset. *See also* capture; frame.

capture password Required to be able to capture statistics from the network and to display captured data using Network Monitor.

capture trigger Performs a specified action (such as starting an executable file) when Network Monitor detects a particular set of conditions on the network.

catalog *See* backup catalog.

CBCP Acronym for Callback Control Protocol, which negotiates callback information with a remote client.

CCP Acronym for Compression Control Protocol, which negotiates compression with a remote client.

centralized network administration A centralized view of the entire network from any workstation on the network that provides the ability to track and manage information on users, groups, and resources in a distributed network.

change log An inventory of the most recent changes made to the directory database such as new or changed passwords, new or changed user and group accounts, and any changes to associated group memberships and user rights. Change logs provide fault tolerance, so if your system crashes before a write completes, Windows NT can complete the write the next time you boot. This log holds only a certain number of changes, however, so when a new change is added, the oldest change is deleted. *See also* directory database; fault tolerance.

CHAP Acronym for Challenge Handshake Authentication Protocol, used by Microsoft RAS to negotiate the most secure form of encrypted authentication supported by both server and client. *See also* encryption.

check box A small box in a dialog box or property page that can be selected or cleared. Check boxes represent an option that you can turn on or off. When a check box is selected, an X or a check mark appears in the box.

checksum The mathematical computation used to verify the accuracy of data in TCP/IP packets. *See also* packet; TCP/IP.

choose To pick an item that begins an action in Windows NT. You often click a command on a menu to perform a task, and you click an icon to start an application.

Chooser The Macintosh desk accessory with which users select the network server and printers they want to use.

Chooser Pack A collection of files, some of which contain PostScript information. When a Macintosh sends a print job to a PostScript printer, the printer uses a Chooser Pack to interpret PostScript commands in the print job. *See* PostScript printer; print processor.

clear To turn off an option by removing the X or check mark from a check box. You clear a check box by clicking it, or by selecting it and then pressing the SPACEBAR.

cleartext passwords Passwords that are not scrambled, thus making them more susceptible to network sniffers. *See also* network sniffer.

click To press and release a mouse button quickly.

client A computer that accesses shared network resources provided by another computer, called a server. *See also* server; workstation.

client application A Windows NT application that can display and store linked or embedded objects. For distributed applications, the application that imitates a request to a server application. *See also* server application, DCOM, DCOM Configuration tool.

Client Service for NetWare Included with Windows NT Workstation, enabling workstations to make direct connections to file and printer resources at NetWare servers running NetWare 2.x or later.

Clipboard A temporary storage area in memory, used to transfer information. You can cut or copy information onto the Clipboard and then paste it into another document or application.

close To remove a window or dialog box, or quit an application. You close a window by clicking **Close** on the **Control** menu, or by clicking on the close button icon in the upper right corner of the dialog box. When you close an application window, you quit the application.

collapse To hide additional directory levels below a selected directory in the directory tree.

color scheme A combination of complementary colors for screen elements.

command A word or phrase, usually found on a menu, that you click to carry out an action. You click a command on a menu or type a command at the Windows NT command prompt. You can also type a command in the **Run** dialog box, which you open by clicking **Run** on the **Start** menu.

command button A button in a dialog box that carries out or cancels the selected action. Two common command buttons are **OK** and **Cancel**. Clicking a command button that contains an ellipsis (for example, Browse...) causes another dialog box to appear.

common groups Common groups appear in the program list on the **Start** menu for all users who log on to the computer. Only Administrators can create or change common groups.

communications settings Settings that specify how information is transferred from your computer to a device (usually a printer or modem).

community names A group of hosts to which a server belongs that is running the SNMP service. The community name is placed in the SNMP packet when the trap is sent. Typically, all hosts belong to Public, which is the standard name for the common community of all hosts. *See also* SNMP; packet; trap.

compact A command-line utility used to compress files on NTFS volumes. To *See* command line options, type compact /? at the command prompt. This utility can also be accessed by right-clicking any file or directory on an NTFS volume in Windows NT Explorer and clicking Properties to compress or uncompress the files.

compound device A device that plays specific media files. For example, to run a compound device such as a MIDI sequencer, you must specify a MIDI file.

computer account Each computer running Windows NT Workstation and Windows NT Server that participates in a domain has its own account in the directory database. A computer account is created when the computer is first identified to the domain during network setup at installation time.

Computer Browser service Maintains an up-to-date list of computers, and provides the list to applications when requested. Provides the computer lists displayed in the **Network Neighborhood**, **Select Computer,** and **Select Domain** dialog boxes; and (for Windows NT Server only) in the Server Manager window.

computer name A unique name of up to 15 uppercase characters that identifies a computer to the network. The name cannot be the same as any other computer or domain name in the network.

configure To change the initial setup of a client, a Macintosh-accessible volume, a server, or a network.

connect To assign a drive letter, port, or computer name to a shared resource so that you can use it with Windows NT.

connected user A user accessing a computer or a resource across the network.

connection A software link between a client and a shared resource such as a printer or a shared directory on a server. Connections require a network card or modem.

control codes Codes that specify terminal commands or formatting instructions (such as linefeeds or carriage returns) in a text file. Control codes are usually preceded by a caret (^).

controller *See* primary domain controller; backup domain controller.

Control menu *See* window menu.

conventional memory Up to the first 640K of memory in your computer. MS-DOS uses this memory to run applications.

current directory The directory that you are currently working in. Also called current folder.

D

DACL Acronym for discretionary access control list. *See* discretionary access control; SACL.

daemon A networking program that runs in the background.

data carrier In communications, either a specified frequency that can be modulated to convey information or a company that provides telephone and other communications services to consumers.

database query The process of extracting data from a database and presenting it for use.

data fork The part of a Macintosh file that holds most of the file's information. The data fork is the part of the file shared between Macintosh and PC clients.

datagram A packet of data and other delivery information that is routed through a packet-switched network or transmitted on a local area network. *See also* packet.

data stream Windows NT Network Monitor monitors the network data stream, which consists of all information transferred over a network at any given time.

DCD Acronym for Data Carrier Detect, which tracks the presence of a data carrier. *See also* data carrier.

DCE Acronym for data communications equipment, an elaborate worldwide network of packet-forwarding nodes that participate in delivering an X.25 packet to its designated address, for example, a modem. *See also* node; packet; X.25.

DCOM Acronym for Distributed Component Object Model. Use the DCOM Configuration tool to integrate client/server applications across multiple computers. DCOM can also be used to integrate robust Web browser applications.

DCOM Configuration tool A Windows NT Server Utility that can be used to configure 32-bit applications for DCOM communication over the network. *See also* DCOM.

DDE *See* dynamic data exchange.

decision tree A geographical representation of a filter's logic used by Windows NT Network Monitor. When you include or exclude information from your capture specifications, the decision tree reflects these specifications.

default button In some dialog boxes, the command button that is selected or highlighted when the dialog box is initially displayed. The default button has a bold border, indicating that it will be chosen automatically if you press ENTER. You can override a default button by clicking **Cancel** or another command button.

default gateway In TCP/IP, the intermediate network device on the local network that has knowledge of the network IDs of the other networks in the internet, so it can forward the packets to other gateways until the packet is eventually delivered to a gateway connected to the specified destination. *See also* gateway; network ID; packet.

default network In the Macintosh environment, this refers to physical network on which a server's processes reside as nodes and on which the server appears to users. A server's default network must be one to which that server is attached. Only servers on AppleTalk Phase 2 internets have default networks.

default owner The person assigned ownership of a folder on the server when the account of the folder or volume's previous owner expires or is deleted. Each server has one default owner; you can specify the owner.

default printer The printer that is used if you choose the Print command without first specifying which printer you want to use with an application. You can have only one default printer; it should be the printer you use most often.

default profile *See* system default profile; user default profile.

default user Every user profile begins as a copy of default user (a default user profile stored on each computer running Windows NT Workstation or Windows NT Server).

default zone The zone to which all Macintosh clients on the network are assigned by default.

dependent service A service that requires support of another service. For example, the Alerter service is dependent on the Messenger service. *See also* Alerter service; Messenger service.

DES Acronym for Data Encryption Standard, a type of encryption (the U.S. government standard) designed to protect against password discovery and playback. Microsoft RAS uses DES encryption when both the client and the server are using RAS.

descendent key All the subkeys that appear when a key in the registry is expanded. A descendent key is the same thing as a subkey. *See also* key; subkey; Windows NT Registry.

desired zone The zone in which Services for Macintosh appears on the network. *See also* default zone.

desktop The background of your screen, on which windows, icons, and dialog boxes appear.

desktop pattern A design that appears across your desktop. You can create your own pattern or select a pattern provided by Windows NT.

destination directory The directory to which you intend to copy or move one or more files.

destination document The document into which a package or a linked or embedded object is being inserted. For an embedded object, this is sometimes also called the container document. *See also* embedded object; linked object; package.

device Any piece of equipment that can be attached to a network—for example, a computer, a printer, or any other peripheral equipment.

device contention The way Windows NT allocates access to peripheral devices, such as modems or a printers, when more than one application is trying to use the same device.

device driver A program that enables a specific piece of hardware (device) to communicate with Windows NT. Although a device may be installed on your system, Windows NT cannot recognize the device until you have installed and configured the appropriate driver. If a device is listed in the Hardware Compatibility List, a driver is usually included with Windows NT. Drivers are installed when you run the Setup program (for a manufacturer's supplied driver) or by using Devices in Control Panel. *See also* HCL.

DHCP Acronym for Dynamic Host Configuration Protocol, which offers dynamic configuration of IP addresses and related information. DHCP provides safe, reliable, and simple TCP/IP network configuration, prevents address conflicts, and helps conserve the use of IP addresses through centralized management of address allocation. *See also* IP address.

DHCP Relay Agent The component responsible for relaying DHCP and BOOTP broadcast messages between a DHCP server and a client across an IP router. *See also* BOOTP; DHCP.

dialog box A window that is displayed to request or supply information. Many dialog boxes have options you must select before Windows NT can carry out a command.

dial-up line A standard dial-up connection such as telephone and ISDN lines.

dial-up networking The client version of Windows NT Remote Access Service (RAS), enabling users to connect to remote networks.

directory Part of a structure for organizing your files on a disk, a directory (also called a folder) is represented by the folder icon in Windows NT, Windows 95, and on Macintosh computers. A directory can contain files and other directories, called subdirectories or folders within folders.

With Services for Macintosh, directories on the computer running Windows NT Server appear to Macintosh users as volumes and folders if they are designated as Macintosh accessible.

See also directory tree; folder.

directory database A database of security information such as user account names and passwords, and the security policy settings. For Windows NT Workstation, the directory database is managed using User Manager. For a Windows NT Server domain, it is managed using User Manager for Domains. (Other Windows NT documents may refer to the directory database as the "Security Accounts Manager (SAM) database.")

directory replication The copying of a master set of directories from a server (called an export server) to specified servers or workstations (called import computers) in the same or other domains. Replication simplifies the task of maintaining identical sets of directories and files on multiple computers, because only a single master copy of the data must be maintained. Files are replicated when they are added to an exported directory, and every time a change is saved to the file. *See also* Directory Replicator service.

Directory Replicator service Replicates directories, and the files in those directories, between computers. *See also* directory replication.

directory services *See* Windows NT Directory Services.

directory tree A graphical display of a disk's directory hierarchy. The directories and folders on the disk are shown as a branching structure. The top-level directory is the root directory.

disabled user account A user account that does not permit logons. The account appears in the user account list of the User Manager or User Manager for Domains window and can be re-enabled at any time. *See also* user account.

discovery A process by which the Windows NT Net Logon service attempts to locate a domain controller running Windows NT Server in the trusted domain. Once a domain controller has been discovered, it is used for subsequent user account authentication.

discretionary access control Allows the network administrator to allow some users to connect to a resource or perform an action while preventing other users from doing so. *See also* DACL; SACL.

disjoint networks Networks that are not connected to each other.

disk configuration information The Windows NT registry includes the following information on the configuration of your disk(s): assigned drive letters, stripe sets, mirror sets, volume sets, and stripe sets with parity. Disk configuration can be changed using Disk Administrator. If you choose to create an Emergency Repair disk, disk configuration information will be stored there, as well as in the registry.

display filter Functions like a database query, allowing you to single out specific types of information. Because a display filter operates on data that has already been captured, it does not affect the contents of the Network Monitor capture buffer. *See also* capture buffer.

display password Required to be able to open previously saved capture (.cap) files in Network Monitor.

distributed server system In Windows NT, a system in which individual departments or workgroups set up and maintain their own remote access domains.

DLL *See* dynamic-link library.

DNS *See* Domain Name System (DNS).

DNS name servers In the DNS client-server model, the servers containing information about a portion of the DNS database, which makes computer names available to client resolvers querying for name resolution across the internet. *See also* Domain Name System (DNS).

document A self-contained file created with an application program and, if saved on disk, given a unique filename by which it can be retrieved. A document can be a text file, a spreadsheet, or an image file, for example.

document file A file that is associated with an application. When you open a document file, the application starts and loads the file. *See also* associate.

Document file icon Represents a file that is associated with an application. When you double-click a document file icon, the application starts and loads the file. *See also* associate.

document icon Located at the left of a document window title bar, the document icon represents the open document. Clicking the document icon opens the window menu. Also known as the control menu box.

domain In Windows NT, a collection of computers defined by the administrator of a Windows NT Server network that share a common directory database. A domain provides access to the centralized user accounts and group accounts maintained by the domain administrator. Each domain has a unique name. *See also* workgroup. *See also* directory database; user account; workgroup.

domain controller In a Windows NT Server domain, refers to the computer running Windows NT Server that manages all aspects of user-domain interactions, and uses information in the directory database to authenticate users logging on to domain accounts. One shared directory database is used to store security and user account information for the entire domain. A domain has one primary domain controller (PDC) and one or more backup domain controllers (BDCs). *See also* directory database; member server; PDC; BDC.

domain database *See* directory database.

domain model A grouping of one or more domains with administration and communication links between them that are arranged for the purpose of user and resource management.

domain name Part of the Domain Name System (DNS) naming structure, a domain name is the name by which a domain is known to the network. Domain names consist of a sequence of labels separated by periods. *See also* Domain Name System (DNS); FQDN.

domain name space The database structure used by the Domain Name System (DNS). *See also* Domain Name System (DNS).

Domain Name System (DNS) Sometimes referred to as the BIND service in BSD UNIX, DNS offers a static, hierarchical name service for TCP/IP hosts. The network administrator configures the DNS with a list of *hostnames* and IP addresses, allowing users of workstations configured to query the DNS to specify remote systems by *hostnames* rather than IP addresses. For example, a workstation configured to use DNS name resolution could use the command **ping remotehost** rather than **ping 172.16.16.235** if the mapping for the system named remotehost was contained in the DNS database. DNS domains should not be confused with Windows NT networking domains. *See also* ping; IP address.

domain synchronization *See* synchronize.

dots per inch (DPI) The standard used to measure print device resolution. The greater the DPI, the better the resolution.

double-click To rapidly press and release a mouse button twice without moving the mouse. Double-clicking carries out an action, such as starting an application.

downloaded fonts Fonts that you send to your printer either before or during the printing of your documents. When you send a font to your printer, it is stored in printer memory until it is needed for printing. *See also* font; font types.

DPI *See* dots per inch.

drag To move an item on the screen by selecting the item and then pressing and holding down the mouse button while moving the mouse. For example, you can move a window to another location on the screen by dragging its title bar.

drive icon An icon in the All Folders column in Windows NT Explorer or the Names Column in My Computer that represents a disk drive on your system. Different icons depict floppy disk drives, hard disk drives, network drives, RAM drives, and CD-ROM drives.

driver *See* device driver.

drop folder In the Macintosh environment this refers to a folder for which you have the Make Changes permission but not the See Files or See Folders permission. You can copy files into a drop folder, but you cannot see what files and subfolders the drop folder contains.

DSDM Acronym for DDE share database manager. *See also* DDE; Network DDE DSDM service.

DSR Acronym for Data Set Ready signal, used in serial communications. A DSR is sent by a modem to the computer to which it's attached to indicate that it is ready to operate. DSRs are hardware signals sent over line 6 in RS-232-C connections.

DTE Acronym for Data Terminal Equipment, for example a RAS server or client. *See also* Remote Access Service (RAS).

dual boot A computer that can boot two different operating systems. *See also* multiple-boot.

DWORD A data type composed of hexadecimal data with a maximum allotted space of 4 bytes.

dynamic data exchange (DDE) A form of interprocess communication (IPC) implemented in the Microsoft Windows family of operating systems. Two or more programs that support dynamic data exchange (DDE) can exchange information and commands. *See also* IPC.

dynamic-link library (DLL) An operating system feature which allows executable routines (generally serving a specific function or set of functions) to be stored separately as files with DLL extensions and to be loaded only when needed by the program that calls them.

dynamic routing Dynamic routing automatically updates the routing tables, reducing administrative overhead (but increasing traffic in large networks). *See also* routing table.

E

EISA *See* Extended Industry Standard Architecture.

embedded object Presents information created in another application which has been pasted inside your document. Information in the embedded object does not exist in another file outside your document.

EMS Acronym for expanded memory, which describes a technique for adding memory to IBM PC systems. EMS bypasses the limits on the maximum amount of usable memory in a computer system by supporting memory boards containing a number of 16 KB banks of RAM that can be enabled or disabled by software. *See also* memory.

encapsulated PostScript (EPS) file
A file that prints at the highest possible resolution for your printer. An EPS file may print faster than other graphical representations. Some Windows NT and non-Windows NT graphical applications can import EPS files. *See also* font types; PostScript printer; print processor.

encryption The process of making information indecipherable to protect it from unauthorized viewing or use, especially during transmission or when it is stored on a transportable magnetic medium.

enterprise server Refers to the server to which multiple primary domain controllers (PDCs) in a large organization will replicate. *See also* primary domain controller (PDC).

environment variable A string consisting of environment information, such as a drive, path, or filename, associated with a symbolic name that can be used by Windows NT. You use the **System** option in Control Panel or the **Set** command from the Windows NT command prompt to define environment variables.

event Any significant occurrence in the system or an application that requires users to be notified, or an entry to be added to a log.

Event Log service Records events in the system, security, and application logs. Event Log Service is located in Event Viewer.

expand To show hidden directory levels in the directory tree. With My Computer or Windows NT Explorer, directories that can expand have plus-sign icons which you click to expand.

expanded memory A type of memory, up to 8 megabytes, that can be added to an 8086 or 8088 computer, or to an 80286, 80386, 80486, or Pentium computer. The use of expanded memory is defined by the Expanded Memory Specification (EMS). Note: Windows NT requires a 80486 or higher computer.

Explorer Microsoft Windows NT Explorer is a program that enables you to view and manage the files and folders on your computer and make network connections to other shared resources, such as a hard disk on a server. Windows NT Explorer replaces Program Manager and File Manger, which were programs available in earlier versions of Windows NT. Program Manager and File Manager are still available, and can be started in the same way you start other Windows-based programs.

export path In directory replication, a path from which subdirectories, and the files in those subdirectories, are automatically exported from an export server. *See also* directory replication.

export server In directory replication, a server from which a master set of directories is exported to specified servers or workstations (called import computers) in the same or other domains. *See also* directory replication.

Extended Industry Standard Architecture (EISA) A 32-bit bus standard introduced in 1988 by a consortium of nine computer industry companies. EISA maintains compatibility with the earlier Industry Standard Architecture (ISA) but provides for additional features.

extended memory Memory beyond one megabyte in 80286, 80386, 80486, and Pentium computers. Note: Windows NT requires a 80486 or higher computer.

extended partition Created from free space on a hard disk, an extended partition can be subpartitioned into zero or more logical drives. Only one of the four partitions allowed per physical disk can be an extended partition, and no primary partition needs to be present to create an extended partition. *See also* free space; logical drives; primary partition.

extension An extension usually indicates the type of file or directory, or the type of application associated with a file. In MS-DOS, this includes a period and up to three characters at the end of a filename. Windows NT supports long filenames up to the filename limit of 255 characters.

extension-type associations The association of an MS-DOS filename extension with a Macintosh file type and file creator. Extension-type associations allow users of the PC and Macintosh versions of the same application to share the same data files on the server. Services for Macintosh has many predefined extension-type associations; you can also use the Associate command in the MacFile menu in File Manager to add more mappings. *See also* name mapping.

external command A command that is stored in its own file and loaded from disk when you use the command.

F

family set A collection of related tapes containing several backup sets. *See also* backup sets.

FAT *See* file allocation table (FAT).

fault tolerance Ensures data integrity when hardware failures occur. In Windows NT, fault tolerance is provided by the FTDISK.SYS driver. In Disk Administrator, fault tolerance is provided using mirror sets, stripe sets with parity, and volume sets. *See also* mirror sets; stripe sets with parity; volume sets.

FCB Acronym for file control block, a small block of memory temporarily assigned by a computer's operating system to hold information about a file that has been opened for use. An FCB typically contains such information as the file's identification, its location on disk, and a pointer that marks the user's current (or last) position in the file.

FDDI (Fiber Distributed Data Interface) A type of network media designed to be used with fiber-optic cabling. *See also* LocalTalk, and Token Ring.

file A collection of information that has been given a name and is stored on a disk. This information can be a document or an application.

file allocation table (FAT) A table or list maintained by some operating systems to keep track of the status of various segments of disk space used for file storage. Also referred to as the FAT file system.

file creator A four-character sequence that tells the Macintosh Finder the name of the application that created a file. With Services for Macintosh, you can create extension-type associations that map PC filename extensions with Macintosh file creators and file types. These associations allow both PC and Macintosh users to share the same data files on the server. *See also* extension-type associations.

file fork One of two subfiles of a Macintosh file. When Macintosh files are stored on a computer running Windows NT Server, each fork is stored as a separate file. Each fork can be independently opened by Macintosh users.

filename The name of a file. MS-DOS supports the 8.3 naming convention of up to eight characters followed by a period and a three-character extension. Windows NT supports the FAT and NTFS file systems with filenames up to 255 characters. Since MS-DOS cannot recognize long filenames, Windows NT Server automatically translates long names of files and folders to 8.3 names for MS-DOS users. *See also* name mapping; long name; short name.

filename extension The characters that follow the period in a filename, following the FAT naming conventions. Filename extensions can have as many as three characters and are often used to identify the type of file and the application used to create the file (for example, spreadsheet files created by Microsoft Excel have the extension .xls). With Services for Macintosh, you can create extension-type associations that map PC filename extensions with Macintosh file creators and types.

file replication service A Windows NT service that allows specified file(s) to be replicated to remote systems, ensuring that copies on each system are kept in synchronization. The system that maintains the master copy is called the exporter, and the systems that receive updates are known as importers.

File Server for Macintosh A Services for Macintosh service that enables Macintosh clients and PC clients to share files. Also called MacFile.

file sharing The ability for a Windows NT computer to share parts (or all) of its local file system(s) with remote computers. An administrator creates share points by using either the file sharing command in My Computer or Windows NT Explorer or by using the **net share** command from the command prompt.

file system In an operating system, the overall structure in which files are named, stored, and organized. NTFS and FAT are types of file systems.

file transfer protocol (FTP) A service supporting file transfers between local and remote systems that support this protocol. FTP supports several commands that allow bidirectional transfer of binary and ASCII files between systems. The FTP Server service is part of the Internet Information Server (IIS). The FTP client is installed with TCP/IP connectivity utilities.

file type In the Macintosh environment this refers to a four-character sequence that identifies the type of a Macintosh file. The file type and file creator are used by the Macintosh Finder to determine the appropriate desktop icon for that file.

find tab Displays the words you can use to search for related topics. Use this tab to look for topics related to a particular word. It is located in the Help button bar near the top of the Help window.

flat name space A naming system in which computer names are created from a short sequence of characters without any additional structure superimposed.

floppy disk A disk that can be inserted in and removed from a disk drive. Floppies are most commonly available in a 3.5 or 5.25 inch format.

flow control An exchange of signals, over specific wires, in which each device signals its readiness to send or receive data.

folder A grouping of files or other folders, graphically represented by a folder icon, in both the Windows NT and Macintosh environments. A folder is analogous to a PC's file system directory, and many folders are, in fact, directories. A folder may contain other folders as well as file objects. *See also* directory.

font A graphic design applied to a collection of numbers, symbols, and characters. A font describes a certain typeface along with other qualities such as size, spacing, and pitch. *See also* font set; font types.

font set A collection of font sizes for one font, customized for a particular display and printer. Font sets determine what text looks like on the screen and when printed. *See also* font.

font types:

device fonts Reside in the hardware of your print device. They can be built into the print device itself or can be provided by a font cartridge or font card.

downloadable soft fonts Fonts that are stored on disk and downloaded as needed to the print device.

PostScript fonts Fonts that are defined in terms of the PostScript page-description language rules from Adobe Systems. When a document displayed in a screen font is sent to a PostScript printer, the printer uses the PostScript version if the font exists. If the font doesn't exist but a version is installed on the computer, that font is downloaded. If there is no PostScript font installed in either the printer or the computer, the bit-mapped font is translated into PostScript and the printer prints text using the bit-mapped font.

raster fonts Fonts that are stored as bitmaps. If a print device does not support raster fonts, it will not print them. Raster fonts cannot be scaled or rotated.

screen fonts Windows NT fonts that can be translated for output to the print device. Most screen fonts (including TrueType fonts) can be printed as well.

TrueType fonts Device-independent fonts that can be reproduced on all print devices. TrueType fonts are stored as outlines and can be scaled and rotated.

vector fonts Fonts that are useful on devices such as pen plotters that cannot reproduce bitmaps. They can be scaled to any size or aspect ratio. *See also* plotter font.

fork *See* data fork; file fork; resource fork.

FQDN *See* fully qualified domain name.

frame In synchronous communication, a package of information transmitted as a single unit from one device to another. *See also* capture.

framing rules Are established between a remote computer and the server, allowing continued communication (frame transfer) to occur. *See also* frame.

free space Free space is an unused and unformatted portion of a hard disk that can be partitioned or subpartitioned. Free space within an extended partition is available for the creation of logical drives. Free space that is not within an extended partition is available for the creation of a partition, with a maximum of four partitions allowed per disk. *See also* extended partition; primary partition; logical drive.

FTP *See* file transfer protocol.

full name A user's complete name, usually consisting of the last name, first name, and middle initial. The full name is information that can be maintained by User Manager and User Manager for Domains as part of the information identifying and defining a user account. *See also* user account.

full-screen application A non-Windows NT application that is displayed in the entire screen, rather than a window, when running in the Windows NT environment.

full synchronization Occurs when a copy of the entire database directory is sent to a backup domain controller (BDC). Full synchronization is performed automatically when changes have been deleted from the change log before replication takes place, and when a new BDC is added to a domain. *See also* BDC; directory database.

fully qualified domain name (FQDN) Part of the TCP/IP naming convention known as the Domain Name System, DNS computer names consist of two parts: host names with their domain names appended to them. For example, a host with host name **corp001** and DNS domain name **trey-research.com** has an FQDN of **corp001.trey-research.com**. (DNS domains should not be confused with Windows NT networking domains.) *See also* Domain Name System.

G

gateway Describes a system connected to multiple physical TCP/IP networks, capable of routing or delivering IP packets between them. A gateway translates between different transport protocols or data formats (for example IPX and IP) and is generally added to a network primarily for its translation ability. Also referred to as an IP router. *See also* IP address; IP router.

Gateway Service for NetWare Included with Windows NT Server, enables a computer running Windows NT Server to connect to NetWare servers. Creating a gateway enables computers running only Microsoft client software to access NetWare resources through the gateway. *See also* gateway.

General MIDI A MIDI specification controlled by the MIDI Manufacturers Association (MMA). The specification provides guidelines that authors of MIDI files can use to create files that sound the same across a variety of different synthesizers.

global account For Windows NT Server, a normal user account in a user's domain. Most user accounts are global accounts. If there are multiple domains in the network, it is best if each user in the network has only one user account, in only one domain, and each user's access to other domains is accomplished through the establishment of domain trust relationships. *See also* local account; trust relationship.

global group For Windows NT Server, a group that can be used in its own domain, member servers and workstations of the domain, and trusting domains. In all those places it can be granted rights and permissions and can become a member of local groups. However, it can only contain user accounts from its own domain. Global groups provide a way to create handy sets of users from inside the domain, available for use both in and out of the domain.

Global groups cannot be created or maintained on computers running Windows NT Workstation. However, for Windows NT Workstation computers that participate in a domain, domain global groups can be granted rights and permissions at those workstations, and can become members of local groups at those workstations. *See also* domain; group; local group; trust relationship.

group In User Manager or User Manager for Domains, an account containing other accounts that are called members. The permissions and rights granted to a group are also provided to its members, making groups a convenient way to grant common capabilities to collections of user accounts. For Windows NT Workstation, groups are managed with User Manager. For Windows NT Server, groups are managed with User Manager for Domains. *See also* built-in groups; global group; local group; user account.

group account A collection of user accounts. Giving a user account membership in a group gives that user all the rights and permissions granted to the group. *See also* user account; local account.

group category One of three categories of users to which you can assign Macintosh permissions for a folder. The permissions assigned to the group category are available to the group associated with the folder.

group memberships The groups to which a user account belongs. Permissions and rights granted to a group are also provided to its members. In most cases, the actions a user can perform in Windows NT are determined by the group memberships of the user account the user is logged on to. *See also* group.

group name A unique name identifying a local group or a global group to Windows NT. A group's name cannot be identical to any other group name or user name of its own domain or computer. *See also* global group; local group.

guest Services for Macintosh users who do not have a user account or who do not provide a password are logged on as a guest, using a user account with guest privileges. When a Macintosh user assigns permissions to everyone, those permissions are given to the group's guests and users.

guest account On computers running Windows NT Workstation or Windows NT Server, a built-in account used for logons by people who do not have a user account on the computer or domain or in any of the domains trusted by the computer's domain.

Guest privilege One of three privilege levels that you can assign to a Windows NT user account. The guest account used for Macintosh guest logons must have the Guest privilege. *See also* user account; Administrator privilege; User privilege.

H

h-node A NetBIOS implementation that uses the p-node protocol first, then the b-node protocol if the name service is unavailable. For registration, it uses the b-node protocol, then the p-node protocol. *See also* p-node; NetBIOS; registration.

handle A handle is a value used to uniquely identify a resource so that a program can access it.

handshaking Refers to flow control in serial communication, which defines a method for the print device to tell Windows NT that its buffer is full. *See also* buffer.

Hardware Compatibility List (HCL)
The Windows NT Hardware Compatibility List lists the devices supported by Windows NT. The latest version of the HCL can be downloaded from the Microsoft Web Page (microsoft.com) on the Internet.

HCL *See* Hardware Compatibility List.

heterogeneous environment An internetwork with servers and workstations running different operating systems, such as Windows NT, Macintosh, or Novell Netware, using a mix of different transport protocols.

hexadecimal A base-16 number system that consists of the digits 0 through 9 and the uppercase and lowercase letters A (equivalent to decimal 10) through F (equivalent to decimal 15).

high memory area The first 64K of extended memory (often referred to as HMA). *See also* memory.

hive A section of the registry that appears as a file on your hard disk. The registry subtree is divided into hives (named for their resemblance to the cellular structure of a beehive). A hive is a discrete body of keys, subkeys, and values that is rooted at the top of the registry hierarchy. A hive is backed by a single file and a .log file which are in the *%SystemRoot%*\system32\config or the *%SystemRoot%*\profiles*username* folders. By default, most hive files (Default, SAM, Security, and System) are stored in the *%SystemRoot%*\system32\config folder.

The *%SystemRoot%*\ profiles folder contains the user profile for each user of the computer. Because a hive is a file, it can be moved from one system to another, but can only be edited using Registry Editor.

home directory A directory that is accessible to the user and contains files and programs for that user. A home directory can be assigned to an individual user or can be shared by many users.

hop Refers to the next router. In IP routing, packets are always forwarded one router at a time. Packets often hop from router to router before reaching their destination. *See also* IP address; packet; router.

host Any device that is attached to the network and uses TCP/IP. *See also* TCP/IP.

host group A set of zero or more hosts identified by a single IP destination address. *See also* host; IP address.

host ID The portion of the IP address that identifies a computer within a particular network ID. *See also* IP address; network ID.

host name The name of a device on a network. For a device on a Windows or Windows NT network, this can be the same as the computername, but it may not be. The host name must be in the host table or be known by a DNS server for that host to be found by another computer attempting to communicate with it. *See also* DNS; host table.

host table The HOSTS and LMHOSTS files, which contain mappings of known IP addresses mapped to host names.

HOSTS file A local text file in the same format as the 4.3 Berkeley Software Distribution (BSD) UNIX *etc**hosts* file. This file maps *host names* to IP addresses. In Windows NT, this file is stored in the *systemroot*\System32\Drivers\Etc directory. *See also* IP address.

HTML Acronym for Hypertext Markup Language, a simple markup language used to create hypertext documents that are portable from one platform to another. HTML files are simple ASCII text files with codes embedded (indicated by markup tags) to indicate formatting and hypertext links. HTML is used for formatting documents on the World Wide Web.

hue The position of a color along the color spectrum. For example, green is between yellow and blue. This attribute can be set using desktop in Control Panel.

I

ICMP *See* internet control message protocol.

icon A graphical representation of an element in Windows NT, such as a disk drive, directory, group, application, or document. You can enlarge an application icon to a window when you want to use the application by clicking on the icon. Within applications, there are also toolbar icons for commands such as cut, copy, paste etc.

IDE Acronym for integrated device electronics, a type of disk-drive interface in which the controller electronics reside on the drive itself, eliminating the need for a separate adapter card.

IETF *See* Internet Engineering Task Force.

IGMP Acronym for Internet Group Management Protocol, used by workgroup software products and supported by Microsoft TCP/IP.

IIS Acronym for Microsoft Internet Information Server, a tool for identifying your computer as an Internet server.

impersonation Impersonation occurs when Windows NT Server allows one process to take on the security attributes of another.

import To create a package by inserting an existing file into Object Packager. When you import a file, the icon of the application you used to create the file appears in the Appearance window, and the name of the file appears in the Contents window. *See also* package.

import computers In directory replication, the servers or workstations that receive copies of the master set of directories from an export server. *See also* directory replication; export server.

import path In directory replication, the path to which imported subdirectories, and the files in those subdirectories, will be stored on an import computer. *See also* directory replication; import computer.

input/output activity (I/O) Read or write actions that your computer performs. Your computer performs a "read" when you type information on your keyboard or you select and choose items by using your mouse. Also, when you open a file, your computer reads the disk on which the file is located to find and open it.

Your computer performs a "write" whenever it stores, sends, prints, or displays information. For example, your computer performs a write when it stores information on a disk, displays information on your screen, or sends information through a modem or to a printer. *See also* I/O addresses.

insertion point The place where text will be inserted when you type. The insertion point usually appears as a flashing vertical bar in an application's window or in a dialog box.

Integrated Services Digital Network (ISDN) A type of phone line used to enhance WAN speeds, ISDN lines can transmit at speeds of 64 or 128 kilobits per second, as opposed to standard phone lines, which typically transmit at only 9600 bits per second (bps). An ISDN line must be installed by the phone company at both the server site and the remote site. *See also* bps.

interactive logon A network logon from a computer keyboard, when the user types information in the Logon Information dialog box displayed by the computer's operating system. *See also* remote logon.

intermediary devices Microsoft RAS supports various kinds of intermediary devices (security hosts and switches) between the remote access client and the remote access server. These devices include a modem-pool switch or security host. *See also* Remote Access Service (RAS).

internal command Commands that are stored in the file Cmd.exe and that reside in memory at all times.

internet In Windows NT, a collection of two or more private networks, or private inter-enterprise TCP/IP networks.

In Macintosh terminology, refers to two or more physical networks connected by routers, which maintain a map of the physical networks on the internet and forward data received from one physical network to other physical networks. Network users in an internet can share information and network devices. You can use an internet with Services for Macintosh by connecting two or more AppleTalk networks to a computer running Windows NT Server.

Internet The global network of networks. *See also* World Wide Web.

internet control message protocol (ICMP) A maintenance protocol in the TCP/IP suite, required in every TCP/IP implementation, that allows two nodes on an IP network to share IP status and error information. ICMP is used by the ping utility to determine the readability of a remote system. *See also* ping; TCP/IP.

Internet Engineering Task Force (IETF) A consortium that introduces procedures for new technology on the Internet. IETF specifications are released in documents called Requests for Comments (RFCs). *See also* RFC.

internet group name A name known by a DNS server that includes a list of the specific addresses of systems that have registered the name. *See also* DNS.

Internet Protocol (IP) The messenger protocol of TCP/IP, responsible for addressing and sending TCP packets over the network. IP provides a best-effort, connectionless delivery system that does not guarantee that packets arrive at their destination or that they are received in the sequence in which they were sent. *See also* packet; TCP; TCP/IP.

internet router A device that connects networks and directs network information to other networks, usually choosing the most efficient route through other routers. *See also* router.

internetworks Networks that connect local area networks (LANs) together.

interprocess communication (IPC) The ability, provided by a multitasking operating system, of one task or process to exchange data with another. Common IPC methods include pipes, semaphores, shared memory, queues, signals, and mailboxes. *See also* named pipes; queue.

interrupt request lines (IRQ) Hardware lines over which devices can send signals to get the attention of the processor when the device is ready to accept or send information. Typically, each device connected to the computer uses a separate IRQ.

intranet A TCP/IP network that uses Internet technology. May be connected to the Internet. *See also* Internet; TCP/IP.

I/O addresses Locations within the input/output address space of your computer, used by a device such as a printer or modem. *See* also input/output activity (I/O).

IP *See* Internet Protocol.

IP address Used to identify a node on a network and to specify routing information. Each node on the network must be assigned a unique IP address, which is made up of the *network ID*, plus a unique *host ID* assigned by the network administrator. This address is typically represented in dotted-decimal notation, with the decimal value of each octet separated by a period (for example, 138.57.7.27).

In Windows NT, the IP address can be configured statically on the client or configured dynamically through DHCP. *See also* DHCP; node; octet.

IPC *See* interprocess communication.

IPCP Acronym for Internet Protocol Control Protocol, specified by RFC 1332. Responsible for configuring, enabling, and disabling the IP protocol modules on both ends of the point-to-point (PPP) link. *See also* PPP; RFC.

IP datagrams The basic internet protocol (IP) information unit. *See also* datagram; Internet Protocol (IP).

IP router A system connected to multiple physical TCP/IP networks that can route or deliver IP packets between the networks. *See also* packet; routing; TCP/IP.

IPX *See* IPX/SPX.

IPX/SPX Acronym for Internetwork Packet Exchange/Sequenced Packet Exchange, transport protocols used in Novell NetWare networks. Windows NT implements IPX through NWLink.

ISDN *See* integrated services digital network.

ISO Abbreviation for the International Standards Organization, an international association of member countries, each of which is represented by its leading standard-setting organization—for example ANSI (American National Standards Institute) for the United States. The ISO works to establish global standards for communications and information exchange.

ISP Acronym for internet service provider, a company or educational institution that enables remote users to access the Internet by providing dial-up connections or installing leased lines.

iteration One of the three key concepts in DNS name resolution. A local name server keeps the burden of processing on itself and passes only iterative resolution requests to other name servers. An iterative resolution request tells the name server that the requester expects the best answer the name server can provide without help from others. If the name server has the requested data, it returns it, otherwise it returns pointers to name servers that are more likely to have the answer. *See also* Domain Name System.

In programming, iteration is the art of executing one or more statements or instructions repeatedly.

J

jump Text, graphics, or parts of graphics that provide links to other Help topics or to more information about the current topic. The pointer changes shape whenever it is over a jump. If you click a jump that is linked to another topic, that topic appears in the Help window. If you click a jump that is linked to more information, the information appears in a pop-up window on top of the main Help window.

K

Kermit
Protocol for transferring binary files that is somewhat slower than XModem/CRC. However, Kermit allows you to transmit and receive either seven or eight data bits per character. *See also* X/Modem/CRC.

kernel driver A driver that accesses hardware. *See also* device driver.

key A folder that appears in the left pane of a Registry Editor window. A key can contain subkeys and value entries. For example: Environment is a key of KKEY_CURRENT_USER. *See also* subkey.

keyboard buffer A temporary storage area in memory that keeps track of keys you typed, even if the computer did not immediately respond to the keys when you typed them.

key map A mapping assignment that translates key values on synthesizers that do not conform to General MIDI standards. Key maps ensure that the appropriate percussion instrument is played or the appropriate octave for a melodic instrument is played when a MIDI file is played. *See also* MIDI.

L

LAN *See* local area network.

lease In Windows NT, the network administrator controls how long IP addresses are assigned by specifying lease durations that specify how long a computer can use an assigned IP address before having to renew the lease with the DHCP server. *See also* DHCP; IP address.

license group License groups show a relationship (also known as a mapping) between users and computers. A license group is comprised of a single descriptive name for the group; a specified number of Per-Seat licenses assigned to the group; and a specific list of users who are members of the group.

line printer daemon (LPD) A line printer daemon (LPD) service on the print server receives documents (print jobs) from line printer remote (LPR) utilities running on client systems.

linked object A representation or placeholder for an object that is inserted into a destination document. The object still exists in the source file and, when it is changed, the linked object is updated to reflect these changes.

list box In a dialog box, a type of box that lists available choices—for example, a list of all files in a directory. If all the choices do not fit in the list box, there is a scroll bar.

LMHOSTS file A local text file that maps IP addresses to the computer names of Windows NT networking computers outside the local subnet. In Windows NT, this file is stored in the *systemroot*\System32\Drivers\Etc directory. *See also* IP address; subnet.

local account For Windows NT Server, a user account provided in a domain for a user whose global account is not in a trusted domain. Not required where trust relationships exist between domains. *See also* global account; trust relationship; user account.

local area network (LAN) A group of computers and other devices dispersed over a relatively limited area and connected by a communications link that enables any device to interact with any other on the network.

local group
For Windows NT Workstation, a group that can be granted permissions and rights only for its own workstation. However, it can contain user accounts from its own computer and (if the workstation participates in a domain) user accounts and global groups both from its own domain and from trusted domains.

For Windows NT Server, a group that can be granted permissions and rights only for the domain controllers of its own domain. However, it can contain user accounts and global groups both from its own domain and from trusted domains.

Local groups provide a way to create handy sets of users from both inside and outside the domain, to be used only at domain controllers of the domain. *See also* global group; group; trust relationship.

local guest logon Takes effect when a user logs on interactively at a computer running Window NT Workstation or at a member server running Windows NT Server, and specifies Guest as the user name in the Logon Information dialog box. *See also* interactive logon.

local printer A printer that is directly connected to one of the ports on your computer. *See also* port.

LocalTalk The name given by Apple Computer to the Apple networking hardware built into every Macintosh. LocalTalk includes the cables and connector boxes that connect components and network devices that are part of the AppleTalk network system. LocalTalk was formerly known as the AppleTalk Personal Network.

local user profiles User profiles which are created automatically on the computer at logon the first time a user logs on to a computer running Windows NT Workstation or Windows NT Server.

lock
A method used to manage certain features of subdirectory replication by the export server. You can lock a subdirectory to prevent it from being exported to any import computers, or use locks to prevent imports to subdirectories on an import computer. *See also* directory replication; export server; import server; subtree.

log books Are kept by the system administrator to record the backup methods, dates, and contents of each tape in a backup set. *See also* backup set; backup types.

log files Are created by Windows NT Backup and contain a record of the date the tapes were created and the names of files and directories successfully backed up and restored. Performance Monitor also creates log files.

log off To stop using the network and remove your user name from active use until you log on again.

log on To provide a user name and password that identifies you to the network.

logical drive A subpartition of an extended partition on a hard disk. *See also* extended partition.

Logical Unit (LU) A preset unit containing all the configuration information needed for a user or a program to establish a session with a host or peer computer. *See also* host; peer.

logon hours For Windows NT Server, a definition of the days and hours during which a user account can connect to a server. When a user is connected to a server and the logon hours are exceeded, the user will either be disconnected from all server connections or allowed to remain connected but denied any new connections.

logon script
A file that can be assigned to user accounts. Typically a batch file, a logon script runs automatically every time the user logs on. It can be used to configure a user's working environment at every logon, and it allows an administrator to affect a user's environment without managing all aspects of it. A logon script can be assigned to one or more user accounts. *See also* batch file.

logon script path When a user logs on, the computer authenticating the logon locates the specified logon script (if one has been assigned to that user account) by following that computer's local logon script path (usually C:\Winnt\System32\Repl\Imports\Scripts). *See also* authentication; logon script.

logon workstations In Windows NT Server, the computers from which a user is allowed to log on.

long name A folder name or filename longer than the 8.3 filename standard (up to eight characters followed by a period and a three-character extension) of the FAT file system. Windows NT Server automatically translates long names of files and folders to 8.3 names for MS-DOS users. Macintosh users can assign long names to files and folders on the server, and using Services for Macintosh, you can assign long names to Macintosh-accessible volumes when you create them. *See also* FAT; filename; name mapping; short name.

LPD *See* line printer daemon.

luminosity The brightness of a color on a scale from black to white on your monitor.

M

m-node A NetBIOS implementation that uses the b-node protocol first, then the p-node protocol if the broadcast fails to resolve a name to an IP address. *See also* IP address; NetBIOS; p-node.

MAC *See* media access control.

MAC address A unique 48-bit number assigned to the network interface card (NIC) by the manufacturer. MAC addresses (which are physical addresses) are used for mapping in TCP/IP network communication. *See also* media access control (MAC); ARP; ARP request packet.

MacFile *See* File Server for Macintosh.

MacFile menu The menu that appears in the Windows NT Server File Manager and Server Manager when Services for Macintosh is set up. You can create Macintosh-accessible volumes, and set permissions and other options using commands on this menu.

Macintosh-accessible volume Storage space on the server used for folders and files of Macintosh users. A Macintosh-accessible volume is equivalent to a shared directory for PC users. Each Macintosh-accessible volume on a computer running Windows NT Server will correspond to a directory. Both PC users and Macintosh users can be given access to files located in a directory that is designated as both a shared directory and a Macintosh-accessible volume.

Macintosh-style permissions Directory and volume permissions that are similar to the access privileges used on a Macintosh.

MacPrint *See* Print Server for Macintosh.

Mac volume *See* Macintosh-accessible volume.

Make Changes The Macintosh-style permission that gives users the right to make changes to a folder's contents; for example, modifying, renaming, moving, creating, and deleting files. When Services for Macintosh translates access privileges into Windows NT Server permissions, a user who has the Make Changes privilege is given Write and Delete permissions.

management information base (MIB) A set of objects that represent various types of information about a device, used by SNMP to manage devices. Because different network-management services are used for different types of devices or protocols, each service has its own set of objects. The entire set of objects that any service or protocol uses is referred to as its MIB. *See also* SNMP.

mandatory user profile A profile that is downloaded to the user's desktop each time he or she logs on. A mandatory user profile is created by an administrator and assigned to one or more users to create consistent or job-specific user profiles. They cannot be changed by the user and remain the same from one logon session to the next. *See also* user profile; roaming user profile.

mapping In TCP/IP, refers to the relationship between a host or computer name and an IP address, used by DNS and NetBIOS servers on TCP/IP networks. In Windows NT Explorer, to mapping a driver letter to a network drive. In Windows NT License Manager, to the relationship between users and computers in license groups. *See also* DNS; IP address; license groups.

mapping file A file defining exactly which users and groups are to be migrated from NetWare to Windows NT Server, and what new user names and passwords are to be assigned to the migrated users.

master browser A kind of network name server which keeps a browse list of all the servers and domains on the network. Also referred to as browse master. *See also* browse; Windows NT browser system.

master domain In the master domain model, the domain that is trusted by all other domains on the network and acts as the central administrative unit for user and group accounts.

maximize To enlarge a window to its maximum size by using the **Maximize** button (at the right of the title bar) or the **Maximize** command on the window menu.

Maximize button The small button containing a window icon at the right of the title bar. Mouse users can click the **Maximize** button to enlarge a window to its maximum size. Keyboard users can use the **Maximize** command on the window menu.

maximum password age The period of time a password can be used before the system requires the user to change it. *See also* account policy.

media access control (MAC) A layer in the network architecture that deals with network access and collision detection.

media access control (MAC) driver *See* network card driver.

Media Control Interface (MCI) A standard control interface for multimedia devices and files. Using MCI, a multimedia application can control a variety of multimedia devices and files.

member server A computer that runs Windows NT Server but is not a primary domain controller (PDC) or backup domain controller (BDC) of a Windows NT domain. Member servers do not receive copies of the directory database. Also called a stand-alone server. *See also* directory database; PDC, BDC.

memory A temporary storage area for information and applications. *See also* expanded memory; extended memory.

menu A list of available commands in an application window. Menu names appear in the menu bar near the top of the window. The window menu, represented by the program icon at the left end of the title bar, is common to all Windows NT applications. You open a menu by clicking the menu name.

menu bar The horizontal bar containing the names of all the application's menus. It appears below the title bar.

Messenger service Sends and receives messages sent by administrators or by the Alerter service. *See also* Alerter service.

MIB *See* management information base.

MIDI Acronym for Musical Instrument Digital Interface, an interface that enables several devices, instruments, or computers to send and receive messages for the purpose of creating music, sound, or lighting.

MIDI setup Specifies the type of MIDI device you are using, the channel and patch settings needed to play MIDI files, and the port your device is using. *See also* MIDI.

Migration Tool for NetWare Included with Windows NT, enabling you to easily transfer user and group accounts, volumes, folders, and files from a NetWare server to a computer running Windows NT Server.Windows NT applications. You open a menu by clicking the menu name.

minimize To reduce a window to a button on the taskbar by using the **Minimize** button (at the right of the title bar) or the **Minimize** command on the **Control** menu. *See also* maximize.

Minimize button The small button containing a short line at the right of the title bar. Mouse users can click the **Minimize** button to reduce a window to a button on the taskbar. Keyboard users can use the **Minimize** command on the **Control** menu.

minimum password age The period of time a password must be used before the user can change it. *See also* account policy.

minimum password length The fewest characters a password can contain. *See also* account policy.

mirror set A fully redundant or shadow copy of data. Mirror sets provide an identical twin for a selected disk; all data written to the primary disk is also written to the shadow or mirror disk. This enables you to have instant access to another disk with a redundant copy of the information on a failed disk. Mirror sets provide fault tolerance. *See also* fault tolerance.

modem Short for modulator/demodulator, a communications device that enables a computer to transmit information over a standard telephone line.

MS-DOS-based application An application that is designed to run with MS-DOS, and therefore may not be able to take full advantage of all Windows NT features.

multicast datagrams IP multicasting is the transmission of an IP datagram to a host group (a set of zero or more hosts identified by a single IP destination address.) An IP datagram sent to one host is called a unicast datagram. An IP datagram sent to all hosts is called a broadcast datagram. *See also* host; IP address; broadcast datagram.

multihomed computer A system that has multiple network cards, or that has been configured with multiple IP addresses for a single network interface card. *See also* IP address; network interface card.

multihomed system A system with multiple network adapters attached to separate physical networks.

multilink dialing Multilink combines multiple physical links into a logical "bundle." This aggregate link increases your bandwidth. *See also* bandwidth.

multiple-boot A computer that runs two or more operating systems. For example, Windows 95, MS-DOS, and Windows NT operating systems can be installed on the same computer. When the computer is started, any one of the operating systems can be selected. Also known as dual-boot.

MultiProtocol Routing (MPR) Enables routing over IP and IPX networks by connecting LANs or by connecting LANS to WANs. *See also* IPX/SPX; local area network (LAN); wide area network (WAN).

N

named pipe An interprocess communication mechanism that allows one process to communicate with another local or remote process.

name mapping Is provided by Windows NT Server and Windows NT Workstation to ensure access by MS-DOS users to NTFS and FAT volumes (which can have share names of up to 255 characters, as opposed to MS-DOS, which is restricted to eight characters followed by a period and a three-character extension). With name mapping, each file or directory with a name that does not conform the MS-DOS 8.3 standard is automatically given a second name that does. MS-DOS users connecting the file or directory over the network See the name in the 8.3 format; Windows NT Workstation and Windows NT Server users see the long name. *See also* long name; DNS; WINS.

name resolution service TCP/IP internetworks require a name resolution service to convert computer names to IP addresses and IP addresses to computer names. (People use "friendly" names to connect to computers; programs use IP addresses.) *See also* IP address; TCP/IP.

NDIS *See* network device interface specification.

NetBEUI A network protocol usually used in small, department-size local area networks of 1 to 200 clients. It can use Token Ring source routing as its only method of routing. *See also* router; Token Ring.

NetBIOS *See* network basic input/output system.

NetBT Short for NetBIOS over TCP/IP. The session-layer network service that performs name-to-IP address mapping for name resolution. *See also* IP address; name resolution service; network basic input/output system; TCP/IP.

Net Logon service For Windows NT Server, performs authentication of domain logons, and keeps the domain's directory database synchronized between the primary domain controller (PDC) and the other backup domain controllers (BDCs) of the domain. *See also* directory database; PDC; BDC.

network adapter *See* network card.

network adapter card *See* network card.

network administrator A person responsible for planning, configuring, and managing the day-to-day operation of the network. This person may also be referred to as a system administrator.

network basic input/output system (NetBIOS) An application program interface (API) that can be used by application programs on a local area network. NetBIOS provides application programs with a uniform set of commands for requesting the lower-level services required to conduct sessions between nodes on a network and to transmit information back and forth. *See also* API.

network card An expansion card or other device used to connect a computer to a local area network (LAN). Also called a network adapter; network adapter card; adapter card; network interface card (NIC).

network card driver A network device driver that works directly with the network card, acting as an intermediary between the card and the protocol driver. With Services for Macintosh, the AppleTalk Protocol stack on the server is implemented as a protocol driver and is bound to one or more network drivers.

Network DDE DSDM service The Network DDE DSDM (DDE share database manager) service manages shared DDE conversations. It is used by the Network DDE service. *See also* DDE.

Network DDE service The Network DDE (dynamic data exchange) service provides a network transport and security for DDE conversations. *See also* DDE.

network device driver Software that coordinates communication between the network card and the computer's hardware and other software, controlling the physical function of the network cards.

network device interface specification (NDIS) In Windows networking, the Microsoft/3Com specification for the interface of network device drivers. All transport drivers call the NDIS interface to access network cards. With Services for Macintosh, the AppleTalk Protocol stack on the server is implemented as an NDIS-compliant protocol and is bound to an NDIS network driver. All network drivers and protocol drivers shipped with Windows NT Workstation and Windows NT Server conform to NDIS.

network directory *See* shared directory.

network driver *See* network device driver.

Network Driver Interface Specification *See* network device interface specification.

Network File System (NFS) A service for distributed computing systems that provides a distributed file system, eliminating the need for keeping multiple copies of files on separate computers.

network ID The portion of the IP address that identifies a group of computers and devices located on the same logical network.

Network Information Service (NIS) A service for distrbuted computing systems that provides a distributed database system for common configuration files.

network interface card (NIC) *See* network card.

network number In the Macintosh environment, the network number (also referred to as the network range) is the address or range of addresses assigned to the network, which is used by AppleTalk routers to route information to the appropriate network. Each physical network can have a range of network numbers.

network protocol Software that enables computers to communicate over a network. TCP/IP is a network protocol, used on the Internet. *See also* TCP/IP.

network range In the Macintosh environment, a range of network numbers (routing addresses) associated with a physical network in Phase 2. Apple manuals sometimes refer to a network range as a cable range. *See also* network number; routing.

network sniffer A hardware and software diagnostic tool that can also be used to decipher passwords, which may result in unauthorized access to network accounts. Cleartext passwords are susceptible to network sniffers.

NFS *See* Network File System.

NIS *See* Network Information Service.

node In the PC environment, a node is any device that is attached to the internetwork and uses TCP/IP. (A node can also be referred to as a host.) In the Macintosh environment, a node is an addressable entity on a network. Each Macintosh client is a node.

nonpaged memory Memory that cannot be paged to disk. *See also* memory; paging file.

non-Windows NT application Refers to an application that is designed to run with Windows 3.x, MS-DOS, OS/2, or POSIX, but not specifically with Windows NT and that may not be able to take full advantage of all Windows NT features (such as memory management). *See also* POSIX.

NT *See* Windows NT.

NT file system *See* NTFS.

NTFS An advanced file system designed for use specifically within the Windows NT operating system. It supports file system recovery, extremely large storage media, long filenames, and various features for the POSIX subsystem. It also supports object-oriented applications by treating all files as objects with user-defined and system-defined attributes. *See also* POSIX.

NWLink IPX\SPX Compatible Transport
A standard network protocol which supports routing, and can support NetWare client-server applications, where NetWare-aware Sockets-based applications communicate with IPX\SPX Sockets-based applications. *See also* IPX/SPX; Sockets.

O

object
Any piece of information, created by using a Windows-based application, that can be linked or embedded into another document. *See also* embedded object; linked object.

octet In programming, an octet refers to eight bits or one byte. IP addresses, for example, are typically represented in dotted-decimal notation, that is, with the decimal value of each octet of the address separated by a period. *See also* IP address.

offset When specifying a filter in Windows NT Network Monitor based on a pattern match (which limits the capture to only those frames containing a specific pattern of ASCII or hexadecimal data), you must specify where the pattern occurs in the frame. This number of bytes (from the beginning or end of the frame) is known as an offset. *See also* frame; hexadecimal.

OLE A way to transfer and share information between applications. *See also* embedded object; linked object.

one-way trust relationship One domain (the trusting domain) "trusts" the domain controllers in the other domain (the trusted domain) to authenticate user accounts from the trusted domain to use resources in the trusting domain. *See also* trust relationship; user account.

open To display the contents of a directory, a document, or a data file in a window.

orphan A member of a mirror set or a stripe set with parity that has failed in a severe manner, such as in a loss of power or a complete head crash. When this happens, the fault-tolerance driver determines that it can no longer use the orphaned member and directs all new reads and writes to the remaining members of the fault-tolerance volume. *See also* fault tolerance; mirror set; stripe set with parity.

orphaned member *See* orphan.

OSI Acronym for Open Systems Interconnection model. TCP/IP protocols map to a four-layered conceptual model consisting of Application, Transport, Internet, and Network Interface. Each layer in this TCP/IP model corresponds to one or more layers of the International Standards Organization (ISO) seven-layer OSI model consisting of Application, Presentation, Session, Transport, Network, Data-link, and Physical. *See also* ISO.

owner In Windows NT, every file and directory on an NTFS volume has an owner, who controls how permissions are set on the file or directory and who can grant permissions to others.

In the Macintosh environment, an owner is the user responsible for setting permissions for a folder on a server. A Macintosh user who creates a folder on the server automatically becomes the owner of the folder. The owner can transfer ownership to someone else. Each Macintosh-accessible volume on the server also has an owner.

owner category In the Macintosh environment, this refers to the user category to which you assign permissions for the owner of a folder or a Macintosh volume. *See also* Macintosh-accessible volume.

P

p-node A NetBIOS implementation that uses point-to-point communications with a name server to resolve names as IP addresses. *See also* h-node; IP address; NetBIOS.

package An icon that represents an embedded or linked object. When you choose the package, the application used to create the object either plays the object (for example, a sound file) or opens and displays the object. *See also* embedded object; linked object.

packet A transmission unit of fixed maximum size that consists of binary information representing both data and a header containing an ID number, source and destination addresses, and error-control data.

packet header The part of a packet that contains an identification number, source and destination addresses, and—sometimes—error-control data. *See also* packet.

PADs Acronym for packet assemblers/disassemblers, a connection used in X.25 networks. X.25 PAD boards can be used in place of modems when provided with a compatible COM driver. *See also* X.25.

paging file A special file on a PC hard disk. With virtual memory under Windows NT, some of the program code and other information is kept in RAM while other information is temporarily swapped into virtual memory. When that information is required again, Windows NT pulls it back into RAM and, if necessary, swaps other information to virtual memory. Also called a swap file.

PAP Acronym for Password Authentication Protocol, a type of authentication which uses cleartext passwords and is the least sophisticated authentication protocol.

parity Redundant information that is associated with a block of information. In Windows NT Server, stripe sets with parity means that there is one additional parity stripe per row. Therefore, you must use at least three, rather than two, disks to allow for this extra parity information. Parity stripes contain the XOR (the Boolean operation called exclusive OR) of the data in that stripe. Windows NT Server, when regenerating a failed disk, uses the parity information in those stripes in conjunction with the data on the good disks to recreate the data on the failed disk. *See also* fault tolerance; stripe sets; stripe sets with parity.

partial synchronization The automatic, timed delivery to all domain BDCs (backup domain controllers) of only those directory database changes that have occurred since the last synchronization. *See also* BDC; synchronize.

partition A partition is a portion of a physical disk that functions as though it were a physically separate unit. *See also* extended partition; system partition.

pass-through authentication When the user account must be authenticated, but the computer being used for the logon is not a domain controller in the domain where the user account is defined, nor is it is not the computer where the user account is defined, the computer passes the logon information through to a domain controller (directly or indirectly) where the user account is defined. *See also* domain controller; user account.

password A security measure used to restrict logons to user accounts and access to computer systems and resources. A password is a unique string of characters that must be provided before a logon or an access is authorized. For Windows NT, a password for a user account can be up to 14 characters, and is case-sensitive. There are four user-defined parameters to be entered in the Account Policy dialog box in User Manager or User Manager for Domains: maximum password age, minimum password age, minimum password length, password uniqueness.

With Services for Macintosh, each Macintosh user has a user password that he or she must type when accessing the Windows NT Server. You can also assign each Macintosh-accessible volume a volume password if you want, which all users must type to access the volume. *See also* account policy.

password uniqueness The number of new passwords that must be used by a user account before an old password can be reused. *See also* account policy; password.

patch map The part of a channel-map entry that translates instrument sounds, volume settings, and (optionally) key values for a channel.

path A sequence of directory (or folder) names that specifies the location of a directory, file, or folder within the directory tree. Each directory name and filename within the path (except the first) must be preceded by a backslash (\). For example, to specify the path of a file named Readme.Wri located in the Windows directory on drive C, you would type **c:\windows\readme.wri**.

PC Any personal computer (such as an IBM PC or compatible) using the MS-DOS, OS/2, Windows, Windows for Workgroups, Windows 95, Windows NT Workstation, or Windows NT Server operating systems.

peer Any of the devices on a layered communications network that operate on the same protocol level.

pel Also known as a pixel, which is short for picture element, the smallest graphic unit that can be displayed on the screen.

permissions Windows NT Server settings you set on a shared resource that determine which users can use the resource and how they can use it. *See also* access permission.

Services for Macintosh automatically translates between permissions and Macintosh access privileges, so that permissions set on a directory (volume) are enforced for Macintosh users, and access privileges set by Macintosh users are enforced for PC users connected to the computer running Windows NT Server.

personal groups In the Start menu on the programs list, a program group you have created that contains program items. Personal groups are stored with your logon information and each time you log on, your personal groups appear. *See also* groups.

Physical Unit (PU) A network-addressable unit that provides the services needed to use and manage a particular device, such as a communications link device. A PU is implemented with a combination of hardware, software, and microcode.

PIF Acronym for program information file. A PIF provides information to Windows NT about how best to run MS-DOS applications. When you start an MS-DOS application, Windows NT looks for a PIF to use with the application. PIFs contain such items as the name of the file, a start-up directory, and multitasking options.

ping A command used to verify connections to one or more remote hosts. The **ping** utility uses the ICMP echo request and echo reply packets to determine whether a particular IP system on a network is functional. The ping utility is useful for diagnosing IP network or router failures. *See also* ICMP; router.

plotter font A font created by a series of dots connected by lines. Plotter fonts can be scaled to any size and are most often printed on plotters. Some dot-matrix printers also support plotter fonts. *See also* font; font types.

Point-to-Point protocol (PPP) A set of industry-standard framing and authentication protocols that is part of Windows NT RAS to ensure interoperability with third-party remote access software. PPP negotiates configuration parameters for multiple layers of the OSI model. *See also* OSI.

Point-to-Point Tunneling Protocol (PPTP)
PPTP is a new networking technology that supports multiprotocol virtual private networks (VPNs), enabling remote users to access corporate networks securely across the Internet by dialing into an internet service provider (ISP) or by connecting directly to the Internet. *See also* VPN.

pointer
The arrow-shaped cursor on the screen that follows the movement of a mouse (or other pointing device) and indicates which area of the screen will be affected when you press the mouse button. The pointer changes shape during certain tasks.

pop-up menu *See* window menu.

port A location used to pass data in and out of a computing device. This can refer to 1) an adapter card connecting a server to a network; 2) a serial 232 port; 3) a TCP/IP port; 4) a printer port.

port ID The method TCP and UDP use to specify which application running on the system is sending or receiving the data. *See also* TCP; UDP.

POSIX Acronym for Portable Operating System Interface, an IEEE (Institute of Electrical and Electronics Engineers) standard that defines a set of operating-system services. Programs that adhere to the POSIX standard can be easily ported from one system to another.

PostScript printer A printer that uses the PostScript page description language to create text and graphics on the output medium, such as paper or overhead transparency. Examples of PostScript printers include the Apple LaserWriter, the NEC LC-890, and the QMS PS-810. *See also* font types.

POTS Acronym for plain-old telephone service. Also an acronym for point of termination station, which refers to where a telephone call terminates.

power conditioning A feature of an uninterruptible power supply (UPS) which removes spikes, surges, sags, and noise from the power supply. *See also* UPS.

PPP *See* Point-to-Point protocol.

PPTP *See* Point-to-Point Tunneling Protocol.

predefined key The key represented by a registry window, the name of which appears in the window's title bar. *See also* key; registry.

Primary Domain Controller (PDC) In a Windows NT Server domain, the computer running Windows NT Server that authenticates domain logons and maintains the directory database for a domain. The PDC tracks changes made to accounts of all computers on a domain. It is the only computer to receive these changes directly. A domain has only one PDC. *See also* directory database.

primary group The group with which a Macintosh user usually shares documents stored on a server. You specify a user's primary group in the user's account. When a user creates a folder on the server, the user's primary group is set as the folder's associated group (by default).

primary partition A partition is a portion of a physical disk that can be marked for use by an operating system. There can be up to four primary partitions (or up to three, if there is an extended partition) per physical disk. A primary partition cannot be subpartitioned. *See also* partition; extended partition.

print device Refers to the actual hardware device that produces printed output.

print job In the Macintosh environment, a document or image sent from a client to a printer.

print processor A PostScript program that understands the format of a document's image file and how to print the file to a specific printer or class of printers. *See also* encapsulated PostScript (EPS) file.

print server Refers to the computer that receives documents from clients.

Print Server for Macintosh A Services for Macintosh service that enables Macintosh clients to send documents to printers attached to a computer running Windows NT; enables PC clients to send documents to printers anywhere on the AppleTalk network; and enables Macintosh users to spool their documents to the computer running Windows NT Server, thus freeing up their clients to do other tasks. Also called MacPrint.

print sharing The ability for a computer running Windows NT Workstation or Windows NT Server to share a printer on the network. This is done by using the Printers folder or the **net share** command.

print spooler A collection of dynamic link libraries (DLLs) that receive, process, schedule, and distribute documents.

printer Refers to the software interface between the operating system and the print device. The printer defines where the document will go before it reaches the print device (to a local port, to a file, or to a remote print share), when it will go, and various other aspects of the printing process.

printer driver A program that converts graphics commands into a specific printer language, such as PostScript or PCL. *See also* font types.

printer fonts Fonts that are built into your printer. These fonts are usually located in the printer's read-only memory (ROM). *See also* font; font types.

printer permissions Specify the type of access a user or group has to use the printer. The printer permissions are No Access, Print, Manage Documents, and Full Control.

printer window Shows information for one of the printers that you have installed or to which you are connected. For each printer, you can see what documents are waiting to be printed, who owns them, how large they are, and other information.

printing pool Consists of two or more identical print devices associated with one printer.

private volume A Macintosh-accessible volume that is accessible by only one Macintosh user. For a volume to be a private volume, the permissions on its root directory must give the volume's owner all three permissions (Make Changes, See Files, and See Folders), while giving the primary group and everyone categories no permissions at all. When a private volume's owner uses the Chooser to view the volumes available on the server, the private volume is listed; however, no other users can see the private volume when viewing the volumes available on the server. *See also* Macintosh-accessible volume.

privilege level One of three settings (User, Administrator, or Guest) assigned to each user account. The privilege level a user account has determines the actions that the user can perform on the network. *See also* Administrator privilege; Guest privilege; User privilege; user account.

process When a program runs, a Windows NT process is created. A process is an object type which consists of an executable program, a set of virtual memory addresses, and one or more threads.

program file A file that starts an application or program. A program file has an .exe, .pif, .com, or .bat filename extension.

program group On the start menu, a collection of applications. Grouping your applications makes them easier to find when you want to start them. *See also* common group; personal group.

program icon Located at the left of the window title bar, the program icon represents the program being run. Clicking the program icon opens the window menu.

program item An application, accessory, or document represented as an icon in the Start menu or on the desktop.

promiscuous mode A state of a network card in which it passes on to the networking software all the frames that it detects on the network, regardless of the frames' destination address. *See also* frame; network card.

property In Windows NT Network Monitor, a property refers to a field within a protocol header. A protocol's properties, collectively, indicate the purpose of the protocol.

protocol A set of rules and conventions for sending information over a network. These rules govern the content, format, timing, sequencing, and error control of messages exchanged among network devices.

protocol driver A network device driver that implements a protocol, communicating between Windows NT Server and one or more network adapter card drivers. With Services for Macintosh, the AppleTalk Protocol stack is implemented as an NDIS-protocol driver, and is bound to one or more network adapter card drivers.

protocol parser A dynamic-link library (DLL) that identifies the protocols used to send a frame onto the network. *See also* frame; dynamic-link library.

protocol properties Refers to the elements of information that define a protocol's purpose. Because the purpose of protocols vary, properties differ from one protocol to another.

protocol stack The implementation of a specific protocol family in a computer or other node on the network.

proxy A computer that listens to name query broadcasts and responds for those names not on the local subnet. The proxy communicates with the name server to resolve names and then caches them for a time period. *See also* caching; Domain Name Systems; subnet.

PSTN
Acronym for public switched telephone network.

pull partner A WINS server that pulls in replicas from its push partner by requesting it and then accepting the pushed replicas. *See also* Windows Internet Name Service.

push partner A WINS server that sends replicas to its pull partner upon receiving a request from it. *See also* Windows Internet Name Service.

Q

queue In Windows NT terminology, a queue refers to a group of documents waiting to be printed. (In NetWare and OS/2 environments, queues are the primary software interface between the application and print device; users submit documents to a queue. However, with Windows NT, the printer is that interface—the document is sent to a printer, not a queue.)

quick format Deletes the file allocation table (FAT) and root directory of a disk but does not scan the disk for bad areas. This function is available in Disk Administrator or when checking disks for errors. *See also* FAT; root directory.

R

RAID Acronym for Redundant Array of Inexpensive Disks. A method used to standardize and categorize fault-tolerant disk systems. Six levels gauge various mixes of performance, reliability, and cost. Windows NT includes three of the RAID levels: Level 0, Level 1, and Level 5.

RAM An acronym for random-access memory. RAM can be read from or written to by the computer or other devices. Information stored in RAM is lost when you turn off the computer. *See also* memory.

RAS *See* Remote Access Service.

recursion
One of the three key concepts in DNS name resolution. A resolver typically passes a recursive resolution request to its local name server, which tells the name server that the resolver expects a complete answer to the query, not just a pointer to another name server. Recursive resolution effectively puts the workload onto the name server and allows the resolver to be small and simple. *See also* Domain Name Service; iteration.

reduce To minimize a window to an icon by using the **Minimize** button or the **Minimize** command. A minimized application continues running, and you can click the icon on the toolbar to make it the active application.

reduced instruction set computing *See* RISC.

refresh To update displayed information with current data.

registration In Windows NT NetBT name resolution, registration is the process used to register a unique name for each computer (node) on the network. A computer typically registers itself when it starts.

registry The Windows NT registry is a database repository for information about a computer's configuration. It is organized in a hierarchical structure, and is comprised of subtrees and their keys, hives, and value entries. *See also* hive; key; subtree; Windows NT registry.

registry size limit (RSL) The total amount of space that can be consumed by registry data (hives) is restricted by the registry size limit, which is a kind of universal maximum for registry space that prevents an application form filling the paged pool with registry data. *See also* hive; paging file.

Remote Access Service (RAS) A service that provides remote networking for telecommuters, mobile workers, and system administrators who monitor and manage servers at multiple branch offices. Users with RAS on a Windows NT computer can dial in to remotely access their networks for services such as file and printer sharing, electronic mail, scheduling, and SQL database access.

remote administration Administration of one computer by an administrator located at another computer and connected to the first computer across the network.

remote logon Occurs when a user is already logged on to a user account and makes a network connection to another computer. *See also* user account.

remote procedure call (RPC) A message-passing facility that allows a distributed application to call services available on various machines in a network. Used during remote administration of computers. *See also* remote administration.

Remote Procedure Call service *See* RPC service.

renew Client computers are periodically required to renew their NetBIOS name registrations with the WINS server. When a client computer first registers with a WINS server, the WINS server returns a message that indicates when the client will need to renew its registration. *See also* Network Basic Input/Output System; Windows Internet Name Service.

repeaters The most basic LAN connection device, repeaters strengthen the physical transmission signal. A repeater simply takes the electrical signals that reach it and then regenerates them to full strength before passing them on. Repeaters generally extend a single network (rather than link two networks).

replication *See* directory replication.

replicators One of Windows NT's built-in local groups for workstations and member servers, used for directory replication functions. *See also* directory replication.

Requests for Comments (RFCs) The official documents of the IETF (Internet Engineering Task Force) that specify the details for protocols included in the TCP/IP family. *See also* IETF; TCP/IP.

resolution In Windows NetBT name resolution, resolution is the process used to determine the specific address for a computer name.

resolvers DNS clients that query DNS servers for name resolution on networks. *See also* Domain Name Service.

resource Any part of a computer system or a network, such as a disk drive, printer, or memory, that can be allotted to a program or a process while it is running, or shared over a local area network.

resource domain A trusting domain that establishes a one-way trust relationship with the master (account) domain, enabling users with accounts in the master domain to use resources in all the other domains. *See also* domain; trust relationship.

resource fork One of two forks that make up each Macintosh file. The resource fork holds Macintosh operating system resources, such as code, menu, font, and icon definitions. Resource forks have no relevance to PCs, so the resource forks of files on the server are never accessed by PC clients. *See also* data fork.

response In Windows NT RAS, responses are strings expected from the device, which can contain macros.

RFC *See* Requests for Comments.

right *See* user right; permissions.

RIP *See* routing information protocol.

RISC Acronym for reduced instruction set computing. A type of microprocessor design that focuses on rapid and efficient processing of a relatively small set of instructions. RISC architecture limits the number of instructions that are built into the microprocessor, but optimizes each so it can be carried out very rapidly—usually within a single clock cycle.

roaming user profiles Are enabled when an administrator enters a user profile path into the user account. The first time the user logs off, the local user profile is copied to that location. Thereafter, the server copy of the user profile is downloaded each time the user logs on (if it is more current than the local copy) and is updated each time the user logs off. *See also* user profile.

root directory The top-level directory on a computer, a partition, or Macintosh-accessible volume. *See also* directory tree.

router In the Windows NT environment, a router helps LANs and WANs achieve interoperability and connectivity and can link LANs that have different network topologies (such as Ethernet and Token Ring). Routers match packet headers to a LAN segment and choose the best path for the packet, optimizing network performance.

In the Macintosh environment, routers are necessary for computers on different physical networks to communicate with each other. Routers maintain a map of the physical networks on a Macintosh internet (network) and forward data received from one physical network to other physical networks. Computers running Windows NT Server with Services for Macintosh can act as routers, and you can also use third-party routing hardware on a network with Services for Macintosh. *See also* local area network; packet; router; wide area network.

routing
The process of forwarding packets to other routers until the packet is eventually delivered to a router connected to the specified destination. *See also* packet; router.

routing information protocol (RIP)
Enables a router to exchange routing information with a neighboring router. *See also* routing.

routing table Controls the routing decisions made by computers running TCP/IP. Routing tables are built automatically by Windows NT based on the IP configuration of your computer. *See also* routing; dynamic routing table; static routing; TCP/IP.

RPC *See* remote procedure call.

RPC Locator service The Remote Procedure Call Locator service allows distributed applications to use the RPC Name service. The RPC Locator service manages the RPC Name service database.

The server side of a distributed application registers its availability with the RPC Locator service. The client side of a distributed application queries the RPC Locator service to find available compatible server applications. *See also* remote procedure call.

RPC service The Remote Procedure Call service is the RPC subsystem for Microsoft Windows NT. The RPC subsystem includes the endpoint mapper and other miscellaneous RPC services. *See also* remote procedure call.

S

SACL Acronym for system access control list. In Windows NT programming, a data structure that consists of smaller data structures called access control elements (ACE). SACL is used in Windows NT security.

SAM Acronym for Security Accounts Manager. *See* directory database.

SAP In the Windows environment, SAP is an acronym for Service Advertising Protocol, a service that broadcasts shared files, directories, and printers categorized first by domain or workgroup and then by server name.

In the context of routing and IPX, SAP is also an acronym for Service Advertising Protocol, used by servers to advertise their services and addresses on a network. Clients use SAP to determine what network resources are available.

In NetBeui, SAP is an acronym for Service Access Point, in which each link-layer program identifies itself by registering a unique service access point.

Not to be confused with SAP financial database application software for the mainframe computer.

saturation The purity of a color's hue, moving from gray to the pure color.

scavenging Cleaning up the WINS database. *See also* Windows Internet Name Service.

Schedule service Supports and is required for use of the **at** command. The **at** command can schedule commands and programs to run on a computer at a specified time and date.

screen buffer The size reserved in memory for the command prompt display.

screen elements The parts that make up a window or dialog box, such as the title bar, the **Minimize** and **Maximize** buttons, the window borders, and the scroll bars.

screen fonts Fonts displayed on your screen. Soft-font manufacturers often provide screen fonts that closely match the soft fonts for your printer. This ensures that your documents look the same on the screen as they do when printed. *See also* font; font types.

screen saver A moving picture or pattern that appears on your screen when you have not used the mouse or the keyboard for a specified period of time. Use the Display option in Control Panel or right click on the desktop for properties to select a screen saver.

scroll To move through text or graphics (up, down, left, or right) in order to see parts of the file that cannot fit on the screen.

scroll arrow An arrow on either end of a scroll bar that you use to scroll through the contents of the window or list box. Click the scroll arrow to scroll one screen at a time, or continue pressing the mouse button while pointing at the scroll arrow to scroll continuously.

scroll bar A bar that appears at the right and/or bottom edge of a window or list box whose contents are not completely visible. Each scroll bar contains two scroll arrows and a scroll box, which enable you to scroll through the contents of the window or list box.

scroll box In a scroll bar, a small box that shows the position of information currently visible in the window or list box relative to the contents of the entire window.

scroll buffer The area in memory that holds information that does not fit on the screen. You can use the scroll bars to scroll through the information.

SCSI Acronym for small computer system interface, a standard high-speed parallel interface defined by the American National Standards Institute (ANSI). A SCSI interface is used for connecting microcomputers to peripheral devices such as hard disks and printers, and to other computers and local area networks.

Search button *See* find tab.

section header In Windows NT RAS, a section header is a string of up to 32 characters between square brackets which identifies the specific device to which the section applies.

secure attention sequence A series of keystrokes (CTRL+ALT+DEL) which will always display the Windows NT operating system logon screen.

secure communications channel Created when computers at each end of a connection are satisfied that the computer on the other end has identified itself correctly using its computer account. *See also* computer account.

security A means of ensuring that shared files can be accessed only by authorized users.

security accounts manager *See* Windows NT Server Directory Services.

security database *See* directory database.

security host A third-party authentication device that verifies whether a caller from a remote client is authorized to connect to the Remote Access server. This verification supplements security already authorized to connect to the Remote-Access server.

security ID A unique name that identifies a logged-on user to the security system. Security IDs (SIDs) can identify one user, or a group of users.

security identifier *See* security ID.

security log Records security events. This helps track changes to the security system and identify any possible breaches of security. For example, depending on the Audit settings in User Manager or User Manager for Domains, attempts to log on the local computer may be recorded in the security log. The security log contains both valid and invalid logon attempts as well as events related to resource use (such as creating, opening, or deleting files.) *See also* event.

security policies For Windows NT Workstation, the security policies consist of the Account, User Rights, and Audit policies, and are managed using User Manager.

For a Windows NT Server domain, the security policies consist of the Account, User Rights, Audit, and Trust Relationships policies, and are managed using User Manager for Domains.

seed router In the Macintosh environment, a seed router initializes and broadcasts routing information about one or more physical networks. This information tells routers where to send each packet of data. A router on an AppleTalk network that initially defines the network number(s) and zone(s) for a network. Services for Macintosh servers can function as seed routers, and you can also use third-party hardware routers as seed routers. *See also* packet; router.

See Files The Macintosh-style permission that give users the right to open a folder and see the files in the folder. For example, a folder that has See Files and See Folders Macintosh-style permissions is given the Windows NT-style R (Read) permission. *See also* permissions.

See Folders The Macintosh-style permission that gives users the right to open a folder and see the files contained in that folder. *See also* permissions.

select To mark an item so that a subsequent action can be carried out on that item. You usually select an item by clicking it with a mouse or pressing a key. After selecting an item, you choose the action that you want to affect the item.

selection cursor The marking device that shows where you are in a window, menu, or dialog box and what you have selected. The selection cursor can appear as a highlight or as a dotted rectangle around text.

sequence number The identifier with which TCP marks packets before sending them. The sequence numbers allow the receiving system to properly order the packets on the receiving system. *See also* packet; TCP.

Serial Line Internet Protocol (SLIP) An older industry standard that is part of Windows NT RAS to ensure interoperabability with third-party remote access software.

server In general, refers to a computer that provides shared resources to network users. *See also* member server.

server application A Windows NT application that can create objects for linking or embedding into other documents. For distributed applications, the application that responds to a client application. *See also* client application, DCOM, DCOM Configuration tool; embedded object; linked object.

Server Manager In Windows NT Server, an application used to view and administer domains, workgroups, and computers.

Server service Provides RPC (remote procedure call) support, and file, print, and named pipe sharing. *See also* named pipe; remote procedure call.

server zone The AppleTalk zone on which a server appears. On a Phase 2 network, a server appears in the default zone of the server's default network. *See also* default network; default zone; desired zone; zone.

service A process that performs a specific system function and often provides an application programming interface (API) for other processes to call. Windows NT services are RPC-enabled, meaning that their API routines can be called from remote computers. *See also* API; remote procedure call.

Services for Macintosh *See* Windows NT Server Services for Macintosh (SFM).

session A link between two network devices, such as a client and a server. A session between a client and server consists of one or more connections from the client to the server.

SFM Acronym for Windows NT Services for Macintosh.

share To make resources, such as directories and printers, available to others.

shared directory A directory that network users can connect to.

shared network directory *See* shared directory.

shared resource Any device, data, or program that is used by more than one other device or program. For Windows NT, shared resources refer to any resource that is made available to network users, such as directories, files, printers, and named pipes. Also refers to a resource on a server that is available to network users. *See also* named pipe.

share name A name that refers to a shared resource on a server. Each shared directory on a server has a share name, used by PC users to refer to the directory. Users of Macintoshes use the name of the Macintosh-accessible volume that corresponds to a directory, which may be the same as the share name. *See also* Macintosh-accessible volume.

share permissions Are used to restrict a shared resource's availability over the network to only certain users.

shortcut key A key or key combination, available for some commands, that you can press to carry out a command without first selecting a menu. Shortcut keys are listed to the right of commands on a menu.

short name A valid MS-DOS or OS/2 8.3 filename (with up to eight characters followed by a period and a three-character extension) that the computer running Windows NT Server creates for every Macintosh folder name or filename on the server. PC users refer to files on the server by their short names; Macintosh users refer to them by their long names. *See also* long name; name mapping.

SID *See* security ID.

silent mode During IP routing in silent mode, the computer listens to RIP broadcasts and updates its route table but does not advertise its own routes. *See also* RIP; routing; routing table.

simple device A device that you use without specifying a related media file. An audio compact-disc player is a simple device.

Simple Network Management Protocol (SNMP) A protocol used by SNMP consoles and agents to communicate. In Windows NT, the SNMP service is used to get and set status information about a host on a TCP/IP network. *See also* SNMP; TCP/IP.

single user logon Windows NT network users can connect to multiple servers, domains, and applications with a single network logon.

SLIP *See* Serial Line Internet Protocol.

SMB Acronym for Server Message Block, a file sharing protocol designed to allow systems to transparently access files that reside on remote systems.

SMS Acronym for Systems Management Server, part of the Windows NT BackOffice suite. SMS includes desktop management and software distribution that significantly automates the task of upgrading software on client computers.

SMTP Acronym for Simple Mail Transfer Protocol, a member of the TCP/IP suite of protocols that governs the exchange of electronic mail between message transfer agents.

SNA *See* System Network Architecture.

snapshot A copy of main memory or video memory at a given instant, sent to a printer or hard disk. A graphical image of the video screen can be saved by taking a snapshot of video memory, more commonly called a screen dump.

sniffer *See* network sniffer.

Sniffer files Files saved from Network General Sniffer, a third-party protocol analyzer. *See also* network sniffer.

SNMP *See* Simple Network Management Protocol.

socket A bidirectional pipe for incoming and outgoing data between networked computers. The Windows Sockets API is a networking API used by programmers creating TCP/IP-based sockets applications. *See also* API; named pipe.

Sockets Windows Sockets is a Windows implementation of the widely used UC Berkeley sockets API. Microsoft TCP/IP, NWLink, and AppleTalk protocols use this interface. Sockets interfaces between programs and the transport protocol and works as a bi-directional pipe for incoming and outgoing data. *See also* API; named pipe; socket.

source directory The directory that contains the file or files you intend to copy or move.

source document The document where a linked or embedded object was originally created. *See also* embedded object; linked object.

SPAP Acronym for Shiva Password Authentication Protocol, a two-way (reversible) encryption mechanism employed by Shiva. Windows NT Workstation, when connecting to a Shiva LAN Rover, uses SPAP, as does a Shiva client connecting to a Windows NT Server. *See also* encryption.

special access permissions On NTFS volumes, a custom set of permissions. You can customize permissions on files and directories by selecting the individual components of the standard sets of permissions. *See also* access permissions.

split bar Divides Windows NT Explorer into two parts: The directory tree is displayed on the left, and the contents of the current directory are on the right. *See also* directory tree.

spooler Software that accepts documents sent by a user to be printed, and then stores those documents and sends them, one by one, to available printer(s). *See also* spooling.

spooling A process on a server in which print documents are stored on a disk until a printing device is ready to process them. A spooler accepts each document from each client, stores it, then sends it to a printing device when it is ready.

SQL Acronym for structured query language, a database programming language used for accessing, querying, and otherwise managing information in a relational database system.

stabilize During subdirectory replication, when a subdirectory is stabilized, the export server waits two minutes after changes before exporting the subdirectory. The waiting period allows time for subsequent changes to take place so that all intended changes are recorded before being replicated. *See also* directory replication; export server; subtree.

stand-alone server *See* member server.

static object Information that has been pasted into a document. Unlike embedded or linked objects, static objects cannot be changed from within the document. The only way you can change a static object is to delete it from the document, change it in the application used to create it, and paste it into the document again. *See also* embedded object; linked object.

static routing Static routing limits you to fixed routing tables, as opposed to dynamically updating the routing tables. *See also* routing table; dynamic routing.

status bar A line of information related to the application in the window. Usually located at the bottom of a window. Not all windows have a status bar.

string A data structure composed of a sequence of characters, usually representing human-readable text.

stripe set Refers to the saving of data across identical partitions on different drives. A stripe set does not provide fault tolerance; however stripe sets with parity do. *See also* fault tolerance; partition; stripe sets with parity.

stripe sets with parity A method of data protection in which data is striped in large blocks across all the disks in an array. Data redundancy is provided by the parity information. This method provides fault tolerance. *See also* fault tolerance; stripe set.

subdirectory A directory within a directory. Also called a folder within a folder.

subkey A key within a key. Subkeys are analogous to subdirectories in the registry hierarchy. Keys and subkeys are similar to the section heading in .ini files; however subkeys can carry out functions. *See also* key; Windows NT Registry.

subnet A portion of a network, which may be a physically independent network segment, which shares a network address with other portions of the network and is distinguished by a subnet number. A subnet is to a network what a network is to an internet.

subnet mask A 32-bit value that allows the recipient of IP packets to distinguish the network ID portion of the IP address from the host ID. *See also* IP address; packet.

substitution macros Are placeholders that are replaced in command strings.

subtree During directory replication, this refers to the export subdirectory and all of its subdirectories. *See also* directory replication.

swap file *See* paging file.

switched circuit *See* dial-up line.

synchronize To replicate the domain database from the primary domain controller (PDC) to one backup domain controller (BDC) of the domain, or to all the BDCs of a domain. This is usually performed automatically by the system, but can also be invoked manually by an administrator. *See also* domain; BDC; PDC.

syntax The order in which you must type a command and the elements that follow the command. Windows NT commands have up to four elements: command name, parameters, switches, and values.

system default profile In Windows NT Server, the user profile that is loaded when Windows NT is running and no user is logged on. When the **Begin Logon** dialog box is visible, the system default profile is loaded. *See also* user default profile, user profile.

system disk A disk that contains the MS-DOS system files necessary to start MS-DOS.

system log The system log contains events logged by the Windows NT components. For example, the failure of a driver or other system component to load during startup is recorded in the system log. Use Event Viewer to view the system log.

System Network Architecture (SNA)
System Network Architecture is a communications framework developed by IBM. Microsoft System Network Architecture (SNA) is an optional solution that provides a gateway connection between personal computer LANs or WANs and IBM mainframe and AS/400 hosts. *See also* AS/400; gateway.

system partition The volume that has the hardware-specific files needed to load Windows NT. *See also* partition.

system policy Is created with the System Policy Editor to control user work environments and actions, and to enforce system configuration for Windows 95. System policy can be implemented for specific users, groups, computers, or for all users. System policy for users overwrites settings in the current user area of the registry, and system policy for computers overwrites the current local machine area of the registry. *See also* registry.

systemroot The name of the directory that contains Windows NT files. The name of this directory is specified when Windows NT is installed.

Systems Management Server Part of the Windows NT BackOffice suite. SMS includes desktop management and software distribution that significantly automates the task of upgrading software on client computers.

T

tape set
A tape set (sometimes referred to as a tape family) in Windows NT Backup is a sequence of tapes such that each tape is a continuation of the backup on the previous tape. *See also* backup sets; backup types.

TAPI Acronym for telephony API, used by programs to make data/fax/voice calls, including the Windows NT applets HyperTerminal, Dial-up Networking, Phone Dialer, and other Win32® communications applications written for Windows NT.

Task list A window that shows all running applications and their status. View the Task list in the **Applications** tab in Task Manager.

Task Manager Task Manager enables you to start, end, or run applications, end processes (either an application, application component, or system process), and view CPU and memory use data. Task Manager gives you a simple, quick view of how each process (application or service) is using CPU and memory resources. (Note: In previous versions of Windows NT, Task List handled some of these functions).

To run Task Manager, right-click on the toolbar and then click Task Manager.

TCP *See* transmission control protocol.

TCP/IP *See* Transmission Control Protocol/Internet Protocol.

TDI *See* Transport Driver Interface.

template accounts Accounts which are not actually used by real users but serve as a basis for the real accounts (for administrative purposes).

terminate-and-stay-resident program (TSR) A program running under MS-DOS that remains loaded in memory even when it is not running so that it can be quickly invoked for a specific task performed while any other application is operating.

text box In a dialog box, a box in which you type information needed to carry out a command. The text box may be blank or may contain text when the dialog box opens.

text file A file containing text characters (letters, numbers, and symbols) but no formatting information. A text file can be a "plain" ASCII file that most computers can read. Text file can also refer to a word-processing file. *See also* ASCII file.

text-file transfer A method for transferring files from HyperTerminal to a remote computer. With this method, files are transferred as ASCII files with minimal formatting characters, such as linefeeds and carriage returns. All font-formatting information is removed. *See also* ASCII file.

text-only An ASCII file that contains no formatting. *See also* ASCII file.

thread Threads are objects within processes that run program instructions. They allow concurrent operations within a process and enable one process to run different parts of its program on different processors simultaneously.

timeout If a device is not performing a task, the amount of time the computer should wait before detecting it as an error.

time slice The amount of processor time allocated to an application, usually measured in milliseconds.

title bar The horizontal bar (at the top of a window) that contains the title of the window or dialog box. On many windows, the title bar also contains the program icon and the **Maximize, Minimize,** and **Close** buttons.

Token Ring A type of network media that connects clients in a closed ring and uses token passing to enable clients to use the network. *See also* FDDI, and LocalTalk.

toolbar A series of icons or shortcut buttons providing quick access to commands. Usually located directly below the menu bar. Not all windows have a toolbar.

topic Information in the Help window. A Help topic usually begins with a title and contains information about a particular task, command, or dialog box.

Transmission Control Protocol (TCP) A connection-based Internet protocol responsible for breaking data into packets, which the IP protocol sends over the network. This protocol provides a reliable, sequenced communication stream for network communication. *See also* IP; packet.

Transmission Control Protocol/Internet Protocol (TCP/IP) A set of networking protocols that provide communications across interconnected networks made up of computers with diverse hardware architectures and various operating systems. TCP/IP includes standards for how computers communicate and conventions for connecting networks and routing traffic.

transport driver interface (TDI) In Windows networking, the common interface for network components that communicate at the Session layer.

trap In SNMP, a discrete block of data that indicates that the request failed authentication. The SNMP service can send a trap when it receives a request for information that does not contain the correct community name and that does not match an accepted hostname for the service. Trap destinations are the names or IP addresses of hosts to which the SNMP service is to send traps with community names. *See also* IP address; SNMP.

trigger A set of conditions that, when met, initiate an action. For example, before using Network Monitor to capture data from the network, you can set a trigger to stop the capture or to execute a program or command file.

Trojan horse A program that masquerades as another common program in an attempt to receive information. An example of a Trojan horse is a program that masquerades as a system logon to retrieve user names and password information, which the writers of the Trojan horse can use later to break into the system.

TrueType fonts Fonts that are scalable and sometimes generated as bitmaps or soft fonts, depending on the capabilities of your printer. TrueType fonts can be sized to any height, and they print exactly as they appear on the screen.

trust *See* trust relationship.

trust relationship A link between domains that enables pass-through authentication, in which a trusting domain honors the logon authentications of a trusted domain. With trust relationships, a user who has only one user account in one domain can potentially access the entire network. User accounts and global groups defined in a trusted domain can be given rights and resource permissions in a trusting domain, even though those accounts don't exist in the trusting domain's directory database. *See also* directory database; global group; pass-through authentication; user account.

trust relationships policy A security policy that determines which domains are trusted and which domains are trusting domains. *See also* trust relationship.

TSR *See* terminate-and-stay-resident program.

two-way trust relationship Each domain trusts user accounts in the other domain to use its resources. Users can log on from computers in either domain to the domain that contains their account. *See also* trust relationship.

type *See* file type.

Type 1 fonts Scalable fonts designed to work with PostScript devices. *See also* font; font types; PostScript printer.

U

UAM *See* user authentication module.

UDP *See* User Datagram Protocol.

unavailable An unavailable button or command is displayed in light gray instead of black, and it cannot be clicked.

UNC name Acronym for universal naming convention name, a full Windows NT name of a resource on a network. It conforms to the *servername**sharename* syntax, where *servername* is the server's name and *sharename* is the name of the shared resource. UNC names of directories or files can also include the directory path under the share name, with the following syntax: *servername**sharename**directory**filename*.

unicast datagram An IP datagram sent to one host. *See also* Internet Protocol (IP); multicast datagram; broadcast datagram.

uninterruptible power supply (UPS) *See* UPS.

UPS Acronym for uninterruptible power supply, a battery-operated power supply connected to a computer to keep the system running during a power failure.

UPS service Manages an uninterruptible power supply connected to a computer. *See also* UPS.

user account Consists of all the information that defines a user to Windows NT. This includes such things as the user name and password required for the user to log on, the groups in which the user account has membership, and the rights and permissions the user has for using the system and accessing its resources. For Windows NT Workstation, user accounts are managed with User Manager. For Windows NT Server, user accounts are managed with User Manager for Domains. *See also* group.

user account database *See* directory database.

user authentication module Software component that prompts clients for their user names and passwords. *See also* cleartext passwords; encrypted passwords.

User Datagram Protocol (UDP) A TCP complement that offers a connectionless datagram service that guarantees neither delivery nor correct sequencing of delivered packets (much like IP). *See also* datagram; IP; packet.

user default profile In Windows NT Server, the user profile that is loaded by a server when a user's assigned profile cannot be accessed for any reason; when a user without an assigned profile logs on to the computer for the first time; or when a user logs on to the Guest account. *See also* system default profile; user profile.

User Manager A Windows NT Workstation tool used to manage the security for a workstation. User Manager administers user accounts, groups, and security policies.

User Manager for Domains A Windows NT Server tool used to manage security for a domain or an individual computer. User Manager for Domains administers user accounts, groups, and security policies.

user name A unique name identifying a user account to Windows NT. An account's user name cannot be identical to any other group name or user name of its own domain or workgroup. *See also* user account.

user password The password stored in each user's account. Each user generally has a unique user password and must type that password when logging on or accessing a server. *See also* password; volume password.

User privilege One of three privilege levels you can assign to a Windows NT user account. Every user account has one of the three privilege levels (Administrator, Guest, and User). Accounts with User privilege are regular users of the network; most accounts on your network will probably have User privilege. *See also* user account; Administrator privilege; Guest privilege.

user profile Configuration information that can be retained on a user-by-user basis, and is saved in user profiles. This information includes all the per-user settings of the Windows NT environment, such as the desktop arrangement, personal program groups and the program items in those groups, screen colors, screen savers, network connections, printer connections, mouse settings, window size and position, and more. When a user logs on, the user's profile is loaded and the user's Windows NT environment is configured according to that profile. *See also* personal groups; program item.

user rights Define a user's access to a computer or domain and the actions that a user can perform on the computer or domain. User rights permit actions such as logging onto a computer or network, adding or deleting users in a workstation or domain, and so forth.

user rights policy Manages the assignment of rights to groups and user accounts. *See also* user account; user rights.

users In the Macintosh environment, a special group that contains all users who have user permissions on the server. When a Macintosh user assigns permissions to everyone, those permissions are given to the groups users and guests. *See also* guests.

V

value entry The string of data that appears in the right pane of a registry window and which defines the value of the currently selected key. A value entry has three parts: name, datatype, and the value itself. *See also* key; subkey.

Van Jacobsen header compression
A TCP/IP network layer compression technique, VJ compression reduces the size of IP and TCP headers. *See also* Internet Protocol; Transmission Control Protocol; Transmission Control Protocol/ Internet Protocol.

variables In programming, a variable is a named storage location capable of containing a certain type of data that can be modified during program execution. System environment variables are defined by Windows NT Server and are the same no matter who is logged on at the computer. (Administrator group members can add new variables or change the values, however.) User environment variables can be different for each user of a particular computer. They include any environment variables you want to define of variables defined by your applications, such as the path where application files are located.

VDD Acronym for virtual device drivers, which enable MS-DOS-based and 16-bit Windows-based applications to run on Windows NT.

VDM Acronym for virtual DOS machine. Simulates an MS-DOS environment so that MS-DOS-based and Windows-based applications can run on Windows NT.

verify operation Occurs after all files are backed up or restored, if specified. A verify operation compares files on disk to files that have been written to tape. *See also* backup types.

virtual memory The space on your hard disk that Windows NT uses as if it were actually memory. Windows NT does this through the use of paging files. The benefit of using virtual memory is that you can run more applications at one time than your system's physical memory would otherwise allow. The drawbacks are the disk space required for the virtual-memory paging file and the decreased execution speed when paging is required. *See also* paging file.

virtual printer memory In a PostScript printer, a part of memory that stores font information. The memory in PostScript printers is divided into two areas: banded memory and virtual memory. The banded memory contains graphics and page-layout information needed to print your documents. The virtual memory contains any font information that is sent to your printer either when you print a document or when you download fonts. *See also* font types; PostScript printer.

virus A program that attempts to spread from computer to computer and either cause damage (by erasing or corrupting data) or annoy users (by printing messages or altering what is displayed on the screen).

volume A partition or collection of partitions that have been formatted for use by a file system. *See also* Macintosh-accessible volume; partition.

volume password An optional, case-sensitive password you can assign to a Macintosh-accessible volume when you configure the volume. To access the volume, a user must type the volume password. *See also* Macintosh-accessible volume; user password.

volume set A combination of partitions on a physical disk that appear as one logical drive. *See also* logical drive; partition.

VPN Acronym for virtual private network, a remote LAN that can be accessed through the Internet using the new PPTP. *See also* Point-to-Point Tunneling Protocol.

W

wallpaper A picture or drawing stored as a bitmap file (a file that has a .bmp extension).

WAN *See* wide area network

warning beep The sound that your computer makes when you encounter an error or try to perform a task that Windows NT does not recognize.

wide area network (WAN) A communications network that connects geographically separated areas.

wildcard A character that represents one or more characters. The question mark (?) wildcard can be used to represent any single character, and the asterisk (*) wildcard can be used to represent any character or group of characters that might match that position in other filenames.

window A rectangular area on your screen in which you view an application or document. You can open, close, and move windows, and change the size of most windows. You can open several windows at a time, and you can often reduce a window to an icon or enlarge it to fill the entire desktop.

window menu A menu that contains commands you can use to manipulate a window. You click the program icon or document icon at the left of the title bar to open the window menu.

Windows Internet Name Service (WINS) A name resolution service that resolves Windows networking computer names to IP addresses in a routed environment. A WINS server handles name registrations, queries, and releases. *See also* IP address; routing.

Windows NT application Used as a shorthand term to refer to an application that is designed to run with Windows NT and does not run without Windows NT. All Windows NT applications follow similar conventions for arrangement of menus, style of dialog boxes, and keyboard and mouse use.

Windows NT browser system Consists of a master browser, backup browser, and client systems. The master browser maintains the browse list—of all the available domains and servers—and periodically sends copies to the backup browsers. *See also* browse; master browser.

Windows NT Registry A hierarchical database that provides a central repository to store configuration information about hardware and user accounts. It is comprised of subtrees and their keys, hives, and value entries. *See also* hive; key; subtree; user account.

Windows NT Server A superset of Windows NT Workstation, Windows NT Server provides centralized management and security, fault tolerance, and additional connectivity. *See also* fault tolerance; Windows NT Workstation.

Windows NT Server Directory Services A Windows NT protected subsystem that maintains the directory database and provides an application programming interface (API) for accessing the database. *See also* API; directory database.

Windows NT Server Services for Macintosh A software component of Windows NT Server that allows Macintosh users access to the computer running Windows NT Server. The services provided with this component allow PC and Macintosh users to share files and resources, such as printers on the AppleTalk network or those attached to the Windows NT Server. *See also* File Server for Macintosh; Print Server for Macintosh.

Windows NT Workstation The portable, secure, 32-bit, preemptive multitasking member of the Microsoft Windows operating system family.

Windows Sockets *See* Sockets.

WINS *See* Windows Internet Name Service.

workgroup For Windows NT, a workgroup is a collection of computers that are grouped for viewing purposes. Each workgroup is identified by a unique name. *See also* domain.

working set Every program running can use a portion of physical memory, its working set, which is the current number of physical memory bytes used by or allocated by a process.

workstation Any networked Macintosh or PC using server resources. *See also* member server; primary domain controller; backup domain controller.

Workstation service Provides network connections and communications.

World Wide Web (WWW) The software, protocols, conventions, and information that enable hypertext and multimedia publishing of resources on different computers around the world. *See also* Internet; HTML.

WOSA Acronym for Microsoft Windows Open System Architecture, which specifies an open set of APIs for integrating Windows-based computers with back-end services on a broad range of vendor's systems. WOSA consists of an extensible set of APIs that enable Windows-based desktop applications to access available information without having to know anything about the type of network in use, the types of computers in the enterprise, or types of back-end services available. As a result, if the network computers or services change, the desktop applications built using WOSA won't require rewriting. *See also* API.

WOW Acronym for Win16 on Win32. The translation of Windows 3.1-based application calls to standard mode for RISC-based computers and 386 enhanced mode for x86-based computers.

wrap To continue to the next line rather than stopping when the cursor reaches the end of the current line.

X

X.25 A recommendation published by the CCITT international communications standards organization that defines the connection between a terminal and a packet-switching network. An X.25 network is a type of packet-switching network that routes units of information (packets) as specified by X.25 and is used in public data communications networks. *See also* packet.

X.25 smart card A hardware card with a PAD (packet assemblers/disassemblers) embedded in it. *See also* PAD; X.25.

XModem/CRC Protocol for transmitting binary files that uses a cyclic redundancy check (CRC) to detect any transmission errors. Both computers must be set to transmit and receive eight data bits per character.

XOR Acronym for exclusive OR. A Boolean operation in which the Windows NT Server stripe-sets-with-parity form of fault tolerance maintains an XOR of the total data to provide data redundancy. This enables the reconstruction of missing data (on a failed disk or sector) from the remaining disks in the stripe set with parity. *See also* stripe set with parity; fault tolerance.

Z

zone In the Macintosh environment, a zone is a logical grouping which simplifies browsing the network for resources, such as servers and printers. It is similar to a domain in Windows NT Server networking.

In a DNS (Domain Name System) database, a zone is a subtree of the DNS database that is administered as a single separate entity, a DNS name server. This administrative unit can consist of a single domain or a domain with subdomains. A DNS zone administrator sets up one or more name servers for the zone. *See also* DNS; domain.

zone list In the Macintosh environment, a zone list includes all of the zones associated with a particular network. Not to be confused with Windows NT DNS zones.

Index

C

D

E

F

G

H

I

J

K

L

M

N

P

Q

R

S

T

U

V

W

X

Y

Z

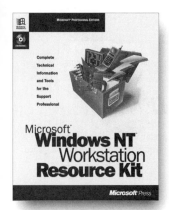

IMPORTANT—READ CAREFULLY BEFORE OPENING SOFTWARE PACKET(S). By opening the sealed packet(s) containing the software, you indicate your acceptance of the following Microsoft License Agreement.

MICROSOFT LICENSE AGREEMENT

(Book Companion CD)

This is a legal agreement between you (either an individual or an entity) and Microsoft Corporation. By opening the sealed software packet(s) you are agreeing to be bound by the terms of this agreement. If you do not agree to the terms of this agreement, promptly return the unopened software packet(s) and any accompanying written materials to the place you obtained them for a full refund.

MICROSOFT SOFTWARE LICENSE

1. GRANT OF LICENSE. Microsoft grants to you the right to use one copy of the Microsoft software program included with this book (the "SOFTWARE") on a single terminal connected to a single computer. The SOFTWARE is in "use" on a computer when it is loaded into the temporary memory (i.e., RAM) or installed into the permanent memory (e.g., hard disk, CD-ROM, or other storage device) of that computer. You may not network the SOFTWARE or otherwise use it on more than one computer or computer terminal at the same time.

2. COPYRIGHT. The SOFTWARE is owned by Microsoft or its suppliers and is protected by United States copyright laws and international treaty provisions. Therefore, you must treat the SOFTWARE like any other copyrighted material (e.g., a book or musical recording) except that you may either (a) make one copy of the SOFTWARE solely for backup or archival purposes, or (b) transfer the SOFTWARE to a single hard disk provided you keep the original solely for backup or archival purposes. You may not copy the written materials accompanying the SOFTWARE.

3. OTHER RESTRICTIONS. You may not rent or lease the SOFTWARE, but you may transfer the SOFTWARE and accompanying written materials on a permanent basis provided you retain no copies and the recipient agrees to the terms of this Agreement. You may not reverse engineer, decompile, or disassemble the SOFTWARE. If the SOFTWARE is an update or has been updated, any transfer must include the most recent update and all prior versions.

4. DUAL MEDIA SOFTWARE. If the SOFTWARE package contains more than one kind of disk (3.5", 5.25", and CD-ROM), then you may use only the disks appropriate for your single-user computer. You may not use the other disks on another computer or loan, rent, lease, or transfer them to another user except as part of the permanent transfer (as provided above) of all SOFTWARE and written materials.

5. SAMPLE CODE. If the SOFTWARE includes Sample Code, then Microsoft grants you a royalty-free right to reproduce and distribute the sample code of the SOFTWARE provided that you: (a) distribute the sample code only in conjunction with and as a part of your software product; (b) do not use Microsoft's or its authors' names, logos, or trademarks to market your software product; (c) include the copyright notice that appears on the SOFTWARE on your product label and as a part of the sign-on message for your software product; and (d) agree to indemnify, hold harmless, and defend Microsoft and its authors from and against any claims or lawsuits, including attorneys' fees, that arise or result from the use or distribution of your software product.

DISCLAIMER OF WARRANTY

The SOFTWARE (including instructions for its use) is provided "AS IS" WITHOUT WARRANTY OF ANY KIND. MICROSOFT FURTHER DISCLAIMS ALL IMPLIED WARRANTIES INCLUDING WITHOUT LIMITATION ANY IMPLIED WARRANTIES OF MERCHANTABILITY OR OF FITNESS FOR A PARTICULAR PURPOSE. THE ENTIRE RISK ARISING OUT OF THE USE OR PERFORMANCE OF THE SOFTWARE AND DOCUMENTATION REMAINS WITH YOU.

IN NO EVENT SHALL MICROSOFT, ITS AUTHORS, OR ANYONE ELSE INVOLVED IN THE CREATION, PRODUCTION, OR DELIVERY OF THE SOFTWARE BE LIABLE FOR ANY DAMAGES WHATSOEVER (INCLUDING, WITHOUT LIMITATION, DAMAGES FOR LOSS OF BUSINESS PROFITS, BUSINESS INTERRUPTION, LOSS OF BUSINESS INFORMATION, OR OTHER PECUNIARY LOSS) ARISING OUT OF THE USE OF OR INABILITY TO USE THE SOFTWARE OR DOCUMENTATION, EVEN IF MICROSOFT HAS BEEN ADVISED OF THE POSSIBILITY OF SUCH DAMAGES. BECAUSE SOME STATES/COUNTRIES DO NOT ALLOW THE EXCLUSION OR LIMITATION OF LIABILITY FOR CONSEQUENTIAL OR INCIDENTAL DAMAGES, THE ABOVE LIMITATION MAY NOT APPLY TO YOU.

U.S. GOVERNMENT RESTRICTED RIGHTS

The SOFTWARE and documentation are provided with RESTRICTED RIGHTS. Use, duplication, or disclosure by the Government is subject to restrictions as set forth in subparagraph (c)(1)(ii) of The Rights in Technical Data and Computer Software clause at DFARS 252.227-7013 or subparagraphs (c)(1) and (2) of the Commercial Computer Software — Restricted Rights 48 CFR 52.227-19, as applicable. Manufacturer is Microsoft Corporation, One Microsoft Way, Redmond, WA 98052-6399.

If you acquired this product in the United States, this Agreement is governed by the laws of the State of Washington.

Should you have any questions concerning this Agreement, or if you desire to contact Microsoft Press for any reason, please write: Microsoft Press, One Microsoft Way, Redmond, WA 98052-6399.

Register Today!

Return this
Microsoft® Windows NT® Workstation
Resource Kit
registration card for a Microsoft Press® catalog

U.S. and Canada addresses only. Fill in information below and mail postage-free. Please mail only the bottom half of this page.

1-57231-343-9A ***MICROSOFT® WINDOWS NT® WORKSTATION RESOURCE KIT*** ***Owner Registration Card***

NAME

INSTITUTION OR COMPANY NAME

ADDRESS

CITY STATE ZIP

NO POSTAGE
NECESSARY
IF MAILED
IN THE
UNITED STATES

BUSINESS REPLY MAIL

FIRST-CLASS MAIL PERMIT NO. 108 REDMOND, WA

POSTAGE WILL BE PAID BY ADDRESSEE

MICROSOFT PRESS REGISTRATION
MICROSOFT® WINDOWS NT®
WORKSTATION RESOURCE KIT
PO BOX 3019
BOTHELL WA 98041-9946

Windows NT 3.51 Architecture

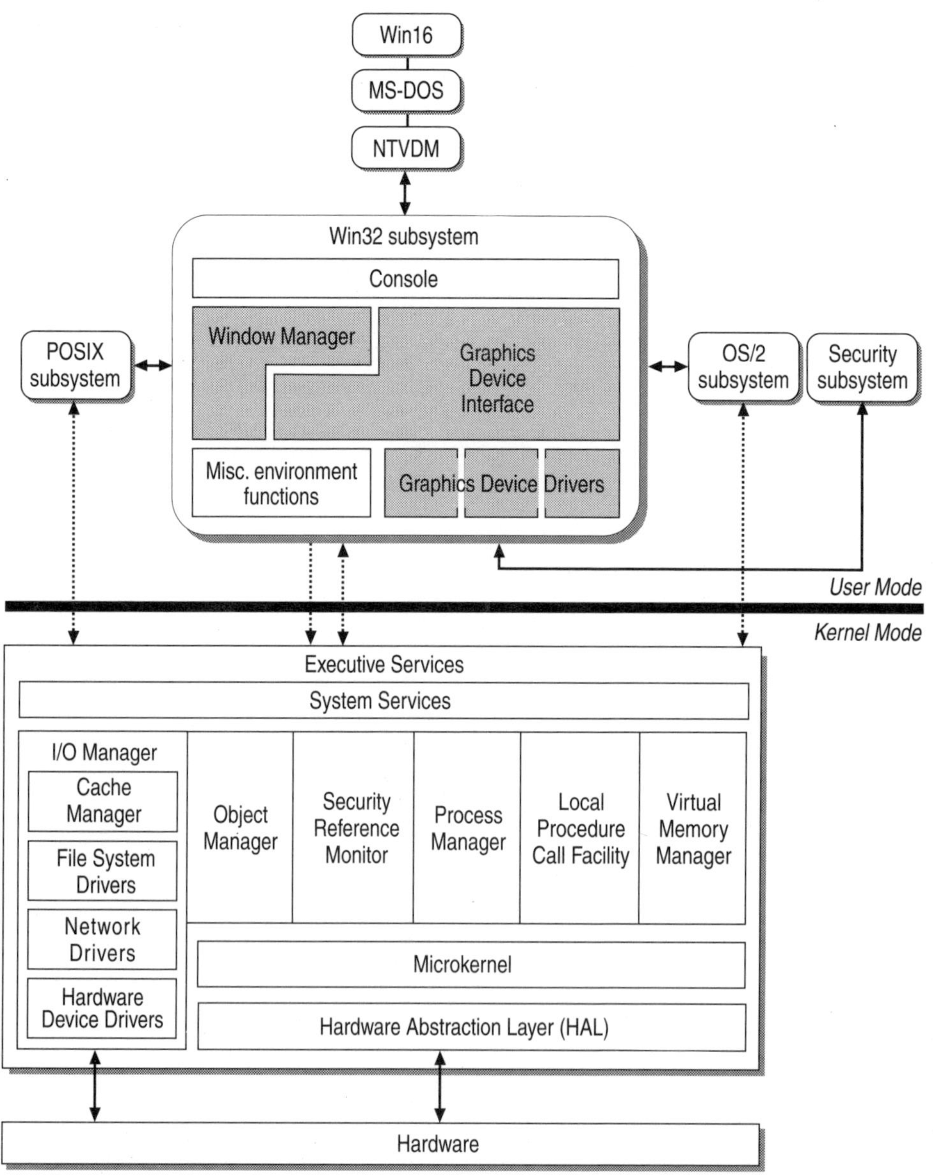